Financial Accounting

Ninth Edition

WEYGANDT • KIMMEL • KIESO

Palm Beach State College
Financial Accounting
ACG 2022

Wiley Custom Learning Solutions

ISBN 978-1-119-04624-0

Printed and bound by Courier Digital Solutions.

10 9 8 7 6 5 4

WileyPLUS

ATTENTION STUDENTS
IMPORTANT REGISTRATION INSTRUCTIONS

Enrollment in this course requires the use of this resource and will be a part of your overall grade in the course. Below are instructions to assist you in registering your WileyPLUS code and gaining access to technical support when needed.

GETTING STARTED:

1. Go to www.wileyplus.com
2. Click **GET STARTED** in the Student section of the homepage.
3. Enter School Name, click **FIND.**
4. Click the Course Name, Find your instructor / class section info.
5. Click the green arrow.
6. Click **CREATE ACCOUNT**.
7. Check "I AGREE TO THESE TERMS" and click **Continue.**
8. Click **+ I HAVE A REGISTRATION CODE.**
9. Enter your unique redemption code when prompted at www.wileyplus.com

NEED HELP?

Login	**www.wileyplus.com**	
View a registration video	**www.wileyplus.com/register**	
Technical Support:	**www.wileyplus.com/support**	**Click LIVE CHAT**

Do not email your instructor for help with WileyPLUS.
Contact Wiley via the technical support live chat link above.

ACCOUNT CLASSIFICATION AND PRESENTATION

Account Title	Classification	Financial Statement	Normal Balance
A			
Accounts Payable	Current Liability	Balance Sheet	Credit
Accounts Receivable	Current Asset	Balance Sheet	Debit
Accumulated Depreciation—Buildings	Plant Asset—Contra	Balance Sheet	Credit
Accumulated Depreciation—Equipment	Plant Asset—Contra	Balance Sheet	Credit
Advertising Expense	Operating Expense	Income Statement	Debit
Allowance for Doubtful Accounts	Current Asset—Contra	Balance Sheet	Credit
Amortization Expense	Operating Expense	Income Statement	Debit
B			
Bad Debt Expense	Operating Expense	Income Statement	Debit
Bonds Payable	Long-Term Liability	Balance Sheet	Credit
Buildings	Plant Asset	Balance Sheet	Debit
C			
Cash	Current Asset	Balance Sheet	Debit
Common Stock	Stockholders' Equity	Balance Sheet	Credit
Copyrights	Intangible Asset	Balance Sheet	Debit
Cost of Goods Sold	Cost of Goods Sold	Income Statement	Debit
D			
Debt Investments	Current Asset/Long-Term Investment	Balance Sheet	Debit
Depreciation Expense	Operating Expense	Income Statement	Debit
Discount on Bonds Payable	Long-Term Liability—Contra	Balance Sheet	Debit
Dividend Revenue	Other Income	Income Statement	Credit
Dividends	Temporary account closed to Retained Earnings	Retained Earnings Statement	Debit
Dividends Payable	Current Liability	Balance Sheet	Credit
E			
Equipment	Plant Asset	Balance Sheet	Debit
F			
Freight-Out	Operating Expense	Income Statement	Debit
G			
Gain on Disposal of Plant Assets	Other Income	Income Statement	Credit
Goodwill	Intangible Asset	Balance Sheet	Debit
I			
Income Summary	Temporary account closed to Retained Earnings	Not Applicable	(1)
Income Tax Expense	Income Tax Expense	Income Statement	Debit
Income Taxes Payable	Current Liability	Balance Sheet	Credit
Insurance Expense	Operating Expense	Income Statement	Debit
Interest Expense	Other Expense	Income Statement	Debit
Interest Payable	Current Liability	Balance Sheet	Credit
Interest Receivable	Current Asset	Balance Sheet	Debit
Interest Revenue	Other Income	Income Statement	Credit
Inventory	Current Asset	Balance Sheet (2)	Debit

Account Title	Classification	Financial Statement	Normal Balance
L			
Land	Plant Asset	Balance Sheet	Debit
Loss on Disposal of Plant Assets	Other Expense	Income Statement	Debit
M			
Maintenance and Repairs Expense	Operating Expense	Income Statement	Debit
Mortgage Payable	Long-Term Liability	Balance Sheet	Credit
N			
Notes Payable	Current Liability/ Long-Term Liability	Balance Sheet	Credit
P			
Patents	Intangible Asset	Balance Sheet	Debit
Paid-in Capital in Excess of Par— Common Stock	Stockholders' Equity	Balance Sheet	Credit
Paid-in Capital in Excess of Par— Preferred Stock	Stockholders' Equity	Balance Sheet	Credit
Preferred Stock	Stockholders' Equity	Balance Sheet	Credit
Premium on Bonds Payable	Long-Term Liability—Adjunct	Balance Sheet	Credit
Prepaid Insurance	Current Asset	Balance Sheet	Debit
Prepaid Rent	Current Asset	Balance Sheet	Debit
R			
Rent Expense	Operating Expense	Income Statement	Debit
Retained Earnings	Stockholders' Equity	Balance Sheet and Retained Earnings Statement	Credit
S			
Salaries and Wages Expense	Operating Expense	Income Statement	Debit
Salaries and Wages Payable	Current Liability	Balance Sheet	Credit
Sales Discounts	Revenue—Contra	Income Statement	Debit
Sales Returns and Allowances	Revenue—Contra	Income Statement	Debit
Sales Revenue	Revenue	Income Statement	Credit
Selling Expenses	Operating Expense	Income Statement	Debit
Service Revenue	Revenue	Income Statement	Credit
Stock Investments	Current Asset/Long-Term Investment	Balance Sheet	Debit
Supplies	Current Asset	Balance Sheet	Debit
Supplies Expense	Operating Expense	Income Statement	Debit
T			
Treasury Stock	Stockholders' Equity	Balance Sheet	Debit
U			
Unearned Service Revenue	Current Liability	Balance Sheet	Credit
Utilities Expense	Operating Expense	Income Statement	Debit

(1) The normal balance for Income Summary will be credit when there is a net income, debit when there is a net loss. The Income Summary account does not appear on any financial statement.

(2) If a periodic system is used, Inventory also appears on the income statement in the calculation of cost of goods sold.

The following is a sample chart of accounts. It does not represent a comprehensive chart of all the accounts used in this textbook but rather those accounts that are commonly used. This sample chart of accounts is for a company that generates both service revenue as well as sales revenue. It uses the perpetual approach to inventory. If a periodic system was used, the following temporary accounts would be needed to record inventory purchases: Purchases; Freight-In; Purchase Returns and Allowances; and Purchase Discounts.

CHART OF ACCOUNTS

Assets	Liabilities	Stockholders' Equity	Revenues	Expenses
Cash	Notes Payable	Common Stock	Service Revenue	Amortization Expense
Accounts Receivable	Accounts Payable	Paid-in Capital in Excess of Par—Common Stock	Sales Revenue	Bad Debt Expense
Allowance for Doubtful Accounts	Unearned Service Revenue	Preferred Stock	Sales Discounts	Cost of Goods Sold
Interest Receivable	Salaries and Wages Payable	Paid-in Capital in Excess of Par—Preferred Stock	Sales Returns and Allowances	Depreciation Expense
Inventory	Interest Payable	Treasury Stock	Interest Revenue	Freight-Out
Supplies	Dividends Payable	Retained Earnings	Gain on Disposal of Plant Assets	Income Tax Expense
Prepaid Insurance	Income Taxes Payable	Dividends		Insurance Expense
Land	Bonds Payable	Income Summary		Interest Expense
Equipment	Discount on Bonds Payable			Loss on Disposal of Plant Assets
Accumulated Depreciation—Equipment	Premium on Bonds Payable			Maintenance and Repairs Expense
Buildings	Mortgage Payable			Rent Expense
Accumulated Depreciation—Buildings				Salaries and Wages Expense
Copyrights				Selling Expenses
Goodwill				Supplies Expense
Patents				Utilities Expense

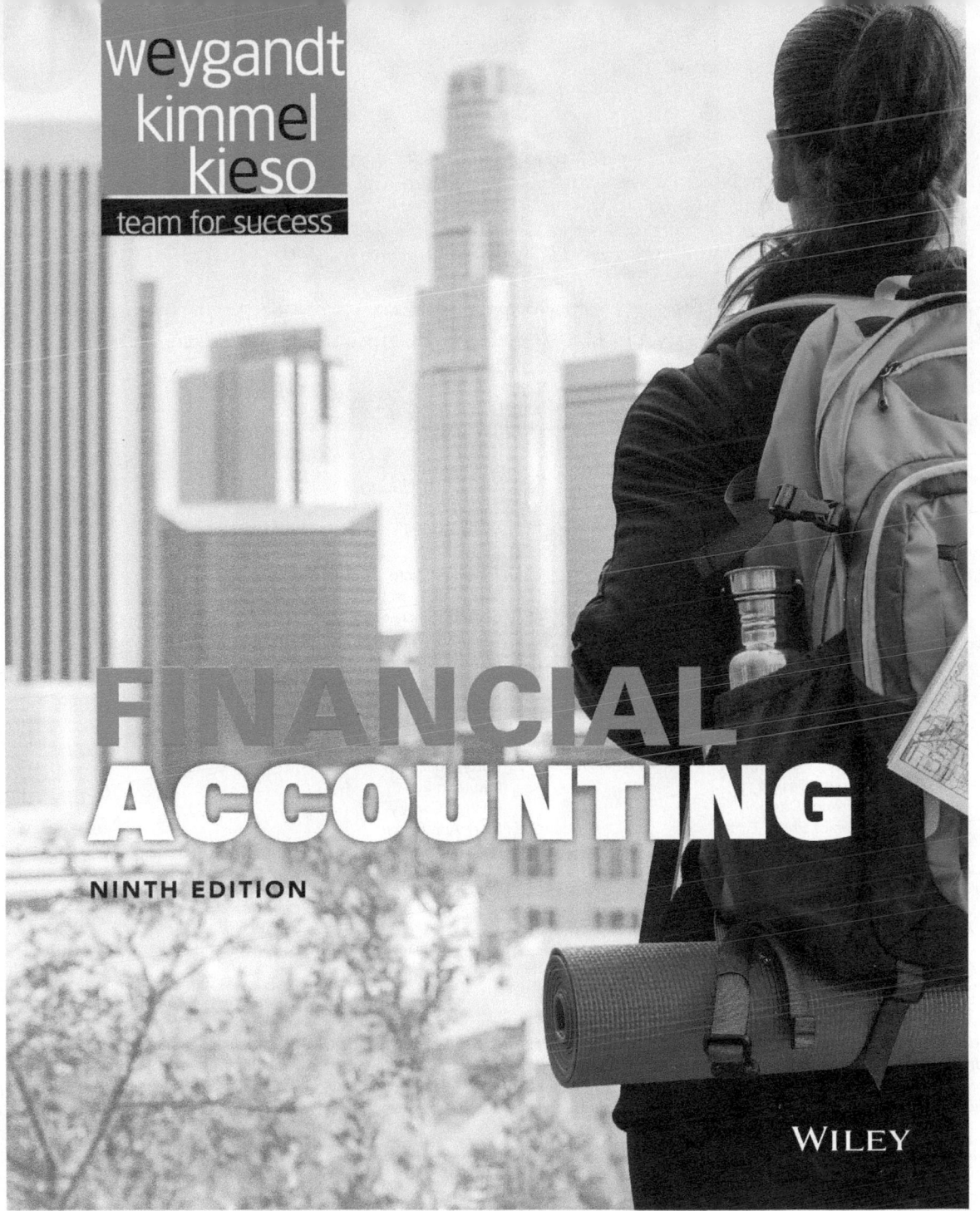

weygandt
kimmel
kieso
team for success

FINANCIAL ACCOUNTING

NINTH EDITION

WILEY

Jerry J. Weygandt PhD, CPA
University of Wisconsin—Madison
Madison, Wisconsin

Paul D. Kimmel PhD, CPA
University of Wisconsin—Milwaukee
Milwaukee, Wisconsin

Donald E. Kieso PhD, CPA
Northern Illinois University
DeKalb, Illinois

WILEY

Dedicated to
the Wiley sales representatives
who sell our books and service our
adopters in a professional and ethical
manner, and to
Enid, Merlynn, and Donna

Vice President & Executive Publisher	George Hoffman
Senior Acquisitions Editor	Michael McDonald
Customer and Market Development Manager	Christopher DeJohn
Editorial Operations Manager	Yana Mermel
Project Editor	Ed Brislin
Senior Development Editor	Terry Ann Tatro
Development Editor	Margaret Thompson
Senior Content Manager	Dorothy Sinclair
Senior Production Editor	Valerie A. Vargas
Director, Marketing	Amy Scholz
Senior Marketing Manager	Karolina Zarychta Honsa
Senior Product Designer	Allison Morris
Product Designer	Greg Chaput
Media Specialist	Daniela DiMaggio
Design Director	Harry Nolan
Cover Design	Maureen Eide
Interior Design	Kristine Carney
Senior Photo Editor	Mary Ann Price
Editorial Assistant	Rebecca Constantini
Marketing Assistant	Mia Brady
Cover and title page	© Predrag Vuckovic/E+/Getty Images

This book was set in New Aster by Aptara®, Inc. and printed and bound by Courier-Kendallville. The cover was printed by Courier-Kendallville.

Founded in 1807, John Wiley & Sons, Inc. has been a valued source of knowledge and understanding for more than 200 years, helping people around the world meet their needs and fulfill their aspirations. Our company is built on a foundation of principles that include responsibility to the communities we serve and where we live and work. In 2008, we launched a Corporate Citizenship Initiative, a global effort to address the environmental, social, economic, and ethical challenges we face in our business. Among the issues we are addressing are carbon impact, paper specifications and procurement, ethical conduct within our business and among our vendors, and community and charitable support. For more information, please visit our website: www.wiley.com/go/citizenship.

ISBN-13 978-1-118-33432-4

Binder-Ready Version ISBN 978-1-118-33843-8

Printed in the United States of America

10 9 8 7 6 5 4 3 2 1

Brief Contents

*Available at the book's companion website, **www.wiley.com/college/weygandt**.

From the Authors

Dear Student,

Why This Course? *Remember your biology course in high school? Did you have one of those "invisible man" models (or maybe something more high-tech than that) that gave you the opportunity to look "inside" the human body? This accounting course offers something similar. To understand a business, you have to understand the financial insides of a business organization. An accounting course will help you understand the essential financial components of businesses. Whether you are looking at a large multinational company like Apple or Starbucks or a single-owner software consulting business or coffee shop, knowing the fundamentals of accounting will help you understand what is happening. As an employee, a manager, an investor, a business owner, or a director of your own personal finances—any of which roles you will have at some point in your life—you will make better decisions for having taken this course.*

> "Whether you are looking at a large multinational company like Apple or Starbucks or a single-owner software consulting business or coffee shop, knowing the fundamentals of accounting will help you understand what is happening."

Why This Book? *Hundreds of thousands of students have used this textbook. Your instructor has chosen it for you because of its trusted reputation. The authors have worked hard to keep the book fresh, timely, and accurate.*

This textbook contains features to help you learn best, whatever your learning style. We invite you to browse through pages xiv–xviii. These pages describe the main features you will find in this textbook and explain their purpose.

How to Succeed? *We've asked many students and many instructors whether there is a secret for success in this course. The nearly unanimous answer turns out to be not much of a secret: "Do the homework." This is one course where doing is learning. The more time you spend on the homework assignments—using the various tools that this textbook provides—the more likely you are to learn the essential concepts, techniques, and methods of accounting. Besides the textbook itself, the book's companion website also offers various support resources.*

Good luck in this course. We hope you enjoy the experience and that you put to good use throughout a lifetime of success the knowledge you obtain in this course. We are sure you will not be disappointed.

Jerry J. Weygandt
Paul D. Kimmel
Donald E. Kieso

Your Team for Success in Accounting

Wiley Accounting is your partner in accounting education. We want to be the first publisher you think of when it comes to quality content, reliable technology, innovative resources, professional training, and unparalleled support for your accounting classroom.

Your Wiley Accounting Team for Success is comprised of three distinctive advantages that you won't find with any other publisher:

Author Commitment
A Proven Author Team of Inspired Teachers

The Team for Success authors bring years of industry and academic experience to the development of each textbook that relates accounting concepts to real-world experiences. This cohesive team brings continuity of writing style, pedagogy, and problem material to each course from Principles to Intermediate so you and your students can seamlessly progress from introductory through advanced courses in accounting.

WileyPLUS
An Engaging System Plus an Experienced Team of Support Professionals

WileyPLUS is a research-based, online environment for effective teaching and learning. The *WileyPLUS* Account Managers understand the time constraints of busy instructors and act as your personal contact for training, course set-up, and other assistance.

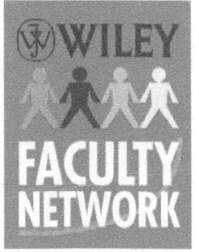

Wiley Faculty Network
A Team of Educators Dedicated to Your Professional Development

The Wiley Faculty Network (WFN) is a global group of seasoned accounting professionals who share best practices in teaching with their peers. Our Virtual Guest Lecture Series provides the opportunity you need for professional development in an online environment that is relevant, convenient, and collaborative. The quality of these seminars and workshops meets the strictest standards, so we are proud to be able to offer valuable CPE credits to attendees.

www.wileyteamforsuccess.com

Author Commitment
Collaboration. Innovation. Experience.

After decades of success as authors of textbooks like this one, Jerry Weygandt, Paul Kimmel, and Don Kieso understand that teaching accounting goes beyond simply presenting data. The authors are truly effective because they know that teaching is about telling compelling stories in ways that make each concept come to life.

Teacher / Author / Professional

Through their textbooks, supplements, online learning tools, and classrooms, these authors have developed a comprehensive pedagogy that engages students in learning and faculty with teaching.

These authors work together throughout the entire process. The end result is a true collaboration where each author brings his individual experience and talent to the development of every paragraph, page, and chapter, thus creating a well-rounded, thorough view on any given accounting topic.

Many Ways in One Direction

Our **Team for Success** has developed a teaching system that addresses every learning style. Each year brings new insights, feedback, ideas, and improvements on how to deliver the material to every student with a passion for the subject in a format that gives them the best chance to succeed.

The key to the team's approach is in understanding that, just as there are many different ways to learn, there are also many different ways to teach.

In Their Own Words

Visit the Wiley **Team for Success** website to hear from the authors first-hand as they discuss their teaching styles, collaboration, and the future of accounting.

www.wileyteamforsuccess.com

Author Commitment

Jerry Weygandt

Jerry J. Weygandt, PhD, CPA, is Arthur Andersen Alumni Emeritus Professor of Accounting at the University of Wisconsin—Madison. He holds a PhD in accounting from the University of Illinois. Articles by Professor Weygandt have appeared in the *Accounting Review, Journal of Accounting Research, Accounting Horizons, Journal of Accountancy*, and other academic and professional journals. These articles have examined such financial reporting issues as accounting for price-level adjustments, pensions, convertible securities, stock option contracts, and interim reports. Professor Weygandt is author of other accounting and financial reporting books and is a member of the American Accounting Association, the American Institute of Certified Public Accountants, and the Wisconsin Society of Certified Public Accountants. He has served on numerous committees of the American Accounting Association and as a member of the editorial board of the Accounting Review; he also has served as President and Secretary-Treasurer of the American Accounting Association. In addition, he has been actively involved with the American Institute of Certified Public Accountants and has been a member of the Accounting Standards Executive Committee (AcSEC) of that organization. He has served on the FASB task force that examined the reporting issues related to accounting for income taxes and served as a trustee of the Financial Accounting Foundation. Professor Weygandt has received the Chancellor's Award for Excellence in Teaching and the Beta Gamma Sigma Dean's Teaching Award. He is the recipient of the Wisconsin Institute of CPA's Outstanding Educator's Award and the Lifetime Achievement Award. In 2001 he received the American Accounting Association's Outstanding Educator Award.

Paul Kimmel

Paul D. Kimmel, PhD, CPA, received his bachelor's degree from the University of Minnesota and his doctorate in accounting from the University of Wisconsin. He is an Associate Professor at the University of Wisconsin—Milwaukee, and has public accounting experience with Deloitte & Touche (Minneapolis). He was the recipient of the UWM School of Business Advisory Council Teaching Award, the Reggie Taite Excellence in Teaching Award, and a three-time winner of the Outstanding Teaching Assistant Award at the University of Wisconsin. He is also a recipient of the Elijah Watts Sells Award for Honorary Distinction for his results on the CPA exam. He is a member of the American Accounting Association and the Institute of Management Accountants and has published articles in *Accounting Review, Accounting Horizons, Advances in Management Accounting, Managerial Finance, Issues in Accounting Education, Journal of Accounting Education*, as well as other journals. His research interests include accounting for financial instruments and innovation in accounting education. He has published papers and given numerous talks on incorporating critical thinking into accounting education, and helped prepare a catalog of critical thinking resources for the Federated Schools of Accountancy.

Don Kieso

Donald E. Kieso, PhD, CPA, received his bachelor's degree from Aurora University and his doctorate in accounting from the University of Illinois. He has served as chairman of the Department of Accountancy and is currently the KPMG Emeritus Professor of Accountancy at Northern Illinois University. He has public accounting experience with Price Waterhouse & Co. (San Francisco and Chicago) and Arthur Andersen & Co. (Chicago) and research experience with the Research Division of the American Institute of Certified Public Accountants (New York). He has done postdoctorate work as a Visiting Scholar at the University of California at Berkeley and is a recipient of NIU's Teaching Excellence Award and four Golden Apple Teaching Awards. Professor Kieso is the author of other accounting and business books and is a member of the American Accounting Association, the American Institute of Certified Public Accountants, and the Illinois CPA Society. He has served as a member of the Board of Directors of the Illinois CPA Society, then AACSB's Accounting Accreditation Committees, the State of Illinois Comptroller's Commission, as Secretary-Treasurer of the Federation of Schools of Accountancy, and as Secretary-Treasurer of the American Accounting Association. Professor Kieso is currently serving on the Board of Trustees and Executive Committee of Aurora University, as a member of the Board of Directors of Kishwaukee Community Hospital, and as Treasurer and Director of Valley West Community Hospital. From 1989 to 1993 he served as a charter member of the national Accounting Education Change Commission. He is the recipient of the Outstanding Accounting Educator Award from the Illinois CPA Society, the FSA's Joseph A. Silvoso Award of Merit, the NIU Foundation's Humanitarian Award for Service to Higher Education, a Distinguished Service Award from the Illinois CPA Society, and in 2003 an honorary doctorate from Aurora University.

WileyPLUS

WileyPLUS is a research-based, online environment for effective teaching and learning.

The market-leading homework experience in *WileyPLUS* offers:

A Blank Sheet of Paper Effect

The *WileyPLUS* homework experience, which includes type-ahead for account title entry, imitates a blank sheet of paper format so that students use recall memory when doing homework and will do better in class, on exams, and in their professions.

A Professional Worksheet Style

The professional, worksheet-style problem layouts help students master accounting skills while doing homework that directly applies to the classroom and the real world.

The Opportunity to Catch Mistakes Earlier

Multi-part problems further help students focus by providing feedback at the part-level. Students can catch their mistakes earlier and access content-specific resources at the point of learning.

WileyPLUS includes a full ebook, videos, interactive tutorials, assessment capabilities, and Blackboard integration.

STARR COMPANY
Trial Balance
June 30, 2014

	Debit	Credit
cal	$	
Cash		
Service Revenue		

Type-ahead feature for account title entry replaces drop-down menus.

WileyPLUS *with* ORION

WileyPLUS with ORION helps students learn by learning about them.

Based on cognitive science, **WileyPLUS with ORION** provides students with a personal, adaptive learning experience so they can build their proficiency on topics and use their study time most effectively.

WileyPLUS with ORION is great as:

- An adaptive pre-lecture tool that assesses your students' conceptual knowledge so they come to class better prepared.

- A personalized study guide that helps students understand both their strengths and the areas where they need to invest more time, especially in preparation for quizzes and exams.

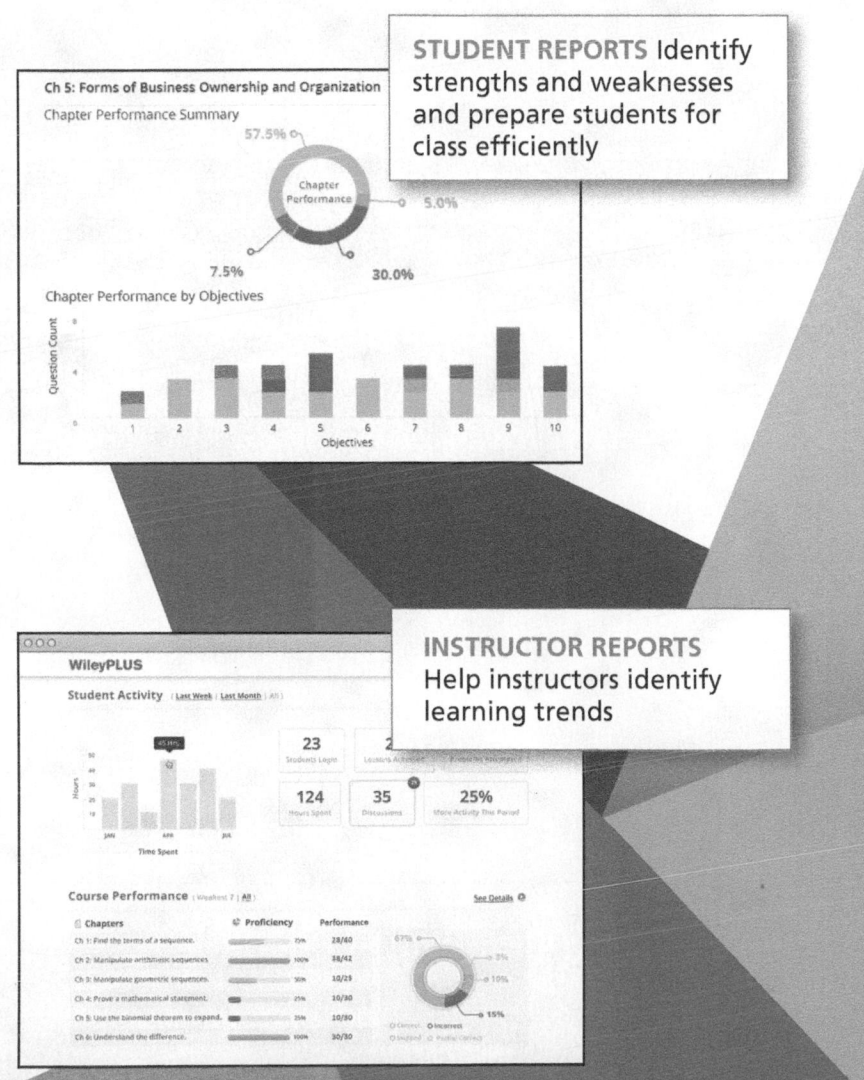

STUDENT REPORTS Identify strengths and weaknesses and prepare students for class efficiently

INSTRUCTOR REPORTS Help instructors identify learning trends

The Wiley Faculty Network

The Place Where Faculty Connect ...

The Wiley Faculty Network is a global community of faculty connected by a passion for teaching and a drive for learning and sharing. Connect with the Wiley Faculty Network to collaborate with your colleagues, find a mentor, attend virtual and live events, and view a wealth of resources all designed to help you grow as an educator. Embrace the art of teaching—great things happen where faculty connect!

Attend

Discover innovative ideas and gain knowledge you can use.

- Training
- Virtual Guest Lectures
- Live Events

View

Explore your resources and development opportunities.

- Teaching Resources
- Archived Guest Lectures
- Recorded Presentations
- Professional Development Modules

Collaborate

Connect with colleagues— your greatest resource.

- Find a Mentor
- Interest Groups
- Blog

Find out more at
www.wiley.com/college/wfn

Virtual Guest Lectures
Connect with recognized leaders across disciplines and collaborate with your peers on timely topics and discipline-specific issues. Many of these lectures offer CPE credit.

Live and Virtual Events
These invitation-only, discipline-specific events organized through a close partnership between WFN, Wiley, and the academic community event location.

Technology Training
Discover a wealth of topic- and technology training presented by subject matter experts, authors, and faculty where and when you

Teaching Resources
Propel your teaching and student learning next level with quality peer-reviewed testimonials, classroom tools, and

Connect with Colleagues
Achieve goals and tackle challenges enlisting the help of your peers and colleagues through the WFN your teaching experience.

WileyPLUS *with* ORION

WileyPLUS with **ORION** helps students learn by learning about them.

Based on cognitive science, **WileyPLUS** with **ORION** provides students with a personal, adaptive learning experience so they can build their proficiency on topics and use their study time most effectively.

WileyPLUS with **ORION** is great as:

- An adaptive pre-lecture tool that assesses your students' conceptual knowledge so they come to class better prepared.

- A personalized study guide that helps students understand both their strengths and the areas where they need to invest more time, especially in preparation for quizzes and exams.

STUDENT REPORTS Identify strengths and weaknesses and prepare students for class efficiently

INSTRUCTOR REPORTS Help instructors identify learning trends

The Wiley Faculty Network

The Place Where Faculty Connect ...

The Wiley Faculty Network is a global community of faculty connected by a passion for teaching and a drive for learning and sharing. Connect with the Wiley Faculty Network to collaborate with your colleagues, find a mentor, attend virtual and live events, and view a wealth of resources all designed to help you grow as an educator. Embrace the art of teaching—great things happen where faculty connect!

Attend

Discover innovative ideas and gain knowledge you can use.

- Training
- Virtual Guest Lectures
- Live Events

View

Explore your resources and development opportunities.

- Teaching Resources
- Archived Guest Lectures
- Recorded Presentations
- Professional Development Modules

Collaborate

Connect with colleagues— your greatest resource.

- Find a Mentor
- Interest Groups
- Blog

Find out more at
www.wiley.com/college/wfn

Virtual Guest Lectures
Connect with recognized leaders across disciplines and collaborate with your peers on timely topics and discipline-specific issues. Many of these lectures offer CPE credit.

Live and Virtual Events
These invitation-only, discipline-specific events are organized through a close partnership between the WFN, Wiley, and the academic community near the event location.

Technology Training
Discover a wealth of topic- and technology-specific training presented by subject matter experts, authors, and faculty where and when you need it.

Teaching Resources
Propel your teaching and student learning to the next level with quality peer-reviewed case studies, testimonials, classroom tools, and checklists.

Connect with Colleagues
Achieve goals and tackle challenges more easily by enlisting the help of your peers. Connecting with colleagues through the WFN can help you improve your teaching experience.

What's New?

The Ninth Edition expands our emphasis on student learning and improves upon a teaching and learning package that instructors and students have rated the highest in customer satisfaction in the following ways:

Continued Emphasis on Helping Students Learn Accounting Concepts

Especially with this edition of the textbook, we carefully scrutinized all chapter material to help students learn accounting concepts. Throughout all chapters, we added more explanations, examples, and illustrations. For example, we added T-accounts in margins to illustrate the effect of accounting procedures, and we discussed how tight credit policies nearly prevented Apple from fulfilling its first sale. Existing explanations were revised and illustrations re-imagined to increase student engagement.

WileyPLUS Enhancements

Over 50 new videos are included in the *WileyPLUS* course for this Ninth Edition. New videos include skill-based videos, narrated PowerPoint presentations, and problem-walkthrough videos.

Orion Adaptive Learning

Available in *WileyPLUS,* Orion is an adaptive study and practice tool that helps students build proficiency in course topics.

Enhanced Homework Material

In each chapter, we updated Self-Test Questions, Questions, Brief Exercises, **DO IT!** Review, Exercises, Problems, and Research Cases. Financial analysis and reporting problems provide students the opportunity to interact with real-world financial statements of Apple, PepsiCo, Coca-Cola, Amazon.com, and Wal-Mart. Finally, Considering People, Planet, and Profit problems are included to offer students experience in evaluating corporate social responsibility.

Updated Illustrations

As over 50% of the textbook is visual, we especially focused on the illustrations in this edition. For example, we added cash flow effects to the transaction analyses as well as revised all of the infographics, which reinforce important textual concepts.

Student-Friendly Companies

One of the goals of this accounting course is to orient students to the application of accounting principles and techniques in practice. Accordingly, we expanded our practice of using numerous examples from real companies throughout the textbook to add more high-interest enterprises that we hope will increase student engagement, such as Clif Bar, Groupon, and REI.

Content Changes by Chapter

Chapter 1: Accounting in Action
- New Feature Story, on Clif Bar and its open-book management program.

Chapter 2: The Recording Process
- Heavily revised Feature Story, now on MF Global's failure to segregate company accounts from customer accounts.
- Added cash flow effects in transaction illustrations, to raise student awareness of how business activities also affect a company's cash.
- New Ethics Insight, on Credit Suisse Group's failure to properly write down the value of its securities.
- New BYP problems: Real-World Focus based on *New York Times* article discussing Green Bay Packers' annual report publication, Ethics Case on résumé fabrications, and Considering People, Planet, and Profit on the role of auditor certifications in the coffee business.

Chapter 3: Adjusting the Accounts
- New Feature Story, on Groupon and the complexity of accounting for its revenues.
- Updated Appendix 3B, Concepts in Action, to reflect current conceptual framework which only includes one constraint, that of cost. Materiality now discussed as an aspect of relevance.

Chapter 5: Accounting for Merchandising Operations
- New Feature Story, on REI and its unique business model.
- Revised Ethics Insight, on improving company clarity of financial disclosures, by citing eBay's sale of Skype.
- Significantly added material to Appendix 5B, Periodic Inventory System, to ensure comprehensive coverage and explanatory material.

Chapter 6: Inventories
- Revised the Accounting Across the Organization on JIT inventory, to illustrate how common events like snowstorms can seriously disrupt inventory levels.
- New Accounting Across the Organization, on Sony's inventory management practices.

Chapter 7: Fraud, Internal Control, and Cash
- New material about rising international economic crime in the *A Look at IFRS* section.

- Updated chapter throughout to include use of more recent technology, such as point-of-sale terminals instead of cash registers.

Chapter 8: Accounting for Receivables
- Added T-account in margin in Percentage-of-Receivables section to assist in student understanding.

Chapter 10: Liabilities
- Expanded discussion and new **DO IT!** in Payroll and Payroll Taxes Payable section.
- New Accounting Across the Organization, about advantages for companies of issuing 30-year bonds.
- Revised Analysis section, for improved discussion on debt to assets ratio and times interest earned.

Chapter 11: Corporations: Organization, Stock Transactions, Dividends, and Retained Earnings
- New Accounting Across the Organization, about Facebook's recent IPO.

Chapter 12: Investments
- Updated Categories of Securities section, to provide more specific information on account titles and debt/stock categories.

Chapter 13: Statement of Cash Flows
- Updated Feature Story, to include more recent information about Apple's cash flow status.
- New Accounting Across the Organization, about Kodak's need to sell plant assets to raise cash.
- Presented appendix on statement of cash flows—direct method before the appendix on preparing a worksheet for the statement of cash flows—indirect method, for improved presentation of topics.

Chapter 14: Financial Statement Analysis
- Revised Feature Story on Warren Buffett, to increase student engagement.
- Used Macy's as example company throughout chapter.

Appendices A-F: Specimen Financial Statements
Now include financial statements for five student-friendly companies—Apple, PepsiCo, Coca-Cola, Amazon.com, and Wal-Mart—as well as instructions for accessing and using their complete annual reports. Appendix F presents the financial statements for Zetar plc, a U.K. manufacturer of candy and natural snacks.

Active Teaching and Learning Supplementary Material

For Instructors

Textbook Companion Website.   On this website, instructors will find electronic versions of the Solutions Manual, Test Bank, Instructor's Manual, Computerized Test Bank, and other resources.

Solutions Manual.   The Solutions Manual contains detailed solutions to all questions, brief exercises, DO IT! review, exercises, and problems in the textbook as well as suggested answers to the questions and *Broadening Your Perspective* problems.

Instructor's Manual.   Included in each chapter are lecture outlines, chapter reviews, and review quizzes.

Test Bank and Computerized Test Bank.
The test bank and computerized test bank allow instructors to tailor examinations according to learning objectives and learning outcomes, including professional standards.

PowerPoint™.   The PowerPoint™ presentations contain a combination of key concepts, images, and problems from the textbook.

For Students

Textbook Companion Website.   On this website, students will find PowerPoint presentations, web quizzing, and other resources. In addition, students can access the B Exercises, Challenge Exercises, C Problems, and Appendices H–J at this site. Finally, a full version of the Continuing Cookie Chronicle problem is included at the student website.

Excel Templates.   These spreadsheets allow students to complete select end-of-chapter exercises and problems identified by a spreadsheet icon in the textbook.

Study Guide.   A useful tool for review, the Study Guide provides an opportunity for practice through problems and multiple-choice exercises. Demonstration problems, multiple-choice questions, true/false, matching, and other exercises are also included.

General Ledger Software.   General ledger software allows students to solve select end-of-chapter text problems using a computerized accounting system. Problems are identified by an icon next to end-of-chapter textbook exercises and problems.

WileyPLUS.   Includes numerous tools that help students review and practice for exams, such as Excel working papers, narrated PowerPoint presentations, videos, and more.

Text Options

The Ninth Edition is available in the following different textbook options:
- *Financial Accounting*, 9e (ISBN: 978-1-118-33432-4)
- *Financial Accounting*, 9e, Binder-Ready Version (ISBN: 978-1-118-33843-8)
- *All Access Pack* (ISBN: 978-1-118-84474-8)

read it!

Feature Stories introduce chapter topics in fun ways using real-world companies that are engaging.

Issues that affect today's business world are highlighted in the textbook.

Comparative Analysis Problem: Amazon.com, Inc. vs. Wal-Mart Stores, Inc.

BYP2-3 Amazon.com, Inc.'s financial statements are presented in Appendix D. Financial statements for Wal-Mart Stores, Inc. are presented in Appendix E. Instructions for accessing and using the complete annual reports of Amazon and Wal-Mart, including the notes to the financial statements, are also provided in Appendices D and E, respectively.

Instructions
(a) Based on the information contained in the financial statements, determine the normal balance of the listed accounts for each company.

Amazon	Wal-Mart
1. Interest Expense	1. Net Sales Revenues
2. Cash and Cash Equivalents	2. Inventories
3. Accounts Payable	3. Cost of Sales

ANATOMY OF A FRAUD

Lawrence Fairbanks, the assistant vice-chancellor of communications at Aesop University, was allowed to make purchases of under $2,500 for his department without external approval. Unfortunately, he also sometimes bought items for himself, such as expensive antiques and other collectibles. How did he do it? He replaced the vendor invoices he received with fake vendor invoices that he created. The fake invoices had descriptions that were more consistent with the communications department's purchases. He submitted these fake invoices to the accounting department as the basis for their journal entries and to the accounts payable department as the basis for payment.

Total take: $475,000

THE MISSING CONTROL
Segregation of duties. The university had not properly segregated related purchasing activities. Lawrence was ordering items, receiving the items, and receiving the invoice. By receiving the invoice, he had control over the documents that were used to account for the purchase and thus was able to substitute a fake invoice.

Source: Adapted from Wells, *Fraud Casebook* (2007), pp. 3–15.

Financial Reporting and Analysis

Financial Reporting Problem: Apple Inc.

BYP3-1 The financial statements of Apple Inc. are presented in Appendix A at the end of this textbook. Instructions for accessing and using the company's complete annual report, including the notes to the financial statements, are also provided in Appendix A.

Insight Boxes highlight real-world company issues through international, ethical, and other examples.

ETHICS INSIGHT

Cooking the Books?

Allegations of abuse of the revenue recognition principle have become all too common in recent years. For example, it was alleged that Krispy Kreme sometimes doubled the number of doughnuts shipped to wholesale customers at the end of a quarter to boost quarterly results. The customers shipped the unsold doughnuts back after the beginning of the next quarter for a refund. Conversely, Computer Associates International was accused of backdating sales—that is, reporting a sale in one period that did not actually occur until the next period in order to achieve the earlier period's sales targets.

 What motivates sales executives and finance and accounting executives to participate in activities that result in inaccurate reporting of revenues? (See page 160.)

© Dean Turner/iStockphoto

A Look at IFRS

Fraud can occur anywhere. Because the three main factors that contribute to fraud are universal in nature, the principles of internal control activities are used globally by companies. While Sarbanes-Oxley (SOX) does not apply to non-U.S. companies, most large international companies have internal controls similar to those indicated in the chapter. IFRS and GAAP are also very similar in accounting for cash. *IAS No. 1 (revised),* "Presentation of Financial Statements," is the only standard that discusses issues specifically related to cash.

LEARNING OBJECTIVE 9
Compare the accounting procedures for fraud, internal control, and cash under GAAP and IFRS.

see it!

CONTENT FOR ALL LEARNING STYLES

In addition to a textbook consistently reviewed as very readable, over 50% of the textbook provides visual presentations and interpretations of content.

Equation Analysis Illustrations visually walk you through the steps of the recording process.

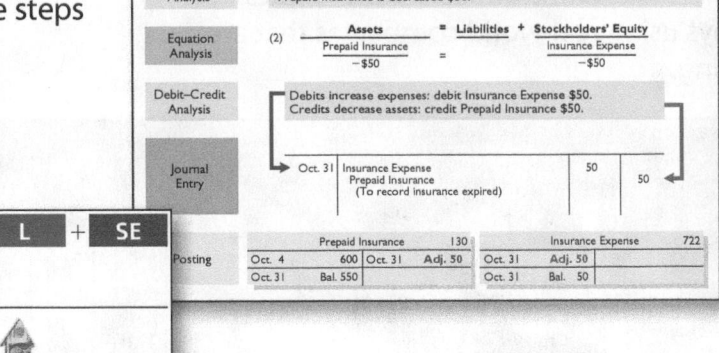

| Basic Analysis | The expense Insurance Expense is increased $50, and the asset Prepaid Insurance is decreased $50. |

Equation Analysis

$$(2) \quad \frac{\text{Assets}}{\text{Prepaid Insurance}} = \text{Liabilities} + \frac{\text{Stockholders' Equity}}{\text{Insurance Expense}}$$
$$-\$50 = -\$50$$

Debit–Credit Analysis: Debits increase expenses: debit Insurance Expense $50. Credits decrease assets: credit Prepaid Insurance $50.

Journal Entry:

Oct. 31	Insurance Expense	50	
	Prepaid Insurance		50
	(To record insurance expired)		

Posting:

Prepaid Insurance			130		Insurance Expense			722
Oct. 4	600	Oct. 31	Adj. 50	Oct. 31	Adj. 50		
Oct. 31	Bal. 550			Oct. 31	Bal. 50		

Cash Flow Analyses visually summarize the effects of transactions on cash flows.

| A | = | L | + | SE |

+200
−200

Cash Flows
+200

Retailer receives cash more quickly from credit card issuer

Infographics reinforce important textual concepts. All infographics are revised in the Ninth Edition.

Kildare Company has just signed a capitalizable lease contract for equipment that requires rental payments of $6,000 each, to be paid at the end of each of the next 5 years. The appropriate discount rate is 12%. What is the present value of the rental payments—that is, the amount used to capitalize the leased equipment?

PV = ? $6,000 $6,000 $6,000 $6,000 $6,000

$i = 12\%$

$n = 5$

Today   1   2   3   4   5 years

Answer: The present value factor from Table 4 is 3.60478 (5 payments at 12%). The present value of 5 payments of $6,000 each discounted at 12% is $21,628.68 ($6,000 × 3.60478).

Illustrations are clearly identified and often present data in a real-world format.

Academy Company.xls

ACADEMY COMPANY
Payroll Register
For the Week Ending January 14, 2014

		Earnings				Deductions					Paid		Account Debited
Employee	Total Hours	Regular	Over-time	Gross	FICA	Federal Income Tax	State Income Tax	United Fund	Union Dues	Total	Net Pay	Check No.	Salaries and Wages Expense
Office Salaries													
Arnold, Patricia	40	580.00		580.00	44.37	61.00	11.60	15.00		131.97	448.03	998	580.00
Canton, Matthew	40	590.00		590.00	45.14	63.00	11.80	20.00		139.94	450.06	999	590.00
Mueller, William	40	530.00		530.00	40.55	54.00	10.60	11.00		116.15	413.85	1000	530.00

www.wileyteamforsuccess.com

do it!

> **DO IT!**

Adjusting Entries for Accruals

Micro Computer Services Inc. began operations on August 1, 2015. At the end of August 2015, management prepares monthly financial statements. The following information relates to August.

1. At August 31, the company owed its employees $800 in salaries and wages that will be paid on September 1.
2. On August 1, the company borrowed $30,000 from a local bank on a 15-year mortgage. The annual interest rate is 10%.
3. Revenue for services performed but unrecorded for August totaled $1,100.

Prepare the adjusting entries needed at August 31, 2015.

Solution

Action Plan

✔ Make adjusting entries at the end of the period to recognize revenues for services performed and for expenses incurred.

✔ Don't forget to make adjusting entries for accruals. Adjusting entries for accruals will increase both a balance sheet and an income statement account.

1. Salaries and Wages Expense	800	
Salaries and Wages Payable		800
(To record accrued salaries)		
2. Interest Expense	250	
Interest Payable		250
(To record accrued interest:		
$30,000 \times 10\% \times \frac{1}{12} = $250)		
3. Accounts Receivable	1,100	
Service Revenue		1,100
(To record revenue for services performed)		

Related exercise material: BE3-2, BE3-7, E3-5, E3-6, E3-7, E3-8, E3-9, **and DO IT! 3-3.**

✔ **The Navigator**

DO IT! exercises in the textbook narrative provide step-by-step applications of a concept at the precise moment you acquire the knowledge. Each **DO IT!** in the textbook narrative includes an **Action Plan**, a **Solution**, and a path of related homework exercises.

Comprehensive DO IT! problems at the end of each chapter apply the **DO IT!** exercises and address **multiple** topics.

> **Comprehensive DO IT!**

The Green Thumb Lawn Care Inc. began operations on April 1. At April 30, the trial balance shows the following balances for selected accounts.

Prepaid Insurance	$ 3,600
Equipment	28,000
Notes Payable	20,000
Unearned Service Revenue	4,200
Service Revenue	1,800

> **DO IT! Review**

Identify timing concepts.
(LO 1, 2)

DO IT! 3-1 Several timing concepts are discussed on pages 104–105. A list of concepts is provided below in the left column, with a description of the concept in the right column. There are more descriptions provided than concepts. Match the description to the concept.

1. ____ Cash-basis accounting.
2. ____ Fiscal year.
3. ____ Revenue recognition principle.
4. ____ Expense recognition principle.

(a) Monthly and quarterly time periods.
(b) Accountants divide the economic life of a business into artificial time periods.
(c) Efforts (expenses) should be matched with accomplishments (revenues).
(d) Companies record revenues when they receive cash and record expenses when they pay out cash.

End-of-chapter **DO IT! Review** exercises provide further practice with alternate versions of the in-chapter **DO IT!** exercises.

get it!

IMPROVE DECISION-MAKING SKILLS

As an employee, manager, or even a director of your own personal finances, you will make better decisions by learning how to analyze and solve business problems using materials provided at the end of each chapter.

Broadening Your Perspective questions help you pull together concepts from a particular chapter and apply them to real-world business situations. Critical thinking, communication, ethics, and other questions are included in this section at the end of each textbook chapter.

Broadening Your **PERSPECTIVE**

Financial Reporting and Analysis

Financial Reporting Problem: Apple Inc.

BYP3-1 The financial statements of Apple Inc. are presented in Appendix A at the end of this textbook. Instructions for accessing and using the company's complete annual report, including the notes to the financial statements, are also provided in Appendix A.

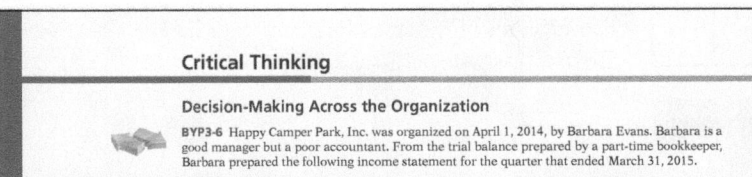

Critical Thinking

Decision-Making Across the Organization

BYP3-6 Happy Camper Park, Inc. was organized on April 1, 2014, by Barbara Evans. Barbara is a good manager but a poor accountant. From the trial balance prepared by a part-time bookkeeper, Barbara prepared the following income statement for the quarter that ended March 31, 2015.

Continuing Cookie Chronicle and **Comprehensive Problems** pull together concepts from multiple chapters and provide a macro perspective of accounting in action.

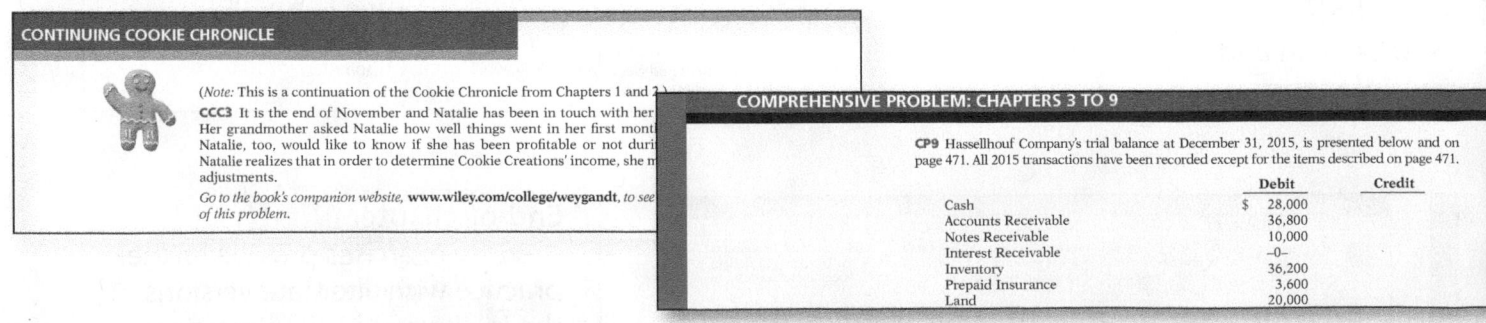

CONTINUING COOKIE CHRONICLE

(*Note:* This is a continuation of the Cookie Chronicle from Chapters 1 and 2.)

CCC3 It is the end of November and Natalie has been in touch with her Her grandmother asked Natalie how well things went in her first mont Natalie, too, would like to know if she has been profitable or not duri Natalie realizes that in order to determine Cookie Creations' income, she n adjustments.

Go to the book's companion website, **www.wiley.com/college/weygandt,** *to see of this problem.*

COMPREHENSIVE PROBLEM: CHAPTERS 3 TO 9

CP9 Hassellhouf Company's trial balance at December 31, 2015, is presented below and on page 471. All 2015 transactions have been recorded except for the items described on page 471.

	Debit	Credit
Cash	$ 28,000	
Accounts Receivable	36,800	
Notes Receivable	10,000	
Interest Receivable	–0–	
Inventory	36,200	
Prepaid Insurance	3,600	
Land	20,000	

kieso
weygandt
kimmel
warfield

team for success

Contents

Acknowledgments

Financial Accounting has benefited greatly from the input of focus group participants, manuscript reviewers, those who have sent comments by letter or e-mail, ancillary authors, and proofers. We greatly appreciate the constructive suggestions and innovative ideas of reviewers and the creativity and accuracy of the ancillary authors and checkers.

Ninth Edition

Shawn Abbott
College of the Siskiyous

Joseph Adamo
Cazenovia College

Pushpa Agrawal
University of Nebraska—Kearney

Sol Ahiarah
SUNY—Buffalo State

Lynn Almond
Virginia Polytechnic Institute

Elizabeth Ammann
Lindenwood University

Timothy Baker
California State University—Fresno

Lisa Banks
Mott Community College

Joyce Barden
DeVry University

Jeffrey Beatty
Fresno City College

Linda Bell
Park University

David Bojarsky
California State University—Long Beach

Jack Borke
University of Wisconsin—Platteville

Anna Boulware
St. Charles Community College

Linda Bressler
University of Houston—Downtown

Robert Brown
Evergreen Valley College

Amy Chang
San Francisco State University

Arthur College
Evergreen Valley College

Steven Day
Dixie State University

Frank Ehresmann
Mercy College

Lori Grady
Bucks County Community College

Andrew Griffith
Iona College

Jeffrey Haber
Iona College

Lynn Krausse
Bakersfield College

Jeffrey T. Kunz
Carroll University

Michael J. MacDonald
University of Wisconsin—Whitewater

Pam Meyer
University of Louisiana—Lafayette

Rosemary Nurre
College of San Mateo

Gary Olsen
Carroll University

Robert Russ
Northern Kentucky University

Susan Sandblom
Scottsdale Community College

Richard Sarkisian
Camden County College

Carl F. Shultz
Rider University

Gregory Sinclair
San Francisco State University

Kathleen J. Smith
University of Nebraska—Kearney

Suzanne Ward
University of Louisiana—Lafayette

Geri B. Wink
Colorado State University—Pueblo

Prior Editions

Dawn Addington
Central New Mexico Community College

Audrey Agnello
Niagara County Community College

John Ahmad
Northern Virginia Community College—Annandale

Matt Anderson
Michigan State University

Joe Anthony
Michigan State University

Art Baja
Ohlone College

Felicia Baldwin
City College of Chicago—Richard J. Daley

Colin Battle
Broward College

Beverly Beatty
Anne Arundel Community College

Jaswinder Bhangal
Chabot College

John Blahnik
Lorain County Community College

Brian Bratten
University of Kentucky—Lexington

Jerry Braun
Daytona State College

Leroy Bugger
Edison State College

Erin Burrell
University of Central Florida

Lisa Capozzoli
College of DuPage

Anne Cardozo
Broward College

Bruce Cassel
SUNY Dutchess Community College

Kimberly Charland
Kansas State University

Milton Chavez-Arias
Ohlone College

Kung Chen
University of Nebraska—Lincoln

Lisa Cole
Johnson County State College

Suzanne Counte
St. Louis Community College—Meramec

Kathy Crusto-Way
Tarrant County College

Robin D'Agati
Palm Beach State College

Karl Dahlberg
Rutgers University—Newark

Dori Danko
Grand Valley State University

Alan Davis
Community College of Philadelphia

Andrew DeJoseph
College of Mount Saint Vincent

Tony Dellarte
Luzerne County Community College

Naman Desai
University of Central Florida

Pam Donahue
Northern Essex Community College

Kathy Dunne
Rider University

Martin Epstein
Central New Mexico Community College

Ann Esarco
McHenry County College

Dora Estes
Volunteer State Community College

Caroline Falconetti
Nassau Community College

Mary Falkey
Prince George's Community College

Roger Gee
San Diego Mesa College

Severin Grabski
Michigan State University

Lori Grady
Bucks County Community College

Joyce Griffin
Kansas City Kansas Community College

Lester Hall
Danville Community College

Becky Hancock
El Paso Community College

Hassan Hefzi
California State Polytechnic University—Pomona

Janice Holmes
Louisiana State University—Baton Rouge

John Hoskins
University of Alabama—Huntsville

Leslie Hubbard
Solano Community College

Daniel Hunt
Ivy Tech Community College

Audrey Hunter
Broward College

John Illig
State College of Florida

Donna Johnston-Blair
Santa Clara University

Naomi Karolinski
Monroe Community College

Nancy Kelly
Middlesex Community College

Ridgway Knight
Santa Monica College

Kenneth Koerber
Bucks County Community College

Sandra Lang
McKendree University

Cathy Xanthaky Larson
Middlesex Community College

David Laurel
South Texas College

Michael Lawrence
Portland Community College

Pamela Legner
College of DuPage

Suneel Maheshwari
Marshall University

Lori Major
Luzerne County Community College

Linda Marquis
Northern Kentucky University

Jim Martin
University of Montevallo

Maureen McBeth
College of DuPage

Evelyn McDowell
Rider University

Jeanette Milius
Iowa Western Community College

Mary Beth Nelson
North Shore Community College

Oluwakemi Onwuchekwa
University of Central Florida

Hong Pak
California State Polytechnic University—Pomona

Glenn Pate
Palm Beach State College

Richard Pettit
Mountain View College

Yvonne Phang
Borough of Manhattan Community College

Mike Prockton
Finger Lakes Community College

Jessica Rakow
Louisiana State University

Raymond Reisig
Pace University—Pleasantville

Richard Sarkisian
Camden County College

Mark Savitskie
Wayne State University

Beth Secrest
Walsh University

William Serafin
Community College of Allegheny County

Walter Silva
Massachusetts Bay Community College

Lois Slutsky
Broward College

Chuck Smith
Iowa Western Community College

Ashley Soliz
Delta State University

Jalal Soroosh
Loyola University Maryland

Frank Stangota
Rutgers University

Dennis Stovall
Grand Valley State University

Grace Stuart-Tuggle
Palm Beach State College

Shafi Ullah
Broward College

Richard Van Ness
Schenectady County Community College

Cynthia Vanoosterum
Ivy Tech Community College

Robert Walsh
University of Dallas

Barbara Warschawski
Schenectady County Community College

Bob Willis
Rogers State University

Jeffrey Wong
Bellevue College

Marj Yuschak
Rutgers University—New Brunswick

WileyPLUS Developers and Reviewers

Carole Brandt-Fink
Laura McNally
Melanie Yon

Ancillary Authors, Contributors, Proofers, and Accuracy Checkers

Ellen Bartley
St. Joseph's College (New York)

LuAnn Bean
Florida Institute of Technology

Jack Borke
University of Wisconsin—Platteville

Sandra Cohen
Columbia College Chicago

Larry Falcetto
Emporia State University

Coby Harmon
University of California—Santa Barbara

Derek Jackson
Saint Mary's University of Minnesota

Douglas Kieso
Aurora University

Jill Misuraca
Central Connecticut State University

Barbara Muller
Arizona State University

Yvonne Phang
Borough of Manhattan Community College

Laura Prosser
Black Hills State University

Lynn Stallworth
Appalachian State University

Teresa Speck
Saint Mary's University of Minnesota

Domenico Tavella
Pittsburgh Technical Institute

Sheila Viel
University of Wisconsin—Milwaukee

Dick Wasson
San Diego State University

We appreciate the exemplary support and commitment given to us by senior acquisitions editor Michael McDonald, customer and market development manager Christopher DeJohn, senior marketing manager Karolina Zarychta Honsa, operations manager Yana Mermel, project editor Ed Brislin, development editors Terry Ann Tatro and Margaret Thompson, senior product designer Allie Morris, product designer Greg Chaput, designers Maureen Eide and Kristine Carney, photo editor Mary Ann Price, Denise Showers at Aptara, Cyndy Taylor, project manager Alverne Bell at Integra, and Steve Martel at SPI Global. All of these professionals provided innumerable services that helped the textbook take shape.

Finally, our thanks to Amy Scholz, Susan Elbe, George Hoffman, Tim Stookesberry, Joe Heider, and Steve Smith for their support and leadership in Wiley's College Division.

We will appreciate suggestions and comments from users—instructors and students alike. You can send your thoughts and ideas about the textbook to us via email at: *wileyauthorfeedback@gmail.com.*

Jerry J. Weygandt   Paul D. Kimmel   Donald E. Kieso
Madison, Wisconsin   Milwaukee, Wisconsin   DeKalb, Illinois

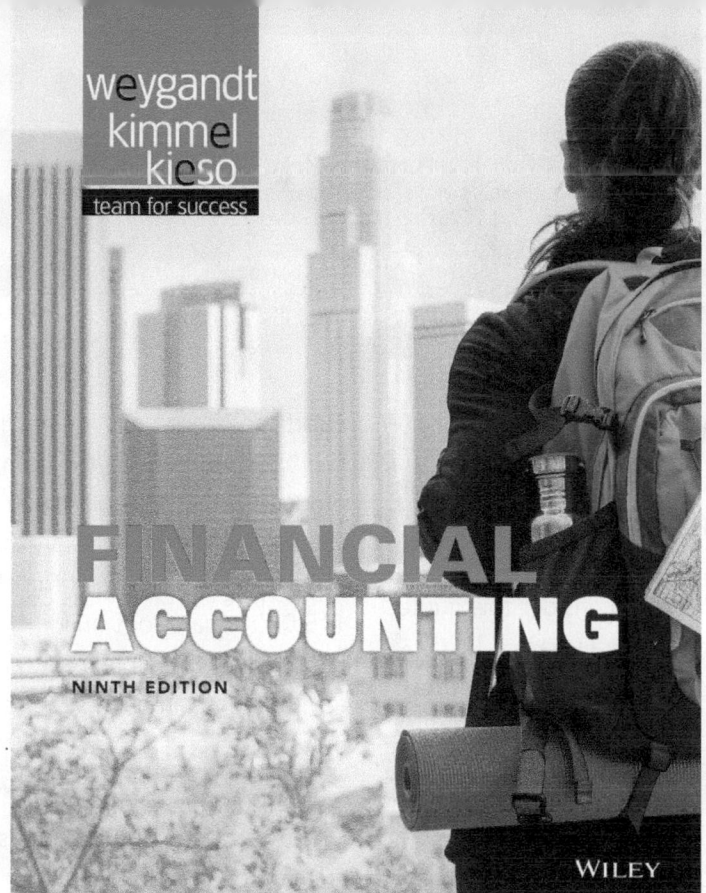

weygandt
kimmel
kieso
team for success

FINANCIAL
ACCOUNTING

NINTH EDITION

WILEY

1 | Accounting in Action

Feature Story

*The **Feature Story** helps you picture how the chapter topic relates to the real world of accounting and business. You will find references to the story throughout the chapter.*

Knowing the Numbers

Many students who take this course do not plan to be accountants. If you are in that group, you might be thinking, "If I'm not going to be an accountant, why do I need to know accounting?" Well, consider this quote from Harold Geneen, the former chairman of IT&T: "To be good at your business, you have to know the numbers—cold." In business, accounting and financial statements are the means for communicating the numbers. If you don't know how to read financial statements, you can't really know your business.

Many businesses agree with this view. They see the value of their employees being able to read financial statements and understand how their actions affect the company's financial results. For example, consider Clif Bar & Company. The original Clif Bar® energy bar was created in 1990 by Gary Erickson and his mother in her kitchen. Today, the company has almost 300 employees.

Clif Bar is guided by what it calls its Five Aspirations— Sustaining Our Business, Our Brands, Our People, Our Community, and the Planet. Its website documents its efforts and accomplishments in these five areas. Just a few examples include the company's use of organic products to protect soil, water, and biodiversity; the "smart" solar array (the largest in North America), which provides nearly all the electrical needs for its 115,000-square foot building; and the incentives Clif Bar provides to employees to reduce their personal environmental impact, such as $6,500 toward the purchase of an efficient car or $1,000 per year for eco-friendly improvements toward their homes.

One of the company's proudest moments was the creation of an employee stock ownership plan (ESOP) in 2010. This plan gives its employees 20% ownership of the company (Gary and his wife Kit own the other 80%). The ESOP also resulted in Clif Bar enacting an open-book management program, including the commitment to educate all employee-owners about its finances. Armed with this basic financial knowledge, employees are more aware of the financial impact of their actions, which leads to better decisions.

Many other companies have adopted this open-book management approach. But even in companies that do

---

*The **Navigator** is a learning system designed to prompt you to use the learning aids in the chapter and set priorities as you study.*

 The Navigator

- ■ Scan Learning Objectives
- ■ Read Feature Story
- ■ Read Preview
- ■ Read text and answer **DO IT!** p. 11
  - ■ p. 14   ■ p. 21   ■ p. 26
- ■ Work Comprehensive **DO IT!** p. 26
- ■ Review Summary of Learning Objectives
- ■ Answer Self-Test Questions
- ■ Complete Assignments
- ■ Go to *WileyPLUS* for practice and tutorials
- Read **A Look at IFRS** p. 50

Learning Objectives give you a framework for learning the specific concepts covered in the chapter.

Learning Objectives   The Navigator

After studying this chapter, you should be able to:

[1] Explain what accounting is.

[2] Identify the users and uses of accounting.

[3] Understand why ethics is a fundamental business concept.

[4] Explain generally accepted accounting principles.

[5] Explain the monetary unit assumption and the economic entity assumption.

[6] State the accounting equation, and define its components.

[7] Analyze the effects of business transactions on the accounting equation.

[8] Understand the four financial statements and how they are prepared.

©Dan Moore/iStockphoto

not practice open-book management, employers generally assume that managers in all areas of the company are "financially literate."

Taking this course will go a long way to making you financially literate. In this textbook, you will learn how to read and prepare financial statements, and how to use basic tools to evaluate financial results. Throughout this textbook, we attempt to increase your familiarity with financial reporting by providing numerous references, questions, and exercises that encourage you to explore the financial statements of well-known companies.

Preview of Chapter 1

The **Preview** *describes and outlines the major topics and subtopics you will see in the chapter.*

 ✔ **The Navigator**

The opening story about Clif Bar & Company highlights the importance of having good financial information and knowing how to use it to make effective business decisions. Whatever your pursuits or occupation, the need for financial information is inescapable. You cannot earn a living, spend money, buy on credit, make an investment, or pay taxes without receiving, using, or dispensing financial information. Good decision-making depends on good information.

The purpose of this chapter is to show you that accounting is the system used to provide useful financial information. The content and organization of Chapter 1 are as follows.

ACCOUNTING IN ACTION

What Is Accounting?	The Building Blocks of Accounting	The Basic Accounting Equation	Using the Accounting Equation	Financial Statements
• Three activities • Who uses accounting data	• Ethics in financial reporting • Generally accepted accounting principles • Measurement principles • Assumptions	• Assets • Liabilities • Stockholders' equity	• Transaction analysis • Summary of transactions	• Income statement • Retained earnings statement • Balance sheet • Statement of cash flows

What Is Accounting?

What consistently ranks as one of the top career opportunities in business? What frequently rates among the most popular majors on campus? What was the undergraduate degree chosen by Nike founder Phil Knight, Home Depot co-founder Arthur Blank, former acting director of the Federal Bureau of Investigation (FBI) Thomas Pickard, and numerous members of Congress? Accounting.[1] Why did these people choose accounting? They wanted to understand what was happening financially to their organizations. Accounting is the financial information system that provides these insights. In short, to understand your organization, you have to know the numbers.

Accounting consists of three basic activities—it **identifies**, **records**, and **communicates** the economic events of an organization to interested users. Let's take a closer look at these three activities.

Three Activities

As a starting point to the accounting process, a company **identifies the economic events relevant to its business**. Examples of economic events are the sale of snack chips by PepsiCo, the provision of telephone services by AT&T, and the payment of wages by Ford Motor Company.

Once a company like PepsiCo identifies economic events, it **records** those events in order to provide a history of its financial activities. Recording consists of keeping a **systematic**, **chronological diary of events**, measured in dollars and cents. In recording, PepsiCo also classifies and summarizes economic events.

Finally, PepsiCo **communicates** the collected information to interested users by means of **accounting reports**. The most common of these reports are called **financial statements**. To make the reported financial information meaningful, PepsiCo reports the recorded data in a standardized way. It accumulates information resulting from similar transactions. For example, PepsiCo accumulates all sales transactions over a certain period of time and reports the data as one amount in the company's financial statements. Such data are said to be reported **in the aggregate**. By presenting the recorded data in the aggregate, the accounting process simplifies a multitude of transactions and makes a series of activities understandable and meaningful.

A vital element in communicating economic events is the accountant's ability to **analyze and interpret** the reported information. Analysis involves use of ratios, percentages, graphs, and charts to highlight significant financial trends and relationships. Interpretation involves **explaining the uses**, **meaning**, **and limitations of reported data**. Appendices A–E show the financial statements of Apple Inc., PepsiCo, Inc., The Coca-Cola Company, Amazon.com, Inc., and Wal-Mart Stores, Inc., respectively. (In addition, in the *A Look at IFRS* section at the end of each chapter, the U.K. company Zetar plc is analyzed.) We refer to these statements at various places throughout the textbook. At this point, these financial statements probably strike you as complex and confusing. By the end of this course, you'll be surprised at your ability to understand, analyze, and interpret them.

Illustration 1-1 summarizes the activities of the accounting process.

---

[1]The appendix to this chapter describes job opportunities for accounting majors and explains why accounting is such a popular major.

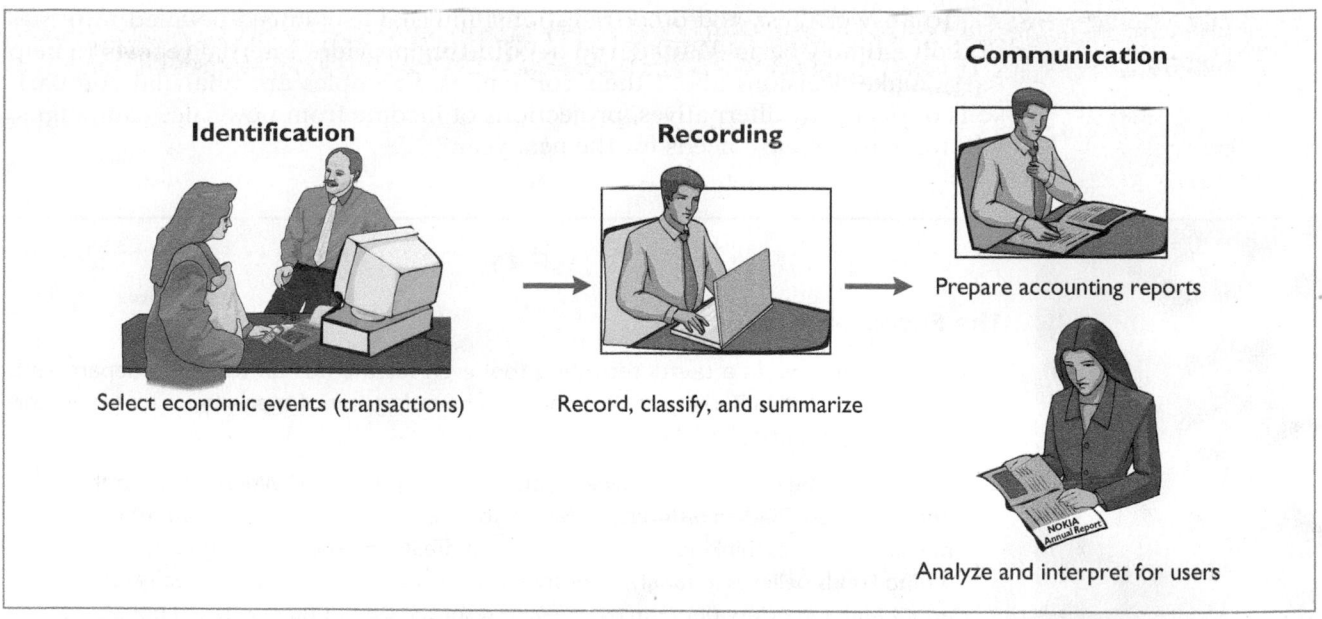

Identification
Select economic events (transactions)

Recording
Record, classify, and summarize

Communication
Prepare accounting reports

Analyze and interpret for users

Illustration 1-1
The activities of the accounting process

Essential terms are printed in blue when they first appear, and are defined in the end-of-chapter glossary.

You should understand that the accounting process **includes** the bookkeeping function. **Bookkeeping** usually involves **only** the recording of economic events. It is therefore just one part of the accounting process. In total, accounting involves **the entire process of identifying, recording, and communicating economic events.**[2]

Who Uses Accounting Data

The financial information that users need depends upon the kinds of decisions they make. There are two broad groups of users of financial information: internal users and external users.

> **LEARNING OBJECTIVE   2**
>
> Identify the users and uses of accounting.

INTERNAL USERS

Internal users of accounting information are managers who plan, organize, and run the business. These include marketing managers, production supervisors, finance directors, and company officers. In running a business, internal users must answer many important questions, as shown in Illustration 1-2.

Questions Asked by Internal Users

Snack chips   Beverages

Finance	**Marketing**	**Human Resources**	**Management**
Is cash sufficient to pay dividends to Microsoft stockholders?	What price should Apple charge for an iPod to maximize the company's net income?	Can General Motors afford to give its employees pay raises this year?	Which PepsiCo product line is the most profitable? Should any product lines be eliminated?

Illustration 1-2
Questions that internal users ask

---

[2]The origins of accounting are generally attributed to the work of Luca Pacioli, an Italian Renaissance mathematician. Pacioli was a close friend and tutor to Leonardo da Vinci and a contemporary of Christopher Columbus. In his 1494 text *Summa de Arithmetica, Geometria, Proportione et Proportionalite*, Pacioli described a system to ensure that financial information was recorded efficiently and accurately.

To answer these and other questions, internal users need detailed information on a timely basis. **Managerial accounting** provides internal reports to help users make decisions about their companies. Examples are financial comparisons of operating alternatives, projections of income from new sales campaigns, and forecasts of cash needs for the next year.

ACCOUNTING ACROSS THE ORGANIZATION

The Scoop on Accounting

Accounting can serve as a useful recruiting tool even for the human resources department. Rhino Foods, located in Burlington, Vermont, is a manufacturer of specialty ice cream. Its corporate website includes the following:

"Wouldn't it be great to work where you were part of a team? Where your input and hard work made a difference? Where you weren't kept in the dark about what management was thinking? . . . Well—it's not a dream! It's the way we do business . . . Rhino Foods believes in family, honesty and open communication—we really care about and appreciate our employees—and it shows. Operating results are posted and monthly group meetings inform all employees about what's happening in the Company. Employees also share in the Company's profits, in addition to having an excellent comprehensive benefits package."

Source: www.rhinofoods.com/workforus/workforus.html.

? What are the benefits to the company and to the employees of making the financial statements available to all employees? (See page 49.)

Accounting Across the Organization boxes demonstrate applications of accounting information in various business functions.

EXTERNAL USERS

External users are individuals and organizations outside a company who want financial information about the company. The two most common types of external users are investors and creditors. **Investors** (owners) use accounting information to decide whether to buy, hold, or sell ownership shares of a company. **Creditors** (such as suppliers and bankers) use accounting information to evaluate the risks of granting credit or lending money. Illustration 1-3 shows some questions that investors and creditors may ask.

Questions Asked by External Users

Investors
Is General Electric earning satisfactory income?

Investors
How does Disney compare in size and profitability with Time Warner?

Creditors
Will United Airlines be able to pay its debts as they come due?

Illustration 1-3
Questions that external users ask

Financial accounting answers these questions. It provides economic and financial information for investors, creditors, and other external users. The information needs of external users vary considerably. **Taxing authorities**, such as the Internal Revenue Service, want to know whether the company complies with tax laws. **Regulatory agencies**, such as the Securities and Exchange Commission or the Federal Trade Commission, want to know whether the company is operating within prescribed rules. **Customers** are interested in whether a company like General Motors will continue to honor product warranties and support its product lines. **Labor unions** such as the Major League Baseball Players Association want to know whether the owners have the ability to pay increased wages and benefits.

The Building Blocks of Accounting

A doctor follows certain standards in treating a patient's illness. An architect follows certain standards in designing a building. An accountant follows certain standards in reporting financial information. For these standards to work, a fundamental business concept must be at work—ethical behavior.

> **LEARNING OBJECTIVE   3**
>
> Understand why ethics is a fundamental business concept.

Ethics in Financial Reporting

People won't gamble in a casino if they think it is "rigged." Similarly, people won't play the stock market if they think stock prices are rigged. In recent years, the financial press has been full of articles about financial scandals at Enron, WorldCom, HealthSouth, AIG, and other companies. As the scandals came to light, mistrust of financial reporting in general grew. One article in the *Wall Street Journal* noted that "repeated disclosures about questionable accounting practices have bruised investors' faith in the reliability of earnings reports, which in turn has sent stock prices tumbling." Imagine trying to carry on a business or invest money if you could not depend on the financial statements to be honestly prepared. Information would have no credibility. There is no doubt that a sound, well-functioning economy depends on accurate and dependable financial reporting.

United States regulators and lawmakers were very concerned that the economy would suffer if investors lost confidence in corporate accounting because of unethical financial reporting. In response, Congress passed the **Sarbanes-Oxley Act (SOX)**. Its intent is to reduce unethical corporate behavior and decrease the likelihood of future corporate scandals. As a result of SOX, top management must now certify the accuracy of financial information. In addition, penalties for fraudulent financial activity are much more severe. Also, SOX increased the independence requirements of the outside auditors who review the accuracy of corporate financial statements and increased the oversight role of boards of directors.

The standards of conduct by which actions are judged as right or wrong, honest or dishonest, fair or not fair, are **ethics**. Effective financial reporting depends on sound ethical behavior. To sensitize you to ethical situations in business and to give you practice at solving ethical dilemmas, we address ethics in a number of ways in this textbook:

1. A number of the *Feature Stories* and other parts of the textbook discuss the central importance of ethical behavior to financial reporting.

> **Ethics Note**
>
> Circus-founder P.T. Barnum is alleged to have said, "Trust everyone, but cut the deck." What Sarbanes-Oxley does is to provide measures that (like cutting the deck of playing cards) help ensure that fraud will not occur.

Ethics Notes help sensitize you to some of the ethical issues in accounting.

2. *Ethics Insight* boxes and marginal *Ethics Notes* highlight ethics situations and issues in actual business settings.

3. Many of the *People, Planet, and Profit Insight* boxes focus on ethical issues that companies face in measuring and reporting social and environmental issues.

4. At the end of the chapter, an *Ethics Case* simulates a business situation and asks you to put yourself in the position of a decision-maker in that case.

When analyzing these various ethics cases, as well as experiences in your own life, it is useful to apply the three steps outlined in Illustration 1-4.

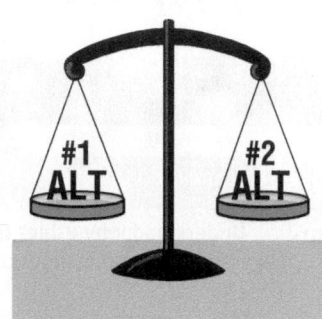

1. Recognize an ethical situation and the ethical issues involved.	**2. Identify and analyze the principal elements in the situation.**	**3. Identify the alternatives, and weigh the impact of each alternative on various stakeholders.**
Use your personal ethics to identify ethical situations and issues. Some businesses and professional organizations provide written codes of ethics for guidance in some business situations.	Identify the **stakeholders**—persons or groups who may be harmed or benefited. Ask the question: What are the responsibilities and obligations of the parties involved?	Select the most ethical alternative, considering all the consequences. Sometimes there will be one right answer. Other situations involve more than one right solution; these situations require an evaluation of each and a selection of the best alternative.

Illustration 1-4
Steps in analyzing ethics cases and situations

Insight boxes provide examples of business situations from various perspectives—ethics, investor, international, and corporate social responsibility. Guideline answers are provided near the end of the chapter.

Gemunu Amarasinghe/AP Photo

ETHICS INSIGHT

The Numbers Behind Not-for-Profit Organizations

Accounting plays an important role for a wide range of business organizations worldwide. Just as the integrity of the numbers matters for business, it matters at least as much at not-for-profit organizations. Proper control and reporting help ensure that money is used the way donors intended. Donors are less inclined to give to an organization if they think the organization is subject to waste or theft. The accounting challenges of some large international not-for-profits rival those of the world's largest businesses. For example, after the Haitian earthquake, the Haitian-born musician Wyclef Jean was criticized for the poor accounting controls in a relief fund that he founded. In response, he hired a new accountant and improved the transparency regarding money raised and spent.

 What benefits does a sound accounting system provide to a not-for-profit organization? (See page 49.)

Generally Accepted Accounting Principles

The accounting profession has developed standards that are generally accepted and universally practiced. This common set of standards is called **generally accepted accounting principles (GAAP)**. These standards indicate how to report economic events.

The primary accounting standard-setting body in the United States is the **Financial Accounting Standards Board (FASB)**. The **Securities and Exchange Commission (SEC)** is the agency of the U.S. government that oversees U.S. financial markets and accounting standard-setting bodies. The SEC relies on the FASB to develop accounting standards, which public companies must follow. Many countries outside of the United States have adopted the accounting standards issued by the **International Accounting Standards Board (IASB)**. These standards are called **International Financial Reporting Standards (IFRS)**.

As markets become more global, it is often desirable to compare the results of companies from different countries that report using different accounting standards. In order to increase comparability, in recent years the two standard-setting bodies have made efforts to reduce the differences between U.S. GAAP and IFRS. This process is referred to as **convergence**. As a result of these convergence efforts, it is likely that someday there will be a single set of high-quality accounting standards that are used by companies around the world. Because convergence is such an important issue, we highlight any major differences between GAAP and IFRS in *International Notes* (as shown in the margin here) and provide a more in-depth discussion in the *A Look at IRFS* section at the end of each chapter.

International Note

Over 100 countries use International Financial Reporting Standards (called IFRS). For example, all companies in the European Union follow international standards. The differences between U.S. and international standards are not generally significant.

International Notes highlight differences between U.S. and international accounting standards.

Measurement Principles

GAAP generally uses one of two measurement principles, the historical cost principle or the fair value principle. Selection of which principle to follow generally relates to trade-offs between relevance and faithful representation. **Relevance** means that financial information is capable of making a difference in a decision. **Faithful representation** means that the numbers and descriptions match what really existed or happened—they are factual.

Helpful Hint
Relevance and *faithful representation* are two primary qualities that make accounting information useful for decision-making.

Helpful Hints further clarify concepts being discussed.

HISTORICAL COST PRINCIPLE
The **historical cost principle** (or cost principle) dictates that companies record assets at their cost. This is true not only at the time the asset is purchased, but also over the time the asset is held. For example, if Best Buy purchases land for $360,000, the company initially reports it in its accounting records at $360,000. But what does Best Buy do if, by the end of the next year, the fair value of the land has increased to $400,000? Under the historical cost principle, it continues to report the land at $360,000.

FAIR VALUE PRINCIPLE
The **fair value principle** states that assets and liabilities should be reported at fair value (the price received to sell an asset or settle a liability). Fair value information may be more useful than historical cost for certain types of assets and liabilities. For example, certain investment securities are reported at fair value because market price information is usually readily available for these types of assets. In determining which measurement principle to use, companies weigh the factual nature of cost figures versus the relevance of fair value. In general, most companies choose to use cost. Only in situations where assets are actively traded, such as investment securities, do companies apply the fair value principle extensively.

INTERNATIONAL INSIGHT

The Korean Discount

If you think that accounting standards don't matter, consider recent events in South Korea. For many years, international investors complained that the financial reports of South Korean companies were inadequate and inaccurate. Accounting practices there often resulted in huge differences between stated revenues and actual revenues. Because investors did not have faith in the accuracy of the numbers, they were unwilling to pay as much for the shares of these companies relative to shares of comparable companies in different countries. This difference in stock price was often referred to as the "Korean discount."

In response, Korean regulators decided that, beginning in 2011, companies would comply with international accounting standards. This change was motivated by a desire to "make the country's businesses more transparent" in order to build investor confidence and spur economic growth. Many other Asian countries, including China, India, Japan, and Hong Kong, have also decided either to adopt international standards or to create standards that are based on the international standards.

Source: Evan Ramstad, "End to 'Korea Discount'?" *Wall Street Journal* (March 16, 2007).

? What is meant by the phrase "make the country's businesses more transparent"? Why would increasing transparency spur economic growth? (See page 49.)

SeongJoonCho/Bloomberg/Getty Images, Inc.

Assumptions

LEARNING OBJECTIVE   5

Explain the monetary unit assumption and the economic entity assumption.

Assumptions provide a foundation for the accounting process. Two main assumptions are the **monetary unit assumption** and the **economic entity assumption**.

MONETARY UNIT ASSUMPTION

The **monetary unit assumption** requires that companies include in the accounting records only transaction data that can be expressed in money terms. This assumption enables accounting to quantify (measure) economic events. The monetary unit assumption is vital to applying the historical cost principle.

This assumption prevents the inclusion of some relevant information in the accounting records. For example, the health of a company's owner, the quality of service, and the morale of employees are not included. The reason: Companies cannot quantify this information in money terms. Though this information is important, companies record only events that can be measured in money.

ECONOMIC ENTITY ASSUMPTION

Ethics Note

The importance of the economic entity assumption is illustrated by scandals involving Adelphia. In this case, senior company employees entered into transactions that blurred the line between the employees' financial interests and those of the company. For example, Adelphia guaranteed over $2 billion of loans to the founding family.

An economic entity can be any organization or unit in society. It may be a company (such as Crocs, Inc.), a governmental unit (the state of Ohio), a municipality (Seattle), a school district (St. Louis District 48), or a church (Southern Baptist). The **economic entity assumption** requires that the activities of the entity be kept separate and distinct from the activities of its owner and all other economic entities. To illustrate, Sally Rider, owner of Sally's Boutique, must keep her personal living costs separate from the expenses of her business. Similarly, McDonald's, Coca-Cola, and Cadbury-Schweppes are segregated into separate economic entities for accounting purposes.

PROPRIETORSHIP A business owned by one person is generally a **proprietorship**. The owner is often the manager/operator of the business.

Small service-type businesses (plumbing companies, beauty salons, and auto repair shops), farms, and small retail stores (antique shops, clothing stores, and used-book stores) are often proprietorships. **Usually, only a relatively small amount of money (capital) is necessary to start in business as a proprietorship. The owner (proprietor) receives any profits, suffers any losses, and is personally liable for all debts of the business.** There is no legal distinction between the business as an economic unit and the owner, but the accounting records of the business activities are kept separate from the personal records and activities of the owner.

PARTNERSHIP A business owned by two or more persons associated as partners is a partnership. In most respects a partnership is like a proprietorship except that more than one owner is involved. Typically, a partnership agreement (written or oral) sets forth such terms as initial investment, duties of each partner, division of net income (or net loss), and settlement to be made upon death or withdrawal of a partner. Each partner generally has unlimited personal liability for the debts of the partnership. **Like a proprietorship, for accounting purposes the partnership transactions must be kept separate from the personal activities of the partners.** Partnerships are often used to organize retail and service-type businesses, including professional practices (lawyers, doctors, architects, and certified public accountants).

CORPORATION A business organized as a separate legal entity under state corporation law and having ownership divided into transferable shares of stock is a corporation. The holders of the shares (stockholders) **enjoy limited liability**; that is, they are not personally liable for the debts of the corporate entity. Stockholders **may transfer all or part of their ownership shares to other investors at any time** (i.e., sell their shares). The ease with which ownership can change adds to the attractiveness of investing in a corporation. Because ownership can be transferred without dissolving the corporation, the corporation **enjoys an unlimited life**.

Although the combined number of proprietorships and partnerships in the United States is more than five times the number of corporations, the revenue produced by corporations is eight times greater. Most of the largest companies in the United States—for example, ExxonMobil, Ford, Wal-Mart Stores, Inc., Citigroup, and Apple—are corporations.

*The **DO IT!** exercises ask you to put newly acquired knowledge to work. They outline the **Action Plan** necessary to complete the exercise, and they show a **Solution**.*

> **DO IT!**

Basic Concepts

Indicate whether each of the five statements presented below is true or false. If false, indicate how to correct the statement.

1. The three steps in the accounting process are identification, recording, and communication.
2. The two most common types of external users are investors and company officers.
3. Congress passed the Sarbanes-Oxley Act to reduce unethical behavior and decrease the likelihood of future corporate scandals.
4. The primary accounting standard-setting body in the United States is the Financial Accounting Standards Board (FASB).
5. The historical cost principle dictates that companies record assets at their cost. In later periods, however, the fair value of the asset must be used if fair value is higher than its cost.

Action Plan

✔ Review the basic concepts learned to date.

✔ Develop an understanding of the key terms used.

Solution

1. True　2. False. The two most common types of external users are investors and creditors. 3. True. 4. True. 5. False. The historical cost principle dictates that companies record assets at their cost. Under the historical cost principle, the company must also use cost in later periods.

Related exercise material: E1-1, E1-2, E1-3, E1-4, **and** DO IT! 1-1.

✔ **The Navigator**

Josef Volavka/iStockphoto

ACCOUNTING ACROSS THE ORGANIZATION

Spinning the Career Wheel

How will the study of accounting help you? A working knowledge of accounting is desirable for virtually every field of business. Some examples of how accounting is used in business careers include:

General management: Managers of Ford Motors, Massachusetts General Hospital, California State University—Fullerton, a McDonald's franchise, and a Trek bike shop all need to understand accounting data in order to make wise business decisions.

Marketing: A marketing specialist at Procter & Gamble must be sensitive to costs and benefits, which accounting helps them quantify and understand. Making a sale is meaningless unless it is a profitable sale.

Finance: Do you want to be a banker for Citicorp, an investment analyst for Goldman Sachs, or a stock broker for Merrill Lynch? These fields rely heavily on accounting knowledge to analyze financial statements. In fact, it is difficult to get a good job in a finance function without two or three courses in accounting.

Real estate: Are you interested in being a real estate broker for Prudential Real Estate? Because a third party—the bank—is almost always involved in financing a real estate transaction, brokers must understand the numbers involved: Can the buyer afford to make the payments to the bank? Does the cash flow from an industrial property justify the purchase price? What are the tax benefits of the purchase?

 How might accounting help you? (See page 49.)

The Basic Accounting Equation

LEARNING OBJECTIVE 6

State the accounting equation, and define its components.

The two basic elements of a business are what it owns and what it owes. **Assets** are the resources a business owns. For example, Google has total assets of approximately $93.8 billion. Liabilities and stockholders' equity are the rights or claims against these resources. Thus, Google has $93.8 billion of claims against its $93.8 billion of assets. Claims of those to whom the company owes money (creditors) are called **liabilities**. Claims of owners are called **stockholders' equity**. Google has liabilities of $22.1 billion and stockholders' equity of $71.7 billion.

We can express the relationship of assets, liabilities, and stockholders' equity as an equation, as shown in Illustration 1-5.

Illustration 1-5
The basic accounting equation

| Assets | = | Liabilities | + | Stockholders' Equity |

This relationship is the **basic accounting equation**. Assets must equal the sum of liabilities and stockholders' equity. Liabilities appear before stockholders' equity in the basic accounting equation because they are paid first if a business is liquidated.

The accounting equation applies to all **economic entities** regardless of size, nature of business, or form of business organization. It applies to a small proprietorship such as a corner grocery store as well as to a giant corporation such as PepsiCo. The equation provides the **underlying framework** for recording and summarizing economic events.

Let's look in more detail at the categories in the basic accounting equation.

Assets

As noted above, **assets** are resources a business owns. The business uses its assets in carrying out such activities as production and sales. The common characteristic possessed by all assets is **the capacity to provide future services or benefits**. In a business, that service potential or future economic benefit eventually results in cash inflows (receipts). For example, consider Campus Pizza, a local restaurant. It owns a delivery truck that provides economic benefits from delivering pizzas. Other assets of Campus Pizza are tables, chairs, jukebox, cash register, oven, tableware, and, of course, cash.

Liabilities

Liabilities are claims against assets—that is, existing debts and obligations. Businesses of all sizes usually borrow money and purchase merchandise on credit. These economic activities result in payables of various sorts:

- Campus Pizza, for instance, purchases cheese, sausage, flour, and beverages on credit from suppliers. These obligations are called **accounts payable**.
- Campus Pizza also has a **note payable** to First National Bank for the money borrowed to purchase the delivery truck.
- Campus Pizza may also have **salaries and wages payable** to employees and **sales and real estate taxes payable** to the local government.

All of these persons or entities to whom Campus Pizza owes money are its **creditors**.

Creditors may legally force the liquidation of a business that does not pay its debts. In that case, the law requires that creditor claims be paid **before** ownership claims.

Stockholders' Equity

The ownership claim on a corporation's total assets is **stockholders' equity**. It is equal to total assets minus total liabilities. Here is why: The assets of a business are claimed by either creditors or stockholders. To find out what belongs to stockholders, we subtract creditors' claims (the liabilities) from the assets. The remainder is the stockholders' claim on the assets—stockholders' equity. It is often referred to as **residual equity**—that is, the equity "left over" after creditors' claims are satisfied.

The stockholders' equity section of a corporation's balance sheet generally consists of (1) common stock and (2) retained earnings.

COMMON STOCK

A corporation may obtain funds by selling shares of stock to investors. **Common stock** is the term used to describe the total amount paid in by stockholders for the shares they purchase.

RETAINED EARNINGS

The **retained earnings** section of the balance sheet is determined by three items: revenues, expenses, and dividends.

Helpful Hint
In some situations, accountants use the term *owner's equity* and in others *owners' equity*. *Owner's* refers to one owner (the case with a sole proprietorship), and *owners'* refers to multiple owners (the case with partnerships). The term *stockholders' equity* refers to ownership in corporations.

REVENUES Revenues **are the gross increases in stockholders' equity resulting from business activities entered into for the purpose of earning income.** Generally, revenues result from selling merchandise, performing services, renting out property, and lending money.

Revenues usually result in an increase in an asset. They may arise from different sources and are called various names depending on the nature of the business. Campus Pizza, for instance, has two categories of sales revenues—pizza sales and beverage sales. Other titles for and sources of revenue common to many businesses are sales, fees, services, commissions, interest, dividends, royalties, and rent.

EXPENSES Expenses **are the cost of assets consumed or services used in the process of earning revenue. They are decreases in stockholders' equity that result from operating the business.** Like revenues, expenses take many forms and are called various names depending on the type of asset consumed or service used. For example, Campus Pizza recognizes the following types of expenses: cost of ingredients (flour, cheese, tomato paste, meat, mushrooms, etc.); cost of beverages; wages expense; utilities expense (electric, gas, and water expense); telephone expense; delivery expense (gasoline, repairs, licenses, etc.); supplies expense (napkins, detergents, aprons, etc.); rent expense; interest expense; and property tax expense.

DIVIDENDS Net income represents an increase in net assets which are then available to distribute to stockholders. The distribution of cash or other assets to stockholders is called a **dividend**. Dividends reduce retained earnings. However, dividends are **not an expense**. A corporation first determines its revenues and expenses and then computes net income or net loss. If it has net income and decides it has no better use for that income, a corporation may decide to distribute a dividend to its owners (the stockholders).

In summary, the principal sources (increases) of stockholders' equity are investments by stockholders and revenues from business operations. In contrast, reductions (decreases) in stockholders' equity result from expenses and dividends. These relationships are shown in Illustration 1-6.

Illustration 1-6
Increases and decreases in stockholders' equity

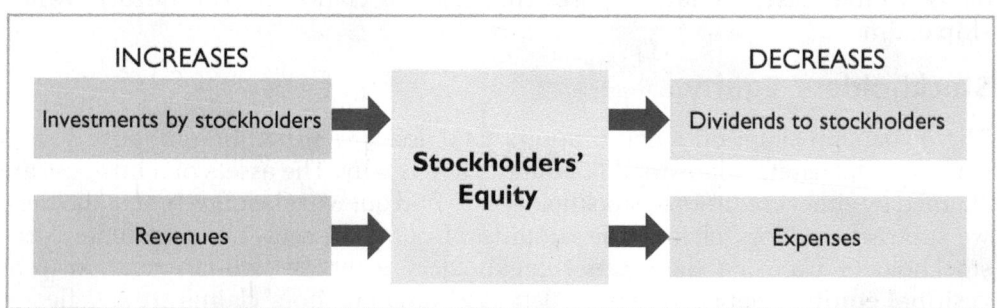

Stockholders' Equity Effects

Action Plan
✔ Understand the sources of revenue.

Classify the following items as issuance of stock (I), dividends (D), revenues (R), or expenses (E). Then indicate whether each item increases or decreases stockholders' equity.

(1) Rent Expense

(2) Service Revenue

(3) Dividends

(4) Salaries and Wages Expense

✔ Understand what causes expenses.

✔ Review the rules for changes in stockholders' equity: Investments and revenues increase stockholders' equity. Expenses and dividends decrease stockholders' equity.

✔ Recognize that dividends are distributions of cash or other assets to stockholders.

Solution

1. Rent Expense is an expense (E); it decreases stockholders' equity. 2. Service Revenue is a revenue (R); it increases stockholders' equity. 3. Dividends is a distribution to stockholders (D); it decreases stockholders' equity. 4. Salaries and Wages Expense is an expense (E); it decreases stockholders' equity.

Related exercise material: BE1-1, BE1-2, BE1-3, BE1-4, BE1-5, E1-5, E1-6, E1-7, **and** DO IT! 1-2.

✔ **The Navigator**

Using the Accounting Equation

Transactions (**business transactions**) are a business's economic events recorded by accountants. Transactions may be external or internal. **External transactions** involve economic events between the company and some outside enterprise. For example, Campus Pizza's purchase of cooking equipment from a supplier, payment of monthly rent to the landlord, and sale of pizzas to customers are external transactions. **Internal transactions** are economic events that occur entirely within one company. The use of cooking and cleaning supplies are internal transactions for Campus Pizza.

Companies carry on many activities that do not represent business transactions. Examples are hiring employees, answering the telephone, talking with customers, and placing merchandise orders. Some of these activities may lead to business transactions: Employees will earn wages, and suppliers will deliver ordered merchandise. The company must analyze each event to find out if it affects the components of the accounting equation. If it does, the company will record the transaction. Illustration 1-7 demonstrates the transaction-identification process.

LEARNING OBJECTIVE 7

Analyze the effects of business transactions on the accounting equation.

Illustration 1-7
Transaction-identification process

Events

Purchase computer

Discuss product design with potential customer

Pay rent

Criterion

Is the financial position (assets, liabilities, or stockholders' equity) of the company changed?

Yes

No

Yes

Record/ Don't Record

Each transaction must have a dual effect on the accounting equation. For example, if an asset is increased, there must be a corresponding (1) decrease in another asset, (2) increase in a specific liability, or (3) increase in stockholders' equity.

Two or more items could be affected. For example, as one asset is increased $10,000, another asset could decrease $6,000 and a liability could increase $4,000. Any change in a liability or ownership claim is subject to similar analysis.

Transaction Analysis

To demonstrate how to analyze transactions in terms of the accounting equation, we will review the business activities of Softbyte Inc., a computer programming business, during its first month of operations. As part of this analysis, we will expand the basic accounting equation. This will allow us to better illustrate the impact of transactions on stockholders' equity. Recall that stockholders' equity is comprised of two parts: common stock and retained earnings. Common stock is affected when the company issues new shares of stock in exchange for cash. Retained earnings is affected when the company earns revenue, incurs expenses, or pays dividends. Illustration 1-8 shows the **expanded accounting equation**.

Illustration 1-8
Expanded accounting equation

Helpful Hint
You will want to study these transactions until you are sure you understand them. They are not difficult, but understanding them is important to your success in this course. The ability to analyze transactions in terms of the basic accounting equation is essential in accounting.

If you are tempted to skip ahead after you've read a few of the following transaction analyses, don't do it. Each has something unique to teach, something you'll need later. (We assure you that we've kept them to the minimum needed!)

TRANSACTION 1. INVESTMENT BY STOCKHOLDERS Ray and Barbara Neal decide to open a computer programming company that they incorporate as Softbyte Inc. On September 1, 2015, they invest $15,000 cash in the business in exchange for $15,000 of common stock. The common stock indicates the ownership interest that the Neals have in Softbyte Inc. This transaction results in an equal increase in both assets and stockholders' equity.

Basic Analysis	The asset Cash increases $15,000, and stockholders' equity (identified as Common Stock) increases $15,000.

	Assets	=	Liabilities	+	Stockholders' Equity
Equation Analysis	Cash	=			Common Stock
	(1) +$15,000	=			+$15,000 Issued Stock

Observe that the equality of the basic equation has been maintained. Note also that the source of the increase in stockholders' equity (in this case, issued stock) is indicated. Why does this matter? Because investments by stockholders do not represent revenues, and they are excluded in determining net income. Therefore, it is necessary to make clear that the increase is an investment rather than revenue from operations. Additional investments (i.e., investments made by stockholders after the corporation has been initially formed) have the same effect on stockholders' equity as the initial investment.

TRANSACTION 2. PURCHASE OF EQUIPMENT FOR CASH Softbyte Inc. purchases computer equipment for $7,000 cash. This transaction results in an equal increase and decrease in total assets, though the composition of assets changes.

Basic Analysis	The asset Cash decreases $7,000, and the asset Equipment increases $7,000.

		Assets		=	Liabilities	+	Stockholders' Equity
		Cash	+	Equipment =			Common Stock
Equation Analysis		$15,000					$15,000
	(2)	−7,000		+$7,000			
		$ 8,000	+	$ 7,000 =			$15,000
			$15,000				

Observe that total assets are still $15,000. Common stock also remains at $15,000, the amount of the original investment.

TRANSACTION 3. PURCHASE OF SUPPLIES ON CREDIT Softbyte Inc. purchases for $1,600 from Acme Supply Company computer paper and other supplies expected to last several months. Acme agrees to allow Softbyte to pay this bill in October. This transaction is a purchase on account (a credit purchase). Assets increase because of the expected future benefits of using the paper and supplies, and liabilities increase by the amount due Acme Company.

Basic Analysis	The asset Supplies increases $1,600, and the liability Accounts Payable increases $1,600.

		Assets					=	Liabilities	+	Stockholders' Equity
		Cash	+	Supplies	+	Equipment =		Accounts Payable	+	Common Stock
Equation Analysis		$8,000				$7,000				$15,000
	(3)			+$1,600				+$1,600		
		$8,000	+	$ 1,600	+	$7,000 =		$ 1,600	+	$15,000
				$16,600				$16,600		

Total assets are now $16,600. This total is matched by a $1,600 creditor's claim and a $15,000 ownership claim.

TRANSACTION 4. SERVICES PERFORMED FOR CASH Softbyte Inc. receives $1,200 cash from customers for programming services it has performed. This transaction represents Softbyte's principal revenue-producing activity. Recall that **revenue increases stockholders' equity**.

Basic Analysis	The asset Cash increases $1,200, and stockholders' equity increases $1,200 due to Service Revenue.						

Equation Analysis

	Assets			= Liabilities +	Stockholders' Equity			
	Cash +	Supplies +	Equipment =	Accounts Payable +	Common Stock +	Retained Earnings		
						Rev. −	Exp. −	Div.
	$8,000	$1,600	$7,000	$1,600	$15,000			
(4)	+1,200					+$1,200		Service Revenue
	$9,200 +	$1,600 +	$7,000 =	$1,600 +	$15,000 +	$1,200		
		$17,800			$17,800			

The two sides of the equation balance at $17,800. Service Revenue is included in determining Softbyte's net income.

Note that we do not have room to give details for each individual revenue and expense account in this illustration. Thus, revenues (and expenses when we get to them) are summarized under one column heading for Revenues and one for Expenses. However, it is important to keep track of the category (account) titles affected (e.g., Service Revenue) as they will be needed when we prepare financial statements later in the chapter.

TRANSACTION 5. PURCHASE OF ADVERTISING ON CREDIT Softbyte Inc. receives a bill for $250 from the *Daily News* for advertising but postpones payment until a later date. This transaction results in an increase in liabilities and a decrease in stockholders' equity.

Basic Analysis	The liability Accounts Payable increases $250, and stockholders' equity decreases $250 due to Advertising Expense.						

Equation Analysis

	Assets			= Liabilities +	Stockholders' Equity			
	Cash +	Supplies +	Equipment =	Accounts Payable +	Common Stock +	Retained Earnings		
						Rev. −	Exp. −	Div.
	$9,200	$1,600	$7,000	$1,600	$15,000	$1,200		
(5)				+250			−$250	Advertising Expense
	$9,200 +	$1,600 +	$7,000 =	$1,850 +	$15,000 +	$1,200 −	$250	
		$17,800			$17,800			

The two sides of the equation still balance at $17,800. Retained Earnings decreases when Softbyte incurs the expense. Expenses do not have to be paid in cash at the time they are incurred. When Softbyte pays at a later date, the liability Accounts Payable will decrease and the asset Cash will decrease (see Transaction 8). The cost of advertising is an expense (rather than an asset) because Softbyte has used the benefits. Advertising Expense is included in determining net income.

TRANSACTION 6. SERVICES PERFORMED FOR CASH AND CREDIT Softbyte Inc. performs $3,500 of programming services for customers. The company receives cash of $1,500 from customers, and it bills the balance of $2,000 on account. This transaction results in an equal increase in assets and stockholders' equity.

Basic Analysis	Three specific items are affected: The asset Cash increases $1,500, the asset Accounts Receivable increases $2,000, and stockholders' equity increases $3,500 due to Service Revenue.

		Assets			=	Liabilities +		Stockholders' Equity		
Equation Analysis	Cash +	Accounts Receivable	+ Supplies +	Equipment =		Accounts Payable	+ Common Stock +	Retained Earnings		
								Rev. − Exp. − Div.		
	$ 9,200		$1,600	$7,000		$1,850	$15,000	$1,200 $250		
	(6) +1,500	+$2,000						+3,500		Service Revenue
	$10,700 +	$ 2,000 +	$1,600 +	$7,000 =		$1,850	+ $15,000 +	$4,700 − $250		
		$21,300						$21,300		

Softbyte recognizes $3,500 in revenues when it performs the service. In exchange for this service, it received $1,500 in Cash and Accounts Receivable of $2,000. This Accounts Receivable represents customers' promises to pay $2,000 to Softbyte in the future. When it later receives collections on account, Softbyte will increase Cash and will decrease Accounts Receivable (see Transaction 9).

TRANSACTION 7. PAYMENT OF EXPENSES Softbyte Inc. pays the following expenses in cash for September: store rent $600, salaries and wages of employees $900, and utilities $200. These payments result in an equal decrease in assets and stockholders' equity.

pay is cash

Basic Analysis	The asset Cash decreases $1,700, and stockholders' equity decreases $1,700 due to the following expenses: Rent Expense, Salaries and Wages Expense, and Utilities Expense.

		Assets			=	Liabilities +		Stockholders' Equity		
Equation Analysis	Cash +	Accounts Receivable	+ Supplies +	Equipment =		Accounts Payable	+ Common Stock +	Retained Earnings		
								Rev. − Exp. − Div.		
	$10,700	$2,000	$1,600	$7,000		$1,850	$15,000	$4,700 $ 250		
	(7) −1,700							−600		Rent Exp.
								−900		Sal./Wages Exp.
								−200		Utilities Exp.
	$ 9,000 +	$2,000 +	$1,600 +	$7,000 =		$1,850	+ $15,000 +	$4,700 − $1,950		
		$19,600						$19,600		

The two sides of the equation now balance at $19,600. Three lines are required in the analysis to indicate the different types of expenses that have been incurred.

TRANSACTION 8. PAYMENT OF ACCOUNTS PAYABLE Softbyte Inc. pays its $250 *Daily News* bill in cash. The company previously (in Transaction 5) recorded the bill as an increase in Accounts Payable and a decrease in stockholders' equity.

Basic Analysis	This cash payment "on account" decreases the asset Cash by $250 and also decreases the liability Accounts Payable by $250.

Equation Analysis

	Assets				=	Liabilities +		Stockholders' Equity		
	Cash +	Accounts Receivable	+ Supplies +	Equipment =		Accounts Payable	+ Common Stock	+	Retained Earnings	
								Rev.	−Exp. −	Div.
	$9,000	$2,000	$1,600	$7,000		$1,850	$15,000	$4,700	$1,950	
(8)	−250					−250				
	$8,750 +	$2,000	+ $1,600 +	$7,000	=	$1,600	+ $15,000	+ $4,700 −	$1,950	
			$19,350					$19,350		

Observe that the payment of a liability related to an expense that has previously been recorded does not affect stockholders' equity. Softbyte recorded the expense (in Transaction 5) and should not record it again.

TRANSACTION 9. RECEIPT OF CASH ON ACCOUNT Softbyte Inc. receives $600 in cash from customers who had been billed for services (in Transaction 6). Transaction 9 does not change total assets, but it changes the composition of those assets.

Basic Analysis	The asset Cash increases $600, and the asset Accounts Receivable decreases $600.

Equation Analysis

	Assets				=	Liabilities +		Stockholders' Equity		
	Cash +	Accounts Receivable	+ Supplies +	Equipment =		Accounts Payable	+ Common Stock	+	Retained Earnings	
								Rev. −	Exp. −	Div.
	$8,750	$2,000	$1,600	$7,000		$1,600	$15,000	$4,700	$1,950	
(9)	+600	−600								
	$9,350 +	$1,400	+ $1,600 +	$7,000	=	$1,600	+ $15,000	+ $4,700 −	$1,950	
			$19,350					$19,350		

Note that the collection of an account receivable for services previously billed and recorded does not affect stockholders' equity. Softbyte already recorded this revenue (in Transaction 6) and should not record it again.

TRANSACTION 10. DIVIDENDS The corporation pays a dividend of $1,300 in cash to Ray and Barbara Neal, the stockholders of Softbyte Inc. This transaction results in an equal decrease in assets and stockholders' equity.

Basic Analysis	The asset Cash decreases $1,300, and stockholders' equity decreases $1,300 due to dividends.

Equation Analysis

	Assets				=	Liabilities +		Stockholders' Equity			
	Cash +	Accounts Receivable	+ Supplies +	Equipment =		Accounts Payable	+ Common Stock	+	Retained Earnings		
								Rev. −	Exp. −	Div.	
	$ 9,350	$1,400	$1,600	$7,000		$1,600	$15,000	$4,700	$1,950		
(10)	−1,300									−$1,300	Dividends
	$ 8,050 +	$1,400	+ $1,600 +	$7,000	=	$1,600	+ $15,000	+$4,700 −	$1,950 −	$ 1,300	
			$18,050					$18,050			

Note that the dividend reduces retained earnings, which is part of stockholders' equity. **Dividends are not expenses.** Like stockholders' investments, dividends are excluded in determining net income.

Summary of Transactions

Illustration 1-9 summarizes the September transactions of Softbyte Inc. to show their cumulative effect on the basic accounting equation. It also indicates the transaction number and the specific effects of each transaction. Finally, Illustration 1-9 demonstrates a number of significant facts:

1. Each transaction must be analyzed in terms of its effect on:
   (a) The three components of the basic accounting equation.
   (b) Specific types (kinds) of items within each component.

2. The two sides of the equation must always be equal.

3. The Common Stock and Retained Earnings columns indicate the causes of each change in the stockholders' claim on assets.

Trans-action		Assets			= Liabilities +		Stockholders' Equity				
	Cash	+ Accounts Receivable	+ Supplies	+ Equipment =	Accounts Payable	+ Common Stock	+ Rev.	Retained Earnings – Exp.	– Div.		
(1)	+$15,000					+ $15,000				Issued Stock
(2)	−7,000			+$7,000						
(3)			+$1,600		+$1,600					
(4)	+1,200						+$1,200			Service Revenue
(5)					+250			−$250		Adver. Expense
(6)	+1,500	+$2,000					+3,500			Service Revenue
(7)	−1,700							−600		Rent Expense
								−900		Sal./Wages Exp.
								−200		Utilities Expense
(8)	−250				−250					
(9)	+600	−600								
(10)	−1,300								−$1,300	Dividends
	$ 8,050 +	$1,400 +	$1,600 +	$7,000 =	$1,600 +	$15,000 +	$4,700 −	$1,950 −	$1,300	
		$18,050					$18,050			

There! You made it through transaction analysis. If you feel a bit shaky on any of the transactions, it might be a good idea at this point to get up, take a short break, and come back again for a brief (10- to 15-minute) review of the transactions, to make sure you understand them before you go on to the next section.

Illustration 1-9
Tabular summary of Softbyte Inc. transactions

> **DO IT!**

Tabular Analysis

Action Plan

✔ Analyze the effects of each transaction on the accounting equation.

✔ Use appropriate category names (not descriptions).

✔ Keep the accounting equation in balance.

Transactions made by Virmari & Co., a public accounting firm, for the month of August are shown below. Prepare a tabular analysis which shows the effects of these transactions on the expanded accounting equation, similar to that shown in Illustration 1-9.

1. Stockholders purchased shares of stock for $25,000 cash.

2. The company purchased $7,000 of office equipment on credit.

3. The company received $8,000 cash in exchange for services performed.

4. The company paid $850 for this month's rent.

5. The company paid a dividend of $1,000 in cash to stockholders.

Solution

Transaction	Assets		=	Liabilities +		Stockholders' Equity				
	Cash	+ Equipment =		Accounts Payable	+	Common Stock	+	Retained Earnings		
								Rev.	− Exp. − Div.	
(1)	+$25,000					+$25,000				
(2)		+$7,000		+$7,000						
(3)	+8,000							+$8,000		Service Revenue
(4)	−850								−$850	Rent Expense
(5)	−1,000								− $1,000	Dividends
	$31,150 +	$7,000	=	$7,000	+	$25,000 +		$8,000 −	$850 − $1,000	
		$38,150					$38,150			

Related exercise material: BE1-6, BE1-7, BE1-8, BE1-9, E1-6, E1-7, E1-8, E1-9, E1-10, **and** DO IT! 1-3.

 The Navigator

Financial Statements

 International Note

The primary types of financial statements required by GAAP and IFRS are the same. In practice, some format differences do exist in presentations employed by GAAP companies compared to IFRS companies.

Helpful Hint
The income statement, retained earnings statement, and statement of cash flows are all for a *period* of time, whereas the balance sheet is for a *point* in time.

Companies prepare four financial statements from the summarized accounting data:

1. An **income statement** presents the revenues and expenses and resulting net income or net loss for a specific period of time.
2. A **retained earnings statement** summarizes the changes in retained earnings for a specific period of time.
3. A **balance sheet** reports the assets, liabilities, and stockholders' equity of a company at a specific date.
4. A **statement of cash flows** summarizes information about the cash inflows (receipts) and outflows (payments) for a specific period of time.

These statements provide relevant financial data for internal and external users. Illustration 1-10 shows the financial statements of Softbyte Inc. Note that the statements shown in Illustration 1-10 are interrelated:

1. Net income of $2,750 on the **income statement** is added to the beginning balance of retained earnings in the **retained earnings statement**.
2. Retained earnings of $1,450 at the end of the reporting period shown in the **retained earnings statement** is reported on the **balance sheet**.
3. Cash of $8,050 on the **balance sheet** is reported on the **statement of cash flows**.

Also, explanatory notes and supporting schedules are an integral part of every set of financial statements. We illustrate these notes and schedules in later chapters of this textbook.

Be sure to carefully examine the format and content of each statement in Illustration 1-10. We describe the essential features of each in the following sections.

Income Statement

The income statement reports the success or profitability of the company's operations over a specific period of time. For example, Softbyte Inc.'s income statement is dated "For the Month Ended September 30, 2015." It is prepared from the data appearing in the revenue and expense columns of Illustration 1-9 (page 21).

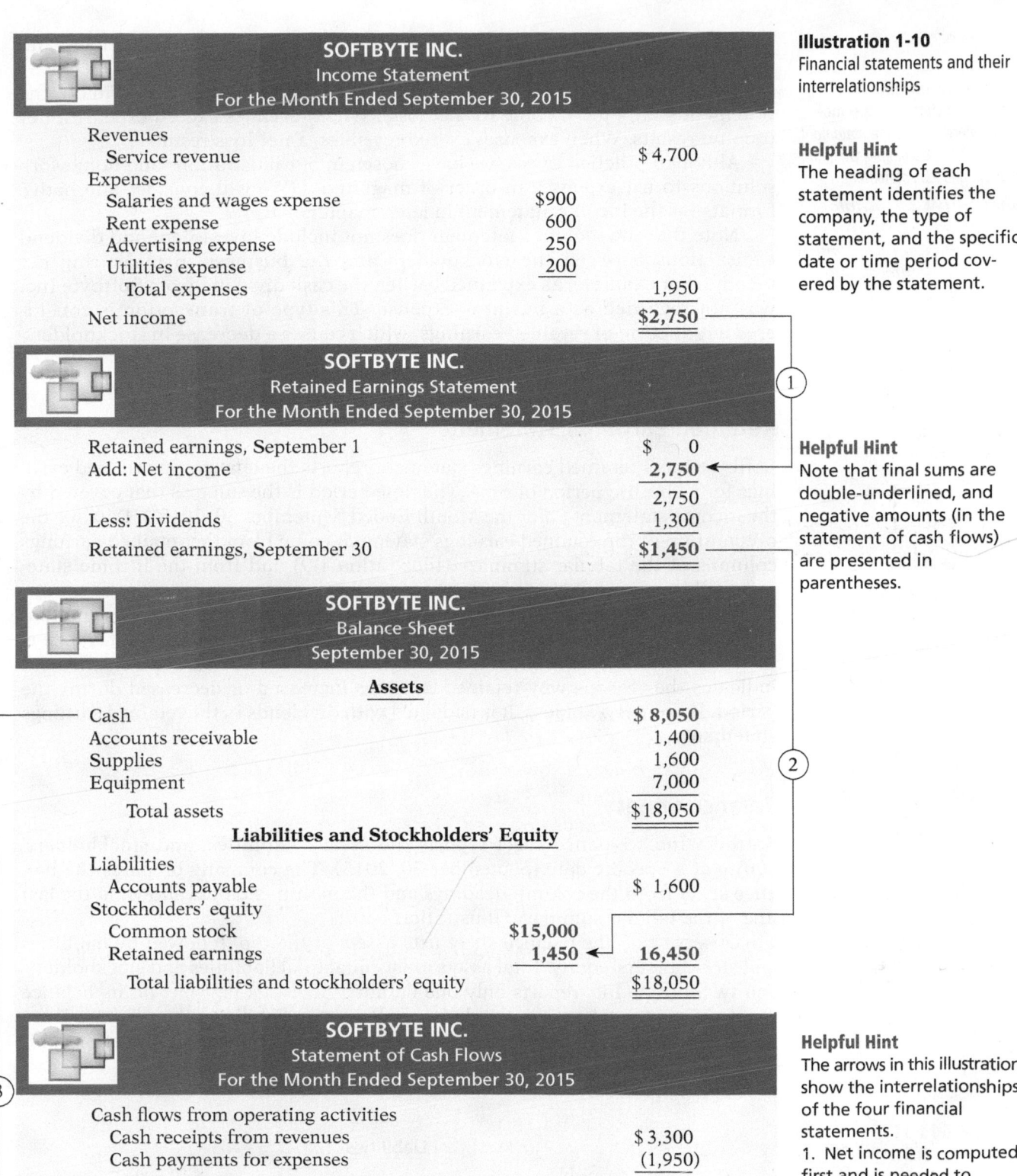

SOFTBYTE INC.
Income Statement
For the Month Ended September 30, 2015

Revenues		
Service revenue		$ 4,700
Expenses		
Salaries and wages expense	$900	
Rent expense	600	
Advertising expense	250	
Utilities expense	200	
Total expenses		1,950
Net income		**$2,750**

SOFTBYTE INC.
Retained Earnings Statement
For the Month Ended September 30, 2015

Retained earnings, September 1	$ 0
Add: Net income	2,750
	2,750
Less: Dividends	1,300
Retained earnings, September 30	**$1,450**

SOFTBYTE INC.
Balance Sheet
September 30, 2015

Assets

Cash	$ 8,050
Accounts receivable	1,400
Supplies	1,600
Equipment	7,000
Total assets	$18,050

Liabilities and Stockholders' Equity

Liabilities		
Accounts payable		$ 1,600
Stockholders' equity		
Common stock	$15,000	
Retained earnings	1,450	16,450
Total liabilities and stockholders' equity		$18,050

SOFTBYTE INC.
Statement of Cash Flows
For the Month Ended September 30, 2015

Cash flows from operating activities		
Cash receipts from revenues	$ 3,300	
Cash payments for expenses	(1,950)	
Net cash provided by operating activities		1,350
Cash flows from investing activities		
Purchase of equipment		(7,000)
Cash flows from financing activities		
Sale of common stock	$15,000	
Payment of cash dividends	(1,300)	13,700
Net increase in cash		8,050
Cash at the beginning of the period		0
Cash at the end of the period		$8,050

Illustration 1-10
Financial statements and their interrelationships

Helpful Hint
The heading of each statement identifies the company, the type of statement, and the specific date or time period covered by the statement.

Helpful Hint
Note that final sums are double-underlined, and negative amounts (in the statement of cash flows) are presented in parentheses.

Helpful Hint
The arrows in this illustration show the interrelationships of the four financial statements.
1. Net income is computed first and is needed to determine the ending balance in retained earnings.
2. The ending balance in retained earnings is needed in preparing the balance sheet.
3. The cash shown on the balance sheet is needed in preparing the statement of cash flows.

Alternative Terminology
The income statement is sometimes referred to as the *statement
of operations, earnings statement,*
or *profit and loss statement.*

*Alternative Terminology
notes present synonymous
terms that you may come
across in practice.*

The heading of the statement identifies the company, the type of statement, and the time period covered by the statement.

The income statement lists revenues first, followed by expenses. Finally, the statement shows net income (or net loss). When revenues exceed expenses, **net income** results. When expenses exceed revenues, a **net loss** results.

Although practice varies, we have chosen in our illustrations and homework solutions to list expenses in order of magnitude. (We will consider alternative formats for the income statement in later chapters.)

Note that the income statement does not include investment and dividend transactions between the stockholders and the business in measuring net income. For example, as explained earlier, the cash dividend from Softbyte Inc. was not regarded as a business expense. This type of transaction is considered a reduction of retained earnings, which causes a decrease in stockholders' equity.

Retained Earnings Statement

Softbyte Inc.'s retained earnings statement reports the changes in retained earnings for a specific period of time. The time period is the same as that covered by the income statement ("For the Month Ended September 30, 2015"). Data for the preparation of the retained earnings statement come from the retained earnings columns of the tabular summary (Illustration 1-9) and from the income statement (Illustration 1-10, page 23).

The first line of the statement shows the beginning retained earnings amount. Then come net income and dividends. The retained earnings ending balance is the final amount on the statement. The information provided by this statement indicates the reasons why retained earnings increased or decreased during the period. If there is a net loss, it is deducted with dividends in the retained earnings statement.

Balance Sheet

Softbyte Inc.'s balance sheet reports the assets, liabilities, and stockholders' equity at a specific date (September 30, 2015). The company prepares the balance sheet from the column headings and the month-end data shown in the last line of the tabular summary (Illustration 1-9).

Observe that the balance sheet lists assets at the top, followed by liabilities and stockholders' equity. Total assets must equal total liabilities and stockholders' equity. Softbyte Inc. reports only one liability, Accounts Payable, on its balance sheet. In most cases, there will be more than one liability. When two or more liabilities are involved, a customary way of listing is as shown in Illustration 1-11.

Illustration 1-11
Presentation of liabilities

Liabilities	
Notes payable	$ 10,000
Accounts payable	63,000
Salaries and wages payable	18,000
Total liabilities	**$91,000**

The balance sheet is like a snapshot of the company's financial condition at a specific moment in time (usually the month-end or year-end).

Statement of Cash Flows

The statement of cash flows provides information on the cash receipts and payments for a specific period of time. The statement of cash flows reports (1) the cash effects of a company's operations during a period, (2) its investing activities, (3) its financing activities, (4) the net increase or decrease in cash during the period, and (5) the cash amount at the end of the period.

Reporting the sources, uses, and change in cash is useful because investors, creditors, and others want to know what is happening to a company's most liquid resource. The statement of cash flows provides answers to the following simple but important questions.

1. Where did cash come from during the period?
2. What was cash used for during the period?
3. What was the change in the cash balance during the period?

As shown in Softbyte Inc.'s statement of cash flows in Illustration 1-10, cash increased $8,050 during the period. Net cash provided by operating activities increased cash $1,350. Cash flow from investing activities decreased cash $7,000, while cash flow from financing activities increased cash $13,700. At this time, you need not be concerned with how these amounts are determined. Chapter 13 will examine in detail how the statement is prepared.

Helpful Hint
Investing activities pertain to investments made by the company, not investments made by the owners.

PEOPLE, PLANET, AND PROFIT INSIGHT

Beyond Financial Statements

Should we expand our financial statements beyond the income statement, retained earnings statement, balance sheet, and statement of cash flows? Some believe we should take into account ecological and social performance, in addition to financial results, in evaluating a company. The argument is that a company's responsibility lies with anyone who is influenced by its actions. In other words, a company should be interested in benefiting many different parties, instead of only maximizing stockholders' interests.

A socially responsible business does not exploit or endanger any group of individuals. It follows fair trade practices, provides safe environments for workers, and bears responsibility for environmental damage. Granted, measurement of these factors is difficult. How to report this information is also controversial. But, many interesting and useful efforts are underway. Throughout this textbook, we provide additional insights into how companies are attempting to meet the challenge of measuring and reporting their contributions to society, as well as their financial results, to stockholders.

 Why might a company's stockholders be interested in its environmental and social performance? (See page 49.)

> DO IT!

Financial Statement Items

Presented below is selected information related to Flanagan Corporation at December 31, 2015. Flanagan reports financial information monthly.

Equipment	$10,000	Utilities Expense	$ 4,000
Cash	8,000	Accounts Receivable	9,000
Service Revenue	36,000	Salaries and Wages Expense	7,000
Rent Expense	11,000	Notes Payable	16,500
Accounts Payable	2,000	Dividends	5,000

(a) Determine the total assets of Flanagan at December 31, 2015.

(b) Determine the net income that Flanagan reported for December 2015.

(c) Determine the stockholders' equity of Flanagan at December 31, 2015.

Solution

Action Plan

✔ Remember the basic accounting equation: assets must equal liabilities plus stockholders' equity.

✔ Review previous financial statements to determine how total assets, net income, and stockholders' equity are computed.

(a) The total assets are $27,000, comprised of Cash $8,000, Accounts Receivable $9,000, and Equipment $10,000.

(b) Net income is $14,000, computed as follows.

Revenues		
Service revenue		$36,000
Expenses		
Rent expense	$11,000	
Salaries and wages expense	7,000	
Utilities expense	4,000	
Total expenses		22,000
Net income		$14,000

(c) The ending stockholders' equity of Flanagan Corporation is $8,500. By rewriting the accounting equation, we can compute stockholders' equity as assets minus liabilities, as follows.

Total assets [as computed in (a)]		$27,000
Less: Liabilities		
Notes payable	$16,500	
Accounts payable	2,000	18,500
Stockholders' equity		$ 8,500

Note that it is not possible to determine the corporation's stockholders' equity in any other way, because the beginning total for stockholders' equity is not provided.

Related exercise material: BE1-10, BE1-11, E1-9, E1-12, E1-13, E1-14, E1-15, E1-16, **and** DO IT! 1-4.

✔ **The Navigator**

*The **Comprehensive DO IT!** is a final review of the chapter. The **Action Plan** gives tips about how to approach the problem, and the **Solution** demonstrates both the form and content of complete answers.*

> Comprehensive DO IT!

Legal Services Inc. was incorporated on July 1, 2015. During the first month of operations, the following transactions occurred.

1. Stockholders invested $10,000 in cash in exchange for common stock of Legal Services Inc.

2. Paid $800 for July rent on office space.

3. Purchased office equipment on account $3,000.

4. Performed legal services for clients for cash $1,500.
5. Borrowed $700 cash from a bank on a note payable.
6. Performed legal services for client on account $2,000.
7. Paid monthly expenses: salaries $500, utilities $300, and advertising $100.

Instructions
(a) Prepare a tabular summary of the transactions.

(b) Prepare the income statement, retained earnings statement, and balance sheet at July 31 for Legal Services Inc.

Solution to Comprehensive DO IT!

(a)

Trans-action	Cash	+	Accounts Receivable	+	Equipment	=	Notes Payable	+	Accounts Payable	+	Common Stock	+	Rev.	−	Exp.	−	Div.	
													Retained Earnings					
(1)	+$10,000					=					+$10,000							Issued Stock
(2)	−800														−$800			Rent Expense
(3)					+$3,000	=			+$3,000									
(4)	+1,500												+$1,500					Service Revenue
(5)	+700						+$700											
(6)			+$2,000										+2,000					Service Revenue
(7)	−500														−500			Sal./Wages Exp.
	−300														−300			Utilities Expense
	−100														−100			Advertising Expense
	$10,500	+	$2,000	+	$3,000	=	$700	+	$3,000	+	$10,000	+	$3,500	−	$1,700			
			$15,500								$15,500							

(b)

LEGAL SERVICES INC.
Income Statement
For the Month Ended July 31, 2015

Revenues		
Service revenue		$3,500
Expenses		
Rent expense	$800	
Salaries and wages expense	500	
Utilities expense	300	
Advertising expense	100	
Total expenses		1,700
Net income		$1,800

LEGAL SERVICES INC.
Retained Earnings Statement
For the Month Ended July 31, 2015

Retained earnings, July 1	$ –0–
Add: Net income	1,800
Retained earnings, July 31	$1,800

Action Plan
✔ Make sure that assets equal liabilities plus stockholders' equity after each transaction.

✔ Investments and revenues increase stockholders' equity. Dividends and expenses decrease stockholders' equity.

✔ Prepare the financial statements in the order listed.

✔ The income statement shows revenues and expenses for a period of time.

✔ The retained earnings statement shows the changes in retained earnings for the same period of time as the income statement.

✔ The balance sheet reports assets, liabilities, and stockholders' equity at a specific date.

LEGAL SERVICES INC.
Balance Sheet
July 31, 2015

Assets

Cash	$10,500
Accounts receivable	2,000
Equipment	3,000
Total assets	$15,500

Liabilities and Stockholders' Equity

Liabilities		
Notes payable	$ 700	
Accounts payable	3,000	
Total liabilities		$ 3,700
Stockholders' equity		
Common stock	10,000	
Retained earnings	1,800	11,800
Total liabilities and stockholders' equity		$15,500

 ✔ The Navigator

SUMMARY OF LEARNING OBJECTIVES

✔ The Navigator

1 **Explain what accounting is.** Accounting is an information system that identifies, records, and communicates the economic events of an organization to interested users.

2 **Identify the users and uses of accounting.** The major users and uses of accounting are as follows. (a) Management uses accounting information to plan, organize, and run the business. (b) Investors (owners) decide whether to buy, hold, or sell their financial interests on the basis of accounting data. (c) Creditors (suppliers and bankers) evaluate the risks of granting credit or lending money on the basis of accounting information. Other groups that use accounting information are taxing authorities, regulatory agencies, customers, and labor unions.

3 **Understand why ethics is a fundamental business concept.** Ethics are the standards of conduct by which actions are judged as right or wrong. Effective financial reporting depends on sound ethical behavior.

4 **Explain generally accepted accounting principles.** Generally accepted accounting principles are a common set of standards used by accountants.

5 **Explain the monetary unit assumption and the economic entity assumption.** The monetary unit assumption requires that companies include in the accounting records only transaction data that can be expressed in terms of money. The economic entity assumption requires that the activities of each economic entity be kept separate from the activities of its owner(s) and other economic entities.

6 **State the accounting equation, and define its components.** The basic accounting equation is:

Assets = Liabilities + Stockholders' Equity

Assets are resources a business owns. Liabilities are creditorship claims on total assets. Stockholders' equity is the ownership claim on total assets.

The expanded accounting equation is:

Assets = Liabilities + Common Stock
+ Revenues − Expenses − Dividends

Common stock is affected when the company issues new shares of stock in exchange for cash. Revenues are increases in assets resulting from income-earning activities. Expenses are the costs of assets consumed or services used in the process of earning revenue. Dividends are payments the company makes to its stockholders.

7 **Analyze the effects of business transactions on the accounting equation.** Each business transaction must have a dual effect on the accounting equation. For example, if an individual asset increases, there must be a corresponding (1) decrease in another asset, or (2) increase in a specific liability, or (3) increase in stockholders' equity.

8 **Understand the four financial statements and how they are prepared.** An income statement presents the revenues and expenses and resulting net income or net loss for a specific period of time. A retained earnings statement summarizes the changes in retained earnings for a specific period of time. A balance sheet reports the assets, liabilities, and stockholders' equity at a specific date. A statement of cash flows summarizes information about the cash inflows (receipts) and outflows (payments) for a specific period of time.

Accounting The information system that identifies, records, and communicates the economic events of an organization to interested users. (p. 4).

Assets Resources a business owns. (p. 13).

Balance sheet A financial statement that reports the assets, liabilities, and stockholders' equity at a specific date. (p. 22).

Basic accounting equation Assets = Liabilities + Stockholders' Equity. (p. 13).

Bookkeeping A part of accounting that involves only the recording of economic events. (p. 5).

Common stock Term used to describe the total amount paid in by stockholders for the shares they purchase. (p. 13).

Convergence The process of reducing the differences between U.S. GAAP and IFRS. (p. 9).

Corporation A business organized as a separate legal entity under state corporation law, having ownership divided into transferable shares of stock. (p. 11).

Dividend A distribution by a corporation to its stockholders. (p. 14).

Economic entity assumption An assumption that requires that the activities of the entity be kept separate and distinct from the activities of its owner and all other economic entities. (p. 10).

Ethics The standards of conduct by which one's actions are judged as right or wrong, honest or dishonest, fair or not fair. (p. 7).

Expanded accounting equation Assets = Liabilities + Common Stock + Revenues − Expenses − Dividends. (p. 16).

Expenses The cost of assets consumed or services used in the process of earning revenue. (p. 14).

Fair value principle An accounting principle stating that assets and liabilities should be reported at fair value (the price received to sell an asset or settle a liability). (p. 9).

Faithful representation Numbers and descriptions match what really existed or happened—they are factual. (p. 9).

Financial accounting The field of accounting that provides economic and financial information for investors, creditors, and other external users. (p. 6).

Financial Accounting Standards Board (FASB) A private organization that establishes generally accepted accounting principles in the United States (GAAP). (p. 9).

Generally accepted accounting principles (GAAP) Common standards that indicate how to report economic events. (p. 8).

Historical cost principle An accounting principle that states that companies should record assets at their cost. (p. 9).

Income statement A financial statement that presents the revenues and expenses and resulting net income or net loss of a company for a specific period of time. (p. 22).

International Accounting Standards Board (IASB) An accounting standard-setting body that issues standards adopted by many countries outside of the United States. (p. 9).

International Financial Reporting Standards (IFRS) International accounting standards set by the International Accounting Standards Board (IASB). (p. 9).

Liabilities Creditor claims against total assets. (p. 13).

Managerial accounting The field of accounting that provides internal reports to help users make decisions about their companies. (p. 6).

Monetary unit assumption An assumption stating that companies include in the accounting records only transaction data that can be expressed in terms of money. (p. 10).

Net income The amount by which revenues exceed expenses. (p. 24).

Net loss The amount by which expenses exceed revenues. (p. 24).

Partnership A business owned by two or more persons associated as partners. (p. 11).

Proprietorship A business owned by one person. (p. 10).

Relevance Financial information that is capable of making a difference in a decision. (p. 9).

Retained earnings statement A financial statement that summarizes the changes in retained earnings for a specific period of time. (p. 22).

Revenues The gross increase in stockholders' equity resulting from business activities entered into for the purpose of earning income. (p. 14).

Sarbanes-Oxley Act (SOX) Law passed by Congress intended to reduce unethical corporate behavior. (p. 7).

Securities and Exchange Commission (SEC) A governmental agency that oversees U.S. financial markets and accounting standard-setting bodies. (p. 9).

Statement of cash flows A financial statement that summarizes information about the cash inflows (receipts) and cash outflows (payments) for a specific period of time. (p. 22).

Stockholders' equity The ownership claim on a corporation's total assets. (p. 13).

Transactions The economic events of a business that are recorded by accountants. (p. 15).

APPENDIX 1A   Accounting Career Opportunities

Why is accounting such a popular major and career choice? First, there are a lot of jobs. In many cities in recent years, the demand for accountants exceeded the supply. Not only are there a lot of jobs, but there are a wide array of opportunities. As one accounting organization observed, "accounting is one degree with 360 degrees of opportunity."

Accounting is also hot because it is obvious that accounting matters. Interest in accounting has increased, ironically, because of the attention caused by the accounting failures of companies such as Enron and WorldCom. These widely publicized scandals revealed the important role that accounting plays in society. Most people want to make a difference, and an accounting career provides many opportunities to contribute to society. Finally, the Sarbanes-Oxley Act (SOX) (see page 7) significantly increased the accounting and internal control requirements for corporations. This dramatically increased demand for professionals with accounting training.

Accountants are in such demand that it is not uncommon for accounting students to have accepted a job offer a year before graduation. As the following discussion reveals, the job options of people with accounting degrees are virtually unlimited.

Public Accounting

Individuals in **public accounting** offer expert service to the general public, in much the same way that doctors serve patients and lawyers serve clients. A major portion of public accounting involves **auditing**. In auditing, a certified public accountant (CPA) examines company financial statements and provides an opinion as to how accurately the financial statements present the company's results and financial position. Analysts, investors, and creditors rely heavily on these "audit opinions," which CPAs have the exclusive authority to issue.

Taxation is another major area of public accounting. The work that tax specialists perform includes tax advice and planning, preparing tax returns, and representing clients before governmental agencies such as the Internal Revenue Service.

A third area in public accounting is **management consulting**. It ranges from installing basic accounting software or highly complex enterprise resource planning systems, to performing support services for major marketing projects and merger and acquisition activities.

Many CPAs are entrepreneurs. They form small- or medium-sized practices that frequently specialize in tax or consulting services.

Private Accounting

Instead of working in public accounting, you might choose to be an employee of a for-profit company such as Starbucks, Google, or PepsiCo. In **private** (or **managerial**) **accounting**, you would be involved in activities such as cost accounting (finding the cost of producing specific products), budgeting, accounting information system design and support, and tax planning and preparation. You might also be a member of your company's internal audit team. In response to SOX, the internal auditors' job of reviewing the company's operations to ensure compliance with company policies and to increase efficiency has taken on increased importance.

Alternatively, many accountants work for not-for-profit organizations such as the Red Cross or the Bill and Melinda Gates Foundation, or for museums, libraries, or performing arts organizations.

Governmental Accounting

Another option is to pursue one of the many accounting opportunities in governmental agencies. For example, the Internal Revenue Service (IRS), Federal Bureau of Investigation (FBI), and the Securities and Exchange Commission (SEC) all employ accountants. The FBI has a stated goal that at least 15 percent of its new agents should be CPAs. There is also a very high demand for accounting educators at public colleges and universities and in state and local governments.

Forensic Accounting

Forensic accounting uses accounting, auditing, and investigative skills to conduct investigations into theft and fraud. It is listed among the top 20 career paths of the future. The job of forensic accountants is to catch the perpetrators of the estimated $600 billion per year of theft and fraud occurring at U.S. companies. This includes tracing money-laundering and identity-theft activities as well as tax evasion. Insurance companies hire forensic accountants to detect frauds such as arson, and law offices employ forensic accountants to identify marital assets in divorces. Forensic accountants often have FBI, IRS, or similar government experience.

"Show Me the Money"

How much can a new accountant make? Take a look at the average salaries for college graduates in public and private accounting. Keep in mind if you also have a CPA license, you'll make 10–15% more when you start out.

Employer	Jr. Level (0–3 yrs.)	Sr. Level (4–6 yrs.)
Public accounting (large firm)	$51,500–$74,250	$71,000–$92,250
Public accounting (small firm)	$42,500–$60,500	$57,000–$74,000
Corporate accounting (large company)	$41,750–$68,500	$67,000–$86,500
Corporate accounting (small company)	$37,000–$56,750	$52,750–$68,500

Illustration 1A-1
Salary estimates for jobs in public and corporate accounting

Serious earning potential over time gives CPAs great job security. Here are some examples of upper-level salaries for managers in corporate accounting. Note that geographic region, experience, education, CPA certification, and company size each play a role in determining salary.

Position	Large Company	Small to Medium Company
Chief financial officer	$189,750–$411,000	$96,750–$190,500
Corporate controller	$128,000–$199,000	$82,750–$144,750
Tax manager	$100,250–$142,500	$79,500–$110,750

Illustration 1A-2
Upper-level management salaries in corporate accounting

For up-to-date salary estimates, as well as a wealth of additional information regarding accounting as a career, check out **www.startheregoplaces.com.**

SUMMARY OF LEARNING OBJECTIVE FOR APPENDIX 1A

 The Navigator

9 **Explain the career opportunities in accounting.** Accounting offers many different jobs in fields such as public and private accounting, governmental accounting, and forensic accounting. Accounting is a popular major because there are many different types of jobs, with unlimited potential for career advancement.

Auditing The examination of financial statements by a certified public accountant in order to express an opinion as to how accurately the financial statements present the company's results and financial position. (p. 30).

Forensic accounting An area of accounting that uses accounting, auditing, and investigative skills to conduct investigations into theft and fraud. (p. 31).

Management consulting An area of public accounting ranging from development of accounting and computer systems to support services for marketing projects and merger and acquisition activities. (p. 30).

Private (or managerial) accounting An area of accounting within a company that involves such activities as cost accounting, budgeting, design and support of accounting information systems, and tax planning and preparation. (p. 30).

Public accounting An area of accounting in which the accountant offers expert service to the general public. (p. 30).

Taxation An area of public accounting involving tax advice, tax planning, preparing tax returns, and representing clients before governmental agencies. (p. 30).

WileyPLUS Self-Test, Brief Exercises, Exercises, Problem Set A, and many more components are available for practice in *WileyPLUS*.

*Note: All asterisked Questions, Exercises, and Problems relate to material in the appendix to the chapter.

SELF-TEST QUESTIONS

Answers are on page 49.

(LO 1) **1.** Which of the following is **not** a step in the accounting process?
(a) Identification.   (c) Recording.
(b) Verification.   (d) Communication.

(LO 2) **2.** Which of the following statements about users of accounting information is **incorrect**?
(a) Management is an internal user.
(b) Taxing authorities are external users.
(c) Present creditors are external users.
(d) Regulatory authorities are internal users.

(LO 4) **3.** The historical cost principle states that:
(a) assets should be initially recorded at cost and adjusted when the fair value changes.
(b) activities of an entity are to be kept separate and distinct from its owner.
(c) assets should be recorded at their cost.
(d) only transaction data capable of being expressed in terms of money be included in the accounting records.

(LO 5) **4.** Which of the following statements about basic assumptions is **correct**?
(a) Basic assumptions are the same as accounting principles.
(b) The economic entity assumption states that there should be a particular unit of accountability.
(c) The monetary unit assumption enables accounting to measure employee morale.
(d) Partnerships are not economic entities.

(LO 5) **5.** The three types of business entities are:
(a) proprietorships, small businesses, and partnerships.
(b) proprietorships, partnerships, and corporations.

(c) proprietorships, partnerships, and large businesses.
(d) financial, manufacturing, and service companies.

(LO 6) **6.** Net income will result during a time period when:
(a) assets exceed liabilities.
(b) assets exceed revenues.
(c) expenses exceed revenues.
(d) revenues exceed expenses.

(LO 6) **7.** As of December 31, 2015, Reed Company has assets of $3,500 and stockholders' equity of $1,500. What are the liabilities for Reed Company as of December 31, 2015?
(a) $1,500.   (c) $2,500.
(b) $1,000.   (d) $2,000.

(LO 7) **8.** Performing services on account will have the following effects on the components of the basic accounting equation:
(a) increase assets and decrease stockholders' equity.
(b) increase assets and increase stockholders' equity.
(c) increase assets and increase liabilities.
(d) increase liabilities and increase stockholders' equity.

(LO 7) **9.** Which of the following events is **not** recorded in the accounting records?
(a) Equipment is purchased on account.
(b) An employee is terminated.
(c) A cash investment is made into the business.
(d) The company pays a cash dividend.

(LO 7) **10.** During 2015, Seisor Company's assets decreased $50,000 and its liabilities decreased $90,000. Its stockholders' equity therefore:
(a) increased $40,000.   (c) decreased $40,000.
(b) decreased $140,000. (d) increased $140,000.

(LO 7) **11.** Payment of an account payable affects the components of the accounting equation in the following way.

(a) Decreases stockholders' equity and decreases liabilities.
(b) Increases assets and decreases liabilities.
(c) Decreases assets and increases stockholders' equity.
(d) Decreases assets and decreases liabilities.

(LO 8) **12.** Which of the following statements is **false**?
(a) A statement of cash flows summarizes information about the cash inflows (receipts) and outflows (payments) for a specific period of time.
(b) A balance sheet reports the assets, liabilities, and stockholders' equity at a specific date.
(c) An income statement presents the revenues, expenses, changes in stockholders' equity, and resulting net income or net loss for a specific period of time.
(d) A retained earnings statement summarizes the changes in retained earnings for a specific period of time.

13. On the last day of the period, Alan Cesska Company buys (LO 8) a $900 machine on credit. This transaction will affect the:
(a) income statement only.
(b) balance sheet only.
(c) income statement and retained earnings statement only.
(d) income statement, retained earnings statement, and balance sheet.

14. The financial statement that reports assets, liabilities, (LO 8) and stockholders' equity is the:
(a) income statement.
(b) retained earnings statement.
(c) balance sheet.
(d) statement of cash flows.

*15. Services performed by a public accountant include: (LO 9)
(a) auditing, taxation, and management consulting.
(b) auditing, budgeting, and management consulting.
(c) auditing, budgeting, and cost accounting.
(d) internal auditing, budgeting, and management consulting.

Go to the book's companion website, www.wiley.com/college/weygandt, for additional Self-Test Questions.

QUESTIONS

1. "Accounting is ingrained in our society and it is vital to our economic system." Do you agree? Explain.
2. Identify and describe the steps in the accounting process.
3. (a) Who are internal users of accounting data?
(b) How does accounting provide relevant data to these users?
4. What uses of financial accounting information are made by (a) investors and (b) creditors?
5. "Bookkeeping and accounting are the same." Do you agree? Explain.
6. Harper Travel Agency purchased land for $85,000 cash on December 10, 2015. At December 31, 2015, the land's value has increased to $93,000. What amount should be reported for land on Harper's balance sheet at December 31, 2015? Explain.
7. What is the monetary unit assumption?
8. What is the economic entity assumption?
9. What are the three basic forms of profit-oriented business organizations?
10. Juana Perez is the owner of a successful printing shop. Recently, her business has been increasing, and Juana has been thinking about changing the organization of her business from a proprietorship to a corporation. Discuss some of the advantages Juana would enjoy if she were to incorporate her business.
11. What is the basic accounting equation?
12. (a) Define the terms assets, liabilities, and stockholders' equity.
(b) What items affect stockholders' equity?

13. Which of the following items are liabilities of jewelry stores?
(a) Cash.
(b) Accounts payable.
(c) Dividends.
(d) Accounts receivable.
(e) Supplies.
(f) Equipment.
(h) Service revenue.
(g) Salaries and wages payable.
(i) Rent expense.
14. Can a business enter into a transaction in which only the left side of the basic accounting equation is affected? If so, give an example.
15. Are the following events recorded in the accounting records? Explain your answer in each case.
(a) The president of the company dies.
(b) Supplies are purchased on account.
(c) An employee is fired.
16. Indicate how the following business transactions affect the basic accounting equation.
(a) Paid cash for janitorial services.
(b) Purchased equipment for cash.
(c) Invested cash in the business for stock.
(d) Paid accounts payable in full.
17. Listed below are some items found in the financial statements of Jonas Co. Indicate in which financial statement(s) the following items would appear.
(a) Service revenue.
(b) Equipment.
(c) Advertising expense.
(d) Accounts receivable.
(e) Retained earnings.
(f) Salaries and wages payable.
18. In February 2015, Rachel Paige invested an additional $10,000 in Drumlin Company. Drumlin's accountant,

Liz Cooke, recorded this receipt as an increase in cash and revenues. Is this treatment appropriate? Why or why not?

19. "A company's net income appears directly on the income statement and the retained earnings statement, and it is included indirectly in the company's balance sheet." Do you agree? Explain.

20. Monique Enterprises had a stockholders' equity balance of $158,000 at the beginning of the period. At the end of the accounting period, the stockholders' equity balance was $198,000.

   (a) Assuming no additional investment or distributions during the period, what is the net income for the period?

   (b) Assuming an additional investment of $16,000 but no distributions during the period, what is the net income for the period?

21. Summarized operations for Lakeview Co. for the month of July are as follows.

   Revenues recognized: for cash $30,000; on account $70,000.

   Expenses incurred: for cash $26,000; on account $38,000.

   Indicate for Lakeview Co. (a) the total revenues, (b) the total expenses, and (c) net income for the month of July.

22. The basic accounting equation is Assets = Liabilities + Stockholders' Equity. Replacing the words in that equation with dollar amounts, what is Apple's accounting equation at September 24, 2011?

BRIEF EXERCISES

Use basic accounting equation.

(LO 6)

BE1-1 Presented below is the basic accounting equation. Determine the missing amounts.

	Assets	=	Liabilities	+	Stockholders' Equity
(a)	$78,000		$50,000		?
(b)	?		$45,000		$70,000
(c)	$94,000		?		$60,000

Use basic accounting equation.

(LO 6)

BE1-2 Given the accounting equation, answer each of the following questions.

(a) The liabilities of Holland Company are $120,000 and its stockholders' equity is $232,000. What is the amount of Holland Company's total assets?

(b) The total assets of Holland Company are $190,000 and its stockholders' equity is $86,000. What is the amount of its total liabilities?

(c) The total assets of Holland Company are $600,000 and its liabilities are equal to one-half of its total assets. What is the amount of Holland Company's stockholders' equity?

Use basic accounting equation.

(LO 6)

BE1-3 At the beginning of the year, Canon Company had total assets of $870,000 and total liabilities of $500,000. Answer the following questions.

(a) If total assets increased $150,000 during the year and total liabilities decreased $80,000, what is the amount of stockholders' equity at the end of the year?

(b) During the year, total liabilities increased $100,000 and stockholders' equity decreased $66,000. What is the amount of total assets at the end of the year?

(c) If total assets decreased $80,000 and stockholders' equity increased $120,000 during the year, what is the amount of total liabilities at the end of the year?

Solve accounting equation.

(LO 6)

BE1-4 Use the accounting equation to answer each of the following questions.

(a) The liabilities of Olga Company are $90,000. Common stock account is $150,000; dividends are $40,000; revenues, $450,000; and expenses, $320,000. What is the amount of Olga Company's total assets?

(b) The total assets of Lafayette Company are $57,000. Common stock account is $23,000; dividends are $7,000; revenues, $50,000; and expenses, $35,000. What is the amount of the company's total liabilities?

(c) The total assets of Dierdorf Co. are $600,000 and its liabilities are equal to two-thirds of its total assets. What is the amount of Dierdorf Co.'s stockholders' equity?

Identify assets, liabilities, and stockholders' equity.

(LO 6)

BE1-5 Indicate whether each of the following items is an asset (A), liability (L), or part of stockholders' equity (SE).

_____	(a) Accounts receivable	_____	(d) Supplies
_____	(b) Salaries and wages payable	_____	(e) Owner's investment
_____	(c) Equipment	_____	(f) Notes payable

Determine effect of transactions on basic accounting equation.

(LO 7)

BE1-6 Presented on the next page are three business transactions. On a sheet of paper, list the letters (a), (b), and (c) with columns for assets, liabilities, and stockholders' equity. For each column, indicate whether the transactions increased (+), decreased (−), or had no effect (NE) on assets, liabilities, and stockholders' equity.

(a) Purchased supplies on account.

(b) Received cash for performing a service.

(c) Paid expenses in cash.

BE1-7 Follow the same format as BE1-6 above. Determine the effect on assets, liabilities, and stockholders' equity of the following three transactions.

(a) Stockholders invested cash in the business for common stock.

(b) Paid a cash dividend.

(c) Received cash from a customer who had previously been billed for services performed.

Determine effect of transactions on accounting equation.

(LO 7)

BE1-8 Classify each of the following items as dividends (D), revenue (R), or expense (E).

_____ **(a)** Advertising expense

_____ **(b)** Service revenue

_____ **(c)** Insurance expense

_____ **(d)** Salaries and wages expense

_____ **(e)** Dividends

_____ **(f)** Rent revenue

_____ **(g)** Utilities expense

Classify items affecting stockholders' equity.

(LO 6)

BE1-9 Presented below are three transactions. Mark each transaction as affecting common stock (C), dividends (D), revenue (R), expense (E), or not affecting stockholders' equity (NSE).

_____ **(a)** Received cash for services performed.

_____ **(b)** Paid cash to purchase equipment.

_____ **(c)** Paid employee salaries.

Determine effect of transactions on stockholders' equity.

(LO 6)

BE1-10 In alphabetical order below are balance sheet items for Ellerby Company at December 31, 2015. Prepare a balance sheet, following the format of Illustration 1-10.

Accounts payable	$85,000
Accounts receivable	$72,500
Cash	$44,000
Common stock	$31,500

Prepare a balance sheet.

(LO 8)

BE1-11 Indicate whether the following items would appear on the income statement (IS), balance sheet (BS), or retained earnings statement (RE).

_____ **(a)** Notes payable

_____ **(b)** Advertising expense

_____ **(c)** Common stock

_____ **(d)** Cash

_____ **(e)** Service revenue

_____ **(f)** Dividends

Determine where items appear on financial statements.

(LO 8)

> DO IT! Review

DO IT! 1-1 Indicate whether each of the five statements presented below is true or false. If false, indicate how to correct the statement.

Review basic concepts.

(LO 1, 2, 4)

1. The three steps in the accounting process are identification, recording, and examination.

2. The two most common types of external users are investors and creditors.

3. Congress passed the Sarbanes-Oxley Act to ensure that investors invest only in companies that will be profitable.

4. The primary accounting standard-setting body in the United States is the Securities and Exchange Commission (SEC).

5. The historical cost principle dictates that companies record assets at their cost and continue to report them at their cost over the time the asset is held.

DO IT! 1-2 Classify the following items as issuance of stock (I), dividends (D), revenues (R), or expenses (E). Then indicate whether each item increases or decreases stockholders' equity.

Evaluate effects of transactions on stockholders' equity.

(LO 6)

1. Dividends.

2. Rent revenue.

3. Advertising expense.

4. Stockholders invest cash in the business.

DO IT! 1-3 Transactions made by Morlan and Co., a law firm, for the month of March are shown on the next page. Prepare a tabular analysis which shows the effects of these transactions on the accounting equation, similar to that shown in Illustration 1-9 (page 21).

Prepare tabular analysis.

(LO 7)

1. The company performed $23,000 of services for customers, on credit.

2. The company received $23,000 in cash from customers who had been billed for services (in transaction 1).

3. The company received a bill for $1,800 of advertising, but will not pay it until a later date.

4. The company paid a dividend of $5,000 in cash to stockholders.

Calculate effects of transactions on financial statement items.

(LO 8)

DO IT! 1-4 Presented below is selected information related to Garryowen Company at December 31, 2015. Garryowen reports financial information monthly.

Accounts Payable	$ 3,000	Salaries and Wages Expense	$16,500
Cash	9,000	Notes Payable	25,000
Advertising Expense	6,000	Rent Expense	9,800
Service Revenue	54,000	Accounts Receivable	13,500
Equipment	29,000	Dividends	7,500

(a) Determine the total assets of Garryowen Company at December 31, 2015.
(b) Determine the net income that Garryowen Company reported for December 2015.
(c) Determine the stockholders' equity of Garryowen Company at December 31, 2015.

EXERCISES

Classify the three activities of accounting.

(LO 1)

E1-1 Callison Company performs the following accounting tasks during the year.

_____Analyzing and interpreting information.
_____Classifying economic events.
_____Explaining uses, meaning, and limitations of data.
_____Keeping a systematic chronological diary of events.
_____Measuring events in dollars and cents.
_____Preparing accounting reports.
_____Reporting information in a standard format.
_____Selecting economic activities relevant to the company.
_____Summarizing economic events.

Accounting is "an information system that **identifies**, **records**, and **communicates** the economic events of an organization to interested users."

Instructions
Categorize the accounting tasks performed by Callison as relating to either the identification (I), recording (R), or communication (C) aspects of accounting.

Identify users of accounting information.

(LO 2)

E1-2 (a) The following are users of financial statements.

_____Customers	_____Securities and Exchange Commission
_____Internal Revenue Service	_____Store manager
_____Labor unions	_____Suppliers
_____Marketing manager	_____Vice president of finance
_____Production supervisor	

Instructions
Identify the users as being either **external users (E)** or **internal users (I)**.

(b) The following questions could be asked by an internal user or an external user.

_____ Can we afford to give our employees a pay raise?
_____ Did the company earn a satisfactory income?
_____ Do we need to borrow in the near future?
_____ How does the company's profitability compare to other companies?
_____ What does it cost us to manufacture each unit produced?
_____ Which product should we emphasize?
_____ Will the company be able to pay its short-term debts?

Instructions
Identify each of the questions as being more likely asked by an **internal user (I)** or an **external user (E)**.

E1-3 Sam Cresco, president of Cresco Company, has instructed Sharon Gross, the head of the accounting department for Cresco Company, to report the company's land in the company's accounting reports at its fair value of $170,000 instead of its cost of $100,000. Cresco says, "Showing the land at $170,000 will make our company look like a better investment when we try to attract new investors next month."

Discuss ethics and the historical cost principle.
(LO 3)

Instructions
Explain the ethical situation involved for Sharon Gross, identifying the stakeholders and the alternatives.

E1-4 The following situations involve accounting principles and assumptions.

Use accounting concepts.
(LO 4, 5)

1. Tina Company owns buildings that are worth substantially more than they originally cost. In an effort to provide more relevant information, Tina reports the buildings at fair value in its accounting reports.
2. Fayette Company includes in its accounting records only transaction data that can be expressed in terms of money.
3. Omar Shariff, president of Omar's Oasis, records his personal living costs as expenses of Oasis.

Instructions
For each of the three situations, state if the accounting method used is correct or incorrect. If correct, identify which principle or assumption supports the method used. If incorrect, identify which principle or assumption has been violated.

E1-5 Bailey Cleaners has the following balance sheet items.

Classify accounts as assets, liabilities, and stockholders' equity.
(LO 6)

Accounts payable	Accounts receivable
Cash	Notes payable
Equipment	Salaries and wages payable
Supplies	Common stock

Instructions
Classify each item as an asset, liability, or stockholders' equity.

E1-6 Selected transactions for Verdent Lawn Care Company are listed below.

Analyze the effect of transactions.
(LO 6, 7)

1. Sold common stock for cash to start business.
2. Paid monthly rent.
3. Purchased equipment on account.
4. Billed customers for services performed.
5. Paid dividends.
6. Received cash from customers billed in (4).
7. Incurred advertising expense on account.
8. Purchased additional equipment for cash.
9. Received cash from customers when service was performed.

Instructions
List the numbers of the above transactions and describe the effect of each transaction on assets, liabilities, and stockholders' equity. For example, the first answer is (1) Increase in assets and increase in stockholders' equity.

E1-7 Keystone Computer Timeshare Company entered into the following transactions during May 2015.

Analyze the effect of transactions on assets, liabilities, and stockholders' equity.
(LO 6, 7)

1. Purchased computer terminals for $20,000 from Data Equipment on account.
2. Paid $3,000 cash for May rent on storage space.
3. Received $15,000 cash from customers for contracts billed in April.
4. Performed computer services for Ryan Construction Company for $2,700 cash.
5. Paid Midland Power Co. $11,000 cash for energy usage in May.
6. Stockholders invested an additional $32,000 in the business.
7. Paid Data Equipment for the terminals purchased in (1) above.
8. Incurred advertising expense for May of $840 on account.

Instructions

Indicate with the appropriate letter whether each of the transactions results in:

(a) An increase in assets and a decrease in assets.
(b) An increase in assets and an increase in stockholders' equity.
(c) An increase in assets and an increase in liabilities.
(d) A decrease in assets and a decrease in stockholders' equity.
(e) A decrease in assets and a decrease in liabilities.
(f) An increase in liabilities and a decrease in stockholders' equity.
(g) An increase in stockholders' equity and a decrease in liabilities.

Analyze transactions and compute net income.
(LO 7, 8)

E1-8 An analysis of the transactions made by Foley & Co., a certified public accounting firm, for the month of August is shown below. Each increase and decrease in stockholders' equity is explained.

	Cash	+	Accounts Receivable	+ Supplies	+ Equipment =	Accounts Payable	+ Common Stock	+ Rev.	− Exp.	− Div.	
1.	+$15,000						+$15,000				
2.	−2,000				+$5,000	+$3,000					
3.	−750			+$750							
4.	+4,900		+$4,500					+$9,400			Service Revenue
5.	−1,500					−1,500					
6.	−2,000									−$2,000	
7.	−850								−$850		Rent Expense
8.	+450		−450								
9.	−3,900								−3,900		Sal./Wages Expense
10.						+500			−500		Utilities Expense

With column group headers: **Assets** spans Cash, Accounts Receivable, Supplies, Equipment. **= Liabilities +** spans Accounts Payable. **Stockholders' Equity** spans Common Stock and **Retained Earnings** (Rev. − Exp. − Div.).

Instructions

(a) ▬▬▶ Describe each transaction that occurred for the month.
(b) Determine how much stockholders' equity increased for the month.
(c) Compute the amount of net income for the month.

Prepare financial statements.
(LO 8)

E1-9 An analysis of transactions for Foley & Co. was presented in E1–8. Assume that August is the company's first month of business.

Instructions

Prepare an income statement and a retained earnings statement for August and a balance sheet at August 31, 2015.

Determine net income (or loss).
(LO 7)

E1-10 Toth Company had the following assets and liabilities on the dates indicated.

December 31	Total Assets	Total Liabilities
2014	$400,000	$260,000
2015	$480,000	$300,000
2016	$590,000	$400,000

Toth began business on January 1, 2014, with an investment of $100,000 from stockholders.

Instructions

From an analysis of the change in stockholders' equity during the year, compute the net income (or loss) for:

(a) 2014, assuming Toth paid $15,000 in dividends for the year.
(b) 2015, assuming stockholders made an additional investment of $50,000 and Toth paid no dividends in 2015.
(c) 2016, assuming stockholders made an additional investment of $15,000 and Toth paid dividends of $30,000 in 2016.

Analyze financial statement items.
(LO 6, 7, 8)

E1-11 Two items are omitted from each of the following summaries of balance sheet and income statement data for two corporations for the year 2015, Plunkett Co. and Herring Enterprises.

	Plunkett Co.	Herring Enterprises
Beginning of year:		
Total assets	$ 97,000	$122,000
Total liabilities	85,000	(c)
Total stockholders' equity	(a)	75,000
End of year:		
Total assets	160,000	180,000
Total liabilities	120,000	50,000
Total stockholders' equity	40,000	130,000
Changes during year in stockholders' equity:		
Additional investment	(b)	25,000
Dividends	15,000	(d)
Total revenues	215,000	100,000
Total expenses	175,000	55,000

Instructions

Determine the missing amounts.

E1-12 The following information relates to La Greca Co. for the year 2015.

Prepare income statement and retained earnings statement.
(LO 8)

Retained earnings, January 1, 2015	$48,000	Advertising expense	$ 1,800
Dividends during 2015	5,000	Rent expense	10,400
Service revenue	62,500	Utilities expense	3,100
Salaries and wages expense	28,000		

Instructions

After analyzing the data, prepare an income statement and a retained earnings statement for the year ending December 31, 2015.

E1-13 Robyn Howser is the bookkeeper for Madison Company. Robyn has been trying to get the balance sheet of Madison Company to balance. Madison's balance sheet is shown below.

Correct an incorrectly prepared balance sheet.
(LO 8)

MADISON COMPANY
Balance Sheet
December 31, 2015

Assets		Liabilities	
Cash	$14,000	Accounts payable	$15,000
Supplies	3,000	Accounts receivable	(8,500)
Equipment	48,000	Common stock	50,000
Dividends	9,000	Retained earnings	17,500
Total assets	$74,000	Total liabilities and stockholders' equity	$74,000

Instructions

Prepare a correct balance sheet.

E1-14 Wyco Park, a public camping ground near the Four Corners National Recreation Area, has compiled the following financial information as of December 31, 2015.

Compute net income and prepare a balance sheet.
(LO 8)

Revenues during 2015—camping fees	$140,000	Notes payable	$ 60,000
Revenues during 2015—general store	47,000	Expenses during 2015	150,000
Accounts payable	11,000	Supplies on hand	2,500
Cash on hand	20,000	Common stock	20,000
Original cost of equipment	105,500	Retained earnings	?
Fair value of equipment	140,000		

Instructions

(a) Determine Wyco Park's net income for 2015.
(b) Prepare a balance sheet for Wyco Park as of December 31, 2015.

Prepare an income statement.
(LO 8)

E1-15 Presented below is financial information related to the 2015 operations of Louisa Cruise Company.

Maintenance and repairs expense	$ 92,000
Utilities expense	10,000
Salaries and wages expense	142,000
Advertising expense	3,500
Ticket revenue	328,000

Instructions
Prepare the 2015 income statement for Louisa Cruise Company.

Prepare a retained earnings statement.
(LO 8)

E1-16 Presented below is information related to Alexis and Ryans, Attorneys at Law.

Retained earnings, January 1, 2015	$ 23,000
Legal service revenue—2015	340,000
Total expenses—2015	211,000
Assets, January 1, 2015	85,000
Liabilities, January 1, 2015	62,000
Assets, December 31, 2015	168,000
Liabilities, December 31, 2015	80,000
Dividends—2015	64,000

Instructions
Prepare the 2015 retained earnings statement for Alexis and Ryans, Attorneys at Law.

Prepare a cash flow statement.
(LO 8)

E1-17 This information is for Paulo Company for the year ended December 31, 2015.

Cash received from revenues from customers	$600,000
Cash received for issuance of common stock	280,000
Cash paid for new equipment	115,000
Cash dividends paid	18,000
Cash paid for expenses	430,000
Cash balance 1/1/15	30,000

Instructions
Prepare the 2015 statement of cash flows for Paulo Company.

EXERCISES: SET B AND CHALLENGE EXERCISES

Visit the book's companion website, at **www.wiley.com/college/weygandt,** and choose the Student Companion site to access Exercise Set B and Challenge Exercises.

PROBLEMS: SET A

Analyze transactions and compute net income.
(LO 6, 7)

P1-1A Fredonia Repair Inc. was started on May 1. A summary of May transactions is presented below.

1. Stockholders invested $10,000 cash in the business in exchange for common stock.
2. Purchased equipment for $5,000 cash.
3. Paid $400 cash for May office rent.
4. Paid $300 cash for supplies.
5. Incurred $250 of advertising costs in the *Beacon News* on account.
6. Received $4,700 in cash from customers for repair service.
7. Declared and paid a $700 cash dividend.
8. Paid part-time employee salaries $1,000.
9. Paid utility bills $140.
10. Performed repair services worth $1,100 on account.
11. Collected cash of $120 for services billed in transaction (10).

Instructions

(a) Prepare a tabular analysis of the transactions using the following column headings: Cash, Accounts Receivable, Supplies, Equipment, Accounts Payable, Common Stock, and Retained Earnings (with separate columns for Revenues, Expenses, and Dividends). Include margin explanations for any changes in Retained Earnings. Revenue is called Service Revenue.

(b) From an analysis of the Retained Earnings columns, compute the net income or net loss for May.

P1-2A On August 31, the balance sheet of La Brava Veterinary Clinic showed Cash $9,000, Accounts Receivable $1,700, Supplies $600, Equipment $6,000, Accounts Payable $3,600, Common Stock $13,000, and Retained Earnings $700. During September, the following transactions occurred.

1. Paid $2,900 cash for accounts payable due.
2. Collected $1,300 of accounts receivable.
3. Purchased additional equipment for $2,100, paying $800 in cash and the balance on account.
4. Recognized revenue of $7,300, of which $2,500 is collected in cash and the balance is due in October.
5. Declared and paid a $400 cash dividend.
6. Paid salaries $1,700, rent for September $900, and advertising expense $200.
7. Incurred utilities expense for month on account $170.
8. Received $10,000 from Capital Bank on a 6-month note payable.

Instructions

(a) Prepare a tabular analysis of the September transactions beginning with August 31 balances. The column headings should be as follows: Cash + Accounts Receivable + Supplies + Equipment = Notes Payable + Accounts Payable + Common Stock + Retained Earnings + Revenues − Expenses − Dividends.

(b) Prepare an income statement for September, a retained earnings statement for September, and a balance sheet at September 30.

P1-3A On May 1, Nimbus Flying School, a company that provides flying lessons, was started with an investment of $45,000 cash in the business. Following are the assets and liabilities of the company on May 31, 2015, and the revenues and expenses for the month of May.

Cash	$ 4,650	Notes Payable	$28,000
Accounts Receivable	7,400	Rent Expense	900
Equipment	64,000	Maintenance and	
Service Revenue	6,800	Repairs Expense	350
Advertising Expense	500	Gasoline Expense	2,500
Accounts Payable	1,400	Utilities Expense	400

No additional investments were made in May, but the company paid dividends of $500 during the month.

Instructions

(a) Prepare an income statement and a retained earnings statement for the month of May and a balance sheet at May 31.

(b) Prepare an income statement and a retained earnings statement for May assuming the following data are not included above: (1) $900 worth of services were performed and billed but not collected at May 31, and (2) $1,500 of gasoline expense was incurred but not paid.

P1-4A Nancy Tercek started a delivery service, Tercek Deliveries, on June 1, 2015. The following transactions occurred during the month of June.

June 1 Stockholders invested $10,000 cash in the business in exchange for common stock.
2 Purchased a used van for deliveries for $14,000. Nancy paid $2,000 cash and signed a note payable for the remaining balance.
3 Paid $500 for office rent for the month.
5 Performed $4,800 of services on account.

(a) Total assets $13,560

Check figures let you know if you are on the right track with your solution.

(b) Net income $4,010

Analyze transactions and prepare income statement, retained earnings statement, and balance sheet.
(LO 6, 7, 8)

(a) Ending cash $15,900

(b) Net income $4,330
Total assets $29,800

Prepare income statement, retained earnings statement, and balance sheet.
(LO 8)

(a) Net income $2,150
Total assets $76,050
(b) Net income $1,550

Analyze transactions and prepare financial statements.
(LO 6, 7, 8)

June 9   Declared and paid $300 in cash dividends.
     12   Purchased supplies for $150 on account.
     15   Received a cash payment of $1,250 for services performed on June 5.
     17   Purchased gasoline for $100 on account.
     20   Received a cash payment of $1,500 for services performed.
     23   Made a cash payment of $500 on the note payable.
     26   Paid $250 for utilities.
     29   Paid for the gasoline purchased on account on June 17.
     30   Paid $1,000 for employee salaries.

Instructions

(a) Total assets $25,800

(a) Show the effects of the previous transactions on the accounting equation using the following format.

		Assets			=	Liabilities	+		Stockholders' Equity		
Date	Cash +	Accounts Receivable	+ Supplies +	Equipment =		Notes Payable	+ Accounts Payable +	Common Stock	+	Retained Earnings	
									Rev. −	Exp. −	Div.

Include margin explanations for any changes in the Retained Earnings account in your analysis.

(b) Net income $4,450

(c) Cash $8,100

(b) Prepare an income statement for the month of June.

(c) Prepare a balance sheet at June 30, 2015.

Determine financial statement amounts and prepare retained earnings statement.

(LO 7, 8)

P1-5A Financial statement information about four different companies is as follows.

	Donatello Company	Leonardo Company	Michelangelo Company	Raphael Company
January 1, 2015				
Assets	$ 75,000	$110,000	(g)	$150,000
Liabilities	48,000	(d)	$ 75,000	(j)
Stockholders' equity	(a)	60,000	45,000	100,000
December 31, 2015				
Assets	(b)	137,000	200,000	(k)
Liabilities	55,000	75,000	(h)	80,000
Stockholders' equity	40,000	(e)	130,000	140,000
Stockholders' equity changes in year				
Additional investment	(c)	15,000	10,000	15,000
Dividends	6,000	(f)	14,000	10,000
Total revenues	350,000	420,000	(i)	500,000
Total expenses	335,000	382,000	342,000	(l)

Instructions

(a) Determine the missing amounts. (*Hint:* For example, to solve for (a), Assets − Liabilities = Stockholders' Equity = $27,000.)

(b) Prepare the retained earnings statement for Leonardo Company. Assume beginning retained earnings was $20,000.

(c) ━━━ Write a memorandum explaining the sequence for preparing financial statements and the interrelationship of the retained earnings statement to the income statement and balance sheet.

PROBLEMS: SET B

Analyze transactions and compute net income.

(LO 6, 7)

P1-1B On April 1, Bill Taylor established Taylor Made Travel Agency. The following transactions were completed during the month.

1. Stockholders invested $8,000 cash in the business in exchange for common stock.
2. Paid $400 cash for April office rent.
3. Purchased office equipment for $2,500 cash.
4. Incurred $300 of advertising costs in the *Chicago Tribune*, on account.

5. Paid $500 cash for office supplies.
6. Performed services worth $8,500: $2,000 cash is received from customers, and the balance of $6,500 is billed to customers on account.
7. Declared and paid a $200 cash dividend.
8. Paid *Chicago Tribune* amount due in transaction (4).
9. Paid employees' salaries $2,000.
10. Received $5,700 in cash from customers billed previously in transaction (6).

Instructions

(a) Prepare a tabular analysis of the transactions using the following column headings: Cash, Accounts Receivable, Supplies, Equipment, Accounts Payable, Common Stock, and Retained Earnings (with separate columns for Revenues, Expenses, and Dividends). Include margin explanation for any changes in Retained Earnings.

(a) Ending cash $9,800

(b) From an analysis of the Retained Earnings columns, compute the net income or net loss for April.

(b) Net income $5,800

P1-2B Randy Coburn opened a law office, Randy Coburn, Attorney at Law, on July 1, 2015. On July 31, the balance sheet showed Cash $4,000, Accounts Receivable $1,500, Supplies $400, Equipment $5,000, Accounts Payable $4,200, Common Stock $6,000, and Retained Earnings $700. During August, the following transactions occurred.

Analyze transactions and prepare income statement, retained earnings statement, and balance sheet.

(LO 6, 7, 8)

1. Collected $1,400 of accounts receivable due from clients.
2. Paid $2,700 cash for accounts payable due.
3. Recognized revenue of $7,900 of which $3,000 is collected in cash and the balance is due in September.
4. Purchased additional equipment for $1,000, paying $400 in cash and the balance on account.
5. Paid salaries $3,000, rent for August $900, and advertising expenses $250.
6. Declared and paid a $450 cash dividend.
7. Received $2,000 from Standard Federal Bank; the money was borrowed on a 4-month note payable.
8. Incurred utility expenses for month on account $180.

Instructions

(a) Prepare a tabular analysis of the August transactions beginning with July 31 balances. The column headings should be as follows: Cash + Accounts Receivable + Supplies + Equipment = Notes Payable + Accounts Payable + Common Stock + Retained Earnings + Revenues − Expenses − Dividends.

(a) Ending expenses $4,330

(b) Prepare an income statement for August, a retained earnings statement for August, and a balance sheet at August 31.

(b) Net income $3,570
    Total assets $14,100

P1-3B Blushe Cosmetics Co., a company that provides individual skin care treatment, was started on June 1 with an investment of $22,000 cash. Following are the assets and liabilities of the company at June 30 and the revenues and expenses for the month of June.

Prepare income statement, retained earnings statement, and balance sheet.

(LO 8)

Cash	$ 8,000	Notes Payable	$13,000
Accounts Receivable	4,000	Accounts Payable	1,400
Service Revenue	5,300	Rent Expense	1,200
Supplies	1,300	Gasoline Expense	600
Advertising Expense	500	Utilities Expense	300
Equipment	25,000		

Stockholders made no additional investments in June. The company paid a cash dividend of $800 during the month.

Instructions

(a) Prepare an income statement and a retained earnings statement for the month of June and a balance sheet at June 30, 2015.

(a) Net income $1,900
    Total assets $38,300

(b) Prepare an income statement and a retained earnings statement for June assuming the following data are not included above: (1) $800 worth of services were performed and billed but not collected at June 30, and (2) $100 of gasoline expense was incurred but not paid.

(b) Net income $3,400

Analyze transactions and prepare financial statements.

(LO 6, 7, 8)

P1-4B Gloria Rodd started a consulting firm, Rodd Consulting, on May 1, 2015. The following transactions occurred during the month of May.

May	1	Rodd invested $8,000 cash in the business in exchange for stock.
	2	Paid $800 for office rent for the month.
	3	Purchased $500 of supplies on account.
	5	Paid $90 to advertise in the *County News*.
	9	Received $3,000 cash for services performed.
	12	Declared and paid a $700 cash dividend.
	15	Performed $3,500 of services on account.
	17	Paid $2,100 for employee salaries.
	20	Paid for the supplies purchased on account on May 3.
	23	Received a cash payment of $2,500 for services performed on account on May 15.
	26	Borrowed $5,000 from the bank on a note payable.
	29	Purchased equipment for $2,600 on account.
	30	Paid $150 for utilities.

Instructions

(a) Total assets $18,260

(a) Show the effects of the previous transactions on the accounting equation using the following format.

			Assets		=	Liabilities	+		Stockholders' Equity	
Date	Cash +	Accounts Receivable	+ Supplies +	Equipment =		Notes Payable	+ Accounts Payable	+	Common Stock	+ Retained Earnings Rev. − Exp. − Div.

Include margin explanations for any changes in the Retained Earnings account in your analysis.

(b) Net income $3,360
(c) Cash $14,160

(b) Prepare an income statement for the month of May.
(c) Prepare a balance sheet at May 31, 2015.

Determine financial statement amounts and prepare retained earnings statement.

(LO 7, 8)

P1-5B Financial statement information about four different companies is shown below.

	Chico Company	Harpo Company	Groucho Company	Zeppo Company
January 1, 2015				
Assets	$ 78,000	$ 90,000	(g)	$150,000
Liabilities	50,000	(d)	$ 75,000	(j)
Stockholders' equity	(a)	46,000	54,000	100,000
December 31, 2015				
Assets	(b)	117,000	180,000	(k)
Liabilities	55,000	79,000	(h)	80,000
Stockholders' equity	40,000	(e)	100,000	160,000
Stockholders' equity changes in year				
Additional investment	(c)	8,000	10,000	15,000
Dividends	10,000	(f)	12,000	10,000
Total revenues	350,000	390,000	(i)	500,000
Total expenses	335,000	400,000	360,000	(l)

Instructions

(a) Determine the missing amounts. (*Hint:* For example, to solve for (a), Assets − Liabilities = Stockholders' Equity = $28,000.)
(b) Prepare the retained earnings statement for Chico Company. Assume beginning retained earnings was $0.
(c) ━━━━ Write a memorandum explaining the sequence for preparing financial statements and the interrelationship of the retained earnings statement to the income statement and balance sheet.

PROBLEMS: SET C

Visit the book's website, at **www.wiley.com/college/weygandt**, and choose the Student Companion site to access Problem Set C.

CONTINUING COOKIE CHRONICLE

CCC1 Natalie Koebel spent much of her childhood learning the art of cookie-making from her grandmother. They passed many happy hours mastering every type of cookie imaginable and later creating new recipes that were both healthy and delicious. Now at the start of her second year in college, Natalie is investigating various possibilities for starting her own business as part of the requirements of the entrepreneurship program in which she is enrolled.

A long-time friend insists that Natalie has to somehow include cookies in her business plan. After a series of brainstorming sessions, Natalie settles on the idea of operating a cookie-making school. She will start on a part-time basis and offer her services in people's homes. Now that she has started thinking about it, the possibilities seem endless. During the fall, she will concentrate on holiday cookies. She will offer individual lessons and group sessions (which will probably be more entertainment than education for the participants). Natalie also decides to include children in her target market.

The Continuing Cookie Chronicle starts in this chapter and continues in every chapter. You also can find this problem at the book's companion website.

The first difficult decision is coming up with the perfect name for her business. In the end, she settles on "Cookie Creations" and then moves on to more important issues.

Instructions

(a) What form of business organization—proprietorship, partnership, or corporation—do you recommend that Natalie use for her business? Discuss the benefits and weaknesses of each form and give the reasons for your choice.

(b) Will Natalie need accounting information? If yes, what information will she need and why? How often will she need this information?

(c) Identify specific asset, liability, and stockholders' equity accounts that Cookie Creations will likely use to record its business transactions.

(d) Should Natalie open a separate bank account for the business? Why or why not?

Broadening Your PERSPECTIVE

Financial Reporting and Analysis

Financial Reporting Problem: Apple Inc.

BYP1-1 The actual financial statements of Apple Inc. for 2011 are presented in Appendix A. Instructions for accessing and using the company's complete annual report, including the notes to the financial statements, are also provided in Appendix A.

Instructions

Refer to Apple's financial statements and answer the following questions.

(a) What were Apple's total assets at September 24, 2011? At September 25, 2010?

(b) How much cash (and cash equivalents) did Apple have on September 24, 2011?

(c) What amount of accounts payable did Apple report on September 24, 2011? On September 25, 2010?

(d) What were Apple's net sales in 2009? In 2010? In 2011?

(e) What is the amount of the change in Apple's net income from 2010 to 2011?

Comparative Analysis Problem:
PepsiCo, Inc. vs. The Coca-Cola Company

BYP1-2 PepsiCo's financial statements are presented in Appendix B. Financial statements of The Coca-Cola Company are presented in Appendix C. Instructions for accessing and using the complete annual reports of PepsiCo and Coca-Cola, including the notes to the financial statements, are also provided in Appendices B and C, respectively.

Instructions
(a) Based on the information contained in these financial statements, determine the following for each company.
   (1) Total assets at December 31, 2011, for PepsiCo and for Coca-Cola at December 31, 2011.
   (2) Accounts (notes) receivable, net at December 31, 2011, for PepsiCo and at December 31, 2011, for Coca-Cola.
   (3) Net revenues for the year ended in 2011.
   (4) Net income for the year ended in 2011.
(b) What conclusions concerning the two companies can be drawn from these data?

Comparative Analysis Problem:
Amazon.com, Inc. vs. Wal-Mart Stores, Inc.

BYP1-3 Amazon.com, Inc.'s financial statements are presented in Appendix D. Financial statements for Wal-Mart Stores, Inc. are presented in Appendix E. Instructions for accessing and using the complete annual reports of Amazon and Wal-Mart, including the notes to the financial statements, are also provided in Appendices D and E, respectively.

Instructions
(a) Based on the information contained in these financial statements, determine the following for each company.
   (1) Total assets at December 31, 2011, for Amazon and for Wal-Mart at January 31, 2012.
   (2) Receivables (net) at December 31, 2011, for Amazon and for Wal-Mart at January 31, 2012.
   (3) Net sales (product only) for the year ended in 2011 (2012 for Wal-Mart).
   (4) Net income for the year ended in 2011 (2012 for Wal-Mart).
(b) What conclusions concerning these two companies can be drawn from these data?

Real-World Focus

BYP1-4 This exercise will familiarize you with skill requirements, job descriptions, and salaries for accounting careers.

Address: **www.careers-in-accounting.com**, or go to **www.wiley.com/college/weygandt**

Instructions
Go to the site shown above. Answer the following questions.

(a) What are the three broad areas of accounting (from "Skills and Talents")?
(b) List eight skills required in accounting.
(c) How do the three accounting areas differ in terms of these eight required skills?
(d) Explain one of the key job options in accounting.
(e) What is the overall salary range for a junior staff accountant?

Critical Thinking

Decision-Making Across the Organization

BYP1-5 Kathy and James Mohr, local golf stars, opened the Chip-Shot Driving Range Company on March 1, 2015. They invested $25,000 cash and received common stock in exchange for their investment. A caddy shack was constructed for cash at a cost of $8,000, and $800 was spent on golf balls and golf clubs. The Mohrs leased five acres of land at a cost of $1,000 per month and paid the first month's rent. During the first month, advertising costs totaled $750, of which $150 was unpaid

at March 31, and $400 was paid to members of the high-school golf team for retrieving golf balls. All revenues from customers were deposited in the company's bank account. On March 15, Kathy and James received a dividend of $1,000. A $100 utility bill was received on March 31 but was not paid. On March 31, the balance in the company's bank account was $18,900.

Kathy and James thought they had a pretty good first month of operations. But, their estimates of profitability ranged from a loss of $6,100 to net income of $2,450.

Instructions

With the class divided into groups, answer the following.

(a) How could the Mohrs have concluded that the business operated at a loss of $6,100? Was this a valid basis on which to determine net income?

(b) How could the Mohrs have concluded that the business operated at a net income of $2,450? (*Hint:* Prepare a balance sheet at March 31.) Was this a valid basis on which to determine net income?

(c) Without preparing an income statement, determine the actual net income for March.

(d) What was the revenue recognized in March?

Communication Activity

BYP1-6 Ashley Hirano, the bookkeeper for New York Company, has been trying to get the balance sheet to balance. The company's balance sheet is shown below.

NEW YORK COMPANY			
Balance Sheet			
For the Month Ended December 31, 2015			
Assets		**Liabilities**	
Equipment	$25,500	Common stock	$26,000
Cash	9,000	Accounts receivable	(6,000)
Supplies	2,000	Retained earnings	(2,000)
Accounts payable	(8,000)	Notes payable	10,500
	$28,500		$28,500

Instructions

Explain to Ashley Hirano in a memo why the original balance sheet is incorrect, and what should be done to correct it.

Ethics Case

BYP1-7 After numerous campus interviews, Greg Thorpe, a senior at Great Northern College, received two office interview invitations from the Baltimore offices of two large firms. Both firms offered to cover his out-of-pocket expenses (travel, hotel, and meals). He scheduled the interviews for both firms on the same day, one in the morning and one in the afternoon. At the conclusion of each interview, he submitted to both firms his total out-of-pocket expenses for the trip to Baltimore: mileage $112 (280 miles at $0.40), hotel $130, meals $36, and parking and tolls $18, for a total of $296. He believes this approach is appropriate. If he had made two trips, his cost would have been two times $296. He is also certain that neither firm knew he had visited the other on that same trip. Within 10 days, Greg received two checks in the mail, each in the amount of $296.

Instructions

(a) Who are the stakeholders (affected parties) in this situation?

(b) What are the ethical issues in this case?

(c) What would you do in this situation?

All About You

BYP1-8 Some people are tempted to make their finances look worse to get financial aid. Companies sometimes also manage their financial numbers in order to accomplish certain goals. Earnings management is the planned timing of revenues, expenses, gains, and losses to smooth out bumps in net income. In managing earnings, companies' actions vary from being within the range of ethical activity, to being both unethical and illegal attempts to mislead investors and creditors.

Instructions
Provide responses for each of the following questions.

(a) Discuss whether you think each of the following actions (adapted from **www.finaid.org/fafsa/maximize.phtml**) to increase the chances of receiving financial aid is ethical.

   (1) Spend down the student's assets and income first, before spending parents' assets and income.

   (2) Accelerate necessary expenses to reduce available cash. For example, if you need a new car, buy it before applying for financial aid.

   (3 State that a truly financially dependent child is independent.

   (4) Have a parent take an unpaid leave of absence for long enough to get below the "threshold" level of income.

(b) What are some reasons why a **company** might want to overstate its earnings?

(c) What are some reasons why a **company** might want to understate its earnings?

(d) Under what circumstances might an otherwise ethical person decide to illegally overstate or understate earnings?

BYP1-9 When companies need money, they go to investors or creditors. Before investors or creditors will give a company cash, they want to know the company's financial position and performance. They want to see the company's financial statements—the balance sheet and the income statement. When students need money for school, they often apply for financial aid. When you apply for financial aid, you must submit your own version of a financial statement—the Free Application for Federal Student Aid (FAFSA) form.

Suppose you have $4,000 in cash and $4,000 in credit card bills. The more cash and other assets that you have, the less likely you are to get financial aid. Also, if you have a lot of consumer debt (credit card bills), schools are not more likely to loan you money. To increase your chances of receiving aid, should you use the cash to pay off your credit card bills and therefore make yourself look "worse off" to the financial aid decision-makers?

YES: You are playing within the rules. You are not hiding assets. You are simply restructuring your assets and liabilities to best conform with the preferences that are built into the federal aid formulas.

NO: You are engaging in a transaction solely to take advantage of a loophole in the federal aid rules. In doing so, you are potentially depriving someone who is actually worse off than you from receiving aid.

Instructions
Write a response indicating your position regarding this situation. Provide support for your view.

FASB Codification Activity

BYP1-10 The FASB has developed the Financial Accounting Standards Board Accounting Standards Codification (or more simply "the Codification"). The FASB's primary goal in developing the Codification is to provide in one place all the authoritative literature related to a particular topic. To provide easy access to the Codification, the FASB also developed the Financial Accounting Standards Board Codification Research System (CRS). CRS is an online, real-time database that provides easy access to the Codification. The Codification and the related CRS provide a topically organized structure, subdivided into topic, subtopics, sections, and paragraphs, using a numerical index system.

You may find this system useful in your present and future studies, and so we have provided an opportunity to use this online system as part of the *Broadening Your Perspective* section.

Instructions
Academic access to the FASB Codification is available through university subscriptions, obtained from the American Accounting Association (at **http://aaahq.org/FASB/Access.cfm**), for an annual fee of $250. This subscription covers an unlimited number of students within a single institution. Once this access has been obtained by your school, you should log in (at **http://aaahq.org/ascLogin.cfm**) and familiarize yourself with the resources that are accessible at the FASB Codification site.

Considering People, Planet, and Profit

BYP1-11 This chapter's Feature Story discusses the fact that although Clif Bar & Company is not a public company, it does share its financial information with its employees as part of its open-book management approach. Further, although it does not publicly share its financial information, it does provide a different form of an annual report to external users. In this report, the company provides information regarding its sustainability efforts.

Address: **www.clifbar.com/uploads/default/ClifBar_AA2010.pdf**

Instructions
Access the 2010 annual report of Clif Bar & Company at the site shown above and then answer the following questions.

(a) What are the Five Aspirations?
(b) What are the four key goals of the company's sustainability efforts related to the planet? Give one example of a recent initiative, and a measurable outcome for that initiative, that the company has taken related to each goal.

Answers to Chapter Questions

Answers to Insight and Accounting Across the Organization Questions

p. 6 The Scoop on Accounting   Q: What are the benefits to the company and to the employees of making the financial statements available to all employees? **A:** If employees can read and use financial reports, a company will benefit in the following ways. The **marketing department** will make better decisions about products to offer and prices to charge. The **finance department** will make better decisions about debt and equity financing and how much to distribute in dividends. The **production department** will make better decisions about when to buy new equipment and how much inventory to produce. The **human resources department** will be better able to determine whether employees can be given raises. Finally, **all employees** will be better informed about the basis on which they are evaluated, which will increase employee morale.

p. 8 The Numbers Behind Not-for-Profit Organizations   Q: What benefits does a sound accounting system provide to a not-for-profit organization? **A:** Accounting provides at least two benefits to not-for-profit organizations. First, it helps to ensure that money is used in the way that donors intended. Second, it assures donors that their money is not going to waste and thus increases the likelihood of future donations.

p. 10 The Korean Discount   Q: What is meant by the phrase "make the country's businesses more transparent"? Why would increasing transparency spur economic growth? **A:** Transparency refers to the extent to which outsiders have knowledge regarding a company's financial performance and financial position. If a company lacks transparency, its financial reports do not adequately inform investors of critical information that is needed to make investment decisions. If corporate transparency is increased, investors would be more willing to supply the financial capital that businesses need in order to grow, which would spur the country's economic growth.

p. 12 Spinning the Career Wheel   Q: How might accounting help you? **A:** You will need to understand financial reports in any enterprise with which you are associated. Whether you become a manager, a doctor, a lawyer, a social worker, a teacher, an engineer, an architect, or an entrepreneur, a working knowledge of accounting is relevant.

p. 25 Beyond Financial Statements   Q: Why might a company's stockholders be interested in its environmental and social performance? **A:** Many companies now recognize that being a socially responsible organization is not only the right thing to do, but it also is good for business. Many investment professionals understand, for example, that environmental, social, and proper corporate governance of companies affects the performance of their investment portfolios. For example, British Petroleum's oil spill disaster is a classic example of the problems that can occur for a company and its stockholders. BP's stock price was slashed, its dividend reduced, its executives replaced, and its reputation badly damaged. It is interesting that socially responsible investment funds are now gaining momentum in the marketplace such that companies now recognize this segment as an important investment group.

Answers to Self-Test Questions

1. b **2.** d **3.** c **4.** b **5.** b **6.** d **7.** d ($3,500 − $1,500) **8.** b **9.** b **10.** a ($90,000 − $50,000) **11.** d **12.** c **13.** b **14.** c ***15.** a

A Look at IFRS

LEARNING OBJECTIVE   10

Describe the impact of international accounting standards on U.S. financial reporting.

Most agree that there is a need for one set of international accounting standards. Here is why:

Multinational corporations. Today's companies view the entire world as their market. For example, Coca-Cola, Intel, and McDonald's generate more than 50% of their sales outside the United States, and many foreign companies, such as Toyota, Nestlé, and Sony, find their largest market to be the United States.

Mergers and acquisitions. The mergers between Fiat/Chrysler and Vodafone/Mannesmann suggest that we will see even more such business combinations of companies from different countries in the future.

Information technology. As communication barriers continue to topple through advances in technology, companies and individuals in different countries and markets are becoming more comfortable buying and selling goods and services from one another.

Financial markets. Financial markets are of international significance today. Whether it is currency, equity securities (stocks), bonds, or derivatives, there are active markets throughout the world trading these types of instruments.

Key Points

- International standards are referred to as **International Financial Reporting Standards (IFRS)**, developed by the International Accounting Standards Board (IASB).

- Recent events in the global capital markets have underscored the importance of financial disclosure and transparency not only in the United States but in markets around the world. As a result, many are examining which accounting and financial disclosure rules should be followed. As indicated in the graphic below, much of the world has voted for the standards issued by the IASB. Over 115 countries require or permit use of IFRS.

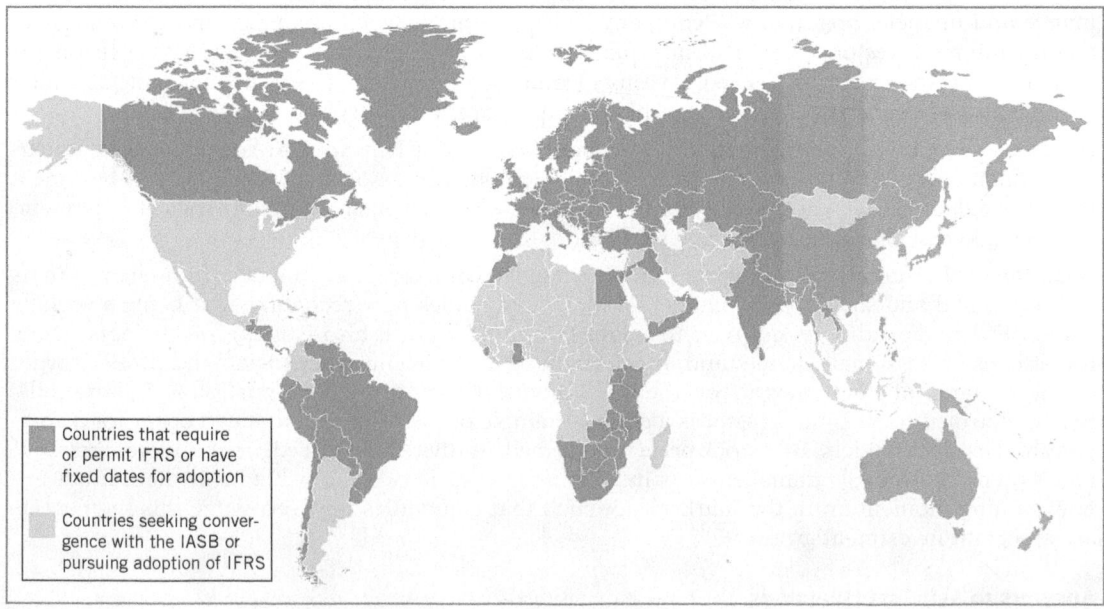

Countries that require or permit IFRS or have fixed dates for adoption

Countries seeking convergence with the IASB or pursuing adoption of IFRS

Source: http://www.pwc.com/us/en/issues/ifrs-reporting/country-adoption/index.html.

- U.S standards, referred to as generally accepted accounting principles (GAAP), are developed by the Financial Accounting Standards Board (FASB). The fact that there are differences between what is in this textbook (which is based on U.S. standards) and IFRS should not be surprising because the FASB and IASB have responded to different user needs. In some countries, the primary users of financial statements are private investors; in others, the primary users are tax authorities or central government planners. It appears that the United States and the international standard-setting environment are primarily driven by meeting the needs of investors and creditors.

- The internal control standards applicable to Sarbanes-Oxley (SOX) apply only to large public companies listed on U.S. exchanges. There is a continuing debate as to whether non-U.S. companies should have to comply with this extra layer of regulation. Debate about international companies (non-U.S.) adopting SOX-type standards centers on whether the benefits exceed the costs. The concern is that the higher costs of SOX compliance are making the U.S. securities markets less competitive.

- The textbook mentions a number of ethics violations, such as Enron, WorldCom, and AIG. These problems have also occurred internationally, for example, at Satyam Computer Services (India), Parmalat (Italy), and Royal Ahold (the Netherlands).

- IFRS tends to be simpler in its accounting and disclosure requirements; some people say more "principles-based." GAAP is more detailed; some people say it is more "rules-based." This difference in approach has resulted in a debate about the merits of "principles-based" versus "rules-based" standards.

- U.S. regulators have recently eliminated the need for foreign companies that trade shares in U.S. markets to reconcile their accounting with GAAP.

- The three most common forms of business organization, proprietorships, partnerships, and corporations, are also found in countries that use IFRS. Because the choice of business organization is influenced by factors such as legal environment, tax rates and regulations, and degree of entrepreneurism, the relative use of each form will vary across countries.

- The conceptual framework that underlies IFRS is very similar to that used to develop GAAP. The basic definitions provided in this textbook for the key elements of financial statements, that is, assets, liabilities, equity, revenues (**referred to as income**), and expenses, are simplified versions of the official definitions provided by the FASB. The more substantive definitions, using the IASB definitional structure, are as follows.

    Assets. A resource controlled by the entity as a result of past events and from which future economic benefits are expected to flow to the entity.

    Liabilities. A present obligation of the entity arising from past events, the settlement of which is expected to result in an outflow from the entity of resources embodying economic benefits. Liabilities may be legally enforceable via a contract or law, but need not be, i.e., they can arise due to normal business practice or customs.

    Equity. A residual interest in the assets of the entity after deducting all its liabilities.

    Income. Increases in economic benefits that result in increases in equity (other than those related to contributions from shareholders). Income includes both revenues (resulting from ordinary activities) and gains.

    Expenses. Decreases in economic benefits that result in decreases in equity (other than those related to distributions to shareholders). Expenses includes losses that are not the result of ordinary activities.

Looking to the Future

Both the IASB and the FASB are hard at work developing standards that will lead to the elimination of major differences in the way certain transactions are accounted for and reported. In fact, at one time the IASB stated that no new major standards would be issued for a period of time. The major reason for this policy was to provide companies the time to translate and implement IFRS into practice, as much has happened in a very short period of time. Consider, for example, that as a result of a joint project on the conceptual framework, the definitions of the most fundamental elements (assets, liabilities, equity, revenues, and expenses) may actually change. However, whether the IASB adopts internal control provisions similar to those in SOX remains to be seen.

IFRS Practice

IFRS Self-Test Questions

1. Which of the following is **not** a reason why a single set of high-quality international accounting standards would be beneficial?
   (a) Mergers and acquisition activity.
   (b) Financial markets.
   (c) Multinational corporations.
   (d) GAAP is widely considered to be a superior reporting system.

2. The Sarbanes-Oxley Act determines:
   (a) international tax regulations.
   (b) internal control standards as enforced by the IASB.
   (c) internal control standards of U.S. publicly traded companies.
   (d) U.S. tax regulations.

3. IFRS is considered to be more:
   (a) principles-based and less rules-based than GAAP.
   (b) rules-based and less principles-based than GAAP.
   (c) detailed than GAAP.
   (d) None of the above.

4. Which of the following statements is **false**?
   (a) IFRS is based on a conceptual framework that is similar to that used to develop GAAP.
   (b) Assets are defined by the IASB as resources controlled by the entity as a result of past events and from which future economic benefits are expected to flow to the entity.
   (c) Non-U.S. companies that trade shares in U.S. markets must reconcile their accounting with GAAP.
   (d) Proprietorships, partnerships, and corporations are also found in countries that use IFRS.

5. Which of the following statements is **true**?
   (a) Under IFRS, the term income refers to what would be called revenues and gains under GAAP.
   (b) The term income is not used under IFRS.
   (c) The term income refers only to gains on investments.
   (d) Under IFRS, expenses include distributions to owners.

IFRS Exercises

IFRS1-1 Who are the two key international players in the development of international accounting standards? Explain their role.

IFRS1-2 What might explain the fact that different accounting standard-setters have developed accounting standards that are sometimes quite different in nature?

IFRS1-3 What is the benefit of a single set of high-quality accounting standards?

IFRS1-4 Discuss the potential advantages and disadvantages that countries outside the United States should consider before adopting regulations, such as those in the Sarbanes-Oxley Act, that increase corporate internal control requirements.

International Financial Reporting Problem: Zetar plc

IFRS1-5 The financial statements of Zetar plc are presented in Appendix F. Instructions for accessing and using the company's complete annual report, including the notes to its financial statements, are also provided in Appendix F.

Instructions

Visit Zetar's corporate website and answer the following questions from Zetar's 2011 annual report.

(a) What accounting firm performed the audit of Zetar's financial statements?

(b) What is the address of the company's corporate headquarters?

(c) What is the company's reporting currency?

(d) What two segments does the company operate in, and what were the sales for each segment in the year ended April 30, 2011?

Answers to IFRS Self-Test Questions

1. d **2.** c **3.** a **4.** c **5.** a

2 | The Recording Process

Accidents Happen

How organized are you financially? Take a short quiz. Answer yes or no to each question:

- Does your wallet contain so many cash machine receipts that you've been declared a walking fire hazard?
- Do you wait until your debit card is denied before checking the status of your funds?
- Was Aaron Rodgers (the quarterback for the Green Bay Packers) playing high school football the last time you verified the accuracy of your bank account?

If you think it is hard to keep track of the many transactions that make up your life, imagine how difficult it is for a big corporation to do so. Not only that, but now consider how important it is for a large company to have good accounting records, especially if

it has control of your life savings. MF Global Holdings Ltd is such a company. As a big investment broker, it held billions of dollars of investments for clients. If you had your life savings invested at MF Global, you might be slightly displeased if you heard this from one of its representatives: "You know, I kind of remember an account for someone with a name like yours—now what did we do with that?"

Unfortunately, that is almost exactly what happened to MF Global's clients shortly before it filed for bankruptcy. During the days immediately following the bankruptcy filing, regulators and auditors struggled to piece things together. In the words of one regulator, "Their books are a disaster . . . we're trying to figure out what numbers are real numbers." One company that considered buying an interest in MF Global walked away from the deal because it "couldn't get a sense of what was on the balance sheet." That company said the information

 The Navigator

- ■ Scan Learning Objectives
- ■ Read Feature Story
- ■ Read Preview
- ■ Read text and answer **DO IT!** p. 61
    - ■ p. 64   ■ p. 74   ■ p. 78
- ■ Work Comprehensive **DO IT!** p. 78
- ■ Review Summary of Learning Objectives
- ■ Answer Self-Test Questions
- ■ Complete Assignments
- ■ Go to *WileyPLUS* for practice and tutorials
- 🌐 Read **A Look at IFRS** p. 100

Learning Objectives ✔ **The Navigator**

After studying this chapter, you should be able to:

[1] Explain what an account is and how it helps in the recording process.

[2] Define debits and credits and explain their use in recording business transactions.

[3] Identify the basic steps in the recording process.

[4] Explain what a journal is and how it helps in the recording process.

[5] Explain what a ledger is and how it helps in the recording process.

[6] Explain what posting is and how it helps in the recording process.

[7] Prepare a trial balance and explain its purposes.

Nick Laham/Getty Images, Inc.

that should have been instantly available instead took days to produce.

It now appears that MF Global did not properly segregate customer accounts from company accounts. And, because of its sloppy record-keeping, customers were not protected when the company had financial troubles. Total customer losses were approximately $1 billion. As you can see, accounting matters!

Source: S. Patterson and A. Lucchetti, "Inside the Hunt for MF Global Cash," *Wall Street Journal Online* (November 11, 2011).

Preview of Chapter 2

✔ **The Navigator**

In Chapter 1, we analyzed business transactions in terms of the accounting equation, and we presented the cumulative effects of these transactions in tabular form. Imagine a company like MF Global (as in the Feature Story) using the same tabular format as Softbyte Inc. to keep track of its transactions. In a single day, MF Global engaged in thousands of business transactions. To record each transaction this way would be impractical, expensive, and unnecessary. Instead, companies use a set of procedures and records to keep track of transaction data more easily. This chapter introduces and illustrates these basic procedures and records.

The content and organization of Chapter 2 are as follows.

THE RECORDING PROCESS

The Account	Steps in the Recording Process	The Trial Balance
• Debits and credits	• Journal	• Limitations of a trial balance
• Stockholders' equity relationships	• Ledger	• Locating errors
• Summary of debit/credit rules	• Posting	• Use of dollar signs
	• The recording process illustrated	

The Account

LEARNING OBJECTIVE　1

Explain what an account is and how it helps in the recording process.

An **account** is an individual accounting record of increases and decreases in a specific asset, liability, or stockholders' equity item. For example, Softbyte Inc. (the company discussed in Chapter 1) would have separate accounts for Cash, Accounts Receivable, Accounts Payable, Service Revenue, Salaries and Wages Expense, and so on. (Note that whenever we are referring to a specific account, we capitalize the name.)

In its simplest form, an account consists of three parts: (1) a title, (2) a left or debit side, and (3) a right or credit side. Because the format of an account resembles the letter T, we refer to it as a **T-account**. Illustration 2-1 shows the basic form of an account.

Illustration 2-1
Basic form of account

We use this form often throughout this textbook to explain basic accounting relationships.

Debits and Credits

LEARNING OBJECTIVE　2

Define debits and credits and explain their use in recording business transactions.

The term **debit** indicates the left side of an account, and **credit** indicates the right side. They are commonly abbreviated as **Dr.** for debit and **Cr.** for credit. They **do not** mean increase or decrease, as is commonly thought. We use the terms **debit** and **credit** repeatedly in the recording process to describe **where** entries are made in accounts. For example, the act of entering an amount on the left side of an account is called **debiting** the account. Making an entry on the right side is **crediting** the account.

When comparing the totals of the two sides, an account shows a **debit balance** if the total of the debit amounts exceeds the credits. An account shows a **credit balance** if the credit amounts exceed the debits. Note the position of the debit side and credit side in Illustration 2-1.

The procedure of recording debits and credits in an account is shown in Illustration 2-2 for the transactions affecting the Cash account of Softbyte Inc. The data are taken from the Cash column of the tabular summary in Illustration 1-9 (page 21).

Illustration 2-2
Tabular summary and account form for Softbyte's Cash account

Tabular Summary	Account Form			
Cash	**Cash**			
$15,000	**(Debits)**	15,000	**(Credits)**	7,000
−7,000		1,200		1,700
1,200		1,500		250
1,500		600		1,300
−1,700				
−250	**Balance**	8,050		
600	**(Debit)**			
−1,300				
$ 8,050				

Every positive item in the tabular summary represents a receipt of cash. Every negative amount represents a payment of cash. **Notice that in the account form, we record the increases in cash as debits and the decreases in cash as credits.** For example, the $15,000 receipt of cash (in red) is debited to Cash, and the −$7,000 payment of cash (in blue) is credited to Cash.

Having increases on one side and decreases on the other reduces recording errors and helps in determining the totals of each side of the account as well as the account balance. The balance is determined by netting the two sides (subtracting one amount from the other). The account balance, a debit of $8,050, indicates that Softbyte had $8,050 more increases than decreases in cash. In other words, Softbyte started with a balance of zero and now has $8,050 in its Cash account.

DEBIT AND CREDIT PROCEDURE

In Chapter 1, you learned the effect of a transaction on the basic accounting equation. Remember that each transaction must affect two or more accounts to keep the basic accounting equation in balance. In other words, for each transaction, debits must equal credits. The equality of debits and credits provides the basis for the **double-entry system** of recording transactions.

Under the double-entry system, the dual (two-sided) effect of each transaction is recorded in appropriate accounts. This system provides a logical method for recording transactions. As discussed in the Feature Story about MF Global, the double-entry system also helps ensure the accuracy of the recorded amounts as well as the detection of errors. If every transaction is recorded with equal debits and credits, the sum of all the debits to the accounts must equal the sum of all the credits.

The double-entry system for determining the equality of the accounting equation is much more efficient than the plus/minus procedure used in Chapter 1. The following discussion illustrates debit and credit procedures in the double-entry system.

> **International Note**
>
> Rules for accounting for specific events sometimes differ across countries. For example, European companies rely less on historical cost and more on fair value than U.S. companies. Despite the differences, the double-entry accounting system is the basis of accounting systems worldwide.

DR./CR. PROCEDURES FOR ASSETS AND LIABILITIES

In Illustration 2-2 for Softbyte Inc., increases in Cash—an asset—were entered on the left side, and decreases in Cash were entered on the right side. We know that both sides of the basic equation (Assets = Liabilities + Stockholders' Equity) must be equal. It therefore follows that increases and decreases in liabilities will have to be recorded **opposite from** increases and decreases in assets. Thus, increases in liabilities must be entered on the right or credit side, and decreases in liabilities must be entered on the left or debit side. The effects that debits and credits have on assets and liabilities are summarized in Illustration 2-3.

Debits	Credits
Increase assets	Decrease assets
Decrease liabilities	Increase liabilities

Illustration 2-3
Debit and credit effects—assets and liabilities

Asset accounts normally show debit balances. That is, debits to a specific asset account should exceed credits to that account. Likewise, **liability accounts normally show credit balances.** That is, credits to a liability account should exceed debits to that account. The **normal balance** of an account is on the side where an increase in the account is recorded. Illustration 2-4 (page 58) shows the normal balances for assets and liabilities.

Illustration 2-4
Normal balances—assets
and liabilities

Knowing the normal balance in an account may help you trace errors. For example, a credit balance in an asset account such as Land or a debit balance in a liability account such as Salaries and Wages Payable usually indicates an error. Occasionally, though, an abnormal balance may be correct. The Cash account, for example, will have a credit balance when a company has overdrawn its bank balance (i.e., written a check that "bounced").

STOCKHOLDERS' EQUITY

As Chapter 1 indicated, there are five subdivisions of stockholders' equity: common stock, retained earnings, dividends, revenues, and expenses. In a double-entry system, companies keep accounts for each of these subdivisions, as explained below.

COMMON STOCK Companies issue **common stock** in exchange for the owners' investment paid in to the corporation. Credits increase the Common Stock account, and debits decrease it. For example, when an owner invests cash in the business in exchange for shares of the corporation's stock, the company debits (increases) Cash and credits (increases) Common Stock.

Illustration 2-5 shows the rules of debit and credit for the Common Stock account.

Illustration 2-5
Debit and credit effects—
common stock

Debits	Credits
Decrease Common Stock	Increase Common Stock

We can diagram the normal balance in Common Stock as follows.

Illustration 2-6
Normal balance—common
stock

Helpful Hint
The rules for debit and credit and the normal balances of common stock and retained earnings are the same as for liabilities.

RETAINED EARNINGS **Retained earnings** is net income that is kept (retained) in the business. It represents the portion of stockholders' equity that the company has accumulated through the profitable operation of the business. Credits (net income) increase the Retained Earnings account, and debits (dividends or net losses) decrease it, as Illustration 2-7 shows.

Illustration 2-7
Debit and credit effects and normal balance—retained earnings

Retained Earnings

Debit for decrease	Credit for increase
	Normal balance

DIVIDENDS A **dividend** is a company's distribution to its stockholders on a pro rata (equal) basis. The most common form of a distribution is a **cash dividend**. Dividends reduce the stockholders' claims on retained earnings. Debits increase the Dividends account, and credits decrease it. Illustration 2-8 shows that this account normally has a debit balance.

Illustration 2-8
Debit and credit effect and normal balance—dividends

Dividends	
Debit for increase	Credit for decrease
Normal balance	

INVESTOR INSIGHT

Keeping Score

The Chicago Cubs baseball team probably has these major revenue and expense accounts:

Revenues	Expenses
Admissions (ticket sales)	Players' salaries
Concessions	Administrative salaries
Television and radio	Travel
Advertising	Ballpark maintenance

 Do you think that the Chicago Bears football team would be likely to have the same major revenue and expense accounts as the Cubs? (See page 99.)

Jonathan Daniel/Getty Images, Inc.

REVENUES AND EXPENSES The purpose of earning revenues is to benefit the stockholders of the business. When a company recognizes revenues, stockholders' equity increases. Revenues are a subdivision of stockholders' equity that provides information as to **why** stockholders' equity increased. Credits increase revenue accounts and debits decrease them. Therefore, **the effect of debits and credits on revenue accounts is the same as their effect on stockholders' equity**.

Expenses have the opposite effect. Expenses decrease stockholders' equity. Since expenses decrease net income and revenues increase it, it is logical that the increase and decrease sides of expense accounts should be the opposite of revenue accounts. Thus, expense accounts are increased by debits and decreased by credits. Illustration 2-9 shows the rules of debits and credits for revenues and expenses.

Helpful Hint
Because revenues increase stockholders' equity, a revenue account has the same debit/credit rules as the Common Stock account. Expenses have the opposite effect.

Illustration 2-9
Debit and credit effects—revenues and expenses

Debits	Credits
Decrease revenues	Increase revenues
Increase expenses	Decrease expenses

Credits to revenue accounts should exceed debits. Debits to expense accounts should exceed credits. Thus, revenue accounts normally show credit balances, and expense accounts normally show debit balances. We can diagram the normal balances as follows.

Illustration 2-10
Normal balances—revenues and expenses

Stockholders' Equity Relationships

As Chapter 1 indicated, companies report common stock and retained earnings in the stockholders' equity section of the balance sheet. They report dividends on the retained earnings statement. And they report revenues and expenses on the income statement. Dividends, revenues, and expenses are eventually transferred to retained earnings at the end of the period. As a result, a change in any one of these three items affects stockholders' equity. Illustration 2-11 shows the relationships related to stockholders' equity.

Illustration 2-11
Stockholders' equity relationships

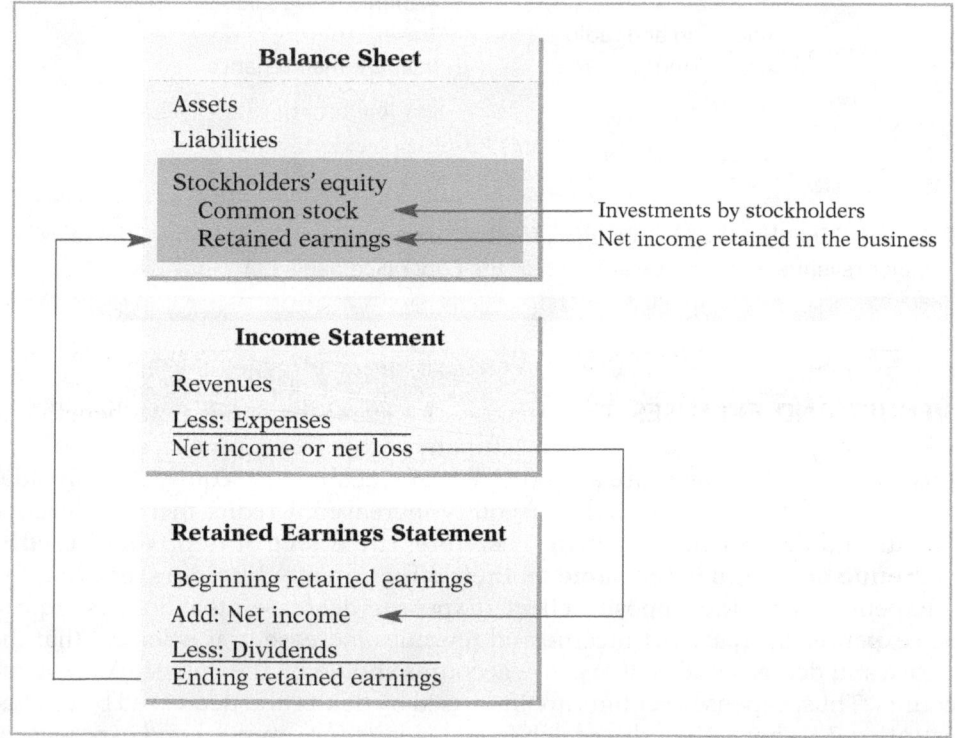

Helpful Hint
You may want to bookmark Illustration 2-12. You probably will refer to it often.

Summary of Debit/Credit Rules

Illustration 2-12 shows a summary of the debit/credit rules and effects on each type of account. Study this diagram carefully. It will help you understand the fundamentals of the double-entry system.

Illustration 2-12
Summary of debit/credit rules

> **DO IT!**

Normal Balances

Action Plan

✔ Determine the types of accounts needed. Kate will need asset accounts for each different type of asset she invests in the business, and liability accounts for any debts she incurs.

✔ Understand the types of stockholders' equity accounts. When Kate begins the business, she will need only Common Stock. Later, she will need other stockholders' equity accounts.

Kate Browne, president of Hair It Is, Inc. has just rented space in a shopping mall in which she will open and operate a beauty salon. A friend has advised Kate to set up a double-entry set of accounting records in which to record all of her business transactions.

Identify the balance sheet accounts that Hair It Is, Inc. will likely use to record the transactions needed to establish and open the business. Also, indicate whether the normal balance of each account is a debit or a credit.

Solution

Hair It Is, Inc. would likely use the following accounts to record the transactions needed to ready the beauty salon for opening day:

Cash (debit balance)   Equipment (debit balance)
Supplies (debit balance)   Accounts Payable (credit balance)
Notes Payable (credit balance),   Common Stock (credit balance)
   if the business borrows money

Related exercise material: BE2-1, BE2-2, BE2-5, E2-1, E2-2, E2-4, **and** DO IT! 2-1.

 The Navigator

Steps in the Recording Process

Although it is possible to enter transaction information directly into the accounts without using a journal, few businesses do so. Practically every business uses three basic steps in the recording process:

LEARNING OBJECTIVE 3

Identify the basic steps in the recording process.

1. Analyze each transaction for its effects on the accounts.

2. Enter the transaction information in a **journal**.

3. Transfer the journal information to the appropriate accounts in the **ledger**.

The recording process begins with the transaction. **Business documents**, such as a sales slip, a check, or a bill provide evidence of the transaction. The company analyzes this evidence to determine the transaction's effects on specific accounts. The company then enters the transaction in the journal. Finally, it transfers the journal entry to the designated accounts in the ledger. Illustration 2-13 (page 62) shows the recording process.

Ethics Note

International Outsourcing Services, LLC was accused of submitting fraudulent documents (store coupons) to companies for reimbursement of as much as $250 million. Use of proper business documents reduces the likelihood of fraudulent activity.

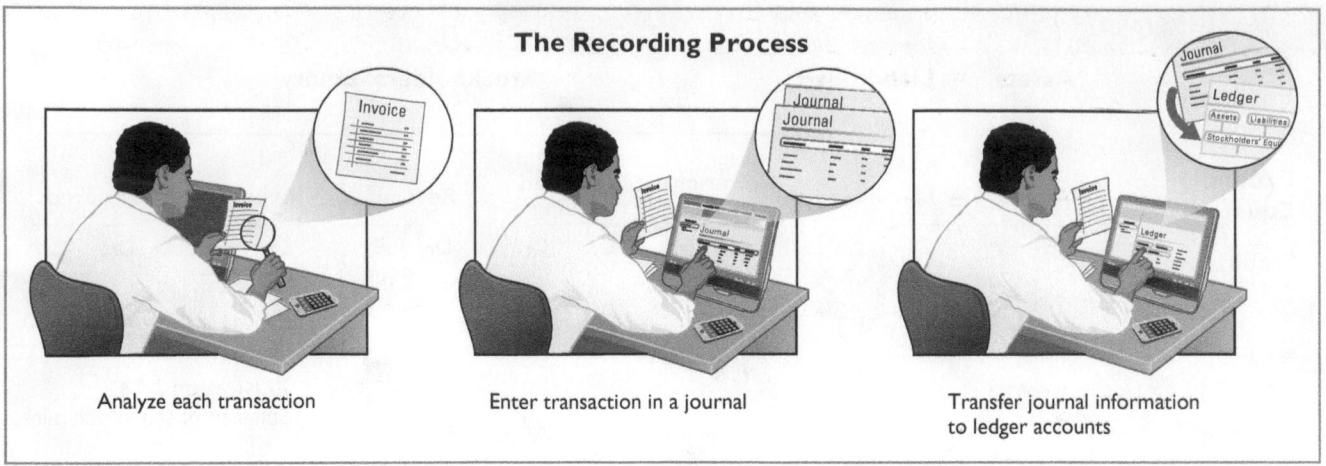

Illustration 2-13
The recording process

The steps in the recording process occur repeatedly. In Chapter 1, we illustrated the first step, the analysis of transactions, and will give further examples in this and later chapters. The other two steps in the recording process are explained in the next sections.

The Journal

Companies initially record transactions in chronological order (the order in which they occur). Thus, the **journal** is referred to as the book of original entry. For each transaction, the journal shows the debit and credit effects on specific accounts.

Companies may use various kinds of journals, but every company has the most basic form of journal, a **general journal**. Typically, a general journal has spaces for dates, account titles and explanations, references, and two amount columns. See the format of the journal in Illustration 2-14 (page 63). *Whenever we use the term "journal" in this textbook, we mean the general journal unless we specify otherwise.*

The journal makes several significant contributions to the recording process:

1. It discloses in one place the **complete effects of a transaction**.

2. It provides a **chronological record** of transactions.

3. It helps to **prevent or locate errors** because the debit and credit amounts for each entry can be easily compared.

JOURNALIZING

Entering transaction data in the journal is known as **journalizing**. Companies make separate journal entries for each transaction. A complete entry consists of (1) the date of the transaction, (2) the accounts and amounts to be debited and credited, and (3) a brief explanation of the transaction.

Illustration 2-14 shows the technique of journalizing, using the first two transactions of Softbyte Inc. On September 1, stockholders invested $15,000 cash in the corporation in exchange for shares of stock, and Softbyte purchased computer equipment for $7,000 cash. The number J1 indicates that these two entries are recorded on the first page of the journal. Illustration 2-14 shows the standard form of journal entries for these two transactions. (The boxed numbers correspond to explanations in the list below the illustration.)

GENERAL JOURNAL				J1
Date	Account Titles and Explanation	Ref.	Debit	Credit
2015		[5]		
Sept. 1 [2]	Cash		15,000	
[1] [3]	Common Stock			15,000
[4]	(Issued shares of stock for cash)			
1	Equipment		7,000	
	Cash			7,000
	(Purchase of equipment for cash)			

Illustration 2-14
Technique of journalizing

[1] The date of the transaction is entered in the Date column.

[2] The debit account title (that is, the account to be debited) is entered first at the extreme left margin of the column headed "Account Titles and Explanation," and the amount of the debit is recorded in the Debit column.

[3] The credit account title (that is, the account to be credited) is indented and entered on the next line in the column headed "Account Titles and Explanation," and the amount of the credit is recorded in the Credit column.

[4] A brief explanation of the transaction appears on the line below the credit account title. A space is left between journal entries. The blank space separates individual journal entries and makes the entire journal easier to read.

[5] The column titled Ref. (which stands for Reference) is left blank when the journal entry is made. This column is used later when the journal entries are transferred to the ledger accounts.

It is important to use correct and specific account titles in journalizing. Erroneous account titles lead to incorrect financial statements. However, some flexibility exists initially in selecting account titles. The main criterion is that each title must appropriately describe the content of the account. Once a company chooses the specific title to use, it should record under that account title all later transactions involving the account.[1]

SIMPLE AND COMPOUND ENTRIES

Some entries involve only two accounts, one debit and one credit. (See, for example, the entries in Illustration 2-14.) An entry like these is considered a **simple entry**. Some transactions, however, require more than two accounts in journalizing. An entry that requires three or more accounts is a **compound entry**. To illustrate, assume that on July 1, Butler Company purchases a delivery truck costing $14,000. It pays $8,000 cash now and agrees to pay the remaining $6,000 on account (to be paid later). The compound entry is as follows.

GENERAL JOURNAL				J1
Date	Account Titles and Explanation	Ref.	Debit	Credit
2015				
July 1	Equipment		14,000	
	Cash			8,000
	Accounts Payable			6,000
	(Purchased truck for cash with			
	balance on account)			

Illustration 2-15
Compound journal entry

---

[1]*In homework problems, you should use specific account titles when they are given.* When account titles are not given, you may select account titles that identify the nature and content of each account. The account titles used in journalizing should not contain explanations such as Cash Paid or Cash Received.

In a compound entry, the standard format requires that all debits be listed before the credits.

© flyfloor/iStockphoto

ACCOUNTING ACROSS THE ORGANIZATION

Boosting Microsoft's Profits

At one time, Microsoft's Home and Entertainment Division lost over $4 billion, mostly due to losses on the original Xbox videogame console. With the Xbox 360 videogame console, the division's head of finance, Bryan Lee, hoped the division would become profitable. He set strict goals for sales, revenue, and profit. "A manager seeking to spend more on a feature such as a disk drive has to find allies in the group to cut spending elsewhere, or identify new revenue to offset the increase," he explained.

For example, Microsoft originally designed the Xbox 360 to have 256 megabytes of memory. But the design department said that amount of memory wouldn't support the best special effects. The purchasing department said that adding more memory would cost $30—which was 10% of the estimated selling price of $300. The marketing department, however, "determined that adding the memory would let Microsoft reduce marketing costs and attract more game developers, boosting royalty revenue. It would also extend the life of the console, generating more sales." As a result, Microsoft doubled the memory to 512 megabytes. Today, the division enjoys great success.

Source: Robert A. Guth, "New Xbox Aim for Microsoft: Profitability," *Wall Street Journal* (May 24, 2005), p. C1.

 In what ways is this Microsoft division using accounting to assist in its effort to become more profitable? (See page 99.)

> DO IT!

Recording Business Activities

As president and sole stockholder, Kate Browne engaged in the following activities in establishing her salon, Hair It Is, Inc.

1. Opened a bank account in the name of Hair It Is, Inc. and deposited $20,000 of her own money in this account in exchange for shares of common stock.

2. Purchased equipment on account (to be paid in 30 days) for a total cost of $4,800.

3. Interviewed three persons for the position of hair stylist.

In what form (type of record) should Kate record these three activities? Prepare the entries to record the transactions.

Action Plan

✔ Understand which activities need to be recorded and which do not. Any that affect assets, liabilities, or stockholders' equity should be recorded in a journal.

✔ Analyze the effects of transactions on asset, liability, and stockholders' equity accounts.

Solution

Each transaction that is recorded is entered in the general journal. The three activities would be recorded as follows.

1. Cash	20,000	
Common Stock		20,000
(Issued shares of stock for cash)		
2. Equipment	4,800	
Accounts Payable		4,800
(Purchase of equipment on account)		
3. No entry because no transaction has occurred.		

Related exercise material: BE2-3, BE2-6, E2-3, E2-5, E2-6, E2-7, **and** DO IT! 2-2.

 The Navigator

The Ledger

The entire group of accounts maintained by a company is the **ledger**. The ledger provides the balance in each of the accounts as well as keeps track of changes in these balances.

Companies may use various kinds of ledgers, but every company has a general ledger. A **general ledger** contains all the asset, liability, and stockholders' equity accounts, as shown in Illustration 2-16 for J. Lind Company. *Whenever we use the term "ledger" in this textbook, we are referring to the general ledger unless we specify otherwise.*

LEARNING OBJECTIVE   **5**

Explain what a ledger is and how it helps in the recording process.

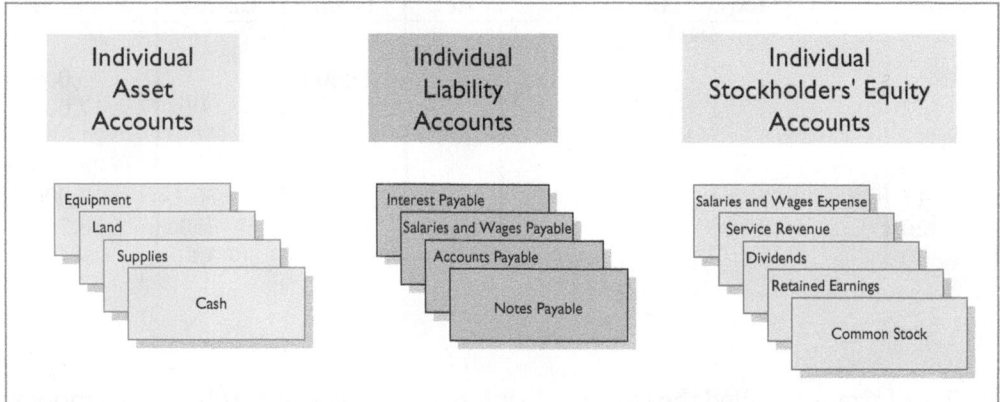

Illustration 2-16
The general ledger, which contains all of a company's accounts

Companies arrange the ledger in the sequence in which they present the accounts in the financial statements, beginning with the balance sheet accounts. First in order are the asset accounts, followed by liability accounts, stockholders' equity accounts, revenues, and expenses. Each account is numbered for easier identification.

The ledger provides the balance in each of the accounts. For example, the Cash account shows the amount of cash available to meet current obligations. The Accounts Receivable account shows amounts due from customers. The Accounts Payable account shows amounts owed to creditors.

ETHICS INSIGHT

A Convenient Overstatement

Sometimes a company's investment securities suffer a permanent decline in value below their original cost. When this occurs, the company is supposed to reduce the recorded value of the securities on its balance sheet ("write-them down" in common financial lingo) and record a loss. It appears, however, that during the financial crisis, employees at some financial institutions chose to look the other way as the value of their investments skidded. A number of Wall Street traders that worked for the investment bank Credit Suisse Group were charged with intentionally overstating the value of securities that had suffered declines of approximately $2.85 billion. One reason that they may have been reluctant to record the losses is out of fear that the company's shareholders and clients would panic if they saw the magnitude of the losses. However, personal self-interest might have been equally to blame—the bonuses of the traders were tied to the value of the investment securities.

Source: S. Pulliam, J. Eaglesham, and M. Siconolfi, "U.S. Plans Changes on Bond Fraud," *Wall Street Journal Online* (February 1, 2012).

? What incentives might employees have had to overstate the value of these investment securities on the company's financial statements? (See page 99.)

© Nuno Silva/iStockphoto

STANDARD FORM OF ACCOUNT

The simple T-account form used in accounting textbooks is often very useful for illustration purposes. However, in practice, the account forms used in ledgers are much more structured. Illustration 2-17 shows a typical form, using assumed data from a cash account.

Illustration 2-17
Three-column form of account

CASH					NO. 101
Date	Explanation	Ref.	Debit	Credit	Balance
2015					
June 1			25,000		25,000
2				8,000	17,000
3			4,200		21,200
9			7,500		28,700
17				11,700	17,000
20				250	16,750
30				7,300	9,450

This format is called the **three-column form of account**. It has three money columns—debit, credit, and balance. The balance in the account is determined after each transaction. Companies use the explanation space and reference columns to provide special information about the transaction.

Posting

LEARNING OBJECTIVE   6

Explain what posting is and how it helps in the recording process.

Transferring journal entries to the ledger accounts is called **posting**. This phase of the recording process accumulates the effects of journalized transactions into the individual accounts. Posting involves the following steps.

1. In the **ledger**, in the appropriate columns of the account(s) debited, enter the date, journal page, and debit amount shown in the journal.

2. In the reference column of the **journal**, write the account number to which the debit amount was posted.

3. In the **ledger**, in the appropriate columns of the account(s) credited, enter the date, journal page, and credit amount shown in the journal.

4. In the reference column of the **journal**, write the account number to which the credit amount was posted.

Illustration 2-18 shows these four steps using Softbyte Inc.'s first journal entry. The boxed numbers indicate the sequence of the steps.

Posting should be performed in chronological order. That is, the company should post all the debits and credits of one journal entry before proceeding to the next journal entry. Postings should be made on a timely basis to ensure that the ledger is up to date.[2]

---

[2]*In homework problems, you can journalize all transactions before posting any of the journal entries.*

Illustration 2-18
Posting a journal entry

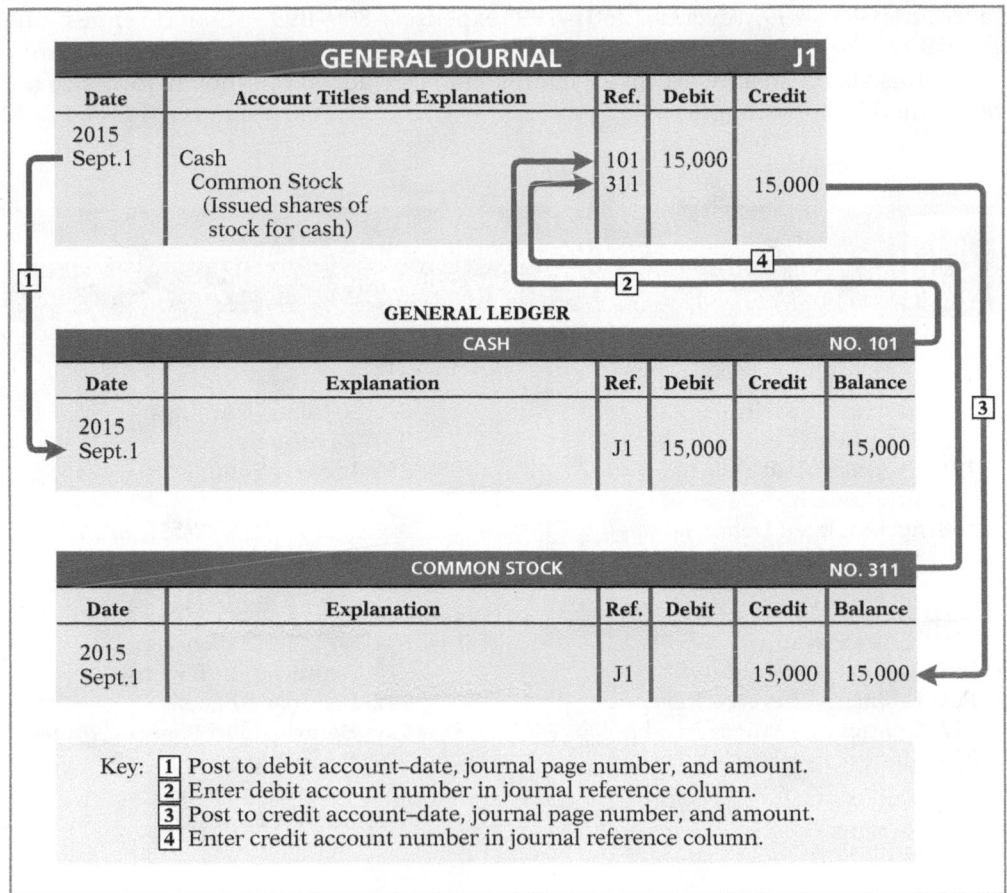

GENERAL JOURNAL				J1
Date	Account Titles and Explanation	Ref.	Debit	Credit
2015 Sept.1	Cash	101	15,000	
	Common Stock	311		15,000
	(Issued shares of stock for cash)			

GENERAL LEDGER

CASH					NO. 101
Date	Explanation	Ref.	Debit	Credit	Balance
2015 Sept.1		J1	15,000		15,000

COMMON STOCK					NO. 311
Date	Explanation	Ref.	Debit	Credit	Balance
2015 Sept.1		J1		15,000	15,000

Key: 1 Post to debit account–date, journal page number, and amount.
      2 Enter debit account number in journal reference column.
      3 Post to credit account–date, journal page number, and amount.
      4 Enter credit account number in journal reference column.

The reference column of a ledger account indicates the journal page from which the transaction was posted.[3] The explanation space of the ledger account is used infrequently because an explanation already appears in the journal.

CHART OF ACCOUNTS

The number and type of accounts differ for each company. The number of accounts depends on the amount of detail management desires. For example, the management of one company may want a single account for all types of utility expense. Another may keep separate expense accounts for each type of utility, such as gas, electricity, and water. Similarly, a small company like Softbyte Inc. will have fewer accounts than a corporate giant like Dell. Softbyte may be able to manage and report its activities in 20 to 30 accounts, while Dell may require thousands of accounts to keep track of its worldwide activities.

Most companies have a **chart of accounts**. This chart lists the accounts and the account numbers that identify their location in the ledger. The numbering system that identifies the accounts usually starts with the balance sheet accounts and follows with the income statement accounts.

In this and the next two chapters, we will be explaining the accounting for Pioneer Advertising Agency Inc. (a service company). Accounts 101–199 indicate asset accounts; 200–299 indicate liabilities; 301–350 indicate stockholders' equity

Helpful Hint
On the textbook's front endpapers, you also will find an expanded chart of accounts.

---

[3]After the last entry has been posted, the accountant should scan the reference column **in the journal**, to confirm that all postings have been made.

accounts; 400–499, revenues; 601–799, expenses; 800–899, other revenues; and 900–999, other expenses. Illustration 2-19 shows Pioneer's chart of accounts. Accounts listed in red are used in this chapter; accounts shown in black are explained in later chapters.

Illustration 2-19
Chart of accounts for Pioneer Advertising Agency Inc.

PIONEER ADVERTISING AGENCY INC.
Chart of Accounts

Assets	Stockholders' Equity
101 Cash	311 Common Stock
112 Accounts Receivable	320 Retained Earnings
126 Supplies	332 Dividends
130 Prepaid Insurance	350 Income Summary
157 Equipment	
158 Accumulated Depreciation— Equipment	**Revenues**
	400 Service Revenue
Liabilities	**Expenses**
200 Notes Payable	631 Supplies Expense
201 Accounts Payable	711 Depreciation Expense
209 Unearned Service Revenue	722 Insurance Expense
212 Salaries and Wages Payable	726 Salaries and Wages Expense
230 Interest Payable	729 Rent Expense
	732 Utilities Expense
	905 Interest Expense

You will notice that there are gaps in the numbering system of the chart of accounts for Pioneer Advertising. Companies leave gaps to permit the insertion of new accounts as needed during the life of the business.

The Recording Process Illustrated

Illustrations 2-20 through 2-29 (pages 69–73) show the basic steps in the recording process, using the October transactions of Pioneer Advertising Agency Inc. Pioneer's accounting period is a month. In these illustrations, a basic analysis, an equation analysis, and a debit-credit analysis precede the journal entry and posting of each transaction. For simplicity, we use the T-account form to show the posting instead of the standard account form.

Study these transaction analyses carefully. **The purpose of transaction analysis is first to identify the type of account involved, and then to determine whether to make a debit or a credit to the account.** You should always perform this type of analysis before preparing a journal entry. Doing so will help you understand the journal entries discussed in this chapter as well as more complex journal entries in later chapters.

In addition, an Accounting Cycle Tutorial is available in *WileyPLUS*. It provides an interactive presentation of the steps in the accounting cycle, using the examples in the illustrations on the following pages.

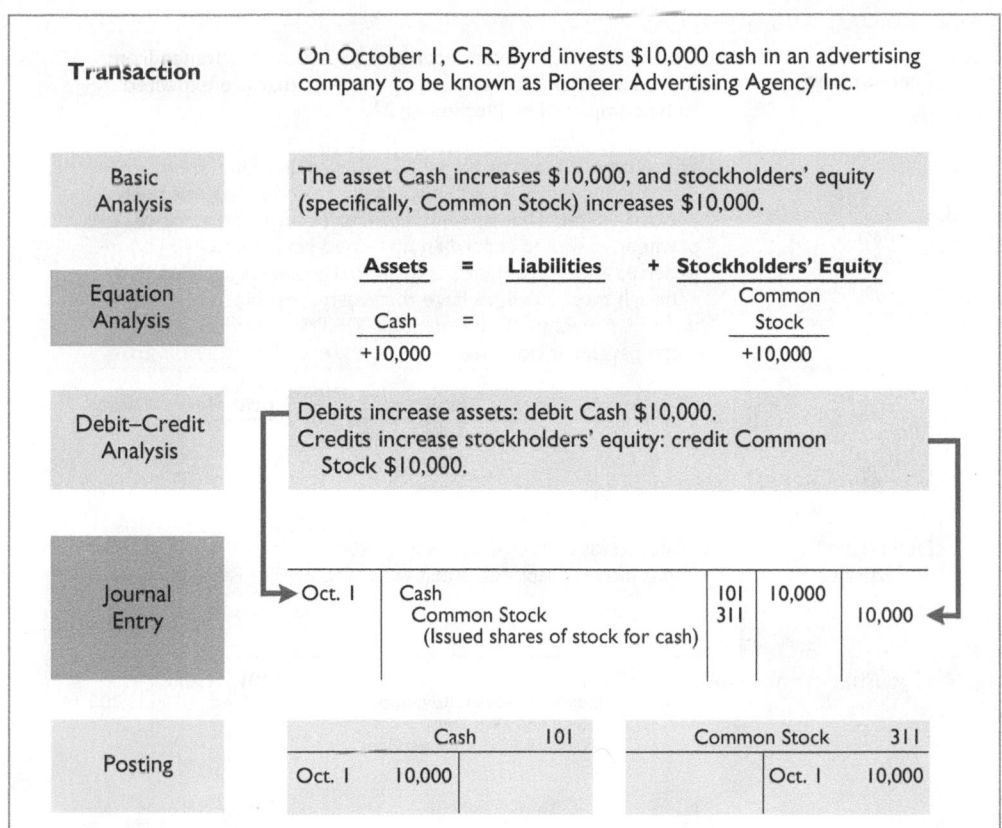

Transaction	On October 1, C. R. Byrd invests $10,000 cash in an advertising company to be known as Pioneer Advertising Agency Inc.
Basic Analysis	The asset Cash increases $10,000, and stockholders' equity (specifically, Common Stock) increases $10,000.

Equation Analysis

Assets	=	Liabilities	+	Stockholders' Equity
				Common
Cash	=			Stock
+10,000				+10,000

Debit–Credit Analysis

Debits increase assets: debit Cash $10,000.
Credits increase stockholders' equity: credit Common Stock $10,000.

Journal Entry

Oct. 1	Cash	101	10,000	
	Common Stock	311		10,000
	(Issued shares of stock for cash)			

Posting

Cash	101		Common Stock	311
Oct. 1	10,000			Oct. 1	10,000

Illustration 2-20
Investment of cash by stockholders

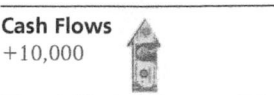

Cash Flows
+10,000

Helpful Hint
Follow these steps:
1. Determine what type of account is involved.
2. Determine what items increased or decreased and by how much.
3. Translate the increases and decreases into debits and credits.

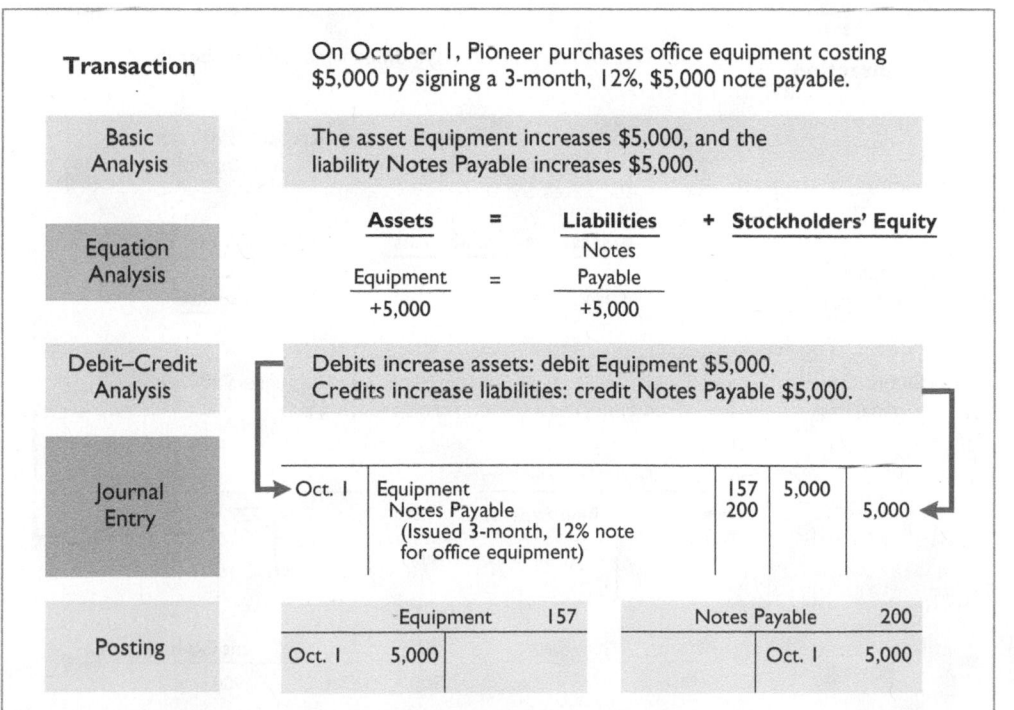

Transaction	On October 1, Pioneer purchases office equipment costing $5,000 by signing a 3-month, 12%, $5,000 note payable.
Basic Analysis	The asset Equipment increases $5,000, and the liability Notes Payable increases $5,000.

Equation Analysis

Assets	=	Liabilities	+	Stockholders' Equity
		Notes		
Equipment	=	Payable		
+5,000		+5,000		

Debit–Credit Analysis

Debits increase assets: debit Equipment $5,000.
Credits increase liabilities: credit Notes Payable $5,000.

Journal Entry

Oct. 1	Equipment	157	5,000	
	Notes Payable	200		5,000
	(Issued 3-month, 12% note for office equipment)			

Posting

Equipment	157		Notes Payable	200
Oct. 1	5,000			Oct. 1	5,000

Illustration 2-21
Purchase of office equipment

Cash Flows
no effect

Illustration 2-22
Receipt of cash for future service

Cash Flows
+1,200

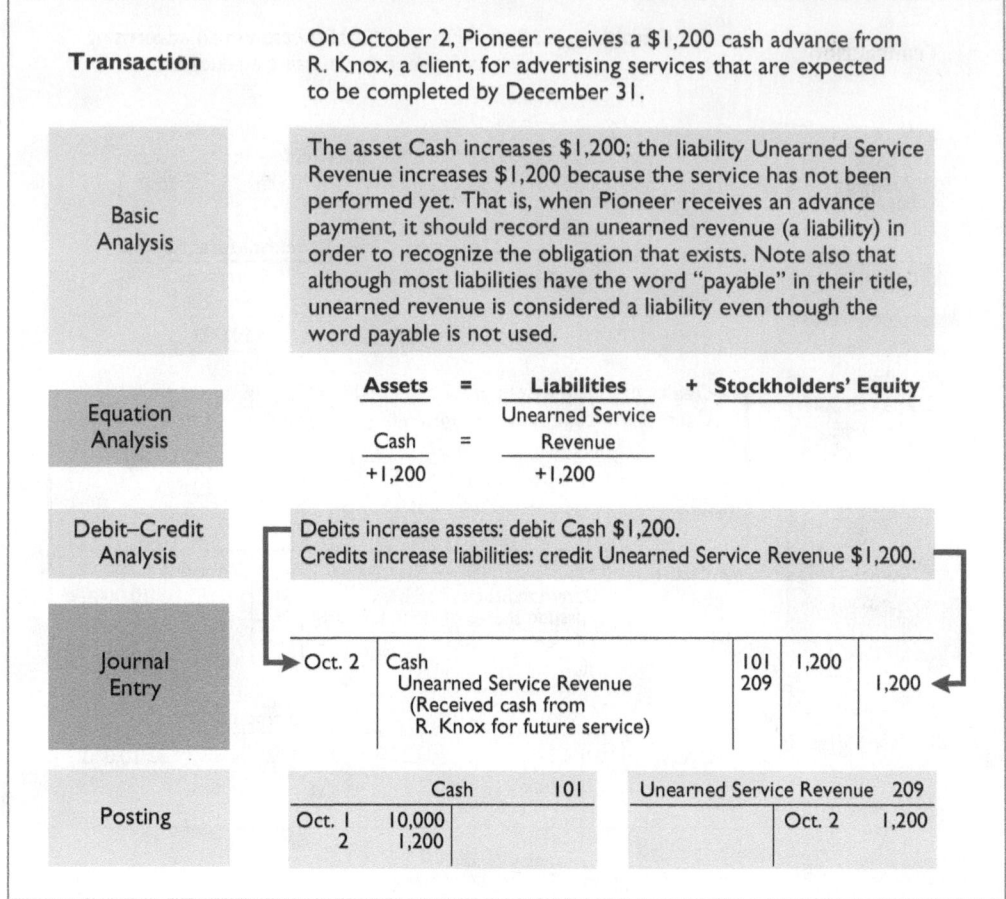

Transaction	On October 2, Pioneer receives a $1,200 cash advance from R. Knox, a client, for advertising services that are expected to be completed by December 31.	
Basic Analysis	The asset Cash increases $1,200; the liability Unearned Service Revenue increases $1,200 because the service has not been performed yet. That is, when Pioneer receives an advance payment, it should record an unearned revenue (a liability) in order to recognize the obligation that exists. Note also that although most liabilities have the word "payable" in their title, unearned revenue is considered a liability even though the word payable is not used.	

Equation Analysis

Assets	=	Liabilities	+	Stockholders' Equity
		Unearned Service		
Cash	=	Revenue		
+1,200		+1,200		

Debit–Credit Analysis

Debits increase assets: debit Cash $1,200.
Credits increase liabilities: credit Unearned Service Revenue $1,200.

Journal Entry

Oct. 2	Cash	101	1,200	
	Unearned Service Revenue	209		1,200
	(Received cash from R. Knox for future service)			

Posting

Cash		101		Unearned Service Revenue	209
Oct. 1	10,000			Oct. 2	1,200
2	1,200				

Illustration 2-23
Payment of monthly rent

Cash Flows
−900

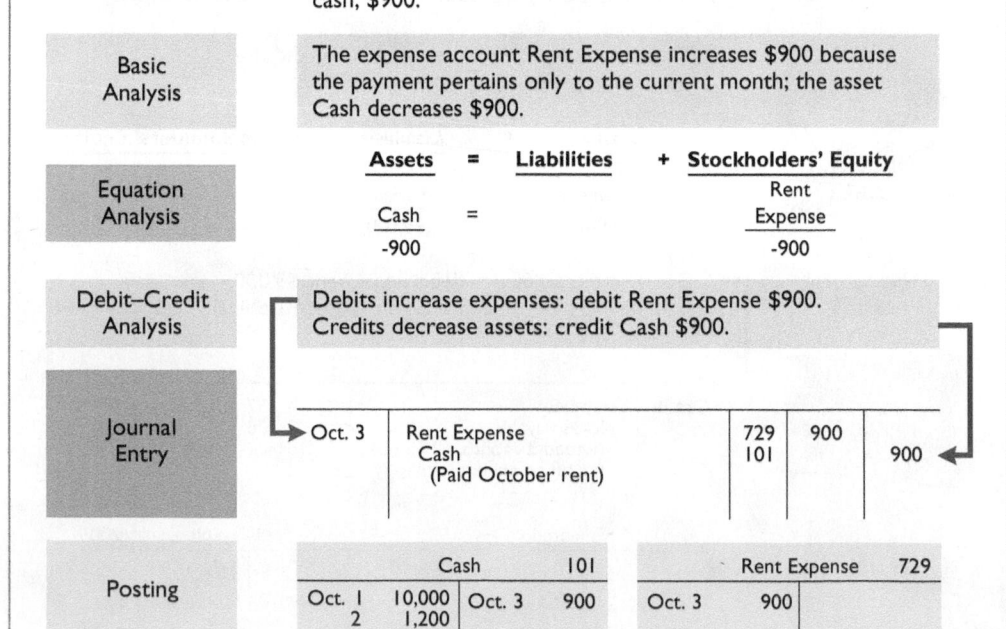

Transaction	On October 3, Pioneer pays office rent for October in cash, $900.
Basic Analysis	The expense account Rent Expense increases $900 because the payment pertains only to the current month; the asset Cash decreases $900.

Equation Analysis

Assets	=	Liabilities	+	Stockholders' Equity
				Rent
Cash	=			Expense
-900				-900

Debit–Credit Analysis

Debits increase expenses: debit Rent Expense $900.
Credits decrease assets: credit Cash $900.

Journal Entry

Oct. 3	Rent Expense	729	900	
	Cash	101		900
	(Paid October rent)			

Posting

Cash		101		Rent Expense		729
Oct. 1	10,000	Oct. 3 900		Oct. 3	900	
2	1,200					

Illustration 2-24
Payment for insurance

Transaction	On October 4, Pioneer pays $600 for a one-year insurance policy that will expire next year on September 30.
Basic Analysis	The asset Prepaid Insurance increases $600 because the payment extends to more than the current month; the asset Cash decreases $600. Payments of expenses that will benefit more than one accounting period are prepaid expenses or prepayments. When a company makes a payment, it debits an asset account in order to show the service or benefit that will be received in the future.

Equation Analysis

	Assets	=	Liabilities	+	Stockholders' Equity
	Prepaid				
Cash +	Insurance				
-600	+600				

Debit–Credit Analysis

Debits increase assets: debit Prepaid Insurance $600.
Credits decrease assets: credit Cash $600.

Cash Flows
−600

Journal Entry

Oct. 4	Prepaid Insurance	130	600	
	Cash	101		600
	(Paid one-year policy; effective date October 1)			

Posting

Cash			101		Prepaid Insurance	130
Oct. 1	10,000	Oct. 3	900	Oct. 4	600	
2	1,200	4	600			

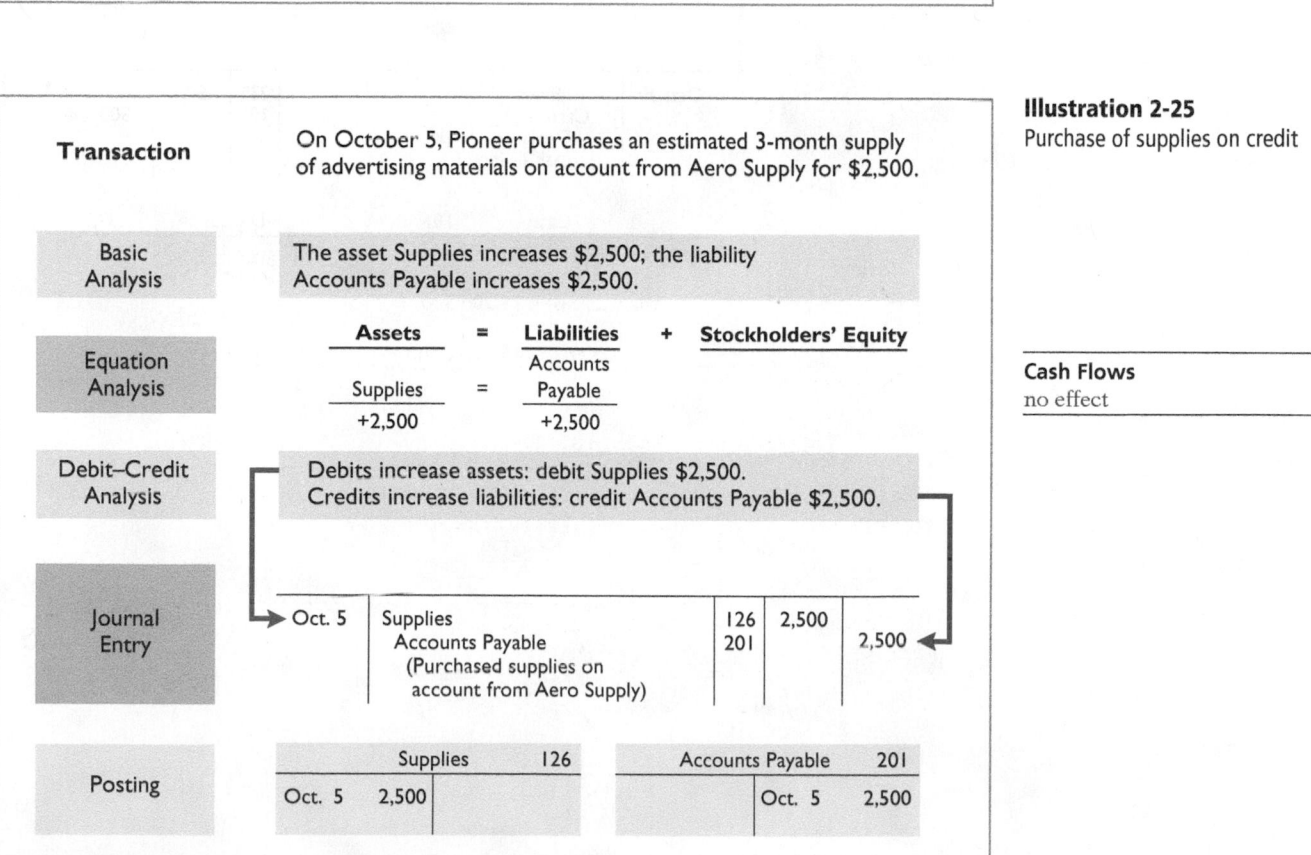

Illustration 2-25
Purchase of supplies on credit

Transaction	On October 5, Pioneer purchases an estimated 3-month supply of advertising materials on account from Aero Supply for $2,500.
Basic Analysis	The asset Supplies increases $2,500; the liability Accounts Payable increases $2,500.

Equation Analysis

	Assets	=	Liabilities	+	Stockholders' Equity
			Accounts		
	Supplies	=	Payable		
	+2,500		+2,500		

Debit–Credit Analysis

Debits increase assets: debit Supplies $2,500.
Credits increase liabilities: credit Accounts Payable $2,500.

Cash Flows
no effect

Journal Entry

Oct. 5	Supplies	126	2,500	
	Accounts Payable	201		2,500
	(Purchased supplies on account from Aero Supply)			

Posting

Supplies		126		Accounts Payable		201
Oct. 5	2,500				Oct. 5	2,500

Illustration 2-26
Hiring of employees

Cash Flows
no effect

Event	On October 9, Pioneer hires four employees to begin work on October 15. Each employee is to receive a weekly salary of $500 for a 5-day work week, payable every 2 weeks—first payment made on October 26.
Basic Analysis	A business transaction has not occurred. There is only an agreement between the employer and the employees to enter into a business transaction beginning on October 15. Thus, a debit–credit analysis is not needed because there is no accounting entry. (See transaction of October 26 for first entry.)

Illustration 2-27
Declaration and payment of dividend

Cash Flows
−500

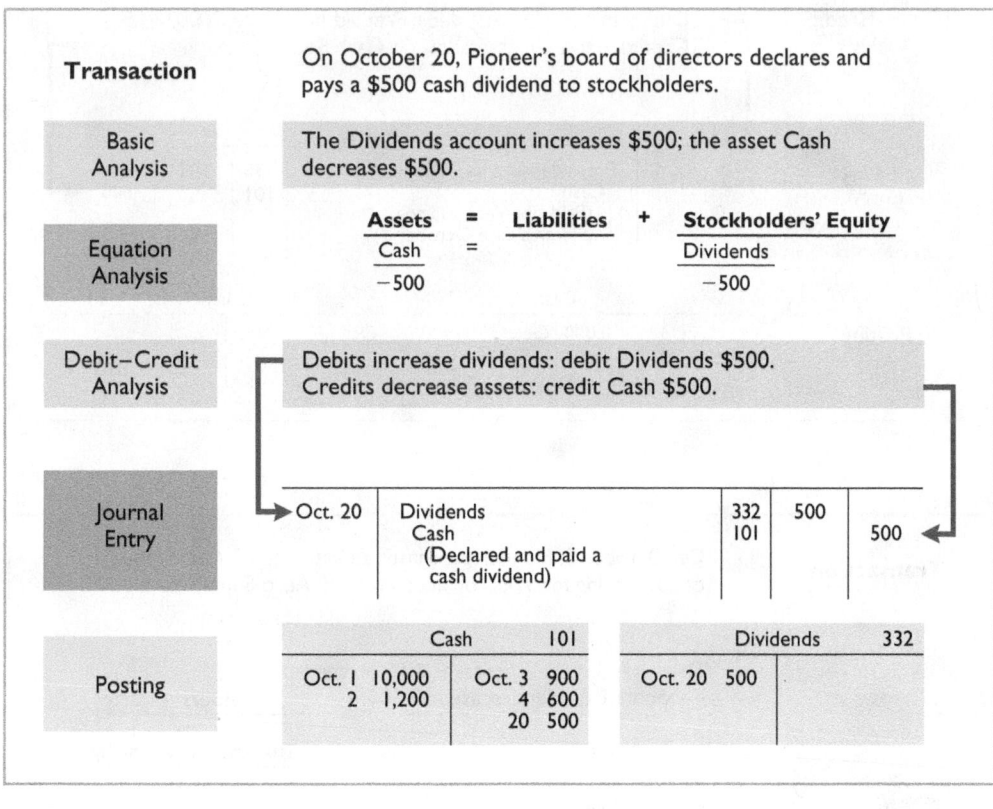

Transaction	On October 20, Pioneer's board of directors declares and pays a $500 cash dividend to stockholders.
Basic Analysis	The Dividends account increases $500; the asset Cash decreases $500.

Assets	=	Liabilities	+	Stockholders' Equity
Cash	=			Dividends
−500				−500

Debit–Credit Analysis	Debits increase dividends: debit Dividends $500. Credits decrease assets: credit Cash $500.

Journal Entry	Oct. 20	Dividends		332	500	
		Cash		101		500
		(Declared and paid a cash dividend)				

Posting

	Cash		101		Dividends		332
Oct. 1	10,000	Oct. 3	900	Oct. 20	500		
2	1,200	4	600				
		20	500				

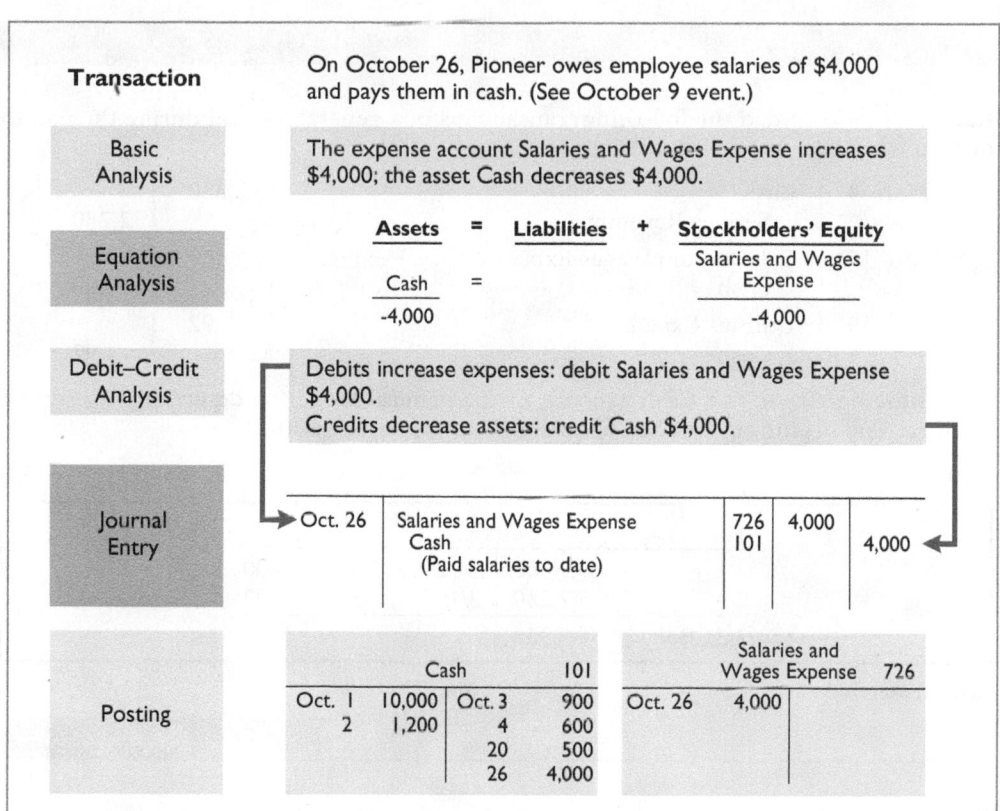

Illustration 2-28
Payment of salaries

| Transaction | On October 26, Pioneer owes employee salaries of $4,000 and pays them in cash. (See October 9 event.) |

| Basic Analysis | The expense account Salaries and Wages Expense increases $4,000; the asset Cash decreases $4,000. |

Equation Analysis

Assets	=	**Liabilities**	+	**Stockholders' Equity**
Cash	=			Salaries and Wages Expense
-4,000				-4,000

Debit–Credit Analysis

Debits increase expenses: debit Salaries and Wages Expense $4,000.
Credits decrease assets: credit Cash $4,000.

Journal Entry

Oct. 26	Salaries and Wages Expense	726	4,000	
	Cash	101		4,000
	(Paid salaries to date)			

Posting

	Cash		101		Salaries and Wages Expense		726
Oct. 1	10,000	Oct. 3	900	Oct. 26	4,000		
2	1,200	4	600				
		20	500				
		26	4,000				

Cash Flows
−4,000

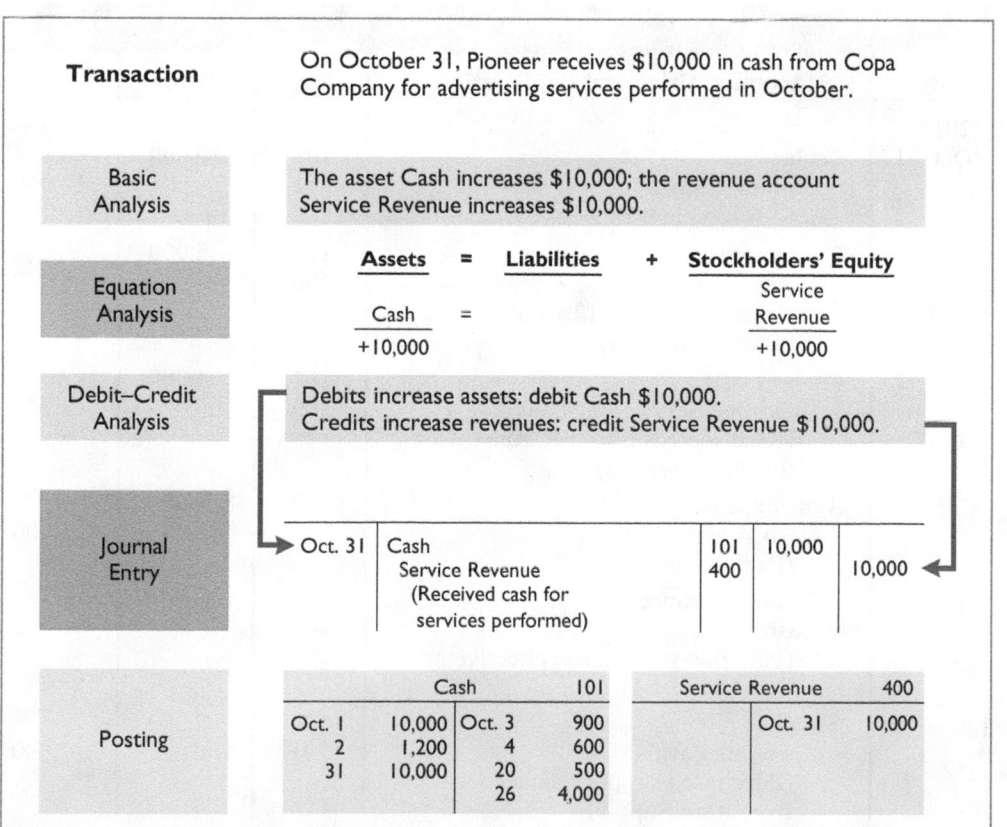

Illustration 2-29
Receipt of cash for services performed

| Transaction | On October 31, Pioneer receives $10,000 in cash from Copa Company for advertising services performed in October. |

| Basic Analysis | The asset Cash increases $10,000; the revenue account Service Revenue increases $10,000. |

Equation Analysis

Assets	=	**Liabilities**	+	**Stockholders' Equity**
Cash	=			Service Revenue
+10,000				+10,000

Debit–Credit Analysis

Debits increase assets: debit Cash $10,000.
Credits increase revenues: credit Service Revenue $10,000.

Journal Entry

Oct. 31	Cash	101	10,000	
	Service Revenue	400		10,000
	(Received cash for services performed)			

Posting

	Cash		101		Service Revenue		400
Oct. 1	10,000	Oct. 3	900			Oct. 31	10,000
2	1,200	4	600				
31	10,000	20	500				
		26	4,000				

Cash Flows
+10,000

Posting

Kate Browne recorded the following transactions in a general journal during the month of March.

Mar. 4	Cash	2,280	
	Service Revenue		2,280
15	Salaries and Wages Expense	400	
	Cash		400
19	Utilities Expense	92	
	Cash		92

Post these entries to the Cash account of the general ledger to determine its ending balance. The beginning balance of Cash on March 1 was $600.

Action Plan

✔ Recall that posting involves transferring the journalized debits and credits to specific accounts in the ledger.

✔ Determine the ending balance by netting the total debits and credits.

Solution

		Cash		
3/1	600	3/15	400
3/4	2,280	3/19	92
3/31 Bal.	2,388		

Related exercise material: BE2-7, BE2-8, E2-8, E2-12, **and** DO IT! 2-3.

✔ **The Navigator**

Summary Illustration of Journalizing and Posting

Illustration 2-30 shows the journal for Pioneer Advertising Agency Inc. for October.

Illustration 2-30
General journal entries

GENERAL JOURNAL				PAGE J1
Date	**Account Titles and Explanation**	**Ref.**	**Debit**	**Credit**
2015 Oct. 1	Cash	101	10,000	
	Common Stock	311		10,000
	(Issued shares of stock for cash)			
1	Equipment	157	5,000	
	Notes Payable	200		5,000
	(Issued 3-month, 12% note for office equipment)			
2	Cash	101	1,200	
	Unearned Service Revenue	209		1,200
	(Received cash from R. Knox for future service)			
3	Rent Expense	729	900	
	Cash	101		900
	(Paid October rent)			
4	Prepaid Insurance	130	600	
	Cash	101		600
	(Paid one-year policy; effective date October 1)			
5	Supplies	126	2,500	
	Accounts Payable	201		2,500
	(Purchased supplies on account from Aero Supply)			

(continued)

Illustration 2-30
(continued)

Date	Account Titles and Explanation	Ref.	Debit	Credit
20	Dividends	332	500	
	Cash	101		500
	(Declared and paid a cash dividend)			
26	Salaries and Wages Expense	726	4,000	
	Cash	101		4,000
	(Paid salaries to date)			
31	Cash	101	10,000	
	Service Revenue	400		10,000
	(Received cash for services performed)			

Illustration 2-31 shows the ledger, with all balances in red.

Illustration 2-31
General ledger

GENERAL LEDGER

Cash No. 101

Date	Explanation	Ref.	Debit	Credit	Balance
2015					
Oct. 1		J1	10,000		10,000
2		J1	1,200		11,200
3		J1		900	10,300
4		J1		600	9,700
20		J1		500	9,200
26		J1		4,000	5,200
31		J1	10,000		15,200

Supplies No. 126

Date	Explanation	Ref.	Debit	Credit	Balance
2015					
Oct. 5		J1	2,500		2,500

Prepaid Insurance No. 130

Date	Explanation	Ref.	Debit	Credit	Balance
2015					
Oct. 4		J1	600		600

Equipment No. 157

Date	Explanation	Ref.	Debit	Credit	Balance
2015					
Oct. 1		J1	5,000		5,000

Notes Payable No. 200

Date	Explanation	Ref.	Debit	Credit	Balance
2015					
Oct. 1		J1		5,000	5,000

Accounts Payable No. 201

Date	Explanation	Ref.	Debit	Credit	Balance
2015					
Oct. 5		J1		2,500	2,500

Unearned Service Revenue No. 209

Date	Explanation	Ref.	Debit	Credit	Balance
2015					
Oct. 2		J1		1,200	1,200

Common Stock No. 311

Date	Explanation	Ref.	Debit	Credit	Balance
2015					
Oct. 1		J1		10,000	10,000

Dividends No. 332

Date	Explanation	Ref.	Debit	Credit	Balance
2015					
Oct. 20		J1	500		500

Service Revenue No. 400

Date	Explanation	Ref.	Debit	Credit	Balance
2015					
Oct. 31		J1		10,000	10,000

Salaries and Wages Expense No. 726

Date	Explanation	Ref.	Debit	Credit	Balance
2015					
Oct. 26		J1	4,000		4,000

Rent Expense No. 729

Date	Explanation	Ref.	Debit	Credit	Balance
2015					
Oct. 3		J1	900		900

The Trial Balance

A **trial balance** is a list of accounts and their balances at a given time. Customarily, companies prepare a trial balance at the end of an accounting period. They list accounts in the order in which they appear in the ledger. Debit balances appear in the left column and credit balances in the right column.

LEARNING OBJECTIVE 7

Prepare a trial balance and explain its purposes.

The trial balance proves the mathematical equality of debits and credits after posting. Under the double-entry system, this equality occurs when the sum of the debit account balances equals the sum of the credit account balances. **A trial balance may also uncover errors in journalizing and posting.** For example, a trial balance may well have detected the error at MF Global discussed in the Feature Story. **In addition, a trial balance is useful in the preparation of financial statements**, as we will explain in the next two chapters.

The steps for preparing a trial balance are:

1. List the account titles and their balances in the appropriate debit or credit column.

2. Total the debit and credit columns.

3. Prove the equality of the two columns.

Illustration 2-32 shows the trial balance prepared from Pioneer Advertising's ledger. Note that the total debits equal the total credits.

Illustration 2-32
A trial balance

Helpful Hint
Note that the order of presentation in the trial balance is:
　Assets
　Liabilities
　Stockholders' equity
　Revenues
　Expenses

PIONEER ADVERTISING AGENCY INC.
Trial Balance
October 31, 2015

	Debit	Credit
Cash	$ 15,200	
Supplies	2,500	
Prepaid Insurance	600	
Equipment	5,000	
Notes Payable		$ 5,000
Accounts Payable		2,500
Unearned Service Revenue		1,200
Common Stock		10,000
Dividends	500	
Service Revenue		10,000
Salaries and Wages Expense	4,000	
Rent Expense	900	
	$28,700	$28,700

A trial balance is a necessary checkpoint for uncovering certain types of errors. For example, if only the debit portion of a journal entry has been posted, the trial balance would bring this error to light.

Limitations of a Trial Balance

Ethics Note

An *error* is the result of an unintentional mistake; it is neither ethical nor unethical. An *irregularity* is an intentional misstatement, which *is* viewed as unethical.

A trial balance does not guarantee freedom from recording errors, however. Numerous errors may exist even though the totals of the trial balance columns agree. For example, the trial balance may balance even when:

1. A transaction is not journalized.

2. A correct journal entry is not posted.

3. A journal entry is posted twice.

4. Incorrect accounts are used in journalizing or posting.

5. Offsetting errors are made in recording the amount of a transaction.

As long as equal debits and credits are posted, even to the wrong account or in the wrong amount, the total debits will equal the total credits. **The trial balance does not prove that the company has recorded all transactions or that the ledger is correct.**

Locating Errors

Errors in a trial balance generally result from mathematical mistakes, incorrect postings, or simply transcribing data incorrectly. What do you do if you are faced with a trial balance that does not balance? First, determine the amount of the difference between the two columns of the trial balance. After this amount is known, the following steps are often helpful:

1. If the error is $1, $10, $100, or $1,000, re-add the trial balance columns and recompute the account balances.

2. If the error is divisible by 2, scan the trial balance to see whether a balance equal to half the error has been entered in the wrong column.

3. If the error is divisible by 9, retrace the account balances on the trial balance to see whether they are incorrectly copied from the ledger. For example, if a balance was $12 and it was listed as $21, a $9 error has been made. Reversing the order of numbers is called a **transposition error**.

4. If the error is not divisible by 2 or 9, scan the ledger to see whether an account balance in the amount of the error has been omitted from the trial balance, and scan the journal to see whether a posting of that amount has been omitted.

Use of Dollar Signs

Note that dollar signs do not appear in journals or ledgers. Dollar signs are typically used only in the trial balance and the financial statements. Generally, a dollar sign is shown only for the first item in the column and for the total of that column. A single line (a totaling rule) is placed under the column of figures to be added or subtracted. Total amounts are double-underlined to indicate they are final sums.

INVESTOR INSIGHT

Why Accuracy Matters

While most companies record transactions very carefully, the reality is that mistakes still happen. For example, bank regulators fined Bank One Corporation (now Chase) $1.8 million because they felt that the unreliability of the bank's accounting system caused it to violate regulatory requirements.

Also, in recent years Fannie Mae, the government-chartered mortgage association, announced a series of large accounting errors. These announcements caused alarm among investors, regulators, and politicians because they fear that the errors may suggest larger, undetected problems. This is important because the home mortgage market depends on Fannie Mae to buy hundreds of billions of dollars of mortgages each year from banks, thus enabling the banks to issue new mortgages.

Finally, before a major overhaul of its accounting system, the financial records of Waste Management Inc. were in such disarray that of the company's 57,000 employees, 10,000 were receiving pay slips that were in error.

The Sarbanes-Oxley Act was created to minimize the occurrence of errors like these by increasing every employee's responsibility for accurate financial reporting.

 In order for these companies to prepare and issue financial statements, their accounting equations (debits and credits) must have been in balance at year-end. How could these errors or misstatements have occurred? (See page 100.)

> **DO IT!**

Trial Balance

The following accounts come from the ledger of SnowGo Corporation at December 31, 2015.

157	Equipment	$88,000		311	Common Stock	$20,000
332	Dividends	8,000		212	Salaries and	
201	Accounts Payable	22,000			Wages Payable	2,000
726	Salaries and			200	Notes Payable	19,000
	Wages Expense	42,000		732	Utilities Expense	3,000
112	Accounts Receivable	4,000		130	Prepaid Insurance	6,000
400	Service Revenue	95,000		101	Cash	7,000

Prepare a trial balance in good form.

Solution

Action Plan

✔ Determine normal balances and list accounts in the order they appear in the ledger.

✔ Accounts with debit balances appear in the left column, and those with credit balances in the right column.

✔ Total the debit and credit columns to prove equality.

SNOWGO CORPORATION		
Trial Balance		
December 31, 2015		
	Debit	**Credit**
Cash	$ 7,000	
Accounts Receivable	4,000	
Prepaid Insurance	6,000	
Equipment	88,000	
Notes Payable		$ 19,000
Accounts Payable		22,000
Salaries and Wages Payable		2,000
Common Stock		20,000
Dividends	8,000	
Service Revenue		95,000
Utilities Expense	3,000	
Salaries and Wages Expense	42,000	
	$158,000	$158,000

Related exercise material: BE2-9, BE2-10, E2-9, E2-10, E2-11, E2-13, E2-14, **and** DO IT! 2-4.

✔ **The Navigator**

> **Comprehensive DO IT!**

Bob Sample and other student investors opened Campus Laundromat Inc. on September 1, 2015. During the first month of operations, the following transactions occurred.

Sept. 1   Stockholders invested $20,000 cash in the business.
2   The company paid $1,000 cash for store rent for September.
3   Purchased washers and dryers for $25,000, paying $10,000 in cash and signing a $15,000, 6-month, 12% note payable.
4   Paid $1,200 for a one-year accident insurance policy.
10   Received a bill from the *Daily News* for advertising the opening of the laundromat $200.
20   Declared and paid a cash dividend to stockholders $700.
30   The company determined that cash receipts for laundry services for the month were $6,200.

The chart of accounts for the company is the same as that for Pioneer Advertising Agency Inc. (page 68), plus No. 610 Advertising Expense.

Instructions

(a) Journalize the September transactions. (Use J1 for the journal page number.)
(b) Open ledger accounts and post the September transactions.
(c) Prepare a trial balance at September 30, 2015.

Solution to Comprehensive DO IT!

(a)

	GENERAL JOURNAL			J1
Date	Account Titles and Explanation	Ref.	Debit	Credit
2015				
Sept. 1	Cash	101	20,000	
	Common Stock	311		20,000
	(Stockholders' investment of cash in business)			
2	Rent Expense	729	1,000	
	Cash	101		1,000
	(Paid September rent)			
3	Equipment	157	25,000	
	Cash	101		10,000
	Notes Payable	200		15,000
	(Purchased laundry equipment for cash and 6-month, 12% note payable)			
4	Prepaid Insurance	130	1,200	
	Cash	101		1,200
	(Paid one-year insurance policy)			
10	Advertising Expense	610	200	
	Accounts Payable	201		200
	(Received bill from *Daily News* for advertising)			
20	Dividends	332	700	
	Cash	101		700
	(Declared and paid a cash dividend)			
30	Cash	101	6,200	
	Service Revenue	400		6,200
	(Received cash for services performed)			

Action Plan

✔ Make separate journal entries for each transaction.

✔ In journalizing, make sure debits equal credits.

✔ In journalizing, use specific account titles taken from the chart of accounts.

✔ Provide appropriate description of each journal entry.

✔ Arrange ledger in statement order, beginning with the balance sheet accounts.

✔ Post in chronological order.

✔ Use numbers in the reference column to indicate the amount has been posted.

✔ In the trial balance, list accounts in the order in which they appear in the ledger.

✔ List debit balances in the left column, and credit balances in the right column.

(b) GENERAL LEDGER

Cash No. 101

Date	Explanation	Ref.	Debit	Credit	Balance
2015					
Sept. 1		J1	20,000		20,000
2		J1		1,000	19,000
3		J1		10,000	9,000
4		J1		1,200	7,800
20		J1		700	7,100
30		J1	6,200		13,300

Prepaid Insurance No. 130

Date	Explanation	Ref.	Debit	Credit	Balance
2015					
Sept. 4		J1	1,200		1,200

Equipment No. 157

Date	Explanation	Ref.	Debit	Credit	Balance
2015					
Sept. 3		J1	25,000		25,000

Notes Payable No. 200

Date	Explanation	Ref.	Debit	Credit	Balance
2015					
Sept. 3		J1		15,000	15,000

Accounts Payable No. 201

Date	Explanation	Ref.	Debit	Credit	Balance
2015					
Sept. 10		J1		200	200

Common Stock No. 311

Date	Explanation	Ref.	Debit	Credit	Balance
2015					
Sept. 1		J1		20,000	20,000

Dividends No. 332

Date	Explanation	Ref.	Debit	Credit	Balance
2015					
Sept. 20		J1	700		700

(b)   **GENERAL LEDGER** (continued)

Service Revenue					No. 400
Date	Explanation	Ref.	Debit	Credit	Balance
2015					
Sept. 30		J1		6,200	6,200

Advertising Expense					No. 610
Date	Explanation	Ref.	Debit	Credit	Balance
2015					
Sept. 10		J1	200		200

Rent Expense					No. 729
Date	Explanation	Ref.	Debit	Credit	Balance
2015					
Sept. 2		J1	1,000		1,000

(c)

CAMPUS LAUNDROMAT INC.
Trial Balance
September 30, 2015

	Debit	Credit
Cash	$13,300	
Prepaid Insurance	1,200	
Equipment	25,000	
Notes Payable		$15,000
Accounts Payable		200
Common Stock		20,000
Dividends	700	
Service Revenue		6,200
Advertising Expense	200	
Rent Expense	1,000	
	$41,400	$41,400

✔ The Navigator

SUMMARY OF LEARNING OBJECTIVES   ✔ The Navigator

1 **Explain what an account is and how it helps in the recording process.** An account is a record of increases and decreases in specific asset, liability, and stockholders' equity items.

2 **Define debits and credits and explain their use in recording business transactions.** The terms debit and credit are synonymous with left and right. Assets, dividends, and expenses are increased by debits and decreased by credits. Liabilities, common stock, retained earnings, and revenues are increased by credits and decreased by debits.

3 **Identify the basic steps in the recording process.** The basic steps in the recording process are (a) analyze each transaction for its effects on the accounts, (b) enter the transaction information in a journal, and (c) transfer the journal information to the appropriate accounts in the ledger.

4 **Explain what a journal is and how it helps in the recording process.** The initial accounting record of a transaction is entered in a journal before the data are entered in the accounts. A journal (a) discloses in one place the complete effects of a transaction, (b) provides a chronological record of transactions, and (c) prevents or locates errors because the debit and credit amounts for each entry can be easily compared.

5 **Explain what a ledger is and how it helps in the recording process.** The ledger is the entire group of accounts maintained by a company. The ledger provides the balance in each of the accounts as well as keeps track of changes in these balances.

6 **Explain what posting is and how it helps in the recording process.** Posting is the transfer of journal entries to the ledger accounts. This phase of the recording process accumulates the effects of journalized transactions in the individual accounts.

7 **Prepare a trial balance and explain its purposes.** A trial balance is a list of accounts and their balances at a given time. Its primary purpose is to prove the equality of debits and credits after posting. A trial balance also uncovers errors in journalizing and posting and is useful in preparing financial statements.

GLOSSARY

Account A record of increases and decreases in specific asset, liability, or stockholders' equity items. (p. 56).

Chart of accounts A list of accounts and the account numbers that identify their location in the ledger. (p. 67).

Common stock Issued in exchange for the owners' investment paid in to corporation. (p. 58)

Compound entry A journal entry that involves three or more accounts. (p. 63).

Credit The right side of an account. (p. 56).

Debit The left side of an account. (p. 56).

Dividend A distribution by a corporation to its stockholders on a pro rata (equal) basis. (p. 59).

Double-entry system A system that records in appropriate accounts the dual effect of each transaction. (p. 57).

General journal The most basic form of journal. (p. 62).

General ledger A ledger that contains all asset, liability, and stockholders' equity accounts. (p. 65).

Journal An accounting record in which transactions are initially recorded in chronological order. (p. 62).

Journalizing The entering of transaction data in the journal. (p. 62).

Ledger The entire group of accounts maintained by a company. (p. 65).

Normal balance An account balance on the side where an increase in the account is recorded. (p. 57).

Posting The procedure of transferring journal entries to the ledger accounts. (p. 66).

Retained earnings Net income that is kept (retained) in the business. (p. 58).

Simple entry A journal entry that involves only two accounts. (p. 63).

T-account The basic form of an account. (p. 56).

Three-column form of account A form with columns for debit, credit, and balance amounts in an account. (p. 66).

Trial balance A list of accounts and their balances at a given time. (p. 75).

WileyPLUS Self-Test, Brief Exercises, Exercises, Problem Set A, and many more components are available for practice in *WileyPLUS*.

SELF-TEST QUESTIONS

Answers are on page 100.

(LO 1) **1.** Which of the following statements about an account is **true**?
(a) In its simplest form, an account consists of two parts.
(b) An account is an individual accounting record of increases and decreases in specific asset, liability, and stockholders' equity items.
(c) There are separate accounts for specific assets and liabilities but only one account for stockholders' equity items.
(d) The left side of an account is the credit or decrease side.

(LO 2) **2.** Debits:
(a) increase both assets and liabilities.
(b) decrease both assets and liabilities.
(c) increase assets and decrease liabilities.
(d) decrease assets and increase liabilities.

(LO 2) **3.** A revenue account:
(a) is increased by debits.
(b) is decreased by credits.
(c) has a normal balance of a debit.
(d) is increased by credits.

(LO 2) **4.** Accounts that normally have debit balances are:
(a) assets, expenses, and revenues.
(b) assets, expenses, and common stock.
(c) assets, liabilities, and dividends.
(d) assets, dividends, and expenses.

(LO 2) **5.** The expanded accounting equation is:
(a) Assets + Liabilities = Common Stock + Retained Earnings + Revenues + Expenses + Dividends.
(b) Assets = Liabilities + Common Stock + Retained Earnings + Revenues − Expenses + Dividends.
(c) Assets = Liabilities − Common Stock − Retained Earnings − Revenues − Expenses − Dividends.
(d) Assets = Liabilities + Common Stock + Retained Earnings + Revenues − Expenses − Dividends.

(LO 3) **6.** Which of the following is **not** part of the recording process?
(a) Analyzing transactions.
(b) Preparing a trial balance.
(c) Entering transactions in a journal.
(d) Posting transactions.

(LO 4) **7.** Which of the following statements about a journal is **false**?
(a) It is not a book of original entry.
(b) It provides a chronological record of transactions.
(c) It helps to locate errors because the debit and credit amounts for each entry can be readily compared.
(d) It discloses in one place the complete effect of a transaction.

(LO 4)　**8.** The purchase of supplies on account should result in:
  (a) a debit to Supplies Expense and a credit to Cash.
  (b) a debit to Supplies Expense and a credit to Accounts Payable.
  (c) a debit to Supplies and a credit to Accounts Payable.
  (d) a debit to Supplies and a credit to Accounts Receivable.

(LO 5)　**9.** The order of the accounts in the ledger is:
  (a) assets, revenues, expenses, liabilities, common stock, dividends.
  (b) assets, liabilities, common stock, dividends, revenues, expenses.
  (c) common stock, assets, revenues, expenses, liabilities, dividends.
  (d) revenues, assets, expenses, liabilities, common stock, dividends.

(LO 5)　**10.** A ledger:
  (a) contains only asset and liability accounts.
  (b) should show accounts in alphabetical order.
  (c) is a collection of the entire group of accounts maintained by a company.
  (d) is a book of original entry.

(LO 6)　**11.** Posting:
  (a) normally occurs before journalizing.
  (b) transfers ledger transaction data to the journal.
  (c) is an optional step in the recording process.
  (d) transfers journal entries to ledger accounts.

12. Before posting a payment of $5,000, the Accounts (LO 6) Payable of Chola Corporation had a normal balance of $18,000. The balance after posting this transaction was:
  (a) $13,000.　　　　**(c)** $23,000.
  (b) $5,000.　　　　**(d)** Cannot be determined.

13. A trial balance: (LO 7)
  (a) is a list of accounts with their balances at a given time.
  (b) proves the mathematical accuracy of journalized transactions.
  (c) will not balance if a correct journal entry is posted twice.
  (d) proves that all transactions have been recorded.

14. A trial balance will not balance if: (LO 7)
  (a) a correct journal entry is posted twice.
  (b) the purchase of supplies on account is debited to Supplies and credited to Cash.
  (c) a $100 cash dividend is debited to Dividends for $1,000 and credited to Cash for $100.
  (d) a $450 payment on account is debited to Accounts Payable for $45 and credited to Cash for $45.

15. The trial balance of Stevens Corporation had accounts (LO 7) with the following normal balances: Cash $5,000, Service Revenue $85,000, Salaries and Wages Payable $4,000, Salaries and Wages Expense $40,000, Rent Expense $10,000, Common Stock $42,000, Dividends $13,000, and Equipment $61,000. In preparing a trial balance, the total in the debit column is:
  (a) $116,000.　　　　**(c)** $129,000.
  (b) $118,000.　　　　**(d)** $131,000.

Go to the book's companion website, www.wiley.com/college/weygandt, for additional Self-Test Questions.

QUESTIONS

1. Describe the parts of a T-account.
2. "The terms debit and credit mean increase and decrease, respectively." Do you agree? Explain.
3. Tom Dingel, a fellow student, contends that the double-entry system means each transaction must be recorded twice. Is Tom correct? Explain.
4. Olga Conrad, a beginning accounting student, believes debit balances are favorable and credit balances are unfavorable. Is Olga correct? Discuss.
5. State the rules of debit and credit as applied to (a) asset accounts, (b) liability accounts, and (c) the stockholders' equity accounts (revenue, expenses, dividends, common stock, and retained earnings).
6. What is the normal balance for each of the following accounts? (a) Accounts Receivable. (b) Cash. (c) Dividends. (d) Accounts Payable. (e) Service Revenue. (f) Salaries and Wages Expense. (g) Common Stock.
7. Indicate whether each of the following accounts is an asset, a liability, or a stockholders' equity account

and whether it has a normal debit or credit balance: (a) Accounts Receivable. (b) Accounts Payable. (c) Equipment. (d) Dividends. (e) Supplies.
8. For the following transactions, indicate the account debited and the account credited.
  (a) Supplies are purchased on account.
  (b) Cash is received on signing a note payable.
  (c) Employees are paid salaries in cash.
9. Indicate whether the following accounts generally will have (a) debit entries only, (b) credit entries only, or (c) both debit and credit entries.
  (1) Cash.
  (2) Accounts Receivable.
  (3) Dividends.
  (4) Accounts Payable.
  (5) Salaries and Wages Expense.
  (6) Service Revenue.
10. What are the basic steps in the recording process?

11. What are the advantages of using a journal in the recording process?
12. (a) When entering a transaction in the journal, should the debit or credit be written first?
    (b) Which should be indented, the debit or credit?
13. Describe a compound entry, and provide an example.
14. (a) Should business transaction debits and credits be recorded directly in the ledger accounts?
    (b) What are the advantages of first recording transactions in the journal and then posting to the ledger?
15. The account number is entered as the last step in posting the amounts from the journal to the ledger. What is the advantage of this step?
16. Journalize the following business transactions.
    (a) Mark Stein invests $9,000 cash in the business in exchange for shares of common stock.
    (b) Insurance of $800 is paid for the year.
    (c) Supplies of $2,000 are purchased on account.
    (d) Cash of $7,800 is received for services performed.
17. (a) What is a ledger?
    (b) What is a chart of accounts and why is it important?
18. What is a trial balance and what are its purposes?

19. Juan Kirby is confused about how accounting information flows through the accounting system. He believes the flow of information is as follows.
    (a) Debits and credits posted to the ledger.
    (b) Business transaction occurs.
    (c) Information entered in the journal.
    (d) Financial statements are prepared.
    (e) Trial balance is prepared.
    Is Juan correct? If not, indicate to Juan the proper flow of the information.
20. Two students are discussing the use of a trial balance. They wonder whether the following errors, each considered separately, would prevent the trial balance from balancing. What would you tell them?
    (a) The bookkeeper debited Cash for $600 and credited Salaries and Wages Expense for $600 for payment of wages.
    (b) Cash collected on account was debited to Cash for $900 and Service Revenue was credited for $90.
21. What are the normal balances for Apple's Cash, Accounts Payable, and Interest Expense accounts?

BRIEF EXERCISES

BE2-1 For each of the following accounts indicate the effects of (a) a debit and (b) a credit on the accounts and (c) the normal balance of the account.

Indicate debit and credit effects and normal balance.

(LO 2)

1. Accounts Payable.
2. Advertising Expense.
3. Service Revenue.
4. Accounts Receivable.
5. Common Stock.
6. Dividends.

BE2-2 Transactions for the Sheldon Cooper Company, which provides welding services, for the month of June are presented below. Identify the accounts to be debited and credited for each transaction.

Identify accounts to be debited and credited.

(LO 2)

June 1 Sheldon Cooper invests $4,000 cash in exchange for shares of common stock in a small welding business.
     2 Purchases equipment on account for $1,200.
     3 $800 cash is paid to landlord for June rent.
    12 Bills P. Leonard $300 for welding work done on account.

BE2-3 Using the data in BE2-2, journalize the transactions. (You may omit explanations.)

Journalize transactions.
(LO 4)

BE2-4 ⊂━━━▶ Evan Saunders, a fellow student, is unclear about the basic steps in the recording process. Identify and briefly explain the steps in the order in which they occur.

Identify and explain steps in recording process.
(LO 3)

BE2-5 Bombeck Inc. has the following transactions during August of the current year. Indicate (a) the effect on the accounting equation and (b) the debit-credit analysis illustrated on pages 69–73 of the textbook.

Indicate basic and debit-credit analysis.
(LO 2)

Aug. 1 Opens an office as a financial advisor, investing $5,000 in cash in exchange for common stock.
     4 Pays insurance in advance for 6 months, $1,800 cash.
    16 Receives $1,900 from clients for services performed.
    27 Pays secretary $1,000 salary.

BE2-6 Using the data in BE2-5, journalize the transactions. (You may omit explanations.)

Journalize transactions.
(LO 4)

Post journal entries to T-accounts.

(LO 6)

BE2-7 Selected transactions for the Nikolai Company are presented in journal form below. Post the transactions to T-accounts. Make one T-account for each item and determine each account's ending balance.

			J1		
Date	Account Titles and Explanation	Ref.	Debit	Credit
May 5	Accounts Receivable		5,000	
	Service Revenue			5,000
	(Billed for services performed)			
12	Cash	.	2,100	
	Accounts Receivable			2,100
	(Received cash in payment of account)			
15	Cash		3,200	
	Service Revenue			3,200
	(Received cash for services performed)			

Post journal entries to standard form of account.

(LO 6)

BE2-8 Selected journal entries for the Nikolai Company are presented in BE2-7. Post the transactions using the standard form of account.

Prepare a trial balance.

(LO 7)

BE2-9 From the ledger balances given below, prepare a trial balance for the Favre Company at June 30, 2015. List the accounts in the order shown on page 76 of the textbook. All account balances are normal.

Accounts Payable $7,000, Cash $5,200, Common Stock $20,000, Dividends $800, Equipment $17,000, Service Revenue $6,000, Accounts Receivable $3,000, Salaries and Wages Expense $6,000, and Rent Expense $1,000.

Prepare a correct trial balance.

(LO 7)

BE2-10 An inexperienced bookkeeper prepared the following trial balance. Prepare a correct trial balance, assuming all account balances are normal.

ERIKA COMPANY
Trial Balance
December 31, 2015

	Debit	Credit
Cash	$16,800	
Prepaid Insurance		$ 3,500
Accounts Payable		3,000
Unearned Service Revenue	4,200	
Common Stock		13,000
Dividends		4,500
Service Revenue		25,600
Salaries and Wages Expense	18,600	
Rent Expense		2,400
	$39,600	$52,000

> **DO IT! Review**

Identify normal balances.

(LO 2)

DO IT! 2-1 James Mayaguez has just rented space in a strip mall. In this space, he will open a photography studio, to be called "Picture This!" A friend has advised James to set up a double-entry set of accounting records in which to record all of his business transactions.

Identify the balance sheet accounts that James will likely need to record the transactions needed to open his business (a corporation). Indicate whether the normal balance of each account is a debit or credit.

DO IT! 2-2 James Mayaguez engaged in the following activities in establishing his photography studio, Picture This!:

1. Opened a bank account in the name of Picture This! and deposited $8,000 of his own money into this account in exchange for common stock.

2. Purchased photography supplies at a total cost of $1,600. The business paid $300 in cash and the balance is on account.

3. Obtained estimates on the cost of photography equipment from three different manufacturers.

In what form (type of record) should James record these three activities? Prepare the entries to record the transactions.

Record business activities.
(LO 4)

DO IT! 2-3 James Mayaguez recorded the following transactions during the month of April.

Post transactions.
(LO 6)

April 3	Cash	3,900	
	Service Revenue		3,900
April 16	Rent Expense	600	
	Cash		600
April 20	Salaries and Wages Expense	500	
	Cash		500

Post these entries to the Cash T-account of the general ledger to determine the ending balance in cash. The beginning balance in cash on April 1 was $1,600.

DO IT! 2-4 The following accounts are taken from the ledger of Chillin' Company at December 31, 2015.

Prepare a trial balance.
(LO 7)

200	Notes Payable	$20,000	101	Cash	$6,000
311	Common Stock	25,000	120	Supplies	5,000
157	Equipment	76,000	522	Rent Expense	2,000
332	Dividends	8,000	220	Salaries and	
726	Salaries and			Wages Payable	3,000
	Wages Expense	38,000	201	Accounts Payable	9,000
400	Service Revenue	86,000	112	Accounts Receivable	8,000

Prepare a trial balance in good form.

EXERCISES

E2-1 Faith Dillon has prepared the following list of statements about accounts.

1. An account is an accounting record of either a specific asset or a specific liability.
2. An account shows only increases, not decreases, in the item it relates to.
3. Some items, such as cash and accounts receivable, are combined into one account.
4. An account has a left, or credit side, and a right, or debit side.
5. A simple form of an account consisting of just the account title, the left side, and the right side, is called a T-account.

Analyze statements about accounting and the recording process.
(LO 1)

Instructions
Identify each statement as true or false. If false, indicate how to correct the statement.

E2-2 Selected transactions for L. Takemoto, an interior decorating firm, in its first month of business, are shown below and on page 86.

Identify debits, credits, and normal balances.
(LO 2)

Jan.	2	Invested $15,000 cash in the business in exchange for common stock.
	3	Purchased used car for $8,200 cash for use in the business.
	9	Purchased supplies on account for $500.
	11	Billed customers $1,800 for services performed.

Jan. 16 Paid $200 cash for advertising.
　　 20 Received $780 cash from customers billed on January 11.
　　 23 Paid creditor $300 cash on balance owed.
　　 28 Declared and paid a $500 cash dividend.

Instructions

For each transaction indicate the following.

(a) The basic type of account debited and credited (asset, liability, stockholders' equity).
(b) The specific account debited and credited (Cash, Rent Expense, Service Revenue, etc.).
(c) Whether the specific account is increased or decreased.
(d) The normal balance of the specific account.

Use the following format, in which the January 2 transaction is given as an example.

	Account Debited				Account Credited			
	(a)	**(b)**	**(c)**	**(d)**	**(a)**	**(b)**	**(c)**	**(d)**
Date	**Basic Type**	**Specific Account**	**Effect**	**Normal Balance**	**Basic Type**	**Specific Account**	**Effect**	**Normal Balance**
Jan. 2	Asset	Cash	Increase	Debit	Stockholders' Equity	Common Stock	Increase	Credit

Journalize transactions.

(LO 4)

E2-3 Data for L. Takemoto, interior decorating, are presented in E2-2.

Instructions

Journalize the transactions using journal page J1. (You may omit explanations.)

Analyze transactions and determine their effect on accounts.

(LO 2)

E2-4 Presented below is information related to Lexington Real Estate Agency.

Oct. 1 Diane Lexington begins business as a real estate agent with a cash investment of $20,000 in exchange for common stock.
　　 2 Hires an administrative assistant.
　　 3 Purchases office furniture for $2,300, on account.
　　 6 Sells a house and lot for N. Fennig; bills N. Fennig $3,600 for realty services performed.
　　 27 Pays $850 on the balance related to the transaction of October 3.
　　 30 Pays the administrative assistant $2,500 in salary for October.

Instructions

Prepare the debit-credit analysis for each transaction as illustrated on pages 69–73.

Journalize transactions.

(LO 4)

E2-5 Transaction data for Lexington Real Estate Agency are presented in E2-4.

Instructions

Journalize the transactions. (You may omit explanations.)

Analyze transactions and journalize.

(LO 2, 3, 4)

E2-6 Fredo Industries had the following transactions.

1. Borrowed $5,000 from the bank by signing a note.
2. Paid $2,500 cash for a computer.
3. Purchased $450 of supplies on account.

Instructions

(a) Indicate what accounts are increased and decreased by each transaction.
(b) Journalize each transaction. (Omit explanations.)

Analyze transactions and journalize.

(LO 2, 3, 4)

E2-7 Leppard Enterprises had the following selected transactions.

1. Kim Leppard invested $5,000 cash in the business in exchange for common stock.
2. Paid office rent of $950.
3. Performed consulting services and billed a client $4,700.
4. Declared and paid a $600 cash dividend.

Instructions

(a) Indicate the effect each transaction has on the accounting equation (Assets = Liabilities + Stockholders' Equity), using plus and minus signs.
(b) Journalize each transaction. (Omit explanations.)

E2-8 Meghan Selzer has prepared the following list of statements about the general ledger.

1. The general ledger contains all the asset and liability accounts, but no stockholders' equity accounts.
2. The general ledger is sometimes referred to as simply the ledger.
3. The accounts in the general ledger are arranged in alphabetical order.
4. Each account in the general ledger is numbered for easier identification.
5. The general ledger is a book of original entry.

Analyze statements about the ledger.

(LO 5)

Instructions

Identify each statement as true or false. If false, indicate how to correct the statement.

E2-9 Selected transactions from the journal of Kati Tillman, investment broker, are presented below.

Post journal entries and prepare a trial balance.

(LO 6, 7)

Date	Account Titles and Explanation	Ref.	Debit	Credit
Aug. 1	Cash		6,000	
	Common Stock			6,000
	(Investment of cash for stock)			
10	Cash		2,700	
	Service Revenue			2,700
	(Received cash for services performed)			
12	Equipment		5,000	
	Cash			800
	Notes Payable			4,200
	(Purchased office equipment for cash and notes payable)			
25	Account Receivable		1,600	
	Service Revenue			1,600
	(Billed clients for services performed)			
31	Cash		880	
	Accounts Receivable			880
	(Receipt of cash on account)			

Instructions

(a) Post the transactions to T-accounts.
(b) Prepare a trial balance at August 31, 2015.

E2-10 The T-accounts below summarize the ledger of Santana Landscaping Company at the end of its first month of operations.

Journalize transactions from account data and prepare a trial balance.

(LO 4, 7)

Cash			No. 101
4/1	10,000	4/15	720
4/12	900	4/25	1,500
4/29	400		
4/30	1,000		

Accounts Receivable			No. 112
4/7	3,200	4/29	400

Supplies			No. 126
4/4	1,800		

Accounts Payable			No. 201
4/25	1,500	4/4	1,800

Unearned Service Revenue			No. 209
		4/30	1,000

Common Stock			No. 311
		4/1	10,000

Service Revenue			No. 400
		4/7	3,200
		4/12	900

Salaries and Wages Expense			No. 726
4/15	720		

Instructions

(a) Prepare the complete general journal (including explanations) from which the postings to Cash were made.

(b) Prepare a trial balance at April 30, 2015.

Journalize transactions from account data and prepare a trial balance.

(LO 4, 7)

E2-11 Presented below is the ledger for Higgs Co.

Cash			No. 101
10/1	5,000	10/4	400
10/10	730	10/12	1,500
10/10	3,000	10/15	280
10/20	500	10/30	300
10/25	2,000	10/31	500

Accounts Receivable			No. 112
10/6	800	10/20	500
10/20	910		

Supplies			No. 126
10/4	400		

Equipment			No. 157
10/3	2,000		

Notes Payable			No. 200
		10/10	3,000

Accounts Payable			No. 201
10/12	1,500	10/3	2,000

Common Stock			No. 311
		10/1	5,000
		10/25	2,000

Dividends			No. 332
10/30	300		

Service Revenue			No. 400
		10/6	800
		10/10	730
		10/20	910

Salaries and Wages Expense			No. 726
10/31	500		

Rent Expense			No. 729
10/15	280		

Instructions

(a) Reproduce the journal entries for the transactions that occurred on October 1, 10, and 20, and provide explanations for each.

(b) Determine the October 31 balance for each of the accounts above, and prepare a trial balance at October 31, 2015.

Prepare journal entries and post using standard account form.

(LO 4, 6)

E2-12 Selected transactions for Alvarado Company during its first month in business are presented below.

Sept.　1　Invested $10,000 cash in the business in exchange for common stock.
　　　　5　Purchased equipment for $12,000 paying $4,000 in cash and the balance on account.
　　　25　Paid $2,400 cash on balance owed for equipment.
　　　30　Declared and paid a $500 cash dividend.

Alvarado's chart of accounts shows No. 101 Cash, No. 157 Equipment, No. 201 Accounts Payable, No. 311 Common Stock, and No. 332 Dividends.

Instructions

(a) Journalize the transactions on page J1 of the journal. (Omit explanations.)

(b) Post the transactions using the standard account form.

Analyze errors and their effects on trial balance.

(LO 7)

E2-13 The bookkeeper for Brooks Equipment Repair made a number of errors in journalizing and posting, as described below.

1. A credit posting of $450 to Accounts Receivable was omitted.
2. A debit posting of $750 for Prepaid Insurance was debited to Insurance Expense.
3. A collection from a customer of $100 in payment of its account owed was journalized and posted as a debit to Cash $100 and a credit to Service Revenue $100.
4. A credit posting of $300 to Property Taxes Payable was made twice.
5. A cash purchase of supplies for $250 was journalized and posted as a debit to Supplies $25 and a credit to Cash $25.
6. A debit of $525 to Advertising Expense was posted as $552.

Instructions

For each error:

(a) Indicate whether the trial balance will balance.

(b) If the trial balance will not balance, indicate the amount of the difference.

(c) Indicate the trial balance column that will have the larger total.

Consider each error separately. Use the following form, in which error (1) is given as an example.

Error	(a) In Balance	(b) Difference	(c) Larger Column
(1)	No	$450	debit

E2-14 The accounts in the ledger of Time Is Money Delivery Service contain the following balances on July 31, 2015.

Prepare a trial balance.
(LO 2, 7)

Accounts Receivable	$10,642	Prepaid Insurance	$ 1,968
Accounts Payable	8,396	Maintenance and Repairs Expense	961
Cash	?	Service Revenue	10,610
Equipment	49,360	Dividends	700
Gasoline Expense	758	Common Stock	40,000
Utilities Expense	523	Salaries and Wages Expense	4,428
Notes Payable	26,450	Salaries and Wages Payable	815
		Retained Earnings	4,636

Instructions

Prepare a trial balance with the accounts arranged as illustrated in the chapter and fill in the missing amount for Cash.

E2-15 The statement of cash flows classifies each transaction as an operating activity, an investing activity, or a financing activity. Operating activities are the types of activities the company performs to generate profits. Investing activities include the purchase of long-lived assets such as equipment or the purchase of investment securities. Financing activities are borrowing money, issuing shares of stock, and paying dividends.

Identify cash flow activities.
(LO 7)

Presented below are the following transactions.

1. Issued stock for $20,000 cash.
2. Issued note payable for $12,000 cash.
3. Purchased office equipment for $11,000 cash.
4. Received $15,000 cash for services performed.
5. Paid $1,000 cash for rent.
6. Paid $600 cash dividend to stockholders.
7. Paid $5,700 cash for salaries.

Instructions

Classify each of these transactions as operating, investing, or financing activities.

EXERCISES: SET B AND CHALLENGE EXERCISES

Visit the book's companion website, at **www.wiley.com/college/weygandt**, and choose the Student Companion site to access Exercise Set B and Challenge Exercises.

PROBLEMS: SET A

P2-1A Grandview Park was started on April 1 by R. S. Francis and associates. The following selected events and transactions occurred during April.

Journalize a series of transactions.
(LO 2, 4)

Apr. 1   Stockholders invested $50,000 cash in the business in exchange for common stock.
     4   Purchased land costing $34,000 for cash.
     8   Incurred advertising expense of $1,800 on account.

Apr. 11   Paid salaries to employees $1,500.
    12   Hired park manager at a salary of $3,500 per month, effective May 1.
    13   Paid $2,400 cash for a one-year insurance policy.
    17   Declared and paid a $1,400 cash dividend.
    20   Received $5,700 in cash for admission fees.
    25   Sold 100 coupon books for $30 each. Each book contains 10 coupons that entitle the holder to one admission to the park.
    30   Received $8,900 in cash admission fees.
    30   Paid $840 on balance owed for advertising incurred on April 8.

Grandview uses the following accounts: Cash, Prepaid Insurance, Land, Accounts Payable, Unearned Service Revenue, Common Stock, Dividends, Service Revenue, Advertising Expense, and Salaries and Wages Expense.

Instructions
Journalize the April transactions.

Journalize transactions, post, and prepare a trial balance.

(LO 2, 4, 6, 7)

P2-2A Julia Dumars is a licensed CPA. During the first month of operations of her business, Julia Dumars, Inc., the following events and transactions occurred.

May 1   Stockholders invested $20,000 cash in exchange for common stock.
    2   Hired a secretary-receptionist at a salary of $2,000 per month.
    3   Purchased $1,500 of supplies on account from Vincent Supply Company.
    7   Paid office rent of $900 cash for the month.
    11   Completed a tax assignment and billed client $2,800 for services performed.
    12   Received $3,500 advance on a management consulting engagement.
    17   Received cash of $1,200 for services performed for Orville Co.
    31   Paid secretary-receptionist $2,000 salary for the month.
    31   Paid 40% of balance due Vincent Supply Company.

Julia uses the following chart of accounts: No. 101 Cash, No. 112 Accounts Receivable, No. 126 Supplies, No. 201 Accounts Payable, No. 209 Unearned Service Revenue, No. 311 Common Stock, No. 400 Service Revenue, No. 726 Salaries and Wages Expense, and No. 729 Rent Expense.

Instructions
(a) Journalize the transactions.
(b) Post to the ledger accounts.
(c) Prepare a trial balance on May 31, 2015.

(c) Trial balance totals $28,400

Journalize and post transactions and prepare a trial balance.

(LO 2, 4, 6, 7)

P2-3A Tom Zopf owns and manages a computer repair service, which had the following trial balance on December 31, 2014 (the end of its fiscal year).

TABLETTE REPAIR SERVICE, INC.
Trial Balance
December 31, 2014

	Debit	Credit
Cash	$ 8,000	
Accounts Receivable	15,000	
Supplies	11,000	
Prepaid Rent	3,000	
Equipment	21,000	
Accounts Payable		$17,000
Common Stock		30,000
Retained Earnings		11,000
	$58,000	$58,000

Summarized transactions for January 2015 were as follows.

1. Advertising costs, paid in cash, $1,000.
2. Additional supplies acquired on account $3,600.
3. Miscellaneous expenses, paid in cash, $1,700.
4. Cash collected from customers in payment of accounts receivable $13,000.
5. Cash paid to creditors for accounts payable due $14,400.

6. Repair services performed during January: for cash $5,000; on account $9,000.
7. Wages for January, paid in cash, $3,000.
8. Dividends during January were $1,600.

Instructions
(a) Open T-accounts for each of the accounts listed in the trial balance, and enter the opening balances for 2015.
(b) Prepare journal entries to record each of the January transactions. (Omit explanations.)
(c) Post the journal entries to the accounts in the ledger. (Add accounts as needed.)
(d) Prepare a trial balance as of January 31, 2015.

(d) Trial balance totals $61,200

P2-4A The trial balance of Dominic Company shown below does not balance.

Prepare a correct trial balance.
(LO 7)

DOMINIC COMPANY
Trial Balance
May 31, 2015

	Debit	Credit
Cash	$ 3,850	
Accounts Receivable		$ 2,750
Prepaid Insurance	700	
Equipment	12,000	
Accounts Payable		4,500
Unearned Service Revenue	560	
Common Stock		11,700
Service Revenue	8,690	
Salaries and Wages Expense	4,200	
Advertising Expense		1,100
Utilities Expense	800	
	$30,800	$20,050

Your review of the ledger reveals that each account has a normal balance. You also discover the following errors.

1. The totals of the debit sides of Prepaid Insurance, Accounts Payable, and Utilities Expense were each understated $100.
2. Transposition errors were made in Accounts Receivable and Service Revenue. Based on postings made, the correct balances were $2,570 and $8,960, respectively.
3. A debit posting to Salaries and Wages Expense of $200 was omitted.
4. A $1,000 cash dividend was debited to Common Stock for $1,000 and credited to Cash for $1,000.
5. A $520 purchase of supplies on account was debited to Equipment for $520 and credited to Cash for $520.
6. A cash payment of $450 for advertising was debited to Advertising Expense for $45 and credited to Cash for $45.
7. A collection from a customer for $420 was debited to Cash for $420 and credited to Accounts Payable for $420.

Instructions
Prepare a correct trial balance. Note that the chart of accounts includes the following: Dividends and Supplies. (*Hint:* It helps to prepare the correct journal entry for the transaction described and compare it to the mistake made.)

Trial balance totals $26,720

P2-5A The Palace Theater opened on April 1. All facilities were completed on March 31. At this time, the ledger showed No. 101 Cash $6,000, No. 140 Land $12,000, No. 145 Buildings (concession stand, projection room, ticket booth, and screen) $8,000, No. 157 Equipment $6,000, No. 201 Accounts Payable $2,000, No. 275 Mortgage Payable $10,000, and No. 311 Common Stock $20,000. During April, the following events and transactions occurred.

Journalize transactions, post, and prepare a trial balance.
(LO 2, 4, 6, 7)

Apr. 2 Paid film rental of $800 on first movie.
    3 Ordered two additional films at $950 each.
    9 Received $1,800 cash from admissions.
    10 Made $2,000 payment on mortgage and $1,000 for accounts payable due.

Apr. 11   Palace Theater contracted with Dever Company to operate the concession stand. Dever is to pay 18% of gross concession receipts (payable monthly) for the rental of the concession stand.

12   Paid advertising expenses $320.

20   Received one of the films ordered on April 3 and was billed $950. The film will be shown in April.

25   Received $5,200 cash from admissions.

29   Paid salaries $1,600.

30   Received statement from Dever showing gross concession receipts of $1,000 and the balance due to The Palace Theater of $180 ($1,000 × 18%) for April. Dever paid one-half of the balance due and will remit the remainder on May 5.

30   Prepaid $1,000 rental on special film to be run in May.

In addition to the accounts identified above, the chart of accounts shows No. 112 Accounts Receivable, No. 136 Prepaid Rent, No. 400 Service Revenue, No. 429 Rent Revenue, No. 610 Advertising Expense, No. 726 Salaries and Wages Expense, and No. 729 Rent Expense.

Instructions

(a) Enter the beginning balances in the ledger as of April 1. Insert a check mark (✓) in the reference column of the ledger for the beginning balance.

(b) Journalize the April transactions.

(c) Post the April journal entries to the ledger. Assume that all entries are posted from page 1 of the journal.

(d) Trial balance totals $37,130   **(d)** Prepare a trial balance on April 30, 2015.

PROBLEMS: SET B

Journalize a series of transactions.

(LO 2, 4)

P2-1B Surepar Disc Golf Course was opened on March 1 by Brian Lando. The following selected events and transactions occurred during March:

Mar. 1   Invested $60,000 cash in the business in exchange for common stock.

3   Purchased Arnie's Golf Land for $38,000 cash. The price consists of land $26,000, shed $8,000, and equipment $4,000. (Make one compound entry.)

5   Advertised the opening of the driving range and miniature golf course, paying advertising expenses of $1,600.

6   Paid cash $3,800 for a one-year insurance policy.

10   Purchased golf discs and other equipment for $1,050 from Wheeler Company payable in 30 days.

18   Received $420 in cash for golf fees.

19   Sold 100 coupon books for $18 each. Each book contains 4 coupons that enable the holder to play one round of disc golf.

25   Declared and paid an $800 cash dividend.

30   Paid salaries of $280.

30   Paid Wheeler Company in full.

31   Received $200 cash for golf fees.

Surepar uses the following accounts: Cash, Prepaid Insurance, Land, Buildings, Equipment, Accounts Payable, Unearned Service Revenue, Common Stock, Dividends, Service Revenue, Advertising Expense, and Salaries and Wages Expense.

Instructions

Journalize the March transactions.

Journalize transactions, post, and prepare a trial balance.

(LO 2, 4, 6, 7)

P2-2B Alicia Hiram is a licensed dentist. During the first month of the operation of her business, the following events and transactions occurred.

April 1   Stockholders invested $40,000 cash in exchange for common stock.

1   Hired a secretary-receptionist at a salary of $600 per week payable monthly.

2   Paid office rent for the month $1,700.

3   Purchased dental supplies on account from Jennings Company $5,200.

10   Performed dental services and billed insurance companies $6,600.

11   Received $1,200 cash advance from Bob Carow for an implant.
20   Received $2,100 cash for dental services performed for Ryan Banks.
30   Paid secretary-receptionist for the month $2,400.
30   Paid $2,200 to Jennings Company for accounts payable due.

Alicia uses the following chart of accounts: No. 101 Cash, No. 112 Accounts Receivable, No. 126 Supplies, No. 201 Accounts Payable, No. 209 Unearned Service Revenue, No. 311 Common Stock, No. 400 Service Revenue, No. 726 Salaries and Wages Expense, and No. 729 Rent Expense.

Instructions
(a) Journalize the transactions.
(b) Post to the ledger accounts.
(c) Prepare a trial balance on April 30, 2015.

(c) Trial balance totals $52,900

P2-3B Hillsborough Services was formed on May 1, 2015. The following transactions took place during the first month.

Journalize transactions, post, and prepare a trial balance.

(LO 2, 4, 6, 7)

Transactions on May 1:

1. Stockholders invested $50,000 cash in exchange for common stock.
2. Hired two employees to work in the warehouse. They will each be paid a salary of $2,800 per month.
3. Signed a 2-year rental agreement on a warehouse; paid $24,000 cash in advance for the first year.
4. Purchased furniture and equipment costing $28,000. A cash payment of $5,000 was made immediately; the remainder will be paid in 6 months.
5. Paid $2,640 cash for a one-year insurance policy on the furniture and equipment.

Transactions during the remainder of the month:

6. Purchased basic office supplies for $750 cash.
7. Purchased more office supplies for $1,300 on account.
8. Total revenues were $18,000—$6,000 cash and $12,000 on account.
9. Paid $400 to suppliers for accounts payable due.
10. Received $3,200 from customers in payment of accounts receivable.
11. Received utility bills in the amount of $260, to be paid next month.
12. Paid the monthly salaries of the two employees, totaling $5,600.

Instructions
(a) Prepare journal entries to record each of the events listed. (Omit explanations.)
(b) Post the journal entries to T-accounts.
(c) Prepare a trial balance as of May 31, 2015.

(c) Trial balance totals $92,160

P2-4B The trial balance of Zoop Co. shown below does not balance.

Prepare a correct trial balance.

(LO 7)

ZOOP CO.
Trial Balance
June 30, 2015

	Debit	Credit
Cash		$ 3,960
Accounts Receivable	$ 2,648	
Supplies	800	
Equipment	3,000	
Accounts Payable		2,666
Unearned Service Revenue	2,200	
Common Stock		9,000
Dividends	800	
Service Revenue		2,367
Salaries and Wages Expense	3,400	
Utilities Expense	910	
	$13,758	$17,993

Each of the listed accounts has a normal balance per the general ledger. An examination of the ledger and journal reveals the following errors.

1. Cash received from a customer in payment of its account was debited for $690, and Accounts Receivable was credited for the same amount. The actual collection was for $960.
2. The purchase of a computer on account for $620 was recorded as a debit to Supplies for $620 and a credit to Accounts Payable for $620.
3. Services were performed on account for a client for $760. Accounts Receivable was debited for $760, and Service Revenue was credited for $76.
4. A debit posting to Salaries and Wages Expense of $700 was omitted.
5. A payment of a balance due for $309 was credited to Cash for $309 and credited to Accounts Payable for $390.
6. The payment of a $600 cash dividend was debited to Salaries and Wages Expense for $600 and credited to Cash for $600.

Trial balance totals $16,218

Instructions

Prepare a correct trial balance. (*Hint:* It helps to prepare the correct journal entry for the transaction described and compare it to the mistake made.)

Journalize transactions, post, and prepare a trial balance.

(LO 2, 4, 6, 7)

GLS

P2-5B The Hart Theater, owned by Paul Hart, will begin operations in March. The Hart will be unique in that it will show only triple features of sequential theme movies. As of March 1, the ledger of Hart showed No. 101 Cash $8,000, No. 140 Land $22,000, No. 145 Buildings (concession stand, projection room, ticket booth, and screen) $10,000, No. 157 Equipment $8,000, No. 201 Accounts Payable $6,000, and No. 311 Common Stock $42,000. During the month of March, the following events and transactions occurred.

Mar. 2   Rented the three *Indiana Jones* movies to be shown for the first 3 weeks of March. The film rental was $3,500; $1,000 was paid in cash and $2,500 will be paid on March 10.

3   Ordered the *Lord of the Rings* movies to be shown the last 10 days of March. It will cost $260 per night.

9   Received $4,000 cash from admissions.

10   Paid balance due on *Indiana Jones* movies rental and $900 on March 1 accounts payable.

11   Hart Theater contracted with D. Sarazan to operate the concession stand. Sarazan is to pay 15% of gross concession receipts (payable monthly) for the right to operate the concession stand.

12   Paid advertising expenses $450.

20   Received $5,400 cash from customers for admissions.

20   Received the *Lord of Rings* movies and paid the rental fee of $2,600.

31   Paid salaries of $2,500.

31   Received statement from D. Sarazan showing gross receipts from concessions of $5,000 and the balance due to Hart Theater of $750 ($5,000 × 15%) for March. Sarazan paid one-half the balance due and will remit the remainder on April 5.

31   Received $9,000 cash from customers for admissions.

In addition to the accounts identified above, the chart of accounts includes No. 112 Accounts Receivable, No. 400 Service Revenue, No. 429 Rent Revenue, No. 610 Advertising Expense, No. 729 Rent Expense, and No. 726 Salaries and Wages Expense.

Instructions

(a) Enter the beginning balances in the ledger. Insert a check mark (✓) in the reference column of the ledger for the beginning balance.
(b) Journalize the March transactions.
(c) Post the March journal entries to the ledger. Assume that all entries are posted from page 1 of the journal.

(d) Trial balance totals $66,250

(d) Prepare a trial balance on March 31, 2015.

PROBLEMS: SET C

Visit the book's companion website, at **www.wiley.com/college/weygandt**, and choose the Student Companion site to access Problem Set C.

CONTINUING COOKIE CHRONICLE

(*Note:* This is a continuation of the Cookie Chronicle from Chapter 1.)

CCC2 After researching the different forms of business organization. Natalie Koebel decides to operate "Cookie Creations" as a corporation. She then starts the process of getting the business running.

Go to the book's companion website, **www.wiley.com/college/weygandt***, to see the completion of this problem.*

Broadening Your PERSPECTIVE

Financial Reporting and Analysis

Financial Reporting Problem: Apple Inc.

BYP2-1 The financial statements of Apple Inc. are presented in Appendix A. Instructions for accessing and using the company's complete annual report, including the notes to the financial statements, are also provided in Appendix A.

Apple's financial statements contain the following selected accounts, stated in millions of dollars.

Accounts Payable	Cash and Cash Equivalents
Accounts Receivable	Research and Development Expense
Property, Plant, and Equipment	Inventories

Instructions

(a) Answer the following questions.
  (1) What is the increase and decrease side for each account?
  (2) What is the normal balance for each account?

(b) Identify the probable other account in the transaction and the effect on that account when:
  (1) Accounts Receivable is decreased.
  (2) Accounts Payable is decreased.
  (3) Inventories are increased.

(c) Identify the other account(s) that ordinarily would be involved when:
  (1) Research and Development Expense is increased.
  (2) Property, Plant, and Equipment is increased.

Comparative Analysis Problem:
PepsiCo, Inc. vs. The Coca-Cola Company

BYP2-2 PepsiCo's financial statements are presented in Appendix B. Financial statements of The Coca-Cola Company are presented in Appendix C. Instructions for accessing and using the complete annual reports of PepsiCo and Coca-Cola, including the notes to the financial statements, are also provided in Appendices B and C, respectively.

Instructions

(a) Based on the information contained in the financial statements, determine the normal balance of the listed accounts for each company.

PepsiCo	Coca-Cola
1. Inventory	**1.** Accounts Receivable
2. Property, Plant, and Equipment	**2.** Cash and Cash Equivalents
3. Accounts Payable	**3.** Cost of Goods Sold (expense)
4. Interest Expense	**4.** Sales (revenue)

(b) Identify the other account ordinarily involved when:

(1) Accounts Receivable is increased.
(2) Salaries and Wages Payable is decreased.
(3) Property, Plant, and Equipment is increased.
(4) Interest Expense is increased.

Comparative Analysis Problem: Amazon.com, Inc. vs. Wal-Mart Stores, Inc.

BYP2-3 Amazon.com, Inc.'s financial statements are presented in Appendix D. Financial statements for Wal-Mart Stores, Inc. are presented in Appendix E. Instructions for accessing and using the complete annual reports of Amazon and Wal-Mart, including the notes to the financial statements, are also provided in Appendices D and E, respectively.

Instructions

(a) Based on the information contained in the financial statements, determine the normal balance of the listed accounts for each company.

Amazon	Wal-Mart
1. Interest Expense	1. Net Sales Revenues
2. Cash and Cash Equivalents	2. Inventories
3. Accounts Payable	3. Cost of Sales

(b) Identify the other account ordinarily involved when:

(1) Accounts Receivable is increased.
(2) Interest Expense is increased.
(3) Salaries and Wages Payable is decreased.
(4) Service Revenue is increased.

Real-World Focus

BYP2-4 Much information about specific companies is available on the Internet. Such information includes basic descriptions of the company's location, activities, industry, financial health, and financial performance.

Address: **biz.yahoo.com/i,** or go to **www.wiley.com/college/weygandt**

Steps
1. Type in a company name, or use the index to find a company name.
2. Choose **Profile**. Perform instructions (a)–(c) below.
3. Click on the company's specific industry to identify competitors. Perform instructions (d)–(g) below.

Instructions
Answer the following questions.

(a) What is the company's industry?
(b) What are the company's total sales?
(c) What is the company's net income?
(d) What are the names of four of the company's competitors?
(e) Choose one of these competitors.
(f) What is this competitor's name? What are its sales? What is its net income?
(g) Which of these two companies is larger by size of sales? Which one reported higher net income?

BYP2-5 The January 27, 2011, edition of the *New York Times* contains an article by Richard Sandomir entitled "N.F.L. Finances, as Seen Through Packers' Records." The article discusses the fact that the Green Bay Packers are the only NFL team that publicly publishes its annual report.

Instructions
Read the article and answer the following questions.

(a) Why are the Green Bay Packers the only professional football team to publish and distribute an annual report?
(b) Why is the football players' labor union particularly interested in the Packers' annual report?

(c) In addition to the players' labor union, what other outside party might be interested in the annual report?

(d) Even though the Packers' revenue increased in recent years, the company's operating profit fell significantly. How does the article explain this decline?

Critical Thinking

Decision-Making Across the Organization

BYP2-6 Dyanna Craig operates Craig Riding Academy. The academy's primary sources of revenue are riding fees and lesson fees, which are paid on a cash basis. Dyanna also boards horses for owners, who are billed monthly for boarding fees. In a few cases, boarders pay in advance of expected use. For its revenue transactions, the academy maintains the following accounts: Cash, Accounts Receivable, and Service Revenue.

The academy owns 10 horses, a stable, a riding corral, riding equipment, and office equipment. These assets are accounted for in these accounts: Horses, Buildings, and Equipment.

The academy also maintains the following accounts: Supplies, Prepaid Insurance, Accounts Payable, Salaries and Wages Expense, Advertising Expense, Utilities Expense, and Maintenance and Repairs Expense.

Dyanna makes periodic withdrawals of cash dividends to stockholders. To record stockholders' equity in the business and dividends, three accounts are maintained: Common Stock, Retained Earnings, and Dividends.

During the first month of operations, an inexperienced bookkeeper was employed. Dyanna Craig asks you to review the following eight entries of the 50 entries made during the month. In each case, the explanation for the entry is correct.

Date	Account	Debit	Credit
May 1	Cash	18,000	
	Common Stock		18,000
	(Invested $18,000 cash in exchange for stock)		
5	Cash	250	
	Service Revenue		250
	(Received $250 cash for lessons provided)		
7	Cash	300	
	Service Revenue		300
	(Received $300 for boarding of horses beginning June 1)		
14	Equipment	80	
	Cash		800
	(Purchased desk and other office equipment for $800 cash)		
15	Salaries and Wages Expense	400	
	Cash		400
	(Issued dividend checks to stockholders)		
20	Cash	148	
	Service Revenue		184
	(Received $184 cash for riding fees)		
30	Maintenance and Repairs Expense	75	
	Accounts Payable		75
	(Received bill of $75 from carpenter for repair services performed)		
31	Supplies	1,700	
	Cash		1,700
	(Purchased an estimated 2 months' supply of feed and hay for $1,700 on account)		

Instructions

With the class divided into groups, answer the following.

(a) Identify each journal entry that is correct. For each journal entry that is incorrect, prepare the entry that should have been made by the bookkeeper.

(b) Which of the incorrect entries would prevent the trial balance from balancing?

(c) What was the correct net income for May, assuming the bookkeeper reported net income of $4,500 after posting all 50 entries?

(d) What was the correct cash balance at May 31, assuming the bookkeeper reported a balance of $12,475 after posting all 50 entries (and the only errors occurred in the items listed above)?

Communication Activity

BYP2-7 Keller's Maid Company offers home-cleaning service. Two recurring transactions for the company are billing customers for services performed and paying employee salaries. For example, on March 15, bills totaling $6,000 were sent to customers and $2,000 was paid in salaries to employees.

Instructions

Write a memo to your instructor that explains and illustrates the steps in the recording process for each of the March 15 transactions. Use the format illustrated in the textbook under the heading, "The Recording Process Illustrated" (p. 68).

Ethics Cases

BYP2-8 Meredith Ward is the assistant chief accountant at Frazier Company, a manufacturer of computer chips and cellular phones. The company presently has total sales of $20 million. It is the end of the first quarter. Meredith is hurriedly trying to prepare a trial balance so that quarterly financial statements can be prepared and released to management and the regulatory agencies. The total credits on the trial balance exceed the debits by $1,000. In order to meet the 4 p.m. deadline, Meredith decides to force the debits and credits into balance by adding the amount of the difference to the Equipment account. She chooses Equipment because it is one of the larger account balances; percentage-wise, it will be the least misstated. Meredith "plugs" the difference! She believes that the difference will not affect anyone's decisions. She wishes that she had another few days to find the error but realizes that the financial statements are already late.

Instructions

(a) Who are the stakeholders in this situation?

(b) What are the ethical issues involved in this case?

(c) What are Meredith's alternatives?

BYP2-9 If you haven't already done so, in the not-too-distant future you will prepare a résumé. In some ways, your résumé is like a company's annual report. Its purpose is to enable others to evaluate your past, in an effort to predict your future.

A résumé is your opportunity to create a positive first impression. It is important that it be impressive—but it should also be accurate. In order to increase their job prospects, some people are tempted to "inflate" their résumés by overstating the importance of some past accomplishments or positions. In fact, you might even think that "everybody does it" and that if you don't do it, you will be at a disadvantage.

David Edmondson, the president and CEO of well-known electronics retailer Radio Shack, overstated his accomplishments by claiming that he had earned a bachelor of science degree, when in fact he had not. Apparently, his employer had not done a background check to ensure the accuracy of his résumé. Should Radio Shack have fired him?

YES: Radio Shack is a publicly traded company. Investors, creditors, employees, and others doing business with the company will not trust it if its leader is known to have poor integrity. The "tone at the top" is vital to creating an ethical organization.

NO: Mr. Edmondson had been a Radio Shack employee for 11 years. He had served the company in a wide variety of positions, and had earned the position of CEO through exceptional performance. While the fact that he lied 11 years earlier on his résumé was unfortunate, his service since then made this past transgression irrelevant. In addition, the company was in the midst of a massive restructuring, which included closing 700 of its 7,000 stores. It could not afford additional upheaval at this time.

Instructions

Write a response indicating your position regarding this situation. Provide support for your view.

All About You

BYP2-10 Every company needs to plan in order to move forward. Its top management must consider where it wants the company to be in three to five years. Like a company, you need to think about where you want to be three to five years from now, and you need to start taking steps now in order to get there.

Instructions
Provide responses to each of the following items.

(a) Where would you like to be working in three to five years? Describe your plan for getting there by identifying between five and 10 specific steps that you need to take.

(b) In order to get the job you want, you will need a résumé. Your résumé is the equivalent of a company's annual report. It needs to provide relevant and reliable information about your past accomplishments so that employers can decide whether to "invest" in you. Do a search on the Internet to find a good résumé format. What are the basic elements of a résumé?

(c) A company's annual report provides information about a company's accomplishments. In order for investors to use the annual report, the information must be reliable; that is, users must have faith that the information is accurate and believable. How can you provide assurance that the information on your résumé is reliable?

(d) Prepare a résumé assuming that you have accomplished the five to 10 specific steps you identified in part (a). Also, provide evidence that would give assurance that the information is reliable.

Considering People, Planet, and Profit

BYP2-11 Auditors provide a type of certification of corporate financial statements. Certification is used in many other aspects of business as well. For example, it plays a critical role in the sustainability movement. The February 7, 2012, issue of the *New York Times* contained an article by S. Amanda Caudill entitled "Better Lives in Better Coffee," which discusses the role of certification in the coffee business.

Address: **http://scientistatwork.blogs.nytimes.com/2012/02/07/better-lives-in-better-coffee**

Instructions
Read the article and answer the following questions.

(a) The article mentions three different certification types that coffee growers can obtain from three different certification bodies. Using financial reporting as an example, what potential problems might the existence of multiple certification types present to coffee purchasers?

(b) According to the author, which certification is most common among coffee growers? What are the possible reasons for this?

(c) What social and environmental benefits are coffee certifications trying to achieve? Are there also potential financial benefits to the parties involved?

Answers to Chapter Questions

Answers to Insight and Accounting Across the Organization Questions

p. 59 Keeping Score   Q: Do you think that the Chicago Bears football team would be likely to have the same major revenue and expense accounts as the Cubs? **A:** Because their businesses are similar—professional sports—many of the revenue and expense accounts for the baseball and football teams might be similar.

p. 64 Boosting Microsoft's Profits   Q: In what ways is this Microsoft division using accounting to assist in its effort to become more profitable? **A:** The division has used accounting to set very strict sales, revenue, and profit goals. In addition, the managers in this division use accounting to keep a tight rein on product costs. Also, accounting serves as the basis of communication so that the marketing managers and product designers can work with production managers, engineers, and accountants to create an exciting product within specified cost constraints.

p. 65 A Convenient Overstatement   Q: What incentives might employees have had to overstate the value of these investment securities on the company's financial statements? **A:** One reason that they may have been reluctant to record the losses is out of fear that the company's shareholders and clients would panic if they saw the magnitude of the losses. However, personal self-interest might have been equally to blame—the bonuses of the traders were tied to the value of the investment securities.

p. 77 Why Accuracy Matters   Q: In order for these companies to prepare and issue financial statements, their accounting equations (debits and credits) must have been in balance at year-end. How could these errors or misstatements have occurred? **A:** A company's accounting equation (its books) can be in balance yet its financial statements have errors or misstatements because of the following: entire transactions were not recorded; transactions were recorded at wrong amounts; transactions were recorded in the wrong accounts; transactions were recorded in the wrong accounting period. Audits of financial statements uncover some but obviously not all errors or misstatements.

Answers to Self-Test Questions

1. b   **2.** c   **3.** d   **4.** d   **5.** d   **6.** b   **7.** a   **8.** c   **9.** b   **10.** c   **11.** d   **12.** a ($18,000 − $5,000)   **13.** a
14. c   **15.** c ($5,000 + $40,000 + $10,000 + $13,000 + $61,000)

A Look at IFRS

LEARNING OBJECTIVE	8

Compare the procedures for the accounting process under GAAP and IFRS.

International companies use the same set of procedures and records to keep track of transaction data. Thus, the material in Chapter 2 dealing with the account, general rules of debit and credit, and steps in the recording process—the journal, ledger, and chart of accounts—is the same under both GAAP and IFRS.

Key Points

- Transaction analysis is the same under IFRS and GAAP but, as you will see in later chapters, different standards sometimes impact how transactions are recorded.

- Rules for accounting for specific events sometimes differ across countries. For example, European companies rely less on historical cost and more on fair value than U.S. companies. Despite the differences, the double-entry accounting system is the basis of accounting systems worldwide.

- Both the IASB and FASB go beyond the basic definitions provided in this textbook for the key elements of financial statements, that is, assets, liabilities, equity, revenues, and expenses. The more substantive definitions, using the IASB definitional structure, are provided in the Chapter 1 *A Look at IFRS* discussion.

- A trial balance under IFRS follows the same format as shown in the textbook.

- As shown in the textbook, dollars signs are typically used only in the trial balance and the financial statements. The same practice is followed under IFRS, using the currency of the country that the reporting company is headquartered.

- In February 2010, the SEC expressed a desire to continue working toward a single set of high-quality standards. In deciding whether the United States should adopt IFRS, some of the issues the SEC said should be considered are:

  ♦ Whether IFRS is sufficiently developed and consistent in application.

  ♦ Whether the IASB is sufficiently independent.

  ♦ Whether IFRS is established for the benefit of investors.

  ♦ The issues involved in educating investors about IFRS.

  ♦ The impact of a switch to IFRS on U.S. laws and regulations.

  ♦ The impact on companies including changes to their accounting systems, contractual arrangements, corporate governance, and litigation.

  ♦ The issues involved in educating accountants, so they can prepare financial statements under IFRS.

Looking to the Future

The basic recording process shown in this textbook is followed by companies around the globe. It is unlikely to change in the future. The definitional structure of assets, liabilities, equity, revenues, and expenses may change over time as the IASB and FASB evaluate their overall conceptual framework for establishing accounting standards.

IFRS Practice

IFRS Self-Test Questions

1. Which statement is **correct** regarding IFRS?
   (a) IFRS reverses the rules of debits and credits, that is, debits are on the right and credits are on the left.
   (b) IFRS uses the same process for recording transactions as GAAP.
   (c) The chart of accounts under IFRS is different because revenues follow assets.
   (d) None of the above statements are correct.

2. The expanded accounting equation under IFRS is as follows:
   (a) Assets = Liabilities + Common Stock + Retained Earnings + Revenues − Expenses + Dividends.
   (b) Assets + Liabilities = Common Stock + Retained Earnings + Revenues − Expenses − Dividends.
   (c) Assets = Liabilities + Common Stock + Retained Earnings + Revenues − Expenses − Dividends.
   (d) Assets = Liabilities + Common Stock + Retained Earnings − Revenues − Expenses − Dividends.

3. A trial balance:
   (a) is the same under IFRS and GAAP.
   (b) proves that transactions are recorded correctly.
   (c) proves that all transactions have been recorded.
   (d) will not balance if a correct journal entry is posted twice.

4. One difference between IFRS and GAAP is that:
   (a) GAAP uses accrual-accounting concepts and IFRS uses primarily the cash basis of accounting.
   (b) IFRS uses a different posting process than GAAP.
   (c) IFRS uses more fair value measurements than GAAP.
   (d) the limitations of a trial balance are different between IFRS and GAAP.

5. The general policy for using proper currency signs (dollar, yen, pound, etc.) is the same for both IFRS and this textbook. This policy is as follows:
   (a) Currency signs only appear in ledgers and journal entries.
   (b) Currency signs are only shown in the trial balance.
   (c) Currency signs are shown for all compound journal entries.
   (d) Currency signs are shown in trial balances and financial statements.

IFRS Exercise

IFRS2-1 Describe some of the issues the SEC must consider in deciding whether the United States should adopt IFRS.

International Financial Reporting Problem: Zetar plc

IFRS2-2 The financial statements of Zetar plc are presented in Appendix F. Instructions for accessing and using the company's complete annual report, including the notes to its financial statements, are also provided in Appendix F.

Instructions
Describe in which statement each of the following items is reported, and the position in the statement (e.g., current asset).

(a) Other administrative expenses.
(b) Cash at bank.
(c) Borrowings and overdrafts.
(d) Finance costs.

Answers to IFRS Self-Test Questions
1. b   2. c   3. a   4. c   5. d

 The Navigator

✔ Remember to go back to The Navigator box on the chapter opening page and check off your completed work.

Feature Story

✔ The Navigator

Keeping Track of Groupons

Who doesn't like buying things at a discount? That's why it's not surprising that three years after it started as a company, Groupon was estimated to be worth $16 billion. This translates into an average increase in value of almost $15 million per day.

Now consider that Groupon had previously been estimated to be worth even more than that. What happened? Well, accounting regulators and investors began to question the way that Groupon had accounted for some of its transactions. But if Groupon sells only coupons ("groupons"), you're probably wondering how hard can it be to accurately account for that? It turns out that accounting for coupons is not as easy as you might think.

First, consider what happens when Groupon makes a sale. Suppose it sells a groupon for $30 for Highrise Hamburgers. When it receives the $30 from the customer, it must turn over half of that amount ($15) to Highrise Hamburgers. So should Groupon record revenue for the full $30 or just $15? Until recently,

Groupon recorded the full $30. But, in response to an SEC ruling on the issue, Groupon now records revenue of $15 instead.

A second issue is a matter of timing. When should Groupon record this $15 revenue? Should it record the revenue when it sells the groupon, or must it wait until the customer uses the groupon at Highrise Hamburgers? You can find the answer to this question in the notes to Groupon's financial statements. It recognizes the revenue once "the number of customers who purchase the daily deal exceeds the predetermined threshold, the Groupon has been electronically delivered to the purchaser and a listing of Groupons sold has been made available to the merchant."

The accounting becomes even more complicated when you consider the company's loyalty programs. Groupon offers free or discounted groupons to its subscribers for doing things such as referring new customers or participating in promotions. These groupons are to be used for future purchases, yet the company must record the expense at the time the customer receives the

✔ The Navigator

- Scan Learning Objectives
- Read Feature Story
- Read Preview
- Read text and answer **DO IT!** p. 106
  - p. 114   ■ p. 120   ■ p. 125
- Work Comprehensive **DO IT!** p. 126
- Review Summary of Learning Objectives
- Answer Self-Test Questions
- Complete Assignments
- Go to *WileyPLUS* for practice and tutorials
- Read **A Look at IFRS** p. 161

Learning Objectives
✔ The Navigator

After studying this chapter, you should be able to:

[1] Explain the time period assumption.

[2] Explain the accrual basis of accounting.

[3] Explain the reasons for adjusting entries and identify the major types of adjusting entries.

[4] Prepare adjusting entries for deferrals.

[5] Prepare adjusting entries for accruals.

[6] Describe the nature and purpose of an adjusted trial balance.

Rudy Archuleta/Redux Pictures

groupon. The cost of these programs is huge for Groupon, so the timing of this expense can definitely affect its reported income.

The final kicker is that Groupon, like all other companies, must rely on many estimates in its financial reporting. For example, Groupon reports that "estimates are utilized for, but not limited to, stock-based compensation, income taxes, valuation of acquired goodwill and intangible assets, customer refunds, contingent liabilities and the depreciable lives of fixed assets." It concludes by saying that "actual results could differ materially from those estimates." So, next time you use a coupon, think about what that means for the company's accountants!

Preview of Chapter 3

✔ **The Navigator**

In Chapter 1, you learned a neat little formula: Net income = Revenues − Expenses. In Chapter 2, you learned some rules for recording revenue and expense transactions. Guess what? Things are not really that nice and neat. In fact, it is often difficult for companies to determine in what time period they should report some revenues and expenses. In other words, in measuring net income, timing is everything.

The content and organization of Chapter 3 are as follows.

ADJUSTING THE ACCOUNTS

Timing Issues	The Basics of Adjusting Entries	The Adjusted Trial Balance and Financial Statements
• Fiscal and calendar years • Accrual- vs. cash-basis accounting • Recognizing revenues and expenses	• Types of adjusting entries • Adjusting entries for deferrals • Adjusting entries for accruals • Summary of basic relationships	• Preparing the adjusted trial balance • Preparing financial statements

Timing Issues

Time Period Assumption

Year 1   Year 10

Year 6

Alternative Terminology
The time period assumption is also called the *periodicity assumption.*

If we could wait to prepare financial statements until a company ended its operations, no adjustments would be needed. At that point, we could easily determine its final balance sheet and the amount of lifetime income it earned.

However, most companies need immediate feedback about how well they are doing. For example, management usually wants monthly financial statements. The Internal Revenue Service requires all businesses to file annual tax returns. Therefore, **accountants divide the economic life of a business into artificial time periods**. This convenient assumption is referred to as the **time period assumption**.

Many business transactions affect more than one of these arbitrary time periods. For example, the airplanes purchased by Southwest Airlines five years ago are still in use today. We must determine the relevance of each business transaction to specific accounting periods. (How much of the cost of an airplane contributed to operations this year?)

Fiscal and Calendar Years

Both small and large companies prepare financial statements periodically in order to assess their financial condition and results of operations. **Accounting time periods are generally a month, a quarter, or a year.** Monthly and quarterly time periods are called **interim periods**. Most large companies must prepare both quarterly and annual financial statements.

An accounting time period that is one year in length is a **fiscal year**. A fiscal year usually begins with the first day of a month and ends 12 months later on the last day of a month. Most businesses use the **calendar year** (January 1 to December 31) as their accounting period. Some do not. Companies whose fiscal year differs from the calendar year include Delta Air Lines, June 30, and Walt Disney Productions, September 30. Sometimes a company's year-end will vary from year to year. For example, PepsiCo's fiscal year ends on the Friday closest to December 31, which was December 31 in 2011 and December 29 in 2012.

Accrual- versus Cash-Basis Accounting

What you will learn in this chapter is **accrual-basis accounting**. Under the accrual basis, companies record transactions that change a company's financial statements **in the periods in which the events occur**. For example, using the accrual basis to determine net income means companies recognize revenues when they perform services (rather than when they receive cash). It also means recognizing expenses when incurred (rather than when paid).

An alternative to the accrual basis is the cash basis. Under **cash-basis accounting**, companies record revenue when they receive cash. They record an expense when they pay out cash. The cash basis seems appealing due to its simplicity, but it often produces misleading financial statements. It fails to record revenue for a company that has performed services but for which it has not received the cash. As a result, it does not match expenses with revenues. **Cash-basis accounting is not in accordance with generally accepted accounting principles (GAAP).**

Individuals and some small companies do use cash-basis accounting. The cash basis is justified for small businesses because they often have few receivables and payables. Medium and large companies use accrual-basis accounting.

Recognizing Revenues and Expenses

It can be difficult to determine when to report revenues and expenses. The revenue recognition principle and the expense recognition principle help in this task.

REVENUE RECOGNITION PRINCIPLE

When a company agrees to perform a service or sell a product to a customer, it has a **performance obligation**. When the company meets this performance obligation, it recognizes revenue. The **revenue recognition principle** therefore requires that companies recognize revenue in the accounting period in which the performance obligation is satisfied. To illustrate, assume that Dave's Dry Cleaning cleans clothing on June 30 but customers do not claim and pay for their clothes until the first week of July. Dave's should record revenue in June when it performed the service (satisfied the performance obligation) rather than in July when it received the cash. At June 30, Dave's would report a receivable on its balance sheet and revenue in its income statement for the service performed.

EXPENSE RECOGNITION PRINCIPLE

Accountants follow a simple rule in recognizing expenses: "Let the expenses follow the revenues." Thus, expense recognition is tied to revenue recognition. In the dry cleaning example, this means that Dave's should report the salary expense incurred in performing the June 30 cleaning service in the same period in which it recognizes the service revenue. The critical issue in expense recognition is when the expense makes its contribution to revenue. This may or may not be the same period in which the expense is paid. If Dave's does not pay the salary incurred on June 30 until July, it would report salaries payable on its June 30 balance sheet.

This practice of expense recognition is referred to as the **expense recognition principle** (often referred to as the **matching principle**). It dictates that efforts (expenses) be matched with results (revenues). Illustration 3-1 summarizes the revenue and expense recognition principles.

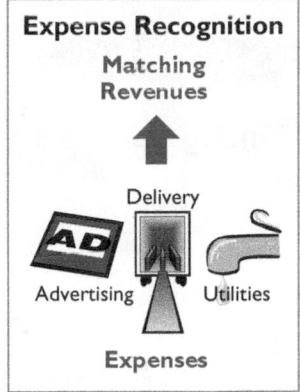

Illustration 3-1
GAAP relationships in revenue and expense recognition

ETHICS INSIGHT

Cooking the Books?

Allegations of abuse of the revenue recognition principle have become all too common in recent years. For example, it was alleged that Krispy Kreme sometimes doubled the number of doughnuts shipped to wholesale customers at the end of a quarter to boost quarterly results. The customers shipped the unsold doughnuts back after the beginning of the next quarter for a refund. Conversely, Computer Associates International was accused of backdating sales—that is, reporting a sale in one period that did not actually occur until the next period in order to achieve the earlier period's sales targets.

 What motivates sales executives and finance and accounting executives to participate in activities that result in inaccurate reporting of revenues? (See page 160.)

© Dean Turner/iStockphoto

> ## > DO IT!

Timing Concepts

Several timing concepts are discussed on pages 104–105. A list of concepts is provided in the left column below, with a description of the concept in the right column below. There are more descriptions provided than concepts. Match the description of the concept to the concept.

1. ____Accrual-basis accounting.
2. ____Calendar year.
3. ____Time period assumption.
4. ____Expense recognition principle.

(a) Monthly and quarterly time periods.
(b) Efforts (expenses) should be matched with results (revenues).
(c) Accountants divide the economic life of a business into artificial time periods.
(d) Companies record revenues when they receive cash and record expenses when they pay out cash.
(e) An accounting time period that starts on January 1 and ends on December 31.
(f) Companies record transactions in the period in which the events occur.

Action Plan

✔ Review the glossary terms identified on pages 104–105 and 128.

✔ Study carefully the revenue recognition principle, the expense recognition principle, and the time period assumption.

Solution

1. f   2. e   3. c   4. b

Related exercise material: E3-1, E3-2, E3-3, **and** DO IT! 3-1.

 The Navigator

The Basics of Adjusting Entries

LEARNING OBJECTIVE   3

Explain the reasons for adjusting entries and identify the major types of adjusting entries.

In order for revenues to be recorded in the period in which services are performed and for expenses to be recognized in the period in which they are incurred, companies make adjusting entries. **Adjusting entries ensure that the revenue recognition and expense recognition principles are followed.**

Adjusting entries are necessary because the **trial balance**—the first pulling together of the transaction data—may not contain up-to-date and complete data. This is true for several reasons:

1. Some events are not recorded daily because it is not efficient to do so. Examples are the use of supplies and the earning of wages by employees.

2. Some costs are not recorded during the accounting period because these costs expire with the passage of time rather than as a result of recurring daily transactions. Examples are charges related to the use of buildings and equipment, rent, and insurance.

3. Some items may be unrecorded. An example is a utility service bill that will not be received until the next accounting period.

Adjusting entries are required every time a company prepares financial statements. The company analyzes each account in the trial balance to determine whether it is complete and up to date for financial statement purposes. **Every adjusting entry will include one income statement account and one balance sheet account.**

International Note

Internal controls are a system of checks and balances designed to detect and prevent fraud and errors. The Sarbanes-Oxley Act requires U.S. companies to enhance their systems of internal control. However, many foreign companies do not have to meet strict internal control requirements. Some U.S. companies believe that this gives foreign firms an unfair advantage because developing and maintaining internal controls can be very expensive.

Types of Adjusting Entries

Adjusting entries are classified as either **deferrals** or **accruals**. As Illustration 3-2 shows, each of these classes has two subcategories.

Deferrals:

1. Prepaid expenses: Expenses paid in cash before they are used or consumed.
2. Unearned revenues: Cash received before services are performed.

Accruals:

1. Accrued revenues: Revenues for services performed but not yet received in cash or recorded.
2. Accrued expenses: Expenses incurred but not yet paid in cash or recorded.

Illustration 3-2
Categories of adjusting entries

Subsequent sections give examples of each type of adjustment. Each example is based on the October 31 trial balance of Pioneer Advertising Agency Inc. from Chapter 2, reproduced in Illustration 3-3.

Illustration 3-3
Trial balance

PIONEER ADVERTISING AGENCY INC.
Trial Balance
October 31, 2015

	Debit	Credit
Cash	$ 15,200	
Supplies	2,500	
Prepaid Insurance	600	
Equipment	5,000	
Notes Payable		$ 5,000
Accounts Payable		2,500
Unearned Service Revenue		1,200
Common Stock		10,000
Retained Earnings		–0–
Dividends	500	
Service Revenue		10,000
Salaries and Wages Expense	4,000	
Rent Expense	900	
	$28,700	$28,700

We assume that Pioneer Advertising uses an accounting period of one month. Thus, monthly adjusting entries are made. The entries are dated October 31.

Adjusting Entries for Deferrals

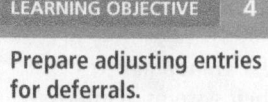

To defer means to postpone or delay. **Deferrals** are expenses or revenues that are recognized at a date later than the point when cash was originally exchanged. The two types of deferrals are prepaid expenses and unearned revenues.

PREPAID EXPENSES

When companies record payments of expenses that will benefit more than one accounting period, they record an asset called **prepaid expenses** or **prepayments**. When expenses are prepaid, an asset account is increased (debited) to show the service or benefit that the company will receive in the future. Examples of common prepayments are insurance, supplies, advertising, and rent. In addition, companies make prepayments when they purchase buildings and equipment.

Prepaid expenses are costs that expire either with the passage of time (e.g., rent and insurance) **or through use** (e.g., supplies). The expiration of these costs does not require daily entries, which would be impractical and unnecessary. Accordingly, companies postpone the recognition of such cost expirations until they prepare financial statements. At each statement date, they make adjusting entries to record the expenses applicable to the current accounting period and to show the remaining amounts in the asset accounts.

Prior to adjustment, assets are overstated and expenses are understated. Therefore, as shown in Illustration 3-4, **an adjusting entry for prepaid expenses results in an increase (a debit) to an expense account and a decrease (a credit) to an asset account**.

Illustration 3-4
Adjusting entries for prepaid expenses

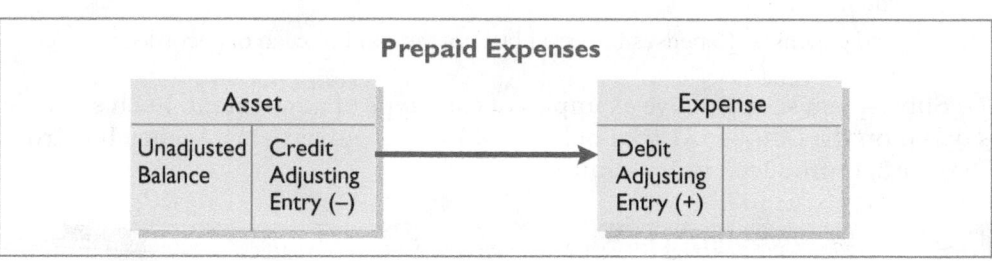

Let's look in more detail at some specific types of prepaid expenses, beginning with supplies.

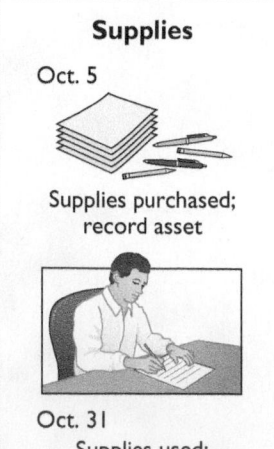

Supplies

Oct. 5

Supplies purchased; record asset

Oct. 31
Supplies used; record supplies expense

SUPPLIES The purchase of supplies, such as paper and envelopes, results in an increase (a debit) to an asset account. During the accounting period, the company uses supplies. Rather than record supplies expense as the supplies are used, companies recognize supplies expense at the **end** of the accounting period. At the end of the accounting period, the company counts the remaining supplies. As shown in Illustration 3-5, the difference between the unadjusted balance in the Supplies (asset) account and the actual cost of supplies on hand represents the supplies used (an expense) for that period.

Recall from Chapter 2 that Pioneer Advertising Agency Inc. purchased supplies costing $2,500 on October 5. Pioneer recorded the purchase by increasing (debiting) the asset Supplies. This account shows a balance of $2,500 in the October 31 trial balance. An inventory count at the close of business on October 31 reveals that $1,000 of supplies are still on hand. Thus, the cost of supplies used is $1,500

($2,500 − $1,000). This use of supplies decreases an asset, Supplies. It also decreases stockholders' equity by increasing an expense account, Supplies Expense. This is shown in Illustration 3-5.

Basic Analysis	The expense Supplies Expense is increased $1,500, and the asset Supplies is decreased $1,500.

Equation Analysis

(1)

Assets	**=**	**Liabilities**	**+**	**Stockholders' Equity**
Supplies				Supplies Expense
−$1,500	**=**			−$1,500

Debit–Credit Analysis

Debits Increase expenses: debit Supplies Expense $1,500.
Credits decrease assets: credit Supplies $1,500.

Journal Entry

Oct. 31	Supplies Expense	1,500	
	Supplies		1,500
	(To record supplies used)		

Posting

Supplies		126		Supplies Expense		631
Oct. 5	2,500	Oct. 31 Adj. 1,500	Oct. 31	Adj. 1,500		
Oct. 31 Bal. 1,000			Oct. 31	Bal. 1,500		

Illustration 3-5
Adjustment for supplies

After adjustment, the asset account Supplies shows a balance of $1,000, which is equal to the cost of supplies on hand at the statement date. In addition, Supplies Expense shows a balance of $1,500, which equals the cost of supplies used in October. **If Pioneer does not make the adjusting entry, October expenses are understated and net income is overstated by $1,500. Moreover, both assets and stockholders' equity will be overstated by $1,500 on the October 31 balance sheet.**

INSURANCE Companies purchase insurance to protect themselves from losses due to fire, theft, and unforeseen events. Insurance must be paid in advance, often for more than one year. The cost of insurance (premiums) paid in advance is recorded as an increase (debit) in the asset account Prepaid Insurance. At the financial statement date, companies increase (debit) Insurance Expense and decrease (credit) Prepaid Insurance for the cost of insurance that has expired during the period.

On October 4, Pioneer Advertising paid $600 for a one-year fire insurance policy. Coverage began on October 1. Pioneer recorded the payment by increasing (debiting) Prepaid Insurance. This account shows a balance of $600 in the October 31 trial balance. Insurance of $50 ($600 ÷ 12) expires each month. The expiration of prepaid insurance decreases an asset, Prepaid Insurance. It also decreases stockholders' equity by increasing an expense account, Insurance Expense.

As shown in Illustration 3-6 (page 110), the asset Prepaid Insurance shows a balance of $550, which represents the unexpired cost for the remaining 11 months of coverage. At the same time, the balance in Insurance Expense equals the insurance cost that expired in October. **If Pioneer does not make this adjustment, October expenses are understated by $50 and net income is overstated by $50. Moreover, both assets and stockholders' equity will be overstated by $50 on the October 31 balance sheet.**

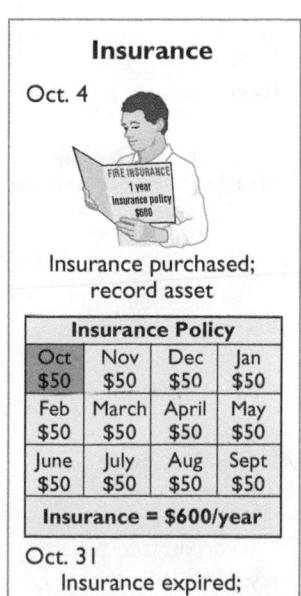

Insurance

Oct. 4

Insurance purchased;
record asset

Insurance Policy			
Oct	Nov	Dec	Jan
$50	$50	$50	$50
Feb	March	April	May
$50	$50	$50	$50
June	July	Aug	Sept
$50	$50	$50	$50
Insurance = $600/year			

Oct. 31
  Insurance expired;
record insurance expense

Illustration 3-6
Adjustment for insurance

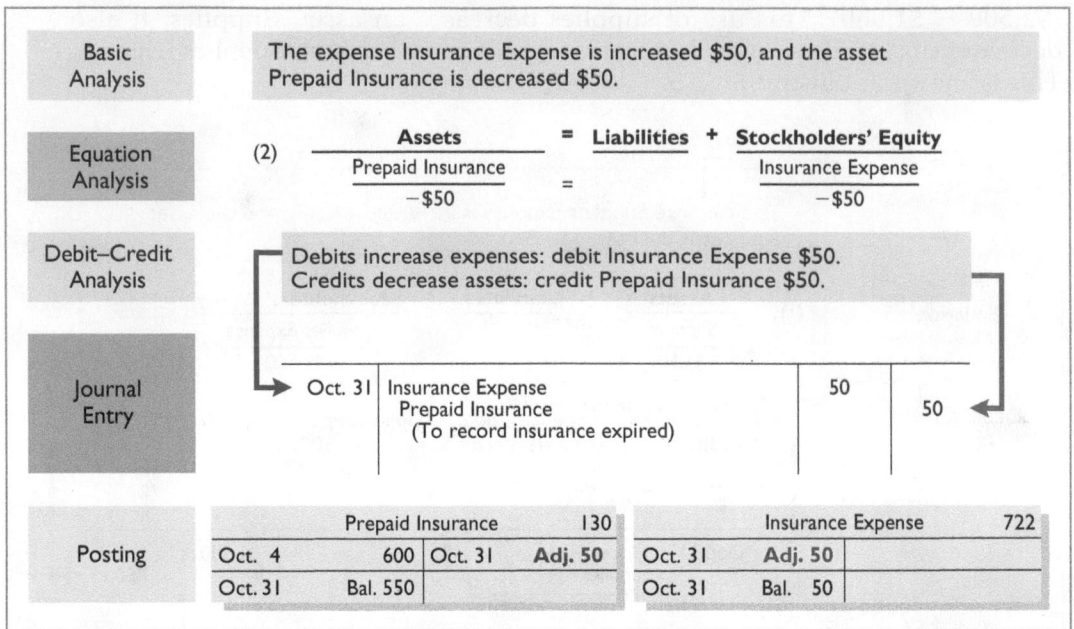

Basic Analysis	The expense Insurance Expense is increased $50, and the asset Prepaid Insurance is decreased $50.
Equation Analysis	(2) $\dfrac{\text{Assets}}{\substack{\text{Prepaid Insurance} \\ -\$50}} \overset{=}{=} \text{Liabilities} + \dfrac{\text{Stockholders' Equity}}{\substack{\text{Insurance Expense} \\ -\$50}}$
Debit–Credit Analysis	Debits increase expenses: debit Insurance Expense $50. Credits decrease assets: credit Prepaid Insurance $50.

Journal Entry	Oct. 31 Insurance Expense 50
	                  Prepaid Insurance 50
	                  (To record insurance expired)

Posting	Prepaid Insurance 130			Insurance Expense 722	
	Oct. 4	600	Oct. 31 **Adj. 50**	Oct. 31 **Adj. 50**	
	Oct. 31	Bal. 550		Oct. 31 Bal. 50	

Depreciation

Oct. 2

Equipment purchased; record asset

Equipment			
Oct $40	Nov $40	Dec $40	Jan $40
Feb $40	March $40	April $40	May $40
June $40	July $40	Aug $40	Sept $40
Depreciation = $480/year			

Oct. 31
Depreciation recognized; record depreciation expense

DEPRECIATION A company typically owns a variety of assets that have long lives, such as buildings, equipment, and motor vehicles. The period of service is referred to as the **useful life** of the asset. Because a building is expected to provide service for many years, it is recorded as an asset, rather than an expense, on the date it is acquired. As explained in Chapter 1, companies record such assets **at cost**, as required by the historical cost principle. To follow the expense recognition principle, companies allocate a portion of this cost as an expense during each period of the asset's useful life. **Depreciation** is the process of allocating the cost of an asset to expense over its useful life.

Need for Adjustment. The acquisition of long-lived assets is essentially a long-term prepayment for the use of an asset. An adjusting entry for depreciation is needed to recognize the cost that has been used (an expense) during the period and to report the unused cost (an asset) at the end of the period. One very important point to understand: **Depreciation is an allocation concept, not a valuation concept.** That is, depreciation **allocates an asset's cost to the periods in which it is used. Depreciation does not attempt to report the actual change in the value of the asset.**

For Pioneer Advertising, assume that depreciation on the equipment is $480 a year, or $40 per month. As shown in Illustration 3-7, rather than decrease (credit) the asset account directly, Pioneer instead credits Accumulated Depreciation— Equipment. Accumulated Depreciation is called a **contra asset account**. Such an account is offset against an asset account on the balance sheet. Thus, the Accumulated Depreciation—Equipment account offsets the asset account Equipment. This account keeps track of the total amount of depreciation expense taken over the life of the asset. To keep the accounting equation in balance, Pioneer decreases stockholders' equity by increasing an expense account, Depreciation Expense.

The balance in the Accumulated Depreciation—Equipment account will increase $40 each month, and the balance in Equipment remains $5,000.

Statement Presentation. As indicated, Accumulated Depreciation—Equipment is a contra asset account. It is offset against Equipment on the balance sheet. The normal balance of a contra asset account is a credit. A theoretical alternative to using a contra asset account would be to decrease (credit) the asset account by the amount of depreciation each period. But using the contra account is preferable for a simple reason: It discloses **both** the original cost of the equipment **and** the

Helpful Hint
All contra accounts have increases, decreases, and normal balances opposite to the account to which they relate.

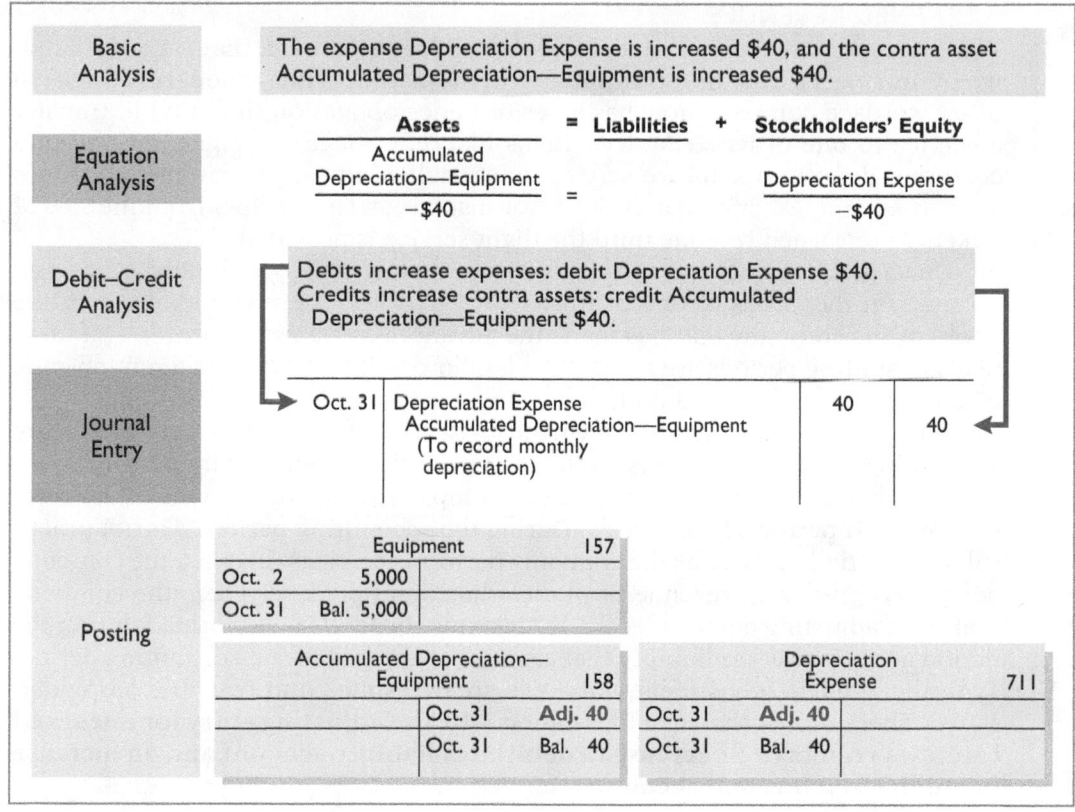

Basic Analysis	The expense Depreciation Expense is increased $40, and the contra asset Accumulated Depreciation—Equipment is increased $40.

Equation Analysis	$$\frac{\text{Assets}}{\substack{\text{Accumulated} \\ \text{Depreciation—Equipment} \\ -\$40}} = \text{Liabilities} + \frac{\text{Stockholders' Equity}}{\substack{\text{Depreciation Expense} \\ -\$40}}$$

Debit–Credit Analysis	Debits increase expenses: debit Depreciation Expense $40. Credits increase contra assets: credit Accumulated Depreciation—Equipment $40.

Journal Entry	Oct. 31	Depreciation Expense
		   Accumulated Depreciation—Equipment
		   (To record monthly depreciation)
			40	40

Posting

Equipment		157
Oct. 2	5,000	
Oct. 31	Bal. 5,000	

Accumulated Depreciation—Equipment		158
	Oct. 31	Adj. 40
	Oct. 31	Bal. 40

Depreciation Expense		711
Oct. 31	Adj. 40	
Oct. 31	Bal. 40	

Illustration 3-7
Adjustment for depreciation

total cost that has been expensed to date. Thus, in the balance sheet, Pioneer deducts Accumulated Depreciation—Equipment from the related asset account, as shown in Illustration 3-8.

Equipment	$ 5,000
Less: Accumulated depreciation—equipment	40
	$4,960

Illustration 3-8
Balance sheet presentation of accumulated depreciation

Book value is the difference between the cost of any depreciable asset and its related accumulated depreciation. In Illustration 3-8, the book value of the equipment at the balance sheet date is $4,960. The book value and the fair value of the asset are generally two different values. As noted earlier, **the purpose of depreciation is not valuation but a means of cost allocation**.

Depreciation expense identifies the portion of an asset's cost that expired during the period (in this case, in October). The accounting equation shows that **without this adjusting entry, total assets, total stockholders' equity, and net income are overstated by $40 and depreciation expense is understated by $40**.

Illustration 3-9 summarizes the accounting for prepaid expenses.

Alternative Terminology
Book value is also referred to as *carrying value*.

Illustration 3-9
Accounting for prepaid expenses

ACCOUNTING FOR PREPAID EXPENSES			
Examples	**Reason for Adjustment**	**Accounts Before Adjustment**	**Adjusting Entry**
Insurance, supplies, advertising, rent, depreciation	Prepaid expenses recorded in asset accounts have been used.	Assets overstated. Expenses understated.	Dr. Expenses Cr. Assets or Contra Assets

Unearned Revenues

Oct. 2

Thank you in advance for your work

I will finish by Dec. 31

$1,200

Cash is received in advance; liability is recorded

Oct. 31
Some service has been performed; some revenue is recorded

UNEARNED REVENUES

When companies receive cash before services are performed, they record a liability by increasing (crediting) a liability account called **unearned revenues**. In other words, a company now has a performance obligation (liability) to transfer a service to one of its customers. Items like rent, magazine subscriptions, and customer deposits for future service may result in unearned revenues. Airlines such as United, American, and Delta, for instance, treat receipts from the sale of tickets as unearned revenue until the flight service is provided.

Unearned revenues are the opposite of prepaid expenses. Indeed, unearned revenue on the books of one company is likely to be a prepaid expense on the books of the company that has made the advance payment. For example, if identical accounting periods are assumed, a landlord will have unearned rent revenue when a tenant has prepaid rent.

When a company receives payment for services to be performed in a future accounting period, it increases (credits) an unearned revenue (a liability) account to recognize the liability that exists. The company subsequently recognizes revenues when it performs the service. During the accounting period, it is not practical to make daily entries as the company performs services. Instead, the company delays recognition of revenue until the adjustment process. Then, the company makes an adjusting entry to record the revenue for services performed during the period and to show the liability that remains at the end of the accounting period. Typically, prior to adjustment, liabilities are overstated and revenues are understated. Therefore, as shown in Illustration 3-10, **the adjusting entry for unearned revenues results in a decrease (a debit) to a liability account and an increase (a credit) to a revenue account**.

Illustration 3-10
Adjusting entries for unearned revenues

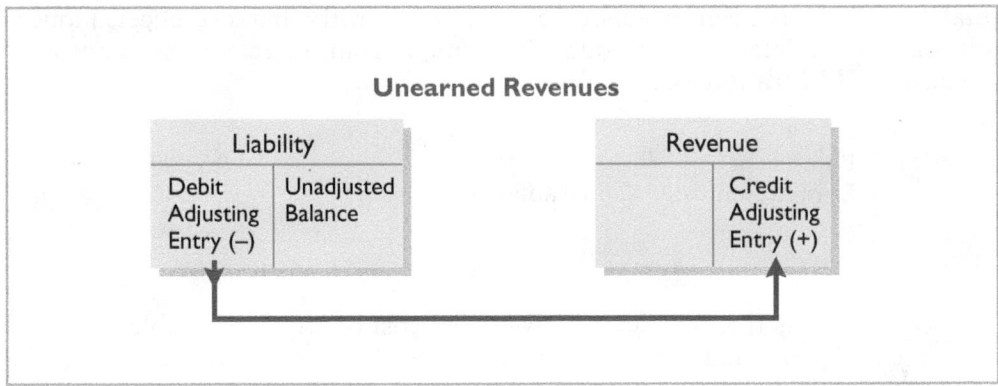

Pioneer Advertising received $1,200 on October 2 from R. Knox for advertising services expected to be completed by December 31. Pioneer credited the payment to Unearned Service Revenue. This liability account shows a balance of $1,200 in the October 31 trial balance. From an evaluation of the service Pioneer performed for Knox during October, the company determines that it should recognize $400 of revenue in October. The liability (Unearned Service Revenue) is therefore decreased, and stockholders' equity (Service Revenue) is increased.

As shown in Illustration 3-11, the liability Unearned Service Revenue now shows a balance of $800. That amount represents the remaining advertising services expected to be performed in the future. At the same time, Service Revenue shows total revenue recognized in October of $10,400. **Without this adjustment, revenues and net income are understated by $400 in the income statement. Moreover, liabilities will be overstated and stockholders' equity will be understated by $400 on the October 31 balance sheet.**

The Basics of Adjusting Er

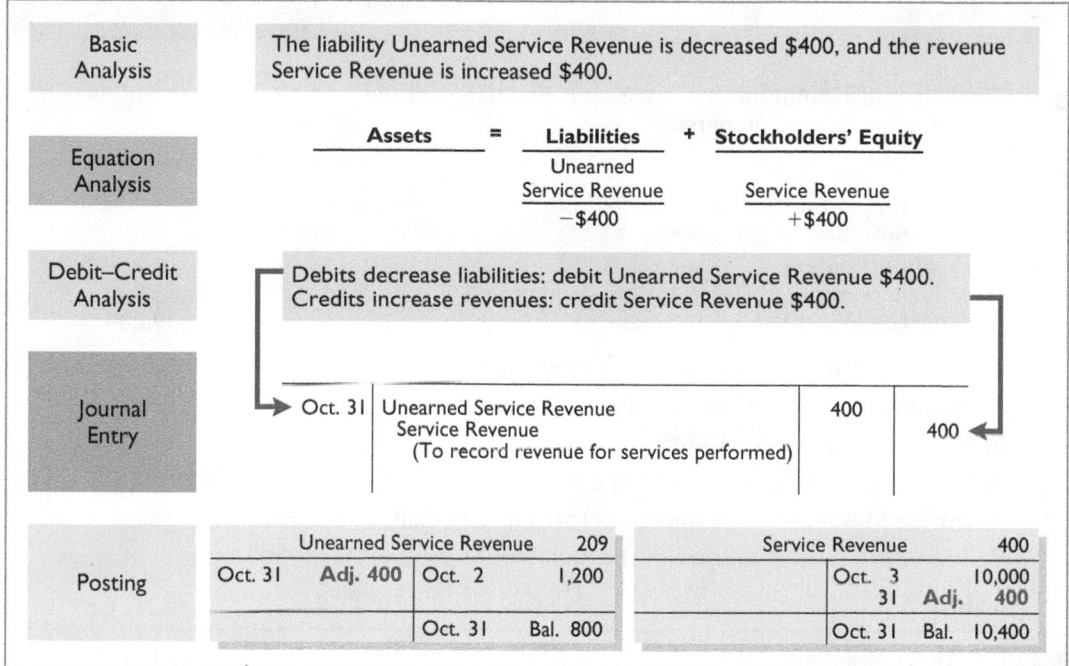

Basic Analysis	The liability Unearned Service Revenue is decreased $400, and the revenue Service Revenue is increased $400.

Equation Analysis

Assets	=	Liabilities	+	Stockholders' Equity
		Unearned Service Revenue −$400		Service Revenue +$400

Debit–Credit Analysis

Debits decrease liabilities: debit Unearned Service Revenue $400.
Credits increase revenues: credit Service Revenue $400.

Journal Entry

Oct. 31	Unearned Service Revenue	400	
	Service Revenue		400
	(To record revenue for services performed)		

Posting

Unearned Service Revenue	209		Service Revenue	400
Oct. 31 Adj. 400	Oct. 2 1,200			Oct. 3 10,000
				31 Adj. 400
	Oct. 31 Bal. 800			Oct. 31 Bal. 10,400

Illustration 3-12 summarizes the accounting for unearned revenues.

Illustration 3-11
Service revenue accounts after adjustment

Illustration 3-12
Accounting for unearned revenues

ACCOUNTING FOR UNEARNED REVENUES

Examples	Reason for Adjustment	Accounts Before Adjustment	Adjusting Entry
Rent, magazine subscriptions, customer deposits for future service	Unearned revenues recorded in liability accounts are now recognized as revenue for services performed.	Liabilities overstated. Revenues understated.	Dr. Liabilities Cr. Revenues

ACCOUNTING ACROSS THE ORGANIZATION

Turning Gift Cards into Revenue

Those of you who are marketing majors (and even most of you who are not) know that gift cards are among the hottest marketing tools in merchandising today. Customers purchase gift cards and give them to someone for later use. In a recent year, gift-card sales topped $95 billion.

Although these programs are popular with marketing executives, they create accounting questions. Should revenue be recorded at the time the gift card is sold, or when it is exercised? How should expired gift cards be accounted for? In a recent balance sheet, Best Buy reported unearned revenue related to gift cards of $479 million.

Source: Robert Berner, "Gift Cards: No Gift to Investors," *BusinessWeek* (March 14, 2005), p. 86.

 Suppose that Robert Jones purchases a $100 gift card at Best Buy on December 24, 2014, and gives it to his wife, Mary Jones, on December 25, 2014. On January 3, 2015, Mary uses the card to purchase $100 worth of CDs. When do you think Best Buy should recognize revenue and why? (See page 160.)

> **DO IT!**

Adjusting Entries for Deferrals

The ledger of Hammond Inc., on March 31, 2015, includes these selected accounts before adjusting entries are prepared.

	Debit	Credit
Prepaid Insurance	$ 3,600	
Supplies	2,800	
Equipment	25,000	
Accumulated Depreciation—Equipment		$5,000
Unearned Service Revenue		9,200

An analysis of the accounts shows the following.

1. Insurance expires at the rate of $100 per month.
2. Supplies on hand total $800.
3. The equipment depreciates $200 a month.
4. During March, services were performed for one-half of the unearned service revenue.

Prepare the adjusting entries for the month of March.

Solution

Action Plan

✔ Make adjusting entries at the end of the period for revenues recognized and expenses incurred in the period.

✔ Don't forget to make adjusting entries for deferrals. Failure to adjust for deferrals leads to overstatement of the asset or liability and understatement of the related expense or revenue.

	Debit	Credit
1. Insurance Expense	100	
Prepaid Insurance		100
(To record insurance expired)		
2. Supplies Expense	2,000	
Supplies		2,000
(To record supplies used)		
3. Depreciation Expense	200	
Accumulated Depreciation—Equipment		200
(To record monthly depreciation)		
4. Unearned Service Revenue	4,600	
Service Revenue		4,600
(To record revenue for services performed)		

Related exercise material: BE3-3, BE3-4, BE3-5, BE3-6, **and** DO IT! 3-2.

✔ **The Navigator**

Adjusting Entries for Accruals

LEARNING OBJECTIVE 5

Prepare adjusting entries for accruals.

The second category of adjusting entries is **accruals**. Prior to an accrual adjustment, the revenue account (and the related asset account) or the expense account (and the related liability account) are understated. Thus, the adjusting entry for accruals will **increase both a balance sheet and an income statement account**.

ACCRUED REVENUES

Revenues for services performed but not yet recorded at the statement date are **accrued revenues**. Accrued revenues may accumulate (accrue) with the passing of time, as in the case of interest revenue. These are unrecorded because the earning of interest does not involve daily transactions. Companies do not record interest revenue on a daily basis because it is often impractical to do so. Accrued revenues also may result from services that have been performed but not yet billed nor collected, as in the case of commissions and fees. These may be unrecorded because only a portion of the total service has been performed and the clients will not be billed until the service has been completed.

An adjusting entry records the receivable that exists at the balance sheet date and the revenue for the services performed during the period. Prior to adjustment, both assets and revenues are understated. As shown in Illustration 3-13, **an adjusting entry for accrued revenues results in an increase (a debit) to an asset account and an increase (a credit) to a revenue account**.

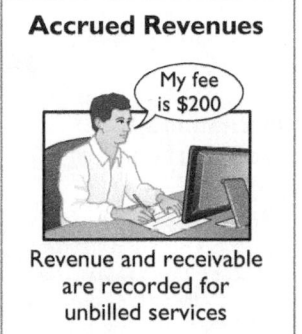

Accrued Revenues

Revenue and receivable are recorded for unbilled services

Illustration 3-13
Adjusting entries for accrued revenues

In October, Pioneer Advertising Agency Inc. performed services worth $200 that were not billed to clients on or before October 31. Because these services are not billed, they are not recorded. The accrual of unrecorded service revenue increases an asset account, Accounts Receivable. It also increases stockholders' equity by increasing a revenue account, Service Revenue, as shown in Illustration 3-14.

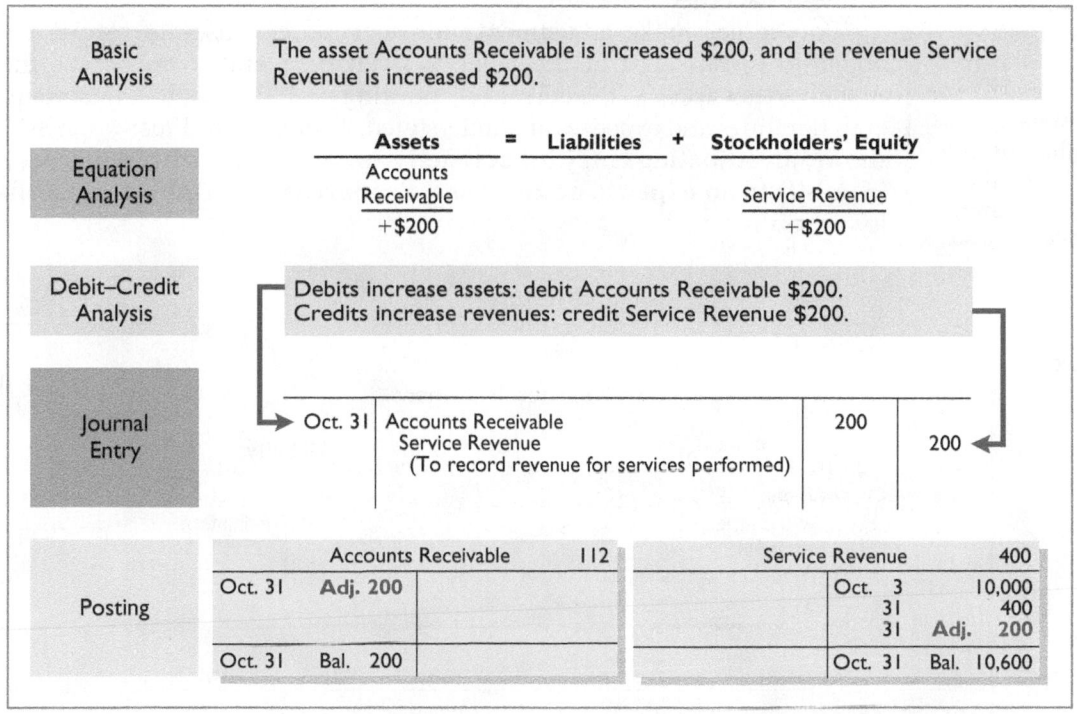

Illustration 3-14
Adjustment for accrued revenue

The asset Accounts Receivable shows that clients owe Pioneer $200 at the balance sheet date. The balance of $10,600 in Service Revenue represents the total revenue for services performed by Pioneer during the month ($10,000 + $400 + $200). **Without the adjusting entry, assets and stockholders' equity on the balance sheet and revenues and net income on the income statement are understated.**

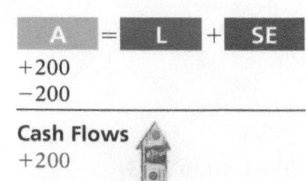

+200
−200
_____

Cash Flows
+200

Equation analyses summarize the effects of transactions on the three elements of the accounting equation, as well as the effect on cash flows.

Illustration 3-15
Accounting for accrued revenues

On November 10, Pioneer receives cash of $200 for the services performed in October and makes the following entry.

Nov. 10	Cash	200	
	Accounts Receivable		200
	(To record cash collected on account)		

The company records the collection of the receivables by a debit (increase) to Cash and a credit (decrease) to Accounts Receivable.

Illustration 3-15 summarizes the accounting for accrued revenues.

ACCOUNTING FOR ACCRUED REVENUES			
Examples	**Reason for Adjustment**	**Accounts Before Adjustment**	**Adjusting Entry**
Interest, rent, services	Services performed but not yet received in cash or recorded.	Assets understated. Revenues understated.	Dr. Assets Cr. Revenues

Ethics Note

A report released by Fannie Mae's board of directors stated that improper adjusting entries at the mortgage-finance company resulted in delayed recognition of expenses caused by interest rate changes. The motivation for such accounting apparently was the desire to hit earnings estimates.

ACCRUED EXPENSES

Expenses incurred but not yet paid or recorded at the statement date are called **accrued expenses**. Interest, taxes, and salaries are common examples of accrued expenses.

Companies make adjustments for accrued expenses to record the obligations that exist at the balance sheet date and to recognize the expenses that apply to the current accounting period. Prior to adjustment, both liabilities and expenses are understated. Therefore, as Illustration 3-16 shows, **an adjusting entry for accrued expenses results in an increase (a debit) to an expense account and an increase (a credit) to a liability account**.

Illustration 3-16
Adjusting entries for accrued expenses

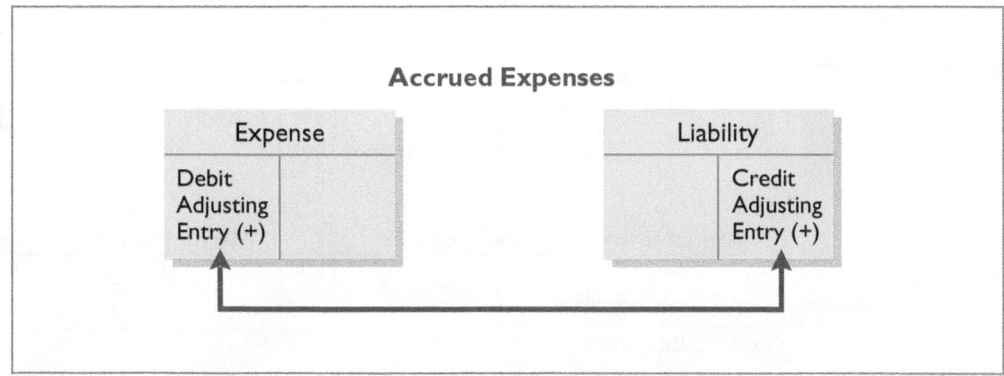

Let's look in more detail at some specific types of accrued expenses, beginning with accrued interest.

ACCRUED INTEREST Pioneer Advertising signed a three-month note payable in the amount of $5,000 on October 1. The note requires Pioneer to pay interest at an annual rate of 12%.

The amount of the interest recorded is determined by three factors: (1) the face value of the note; (2) the interest rate, which is always expressed as an annual rate; and (3) the length of time the note is outstanding. For Pioneer, the total interest due on the $5,000 note at its maturity date three months in the future is $150 ($5,000 × 12% × $\frac{3}{12}$), or $50 for one month. Illustration 3-17 shows the formula for computing interest and its application to Pioneer for the month of October.

Face Value of Note	×	Annual Interest Rate	×	Time in Terms of One Year	=	Interest
$5,000	×	12%	×	$\frac{1}{12}$	=	$50

Illustration 3-17
Formula for computing interest

Helpful Hint
In computing interest, we express the time period as a fraction of a year.

As Illustration 3-18 shows, the accrual of interest at October 31 increases a liability account, Interest Payable. It also decreases stockholders' equity by increasing an expense account, Interest Expense.

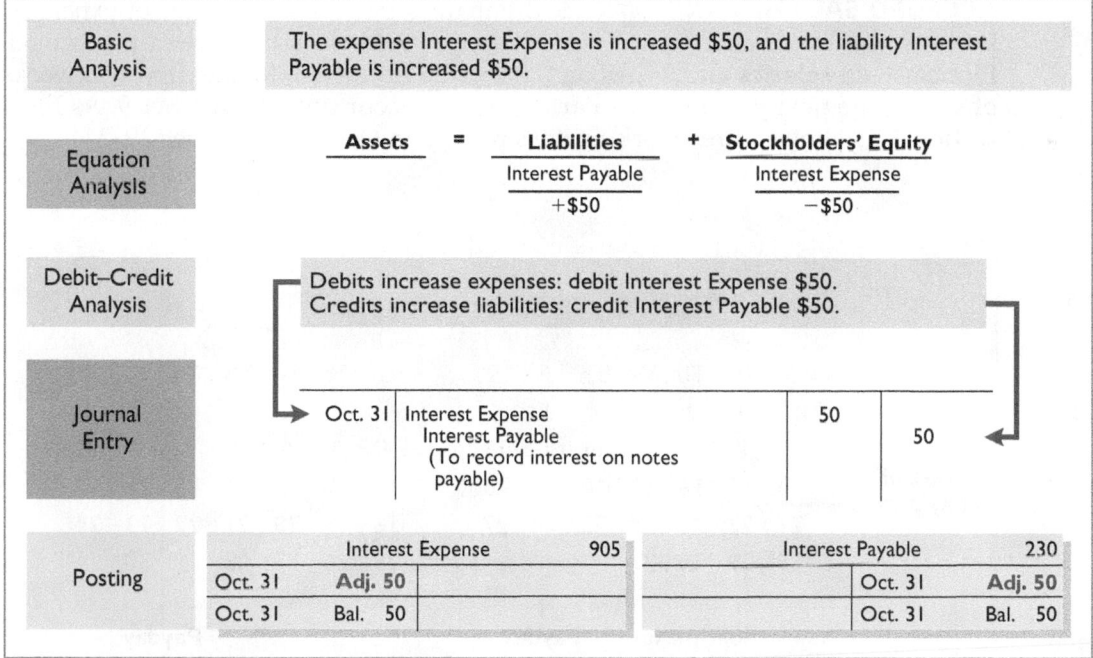

Illustration 3-18
Adjustment for accrued interest

Interest Expense shows the interest charges for the month of October. Interest Payable shows the amount of interest the company owes at the statement date. Pioneer will not pay the interest until the note comes due at the end of three months. Companies use the Interest Payable account, instead of crediting Notes Payable, to disclose the two different types of obligations—interest and principal—in the accounts and statements. **Without this adjusting entry, liabilities and interest expense are understated, and net income and stockholders' equity are overstated.**

INTERNATIONAL INSIGHT

Cashing In on Accrual Accounting

The Chinese government, like most governments, uses cash accounting. A recent report, however, noted that it decided to use accrual accounting versus cash accounting for about $38 billion of expenditures in a recent budget projection. The Chinese government decided to expense the amount in the year in which it was originally allocated rather than when the payments would be made. Why did the Chinese government do this? It enabled the government to keep its projected budget deficit below a 3% threshold. While the Chinese government was able to keep its projected shortfall below 3%, it did suffer some criticism for its inconsistent accounting. Critics charge that this inconsistent treatment reduces the transparency of China's accounting information. That is, it is not easy for outsiders to accurately evaluate what is really going on.

Source: Andrew Batson, "China Altered Budget Accounting to Reduce Deficit Figure," *Wall Street Journal Online* (March 15, 2010).

? Accrual accounting is often considered superior to cash accounting. Why, then, were some people critical of China's use of accrual accounting in this instance? (See page 161.)

ACCRUED SALARIES AND WAGES Companies pay for some types of expenses, such as employee salaries and wages, after the services have been performed. Pioneer paid salaries and wages on October 26 for its employees' first two weeks of work. The next payment of salaries will not occur until November 9. As Illustration 3-19 shows, three working days remain in October (October 29–31).

Illustration 3-19
Calendar showing Pioneer's pay periods

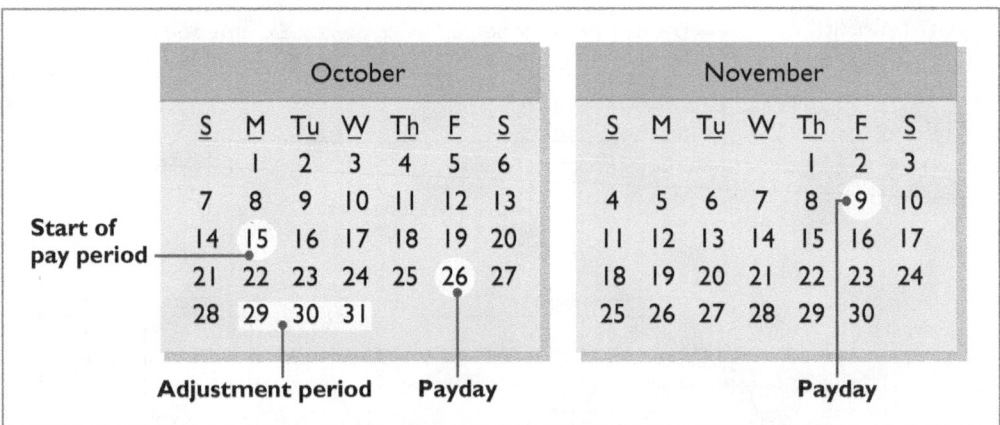

At October 31, the salaries and wages for these three days represent an accrued expense and a related liability to Pioneer. The employees receive total salaries and wages of $2,000 for a five-day work week, or $400 per day. Thus, accrued salaries and wages at October 31 are $1,200 ($400 × 3). This accrual increases a liability, Salaries and Wages Payable. It also decreases stockholders' equity by increasing an expense account, Salaries and Wages Expense, as shown in Illustration 3-20.

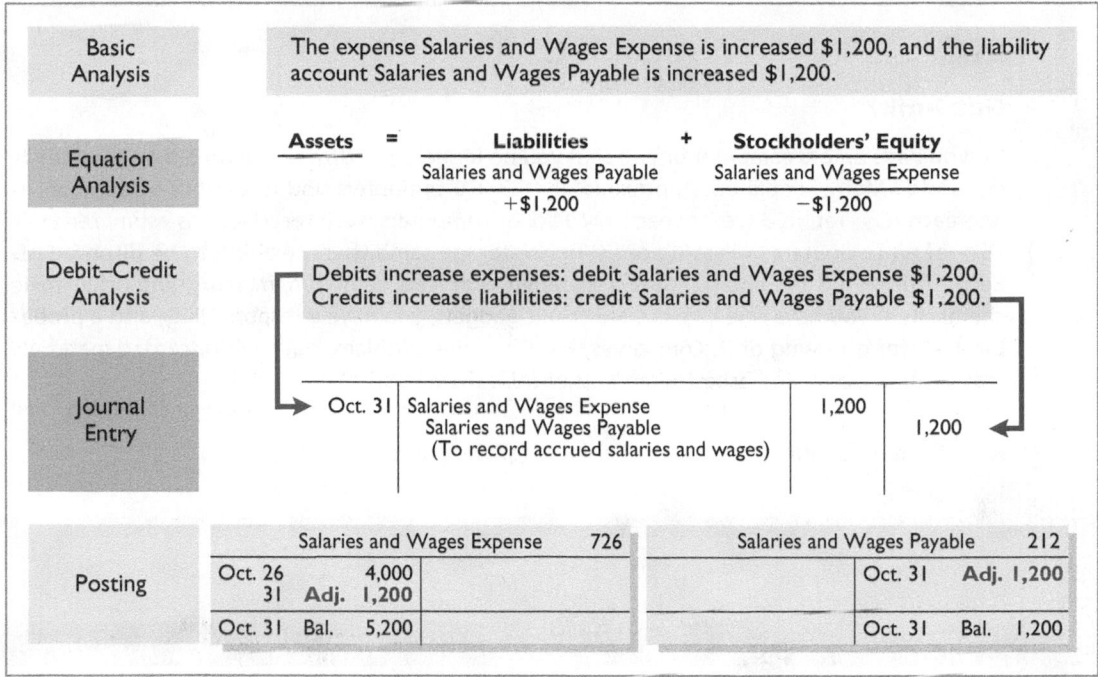

Basic Analysis	The expense Salaries and Wages Expense is increased $1,200, and the liability account Salaries and Wages Payable is increased $1,200.

Equation Analysis	

Assets	**=**	**Liabilities**	**+**	**Stockholders' Equity**
		Salaries and Wages Payable		Salaries and Wages Expense
		+$1,200		−$1,200

Debit–Credit Analysis	Debits increase expenses: debit Salaries and Wages Expense $1,200. Credits increase liabilities: credit Salaries and Wages Payable $1,200.

Journal Entry	Oct. 31	Salaries and Wages Expense	1,200	
		Salaries and Wages Payable		1,200
		(To record accrued salaries and wages)		

Posting

Salaries and Wages Expense	726		Salaries and Wages Payable	212
Oct. 26 4,000				Oct. 31 Adj. 1,200
31 Adj. 1,200				
Oct. 31 Bal. 5,200				Oct. 31 Bal. 1,200

Illustration 3-20
Adjustment for accrued salaries and wages

After this adjustment, the balance in Salaries and Wages Expense of $5,200 (13 days × $400) is the actual salary and wages expense for October. The balance in Salaries and Wages Payable of $1,200 is the amount of the liability for salaries and wages Pioneer owes as of October 31. **Without the $1,200 adjustment for salaries and wages, Pioneer's expenses are understated $1,200 and its liabilities are understated $1,200.**

Pioneer Advertising pays salaries and wages every two weeks. Consequently, the next payday is November 9, when the company will again pay total salaries and wages of $4,000. The payment consists of $1,200 of salaries and wages payable at October 31 plus $2,800 of salaries and wages expense for November (7 working days, as shown in the November calendar × $400). Therefore, Pioneer makes the following entry on November 9.

Nov. 9	Salaries and Wages Payable	1,200	
	Salaries and Wages Expense	2,800	
	Cash		4,000
	(To record November 9 payroll)		

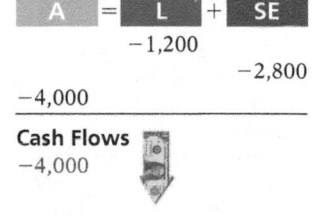

A	=	L	+	SE
		−1,200		
				−2,800
−4,000				

Cash Flows
−4,000

This entry eliminates the liability for Salaries and Wages Payable that Pioneer recorded in the October 31 adjusting entry, and it records the proper amount of Salaries and Wages Expense for the period between November 1 and November 9.

Illustration 3-21 summarizes the accounting for accrued expenses.

ACCOUNTING FOR ACCRUED EXPENSES			
Examples	**Reason for Adjustment**	**Accounts Before Adjustment**	**Adjusting Entry**
Interest, rent, salaries	Expenses have been incurred but not yet paid in cash or recorded.	Expenses understated. Liabilities understated.	Dr. Expenses Cr. Liabilities

Illustration 3-21
Accounting for accrued expenses

© Nathan Gleave/iStockphoto

PEOPLE, PLANET, AND PROFIT INSIGHT

Got Junk?

Do you have an old computer or two that you no longer use? How about an old TV that needs replacing? Many people do. Approximately 163,000 computers and televisions become obsolete each day. Yet, in a recent year, only 11% of computers were recycled. It is estimated that 75% of all computers ever sold are sitting in storage somewhere, waiting to be disposed of. Each of these old TVs and computers is loaded with lead, cadmium, mercury, and other toxic chemicals. If you have one of these electronic gadgets, you have a responsibility, and a probable cost, for disposing of it. Companies have the same problem, but their discarded materials may include lead paint, asbestos, and other toxic chemicals.

 What accounting issue might this cause for companies? (See page 161.)

> **DO IT!**

Adjusting Entries for Accruals

Micro Computer Services Inc. began operations on August 1, 2015. At the end of August 2015, management prepares monthly financial statements. The following information relates to August.

1. At August 31, the company owed its employees $800 in salaries and wages that will be paid on September 1.

2. On August 1, the company borrowed $30,000 from a local bank on a 15-year mortgage. The annual interest rate is 10%.

3. Revenue for services performed but unrecorded for August totaled $1,100.

Prepare the adjusting entries needed at August 31, 2015.

Solution

Action Plan

✔ Make adjusting entries at the end of the period to recognize revenues for services performed and for expenses incurred.

✔ Don't forget to make adjusting entries for accruals. Adjusting entries for accruals will increase both a balance sheet and an income statement account.

1. Salaries and Wages Expense	800	
Salaries and Wages Payable		800
(To record accrued salaries)		
2. Interest Expense	250	
Interest Payable		250
(To record accrued interest:		
$30,000 \times 10\% \times \frac{1}{12} = \$250$)		
3. Accounts Receivable	1,100	
Service Revenue		1,100
(To record revenue for services performed)		

Related exercise material: BE3-2, BE3-7, E3-5, E3-6, E3-7, E3-8, E3-9, **and** DO IT! 3-3.

 The Navigator

Summary of Basic Relationships

Illustration 3-22 summarizes the four basic types of adjusting entries. Take some time to study and analyze the adjusting entries. Be sure to note that **each adjusting entry affects one balance sheet account and one income statement account.**

Type of Adjustment	Accounts Before Adjustment	Adjusting Entry
Prepaid expenses	Assets overstated Expenses understated	Dr. Expenses Cr. Assets or Contra Assets
Unearned revenues	Liabilities overstated Revenues understated	Dr. Liabilities Cr. Revenues
Accrued revenues	Assets understated Revenues understated	Dr. Assets Cr. Revenues
Accrued expenses	Expenses understated Liabilities understated	Dr. Expenses Cr. Liabilities

Illustration 3-22
Summary of adjusting entries

Illustrations 3-23 (below) and 3-24 (on page 122) show the journalizing and posting of adjusting entries for Pioneer Advertising Agency Inc. on October 31. The ledger identifies all adjustments by the reference J2 because they have been recorded on page 2 of the general journal. The company may insert a center caption "Adjusting Entries" between the last transaction entry and the first adjusting entry in the journal. When you review the general ledger in Illustration 3-24, note that the entries highlighted in color are the adjustments.

GENERAL JOURNAL				J2
Date	**Account Titles and Explanation**	**Ref.**	**Debit**	**Credit**

2015
Oct. 31
	Adjusting Entries
	Supplies Expense
	    Supplies
	      (To record supplies used)
		631
		126
			1,500	1,500

31	Insurance Expense
	    Prepaid Insurance
	      (To record insurance expired)
		722
		130
			50	50

31	Depreciation Expense
	    Accumulated Depreciation—Equipment
	      (To record monthly depreciation)
		711
		158
			40	40

31	Unearned Service Revenue
	    Service Revenue
	      (To record revenue for services
	      performed)
		209
		400
			400	400

31	Accounts Receivable
	    Service Revenue
	      (To record revenue for services
	      performed)
		112
		400
			200	200

31	Interest Expense
	    Interest Payable
	      (To record interest on notes payable)
		905
		230
			50	50

31	Salaries and Wages Expense
	    Salaries and Wages Payable
	      (To record accrued salaries
	      and wages)
		726
		212
			1,200	1,200

Illustration 3-23
General journal showing adjusting entries

Helpful Hint
(1) Adjusting entries should not involve debits or credits to Cash.
(2) Evaluate whether the adjustment makes sense. For example, an adjustment to recognize supplies used should increase Supplies Expense.
(3) Double-check all computations.
(4) Each adjusting entry affects one balance sheet account and one income statement account.

Illustration 3-24
General ledger after adjustment

GENERAL LEDGER

Cash — No. 101

Date	Explanation	Ref.	Debit	Credit	Balance
2015					
Oct. 1		J1	10,000		10,000
2		J1	1,200		11,200
3		J1		900	10,300
4		J1		600	9,700
20		J1		500	9,200
26		J1		4,000	5,200
31		J1	10,000		15,200

Accounts Receivable — No. 112

Date	Explanation	Ref.	Debit	Credit	Balance
2015					
Oct. 31	Adj. entry	J2	200		200

Supplies — No. 126

Date	Explanation	Ref.	Debit	Credit	Balance
2015					
Oct. 5		J1	2,500		2,500
31	Adj. entry	J2		1,500	1,000

Prepaid Insurance — No. 130

Date	Explanation	Ref.	Debit	Credit	Balance
2015					
Oct. 4		J1	600		600
31	Adj. entry	J2		50	550

Equipment — No. 157

Date	Explanation	Ref.	Debit	Credit	Balance
2015					
Oct. 1		J1	5,000		5,000

Accumulated Depreciation—Equipment — No. 158

Date	Explanation	Ref.	Debit	Credit	Balance
2015					
Oct. 31	Adj. entry	J2		40	40

Notes Payable — No. 200

Date	Explanation	Ref.	Debit	Credit	Balance
2015					
Oct. 1		J1		5,000	5,000

Accounts Payable — No. 201

Date	Explanation	Ref.	Debit	Credit	Balance
2015					
Oct. 5		J1		2,500	2,500

Unearned Service Revenue — No. 209

Date	Explanation	Ref.	Debit	Credit	Balance
2015					
Oct. 2		J1		1,200	1,200
31	Adj. entry	J2	400		800

Salaries and Wages Payable — No. 212

Date	Explanation	Ref.	Debit	Credit	Balance
2015					
Oct. 31	Adj. entry	J2		1,200	1,200

Interest Payable — No. 230

Date	Explanation	Ref.	Debit	Credit	Balance
2015					
Oct. 31	Adj. entry	J2		50	50

Common Stock — No. 311

Date	Explanation	Ref.	Debit	Credit	Balance
2015					
Oct. 1		J1		10,000	10,000

Retained Earnings — No. 320

Date	Explanation	Ref.	Debit	Credit	Balance
2015					

Dividends — No. 332

Date	Explanation	Ref.	Debit	Credit	Balance
2015					
Oct. 20		J1	500		500

Service Revenue — No. 400

Date	Explanation	Ref.	Debit	Credit	Balance
2015					
Oct. 31		J1		10,000	10,000
31	Adj. entry	J2		400	10,400
31	Adj. entry	J2		200	10,600

Supplies Expense — No. 631

Date	Explanation	Ref.	Debit	Credit	Balance
2015					
Oct. 31	Adj. entry	J2	1,500		1,500

Depreciation Expense — No. 711

Date	Explanation	Ref.	Debit	Credit	Balance
2015					
Oct. 31	Adj. entry	J2	40		40

Insurance Expense — No. 722

Date	Explanation	Ref.	Debit	Credit	Balance
2015					
Oct. 31	Adj. entry	J2	50		50

Salaries and Wages Expense — No. 726

Date	Explanation	Ref.	Debit	Credit	Balance
2015					
Oct. 26		J1	4,000		4,000
31	Adj. entry	J2	1,200		5,200

Rent Expense — No. 729

Date	Explanation	Ref.	Debit	Credit	Balance
2015					
Oct. 3		J1	900		900

Interest Expense — No. 905

Date	Explanation	Ref.	Debit	Credit	Balance
2015					
Oct. 31	Adj. entry	J2	50		50

The Adjusted Trial Balance and Financial Statements

After a company has journalized and posted all adjusting entries, it prepares another trial balance from the ledger accounts. This trial balance is called an **adjusted trial balance**. It shows the balances of all accounts, including those adjusted, at the end of the accounting period. The purpose of an adjusted trial balance is to **prove the equality** of the total debit balances and the total credit balances in the ledger after all adjustments. Because the accounts contain all data needed for financial statements, the adjusted trial balance is the **primary basis for the preparation of financial statements**.

LEARNING OBJECTIVE   6

Describe the nature and purpose of an adjusted trial balance.

Preparing the Adjusted Trial Balance

Illustration 3-25 presents the adjusted trial balance for Pioneer Advertising Agency Inc. prepared from the ledger accounts in Illustration 3-24. The amounts affected by the adjusting entries are highlighted in color. Compare these amounts to those in the unadjusted trial balance in Illustration 3-3 on page 107. In this comparison, you will see that there are more accounts in the adjusted trial balance as a result of the adjusting entries made at the end of the month.

PIONEER ADVERTISING AGENCY INC.
Adjusted Trial Balance
October 31, 2015

Illustration 3-25
Adjusted trial balance

	Dr.	Cr.
Cash	$ 15,200	
Accounts Receivable	200	
Supplies	1,000	
Prepaid Insurance	550	
Equipment	5,000	
Accumulated Depreciation—Equipment		$ 40
Notes Payable		5,000
Accounts Payable		2,500
Interest Payable		50
Unearned Service Revenue		800
Salaries and Wages Payable		1,200
Common Stock		10,000
Retained Earnings		–0–
Dividends	500	
Service Revenue		10,600
Salaries and Wages Expense	5,200	
Supplies Expense	1,500	
Rent Expense	900	
Insurance Expense	50	
Interest Expense	50	
Depreciation Expense	40	
	$30,190	$30,190

Preparing Financial Statements

Companies can prepare financial statements directly from the adjusted trial balance. Illustrations 3-26 (page 124) and 3-27 (page 125) present the interrelationships of data in the adjusted trial balance and the financial statements.

As Illustration 3-26 shows, companies prepare the income statement from the revenue and expense accounts. Next, they use the Retained Earnings and Dividends accounts and the net income (or net loss) from the income statement to prepare the retained earnings statement.

Illustration 3-26
Preparation of the income statement and retained earnings statement from the adjusted trial balance

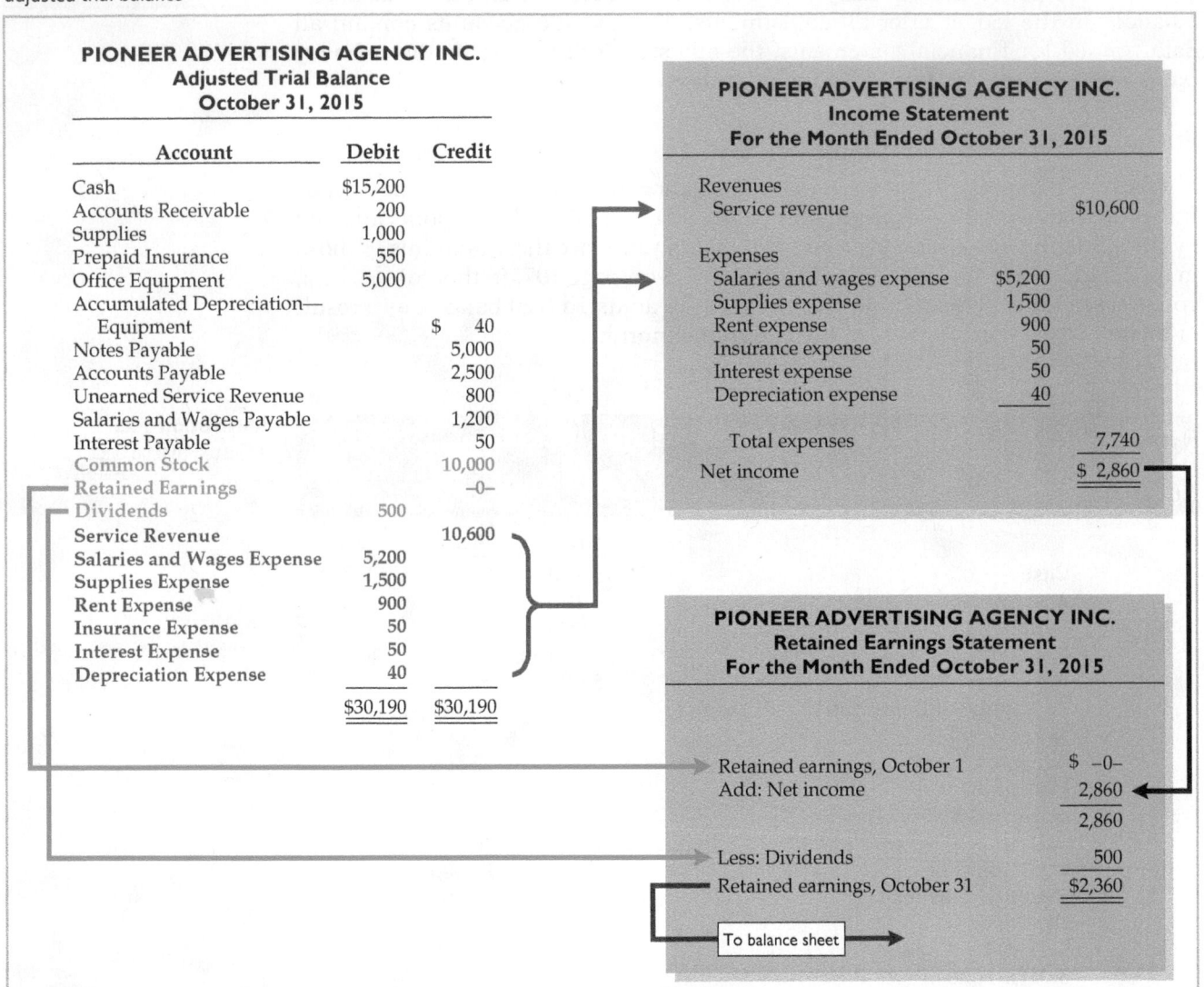

As Illustration 3-27 shows, companies then prepare the balance sheet from the asset and liability accounts and the ending retained earnings balance as reported in the retained earnings statement.

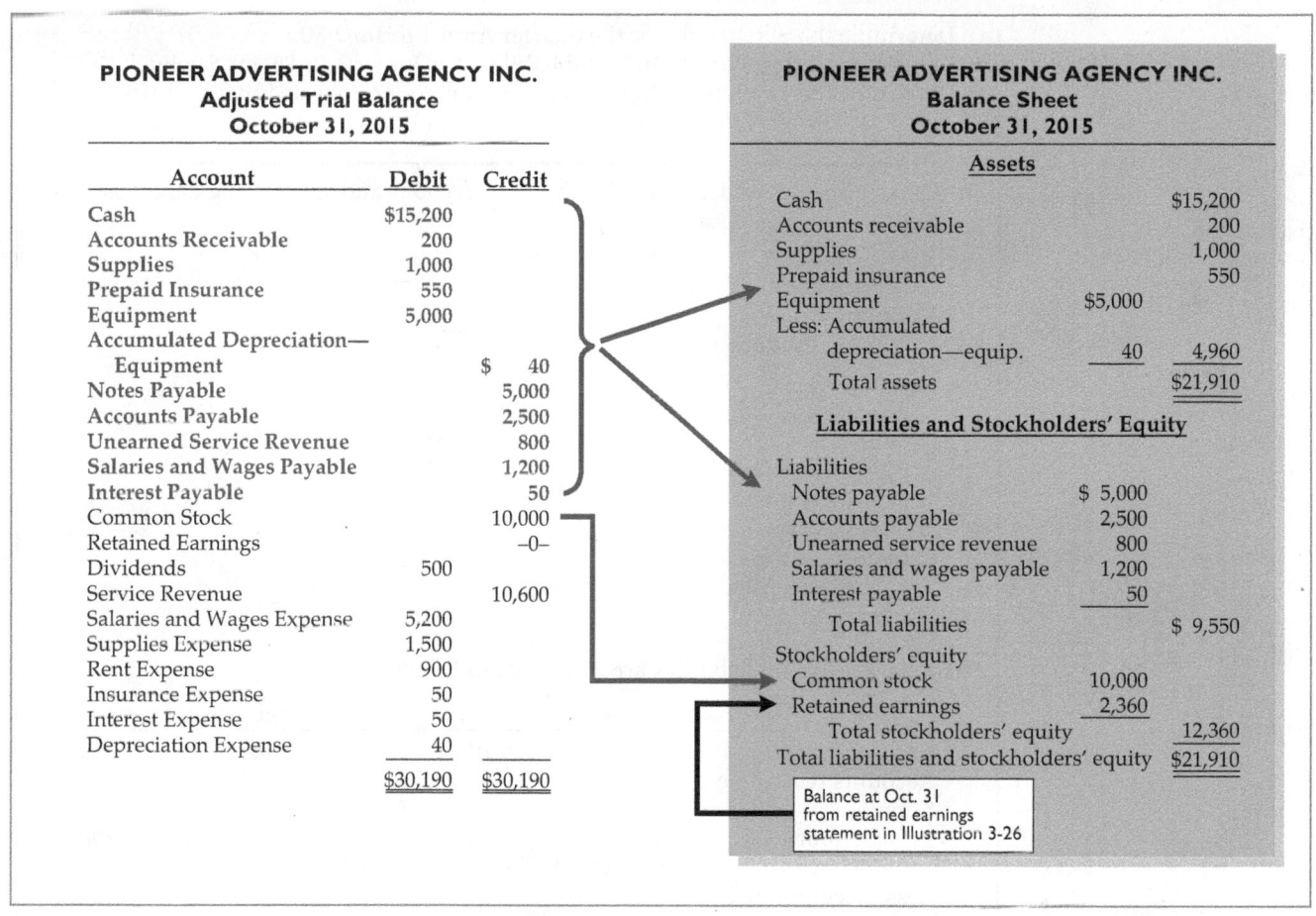

PIONEER ADVERTISING AGENCY INC. Adjusted Trial Balance October 31, 2015		
Account	**Debit**	**Credit**
Cash	$15,200	
Accounts Receivable	200	
Supplies	1,000	
Prepaid Insurance	550	
Equipment	5,000	
Accumulated Depreciation— Equipment		$ 40
Notes Payable		5,000
Accounts Payable		2,500
Unearned Service Revenue		800
Salaries and Wages Payable		1,200
Interest Payable		50
Common Stock		10,000
Retained Earnings		–0–
Dividends	500	
Service Revenue		10,600
Salaries and Wages Expense	5,200	
Supplies Expense	1,500	
Rent Expense	900	
Insurance Expense	50	
Interest Expense	50	
Depreciation Expense	40	
	$30,190	$30,190

PIONEER ADVERTISING AGENCY INC.
Balance Sheet
October 31, 2015

Assets

Cash		$15,200
Accounts receivable		200
Supplies		1,000
Prepaid insurance		550
Equipment	$5,000	
Less: Accumulated depreciation—equip.	40	4,960
Total assets		$21,910

Liabilities and Stockholders' Equity

Liabilities		
Notes payable	$ 5,000	
Accounts payable	2,500	
Unearned service revenue	800	
Salaries and wages payable	1,200	
Interest payable	50	
Total liabilities		$ 9,550
Stockholders' equity		
Common stock	10,000	
Retained earnings	2,360	
Total stockholders' equity		12,360
Total liabilities and stockholders' equity		$21,910

Balance at Oct. 31 from retained earnings statement in Illustration 3-26

Illustration 3-27
Preparation of the balance sheet from the adjusted trial balance

---

> **DO IT!**

Trial Balance

Skolnick Co. was organized on April 1, 2015. The company prepares quarterly financial statements. The adjusted trial balance amounts at June 30 are shown below.

	Debit		Credit
Cash	$ 6,700	Accumulated Depreciation—	
Accounts Receivable	600	Equipment	$ 850
Prepaid Rent	900	Notes Payable	5,000
Supplies	1,000	Accounts Payable	1,510
Equipment	15,000	Salaries and Wages Payable	400
Dividends	600	Interest Payable	50
Salaries and Wages Expense	9,400	Unearned Rent Revenue	500
Rent Expense	1,500	Common Stock	14,000
Depreciation Expense	850	Service Revenue	14,200
Supplies Expense	200	Rent Revenue	800
Utilities Expense	510		
Interest Expense	50		
	$37,310		$37,310

(a) Determine the net income for the quarter April 1 to June 30.
(b) Determine the total assets and total liabilities at June 30, 2015, for Skolnick Co.
(c) Determine the amount that appears for Retained Earnings at June 30, 2015.

Solution

Action Plan

✔ In an adjusted trial balance, make sure all asset, liability, revenue, and expense accounts are properly stated.

✔ To determine the ending balance in Retained Earnings, add net income and subtract dividends.

(a) The net income is determined by adding revenues and subtracting expenses. The net income is computed as follows.

Revenues		
Service revenue	$14,200	
Rent revenue	800	
Total revenues		$15,000
Expenses		
Salaries and wages expense	9,400	
Rent expense	1,500	
Depreciation expense	850	
Utilities expense	510	
Supplies expense	200	
Interest expense	50	
Total expenses		12,510
Net income		$ 2,490

(b) Total assets and liabilities are computed as follows.

Assets			Liabilities	
Cash		$ 6,700	Notes payable	$5,000
Accounts receivable		600	Accounts payable	1,510
Supplies		1,000	Unearned rent	
Prepaid rent		900	revenue	500
Equipment	$15,000		Salaries and wages	
Less: Accumulated			payable	400
depreciation—			Interest payable	50
equipment	850	14,150		
Total assets		$23,350	Total liabilities	$7,460

(c)

Retained earnings, April 1	$ 0
Add: Net income	2,490
Less: Dividends	600
Retained earnings, June 30	$ 1,890

Related exercise material: BE3-9, BE3-10, E3-11, E3-12, E3-13, **and** DO IT! 3-4.

 The Navigator

> Comprehensive DO IT!

The Green Thumb Lawn Care Inc. began operations on April 1. At April 30, the trial balance shows the following balances for selected accounts.

Prepaid Insurance	$ 3,600
Equipment	28,000
Notes Payable	20,000
Unearned Service Revenue	4,200
Service Revenue	1,800

Analysis reveals the following additional data.

1. Prepaid insurance is the cost of a 2-year insurance policy, effective April 1.
2. Depreciation on the equipment is $500 per month.
3. The note payable is dated April 1. It is a 6-month, 12% note.
4. Seven customers paid for the company's 6-month lawn service package of $600 beginning in April. The company performed services for these customers in April.
5. Lawn services performed for other customers but not recorded at April 30 totaled $1,500.

Instructions
Prepare the adjusting entries for the month of April. Show computations.

Solution to Comprehensive DO IT!

Action Plan

✔ Note that adjustments are being made for one month.

✔ Make computations carefully.

✔ Select account titles carefully.

✔ Make sure debits are made first and credits are indented.

✔ Check that debits equal credits for each entry.

	GENERAL JOURNAL			**J1**
Date	**Account Titles and Explanation**	**Ref.**	**Debit**	**Credit**
	Adjusting Entries			
Apr. 30	Insurance Expense		150	
	Prepaid Insurance			150
	(To record insurance expired: $3,600 ÷ 24 = $150 per month)			
30	Depreciation Expense		500	
	Accumulated Depreciation—Equipment			500
	(To record monthly depreciation)			
30	Interest Expense		200	
	Interest Payable			200
	(To record interest on notes payable: $20,000 × 12% × 1/12 = $200)			
30	Unearned Service Revenue		700	
	Service Revenue			700
	(To record revenue for services performed: $600 ÷ 6 = $100; $100 per month × 7 = $700)			
30	Accounts Receivable		1,500	
	Service Revenue			1,500
	(To record revenue for services performed)			

 The Navigator

SUMMARY OF LEARNING OBJECTIVES

✔ The Navigator

1 **Explain the time period assumption.** The time period assumption assumes that the economic life of a business is divided into artificial time periods.

2 **Explain the accrual basis of accounting.** Accrual-basis accounting means that companies record events that change a company's financial statements in the periods in which those events occur, rather than in the periods in which the company receives or pays cash.

3 **Explain the reasons for adjusting entries and identify the major types of adjusting entries.** Companies make adjusting entries at the end of an accounting period. Such entries ensure that companies recognize revenues in the period in which the performance obligation is satisfied and recognize expenses in the period in which they are incurred.

The major types of adjusting entries are deferrals (prepaid expenses and unearned revenues) and accruals (accrued revenues and accrued expenses).

4 Prepare adjusting entries for deferrals. Deferrals are either prepaid expenses or unearned revenues. Companies make adjusting entries for deferrals to record the portion of the prepayment that represents the expense incurred or the revenue for services performed in the current accounting period.

5 Prepare adjusting entries for accruals. Accruals are either accrued revenues or accrued expenses. Companies make adjusting entries for accruals to record revenues for services performed and expenses incurred in the current accounting period that have not been recognized through daily entries.

6 Describe the nature and purpose of an adjusted trial balance. An adjusted trial balance shows the balances of all accounts, including those that have been adjusted, at the end of an accounting period. Its purpose is to prove the equality of the total debit balances and total credit balances in the ledger after all adjustments.

GLOSSARY

Accrual-basis accounting Accounting basis in which companies record transactions that change a company's financial statements in the periods in which the events occur. (p. 104).

Accruals Adjusting entries for either accrued revenues or accrued expenses. (p. 107).

Accrued expenses Expenses incurred but not yet paid in cash or recorded. (p. 116).

Accrued revenues Revenues for services performed but not yet received in cash or recorded. (p. 114).

Adjusted trial balance A list of accounts and their balances after the company has made all adjustments. (p. 123).

Adjusting entries Entries made at the end of an accounting period to ensure that companies follow the revenue recognition and expense recognition principles. (p. 106).

Book value The difference between the cost of a depreciable asset and its related accumulated depreciation. (p. 111).

Calendar year An accounting period that extends from January 1 to December 31. (p. 104).

Cash-basis accounting Accounting basis in which companies record revenue when they receive cash and an expense when they pay cash. (p. 104).

Contra asset account An account offset against an asset account on the balance sheet. (p. 110).

Deferrals Adjusting entries for either prepaid expenses or unearned revenues. (p. 107).

Depreciation The process of allocating the cost of an asset to expense over its useful life. (p. 110).

Expense recognition principle (matching principle) The principle that companies match efforts (expenses) with accomplishments (revenues). (p. 105).

Fiscal year An accounting period that is one year in length. (p. 104).

Interim periods Monthly or quarterly accounting time periods. (p. 104).

Prepaid expenses (prepayments) Expenses paid in cash before they are used or consumed. (p. 108).

Revenue recognition principle The principle that companies recognize revenue in the accounting period in which the performance obligation is satisfied. (p. 105).

Time period assumption An assumption that accountants can divide the economic life of a business into artificial time periods. (p. 104).

Unearned revenues A liability recorded for cash received before services are performed. (p. 112).

Useful life The length of service of a long-lived asset. (p. 110).

APPENDIX 3A Alternative Treatment of Prepaid Expenses and Unearned Revenues

LEARNING OBJECTIVE 7

Prepare adjusting entries for the alternative treatment of deferrals.

In discussing adjusting entries for prepaid expenses and unearned revenues, we illustrated transactions for which companies made the initial entries to balance sheet accounts. In the case of prepaid expenses, the company debited the prepayment to an asset account. In the case of unearned revenue, the company credited a liability account to record the cash received.

Some companies use an alternative treatment. (1) When a company prepays an expense, it debits that amount to an expense account. (2) When it receives payment for future services, it credits the amount to a revenue account. In this appendix, we describe the circumstances that justify such entries and the different adjusting entries that may be required. This alternative treatment of prepaid expenses and unearned revenues has the same effect on the financial statements as the procedures described in the chapter.

Prepaid Expenses

Prepaid expenses become expired costs either through the passage of time (e.g., insurance) or through consumption (e.g., advertising supplies). If at the time of purchase the company expects to consume the supplies before the next financial statement date, **it may choose to debit (increase) an expense account rather than an asset account. This alternative treatment is simply more convenient.**

Assume that Pioneer Advertising Agency Inc. expects that it will use before the end of the month all of the supplies purchased on October 5. A debit of $2,500 to Supplies Expense (rather than to the asset account Supplies) on October 5 will eliminate the need for an adjusting entry on October 31. At October 31, the Supplies Expense account will show a balance of $2,500, which is the cost of supplies used between October 5 and October 31.

But what if the company does not use all the supplies? For example, what if an inventory of $1,000 of advertising supplies remains on October 31? Obviously, the company would need to make an adjusting entry. Prior to adjustment, the expense account Supplies Expense is overstated $1,000, and the asset account Supplies is understated $1,000. Thus, Pioneer makes the following adjusting entry.

Oct. 31	Supplies	1,000	
	Supplies Expense		1,000
	(To record supplies inventory)		

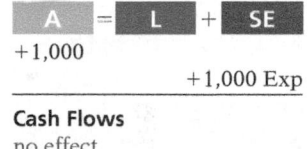

A = L + SE
+1,000
+1,000 Exp

Cash Flows
no effect

After the company posts the adjusting entry, the accounts show:

Supplies			**Supplies Expense**			
10/31 Adj.	1,000		10/5	2,500	10/31 Adj.	1,000
			10/31 Bal.	1,500		

Illustration 3A-1
Prepaid expenses accounts after adjustment

After adjustment, the asset account Supplies shows a balance of $1,000, which is equal to the cost of supplies on hand at October 31. In addition, Supplies Expense shows a balance of $1,500. This is equal to the cost of supplies used between October 5 and October 31. Without the adjusting entry, expenses are overstated and net income is understated by $1,000 in the October income statement. Also, both assets and stockholders' equity are understated by $1,000 on the October 31 balance sheet.

Illustration 3A-2 compares the entries and accounts for advertising supplies in the two adjustment approaches.

Illustration 3A-2
Adjustment approaches—a comparison

Prepayment Initially Debited to Asset Account (per chapter)			**Prepayment Initially Debited to Expense Account (per appendix)**		
Oct. 5 Supplies	2,500		Oct. 5 Supplies Expense	2,500	
Accounts Payable		2,500	Accounts Payable		2,500
Oct. 31 Supplies Expense	1,500		Oct. 31 Supplies	1,000	
Supplies		1,500	Supplies Expense		1,000

After Pioneer posts the entries, the accounts appear as follows.

Illustration 3A-3
Comparison of accounts

	(per chapter) Supplies			(per appendix) Supplies	
10/5	2,500	10/31 Adj. 1,500	10/31 Adj.	1,000	
10/31 Bal.	1,000				

	Supplies Expense			Supplies Expense	
10/31 Adj.	1,500		10/5	2,500	10/31 Adj. 1,000
			10/31 Bal.	1,500	

Note that the account balances under each alternative are the same at October 31: Supplies $1,000 and Supplies Expense $1,500.

Unearned Revenues

Unearned revenues are recognized as revenue at the time services are performed. Similar to the case for prepaid expenses, companies may credit (increase) a revenue account when they receive cash for future services.

Helpful Hint
The required adjusted balances here are Service Revenue $400 and Unearned Service Revenue $800.

To illustrate, assume that Pioneer Advertising Inc. received $1,200 for future services on October 2. Pioneer expects to perform the services before October 31.[1] In such a case, the company credits Service Revenue. If Pioneer in fact performs the service before October 31, no adjustment is needed.

However, if at the statement date Pioneer has not performed $800 of the services, it would make an adjusting entry. Without the entry, the revenue account Service Revenue is overstated $800, and the liability account Unearned Service Revenue is understated $800. Thus, Pioneer makes the following adjusting entry.

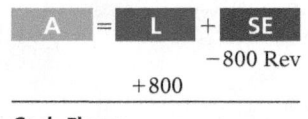
A = L + SE
−800 Rev
+800

Cash Flows
no effect

Oct. 31	Service Revenue	800	
	Unearned Service Revenue		800
	(To record unearned service revenue)		

After Pioneer posts the adjusting entry, the accounts show:

Illustration 3A-4
Unearned service revenue accounts after adjustment

Unearned Service Revenue		Service Revenue	
	10/31 Adj. 800	10/31 Adj. 800	10/2 1,200
			10/31 Bal. 400

The liability account Unearned Service Revenue shows a balance of $800. This equals the services that will be performed in the future. In addition, the balance in Service Revenue equals the services performed in October. Without the adjusting entry, both revenues and net income are overstated by $800 in the October income statement. Also, liabilities are understated by $800 and stockholders' equity is overstated by $800 on the October 31 balance sheet.

---

[1]This example focuses only on the alternative treatment of unearned revenues. For simplicity, we have ignored the entries to Service Revenue pertaining to the immediate recognition of revenue ($10,000) and the adjusting entry for accrued revenue ($200).

Illustration 3A-5 compares the entries and accounts for initially recording unearned service revenue in (1) a liability account or (2) a revenue account.

Illustration 3A-5
Adjustment approaches—a comparison

Unearned Service Revenue Initially Credited to Liability Account (per chapter)			Unearned Service Revenue Initially Credited to Revenue Account (per appendix)		
Oct. 2 Cash	1,200		Oct. 2 Cash	1,200	
Unearned Service Revenue		1,200	Service Revenue		1,200
Oct. 31 Unearned Service Revenue	400		Oct. 31 Service Revenue	800	
Service Revenue		400	Unearned Service Revenue		800

After Pioneer posts the entries, the accounts appear as follows.

Illustration 3A-6
Comparison of accounts

(per chapter)
Unearned Service Revenue

10/31 Adj.	400	10/2	1,200
		10/31 Bal.	800

Service Revenue

		10/31 Adj.	400

(per appendix)
Unearned Service Revenue

		10/31 Adj.	800

Service Revenue

10/31 Adj.	800	10/2	1,200
		10/31 Bal.	400

Note that the balances in the accounts are the same under the two alternatives: Unearned Service Revenue $800 and Service Revenue $400.

Summary of Additional Adjustment Relationships

Illustration 3A-7 provides a summary of basic relationships for deferrals.

Illustration 3A-7
Summary of basic relationships for deferrals

Type of Adjustment	Reason for Adjustment	Account Balances before Adjustment	Adjusting Entry
1. Prepaid expenses	(a) Prepaid expenses initially recorded in asset accounts have been used.	Assets overstated Expenses understated	Dr. Expenses Cr. Assets
	(b) **Prepaid expenses initially recorded in expense accounts have not been used.**	**Assets understated Expenses overstated**	**Dr. Assets Cr. Expenses**
2. Unearned revenues	(a) Unearned revenues initially recorded in liability accounts are now recognized as revenue.	Liabilities overstated Revenues understated	Dr. Liabilities Cr. Revenues
	(b) **Unearned revenues initially recorded in revenue accounts are still unearned.**	**Liabilities understated Revenues overstated**	**Dr. Revenues Cr. Liabilities**

Alternative adjusting entries **do not apply** to accrued revenues and accrued expenses because **no entries occur before companies make these types of adjusting entries**.

---

7 Prepare adjusting entries for the alternative treatment of deferrals. Companies may initially debit prepayments to an expense account. Likewise, they may credit unearned revenues to a revenue account. At the end of the period, these accounts may be overstated.

The adjusting entries for prepaid expenses are a debit to an asset account and a credit to an expense account. Adjusting entries for unearned revenues are a debit to a revenue account and a credit to a liability account.

APPENDIX 3B   Concepts in Action

LEARNING OBJECTIVE   8

Discuss financial reporting concepts.

This appendix provides a summary of the concepts in action used in this textbook. In addition, it provides other useful concepts which accountants use as a basis for recording and reporting financial information.

Qualities of Useful Information

Recently, the FASB completed the first phase of a project in which it developed a conceptual framework to serve as the basis for future accounting standards. The framework begins by stating that the primary objective of financial reporting is to provide financial information that is **useful** to investors and creditors for making decisions about providing capital. Useful information should possess two fundamental qualities, relevance and faithful representation, as shown in Illustration 3B-1.

Illustration 3B-1
Fundamental qualities of useful information

Tell me what I need to know.

BIG SHOT

Relevance Accounting information has relevance if it would make a difference in a business decision. Information is considered relevant if it provides information that has **predictive value**, that is, helps provide accurate expectations about the future, and has **confirmatory value**, that is, confirms or corrects prior expectations. Materiality is a company-specific aspect of relevance. An item is material when its **size** makes it likely to influence the decision of an investor or creditor.

Faithful Representation Faithful representation means that information accurately depicts what really happened. To provide a faithful representation, information must be **complete** (nothing important has been omitted), **neutral** (is not biased toward one position or another), and **free from error**.

ENHANCING QUALITIES

In addition to the two fundamental qualities, the FASB also describes a number of enhancing qualities of useful information. These include **comparability**, **consistency**, **verifiability**, **timeliness**, and **understandability**. In accounting,

comparability results when different companies use the same accounting principles. Another characteristic that enhances comparability is consistency. **Consistency** means that a company uses the same accounting principles and methods from year to year. Information is **verifiable** if independent observers, using the same methods, obtain similar results. For accounting information to have relevance, it must be **timely**. That is, it must be available to decision-makers before it loses its capacity to influence decisions. For example, public companies like Google or Best Buy provide their annual reports to investors within 60 days of their year-end. Information has the quality of **understandability** if it is presented in a clear and concise fashion, so that reasonably informed users of that information can interpret it and comprehend its meaning.

Assumptions in Financial Reporting

To develop accounting standards, the FASB relies on some key assumptions, as shown in Illustration 3B-2. These include assumptions about the monetary unit, economic entity, time period, and going concern.

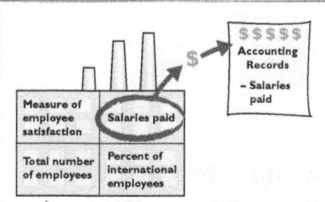 **Monetary Unit Assumption** The monetary unit assumption requires that only those things that can be expressed in money are included in the accounting records. This means that certain important information needed by investors, creditors, and managers, such as customer satisfaction, is not reported in the financial statements.

 Economic Entity Assumption The economic entity assumption states that every economic entity can be separately identified and accounted for. In order to assess a company's performance and financial position accurately, it is important to not blur company transactions with personal transactions (especially those of its managers) or transactions of other companies.

 Time Period Assumption Notice that the income statement, retained earnings statement, and statement of cash flows all cover periods of one year, and the balance sheet is prepared at the end of each year. The time period assumption states that the life of a business can be divided into artificial time periods and that useful reports covering those periods can be prepared for the business.

 Going Concern Assumption The going concern assumption states that the business will remain in operation for the foreseeable future. Of course, many businesses do fail, but in general it is reasonable to assume that the business will continue operating.

Illustration 3B-2
Key assumptions in financial reporting

Principles in Financial Reporting

MEASUREMENT PRINCIPLES

GAAP generally uses one of two measurement principles, the historical cost principle or the fair value principle. Selection of which principle to follow generally relates to trade-offs between relevance and faithful representation.

HISTORICAL COST PRINCIPLE The **historical cost principle** (or cost principle, discussed in Chapter 1) dictates that companies record assets at their cost. This is true not only at the time the asset is purchased but also over the time the asset is held. For example, if land that was purchased for $30,000 increases in value to $40,000, it continues to be reported at $30,000.

FAIR VALUE PRINCIPLE The **fair value principle** (discussed in Chapter 1) indicates that assets and liabilities should be reported at fair value (the price received to sell an asset or settle a liability). Fair value information may be more useful than historical cost for certain types of assets and liabilities. For example, certain investment securities are reported at fair value because market price information is often readily available for these types of assets. In choosing between cost and fair value, two qualities that make accounting information useful for decision-making are used—relevance and faithful representation. In determining which measurement principle to use, the factual nature of cost figures are weighed versus the relevance of fair value. In general, most assets follow the historical cost principle because fair values may not be representationally faithful. Only in situations where assets are actively traded, such as investment securities, is the fair value principle applied.

REVENUE RECOGNITION PRINCIPLE

The **revenue recognition principle** requires that companies recognize revenue in the accounting period in which the performance obligation is satisfied. As discussed earlier in the chapter, in a service company, revenue is recognized at the time the service is performed. In a merchandising company, the performance obligation is generally satisfied when the goods transfer from the seller to the buyer (discussed in Chapter 5). At this point, the sales transaction is complete and the sales price established.

EXPENSE RECOGNITION PRINCIPLE

The **expense recognition principle** (often referred to as the matching principle, discussed earlier in the chapter) dictates that efforts (expenses) be matched with results (revenues). Thus, expenses follow revenues.

FULL DISCLOSURE PRINCIPLE

The **full disclosure principle** (discussed in Chapter 11) requires that companies disclose all circumstances and events that would make a difference to financial statement users. If an important item cannot reasonably be reported directly in one of the four types of financial statements, then it should be discussed in notes that accompany the statements.

Cost Constraint

Providing information is costly. In deciding whether companies should be required to provide a certain type of information, accounting standard-setters consider the **cost constraint**. It weighs the cost that companies will incur to provide the information against the benefit that financial statement users will gain from having the information available.

8 Discuss financial reporting concepts To be judged useful, information should have the primary characteristics of relevance and faithful representation. In addition, it should be comparable, consistent, verifiable, timely, and understandable.

The **monetary unit assumption** requires that companies include in the accounting records only transaction data that can be expressed in terms of money. The **economic entity assumption** states that economic events can be identified with a particular unit of accountability. The **time period assumption** states that the economic life of a business can be divided into artificial time periods and that meaningful accounting reports can be prepared for each period. The **going concern assumption** states that the company will continue in operation long enough to carry out its existing objectives and commitments.

The **historical cost principle** states that companies should record assets at their cost. The **fair value principle** indicates that assets and liabilities should be reported at fair value. The **revenue recognition principle** requires that companies recognize revenue in the accounting period in which the performance obligation is satisfied. The **expense recognition principle** dictates that efforts (expenses) be matched with results (revenues). The **full disclosure principle** requires that companies disclose circumstances and events that matter to financial statement users.

The **cost constraint** weighs the cost that companies incur to provide a type of information against its benefits to financial statement users.

GLOSSARY FOR APPENDIX 3B

Comparability Ability to compare the accounting information of different companies because they use the same accounting principles. (p. 133).

Consistency Use of the same accounting principles and methods from year to year within a company. (p. 133).

Cost constraint Constraint that weighs the cost that companies will incur to provide the information against the benefit that financial statement users will gain from having the information available. (p. 134).

Economic entity assumption An assumption that every economic entity can be separately identified and accounted for. (p. 133).

Expense recognition principle Efforts (expenses) should be matched with results (revenues). (p. 134).

Fair value principle Assets and liabilities should be reported at fair value (the price received to sell an asset or settle a liability). (p. 134).

Faithful representation Information that accurately depicts what really happened. (p. 132).

Full disclosure principle Accounting principle that dictates that companies disclose circumstances and events that make a difference to financial statement users. (p. 134).

Going concern assumption The assumption that the company will continue in operation for the foreseeable future. (p. 133).

Historical cost principle An accounting principle that states that companies should record assets at their cost. (p. 134).

Materiality A company-specific aspect of relevance. An item is material when its size makes it likely to influence the decision of an investor or creditor. (p. 132).

Monetary unit assumption An assumption that requires that only those things that can be expressed in money are included in the accounting records. (p. 133).

Relevance The quality of information that indicates the information makes a difference in a decision. (p. 132).

Revenue recognition principle Companies recognize revenue in the accounting period in which the performance obligation is satisfied. (p. 134).

Timely Information that is available to decision-makers before it loses its capacity to influence decisions. (p. 133).

Time period assumption An assumption that the life of a business can be divided into artificial time periods and that useful reports covering those periods can be prepared for the business. (p. 133).

Understandability Information presented in a clear and concise fashion so that users can interpret it and comprehend its meaning. (p. 133).

Verifiable The quality of information that occurs when independent observers, using the same methods, obtain similar results. (p. 133).

*Note: All asterisked Questions, Exercises, and Problems relate to material in the appendices to the chapter.

SELF-TEST QUESTIONS

Answers are on page 161.

(LO 1) **1.** The revenue recognition principle states that:
  (a) revenue should be recognized in the accounting period in which a performance obligation is satisfied.
  (b) expenses should be matched with revenues.
  (c) the economic life of a business can be divided into artificial time periods.
  (d) the fiscal year should correspond with the calendar year.

(LO 2) **2.** The time period assumption states that:
  (a) companies must wait until the calendar year is completed to prepare financial statements.
  (b) companies use the fiscal year to report financial information.
  (c) the economic life of a business can be divided into artificial time periods.
  (d) companies record information in the time period in which the events occur.

(LO 2) **3.** Which of the following statements about the accrual basis of accounting is **false**?
  (a) Events that change a company's financial statements are recorded in the periods in which the events occur.
  (b) Revenue is recognized in the period in which services are performed.
  (c) This basis is in accord with generally accepted accounting principles.
  (d) Revenue is recorded only when cash is received, and expense is recorded only when cash is paid.

(LO 2) **4.** The principle or assumption dictating that efforts (expenses) be matched with accomplishments (revenues) is the:
  (a) expense recognition principle.
  (b) cost assumption.
  (c) time period assumption.
  (d) revenue recognition principle.

(LO 3) **5.** Adjusting entries are made to ensure that:
  (a) expenses are recognized in the period in which they are incurred.
  (b) revenues are recorded in the period in which services are performed.
  (c) balance sheet and income statement accounts have correct balances at the end of an accounting period.
  (d) All the responses above are correct.

(LO 3) **6.** Each of the following is a major type (or category) of adjusting entries **except**:
  (a) prepaid expenses.
  (b) accrued revenues.
  (c) accrued expenses.
  (d) recognized revenues.

(LO 4) **7.** The trial balance shows Supplies $1,350 and Supplies Expense $0. If $600 of supplies are on hand at the end of the period, the adjusting entry is:
  (a) Supplies   600
        Supplies Expense   600
  (b) Supplies   750
        Supplies Expense   750
  (c) Supplies Expense   750
        Supplies   750
  (d) Supplies Expense   600
        Supplies   600

(LO 4) **8.** Adjustments for prepaid expenses:
  (a) decrease assets and increase revenues.
  (b) decrease expenses and increase assets.
  (c) decrease assets and increase expenses.
  (d) decrease revenues and increase assets.

(LO 4) **9.** Accumulated Depreciation is:
  (a) a contra asset account.
  (b) an expense account.
  (c) a stockholders' equity account.
  (d) a liability account.

(LO 4) **10.** Rivera Company computes depreciation on delivery equipment at $1,000 for the month of June. The adjusting entry to record this depreciation is as follows.
  (a) Depreciation Expense   1,000
        Accumulated Depreciation—
          Rivera Company   1,000
  (b) Depreciation Expense   1,000
        Equipment   1,000
  (c) Depreciation Expense   1,000
        Accumulated Depreciation—
          Equipment   1,000
  (d) Equipment Expense   1,000
        Accumulated Depreciation—
          Equipment   1,000

(LO 4) **11.** Adjustments for unearned revenues:
  (a) decrease liabilities and increase revenues.
  (b) have an assets and revenues account relationship.
  (c) increase assets and increase revenues.
  (d) decrease revenues and decrease assets.

(LO 5) **12.** Adjustments for accrued revenues:
  (a) have a liabilities and revenues account relationship.
  (b) have an assets and revenues account relationship.
  (c) decrease assets and revenues.
  (d) decrease liabilities and increase revenues.

(LO 5) **13.** Anika Wilson earned a salary of $400 for the last week of September. She will be paid on October 1. The adjusting entry for Anika's employer at September 30 is:
  (a) No entry is required.
  (b) Salaries and Wages Expense   400
        Salaries and Wages Payable   400

(c) Salaries and Wages Expense | 400 |
    Cash | | 400
(d) Salaries and Wages Payable | 400 |
    Cash | | 400

(LO 6) **14.** Which of the following statements is **incorrect** concerning the adjusted trial balance?

    (a) An adjusted trial balance proves the equality of the total debit balances and the total credit balances in the ledger after all adjustments are made.

    (b) The adjusted trial balance provides the primary basis for the preparation of financial statements.

    (c) The adjusted trial balance lists the account balances segregated by assets and liabilities.

    (d) The adjusted trial balance is prepared after the adjusting entries have been journalized and posted.

(LO 7)***15.** The trial balance shows Supplies $0 and Supplies Expense $1,500. If $800 of supplies are on hand at the end of the period, the adjusting entry is:

(a) Debit Supplies $800 and credit Supplies Expense $800.

(b) Debit Supplies Expense $800 and credit Supplies $800.

(c) Debit Supplies $700 and credit Supplies Expense $700.

(d) Debit Supplies Expense $700 and credit Supplies $700.

*16. Neutrality is an ingredient of: (LO 8)

	Faithful Representation	Relevance
(a)	Yes	Yes
(b)	No	No
(c)	Yes	No
(d)	No	Yes

*17. Which item is a constraint in financial accounting?   (LO 8)
(a) Comparability.   **(c)** Cost.
(b) Materiality.   **(d)** Consistency.

Go to the book's companion website, www.wiley.com/college/weygandt, for additional Self-Test Questions.

 ✔ **The Navigator**

QUESTIONS

1. (a) How does the time period assumption affect an accountant's analysis of business transactions?

    (b) Explain the terms fiscal year, calendar year, and interim periods.

2. Define two generally accepted accounting principles that relate to adjusting the accounts.

3. Susan Zupan, a lawyer, accepts a legal engagement in March, performs the work in April, and is paid in May. If Zupan's law firm prepares monthly financial statements, when should it recognize revenue from this engagement? Why?

4. Why do accrual-basis financial statements provide more useful information than cash-basis statements?

5. In completing the engagement in Question 3, Zupan pays no costs in March, $2,000 in April, and $2,500 in May (incurred in April). How much expense should the firm deduct from revenues in the month when it recognizes the revenue? Why?

6. "Adjusting entries are required by the historical cost principle of accounting." Do you agree? Explain.

7. Why may a trial balance not contain up-to-date and complete financial information?

8. Distinguish between the two categories of adjusting entries, and identify the types of adjustments applicable to each category.

9. What is the debit/credit effect of a prepaid expense adjusting entry?

10. "Depreciation is a valuation process that results in the reporting of the fair value of the asset." Do you agree? Explain.

11. Explain the differences between depreciation expense and accumulated depreciation.

12. J. Brownlee Company purchased equipment for $18,000. By the current balance sheet date, $6,000 had been depreciated. Indicate the balance sheet presentation of the data.

13. What is the debit/credit effect of an unearned revenue adjusting entry?

14. A company fails to recognize revenue for services performed but not yet received in cash or recorded. Which of the following accounts are involved in the adjusting entry: (a) asset, (b) liability, (c) revenue, or (d) expense? For the accounts selected, indicate whether they would be debited or credited in the entry.

15. A company fails to recognize an expense incurred but not paid. Indicate which of the following accounts is debited and which is credited in the adjusting entry: (a) asset, (b) liability, (c) revenue, or (d) expense.

16. A company makes an accrued revenue adjusting entry for $900 and an accrued expense adjusting entry for $700. How much was net income understated prior to these entries? Explain.

17. On January 9, a company pays $5,000 for salaries and wages of which $2,000 was reported as Salaries and Wages Payable on December 31. Give the entry to record the payment.

18. For each of the following items before adjustment, indicate the type of adjusting entry (prepaid expense, unearned revenue, accrued revenue, or accrued expense) that is needed to correct the misstatement. If an item could result in more than one type of adjusting entry, indicate each of the types.

    (a) Assets are understated.
    (b) Liabilities are overstated.
    (c) Liabilities are understated.
    (d) Expenses are understated.
    (e) Assets are overstated.
    (f) Revenue is understated.

19. One-half of the adjusting entry is given below. Indicate the account title for the other half of the entry.
    (a) Salaries and Wages Expense is debited.
    (b) Depreciation Expense is debited.
    (c) Interest Payable is credited.
    (d) Supplies is credited.
    (e) Accounts Receivable is debited.
    (f) Unearned Service Revenue is debited.
20. "An adjusting entry may affect more than one balance sheet or income statement account." Do you agree? Why or why not?
21. Why is it possible to prepare financial statements directly from an adjusted trial balance?
*22. Dashan Company debits Supplies Expense for all purchases of supplies and credits Rent Revenue for all advanced rentals. For each type of adjustment, give the adjusting entry.
*23. (a) What is the primary objective of financial reporting?
     (b) Identify the characteristics of useful accounting information.

*24. Dan Fineman, the president of King Company, is pleased. King substantially increased its net income in 2015 while keeping its unit inventory relatively the same. Howard Gross, chief accountant, cautions Dan, however. Gross says that since King changed its method of inventory valuation, there is a consistency problem and it is difficult to determine whether King is better off. Is Gross correct? Why or why not?
*25. What is the distinction between comparability and consistency?
*26. Describe the constraint inherent in the presentation of accounting information.
*27. Laurie Belk is president of Better Books. She has no accounting background. Belk cannot understand why fair value is not used as the basis for all accounting measurement and reporting. Discuss.
*28. What is the economic entity assumption? Give an example of its violation.

BRIEF EXERCISES

Indicate why adjusting entries are needed.
(LO 3)

BE3-1 The ledger of Jung Company includes the following accounts. Explain why each account may require adjustment.
(a) Prepaid Insurance.
(b) Depreciation Expense.
(c) Unearned Service Revenue.
(d) Interest Payable.

Identify the major types of adjusting entries.
(LO 3, 4, 5)

BE3-2 Moteki Company accumulates the following adjustment data at December 31. Indicate (a) the type of adjustment (prepaid expense, accrued revenues and so on), and (b) the status of accounts before adjustment (overstated or understated).
1. Supplies of $100 are on hand.
2. Services performed but not recorded total $900.
3. Interest of $200 has accumulated on a note payable.
4. Rent collected in advance totaling $650 has been earned.

Prepare adjusting entry for supplies.
(LO 4)

BE3-3 Ritter Advertising Company's trial balance at December 31 shows Supplies $6,700 and Supplies Expense $0. On December 31, there are $2,500 of supplies on hand. Prepare the adjusting entry at December 31, and using T-accounts, enter the balances in the accounts, post the adjusting entry, and indicate the adjusted balance in each account.

Prepare adjusting entry for depreciation.
(LO 4)

BE3-4 At the end of its first year, the trial balance of Nygaard Company shows Equipment $30,000 and zero balances in Accumulated Depreciation—Equipment and Depreciation Expense. Depreciation for the year is estimated to be $4,000. Prepare the adjusting entry for depreciation at December 31, post the adjustments to T-accounts, and indicate the balance sheet presentation of the equipment at December 31.

Prepare adjusting entry for prepaid expense.
(LO 4)

BE3-5 On July 1, 2015, Dobbs Co. pays $14,400 to Kalter Insurance Co. for a 3-year insurance contract. Both companies have fiscal years ending December 31. For Dobbs Co., journalize and post the entry on July 1 and the adjusting entry on December 31.

Prepare adjusting entry for unearned revenue.
(LO 4)

BE3-6 Using the data in BE3-5, journalize and post the entry on July 1 and the adjusting entry on December 31 for Kalter Insurance Co. Kalter uses the accounts Unearned Service Revenue and Service Revenue.

Prepare adjusting entries for accruals.
(LO 5)

BE3-7 The bookkeeper for Bradbury Company asks you to prepare the following accrued adjusting entries at December 31.
1. Interest on notes payable of $400 is accrued.
2. Services performed but not recorded total $1,900.
3. Salaries earned by employees of $900 have not been recorded.

Use the following account titles: Service Revenue, Accounts Receivable, Interest Expense, Interest Payable, Salaries and Wages Expense, and Salaries and Wages Payable.

BE3-8 The trial balance of Yewlett Company includes the following balance sheet accounts, which may require adjustment. For each account that requires adjustment, indicate (a) the type of adjusting entry (prepaid expenses, unearned revenues, accrued revenues, and accrued expenses) and (b) the related account in the adjusting entry.

Analyze accounts in an unadjusted trial balance.

(LO 3, 4, 5)

Accounts Receivable	Interest Payable
Prepaid Insurance	Unearned Service Revenue
Accumulated Depreciation—Equipment	

BE3-9 The adjusted trial balance of Parsons Company at December 31, 2015, includes the following accounts: Common Stock $15,600, Dividends $7,000, Service Revenue $37,000, Salaries and Wages Expense $16,000, Insurance Expense $2,000, Rent Expense $4,000, Supplies Expense $1,500, and Depreciation Expense $1,300. Prepare an income statement for the year.

Prepare an income statement from an adjusted trial balance.

(LO 6)

BE3-10 Partial adjusted trial balance data for Parsons Company is presented in BE3-9. The balance in Common Stock is the balance as of January 1. Prepare a retained earnings statement for the year assuming net income is $12,200 for the year and Retained Earnings is $7,240 on January 1.

Prepare a retained earnings statement from an adjusted trial balance.

(LO 6)

*****BE3-11** Mayes Company records all prepayments in income statement accounts. At April 30, the trial balance shows Supplies Expense $2,800, Service Revenue $9,200, and zero balances in related balance sheet accounts. Prepare the adjusting entries at April 30 assuming (a) $700 of supplies on hand and (b) $3,000 of service revenue should be reported as unearned.

Prepare adjusting entries under alternative treatment of deferrals.

(LO 7)

*****BE3-12** The accompanying chart shows the qualitative characteristics of useful accounting information. Fill in the blanks.

Identify characteristics of useful information.

(LO 8)

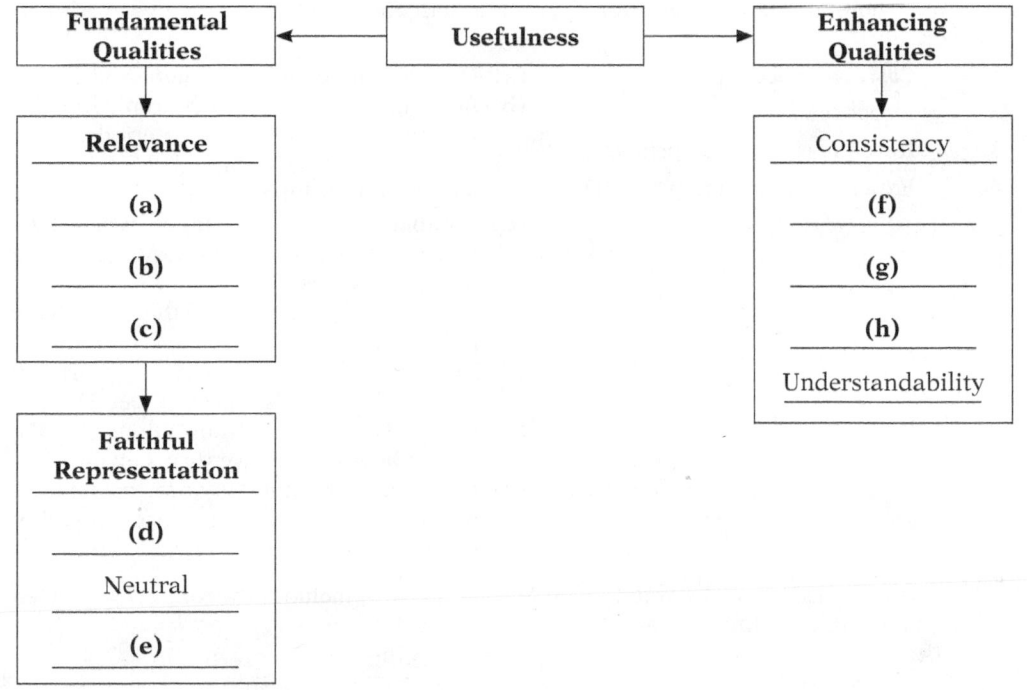

*****BE3-13** Given the characteristics of useful accounting information, complete each of the following statements.

Identify characteristics of useful information.

(LO 8)

(a) For information to be _____, it should have predictive value, confirmatory value, and be material.

(b) _____ is the quality of information that gives assurance that the information accurately depicts what really happened.

(c) _____ means using the same accounting principles and methods from year to year within a company.

Identify characteristics of useful information.
(LO 8)

*BE3-14 Here are some qualitative characteristics of useful accounting information:

1. Predictive value   3. Verifiable
2. Neutral   4. Timely

Match each qualitative characteristic to one of the following statements.

_____ **(a)** Accounting information should help provide accurate expectations about future events.

_____ **(b)** Accounting information cannot be selected, prepared, or presented to favor one set of interested users over another.

_____ **(c)** The quality of information that occurs when independent observers, using the same methods, obtain similar results.

_____ **(d)** Accounting information must be available to decision-makers before it loses its capacity to influence their decisions.

Define full disclosure principle.
(LO 8)

*BE3-15 The full disclosure principle dictates that:

(a) financial statements should disclose all assets at their cost.

(b) financial statements should disclose only those events that can be measured in currency.

(c) financial statements should disclose all events and circumstances that would matter to users of financial statements.

(d) financial statements should not be relied on unless an auditor has expressed an unqualified opinion on them.

> DO IT! Review

Identify timing concepts.
(LO 1, 2)

DO IT! 3-1 Several timing concepts are discussed on pages 104–105. A list of concepts is provided below in the left column, with a description of the concept in the right column. There are more descriptions provided than concepts. Match the description to the concept.

1. ____ Cash-basis accounting.
2. ____ Fiscal year.
3. ____ Revenue recognition principle.
4. ____ Expense recognition principle.

(a) Monthly and quarterly time periods.
(b) Accountants divide the economic life of a business into artificial time periods.
(c) Efforts (expenses) should be matched with accomplishments (revenues).
(d) Companies record revenues when they receive cash and record expenses when they pay out cash.
(e) An accounting time period that is one year in length.
(f) An accounting time period that starts on January 1 and ends on December 31.
(g) Companies record transactions in the period in which the events occur.
(h) Recognize revenue in the accounting period in which a performance obligation is satisfied.

Prepare adjusting entries for deferrals.
(LO 4)

DO IT! 3-2 The ledger of Herrera, Inc. on March 31, 2015, includes the following selected accounts before adjusting entries.

	Debit	Credit
Prepaid Insurance	2,400	
Supplies	2,500	
Equipment	30,000	
Unearned Service Revenue		9,000

An analysis of the accounts shows the following.

1. Insurance expires at the rate of $300 per month.
2. Supplies on hand total $1,100.

3. The equipment depreciates $500 per month.

4. During March, services were performed for two-fifths of the unearned service revenue.

Prepare the adjusting entries for the month of March.

DO IT! 3-3 Javier Computer Services began operations in July 2015. At the end of the month, the company prepares monthly financial statements. It has the following information for the month.

Prepare adjusting entries for accruals.
(LO 5)

1. At July 31, the company owed employees $1,300 in salaries that the company will pay in August.

2. On July 1, the company borrowed $20,000 from a local bank on a 10-year note. The annual interest rate is 12%.

3. Service revenue unrecorded in July totaled $2,400.

Prepare the adjusting entries needed at July 31, 2015.

DO IT! 3-4 Lumina Co. was organized on April 1, 2015. The company prepares quarterly financial statements. The adjusted trial balance amounts at June 30 are shown below.

Calculate amounts from trial balance.
(LO 6)

	Debit		Credit
Cash	$ 5,360	Accumulated Depreciation—	
Accounts Receivable	480	Equipment	$ 700
Prepaid Rent	720	Notes Payable	4,000
Supplies	920	Accounts Payable	790
Equipment	12,000	Salaries and Wages Payable	300
Dividends	500	Interest Payable	40
Salaries and Wages Expense	7,400	Unearned Rent Revenue	400
Rent Expense	1,200	Common Stock	11,200
Depreciation Expense	700	Service Revenue	11,360
Supplies Expense	160	Rent Revenue	1,100
Utilities Expense	410		$29,890
Interest Expense	40		
	$29,890		

(a) Determine the net income for the quarter April 1 to June 30.
(b) Determine the total assets and total liabilities at June 30, 2015, for Lumina Company.
(c) Determine the amount that appears for Retained Earnings at June 30, 2015.

EXERCISES

E3-1 Ian Muse has prepared the following list of statements about the time period assumption.

Explain the time period assumption.
(LO 1)

1. Adjusting entries would not be necessary if a company's life were not divided into artificial time periods.
2. The IRS requires companies to file annual tax returns.
3. Accountants divide the economic life of a business into artificial time periods, but each transaction affects only one of these periods.
4. Accounting time periods are generally a month, a quarter, or a year.
5. A time period lasting one year is called an interim period.
6. All fiscal years are calendar years, but not all calendar years are fiscal years.

Instructions
Identify each statement as true or false. If false, indicate how to correct the statement.

E3-2 On numerous occasions, proposals have surfaced to put the federal government on the accrual basis of accounting. This is no small issue. If this basis were used, it would mean that billions in unrecorded liabilities would have to be booked, and the federal deficit would increase substantially.

Distinguish between cash and accrual basis of accounting.
(LO 2)

Instructions
(a) What is the difference between accrual-basis accounting and cash-basis accounting?
(b) Why would politicians prefer the cash basis over the accrual basis?
(c) Write a letter to your senator explaining why the federal government should adopt the accrual basis of accounting.

Compute cash and accrual accounting income.
(LO 2)

E3-3 Primo Industries collected $105,000 from customers in 2015. Of the amount collected, $25,000 was for services performed in 2014. In addition, Primo performed services worth $40,000 in 2015, which will not be collected until 2016.

Primo Industries also paid $72,000 for expenses in 2015. Of the amount paid, $30,000 was for expenses incurred on account in 2014. In addition, Primo incurred $42,000 of expenses in 2015, which will not be paid until 2016.

Instructions
(a) Compute 2015 cash-basis net income.
(b) Compute 2015 accrual-basis net income.

Identify the type of adjusting entry needed.
(LO 3, 4, 5)

E3-4 Hart Corporation encounters the following situations:

1. Hart collects $1,300 from a customer in 2015 for services to be performed in 2016.
2. Hart incurs utility expense which is not yet paid in cash or recorded.
3. Hart's employees worked 3 days in 2015 but will not be paid until 2016.
4. Hart performs services for customers but has not yet received cash or recorded the transaction.
5. Hart paid $2,400 rent on December 1 for the 4 months starting December 1.
6. Hart received cash for future services and recorded a liability until the service was performed.
7. Hart performed consulting services for a client in December 2015. On December 31, it had not billed the client for services performed of $1,200.
8. Hart paid cash for an expense and recorded an asset until the item was used up.
9. Hart purchased $900 of supplies in 2015; at year-end, $400 of supplies remain unused.
10. Hart purchased equipment on January 1, 2015; the equipment will be used for 5 years.
11. Hart borrowed $10,000 on October 1, 2015, signing an 8% one-year note payable.

Instructions
Identify what type of adjusting entry (prepaid expense, unearned revenue, accrued expense, or accrued revenue) is needed in each situation at December 31, 2015.

Prepare adjusting entries from selected data.
(LO 4, 5)

E3-5 Verne Cova Company has the following balances in selected accounts on December 31, 2015.

Accounts Receivable	$ –0–
Accumulated Depreciation—Equipment	–0–
Equipment	7,000
Interest Payable	–0–
Notes Payable	10,000
Prepaid Insurance	2,100
Salaries and Wages Payable	–0–
Supplies	2,450
Unearned Service Revenue	30,000

All the accounts have normal balances. The information below has been gathered at December 31, 2015.

1. Verne Cova Company borrowed $10,000 by signing a 12%, one-year note on September 1, 2015.
2. A count of supplies on December 31, 2015, indicates that supplies of $900 are on hand.
3. Depreciation on the equipment for 2015 is $1,000.
4. Verne Cova Company paid $2,100 for 12 months of insurance coverage on June 1, 2015.
5. On December 1, 2015, Verne Cova collected $30,000 for consulting services to be performed from December 1, 2015, through March 31, 2016.
6. Verne Cova performed consulting services for a client in December 2015. The client will be billed $4,200.
7. Verne Cova Company pays its employees total salaries of $9,000 every Monday for the preceding 5-day week (Monday through Friday). On Monday, December 29, employees were paid for the week ending December 26. All employees worked the last 3 days of 2015.

Instructions
Prepare adjusting entries for the seven items described above.

E3-6 Lei Company accumulates the following adjustment data at December 31.

1. Services performed but not recorded total $1,000.
2. Supplies of $300 have been used.
3. Utility expenses of $225 are unpaid.
4. Services related to unearned service revenue of $260 were performed.
5. Salaries of $800 are unpaid.
6. Prepaid insurance totaling $350 has expired.

Instructions
For each of the above items indicate the following.

(a) The type of adjustment (prepaid expense, unearned revenue, accrued revenue, or accrued expense).
(b) The status of accounts before adjustment (overstatement or understatement).

E3-7 The ledger of Perez Rental Agency on March 31 of the current year includes the selected accounts, shown below, before quarterly adjusting entries have been prepared.

	Debit	Credit
Prepaid Insurance	$ 3,600	
Supplies	2,800	
Equipment	25,000	
Accumulated		
Depreciation—Equipment		$ 8,400
Notes Payable		20,000
Unearned Rent Revenue		10,200
Rent Revenue		60,000
Interest Expense	–0–	
Salaries and Wages Expense	14,000	

An analysis of the accounts shows the following.

1. The equipment depreciates $400 per month.
2. One-third of the unearned rent revenue was earned during the quarter.
3. Interest totaling $500 is accrued on the notes payable for the quarter.
4. Supplies on hand total $900.
5. Insurance expires at the rate of $200 per month.

Instructions
Prepare the adjusting entries at March 31, assuming that adjusting entries are made **quarterly**. Additional accounts are Depreciation Expense, Insurance Expense, Interest Payable, and Supplies Expense.

E3-8 Robin Shalit, D.D.S., opened a dental practice on January 1, 2015. During the first month of operations, the following transactions occurred.

1. Performed services for patients who had dental plan insurance. At January 31, $875 of such services were performed but not yet recorded.
2. Utility expenses incurred but not paid prior to January 31 totaled $650.
3. Purchased dental equipment on January 1 for $80,000, paying $20,000 in cash and signing a $60,000, 3-year note payable. The equipment depreciates $400 per month. Interest is $500 per month.
4. Purchased a one-year malpractice insurance policy on January 1 for $24,000.
5. Purchased $1,600 of dental supplies. On January 31, determined that $400 of supplies were on hand.

Instructions
Prepare the adjusting entries on January 31. Account titles are Accumulated Depreciation—Equipment, Depreciation Expense, Service Revenue, Accounts Receivable, Insurance Expense, Interest Expense, Interest Payable, Prepaid Insurance, Supplies, Supplies Expense, Utilities Expense, and Utilities Payable.

E3-9 The trial balance for Pioneer Advertising Agency Inc. is shown in Illustration 3-3 (page 107). Instead of the adjusting entries shown in the text at October 31, assume the following adjustment data.

Identify types of adjustments and account relationships.
(LO 3, 4, 5)

Prepare adjusting entries from selected account data.
(LO 4, 5)

Prepare adjusting entries.
(LO 4, 5)

Prepare adjusting entries.
(LO 4, 5)

1. Supplies on hand at October 31 total $500.
2. Expired insurance for the month is $100.
3. Depreciation for the month is $50.
4. Services related to unearned service revenue in October worth $600 were performed.
5. Services performed but not recorded at October 31 are $300.
6. Interest accrued at October 31 is $95.
7. Accrued salaries at October 31 are $1,625.

Instructions
Prepare the adjusting entries for the items above.

Prepare correct income statement.

(LO 2, 4, 5, 6)

E3-10 The income statement of Gopitkumar Co. for the month of July shows net income of $1,400 based on Service Revenue $5,500, Salaries and Wages Expense $2,300, Supplies Expense $1,200, and Utilities Expense $600. In reviewing the statement, you discover the following.

1. Insurance expired during July of $400 was omitted.
2. Supplies expense includes $250 of supplies that are still on hand at July 31.
3. Depreciation on equipment of $150 was omitted.
4. Accrued but unpaid salaries and wages at July 31 of $300 were not included.
5. Services performed but unrecorded totaled $650.

Instructions
Prepare a correct income statement for July 2015.

Analyze adjusted data.

(LO 3, 4, 5, 6)

E3-11 A partial adjusted trial balance of Gehring Company at January 31, 2015, shows the following.

GEHRING COMPANY
Adjusted Trial Balance
January 31, 2015

	Debit	Credit
Supplies	$ 850	
Prepaid Insurance	2,400	
Salaries and Wages Payable		$ 800
Unearned Service Revenue		750
Supplies Expense	950	
Insurance Expense	400	
Salaries and Wages Expense	2,900	
Service Revenue		2,000

Instructions
Answer the following questions, assuming the year begins January 1.

(a) If the amount in Supplies Expense is the January 31 adjusting entry, and $1,000 of supplies was purchased in January, what was the balance in Supplies on January 1?
(b) If the amount in Insurance Expense is the January 31 adjusting entry, and the original insurance premium was for one year, what was the total premium and when was the policy purchased?
(c) If $3,500 of salaries was paid in January, what was the balance in Salaries and Wages Payable at December 31, 2014?

Journalize basic transactions and adjusting entries.

(LO 4, 5, 6)

E3-12 Selected accounts of Koffman Company are as follows.

Supplies Expense

7/31	800	

Supplies

7/1 Bal.	1,100	7/31	800
7/10	650		

Salaries and Wages Payable

		7/31	1,200

Accounts Receivable			Unearned Service Revenue		
7/31	500		7/31	1,150	7/1 Bal. 1,500
					7/20 1,000

Salaries and Wages Expense			Service Revenue		
7/15	1,200				7/14 2,000
7/31	1,200				7/31 1,150
					7/31 500

Instructions

After analyzing the accounts, journalize (a) the July transactions and (b) the adjusting entries that were made on July 31. (*Hint:* July transactions were for cash.)

E3-13 The trial balances before and after adjustment for Frinzi Company at the end of its fiscal year are presented below.

Prepare adjusting entries from analysis of trial balances.

(LO 4, 5, 6)

FRINZI COMPANY
Trial Balance
August 31, 2015

	Before Adjustment		After Adjustment	
	Dr.	Cr.	Dr.	Cr.
Cash	$10,400		$10,400	
Accounts Receivable	8,800		10,800	
Supplies	2,300		900	
Prepaid Insurance	4,000		2,500	
Equipment	14,000		14,000	
Accumulated Depreciation—Equipment		$ 3,600		$ 4,500
Accounts Payable		5,800		5,800
Salaries and Wages Payable		–0–		1,100
Unearned Rent Revenue		1,500		600
Common Stock		12,000		12,000
Retained Earnings		3,600		3,600
Service Revenue		34,000		36,000
Rent Revenue		11,000		11,900
Salaries and Wages Expense	17,000		18,100	
Supplies Expense	–0–		1,400	
Rent Expense	15,000		15,000	
Insurance Expense	–0–		1,500	
Depreciation Expense	–0–		900	
	$71,500	$71,500	$75,500	$75,500

Instructions

Prepare the adjusting entries that were made.

E3-14 The adjusted trial balance for Frinzi Company is given in E3-13.

Prepare financial statements from adjusted trial balance.

(LO 6)

Instructions

Prepare the income and retained earnings statements for the year and the balance sheet at August 31.

E3-15 The following data are taken from the comparative balance sheets of Cascade Billiards Club, which prepares its financial statements using the accrual basis of accounting.

Record transactions on accrual basis; convert revenue to cash receipts.

(LO 4, 5)

December 31	2015	2014
Accounts receivable from members	$14,000	$ 9,000
Unearned service revenue	17,000	25,000

Members are billed based upon their use of the club's facilities. Unearned service revenues arise from the sale of gift certificates, which members can apply to their future use of club facilities. The 2015 income statement for the club showed that service revenue of $161,000 was recorded during the year.

Instructions

(*Hint:* You will probably find it helpful to use T-accounts to analyze these data.)

(a) Prepare journal entries for each of the following events that took place during 2015.

    (1) Accounts receivable from 2014 were all collected.

    (2) Gift certificates outstanding at the end of 2014 were all redeemed.

    (3) An additional $38,000 worth of gift certificates were sold during 2015. A portion of these was used by the recipients during the year; the remainder was still outstanding at the end of 2015.

    (4) Services performed for members for 2015 were billed to members.

    (5) Accounts receivable for 2015 (i.e., those billed in item [4] above) were partially collected.

(b) Determine the amount of cash received by the club, with respect to member services, during 2015.

Journalize adjusting entries.
(LO 7)

*E3-16 Aaron Lynch Company has the following balances in selected accounts on December 31, 2015.

Service Revenue	$40,000
Insurance Expense	2,700
Supplies Expense	2,450

All the accounts have normal balances. Aaron Lynch Company debits prepayments to expense accounts when paid, and credits unearned revenues to revenue accounts when received. The following information below has been gathered at December 31, 2015.

1. Aaron Lynch Company paid $2,700 for 12 months of insurance coverage on June 1, 2015.

2. On December 1, 2015, Aaron Lynch Company collected $40,000 for consulting services to be performed from December 1, 2015, through March 31, 2016.

3. A count of supplies on December 31, 2015, indicates that supplies of $900 are on hand.

Instructions

Prepare the adjusting entries needed at December 31, 2015.

Journalize transactions and adjusting entries.
(LO 7)

*E3-17 At Cambridge Company, prepayments are debited to expense when paid, and unearned revenues are credited to revenue when cash is received. During January of the current year, the following transactions occurred.

Jan. 2 Paid $1,920 for fire insurance protection for the year.
     10 Paid $1,700 for supplies.
     15 Received $6,100 for services to be performed in the future.

On January 31, it is determined that $2,500 of the services were performed and that there are $650 of supplies on hand.

Instructions

(a) Journalize and post the January transactions. (Use T-accounts.)

(b) Journalize and post the adjusting entries at January 31.

(c) Determine the ending balance in each of the accounts.

Identify accounting assumptions and principles.
(LO 8)

*E3-18 Presented below are the assumptions and principles discussed in Appendix 3B.

1. Full disclosure principle.   **4.** Time period assumption.

2. Going concern assumption.   **5.** Historical cost principle.

3. Monetary unit assumption.   **6.** Economic entity assumption.

Instructions

Identify by number the accounting assumption or principle that is described below. Do not use a number more than once.

_____ **(a)** Is the rationale for why plant assets are not reported at liquidation value. (*Note:* Do not use the historical cost principle.)

_____ **(b)** Indicates that personal and business record-keeping should be separately maintained.

_____ **(c)** Assumes that the monetary unit is the "measuring stick" used to report on financial performance.

_____ **(d)** Separates financial information into time periods for reporting purposes.

_____ **(e)** Measurement basis used when a reliable estimate of fair value is not available.

_____ **(f)** Dictates that companies should disclose all circumstances and events that make a difference to financial statement users.

*E3-19 Rosman Co. had three major business transactions during 2015.

(a) Reported at its fair value of $260,000 merchandise inventory with a cost of $208,000.

(b) The president of Rosman Co., Jay Rosman, purchased a truck for personal use and charged it to his Salaries and Wages Expense account.

(c) Rosman Co. wanted to make its 2015 income look better, so it added 2 more weeks to the year (a 54-week year). Previous years were 52 weeks.

Identify the assumption or principle that has been violated.

(LO 8)

Instructions

In each situation, identify the assumption or principle that has been violated, if any, and discuss what the company should have done.

*E3-20 The following characteristics, assumptions, principles, or constraint guide the FASB when it creates accounting standards.

Identity financial accounting concepts and principles.

(LO 8)

> Relevance
> Faithful representation
> Comparability
> Consistency
> Monetary unit assumption
> Economic entity assumption
>
> Expense recognition principle
> Time period assumption
> Going concern assumption
> Historical cost principle
> Full disclosure principle
> Materiality

Match each item above with a description below.

1. _____ Ability to easily evaluate one company's results relative to another's.

2. _____ Belief that a company will continue to operate for the foreseeable future.

3. _____ The judgment concerning whether an item's size is large enough to matter to decision-makers.

4. _____ The reporting of all information that would make a difference to financial statement users.

5. _____ The practice of preparing financial statements at regular intervals.

6. _____ The quality of information that indicates the information makes a difference in a decision.

7. _____ A belief that items should be reported on the balance sheet at the price that was paid to acquire them.

8. _____ A company's use of the same accounting principles and methods from year to year.

9. _____ Tracing accounting events to particular companies.

10. _____ The desire to minimize bias in financial statements.

11. _____ Reporting only those things that can be measured in monetary units.

12. _____ Dictates that efforts (expenses) be matched with results (revenues).

*E3-21 Net Nanny Software International Inc., headquartered in Vancouver, Canada, specializes in Internet safety and computer security products for both the home and commercial markets. In a recent balance sheet, it reported a deficit of US$5,678,288. It has reported only net losses since its inception. In spite of these losses, Net Nanny's shares of stock have traded anywhere from a high of $3.70 to a low of $0.32 on the Canadian Venture Exchange.

Comment on the objective and qualitative characteristics of accounting information.

(LO 8)

Net Nanny's financial statements have historically been prepared in Canadian dollars. Recently, the company adopted the U.S. dollar as its reporting currency.

Instructions

(a) What is the objective of financial reporting? How does this objective meet or not meet Net Nanny's investors' needs?

(b) Why would investors want to buy Net Nanny's shares if the company has consistently reported losses over the last few years? Include in your answer an assessment of the relevance of the information reported on Net Nanny's financial statements.

(c) Comment on how the change in reporting information from Canadian dollars to U.S. dollars likely affected the readers of Net Nanny's financial statements. Include in your answer an assessment of the comparability of the information.

Comment on the objective and qualitative characteristics of financial reporting.

(LO 8)

*E3-22 A friend of yours, Ana Gehrig, recently completed an undergraduate degree in science and has just started working with an international biotechnology company. Ana tells you that the owners of the business are trying to secure new sources of financing which are needed in order for the company to proceed with development of a new health-care product. Ana said that her boss told her that the company must put together a report to present to potential investors.

Ana thought that the company should include in this package the detailed scientific findings related to the Phase I clinical trials for this product. She said, "I know that the biotech industry sometimes has only a 10% success rate with new products, but if we report all the scientific findings, everyone will see what a sure success this is going to be! The president was talking about the importance of following some set of accounting principles. Why do we need to look at some accounting rules? What they need to realize is that we have scientific results that are quite encouraging, some of the most talented employees around, and the start of some really great customer relationships. We haven't made any sales yet, but we will. We just need the funds to get through all the clinical testing and get government approval for our product. Then these investors will be quite happy that they bought in to our company early!"

Instructions

(a) What is accounting information?

(b) Comment on how Ana's suggestions for what should be reported to prospective investors conforms to the qualitative characteristics of accounting information. Do you think that the things that Ana wants to include in the information for investors will conform to financial reporting guidelines?

EXERCISES: SET B AND CHALLENGE EXERCISES

Visit the book's companion website, at **www.wiley.com/college/weygandt**, and choose the Student Companion site to access Exercise Set B and Challenge Exercises.

PROBLEMS: SET A

Prepare adjusting entries, post to ledger accounts, and prepare an adjusted trial balance.

(LO 4, 5, 6)

P3-1A Deanna Nardelli started her own consulting firm, Nardelli Consulting, on May 1, 2015. The trial balance at May 31 is as follows.

NARDELLI CONSULTING
Trial Balance
May 31, 2015

Account Number		Debit	Credit
101	Cash	$ 4,500	
112	Accounts Receivable	6,000	
126	Supplies	1,900	
130	Prepaid Insurance	3,600	
149	Equipment	11,400	
201	Accounts Payable		$ 2,200
209	Unearned Service Revenue		2,000
311	Common Stock		20,000
400	Service Revenue		7,500
726	Salaries and Wages Expense	3,400	
729	Rent Expense	900	
		$31,700	$31,700

In addition to those accounts listed on the trial balance, the chart of accounts for Nardelli Consulting also contains the following accounts and account numbers: No. 150 Accumulated Depreciation—Equipment, No. 212 Salaries and Wages Payable, No. 631 Supplies Expense, No. 717 Depreciation Expense, No. 722 Insurance Expense, and No. 732 Utilities Expense.

Other data:

1. $900 of supplies have been used during the month.
2. Utilities expense incurred but not paid on May 31, 2015, $250.
3. The insurance policy is for 2 years.
4. $400 of the balance in the unearned service revenue account remains unearned at the end of the month.
5. May 31 is a Wednesday, and employees are paid on Fridays. Nardelli Consulting has two employees, who are paid $900 each for a 5-day work week.
6. The equipment has a 5-year life with no salvage value. It is being depreciated at $190 per month for 60 months.
7. Invoices representing $1,700 of services performed during the month have not been recorded as of May 31.

Instructions
(a) Prepare the adjusting entries for the month of May. Use J4 as the page number for your journal.
(b) Enter the totals from the trial balance as beginning account balances and place a check mark in the posting reference column. Post the adjusting entries to the ledger accounts.
(c) Prepare an adjusted trial balance at May 31, 2015.

(c) Adj. trial balance $34,920

P3-2A The Skyline Motel opened for business on May 1, 2015. Its trial balance before adjustment on May 31 is as follows.

Prepare adjusting entries, post, and prepare adjusted trial balance and financial statements.
(LO 4, 5, 6)

SKYLINE MOTEL
Trial Balance
May 31, 2015

Account Number		Debit	Credit
101	Cash	$ 3,500	
126	Supplies	2,080	
130	Prepaid Insurance	2,400	
140	Land	12,000	
141	Buildings	60,000	
149	Equipment	15,000	
201	Accounts Payable		$11,180
208	Unearned Rent Revenue		3,300
275	Mortgage Payable		40,000
311	Common Stock		35,000
429	Rent Revenue		10,300
610	Advertising Expense	600	
726	Salaries and Wages Expense	3,300	
732	Utilities Expense	900	
		$99,780	$99,780

In addition to those accounts listed on the trial balance, the chart of accounts for Skyline Motel also contains the following accounts and account numbers: No. 142 Accumulated Depreciation—Buildings, No. 150 Accumulated Depreciation—Equipment, No. 212 Salaries and Wages Payable, No. 230 Interest Payable, No. 619 Depreciation Expense, No. 631 Supplies Expense, No. 718 Interest Expense, and No. 722 Insurance Expense.

Other data:

1. Prepaid insurance is a 1-year policy starting May 1, 2015.
2. A count of supplies shows $750 of unused supplies on May 31.
3. Annual depreciation is $3,000 on the buildings and $1,500 on equipment.

4. The mortgage interest rate is 12%. (The mortgage was taken out on May 1.)
5. Two-thirds of the unearned rent revenue has been earned.
6. Salaries of $750 are accrued and unpaid at May 31.

Instructions
(a) Journalize the adjusting entries on May 31.

(c) Adj. trial balance $101,305
(d) Net income $4,645
   Ending retained earnings
   $4,645
   Total assets $93,075

(b) Prepare a ledger using the three-column form of account. Enter the trial balance amounts and post the adjusting entries. (Use J1 as the posting reference.)
(c) Prepare an adjusted trial balance on May 31.
(d) Prepare an income statement and a retained earnings statement for the month of May and a balance sheet at May 31.

Prepare adjusting entries and financial statements.
(LO 4, 5, 6)

P3-3A Everett Co. was organized on July 1, 2015. Quarterly financial statements are prepared. The unadjusted and adjusted trial balances as of September 30 are shown below.

EVERETT CO.
Trial Balance
September 30, 2015

	Unadjusted		Adjusted	
	Dr.	Cr.	Dr.	Cr.
Cash	$ 8,700		$ 8,700	
Accounts Receivable	10,400		11,500	
Supplies	1,500		650	
Prepaid Rent	2,200		1,200	
Equipment	18,000		18,000	
Accumulated Depreciation—Equipment		$ –0–		$ 700
Notes Payable		10,000		10,000
Accounts Payable		2,500		2,500
Salaries and Wages Payable		–0–		725
Interest Payable		–0–		100
Unearned Rent Revenue		1,900		1,050
Common Stock		22,000		22,000
Dividends	1,600		1,600	
Service Revenue		16,000		17,100
Rent Revenue		1,410		2,260
Salaries and Wages Expense	8,000		8,725	
Rent Expense	1,900		2,900	
Depreciation Expense			700	
Supplies Expense			850	
Utilities Expense	1,510		1,510	
Interest Expense			100	
	$53,810	$53,810	$56,435	$56,435

(b) Net income $4,575
   Ending retained earnings
   $2,975
   Total assets $39,350

Instructions
(a) Journalize the adjusting entries that were made.
(b) Prepare an income statement and a retained earnings statement for the 3 months ending September 30 and a balance sheet at September 30.
(c) If the note bears interest at 12%, how many months has it been outstanding?

Prepare adjusting entries.
(LO 4, 5)

1. Insurance expense $4,890

P3-4A A review of the ledger of Carmel Company at December 31, 2015, produces the following data pertaining to the preparation of annual adjusting entries.

1. Prepaid Insurance $10,440. The company has separate insurance policies on its buildings and its motor vehicles. Policy B4564 on the building was purchased on April 1, 2014, for $7,920. The policy has a term of 3 years. Policy A2958 on the vehicles was purchased on January 1, 2015, for $4,500. This policy has a term of 2 years.

2. Rent revenue $84,000

2. Unearned Rent Revenue $429,000. The company began subleasing office space in its new building on November 1. At December 31, the company had the following rental contracts that are paid in full for the entire term of the lease.

Date	Term (in months)	Monthly Rent	Number of Leases
Nov. 1	9	$5,000	5
Dec. 1	6	$8,500	4

3. Notes Payable $120,000. This balance consists of a note for 9 months at an annual interest rate of 9%, dated November 1.

4. Salaries and Wages Payable $0. There are eight salaried employees. Salaries are paid every Friday for the current week. Five employees receive a salary of $700 each per week, and three employees earn $500 each per week. Assume December 31 is a Tuesday. Employees do not work weekends. All employees worked the last 2 days of December.

3. Interest expense $1,800

4. Salaries and wages expense $2,000

Instructions
Prepare the adjusting entries at December 31, 2015.

P3-5A On November 1, 2015, the account balances of Schilling Equipment Repair were as follows.

Journalize transactions and follow through accounting cycle to preparation of financial statements.

(LO 4, 5, 6)

No.		Debit	No.		Credit
101	Cash	$ 2,400	154	Accumulated Depreciation—Equipment	$ 2,000
112	Accounts Receivable	4,250	201	Accounts Payable	2,600
126	Supplies	1,800	209	Unearned Service Revenue	1,200
153	Equipment	12,000	212	Salaries and Wages Payable	700
			311	Common Stock	10,000
			320	Retained Earnings	3,950
		$20,450			$20,450

During November, the following summary transactions were completed.

Nov. 8	Paid $1,700 for salaries due employees, of which $700 is for October salaries.
10	Received $3,420 cash from customers on account.
12	Received $3,100 cash for services performed in November.
15	Purchased equipment on account $2,000.
17	Purchased supplies on account $700.
20	Paid creditors on account $2,700.
22	Paid November rent $400.
25	Paid salaries $1,700.
27	Performed services on account and billed customers $1,900 for these services.
29	Received $600 from customers for future service.

Adjustment data consist of:

1. Supplies on hand $1,400.
2. Accrued salaries payable $350.
3. Depreciation for the month is $200.
4. Services related to unearned service revenue of $1,250 were performed.

Instructions
(a) Enter the November 1 balances in the ledger accounts.
(b) Journalize the November transactions.
(c) Post to the ledger accounts. Use J1 for the posting reference. Use the following additional accounts: No. 407 Service Revenue, No. 615 Depreciation Expense, No. 631 Supplies Expense, No. 726 Salaries and Wages Expense, and No. 729 Rent Expense.
(d) Prepare a trial balance at November 30.
(e) Journalize and post adjusting entries.
(f) Prepare an adjusted trial balance.
(g) Prepare an income statement and a retained earnings statement for November and a balance sheet at November 30.

(d) Trial balance $25,350
(f) Adj. trial balance $25,900
(g) Net income $1,500
   Ending retained earnings $5,450
   Total assets $18,950

Prepare adjusting entries,
adjusted trial balance, and
financial statements using
Appendix 3A.
(LO 4, 5, 6, 7)

***P3-6A** Sommer Graphics Company was organized on January 1, 2015, by Krystal Sommer. At the end of the first 6 months of operations, the trial balance contained the accounts shown below.

	Debit		Credit
Cash	$ 8,600	Notes Payable	$ 20,000
Accounts Receivable	14,000	Accounts Payable	9,000
Equipment	45,000	Common Stock	22,000
Insurance Expense	2,700	Sales Revenue	52,100
Salaries and Wages Expense	30,000	Service Revenue	6,000
Supplies Expense	3,700		
Advertising Expense	1,900		
Rent Expense	1,500		
Utilities Expense	1,700		
	$109,100		$109,100

Analysis reveals the following additional data.

1. The $3,700 balance in Supplies Expense represents supplies purchased in January. At June 30, $1,500 of supplies are on hand.
2. The note payable was issued on February 1. It is a 9%, 6-month note.
3. The balance in Insurance Expense is the premium on a one-year policy, dated March 1, 2015.
4. Service revenues are credited to revenue when received. At June 30, services revenue of $1,300 are unearned.
5. Revenue for services performed but unrecorded at June 30 totals $2,000.
6. Depreciation is $2,250 per year.

Instructions

(b) Adj. trial balance $112,975
(c) Net income $18,725
   Ending retained earnings
   $18,725
   Total assets $71,775

(a) Journalize the adjusting entries at June 30. (Assume adjustments are recorded every 6 months.)
(b) Prepare an adjusted trial balance.
(c) Prepare an income statement and a retained earnings statement for the 6 months ended June 30 and a balance sheet at June 30.

PROBLEMS: SET B

Prepare adjusting entries,
post to ledger accounts, and
prepare adjusted trial balance.
(LO 4, 5, 6)

P3-1B Jason Elsner started his own consulting firm, Elsner Company, on June 1, 2015. The trial balance at June 30 is shown below.

ELSNER COMPANY
Trial Balance
June 30, 2015

Account Number		Debit	Credit
101	Cash	$ 7,150	
112	Accounts Receivable	6,000	
126	Supplies	2,000	
130	Prepaid Insurance	3,000	
157	Equipment	15,000	
201	Accounts Payable		$ 6,250
209	Unearned Service Revenue		4,000
311	Common Stock		20,000
400	Service Revenue		7,900
726	Salaries and Wages Expense	4,000	
729	Rent Expense	1,000	
		$38,150	$38,150

In addition to those accounts listed on the trial balance, the chart of accounts for Elsner Company also contains the following accounts and account numbers: No. 158 Accumulated Depreciation—Equipment, No. 212 Salaries and Wages Payable, No. 631 Supplies Expense, No. 711 Depreciation Expense, No. 722 Insurance Expense, and No. 732 Utilities Expense.

Other data:

1. Supplies on hand at June 30 are $750.
2. A utility bill for $150 has not been recorded and will not be paid until next month.
3. The insurance policy is for a year.
4. $2,800 of unearned service revenue is recognized for services performed during the month.
5. Salaries of $2,900 are accrued at June 30.
6. The equipment has a 5-year life with no salvage value. It is being depreciated at $250 per month for 60 months.
7. Invoices representing $1,700 of services performed during the month have not been recorded as of June 30.

Instructions
(a) Prepare the adjusting entries for the month of June. Use J3 as the page number for your journal.
(b) Enter the totals from the trial balance as beginning account balances and place a check mark in the posting reference column. Post the adjusting entries to the ledger accounts.
(c) Prepare an adjusted trial balance at June 30, 2015.

(c) Adj. trial balance $43,150

P3-2B Maquoketa River Resort opened for business on June 1 with eight air-conditioned units. Its trial balance before adjustment on August 31 is as follows.

Prepare adjusting entries, post, and prepare adjusted trial balance and financial statements.

(LO 4, 5, 6)

MAQUOKETA RIVER RESORT
Trial Balance
August 31, 2015

Account Number		Debit	Credit
101	Cash	$ 19,600	
126	Supplies	3,300	
130	Prepaid Insurance	6,000	
140	Land	25,000	
143	Buildings	125,000	
149	Equipment	26,000	
201	Accounts Payable		$ 6,500
208	Unearned Rent Revenue		7,400
275	Mortgage Payable		80,000
311	Common Stock		100,000
332	Dividends	5,000	
429	Rent Revenue		80,000
622	Maintenance and Repairs Expense	3,600	
726	Salaries and Wages Expense	51,000	
732	Utilities Expense	9,400	
		$273,900	$273,900

In addition to those accounts listed on the trial balance, the chart of accounts for Maquoketa River Resort also contains the following accounts and account numbers: No. 112 Accounts Receivable, No. 144 Accumulated Depreciation—Buildings, No. 150 Accumulated Depreciation—Equipment, No. 212 Salaries and Wages Payable, No. 230 Interest Payable, No. 620 Depreciation Expense, No. 631 Supplies Expense, No. 718 Interest Expense, and No. 722 Insurance Expense.

Other data:

1. Insurance expires at the rate of $300 per month.
2. A count on August 31 shows $800 of supplies on hand.

3. Annual depreciation is $6,000 on buildings and $2,400 on equipment.
4. Unearned rent revenue of $4,800 was earned prior to August 31.
5. Salaries of $400 were unpaid at August 31.
6. Rentals of $4,000 were due from tenants at August 31. (Use Accounts Receivable.)
7. The mortgage interest rate is 9% per year. (The mortgage was taken out on August 1.)

Instructions

(c) Adj. trial balance $281,000
(d) Net income $18,300
Ending retained earnings
$13,300
Total assets $203,400

(a) Journalize the adjusting entries on August 31 for the 3-month period June 1–August 31.
(b) Prepare a ledger using the three-column form of account. Enter the trial balance amounts and post the adjusting entries. (Use J1 as the posting reference.)
(c) Prepare an adjusted trial balance on August 31.
(d) Prepare an income statement and a retained earnings statement for the 3 months ending August 31 and a balance sheet as of August 31.

Prepare adjusting entries and financial statements.

(LO 4, 5, 6)

P3-3B Delgado Advertising Agency was founded by Maria Delgado in January of 2014. Presented below are both the adjusted and unadjusted trial balances as of December 31, 2015.

DELGADO ADVERTISING AGENCY
Trial Balance
December 31, 2015

	Unadjusted		Adjusted	
	Dr.	**Cr.**	**Dr.**	**Cr.**
Cash	$ 11,000		$ 11,000	
Accounts Receivable	20,000		23,500	
Supplies	8,600		4,800	
Prepaid Insurance	3,350		2,500	
Equipment	60,000		60,000	
Accumulated Depreciation—Equipment		$ 28,000		$ 32,000
Accounts Payable		5,000		5,000
Interest Payable		–0–		150
Notes Payable		5,000		5,000
Unearned Service Revenue		7,200		5,900
Salaries and Wages Payable		–0–		2,100
Common Stock		20,000		20,000
Retained Earnings		5,500		5,500
Dividends	12,000		12,000	
Service Revenue		58,600		63,400
Salaries and Wages Expense	10,000		12,100	
Insurance Expense			850	
Interest Expense	350		500	
Depreciation Expense			4,000	
Supplies Expense			3,800	
Rent Expense	4,000		4,000	
	$129,300	$129,300	$139,050	$139,050

Instructions

(b) Net income $38,150
Ending retained earnings
$31,650
Total assets $69,800

(c) (1) 6%
(2) $2,500

(a) Journalize the annual adjusting entries that were made.
(b) Prepare an income statement and a retained earnings statement for the year ending December 31, 2015, and a balance sheet at December 31.
(c) Answer the following questions.
 (1) If the note has been outstanding 6 months, what is the annual interest rate on that note?
 (2) If the company paid $12,500 in salaries in 2015, what was the balance in Salaries and Wages Payable on December 31, 2014?

Preparing adjusting entries.

(LO 4, 5)

1. Salaries and wages expense
$2,640

P3-4B A review of the ledger of Almquist Company at December 31, 2015, produces the following data pertaining to the preparation of annual adjusting entries.

1. Salaries and Wages Payable $0. There are eight salaried employees. Salaries are paid every Friday for the current week. Five employees receive a salary of $900 each

per week, and three employees earn $700 each per week. Assume December 31 is a Tuesday. Employees do not work weekends. All employees worked the last 2 days of December.

2. Unearned Rent Revenue $354,000. The company began subleasing office space in its new building on November 1. At December 31, the company had the following rental contracts that are paid in full for the entire term of the lease.

Date	Term (in months)	Monthly Rent	Number of Leases
Nov. 1	6	$5,000	5
Dec. 1	6	$8,500	4

2. Rent revenue $84,000

3. Prepaid Advertising $15,600. This balance consists of payments on two advertising contracts. The contracts provide for monthly advertising in two trade magazines. The terms of the contracts are as follows.

Contract	Date	Amount	Number of Magazine Issues
A650	May 1	$6,000	12
B974	Oct. 1	9,600	24

3. Advertising expense $5,200

The first advertisement runs in the month in which the contract is signed.

4. Notes Payable $120,000. This balance consists of a note for one year at an annual interest rate of 9%, dated June 1.

4. Interest expense $6,300

Instructions

Prepare the adjusting entries at December 31, 2015. (Show all computations.)

P3-5B On September 1, 2015, the account balances of Percy Equipment Repair were as follows.

Journalize transactions and follow through accounting cycle to preparation of financial statements.

(LO 4, 5, 6)

No.		Debit	No.		Credit
101	Cash	$ 4,880	154	Accumulated Depreciation—Equipment	$ 1,500
112	Accounts Receivable	3,520	201	Accounts Payable	3,400
126	Supplies	2,000	209	Unearned Service Revenue	1,400
153	Equipment	15,000	212	Salaries and Wages Payable	500
			311	Common Stock	10,000
			320	Retained Earnings	8,600
		$25,400			$25,400

During September, the following summary transactions were completed.

Sept. 8 Paid $1,400 for salaries due employees, of which $900 is for September.
10 Received $1,200 cash from customers on account.
12 Received $3,400 cash for services performed in September.
15 Purchased store equipment on account $3,000.
17 Purchased supplies on account $1,200.
20 Paid creditors $4,500 on account.
22 Paid September rent $500.
25 Paid salaries $1,750.
27 Performed services on account and billed customers $4,100 for these services.
29 Received $650 from customers for future service.

Adjustment data consist of:

1. Supplies on hand $1,300.
2. Accrued salaries payable $300.
3. Depreciation is $100 per month.
4. Services related to unearned service revenue of $1,450 were performed.

Instructions

(a) Enter the September 1 balances in the ledger accounts.
(b) Journalize the September transactions.
(c) Post to the ledger accounts. Use J1 for the posting reference. Use the following additional accounts: No. 407 Service Revenue, No. 615 Depreciation Expense, No. 631 Supplies Expense, No. 726 Salaries and Wages Expense, and No. 729 Rent Expense.
(d) Prepare a trial balance at September 30.
(e) Journalize and post adjusting entries.
(f) Prepare an adjusted trial balance.
(g) Prepare an income statement and a retained earnings statement for September and a balance sheet at September 30.

(d) Trial balance $32,750
(f) Adj. trial balance $33,150
(g) Net income $3,500
   Ending retained
   earnings $12,100
   Total assets $26,100

PROBLEMS: SET C

Visit the book's companion website, at **www.wiley.com/college/weygandt**, and choose the Student Companion site to access Problem Set C.

CONTINUING COOKIE CHRONICLE

(*Note:* This is a continuation of the Cookie Chronicle from Chapters 1 and 2.)

CCC3 It is the end of November and Natalie has been in touch with her grandmother. Her grandmother asked Natalie how well things went in her first month of business. Natalie, too, would like to know if she has been profitable or not during November. Natalie realizes that in order to determine Cookie Creations' income, she must first make adjustments.

Go to the book's companion website, **www.wiley.com/college/weygandt**, *to see the completion of this problem.*

Broadening Your **PERSPECTIVE**

Financial Reporting and Analysis

Financial Reporting Problem: Apple Inc.

BYP3-1 The financial statements of Apple Inc. are presented in Appendix A at the end of this textbook. Instructions for accessing and using the company's complete annual report, including the notes to the financial statements, are also provided in Appendix A.

Instructions

(a) Using the consolidated financial statements and related information, identify items that may result in adjusting entries for prepayments.

(b) Using the consolidated financial statements and related information, identify items that may result in adjusting entries for accruals.

(c) What has been the trend since 2009 for net income?

Comparative Analysis Problem:
PepsiCo, Inc. vs. The Coca-Cola Company

BYP3-2 PepsiCo's financial statements are presented in Appendix B. Financial statements for The Coca-Cola Company are presented in Appendix C. Instructions for accessing and using the complete annual reports of PepsiCo and Coca-Cola, including the notes to the financial statements, are also provided in Appendices B and C, respectively.

Instructions
Based on information contained in these financial statements, determine the following for each company.

(a) Net increase (decrease) in property, plant, and equipment (net) from 2010 to 2011.

(b) Increase (decrease) in selling, general, and administrative expenses from 2010 to 2011.

(c) Increase (decrease) in long-term debt (obligations) from 2010 to 2011.

(d) Increase (decrease) in net income from 2010 to 2011.

(e) Increase (decrease) in cash and cash equivalents from 2010 to 2011.

Comparative Analysis Problem:
Amazon.com, Inc. vs. Wal-Mart Stores, Inc.

BYP3-3 Amazon.com, Inc.'s financial statements are presented in Appendix D. Financial statements for Wal-Mart Stores, Inc. are presented in Appendix E. Instructions for accessing and using the complete annual reports of Amazon and Wal-Mart, including the notes to the financial statements, are also provided in Appendices D and E, respectively.

Instructions
Based on information contained in these financial statements, determine the following for each company.

1. (a) Increase (decrease) in interest expense from 2010 to 2011.

   (b) Increase (decrease) in net income from 2010 to 2011.

   (c) Increase (decrease) in cash flow from operations from 2010 to 2011.

2. Cash flow from operations and net income for each company is different. What are some possible reasons for these differences?

Real-World Focus

BYP3-4 No financial decision-maker should ever rely solely on the financial information reported in the annual report to make decisions. It is important to keep abreast of financial news. This activity demonstrates how to search for financial news on the Internet.

Address: **http://biz.yahoo.com/i**, or go to **www.wiley.com/college/weygandt**

Steps:
1. Type in either Wal-Mart, Target Corp., or Kmart.
2. Choose **News**.
3. Select an article that sounds interesting to you and that would be relevant to an investor in these companies.

Instructions
(a) What was the source of the article (e.g., Reuters, Businesswire, Prnewswire)?

(b) Assume that you are a personal financial planner and that one of your clients owns stock in the company. Write a brief memo to your client summarizing the article and explaining the implications of the article for their investment.

BYP3-5 The July 6, 2011, edition of the *Wall Street Journal Online* includes an article by Michael Rapoport entitled "U.S. Firms Clash Over Accounting Rules." The article discusses why some U.S. companies favored adoption of International Financial Reporting Standards (**IFRS**) while other companies opposed it.

Instructions
Read the article and answer the following questions.

(a) The articles says that the switch to IFRS tends to be favored by "larger companies, big accounting firms, and rule makers." What reasons are given for favoring the switch?
(b) What two reasons are given by many smaller companies that oppose the switch?
(c) What criticism of IFRS is raised with regard to regulated companies?
(d) Explain what is meant by "condorsement."

Critical Thinking

Decision-Making Across the Organization

BYP3-6 Happy Camper Park, Inc. was organized on April 1, 2014, by Barbara Evans. Barbara is a good manager but a poor accountant. From the trial balance prepared by a part-time bookkeeper, Barbara prepared the following income statement for the quarter that ended March 31, 2015.

HAPPY CAMPER PARK, INC.
Income Statement
For the Quarter Ended March 31, 2015

Revenues		
Rent revenue		$90,000
Operating expenses		
Advertising	$ 5,200	
Salaries and wages	29,800	
Utilities	900	
Depreciation	800	
Maintenance and repairs	4,000	
Total operating expenses		40,700
Net income		$49,300

Barbara thought that something was wrong with the statement because net income had never exceeded $20,000 in any one quarter. Knowing that you are an experienced accountant, she asks you to review the income statement and other data.

You first look at the trial balance. In addition to the account balances reported above in the income statement, the ledger contains the following additional selected balances at March 31, 2015.

Supplies	$ 6,200
Prepaid Insurance	7,200
Notes Payable	12,000

You then make inquiries and discover the following.

1. Rent revenues include advanced rentals for summer occupancy $15,000.
2. There were $1,700 of supplies on hand at March 31.
3. Prepaid insurance resulted from the payment of a one-year policy on January 1, 2015.
4. The mail on April 1, 2015, brought the following bills: advertising for week of March 24, $110; repairs made March 10, $260; and utilities, $180.
5. There are four employees, who receive wages totaling $300 per day. At March 31, 2 days' salaries and wages have been incurred but not paid.
6. The note payable is a 3-month, 10% note dated January 1, 2015.

Instructions

With the class divided into groups, answer the following.

(a) Prepare a correct income statement for the quarter ended March 31, 2015.

(b) Explain to Barbara the generally accepted accounting principles that she did not recognize in preparing her income statement and their effect on her results.

Communication Activity

BYP3-7 In reviewing the accounts of Gloria Jean Co. at the end of the year, you discover that adjusting entries have not been made.

Instructions

Write a memo to Gloria Jean Hall, the owner of Gloria Jean Co., that explains the following: the nature and purpose of adjusting entries, why adjusting entries are needed, and the types of adjusting entries that may be made.

Ethics Case

BYP3-8 Kellner Company is a pesticide manufacturer. Its sales declined greatly this year due to the passage of legislation outlawing the sale of several of Kellner's chemical pesticides. In the coming year, Kellner will have environmentally safe and competitive chemicals to replace these discontinued products. Sales in the next year are expected to greatly exceed any prior year's. The decline in sales and profits appears to be a one-year aberration. But even so, the company president fears a large dip in the current year's profits. He believes that such a dip could cause a significant drop in the market price of Kellner's stock and make the company a takeover target.

To avoid this possibility, the company president calls in Melissa Ray, controller, to discuss this period's year-end adjusting entries. He urges her to accrue every possible revenue and to defer as many expenses as possible. He says to Melissa, "We need the revenues this year, and next year can easily absorb expenses deferred from this year. We can't let our stock price be hammered down!" Melissa didn't get around to recording the adjusting entries until January 17, but she dated the entries December 31 as if they were recorded then. Melissa also made every effort to comply with the president's request.

Instructions

(a) Who are the stakeholders in this situation?

(b) What are the ethical considerations of (1) the president's request and (2) Melissa dating the adjusting entries December 31?

(c) Can Melissa accrue revenues and defer expenses and still be ethical?

All About You

BYP3-9 Companies must report or disclose in their financial statements information about all liabilities, including potential liabilities related to environmental cleanup. There are many situations in which you will be asked to provide personal financial information about your assets, liabilities, revenue, and expenses. Sometimes you will face difficult decisions regarding what to disclose and how to disclose it.

Instructions

Suppose that you are putting together a loan application to purchase a home. Based on your income and assets, you qualify for the mortgage loan, but just barely. How would you address each of the following situations in reporting your financial position for the loan application? Provide responses for each of the following situations.

(a) You signed a guarantee for a bank loan that a friend took out for $20,000. If your friend doesn't pay, you will have to pay. Your friend has made all of the payments so far, and it appears he will be able to pay in the future.

(b) You were involved in an auto accident in which you were at fault. There is the possibility that you may have to pay as much as $50,000 as part of a settlement. The issue will not be resolved before the bank processes your mortgage request.

(c) The company for which you work isn't doing very well, and it has recently laid off employees. You are still employed, but it is quite possible that you will lose your job in the next few months.

Considering People, Planet, and Profit

BYP3-10 Many companies have potential pollution or environmental-disposal problems—not only for electronic gadgets, but also for the lead paint or asbestos they sold. How do we fit these issues into the accounting equation? Are these costs and related liabilities that companies should report?

YES: As more states impose laws holding companies responsible, and as more courts levy pollution-related fines, it becomes increasingly likely that companies will have to pay large amounts in the future.

NO: The amounts still are too difficult to estimate. Putting inaccurate estimates on the financial statements reduces their usefulness. Instead, why not charge the costs later, when the actual environmental cleanup or disposal occurs, at which time the company knows the actual cost?

Instructions

Write a response indicating your position regarding this situation. Provide support for your view.

FASB Codification Activity

BYP3-11 If your school has a subscription to the FASB Codification, go to **http://aaahq.org/asclogin.cfm** to log in and prepare responses to the following.

Instructions

Access the glossary ("Master Glossary") to answer the following.

(a) What is the definition of revenue?
(b) What is the definition of compensation?

Answers to Chapter Questions

Answers to Insight and Accounting Across the Organization Questions

p. 106 Cooking the Books? Q: What motivates sales executives and finance and accounting executives to participate in activities that result in inaccurate reporting of revenues? **A:** Sales executives typically receive bonuses based on their ability to meet quarterly sales targets. In addition, they often face the possibility of losing their jobs if they miss those targets. Executives in accounting and finance are very aware of the earnings targets of Wall Street analysts and investors. If they fail to meet these targets, the company's stock price will fall. As a result of these pressures, executives sometimes knowingly engage in unethical efforts to misstate revenues. As a result of the Sarbanes-Oxley Act, the penalties for such behavior are now much more severe.

p. 113 Turning Gift Cards into Revenue Q: Suppose that Robert Jones purchases a $100 gift card at Best Buy on December 24, 2014, and gives it to his wife, Mary Jones, on December 25, 2014. On January 3, 2015, Mary uses the card to purchase $100 worth of CDs. When do you think Best Buy should recognize revenue and why? **A:** According to the revenue recognition principle, companies should recognize revenue when the performance obligation is satisfied. In this case, revenue results when Best Buy provides the goods. Thus, when Best Buy receives cash in exchange for the gift card on December 24, 2014, it should recognize a liability, Unearned Sales Revenue, for $100. On January 3, 2015, when Mary Jones exchanges the card for merchandise, Best Buy should recognize revenue and eliminate $100 from the balance in the Unearned Sales Revenue account.

p. 118 Cashing In on Accrual Accounting   Q: Accrual accounting is often considered superior to cash accounting. Why, then, were some people critical of China's use of accrual accounting in this instance? **A:** In this case, some people were critical because, in general, China uses cash accounting. By switching to accrual accounting for this transaction, China was not being consistent in its accounting practices. Lack of consistency reduces the transparency and usefulness of accounting information.

p. 120 Got Junk?   Q: What accounting issue might this cause for companies? **A:** The balance sheet should provide a fair representation of what a company owns and what it owes. If significant obligations of the company are not reported on the balance sheet, the company's net worth (its equity) will be overstated. While it is true that it is not possible to estimate the **exact** amount of future environmental cleanup costs, it is becoming clear that companies will be held accountable. Therefore, it seems reasonable to accrue for environmental costs. Recognition of these liabilities provides a more accurate picture of the company's financial position. It also has the potential to improve the environment. As companies are forced to report these amounts on their financial statements, they will start to look for more effective and efficient means to reduce toxic waste and therefore reduce their costs.

Answers to Self-Test Questions

1. a **2.** c **3.** d **4.** a **5.** d **6.** d **7.** c ($1,350 − $600) **8.** c **9.** a **10.** c **11.** a **12.** b **13.** b **14.** c ***15.** a ***16.** c ***17.** c

 # A Look at IFRS

It is often difficult for companies to determine in what time period they should report particular revenues and expenses. Both the IASB and FASB are working on a joint project to develop a common conceptual framework that will enable companies to better use the same principles to record transactions consistently over time.

LEARNING OBJECTIVE	9

Compare the procedures for adjusting entries under GAAP and IFRS.

Key Points

- In this chapter, you learned accrual-basis accounting applied under GAAP. Companies applying IFRS also use accrual-basis accounting to ensure that they record transactions that change a company's financial statements in the period in which events occur.

- Similar to GAAP, cash-basis accounting is not in accordance with IFRS.

- IFRS also divides the economic life of companies into artificial time periods. Under both GAAP and IFRS, this is referred to as the **time period assumption**.

- IFRS requires that companies present a complete set of financial statements, including comparative information, annually.

- The **general** revenue recognition principle required by GAAP that is used in this textbook is similar to that used under IFRS.

- Revenue recognition fraud is a major issue in U.S. financial reporting. The same situation occurs in other countries, as evidenced by revenue recognition breakdowns at Dutch software company Baan NV, Japanese electronics giant NEC, and Dutch grocer Ahold NV.

- Under IFRS, revaluation (using fair value) of items such as land and buildings is permitted. IFRS allows depreciation based on revaluation of assets, which is not permitted under GAAP.

- The terminology used for revenues and gains, and expenses and losses, differs somewhat between IFRS and GAAP. For example, income under IFRS is defined as:

    Increases in economic benefits during the accounting period in the form of inflows or enhancements of assets or decreases of liabilities that result in increases in equity, other than those relating to contributions from shareholders.

Income includes both revenues, which arise during the normal course of operating activities, and gains, which arise from activities outside of the normal sales of goods and services. The term income is not used this way under GAAP. Instead, under GAAP income refers to the net difference between revenues and expenses. Expenses under IFRS are defined as:

    Decreases in economic benefits during the accounting period in the form of outflows or depletions of assets or incurrences of liabilities that result in decreases in equity other than those relating to distributions to shareholders.

Note that under IFRS, expenses include both those costs incurred in the normal course of operations as well as losses that are not part of normal operations. This is in contrast to GAAP, which defines each separately.

Looking to the Future

The IASB and FASB are completing a joint project on revenue recognition. The purpose of this project is to develop comprehensive guidance on when to recognize revenue. It is hoped that this approach will lead to more consistent accounting in this area. For more on this topic, see **www.fasb.org/project/revenue_recognition.shtml**.

IFRS Practice

IFRS Self-Test Questions

1. IFRS:
   (a) uses accrual accounting.
   (b) uses cash-basis accounting.
   (c) allows revenue to be recognized when a customer makes an order.
   (d) requires that revenue not be recognized until cash is received.

2. Which of the following statements is **false**?
   (a) IFRS employs the time period assumption.
   (b) IFRS employs accrual accounting.
   (c) IFRS requires that revenues and costs must be capable of being measured reliably.
   (d) IFRS uses the cash basis of accounting.

3. As a result of the revenue recognition project by the FASB and IASB:
   (a) revenue recognition places more emphasis on when the performance obligation is satisfied.
   (b) revenue recognition places more emphasis on when revenue is realized.
   (c) revenue recognition places more emphasis on when expenses are incurred.
   (d) revenue is no longer recorded unless cash has been received.

4. Which of the following is **false**?
   (a) Under IFRS, the term income describes both revenues and gains.
   (b) Under IFRS, the term expenses includes losses.
   (c) Under IFRS, companies do not engage in the adjusting process.
   (d) Under IFRS, revenue recognition fraud is a major issue.

5. Accrual-basis accounting:
   (a) is optional under IFRS.
   (b) results in companies recording transactions that change a company's financial statements in the period in which events occur.
   (c) has been eliminated as a result of the IASB/FASB joint project on revenue recognition.
   (d) is not consistent with the IASB conceptual framework.

IFRS Exercises

IFRS3-1 Compare and contrast the rules regarding revenue recognition under IFRS versus GAAP.

IFRS3-2 Under IFRS, do the definitions of revenues and expenses include gains and losses? Explain.

International Financial Reporting Problem: Zetar plc

IFRS3-3 The financial statements of Zetar plc are presented in Appendix F. Instructions for accessing and using the company's complete annual report, including the notes to its financial statements, are also provided in Appendix F.

Instructions

Visit Zetar's corporate website and answer the following questions from Zetar's 2011 annual report.

(a) From the notes to the financial statements, how does the company determine the amount of revenue to record at the time of a sale?

(b) From the notes to the financial statements, how does the company determine whether a sale has occurred?

(c) Using the consolidated income statement and consolidated statement of financial position, identify items that may result in adjusting entries for deferrals.

(d) Using the consolidated income statement, identify two items that may result in adjusting entries for accruals.

Answers to IFRS Self-Test Questions
1. a   2. d   3. a   4. c   5. b

 ✔ **The Navigator**

✔ Remember to go back to The Navigator box on the chapter opening page and check off your completed work.

4 | Completing the Accounting Cycle

Everyone Likes to Win

When Ted Castle was a hockey coach at the University of Vermont, his players were self-motivated by their desire to win. Hockey was a game you usually either won or lost. But at Rhino Foods, Inc., a bakery-foods company he founded in Burlington, Vermont, he discovered that manufacturing-line workers were not so self-motivated. Ted thought, what if he turned the food-making business into a game, with rules, strategies, and trophies?

In a game, knowing the score is all-important. Ted felt that only if the employees know the score—know exactly how the business is doing daily, weekly, monthly— could he turn food-making into a game. But Rhino is a closely held, family-owned business, and its financial statements and profits were confidential. Ted wondered, should he open Rhino's books to the employees?

A consultant put Ted's concerns in perspective when he said, "Imagine you're playing touch football. You play for an hour or two, and the whole time I'm sitting there with a book, keeping score. All of a sudden I blow the

whistle, and I say, 'OK, that's it. Everybody go home.' I close my book and walk away. How would you feel?" Ted opened his books and revealed the financial statements to his employees.

The next step was to teach employees the rules and strategies of how to "win" at making food. The first lesson: "Your opponent at Rhino is expenses. You must cut and control expenses." Ted and his staff distilled those lessons into daily scorecards—production reports and income statements—that keep Rhino's employees up-to-date on the game. At noon each day, Ted posts the previous day's results at the entrance to the production room. Everyone checks whether they made or lost money on what they produced the day before. And it's not just an academic exercise: There's a bonus check for each employee at the end of every four-week "game" that meets profitability guidelines.

Rhino has flourished since the first game. Employment has increased from 20 to 130 people, while both revenues and profits have grown dramatically.

- ■ Scan Learning Objectives
- ■ Read Feature Story
- ■ Read Preview
- ■ Read text and answer **DO IT!** p. 171
  - ■ p. 176   ■ p. 185   ■ p. 187
- ■ Work Comprehensive **DO IT!** p. 188
- ■ Review Summary of Learning Objectives
- ■ Answer Self-Test Questions
- ■ Complete Assignments
- ■ Go to *WileyPLUS* for practice and tutorials
- Read **A Look at IFRS** p. 215

Learning Objectives ✔ The Navigator

After studying this chapter, you should be able to:

[1] Prepare a worksheet.

[2] Explain the process of closing the books.

[3] Describe the content and purpose of a post-closing trial balance.

[4] State the required steps in the accounting cycle.

[5] Explain the approaches to preparing correcting entries.

[6] Identify the sections of a classified balance sheet.

Comstock/Getty Images, Inc.

Preview of Chapter 4

 The Navigator

At Rhino Foods, Inc., financial statements help employees understand what is happening in the business. In Chapter 3, we prepared financial statements directly from the adjusted trial balance. However, with so many details involved in the end-of-period accounting procedures, it is easy to make errors. One way to minimize errors in the records and to simplify the end-of-period procedures is to use a worksheet.

In this chapter, we will explain the role of the worksheet in accounting. We also will study the remaining steps in the accounting cycle, especially the closing process, again using Pioneer Advertising Agency Inc. as an example. Then we will consider correcting entries and classified balance sheets. The content and organization of Chapter 4 are as follows.

COMPLETING THE ACCOUNTING CYCLE

Using a Worksheet	Closing the Books	Summary of the Accounting Cycle	Classified Balance Sheet
• Steps in preparation • Preparing financial statements • Preparing adjusting entries	• Preparing closing entries • Posting closing entries • Preparing a post-closing trial balance	• Reversing entries—An optional step • Correcting entries—An avoidable step	• Current assets • Long-term investments • Property, plant, and equipment • Intangible assets • Current liabilities • Long-term liabilities • Stockholders' equity

Using a Worksheet

LEARNING OBJECTIVE   **1**

Prepare a worksheet.

A **worksheet** is a multiple-column form used in the adjustment process and in preparing financial statements. As its name suggests, the worksheet is a working tool. **It is not a permanent accounting record.** It is neither a journal nor a part of the general ledger. The worksheet is merely a device used in preparing adjusting entries and the financial statements. Companies generally computerize worksheets using an electronic spreadsheet program such as Excel.

Illustration 4-1 shows the basic form of a worksheet and the five steps for preparing it. Each step is performed in sequence. **The use of a worksheet is optional.** When a company chooses to use one, it prepares financial statements directly from the worksheet. It enters the adjustments in the worksheet columns and then journalizes and posts the adjustments after it has prepared the financial statements. Thus, worksheets make it possible to provide the financial statements to management and other interested parties at an earlier date.

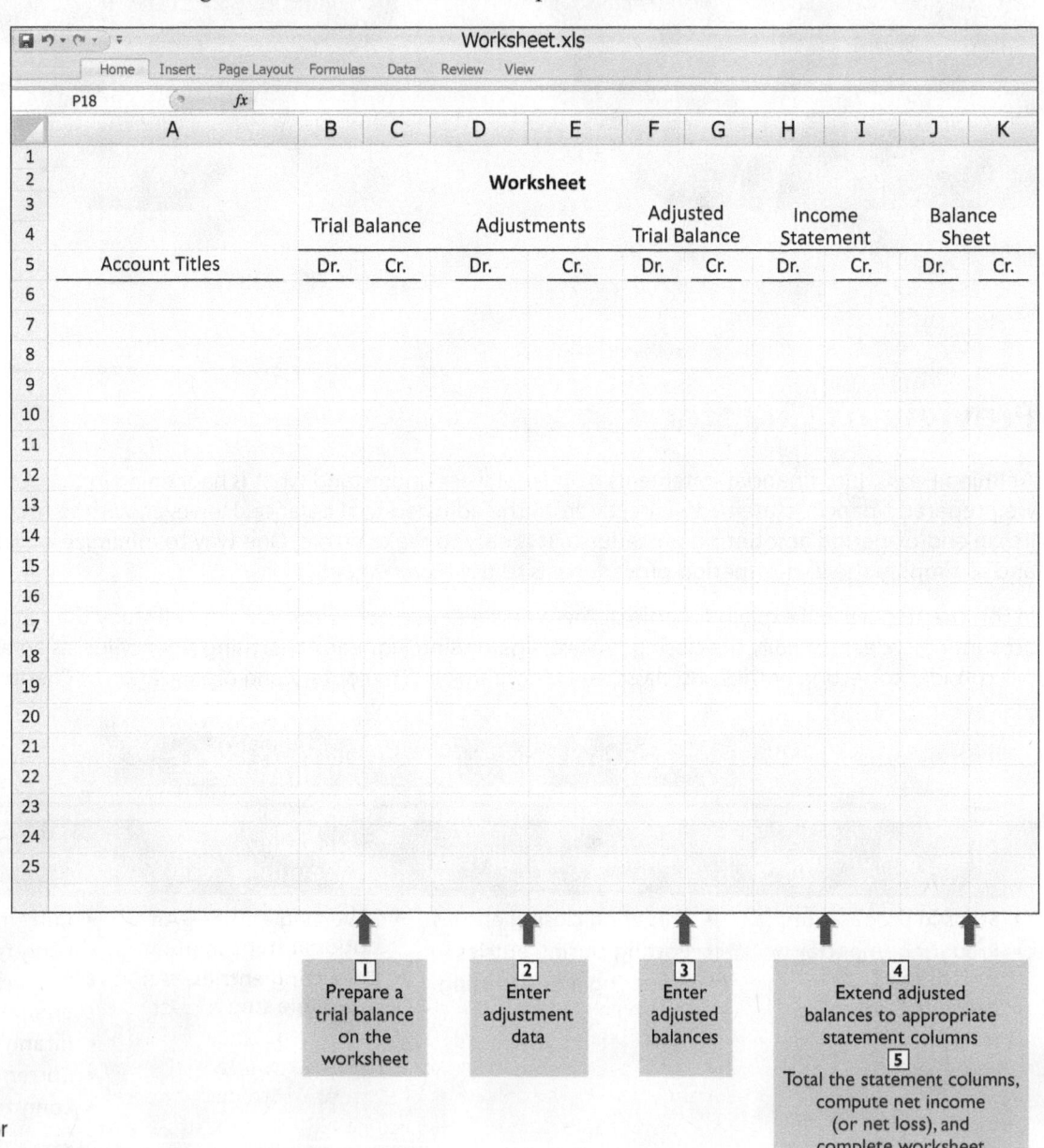

Illustration 4-1
Form and procedure for a worksheet

Steps in Preparing a Worksheet

We will use the October 31 trial balance and adjustment data of Pioneer Advertising Agency Inc. from Chapter 3 to illustrate how to prepare a worksheet. We describe each step of the process and demonstrate these steps in Illustration 4-2 (page 168).

STEP 1. PREPARE A TRIAL BALANCE ON THE WORKSHEET

Enter all ledger accounts with balances in the account titles column. Enter debit and credit amounts from the ledger in the trial balance columns. Illustration 4-2 shows the worksheet trial balance for Pioneer Advertising Agency Inc. This trial balance is the same one that appears in Illustration 2-32 (page 76) and Illustration 3-3 (page 107).

STEP 2. ENTER THE ADJUSTMENTS IN THE ADJUSTMENTS COLUMNS

When using a worksheet, enter all adjustments in the adjustments columns. In entering the adjustments, use applicable trial balance accounts. If additional accounts are needed, insert them on the lines immediately below the trial balance totals. A different letter identifies the debit and credit for each adjusting entry. The term used to describe this process is **keying. Companies do not journalize the adjustments until after they complete the worksheet and prepare the financial statements.**

The adjustments for Pioneer Advertising Agency Inc. are the same as the adjustments in Illustration 3-23 (page 121). They are keyed in the adjustments columns of the worksheet as follows.

(a) Pioneer debits an additional account, Supplies Expense, $1,500 for the cost of supplies used, and credits Supplies $1,500.

(b) Pioneer debits an additional account, Insurance Expense, $50 for the insurance that has expired, and credits Prepaid Insurance $50.

(c) The company needs two additional depreciation accounts. It debits Depreciation Expense $40 for the month's depreciation, and credits Accumulated Depreciation—Equipment $40.

(d) Pioneer debits Unearned Service Revenue $400 for services performed, and credits Service Revenue $400.

(e) Pioneer debits an additional account, Accounts Receivable, $200 for services performed but not billed, and credits Service Revenue $200.

(f) The company needs two additional accounts relating to interest. It debits Interest Expense $50 for accrued interest, and credits Interest Payable $50.

(g) Pioneer debits Salaries and Wages Expense $1,200 for accrued salaries, and credits an additional account, Salaries and Wages Payable, $1,200.

After Pioneer has entered all the adjustments, the adjustments columns are totaled to prove their equality. (See the yellow-shaded area in Illustration 4-2.)

STEP 3. ENTER ADJUSTED BALANCES IN THE ADJUSTED TRIAL BALANCE COLUMNS

Pioneer determines the adjusted balance of an account by combining the amounts entered in the first four columns of the worksheet for each account. For example, the Prepaid Insurance account in the trial balance columns has a $600 debit balance and a $50 credit in the adjustments columns. The result is a $550 debit balance recorded in the adjusted trial balance columns. **For each account, the amount in the adjusted trial balance columns is the balance that will appear in the ledger after journalizing and posting the adjusting entries.** The balances in these columns are the same as those in the adjusted trial balance in Illustration 3-25 (page 123).

Illustration 4-2

Preparing a trial balance

	Home	Insert	Page Layout	Formulas	Data	Review	View

P18   fx

PIONEER ADVERTISING AGENCY INC.
Worksheet
For the Month Ended October 31, 2015

Account Titles	Trial Balance Dr.	Trial Balance Cr.	Adjustments Dr.		Adjustments Cr.		Adjusted Trial Balance Dr.	Adjusted Trial Balance Cr.	Income Statement Dr.	Income Statement Cr.	Balance Sheet Dr.	Balance Sheet Cr.
Cash	15,200						15,200				15,200	
Supplies	2,500				(a)	1,500	1,000				1,000	
Prepaid Insurance	600				(b)	50	550				550	
Equipment	5,000						5,000				5,000	
Notes Payable		5,000						5,000				5,000
Accounts Payable		2,500						2,500				2,500
Unearned Service Revenue		1,200	(d)	400				800				800
Common Stock		10,000						10,000				10,000
Dividends	500						500				500	
Service Revenue		10,000			(d)	400		10,600		10,600		
					(e)	200						
Salaries and Wages Expense	4,000		(g)	1,200			5,200		5,200			
Rent Expense	900						900		900			
Totals	28,700	28,700										
Supplies Expense			(a)	1,500			1,500		1,500			
Insurance Expense			(b)	50			50		50			
Accum. Depreciation—												
Equipment					(c)	40		40				40
Depreciation Expense			(c)	40			40		40			
Accounts Receivable			(e)	200			200				200	
Interest Expense			(f)	50			50		50			
Interest Payable					(f)	50		50				50
Salaries and Wages Payable					(g)	1,200		1,200				1,200
Totals			3,440		3,440		30,190	30,190	7,740	10,600	22,450	19,590
Net Income									2,860			2,860
Totals									10,600	10,600	22,450	22,450

Add additional accounts as needed to complete the adjustments:

(a) Supplies Used.
(b) Insurance Expired.
(c) Depreciation Expensed.
(d) Service Revenue Recognized.
(e) Service Revenue Accrued.
(f) Interest Accrued.
(g) Salaries Accrued.

The difference between the totals of the two income statement columns determines net income or net loss.

Net income is extended to the credit column of the balance sheet columns. (Net loss would be extended to the debit column.)

After Pioneer has entered all account balances in the adjusted trial balance columns, the columns are totaled to prove their equality. (See the blue-shaded area in Illustration 4-2.) If the column totals do not agree, the financial statement columns will not balance and the financial statements will be incorrect.

STEP 4. EXTEND ADJUSTED TRIAL BALANCE AMOUNTS TO APPROPRIATE FINANCIAL STATEMENT COLUMNS

The fourth step is to extend adjusted trial balance amounts to the income statement and balance sheet columns of the worksheet. Pioneer enters balance sheet accounts in the appropriate balance sheet debit and credit columns. For instance, it enters Cash in the balance sheet debit column, and Notes Payable in the balance sheet credit column. Pioneer extends Accumulated Depreciation—Equipment to the balance sheet credit column. The reason is that accumulated depreciation is a contra asset account with a credit balance.

Pioneer extends the balances in Common Stock and Retained Earnings, if any, to the balance sheet credit column. In addition, it extends the balance in Dividends to the balance sheet debit column because it is a stockholders' equity account with a debit balance.

The company enters the expense and revenue accounts such as Salaries and Wages Expense and Service Revenue in the appropriate income statement columns. (See the green-shaded area in Illustration 4-2.)

> **Helpful Hint**
> Every adjusted trial balance amount must be extended to one of the four statement columns.

STEP 5. TOTAL THE STATEMENT COLUMNS, COMPUTE THE NET INCOME (OR NET LOSS), AND COMPLETE THE WORKSHEET

The company now must total each of the financial statement columns. The net income or net loss for the period is the difference between the totals of the two income statement columns. If total credits exceed total debits, the result is net income. In such a case, as shown in Illustration 4-2, the company inserts the words "Net Income" in the account titles space. It then enters the amount in the income statement debit column and the balance sheet credit column. **The debit amount balances the income statement columns; the credit amount balances the balance sheet columns.** In addition, the credit in the balance sheet column indicates the increase in stockholders' equity resulting from net income.

What if total debits exceed total credits in the income statement columns? In that case, the company has a net loss. It enters the amount of the net loss in the income statement credit column and the balance sheet debit column.

After entering the net income or net loss, the company determines new column totals. The totals shown in the debit and credit income statement columns will match. So will the totals shown in the debit and credit balance sheet columns. If either the income statement columns or the balance sheet columns are not equal after the net income or net loss has been entered, there is an error in the worksheet. (See the grey-shaded area in Illustration 4-2.)

Preparing Financial Statements from a Worksheet

After a company has completed a worksheet, it has at hand all the data required for preparation of financial statements. The income statement is prepared from the income statement columns. The balance sheet and retained earnings statement are prepared from the balance sheet columns. Illustration 4-3 (page 170) shows the financial statements prepared from Pioneer's worksheet. At this point, the company has not journalized or posted adjusting entries. Therefore, ledger balances for some accounts are not the same as the financial statement amounts.

Illustration 4-3
Financial statements from a
worksheet

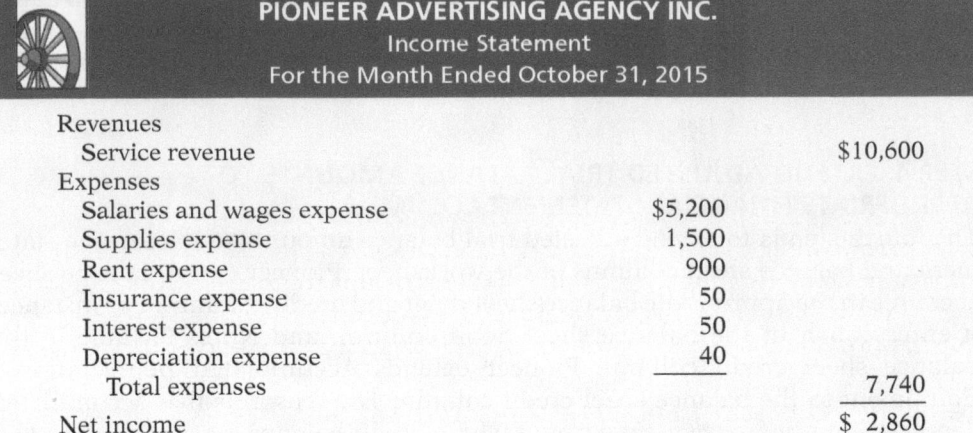

PIONEER ADVERTISING AGENCY INC.
Income Statement
For the Month Ended October 31, 2015

Revenues		
Service revenue		$10,600
Expenses		
Salaries and wages expense	$5,200	
Supplies expense	1,500	
Rent expense	900	
Insurance expense	50	
Interest expense	50	
Depreciation expense	40	
Total expenses		7,740
Net income		$ 2,860

PIONEER ADVERTISING AGENCY INC.
Retained Earnings Statement
For the Month Ended October 31, 2015

Retained earnings, October 1	$ –0–
Add: Net income	2,860
	2,860
Less: Dividends	500
Retained earnings, October 31	$2,360

PIONEER ADVERTISING AGENCY INC.
Balance Sheet
October 31, 2015

Assets

Cash		$15,200
Accounts receivable		200
Supplies		1,000
Prepaid insurance		550
Equipment	$5,000	
Less: Accumulated depreciation—equipment	40	4,960
Total assets		$21,910

Liabilities and Stockholders' Equity

Liabilities		
Notes payable	$5,000	
Accounts payable	2,500	
Interest payable	50	
Unearned service revenue	800	
Salaries and wages payable	1,200	
Total liabilities		$ 9,550
Stockholders' equity		
Common stock	10,000	
Retained earnings	2,360	
Total stockholders' equity		12,360
Total liabilities and stockholders' equity		$21,910

The amount shown for common stock on the worksheet does not change from the beginning to the end of the period unless the company issues additional stock during the period. Because there was no balance in Pioneer's retained earnings, the account is not listed on the worksheet. Only after dividends and net income (or loss) are posted to retained earnings does this account have a balance at the end of the first year of the business.

Using a worksheet, companies can prepare financial statements before they journalize and post adjusting entries. **However, the completed worksheet is not a substitute for formal financial statements.** The format of the data in the financial statement columns of the worksheet is not the same as the format of the financial statements. **A worksheet is essentially a working tool of the accountant**; companies do not distribute it to management and other parties.

Preparing Adjusting Entries from a Worksheet

A worksheet is not a journal, and it cannot be used as a basis for posting to ledger accounts. To adjust the accounts, the company must journalize the adjustments and post them to the ledger. **The adjusting entries are prepared from the adjustments columns of the worksheet.** The reference letters in the adjustments columns and the explanations of the adjustments at the bottom of the worksheet help identify the adjusting entries. The journalizing and posting of adjusting entries **follow** the preparation of financial statements when a worksheet is used. The adjusting entries on October 31 for Pioneer Advertising Agency Inc. are the same as those shown in Illustration 3-23 (page 121).

Helpful Hint
Note that writing the explanation of the adjustment at the bottom of the worksheet is not required.

> **DO IT!**

Worksheet

Susan Elbe is preparing a worksheet. Explain to Susan how she should extend the following adjusted trial balance accounts to the financial statement columns of the worksheet.

Cash	Dividends
Accumulated Depreciation—Equipment	Service Revenue
Accounts Payable	Salaries and Wages Expense

Action Plan

✔ Balance sheet: Extend assets to debit column. Extend liabilities to credit column. Extend contra assets to credit column. Extend Dividends account to debit column.

✔ Income statement: Extend expenses to debit column. Extend revenues to credit column.

Solution

Income statement debit column—Salaries and Wages Expense
Income statement credit column—Service Revenue
Balance sheet debit column—Cash; Dividends
Balance sheet credit column—Accumulated Depreciation—Equipment; Accounts Payable

Related exercise material: BE4-1, BE4-2, BE4-3, E4-1, E4-2, E4-5, E4-6, **and** DO IT! 4-1.

✔ **The Navigator**

Closing the Books

At the end of the accounting period, the company makes the accounts ready for the next period. This is called **closing the books.** In closing the books, the company distinguishes between temporary and permanent accounts.

Temporary accounts relate only to a given accounting period. They include all income statement accounts and the Dividends account. **The company closes all temporary accounts at the end of the period.**

LEARNING OBJECTIVE	2

Explain the process of closing the books.

In contrast, **permanent accounts** relate to one or more future accounting periods. They consist of all balance sheet accounts, including stockholders' equity accounts. **Permanent accounts are not closed from period to period.** Instead, the company carries forward the balances of permanent accounts into the next accounting period. Illustration 4-4 identifies the accounts in each category.

TEMPORARY	PERMANENT
These accounts are closed	These accounts are not closed
All revenue accounts	All asset accounts
All expense accounts	All liability accounts
Dividends	Stockholders' equity

Preparing Closing Entries

At the end of the accounting period, the company transfers temporary account balances to the permanent stockholders' equity account, Retained Earnings, by means of closing entries.

Closing entries formally recognize in the ledger the transfer of net income (or net loss) and Dividends to Retained Earnings. The retained earnings statement shows the results of these entries. **Closing entries also produce a zero balance in each temporary account.** The temporary accounts are then ready to accumulate data in the next accounting period separate from the data of prior periods. Permanent accounts are not closed.

Journalizing and posting closing entries is a required step in the accounting cycle. (See Illustration 4-11 on page 179.) The company performs this step after it has prepared financial statements. In contrast to the steps in the cycle that you have already studied, companies generally journalize and post closing entries **only at the end of the annual accounting period**. Thus, all temporary accounts will contain data for the entire year.

In preparing closing entries, companies could close each income statement account directly to Retained Earnings. However, to do so would result in excessive detail in the permanent Retained Earnings account. Instead, companies close the revenue and expense accounts to another temporary account, **Income Summary**, and they transfer the resulting net income or net loss from this account to Retained Earnings.

Companies **record closing entries in the general journal**. A center caption, Closing Entries, inserted in the journal between the last adjusting entry and the first closing entry, identifies these entries. Then the company posts the closing entries to the ledger accounts.

Companies generally prepare closing entries directly from the adjusted balances in the ledger. They could prepare separate closing entries for each nominal account, but the following four entries accomplish the desired result more efficiently:

1. Debit each revenue account for its balance, and credit Income Summary for total revenues.

2. Debit Income Summary for total expenses, and credit each expense account for its balance.

3. Debit Income Summary and credit Retained Earnings for the amount of net income.

4. Debit Retained Earnings for the balance in the Dividends account, and credit Dividends for the same amount.

Illustration 4-5 presents a diagram of the closing process. In it, the boxed numbers refer to the four entries required in the closing process.

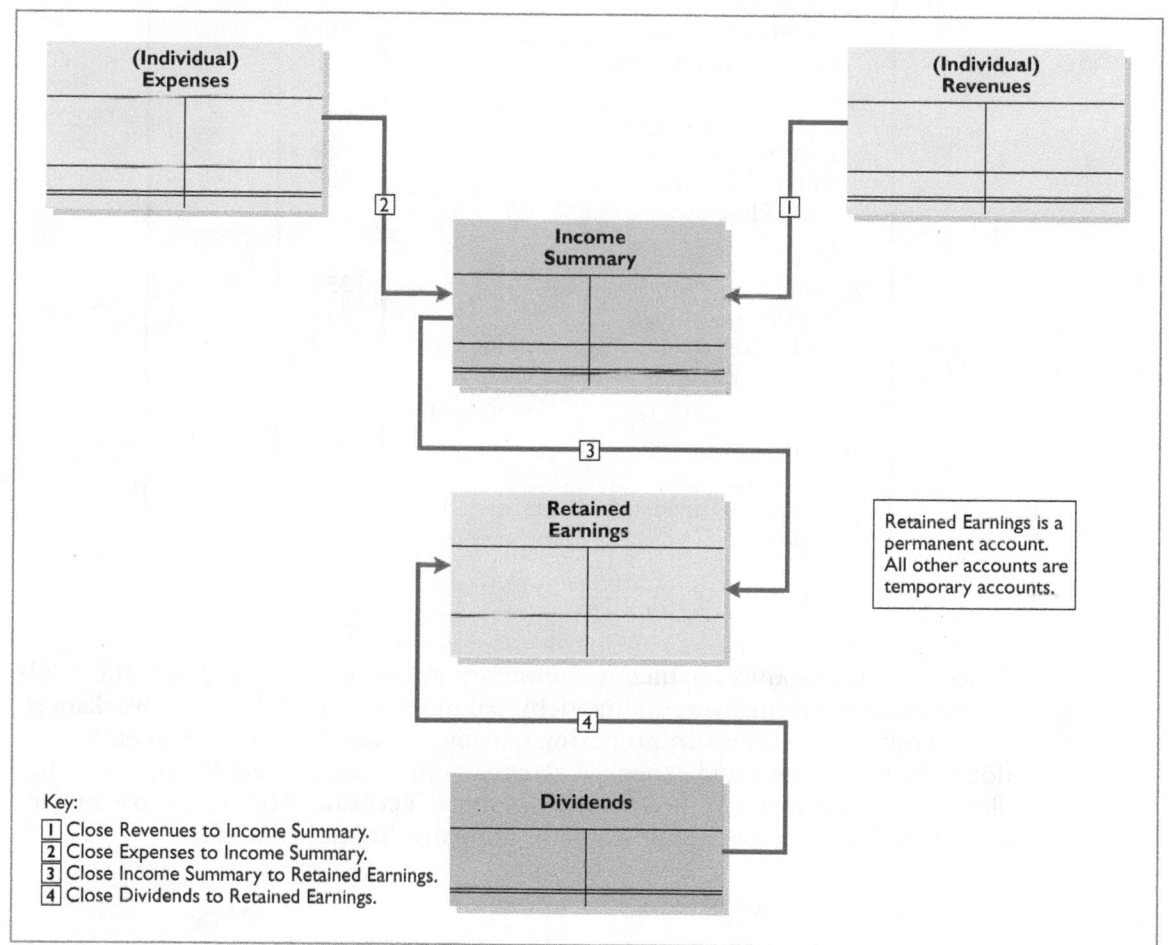

Illustration 4-5
Diagram of closing process—corporation

If there were a net loss (because expenses exceeded revenues), entry 3 in Illustration 4-5 would be reversed: there would be a credit to Income Summary and a debit to Retained Earnings.

CLOSING ENTRIES ILLUSTRATED

In practice, companies generally prepare closing entries only at the end of the annual accounting period. However, to illustrate the journalizing and posting of closing entries, we will assume that Pioneer Advertising Agency Inc. closes its books monthly. Illustration 4-6 (page 174) shows the closing entries at October 31. (The numbers in parentheses before each entry correspond to the four entries diagrammed in Illustration 4-5.)

Illustration 4-6
Closing entries journalized

	GENERAL JOURNAL			J3
Date	Account Titles and Explanation	Ref.	Debit	Credit
	Closing Entries			
2015	(1)			
Oct. 31	Service Revenue	400	10,600	
	Income Summary	350		10,600
	(To close revenue account)			
	(2)			
31	Income Summary	350	7,740	
	Supplies Expense	631		1,500
	Depreciation Expense	711		40
	Insurance Expense	722		50
	Salaries and Wages Expense	726		5,200
	Rent Expense	729		900
	Interest Expense	905		50
	(To close expense accounts)			
	(3)			
31	Income Summary	350	2,860	
	Retained Earnings	320		2,860
	(To close net income to retained earnings)			
	(4)			
31	Retained Earnings	320	500	
	Dividends	332		500
	(To close dividends to retained earnings)			

Note that the amounts for Income Summary in entries (1) and (2) are the totals of the income statement credit and debit columns, respectively, in the worksheet.

A couple of cautions in preparing closing entries: (1) Avoid unintentionally doubling the revenue and expense balances rather than zeroing them. (2) Do not close Dividends through the Income Summary account. **Dividends are not an expense, and they are not a factor in determining net income.**

Posting Closing Entries

Illustration 4-7 shows the posting of the closing entries and the underlining (ruling) of the accounts. Note that all temporary accounts have zero balances after posting the closing entries. In addition, you should realize that the balance in Retained Earnings represents the accumulated undistributed earnings of the corporation at the end of the accounting period. This balance is shown on the balance sheet and is the ending amount reported on the retained earnings statement, as shown in Illustration 4-3 on page 170. Pioneer uses the Income Summary account only in closing. It does not journalize and post entries to this account during the year.

As part of the closing process, Pioneer totals, balances, and double-underlines its temporary accounts—revenues, expenses, and Dividends, as shown in T-account form in Illustration 4-7. It does not close its permanent accounts—assets, liabilities, and stockholders' equity (Common Stock and Retained Earnings). Instead, Pioneer draws a single underline beneath the current-period entries for the permanent accounts. The account balance is then entered below the single underline and is carried forward to the next period. (For example, see Retained Earnings.)

Helpful Hint
The balance in Income Summary before it is closed must equal the net income or net loss for the period.

Supplies Expense		631
1,500	(2)	1,500

Depreciation Expense		711
40	(2)	40

Insurance Expense		722
50	(2)	50

Salaries and Wages Expense		726
4,000	(2)	5,200
1,200		
5,200		5,200

Rent Expense		729
900	(2)	900

Interest Expense		905
50	(2)	50

Service Revenue			400
(1)	10,600		10,000
			400
			200
	10,600		10,600

Income Summary			350
(2)	7,740	(1)	10,600
(3)	2,860		
	10,600		10,600

Retained Earnings			320
(4)	500		
		(3)	2,860
		Bal.	2,360

Dividends			332
	500	(4)	500

Key:
1 Close Revenues to Income Summary.
2 Close Expenses to Income Summary.
3 Close Income Summary to Retained Earnings.
4 Close Dividends to Retained Earnings.

Illustration 4-7
Posting of closing entries

ACCOUNTING ACROSS THE ORGANIZATION

Cisco Performs the Virtual Close

Technology has dramatically shortened the closing process. Recent surveys have reported that the average company now takes only six to seven days to close, rather than 20 days. But a few companies do much better. Cisco Systems can perform a "virtual close"—closing within 24 hours on any day in the quarter. The same is true at Lockheed Martin Corp., which improved its closing time by 85% in just the last few years. Not very long ago, it took 14 to 16 days. Managers at these companies emphasize that this increased speed has not reduced the accuracy and completeness of the data.

This is not just showing off. Knowing exactly where you are financially all of the time allows the company to respond faster than competitors. It also means that the hundreds of people who used to spend 10 to 20 days a quarter tracking transactions can now be more usefully employed on things such as mining data for business intelligence to find new business opportunities.

Source: "Reporting Practices: Few Do It All," *Financial Executive* (November 2003), p. 11.

© Steve Cole/iStockphoto

? Who else benefits from a shorter closing process? (See page 215.)

> **DO IT!**

Closing Entries

Action Plan
✔ Close Income Summary to Retained Earnings.
✔ Close Dividends to Retained Earnings.

The worksheet for Hancock Company shows the following in the financial statement columns:

Dividends $15,000
Common stock $42,000
Net income $18,000

Prepare the closing entries at December 31 that affect stockholders' equity.

Solution

Dec. 31	Income Summary	18,000	
	Retained Earnings		18,000
	(To close net income to retained earnings)		
31	Retained Earnings	15,000	
	Dividends		15,000
	(To close dividends to retained earnings)		

Related exercise material: BE4-4, BE4-5, BE4-6, E4-4, E4-7, E4-8, E4-11, **and** DO IT! 4-2.

 The Navigator

Preparing a Post-Closing Trial Balance

LEARNING OBJECTIVE 3

Describe the content and purpose of a post-closing trial balance.

After Pioneer has journalized and posted all closing entries, it prepares another trial balance, called a **post-closing trial balance**, from the ledger. The post-closing trial balance lists permanent accounts and their balances after the journalizing and posting of closing entries. The purpose of the post-closing trial balance is **to prove the equality of the permanent account balances carried forward into the next accounting period**. Since all temporary accounts will have zero balances, **the post-closing trial balance will contain only permanent—balance sheet—accounts**.

Illustration 4-8 shows the post-closing trial balance for Pioneer Advertising Agency Inc.

Illustration 4-8
Post-closing trial balance

 PIONEER ADVERTISING AGENCY INC.
Post-Closing Trial Balance
October 31, 2015

	Debit	Credit
Cash	$ 15,200	
Accounts Receivable	200	
Supplies	1,000	
Prepaid Insurance	550	
Equipment	5,000	
Accumulated Depreciation—Equipment		$ 40
Notes Payable		5,000
Accounts Payable		2,500
Unearned Service Revenue		800
Salaries and Wages Payable		1,200
Interest Payable		50
Common Stock		10,000
Retained Earnings		2,360
	$21,950	$21,950

Pioneer prepares the post-closing trial balance from the permanent accounts in the ledger. Illustration 4-9 shows the permanent accounts in Pioneer's general ledger.

Illustration 4-9
General ledger, permanent accounts

(Permanent Accounts Only)

GENERAL LEDGER

Cash   No. 101

Date	Explanation	Ref.	Debit	Credit	Balance
2015					
Oct. 1		J1	10,000		10,000
2		J1	1,200		11,200
3		J1		900	10,300
4		J1		600	9,700
20		J1		500	9,200
26		J1		4,000	5,200
31		J1	10,000		**15,200**

Accounts Receivable   No. 112

Date	Explanation	Ref.	Debit	Credit	Balance
2015					
Oct. 31	Adj. entry	J2	**200**		200

Supplies   No. 126

Date	Explanation	Ref.	Debit	Credit	Balance
2015					
Oct. 5		J1	2,500		2,500
31	Adj. entry	J2		**1,500**	1,000

Prepaid Insurance   No. 130

Date	Explanation	Ref.	Debit	Credit	Balance
2015					
Oct. 4		J1	600		600
31	Adj. entry	J2		**50**	550

Equipment   No. 157

Date	Explanation	Ref.	Debit	Credit	Balance
2015					
Oct. 1		J1	5,000		5,000

Accumulated Depreciation—Equipment   No. 158

Date	Explanation	Ref.	Debit	Credit	Balance
2015					
Oct. 31	Adj. entry	J2		**40**	40

Notes Payable   No. 200

Date	Explanation	Ref.	Debit	Credit	Balance
2015					
Oct. 1		J1		5,000	**5,000**

Accounts Payable   No. 201

Date	Explanation	Ref.	Debit	Credit	Balance
2015					
Oct. 5		J1		2,500	**2,500**

Unearned Service Revenue   No. 209

Date	Explanation	Ref.	Debit	Credit	Balance
2015					
Oct. 2		J1		1,200	1,200
31	Adj. entry	J2	400		800

Salaries and Wages Payable   No. 212

Date	Explanation	Ref.	Debit	Credit	Balance
2015					
Oct. 31	Adj. entry	J2		**1,200**	1,200

Interest Payable   No. 230

Date	Explanation	Ref.	Debit	Credit	Balance
2015					
Oct. 31	Adj. entry	J2		**50**	50

Common Stock   No. 311

Date	Explanation	Ref.	Debit	Credit	Balance
2015					
Oct. 1		J1		10,000	10,000

Retained Earnings   No. 320

Date	Explanation	Ref.	Debit	Credit	Balance
2015					
Oct. 1					–0–
31	Closing entry	J3		2,860	2,860
31	Closing entry	J3	500		2,360

Note: The permanent accounts for Pioneer Advertising Agency Inc. are shown here; the temporary accounts are shown in Illustration 4-10. Both permanent and temporary accounts are part of the general ledger; we segregated them here to aid in learning.

A post-closing trial balance provides evidence that the company has properly journalized and posted the closing entries. It also shows that the accounting equation is in balance at the end of the accounting period. However, like the trial balance, it does not prove that Pioneer has recorded all transactions or that the ledger is correct. For example, the post-closing trial balance still will balance even if a transaction is not journalized and posted or if a transaction is journalized and posted twice.

The remaining accounts in the general ledger are temporary accounts, shown in Illustration 4-10. After Pioneer correctly posts the closing entries, each temporary account has a zero balance. These accounts are double-underlined to finalize the closing process.

Illustration 4-10
General ledger, temporary accounts

(Temporary Accounts Only)

GENERAL LEDGER

Dividends — No. 332

Date	Explanation	Ref.	Debit	Credit	Balance
2015					
Oct. 20		J1	500		500
31	Closing entry	J3		500	–0–

Income Summary — No. 350

Date	Explanation	Ref.	Debit	Credit	Balance
2015					
Oct.31	Closing entry	J3		10,600	10,600
31	Closing entry	J3	7,740		2,860
31	Closing entry	J3	2,860		–0–

Service Revenue — No. 400

Date	Explanation	Ref.	Debit	Credit	Balance
2015					
Oct. 31		J1		10,000	10,000
31	Adj. entry	J2		400	10,400
31	Adj. entry	J2		200	10,600
31	Closing entry	J3	10,600		–0–

Supplies Expense — No. 631

Date	Explanation	Ref.	Debit	Credit	Balance
2015					
Oct. 31	Adj. entry	J2	1,500		1,500
31	Closing entry	J3		1,500	–0–

Depreciation Expense — No. 711

Date	Explanation	Ref.	Debit	Credit	Balance
2015					
Oct. 31	Adj. entry	J2	40		40
31	Closing entry	J3		40	–0–

Insurance Expense — No. 722

Date	Explanation	Ref.	Debit	Credit	Balance
2015					
Oct. 31	Adj. entry	J2	50		50
31	Closing entry	J3		50	–0–

Salaries and Wages Expense — No. 726

Date	Explanation	Ref.	Debit	Credit	Balance
2015					
Oct. 26		J1	4,000		4,000
31	Adj. entry	J2	1,200		5,200
31	Closing entry	J3		5,200	–0–

Rent Expense — No. 729

Date	Explanation	Ref.	Debit	Credit	Balance
2015					
Oct. 3		J1	900		900
31	Closing entry	J3		900	–0–

Interest Expense — No. 905

Date	Explanation	Ref.	Debit	Credit	Balance
2015					
Oct. 31	Adj. entry	J2	50		50
31	Closing entry	J3		50	–0–

Note: The temporary accounts for Pioneer Advertising Agency Inc. are shown here. Illustration 4-9 (page 177) shows the permanent accounts. Both permanent and temporary accounts are part of the general ledger; we segregate them here to aid in learning.

Summary of the Accounting Cycle

LEARNING OBJECTIVE **4**

State the required steps in the accounting cycle.

Illustration 4-11 summarizes the steps in the accounting cycle. You can see that the cycle begins with the analysis of business transactions and ends with the preparation of a post-closing trial balance.

Illustration 4-11
Steps in the accounting cycle

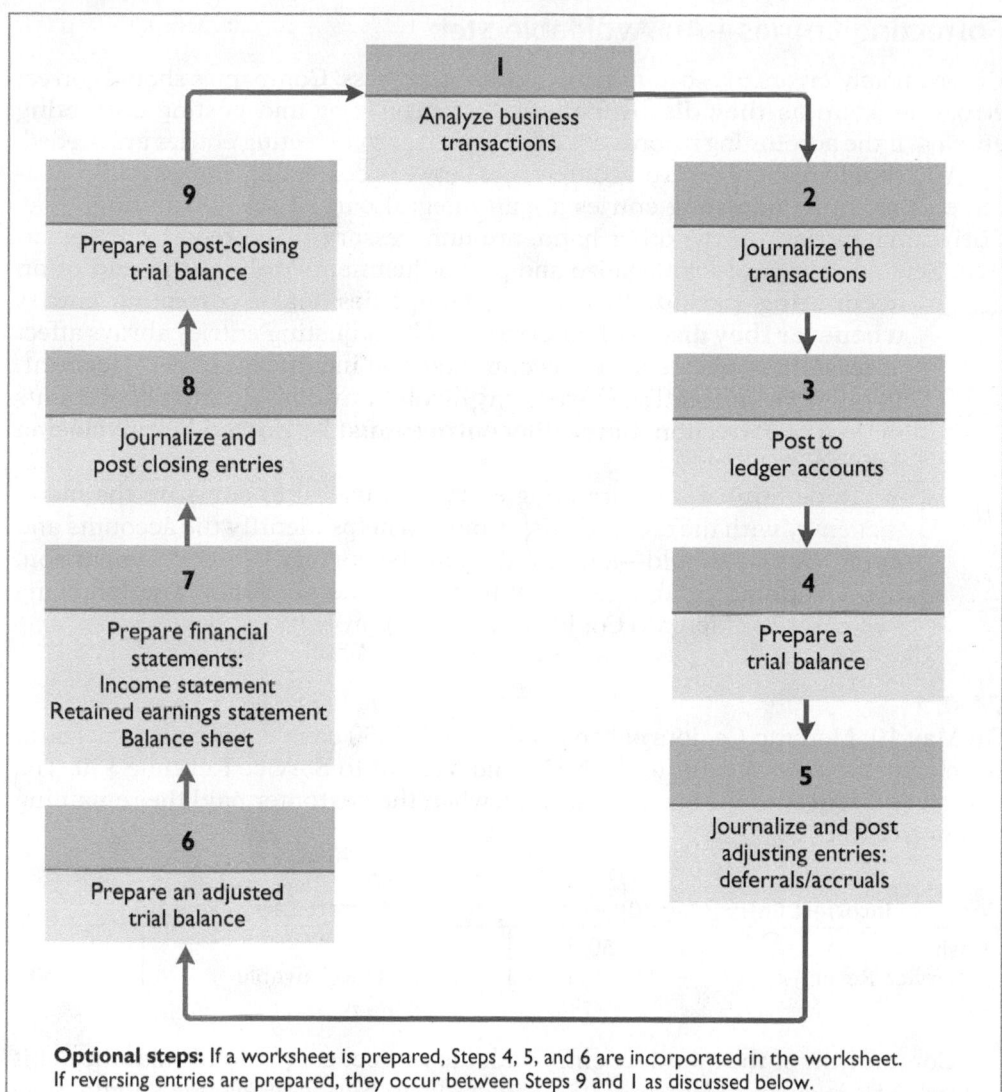

Optional steps: If a worksheet is prepared, Steps 4, 5, and 6 are incorporated in the worksheet. If reversing entries are prepared, they occur between Steps 9 and 1 as discussed below.

Steps 1–3 may occur daily during the accounting period. Companies perform Steps 4–7 on a periodic basis, such as monthly, quarterly, or annually. Steps 8 and 9—closing entries and a post-closing trial balance—usually take place only at the end of a company's **annual** accounting period.

There are also two **optional steps** in the accounting cycle. As you have seen, companies may use a worksheet in preparing adjusting entries and financial statements. In addition, they may use reversing entries, as explained below.

Reversing Entries—An Optional Step

Some accountants prefer to reverse certain adjusting entries by making a **reversing entry** at the beginning of the next accounting period. A reversing entry is the exact opposite of the adjusting entry made in the previous period. **Use of reversing entries is an optional bookkeeping procedure; it is not a required step in the accounting cycle.** Accordingly, we have chosen to cover this topic in Appendix 4A at the end of this chapter.

Correcting Entries—An Avoidable Step

LEARNING OBJECTIVE 5

Explain the approaches to preparing correcting entries.

Unfortunately, errors may occur in the recording process. Companies should correct errors, **as soon as they discover them**, by journalizing and posting **correcting entries**. If the accounting records are free of errors, no correcting entries are needed.

You should recognize several differences between correcting entries and adjusting entries. First, adjusting entries are an integral part of the accounting cycle. Correcting entries, on the other hand, are unnecessary if the records are error-free. Second, companies journalize and post adjustments **only at the end of an accounting period**. In contrast, companies make correcting entries **whenever they discover an error**. Finally, adjusting entries always affect at least one balance sheet account and one income statement account. In contrast, correcting entries may involve any combination of accounts in need of correction. **Correcting entries must be posted before closing entries.**

> ### Ethics Note
>
> When companies find errors in previously released income statements, they restate those numbers. Perhaps because of the increased scrutiny caused by Sarbanes-Oxley, in a recent year companies filed a record 1,195 restatements.

To determine the correcting entry, it is useful to compare the incorrect entry with the correct entry. Doing so helps identify the accounts and amounts that should—and should not—be corrected. After comparison, the accountant makes an entry to correct the accounts. The following two cases for Mercato Co. illustrate this approach.

CASE 1

On May 10, Mercato Co. journalized and posted a $50 cash collection on account from a customer as a debit to Cash $50 and a credit to Service Revenue $50. The company discovered the error on May 20, when the customer paid the remaining balance in full.

Illustration 4-12
Comparison of entries

Incorrect Entry (May 10)			Correct Entry (May 10)		
Cash	50		Cash	50	
Service Revenue		50	Accounts Receivable		50

Comparison of the incorrect entry with the correct entry reveals that the debit to Cash $50 is correct. However, the $50 credit to Service Revenue should have been credited to Accounts Receivable. As a result, both Service Revenue and Accounts Receivable are overstated in the ledger. Mercato makes the following correcting entry.

Illustration 4-13
Correcting entry

A	=	L	+	SE
				−50 Rev
−50				

Cash Flows
no effect

	Correcting Entry		
May 20	Service Revenue	50	
	Accounts Receivable		50
	(To correct entry of May 10)		

CASE 2

On May 18, Mercato purchased on account equipment costing $450. The transaction was journalized and posted as a debit to Equipment $45 and a credit to Accounts Payable $45. The error was discovered on June 3, when Mercato received the monthly statement for May from the creditor.

Illustration 4-14
Comparison of entries

Incorrect Entry (May 18)			Correct Entry (May 18)		
Equipment	45		Equipment	450	
Accounts Payable		45	Accounts Payable		450

Comparison of the two entries shows that two accounts are incorrect. Equipment is understated $405, and Accounts Payable is understated $405. Mercato makes the following correcting entry.

Correcting Entry

June 3	Equipment	405	
	Accounts Payable		405
	(To correct entry of May 18)		

A	=	L	+	SE
+405				
		+405		

Cash Flows
no effect

Illustration 4-15
Correcting entry

Instead of preparing a correcting entry, **it is possible to reverse the incorrect entry and then prepare the correct entry**. This approach will result in more entries and postings than a correcting entry, but it will accomplish the desired result.

ACCOUNTING ACROSS THE ORGANIZATION

Yale Express Loses Some Transportation Bills

Yale Express, a short-haul trucking firm, turned over much of its cargo to local truckers to complete deliveries. Yale collected the entire delivery charge. When billed by the local trucker, Yale sent payment for the final phase to the local trucker. Yale used a cutoff period of 20 days into the next accounting period in making its adjusting entries for accrued liabilities. That is, it waited 20 days to receive the local truckers' bills to determine the amount of the unpaid but incurred delivery charges as of the balance sheet date.

On the other hand, Republic Carloading, a nationwide, long-distance freight forwarder, frequently did not receive transportation bills from truckers to whom it passed on cargo until months after the year-end. In making its year-end adjusting entries, Republic waited for months in order to include all of these outstanding transportation bills.

When Yale Express merged with Republic Carloading, Yale's vice president employed the 20-day cutoff procedure for both firms. As a result, millions of dollars of Republic's accrued transportation bills went unrecorded. When the company detected the error and made correcting entries, these and other errors changed a reported profit of $1.14 million into a loss of $1.88 million!

 What might Yale Express's vice president have done to produce more accurate financial statements without waiting months for Republic's outstanding transportation bills? (See page 215.)

© Christian Lagereek/iStockphoto

The Classified Balance Sheet

The balance sheet presents a snapshot of a company's financial position at a point in time. To improve users' understanding of a company's financial position, companies often use a classified balance sheet. A **classified balance sheet** groups together similar assets and similar liabilities, using a number of standard classifications and sections. This is useful because items within a group have similar economic characteristics. A classified balance sheet generally contains the standard classifications listed in Illustration 4-16.

Assets	Liabilities and Stockholders' Equity
Current assets	Current liabilities
Long-term investments	Long-term liabilities
Property, plant, and equipment	Stockholders' equity
Intangible assets	

Illustration 4-16
Standard balance sheet classifications

These groupings help financial statement readers determine such things as (1) whether the company has enough assets to pay its debts as they come due, and (2) the claims of short- and long-term creditors on the company's total assets. Many of these groupings can be seen in the balance sheet of Franklin Corporation shown in Illustration 4-17 below. In the sections that follow, we explain each of these groupings.

Illustration 4-17
Classified balance sheet

FRANKLIN CORPORATION
Balance Sheet
October 31, 2015

Assets

Current assets			
Cash		$ 6,600	
Debt investments		2,000	
Accounts receivable		7,000	
Notes receivable		1,000	
Inventory		3,000	
Supplies		2,100	
Prepaid insurance		400	
Total current assets			$22,100
Long-term investments			
Stock investments		5,200	
Investment in real estate		2,000	7,200
Property, plant, and equipment			
Land		10,000	
Equipment	$24,000		
Less: Accumulated depreciation—			
equipment	5,000	19,000	29,000
Intangible assets			
Patents			3,100
Total assets			$61,400

Liabilities and Stockholders' Equity

Current liabilities			
Notes payable		$11,000	
Accounts payable		2,100	
Unearned service revenue		900	
Salaries and wages payable		1,600	
Interest payable		450	
Total current liabilities			$16,050
Long-term liabilities			
Mortgage payable		10,000	
Notes payable		1,300	
Total long-term liabilities			11,300
Total liabilities			27,350
Stockholders' equity			
Common stock		20,000	
Retained earnings		14,050	
Total stockholders' equity			34,050
Total liabilities and stockholders' equity			$61,400

Helpful Hint
Recall that the basic accounting equation is Assets = Liabilities + Stockholders' Equity.

Current Assets

Current assets are assets that a company expects to convert to cash or use up within one year or its operating cycle, whichever is longer. In Illustration 4-17, Franklin Corporation had current assets of $22,100. For most businesses, the cutoff for classification as current assets is one year from the balance sheet date. For example, accounts receivable are current assets because the company will collect them and convert them to cash within one year. Supplies is a current asset because the company expects to use them up in operations within one year.

Some companies use a period longer than one year to classify assets and liabilities as current because they have an operating cycle longer than one year. The **operating cycle** of a company is the average time that it takes to purchase inventory, sell it on account, and then collect cash from customers. For most businesses, this cycle takes less than a year, so they use a one-year cutoff. But, for some businesses, such as vineyards or airplane manufacturers, this period may be longer than a year. **Except where noted, we will assume that companies use one year to determine whether an asset or liability is current or long-term.**

Common types of current assets are (1) cash, (2) investments (such as short-term U.S. government securities), (3) receivables (notes receivable, accounts receivable, and interest receivable), (4) inventories, and (5) prepaid expenses (supplies and insurance). **On the balance sheet, companies usually list these items in the order in which they expect to convert them into cash.**

Illustration 4-18 presents the current assets of Southwest Airlines Co.

Real World	SOUTHWEST AIRLINES CO. Balance Sheet (partial) (in millions)	
Current assets		
Cash and cash equivalents		$1,390
Short-term investments		369
Accounts receivable		241
Inventories		181
Prepaid expenses and other current assets		420
Total current assets		$2,601

Illustration 4-18
Current assets section

As explained later in the chapter, a company's current assets are important in assessing its short-term debt-paying ability.

Long-Term Investments

Long-term investments are generally (1) investments in stocks and bonds of other companies that are normally held for many years, (2) long-term assets such as land or buildings that a company is not currently using in its operating activities, and (3) long-term notes receivable. In Illustration 4-17, Franklin Corporation reported total long-term investments of $7,200 on its balance sheet.

Yahoo! Inc. reported long-term investments in its balance sheet as shown in Illustration 4-19.

Alternative Terminology
Long-term investments are often referred to simply as *investments*.

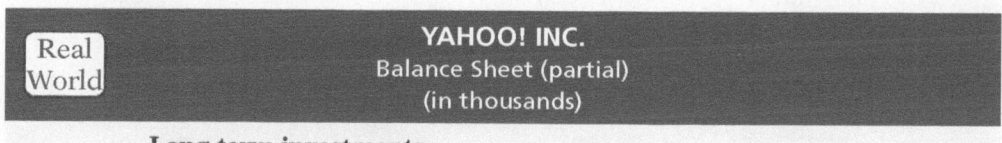

Real World	YAHOO! INC. Balance Sheet (partial) (in thousands)	
Long-term investments		
Investments in securities		$90,266

Illustration 4-19
Long-term investments section

Property, Plant, and Equipment

Property, plant, and equipment are assets with relatively long useful lives that a company is currently using in operating the business. This category includes land, buildings, machinery and equipment, delivery equipment, and furniture. In Illustration 4-17, Franklin Corporation reported property, plant, and equipment of $29,000.

International Note

Recently, China adopted International Financial Reporting Standards (IFRS). This was done in an effort to reduce fraud and increase investor confidence in financial reports. Under these standards, many items, such as property, plant, and equipment, may be reported at current fair values rather than historical cost.

Depreciation is the practice of allocating the cost of assets to a number of years. Companies do this by systematically assigning a portion of an asset's cost as an expense each year (rather than expensing the full purchase price in the year of purchase). The assets that the company depreciates are reported on the balance sheet at cost less accumulated depreciation. The **accumulated depreciation** account shows the total amount of depreciation that the company has expensed thus far in the asset's life. In Illustration 4-17, Franklin Corporation reported accumulated depreciation of $5,000.

Illustration 4-20 presents the property, plant, and equipment of Cooper Tire & Rubber Company.

Illustration 4-20
Property, plant, and equipment section

COOPER TIRE & RUBBER COMPANY		
Real World	Balance Sheet (partial) (in thousands)	
Property, plant, and equipment		
Land and land improvements	$ 41,553	
Buildings	298,706	
Machinery and equipment	1,636,091	
Molds, cores, and rings	268,158	$2,244,508
Less: Accumulated depreciation		1,252,692
		$ 991,816

Intangible Assets

Many companies have long-lived assets that do not have physical substance yet often are very valuable. We call these assets **intangible assets**. One significant intangible asset is goodwill. Others include patents, copyrights, and trademarks or trade names that give the company **exclusive right** of use for a specified period of time. In Illustration 4-17, Franklin Corporation reported intangible assets of $3,100.

Illustration 4-21 shows the intangible assets of media giant Time Warner, Inc.

Illustration 4-21
Intangible assets section

TIME WARNER, INC.	
Real World	Balance Sheet (partial) (in millions)
Intangible assets	
Goodwill	$40,953
Film library	2,690
Customer lists	2,540
Cable television franchises	38,048
Sports franchises	262
Brands, trademarks, and other intangible assets	8,313
	$92,806

PEOPLE, PLANET, AND PROFIT INSIGHT

Regaining Goodwill

After falling to unforeseen lows amidst scandals, recalls, and economic crises, the American public's positive perception of the reputation of corporate America is on the rise. Overall corporate reputation is experiencing rehabilitation as the American public gives high marks overall to corporate America, specific industries, and the largest number of individual companies in a dozen years. This is according to the findings of the *2011 Harris Interactive RQ Study*, which measures the reputations of the 60 most visible companies in the United States.

The survey focuses on six reputational dimensions that influence reputation and consumer behavior. Four of these dimensions, along with the five corporations that ranked highest within each, are as follows.

- **Social Responsibility:** (1) Whole Foods Market, (2) Johnson & Johnson, (3) Google, (4) The Walt Disney Company, (5) Procter & Gamble Co.

- **Emotional Appeal:** (1) Johnson & Johnson, (2) Amazon.com, (3) UPS, (4) General Mills, (5) Kraft Foods

- **Financial Performance:** (1) Google, (2) Berkshire Hathaway, (3) Apple, (4) Intel, (5) The Walt Disney Company

- **Products and Services:** (1) Intel Corporation, (2) 3M Company, (3) Johnson & Johnson, (4) Google, (5) Procter & Gamble Co.

Source: www.harrisinteractive.com.

© Gehring/iStockphoto

? Name two industries today which are probably rated low on the reputational characteristics of "being trusted" and "having high ethical standards." (See page 215.)

> DO IT!

Assets Section of Classified Balance Sheet

Baxter Hoffman recently received the following information related to Hoffman Company's December 31, 2015, balance sheet.

Prepaid insurance	$ 2,300	Inventory	$3,400
Cash	800	Accumulated depreciation—	
Equipment	10,700	equipment	2,700
		Accounts receivable	1,100

Prepare the assets section of Hoffman Company's classified balance sheet.

Solution

Action Plan

✔ Present current assets first. Current assets are cash and other resources that the company expects to convert to cash or use up within one year.

✔ Present current assets in the order in which the company expects to convert them into cash.

✔ Subtract accumulated depreciation—equipment from equipment to determine the book value of equipment.

Assets		
Current assets		
Cash	$ 800	
Accounts receivable	1,100	
Inventory	3,400	
Prepaid insurance	2,300	
Total current assets		$ 7,600
Property, plant, and equipment		
Equipment	10,700	
Less: Accumulated depreciation—equipment	2,700	8,000
Total assets		$15,600

Related exercise material: BE4-10 **and** DO IT! 4-3.

 The Navigator

Current Liabilities

In the liabilities and stockholders' equity section of the balance sheet, the first grouping is current liabilities. **Current liabilities** are obligations that the company is to pay within the coming year or its operating cycle, whichever is longer. Common examples are accounts payable, salaries and wages payable, notes payable, interest payable, and income taxes payable. Also included as current liabilities are current maturities of long-term obligations—payments to be made within the next year on long-term obligations. In Illustration 4-17, Franklin Corporation reported five different types of current liabilities, for a total of $16,050.

Illustration 4-22 shows the current liabilities section adapted from the balance sheet of Marcus Corporation.

Illustration 4-22
Current liabilities section

Liquidity

Illiquidity

MARCUS CORPORATION Balance Sheet (partial) (in thousands)	
Current liabilities	
Notes payable	$ 239
Accounts payable	24,242
Current maturities of long-term debt	57,250
Other current liabilities	27,477
Income taxes payable	11,215
Salaries and wages payable	6,720
Total current liabilities	$127,143

Real World

Users of financial statements look closely at the relationship between current assets and current liabilities. This relationship is important in evaluating a company's **liquidity**—its ability to pay obligations expected to be due within the next year. When current assets exceed current liabilities, the likelihood for paying the liabilities is favorable. When the reverse is true, short-term creditors may not be paid, and the company may ultimately be forced into bankruptcy.

ACCOUNTING ACROSS THE ORGANIZATION

Can a Company Be Too Liquid?

There actually is a point where a company can be too liquid—that is, it can have too much working capital (current assets less current liabilities). While it is important to be liquid enough to be able to pay short-term bills as they come due, a company does not want to tie up its cash in extra inventory or receivables that are not earning the company money.

By one estimate from the REL Consultancy Group, the thousand largest U.S. companies have on their books cumulative excess working capital of $764 billion. Based on this figure, companies could have reduced debt by 36% or increased net income by 9%. Given that managers throughout a company are interested in improving profitability, it is clear that they should have an eye toward managing working capital. They need to aim for a "Goldilocks solution"—not too much, not too little, but just right.

Source: K. Richardson, "Companies Fall Behind in Cash Management," *Wall Street Journal* (June 19, 2007).

 What can various company managers do to ensure that working capital is managed efficiently to maximize net income? (See page 215.)

Long-Term Liabilities

Long-term liabilities are obligations that a company expects to pay **after** one year. Liabilities in this category include bonds payable, mortgages payable, long-term notes payable, lease liabilities, and pension liabilities. Many companies report long-term debt maturing after one year as a single amount in the balance sheet and show the details of the debt in notes that accompany the financial statements. Others list the various types of long-term liabilities. In Illustration 4-17, Franklin Corporation reported long-term liabilities of $11,300.

Illustration 4-23 shows the long-term liabilities that The Procter & Gamble Company reported in its balance sheet.

Illustration 4-23
Long-term liabilities section

Real World	THE PROCTER & GAMBLE COMPANY Balance Sheet (partial) (in millions)	
Long-term liabilities		
Long-term debt		$23,375
Deferred income taxes		12,015
Other noncurrent liabilities		5,147
Total long-term liabilities		$40,537

Stockholders' (Owners') Equity

The content of the owners' equity section varies with the form of business organization. In a proprietorship, there is one capital account. In a partnership, there is a capital account for each partner. Corporations divide owners' equity into two accounts—Common Stock (sometimes referred to as Capital Stock) and Retained Earnings. Corporations record stockholders' investments in the company by debiting an asset account and crediting the Common Stock account. They record in the Retained Earnings account income retained for use in the business. Corporations combine the Common Stock and Retained Earnings accounts and report them on the balance sheet as **stockholders' equity**. (We'll learn more about these corporation accounts in later chapters.) Nordstrom, Inc. recently reported its stockholders' equity section as follows.

Alternative Terminology
Common stock is sometimes called *capital stock*.

Illustration 4-24
Stockholders' equity section

Real World	NORDSTROM, INC. Balance Sheet (partial) ($ in thousands)	
Stockholders' equity		
Common stock, 271,331 shares		$ 685,934
Retained earnings		1,406,747
Total stockholders' equity		$2,092,681

> **DO IT!**

Balance Sheet Classifications

The following accounts were taken from the financial statements of Callahan Company.

_____ Salaries and wages payable
_____ Service revenue
_____ Interest payable
_____ Goodwill
_____ Debt investments (short-term)
_____ Mortgage payable (due in 3 years)

_____ Stock investments (long-term)
_____ Equipment
_____ Accumulated depreciation—equipment
_____ Depreciation expense
_____ Common stock
_____ Unearned service revenue

Match each of the accounts to its proper balance sheet classification, shown below. If the item would not appear on a balance sheet, use "NA."

Current assets (CA)   Current liabilities (CL)
Long-term investments (LTI)   Long-term liabilities (LTL)
Property, plant, and equipment (PPE)   Stockholders' equity (SE)
Intangible assets (IA)

Solution

Action Plan

✔ Analyze whether each financial statement item is an asset, liability, or stockholders' equity.

✔ Determine if asset and liability items are short-term or long-term.

__CL__	Salaries and wages payable	__LTI__	Stock investments (long-term)
__NA__	Service revenue	__PPE__	Equipment
__CL__	Interest payable	__PPE__	Accumulated depreciation—
__IA__	Goodwill		equipment
__CA__	Debt investments (short-term)	__NA__	Depreciation expense
__LTL__	Mortgage payable (due in 3 years)	__SE__	Common stock
		__CL__	Unearned service revenue

Related exercise material: BE4-11, E4-9, E4-14, E4-15, E4-16, E4-17, **and** DO IT! 4-4.

 The Navigator

> ## Comprehensive DO IT!

At the end of its first month of operations, Watson Answering Service Inc. has the following unadjusted trial balance.

Action Plan

✔ In completing the worksheet, be sure to (a) key the adjustments; (b) start at the top of the adjusted trial balance columns and extend adjusted balances to the correct statement columns; and (c) enter net income (or net loss) in the proper columns.

✔ In preparing a classified balance sheet, know the contents of each of the sections.

✔ In journalizing closing entries, remember that there are only four entries and that Dividends are closed to Retained Earnings.

WATSON ANSWERING SERVICE INC.
August 31, 2015
Trial Balance

	Debit	Credit
Cash	$ 5,400	
Accounts Receivable	2,800	
Supplies	1,300	
Prepaid Insurance	2,400	
Equipment	60,000	
Notes Payable		$40,000
Accounts Payable		2,400
Common Stock		30,000
Dividends	1,000	
Service Revenue		4,900
Salaries and Wages Expense	3,200	
Utilities Expense	800	
Advertising Expense	400	
	$77,300	$77,300

Other data:

1. Insurance expires at the rate of $200 per month.
2. $1,000 of supplies are on hand at August 31.
3. Monthly depreciation on the equipment is $900.
4. Interest of $500 on the notes payable has accrued during August.

Instructions
(a) Prepare a worksheet.
(b) Prepare a classified balance sheet assuming $35,000 of the notes payable are long-term.
(c) Journalize the closing entries.

Solution to Comprehensive DO IT!

(a)

WATSON ANSWERING SERVICE INC.
Worksheet for the Month Ended August 31, 2015

Account Titles	Trial Balance Dr.	Trial Balance Cr.	Adjustments Dr.	Adjustments Cr.	Adjusted Trial Balance Dr.	Adjusted Trial Balance Cr.	Income Statement Dr.	Income Statement Cr.	Balance Sheet Dr.	Balance Sheet Cr.
Cash	5,400				5,400				5,400	
Accounts Receivable	2,800				2,800				2,800	
Supplies	1,300			(b) 300	1,000				1,000	
Prepaid Insurance	2,400			(a) 200	2,200				2,200	
Equipment	60,000				60,000				60,000	
Notes Payable		40,000				40,000				40,000
Accounts Payable		2,400				2,400				2,400
Common Stock		30,000				30,000				30,000
Dividends	1,000				1,000				1,000	
Service Revenue		4,900				4,900		4,900		
Salaries and Wages Expense	3,200				3,200		3,200			
Utilities Expense	800				800		800			
Advertising Expense	400				400		400			
Totals	77,300	77,300								
Insurance Expense			(a) 200		200		200			
Supplies Expense			(b) 300		300		300			
Depreciation Expense			(c) 900		900		900			
Accumulated Depreciation—Equipment				(c) 900		900				900
Interest Expense			(d) 500		500		500			
Interest Payable				(d) 500		500				500
Totals			1,900	1,900	78,700	78,700	6,300	4,900	72,400	73,800
Net Loss								1,400	1,400	
Totals							6,300	6,300	73,800	73,800

Explanation: (a) insurance expired, (b) supplies used, (c) depreciation expensed, (d) interest accrued.

(b)

WATSON ANSWERING SERVICE INC.
Balance Sheet
August 31, 2015

Assets

Current assets			
Cash		$ 5,400	
Accounts receivable		2,800	
Supplies		1,000	
Prepaid insurance		2,200	
Total current assets			$11,400
Property, plant, and equipment			
Equipment		60,000	
Less: Accumulated depreciation—equipment		900	59,100
Total assets			$70,500

Liabilities and Stockholders' Equity

Current liabilities			
Notes payable		$ 5,000	
Accounts payable		2,400	
Interest payable		500	
Total current liabilities			$ 7,900
Long-term liabilities			
Notes payable			35,000
Total liabilities			42,900
Stockholders' equity			
Common stock		30,000	
Retained earnings		(2,400)*	
Total stockholders' equity			27,600
Total liabilities and stockholders' equity			$70,500

*Net loss $1,400, plus dividends of $1,000.

(c)

Aug. 31	Service Revenue	4,900	
	Income Summary		4,900
	(To close revenue account)		
31	Income Summary	6,300	
	Salaries and Wages Expense		3,200
	Depreciation Expense		900
	Utilities Expense		800
	Interest Expense		500
	Advertising Expense		400
	Supplies Expense		300
	Insurance Expense		200
	(To close expense accounts)		
31	Retained Earnings	1,400	
	Income Summary		1,400
	(To close net loss to retained earnings)		
31	Retained Earnings	1,000	
	Dividends		1,000
	(To close dividends to retained earnings)		

The Navigator

SUMMARY OF LEARNING OBJECTIVES

1 Prepare a worksheet. The steps in preparing a worksheet are as follows. (a) Prepare a trial balance on the worksheet. (b) Enter the adjustments in the adjustments columns. (c) Enter adjusted balances in the adjusted trial balance columns. (d) Extend adjusted trial balance amounts to appropriate financial statement columns. (e) Total the statement columns, compute net income (or net loss), and complete the worksheet.

2 Explain the process of closing the books. Closing the books occurs at the end of an accounting period. The process is to journalize and post closing entries and then underline and balance all accounts. In closing the books, companies make separate entries to close revenues and expenses to Income Summary, Income Summary to Retained Earnings, and Dividends to Retained Earnings. Only temporary accounts are closed.

3 Describe the content and purpose of a post-closing trial balance. A post-closing trial balance contains the balances in permanent accounts that are carried forward to the next accounting period. The purpose of this trial balance is to prove the equality of these balances.

4 State the required steps in the accounting cycle. The required steps in the accounting cycle are (1) analyze business transactions, (2) journalize the transactions, (3) post to ledger accounts, (4) prepare a trial balance, (5) journalize and post adjusting entries, (6) prepare an adjusted trial balance, (7) prepare financial statements, (8) journalize and post closing entries, and (9) prepare a post-closing trial balance.

5 Explain the approaches to preparing correcting entries. One way to determine the correcting entry is to compare the incorrect entry with the correct entry. After comparison, the company makes a correcting entry to correct the accounts. An alternative to a correcting entry is to reverse the incorrect entry and then prepare the correct entry.

6 Identify the sections of a classified balance sheet. A classified balance sheet categorizes assets as current assets; long-term investments; property, plant, and equipment; and intangibles. Liabilities are classified as either current or long-term. There is also a stockholders' (owners') equity section, which varies with the form of business organization.

GLOSSARY

Classified balance sheet A balance sheet that contains standard classifications or sections. (p. 181).

Closing entries Entries made at the end of an accounting period to transfer the balances of temporary accounts to a permanent stockholders' equity account, Retained Earnings. (p. 172).

Correcting entries Entries to correct errors made in recording transactions. (p. 180).

Current assets Assets that a company expects to convert to cash or use up within one year. (p. 182).

Current liabilities Obligations that a company expects to pay within the coming year or its operating cycle, whichever is longer. (p. 186).

Income Summary A temporary account used in closing revenue and expense accounts. (p. 172).

Intangible assets Noncurrent assets that do not have physical substance. (p. 184).

Liquidity The ability of a company to pay obligations expected to be due within the next year. (p. 186).

Long-term investments Generally, (1) investments in stocks and bonds of other companies that companies normally hold for many years, and (2) long-term assets, such as land and buildings, not currently being used in operations. (p. 183).

Long-term liabilities Obligations that a company expects to pay after one year. (p. 187).

Operating cycle The average time that it takes to purchase inventory, sell it on account, and then collect cash from customers. (p. 183).

Permanent (real) accounts Accounts that relate to one or more future accounting periods. Consist of all balance sheet accounts. Balances are carried forward to the next accounting period. (p. 172).

Post-closing trial balance A list of permanent accounts and their balances after a company has journalized and posted closing entries. (p. 176).

Property, plant, and equipment Assets with relatively long useful lives and currently being used in operations. (p. 184).

Reversing entry An entry, made at the beginning of the next accounting period, that is the exact opposite of the adjusting entry made in the previous period. (p. 179).

Stockholders' equity The ownership claim of shareholders on total assets. It is to a corporation what owner's equity is to a proprietorship. (p. 187).

Temporary (nominal) accounts Accounts that relate only to a given accounting period. Consist of all income statement accounts and the Dividends account. All temporary accounts are closed at the end of the accounting period. (p. 171).

Worksheet A multiple-column form that may be used in making adjusting entries and in preparing financial statements. (p. 166).

APPENDIX 4A   Reversing Entries

After preparing the financial statements and closing the books, it is often helpful to reverse some of the adjusting entries before recording the regular transactions of the next period. Such entries are **reversing entries**. Companies make **a reversing entry at the beginning of the next accounting period**. Each reversing entry **is the exact opposite of the adjusting entry made in the previous period**. The recording of reversing entries is an **optional step** in the accounting cycle.

The purpose of reversing entries is to simplify the recording of a subsequent transaction related to an adjusting entry. For example, in Chapter 3 (page 119), the payment of salaries after an adjusting entry resulted in two debits: one to Salaries and Wages Payable and the other to Salaries and Wages Expense. With reversing entries, the company can debit the entire subsequent payment to Salaries and Wages Expense. **The use of reversing entries does not change the amounts reported in the financial statements**. What it does is simplify the recording of subsequent transactions.

Reversing Entries Example

Companies most often use reversing entries to reverse two types of adjusting entries: accrued revenues and accrued expenses. To illustrate the optional use of reversing entries for accrued expenses, we will use the salaries expense transactions for Pioneer Advertising Agency Inc. as illustrated in Chapters 2, 3, and 4. The transaction and adjustment data are as follows.

1. October 26 (initial salary entry): Pioneer pays $4,000 of salaries and wages earned between October 15 and October 26.

2. October 31 (adjusting entry): Salaries and wages earned between October 29 and October 31 are $1,200. The company will pay these in the November 9 payroll.

3. November 9 (subsequent salary entry): Salaries and wages paid are $4,000. Of this amount, $1,200 applied to accrued salaries and wages payable and $2,800 was earned between November 1 and November 9.

Illustration 4A-1 shows the entries with and without reversing entries.

The first three entries are the same whether or not Pioneer uses reversing entries. The last two entries are different. The November 1 **reversing entry** eliminates the $1,200 balance in Salaries and Wages Payable created by the October 31 adjusting entry. The reversing entry also creates a $1,200 credit balance in the Salaries and Wages Expense account. As you know, it is unusual for an expense account to have a credit balance. The balance is correct in this instance, though, because it anticipates that the entire amount of the first salaries and wages payment in the new accounting period will be debited to Salaries and Wages Expense. This debit will eliminate the credit balance. The resulting debit balance in the expense account will equal the salaries and wages expense incurred in the new accounting period ($2,800 in this example).

If Pioneer makes reversing entries, it can debit all cash payments of expenses to the expense account. This means that on November 9 (and every payday) Pioneer can debit Salaries and Wages Expense for the amount paid, without regard to any accrued salaries and wages payable. Being able to make the **same entry each time** simplifies the recording process. The company can record subsequent transactions as if the related adjusting entry had never been made.

Without Reversing Entries (per chapter)			With Reversing Entries (per appendix)		
Initial Salary Entry			**Initial Salary Entry**		
Oct. 26 Salaries and Wages Expense	4,000		Oct. 26 (Same entry)		
Cash		4,000			
Adjusting Entry			**Adjusting Entry**		
Oct. 31 Salaries and Wages Expense	1,200		Oct. 31 (Same entry)		
Salaries and Wages Payable		1,200			
Closing Entry			**Closing Entry**		
Oct. 31 Income Summary	5,200		Oct. 31 (Same entry)		
Salaries and Wages Expense		5,200			
Reversing Entry			**Reversing Entry**		
Nov. 1 No reversing entry is made.			Nov. 1 **Salaries and Wages Payable**	**1,200**	
			Salaries and Wages Expense		**1,200**
Subsequent Salary Entry			**Subsequent Salary Entry**		
Nov. 9 Salaries and Wages Payable	1,200		Nov. 9 **Salaries and Wages Expense**	**4,000**	
Salaries and Wages Expense	2,800		**Cash**		**4,000**
Cash		4,000			

Illustration 4A-1
Comparative entries—not reversing vs. reversing

Illustration 4A-2 shows the posting of the entries with reversing entries.

Salaries and Wages Expense					Salaries and Wages Payable			
10/26 Paid	4,000	10/31 Closing	5,200		11/1 Reversing	1,200	10/31 Adjusting	1,200
31 Adjusting	1,200							
	5,200		5,200					
11/9 Paid	4,000	11/1 Reversing	1,200					

Illustration 4A-2
Postings with reversing entries

A company can also use reversing entries for accrued revenue adjusting entries. For Pioneer Advertising Agency Inc., the adjusting entry was Accounts Receivable (Dr.) $200 and Service Revenue (Cr.) $200. Thus, the reversing entry on November 1 is:

Nov. 1	Service Revenue	200	
	Accounts Receivable		200
	(To reverse October 31 adjusting entry)		

A	=	L	+	SE
				−200 Rev
−200				

Cash Flows
no effect

When Pioneer collects the accrued service revenue, it debits Cash and credits Service Revenue.

SUMMARY OF LEARNING OBJECTIVE FOR APPENDIX 4A

 The Navigator

7 Prepare reversing entries. Reversing entries are the opposite of the adjusting entries made in the preceding period. Some companies choose to make reversing entries at the beginning of a new accounting period to simplify the recording of later transactions related to the adjusting entries. In most cases, only accrued adjusting entries are reversed.

WileyPLUS Self-Test, Brief Exercises, Exercises, Problem Set A, and many more components are available for practice in *WileyPLUS*.

---

*Note: All asterisked Questions, Exercises, and Problems relate to material in the appendix to the chapter.

SELF-TEST QUESTIONS

Answers are on page 215.

(LO 1)   **1.** Which of the following statements is **incorrect** concerning the worksheet?
  (a) The worksheet is essentially a working tool of the accountant.
  (b) The worksheet is distributed to management and other interested parties.
  (c) The worksheet cannot be used as a basis for posting to ledger accounts.
  (d) Financial statements can be prepared directly from the worksheet before journalizing and posting the adjusting entries.

(LO 1)   **2.** In a worksheet, net income is entered in the following columns:
  (a) income statement (Dr) and balance sheet (Dr).
  (b) income statement (Cr) and balance sheet (Dr).
  (c) income statement (Dr) and balance sheet (Cr).
  (d) income statement (Cr) and balance sheet (Cr).

(LO 1)   **3.** In the unadjusted trial balance of its worksheet for the year ended December 31, 2015, Knox Company reported Equipment of $120,000. The year-end adjusting entries require an adjustment of $15,000 for depreciation expense for the equipment. After adjustment, the following adjusted amount should be reported:
  (a) a debit of $105,000 for Equipment in the balance sheet column.
  (b) a credit of $15,000 for Depreciation Expense—Equipment in the income statement column.
  (c) a debit of $120,000 for Equipment in the balance sheet column.
  (d) a debit of $15,000 for Accumulated Depreciation—Equipment in the balance sheet column.

(LO 2)   **4.** An account that will have a zero balance after closing entries have been journalized and posted is:
  (a) Service Revenue.
  (b) Supplies.
  (c) Prepaid Insurance.
  (d) Accumulated Depreciation—Equipment.

(LO 2)   **5.** When a net loss has occurred, Income Summary is:
  (a) debited and Retained Earnings is credited.
  (b) credited and Retained Earnings is debited.
  (c) debited and Dividends are credited.
  (d) credited and Dividends are is debited.

(LO 2)   **6.** The closing process involves separate entries to close (1) expenses, (2) dividends, (3) revenues, and (4) income summary. The correct sequencing of the entries is:
  (a) (4), (3), (2), (1)   **(c)** (3), (1), (4), (2)
  (b) (1), (2), (3), (4)   **(d)** (3), (2), (1), (4)

(LO 3)   **7.** Which types of accounts will appear in the post-closing trial balance?

  (a) Permanent (real) accounts.
  (b) Temporary (nominal) accounts.
  (c) Accounts shown in the income statement columns of a worksheet.
  (d) None of the above.

(LO 4)   **8.** All of the following are required steps in the accounting cycle **except:**
  (a) journalizing and posting closing entries.
  (b) preparing financial statements.
  (c) journalizing the transactions.
  (d) preparing a worksheet.

(LO 4)   **9.** The proper order of the following steps in the accounting cycle is:
  (a) prepare unadjusted trial balance, journalize transactions, post to ledger accounts, journalize and post adjusting entries.
  (b) journalize transactions, prepare unadjusted trial balance, post to ledger accounts, journalize and post adjusting entries.
  (c) journalize transactions, post to ledger accounts, prepare unadjusted trial balance, journalize and post adjusting entries.
  (d) prepare unadjusted trial balance, journalize and post adjusting entries, journalize transactions, post to ledger accounts.

(LO 5)   **10.** When Ramirez Company purchased supplies worth $500, it incorrectly recorded a credit to Supplies for $5,000 and a debit to Cash for $5,000. Before correcting this error:
  (a) Cash is overstated and Supplies is overstated.
  (b) Cash is understated and Supplies is understated.
  (c) Cash is understated and Supplies is overstated.
  (d) Cash is overstated and Supplies is understated.

(LO 5)   **11.** Cash of $100 received at the time the service was performed was journalized and posted as a debit to Cash $100 and a credit to Accounts Receivable $100. Assuming the incorrect entry is not reversed, the correcting entry is:
  (a) debit Service Revenue $100 and credit Accounts Receivable $100.
  (b) debit Accounts Receivable $100 and credit Service Revenue $100.
  (c) debit Cash $100 and credit Service Revenue $100.
  (d) debit Accounts Receivable $100 and credit Cash $100.

(LO 6)   **12.** The correct order of presentation in a classified balance sheet for the following current assets is:
  (a) accounts receivable, cash, prepaid insurance, inventory.
  (b) cash, inventory, accounts receivable, prepaid insurance.

(c) cash, accounts receivable, inventory, prepaid insurance.

(d) inventory, cash, accounts receivable, prepaid insurance.

(LO 6) **13.** A company has purchased a tract of land. It expects to build a production plant on the land in approximately 5 years. During the 5 years before construction, the land will be idle. The land should be reported as:

(a) property, plant, and equipment.

(b) land expense.

(c) a long-term investment.

(d) an intangible asset.

(LO 6) **14.** In a classified balance sheet, assets are usually classified using the following categories:

(a) current assets; long-term assets; property, plant, and equipment; and intangible assets.

(b) current assets; long-term investments; property, plant, and equipment; and tangible assets.

(c) current assets; long-term investments; tangible assets; and intangible assets.

(d) current assets; long-term investments; property, plant, and equipment; and intangible assets.

15. Current assets are listed: (LO 6)

(a) by expected conversion to cash.

(b) by importance.

(c) by longevity.

(d) alphabetically.

*__16.__ On December 31, Kevin Hartman Company correctly (LO 7) made an adjusting entry to recognize $2,000 of accrued salaries payable. On January 8 of the next year, total salaries of $3,400 were paid. Assuming the correct reversing entry was made on January 1, the entry on January 8 will result in a credit to Cash $3,400 and the following debit(s):

(a) Salaries and Wages Payable $1,400 and Salaries and Wages Expense $2,000.

(b) Salaries and Wages Payable $2,000 and Salaries and Wages Expense $1,400.

(c) Salaries and Wages Expense $3,400.

(d) Salaries and Wages Payable $3,400.

Go to the book's companion website, www.wiley.com/college/weygandt, for additional Self-Test Questions.

QUESTIONS

1. "A worksheet is a permanent accounting record and its use is required in the accounting cycle." Do you agree? Explain.

2. Explain the purpose of the worksheet.

3. What is the relationship, if any, between the amount shown in the adjusted trial balance column for an account and that account's ledger balance?

4. If a company's revenues are $125,000 and its expenses are $113,000, in which financial statement columns of the worksheet will the net income of $12,000 appear? When expenses exceed revenues, in which columns will the difference appear?

5. Why is it necessary to prepare formal financial statements if all of the data are in the statement columns of the worksheet?

6. Identify the account(s) debited and credited in each of the four closing entries, assuming the company has net income for the year.

7. Describe the nature of the Income Summary account and identify the types of summary data that may be posted to this account.

8. What are the content and purpose of a post-closing trial balance?

9. Which of the following accounts would not appear in the post-closing trial balance? Interest Payable; Equipment; Depreciation Expense; Dividends; Unearned Service Revenue; Accumulated Depreciation—Equipment; and Service Revenue.

10. Distinguish between a reversing entry and an adjusting entry. Are reversing entries required?

11. Indicate, in the sequence in which they are made, the three required steps in the accounting cycle that involve journalizing.

12. Identify, in the sequence in which they are prepared, the three trial balances that are often used to report financial information about a company.

13. How do correcting entries differ from adjusting entries?

14. What standard classifications are used in preparing a classified balance sheet?

15. What is meant by the term "operating cycle?"

16. Define current assets. What basis is used for arranging individual items within the current assets section?

17. Distinguish between long-term investments and property, plant, and equipment.

18. (a) What is the term used to describe the owners' equity section of a corporation? (b) Identify the two owners' equity accounts in a corporation and indicate the purpose of each.

19. Using Apple's annual report, determine its current liabilities at September 25, 2010, and September 24, 2011. Were current liabilities higher or lower than current assets in these two years?

*__20.__ Cigale Company prepares reversing entries. If the adjusting entry for interest payable is reversed, what type of an account balance, if any, will there be in Interest Payable and Interest Expense after the reversing entry is posted?

*__21.__ At December 31, accrued salaries payable totaled $3,500. On January 10, total salaries of $8,000 are paid. (a) Assume that reversing entries are made at January 1. Give the January 10 entry, and indicate the Salaries and Wages Expense account balance after the entry is posted. (b) Repeat part (a) assuming reversing entries are not made.

BRIEF EXERCISES

List the steps in preparing a worksheet.

(LO 1)

BE4-1 The steps in using a worksheet are presented in random order below. List the steps in the proper order by placing numbers 1–5 in the blank spaces.

(a) _____ Prepare a trial balance on the worksheet.
(b) _____ Enter adjusted balances.
(c) _____ Extend adjusted balances to appropriate statement columns.
(d) _____ Total the statement columns, compute net income (loss), and complete the worksheet.
(e) _____ Enter adjustment data.

Prepare partial worksheet.

(LO 1)

BE4-2 The ledger of Clayton Company includes the following unadjusted balances: Prepaid Insurance $3,000, Service Revenue $58,000, and Salaries and Wages Expense $25,000. Adjusting entries are required for (a) expired insurance $1,800; (b) services performed $1,100, but unbilled and uncollected; and (c) accrued salaries payable $800. Enter the unadjusted balances and adjustments into a worksheet and complete the worksheet for all accounts. (*Note:* You will need to add the following accounts: Accounts Receivable, Salaries and Wages Payable, and Insurance Expense.)

Identify worksheet columns for selected accounts.

(LO 1)

BE4-3 The following selected accounts appear in the adjusted trial balance columns of the worksheet for Goulet Company: Accumulated Depreciation—Equipment; Depreciation Expense; Common Stock; Dividends; Service Revenue; Supplies; and Accounts Payable. Indicate the financial statement column (income statement Dr., balance sheet Cr., etc.) to which each balance should be extended.

Prepare closing entries from ledger balances.

(LO 2)

BE4-4 The ledger of Rios Company contains the following balances: Retained Earnings $30,000; Dividends $2,000; Service Revenue $50,000; Salaries and Wages Expense $27,000; and Supplies Expense $7,000. Prepare the closing entries at December 31.

Post closing entries; underline and balance T-accounts.

(LO 2)

BE4-5 Using the data in BE4-4, enter the balances in T-accounts, post the closing entries, and underline and balance the accounts.

Journalize and post closing entries using the three-column form of account.

(LO 2)

BE4-6 The income statement for Weeping Willow Golf Club for the month ending July 31 shows Service Revenue $16,400, Salaries and Wages Expense $8,200, Maintenance and Repairs Expense $2,500, and Net Income $5,700. Prepare the entries to close the revenue and expense accounts. Post the entries to the revenue and expense accounts, and complete the closing process for these accounts using the three-column form of account.

Identify post-closing trial balance accounts.

(LO 3)

BE4-7 Using the data in BE4-3, identify the accounts that would be included in a post-closing trial balance.

List the required steps in the accounting cycle in sequence.

(LO 4)

BE4-8 The steps in the accounting cycle are listed in random order below. List the steps in proper sequence, assuming no worksheet is prepared, by placing numbers 1–9 in the blank spaces.

(a) _____ Prepare a trial balance.
(b) _____ Journalize the transactions.
(c) _____ Journalize and post closing entries.
(d) _____ Prepare financial statements.
(e) _____ Journalize and post adjusting entries.
(f) _____ Post to ledger accounts.
(g) _____ Prepare a post-closing trial balance.
(h) _____ Prepare an adjusted trial balance.
(i) _____ Analyze business transactions.

Prepare correcting entries.

(LO 5)

BE4-9 At Creighton Company, the following errors were discovered after the transactions had been journalized and posted. Prepare the correcting entries.

1. A collection on account from a customer for $870 was recorded as a debit to Cash $870 and a credit to Service Revenue $870.
2. The purchase of store supplies on account for $1,570 was recorded as a debit to Supplies $1,750 and a credit to Accounts Payable $1,750.

Prepare the current assets section of a balance sheet.

(LO 6)

BE4-10 The balance sheet debit column of the worksheet for Hamidi Company includes the following accounts: Accounts Receivable $12,500; Prepaid Insurance $3,600; Cash $4,100; Supplies $5,200; and Debt Investments (short-term) $6,700. Prepare the current assets section of the balance sheet, listing the accounts in proper sequence.

BE4-11 The following are the major balance sheet classifications:

Current assets (CA)
Long-term investments (LTI)
Property, plant, and equipment (PPE)
Intangible assets (IA)

Current liabilities (CL)
Long-term liabilities (LTL)
Stockholders' equity (SE)

Classify accounts on balance sheet.
(LO 6)

Match each of the following accounts to its proper balance sheet classification.

_____ Accounts payable
_____ Accounts receivable
_____ Accumulated depreciation—buildings
_____ Buildings
_____ Cash
_____ Copyrights

_____ Income taxes payable
_____ Debt investments (long-term)
_____ Land
_____ Inventory
_____ Patents
_____ Supplies

*BE4-12 At October 31, Burgess Company made an accrued expense adjusting entry of $2,100 for salaries. Prepare the reversing entry on November 1, and indicate the balances in Salaries and Wages Payable and Salaries and Wages Expense after posting the reversing entry.

Prepare reversing entries.
(LO 7)

> DO IT! Review

DO IT! 4-1 Bradley Decker is preparing a worksheet. Explain to Bradley how he should extend the following adjusted trial balance accounts to the financial statement columns of the worksheet.

Prepare a worksheet.
(LO 1)

Service Revenue   Accounts Receivable
Notes Payable   Accumulated Depreciation
Common Stock   Utilities Expense

DO IT! 4-2 The worksheet for Tsai Company shows the following in the financial statement columns.

Prepare closing entries.
(LO 2)

Dividends $22,000
Common Stock   70,000
Net income   41,000

Prepare the closing entries at December 31 that affect stockholders' equity.

DO IT! 4-3 Ryan Newton recently received the following information related to Ryan Company's December 31, 2015, balance sheet.

Prepare assets section of the balance sheet.
(LO 6)

Inventory	$ 2,900	Debt investments (short-term)	$1,200
Cash	4,300	Accumulated depreciation—equip.	5,700
Equipment	21,700	Accounts receivable	4,300
Stock investments (long-term)	6,500		

Prepare the assets section of Ryan Company's classified balance sheet.

DO IT! 4-4 The following accounts were taken from the financial statements of Lee Company.

Match accounts to balance sheet classifications.
(LO 6)

_____ Interest revenue
_____ Utilities payable
_____ Accounts payable
_____ Supplies
_____ Bonds payable
_____ Goodwill

_____ Common stock
_____ Accumulated depreciation—equipment
_____ Equipment
_____ Salaries and wages expense
_____ Debt investments (long-term)
_____ Unearned rent revenue

Match each of the accounts to its proper balance sheet classification, as shown below. If the item would not appear on a balance sheet, use "NA."

Current assets (CA)
Long-term investments (LTI)
Property, plant, and equipment (PPE)
Intangible assets (IA)

Current liabilities (CL)
Long-term liabilities (LTL)
Stockholders' equity (SE)

Complete the worksheet.
(LO 1)

E4-1 The trial balance columns of the worksheet for Nanduri Company at June 30, 2015, are as follows.

NANDURI COMPANY
Worksheet
For the Month Ended June 30, 2015

Account Titles	Trial Balance Dr.	Trial Balance Cr.
Cash	2,320	
Accounts Receivable	2,440	
Supplies	1,880	
Accounts Payable		1,120
Unearned Service Revenue		240
Common Stock		3,600
Service Revenue		2,400
Salaries and Wages Expense	560	
Miscellaneous Expense	160	
	7,360	7,360

Other data:

1. A physical count reveals $500 of supplies on hand.
2. $100 of the unearned revenue is still unearned at month-end.
3. Accrued salaries are $210.

Instructions
Enter the trial balance on a worksheet and complete the worksheet.

Complete the worksheet.
(LO 1)

E4-2 The adjusted trial balance columns of the worksheet for DeSousa Company are as follows.

DESOUSA COMPANY
Worksheet (partial)
For the Month Ended April 30, 2015

Account Titles	Adjusted Trial Balance Dr.	Adjusted Trial Balance Cr.	Income Statement Dr.	Income Statement Cr.	Balance Sheet Dr.	Balance Sheet Cr.
Cash	10,000					
Accounts Receivable	7,840					
Prepaid Rent	2,280					
Equipment	23,050					
Accumulated Depreciation—Equip.		4,921				
Notes Payable		5,700				
Accounts Payable		4,920				
Common Stock		20,000				
Retained Earnings		7,960				
Dividends	3,650					
Service Revenue		15,590				
Salaries and Wages Expense	10,840					
Rent Expense	760					
Depreciation Expense	671					
Interest Expense	57					
Interest Payable		57				
Totals	59,148	59,148				

Instructions
Complete the worksheet.

E4-3 Worksheet data for DeSousa Company are presented in E4-2.

Prepare financial statements from worksheet.

(LO 1, 6)

Instructions

Prepare an income statement, a retained earnings statement, and a classified balance sheet.

E4-4 Worksheet data for DeSousa Company are presented in E4-2.

Journalize and post closing entries and prepare a post-closing trial balance.

(LO 2, 3)

Instructions

(a) Journalize the closing entries at April 30.
(b) Post the closing entries to Income Summary and Retained Earnings. (Use T-accounts.)
(c) Prepare a post-closing trial balance at April 30.

E4-5 The adjustments columns of the worksheet for Misra Company are shown below.

Prepare adjusting entries from a worksheet, and extend balances to worksheet columns.

(LO 1)

	Adjustments	
Account Titles	**Debit**	**Credit**
Accounts Receivable	1,100	
Prepaid Insurance		300
Accumulated Depreciation—Equipment		900
Salaries and Wages Payable		500
Service Revenue		1,100
Salaries and Wages Expense	500	
Insurance Expense	300	
Depreciation Expense	900	
	2,800	2,800

Instructions

(a) Prepare the adjusting entries.
(b) Assuming the adjusted trial balance amount for each account is normal, indicate the financial statement column to which each balance should be extended.

E4-6 Selected worksheet data for Elsayed Company are presented below.

Derive adjusting entries from worksheet data.

(LO 1)

Account Titles	**Trial Balance**		**Adjusted Trial Balance**	
	Dr.	**Cr.**	**Dr.**	**Cr.**
Accounts Receivable	?		34,000	
Prepaid Insurance	26,000		20,000	
Supplies	7,000		?	
Accumulated Depreciation—Equipment		12,000		?
Salaries and Wages Payable		?		5,600
Service Revenue		88,000		97,000
Insurance Expense			?	
Depreciation Expense			10,000	
Supplies Expense			4,500	
Salaries and Wages Expense	?		49,000	

Instructions

(a) Fill in the missing amounts.
(b) Prepare the adjusting entries that were made.

Prepare closing entries, and prepare a post-closing trial balance.

(LO 2, 3)

E4-7 Kay Magill Company had the following adjusted trial balance.

KAY MAGILL COMPANY
Adjusted Trial Balance
For the Month Ended June 30, 2015

Account Titles	Adjusted Trial Balance	
	Debit	Credit
Cash	$ 3,712	
Accounts Receivable	3,904	
Supplies	480	
Accounts Payable		$ 1,556
Unearned Service Revenue		160
Common Stock		4,000
Retained Earnings		1,760
Dividends	628	
Service Revenue		4,300
Salaries and Wages Expense	1,344	
Miscellaneous Expense	256	
Supplies Expense	1,900	
Salaries and Wages Payable		448
	$12,224	$12,224

Instructions
(a) Prepare closing entries at June 30, 2015.
(b) Prepare a post-closing trial balance.

Journalize and post closing entries, and prepare a post-closing trial balance.
(LO 2, 3)

E4-8 Plevin Company ended its fiscal year on July 31, 2015. The company's adjusted trial balance as of the end of its fiscal year is shown below.

PLEVIN COMPANY
Adjusted Trial Balance
July 31, 2015

No.	Account Titles	Debit	Credit
101	Cash	$ 9,840	
112	Accounts Receivable	8,780	
157	Equipment	15,900	
158	Accumulated Depreciation—Equip.		$ 7,400
201	Accounts Payable		4,220
208	Unearned Rent Revenue		1,800
311	Common Stock		20,000
320	Retained Earnings		25,200
332	Dividends	16,000	
400	Service Revenue		64,000
429	Rent Revenue		6,500
711	Depreciation Expense	8,000	
726	Salaries and Wages Expense	55,700	
732	Utilities Expense	14,900	
		$129,120	$129,120

Instructions
(a) Prepare the closing entries using page J15.
(b) Post to the Retained Earnings and No. 350 Income Summary accounts. (Use the three-column form.)
(c) Prepare a post-closing trial balance at July 31.

Prepare financial statements.
(LO 6)

E4-9 The adjusted trial balance for Plevin Company is presented in E4-8.

Instructions
(a) Prepare an income statement and a retained earnings statement for the year.
(b) Prepare a classified balance sheet at July 31.

E4-10 Janis Engle has prepared the following list of statements about the accounting cycle.

Answer questions related to the accounting cycle.
(LO 4)

1. "Journalize the transactions" is the first step in the accounting cycle.
2. Reversing entries are a required step in the accounting cycle.
3. Correcting entries do not have to be part of the accounting cycle.
4. If a worksheet is prepared, some steps of the accounting cycle are incorporated into the worksheet.
5. The accounting cycle begins with the analysis of business transactions and ends with the preparation of a post-closing trial balance.
6. All steps of the accounting cycle occur daily during the accounting period.
7. The step of "post to the ledger accounts" occurs before the step of "journalize the transactions."
8. Closing entries must be prepared before financial statements can be prepared.

Instructions

Identify each statement as true or false. If false, indicate how to correct the statement.

E4-11 Selected accounts for Heather's Salon are presented below. All June 30 postings are from closing entries.

Prepare closing entries.
(LO 2)

Salaries and Wages Expense				Service Revenue				Retained Earnings			
6/10	3,200	6/30	8,800	6/30	18,100	6/15	9,700	6/30	2,500	6/1	12,000
6/28	5,600					6/24	8,400			6/30	5,000
										Bal.	14,500

Supplies Expense				Rent Expense				Dividends			
6/12	600	6/30	1,300	6/1	3,000	6/30	3,000	6/13	1,000	6/30	2,500
6/24	700							6/25	1,500		

Instructions

(a) Prepare the closing entries that were made.
(b) Post the closing entries to Income Summary.

E4-12 Andrew Clark Company discovered the following errors made in January 2015.

Prepare correcting entries.
(LO 5)

1. A payment of Salaries and Wages Expense of $700 was debited to Equipment and credited to Cash, both for $700.
2. A collection of $1,000 from a client on account was debited to Cash $100 and credited to Service Revenue $100.
3. The purchase of equipment on account for $760 was debited to Equipment $670 and credited to Accounts Payable $670.

Instructions

(a) Correct the errors by reversing the incorrect entry and preparing the correct entry.
(b) Correct the errors without reversing the incorrect entry.

E4-13 Keenan Company has an inexperienced accountant. During the first 2 weeks on the job, the accountant made the following errors in journalizing transactions. All entries were posted as made.

Prepare correcting entries.
(LO 5)

1. A payment on account of $840 to a creditor was debited to Accounts Payable $480 and credited to Cash $480.
2. The purchase of supplies on account for $560 was debited to Equipment $56 and credited to Accounts Payable $56.
3. A $500 cash dividend was debited to Salaries and Wages Expense $500 and credited to Cash $500.

Instructions

Prepare the correcting entries.

E4-14 The adjusted trial balance for Martell Bowling Alley at December 31, 2015, contains the following accounts.

Prepare a classified balance sheet.
(LO 6)

	Debit		Credit
Buildings	$128,800	Common Stock	$ 90,000
Accounts Receivable	14,520	Retained Earnings	25,000
Prepaid Insurance	4,680	Accumulated Depreciation—Buildings	42,600
Cash	18,040	Accounts Payable	12,300
Equipment	62,400	Notes Payable	97,780
Land	67,000	Accumulated Depreciation—Equipment	18,720
Insurance Expense	780	Interest Payable	2,600
Depreciation Expense	7,360	Service Revenue	17,180
Interest Expense	2,600		$306,180
	$306,180		

Instructions

(a) Prepare a classified balance sheet; assume that $22,000 of the note payable will be paid in 2016.

(b) ━━━━━➤ Comment on the liquidity of the company.

Classify accounts on balance sheet.

(LO 6)

E4-15 The following are the major balance sheet classifications.

Current assets (CA)	Current liabilities (CL)
Long-term investments (LTI)	Long-term liabilities (LTL)
Property, plant, and equipment (PPE)	Stockholders' equity (SE)
Intangible assets (IA)	

Instructions

Classify each of the following accounts taken from Raman Company's balance sheet.

_____ Accounts payable	_____ Accumulated depreciation—equipment
_____ Accounts receivable	_____ Buildings
_____ Cash	_____ Land (in use)
_____ Common stock	_____ Notes payable (due in 2 years)
_____ Patents	_____ Supplies
_____ Salaries and wages payable	_____ Equipment
_____ Inventory	_____ Prepaid expenses
_____ Stock investments (to be sold in 7 months)	

Prepare a classified balance sheet.

(LO 6)

E4-16 The following items were taken from the financial statements of D. Gygi Company. (All amounts are in thousands.)

Long-term debt	$ 1,000	Accumulated depreciation—equipment	$ 5,655
Prepaid insurance	880	Accounts payable	1,444
Equipment	11,500	Notes payable (due after 2016)	400
Stock investments (long-term)	264	Common stock	10,000
Debt investments (short-term)	3,690	Retained earnings	2,955
Notes payable (due in 2016)	500	Accounts receivable	1,696
Cash	2,668	Inventory	1,256

Instructions

Prepare a classified balance sheet in good form as of December 31, 2015.

Prepare financial statements.

(LO 6)

E4-17 These financial statement items are for Norsted Company at year-end, July 31, 2015.

Salaries and wages payable	$ 2,080	Notes payable (long-term)	$ 1,800
Salaries and wages expense	51,700	Cash	14,200
Utilities expense	22,600	Accounts receivable	9,780
Equipment	30,400	Accumulated depreciation—equipment	6,000
Accounts payable	4,100	Dividends	3,000
Service revenue	62,000	Depreciation expense	4,000
Rent revenue	8,500	Retained earnings (beginning of the year)	21,200
Common stock	30,000		

Instructions

(a) Prepare an income statement and a retained earnings statement for the year.

(b) Prepare a classified balance sheet at July 31.

*E4-18 Reblin Company pays salaries of $12,000 every Monday for the preceding 5-day week (Monday through Friday). Assume December 31 falls on a Tuesday, so Reblin's employees have worked 2 days without being paid.

Use reversing entries.
(LO 7)

Instructions

(a) Assume the company does not use reversing entries. Prepare the December 31 adjusting entry and the entry on Monday, January 6, when Reblin pays the payroll.

(b) Assume the company does use reversing entries. Prepare the December 31 adjusting entry, the January 1 reversing entry, and the entry on Monday, January 6, when Reblin pays the payroll.

*E4-19 On December 31, the adjusted trial balance of Cisneros Employment Agency shows the following selected data.

Prepare closing and reversing entries.
(LO 2, 4, 7)

Accounts Receivable	$24,500	Service Revenue	$92,500
Interest Expense	8,300	Interest Payable	2,000

Analysis shows that adjusting entries were made to (1) accrue $5,000 of service revenue and (2) accrue $2,000 interest expense.

Instructions

(a) Prepare the closing entries for the temporary accounts shown above at December 31.

(b) Prepare the reversing entries on January 1.

(c) Post the entries in (a) and (b), excluding the Income Summary account. Underline and balance the accounts. (Use T-accounts.)

(d) Prepare the entries to record (1) the collection of the accrued revenue on January 10 and (2) the payment of all interest due ($3,000) on January 15.

(e) Post the entries in (d) to the temporary accounts.

EXERCISES: SET B AND CHALLENGE EXERCISES

Visit the book's companion website, at **www.wiley.com/college/weygandt**, and choose the Student Companion site to access Exercise Set B and Challenge Exercises.

PROBLEMS: SET A

P4-1A The trial balance columns of the worksheet for Lampert Roofing at March 31, 2015, are as follows.

Prepare a worksheet, financial statements, and adjusting and closing entries.
(LO 1, 2, 3, 6)

LAMPERT ROOFING
Worksheet
For the Month Ended March 31, 2015

Account Titles	Trial Balance	
	Dr.	Cr.
Cash	4,500	
Accounts Receivable	3,200	
Supplies	2,000	
Equipment	11,000	
Accumulated Depreciation—Equipment		1,250
Accounts Payable		2,500
Unearned Service Revenue		550
Common Stock		10,000
Retained Earnings		2,900
Dividends	1,100	
Service Revenue		6,300
Salaries and Wages Expense	1,300	
Miscellaneous Expense	400	
	23,500	23,500

Other data:

1. A physical count reveals only $550 of roofing supplies on hand.
2. Depreciation for March is $250.
3. Unearned service revenue amounted to $210 at March 31.
4. Accrued salaries are $700.

Instructions

(a) Adjusted trial balance
$24,450

(b) Net income $2,540
Total assets $17,750

(a) Enter the trial balance on a worksheet and complete the worksheet.
(b) Prepare an income statement and a retained earnings statement for the month of March and a classified balance sheet at March 31.
(c) Journalize the adjusting entries from the adjustments columns of the worksheet.
(d) Journalize the closing entries from the financial statement columns of the worksheet.

Complete worksheet; prepare financial statements, closing entries, and post-closing trial balance.

(LO 1, 2, 3, 6)

P4-2A The adjusted trial balance columns of the worksheet for Alshwer Company are as follows.

ALSHWER COMPANY
Worksheet
For the Year Ended December 31, 2015

Account No.	Account Titles	Adjusted Trial Balance Dr.	Cr.
101	Cash	5,300	
112	Accounts Receivable	10,800	
126	Supplies	1,500	
130	Prepaid Insurance	2,000	
157	Equipment	27,000	
158	Accumulated Depreciation—Equipment		5,600
200	Notes Payable		15,000
201	Accounts Payable		6,100
212	Salaries and Wages Payable		2,400
230	Interest Payable		600
311	Common Stock		10,000
320	Retained Earnings		3,000
332	Dividends	7,000	
400	Service Revenue		61,000
610	Advertising Expense	8,400	
631	Supplies Expense	4,000	
711	Depreciation Expense	5,600	
722	Insurance Expense	3,500	
726	Salaries and Wages Expense	28,000	
905	Interest Expense	600	
	Totals	103,700	103,700

Instructions

(a) Net income $10,900

(b) Current assets $19,600
Current liabilities $14,100

(e) Post-closing trial balance $46,600

(a) Complete the worksheet by extending the balances to the financial statement columns.
(b) Prepare an income statement, a retained earnings statement, and a classified balance sheet. (*Note:* $5,000 of the notes payable become due in 2016.)
(c) Prepare the closing entries. Use J14 for the journal page.
(d) Post the closing entries. (Use the three-column form of account.) Income Summary is No. 350.
(e) Prepare a post-closing trial balance.

Prepare financial statements, closing entries, and post-closing trial balance.

(LO 1, 2, 3, 6)

P4-3A The completed financial statement columns of the worksheet for Fleming Company are shown on the next page.

FLEMING COMPANY
Worksheet
For the Year Ended December 31, 2015

Account No.	Account Titles	Income Statement Dr.	Income Statement Cr.	Balance Sheet Dr.	Balance Sheet Cr.
101	Cash			8,900	
112	Accounts Receivable			10,800	
130	Prepaid Insurance			2,800	
157	Equipment			24,000	
158	Accumulated Depreciation—Equip.				4,500
201	Accounts Payable				9,000
212	Salaries and Wages Payable				2,400
311	Common Stock				12,000
320	Retained Earnings				7,500
332	Dividends			11,000	
400	Service Revenue		60,000		
622	Maintenance and Repairs Expense	1,600			
711	Depreciation Expense	3,100			
722	Insurance Expense	1,800			
726	Salaries and Wages Expense	30,000			
732	Utilities Expense	1,400			
	Totals	37,900	60,000	57,500	35,400
	Net Income	22,100			22,100
		60,000	60,000	57,500	57,500

Instructions

(a) Prepare an income statement, a retained earnings statement, and a classified balance sheet.
(b) Prepare the closing entries.
(c) Post the closing entries and underline and balance the accounts. (Use T-accounts.) Income Summary is account No. 350.
(d) Prepare a post-closing trial balance.

(a) Ending retained earnings $18,600
Total current assets $22,500
(d) Post-closing trial balance $46,500

P4-4A Jarmuz Management Services began business on January 1, 2014, with a capital investment of $90,000. The company manages condominiums for owners (service revenue) and rents space in its own office building (rent revenue). The trial balance and adjusted trial balance columns of the worksheet at the end of 2014 are as follows.

Complete worksheet; prepare classified balance sheet, entries, and post-closing trial balance.

(LO 1, 2, 3, 6)

JARMUZ MANAGEMENT SERVICES
Worksheet
For the Year Ended December 31, 2014

Account Titles	Trial Balance Dr.	Trial Balance Cr.	Adjusted Trial Balance Dr.	Adjusted Trial Balance Cr.
Cash	13,800		13,800	
Accounts Receivable	28,300		28,300	
Prepaid Insurance	3,600		2,400	
Land	67,000		67,000	
Buildings	127,000		127,000	
Equipment	59,000		59,000	
Accounts Payable		12,500		12,500
Unearned Rent Revenue		6,000		1,500
Mortgage Payable		120,000		120,000
Common Stock		90,000		90,000
Retained Earnings		54,000		54,000
Dividends	22,000		22,000	
Service Revenue		90,700		90,700
Rent Revenue		29,000		33,500
Salaries and Wages Expense	42,000		42,000	
Advertising Expense	20,500		20,500	
Utilities Expense	19,000		19,000	
Totals	402,200	402,200		

	Trial Balance		Adjusted Trial Balance	
Account Titles	Dr.	Cr.	Dr.	Cr.
Insurance Expense			1,200	
Depreciation Expense			6,600	
Accumulated Depreciation—Buildings				3,000
Accumulated Depreciation—Equipment				3,600
Interest Expense			10,000	
Interest Payable				10,000
Totals			418,800	418,800

Instructions

(a) Net income $24,900

(b) Total current assets $44,500

(e) Post-closing trial balance $297,500

(a) Prepare a complete worksheet.

(b) Prepare a classified balance sheet. (*Note:* $30,000 of the mortgage note payable is due for payment next year.)

(c) Journalize the adjusting entries.

(d) Journalize the closing entries.

(e) Prepare a post-closing trial balance.

Complete all steps in accounting cycle.

(LO 1, 2, 3, 4, 6)

P4-5A Heidi Jara opened Jara's Cleaning Service on July 1, 2015. During July, the following transactions were completed.

July	1	Stockholders invested $20,000 cash in the business in exchange for common stock.
	1	Purchased used truck for $9,000, paying $4,000 cash and the balance on account.
	3	Purchased cleaning supplies for $2,100 on account.
	5	Paid $1,800 cash on a 1-year insurance policy effective July 1.
	12	Billed customers $4,500 for cleaning services.
	18	Paid $1,500 cash on amount owed on truck and $1,400 on amount owed on cleaning supplies.
	20	Paid $2,500 cash for employee salaries.
	21	Collected $3,400 cash from customers billed on July 12.
	25	Billed customers $6,000 for cleaning services.
	31	Paid $350 for the monthly gasoline bill for the truck.
	31	Paid a $5,600 cash dividend.

The chart of accounts for Jara's Cleaning Service contains the following accounts: No. 101 Cash, No. 112 Accounts Receivable, No. 126 Supplies, No. 130 Prepaid Insurance, No. 157 Equipment, No. 158 Accumulated Depreciation—Equipment, No. 201 Accounts Payable, No. 212 Salaries and Wages Payable, No. 311 Common Stock, No. 320 Retained Earnings, No. 332 Dividends, No. 350 Income Summary, No. 400 Service Revenue, No. 631 Supplies Expense, No. 633 Gasoline Expense, No. 711 Depreciation Expense, No. 722 Insurance Expense, and No. 726 Salaries and Wages Expense.

Instructions

(b) Trial balance $34,700

(c) Adjusted trial balance $38,900

(d) Net income $7,200
Total assets $26,800

(g) Post-closing trial balance $27,300

(a) Journalize and post the July transactions. Use page J1 for the journal and the three-column form of account.

(b) Prepare a trial balance at July 31 on a worksheet.

(c) Enter the following adjustments on the worksheet and complete the worksheet.
   (1) Unbilled and uncollected revenue for services performed at July 31 were $2,700.
   (2) Depreciation on equipment for the month was $500.
   (3) One-twelfth of the insurance expired.
   (4) An inventory count shows $600 of cleaning supplies on hand at July 31.
   (5) Accrued but unpaid employee salaries were $1,000.

(d) Prepare an income statement and a retained earnings statement for July and a classified balance sheet at July 31.

(e) Journalize and post adjusting entries. Use page J2 for the journal.

(f) Journalize and post closing entries and complete the closing process. Use page J3 for the journal.

(g) Prepare a post-closing trial balance at July 31.

P4-6A Dao Vang, CPA, was retained by Universal Cable to prepare financial statements for April 2015. Vang accumulated all the ledger balances per Universal's records and found the following.

Analyze errors and prepare correcting entries and trial balance.

(LO 5)

UNIVERSAL CABLE
Trial Balance
April 30, 2015

	Debit	Credit
Cash	$ 4,100	
Accounts Receivable	3,200	
Supplies	800	
Equipment	10,600	
Accumulated Depreciation—Equip.		$ 1,350
Accounts Payable		2,100
Salaries and Wages Payable		700
Unearned Service Revenue		890
Common Stock		10,000
Retained Earnings		2,900
Service Revenue		5,450
Salaries and Wages Expense	3,300	
Advertising Expense	600	
Miscellaneous Expense	290	
Depreciation Expense	500	
	$23,390	$23,390

Dao Vang reviewed the records and found the following errors.

1. Cash received from a customer on account was recorded as $950 instead of $590.
2. A payment of $75 for advertising expense was entered as a debit to Miscellaneous Expense $75 and a credit to Cash $75.
3. The first salary payment this month was for $1,900, which included $700 of salaries payable on March 31. The payment was recorded as a debit to Salaries and Wages Expense $1,900 and a credit to Cash $1,900. (No reversing entries were made on April 1.)
4. The purchase on account of a printer costing $310 was recorded as a debit to Supplies and a credit to Accounts Payable for $310.
5. A cash payment of repair expense on equipment for $96 was recorded as a debit to Equipment $69 and a credit to Cash $69.

Instructions
(a) Prepare an analysis of each error showing (1) the incorrect entry, (2) the correct entry, and (3) the correcting entry. Items 4 and 5 occurred on April 30, 2015.
(b) Prepare a correct trial balance.

(b) Trial balance $22,690

PROBLEMS: SET B

P4-1B Pevnick Inc. began operations as a detective agency on January 1, 2015. The trial balance columns of the worksheet for Pevnick Inc. at March 31 are as follows.

Prepare worksheet, financial statements, and adjusting and closing entries.

(LO 1, 2, 3, 6)

PEVNICK INC.
Worksheet
For the Quarter Ended March 31, 2015

Account Titles	Trial Balance	
	Dr.	Cr.
Cash	11,400	
Accounts Receivable	5,620	
Supplies	1,050	
Prepaid Insurance	2,400	
Equipment	30,000	

	Trial Balance	
Account Titles	**Dr.**	**Cr.**
Notes Payable		10,000
Accounts Payable		12,350
Common Stock		20,000
Dividends	600	
Service Revenue		13,620
Salaries and Wages Expense	2,200	
Travel Expense	1,300	
Rent Expense	1,200	
Miscellaneous Expense	200	
	55,970	55,970

Other data:

1. Supplies on hand total $280.
2. Depreciation is $800 per quarter.
3. Interest accrued on 6-month note payable, issued January 1, $300.
4. Insurance expires at the rate of $200 per month.
5. Services performed but unbilled at March 31 total $2,030.

Instructions

(a) Adjusted trial balance
$59,100

(b) Net income $8,280
Total assets $50,330

(a) Enter the trial balance on a worksheet and complete the worksheet.
(b) Prepare an income statement and a retained earnings statement for the quarter and a classified balance sheet at March 31.
(c) Journalize the adjusting entries from the adjustments columns of the worksheet.
(d) Journalize the closing entries from the financial statement columns of the worksheet.

Complete worksheet; prepare financial statements, closing entries, and post-closing trial balance.

(LO 1, 2, 3, 6)

P4-2B The adjusted trial balance columns of the worksheet for Greenwood Company are as follows.

GREENWOOD COMPANY
Worksheet
For the Year Ended December 31, 2015

Account No.	Account Titles	Adjusted Trial Balance Dr.	Adjusted Trial Balance Cr.
101	Cash	18,800	
112	Accounts Receivable	16,200	
126	Supplies	2,300	
130	Prepaid Insurance	4,400	
157	Equipment	46,000	
158	Accumulated Depreciation—Equipment		20,000
200	Notes Payable		20,000
201	Accounts Payable		8,000
212	Salaries and Wages Payable		2,600
230	Interest Payable		1,000
311	Common Stock		15,000
320	Retained Earnings		11,000
332	Dividends	12,000	
400	Service Revenue		87,800
610	Advertising Expense	10,000	
631	Supplies Expense	3,700	
711	Depreciation Expense	8,000	
722	Insurance Expense	4,000	
726	Salaries and Wages Expense	39,000	
905	Interest Expense	1,000	
	Totals	165,400	165,400

Instructions
(a) Complete the worksheet by extending the balances to the financial statement columns.
(b) Prepare an income statement, a retained earnings statement, and a classified balance sheet. (*Note:* $5,000 of the notes payable become due in 2016.)
(c) Prepare the closing entries. Use J14 for the journal page.
(d) Post the closing entries. (Use the three-column form of account.) Income Summary is account No. 350.
(e) Prepare a post-closing trial balance.

(a) Net income $22,100
(b) Current assets $41,700
     Current liabilities $16,600

(e) Post-closing trial balance
     $87,700

P4-3B The completed financial statement columns of the worksheet for Niho Company are shown below.

Prepare financial statements, closing entries, and post-closing trial balance.
(LO 1, 2, 3, 6)

NIHO COMPANY
Worksheet
For the Year Ended December 31, 2015

Account No.	Account Titles	Income Statement Dr.	Income Statement Cr.	Balance Sheet Dr.	Balance Sheet Cr.
101	Cash			5,200	
112	Accounts Receivable			7,500	
130	Prepaid Insurance			1,800	
157	Equipment			33,000	
158	Accumulated Depreciation—Equip.				8,600
201	Accounts Payable				11,700
212	Salaries and Wages Payable				3,000
311	Common Stock				20,000
320	Retained Earnings				14,000
332	Dividends			7,200	
400	Service Revenue		45,000		
622	Maintenance and Repairs Expense	4,400			
711	Depreciation Expense	2,800			
722	Insurance Expense	1,200			
726	Salaries and Wages Expense	35,200			
732	Utilities Expense	4,000			
	Totals	47,600	45,000	54,700	57,300
	Net Loss		2,600	2,600	
		47,600	47,600	57,300	57,300

Instructions
(a) Prepare an income statement, a retained earnings statement, and a classified balance sheet.
(b) Prepare the closing entries.
(c) Post the closing entries and underline and balance the accounts. (Use T-accounts.) Income Summary is account No. 350.
(d) Prepare a post-closing trial balance.

(a) Net loss $2,600
     Ending retained earnings
     $4,200
     Total assets $38,900
(d) Post-closing trial balance
     $47,500

P4-4B Avalon Amusement Park has a fiscal year ending on September 30. Selected data from the September 30 worksheet are presented below and on the next page.

Complete worksheet; prepare classified balance sheet, entries, and post-closing trial balance.
(LO 1, 2, 3, 6)

AVALON AMUSEMENT PARK
Worksheet
For the Year Ended September 30, 2015

	Trial Balance Dr.	Trial Balance Cr.	Adjusted Trial Balance Dr.	Adjusted Trial Balance Cr.
Cash	41,400		41,400	
Supplies	18,600		2,200	
Prepaid Insurance	31,900		10,900	
Land	80,000		80,000	
Equipment	120,000		120,000	

	Trial Balance		Adjusted Trial Balance	
	Dr.	Cr.	Dr.	Cr.
Accumulated Depreciation—Equip.		36,200		42,200
Accounts Payable		14,600		14,600
Unearned Ticket Revenue		3,700		1,000
Mortgage Payable		50,000		50,000
Common Stock		60,000		60,000
Retained Earnings		49,700		49,700
Dividends	14,000		14,000	
Ticket Revenue		277,500		280,200
Salaries and Wages Expense	105,000		105,000	
Maintenance and Repairs Expense	30,500		30,500	
Advertising Expense	9,400		9,400	
Utilities Expense	16,900		16,900	
Property Tax Expense	18,000		21,000	
Interest Expense	6,000		10,000	
Totals	491,700	491,700		
Insurance Expense			21,000	
Supplies Expense			16,400	
Interest Payable				4,000
Depreciation Expense			6,000	
Property Taxes Payable				3,000
Totals			504,700	504,700

Instructions

(a) Net income $44,000

(a) Prepare a complete worksheet.

(b) Total current assets $54,500

(b) Prepare a classified balance sheet. (*Note:* $15,000 of the mortgage note payable is due for payment in the next fiscal year.)

(c) Journalize the adjusting entries using the worksheet as a basis.

(e) Post-closing trial balance $254,500

(d) Journalize the closing entries using the worksheet as a basis.

(e) Prepare a post-closing trial balance.

Complete all steps in accounting cycle.

(LO 1, 2, 3, 4, 6)

P4-5B Gillian Shaw opened Shaw's Carpet Cleaners on March 1. During March, the following transactions were completed.

Mar.	1	Stockholders invested $10,000 cash in the business in exchange for common stock.
	1	Purchased used truck for $6,000, paying $3,000 cash and the balance on account.
	3	Purchased cleaning supplies for $1,200 on account.
	5	Paid $1,200 cash on a 1-year insurance policy effective March 1.
	14	Billed customers $4,800 for cleaning services.
	18	Paid $1,500 cash on amount owed on truck and $500 on amount owed on cleaning supplies.
	20	Paid $1,800 cash for employee salaries.
	21	Collected $1,400 cash from customers billed on March 14.
	28	Billed customers $4,500 for cleaning services.
	31	Paid $500 for the monthly gasoline bill for the truck.
	31	Paid a $700 cash dividend.

The chart of accounts for Shaw's Carpet Cleaners contains the following accounts: No. 101 Cash, No. 112 Accounts Receivable, No. 126 Supplies, No. 130 Prepaid Insurance, No. 157 Equipment, No. 158 Accumulated Depreciation—Equipment, No. 201 Accounts Payable, No. 212 Salaries and Wages Payable, No. 311 Common Stock, No. 320 Retained Earnings, No. 332 Dividends, No. 350 Income Summary, No. 400 Service Revenue, No. 631 Supplies Expense, No. 633 Gasoline Expense, No. 711 Depreciation Expense, No. 722 Insurance Expense, and No. 726 Salaries and Wages Expense.

Instructions

(a) Journalize and post the March transactions. Use page J1 for the journal and the three-column form of account.

(b) Trial balance $21,500

(b) Prepare a trial balance at March 31 on a worksheet.

(c) Enter the following adjustments on the worksheet and complete the worksheet.
  (1) Unbilled revenue for services performed at March 31 was $500.
  (2) Depreciation on equipment for the month was $300.
  (3) One-twelfth of the insurance expired.
  (4) An inventory count shows $250 of cleaning supplies on hand at March 31.
  (5) Accrued but unpaid employee salaries were $550.
(d) Prepare an income statement and a retained earnings statement for March and a classified balance sheet at March 31.
(e) Journalize and post adjusting entries. Use page J2 for the journal.
(f) Journalize and post closing entries and complete the closing process. Use page J3 for the journal.
(g) Prepare a post-closing trial balance at March 31.

(c) Adjusted trial balance $22,850

(d) Net income $5,600
Total assets $17,650

(g) Post-closing trial balance $17,950

PROBLEMS: SET C

Visit the book's companion website, at **www.wiley.com/college/weygandt**, and choose the Student Companion site to access Problem Set C.

COMPREHENSIVE PROBLEM: CHAPTERS 2 TO 4

CP4 Kristin Malone opened Kristin's Maids Cleaning Service on July 1, 2015. During July, the company completed the following transactions.

July 1 Stockholders invested $14,000 cash in the business in exchange for common stock.
    1 Purchased a used truck for $10,000, paying $3,000 cash and the balance on account.
    3 Purchased cleaning supplies for $800 on account.
    5 Paid $1,800 on a 1-year insurance policy, effective July 1.
   12 Billed customers $3,800 for cleaning services.
   18 Paid $1,000 of amount owed on truck, and $400 of amount owed on cleaning supplies.
   20 Paid $1,600 for employee salaries.
   21 Collected $1,400 from customers billed on July 12.
   25 Billed customers $1,500 for cleaning services.
   31 Paid gasoline for the month on the truck, $400.
   31 Declared and paid a $600 cash dividend.

The chart of accounts for Kristin's Maids Cleaning Service contains the following accounts: No. 101 Cash, No. 112 Accounts Receivable, No. 126 Supplies, No. 130 Prepaid Insurance, No. 157 Equipment, No. 158 Accumulated Depreciation—Equipment, No. 201 Accounts Payable, No. 212 Salaries and Wages Payable, No. 311 Common Stock, No. 320 Retained Earnings, No. 332 Dividends, No. 350 Income Summary, No. 400 Service Revenue, No. 631 Supplies Expense, No. 633 Gasoline Expense, No. 711 Depreciation Expense, No. 722 Insurance Expense, and No. 726 Salaries and Wages Expense.

Instructions
(a) Journalize and post the July transactions. Use page J1 for the journal.
(b) Prepare a trial balance at July 31 on a worksheet.
(c) Enter the following adjustments on the worksheet, and complete the worksheet.
  (1) Unbilled fees for services performed at July 31 were $1,300.
  (2) Depreciation on equipment for the month was $200.
  (3) One-twelfth of the insurance expired.
  (4) An inventory count shows $100 of cleaning supplies on hand at July 31.
  (5) Accrued but unpaid employee salaries were $500.
(d) Prepare an income statement and a retained earnings statement for July, and a classified balance sheet at July 31, 2015.
(e) Journalize and post the adjusting entries. Use page J2 for the journal.
(f) Journalize and post the closing entries, and complete the closing process. Use page J3 for the journal.
(g) Prepare a post-closing trial balance at July 31.

(b) Trial balance $25,700

(d) Net income $3,050
Total assets $23,350

(g) Post-closing trial balance $23,550

(*Note:* This is a continuation of the Cookie Chronicle from Chapters 1 through 3.)

CCC4 Natalie had a very busy December. At the end of the month, after journalizing and posting the December transactions and adjusting entries, Natalie then prepared an adjusted trial balance.

Go to the book's companion website, **www.wiley.com/college/weygandt**, *to see the completion of this problem.*

Broadening Your **PERSPECTIVE**

Financial Reporting and Analysis

Financial Reporting Problem: Apple Inc.

BYP4-1 The financial statements of Apple Inc. are presented in Appendix A at the end of this textbook. Instructions for accessing and using the company's complete annual report, including the notes to the financial statements, are also provided in Appendix A.

Instructions
Answer the questions below using Apple's Consolidated Balance Sheets.

(a) What were Apple's total current assets at September 24, 2011, and September 25, 2010?
(b) Are assets that Apple included under current assets listed in proper order? Explain.
(c) How are Apple's assets classified?
(d) What was Apple's "Cash and cash equivalents" at September 24, 2011?
(e) What were Apple's total current liabilities at September 24, 2011, and September 25, 2010?

Comparative Analysis Problem:
PepsiCo, Inc. vs. The Coca-Cola Company

BYP4-2 PepsiCo's financial statements are presented in Appendix B. Financial statements for The Coca-Cola Company are presented in Appendix C. Instructions for accessing and using the complete annual reports of PepsiCo and Coca-Cola, including the notes to the financial statements, are also provided in Appendices B and C, respectively.

Instructions
(a) Based on the information contained in these financial statements, determine each of the following for PepsiCo at December 31, 2011, and for Coca-Cola at December 31, 2011.
  (1) Total current assets.
  (2) Net amount of property, plant, and equipment (land, buildings, and equipment).
  (3) Total current liabilities.
  (4) Total equity.
(b) What conclusions concerning the companies' respective financial positions can be drawn?

Comparative Analysis Problem:
Amazon.com, Inc. vs. Wal-Mart Stores, Inc.

BYP4-3 Amazon.com, Inc.'s financial statements are presented in Appendix D. Financial statements for Wal-Mart Stores, Inc. are presented in Appendix E. Instructions for accessing and using the complete annual reports of Amazon and Wal-Mart, including the notes to the financial statements, are also provided in Appendices D and E, respectively.

Instructions
(a) Based on the information contained in these financial statements, determine the following for Amazon at December 31, 2011, and Wal-Mart at January 31, 2012.
  (1) Total current assets.
  (2) Net amount of property and equipment (fixed assets), net.

   (3) Total current liabilities.
   (4) Total equity.
(b) What conclusions concerning these two companies can be drawn from these data?

Real-World Focus

BYP4-4 Numerous companies have established home pages on the Internet, e.g., Capt'n Eli Root Beer Company (**www.captneli.com/rootbeer.php**) and Kodak (**www.kodak.com**).

Instructions
Examine the home pages of any two companies and answer the following questions.

(a) What type of information is available?
(b) Is any accounting-related information presented?
(c) Would you describe the home page as informative, promotional, or both? Why?

Critical Thinking

Decision-Making Across the Organization

BYP4-5 Whitegloves Janitorial Service was started 2 years ago by Lynn Sanders. Because business has been exceptionally good, Lynn decided on July 1, 2015, to expand operations by acquiring an additional truck and hiring two more assistants. To finance the expansion, Lynn obtained on July 1, 2015, a $25,000, 10% bank loan, payable $10,000 on July 1, 2016, and the balance on July 1, 2017. The terms of the loan require the borrower to have $10,000 more current assets than current liabilities at December 31, 2015. If these terms are not met, the bank loan will be refinanced at 15% interest. At December 31, 2015, the accountant for Whitegloves Janitorial Service Inc. prepared the following balance sheet.

WHITEGLOVES JANITORIAL SERVICE
Balance Sheet
December 31, 2015

Assets			**Liabilities and Stockholders' Equity**		
Current assets			Current liabilities		
Cash	$ 6,500		Notes payable	$10,000	
Accounts receivable	9,000		Accounts payable	2,500	
Supplies	5,200		Total current liabilities		$12,500
Prepaid insurance	4,800		Long-term liability		
Total current assets		$25,500	Notes payable		15,000
Property, plant, and equipment			Total liabilities		27,500
Equipment (net)	22,000		Stockholders' equity		
Delivery trucks (net)	34,000		Common stock	30,000	
Total property, plant,			Retained earnings	24,000	
and equipment		56,000	Total stockholders' equity		54,000
Total assets		$81,500	Total liabilities and		
			stockholders' equity		$81,500

Lynn presented the balance sheet to the bank's loan officer on January 2, 2016, confident that the company had met the terms of the loan. The loan officer was not impressed. She said, "We need financial statements audited by a CPA." A CPA was hired and immediately realized that the balance sheet had been prepared from a trial balance and not from an adjusted trial balance. The adjustment data at the balance sheet date consisted of the following.

1. Unbilled janitorial services performed were $3,700.
2. Janitorial supplies on hand were $2,500.
3. Prepaid insurance was a 3-year policy dated January 1, 2015.
4. December expenses incurred but unpaid at December 31, $500.
5. Interest on the bank loan was not recorded.
6. The amounts for property, plant, and equipment presented in the balance sheet were reported net of accumulated depreciation (cost less accumulated depreciation). These amounts were $4,000 for cleaning equipment and $5,000 for delivery trucks as of January 1, 2015. Depreciation for 2015 was $2,000 for cleaning equipment and $5,000 for delivery trucks.

Instructions

With the class divided into groups, answer the following.

(a) Prepare a correct balance sheet.

(b) Were the terms of the bank loan met? Explain.

Communication Activity

BYP4-6 The accounting cycle is important in understanding the accounting process.

Instructions

Write a memo to your instructor that lists the steps of the accounting cycle in the order they should be completed. End with a paragraph that explains the optional steps in the cycle.

Ethics Case

BYP4-7 As the controller of Take No Prisoners Perfume Company, you discover a misstatement that overstated net income in the prior year's financial statements. The misleading financial statements appear in the company's annual report which was issued to banks and other creditors less than a month ago. After much thought about the consequences of telling the president, Jeb Wilde, about this misstatement, you gather your courage to inform him. Jeb says, "Hey! What they don't know won't hurt them. But, just so we set the record straight, we'll adjust this year's financial statements for last year's misstatement. We can absorb that misstatement better in this year than in last year anyway! Just don't make such a mistake again."

Instructions

(a) Who are the stakeholders in this situation?

(b) What are the ethical issues in this situation?

(c) What would you do as a controller in this situation?

All About You

BYP4-8 Companies prepare balance sheets in order to know their financial position at a specific point in time. This enables them to make a comparison to their position at previous points in time, and gives them a basis for planning for the future. In order to evaluate your financial position, you need to prepare a personal balance sheet. Assume that you have compiled the following information regarding your finances. (*Hint:* Some of the items might not be used in your personal balance sheet.)

Amount owed on student loan balance (long-term)	$ 5,000
Balance in checking account	1,200
Certificate of deposit (6-month)	3,000
Annual earnings from part-time job	11,300
Automobile	7,000
Balance on automobile loan (current portion)	1,500
Balance on automobile loan (long-term portion)	4,000
Home computer	800
Amount owed to you by younger brother	300
Balance in money market account	1,800
Annual tuition	6,400
Video and stereo equipment	1,250
Balance owed on credit card (current portion)	150
Balance owed on credit card (long-term portion)	1,650

Instructions

Prepare a personal balance sheet using the format you have learned for a classified balance sheet for a company. For the equity account, use Owner's Equity.

FASB Codification Activity

BYP4-9 If your school has a subscription to the FASB Codification, go to **http://aaahq.org/ ascLogin.cfm** to log in and prepare responses to the following.

Instructions

(a) Access the glossary ("Master Glossary") at the FASB Codification website to answer the following.

    (1) What is the definition of current assets?

    (2) What is the definition of current liabilities?

(b) A company wants to offset its accounts payable against its cash account and show a cash amount net of accounts payable on its balance sheet. Identify the criteria (found in the FASB Codification) under which a company has the right of set off. Does the company have the right to offset accounts payable against the cash account?

Answers to Chapter Questions

Answers to Insight and Accounting Across the Organization Questions

p. 175 Cisco Performs the Virtual Close **Q:** Who else benefits from a shorter closing process? **A:** Investors benefit from a shorter closing process. The shorter the closing, the sooner the company can report its financial results. This means that the financial information is more timely and therefore more relevant to investors.

p. 181 Yale Express Loses Some Transportation Bills **Q:** What might Yale Express's vice president have done to produce more accurate financial statements without waiting months for Republic's outstanding transportation bills? **A:** Yale's vice president could have engaged his accountants and auditors to prepare an adjusting entry based on an estimate of the outstanding transportation bills. (The estimate could have been made using past experience and the current volume of business.)

p. 185 Regaining Goodwill **Q:** Name two industries today which are probably rated low on the reputational characteristics of "being trusted" and "having high ethical standards." **A:** Two possible industries are financial companies (Goldman Sachs or AIG) or oil companies (BP).

p. 186 Can a Company Be Too Liquid? **Q:** What can various company managers do to ensure that working capital is managed efficiently to maximize net income? **A:** Marketing and sales managers must understand that by extending generous repayment terms, they are expanding the company's receivables balance and slowing the company's cash flow. Production managers must strive to minimize the amount of excess inventory on hand. Managers must coordinate efforts to speed up the collection of receivables, while also ensuring that the company pays its payables on time but never too early.

Answers to Self-Test Questions

1. b   **2.** c   **3.** c   **4.** a   **5.** b   **6.** c   **7.** a   **8.** d   **9.** c   **10.** d   **11.** b   **12.** c   **13.** c   **14.** d   **15.** a
***16.** c

A Look at IFRS

The classified balance sheet, although generally required internationally, contains certain variations in format when reporting under IFRS.

LEARNING OBJECTIVE 8

Compare the procedures for the closing process under GAAP and IFRS.

Key Points

• The procedures of the closing process are applicable to all companies, whether they are using IFRS or GAAP.

• IFRS recommends but does not require the use of the title "statement of financial position" rather than balance sheet.

- The format of statement of financial position information is often presented differently under IFRS. Although no specific format is required, most companies that follow IFRS present statement of financial position information in this order:
  - ♦ Non-current assets
  - ♦ Current assets
  - ♦ Equity
  - ♦ Non-current liabilities
  - ♦ Current liabilities

- IFRS requires a classified statement of financial position except in very limited situations. IFRS follows the same guidelines as this textbook for distinguishing between current and non-current assets and liabilities.

- Under IFRS, current assets are usually listed in the reverse order of liquidity. For example, under GAAP cash is listed first, but under IFRS it is listed last.

- Some companies report the subtotal **net assets**, which equals total assets minus total liabilities. See, for example, the statement of financial position of Zetar plc in Appendix F.

- IFRS has many differences in terminology from what are shown in your textbook. For example, in the sample statement of financial position illustrated below, notice in the investment category that stock is called shares.

FRANKLIN CORPORATION
Statement of Financial Position
October 31, 2015

Assets

Intangible assets			
Patents			$ 3,100
Property, plant, and equipment			
Land		$10,000	
Equipment	$24,000		
Less: Accumulated depreciation	5,000	19,000	29,000
Long-term investments			
Share investments		5,200	
Investment in real estate		2,000	7,200
Current assets			
Prepaid insurance		400	
Supplies		2,100	
Inventory		3,000	
Notes receivable		1,000	
Accounts receivable		7,000	
Debt investments		2,000	
Cash		6,600	22,100
Total assets			$61,400

Equity and Liabilities

Equity			
Share capital			$34,050
Non-current liabilities			
Mortgage payable		$10,000	
Notes payable		1,300	11,300
Current liabilities			
Notes payable		11,000	
Accounts payable		2,100	
Salaries and wages payable		1,600	
Unearned service revenue		900	
Interest payable		450	16,050
Total equity and liabilities			$61,400

- Both IFRS and GAAP require disclosures about (1) accounting policies followed, (2) judgments that management has made in the process of applying the entity's accounting policies, and (3) the key assumptions and estimation uncertainty that could result in a material adjustment to the carrying amounts of assets and liabilities within the next financial year.

- Comparative prior-period information must be presented and financial statements must be prepared annually.

- Both GAAP and IFRS are increasing the use of fair value to report assets. However, at this point IFRS has adopted it more broadly. As examples, under IFRS companies can apply fair value to property, plant, and equipment; natural resources; and in some cases intangible assets.

Looking to the Future

The IASB and the FASB are working on a project to converge their standards related to financial statement presentation. A key feature of the proposed framework is that each of the statements will be organized in the same format, to separate an entity's financing activities from its operating and investing activities and, further, to separate financing activities into transactions with owners and creditors. Thus, the same classifications used in the statement of financial position would also be used in the income statement and the statement of cash flows. The project has three phases. You can follow the joint financial presentation project at the following link: **http://www.fasb.org/project/financial_statement_presentation.shtml**.

The IASB and the FASB face a difficult task in attempting to update, modify, and complete a converged conceptual framework. For example, how do companies choose between information that is highly relevant but difficult to verify versus information that is less relevant but easy to verify? How do companies define control when developing a definition of an asset? Is a liability the future sacrifice itself or the obligation to make the sacrifice? Should a single measurement method, such as historical cost or fair value, be used, or does it depend on whether it is an asset or liability that is being measured? It appears that the new document will be a significant improvement over its predecessors and will lead to principles-based standards, which will help financial statement users make better decisions.

IFRS Practice

IFRS Self-Test Questions

1. Which of the following statements is **false**?
   (a) Assets equals liabilities plus equity.
   (b) Under IFRS, companies sometimes net liabilities against assets to report "net assets."
   (c) The FASB and IASB are working on a joint conceptual framework project.
   (d) Under IFRS, the statement of financial position is usually referred to as the statement of assets and equity.

2. A company has purchased a tract of land and expects to build a production plant on the land in approximately 5 years. During the 5 years before construction, the land will be idle. Under IFRS, the land should be reported as:
   (a) land expense.
   (b) property, plant, and equipment.
   (c) an intangible asset.
   (d) a long-term investment.

3. Current assets under IFRS are listed generally:
   (a) by importance.
   (b) in the reverse order of their expected conversion to cash.
   (c) by longevity.
   (d) alphabetically.

4. Companies that use IFRS:
   (a) may report all their assets on the statement of financial position at fair value.
   (b) may offset assets against liabilities and show net assets and net liabilities on their statement of financial positions, rather than the underlying detailed line items.
   (c) may report non-current assets before current assets on the statement of financial position.
   (d) do not have any guidelines as to what should be reported on the statement of financial position.

5. Companies that follow IFRS to prepare a statement of financial position generally use the following order of classification:
   (a) current assets, current liabilities, non-current assets, non-current liabilities, equity.
   (b) non-current assets, non-current liabilities, current assets, current liabilities, equity.
   (c) non-current assets, current assets, equity, non-current liabilities, current liabilities.
   (d) equity, non-current assets, current assets, non-current liabilities, current liabilities.

IFRS Exercises

IFRS4-1 In what ways does the format of a statement of financial of position under IFRS often differ from a balance sheet presented under GAAP?

IFRS4-2 What term is commonly used under IFRS in reference to the balance sheet?

IFRS4-3 The statement of financial position for Sundell Company includes the following accounts (in British pounds): Accounts Receivable £12,500; Prepaid Insurance £3,600; Cash £15,400; Supplies £5,200; and Debt Investments (short-term) £6,700. Prepare the current assets section of the statement of financial position, listing the accounts in proper sequence.

IFRS4-4 Glarus Company recently received the following information related to the company's December 31, 2015, statement of financial position (in Swiss francs).

Inventory	CHF 2,900	Debt investments (short-term)	CHF 120
Cash	13,400	Accumulated depreciation—	
Equipment	21,700	equipment	5,700
Share investments		Accounts receivable	4,300
(long-term)	6,500		

Prepare the assets section of the company's classified statement of financial position.

IFRS4-5 The following information is available for Lessila Bowling Alley at December 31, 2015.

Buildings	$128,800	Share Capital	$115,000
Accounts Receivable	14,520	Accumulated Depreciation—Buildings	42,600
Prepaid Insurance	4,680	Accounts Payable	12,300
Cash	18,040	Notes Payable	97,780
Equipment	62,400	Accumulated Depreciation—Equipment	18,720
Land	64,000	Interest Payable	2,600
Insurance Expense	780	Bowling Revenues	14,180
Depreciation Expense	7,360		
Interest Expense	2,600		

Prepare a classified statement of financial position. Assume that $13,900 of the notes payable will be paid in 2016.

IFRS4-6 Nate Roche is interested in comparing the liquidity and solvency of a U.S. software company with a Chinese competitor. Is this possible if the two companies report using different currencies?

International Comparative Analysis Problem:
Apple vs. Zetar plc

IFRS4-7 The financial statements of Zetar plc are presented in Appendix F. Instructions for accessing and using the company's complete annual report, including the notes to its financial statements, are also provided in Appendix F.

Instructions

Identify five differences in the format of the statement of financial position used by Zetar plc compared to a company, such as Apple, that follows GAAP. (Apple's financial statements are available in Appendix A.)

Answers to IFRS Self-Test Questions
1. d   **2.** d   **3.** b   **4.** c   **5.** c

✔ **The Navigator**

✔ Remember to go back to The Navigator box on the chapter opening page and check off your completed work.

5 | Accounting for Merchandising Operations

Buy Now, Vote Later

Have you ever shopped for outdoor gear at an REI (Recreational Equipment Incorporated) store? If so, you might have been surprised if a salesclerk asked if you were a member. A member? What do you mean a member? You soon realize that REI might not be your typical store. In fact, there's a lot about REI that makes it different.

REI is a consumer cooperative, or "co-op" for short. To figure out what that means, consider this quote from the company's annual report:

> As a cooperative, the Company is owned by its members. Each member is entitled to one vote in the election of the Company's Board of Directors. Since January 1, 2008, the nonrefundable, nontransferable, one-time membership fee has been $20 dollars. As of December 31, 2010, there were approximately 10.8 million members.

Voting rights? Now that's something you don't get from shopping at Walmart. REI members get other benefits as well, including sharing in the company's profits through a dividend at the end of the year, which can be used for purchases at REI stores during the next two years. The more you spend, the bigger your dividend.

Since REI is a co-op, you might also wonder whether management's incentives might be a little different than at other stores. For example, is management still concerned about making a profit? The answer is yes, as it ensures the long-term viability of the company. At the same time, REI's members want the company to be run efficiently, so that prices remain low. In order for its members to evaluate just how well management is doing, REI publishes an audited annual report, just like publicly traded companies do. So, while profit maximization might not be the ultimate goal for REI, the accounting and reporting issues are similar to those of a typical corporation.

How well is this business model working for REI? Well, it has consistently been rated as one of the best places to work in the United States. It was ranked 8th on *Fortune*'s 2012 list. Also, REI had sustainable business practices long before social responsibility became

✔ The Navigator

- Scan Learning Objectives
- Read Feature Story
- Read Preview
- Read text and answer **DO IT!** p. 229
    - p. 233   - p. 236   - p. 241
- Work Comprehensive **DO IT!** p. 242
- Review Summary of Learning Objectives
- Answer Self-Test Questions
- Complete Assignments
- Go to *WileyPLUS* for practice and tutorials
- Read **A Look at IFRS** p. 275

Learning Objectives   ✔ The Navigator

After studying this chapter, you should be able to:

[1] Identify the differences between service and merchandising companies.

[2] Explain the recording of purchases under a perpetual inventory system.

[3] Explain the recording of sales revenues under a perpetual inventory system.

[4] Explain the steps in the accounting cycle for a merchandising company.

[5] Distinguish between a multiple-step and a single-step income statement.

popular at other companies. As the CEO's Stewardship Report states, "we reduced the absolute amount of energy we use despite opening four new stores and growing our business; we grew the amount of FSC-certified paper we use to 58.4 percent of our total paper footprint—including our cash register receipt paper; we facilitated 2.2 million volunteer hours and we provided $3.7 million to more than 330 conservation and recreation nonprofits."

So, while REI, like other retailers, closely monitors its financial results, it also strives to succeed in other areas. And, with over 10 million votes at stake, REI's management knows that it has to deliver.

Preview of Chapter 5

✔ The Navigator

Merchandising is one of the largest and most influential industries in the United States. It is likely that a number of you will work for a merchandiser. Therefore, understanding the financial statements of merchandising companies is important. In this chapter, you will learn the basics about reporting merchandising transactions. In addition, you will learn how to prepare and analyze a commonly used form of the income statement—the multiple-step income statement. The content and organization of the chapter are as follows.

ACCOUNTING FOR MERCHANDISING OPERATIONS

Merchandising Operations	Recording Purchases of Merchandise	Recording Sales of Merchandise	Completing the Accounting Cycle	Forms of Financial Statements
• Operating cycles • Flow of costs—perpetual and periodic inventory systems • Advantages of the perpetual system	• Freight costs • Purchase returns and allowances • Purchase discounts • Summary of purchasing transactions	• Sales returns and allowances • Sales discounts	• Adjusting entries • Closing entries • Summary of merchandising entries	• Multiple-step income statement • Single-step income statement • Classified balance sheet

Merchandising Operations

REI, Wal-Mart Stores, Inc., and Amazon.com are called merchandising companies because they buy and sell merchandise rather than perform services as their primary source of revenue. Merchandising companies that purchase and sell directly to consumers are called **retailers**. Merchandising companies that sell to retailers are known as **wholesalers**. For example, retailer Walgreens might buy goods from wholesaler McKesson. Retailer Office Depot might buy office supplies from wholesaler United Stationers. The primary source of revenues for merchandising companies is the sale of merchandise, often referred to simply as **sales revenue** or **sales**. A merchandising company has two categories of expenses: cost of goods sold and operating expenses.

Cost of goods sold is the total cost of merchandise sold during the period. This expense is directly related to the revenue recognized from the sale of goods. Illustration 5-1 shows the income measurement process for a merchandising company. The items in the two blue boxes are unique to a merchandising company; they are not used by a service company.

Illustration 5-1

Income measurement process for a merchandising company

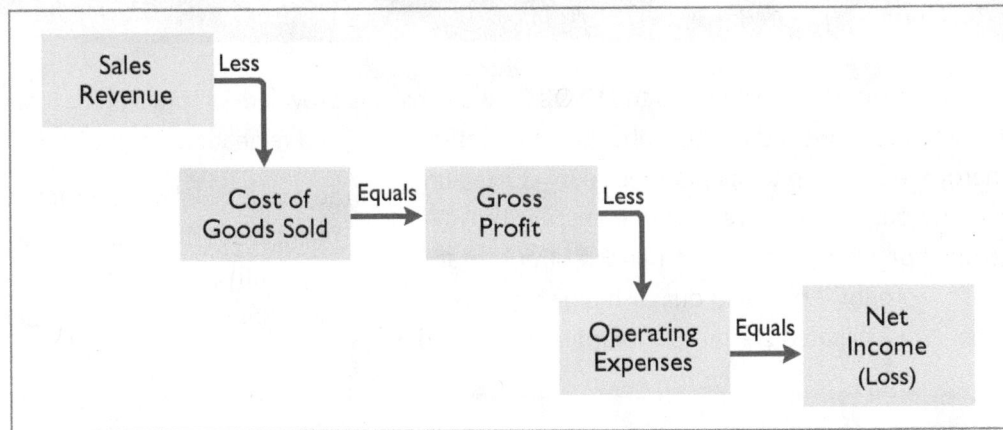

Operating Cycles

The operating cycle of a merchandising company ordinarily is longer than that of a service company. The purchase of merchandise inventory and its eventual sale lengthen the cycle. Illustration 5-2 shows the operating cycle of a service company.

Illustration 5-2

Operating cycle for a service company

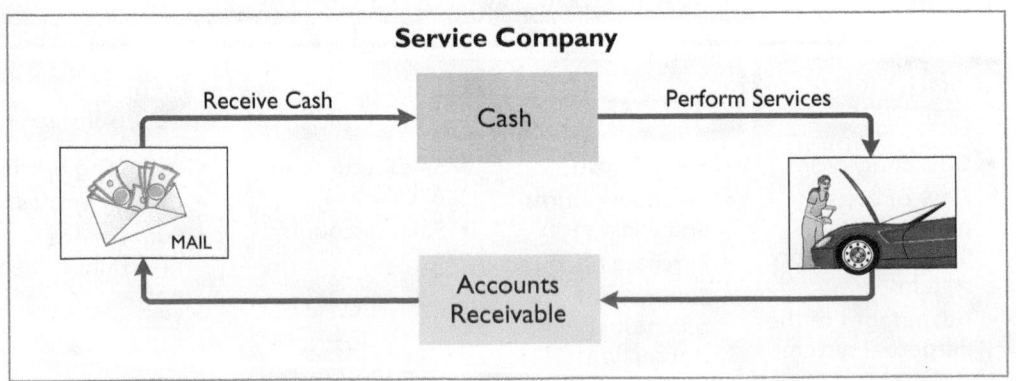

Illustration 5-3 shows the operating cycle of a merchandising company.

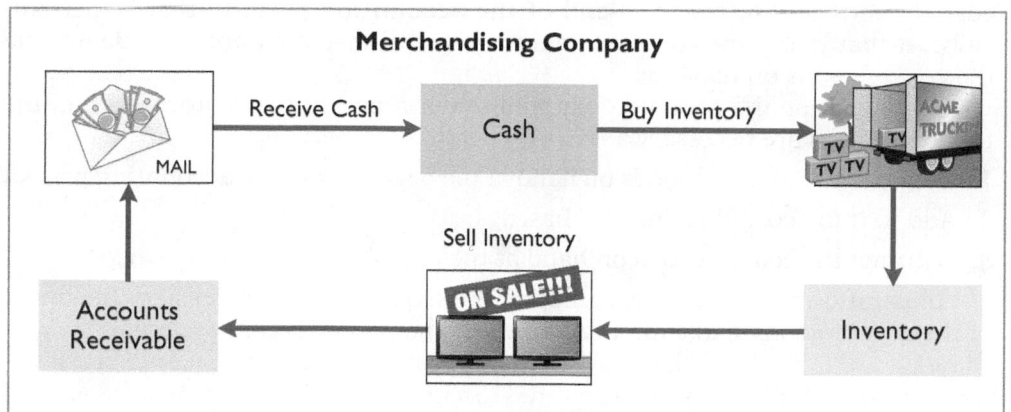

Illustration 5-3
Operating cycle for a
merchandising company

Note that the added asset account for a merchandising company is the Inventory account. Companies report inventory as a current asset on the balance sheet.

Flow of Costs

The flow of costs for a merchandising company is as follows. Beginning inventory plus the cost of goods purchased is the cost of goods available for sale. As goods are sold, they are assigned to cost of goods sold. Those goods that are not sold by the end of the accounting period represent ending inventory. Illustration 5-4 describes these relationships. Companies use one of two systems to account for inventory: a **perpetual inventory system** or a **periodic inventory system**.

Illustration 5-4
Flow of costs

PERPETUAL SYSTEM

In a **perpetual inventory system**, companies keep detailed records of the cost of each inventory purchase and sale. These records continuously—perpetually—show the inventory that should be on hand for every item. For example, a Ford dealership has separate inventory records for each automobile, truck, and van on its lot and showroom floor. Similarly, a Kroger grocery store uses bar codes and optical scanners to keep a daily running record of every box of cereal and every jar of jelly that it buys and sells. Under a perpetual inventory system, a company determines the cost of goods sold **each time a sale occurs**.

Helpful Hint
For control purposes, companies take a physical inventory count under the perpetual system, even though it is not needed to determine cost of goods sold.

PERIODIC SYSTEM

In a **periodic inventory system**, companies do not keep detailed inventory records of the goods on hand throughout the period. Instead, they determine the cost of goods sold **only at the end of the accounting period**—that is, periodically. At that point, the company takes a physical inventory count to determine the cost of goods on hand.

To determine the cost of goods sold under a periodic inventory system, the following steps are necessary:

1. Determine the cost of goods on hand at the beginning of the accounting period.

2. Add to it the cost of goods purchased.

3. Subtract the cost of goods on hand at the end of the accounting period.

Illustration 5-5 graphically compares the sequence of activities and the timing of the cost of goods sold computation under the two inventory systems.

Illustration 5-5
Comparing perpetual and periodic inventory systems

ADVANTAGES OF THE PERPETUAL SYSTEM

Companies that sell merchandise with high unit values, such as automobiles, furniture, and major home appliances, have traditionally used perpetual systems. The growing use of computers and electronic scanners has enabled many more companies to install perpetual inventory systems. The perpetual inventory system is so named because the accounting records continuously—perpetually—show the quantity and cost of the inventory that should be on hand at any time.

A perpetual inventory system provides better control over inventories than a periodic system. Since the inventory records show the quantities that should be on hand, the company can count the goods at any time to see whether the amount of goods actually on hand agrees with the inventory records. If shortages are uncovered, the company can investigate immediately. Although a perpetual inventory system requires both additional clerical work and expense to maintain the subsidiary records, a computerized system can minimize this cost. Much of Amazon.com's success is attributed to its sophisticated inventory system.

Some businesses find it either unnecessary or uneconomical to invest in a sophisticated, computerized perpetual inventory system such as Amazon's.

Many small merchandising businesses find that basic computerized accounting packages provide some of the essential benefits of a perpetual inventory system. Also, managers of some small businesses still find that they can control their merchandise and manage day-to-day operations using a periodic inventory system.

Because of the widespread use of the perpetual inventory system, we illustrate it in this chapter. We discuss and illustrate the periodic system in Appendix 5B.

INVESTOR INSIGHT   %

Morrow Snowboards Improves Its Stock Appeal

Investors are often eager to invest in a company that has a hot new product. However, when snowboard-maker Morrow Snowboards, Inc. issued shares of stock to the public for the first time, some investors expressed reluctance to invest in Morrow because of a number of accounting control problems. To reduce investor concerns, Morrow implemented a perpetual inventory system to improve its control over inventory. In addition, it stated that it would perform a physical inventory count every quarter until it felt that the perpetual inventory system was reliable.

? If a perpetual system keeps track of inventory on a daily basis, why do companies ever need to do a physical count? (See page 274.)

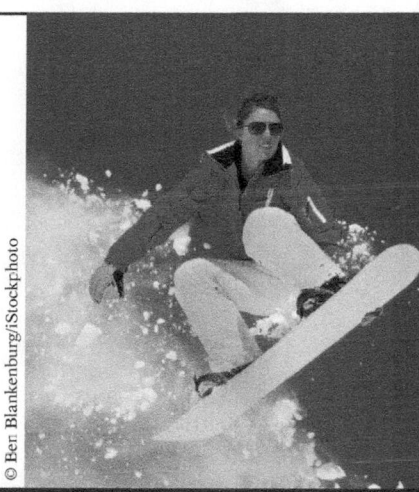

© Ben Blankenburg/iStockphoto

Recording Purchases of Merchandise

Companies purchase inventory using cash or credit (on account). They normally record purchases when they receive the goods from the seller. Every purchase should be supported by business documents that provide written evidence of the transaction. Each cash purchase should be supported by a canceled check or a cash register receipt indicating the items purchased and amounts paid. Companies record cash purchases by an increase in Inventory and a decrease in Cash.

A **purchase invoice** should support each credit purchase. This invoice indicates the total purchase price and other relevant information. However, the purchaser does not prepare a separate purchase invoice. Instead, the purchaser uses as a purchase invoice a copy of the sales invoice sent by the seller. In Illustration 5-6 (page 226), for example, Sauk Stereo (the buyer) uses as a purchase invoice the sales invoice prepared by PW Audio Supply, Inc. (the seller).

Sauk Stereo makes the following journal entry to record its purchase from PW Audio Supply. The entry increases (debits) Inventory and increases (credits) Accounts Payable.

> **LEARNING OBJECTIVE   2**
>
> Explain the recording of purchases under a perpetual inventory system.

May 4	Inventory	3,800	
	Accounts Payable		3,800
	(To record goods purchased on account from PW Audio Supply)		

A	=	L	+	SE
+3,800				
				+3,800

Cash Flows
no effect

Helpful Hint
To better understand the contents of this invoice, identify these items:
1. Seller
2. Invoice date
3. Purchaser
4. Salesperson
5. Credit terms
6. Freight terms
7. Goods sold: catalog number, description, quantity, price per unit
8. Total invoice amount

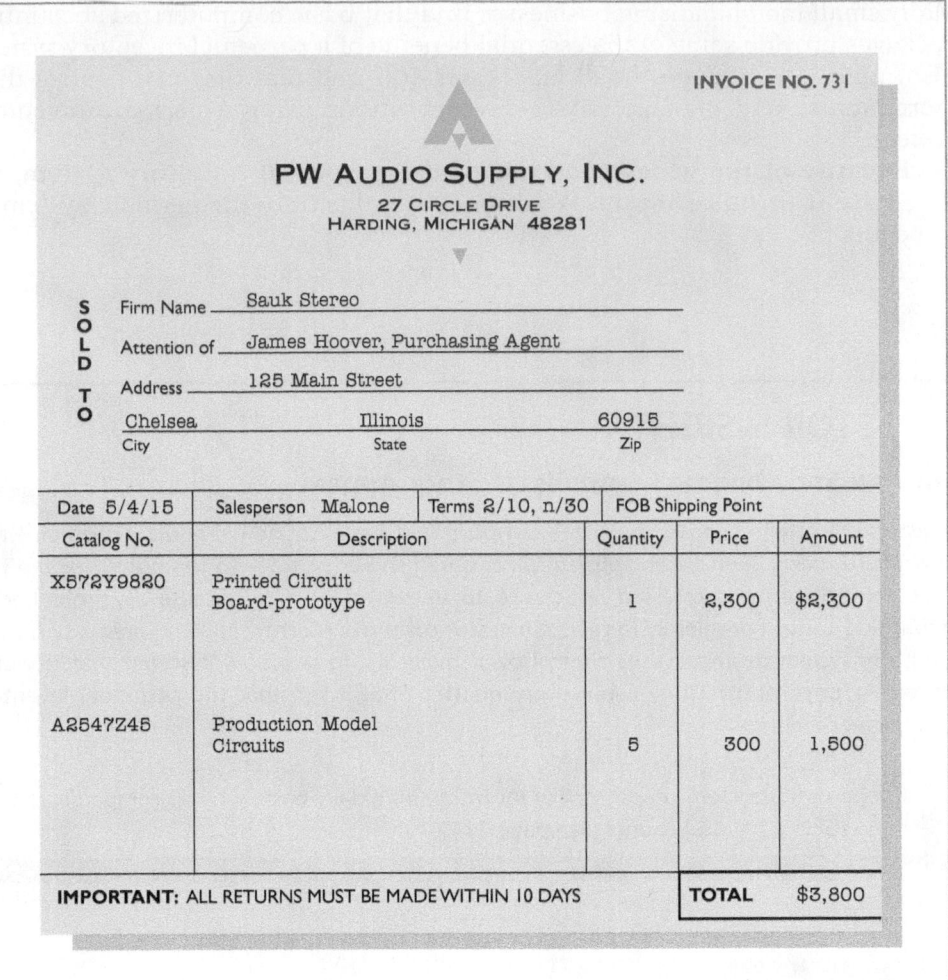

Under the perpetual inventory system, companies record purchases of merchandise for sale in the Inventory account. Thus, REI would increase (debit) Inventory for clothing, sporting goods, and anything else purchased for resale to customers.

Not all purchases are debited to Inventory, however. Companies record purchases of assets acquired for use and not for resale, such as supplies, equipment, and similar items, as increases to specific asset accounts rather than to Inventory. For example, to record the purchase of materials used to make shelf signs or for cash register receipt paper, REI would increase (debit) Supplies.

Freight Costs

The sales agreement should indicate who—the seller or the buyer—is to pay for transporting the goods to the buyer's place of business. When a common carrier such as a railroad, trucking company, or airline transports the goods, the carrier prepares a freight bill in accord with the sales agreement.

Freight terms are expressed as either FOB shipping point or FOB destination. The letters FOB mean **free on board**. Thus, **FOB shipping point** means that the seller places the goods free on board the carrier, and the buyer pays the freight costs. Conversely, **FOB destination** means that the seller places the goods free on board to the buyer's place of business, and the seller pays the freight. For example, the sales invoice in Illustration 5-6 indicates FOB shipping point. Thus, the buyer (Sauk Stereo) pays the freight charges. Illustration 5-7 (on the next page) illustrates these shipping terms.

Illustration 5-7
Shipping terms

FREIGHT COSTS INCURRED BY THE BUYER

When the buyer incurs the transportation costs, these costs are considered part of the cost of purchasing inventory. Therefore, the buyer debits (increases) the Inventory account. For example, if Sauk Stereo (the buyer) pays Public Carrier Co. $150 for freight charges on May 6, the entry on Sauk Stereo's books is:

May 6	Inventory	150	
	Cash		150
	(To record payment of freight on goods purchased)		

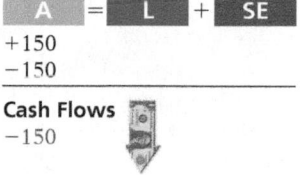

A = L + SE
+150
−150

Cash Flows
−150

Thus, any freight costs incurred by the buyer are part of the cost of merchandise purchased. The reason: Inventory cost should include all costs to acquire the inventory, including freight necessary to deliver the goods to the buyer. Companies recognize these costs as cost of goods sold when inventory is sold.

FREIGHT COSTS INCURRED BY THE SELLER

In contrast, **freight costs incurred by the seller on outgoing merchandise are an operating expense to the seller**. These costs increase an expense account titled Freight-Out (sometimes called Delivery Expense). For example, if the freight terms on the invoice in Illustration 5-6 had required PW Audio Supply (the seller) to pay the freight charges, the entry by PW Audio Supply would be:

May 4	Freight-Out (or Delivery Expense)	150	
	Cash		150
	(To record payment of freight on goods sold)		

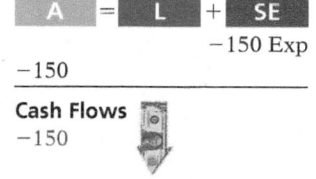

A = L + SE
−150 Exp
−150

Cash Flows
−150

When the seller pays the freight charges, the seller will usually establish a higher invoice price for the goods to cover the shipping expense.

Purchase Returns and Allowances

A purchaser may be dissatisfied with the merchandise received because the goods are damaged or defective, of inferior quality, or do not meet the purchaser's specifications. In such cases, the purchaser may return the goods to the seller for credit if the sale was made on credit, or for a cash refund if the purchase was for cash. This transaction is known as a **purchase return**. Alternatively, the purchaser may choose to keep the merchandise if the seller is willing to grant an allowance (deduction) from the purchase price. This transaction is known as a **purchase allowance**.

Assume that Sauk Stereo returned goods costing $300 to PW Audio Supply on May 8. The following entry by Sauk Stereo for the returned merchandise decreases (debits) Accounts Payable and decreases (credits) Inventory.

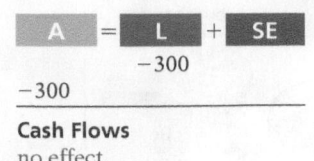

May 8	Accounts Payable	300	
	Inventory		300
	(To record return of goods purchased from PW Audio Supply)		

Because Sauk Stereo increased Inventory when the goods were received, Inventory is decreased when Sauk Stereo returns the goods.

Suppose instead that Sauk Stereo chose to keep the goods after being granted a $50 allowance (reduction in price). It would reduce (debit) Accounts Payable and reduce (credit) Inventory for $50.

Purchase Discounts

The credit terms of a purchase on account may permit the buyer to claim a cash discount for prompt payment. The buyer calls this cash discount a **purchase discount**. This incentive offers advantages to both parties. The purchaser saves money, and the seller is able to shorten the operating cycle by converting the accounts receivable into cash.

Credit terms specify the amount of the cash discount and time period in which it is offered. They also indicate the time period in which the purchaser is expected to pay the full invoice price. In the sales invoice in Illustration 5-6 (page 226), credit terms are 2/10, n/30, which is read "two-ten, net thirty." This means that the buyer may take a 2% cash discount on the invoice price, less ("net of") any returns or allowances, if payment is made within 10 days of the invoice date (the **discount period**). Otherwise, the invoice price, less any returns or allowances, is due 30 days from the invoice date.

Alternatively, the discount period may extend to a specified number of days following the month in which the sale occurs. For example, 1/10 EOM (end of month) means that a 1% discount is available if the invoice is paid within the first 10 days of the next month.

When the seller elects not to offer a cash discount for prompt payment, credit terms will specify only the maximum time period for paying the balance due. For example, the invoice may state the time period as n/30, n/60, or n/10 EOM. This means, respectively, that the buyer must pay the net amount in 30 days, 60 days, or within the first 10 days of the next month.

When the buyer pays an invoice within the discount period, the amount of the discount decreases Inventory. Why? Because companies record inventory at cost, and by paying within the discount period, the buyer has reduced its cost. To illustrate, assume Sauk Stereo pays the balance due of $3,500 (gross invoice price of $3,800 less purchase returns and allowances of $300) on May 14, the last day of the discount period. The cash discount is $70 ($3,500 × 2%), and Sauk Stereo pays $3,430 ($3,500 − $70). The entry Sauk Stereo makes to record its May 14 payment decreases (debits) Accounts Payable by the amount of the gross invoice price, reduces (credits) Inventory by the $70 discount, and reduces (credits) Cash by the net amount owed.

Helpful Hint
The term *net* in "net 30" means the remaining amount due after subtracting any sales returns and allowances and partial payments.

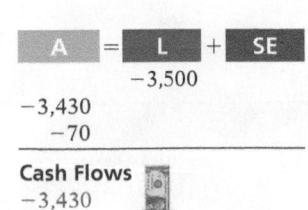

May 14	Accounts Payable	3,500	
	Cash		3,430
	Inventory		70
	(To record payment within discount period)		

If Sauk Stereo failed to take the discount and instead made full payment of $3,500 on June 3, it would debit Accounts Payable and credit Cash for $3,500 each.

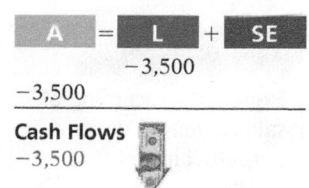

June 3	Accounts Payable	3,500	
	Cash		3,500
	(To record payment with no discount taken)		

A = L + SE
−3,500
−3,500

Cash Flows
−3,500

A merchandising company usually should take all available discounts. Passing up the discount may be viewed as **paying interest** for use of the money. For example, passing up the discount offered by PW Audio Supply would be comparable to Sauk Stereo paying an interest rate of 2% for the use of $3,500 for 20 days. This is the equivalent of an annual interest rate of approximately 36.5% (2% × 365/20). Obviously, it would be better for Sauk Stereo to borrow at prevailing bank interest rates of 6% to 10% than to lose the discount.

Summary of Purchasing Transactions

The following T-account (with transaction descriptions in red) provides a summary of the effect of the previous transactions on Inventory. Sauk Stereo originally purchased $3,800 worth of inventory for resale. It then returned $300 of goods. It paid $150 in freight charges, and finally, it received a $70 discount off the balance owed because it paid within the discount period. This results in a balance in Inventory of $3,580.

	Inventory				
Purchase	May 4	3,800	May 8	300	**Purchase return**
Freight-in	6	150	14	70	**Purchase discount**
Balance		3,580			

> **DO IT!**

Purchase Transactions

On September 5, De La Hoya Company buys merchandise on account from Junot Diaz Company. The selling price of the goods is $1,500, and the cost to Diaz Company was $800. On September 8, De La Hoya returns defective goods with a selling price of $200. Record the transactions on the books of De La Hoya Company.

Solution

Action Plan

✔ Purchaser records goods at cost.

✔ When goods are returned, purchaser reduces Inventory.

Sept. 5	Inventory	1,500	
	Accounts Payable		1,500
	(To record goods purchased on account)		
8	Accounts Payable	200	
	Inventory		200
	(To record return of defective goods)		

Related exercise material: BE5-2, BE5-4, E5-2, E5-3, E5-4, **and** DO IT! 5-1.

✔ **The Navigator**

Recording Sales of Merchandise

In accordance with the revenue recognition principle, companies record sales revenue when the performance obligation is satisfied. Typically, the performance obligation is satisfied when the goods transfer from the seller to the buyer. At this point, the sales transaction is complete and the sales price established.

Sales may be made on credit or for cash. A **business document** should support every sales transaction, to provide written evidence of the sale. **Cash register documents** provide evidence of cash sales. A sales invoice, like the one shown in Illustration 5-6 (page 226), provides support for a credit sale. The original copy of the invoice goes to the customer, and the seller keeps a copy for use in recording the sale. The invoice shows the date of sale, customer name, total sales price, and other relevant information.

The seller makes two entries for each sale. **The first entry records the sale:** The seller increases (debits) Cash (or Accounts Receivable if a credit sale) and also increases (credits) Sales Revenue. **The second entry records the cost of the merchandise sold:** The seller increases (debits) Cost of Goods Sold and also decreases (credits) Inventory for the cost of those goods. As a result, the Inventory account will show at all times the amount of inventory that should be on hand.

To illustrate a credit sales transaction, PW Audio Supply, Inc. records its May 4 sale of $3,800 to Sauk Stereo (see Illustration 5-6) as follows (assume the merchandise cost PW Audio Supply $2,400).

A = L + SE

+3,800

     +3,800 Rev

Cash Flows
no effect

May 4	Accounts Receivable	3,800	
	Sales Revenue		3,800
	(To record credit sale to Sauk Stereo per invoice #731)		

A = L + SE

        −2,400 Exp

−2,400

Cash Flows
no effect

4	Cost of Goods Sold	2,400	
	Inventory		2,400
	(To record cost of merchandise sold on invoice #731 to Sauk Stereo)		

For internal decision-making purposes, merchandising companies may use more than one sales account. For example, PW Audio Supply may decide to keep separate sales accounts for its sales of TV sets, DVD recorders, and cell phones. REI might use separate accounts for camping gear, children's clothing, and ski equipment—or it might have even more narrowly defined accounts. By using separate sales accounts for major product lines, rather than a single combined sales account, company management can more closely monitor sales trends and respond more strategically to changes in sales patterns. For example, if cell-phone sales are increasing while TV sales are decreasing, PW Audio Supply might reevaluate both its advertising and pricing policies on these items to ensure they are optimal.

On its income statement presented to outside investors, a merchandising company normally would provide only a single sales figure—the sum of all of its individual sales accounts. This is done for two reasons. First, providing detail on all of its individual sales accounts would add considerable length to its income statement. Second, companies do not want their competitors to know the details of their operating results. However, Microsoft recently expanded its disclosure of revenue from three to five types. The reason: The additional categories enabled financial statement users to better evaluate the growth of the company's consumer and Internet businesses.

Ethics Note

Many companies are trying to improve the quality of their financial reporting. For example, General Electric now provides more detail on its revenues and operating profits.

At the end of "Anatomy of a Fraud" stories, which describe some recent real-world frauds, we discuss the missing control activities that would likely have prevented or uncovered the fraud.

Sales Returns and Allowances

We now look at the "flip side" of purchase returns and allowances, which the seller records as **sales returns and allowances**. These are transactions where the seller either accepts goods back from the buyer (a return) or grants a reduction in the purchase price (an allowance) so the buyer will keep the goods. PW Audio Supply's entries to record credit for returned goods involve (1) an increase (debit) in Sales Returns and Allowances (a contra account to Sales Revenue) and a decrease (credit) in Accounts Receivable at the $300 selling price, and (2) an increase (debit) in Inventory (assume a $140 cost) and a decrease (credit) in Cost of Goods Sold, as shown below (assuming that the goods were not defective).

May 8	Sales Returns and Allowances	300	
	Accounts Receivable		300
	(To record credit granted to Sauk Stereo for returned goods)		
8	Inventory	140	
	Cost of Goods Sold		140
	(To record cost of goods returned)		

If Sauk Stereo returns goods because they are damaged or defective, then PW Audio Supply's entry to Inventory and Cost of Goods Sold should be for the fair value of the returned goods, rather than their cost. For example, if the returned

---

goods were defective and had a fair value of $50, PW Audio Supply would debit Inventory for $50 and credit Cost of Goods Sold for $50.

What happens if the goods are not returned but the seller grants the buyer an allowance by reducing the purchase price? In this case, the seller debits Sales Returns and Allowances and credits Accounts Receivable for the amount of the allowance. An allowance has no impact on Inventory or Cost of Goods Sold.

As mentioned above, Sales Returns and Allowances is a **contra revenue account** to Sales Revenue. This means that it is offset against a revenue account on the income statement. The normal balance of Sales Returns and Allowances is a debit. Companies use a contra account, instead of debiting Sales Revenue, to disclose in the accounts and in the income statement the amount of sales returns and allowances. Disclosure of this information is important to management. Excessive returns and allowances may suggest problems—inferior merchandise, inefficiencies in filling orders, errors in billing customers, or delivery or shipment mistakes. Moreover, a decrease (debit) recorded directly to Sales Revenue would obscure the relative importance of sales returns and allowances as a percentage of sales. It also could distort comparisons between total sales in different accounting periods.

© Jacob Wackerhausen/iStockphoto

ACCOUNTING ACROSS THE ORGANIZATION

Should Costco Change Its Return Policy?

In most industries, sales returns are relatively minor. But returns of consumer electronics can really take a bite out of profits. At one time, the marketing executives at Costco Wholesale Corp. faced a difficult decision. Costco always prided itself on its generous return policy. Most goods had an unlimited grace period for returns. However, a new policy requires that certain electronics must be returned within 90 days of their purchase. The reason? The cost of returned products such as high-definition TVs, computers, and iPods cut an estimated 8¢ per share off Costco's earnings per share, which was $2.30.

Source: Kris Hudson, "Costco Tightens Policy on Returning Electronics," *Wall Street Journal* (February 27, 2007), p. B4.

 If a company expects significant returns, what are the implications for revenue recognition? (See page 274.)

Sales Discounts

As mentioned in our discussion of purchase transactions, the seller may offer the customer a cash discount—called by the seller a **sales discount**—for the prompt payment of the balance due. Like a purchase discount, a sales discount is based on the invoice price less returns and allowances, if any. The seller increases (debits) the Sales Discounts account for discounts that are taken. For example, PW Audio Supply makes the following entry to record the cash receipt on May 14 from Sauk Stereo within the discount period.

A	=	L	+	SE
+3,430				
				−70 Rev
−3,500				

Cash Flows
+3,430

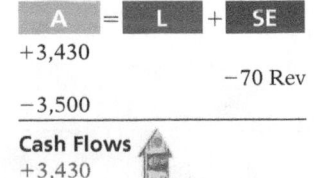

May 14	Cash	3,430	
	Sales Discounts	70	
	Accounts Receivable		3,500
	(To record collection within 2/10, n/30 discount period from Sauk Stereo)		

Like Sales Returns and Allowances, Sales Discounts is a **contra revenue account** to Sales Revenue. Its normal balance is a debit. PW Audio Supply uses this account, instead of debiting Sales Revenue, to disclose the amount of cash discounts taken by customers. If Sauk Stereo does not take the discount, PW Audio Supply increases (debits) Cash for $3,500 and decreases (credits) Accounts Receivable for the same amount at the date of collection.

The following T-accounts summarize the three sales-related transactions and show their combined effect on net sales.

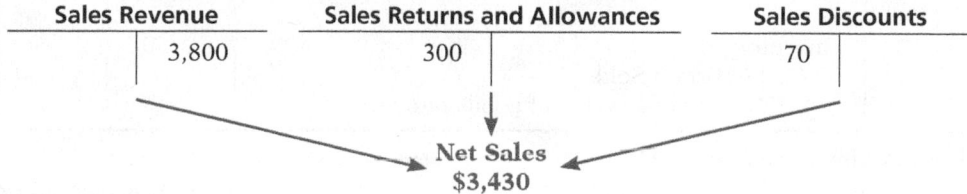

PEOPLE, PLANET, AND PROFIT INSIGHT

Selling Green

Here is a question an executive of PepsiCo was asked: Should PepsiCo market green? The executive indicated that the company should, as he believes it's the No. 1 thing consumers all over the world care about. Here are some of his thoughts on this issue:

"Sun Chips are part of the food business I run. It's a 'healthy snack.' We decided that Sun Chips, if it's a healthy snack, should be made in facilities that have a net-zero footprint. In other words, I want off the electric grid everywhere we make Sun Chips. We did that. Sun Chips should be made in a facility that puts back more water than it uses. It does that. And we partnered with our suppliers and came out with the world's first compostable chip package.

Now, there was an issue with this package: It was louder than the New York subway, louder than jet engines taking off. What would a company that's committed to green do: walk away or stay committed? If your people are passionate, they're going to fix it for you as long as you stay committed. Six months later, the compostable bag has half the noise of our current package.

So the view today is: we should market green, we should be proud to do it . . . it has to be a 360-degree process, both internal and external. And if you do that, you can monetize environmental sustainability for the shareholders."

Source: "Four Problems—and Solutions," *Wall Street Journal* (March 7, 2011), p. R2.

 What is meant by "monetize environmental sustainability" for shareholders? (See page 274.)

> DO IT!

Sales Transactions

On September 5, De La Hoya Company buys merchandise on account from Junot Diaz Company. The selling price of the goods is $1,500, and the cost to Diaz Company was $800. On September 8, De La Hoya returns defective goods with a selling price of $200 and a fair value of $30. Record the transactions on the books of Junot Diaz Company.

Solution

Action Plan

✔ Seller records both the sale and the cost of goods sold at the time of the sale.

Sept. 5	Accounts Receivable	1,500	
	Sales Revenue		1,500
	(To record credit sale)		

Action Plan (cont'd)

✔ When goods are returned, the seller records the return in a contra account, Sales Returns and Allowances, and reduces Accounts Receivable.

✔ Any goods returned increase Inventory and reduce Cost of Goods Sold. Defective or damaged inventory is recorded at fair value (scrap value).

5	Cost of Goods Sold		800	
	Inventory			800
	(To record cost of goods sold on account)			
8	Sales Returns and Allowances		200	
	Accounts Receivable			200
	(To record credit granted for receipt of returned goods)			
8	Inventory		30	
	Cost of Goods Sold			30
	(To record fair value of goods returned)			

Related exercise material: BE5-2, BE5-3, E5-3, E5-4, E5-5, **and** DO IT! 5-2.

✔ The Navigator

Completing the Accounting Cycle

LEARNING OBJECTIVE   4

Explain the steps in the accounting cycle for a merchandising company.

Up to this point, we have illustrated the basic entries for transactions relating to purchases and sales in a perpetual inventory system. Now we consider the remaining steps in the accounting cycle for a merchandising company. Each of the required steps described in Chapter 4 for service companies apply to merchandising companies. Appendix 5A to this chapter shows the use of a worksheet by a merchandiser (an optional step).

Adjusting Entries

A merchandising company generally has the same types of adjusting entries as a service company. However, a merchandiser using a perpetual system will require one additional adjustment to make the records agree with the actual inventory on hand. Here's why: At the end of each period, for control purposes, a merchandising company that uses a perpetual system will take a physical count of its goods on hand. The company's unadjusted balance in Inventory usually does not agree with the actual amount of inventory on hand. The perpetual inventory records may be incorrect due to recording errors, theft, or waste. Thus, the company needs to adjust the perpetual records to make the recorded inventory amount agree with the inventory on hand. **This involves adjusting Inventory and Cost of Goods Sold.**

For example, suppose that PW Audio Supply, Inc. has an unadjusted balance of $40,500 in Inventory. Through a physical count, PW Audio Supply determines that its actual merchandise inventory at year-end is $40,000. The company would make an adjusting entry as follows.

A = L + SE

−500

−500 Exp

Cash Flows
no effect

Cost of Goods Sold		500	
Inventory			500
(To adjust inventory to physical count)			

Closing Entries

A merchandising company, like a service company, closes to Income Summary all accounts that affect net income. In journalizing, the company credits all temporary accounts with debit balances, and debits all temporary accounts with credit balances, as shown on the next page for PW Audio Supply. Note that PW Audio Supply closes Cost of Goods Sold to Income Summary.

Dec. 31	Sales Revenue	480,000	
	Income Summary		480,000
	(To close income statement accounts		
	with credit balances)		
31	Income Summary	450,000	
	Sales Returns and Allowances		12,000
	Sales Discounts		8,000
	Cost of Goods Sold		316,000
	Salaries and Wages Expense		64,000
	Freight-Out		7,000
	Advertising Expense		16,000
	Utilities Expense		17,000
	Depreciation Expense		8,000
	Insurance Expense		2,000
	(To close income statement accounts		
	with debit balances)		
31	Income Summary	30,000	
	Retained Earnings		30,000
	(To close net income to retained earnings)		
31	Retained Earnings	15,000	
	Dividends		15,000
	(To close dividends to retained earnings)		

Helpful Hint
The easiest way to prepare the first two closing entries is to identify the temporary accounts by their balances and then prepare one entry for the credits and one for the debits.

After PW Audio Supply has posted the closing entries, all temporary accounts have zero balances. Also, Retained Earnings has a balance that is carried over to the next period.

Summary of Merchandising Entries

Illustration 5-8 summarizes the entries for the merchandising accounts using a perpetual inventory system.

Illustration 5-8
Daily recurring and adjusting and closing entries

	Transactions	Daily Recurring Entries	Dr.	Cr.
Sales Transactions	Selling merchandise to customers.	Cash or Accounts Receivable	XX	
		Sales Revenue		XX
		Cost of Goods Sold	XX	
		Inventory		XX
	Granting sales returns or allowances to customers.	Sales Returns and Allowances	XX	
		Cash or Accounts Receivable		XX
		Inventory	XX	
		Cost of Goods Sold		XX
	Paying freight costs on sales; FOB destination.	Freight-Out	XX	
		Cash		XX
	Receiving payment from customers within discount period.	Cash	XX	
		Sales Discounts	XX	
		Accounts Receivable		XX
Purchase Transactions	Purchasing merchandise for resale.	Inventory	XX	
		Cash or Accounts Payable		XX
	Paying freight costs on merchandise purchased; FOB shipping point.	Inventory	XX	
		Cash		XX
	Receiving purchase returns or allowances from suppliers.	Cash or Accounts Payable	XX	
		Inventory		XX
	Paying suppliers within discount period.	Accounts Payable	XX	
		Inventory		XX
		Cash		XX

Events	Adjusting and Closing Entries	Dr.	Cr.
Adjust because book amount is higher than the inventory amount determined to be on hand.	Cost of Goods Sold Inventory	XX	XX
Closing temporary accounts with credit balances.	Sales Revenue Income Summary	XX	XX

Closing temporary accounts with debit balances.	Income Summary
	    Sales Returns and Allowances
	    Sales Discounts
	    Cost of Goods Sold
	    Freight-Out
	    Expenses
		XX	XX
			XX
			XX
			XX
			XX

Illustration 5-8
(*continued*)

> DO IT!

Closing Entries

Action Plan

✔ Close all temporary accounts with credit balances to Income Summary by debiting these accounts.

✔ Close all temporary accounts with debit balances, except dividends, to Income Summary by crediting these accounts.

The trial balance of Celine's Sports Wear Shop at December 31 shows Inventory $25,000, Sales Revenue $162,400, Sales Returns and Allowances $4,800, Sales Discounts $3,600, Cost of Goods Sold $110,000, Rent Revenue $6,000, Freight-Out $1,800, Rent Expense $8,800, and Salaries and Wages Expense $22,000. Prepare the closing entries for the above accounts.

Solution

The two closing entries are:

Dec. 31	Sales Revenue	162,400	
	Rent Revenue	6,000	
	Income Summary		168,400
	(To close accounts with credit balances)		
31	Income Summary	151,000	
	Cost of Goods Sold		110,000
	Sales Returns and Allowances		4,800
	Sales Discounts		3,600
	Freight-Out		1,800
	Rent Expense		8,800
	Salaries and Wages Expense		22,000
	(To close accounts with debit balances)		

Related exercise material: BE5-5, BE5-6, E5-6, E5-7, E5-8, **and** DO IT! 5-3.

✔ **The Navigator**

Forms of Financial Statements

LEARNING OBJECTIVE **5**

Distinguish between a multiple-step and a single-step income statement.

Merchandising companies widely use the classified balance sheet introduced in Chapter 4 and one of two forms for the income statement. This section explains the use of these financial statements by merchandisers.

Multiple-Step Income Statement

The **multiple-step income statement** is so named because it shows several steps in determining net income. Two of these steps relate to the company's principal operating activities. A multiple-step statement also distinguishes between

operating and **nonoperating activities**. Finally, the statement highlights intermediate components of income and shows subgroupings of expenses.

INCOME STATEMENT PRESENTATION OF SALES

The multiple-step income statement begins by presenting **sales revenue**. It then deducts contra revenue accounts—sales returns and allowances and sales discounts—from sales revenue to arrive at **net sales**. Illustration 5-9 presents the sales section for PW Audio Supply, Inc., using assumed data.

<table>
<tr><td colspan="3" style="text-align:center">**PW AUDIO SUPPLY, INC.**
Income Statement (partial)</td></tr>
<tr><td>**Sales**</td><td></td><td></td></tr>
<tr><td>Sales revenue</td><td></td><td>$ 480,000</td></tr>
<tr><td>Less: Sales returns and allowances</td><td>$12,000</td><td></td></tr>
<tr><td>Sales discounts</td><td>8,000</td><td>20,000</td></tr>
<tr><td>**Net sales**</td><td></td><td>**$460,000**</td></tr>
</table>

Illustration 5-9
Computation of net sales

GROSS PROFIT

From Illustration 5-1, you learned that companies deduct cost of goods sold from sales revenue to determine **gross profit**. For this computation, companies use **net sales** (which takes into consideration Sales Returns and Allowances and Sales Discounts) as the amount of sales revenue. On the basis of the sales data in Illustration 5-9 (net sales of $460,000) and cost of goods sold under the perpetual inventory system (assume $316,000), PW Audio Supply's gross profit is $144,000, computed as follows.

Alternative Terminology
Gross profit is sometimes referred to as *gross margin*.

Net sales	$ 460,000
Cost of goods sold	316,000
Gross profit	**$144,000**

Illustration 5-10
Computation of gross profit

We also can express a company's gross profit as a percentage, called the **gross profit rate**. To do so, we divide the amount of gross profit by net sales. For PW Audio Supply, the **gross profit rate** is 31.3%, computed as follows.

Gross Profit	÷	Net Sales	=	Gross Profit Rate
$144,000	÷	$460,000	=	31.3%

Illustration 5-11
Gross profit rate formula and computation

Analysts generally consider the gross profit **rate** to be more useful than the gross profit **amount**. The rate expresses a more meaningful (qualitative) relationship between net sales and gross profit. For example, a gross profit of $1,000,000 may sound impressive. But if it is the result of a gross profit rate of only 7%, it is not so impressive. The gross profit rate tells how many cents of each sales dollar go to gross profit.

Gross profit represents the **merchandising profit** of a company. It is not a measure of the overall profitability because operating expenses are not yet deducted. But managers and other interested parties closely watch the amount and trend of gross profit. They compare current gross profit with amounts reported in past periods. They also compare the company's gross profit rate with rates of competitors and with industry averages. Such comparisons provide information about the effectiveness of a company's purchasing function and the soundness of its pricing policies.

OPERATING EXPENSES AND NET INCOME

Operating expenses are the next component in measuring net income for a merchandising company. They are the expenses incurred in the process of earning sales revenue. These expenses are similar in merchandising and service companies. At PW Audio Supply, operating expenses were $114,000. The company determines its net income by subtracting operating expenses from gross profit. Thus, net income is $30,000, as shown below.

Illustration 5-12
Operating expenses in computing net income

Gross profit	$144,000
Operating expenses	**114,000**
Net income	$ 30,000

The net income amount is the so-called "bottom line" of a company's income statement.

NONOPERATING ACTIVITIES

Nonoperating activities consist of various revenues and expenses and gains and losses that are unrelated to the company's main line of operations. When nonoperating items are included, the label "**Income from operations**" (or "Operating income") precedes them. This label clearly identifies the results of the company's normal operations, an amount determined by subtracting cost of goods sold and operating expenses from net sales. The results of nonoperating activities are shown in the categories "**Other revenues and gains**" and "**Other expenses and losses**." Illustration 5-13 lists examples of each.

Illustration 5-13
Other items of nonoperating activities

Other Revenues and Gains
Interest revenue from notes receivable and marketable securities.
Dividend revenue from investments in common stock.
Rent revenue from subleasing a portion of the store.
Gain from the sale of property, plant, and equipment.

Other Expenses and Losses
Interest expense on notes and loans payable.
Casualty losses from recurring causes, such as vandalism and accidents.
Loss from the sale or abandonment of property, plant, and equipment.
Loss from strikes by employees and suppliers.

Ethics Note

Companies manage earnings in various ways. ConAgra Foods recorded a non-recurring gain for $186 million from the sale of Pilgrim's Pride stock to help meet an earnings projection for the quarter.

Merchandising companies report the nonoperating activities in the income statement immediately after the company's operating activities. Illustration 5-14 shows these sections for PW Audio Supply, Inc., using assumed data.

The distinction between operating and nonoperating activities is crucial to many external users of financial data. These users view operating income as sustainable and many nonoperating activities as non-recurring. Therefore, when forecasting next year's income, analysts put the most weight on this year's operating income and less weight on this year's nonoperating activities.

Illustration 5-14
Multiple-step income statement

PW AUDIO SUPPLY, INC. Income Statement For the Year Ended December 31, 2015			

Calculation of gross profit

Sales			
Sales revenue			$480,000
Less: Sales returns and allowances		$12,000	
Sales discounts		8,000	20,000
Net sales			460,000
Cost of goods sold			316,000
Gross profit			144,000

Calculation of income from operations

Operating expenses		
Salaries and wages expense	64,000	
Utilities expense	17,000	
Advertising expense	16,000	
Depreciation expense	8,000	
Freight-out	7,000	
Insurance expense	2,000	
Total operating expenses		114,000
Income from operations		30,000

Results of nonoperating activities

Other revenues and gains		
Interest revenue	3,000	
Gain on disposal of plant assets	600	3,600
Other expenses and losses		
Interest expense	1,800	
Casualty loss from vandalism	200	2,000
Net income		$ 31,600

ETHICS INSIGHT

Disclosing More Details

After Enron, increased investor criticism and regulator scrutiny forced many companies to improve the clarity of their financial disclosures. For example, IBM began providing more detail regarding its "Other gains and losses." It had previously included these items in its selling, general, and administrative expenses, with little disclosure.

Disclosing other gains and losses in a separate line item on the income statement will not have any effect on bottom-line income. However, analysts complained that burying these details in the selling, general, and administrative expense line reduced their ability to fully understand how well IBM was performing. For example, previously if IBM sold off one of its buildings at a gain, it would include this gain in the selling, general, and administrative expense line item, thus reducing that expense. This made it appear that the company had done a better job of controlling operating expenses than it actually had.

As another example, when eBay recently sold the remainder of its investment in Skype to Microsoft, it reported a gain in "Other revenues and gains" of $1.7 billion. Since eBay's total income from operations was $2.4 billion, it was very important that the gain from the Skype sale not be buried in operating income.

ImageRite/Getty Images, Inc.

 Why have investors and analysts demanded more accuracy in isolating "Other gains and losses" from operating items? (See page 274.)

Single-Step Income Statement

Another income statement format is the **single-step income statement**. The statement is so named because only one step—subtracting total expenses from total revenues—is required in determining net income.

In a single-step statement, all data are classified into two categories: (1) **revenues**, which include both operating revenues and other revenues and gains; and (2) **expenses**, which include cost of goods sold, operating expenses, and other expenses and losses. Illustration 5-15 shows a single-step statement for PW Audio Supply, Inc.

Illustration 5-15
Single-step income statement

PW AUDIO SUPPLY, INC.		
Income Statement		
For the Year Ended December 31, 2015		
Revenues		
Net sales		$460,000
Interest revenue		3,000
Gain on disposal of plant assets		600
Total revenues		463,600
Expenses		
Cost of goods sold	$316,000	
Operating expenses	114,000	
Interest expense	1,800	
Casualty loss from vandalism	200	
Total expenses		432,000
Net income		$ 31,600

There are two primary reasons for using the single-step format. (1) A company does not realize any type of profit or income until total revenues exceed total expenses, so it makes sense to divide the statement into these two categories. (2) The format is simpler and easier to read. *For homework problems, however, you should use the single-step format only when specifically instructed to do so.*

Classified Balance Sheet

In the balance sheet, merchandising companies report inventory as a current asset immediately below accounts receivable. Recall from Chapter 4 that companies generally list current asset items in the order of their closeness to cash (liquidity). Inventory is less close to cash than accounts receivable because the goods must first be sold and then collection made from the customer. Illustration 5-16 presents the assets section of a classified balance sheet for PW Audio Supply, Inc.

Illustration 5-16
Assets section of a classified balance sheet

PW AUDIO SUPPLY, INC.		
Balance Sheet (Partial)		
December 31, 2015		
Assets		
Current assets		
Cash		$ 9,500
Accounts receivable		16,100
Inventory		40,000
Prepaid insurance		1,800
Total current assets		67,400
Property, plant, and equipment		
Equipment	$80,000	
Less: Accumulated depreciation—equipment	24,000	56,000
Total assets		$123,400

Helpful Hint
The $40,000 is the cost of the inventory on hand, not its expected selling price.

> DO IT!

Financial Statement Classifications

You are presented with the following list of accounts from the adjusted trial balance for merchandiser Gorman Company. Indicate in which financial statement and under what classification each of the following would be reported.

Accounts Payable
Accounts Receivable
Accumulated Depreciation—Buildings
Accumulated Depreciation—Equipment
Advertising Expense
Buildings
Cash
Common Stock
Depreciation Expense
Dividends
Equipment
Freight-Out
Gain on Disposal of Plant Assets

Insurance Expense
Interest Expense
Interest Payable
Inventory
Land
Notes Payable (due in 3 years)
Property Taxes Payable
Salaries and Wages Expense
Salaries and Wages Payable
Sales Returns and Allowances
Sales Revenue
Utilities Expense

Solution

Action Plan

✔ Review the major sections of the income statement: sales, cost of goods sold, operating expenses, other revenues and gains, and other expenses and losses.

✔ Add net income and investments to beginning retained earnings and deduct dividends to arrive at ending retained earnings in the retained earnings statement.

✔ Review the major sections of the balance sheet, income statement, and retained earnings statement.

Account	Financial Statement	Classification
Accounts Payable	Balance sheet	Current liabilities
Accounts Receivable	Balance sheet	Current assets
Accumulated Depreciation—Buildings	Balance sheet	Property, plant, and equipment
Accumulated Depreciation—Equipment	Balance sheet	Property, plant, and equipment
Advertising Expense	Income statement	Operating expenses
Buildings	Balance sheet	Property, plant, and equipment
Cash	Balance sheet	Current assets
Common Stock	Balance sheet	Stockholders' equity
Depreciation Expense	Income statement	Operating expenses
Dividends	Retained earnings statement	Deduction section
Equipment	Balance sheet	Property, plant, and equipment
Freight-Out	Income statement	Operating expenses
Gain on Disposal of Plant Assets	Income statement	Other revenues and gains
Insurance Expense	Income statement	Operating expenses
Interest Expense	Income statement	Other expenses and losses
Interest Payable	Balance sheet	Current liabilities
Inventory	Balance sheet	Current assets
Land	Balance sheet	Property, plant, and equipment
Notes Payable (due in 3 years)	Balance sheet	Long-term liabilities
Property Taxes Payable	Balance sheet	Current liabilities
Salaries and Wages Expense	Income statement	Operating expenses
Salaries and Wages Payable	Balance sheet	Current liabilities
Sales Returns and Allowances	Income statement	Sales
Sales Revenue	Income statement	Sales
Utilities Expense	Income statement	Operating expenses

Related exercise material: BE5-7, BE5-8, BE5-9, E5-9, E5-10, E5-12, E5-13, E5-14, **and** DO IT! 5-4.

 The Navigator

> **Comprehensive DO IT!**

The adjusted trial balance columns of Falcetto Company's worksheet for the year ended December 31, 2015, are as follows.

	Debit		Credit
Cash	14,500	Accumulated Depreciation—	
Accounts Receivable	11,100	·Equipment	18,000
Inventory	29,000	Notes Payable	25,000
Prepaid Insurance	2,500	Accounts Payable	10,600
Equipment	95,000	Common Stock	50,000
Dividends	12,000	Retained Earnings	31,000
Sales Returns and Allowances	6,700	Sales Revenue	536,800
Sales Discounts	5,000	Interest Revenue	2,500
Cost of Goods Sold	363,400		673,900
Freight-Out	7,600		
Advertising Expense	12,000		
Salaries and Wages Expense	56,000		
Utilities Expense	18,000		
Rent Expense	24,000		
Depreciation Expense	9,000		
Insurance Expense	4,500		
Interest Expense	3,600		
	673,900		

Instructions

Prepare a multiple-step income statement for Falcetto Company.

Solution to Comprehensive DO IT!

Action Plan

✔ Remember that the key components of the income statement are net sales, cost of goods sold, gross profit, total operating expenses, and net income (loss). Report these components in the right-hand column of the income statement.

✔ Put nonoperating items after income from operations.

FALCETTO COMPANY
Income Statement
For the Year Ended December 31, 2015

Sales		
Sales revenue		$536,800
Less: Sales returns and allowances	$ 6,700	
Sales discounts	5,000	11,700
Net sales		525,100
Cost of goods sold		363,400
Gross profit		161,700
Operating expenses		
Salaries and wages expense	56,000	
Rent expense	24,000	
Utilities expense	18,000	
Advertising expense	12,000	
Depreciation expense	9,000	
Freight-out	7,600	
Insurance expense	4,500	
Total operating expenses		131,100
Income from operations		30,600
Other revenues and gains		
Interest revenue	2,500	
Other expenses and losses		
Interest expense	3,600	1,100
Net income		$ 29,500

SUMMARY OF LEARNING OBJECTIVES

1 **Identify the differences between service and merchandising companies.** Because of inventory, a merchandising company has sales revenue, cost of goods sold, and gross profit. To account for inventory, a merchandising company must choose between a perpetual and a periodic inventory system.

2 **Explain the recording of purchases under a perpetual inventory system.** The company debits the Inventory account for all purchases of merchandise and freight-in, and credits it for purchase discounts and purchase returns and allowances.

3 **Explain the recording of sales revenues under a perpetual inventory system.** When a merchandising company sells inventory, it debits Accounts Receivable (or Cash) and credits Sales Revenue for the **selling price** of the merchandise. At the same time, it debits Cost of Goods Sold and credits Inventory for the **cost** of the inventory items sold. Sales Returns and Allowances and Sales Discounts are debited and are contra revenue accounts.

4 **Explain the steps in the accounting cycle for a merchandising company.** Each of the required steps in the accounting cycle for a service company applies to a merchandising company. A worksheet is again an optional step. Under a perpetual inventory system, the company must adjust the Inventory account to agree with the physical count.

5 **Distinguish between a multiple-step and a single-step income statement.** A multiple-step income statement shows numerous steps in determining net income, including nonoperating activities sections. A single-step income statement classifies all data under two categories, revenues or expenses, and determines net income in one step.

GLOSSARY

Contra revenue account An account that is offset against a revenue account on the income statement. (p. 232).

Cost of goods sold The total cost of merchandise sold during the period. (p. 222).

FOB destination Freight terms indicating that the seller places the goods free on board to the buyer's place of business, and the seller pays the freight. (p. 226).

FOB shipping point Freight terms indicating that the seller places goods free on board the carrier, and the buyer pays the freight costs. (p. 226).

Gross profit The excess of net sales over the cost of goods sold. (p. 237).

Gross profit rate Gross profit expressed as a percentage, by dividing the amount of gross profit by net sales. (p. 237).

Income from operations Income from a company's principal operating activity; determined by subtracting cost of goods sold and operating expenses from net sales. (p. 238).

Multiple-step income statement An income statement that shows several steps in determining net income. (p. 236).

Net sales Sales revenue less sales returns and allowances and less sales discounts. (p. 237).

Nonoperating activities Various revenues, expenses, gains, and losses that are unrelated to a company's main line of operations. (p. 238).

Operating expenses Expenses incurred in the process of earning sales revenue. (p. 238).

Other expenses and losses A nonoperating-activities section of the income statement that shows expenses and losses unrelated to the company's main line of operations. (p. 238).

Other revenues and gains A nonoperating-activities section of the income statement that shows revenues and gains unrelated to the company's main line of operations. (p. 238).

Periodic inventory system An inventory system under which the company does not keep detailed inventory records throughout the accounting period but determines the cost of goods sold only at the end of an accounting period. (p. 224).

Perpetual inventory system An inventory system under which the company keeps detailed records of the cost of each inventory purchase and sale, and the records continuously show the inventory that should be on hand. (p. 223).

Purchase allowance A deduction made to the selling price of merchandise, granted by the seller so that the buyer will keep the merchandise. (p. 227).

Purchase discount A cash discount claimed by a buyer for prompt payment of a balance due. (p. 228).

Purchase invoice A document that supports each credit purchase. (p. 225).

Purchase return A return of goods from the buyer to the seller for a cash or credit refund. (p. 227).

Sales discount A reduction given by a seller for prompt payment of a credit sale. (p. 232).

Sales invoice A document that supports each credit sale. (p. 230).

Sales returns and allowances Purchase returns and allowances from the seller's perspective. See *Purchase return* and *Purchase allowance*, above. (p. 231).

Sales revenue (Sales) The primary source of revenue in a merchandising company. (p. 222).

Single-step income statement An income statement that shows only one step in determining net income. (p. 240).

APPENDIX 5A   Worksheet for a Merchandising Company— Perpetual Inventory

LEARNING OBJECTIVE   6

Prepare a worksheet for a merchandising company.

Using a Worksheet

As indicated in Chapter 4, a worksheet enables companies to prepare financial statements before they journalize and post adjusting entries. The steps in preparing a worksheet for a merchandising company are the same as for a service company (see pages 167–169). Illustration 5A-1 shows the worksheet for PW Audio Supply, Inc. (excluding nonoperating items). The unique accounts for a merchandiser using a **perpetual inventory system** are in red.

Illustration 5A-1
Worksheet for merchandising company—perpetual inventory system

	Trial Balance Dr.	Trial Balance Cr.	Adjustments Dr.	Adjustments Cr.	Adjusted Trial Balance Dr.	Adjusted Trial Balance Cr.	Income Statement Dr.	Income Statement Cr.	Balance Sheet Dr.	Balance Sheet Cr.
PW AUDIO SUPPLY, INC. Worksheet For the Year Ended December 31, 2015										
Accounts	Dr.	Cr.	Dr.	Cr.	Dr.	Cr.	Dr.	Cr.	Dr.	Cr.
Cash	9,500				9,500				9,500	
Accounts Receivable	16,100				16,100				16,100	
Inventory	40,500			(a) 500	40,000				40,000	
Prepaid Insurance	3,800			(b) 2,000	1,800				1,800	
Equipment	80,000				80,000				80,000	
Accumulated Depreciation—Equipment		16,000		(c) 8,000		24,000				24,000
Accounts Payable		20,400				20,400				20,400
Common Stock		50,000				50,000				50,000
Retained Earnings		33,000				33,000				33,000
Dividends	15,000				15,000				15,000	
Sales Revenue		480,000				480,000		480,000		
Sales Returns and Allowances	12,000				12,000		12,000			
Sales Discounts	8,000				8,000		8,000			
Cost of Goods Sold	315,500		(a) 500		316,000		316,000			
Freight-Out	7,000				7,000		7,000			
Advertising Expense	16,000				16,000		16,000			
Salaries and Wages Expense	59,000		(d) 5,000		64,000		64,000			
Utilities Expense	17,000				17,000		17,000			
Totals	599,400	599,400								
Insurance Expense			(b) 2,000		2,000		2,000			
Depreciation Expense			(c) 8,000		8,000		8,000			
Salaries and Wages Payable				(d) 5,000		5,000				5,000
Totals			15,500	15,500	612,400	612,400	450,000	480,000	162,400	132,400
Net Income							30,000			30,000
Totals							480,000	480,000	162,400	162,400

Key: (a) Adjustment to inventory on hand. (b) Insurance expired. (c) Depreciation expense. (d) Salaries and wages accrued.

TRIAL BALANCE COLUMNS

Data for the trial balance come from the ledger balances of PW Audio Supply at December 31. The amount shown for Inventory, $40,500, is the year-end inventory amount from the perpetual inventory system.

ADJUSTMENTS COLUMNS

A merchandising company generally has the same types of adjustments as a service company. As you see in the worksheet, adjustments (b), (c), and (d) are for insurance, depreciation, and salaries and wages. Pioneer Advertising Agency Inc., as illustrated in Chapters 3 and 4, also had these adjustments. Adjustment (a) was required to adjust the perpetual inventory carrying amount to the actual count.

After PW Audio Supply enters all adjustments data on the worksheet, it establishes the equality of the adjustments column totals. It then extends the balances in all accounts to the adjusted trial balance columns.

ADJUSTED TRIAL BALANCE

The adjusted trial balance shows the balance of all accounts after adjustment at the end of the accounting period.

INCOME STATEMENT COLUMNS

Next, the merchandising company transfers the accounts and balances that affect the income statement from the adjusted trial balance columns to the income statement columns. PW Audio Supply shows Sales Revenue of $480,000 in the credit column. It shows the contra revenue accounts Sales Returns and Allowances $12,000 and Sales Discounts $8,000 in the debit column. The difference of $460,000 is the net sales shown on the income statement (Illustration 5-14, page 239).

Finally, the company totals all the credits in the income statement column and compares those totals to the total of the debits in the income statement column. If the credits exceed the debits, the company has net income. PW Audio Supply has net income of $30,000. If the debits exceed the credits, the company would report a net loss.

BALANCE SHEET COLUMNS

The major difference between the balance sheets of a service company and a merchandiser is inventory. PW Audio Supply shows the ending inventory amount of $40,000 in the balance sheet debit column. The information to prepare the retained earnings statement is also found in these columns. That is, the retained earnings beginning balance is $33,000. Dividends are $15,000. Net income results when the total of the debit column exceeds the total of the credit column in the balance sheet columns. A net loss results when the total of the credits exceeds the total of the debit balances.

SUMMARY OF LEARNING OBJECTIVE FOR APPENDIX 5A

 The Navigator

6 Prepare a worksheet for a merchandising company. The steps in preparing a worksheet for a merchandising company are the same as for a service company.

The unique accounts for a merchandiser are Inventory, Sales Revenue, Sales Returns and Allowances, Sales Discounts, and Cost of Goods Sold.

APPENDIX 5B Periodic Inventory System

LEARNING OBJECTIVE **7**

Explain the recording of purchases and sales of inventory under a periodic inventory system.

As described in this chapter, companies may use one of two basic systems of accounting for inventories: (1) the perpetual inventory system or (2) the periodic inventory system. In the chapter, we focused on the characteristics of the perpetual inventory system. In this appendix, we discuss and illustrate the **periodic inventory system**. One key difference between the two systems is the point at which the company computes cost of goods sold. For a visual reminder of this difference, refer back to Illustration 5-5 (on page 224).

Determining Cost of Goods Sold Under a Periodic System

Determining cost of goods sold is different when a periodic inventory system is used rather than a perpetual system. As you have seen, a company using a **perpetual system** makes an entry to record cost of goods sold and to reduce inventory each time a sale is made. A company using a **periodic system** does not determine cost of goods sold until the end of the period. At the end of the period, the company performs a count to determine the ending balance of inventory. It then **calculates cost of goods sold by subtracting ending inventory from the goods available for sale**. Goods available for sale is the sum of beginning inventory plus purchases, as shown in Illustration 5B-1.

Illustration 5B-1
Basic formula for cost of goods sold using the periodic system

	Beginning Inventory
+	Cost of Goods Purchased
	Cost of Goods Available for Sale
−	Ending Inventory
	Cost of Goods Sold

Another difference between the two approaches is that the perpetual system directly adjusts the Inventory account for any transaction that affects inventory (such as freight costs, returns, and discounts). The periodic system does not do this. Instead, it creates different accounts for purchases, freight costs, returns, and discounts. These various accounts are shown in Illustration 5B-2, which presents the calculation of cost of goods sold for PW Audio Supply, Inc., using the periodic approach.

Illustration 5B-2
Cost of goods sold for a merchandiser using a periodic inventory system

PW AUDIO SUPPLY, INC.
Cost of Goods Sold
For the Year Ended December 31, 2015

Cost of goods sold			
Inventory, January 1			$ 36,000
Purchases		$325,000	
Less: Purchase returns and			
allowances	$10,400		
Purchase discounts	6,800	17,200	
Net purchases		307,800	
Add: Freight-in		12,200	
Cost of goods purchased			320,000
Cost of goods available for sale			356,000
Inventory, December 31			40,000
Cost of goods sold			**$316,000**

Helpful Hint
The far right column identifies the primary items that make up cost of goods sold of $316,000. The middle column explains cost of goods purchased of $320,000. The left column reports contra purchase items of $17,200.

Note that the basic elements from Illustration 5B-1 are highlighted in Illustration 5B-2. You will learn more in Chapter 6 about how to determine cost of goods sold using the periodic system.

The use of the periodic inventory system does not affect the form of presentation in the balance sheet. As under the perpetual system, a company reports inventory in the current assets section.

Recording Merchandise Transactions

In a **periodic inventory system**, companies record revenues from the sale of merchandise when sales are made, just as in a perpetual system. Unlike the perpetual system, however, companies **do not attempt on the date of sale to record the cost of the merchandise sold**. Instead, they take a physical inventory count at the **end of the period** to determine (1) the cost of the merchandise then on hand and (2) the cost of the goods sold during the period. And, **under a periodic system, companies record purchases of merchandise in the Purchases account rather than in the Inventory account**. Also, in a periodic system, purchase returns and allowances, purchase discounts, and freight costs on purchases are recorded in separate accounts.

To illustrate the recording of merchandise transactions under a periodic inventory system, we will use purchase/sales transactions between PW Audio Supply, Inc. and Sauk Stereo, as illustrated for the perpetual inventory system in this chapter.

Recording Purchases of Merchandise

On the basis of the sales invoice (Illustration 5-6, shown on page 226) and receipt of the merchandise ordered from PW Audio Supply, Sauk Stereo records the $3,800 purchase as follows.

Helpful Hint
Be careful not to debit purchases of equipment or supplies to a Purchases account.

May 4	Purchases	3,800	
	Accounts Payable		3,800
	(To record goods purchased on account		
	from PW Audio Supply)		

Purchases is a temporary account whose normal balance is a debit.

FREIGHT COSTS

When the purchaser directly incurs the freight costs, it debits the account Freight-In (or Transportation-In). For example, if Sauk Stereo pays Public Carrier Co. $150 for freight charges on its purchase from PW Audio Supply on May 6, the entry on Sauk Stereo's books is:

Alternative Terminology
Freight-In is also called *Transportation-In.*

May 6	Freight-In (Transportation-In)	150	
	Cash		150
	(To record payment of freight on goods		
	purchased)		

Like Purchases, Freight-In is a temporary account whose normal balance is a debit. **Freight-In is part of cost of goods purchased.** The reason is that cost of goods purchased should include any freight charges necessary to bring the goods to the purchaser. Freight costs are not subject to a purchase discount. Purchase discounts apply only to the invoice cost of the merchandise.

PURCHASE RETURNS AND ALLOWANCES

Sauk Stereo returns $300 of goods to PW Audio Supply and prepares the following entry to recognize the return.

May 8	Accounts Payable	300	
	Purchase Returns and Allowances		300
	(To record return of goods purchased		
	from PW Audio Supply)		

Purchase Returns and Allowances is a temporary account whose normal balance is a credit.

PURCHASE DISCOUNTS

On May 14, Sauk Stereo pays the balance due on account to PW Audio Supply, taking the 2% cash discount allowed by PW Audio Supply for payment within 10 days. Sauk Stereo records the payment and discount as follows.

May 14	Accounts Payable ($3,800 − $300)	3,500	
	Purchase Discounts ($3,500 × .02)		70
	Cash		3,430
	(To record payment within the		
	discount period)		

Purchase Discounts is a temporary account whose normal balance is a credit.

Recording Sales of Merchandise

The seller, PW Audio Supply, records the sale of $3,800 of merchandise to Sauk Stereo on May 4 (sales invoice No. 731, Illustration 5-6, page 226) as follows.

May 4	Accounts Receivable	3,800	
	Sales Revenue		3,800
	(To record credit sales per invoice #731		
	to Sauk Stereo)		

SALES RETURNS AND ALLOWANCES

To record the returned goods received from Sauk Stereo on May 8, PW Audio Supply records the $300 sales return as follows.

May 8	Sales Returns and Allowances	300	
	Accounts Receivable		300
	(To record credit granted to Sauk Stereo		
	for returned goods)		

SALES DISCOUNTS

On May 14, PW Audio Supply receives payment of $3,430 on account from Sauk Stereo. PW Audio Supply honors the 2% cash discount and records the payment of Sauk Stereo's account receivable in full as follows.

May 14	Cash	3,430	
	Sales Discounts ($3,500 × .02)	70	
	Accounts Receivable ($3,800 − $300)		3,500
	(To record collection within 2/10, n/30		
	discount period from Sauk Stereo)		

COMPARISON OF ENTRIES—PERPETUAL VS. PERIODIC

Illustration 5B-3 summarizes the periodic inventory entries shown in this appendix and compares them to the perpetual system entries from the chapter. Entries that differ in the two systems are shown in color.

ENTRIES ON SAUK STEREO'S BOOKS						
Transaction	**Perpetual Inventory System**			**Periodic Inventory System**		
May 4 Purchase of merchandise on credit.	Inventory Accounts Payable	3,800	3,800	Purchases Accounts Payable	3,800	3,800
6 Freight costs on purchases.	Inventory Cash	150	150	Freight-In Cash	150	150
8 Purchase returns and allowances.	Accounts Payable Inventory	300	300	Accounts Payable Purchase Returns and Allowances	300	300
14 Payment on account with a discount.	Accounts Payable Cash Inventory	3,500	3,430 70	Accounts Payable Cash Purchase Discounts	3,500	3,430 70

ENTRIES ON PW AUDIO SUPPLY'S BOOKS						
Transaction	**Perpetual Inventory System**			**Periodic Inventory System**		
May 4 Sale of merchandise on credit.	Accounts Receivable Sales Revenue	3,800	3,800	Accounts Receivable Sales Revenue	3,800	3,800
	Cost of Goods Sold Inventory	2,400	2,400	No entry for cost of goods sold		
8 Return of merchandise sold.	Sales Returns and Allowances Accounts Receivable	300	300	Sales Returns and Allowances Accounts Receivable	300	300
	Inventory Cost of Goods Sold	140	140	No entry		
14 Cash received on account with a discount.	Cash Sales Discounts Accounts Receivable	3,430 70	3,500	Cash Sales Discounts Accounts Receivable	3,430 70	3,500

Illustration 5B-3
Comparison of entries for perpetual and periodic inventory systems

Journalizing and Posting Closing Entries

For a merchandising company, like a service company, all accounts that affect the determination of net income are closed to Income Summary. Data for the preparation of closing entries may be obtained from the income statement columns of the worksheet. In journalizing, all debit column amounts are credited, and all credit columns amounts are debited. To close the merchandise inventory in a periodic inventory system:

1. The beginning inventory balance is debited to Income Summary and credited to Inventory.

2. The ending inventory balance is debited to Inventory and credited to Income Summary.

The two entries for PW Audio Supply are:

(1)

Dec. 31	Income Summary	36,000	
	Inventory		36,000
	(To close beginning inventory)		

(2)

31	Inventory	40,000	
	Income Summary		40,000
	(To record ending inventory)		

After posting, the Inventory and Income Summary accounts will show the following.

Illustration 5B-4
Posting closing entries for merchandise inventory

Inventory				Income Summary			
1/1	Bal.	36,000	12/31 Close **36,000**	12/31 Close **36,000**	12/31 Close **40,000**		
12/31	Close	**40,000**					
12/31	Bal.	**40,000**					

Often, the closing of Inventory is included with other closing entries, as shown below for PW Audio Supply.

Helpful Hint
Except for merchandise inventory, the easiest way to prepare the first two closing entries is to identify the temporary accounts by their balances and then prepare one entry for the credits and one for the debits.

Helpful Hint
Close Inventory with other accounts in homework problems unless stated otherwise.

Dec. 31		**Inventory (Dec. 31)**	**40,000**	
		Sales Revenue	480,000	
		Purchase Returns and Allowances	10,400	
		Purchase Discounts	6,800	
		Income Summary		537,200
		(To record ending inventory and close		
		accounts with credit balances)		
	31	Income Summary	507,200	
		Inventory (Jan. 1)		**36,000**
		Sales Returns and Allowances		12,000
		Sales Discounts		8,000
		Purchases		325,000
		Freight-In		12,200
		Salaries and Wages Expense		64,000
		Freight-Out		7,000
		Advertising Expense		16,000
		Utilities Expense		17,000
		Depreciation Expense		8,000
		Insurance Expense		2,000
		(To close beginning inventory and		
		other income statement accounts with		
		debit balances)		
	31	Income Summary	30,000	
		Retained Earnings		30,000
		(To transfer net income to		
		retained earnings)		
	31	Retained Earnings	15,000	
		Dividends		15,000
		(To close dividends to retained earnings)		

After the closing entries are posted, all temporary accounts have zero balances. In addition, Retained Earnings has a credit balance of $48,000: beginning balance + net income − dividends ($33,000 + $30,000 − $15,000).

Using a Worksheet

As indicated in Chapter 4, a worksheet enables companies to prepare financial statements before journalizing and posting adjusting entries. The steps in preparing a worksheet for a merchandising company are the same as they are for a service company (see pages 167–169).

TRIAL BALANCE COLUMNS
Data for the trial balance come from the ledger balances of PW Audio Supply at December 31. The amount shown for Inventory, $36,000, is the beginning inventory amount from the periodic inventory system.

ADJUSTMENTS COLUMNS

A merchandising company generally has the same types of adjustments as a service company. As you see in the worksheet in Illustration 5B-5, adjustments (a), (b), and (c) are for insurance, depreciation, and salaries and wages. These adjustments were also required for Pioneer Advertising Agency Inc., as illustrated in Chapters 3 and 4. The unique accounts for a merchandiser using a **periodic inventory system** are shown in capital red letters. Note, however, that the worksheet excludes nonoperating items.

Illustration 5B-5

Worksheet for merchandising company—periodic inventory system

PW Audio Supply.xls

Home   Insert   Page Layout   Formulas   Data   Review   View

P18   fx

PW AUDIO SUPPLY, INC.
Worksheet
For the Year Ended December 31, 2015

	A	Trial Balance Dr.	Trial Balance Cr.	Adjustments Dr.	Adjustments Cr.	Adjusted Trial Balance Dr.	Adjusted Trial Balance Cr.	Income Statement Dr.	Income Statement Cr.	Balance Sheet Dr.	Balance Sheet Cr.
7	Accounts	Dr.	Cr.	Dr.	Cr.	Dr.	Cr.	Dr.	Cr.	Dr.	Cr.
8	Cash	9,500				9,500				9,500	
9	Accounts Receivable	16,100				16,100				16,100	
10	INVENTORY	36,000				36,000		36,000	40,000	40,000	
11	Prepaid Insurance	3,800			(a) 2,000	1,800				1,800	
12	Equipment	80,000				80,000				80,000	
13	Accumulated Depreciation—Equipment		16,000		(b) 8,000		24,000				24,000
14	Accounts Payable		20,400				20,400				20,400
15	Common Stock		50,000				50,000				50,000
16	Retained Earnings		33,000				33,000				33,000
17	Dividends	15,000				15,000				15,000	
18	SALES REVENUE		480,000				480,000		480,000		
19	SALES RETURNS AND ALLOWANCES	12,000				12,000		12,000			
20	SALES DISCOUNTS	8,000				8,000		8,000			
21	PURCHASES	325,000				325,000		325,000			
22	PURCHASE RETURNS AND ALLOWANCES		10,400				10,400		10,400		
23	PURCHASE DISCOUNTS		6,800				6,800		6,800		
24	FREIGHT-IN	12,200				12,200		12,200			
25	Freight-Out	7,000				7,000		7,000			
26	Advertising Expense	16,000				16,000		16,000			
27	Salaries and Wages Expense	59,000		(c) 5,000		64,000		64,000			
28	Utilities Expense	17,000				17,000		17,000			
29	Totals	616,600	616,600								
30	Insurance Expense			(a) 2,000		2,000		2,000			
31	Depreciation Expense			(b) 8,000		8,000		8,000			
32	Salaries and Wages Payable				(c) 5,000		5,000				5,000
33	Totals			15,000	15,000	629,600	629,600	507,200	537,200	162,400	132,400
34	Net Income							30,000			30,000
35	Totals							537,200	537,200	162,400	162,400
36											
37											

Key: (a) Insurance expired. (b) Depreciation expense. (c) Salaries and wages accrued.

After all adjustment data are entered on the worksheet, the equality of the adjustment column totals is established. The balances in all accounts are then extended to the adjusted trial balance columns.

INCOME STATEMENT COLUMNS

Next, PW Audio Supply transfers the accounts and balances that affect the income statement from the adjusted trial balance columns to the income statements columns. The company shows Sales Revenue of $480,000 in the credit column. It shows the contra revenue accounts, Sales Returns and Allowances of $12,000 and Sales Discounts of $8,000, in the debit column. The difference of $460,000 is the net sales shown on the income statement (Illustration 5-9, page 237). Similarly, Purchases of $325,000 and Freight-In of $12,200 are extended to the debit column. The contra purchase accounts, Purchase Returns and Allowances of $10,400 and Purchase Discounts of $6,800, are extended to the credit columns.

The worksheet procedures for the Inventory account merit specific comment. The procedures are:

1. The beginning balance, $36,000, is extended from the adjusted trial balance column to the **income statement debit column**. From there it can be added in reporting cost of goods available for sale in the income statement.
2. The ending inventory, $40,000, is added to the worksheet by an **income statement credit and a balance sheet debit**. The credit makes it possible to deduct ending inventory from the cost of goods available for sale in the income statement to determine cost of goods sold. The debit means the ending inventory can be reported as an asset on the balance sheet.

These two procedures are specifically illustrated below:

Illustration 5B-6
Worksheet procedures for inventories

	Income Statement		Balance Sheet	
	Dr.	Cr.	Dr.	Cr.
Inventory	(1) 36,000	40,000 ◄——— (2) ——→ 40,000		

The computation for cost of goods sold, taken from the income statement column in Illustration 5B-5, is as follows.

Illustration 5B-7
Computation of cost of goods sold from worksheet columns

Debit Column		Credit Column	
Beginning inventory	$ 36,000	Ending inventory	$40,000
Purchases	325,000	Purchase returns and allowances	10,400
Freight-in	12,200	Purchase discounts	6,800
Total debits	373,200	Total credits	$57,200
Less: Total credits	57,200		
Cost of goods sold	**$316,000**		

Helpful Hint
In a periodic system, cost of goods sold is a computation—it is not a separate account with a balance.

Finally, PW Audio Supply totals all the credits in the income statement column and compares these totals to the total of the debits in the income statement column. If the credits exceed the debits, the company has net income. PW Audio Supply has net income of $30,000. If the debits exceed the credits, the company would report a net loss.

BALANCE SHEET COLUMNS

The major difference between the balance sheets of a service company and a merchandising company is inventory. PW Audio Supply shows ending inventory of $40,000 in the balance sheet debit column. The information to prepare the retained earnings statement is also found in these columns. That is, the retained earnings beginning balance is $33,000. Dividends are $15,000. Net income results when the total of the debit column exceeds the total of the credit column in the balance sheet columns. A net loss results when the total of the credits exceeds the total of the debit balances.

SUMMARY OF LEARNING OBJECTIVE FOR APPENDIX 5B

 The Navigator

7 Explain the recording of purchases and sales of inventory under a periodic inventory system. In recording purchases under a periodic system, companies must make entries for (a) cash and credit purchases, (b) purchase returns and allowances, (c) purchase discounts, and (d) freight costs. In recording sales, companies must make entries for (a) cash and credit sales, (b) sales returns and allowances, and (c) sales discounts.

WileyPLUS Self-Test, Brief Exercises, Exercises, Problem Set A, and many more components are available for practice in *WileyPLUS*.

*Note: All asterisked Questions, Exercises, and Problems relate to material in the appendices to the chapter.

SELF-TEST QUESTIONS

Answers are on page 275.

(LO 1) **1.** Gross profit will result if:
 (a) operating expenses are less than net income.
 (b) sales revenues are greater than operating expenses.
 (c) sales revenues are greater than cost of goods sold.
 (d) operating expenses are greater than cost of goods sold.

(LO 2) **2.** Under a perpetual inventory system, when goods are purchased for resale by a company:
 (a) purchases on account are debited to Inventory.
 (b) purchases on account are debited to Purchases.
 (c) purchase returns are debited to Purchase Returns and Allowances.
 (d) freight costs are debited to Freight-Out.

(LO 3) **3.** The sales accounts that normally have a debit balance are:
 (a) Sales Discounts.
 (b) Sales Returns and Allowances.
 (c) Both (a) and (b).
 (d) Neither (a) nor (b).

(LO 3) **4.** A credit sale of $750 is made on June 13, terms 2/10, net/30. A return of $50 is granted on June 16. The amount received as payment in full on June 23 is:
 (a) $700. (c) $685.
 (b) $686. (d) $650.

(LO 2) **5.** Which of the following accounts will normally appear in the ledger of a merchandising company that uses a perpetual inventory system?
 (a) Purchases. (c) Cost of Goods Sold.
 (b) Freight-In. (d) Purchase Discounts.

(LO 3) **6.** To record the sale of goods for cash in a perpetual inventory system:
 (a) only one journal entry is necessary to record cost of goods sold and reduction of inventory.
 (b) only one journal entry is necessary to record the receipt of cash and the sales revenue.
 (c) two journal entries are necessary: one to record the receipt of cash and sales revenue, and one to record the cost of goods sold and reduction of inventory.
 (d) two journal entries are necessary: one to record the receipt of cash and reduction of inventory, and one to record the cost of goods sold and sales revenue.

7. The steps in the accounting cycle for a merchandising (LO 4) company are the same as those in a service company **except:**
 (a) an additional adjusting journal entry for inventory may be needed in a merchandising company.
 (b) closing journal entries are not required for a merchandising company.
 (c) a post-closing trial balance is not required for a merchandising company.
 (d) a multiple-step income statement is required for a merchandising company.

8. The multiple-step income statement for a merchandising (LO 5) company shows each of the following features **except:**
 (a) gross profit.
 (b) cost of goods sold.
 (c) a sales revenue section.
 (d) an investing activities section.

9. If sales revenues are $400,000, cost of goods sold is (LO 5) $310,000, and operating expenses are $60,000, the gross profit is:
 (a) $30,000. (c) $340,000.
 (b) $90,000. (d) $400,000.

10. A single-step income statement: (LO 5)
 (a) reports gross profit.
 (b) does not report cost of goods sold.
 (c) reports sales revenues and "Other revenues and gains" in the revenues section of the income statement.
 (d) reports operating income separately.

(LO 5) **11.** Which of the following appears on both a single-step and a multiple-step income statement?
   (a) Inventory.
   (b) Gross profit.
   (c) Income from operations.
   (d) Cost of goods sold.

(LO 6) ***12.** In a worksheet using a perpetual inventory system, Inventory is shown in the following columns:
   (a) adjusted trial balance debit and balance sheet debit.
   (b) income statement debit and balance sheet debit.
   (c) income statement credit and balance sheet debit.
   (d) income statement credit and adjusted trial balance debit.

(LO 7) ***13.** In determining cost of goods sold in a periodic system:
   (a) purchase discounts are deducted from net purchases.
   (b) freight-out is added to net purchases.
   (c) purchase returns and allowances are deducted from net purchases.
   (d) freight-in is added to net purchases.

*14. If beginning inventory is $60,000, cost of goods purchased is $380,000, and ending inventory is $50,000, cost of goods sold is: (LO 7)
   (a) $390,000.   **(c)** $330,000.
   (b) $370,000.   **(d)** $420,000.

*15. When goods are purchased for resale by a company (LO 7) using a periodic inventory system:
   (a) purchases on account are debited to Inventory.
   (b) purchases on account are debited to Purchases.
   (c) purchase returns are debited to Purchase Returns and Allowances.
   (d) freight costs are debited to Purchases.

Go to the book's companion website, www.wiley.com/college/weygandt, for additional Self-Test Questions.

 ✔ The Navigator

QUESTIONS

1. (a) "The steps in the accounting cycle for a merchandising company are different from the accounting cycle for a service company." Do you agree or disagree? (b) Is the measurement of net income for a merchandising company conceptually the same as for a service company? Explain.

2. Why is the normal operating cycle for a merchandising company likely to be longer than for a service company?

3. (a) How do the components of revenues and expenses differ between merchandising and service companies? (b) Explain the income measurement process in a merchandising company.

4. How does income measurement differ between a merchandising and a service company?

5. When is cost of goods sold determined in a perpetual inventory system?

6. Distinguish between FOB shipping point and FOB destination. Identify the freight terms that will result in a debit to Inventory by the buyer and a debit to Freight-Out by the seller.

7. Explain the meaning of the credit terms 2/10, n/30.

8. Goods costing $2,000 are purchased on account on July 15 with credit terms of 2/10, n/30. On July 18, a $200 credit memo is received from the supplier for damaged goods. Give the journal entry on July 24 to record payment of the balance due within the discount period using a perpetual inventory system.

9. Ming Xu believes revenues from credit sales may be recorded before they are collected in cash. Do you agree? Explain.

10. (a) What is the primary source document for recording (1) cash sales and (2) credit sales? (b) Using XXs for amounts, give the journal entry for each of the transactions in part (a).

11. A credit sale is made on July 10 for $900, terms 2/10, n/30. On July 12, $100 of goods are returned for credit. Give the journal entry on July 19 to record the receipt of the balance due within the discount period.

12. Explain why the Inventory account will usually require adjustment at year-end.

13. Prepare the closing entries for the Sales Revenue account, assuming a balance of $200,000 and the Cost of Goods Sold account with a $145,000 balance.

14. What merchandising account(s) will appear in the post-closing trial balance?

15. Minnick Co. has sales revenue of $105,000, cost of goods sold of $70,000, and operating expenses of $20,000. What is its gross profit and its gross profit rate?

16. Paul Scott Company reports net sales of $800,000, gross profit of $370,000, and net income of $240,000. What are its operating expenses?

17. Identify the distinguishing features of an income statement for a merchandising company.

18. Identify the sections of a multiple-step income statement that relate to (a) operating activities, and (b) nonoperating activities.

19. How does the single-step form of income statement differ from the multiple-step form?

20. Determine Apple's gross profit rate for 2011 and 2010. Indicate whether it increased or decreased from 2010 to 2011.

*21. Indicate the columns of the worksheet in a perpetual system in which (a) inventory and (b) cost of goods sold will be shown.

*22. Identify the accounts that are added to or deducted from Purchases in a periodic system to determine the cost of goods purchased. For each account, indicate whether it is added or deducted.

*23. Goods costing $3,000 are purchased on account on July 15 with credit terms of 2/10, n/30. On July 18, a $200 credit was received from the supplier for damaged goods. Give the journal entry on July 24 to record payment of the balance due within the discount period, assuming a periodic inventory system.

BRIEF EXERCISES

BE5-1 Presented below are the components in Gates Company's income statement. Determine the missing amounts.

Compute missing amounts in determining net income.

(LO 1)

	Sales Revenue	Cost of Goods Sold	Gross Profit	Operating Expenses	Net Income
(a)	$75,000	?	$30,000	?	$10,800
(b)	$108,000	$70,000	?	?	$29,500
(c)	?	$83,900	$79,600	$39,500	?

BE5-2 Radomir Company buys merchandise on account from Lemke Company. The selling price of the goods is $780, and the cost of the goods is $470. Both companies use perpetual inventory systems. Journalize the transaction on the books of both companies.

Journalize perpetual inventory entries.

(LO 2, 3)

BE5-3 Prepare the journal entries to record the following transactions on Kwang Company's books using a perpetual inventory system.

Journalize sales transactions.

(LO 3)

(a) On March 2, Kwang Company sold $900,000 of merchandise to Sensat Company, terms 2/10, n/30. The cost of the merchandise sold was $620,000.

(b) On March 6, Sensat Company returned $90,000 of the merchandise purchased on March 2. The cost of the returned merchandise was $62,000.

(c) On March 12, Kwang Company received the balance due from Sensat Company.

BE5-4 From the information in BE5-3, prepare the journal entries to record these transactions on Sensat Company's books under a perpetual inventory system.

Journalize purchase transactions.

(LO 2)

BE5-5 At year-end, the perpetual inventory records of Litwin Company showed merchandise inventory of $98,000. The company determined, however, that its actual inventory on hand was $95,700. Record the necessary adjusting entry.

Prepare adjusting entry for inventory.

(LO 4)

BE5-6 Hudson Company has the following account balances: Sales Revenue $195,000, Sales Discounts $2,000, Cost of Goods Sold $117,000, and Inventory $40,000. Prepare the entries to record the closing of these items to Income Summary.

Prepare closing entries for accounts.

(LO 4)

BE5-7 Arndt Company provides the following information for the month ended October 31, 2015: sales on credit $280,000, cash sales $100,000, sales discounts $5,000, and sales returns and allowances $11,000. Prepare the sales section of the income statement based on this information.

Prepare sales section of income statement.

(LO 5)

BE5-8 ⇒ Explain where each of the following items would appear on (1) a multiple-step income statement, and on (2) a single-step income statement: (a) gain on sale of equipment, (b) interest expense, (c) casualty loss from vandalism, and (d) cost of goods sold.

Contrast presentation in multiple-step and single-step income statements.

(LO 5)

BE5-9 Assume Kader Company has the following reported amounts: Sales revenue $510,000, Sales returns and allowances $15,000, Cost of goods sold $330,000, and Operating expenses $110,000. Compute the following: (a) net sales, (b) gross profit, (c) income from operations, and (d) gross profit rate. (Round to one decimal place.)

Compute net sales, gross profit, income from operations, and gross profit rate.

(LO 5)

*BE5-10 Presented below is the format of the worksheet using the perpetual inventory system presented in Appendix 5A.

Identify worksheet columns for selected accounts.

(LO 6)

Trial Balance		Adjustments		Adjusted Trial Balance		Income Statement		Balance Sheet	
Dr.	Cr.	Dr.	Cr.	Dr.	Cr.	Dr.	Cr.	Dr.	Cr.

Indicate where the following items will appear on the worksheet: (a) Cash, (b) Inventory, (c) Sales revenue, and (d) Cost of goods sold.

Example:
Cash: Trial balance debit column; Adjusted trial balance debit column; and Balance sheet debit column.

Compute net purchases and cost of goods purchased.
(LO 7)

*BE5-11 Assume that Gallant Company uses a periodic inventory system and has these account balances: Purchases $450,000, Purchase Returns and Allowances $13,000, Purchase Discounts $8,000, and Freight-In $16,000. Determine net purchases and cost of goods purchased.

Compute cost of goods sold and gross profit.
(LO 7)

*BE5-12 Assume the same information as in BE5-11 and also that Gallant Company has beginning inventory of $60,000, ending inventory of $90,000, and net sales of $730,000. Determine the amounts to be reported for cost of goods sold and gross profit.

Journalize purchase transactions.
(LO 7)

*BE5-13 Prepare the journal entries to record these transactions on Nimmer Company's books using a periodic inventory system.

(a) On March 2, Nimmer Company purchased $900,000 of merchandise from Sen Company, terms 2/10, n/30.
(b) On March 6, Nimmer Company returned $130,000 of the merchandise purchased on March 2.
(c) On March 12, Nimmer Company paid the balance due to Sen Company.

Prepare closing entries for merchandise accounts.
(LO 7)

*BE5-14 A. Hall Company has the following merchandise account balances: Sales Revenue $180,000, Sales Discounts $2,000, Purchases $120,000, and Purchases Returns and Allowances $30,000. In addition, it has a beginning inventory of $40,000 and an ending inventory of $30,000. Prepare the entries to record the closing of these items to Income Summary using the periodic inventory system.

Identify worksheet columns for selected accounts
(LO 7)

*BE5-15 Presented below is the format of the worksheet using the periodic inventory system presented in Appendix 5B.

Trial Balance		Adjustments		Adjusted Trial Balance		Income Statement		Balance Sheet	
Dr.	Cr.	Dr.	Cr.	Dr.	Cr.	Dr.	Cr.	Dr.	Cr.

Indicate where the following items will appear on the worksheet: (a) Cash, (b) Beginning inventory, (c) Accounts payable, (d) Ending inventory.

Example
Cash: Trial balance debit column; Adjustment trial balance debit column; and Balance sheet debit column.

> DO IT! Review

Record transactions of purchasing company.
(LO 2)

DO IT! 5-1 On October 5, Loomis Company buys merchandise on account from Brooke Company. The selling price of the goods is $5,000, and the cost to Brooke Company is $3,100. On October 8, Loomis returns defective goods with a selling price of $650 and a fair value of $100. Record the transactions on the books of Loomis Company.

Record transactions of selling company.
(LO 3)

DO IT! 5-2 Assume information similar to that in **DO IT!** 5-1: On October 5, Loomis Company buys merchandise on account from Brooke Company. The selling price of the goods is $5,000, and the cost to Brooke Company is $3,100. On October 8, Loomis returns defective goods with a selling price of $650 and a fair value of $100. Record the transactions on the books of Brooke Company.

Prepare closing entries for a merchandising company.
(LO 4)

DO IT! 5-3 The trial balance of Optique Boutique at December 31 shows Inventory $21,000, Sales Revenue $156,000, Sales Returns and Allowances $4,000, Sales Discounts $3,000, Cost of Goods Sold $92,400, Interest Revenue $5,000, Freight-Out $1,500, Utilities Expense $7,400, and Salaries and Wages Expense $19,500. Prepare the closing entries for Optique.

Classify financial statement accounts.
(LO 5)

DO IT! 5-4 Estes Company is preparing its multiple-step income statement, retained earnings statement, and classified balance sheet. Using the column heads **Account**, **Financial Statement**, and **Classification**, indicate in which financial statement and under what classification each of the following would be reported.

Account	Financial Statement	Classification
Accounts Payable		
Accounts Receivable		
Accumulated Depreciation—Buildings		
Cash		
Casualty Loss from Vandalism		
Common Stock		
Cost of Goods Sold		
Depreciation Expense		
Dividends		
Equipment		
Freight-Out		
Insurance Expense		
Interest Payable		
Inventory		
Land		
Notes Payable (due in 5 years)		
Property Taxes Payable		
Salaries and Wages Expense		
Salaries and Wages Payable		
Sales Returns and Allowances		
Sales Revenue		
Unearned Rent Revenue		
Utilities Expense		

EXERCISES

E5-1 Mr. Etemadi has prepared the following list of statements about service companies and merchandisers.

Answer general questions about merchandisers.
(LO 1)

1. Measuring net income for a merchandiser is conceptually the same as for a service company.
2. For a merchandiser, sales less operating expenses is called gross profit.
3. For a merchandiser, the primary source of revenues is the sale of inventory.
4. Sales salaries and wages is an example of an operating expense.
5. The operating cycle of a merchandiser is the same as that of a service company.
6. In a perpetual inventory system, no detailed inventory records of goods on hand are maintained.
7. In a periodic inventory system, the cost of goods sold is determined only at the end of the accounting period.
8. A periodic inventory system provides better control over inventories than a perpetual system.

Instructions
Identify each statement as true or false. If false, indicate how to correct the statement.

E5-2 Information related to Harwick Co. is presented below.

Journalize purchase transactions.
(LO 2)

1. On April 5, purchased merchandise from Botham Company for $23,000, terms 2/10, net/30, FOB shipping point.
2. On April 6, paid freight costs of $900 on merchandise purchased from Botham.
3. On April 7, purchased equipment on account for $26,000.
4. On April 8, returned damaged merchandise to Botham Company and was granted a $3,000 credit for returned merchandise.
5. On April 15, paid the amount due to Botham Company in full.

Instructions
(a) Prepare the journal entries to record these transactions on the books of Harwick Co. under a perpetual inventory system.
(b) Assume that Harwick Co. paid the balance due to Botham Company on May 4 instead of April 15. Prepare the journal entry to record this payment.

Journalize perpetual inventory entries.
(LO 2, 3)

E5-3 On September 1, Boylan Office Supply had an inventory of 30 calculators at a cost of $18 each. The company uses a perpetual inventory system. During September, the following transactions occurred.

Sept. 6	Purchased with cash 80 calculators at $20 each from Guthrie Co.
9	Paid freight of $80 on calculators purchased from Guthrie Co.
10	Returned 3 calculators to Guthrie Co. for $63 credit (including freight) because they did not meet specifications.
12	Sold 26 calculators costing $21 (including freight) for $31 each to Lee Book Store, terms n/30.
14	Granted credit of $31 to Lee Book Store for the return of one calculator that was not ordered.
20	Sold 30 calculators costing $21 for $32 each to Orr's Card Shop, terms n/30.

Instructions
Journalize the September transactions.

Prepare purchase and sale entries.
(LO 2, 3)

E5-4 On June 10, Tuzun Company purchased $8,000 of merchandise from Epps Company, FOB shipping point, terms 2/10, n/30. Tuzun pays the freight costs of $400 on June 11. Damaged goods totaling $300 are returned to Epps for credit on June 12. The fair value of these goods is $70. On June 19, Tuzun pays Epps Company in full, less the purchase discount. Both companies use a perpetual inventory system.

Instructions
(a) Prepare separate entries for each transaction on the books of Tuzun Company.
(b) Prepare separate entries for each transaction for Epps Company. The merchandise purchased by Tuzun on June 10 had cost Epps $4,800.

Journalize sales transactions.
(LO 3)

E5-5 Presented below are transactions related to Bogner Company.

1. On December 3, Bogner Company sold $570,000 of merchandise to Maris Co., terms 2/10, n/30, FOB shipping point. The cost of the merchandise sold was $350,000.
2. On December 8, Maris Co. was granted an allowance of $20,000 for merchandise purchased on December 3.
3. On December 13, Bogner Company received the balance due from Maris Co.

Instructions
(a) Prepare the journal entries to record these transactions on the books of Bogner Company using a perpetual inventory system.
(b) Assume that Bogner Company received the balance due from Maris Co. on January 2 of the following year instead of December 13. Prepare the journal entry to record the receipt of payment on January 2.

Prepare sales section and closing entries.
(LO 4, 5)

E5-6 The adjusted trial balance of Tsai Company shows the following data pertaining to sales at the end of its fiscal year October 31, 2015: Sales Revenue $820,000, Freight-Out $16,000, Sales Returns and Allowances $25,000, and Sales Discounts $13,000.

Instructions
(a) Prepare the sales section of the income statement.
(b) Prepare separate closing entries for (1) sales revenue, and (2) the contra accounts to sales revenue.

Prepare adjusting and closing entries.
(LO 4)

E5-7 Juan Morales Company had the following account balances at year-end: Cost of Goods Sold $60,000, Inventory $15,000, Operating Expenses $29,000, Sales Revenue $115,000, Sales Discounts $1,200, and Sales Returns and Allowances $1,700. A physical count of inventory determines that merchandise inventory on hand is $13,900.

Instructions
(a) Prepare the adjusting entry necessary as a result of the physical count.
(b) Prepare closing entries.

Prepare adjusting and closing entries.
(LO 4)

E5-8 Presented below is information related to Garland Co. for the month of January 2015.

Ending inventory per perpetual records	$ 21,600	Insurance expense	$ 12,000
		Rent expense	20,000
Ending inventory actually on hand	21,000	Salaries and wages expense	55,000
		Sales discounts	10,000
Cost of goods sold	218,000	Sales returns and allowances	13,000
Freight-out	7,000	Sales revenue	380,000

Instructions
(a) Prepare the necessary adjusting entry for inventory.
(b) Prepare the necessary closing entries.

E5-9 Presented below is information for Furlow Company for the month of March 2015.

Cost of goods sold	$212,000	Rent expense	$ 32,000
Freight-out	7,000	Sales discounts	8,000
Insurance expense	6,000	Sales returns and allowances	13,000
Salaries and wages expense	58,000	Sales revenue	380,000

Prepare multiple-step income statement.

(LO 5)

Instructions
(a) Prepare a multiple-step income statement.
(b) Compute the gross profit rate.

E5-10 In its income statement for the year ended December 31, 2015, Lemere Company reported the following condensed data.

Operating expenses	$ 725,000	Interest revenue	$ 28,000
Cost of goods sold	1,289,000	Loss on disposal of plant assets	17,000
Interest expense	70,000	Net sales	2,200,000

Prepare multiple-step and single-step income statements.

(LO 5)

Instructions
(a) Prepare a multiple-step income statement.
(b) Prepare a single-step income statement.

E5-11 An inexperienced accountant for Huang Company made the following errors in recording merchandising transactions.

1. A $195 refund to a customer for faulty merchandise was debited to Sales Revenue $195 and credited to Cash $195.
2. A $180 credit purchase of supplies was debited to Inventory $180 and credited to Cash $180.
3. A $215 sales discount was debited to Sales Revenue.
4. A cash payment of $20 for freight on merchandise purchases was debited to Freight-Out $200 and credited to Cash $200.

Prepare correcting entries for sales and purchases.

(LO 2, 3)

Instructions
Prepare separate correcting entries for each error, assuming that the incorrect entry is not reversed. (Omit explanations.)

E5-12 In 2015, Matt Cruz Company had net sales of $900,000 and cost of goods sold of $522,000. Operating expenses were $225,000, and interest expense was $11,000. Cruz prepares a multiple-step income statement.

Compute various income measures.

(LO 5)

Instructions
(a) Compute Cruz's gross profit.
(b) Compute the gross profit rate. Why is this rate computed by financial statement users?
(c) What is Cruz's income from operations and net income?
(d) If Cruz prepared a single-step income statement, what amount would it report for net income?
(e) In what section of its classified balance sheet should Cruz report inventory?

E5-13 Presented below is financial information for two different companies.

	May Company	Reed Company
Sales revenue	$90,000	$ (d)
Sales returns	(a)	5,000
Net sales	87,000	102,000
Cost of goods sold	56,000	(e)
Gross profit	(b)	41,500
Operating expenses	15,000	(f)
Net income	(c)	15,000

Compute missing amounts and compute gross profit rate.

(LO 5)

Instructions
(a) Determine the missing amounts.
(b) Determine the gross profit rates. (Round to one decimal place.)

Compute missing amounts.
(LO 5)

E5-14 Financial information is presented below for three different companies.

	Allen Cosmetics	Bast Grocery	Corr Wholesalers
Sales revenue	$90,000	$ (e)	$122,000
Sales returns and allowances	(a)	5,000	12,000
Net sales	86,000	95,000	(i)
Cost of goods sold	56,000	(f)	(j)
Gross profit	(b)	38,000	24,000
Operating expenses	15,000	(g)	18,000
Income from operations	(c)	(h)	(k)
Other expenses and losses	4,000	7,000	(l)
Net income	(d)	11,000	5,000

Instructions
Determine the missing amounts.

Complete worksheet using a perpetual inventory system.
(LO 6)

*E5-15 Presented below are selected accounts for Salazar Company as reported in the worksheet using a perpetual inventory system at the end of May 2015.

Accounts	Adjusted Trial Balance		Income Statement		Balance Sheet	
	Dr.	Cr.	Dr.	Cr.	Dr.	Cr.
Cash	11,000					
Inventory	76,000					
Sales Revenue		480,000				
Sales Returns and Allowances	10,000					
Sales Discounts	9,000					
Cost of Goods Sold	300,000					

Instructions
Complete the worksheet by extending amounts reported in the adjusted trial balance to the appropriate columns in the worksheet. Do not total individual columns.

Prepare a worksheet using a perpetual inventory system.
(LO 6)

*E5-16 The trial balance columns of the worksheet using a perpetual inventory system for Marquez Company at June 30, 2015, are as follows.

MARQUEZ COMPANY
Worksheet
For the Month Ended June 30, 2015

	Trial Balance	
Account Titles	Debit	Credit
Cash	1,920	
Accounts Receivable	2,440	
Inventory	11,640	
Accounts Payable		1,120
Common Stock		3,500
Sales Revenue		42,500
Cost of Goods Sold	20,560	
Operating Expenses	10,560	
	47,120	47,120

Other data:
Operating expenses incurred on account, but not yet recorded, total $1,500.

Instructions
Enter the trial balance on a worksheet and complete the worksheet.

*E5-17 The trial balance of D. Savage Company at the end of its fiscal year, August 31, 2015, includes these accounts: Inventory $17,200, Purchases $149,000, Sales Revenue $190,000, Freight-In $5,000, Sales Returns and Allowances $3,000, Freight-Out $1,000, and Purchase Returns and Allowances $2,000. The ending merchandise inventory is $23,000.

Prepare cost of goods sold section.

(LO 7)

Instructions
Prepare a cost of goods sold section for the year ending August 31 (periodic inventory).

*E5-18 On January 1, 2015, Christel Madan Corporation had inventory of $50,000. At December 31, 2015, Christel Madan had the following account balances.

Compute various income statement items.

(LO 7)

Freight-in	$ 4,000
Purchases	509,000
Purchase discounts	6,000
Purchase returns and allowances	2,000
Sales revenue	840,000
Sales discounts	5,000
Sales returns and allowances	10,000

At December 31, 2015, Christel Madan determines that its ending inventory is $60,000.

Instructions
(a) Compute Christel Madan's 2015 gross profit.
(b) Compute Christel Madan's 2015 operating expenses if net income is $130,000 and there are no nonoperating activities.

*E5-19 Below is a series of cost of goods sold sections for companies B, F, L, and R.

Prepare cost of goods sold section.

(LO 7)

	B	F	L	R
Beginning inventory	$ 150	$ 70	$1,000	$ (j)
Purchases	1,620	1,060	(g)	43,590
Purchase returns and allowances	40	(d)	290	(k)
Net purchases	(a)	1,030	6,210	41,090
Freight-in	110	(e)	(h)	2,240
Cost of goods purchased	(b)	1,280	7,940	(l)
Cost of goods available for sale	1,840	1,350	(i)	49,530
Ending inventory	310	(f)	1,450	6,230
Cost of goods sold	(c)	1,230	7,490	43,300

Instruction
Fill in the lettered blanks to complete the cost of goods sold sections.

*E5-20 This information relates to Rana Co.

Journalize purchase transactions.

(LO 7)

1. On April 5, purchased merchandise from Craig Company for $25,000, terms 2/10, net/30, FOB shipping point.
2. On April 6, paid freight costs of $900 on merchandise purchased from Craig Company.
3. On April 7, purchased equipment on account for $30,000.
4. On April 8, returned some of April 5 merchandise, which cost $2,800, to Craig Company.
5. On April 15, paid the amount due to Craig Company in full.

Instructions
(a) Prepare the journal entries to record these transactions on the books of Rana Co. using a periodic inventory system.
(b) Assume that Rana Co. paid the balance due to Craig Company on May 4 instead of April 15. Prepare the journal entry to record this payment.

*E5-21 Presented below is information related to Lor Co.

Journalize purchase transactions.

(LO 7)

1. On April 5, purchased merchandise from Garcia Company for $19,000, terms 2/10, net/30, FOB shipping point.
2. On April 6, paid freight costs of $800 on merchandise purchased from Garcia.
3. On April 7, purchased equipment on account from Holifield Mfg. Co. for $23,000.
4. On April 8, returned merchandise, which cost $4,000, to Garcia Company.
5. On April 15, paid the amount due to Garcia Company in full.

Instructions

(a) Prepare the journal entries to record the preceding transactions on the books of Lor Co. using a periodic inventory system.

(b) Assume that Lor Co. paid the balance due to Garcia Company on May 4 instead of April 15. Prepare the journal entry to record this payment.

Complete worksheet.
(LO 7)

*E5-22 Presented below are selected accounts for B. Midler Company as reported in the worksheet at the end of May 2015. Ending inventory is $75,000.

Accounts	Adjusted Trial Balance		Income Statement		Balance Sheet	
	Dr.	Cr.	Dr.	Cr.	Dr.	Cr.
Cash	9,000					
Inventory	80,000					
Purchases	240,000					
Purchase Returns and Allowances		30,000				
Sales Revenue		450,000				
Sales Returns and Allowances	10,000					
Sales Discounts	5,000					
Rent Expense	42,000					

Instructions

Complete the worksheet by extending amounts reported in the adjusted trial balance to the appropriate columns in the worksheet. The company uses the periodic inventory system.

EXERCISES: SET B AND CHALLENGE EXERCISES

Visit the book's companion website, at **www.wiley.com/college/weygandt**, and choose the Student Companion site to access Exercise Set B and Challenge Exercises.

PROBLEMS: SET A

Journalize purchase and sales transactions under a perpetual inventory system.
(LO 2, 3)

P5-1A Powell's Book Warehouse distributes hardcover books to retail stores and extends credit terms of 2/10, n/30 to all of its customers. At the end of May, Powell's inventory consisted of books purchased for $1,800. During June, the following merchandising transactions occurred.

June 1   Purchased books on account for $1,600 from Kline Publishers, FOB destination, terms 2/10, n/30. The appropriate party also made a cash payment of $50 for the freight on this date.

      3   Sold books on account to Reading Rainbow for $2,500. The cost of the books sold was $1,440.

      6   Received $100 credit for books returned to Kline Publishers.

      9   Paid Kline Publishers in full, less discount.

    15   Received payment in full from Reading Rainbow.

    17   Sold books on account to Blanco Books for $1,800. The cost of the books sold was $1,080.

20   Purchased books on account for $1,500 from Dietz Publishers, FOB destination, terms 2/15, n/30. The appropriate party also made a cash payment of $50 for the freight on this date.

24   Received payment in full from Blanco Books.

26   Paid Dietz Publishers in full, less discount.

28   Sold books on account to Reddy Bookstore for $1,400. The cost of the books sold was $850.

30   Granted Reddy Bookstore $120 credit for books returned costing $72.

Powell's Book Warehouse's chart of accounts includes the following: No. 101 Cash, No. 112 Accounts Receivable, No. 120 Inventory, No. 201 Accounts Payable, No. 401 Sales Revenue, No. 412 Sales Returns and Allowances, No. 414 Sales Discounts, and No. 505 Cost of Goods Sold.

Instructions

Journalize the transactions for the month of June for Powell's Book Warehouse using a perpetual inventory system.

P5-2A Latona Hardware Store completed the following merchandising transactions in the month of May. At the beginning of May, the ledger of Latona showed Cash of $5,000 and Common Stock of $5,000.

Journalize, post, and prepare a partial income statement.

(LO 2, 3, 5)

GLS

May 1   Purchased merchandise on account from Gray's Wholesale Supply $4,200, terms 2/10, n/30.

2   Sold merchandise on account $2,100, terms 1/10, n/30. The cost of the merchandise sold was $1,300.

5   Received credit from Gray's Wholesale Supply for merchandise returned $300.

9   Received collections in full, less discounts, from customers billed on sales of $2,100 on May 2.

10   Paid Gray's Wholesale Supply in full, less discount.

11   Purchased supplies for cash $400.

12   Purchased merchandise for cash $1,400.

15   Received refund for poor quality merchandise from supplier on cash purchase $150.

17   Purchased merchandise from Amland Distributors $1,300, FOB shipping point, terms 2/10, n/30.

19   Paid freight on May 17 purchase $130.

24   Sold merchandise for cash $3,200. The merchandise sold had a cost of $2,000.

25   Purchased merchandise from Horvath, Inc. $620, FOB destination, terms 2/10, n/30.

27   Paid Amland Distributors in full, less discount.

29   Made refunds to cash customers for defective merchandise $70. The returned merchandise had a fair value of $30.

31   Sold merchandise on account $1,000 terms n/30. The cost of the merchandise sold was $560.

Latona Hardware's chart of accounts includes the following: No. 101 Cash, No. 112 Accounts Receivable, No. 120 Inventory, No. 126 Supplies, No. 201 Accounts Payable, No. 311 Common Stock, No. 401 Sales Revenue, No. 412 Sales Returns and Allowances, No. 414 Sales Discounts, and No. 505 Cost of Goods Sold.

Instructions

(a) Journalize the transactions using a perpetual inventory system.

(b) Enter the beginning cash and common stock balances and post the transactions. (Use J1 for the journal reference.)

(c) Prepare an income statement through gross profit for the month of May 2015.

(c) Gross profit $2,379

P5-3A The Deluxe Store is located in midtown Madison. During the past several years, net income has been declining because of suburban shopping centers. At the end of the company's fiscal year on November 30, 2015, the following accounts appeared in two of its trial balances.

Prepare financial statements and adjusting and closing entries.

(LO 4, 5)

	Unadjusted	Adjusted		Unadjusted	Adjusted
Accounts Payable	$ 25,200	$ 25,200	Inventory	$ 29,000	$ 29,000
Accounts Receivable	30,500	30,500	Notes Payable	37,000	37,000
Accumulated Depr.—Equip.	34,000	45,000	Prepaid Insurance	10,500	3,500
Cash	26,000	26,000	Property Tax Expense		2,500
Common Stock	40,000	40,000	Property Taxes Payable		2,500
Cost of Goods Sold	507,000	507,000	Rent Expense	15,000	15,000
Dividends	10,000	10,000	Retained Earnings	61,700	61,700
Freight-Out	6,500	6,500	Salaries and Wages Expense	96,000	96,000
Equipment	146,000	146,000	Sales Commissions Expense	6,500	11,000
Depreciation Expense		11,000	Sales Commissions Payable		4,500
Insurance Expense		7,000	Sales Returns and Allowances	8,000	8,000
Interest Expense	6,400	6,400	Sales Revenue	700,000	700,000
Interest Revenue	8,000	8,000	Utilities Expense	8,500	8,500

(a) Net income $29,100
   Retained earnings $80,800
   Total assets $190,000

Instructions

(a) Prepare a multiple-step income statement, a retained earnings statement, and a classified balance sheet. Notes payable are due in 2018.

(b) Journalize the adjusting entries that were made.

(c) Journalize the closing entries that are necessary.

Journalize, post, and prepare a trial balance.

(LO 2, 3, 4)

P5-4A Adam Nichols, a former disc golf star, operates Adam's Discorama. At the beginning of the current season on April 1, the ledger of Adam's Discorama showed Cash $1,800, Inventory $2,500, and Common Stock $4,300. The following transactions were completed during April.

Apr.	5	Purchased golf discs, bags, and other inventory on account from Rayford Co. $1,200, FOB shipping point, terms 2/10, n/60.
	7	Paid freight on the Rayford purchase $50.
	9	Received credit from Rayford Co. for merchandise returned $100.
	10	Sold merchandise on account for $900, terms n/30. The merchandise sold had a cost of $540.
	12	Purchased disc golf shirts and other accessories on account from Galaxy Sportswear $670, terms 1/10, n/30.
	14	Paid Rayford Co. in full, less discount.
	17	Received credit from Galaxy Sportswear for merchandise returned $70.
	20	Made sales on account for $610, terms n/30. The cost of the merchandise sold was $370.
	21	Paid Galaxy Sportswear in full, less discount.
	27	Granted an allowance to customers for clothing that was flawed $20.
	30	Received payments on account from customers $900.

The chart of accounts for the store includes the following: No. 101 Cash, No. 112 Accounts Receivable, No. 120 Inventory, No. 201 Accounts Payable, No. 311 Common Stock, No. 401 Sales Revenue, No. 412 Sales Returns and Allowances, and No. 505 Cost of Goods Sold.

Instructions

(a) Journalize the April transactions using a perpetual inventory system.

(b) Enter the beginning balances in the ledger accounts and post the April transactions. (Use J1 for the journal reference.)

(c) Total debits $5,810

(c) Prepare a trial balance on April 30, 2015.

Complete accounting cycle beginning with a worksheet.

(LO 4, 5, 6)

*P5-5A The trial balance of Valdez Fashion Center contained the following accounts at November 30, the end of the company's fiscal year.

VALDEZ FASHION CENTER
Trial Balance
November 30, 2015

	Debit	Credit
Cash	$ 8,700	
Accounts Receivable	30,700	
Inventory	44,700	
Supplies	6,200	
Equipment	133,000	
Accumulated Depreciation—Equipment		$ 28,000
Notes Payable		51,000
Accounts Payable		48,500
Common Stock		50,000
Retained Earnings		40,000
Dividends	12,000	
Sales Revenue		755,200
Sales Returns and Allowances	8,800	
Cost of Goods Sold	497,400	
Salaries and Wages Expense	140,000	
Advertising Expense	24,400	
Utilities Expense	14,000	
Maintenance and Repairs Expense	12,100	
Freight-Out	16,700	
Rent Expense	24,000	
Totals	$972,700	$972,700

Adjustment data:
1. Supplies on hand totaled $2,000.
2. Depreciation is $11,500 on the equipment.
3. Interest of $4,000 is accrued on notes payable at November 30.
4. Inventory actually on hand is $44,400.

Instructions
(a) Enter the trial balance on a worksheet, and complete the worksheet.
(b) Prepare a multiple-step income statement and a retained earnings statement for the year, and a classified balance sheet as of November 30, 2015. Notes payable of $20,000 are due in January 2016.
(c) Journalize the adjusting entries.
(d) Journalize the closing entries.
(e) Prepare a post-closing trial balance.

(a) Adj. trial balance $988,200
    Net loss $2,200
(b) Gross profit $248,700
    Total assets $179,300

*P5-6A At the end of Dayton Department Store's fiscal year on November 30, 2015, these accounts appeared in its adjusted trial balance.

Freight-In	$ 7,500
Inventory	40,000
Purchases	585,000
Purchase Discounts	6,300
Purchase Returns and Allowances	2,700
Sales Revenue	1,000,000
Sales Returns and Allowances	20,000

Determine cost of goods sold and gross profit under periodic approach.

(LO 5, 7)

Additional facts:
1. Merchandise inventory on November 30, 2015, is $52,600.
2. Dayton Department Store uses a periodic system.

Instructions
Prepare an income statement through gross profit for the year ended November 30, 2015.

Gross profit $409,100

Calculate missing amounts and assess profitability.
(LO 5, 7)

*P5-7A Alana Inc. operates a retail operation that purchases and sells home entertainment products. The company purchases all merchandise inventory on credit and uses a periodic inventory system. The Accounts Payable account is used for recording inventory purchases only; all other current liabilities are accrued in separate accounts. You are provided with the following selected information for the fiscal years 2012 through 2015, inclusive.

	2012	2013	2014	2015
Income Statement Data				
Sales revenue		$55,000	$ (e)	$47,000
Cost of goods sold		(a)	13,800	14,300
Gross profit		38,300	35,200	(i)
Operating expenses		34,900	(f)	28,600
Net income		$ (b)	$ 2,500	$ (j)
Balance Sheet Data				
Inventory	$7,200	$ (c)	$ 8,100	$ (k)
Accounts payable	3,200	3,600	2,500	(l)
Additional Information				
Purchases of merchandise inventory on account		$14,200	$ (g)	$13,200
Cash payments to suppliers		(d)	(h)	13,600

(c) $4,700

(g) $17,200

(i) $32,700

Instructions

(a) Calculate the missing amounts.

(b) Sales declined over the 3-year fiscal period, 2013–2015. Does that mean that profitability necessarily also declined? Explain, computing the gross profit rate and the profit margin for each fiscal year to help support your answer. (Round to one decimal place.)

Journalize, post, and prepare trial balance and partial income statement using periodic approach.
(LO 7)

*P5-8A At the beginning of the current season on April 1, the ledger of Kokott Pro Shop showed Cash $3,000, Inventory $4,000, and Common Stock $7,000. These transactions occurred during April 2015.

Apr. 5   Purchased golf bags, clubs, and balls on account from Hogan Co. $1,200, FOB shipping point, terms 2/10, n/60.
     7   Paid freight on Hogan Co. purchases $50.
     9   Received credit from Hogan Co. for merchandise returned $100.
    10   Sold merchandise on account to customers $600, terms n/30.
    12   Purchased golf shoes, sweaters, and other accessories on account from Duffer Sportswear $450, terms 1/10, n/30.
    14   Paid Hogan Co. in full.
    17   Received credit from Duffer Sportswear for merchandise returned $50.
    20   Made sales on account to customers $600, terms n/30.
    21   Paid Duffer Sportswear in full.
    27   Granted credit to customers for clothing that had flaws $35.
    30   Received payments on account from customers $600.

The chart of accounts for the pro shop includes Cash, Accounts Receivable, Inventory, Accounts Payable, Common Stock, Sales Revenue, Sales Returns and Allowances, Purchases, Purchase Returns and Allowances, Purchase Discounts, and Freight-In.

Instructions

(a) Journalize the April transactions using a periodic inventory system.

(b) Using T-accounts, enter the beginning balances in the ledger accounts and post the April transactions.

(c) Tot. trial balance $8,376
    Gross profit $465

(c) Prepare a trial balance on April 30, 2015.

(d) Prepare an income statement through gross profit, assuming merchandise inventory on hand at April 30 is $4,824.

PROBLEMS: SET B

P5-1B Urdan Co. distributes suitcases to retail stores and extends credit terms of 1/10, n/30 to all of its customers. At the end of June, Urdan's inventory consisted of suitcases costing $1,200. During the month of July, the following merchandising transactions occurred.

Journalize purchase and sales transactions under a perpetual inventory system.
(LO 2, 3)

July 1 Purchased suitcases on account for $1,800 from Hostad Manufacturers, FOB destination, terms 2/10, n/30. The appropriate party also made a cash payment of $100 for freight on this date.

     3 Sold suitcases on account to Kaye Satchels for $2,000. The cost of suitcases sold is $1,200.

     9 Paid Hostad Manufacturers in full.

   12 Received payment in full from Kaye Satchels.

   17 Sold suitcases on account to The Going Concern for $1,800. The cost of the suitcases sold was $1,080.

   18 Purchased suitcases on account for $1,900 from Nelson Manufacturers, FOB shipping point, terms 1/10, n/30. The appropriate party also made a cash payment of $125 for freight on this date.

   20 Received $300 credit (including freight) for suitcases returned to Nelson Manufacturers.

   21 Received payment in full from The Going Concern.

   22 Sold suitcases on account to Wopat's for $2,250. The cost of suitcases sold was $1,350.

   30 Paid Nelson Manufacturers in full.

   31 Granted Wopat's $200 credit for suitcases returned costing $120.

Urdan's chart of accounts includes the following: No. 101 Cash, No. 112 Accounts Receivable, No. 120 Inventory, No. 201 Accounts Payable, No. 401 Sales Revenue, No. 412 Sales Returns and Allowances, No. 414 Sales Discounts, and No. 505 Cost of Goods Sold.

Instructions
Journalize the transactions for the month of July for Urdan using a perpetual inventory system.

P5-2B Rose Distributing Company completed the following merchandising transactions in the month of April. At the beginning of April, the ledger of Rose showed Cash of $9,000 and Common Stock of $9,000.

Journalize, post, and prepare a partial income statement.
(LO 2, 3, 5)

Apr. 2 Purchased merchandise on account from Kwon Supply Co. $6,900, terms 1/10, n/30.

     4 Sold merchandise on account $6,500, FOB destination, terms 1/10, n/30. The cost of the merchandise sold was $3,900.

     5 Paid $240 freight on April 4 sale.

     6 Received credit from Kwon Supply Co. for merchandise returned $500.

   11 Paid Kwon Supply Co. in full, less discount.

   13 Received collections in full, less discounts, from customers billed on April 4.

   14 Purchased merchandise for cash $3,800.

   16 Received refund from supplier for returned goods on cash purchase of April 14, $500.

   18 Purchased merchandise from Davis Distributors $4,500, FOB shipping point, terms 2/10, n/30.

   20 Paid freight on April 18 purchase $100.

   23 Sold merchandise for cash $7,400. The merchandise sold had a cost of $4,120.

   26 Purchased merchandise for cash $2,300.

   27 Paid Davis Distributors in full, less discount.

   29 Made refunds to cash customers for defective merchandise $90. The returned merchandise had a fair value of $30.

   30 Sold merchandise on account $3,700, terms n/30. The cost of the merchandise sold was $2,800.

Rose Distributing Company's chart of accounts includes the following: No. 101 Cash, No. 112 Accounts Receivable, No. 120 Inventory, No. 201 Accounts Payable, No. 311 Common Stock, No. 401 Sales Revenue, No. 412 Sales Returns and Allowances, No. 414 Sales Discounts, No. 505 Cost of Goods Sold, and No. 644 Freight-Out.

Instructions
(a) Journalize the preceding transactions using a perpetual inventory system.
(b) Enter the beginning cash and common stock balances, and post the transactions. (Use J1 for the journal reference.)

(c) Gross profit $6,655

(c) Prepare the income statement through gross profit for the month of April 2015.

Prepare financial statements and adjusting and closing entries.
(LO 4, 5)

P5-3B Mackey Department Store is located near the Village Shopping Mall. At the end of the company's calendar year on December 31, 2015, the following accounts appeared in two of its trial balances.

	Unadjusted	Adjusted		Unadjusted	Adjusted
Accounts Payable	$ 79,300	$ 80,300	Interest Revenue	$ 4,000	$ 4,000
Accounts Receivable	50,300	50,300	Inventory	75,000	75,000
Accumulated Depr.—Buildings	42,100	52,500	Mortgage Payable	80,000	80,000
Accumulated Depr.—Equipment	29,600	42,900	Prepaid Insurance	9,600	2,400
Buildings	290,000	290,000	Property Tax Expense		4,800
Cash	23,800	23,800	Property Taxes Payable		4,800
Common Stock	112,000	112,000	Retained Earnings	64,600	64,600
Cost of Goods Sold	412,700	412,700	Salaries and Wages Expense	108,000	108,000
Depreciation Expense		23,700	Sales Commissions Expense	10,200	14,500
Dividends	28,000	28,000	Sales Commissions Payable		4,300
Equipment	110,000	110,000	Sales Returns and Allowances	8,000	8,000
Insurance Expense		7,200	Sales Revenue	728,000	728,000
Interest Expense	3,000	12,000	Utilities Expense	11,000	12,000
Interest Payable		9,000			

Instructions

(a) Net income $129,100
    Retained earnings $165,700
    Total assets $456,100

(a) Prepare a multiple-step income statement, a retained earnings statement, and a classified balance sheet. $25,000 of the mortgage payable is due for payment next year.
(b) Journalize the adjusting entries that were made.
(c) Journalize the closing entries that are necessary.

Journalize, post, and prepare a trial balance.
(LO 2, 3, 4)

P5-4B Alex Diaz, a former professional tennis star, operates Diaz Tennis Shop at the Cedar Lake Resort. At the beginning of the current season, the ledger of Diaz Tennis Shop showed Cash $2,500, Inventory $1,700, and Common Stock $4,200. The following transactions were completed during April.

Apr. 4   Purchased racquets and balls from Marx Co. $840, FOB shipping point, terms 2/10, n/30.
       6   Paid freight on purchase from Marx Co. $40.
       8   Sold merchandise to members $1,150, terms n/30. The merchandise sold had a cost of $790.
      10   Received credit of $40 from Marx Co. for a racquet that was returned.
      11   Purchased tennis shoes from Rupp Sports for cash, $420.
      13   Paid Marx Co. in full.
      14   Purchased tennis shirts and shorts from Hayley's Sportswear $900, FOB shipping point, terms 3/10, n/60.
      15   Received cash refund of $50 from Rupp Sports for damaged merchandise that was returned.
      17   Paid freight on Hayley's Sportswear purchase $30.
      18   Sold merchandise to members $900, terms n/30. The cost of the merchandise sold was $540.
      20   Received $600 in cash from customers in settlement of their accounts.
      21   Paid Hayley's Sportswear in full.
      27   Granted an allowance of $40 to members for tennis clothing that did not fit properly.
      30   Received cash payments on account from customers, $710.

The chart of accounts for the tennis shop includes the following: No. 101 Cash, No. 112 Accounts Receivable, No. 120 Inventory, No. 201 Accounts Payable, No. 311 Common Stock, No. 401 Sales Revenue, No. 412 Sales Returns and Allowances, and No. 505 Cost of Goods Sold.

Instructions

(a) Journalize the April transactions using a perpetual inventory system.

(b) Enter the beginning balances in the ledger accounts and post the April transactions. (Use J1 for the journal reference.)

(c) Prepare a trial balance on April 30, 2015.

(c) Total debits $6,250

*P5-5B At the end of Roshek Department Store's fiscal year on December 31, 2015, these accounts appeared in its adjusted trial balance.

Determine cost of goods sold and gross profit under periodic approach.

(LO 5, 7)

Freight-In	$ 5,600
Inventory	40,500
Purchases	447,000
Purchase Discounts	12,000
Purchase Returns and Allowances	6,400
Sales Revenue	725,000
Sales Returns and Allowances	11,000

Additional facts:

1. Merchandise inventory on December 31, 2015, is $65,000.

2. Roshek Department Store uses a periodic system.

Instructions

Prepare an income statement through gross profit for the year ended December 31, 2015.

Gross profit $304,300

*P5-6B Val Knight operates a retail clothing operation. She purchases all merchandise inventory on credit and uses a periodic inventory system. The Accounts Payable account is used for recording inventory purchases only; all other current liabilities are accrued in separate accounts. You are provided with the following selected information for the fiscal years 2012–2015.

Calculate missing amounts and assess profitability.

(LO 5, 7)

	2012	2013	2014	2015
Inventory (ending)	$13,000	$ 11,300	$ 14,700	$ 12,200
Accounts payable (ending)	20,000			
Sales revenue		239,000	237,000	235,000
Purchases of merchandise inventory on account		146,000	145,000	129,000
Cash payments to suppliers		135,000	161,000	127,000

Instructions

(a) Calculate cost of goods sold for each of the 2013, 2014, and 2015 fiscal years.

(b) Calculate the gross profit for each of the 2013, 2014, and 2015 fiscal years.

(c) Calculate the ending balance of accounts payable for each of the 2013, 2014, and 2015 fiscal years.

(d) Sales declined in fiscal 2015. Does that mean that profitability, as measured by the gross profit rate, necessarily also declined? Explain, calculating the gross profit rate for each fiscal year to help support your answer. (Round to one decimal place.)

(a) 2014 $141,600

(c) 2014 Ending accts payable $15,000

*P5-7B At the beginning of the current season, the ledger of Everett Tennis Shop showed Cash $2,500; Inventory $1,700; and Common Stock $4,200. The following transactions were completed during April.

Journalize, post, and prepare trial balance and partial income statement using periodic approach.

(LO 7)

Apr.	4	Purchased racquets and balls from Riggs Co. $740, terms 3/10, n/30.
	6	Paid freight on Riggs Co. purchase $60.
	8	Sold merchandise to customers $900, terms n/30.
	10	Received credit of $40 from Riggs Co. for a racquet that was returned.
	11	Purchased tennis shoes from King Sports for cash $300.
	13	Paid Riggs Co. in full.
	14	Purchased tennis shirts and shorts from BJ Sportswear $700, terms 2/10, n/60.
	15	Received cash refund of $50 from King Sports for damaged merchandise that was returned.

17 Paid freight on BJ Sportswear purchase $30.
18 Sold merchandise to customers $1,000, terms n/30.
20 Received $500 in cash from customers in settlement of their accounts.
21 Paid BJ Sportswear in full.
27 Granted an allowance of $25 to customers for tennis clothing that did not fit properly.
30 Received cash payments on account from customers $550.

The chart of accounts for the tennis shop includes Cash, Accounts Receivable, Inventory, Accounts Payable, Common Stock, Sales Revenue, Sales Returns and Allowances, Purchases, Purchase Returns and Allowances, Purchase Discounts, and Freight-In.

Instructions
(a) Journalize the April transactions using a periodic inventory system.
(b) Using T-accounts, enter the beginning balances in the ledger accounts and post the April transactions.
(c) Tot. trial balance $6,225
(d) Gross profit $766
(c) Prepare a trial balance on April 30, 2015.
(d) Prepare an income statement through gross profit, assuming inventory on hand at April 30 is $2,296.

PROBLEMS: SET C

Visit the book's companion website, at **www.wiley.com/college/weygandt**, and choose the Student Companion site to access Problem Set C.

COMPREHENSIVE PROBLEM

CP5 On December 1, 2015, Prosen Distributing Company had the following account balances.

	Debit		Credit
Cash	$ 7,200	Accumulated Depreciation—	
Accounts Receivable	4,600	Equipment	$ 2,200
Inventory	12,000	Accounts Payable	4,500
Supplies	1,200	Salaries and Wages Payable	1,000
Equipment	22,000	Common Stock	30,000
	$47,000	Retained Earnings	9,300
			$47,000

During December, the company completed the following summary transactions.

Dec. 6 Paid $1,600 for salaries and wages due employees, of which $600 is for December and $1,000 is for November salaries and wages payable.
8 Received $1,900 cash from customers in payment of account (no discount allowed).
10 Sold merchandise for cash $6,300. The cost of the merchandise sold was $4,100.
13 Purchased merchandise on account from Maglio Co. $9,000, terms 2/10, n/30.
15 Purchased supplies for cash $2,000.
18 Sold merchandise on account $12,000, terms 3/10, n/30. The cost of the merchandise sold was $8,000.
20 Paid salaries and wages $1,800.
23 Paid Maglio Co. in full, less discount.
27 Received collections in full, less discounts, from customers billed on December 18.

Adjustment data:

1. Accrued salaries and wages payable $800.
2. Depreciation $200 per month.
3. Supplies on hand $1,500.

Instructions

(a) Journalize the December transactions using a perpetual inventory system.

(b) Enter the December 1 balances in the ledger T-accounts and post the December transactions. Use Cost of Goods Sold, Depreciation Expense, Salaries and Wages Expense, Sales Revenue, Sales Discounts, and Supplies Expense.

(c) Journalize and post adjusting entries.

(d) Prepare an adjusted trial balance.

(d) Totals $65,300

(e) Prepare an income statement and a retained earnings statement for December and a classified balance sheet at December 31.

(e) Net income $740

CONTINUING COOKIE CHRONICLE

(*Note:* This is a continuation of the Cookie Chronicle from Chapters 1 through 4.)

CCC5 Because Natalie has had such a successful first few months, she is considering other opportunities to develop her business. One opportunity is the sale of fine European mixers. The owner of Kzinski Supply Company has approached Natalie to become the exclusive U.S. distributor of these fine mixers. The current cost of a mixer is approximately $525 (U.S.), and Natalie would sell each one for $1,050. Natalie comes to you for advice on how to account for these mixers.

Go to the book's companion website, **www.wiley.com/college/weygandt**, *to see the completion of this problem.*

Broadening Your **PERSPECTIVE**

Financial Reporting and Analysis

Financial Reporting Problem: Apple Inc.

BYP5-1 The financial statements of Apple Inc. are presented in Appendix A at the end of this textbook. Instructions for accessing and using the company's complete annual report, including the notes to the financial statements, are also provided in Appendix A.

Instructions

Answer the following questions using Apple's Consolidated Statement of Income.

(a) What was the percentage change in (1) sales and in (2) net income from 2009 to 2010 and from 2010 to 2011?

(b) What was the company's gross profit rate in 2009, 2010, and 2011?

(c) What was the company's percentage of net income to net sales in 2009, 2010, and 2011? Comment on any trend in this percentage.

Comparative Analysis Problem:
PepsiCo, Inc. vs. The Coca-Cola Company

BYP5-2 PepsiCo's financial statements are presented in Appendix B. Financial statements of The Coca-Cola Company are presented in Appendix C. Instructions for accessing and using the complete annual reports of PepsiCo and Coca-Cola, including the notes to the financial statements, are also provided in Appendices B and C, respectively.

Instructions

(a) Based on the information contained in these financial statements, determine each of the following for each company.

    (1) Gross profit for 2011.

    (2) Gross profit rate for 2011.

  (3) Operating income for 2011.

  (4) Percentage change in operating income from 2010 to 2011.

(b) What conclusions concerning the relative profitability of the two companies can you draw from these data?

Comparative Analysis Problem:
Amazon.com, Inc. vs. Wal-Mart Stores, Inc.

BYP5-3 Amazon.com, Inc.'s financial statements are presented in Appendix D. Financial statements of Wal-Mart Stores, Inc. are presented in Appendix E. (Use Wal-Mart's January 31, 2012, financial statements for comparative purposes.) Instructions for accessing and using the complete annual reports of Amazon and Wal-Mart, including the notes to the financial statements, are also provided in Appendices D and E, respectively.

Instructions

(a) Based on the information contained in these financial statements, determine each of the following for each company. Use Amazon's net product sales to compute gross profit information.

  (1) Gross profit for 2011.

  (2) Gross profit rate for 2011.

  (3) Operating income for 2011.

  (4) Percentage change in operating income from 2010 to 2011.

(b) What conclusions concerning the relative profitability of the two companies can you draw from these data?

Real-World Focus

BYP5-4 No financial decision-maker should ever rely solely on the financial information reported in the annual report to make decisions. It is important to keep abreast of financial news. This activity demonstrates how to search for financial news on the Internet.

Address: **biz.yahoo.com/i**, or go to **www.wiley.com/college/weygandt**

Steps:

1. Type in either PepsiCo or Coca-Cola.

2. Choose **News**.

3. Select an article that sounds interesting to you.

Instructions

(a) What was the source of the article (e.g., Reuters, Businesswire, PR Newswire)?

(b) Assume that you are a personal financial planner and that one of your clients owns stock in the company. Write a brief memo to your client, summarizing the article and explaining the implications of the article for his or her investment.

Critical Thinking

Decision-Making Across the Organization

BYP5-5 Three years ago, Dana Mann and her brother-in-law Eric Boldt opened Family Department Store. For the first two years, business was good, but the following condensed income results for 2014 were disappointing.

FAMILY DEPARTMENT STORE
Income Statement
For the Year Ended December 31, 2014

Net sales		$700,000
Cost of goods sold		553,000
Gross profit		147,000
Operating expenses		
Selling expenses	$100,000	
Administrative expenses	20,000	120,000
Net income		$ 27,000

Dana believes the problem lies in the relatively low gross profit rate (gross profit divided by net sales) of 21%. Eric believes the problem is that operating expenses are too high.

Dana thinks the gross profit rate can be improved by making both of the following changes. She does not anticipate that these changes will have any effect on operating expenses.

1. Increase average selling prices by 17%. This increase is expected to lower sales volume so that total sales will increase only 6%.
2. Buy merchandise in larger quantities and take all purchase discounts. These changes are expected to increase the gross profit rate by 3 percentage points.

Eric thinks expenses can be cut by making both of the following changes. He feels that these changes will not have any effect on net sales.

1. Cut 2014 sales salaries of $60,000 in half and give sales personnel a commission of 2% of net sales.
2. Reduce store deliveries to one day per week rather than twice a week. This change will reduce 2014 delivery expenses of $30,000 by 40%.

Dana and Eric come to you for help in deciding the best way to improve net income.

Instructions
With the class divided into groups, answer the following.

(a) Prepare a condensed income statement for 2015, assuming (1) Dana's changes are implemented and (2) Eric's ideas are adopted.
(b) What is your recommendation to Dana and Eric?
(c) Prepare a condensed income statement for 2015, assuming both sets of proposed changes are made.

Communication Activity

BYP5-6 The following situation is in chronological order.

1. Connor decides to buy a surfboard.
2. He calls Surfing USA Co. to inquire about its surfboards.
3. Two days later, he requests Surfing USA Co. to make a surfboard.
4. Three days later, Surfing USA Co. sends him a purchase order to fill out.
5. He sends back the purchase order.
6. Surfing USA Co. receives the completed purchase order.
7. Surfing USA Co. completes the surfboard.
8. Connor picks up the surfboard.
9. Surfing USA Co. bills Connor.
10. Surfing USA Co. receives payment from Connor.

Instructions
In a memo to the president of Surfing USA Co., answer the following.

(a) When should Surfing USA Co. record the sale?
(b) Suppose that with his purchase order, Connor is required to make a down payment. Would that change your answer?

Ethics Case

BYP5-7 Jacquie Boynton was just hired as the assistant treasurer of Key West Stores. The company is a specialty chain store with nine retail stores concentrated in one metropolitan area. Among other things, the payment of all invoices is centralized in one of the departments Jacquie will manage. Her primary responsibility is to maintain the company's high credit rating by paying all bills when due and to take advantage of all cash discounts.

Phelan Carter, the former assistant treasurer who has been promoted to treasurer, is training Jacquie in her new duties. He instructs Jacquie that she is to continue the practice of preparing all checks "net of discount" and dating the checks the last day of the discount period. "But," Phelan continues, "we always hold the checks at least 4 days beyond the discount period before mailing them. That way, we get another 4 days of interest on our money. Most of our creditors need our business and don't complain. And, if they scream about our missing the discount period, we blame it on the mail room or the post office. We've only lost one discount out of every hundred we take that way. I think everybody does it. By the way, welcome to our team!"

Instructions
(a) What are the ethical considerations in this case?
(b) Who are the stakeholders that are harmed or benefitted in this situation?
(c) Should Jacquie continue the practice started by Phelan? Does she have any choice?

All About You

BYP5-8 There are many situations in business where it is difficult to determine the proper period in which to record revenue. Suppose that after graduation with a degree in finance, you take a job as a manager at a consumer electronics store called Impact Electronics. The company has expanded rapidly in order to compete with Best Buy. Impact has also begun selling gift cards for its electronic products. The cards are available in any dollar amount and allow the holder of the card to purchase an item for up to 2 years from the time the card is purchased. If the card is not used during that 2 years, it expires.

Instructions
Answer the following questions.

At what point should the revenue from the gift cards be recognized? Should the revenue be recognized at the time the card is sold, or should it be recorded when the card is redeemed? Explain the reasoning to support your answers.

FASB Codification Activity

BYP5-9 If your school has a subscription to the FASB Codification, go to **http://aaahq.org/ascLogin.cfm** to log in and prepare responses to the following.

Instructions
(a) Access the glossary ("Master Glossary") to answer the following:
  (1) What is the definition provided for inventory?
  (2) What is a customer?
(b) What guidance does the Codification provide concerning reporting inventories above cost?

Answers to Chapter Questions

Answers to Insight and Accounting Across the Organization Questions

p. 225 Morrow Snowboards Improves Its Stock Appeal **Q:** If a perpetual system keeps track of inventory on a daily basis, why do companies ever need to do a physical count? **A:** A perpetual system keeps track of all sales and purchases on a continuous basis. This provides a constant record of the number of units in the inventory. However, if employees make errors in recording sales or purchases, or if there is theft, the inventory value will not be correct. As a consequence, all companies do a physical count of inventory at least once a year.

p. 232 Should Costco Change Its Return Policy? **Q:** If a company expects significant returns, what are the implications for revenue recognition? **A:** If a company expects significant returns, it should make an adjusting entry at the end of the year, reducing sales by the estimated amount of sales returns. This is necessary so as not to overstate the amount of revenue recognized in the period.

p. 233 Selling Green **Q:** What is meant by "monetize environmental sustainability" for shareholders? **A:** By marketing green, not only does PepsiCo help the environment in the long run, but it also leads to long-term profitability as well. In other words, sound sustainability practices are good business and lead to sound financial results.

p. 239 Disclosing More Details **Q:** Why have investors and analysts demanded more accuracy in isolating "Other gains and losses" from operating items? **A:** Greater accuracy in the classification of operating versus nonoperating ("Other gains and losses") items permits investors and analysts to judge the real operating margin, the results of continuing operations, and management's ability to control operating expenses.

A Look at IFRS

The basic accounting entries for merchandising are the same under both GAAP and IFRS. The income statement is a required statement under both sets of standards. The basic format is similar although some differences do exist.

Key Points

- Under both GAAP and IFRS, a company can choose to use either a perpetual or a periodic system.

- Inventories are defined by IFRS as held-for-sale in the ordinary course of business, in the process of production for such sale, or in the form of materials or supplies to be consumed in the production process or in the performance of services.

- Under GAAP, companies generally classify income statement items by function. Classification by function leads to descriptions like administration, distribution, and manufacturing. Under IFRS, companies must classify expenses either by nature or by function. Classification by nature leads to descriptions such as the following: salaries, depreciation expense, and utilities expense. If a company uses the functional-expense method on the income statement, disclosure by nature is required in the notes to the financial statements.

- Presentation of the income statement under GAAP follows either a single-step or multiple-step format. IFRS does not mention a single-step or multiple-step approach.

- Under IFRS, revaluation of land, buildings, and intangible assets is permitted. The initial gains and losses resulting from this revaluation are reported as adjustments to equity, often referred to as **other comprehensive income**. The effect of this difference is that the use of IFRS results in more transactions affecting equity (other comprehensive income) but not net income.

- *IAS 1*, "Presentation of Financial Statements," provides general guidelines for the reporting of income statement information. Subsequently, a number of international standards have been issued that provide additional guidance to issues related to income statement presentation.

- Similar to GAAP, comprehensive income under IFRS includes unrealized gains and losses (such as those on so-called "non-trading securities") that are not included in the calculation of net income.

- IFRS requires that two years of income statement information be presented, whereas GAAP requires three years.

Looking to the Future

The IASB and FASB are working on a project that would rework the structure of financial statements. Specifically, this project will address the issue of how to classify various items in the income statement. A main goal of this new approach is to provide information that better represents how businesses are run. In addition, this approach draws attention away from just one number—net income. It will adopt major groupings similar to those currently used by the statement of cash flows (operating, investing, and financing), so that numbers can be more readily traced across statements. For example, the amount of income that is generated by operations would be traceable to the assets and liabilities used to generate the income. Finally, this approach would also provide detail, beyond that currently seen in most statements (either GAAP or IFRS), by requiring that line items be presented both by function and by nature. The new financial statement format was heavily influenced by suggestions from financial statement analysts.

IFRS Practice

IFRS Self-Test Questions

1. Which of the following would **not** be included in the definition of inventory under IFRS?
   (a) Photocopy paper held for sale by an office-supply store.
   (b) Stereo equipment held for sale by an electronics store.
   (c) Used office equipment held for sale by the human relations department of a plastics company.
   (d) All of the above would meet the definition.

2. Which of the following would **not** be a line item of a company reporting costs by nature?
   (a) Depreciation expense.
   (b) Salaries expense.
   (c) Interest expense.
   (d) Manufacturing expense.

3. Which of the following would **not** be a line item of a company reporting costs by function?
   (a) Administration.
   (b) Manufacturing.
   (c) Utilities expense.
   (d) Distribution.

4. Which of the following statements is **false**?
   (a) IFRS specifically requires use of a multiple-step income statement.
   (b) Under IFRS, companies can use either a perpetual or periodic system.
   (c) The proposed new format for financial statements was heavily influenced by the suggestions of financial statement analysts.
   (d) The new income statement format will try to de-emphasize the focus on the "net income" line item.

5. Under the new format for financial statements being proposed under a joint IASB/FASB project:
   (a) all financial statements would adopt headings similar to the current format of the balance sheet.
   (b) financial statements would be presented consistent with the way management usually run companies.
   (c) companies would be required to report income statement line items by function only.
   (d) the amount of detail shown in the income statement would decrease compared to current presentations.

IFRS Exercises

IFRS5-1 Explain the difference between the "nature-of-expense" and "function-of-expense" classifications.

IFRS5-2 For each of the following income statement line items, state whether the item is a "by nature" expense item or a "by function" expense item.

_____ Cost of goods sold
_____ Depreciation expense
_____ Salaries and wages expense
_____ Selling expenses
_____ Utilities expense
_____ Delivery expense
_____ General and administrative expenses

IFRS5-3 Matilda Company reported the following amounts (in euros) in 2015: Net income, €150,000; Unrealized gain related to revaluation of buildings, €10,000; and Unrealized loss on non-trading securities, €(35,000). Determine Matilda's total comprehensive income for 2015.

International Financial Reporting Problem: Zetar plc

IFRS5-4 The financial statements of Zetar plc are presented in Appendix F. Instructions for accessing and using the company's complete annual report, including the notes to its financial statements, are also provided in Appendix F.

Instructions

Use Zetar's annual report to answer the following questions.

(a) Does Zetar use a multiple-step or a single-step income statement format? Explain how you made your determination.

(b) Instead of "interest expense," what label does Zetar use for interest costs that it incurs?

(c) Using the notes to the company's financial statements, explain what each of the following are:

   (1) Adjusted results.

   (2) One-off items.

Answers to IFRS Self-Test Questions
1. c   2. d   3. c   4. a   5. b

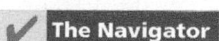 The Navigator

6 | Inventories

Feature Story

"Where Is That Spare Bulldozer Blade?"

Let's talk inventory—big, bulldozer-size inventory. Caterpillar Inc. is the world's largest manufacturer of construction and mining equipment, diesel and natural gas engines, and industrial gas turbines. It sells its products in over 200 countries, making it one of the most successful U.S. exporters. More than 70% of its productive assets are located domestically, and nearly 50% of its sales are foreign.

In the past, Caterpillar's profitability suffered, but today it is very successful. A big part of this turnaround can be attributed to effective management of its inventory. Imagine what it costs Caterpillar to have too many bulldozers sitting around in inventory—a situation the company definitely wants to avoid. Conversely, Caterpillar must make sure it has enough inventory to meet demand.

At one time during a 7-year period, Caterpillar's sales increased by 100%, while its inventory increased by only 50%. To achieve this dramatic reduction in the amount of resources tied up in inventory, while continuing to meet customers' needs, Caterpillar used a two-pronged approach. First, it completed a factory modernization program, which greatly increased its production efficiency. The program reduced by 60% the amount of inventory the company processed at any one time. It also reduced by an incredible 75% the time it takes to manufacture a part.

Second, Caterpillar dramatically improved its parts distribution system. It ships more than 100,000 items daily from its 23 distribution centers strategically located around the world (10 million square feet of warehouse space—remember, we're talking bulldozers). The company can virtually guarantee that it can get any part to anywhere in the world within 24 hours.

After these changes, Caterpillar had record exports, profits, and revenues. It would seem that things couldn't be better. But industry analysts, as well as the company's managers, thought otherwise. In order to maintain Caterpillar's position as the industry leader, management

✔ The Navigator

- Scan Learning Objectives
- Read Feature Story
- Read Preview
- Read text and answer **DO IT!** p. 284
  - p. 290 ■ p. 295 ■ p. 298
- Work Comprehensive **DO IT!** **1** p. 298
  - **2** p. 303
- Review Summary of Learning Objectives
- Answer Self-Test Questions
- Complete Assignments
- Go to *WileyPLUS* for practice and tutorials
- Read **A Look at IFRS** p. 328

Learning Objectives
 ✔ The Navigator

After studying this chapter, you should be able to:

[1] Determine how to classify inventory and inventory quantities.

[2] Explain the accounting for inventories and apply the inventory cost flow methods.

[3] Explain the financial effects of the inventory cost flow assumptions.

[4] Explain the lower-of-cost-or-market basis of accounting for inventories.

[5] Indicate the effects of inventory errors on the financial statements.

[6] Discuss the presentation and analysis of inventory.

began another major overhaul of inventory production and inventory management processes. The goal: to cut the number of repairs in half, increase productivity by 20%, and increase inventory turnover by 40%.

In short, Caterpillar's ability to manage its inventory has been a key reason for its past success, and inventory management will very likely play a huge part in its ability to succeed in the future.

Preview of Chapter 6

✔ The Navigator

In the previous chapter, we discussed the accounting for merchandise inventory using a perpetual inventory system. In this chapter, we explain the methods used to calculate the cost of inventory on hand at the balance sheet date and the cost of goods sold.

The content and organization of this chapter are as follows.

INVENTORIES			
Classifying and Determining Inventory	**Inventory Costing**	**Inventory Errors**	**Statement Presentation and Analysis**
• Classifying inventory • Determining inventory quantities	• Specific identification • Cost flow assumptions • Financial statement and tax effects • Consistent use • Lower-of-cost-or-market	• Income statement effects • Balance sheet effects	• Presentation • Analysis

Classifying and Determining Inventory

LEARNING OBJECTIVE   1

Determine how to classify inventory and inventory quantities.

Two important steps in the reporting of inventory at the end of the accounting period are the classification of inventory based on its degree of completeness and the determination of inventory amounts.

Classifying Inventory

How a company classifies its inventory depends on whether the firm is a merchandiser or a manufacturer. In a **merchandising** company, such as those described in Chapter 5, inventory consists of many different items. For example, in a grocery store, canned goods, dairy products, meats, and produce are just a few of the inventory items on hand. These items have two common characteristics: (1) They are owned by the company, and (2) they are in a form ready for sale to customers in the ordinary course of business. Thus, merchandisers need only one inventory classification, **merchandise inventory**, to describe the many different items that make up the total inventory.

In a **manufacturing** company, some inventory may not yet be ready for sale. As a result, manufacturers usually classify inventory into three categories: finished goods, work in process, and raw materials. **Finished goods inventory** is manufactured items that are completed and ready for sale. **Work in process** is that portion of manufactured inventory that has been placed into the production process but is not yet complete. **Raw materials** are the basic goods that will be used in production but have not yet been placed into production.

For example, Caterpillar classifies earth-moving tractors completed and ready for sale as **finished goods**. It classifies the tractors on the assembly line in various stages of production as **work in process**. The steel, glass, tires, and other components that are on hand waiting to be used in the production of tractors are identified as **raw materials**. Illustration 6-1 shows an excerpt from Note 7 of Caterpillar's annual report, which shows the significant increases in each type of Caterpillar's inventory levels as the economy began to recover during this period.

Helpful Hint
Regardless of the classification, companies report all inventories under Current Assets on the balance sheet.

Illustration 6-1
Composition of Caterpillar's inventory

(millions of dollars)	December 31		
	2012	**2011**	**2010**
Raw materials	$ 3,573	$ 3,766	$ 2,766
Work-in-process	2,920	2,959	1,483
Finished goods	8,767	7,562	5,098
Supplies	287	257	240
Total inventories	**$15,547**	**$14,544**	**$9,587**

By observing the levels and changes in the levels of these three inventory types, financial statement users can gain insight into management's production plans. For example, low levels of raw materials and high levels of finished goods suggest that management believes it has enough inventory on hand, and production will be slowing down—perhaps in anticipation of a recession. On the other hand, high levels of raw materials and low levels of finished goods probably signal that management is planning to step up production.

Many companies have significantly lowered inventory levels and costs using **just-in-time (JIT) inventory** methods. Under a just-in-time method, companies manufacture or purchase goods just in time for use. Dell is famous for having developed a system for making computers in response to individual customer requests. Even though it makes each computer to meet each customer's particular specifications, Dell is able to assemble the computer and put it on a truck in less than 48 hours. The success of the JIT system depends on reliable suppliers. By integrating its information systems with those of its suppliers, Dell reduced its inventories to nearly zero. This is a huge advantage in an industry where products become obsolete nearly overnight.

The accounting concepts discussed in this chapter apply to the inventory classifications of both merchandising and manufacturing companies. Our focus here is on merchandise inventory.

ACCOUNTING ACROSS THE ORGANIZATION

A Big Hiccup

JIT can save a company a lot of money, but it isn't without risk. An unexpected disruption in the supply chain can cost a company a lot of money. Japanese automakers experienced just such a disruption when a 6.8-magnitude earthquake caused major damage to the company that produces 50% of their piston rings. The rings themselves cost only $1.50, but without them you cannot make a car. No other supplier could quickly begin producing sufficient quantities of the rings to match the desired specifications. As a result, the automakers were forced to shut down production for a few days—a loss of tens of thousands of cars.

Similarly, a major snowstorm halted production at Canadian plants of General Motors and Ford. A Ford spokesperson said, "Because the plants run with just-in-time inventory, we don't have large stockpiles of parts sitting around. When you have a somewhat significant disruption, you can pretty quickly run out of parts."

Sources: Amy Chozick, "A Key Strategy of Japan's Car Makers Backfires," *Wall Street Journal* (July 20, 2007); Kate Linebaugh, "Canada Military Evacuates Motorists Stranded by Snow," *Wall Street Journal* (December 15, 2010).

? What steps might the companies take to avoid such a serious disruption in the future? (See page 328.)

Determining Inventory Quantities

No matter whether they are using a periodic or perpetual inventory system, all companies need to determine inventory quantities at the end of the accounting period. If using a perpetual system, companies take a physical inventory for the following reasons:

1. To check the accuracy of their perpetual inventory records.
2. To determine the amount of inventory lost due to wasted raw materials, shoplifting, or employee theft.

Companies using a periodic inventory system take a physical inventory for **two different purposes**: to determine the inventory on hand at the balance sheet date, and to determine the cost of goods sold for the period.

Determining inventory quantities involves two steps: (1) taking a physical inventory of goods on hand and (2) determining the ownership of goods.

TAKING A PHYSICAL INVENTORY

Companies take a physical inventory at the end of the accounting period. Taking a physical inventory involves actually counting, weighing, or measuring each kind of inventory on hand. In many companies, taking an

Ethics Note

In a famous fraud, a salad oil company filled its storage tanks mostly with water. The oil rose to the top, so auditors thought the tanks were full of oil. The company also said it had more tanks than it really did: It repainted numbers on the tanks to confuse auditors.

inventory is a formidable task. Retailers such as Target, True Value Hardware, or Home Depot have thousands of different inventory items. An inventory count is generally more accurate when goods are not being sold or received during the counting. Consequently, companies often "take inventory" when the business is closed or when business is slow. Many retailers close early on a chosen day in January—after the holiday sales and returns, when inventories are at their lowest level—to count inventory. Wal-Mart Stores, Inc., for example, has a year-end of January 31.

© Greg Brookes/iStockphoto

ETHICS INSIGHT

Falsifying Inventory to Boost Income

Managers at women's apparel maker Leslie Fay were convicted of falsifying inventory records to boost net income—and consequently to boost management bonuses. In another case, executives at Craig Consumer Electronics were accused of defrauding lenders by manipulating inventory records. The indictment said the company classified "defective goods as new or refurbished" and claimed that it owned certain shipments "from overseas suppliers" when, in fact, Craig either did not own the shipments or the shipments did not exist.

? What effect does an overstatement of inventory have on a company's financial statements? (See page 328.)

DETERMINING OWNERSHIP OF GOODS

One challenge in computing inventory quantities is determining what inventory a company owns. To determine ownership of goods, two questions must be answered: Do all of the goods included in the count belong to the company? Does the company own any goods that were not included in the count?

GOODS IN TRANSIT A complication in determining ownership is **goods in transit** (on board a truck, train, ship, or plane) at the end of the period. The company may have purchased goods that have not yet been received, or it may have sold goods that have not yet been delivered. To arrive at an accurate count, the company must determine ownership of these goods.

Goods in transit should be included in the inventory of the company that has legal title to the goods. Legal title is determined by the terms of the sale, as shown in Illustration 6-2 and described below.

Illustration 6-2
Terms of sale

1. When the terms are **FOB (free on board) shipping point**, ownership of the goods passes to the buyer when the public carrier accepts the goods from the seller.
2. When the terms are **FOB destination**, ownership of the goods remains with the seller until the goods reach the buyer.

If goods in transit at the statement date are ignored, inventory quantities may be seriously miscounted. Assume, for example, that Hargrove Company has 20,000 units of inventory on hand on December 31. It also has the following goods in transit:

1. Sales of 1,500 units shipped December 31 FOB destination.
2. Purchases of 2,500 units shipped FOB shipping point by the seller on December 31.

Hargrove has legal title to both the 1,500 units sold and the 2,500 units purchased. If the company ignores the units in transit, it would understate inventory quantities by 4,000 units (1,500 + 2,500).

As we will see later in the chapter, inaccurate inventory counts affect not only the inventory amount shown on the balance sheet but also the cost of goods sold calculation on the income statement.

CONSIGNED GOODS In some lines of business, it is common to hold the goods of other parties and try to sell the goods for them for a fee, but without taking ownership of the goods. These are called **consigned goods**.

For example, you might have a used car that you would like to sell. If you take the item to a dealer, the dealer might be willing to put the car on its lot and charge you a commission if it is sold. Under this agreement, the dealer **would not take ownership** of the car, which would still belong to you. Therefore, if an inventory count were taken, the car would not be included in the dealer's inventory because the dealer does not own it.

Many car, boat, and antique dealers sell goods on consignment to keep their inventory costs down and to avoid the risk of purchasing an item that they will not be able to sell. Today, even some manufacturers are making consignment agreements with their suppliers in order to keep their inventory levels low.

ANATOMY OF A FRAUD

Ted Nickerson, CEO of clock manufacturer Dally Industries, was feared by all of his employees. Ted also had expensive tastes. To support this habit, Ted took out large loans, which he collateralized with his shares of Dally Industries stock. If the price of Dally's stock fell, he was required to provide the bank with more shares of stock. To achieve target net income figures and thus maintain the stock price, Ted coerced employees in the company to alter inventory figures. Inventory quantities were manipulated by changing the amounts on inventory control tags after the year-end physical inventory count. For example, if a tag said there were 20 units of a particular item, the tag was changed to 220. Similarly, the unit costs that were used to determine the value of ending inventory were increased from, for example, $125 per unit to $1,250. Both of these fraudulent changes had the effect of increasing the amount of reported ending inventory. This reduced cost of goods sold and increased net income.

Total take: $245,000

THE MISSING CONTROL

Independent internal verification. The company should have spot-checked its inventory records periodically, verifying that the number of units in the records agreed with the amount on hand and that the unit costs agreed with vendor price sheets.

Source: Adapted from Wells, *Fraud Casebook* (2007), pp. 502–509.

> DO IT!

Rules of Ownership

Hasbeen Company completed its inventory count. It arrived at a total inventory value of $200,000. As a new member of Hasbeen's accounting department, you have been given the information listed below. Discuss how this information affects the reported cost of inventory.

1. Hasbeen included in the inventory goods held on consignment for Falls Co., costing $15,000.

2. The company did not include in the count purchased goods of $10,000 which were in transit (terms: FOB shipping point).

3. The company did not include in the count sold inventory with a cost of $12,000 which was in transit (terms: FOB shipping point).

Solution

Action Plan

✔ Apply the rules of ownership to goods held on consignment.

✔ Apply the rules of ownership to goods in transit.

> The goods of $15,000 held on consignment should be deducted from the inventory count. The goods of $10,000 purchased FOB shipping point should be added to the inventory count. Sold goods of $12,000 which were in transit FOB shipping point should not be included in the ending inventory. Thus, inventory should be carried at $195,000 ($200,000 − $15,000 + $10,000).

Related exercise material: BE6-1, E6-1, E6-2, **and** DO IT! 6-1.

✔ The Navigator

Inventory Costing

LEARNING OBJECTIVE   2

Explain the accounting for inventories and apply the inventory cost flow methods.

Inventory is accounted for at cost. Cost includes all expenditures necessary to acquire goods and place them in a condition ready for sale. For example, freight costs incurred to acquire inventory are added to the cost of inventory, but the cost of shipping goods to a customer are a selling expense.

After a company has determined the quantity of units of inventory, it applies unit costs to the quantities to compute the total cost of the inventory and the cost of goods sold. This process can be complicated if a company has purchased inventory items at different times and at different prices.

For example, assume that Crivitz TV Company purchases three identical 50-inch TVs on different dates at costs of $700, $750, and $800. During the year, Crivitz sold two sets at $1,200 each. These facts are summarized in Illustration 6-3.

Illustration 6-3
Data for inventory costing example

Purchases

February 3	1 TV	at	$700
March 5	1 TV	at	$750
May 22	1 TV	at	$800

Sales

June 1	2 TVs	for	$2,400 ($1,200 × 2)

Cost of goods sold will differ depending on which two TVs the company sold. For example, it might be $1,450 ($700 + $750), or $1,500 ($700 + $800), or $1,550 ($750 + $800). In this section, we discuss alternative costing methods available to Crivitz.

Specific Identification

If Crivitz can positively identify which particular units it sold and which are still in ending inventory, it can use the **specific identification method** of inventory costing. For example, if Crivitz sold the TVs it purchased on February 3 and May 22, then its cost of goods sold is $1,500 ($700 + $800), and its ending inventory is $750 (see Illustration 6-4). Using this method, companies can accurately determine ending inventory and cost of goods sold.

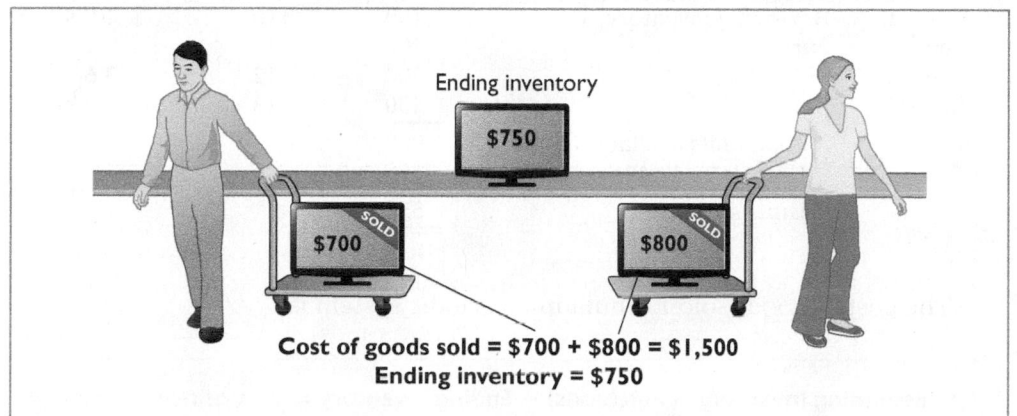

Cost of goods sold = $700 + $800 = $1,500
Ending inventory = $750

Illustration 6-4
Specific identification method

Specific identification requires that companies keep records of the original cost of each individual inventory item. Historically, specific identification was possible only when a company sold a limited variety of high-unit-cost items that could be identified clearly from the time of purchase through the time of sale. Examples of such products are cars, pianos, or expensive antiques.

Today, bar coding, electronic product codes, and radio frequency identification make it theoretically possible to do specific identification with nearly any type of product. The reality is, however, that this practice is still relatively rare. Instead, rather than keep track of the cost of each particular item sold, most companies make assumptions, called **cost flow assumptions**, about which units were sold.

Ethics Note

A major disadvantage of the specific identification method is that management may be able to manipulate net income. For example, it can boost net income by selling units purchased at a low cost, or reduce net income by selling units purchased at a high cost.

Cost Flow Assumptions

Because specific identification is often impractical, other cost flow methods are permitted. These differ from specific identification in that they **assume** flows of costs that may be unrelated to the physical flow of goods. There are three assumed cost flow methods:

1. First-in, first-out (FIFO)
2. Last-in, first-out (LIFO)
3. Average-cost

There is no accounting requirement that the cost flow assumption be consistent with the physical movement of the goods. Company management selects the appropriate cost flow method.

To demonstrate the three cost flow methods, we will use a **periodic** inventory system. We assume a periodic system because **very few companies use** *perpetual* **LIFO, FIFO, or average-cost** to cost their inventory and related cost of goods sold. Instead, companies that use perpetual systems often use an assumed cost (called a standard cost) to record cost of goods sold at the time of sale. Then, at the end of the period when they count their inventory, they **recalculate cost of** goods sold using *periodic* **FIFO, LIFO, or average-cost** as shown in this chapter and adjust cost of goods sold to this recalculated number.[1]

To illustrate the three inventory cost flow methods, we will use the data for Houston Electronics' Astro condensers, shown in Illustration 6-5.

Illustration 6-5
Data for Houston Electronics

HOUSTON ELECTRONICS				
Astro Condensers				
Date	**Explanation**	**Units**	**Unit Cost**	**Total Cost**
Jan. 1	Beginning inventory	100	$10	$ 1,000
Apr. 15	Purchase	200	11	2,200
Aug. 24	Purchase	300	12	3,600
Nov. 27	Purchase	400	13	5,200
	Total units available for sale	1,000		$12,000
	Units in ending inventory	(450)		
	Units sold	550		

The cost of goods sold formula in a periodic system is:

> **(Beginning Inventory + Purchases) − Ending Inventory = Cost of Goods Sold**

Houston Electronics had a total of 1,000 units available to sell during the period (beginning inventory plus purchases). The total cost of these 1,000 units is $12,000, referred to as **cost of goods available for sale**. A physical inventory taken at December 31 determined that there were 450 units in ending inventory. Therefore, Houston sold 550 units (1,000 − 450) during the period. To determine the cost of the 550 units that were sold (the cost of goods sold), we assign a cost to the ending inventory and subtract that value from the cost of goods available for sale. The value assigned to the ending inventory **will depend on which cost flow method we use**. No matter which cost flow assumption we use, though, the sum of cost of goods sold plus the cost of the ending inventory must equal the cost of goods available for sale—in this case, $12,000.

FIRST-IN, FIRST-OUT (FIFO)

The **first-in, first-out (FIFO) method** assumes that the **earliest goods** purchased are the first to be sold. FIFO often parallels the actual physical flow of merchandise. That is, it generally is good business practice to sell the oldest units first. Under the FIFO method, therefore, the **costs** of the earliest goods purchased are the first to be recognized in determining cost of goods sold. (This does not necessarily mean that the oldest units **are** sold first, but that the costs of the oldest units are **recognized** first. In a bin of picture hangers at the hardware store, for example, no one really knows, nor would it matter, which hangers are sold first.) Illustration 6-6 shows the allocation of the cost of goods available for sale at Houston Electronics under FIFO.

---

[1]Also, some companies use a perpetual system to keep track of units, but they do not make an entry for perpetual cost of goods sold. In addition, firms that employ LIFO tend to use **dollar-value LIFO**, a method discussed in upper-level courses. FIFO periodic and FIFO perpetual give the same result. Therefore, companies should not incur the additional cost to use FIFO perpetual. Few companies use perpetual average-cost because of the added cost of record-keeping. Finally, for instructional purposes, we believe it is easier to demonstrate the cost flow assumptions under the periodic system, which makes it more pedagogically appropriate.

COST OF GOODS AVAILABLE FOR SALE				
Date	Explanation	Units	Unit Cost	Total Cost
Jan. 1	Beginning inventory	100	$10	$ 1,000
Apr. 15	Purchase	200	11	2,200
Aug. 24	Purchase	300	12	3,600
Nov. 27	Purchase	400	13	5,200
	Total	1,000		$12,000

Illustration 6-6
Allocation of costs—FIFO method

Helpful Hint
Note the sequencing of the allocation: (1) Compute ending inventory, and (2) determine cost of goods sold.

STEP 1: ENDING INVENTORY				STEP 2: COST OF GOODS SOLD	
Date	Units	Unit Cost	Total Cost		
Nov. 27	400	$13	$ 5,200	Cost of goods available for sale	$12,000
Aug. 24	50	12	600	Less: Ending inventory	5,800
Total	450		$5,800	Cost of goods sold	$ 6,200

Helpful Hint
Another way of thinking about the calculation of FIFO ending inventory is the *LISH assumption*—last in still here.

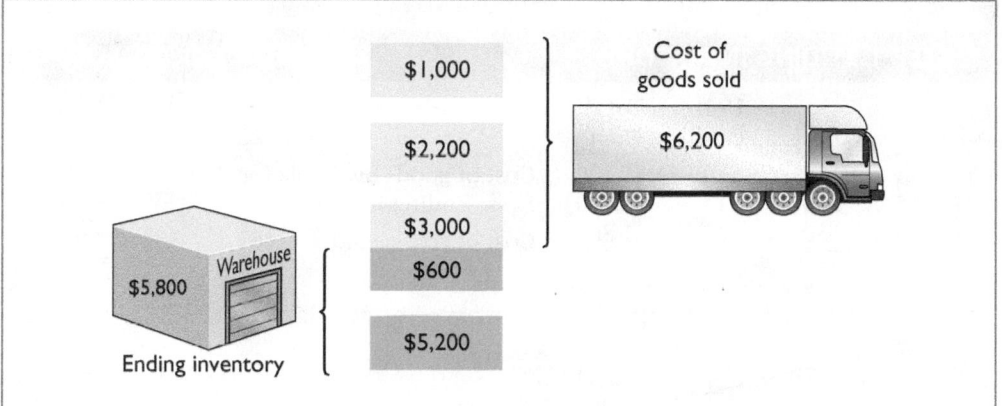

Under FIFO, since it is assumed that the first goods purchased were the first goods sold, ending inventory is based on the prices of the most recent units purchased. That is, **under FIFO, companies obtain the cost of the ending inventory by taking the unit cost of the most recent purchase and working backward until all units of inventory have been costed**. In this example, Houston Electronics prices the 450 units of ending inventory using the **most recent** prices. The last purchase was 400 units at $13 on November 27. The remaining 50 units are priced using the unit cost of the second most recent purchase, $12, on August 24. Next, Houston Electronics calculates cost of goods sold by subtracting the cost of the units **not sold** (ending inventory) from the cost of all goods available for sale.

Illustration 6-7 demonstrates that companies also can calculate cost of goods sold by pricing the 550 units sold using the prices of the first 550 units acquired. Note that of the 300 units purchased on August 24, only 250 units are assumed sold. This agrees with our calculation of the cost of ending inventory, where 50 of these units were assumed unsold and thus included in ending inventory.

Date	Units	Unit Cost	Total Cost
Jan. 1	100	$10	$ 1,000
Apr. 15	200	11	2,200
Aug. 24	250	12	3,000
Total	550		$6,200

Illustration 6-7
Proof of cost of goods sold

LAST-IN, FIRST-OUT (LIFO)

The **last-in, first-out (LIFO) method** assumes that the **latest goods** purchased are the first to be sold. LIFO seldom coincides with the actual physical flow of inventory. (Exceptions include goods stored in piles, such as coal or hay, where goods are removed from the top of the pile as they are sold.) Under the LIFO method, the **costs** of the latest goods purchased are the first to be recognized in determining cost of goods sold. Illustration 6-8 shows the allocation of the cost of goods available for sale at Houston Electronics under LIFO.

Illustration 6-8
Allocation of costs—LIFO method

COST OF GOODS AVAILABLE FOR SALE				
Date	**Explanation**	**Units**	**Unit Cost**	**Total Cost**
Jan. 1	Beginning inventory	100	$10	$ 1,000
Apr. 15	Purchase	200	11	2,200
Aug. 24	Purchase	300	12	3,600
Nov. 27	Purchase	400	13	5,200
	Total	1,000		$12,000

STEP 1: ENDING INVENTORY				STEP 2: COST OF GOODS SOLD	
Date	**Units**	**Unit Cost**	**Total Cost**		
Jan. 1	100	$10	$1,000	Cost of goods available for sale	$12,000
Apr. 15	200	11	2,200	Less: Ending inventory	5,000
Aug. 24	150	12	1,800	Cost of goods sold	$ 7,000
Total	450		$5,000		

Helpful Hint
Another way of thinking about the calculation of LIFO **ending inventory** is the *FISH assumption*—first in still here.

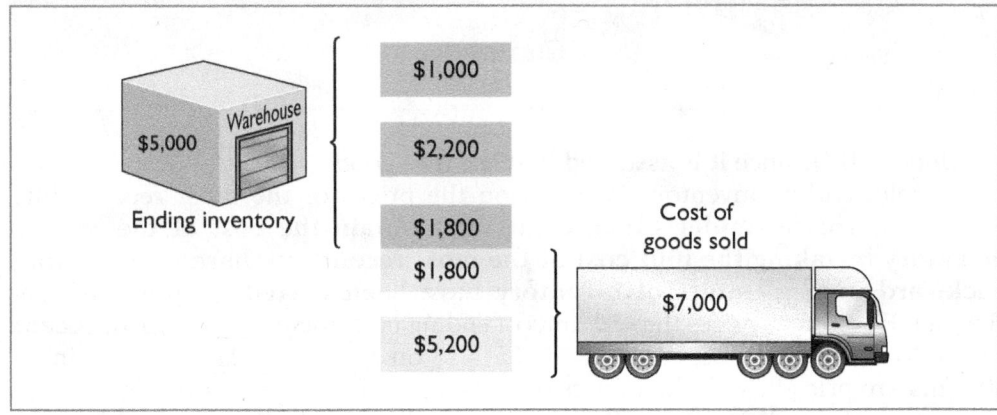

Under LIFO, since it is assumed that the first goods sold were those that were most recently purchased, ending inventory is based on the prices of the oldest units purchased. That is, **under LIFO, companies obtain the cost of the ending inventory by taking the unit cost of the earliest goods available for sale and working forward until all units of inventory have been costed**. In this example, Houston Electronics prices the 450 units of ending inventory using the **earliest** prices. The first purchase was 100 units at $10 in the January 1 beginning inventory. Then, 200 units were purchased at $11. The remaining 150 units needed are priced at $12 per unit (August 24 purchase). Next, Houston Electronics calculates cost of goods sold by subtracting the cost of the units **not sold** (ending inventory) from the cost of all goods available for sale.

Illustration 6-9 demonstrates that companies also can calculate cost of goods sold by pricing the 550 units sold using the prices of the last 550 units acquired. Note that of the 300 units purchased on August 24, only 150 units are assumed sold. This agrees with our calculation of the cost of ending inventory, where 150 of these units were assumed unsold and thus included in ending inventory.

Illustration 6-9
Proof of cost of goods sold

Date	Units	Unit Cost	Total Cost
Nov. 27	400	$13	$ 5,200
Aug. 24	150	12	1,800
Total	550		$7,000

Under a periodic inventory system, which we are using here, **all goods purchased during the period are assumed to be available for the first sale, regardless of the date of purchase**.

AVERAGE-COST

The **average-cost method** allocates the cost of goods available for sale on the basis of the **weighted-average unit cost** incurred. The average-cost method assumes that goods are similar in nature. Illustration 6-10 presents the formula and a sample computation of the weighted-average unit cost.

Illustration 6-10
Formula for weighted-average
unit cost

Cost of Goods Available for Sale	÷	Total Units Available for Sale	=	Weighted-Average Unit Cost
$12,000	÷	1,000	=	$12

The company then applies the weighted-average unit cost to the units on hand to determine the cost of the ending inventory. Illustration 6-11 shows the allocation of the cost of goods available for sale at Houston Electronics using average-cost.

Illustration 6-11
Allocation of costs—average-
cost method

COST OF GOODS AVAILABLE FOR SALE

Date	Explanation	Units	Unit Cost	Total Cost
Jan. 1	Beginning inventory	100	$10	$ 1,000
Apr. 15	Purchase	200	11	2,200
Aug. 24	Purchase	300	12	3,600
Nov. 27	Purchase	400	13	5,200
	Total	1,000		$12,000

STEP 1: ENDING INVENTORY

$12,000 ÷ 1,000 = $12

Units	Unit Cost	Total Cost
450	$12	$5,400

STEP 2: COST OF GOODS SOLD

Cost of goods available for sale	$12,000
Less: Ending inventory	5,400
Cost of goods sold	$ 6,600

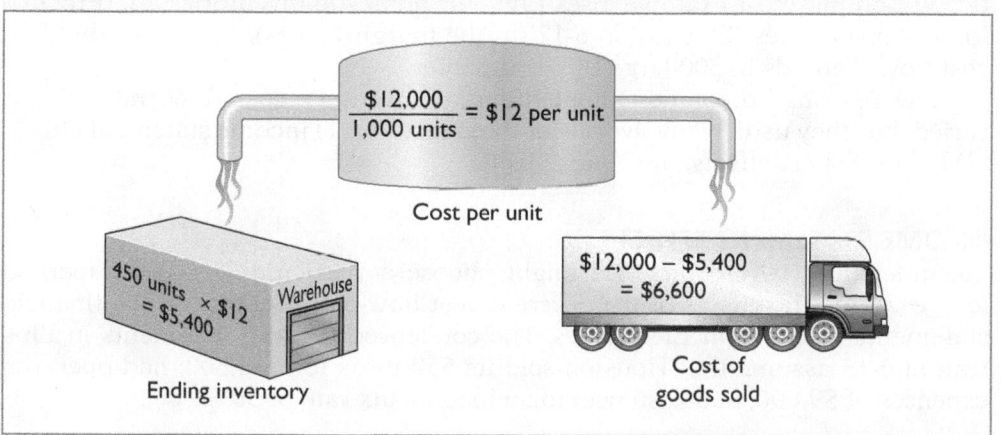

We can verify the cost of goods sold under this method by multiplying the units sold times the weighted-average unit cost (550 × $12 = $6,600). Note that this method does not use the average of the unit costs. That average is $11.50 ($10 + $11 + $12 + $13 = $46; $46 ÷ 4). The average-cost method instead uses the average **weighted by** the quantities purchased at each unit cost.

> DO IT!

Cost Flow Methods

Action Plan

✔ Understand the periodic inventory system.

✔ Allocate costs between goods sold and goods on hand (ending inventory) for each cost flow method.

✔ Compute cost of goods sold for each method.

The accounting records of Shumway Ag Implements show the following data.

Beginning inventory	4,000 units at $ 3
Purchases	6,000 units at $ 4
Sales	7,000 units at $12

Determine the cost of goods sold during the period under a periodic inventory system using (a) the FIFO method, (b) the LIFO method, and (c) the average-cost method.

Solution

Cost of goods available for sale = (4,000 × $3) + (6,000 × $4) = $36,000

Ending inventory = 10,000 − 7,000 = 3,000 units

(a) FIFO: $36,000 − (3,000 × $4) = $24,000

(b) LIFO: $36,000 − (3,000 × $3) = $27,000

(c) Average cost per unit: [(4,000 @ $3) + (6,000 @ $4)] ÷ 10,000 = $3.60
Average-cost: $36,000 − (3,000 × $3.60) = $25,200

Related exercise material: BE6-3, BE6-4, BE6-5, E6-3, E6-4, E6-5, E6-6, E6-7, E6-8, **and** DO IT! 6-2.

✔ **The Navigator**

Financial Statement and Tax Effects of Cost Flow Methods

LEARNING OBJECTIVE   **3**

Explain the financial effects of the inventory cost flow assumptions.

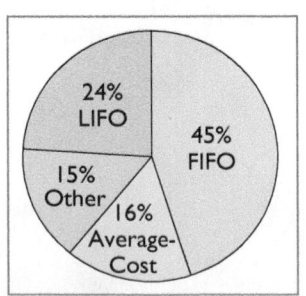

Illustration 6-12
Use of cost flow methods in major U.S. companies

Each of the three assumed cost flow methods is acceptable for use. For example, Reebok International Ltd. and Wendy's International currently use the FIFO method of inventory costing. Campbell Soup Company, Krogers, and Walgreen Drugs use LIFO for part or all of their inventory. Bristol-Myers Squibb, Starbucks, and Motorola use the average-cost method. In fact, a company may also use more than one cost flow method at the same time. Stanley Black & Decker Manufacturing Company, for example, uses LIFO for domestic inventories and FIFO for foreign inventories. Illustration 6-12 (in the margin) shows the use of the three cost flow methods in 500 large U.S. companies.

The reasons companies adopt different inventory cost flow methods are varied, but they usually involve one of three factors: (1) income statement effects, (2) balance sheet effects, or (3) tax effects.

INCOME STATEMENT EFFECTS

To understand why companies might choose a particular cost flow method, let's examine the effects of the different cost flow assumptions on the financial statements of Houston Electronics. The condensed income statements in Illustration 6-13 assume that Houston sold its 550 units for $18,500, had operating expenses of $9,000, and is subject to an income tax rate of 30%.

HOUSTON ELECTRONICS Condensed Income Statements			
	FIFO	**LIFO**	**Average-Cost**
Sales revenue	$18,500	$18,500	$18,500
Beginning inventory	1,000	1,000	1,000
Purchases	11,000	11,000	11,000
Cost of goods available for sale	12,000	12,000	12,000
Ending inventory	**5,800**	**5,000**	**5,400**
Cost of goods sold	6,200	7,000	6,600
Gross profit	12,300	11,500	11,900
Operating expenses	9,000	9,000	9,000
Income before income taxes*	3,300	2,500	2,900
Income tax expense (30%)	990	750	870
Net income	**$ 2,310**	**$ 1,750**	**$ 2,030**

*We are assuming that Houston Electronics is a corporation, and corporations are required to pay income taxes.

Illustration 6-13
Comparative effects of cost flow methods

Note the cost of goods available for sale ($12,000) is the same under each of the three inventory cost flow methods. However, the ending inventories and the costs of goods sold are different. This difference is due to the unit costs that the company allocated to cost of goods sold and to ending inventory. Each dollar of difference in ending inventory results in a corresponding dollar difference in income before income taxes. For Houston, an $800 difference exists between FIFO and LIFO cost of goods sold.

In periods of changing prices, the cost flow assumption can have a significant impact on income and on evaluations based on income. In most instances, prices are rising (inflation). In a period of inflation, FIFO produces a higher net income because the lower unit costs of the first units purchased are matched against revenues. In a period of rising prices (as is the case in the Houston example), FIFO reports the highest net income ($2,310) and LIFO the lowest ($1,750); average-cost falls in the middle ($2,030). If prices are falling, the results from the use of FIFO and LIFO are reversed. FIFO will report the lowest net income and LIFO the highest.

To management, higher net income is an advantage. It causes external users to view the company more favorably. In addition, management bonuses, if based on net income, will be higher. Therefore, when prices are rising (which is usually the case), companies tend to prefer FIFO because it results in higher net income.

Some argue that the use of LIFO in a period of inflation enables the company to avoid reporting **paper** (or **phantom**) **profit** as economic gain. To illustrate, assume that Kralik Company buys 200 units of a product at $20 per unit on January 10 and 200 more on December 31 at $24 each. During the year, Kralik sells 200 units at $30 each. Illustration 6-14 shows the results under FIFO and LIFO.

	FIFO	LIFO
Sales revenue (200 × $30)	$6,000	$6,000
Cost of goods sold	4,000 (200 × $20)	4,800 (200 × $24)
Gross profit	$2,000	$1,200

Illustration 6-14
Income statement effects compared

Under LIFO, Kralik Company has recovered the current replacement cost ($4,800) of the units sold. Thus, the gross profit in economic terms is real. However, under FIFO, the company has recovered only the January 10 cost ($4,000). To replace the units sold, it must reinvest $800 (200 × $4) of the gross profit. Thus, $800 of the gross profit is said to be phantom or illusory. As a result, reported net income is also overstated in real terms.

BALANCE SHEET EFFECTS

A major advantage of the FIFO method is that in a period of inflation, the costs allocated to ending inventory will approximate their current cost. For example, for Houston Electronics, 400 of the 450 units in the ending inventory are costed under FIFO at the higher November 27 unit cost of $13.

Conversely, a major shortcoming of the LIFO method is that in a period of inflation, the costs allocated to ending inventory may be significantly understated in terms of current cost. The understatement becomes greater over prolonged periods of inflation if the inventory includes goods purchased in one or more prior accounting periods. For example, Caterpillar has used LIFO for more than 50 years. Its balance sheet shows ending inventory of $14,544 million. But the inventory's actual current cost if FIFO had been used is $16,966 million.

TAX EFFECTS

Helpful Hint
A tax rule, often referred to as the *LIFO conformity rule*, requires that if companies use LIFO for tax purposes they must also use it for financial reporting purposes. This means that if a company chooses the LIFO method to reduce its tax bills, it will also have to report lower net income in its financial statements.

We have seen that both inventory on the balance sheet and net income on the income statement are higher when companies use FIFO in a period of inflation. Yet, many companies have selected LIFO. Why? The reason is that LIFO results in the lowest income taxes (because of lower net income) during times of rising prices. For example, at Houston Electronics, income taxes are $750 under LIFO, compared to $990 under FIFO. The tax savings of $240 makes more cash available for use in the business.

Using Inventory Cost Flow Methods Consistently

Whatever cost flow method a company chooses, it should use that method consistently from one accounting period to another. This approach is often referred to as the **consistency concept**, which means that a company uses the same accounting principles and methods from year to year. Consistent application enhances the comparability of financial statements over successive time periods. In contrast, using the FIFO method one year and the LIFO method the next year would make it difficult to compare the net incomes of the two years.

Although consistent application is preferred, it does not mean that a company may never change its inventory costing method. When a company adopts a different method, it should disclose in the financial statements the change and its effects on net income. Illustration 6-15 shows a typical disclosure, using information from recent financial statements of Quaker Oats (now a unit of PepsiCo).

Illustration 6-15
Disclosure of change in cost flow method

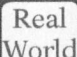   **QUAKER OATS**
Notes to the Financial Statements

Note 1: Effective July 1, the Company adopted the LIFO cost flow assumption for valuing the majority of U.S. Grocery Products inventories. The Company believes that the use of the LIFO method better matches current costs with current revenues. The effect of this change on the current year was to decrease net income by $16.0 million.

INTERNATIONAL INSIGHT

Is LIFO Fair?

ExxonMobil Corporation, like many U.S. companies, uses LIFO to value its inventory for financial reporting and tax purposes. In one recent year, this resulted in a cost of goods sold figure that was $5.6 billion higher than under FIFO. By increasing cost of goods sold, ExxonMobil reduces net income, which reduces taxes. Critics say that LIFO provides an unfair "tax dodge." As Congress looks for more sources of tax revenue, some lawmakers favor the elimination of LIFO. Supporters of LIFO argue that the method is conceptually sound because it matches current costs with current revenues. In addition, they point out that this matching provides protection against inflation.

International accounting standards do not allow the use of LIFO. Because of this, the net income of foreign oil companies such as BP and Royal Dutch Shell are not directly comparable to U.S. companies, which makes analysis difficult.

Source: David Reilly, "Big Oil's Accounting Methods Fuel Criticism," *Wall Street Journal* (August 8, 2006), p. C1.

? What are the arguments for and against the use of LIFO? (See page 328.)

Bloomberg/Getty Images

Lower-of-Cost-or-Market

The value of inventory for companies selling high-technology or fashion goods can drop very quickly due to changes in technology or fashion. These circumstances sometimes call for inventory valuation methods other than those presented so far. For example, at one time purchasing managers at Ford decided to make a large purchase of palladium, a precious metal used in vehicle emission devices. They made this purchase because they feared a future shortage. The shortage did not materialize, and by the end of the year the price of palladium had plummeted. Ford's inventory was then worth $1 billion less than its original cost. Do you think Ford's inventory should have been stated at cost, in accordance with the historical cost principle, or at its lower replacement cost?

As you probably reasoned, this situation requires a departure from the cost basis of accounting. This is done by valuing the inventory at the **lower-of-cost-or-market (LCM)** in the period in which the price decline occurs. LCM is a basis whereby inventory is stated at the lower of either its cost or market value as determined by current replacement cost. LCM is an example of the accounting convention of **conservatism**. Conservatism means that the approach adopted among accounting alternatives is the method that is least likely to overstate assets and net income.

Companies apply LCM to the items in inventory after they have used one of the cost flow methods (specific identification, FIFO, LIFO, or average-cost) to determine cost. Under the LCM basis, market is defined as **current replacement cost**, not selling price. For a merchandising company, current replacement cost is the cost of purchasing the same goods at the present time from the usual suppliers in the usual quantities. Current replacement cost is used because a decline in the replacement cost of an item usually leads to a decline in the selling price of the item.

To illustrate the application of LCM, assume that Ken Tuckie TV has the following lines of merchandise with costs and market values as indicated. LCM produces the results shown in Illustration 6-16 (page 294). Note that the amounts shown in the final column are the lower-of-cost-or-market amounts for each item.

> **LEARNING OBJECTIVE   4**
>
> Explain the lower-of-cost-or-market basis of accounting for inventories.

> **International Note**
>
> Under U.S. GAAP, companies cannot reverse inventory write-downs if inventory increases in value in subsequent periods. IFRS permits companies to reverse write-downs in some circumstances.

Illustration 6-16
Computation of lower-of-cost-or-market

	Cost	Market	Lower-of-Cost-or-Market
Flat-screen TVs	$60,000	$55,000	$ 55,000
Satellite radios	45,000	52,000	45,000
DVD recorders	48,000	45,000	45,000
DVDs	15,000	14,000	14,000
Total inventory			$159,000

Inventory Errors

LEARNING OBJECTIVE 5

Indicate the effects of inventory errors on the financial statements.

Unfortunately, errors occasionally occur in accounting for inventory. In some cases, errors are caused by failure to count or price the inventory correctly. In other cases, errors occur because companies do not properly recognize the transfer of legal title to goods that are in transit. When errors occur, they affect both the income statement and the balance sheet.

Income Statement Effects

Under a periodic inventory system, both the beginning and ending inventories appear in the income statement. The ending inventory of one period automatically becomes the beginning inventory of the next period. Thus, inventory errors affect the computation of cost of goods sold and net income in two periods.

The effects on cost of goods sold can be computed by entering incorrect data in the formula in Illustration 6-17 and then substituting the correct data.

Illustration 6-17
Formula for cost of goods sold

Beginning Inventory	+	Cost of Goods Purchased	−	Ending Inventory	=	Cost of Goods Sold

If the error understates **beginning** inventory, cost of goods sold will be understated. If the error understates **ending** inventory, cost of goods sold will be overstated. Illustration 6-18 shows the effects of inventory errors on the current year's income statement.

Illustration 6-18
Effects of inventory errors on current year's income statement

When Inventory Error:	Cost of Goods Sold Is:	Net Income Is:
Understates beginning inventory	Understated	Overstated
Overstates beginning inventory	Overstated	Understated
Understates ending inventory	Overstated	Understated
Overstates ending inventory	Understated	Overstated

> **Ethics Note**
>
> Inventory fraud increases during recessions. Such fraud includes pricing inventory at amounts in excess of its actual value, or claiming to have inventory when no inventory exists. Inventory fraud usually overstates ending inventory, thereby understating cost of goods sold and creating higher income.

So far, the effects of inventory errors are fairly straightforward. Now, though, comes the (at first) surprising part: An error in the ending inventory of the current period will have a **reverse effect on net income of the next accounting period**. Illustration 6-19 shows this effect. As you study the illustration, you will see that the reverse effect comes from the fact that understating ending inventory in 2014 results in understating beginning inventory in 2015 and overstating net income in 2015.

Over the two years, though, total net income is correct because the errors **offset each other**. Notice that total income using incorrect data is $35,000 ($22,000 + $13,000), which is the same as the total income of

SAMPLE COMPANY
Condensed Income Statements

	2014			2015		
	Incorrect		**Correct**	**Incorrect**		**Correct**
Sales revenue		$80,000	$80,000		$90,000	$90,000
Beginning inventory	$20,000		$20,000	$12,000	$15,000	
Cost of goods purchased	40,000		40,000	68,000	68,000	
Cost of goods available for sale	60,000		60,000	80,000	83,000	
Ending inventory	12,000		15,000	23,000	23,000	
Cost of goods sold		48,000	45,000	57,000		60,000
Gross profit		32,000	35,000	33,000		30,000
Operating expenses		10,000	10,000	20,000		20,000
Net income		$22,000	$25,000	$13,000		$10,000

$(3,000)
Net income
understated

$3,000
Net income
overstated

The errors cancel. Thus, the combined total
income for the 2-year period is correct.

Illustration 6-19
Effects of inventory errors on
two years' income statements

$35,000 ($25,000 + $10,000) using correct data. Also note in this example that an error in the beginning inventory does not result in a corresponding error in the ending inventory for that period. The correctness of the ending inventory depends entirely on the accuracy of taking and costing the inventory at the balance sheet date under the periodic inventory system.

Balance Sheet Effects

Companies can determine the effect of ending inventory errors on the balance sheet by using the basic accounting equation: Assets = Liabilities + Stockholders' Equity. Errors in the ending inventory have the effects shown in Illustration 6-20.

Illustration 6-20
Effects of ending inventory
errors on balance sheet

Ending Inventory Error	Assets	Liabilities	Stockholders' Equity
Overstated	Overstated	No effect	Overstated
Understated	Understated	No effect	Understated

The effect of an error in ending inventory on the subsequent period was shown in Illustration 6-19. Recall that if the error is not corrected, the combined total net income for the two periods would be correct. Thus, total stockholders' equity reported on the balance sheet at the end of 2015 will also be correct.

> ## DO IT!

LCM Basis; Inventory Errors

(a) Tracy Company sells three different types of home heating stoves (gas, wood, and pellet). The cost and market value of its inventory of stoves are as follows.

	Cost	Market
Gas	$ 84,000	$ 79,000
Wood	250,000	280,000
Pellet	112,000	101,000

Determine the value of the company's inventory under the lower-of-cost-or-market approach.

Solution

> The lowest value for each inventory type is gas $79,000, wood $250,000, and pellet $101,000. The total inventory value is the sum of these amounts, $430,000.

(b) Visual Company overstated its 2014 ending inventory by $22,000. Determine the impact this error has on ending inventory, cost of goods sold, and stockholders' equity in 2014 and 2015.

Solution

	2014	2015
Ending inventory	$22,000 overstated	No effect
Cost of goods sold	$22,000 understated	$22,000 overstated
Stockholders' equity	$22,000 overstated	No effect

Related exercise material: BE6-7, BE6-8, E6-9, E6-10, E6-11, E6-12, **and** DO IT! 6-3.

✔ **The Navigator**

Statement Presentation and Analysis

Presentation

As indicated in Chapter 5, inventory is classified in the balance sheet as a current asset immediately below receivables. In a multiple-step income statement, cost of goods sold is subtracted from sales. There also should be disclosure of (1) the major inventory classifications, (2) the basis of accounting (cost, or lower-of-cost-or-market), and (3) the cost method (FIFO, LIFO, or average-cost).

Wal-Mart Stores, Inc., for example, in its January 31, 2011, balance sheet reported inventories of $36,318 million under current assets. The accompanying notes to the financial statements, as shown in Illustration 6-21, disclosed the following information.

Illustration 6-21
Inventory disclosures by Wal-Mart

 Real World

WAL-MART STORES, INC.
Notes to the Financial Statements

Note 1. Summary of Significant Accounting Policies

Inventories

The Company values inventories at the lower of cost or market as determined primarily by the retail method of accounting, using the last-in, first-out ("LIFO") method for substantially all of the WalMart U.S. segment's merchandise inventories. The retail method of accounting results in inventory being valued at the lower of cost or market since permanent markdowns are currently taken as a reduction of the retail value of inventory. The Sam's Club segment's merchandise is valued based on the weighted-average cost using the LIFO method. Inventories for the Walmart International operations are primarily valued by the retail method of accounting and are stated using the first-in, first-out ("FIFO") method. At January 31, 2011 and 2010, our inventories valued at LIFO approximate those inventories as if they were valued at FIFO.

As indicated in this note, Wal-Mart values its inventories at the lower-of-cost-or-market using LIFO and FIFO.

Analysis

The amount of inventory carried by a company has significant economic consequences. And inventory management is a double-edged sword that requires constant attention. On the one hand, management wants to have a great variety and quantity on hand so that customers have a wide selection and items are always in stock. But, such a policy may incur high carrying costs (e.g., investment, storage, insurance, obsolescence, and damage). On the other hand, low inventory levels lead to stock-outs and lost sales. Common ratios used to manage and evaluate inventory levels are inventory turnover and a related measure, days in inventory.

Inventory turnover measures the number of times on average the inventory is sold during the period. Its purpose is to measure the liquidity of the inventory. The inventory turnover is computed by dividing cost of goods sold by the average inventory during the period. Unless seasonal factors are significant, average inventory can be computed from the beginning and ending inventory balances. For example, Wal-Mart reported in its 2011 annual report a beginning inventory of $32,713 million, an ending inventory of $36,318 million, and cost of goods sold for the year ended January 31, 2011, of $315,287 million. The inventory turnover formula and computation for Wal-Mart are shown below.

Cost of Goods Sold	÷	Average Inventory	=	Inventory Turnover
$315,287	÷	$\dfrac{\$36,318 + \$32,713}{2}$	=	9.1 times

Illustration 6-22
Inventory turnover formula and computation for Wal-Mart

A variant of the inventory turnover is **days in inventory**. This measures the average number of days inventory is held. It is calculated as 365 divided by the inventory turnover. For example, Wal-Mart's inventory turnover of 9.1 times divided into 365 is 40.1 days. This is the approximate time that it takes a company to sell the inventory once it arrives at the store.

There are typical levels of inventory in every industry. Companies that are able to keep their inventory at lower levels and higher turnovers and still satisfy customer needs are the most successful.

ACCOUNTING ACROSS THE ORGANIZATION

Too Many TVs or Too Few?

Financial analysts closely monitored the inventory management practices of companies during the recent recession. For example, some analysts following Sony expressed concern because the company built up its inventory of televisions in an attempt to sell 25 million liquid crystal display (LCD) TVs—a 60% increase over the prior year. A year earlier, Sony had cut its inventory levels so that its quarterly days in inventory was down to 38 days, compared to 61 days for the same quarter a year before that. But now, as a result of its inventory build-up, days in inventory rose to 59 days. While management was saying that it didn't think that Sony's inventory levels were now too high, analysts were concerned that the company would have to engage in very heavy discounting in order to sell off its inventory. Analysts noted that the losses from discounting can be "punishing."

Source: Daisuke Wakabayashi, "Sony Pledges to Corral Inventory," *Wall Street Journal Online* (November 2, 2010).

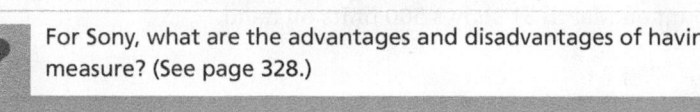

? For Sony, what are the advantages and disadvantages of having a low days in inventory measure? (See page 328.)

© Dmitry Kutlayev/iStockphoto

> DO IT!

Inventory Turnover

Early in 2015, Westmoreland Company switched to a just-in-time inventory system. Its sales revenue, cost of goods sold, and inventory amounts for 2014 and 2015 are shown below.

	2014	2015
Sales revenue	$2,000,000	$1,800,000
Cost of goods sold	1,000,000	910,000
Beginning inventory	290,000	210,000
Ending inventory	210,000	50,000

Determine the inventory turnover and days in inventory for 2014 and 2015. Discuss the changes in the amount of inventory, the inventory turnover and days in inventory, and the amount of sales across the two years.

Solution

Action Plan

✔ To find the inventory turnover, divide cost of goods sold by average inventory.

✔ To determine days in inventory, divide 365 days by the inventory turnover.

✔ Just-in-time inventory reduces the amount of inventory on hand, which reduces carrying costs. Reducing inventory levels by too much has potential negative implications for sales.

	2014	2015
Inventory turnover	$\dfrac{\$1,000,000}{(\$290,000 + \$210,000)/2} = 4$	$\dfrac{\$910,000}{(\$210,000 + \$50,000)/2} = 7$
Days in inventory	$365 \div 4 = 91.3$ days	$365 \div 7 = 52.1$ days

The company experienced a very significant decline in its ending inventory as a result of the just-in-time inventory. This decline improved its inventory turnover and its days in inventory. However, its sales declined by 10%. It is possible that this decline was caused by the dramatic reduction in the amount of inventory that was on hand, which increased the likelihood of "stock-outs." To determine the optimal inventory level, management must weigh the benefits of reduced inventory against the potential lost sales caused by stock-outs.

Related exercise material: BE6-9, E6-13, E6-14, **and** DO IT! 6-4.

 The Navigator

> Comprehensive DO IT! 1

Gerald D. Englehart Company has the following inventory, purchases, and sales data for the month of March.

Inventory:	March 1	200 units @ $4.00	$ 800
Purchases:			
	March 10	500 units @ $4.50	2,250
	March 20	400 units @ $4.75	1,900
	March 30	300 units @ $5.00	1,500
Sales:			
	March 15	500 units	
	March 25	400 units	

The physical inventory count on March 31 shows 500 units on hand.

Instructions

Under a **periodic inventory system**, determine the cost of inventory on hand at March 31 and the cost of goods sold for March under (a) FIFO, (b) LIFO, and (c) average-cost.

Solution to Comprehensive DO IT! 1

Action Plan

✔ Compute the total goods available for sale, in both units and dollars.

✔ Compute the cost of ending inventory under the periodic FIFO method by allocating to the units on hand the **latest costs**.

✔ Compute the cost of ending inventory under the periodic LIFO method by allocating to the units on hand the **earliest costs**.

✔ Compute the cost of ending inventory under the periodic average-cost method by allocating to the units on hand a **weighted-average cost**.

The cost of goods available for sale is $6,450, as follows.

Inventory:		200 units @ $4.00	$ 800
Purchases:			
	March 10	500 units @ $4.50	2,250
	March 20	400 units @ $4.75	1,900
	March 30	300 units @ $5.00	1,500
Total:		1,400	$6,450

Under a **periodic inventory system**, the cost of goods sold under each cost flow method is as follows.

(a)   **FIFO Method**

Ending inventory:

Date	Units	Unit Cost	Total Cost	
March 30	300	$5.00	$1,500	
March 20	200	4.75	950	$2,450

Cost of goods sold: $6,450 − $2,450 = $4,000

(b)   **LIFO Method**

Ending inventory:

Date	Units	Unit Cost	Total Cost	
March 1	200	$4.00	$ 800	
March 10	300	4.50	1,350	$2,150

Cost of goods sold: $6,450 − $2,150 = $4,300

(c)   **Average-Cost Method**

Average unit cost: $6,450 ÷ 1,400 = $4.607
Ending inventory: 500 × $4.607 = $2,303.50

Cost of goods sold: $6,450 − $2,303.50 = $4,146.50

 The Navigator

SUMMARY OF LEARNING OBJECTIVES

 The Navigator

1 Determine how to classify inventory and inventory quantities. Merchandisers need only one inventory classification, merchandise inventory, to describe the different items that make up total inventory. Manufacturers, on the other hand, usually classify inventory into three categories: finished goods, work in process, and raw materials. To determine inventory quantities, manufacturers (1) take a physical inventory of goods on hand and (2) determine the ownership of goods in transit or on consignment.

2 Explain the accounting for inventories and apply the inventory cost flow methods. The primary basis of accounting for inventories is cost. Cost of goods available for sale includes (a) cost of beginning inventory and (b) cost of goods purchased. The inventory cost flow methods are specific identification and three assumed cost flow methods—FIFO, LIFO, and average-cost.

3 Explain the financial effects of the inventory cost flow assumptions. Companies may allocate the cost of goods available for sale to cost of goods sold and ending inventory by specific identification or by a method based on an assumed cost flow. When prices are rising, the first-in, first-out (FIFO) method results in lower cost of goods sold and higher net income than the other methods. The reverse is true when prices are falling. In the balance sheet, FIFO results in an ending inventory that is closest to current value. Inventory under LIFO is the farthest from current value. LIFO results in the lowest income taxes.

4 Explain the lower-of-cost-or-market basis of accounting for inventories. Companies use the lower-of-cost-or-market (LCM) basis when the current replacement cost (market) is less than cost. Under LCM, companies recognize the loss in the period in which the price decline occurs.

5 Indicate the effects of inventory errors on the financial statements. In the income statement of the current year: (a) An error in beginning inventory will have a reverse effect on net income. (b) An error in ending inventory will have a similar effect on net income. In the following period, its effect on net income for that period is reversed, and total net income for the two years will be correct.

In the balance sheet: Ending inventory errors will have the same effect on total assets and total stockholders' equity and no effect on liabilities.

6 Discuss the presentation and analysis of inventory. Inventory is classified in the balance sheet as a current asset immediately below receivables. There also should be disclosure of (1) the major inventory classifications, (2) the basis of accounting, and (3) the cost method.

The inventory turnover is cost of goods sold divided by average inventory. To convert it to average days in inventory, divide 365 days by the inventory turnover.

GLOSSARY

Average-cost method Inventory costing method that uses the weighted-average unit cost to allocate to ending inventory and cost of goods sold the cost of goods available for sale. (p. 289).

Consigned goods Goods held for sale by one party although ownership of the goods is retained by another party. (p. 283).

Consistency concept Dictates that a company use the same accounting principles and methods from year to year. (p. 292).

Current replacement cost The current cost to replace an inventory item. (p. 293).

Days in inventory Measure of the average number of days inventory is held; calculated as 365 divided by inventory turnover. (p. 297).

Finished goods inventory Manufactured items that are completed and ready for sale. (p. 280).

First-in, first-out (FIFO) method Inventory costing method that assumes that the costs of the earliest goods purchased are the first to be recognized as cost of goods sold. (p. 286).

FOB (free on board) destination Freight terms indicating that ownership of the goods remains with the seller until the goods reach the buyer. (p. 282).

FOB (free on board) shipping point Freight terms indicating that ownership of the goods passes to the buyer when the public carrier accepts the goods from the seller. (p. 282).

Inventory turnover A ratio that measures the number of times on average the inventory sold during the period; computed by dividing cost of goods sold by the average inventory during the period. (p. 297).

Just-in-time (JIT) inventory Inventory system in which companies manufacture or purchase goods just in time for use. (p. 280).

Last-in, first-out (LIFO) method Inventory costing method that assumes the costs of the latest units purchased are the first to be allocated to cost of goods sold. (p. 288).

Lower-of-cost-or-market (LCM) A basis whereby inventory is stated at the lower of either its cost or its market value as determined by current replacement cost. (p. 293).

Raw materials Basic goods that will be used in production but have not yet been placed into production. (p. 280).

Specific identification method An actual physical flow costing method in which items still in inventory are specifically costed to arrive at the total cost of the ending inventory. (p. 285).

Weighted-average unit cost Average cost that is weighted by the number of units purchased at each unit cost. (p. 289).

Work in process That portion of manufactured inventory that has been placed into the production process but is not yet complete. (p. 280).

APPENDIX 6A   Inventory Cost Flow Methods in Perpetual Inventory Systems

What inventory cost flow methods do companies employ if they use a perpetual inventory system? Simple—they can use any of the inventory cost flow methods described in the chapter. To illustrate the application of the three assumed cost flow methods (FIFO, LIFO, and average-cost), we will use the data shown in Illustration 6A-1 and in this chapter for Houston Electronics' Astro condensers.

LEARNING OBJECTIVE   7

Apply the inventory cost flow methods to perpetual inventory records.

Illustration 6A-1
Inventoriable units and costs

HOUSTON ELECTRONICS
Astro Condensers

Date	Explanation	Units	Unit Cost	Total Cost	Balance in Units
1/1	Beginning inventory	100	$10	$ 1,000	100
4/15	Purchases	200	11	2,200	300
8/24	Purchases	300	12	3,600	600
9/10	Sale	550			50
11/27	Purchases	400	13	5,200	450
				$12,000	

First-In, First-Out (FIFO)

Under perpetual FIFO, the company charges to cost of goods sold the cost of the earliest goods on hand **prior to each sale**. Therefore, the cost of goods sold on September 10 consists of the units on hand January 1 and the units purchased April 15 and August 24. Illustration 6A-2 shows the inventory under a FIFO method perpetual system.

Illustration 6A-2
Perpetual system—FIFO

Date	Purchases		Cost of Goods Sold	Balance (in units and cost)	
January 1				(100 @ $10)	$ 1,000
April 15	(200 @ $11)	$2,200		(100 @ $10) ⎱ (200 @ $11) ⎰	$ 3,200
August 24	(300 @ $12)	$3,600		(100 @ $10) ⎱ (200 @ $11) ⎱ (300 @ $12) ⎰	$ 6,800
September 10			(100 @ $10) (200 @ $11) (250 @ $12)	(50 @ $12)	$ 600
			$6,200		**Cost of goods sold**
November 27	(400 @ $13)	$5,200		(50 @ $12) ⎱ (400 @ $13) ⎰ $5,800	**Ending inventory**

The ending inventory in this situation is $5,800, and the cost of goods sold is $6,200 [(100 @ $10) + (200 @ $11) + (250 @ $12)].

Compare Illustrations 6-6 (page 287) and 6A-2. You can see that the results under FIFO in a perpetual system are the **same as in a periodic system**. In both cases, the ending inventory is $5,800 and cost of goods sold is $6,200. Regardless of the system, the first costs in are the costs assigned to cost of goods sold.

Last-In, First-Out (LIFO)

Under the LIFO method using a perpetual system, the company charges to cost of goods sold the cost of the most recent purchase prior to sale. Therefore, the cost of the goods sold on September 10 consists of all the units from the August 24 and April 15 purchases plus 50 of the units in beginning inventory. Illustration 6A-3 shows the computation of the ending inventory under the LIFO method.

Illustration 6A-3
Perpetual system—LIFO

Date	Purchases		Cost of Goods Sold	Balance (in units and cost)	
January 1				(100 @ $10)	$ 1,000
April 15	(200 @ $11)	$2,200		(100 @ $10) (200 @ $11) }	$ 3,200
August 24	(300 @ $12)	$3,600		(100 @ $10) (200 @ $11) (300 @ $12) }	$ 6,800
September 10			(300 @ $12) (200 @ $11) (50 @ $10)	(50 @ $10)	$ 500
Cost of goods sold			**$6,300**		
November 27	(400 @ $13)	$5,200		(50 @ $10) (400 @ $13) }	**$5,700**
Ending inventory					

The use of LIFO in a perpetual system will usually produce cost allocations that differ from those using LIFO in a periodic system. In a perpetual system, the company allocates the latest units purchased **prior to each sale** to cost of goods sold. In contrast, in a periodic system, the latest units purchased **during the period** are allocated to cost of goods sold. Thus, when a purchase is made after the last sale, the LIFO periodic system will apply this purchase to the previous sale. Compare Illustrations 6-8 (page 288) and 6A-3. Illustration 6-8 shows that the 400 units at $13 purchased on November 27 applied to the sale of 550 units on September 10. Under the LIFO perpetual system in Illustration 6A-3, the 400 units at $13 purchased on November 27 are all applied to the ending inventory.

The ending inventory in this LIFO perpetual illustration is $5,700, and cost of goods sold is $6,300, as compared to the LIFO periodic Illustration 6-8 (on page 288) where the ending inventory is $5,000 and cost of goods sold is $7,000.

Average-Cost

The average-cost method in a perpetual inventory system is called the **moving-average method**. Under this method, the company computes a new average **after each purchase**, by dividing the cost of goods available for sale by the units on hand. The average cost is then applied to (1) the units sold, to determine the cost of goods sold, and (2) the remaining units on hand, to determine the ending inventory amount. Illustration 6A-4 shows the application of the moving-average cost method by Houston Electronics.

Illustration 6A-4
Perpetual system—
moving-average method

Date	Purchases		Cost of Goods Sold	Balance (in units and cost)	
January 1				(100 @ $10)	$ 1,000
April 15	(200 @ $11)	$2,200		(300 @ $10.667)	$ 3,200
August 24	(300 @ $12)	$3,600		(600 @ $11.333)	$ 6,800
September 10			(550 @ $11.333)	(50 @ $11.333)	$ 567
Cost of goods sold			**$6,233**		
November 27	(400 @ $13)	$5,200		(450 @ $12.816)	**$5,767**
Ending inventory					

As indicated, Houston Electronics computes **a new average each time it makes a purchase**. On April 15, after it buys 200 units for $2,200, a total of 300 units costing $3,200 ($1,000 + $2,200) are on hand. The average unit cost is $10.667 ($3,200 ÷ 300). On August 24, after Houston Electronics buys 300 units for $3,600, a total of 600 units costing $6,800 ($1,000 + $2,200 + $3,600) are on hand, at an average cost per unit of $11.333 ($6,800 ÷ 600). Houston Electronics uses this unit cost of $11.333 in costing sales until it makes another purchase, when the company computes a new unit cost. Accordingly, the unit cost of the 550 units sold on September 10 is $11.333, and the total cost of goods sold is $6,233. On November 27, following the purchase of 400 units for $5,200, there are 450 units on hand costing $5,767 ($567 + $5,200) with a new average cost of $12.816 ($5,767 ÷ 450).

Compare this moving-average cost under the perpetual inventory system to Illustration 6-11 (on page 289) showing the average-cost method under a periodic inventory system.

> Comprehensive DO IT! 2

Comprehensive DO IT! 1 on page 298 showed cost of goods sold computations under a periodic inventory system. Now let's assume that Gerald D. Englehart Company uses a perpetual inventory system. The company has the same inventory, purchases, and sales data for the month of March as shown earlier:

Inventory:	March 1	200 units @ $4.00	$ 800
Purchases:			
	March 10	500 units @ $4.50	2,250
	March 20	400 units @ $4.75	1,900
	March 30	300 units @ $5.00	1,500
Sales:			
	March 15	500 units	
	March 25	400 units	

The physical inventory count on March 31 shows 500 units on hand.

Action Plan

✔ Compute the cost of goods sold under the perpetual FIFO method by allocating to the goods sold the **earliest** cost of goods purchased.

✔ Compute the cost of goods sold under the perpetual LIFO method by allocating to the goods sold the **latest** cost of goods purchased.

✔ Compute the cost of goods sold under the perpetual average-cost method by allocating to the goods sold a **moving-average** cost.

Instructions

Under a **perpetual inventory system**, determine the cost of inventory on hand at March 31 and the cost of goods sold for March under (a) FIFO, (b) LIFO, and (c) moving-average cost.

Solution to Comprehensive DO IT! 2

The cost of goods available for sale is $6,450, as follows.

Inventory:	200 units @ $4.00	$ 800
Purchases:		
March 10	500 units @ $4.50	2,250
March 20	400 units @ $4.75	1,900
March 30	300 units @ $5.00	1,500
Total:	1,400	$6,450

Under a **perpetual inventory system**, the cost of goods sold under each cost flow method is as follows.

(a)   **FIFO Method**

Date	Purchases	Cost of Goods Sold	Balance
March 1			(200 @ $4.00) $ 800
March 10	(500 @ $4.50) $2,250		(200 @ $4.00)⎱ $3,050 (500 @ $4.50)⎰
March 15		(200 @ $4.00) (300 @ $4.50) ——————— $2,150	(200 @ $4.50) $ 900
March 20	(400 @ $4.75) $1,900		(200 @ $4.50)⎱ $2,800 (400 @ $4.75)⎰
March 25		(200 @ $4.50) (200 @ $4.75) ——————— $1,850	(200 @ $4.75) $ 950
March 30	(300 @ $5.00) $1,500		(200 @ $4.75)⎱ $2,450 (300 @ $5.00)⎰
	Ending inventory $2,450	Cost of goods sold: $2,150 + $1,850 = $4,000	

(b)   **LIFO Method**

Date	Purchases	Cost of Goods Sold	Balance
March 1			(200 @ $4.00) $ 800
March 10	(500 @ $4.50) $2,250		(200 @ $4.00)⎱ $3,050 (500 @ $4.50)⎰
March 15		(500 @ $4.50) $2,250	(200 @ $4.00) $ 800
March 20	(400 @ $4.75) $1,900		(200 @ $4.00)⎱ $2,700 (400 @ $4.75)⎰
March 25		(400 @ $4.75) $1,900	(200 @ $4.00) $ 800
March 30	(300 @ $5.00) $1,500		(200 @ $4.00)⎱ $2,300 (300 @ $5.00)⎰
	Ending inventory $2,300	Cost of goods sold: $2,250 + $1,900 = $4,150	

(c)   **Moving-Average Cost Method**

Date	Purchases	Cost of Goods Sold	Balance
March 1			(200 @ $ 4.00) $ 800
March 10	(500 @ $4.50) $2,250		(700 @ $4.357) $3,050
March 15		(500 @ $4.357) $2,179	(200 @ $4.357) $ 871
March 20	(400 @ $4.75) $1,900		(600 @ $4.618) $2,771
March 25		(400 @ $4.618) $1,847	(200 @ $4.618) $ 924
March 30	(300 @ $5.00) $1,500		(500 @ $4.848) $2,424
	Ending inventory $2,424	Cost of goods sold: $2,179 + $1,847 = $4,026	

 ✔ The Navigator

SUMMARY OF LEARNING OBJECTIVE FOR APPENDIX 6A   ✔ The Navigator

7 Apply the inventory cost flow methods to perpetual inventory records. Under FIFO and a perpetual inventory system, companies charge to cost of goods sold the cost of the earliest goods on hand prior to each sale. Under LIFO and a perpetual system, companies charge to cost of goods sold the cost of the most recent purchase prior to sale. Under the moving-average (average-cost) method and a perpetual system, companies compute a new average cost after each purchase.

APPENDIX 6B   Estimating Inventories

In the chapter, we assumed that a company would be able to physically count its inventory. What if it cannot? What if the inventory were destroyed by fire or flood, for example? In that case, the company would use an estimate.

Two circumstances explain why companies sometimes estimate inventories. First, a casualty such as fire, flood, or earthquake may make it impossible to take a physical inventory. Second, managers may want monthly or quarterly financial statements, but a physical inventory is taken only annually. The need for estimating inventories occurs primarily with a periodic inventory system because of the absence of perpetual inventory records.

There are two widely used methods of estimating inventories: (1) the gross profit method, and (2) the retail inventory method.

> **LEARNING OBJECTIVE 8**
> Describe the two methods of estimating inventories.

Gross Profit Method

The **gross profit method** estimates the cost of ending inventory by applying a gross profit rate to net sales. This method is relatively simple but effective. Accountants, auditors, and managers frequently use the gross profit method to test the reasonableness of the ending inventory amount. It will detect large errors.

To use this method, a company needs to know its net sales, cost of goods available for sale, and gross profit rate. The company then can estimate its gross profit for the period. Illustration 6B-1 shows the formulas for using the gross profit method.

Step 1: Net Sales − Estimated Gross Profit = Estimated Cost of Goods Sold

Step 2: Cost of Goods Available for Sale − Estimated Cost of Goods Sold = Estimated Cost of Ending Inventory

Illustration 6B-1
Gross profit method formulas

To illustrate, assume that Kishwaukee Company wishes to prepare an income statement for the month of January. Its records show net sales of $200,000, beginning inventory $40,000, and cost of goods purchased $120,000. In the preceding year, the company realized a 30% gross profit rate. It expects to earn the same rate this year. Given these facts and assumptions, Kishwaukee can compute the estimated cost of the ending inventory at January 31 under the gross profit method as follows.

Step 1:

Net sales	$200,000
Less: Estimated gross profit (30% × $200,000)	60,000
Estimated cost of goods sold	**$140,000**

Step 2:

Beginning inventory	$40,000
Cost of goods purchased	120,000
Cost of goods available for sale	160,000
Less: Estimated cost of goods sold	140,000
Estimated cost of ending inventory	**$20,000**

Illustration 6B-2
Example of gross profit method

The gross profit method is based on the assumption that the gross profit rate will remain constant. But, it may not remain constant, due to a change in merchandising policies or in market conditions. In such cases, the company should adjust the rate to reflect current operating conditions. In some cases, companies can obtain a more accurate estimate by applying this method on a department or product-line basis.

Note that companies should not use the gross profit method to prepare financial statements at the end of the year. These statements should be based on a physical inventory count.

Retail Inventory Method

A retail store such as Home Depot, Ace Hardware, or Walmart has thousands of different types of merchandise at low unit costs. In such cases, it is difficult and time-consuming to apply unit costs to inventory quantities. An alternative is to use the **retail inventory method** to estimate the cost of inventory. Most retail companies can establish a relationship between cost and sales price. The company then applies the cost-to-retail percentage to the ending inventory at retail prices to determine inventory at cost.

Under the retail inventory method, a company's records must show both the cost and retail value of the goods available for sale. Illustration 6B-3 presents the formulas for using the retail inventory method.

Illustration 6B-3
Retail inventory method formulas

Step 1:	Goods Available for Sale at Retail	−	Net Sales	=	Ending Inventory at Retail
Step 2:	Goods Available for Sale at Cost	÷	Goods Available for Sale at Retail	=	Cost-to-Retail Ratio
Step 3:	Ending Inventory at Retail	×	Cost-to-Retail Ratio	=	Estimated Cost of Ending Inventory

We can demonstrate the logic of the retail method by using unit-cost data. Assume that Ortiz Inc. has marked 10 units purchased at $7 to sell for $10 per unit. Thus, the cost-to-retail ratio is 70% ($70 ÷ $100). If four units remain unsold, their retail value is $40 (4 × $10), and their cost is $28 ($40 × 70%). This amount agrees with the total cost of goods on hand on a per unit basis (4 × $7).

Illustration 6B-4 shows application of the retail method for Valley West. Note that it is not necessary to take a physical inventory to determine the estimated cost of goods on hand at any given time.

Illustration 6B-4
Application of retail inventory method

	At Cost	At Retail
Beginning inventory	$14,000	$ 21,500
Goods purchased	61,000	78,500
Goods available for sale	$75,000	100,000
Less: Net sales		70,000
Step (1) Ending inventory at retail =		$ 30,000

Step (2) Cost-to-retail ratio = $75,000 ÷ $100,000 = 75%
Step (3) Estimated cost of ending inventory = $30,000 × 75% = $22,500

Helpful Hint
In determining inventory at retail, companies use selling prices of the units.

The retail inventory method also facilitates taking a physical inventory at the end of the year. Valley West can value the goods on hand at the prices marked on the merchandise, and then apply the cost-to-retail ratio to the goods on hand at retail to determine the ending inventory at cost.

The major disadvantage of the retail method is that it is an averaging technique. Thus, it may produce an incorrect inventory valuation if the mix of the ending inventory is not representative of the mix in the goods available for sale. Assume, for example, that the cost-to-retail ratio of 75% for Valley West consists of equal proportions of inventory items that have cost-to-retail ratios of 70%, 75%, and 80%. If the ending inventory contains only items with a 70% ratio, an incorrect inventory cost will result. Companies can minimize this problem by applying the retail method on a department or product-line basis.

SUMMARY OF LEARNING OBJECTIVE FOR APPENDIX 6B

 The Navigator

8 Describe the two methods of estimating inventories. The two methods of estimating inventories are the gross profit method and the retail inventory method. Under the gross profit method, companies apply a gross profit rate to net sales to determine estimated cost of goods sold. They then subtract estimated cost of goods sold from cost of goods available for sale to determine the estimated cost of the ending inventory.

Under the retail inventory method, companies compute a cost-to-retail ratio by dividing the cost of goods available for sale by the retail value of the goods available for sale. They then apply this ratio to the ending inventory at retail to determine the estimated cost of the ending inventory.

GLOSSARY FOR APPENDIX 6B

Gross profit method A method for estimating the cost of the ending inventory by applying a gross profit rate to net sales and subtracting estimated cost of goods sold from cost of goods available for sale. (p. 305).

Retail inventory method A method for estimating the cost of the ending inventory by applying a cost-to-retail ratio to the ending inventory at retail. (p. 306).

WileyPLUS   Self-Test, Brief Exercises, Exercises, Problem Set A, and many more components are available for practice in *WileyPLUS*.

*Note: All asterisked Questions, Exercises, and Problems relate to material in the appendices to the chapter.

SELF-TEST QUESTIONS

Answers are on page 328.

(LO 1) **1.** Which of the following should **not** be included in the physical inventory of a company?
  (a) Goods held on consignment from another company.
  (b) Goods shipped on consignment to another company.
  (c) Goods in transit from another company shipped FOB shipping point.
  (d) None of the above.

(LO 1) **2.** As a result of a thorough physical inventory, Railway Company determined that it had inventory worth $180,000 at December 31, 2015. This count did not take into consideration the following facts: Rogers Consignment store currently has goods worth $35,000 on its sales floor that belong to Railway but are being sold on consignment by Rogers. The selling price of these goods is $50,000. Railway purchased $13,000 of goods that were shipped on December 27, FOB destination, that will be received by Railway on January 3. Determine the correct amount of inventory that Railway should report.
  (a) $230,000.   **(c)** $228,000.
  (b) $215,000.   **(d)** $193,000.

(LO 2) **3.** Cost of goods available for sale consists of two elements: beginning inventory and:
  (a) ending inventory.
  (b) cost of goods purchased.
  (c) cost of goods sold.
  (d) All of the above.

(LO 2) **4.** Poppins Company has the following:

	Units	Unit Cost
Inventory, Jan. 1	8,000	$11
Purchase, June 19	13,000	12
Purchase, Nov. 8	5,000	13

If Poppins has 9,000 units on hand at December 31, the cost of the ending inventory under FIFO is:
(a) $99,000.   (c) $113,000.
(b) $108,000.   (d) $117,000.

(LO 2) **5.** Using the data in Question 4 above, the cost of the ending inventory under LIFO is:
(a) $113,000.   (c) $99,000.
(b) $108,000.   (d) $100,000.

(LO 2) **6.** Hansel Electronics has the following:

	Units	Unit Cost
Inventory, Jan. 1	5,000	$ 8
Purchase, April 2	15,000	$10
Purchase, Aug. 28	20,000	$12

If Hansel has 7,000 units on hand at December 31, the cost of ending inventory under the average-cost method is:
(a) $84,000.   (c) $56,000.
(b) $70,000.   (d) $75,250.

(LO 3) **7.** In periods of rising prices, LIFO will produce:
(a) higher net income than FIFO.
(b) the same net income as FIFO.
(c) lower net income than FIFO.
(d) higher net income than average-cost.

(LO 3) **8.** Factors that affect the selection of an inventory costing method do **not** include:
(a) tax effects.
(b) balance sheet effects.
(c) income statement effects.
(d) perpetual vs. periodic inventory system.

(LO 4) **9.** Norton Company purchased 1,000 widgets and has 200 widgets in its ending inventory at a cost of $91 each and a current replacement cost of $80 each. The ending inventory under lower-of-cost-or-market is:
(a) $91,000.   (c) $18,200.
(b) $80,000.   (d) $16,000.

(LO 5) **10.** Falk Company's ending inventory is understated $4,000. The effects of this error on the current year's cost of goods sold and net income, respectively, are:

(a) understated, overstated.
(b) overstated, understated.
(c) overstated, overstated.
(d) understated, understated.

11. Pauline Company overstated its inventory by $15,000 (LO 4) at December 31, 2014. It did not correct the error in 2014 or 2015. As a result, Pauline's stockholders' equity was:
(a) overstated at December 31, 2014, and understated at December 31, 2015.
(b) overstated at December 31, 2014, and properly stated at December 31, 2015.
(c) understated at December 31, 2014, and understated at December 31, 2015.
(d) overstated at December 31, 2014, and overstated at December 31, 2015.

12. Santana Company had beginning inventory of (LO 5) $80,000, ending inventory of $110,000, cost of goods sold of $285,000, and sales of $475,000. Santana's days in inventory is:
(a) 73 days.   (c) 102.5 days.
(b) 121.7 days.   (d) 84.5 days.

13. Which of these would cause the inventory turnover to (LO 6) increase the most?
(a) Increasing the amount of inventory on hand.
(b) Keeping the amount of inventory on hand constant but increasing sales.
(c) Keeping the amount of inventory on hand constant but decreasing sales.
(d) Decreasing the amount of inventory on hand and increasing sales.

*****14.** In a perpetual inventory system: (LO 7)
(a) LIFO cost of goods sold will be the same as in a periodic inventory system.
(b) average costs are a simple average of unit costs incurred.
(c) a new average is computed under the average-cost method after each sale.
(d) FIFO cost of goods sold will be the same as in a periodic inventory system.

*****15.** King Company has sales of $150,000 and cost of goods (LO 8) available for sale of $135,000. If the gross profit rate is 30%, the estimated cost of the ending inventory under the gross profit method is:
(a) $15,000.   (c) $45,000.
(b) $30,000.   (d) $75,000.

Go to the book's companion website, www.wiley.com/college/weygandt, for additional Self-Test Questions.

QUESTIONS

1. "The key to successful business operations is effective inventory management." Do you agree? Explain.
2. An item must possess two characteristics to be classified as inventory by a merchandiser. What are these two characteristics?

3. Your friend Theo Dolan has been hired to help take the physical inventory in Silker Hardware Store. Explain to Theo Dolan what this job will entail.
4. (a) Rochelle Company ships merchandise to Jay Company on December 30. The merchandise

reaches the buyer on January 6. Indicate the terms of sale that will result in the goods being included in (1) Rochelle's December 31 inventory, and (2) Jay's December 31 inventory.

(b) Under what circumstances should Rochelle Company include consigned goods in its inventory?

5. Katz Hat Shop received a shipment of hats for which it paid the wholesaler $2,970. The price of the hats was $3,000, but Katz was given a $30 cash discount and required to pay freight charges of $50. In addition, Katz paid $130 to cover the travel expenses of an employee who negotiated the purchase of the hats. What amount will Katz record for inventory? Why?

6. Explain the difference between the terms FOB shipping point and FOB destination.

7. Kyle Ebert believes that the allocation of inventoriable costs should be based on the actual physical flow of the goods. Explain to Kyle why this may be both impractical and inappropriate.

8. What is a major advantage and a major disadvantage of the specific identification method of inventory costing?

9. "The selection of an inventory cost flow method is a decision made by accountants." Do you agree? Explain. Once a method has been selected, what accounting requirement applies?

10. Which assumed inventory cost flow method:
(a) usually parallels the actual physical flow of merchandise?
(b) assumes that goods available for sale during an accounting period are identical?
(c) assumes that the latest units purchased are the first to be sold?

11. In a period of rising prices, the inventory reported in Gumby Company's balance sheet is close to the current cost of the inventory. Pokey Company's inventory is considerably below its current cost. Identify the inventory cost flow method being used by each company. Which company has probably been reporting the higher gross profit?

12. Davey Company has been using the FIFO cost flow method during a prolonged period of rising prices. During the same time period, Davey has been paying out all of its net income as dividends. What adverse effects may result from this policy?

13. Josh Kuchin is studying for the next accounting midterm examination. What should Josh know about (a) departing from the cost basis of accounting for inventories and (b) the meaning of "market" in the lower-of-cost-or-market method?

14. Taylor Music Center has 5 CD players on hand at the balance sheet date. Each costs $400. The current replacement cost is $380 per unit. Under the lower-of-cost-or-market basis of accounting for inventories, what value should be reported for the CD players on the balance sheet? Why?

15. Bonnie Stores has 20 toasters on hand at the balance sheet date. Each costs $27. The current replacement cost is $30 per unit. Under the lower-of-cost-or-market basis of accounting for inventories, what value should Bonnie report for the toasters on the balance sheet? Why?

16. Kuzu Company discovers in 2015 that its ending inventory at December 31, 2014, was $7,000 understated. What effect will this error have on (a) 2014 net income, (b) 2015 net income, and (c) the combined net income for the 2 years?

17. Ryder Company's balance sheet shows Inventory $162,800. What additional disclosures should be made?

18. Under what circumstances might inventory turnover be too high? That is, what possible negative consequences might occur?

19. What inventory cost flow does Apple use for its inventories? (Hint: You will need to examine the notes for Apple's financial statements.)

*20. "When perpetual inventory records are kept, the results under the FIFO and LIFO methods are the same as they would be in a periodic inventory system." Do you agree? Explain.

*21. How does the average-cost method of inventory costing differ between a perpetual inventory system and a periodic inventory system?

*22. When is it necessary to estimate inventories?

*23. Both the gross profit method and the retail inventory method are based on averages. For each method, indicate the average used, how it is determined, and how it is applied.

*24. Wiggins Company has net sales of $400,000 and cost of goods available for sale of $300,000. If the gross profit rate is 35%, what is the estimated cost of the ending inventory? Show computations.

*25. Emporia Shoe Shop had goods available for sale in 2015 with a retail price of $120,000. The cost of these goods was $84,000. If sales during the period were $80,000, what is the estimated cost of ending inventory using the retail inventory method?

BRIEF EXERCISES

BE6-1 Farley Company identifies the following items for possible inclusion in the taking of a physical inventory. Indicate whether each item should be included or excluded from the inventory taking.

(a) Goods shipped on consignment by Farley to another company.
(b) Goods in transit from a supplier shipped FOB destination.
(c) Goods sold but being held for customer pickup.
(d) Goods held on consignment from another company.

Identify items to be included in taking a physical inventory.

(LO 1)

BE6-2 Wilbur Company has the following items: (a) Freight-In, (b) Purchase Returns and Allowances, (c) Purchases, (d) Sales Discounts, and (e) Purchase Discounts. Identify which items are included in goods available for sale.

BE6-3 In its first month of operations, Bethke Company made three purchases of merchandise in the following sequence: (1) 300 units at $6, (2) 400 units at $7, and (3) 200 units at $8. Assuming there are 360 units on hand, compute the cost of the ending inventory under the (a) FIFO method and (b) LIFO method. Bethke uses a periodic inventory system.

BE6-4 Data for Bethke Company are presented in BE6-3. Compute the cost of the ending inventory under the average-cost method, assuming there are 360 units on hand. (Round average cost per unit to nearest cent.)

BE6-5 The management of Svetlana Corp. is considering the effects of inventory-costing methods on its financial statements and its income tax expense. Assuming that the price the company pays for inventory is increasing, which method will:

(a) Provide the highest net income?
(b) Provide the highest ending inventory?
(c) Result in the lowest income tax expense?
(d) Result in the most stable earnings over a number of years?

BE6-6 In its first month of operation, Franklin Company purchased 120 units of inventory for $6, then 200 units for $7, and finally 140 units for $8. At the end of the month, 180 units remained. Compute the amount of phantom profit that would result if the company used FIFO rather than LIFO. Explain why this amount is referred to as **phantom profit**. The company uses the periodic method.

BE6-7 Central Appliance Center accumulates the following cost and market data at December 31.

Inventory Categories	Cost Data	Market Data
Cameras	$12,000	$12,100
Camcorders	9,500	9,700
DVD players	14,000	12,800

Compute the lower-of-cost-or-market valuation for the company's total inventory.

BE6-8 Pettit Company reports net income of $90,000 in 2015. However, ending inventory was understated $7,000. What is the correct net income for 2015? What effect, if any, will this error have on total assets as reported in the balance sheet at December 31, 2015?

BE6-9 At December 31, 2015, the following information was available for A. Kamble Company: ending inventory $40,000, beginning inventory $60,000, cost of goods sold $270,000, and sales revenue $380,000. Calculate inventory turnover and days in inventory for A. Kamble Company.

*BE6-10 Gregory Department Store uses a perpetual inventory system. Data for product E2-D2 include the following purchases.

Date	Number of Units	Unit Price
May 7	50	$10
July 28	30	13

On June 1, Gregory sold 26 units, and on August 27, 40 more units. Prepare the perpetual inventory schedule for the above transactions using (a) FIFO, (b) LIFO, and (c) moving-average cost. (Round average cost per unit to nearest cent.)

*BE6-11 At May 31, Suarez Company has net sales of $330,000 and cost of goods available for sale of $230,000. Compute the estimated cost of the ending inventory, assuming the gross profit rate is 35%.

*BE6-12 On June 30, Calico Fabrics has the following data pertaining to the retail inventory method. Goods available for sale: at cost $38,000; at retail $50,000; net sales $40,000; and ending inventory at retail $10,000. Compute the estimated cost of the ending inventory using the retail inventory method.

> DO IT! Review

DO IT! 6-1 Gomez Company just took its physical inventory. The count of inventory items on hand at the company's business locations resulted in a total inventory cost of $300,000. In reviewing the details of the count and related inventory transactions, you have discovered the following.

Apply rules of ownership to determine inventory cost.
(LO 1)

1. Gomez has sent inventory costing $26,000 on consignment to Kako Company. All of this inventory was at Kako's showrooms on December 31.

2. The company did not include in the count inventory (cost, $20,000) that was sold on December 28, terms FOB shipping point. The goods were in transit on December 31.

3. The company did not include in the count inventory (cost, $17,000) that was purchased with terms of FOB shipping point. The goods were in transit on December 31.

Compute the correct December 31 inventory.

DO IT! 6-2 The accounting records of Old Towne Electronics show the following data.

Compute cost of goods sold under different cost flow methods.
(LO 2)

Beginning inventory	3,000 units at $5
Purchases	8,000 units at $7
Sales	9,400 units at $10

Determine cost of goods sold during the period under a periodic inventory system using (a) the FIFO method, (b) the LIFO method, and (c) the average-cost method. (Round unit cost to nearest tenth of a cent.)

DO IT! 6-3 (a) Moberg Company sells three different categories of tools (small, medium, and large). The cost and market value of its inventory of tools are as follows.

Compute inventory value under LCM.
(LO 4)

	Cost	Market Value
Small	$ 64,000	$ 73,000
Medium	290,000	260,000
Large	152,000	171,000

Determine the value of the company's inventory under the lower-of-cost-or-market approach.

(b) Janus Company understated its 2014 ending inventory by $31,000. Determine the impact this error has on ending inventory, cost of goods sold, and stockholders' equity in 2014 and 2015.

DO IT! 6-4 Early in 2015, Chien Company switched to a just-in-time inventory system. Its sales revenue, cost of goods sold, and inventory amounts for 2014 and 2015 are shown below.

Compute inventory turnover and assess inventory level.
(LO 6)

	2014	2015
Sales revenue	$3,120,000	$3,713,000
Cost of goods sold	1,200,000	1,425,000
Beginning inventory	180,000	220,000
Ending inventory	220,000	100,000

Determine the inventory turnover and days in inventory for 2014 and 2015. Discuss the changes in the amount of inventory, the inventory turnover and days in inventory, and the amount of sales revenue across the two years.

EXERCISES

E6-1 Tri-State Bank and Trust is considering giving Josef Company a loan. Before doing so, management decides that further discussions with Josef's accountant may be desirable. One area of particular concern is the inventory account, which has a year-end balance of $297,000. Discussions with the accountant reveal the following.

Determine the correct inventory amount.
(LO 1)

1. Josef sold goods costing $38,000 to Sorci Company, FOB shipping point, on December 28. The goods are not expected to arrive at Sorci until January 12. The goods were not included in the physical inventory because they were not in the warehouse.

2. The physical count of the inventory did not include goods costing $95,000 that were shipped to Josef FOB destination on December 27 and were still in transit at year-end.

3. Josef received goods costing $22,000 on January 2. The goods were shipped FOB shipping point on December 26 by Solita Co. The goods were not included in the physical count.

4. Josef sold goods costing $35,000 to Natali Co., FOB destination, on December 30. The goods were received at Natali on January 8. They were not included in Josef's physical inventory.

5. Josef received goods costing $44,000 on January 2 that were shipped FOB destination on December 29. The shipment was a rush order that was supposed to arrive December 31. This purchase was included in the ending inventory of $297,000.

Instructions
Determine the correct inventory amount on December 31.

Determine the correct inventory amount.
(LO 1)

E6-2 Rachel Warren, an auditor with Laplante CPAs, is performing a review of Schuda Company's inventory account. Schuda did not have a good year, and top management is under pressure to boost reported income. According to its records, the inventory balance at year-end was $740,000. However, the following information was not considered when determining that amount.

1. Included in the company's count were goods with a cost of $250,000 that the company is holding on consignment. The goods belong to Harmon Corporation.

2. The physical count did not include goods purchased by Schuda with a cost of $40,000 that were shipped FOB destination on December 28 and did not arrive at Schuda's warehouse until January 3.

3. Included in the inventory account was $14,000 of office supplies that were stored in the warehouse and were to be used by the company's supervisors and managers during the coming year.

4. The company received an order on December 29 that was boxed and sitting on the loading dock awaiting pick-up on December 31. The shipper picked up the goods on January 1 and delivered them on January 6. The shipping terms were FOB shipping point. The goods had a selling price of $40,000 and a cost of $28,000. The goods were not included in the count because they were sitting on the dock.

5. On December 29, Schuda shipped goods with a selling price of $80,000 and a cost of $60,000 to Reza Sales Corporation FOB shipping point. The goods arrived on January 3. Reza Sales had only ordered goods with a selling price of $10,000 and a cost of $8,000. However, a sales manager at Schuda had authorized the shipment and said that if Reza wanted to ship the goods back next week, it could.

6. Included in the count was $40,000 of goods that were parts for a machine that the company no longer made. Given the high-tech nature of Schuda's products, it was unlikely that these obsolete parts had any other use. However, management would prefer to keep them on the books at cost, "since that is what we paid for them, after all."

Instructions
Prepare a schedule to determine the correct inventory amount. Provide explanations for each item above, saying why you did or did not make an adjustment for each item.

Calculate cost of goods sold using specific identification and FIFO.
(LO 2, 3)

E6-3 On December 1, Marzion Electronics Ltd. has three DVD players left in stock. All are identical, all are priced to sell at $150. One of the three DVD players left in stock, with serial #1012, was purchased on June 1 at a cost of $100. Another, with serial #1045, was purchased on November 1 for $90. The last player, serial #1056, was purchased on November 30 for $80.

Instructions
(a) Calculate the cost of goods sold using the FIFO periodic inventory method assuming that two of the three players were sold by the end of December, Marzion Electronics' year-end.

(b) If Marzion Electronics used the specific identification method instead of the FIFO method, how might it alter its earnings by "selectively choosing" which particular players to sell to the two customers? What would Marzion's cost of goods sold be if the company wished to minimize earnings? Maximize earnings?

(c) Which of the two inventory methods do you recommend that Marzion use? Explain why.

E6-4 Linda's Boards sells a snowboard, Xpert, that is popular with snowboard enthusiasts. Information relating to Linda's purchases of Xpert snowboards during September is shown below. During the same month, 121 Xpert snowboards were sold. Linda's uses a periodic inventory system.

Compute inventory and cost of goods sold using FIFO and LIFO.

(LO 2)

Date	Explanation	Units	Unit Cost	Total Cost
Sept. 1	Inventory	26	$ 97	$ 2,522
Sept. 12	Purchases	45	102	4,590
Sept. 19	Purchases	20	104	2,080
Sept. 26	Purchases	50	105	5,250
	Totals	141		$14,442

Instructions

(a) Compute the ending inventory at September 30 and cost of goods sold using the FIFO and LIFO methods. Prove the amount allocated to cost of goods sold under each method.

(b) For both FIFO and LIFO, calculate the sum of ending inventory and cost of goods sold. What do you notice about the answers you found for each method?

E6-5 Xiong Co. uses a periodic inventory system. Its records show the following for the month of May, in which 65 units were sold.

Compute inventory and cost of goods sold using FIFO and LIFO.

(LO 2)

		Units	Unit Cost	Total Cost
May 1	Inventory	30	$ 8	$240
15	Purchases	25	11	275
24	Purchases	35	12	420
	Totals	90		$935

Instructions

Compute the ending inventory at May 31 and cost of goods sold using the FIFO and LIFO methods. Prove the amount allocated to cost of goods sold under each method.

E6-6 Kaleta Company reports the following for the month of June.

Compute inventory and cost of goods sold using FIFO and LIFO.

(LO 2, 3)

		Units	Unit Cost	Total Cost
June 1	Inventory	200	$5	$1,000
12	Purchase	400	6	2,400
23	Purchase	300	7	2,100
30	Inventory	100		

Instructions

(a) Compute the cost of the ending inventory and the cost of goods sold under (1) FIFO and (2) LIFO.

(b) Which costing method gives the higher ending inventory? Why?

(c) Which method results in the higher cost of goods sold? Why?

E6-7 Lisa Company had 100 units in beginning inventory at a total cost of $10,000. The company purchased 200 units at a total cost of $26,000. At the end of the year, Lisa had 80 units in ending inventory.

Compute inventory under FIFO, LIFO, and average-cost.

(LO 2, 3)

Instructions

(a) Compute the cost of the ending inventory and the cost of goods sold under (1) FIFO, (2) LIFO, and (3) average-cost.

(b) Which cost flow method would result in the highest net income?

(c) Which cost flow method would result in inventories approximating current cost in the balance sheet?

(d) Which cost flow method would result in Lisa paying the least taxes in the first year?

E6-8 Inventory data for Kaleta Company are presented in E6-6.

Compute inventory and cost of goods sold using average-cost.

(LO 2, 3)

Instructions

(a) Compute the cost of the ending inventory and the cost of goods sold using the average-cost method. (Round average cost per unit to nearest cent.)

(b) Will the results in (a) be higher or lower than the results under (1) FIFO and (2) LIFO?

(c) Why is the average unit cost not $6?

Determine ending inventory under LCM.

(LO 4)

E6-9 Optix Camera Shop uses the lower-of-cost-or-market basis for its inventory. The following data are available at December 31.

Item	Units	Unit Cost	Market
Cameras:			
Minolta	5	$170	$156
Canon	6	150	152
Light meters:			
Vivitar	12	125	115
Kodak	14	120	135

Instructions

Determine the amount of the ending inventory by applying the lower-of-cost-or-market basis.

Compute lower-of-cost-or-market.

(LO 4)

E6-10 Serebin Company applied FIFO to its inventory and got the following results for its ending inventory.

Cameras	100 units at a cost per unit of $65
DVD players	150 units at a cost per unit of $75
iPods	125 units at a cost per unit of $80

The cost of purchasing units at year-end was cameras $71, DVD players $67, and iPods $78.

Instructions

Determine the amount of ending inventory at lower-of-cost-or-market.

Determine effects of inventory errors.

(LO 5)

E6-11 Hamid's Hardware reported cost of goods sold as follows.

	2014	**2015**
Beginning inventory	$ 20,000	$ 30,000
Cost of goods purchased	150,000	175,000
Cost of goods available for sale	170,000	205,000
Ending inventory	30,000	35,000
Cost of goods sold	$140,000	$170,000

Hamid's made two errors: (1) 2014 ending inventory was overstated $3,000, and (2) 2015 ending inventory was understated $6,000.

Instructions

Compute the correct cost of goods sold for each year.

Prepare correct income statements.

(LO 5)

E6-12 Rulix Watch Company reported the following income statement data for a 2-year period.

	2014	**2015**
Sales revenue	$220,000	$250,000
Cost of goods sold		
Beginning inventory	32,000	44,000
Cost of goods purchased	173,000	202,000
Cost of goods available for sale	205,000	246,000
Ending inventory	44,000	52,000
Cost of goods sold	161,000	194,000
Gross profit	$ 59,000	$ 56,000

Rulix uses a periodic inventory system. The inventories at January 1, 2014, and December 31, 2015, are correct. However, the ending inventory at December 31, 2014, was overstated $6,000.

Instructions

(a) Prepare correct income statement data for the 2 years.
(b) What is the cumulative effect of the inventory error on total gross profit for the 2 years?
(c) ━━━ Explain in a letter to the president of Rulix Watch Company what has happened, i.e., the nature of the error and its effect on the financial statements.

E6-13 This information is available for Quick's Photo Corporation for 2013, 2014, and 2015.

	2013	2014	2015
Beginning inventory	$ 100,000	$ 300,000	$ 400,000
Ending inventory	300,000	400,000	480,000
Cost of goods sold	900,000	1,120,000	1,300,000
Sales revenue	1,200,000	1,600,000	1,900,000

Compute inventory turnover, days in inventory, and gross profit rate.

(LO 6)

Instructions
Calculate inventory turnover, days in inventory, and gross profit rate (from Chapter 5) for Quick's Photo Corporation for 2013, 2014, and 2015. Comment on any trends.

E6-14 The cost of goods sold computations for Alpha Company and Omega Company are shown below.

Compute inventory turnover and days in inventory.

(LO 6)

	Alpha Company	Omega Company
Beginning inventory	$ 45,000	$ 71,000
Cost of goods purchased	200,000	290,000
Cost of goods available for sale	245,000	361,000
Ending inventory	55,000	69,000
Cost of goods sold	$190,000	$292,000

Instructions
(a) Compute inventory turnover and days in inventory for each company.
(b) Which company moves its inventory more quickly?

*E6-15 Bufford Appliance uses a perpetual inventory system. For its flat-screen television sets, the January 1 inventory was 3 sets at $600 each. On January 10, Bufford purchased 6 units at $660 each. The company sold 2 units on January 8 and 4 units on January 15.

Apply cost flow methods to perpetual records.

(LO 7)

Instructions
Compute the ending inventory under (a) FIFO, (b) LIFO, and (c) moving-average cost. (Round average cost per unit to nearest cent.)

*E6-16 Kaleta Company reports the following for the month of June.

Calculate inventory and cost of goods sold using three cost flow methods in a perpetual inventory system.

(LO 7)

Date	Explanation	Units	Unit Cost	Total Cost
June 1	Inventory	200	$5	$1,000
12	Purchase	400	6	2,400
23	Purchase	300	7	2,100
30	Inventory	100		

Instructions
(a) Calculate the cost of the ending inventory and the cost of goods sold for each cost flow assumption, using a perpetual inventory system. Assume a sale of 440 units occurred on June 15 for a selling price of $8 and a sale of 360 units on June 27 for $9. (Round average cost per unit to 3 decimal places.)
(b) How do the results differ from E6-6 and E6-8?
(c) Why is the average unit cost not $6 [($5 + $6 + $7) ÷ 3 = $6]?

*E6-17 Information about Linda's Boards is presented in E6-4. Additional data regarding Linda's sales of Xpert snowboards are provided below. Assume that Linda's uses a perpetual inventory system.

Apply cost flow methods to perpetual records.

(LO 7)

Date		Units	Unit Price	Total Revenue
Sept. 5	Sale	12	$199	$ 2,388
Sept. 16	Sale	50	199	9,950
Sept. 29	Sale	59	209	12,331
	Totals	121		$24,669

Instructions
(a) Compute ending inventory at September 30 using FIFO, LIFO, and moving-average cost. (Round average cost per unit to nearest cent.)
(b) Compare ending inventory using a perpetual inventory system to ending inventory using a periodic inventory system (from E6-4).
(c) Which inventory cost flow method (FIFO, LIFO) gives the same ending inventory value under both periodic and perpetual? Which method gives different ending inventory values?

Use the gross profit method to estimate inventory.
(LO 8)

*E6-18 Brenda Company reported the following information for November and December 2015.

	November	December
Cost of goods purchased	$536,000	$ 610,000
Inventory, beginning-of-month	130,000	120,000
Inventory, end-of-month	120,000	?
Sales revenue	840,000	1,000,000

Brenda's ending inventory at December 31 was destroyed in a fire.

Instructions
(a) Compute the gross profit rate for November.
(b) Using the gross profit rate for November, determine the estimated cost of inventory lost in the fire.

Determine merchandise lost using the gross profit method of estimating inventory.
(LO 8)

*E6-19 The inventory of Hauser Company was destroyed by fire on March 1. From an examination of the accounting records, the following data for the first 2 months of the year are obtained: Sales Revenue $51,000, Sales Returns and Allowances $1,000, Purchases $31,200, Freight-In $1,200, and Purchase Returns and Allowances $1,400.

Instructions
Determine the merchandise lost by fire, assuming:

(a) A beginning inventory of $20,000 and a gross profit rate of 40% on net sales.
(b) A beginning inventory of $30,000 and a gross profit rate of 30% on net sales.

Determine ending inventory at cost using retail method.
(LO 8)

*E6-20 Gepetto Shoe Store uses the retail inventory method for its two departments, Women's Shoes and Men's Shoes. The following information for each department is obtained.

Item	Women's Shoes	Men's Shoes
Beginning inventory at cost	$ 25,000	$ 45,000
Cost of goods purchased at cost	110,000	136,300
Net sales	178,000	185,000
Beginning inventory at retail	46,000	60,000
Cost of goods purchased at retail	179,000	185,000

Instructions
Compute the estimated cost of the ending inventory for each department under the retail inventory method.

EXERCISES: SET B AND CHALLENGE EXERCISES

Visit the book's companion website, at **www.wiley.com/college/weygandt**, and choose the Student Companion site to access Exercise Set B and Challenge Exercises.

PROBLEMS: SET A

Determine items and amounts to be recorded in inventory.
(LO 1)

P6-1A Austin Limited is trying to determine the value of its ending inventory as of February 28, 2015, the company's year-end. The following transactions occurred, and the accountant asked your help in determining whether they should be recorded or not.

(a) On February 26, Austin shipped goods costing $800 to a customer and charged the customer $1,000. The goods were shipped with terms FOB shipping point and the receiving report indicates that the customer received the goods on March 2.
(b) On February 26, Louis Inc. shipped goods to Austin under terms FOB shipping point. The invoice price was $450 plus $30 for freight. The receiving report indicates that the goods were received by Austin on March 2.
(c) Austin had $650 of inventory isolated in the warehouse. The inventory is designated for a customer who has requested that the goods be shipped on March 10.

(d) Also included in Austin's warehouse is $700 of inventory that Ryhn Producers shipped to Austin on consignment.

(e) On February 26, Austin issued a purchase order to acquire goods costing $900. The goods were shipped with terms FOB destination on February 27. Austin received the goods on March 2.

(f) On February 26, Austin shipped goods to a customer under terms FOB destination. The invoice price was $350; the cost of the items was $200. The receiving report indicates that the goods were received by the customer on March 2.

Instructions

For each of the preceding transactions, specify whether the item in question should be included in ending inventory, and if so, at what amount.

P6-2A Express Distribution markets CDs of the performing artist Fishe. At the beginning of October, Express had in beginning inventory 2,000 of Fishe's CDs with a unit cost of $7. During October, Express made the following purchases of Fishe's CDs.

Oct. 3	2,500 @ $8	Oct. 19	3,000 @ $10
Oct. 9	3,500 @ $9	Oct. 25	4,000 @ $11

Determine cost of goods sold and ending inventory using FIFO, LIFO, and average-cost with analysis.

(LO 2, 3)

During October, 10,900 units were sold. Express uses a periodic inventory system.

Instructions

(a) Determine the cost of goods available for sale.

(b) Determine (1) the ending inventory and (2) the cost of goods sold under each of the assumed cost flow methods (FIFO, LIFO, and average cost). Prove the accuracy of the cost of goods sold under the FIFO and LIFO methods.

(c) Which cost flow method results in (1) the highest inventory amount for the balance sheet and (2) the highest cost of goods sold for the income statement?

(b)(2) Cost of goods sold:
FIFO $ 94,500
LIFO $108,700
Average $101,370

P6-3A Ziad Company had a beginning inventory on January 1 of 150 units of Product 4-18-15 at a cost of $20 per unit. During the year, the following purchases were made.

Mar. 15	400 units at $23	Sept. 4	350 units at $26
July 20	250 units at $24	Dec. 2	100 units at $29

Determine cost of goods sold and ending inventory using FIFO, LIFO, and average-cost with analysis.

(LO 2, 3)

1,000 units were sold. Ziad Company uses a periodic inventory system.

Instructions

(a) Determine the cost of goods available for sale.

(b) Determine (1) the ending inventory, and (2) the cost of goods sold under each of the assumed cost flow methods (FIFO, LIFO, and average-cost). Prove the accuracy of the cost of goods sold under the FIFO and LIFO methods.

(c) Which cost flow method results in (1) the highest inventory amount for the balance sheet, and (2) the highest cost of goods sold for the income statement?

(b)(2) Cost of goods sold:
FIFO $23,400
LIFO $24,900
Average $24,160

P6-4A The management of Felipe Inc. is reevaluating the appropriateness of using its present inventory cost flow method, which is average-cost. The company requests your help in determining the results of operations for 2015 if either the FIFO or the LIFO method had been used. For 2015, the accounting records show these data:

Compute ending inventory, prepare income statements, and answer questions using FIFO and LIFO.

(LO 2, 3)

Inventories		Purchases and Sales	
Beginning (7,000 units)	$14,000	Total net sales (180,000 units)	$747,000
Ending (17,000 units)		Total cost of goods purchased	
		(190,000 units)	466,000

Purchases were made quarterly as follows.

Quarter	Units	Unit Cost	Total Cost
1	50,000	$2.20	$110,000
2	40,000	2.35	94,000
3	40,000	2.50	100,000
4	60,000	2.70	162,000
	190,000		$466,000

Operating expenses were $130,000, and the company's income tax rate is 40%.

Instructions

(a) Prepare comparative condensed income statements for 2015 under FIFO and LIFO. (Show computations of ending inventory.)

(a) Gross profit:
FIFO $312,900
LIFO $303,000

(b) ──── Answer the following questions for management.
  (1) Which cost flow method (FIFO or LIFO) produces the more meaningful inventory amount for the balance sheet? Why?
  (2) Which cost flow method (FIFO or LIFO) produces the more meaningful net income? Why?
  (3) Which cost flow method (FIFO or LIFO) is more likely to approximate the actual physical flow of goods? Why?
  (4) How much more cash will be available for management under LIFO than under FIFO? Why?
  (5) Will gross profit under the average-cost method be higher or lower than FIFO? Than LIFO? (*Note:* It is not necessary to quantify your answer.)

Calculate ending inventory, cost of goods sold, gross profit, and gross profit rate under periodic method; compare results.

(LO 2, 3)

P6-5A You are provided with the following information for Najera Inc. for the month ended June 30, 2015. Najera uses the periodic method for inventory.

Date	Description	Quantity	Unit Cost or Selling Price
June 1	Beginning inventory	40	$40
June 4	Purchase	135	44
June 10	Sale	110	70
June 11	Sale return	15	70
June 18	Purchase	55	46
June 18	Purchase return	10	46
June 25	Sale	65	75
June 28	Purchase	30	50

Instructions

(a)(iii) Gross profit:
  LIFO $4,215
  FIFO $4,645
  Average $4,414.60

(a) Calculate (i) ending inventory, (ii) cost of goods sold, (iii) gross profit, and (iv) gross profit rate under each of the following methods.
  (1) LIFO.   **(2)** FIFO.   **(3)** Average-cost.
(b) Compare results for the three cost flow assumptions.

Compare specific identification, FIFO, and LIFO under periodic method; use cost flow assumption to justify price increase.

(LO 2, 3)

P6-6A You are provided with the following information for Barton Inc. Barton Inc. uses the periodic method of accounting for its inventory transactions.

March 1	Beginning inventory 2,000 liters at a cost of 60¢ per liter.
March 3	Purchased 2,500 liters at a cost of 65¢ per liter.
March 5	Sold 2,300 liters for $1.05 per liter.
March 10	Purchased 4,000 liters at a cost of 72¢ per liter.
March 20	Purchased 2,500 liters at a cost of 80¢ per liter.
March 30	Sold 5,200 liters for $1.25 per liter.

Instructions

(a) Prepare partial income statements through gross profit, and calculate the value of ending inventory that would be reported on the balance sheet, under each of the following cost flow assumptions. (Round ending inventory and cost of goods sold to the nearest dollar.)

(a) Gross profit:
  (1) Specific identification
          $3,715

  (1) Specific identification method assuming:
    (i) The March 5 sale consisted of 1,000 liters from the March 1 beginning inventory and 1,300 liters from the March 3 purchase; and
    (ii) The March 30 sale consisted of the following number of units sold from beginning inventory and each purchase: 450 liters from March 1; 550 liters from March 3; 2,900 liters from March 10; and 1,300 liters from March 20.

  (2) FIFO $3,930
  (3) LIFO $3,385

  (2) FIFO.
  (3) LIFO.

(b) How can companies use a cost flow method to justify price increases? Which cost flow method would best support an argument to increase prices?

Compute ending inventory, prepare income statements, and answer questions using FIFO and LIFO.

(LO 2, 3)

P6-7A The management of Sherlynn Co. asks your help in determining the comparative effects of the FIFO and LIFO inventory cost flow methods. For 2015, the accounting records provide the following data.

Inventory, January 1 (10,000 units)	$ 45,000
Cost of 100,000 units purchased	532,000
Selling price of 80,000 units sold	700,000
Operating expenses	140,000

Units purchased consisted of 35,000 units at $5.10 on May 10; 35,000 units at $5.30 on August 15; and 30,000 units at $5.60 on November 20. Income taxes are 30%.

Instructions

(a) Prepare comparative condensed income statements for 2015 under FIFO and LIFO. (Show computations of ending inventory.)

(b) ━━━► Answer the following questions for management.

    (1) Which inventory cost flow method produces the most meaningful inventory amount for the balance sheet? Why?

    (2) Which inventory cost flow method produces the most meaningful net income? Why?

    (3) Which inventory cost flow method is most likely to approximate actual physical flow of the goods? Why?

    (4) How much additional cash will be available for management under LIFO than under FIFO? Why?

    (5) How much of the gross profit under FIFO is illusory in comparison with the gross profit under LIFO?

(a) Net income:
FIFO $105,700
LIFO $91,000

*P6-8A Mercer Inc. is a retailer operating in British Columbia. Mercer uses the perpetual inventory method. All sales returns from customers result in the goods being returned to inventory; the inventory is not damaged. Assume that there are no credit transactions; all amounts are settled in cash. You are provided with the following information for Mercer Inc. for the month of January 2015.

Calculate cost of goods sold and ending inventory under LIFO, FIFO, and moving-average cost under the perpetual system; compare gross profit under each assumption.

(LO 7)

Date	Description	Quantity	Unit Cost or Selling Price
January 1	Beginning inventory	100	$15
January 5	Purchase	140	18
January 8	Sale	110	28
January 10	Sale return	10	28
January 15	Purchase	55	20
January 16	Purchase return	5	20
January 20	Sale	90	32
January 25	Purchase	20	22

Instructions

(a) For each of the following cost flow assumptions, calculate (i) cost of goods sold, (ii) ending inventory, and (iii) gross profit.

    (1) LIFO.

    (2) FIFO.

    (3) Moving-average cost. (Round average cost per unit to 3 decimal places.)

(b) Compare results for the three cost flow assumptions.

(a)(iii) Gross profit:
LIFO $2,160
FIFO $2,560
Average $2,421

*P6-9A Terando Co. began operations on July 1. It uses a perpetual inventory system. During July, the company had the following purchases and sales.

Determine ending inventory under a perpetual inventory system.

(LO 7)

	Purchases		
Date	Units	Unit Cost	Sales Units
July 1	5	$120	
July 6			4
July 11	7	$136	
July 14			3
July 21	8	$147	
July 27			6

Instructions

(a) Determine the ending inventory under a perpetual inventory system using (1) FIFO, (2) moving-average cost, and (3) LIFO.

(b) Which costing method produces the highest ending inventory valuation?

(a) Ending inventory:
FIFO $1,029
Average $994
LIFO $958

Compute gross profit rate and inventory loss using gross profit method.

(LO 8)

XLS

*P6-10A Suzuki Company lost all of its inventory in a fire on December 26, 2015. The accounting records showed the following gross profit data for November and December.

	November	December (to 12/26)
Net sales	$600,000	$700,000
Beginning inventory	32,000	36,000
Purchases	389,000	420,000
Purchase returns and allowances	13,300	14,900
Purchase discounts	8,500	9,500
Freight-in	8,800	9,900
Ending inventory	36,000	?

Suzuki is fully insured for fire losses but must prepare a report for the insurance company.

Instructions

(a) Gross profit rate 38%

(a) Compute the gross profit rate for November.

(b) Using the gross profit rate for November, determine the estimated cost of the inventory lost in the fire.

Compute ending inventory using retail method.

(LO 8)

*P6-11A Dixon Books uses the retail inventory method to estimate its monthly ending inventories. The following information is available for two of its departments at October 31, 2015.

	Hardcovers		Paperbacks	
	Cost	Retail	Cost	Retail
Beginning inventory	$ 420,000	$ 700,000	$ 280,000	$ 360,000
Purchases	2,135,000	3,200,000	1,155,000	1,540,000
Freight-in	24,000		12,000	
Purchase discounts	44,000		22,000	
Net sales		3,100,000		1,570,000

At December 31, Dixon Books takes a physical inventory at retail. The actual retail values of the inventories in each department are Hardcovers $790,000 and Paperbacks $335,000.

Instructions

(a) Hardcovers: end. inv. $520,000

(a) Determine the estimated cost of the ending inventory for each department at **October 31**, 2015, using the retail inventory method.

(b) Compute the ending inventory at cost for each department at **December 31**, assuming the cost-to-retail ratios for the year are 65% for Hardcovers and 75% for Paperbacks.

PROBLEMS: SET B

Determine items and amounts to be recorded in inventory.

(LO 1)

P6-1B Weber Limited is trying to determine the value of its ending inventory at February 28, 2015, the company's year-end. The accountant counted everything that was in the warehouse as of February 28, which resulted in an ending inventory valuation of $48,000. However, she didn't know how to treat the following transactions so she didn't record them.

(a) On February 26, Weber shipped to a customer goods costing $800. The goods were shipped FOB shipping point, and the receiving report indicates that the customer received the goods on March 2.

(b) On February 26, Gretel Inc. shipped goods to Weber FOB destination. The invoice price was $350. The receiving report indicates that the goods were received by Weber on March 2.

(c) Weber had $500 of inventory at a customer's warehouse "on approval." The customer was going to let Weber know whether it wanted the merchandise by the end of the week, March 4.

(d) Weber also had $400 of inventory on consignment at a Roslyn craft shop.

(e) On February 26, Weber ordered goods costing $750. The goods were shipped FOB shipping point on February 27. Weber received the goods on March 1.

(f) On February 28, Weber packaged goods and had them ready for shipping to a customer FOB destination. The invoice price was $350; the cost of the items was $250. The receiving report indicates that the goods were received by the customer on March 2.

(g) Weber had damaged goods set aside in the warehouse because they are no longer salable. These goods cost $400, and Weber originally expected to sell these items for $600.

Instructions

For each of the preceding transactions, specify whether the item in question should be included in ending inventory and, if so, at what amount. For each item that is not included in ending inventory, indicate who owns it and in what account, if any, it should have been recorded.

P6-2B Xinxin Distribution markets CDs of the performing artist Carly. At the beginning of March, Xinxin had in beginning inventory 1,500 Carly CDs with a unit cost of $7. During March Xinxin made the following purchases of Carly CDs.

Determine cost of goods sold and ending inventory using FIFO, LIFO, and average-cost with analysis.

(LO 2, 3)

| March 5 | 3,000 @ $8 | March 21 | 4,000 @ $10 |
| March 13 | 4,500 @ $9 | March 26 | 2,500 @ $11 |

During March, 12,000 units were sold. Xinxin uses a periodic inventory system.

Instructions

(a) Determine the cost of goods available for sale.

(b) Determine (1) the ending inventory and (2) the cost of goods sold under each of the assumed cost flow methods (FIFO, LIFO, and average-cost). Prove the accuracy of the cost of goods sold under the FIFO and LIFO methods. (Round average cost per unit to 3 decimal places.)

(c) Which cost flow method results in (1) the highest inventory amount for the balance sheet and (2) the highest cost of goods sold for the income statement?

(b)(2) Cost of goods sold:
FIFO $105,000
LIFO $116,000
Average $110,321

P6-3B Walz Company had a beginning inventory of 400 units of Product Ribo at a cost of $8 per unit. During the year, purchases were:

Determine cost of goods sold and ending inventory using FIFO, LIFO, and average-cost with analysis.

(LO 2, 3)

| Feb. 20 | 600 units at $9 | Aug. 12 | 300 units at $11 |
| May 5 | 500 units at $10 | Dec. 8 | 200 units at $12 |

Walz Company uses a periodic inventory system. Sales totaled 1,500 units.

Instructions

(a) Determine the cost of goods available for sale.

(b) Determine (1) the ending inventory and (2) the cost of goods sold under each of the assumed cost flow methods (FIFO, LIFO, and average-cost). Prove the accuracy of the cost of goods sold under the FIFO and LIFO methods.

(c) Which cost flow method results in (1) the lowest inventory amount for the balance sheet, and (2) the lowest cost of goods sold for the income statement?

(b)(2) Cost of goods sold:
FIFO $13,600
LIFO $15,200
Average $14,475

P6-4B The management of Patel Co. is reevaluating the appropriateness of using its present inventory cost flow method, which is average-cost. They request your help in determining the results of operations for 2015 if either the FIFO method or the LIFO method had been used. For 2015, the accounting records show the following data.

Compute ending inventory, prepare income statements, and answer questions using FIFO and LIFO.

(LO 2, 3)

Inventories		Purchases and Sales	
Beginning (15,000 units)	$32,000	Total net sales (217,000 units)	$865,000
Ending (28,000 units)		Total cost of goods purchased (230,000 units)	600,000

Purchases were made quarterly as follows.

Quarter	Units	Unit Cost	Total Cost
1	60,000	$2.40	$144,000
2	50,000	2.50	125,000
3	50,000	2.70	135,000
4	70,000	2.80	196,000
	230,000		$600,000

Operating expenses were $147,000, and the company's income tax rate is 34%.

(a) Net income:
FIFO $108,504
LIFO $98,472

Instructions

(a) Prepare comparative condensed income statements for 2015 under FIFO and LIFO. (Show computations of ending inventory.)

(b) ━━━━ Answer the following questions for management.

(1) Which cost flow method (FIFO or LIFO) produces the more meaningful inventory amount for the balance sheet? Why?

(2) Which cost flow method (FIFO or LIFO) produces the more meaningful net income? Why?

(3) Which cost flow method (FIFO or LIFO) is more likely to approximate actual physical flow of the goods? Why?

(b)(4) $5,168

(4) How much additional cash will be available for management under LIFO than under FIFO? Why?

(5) Will gross profit under the average-cost method be higher or lower than (i) FIFO and (ii) LIFO? (*Note:* It is not necessary to quantify your answer.)

Calculate ending inventory, cost of goods sold, gross profit, and gross profit rate under periodic method; compare results.

(LO 2, 3)

P6-5B You are provided with the following information for Perkins Inc. for the month ended October 31, 2015. Perkins uses a periodic method for inventory.

Date	Description	Units	Unit Cost or Selling Price
October 1	Beginning inventory	60	$25
October 9	Purchase	120	26
October 11	Sale	100	35
October 17	Purchase	70	27
October 22	Sale	60	40
October 25	Purchase	80	28
October 29	Sale	110	40

Instructions

(a)(iii) Gross profit:
LIFO $3,050
FIFO $3,230
Average $3,141

(a) Calculate (i) ending inventory, (ii) cost of goods sold, (iii) gross profit, and (iv) gross profit rate under each of the following methods.

(1) LIFO.

(2) FIFO.

(3) Average-cost. (Round average cost per unit to 3 decimal places.)

(b) Compare results for the three cost flow assumptions.

Compare specific identification, FIFO, and LIFO under periodic method; use cost flow assumption to influence earnings.

(LO 2, 3)

P6-6B You have the following information for Princess Diamonds. Princess Diamonds uses the periodic method of accounting for its inventory transactions. Princess only carries one brand and size of diamonds—all are identical. Each batch of diamonds purchased is carefully coded and marked with its purchase cost.

March 1   Beginning inventory 150 diamonds at a cost of $300 per diamond.
March 3   Purchased 200 diamonds at a cost of $360 each.
March 5   Sold 180 diamonds for $600 each.
March 10   Purchased 350 diamonds at a cost of $380 each.
March 25   Sold 400 diamonds for $650 each.

Instructions

(a) Gross profit:
(1) Maximum $163,600

(2) Minimum $154,000

(a) Assume that Princess Diamonds uses the specific identification cost flow method.

(1) Demonstrate how Princess Diamonds could maximize its gross profit for the month by specifically selecting which diamonds to sell on March 5 and March 25.

(2) Demonstrate how Princess Diamonds could minimize its gross profit for the month by selecting which diamonds to sell on March 5 and March 25.

(b) Assume that Princess Diamonds uses the FIFO cost flow assumption. Calculate cost of goods sold. How much gross profit would Princess Diamonds report under this cost flow assumption?

(c) Assume that Princess Diamonds uses the LIFO cost flow assumption. Calculate cost of goods sold. How much gross profit would the company report under this cost flow assumption?

Compute ending inventory, prepare income statements, and answer questions using FIFO and LIFO.

(LO 2, 3)

(d) Which cost flow method should Princess Diamonds select? Explain.

P6-7B The management of Chelsea Inc. asks your help in determining the comparative effects of the FIFO and LIFO inventory cost flow methods. For 2015, the accounting records provide the following data.

Inventory, January 1 (10,000 units)	$ 35,000
Cost of 120,000 units purchased	504,500
Selling price of 100,000 units sold	665,000
Operating expenses	130,000

Units purchased consisted of 35,000 units at $4.00 on May 10; 60,000 units at $4.20 on August 15; and 25,000 units at $4.50 on November 20. Income taxes are 28%.

Instructions

(a) Prepare comparative condensed income statements for 2015 under FIFO and LIFO. (Show computations of ending inventory.)

(b) ——— Answer the following questions for management in the form of a business letter.

(1) Which inventory cost flow method produces the most meaningful inventory amount for the balance sheet? Why?

(2) Which inventory cost flow method produces the most meaningful net income? Why?

(3) Which inventory cost flow method is most likely to approximate the actual physical flow of the goods? Why?

(4) How much more cash will be available for management under LIFO than under FIFO? Why?

(5) How much of the gross profit under FIFO is illusionary in comparison with the gross profit under LIFO?

(a) Gross profit:
FIFO $259,000
LIFO $240,500

*P6-8B Minsoo Ltd. is a retailer operating in Edmonton, Alberta. Minsoo uses the perpetual inventory method. All sales returns from customers result in the goods being returned to inventory; the inventory is not damaged. Assume that there are no credit transactions; all amounts are settled in cash. You are provided with the following information for Minsoo Ltd. for the month of January 2015.

Calculate cost of goods sold and ending inventory for FIFO, moving-average cost, and LIFO under the perpetual system; compare gross profit under each assumption.

(LO 7)

Date	Description	Quantity	Unit Cost or Selling Price
December 31	Ending inventory	160	$17
January 2	Purchase	100	21
January 6	Sale	150	40
January 9	Sale return	10	40
January 9	Purchase	80	24
January 10	Purchase return	10	24
January 10	Sale	60	45
January 23	Purchase	100	28
January 30	Sale	110	50

Instructions

(a) For each of the following cost flow assumptions, calculate (i) cost of goods sold, (ii) ending inventory, and (iii) gross profit.
(1) LIFO.
(2) FIFO.
(3) Moving-average cost. (Round average cost per unit to 3 decimal places.)
(b) Compare results for the three cost flow assumptions.

(a)(iii) Gross profit:
LIFO $6,540
FIFO $7,780
Average $7,354

*P6-9B Buffet Appliance Mart began operations on May 1. It uses a perpetual inventory system. During May, the company had the following purchases and sales for its Model 25 Sureshot camera.

Determine ending inventory under a perpetual inventory system.

(LO 7)

Date	Purchases Units	Purchases Unit Cost	Sales Units
May 1	7	$150	
4			4
8	8	$170	
12			5
15	6	$185	
20			3
25			4

Instructions

(a) Determine the ending inventory under a perpetual inventory system using (1) FIFO, (2) moving-average cost, and (3) LIFO. (Round average cost per unit to 3 decimal places.)
(b) Which costing method produces (1) the highest ending inventory valuation and (2) the lowest ending inventory valuation?

(a) Ending inventory:
FIFO $925
Average $874
LIFO $790

Estimate inventory loss using gross profit method.

(LO 8)

*P6-10B Liis Company lost 70% of its inventory in a fire on March 25, 2015. The accounting records showed the following gross profit data for February and March.

	February	March (to 3/25)
Net sales	$300,000	$250,000
Net purchases	176,800	139,000
Freight-in	3,900	3,000
Beginning inventory	4,500	20,200
Ending inventory	20,200	?

Liis Company is fully insured for fire losses but must prepare a report for the insurance company.

Instructions

(a) Gross profit rate 45%

(a) Compute the gross profit rate for the month of February.

(b) Using the gross profit rate for February, determine both the estimated total inventory and inventory lost in the fire in March.

Compute ending inventory using retail method.

(LO 8)

*P6-11B Belden Department Store uses the retail inventory method to estimate its monthly ending inventories. The following information is available for two of its departments at August 31, 2015.

	Sporting Goods		Jewelry and Cosmetics	
	Cost	Retail	Cost	Retail
Net sales		$1,000,000		$1,160,000
Purchases	$675,000	1,066,000	$741,000	1,158,000
Purchase returns	(26,000)	(40,000)	(12,000)	(20,000)
Purchase discounts	(12,360)	—	(2,440)	—
Freight-in	9,000	—	14,000	—
Beginning inventory	47,360	74,000	39,440	62,000

At December 31, Belden Department Store takes a physical inventory at retail. The actual retail values of the inventories in each department are Sporting Goods $95,000 and Jewelry and Cosmetics $44,000.

Instructions

(a) Determine the estimated cost of the ending inventory for each department on **August 31**, 2015, using the retail inventory method.

(b) Sporting Goods: end. inv. $63,000

(b) Compute the ending inventory at cost for each department at **December 31**, assuming the cost-to-retail ratios are 60% for Sporting Goods and 64% for Jewelry and Cosmetics.

PROBLEMS: SET C

Visit the book's companion website, at **www.wiley.com/college/weygandt**, and choose the Student Companion site to access Problem Set C.

COMPREHENSIVE PROBLEM

CP6 On December 1, 2015, Matthias Company had the account balances shown below.

	Debit		Credit
Cash	$ 4,800	Accumulated Depreciation—Equipment	$ 1,500
Accounts Receivable	3,900	Accounts Payable	3,000
Inventory	1,800*	Common Stock	20,000
Equipment	21,000	Retained Earnings	7,000
	$31,500		$31,500

*(3,000 × $0.60)

The following transactions occurred during December.

Dec.	3	Purchased 4,000 units of inventory on account at a cost of $0.72 per unit.
	5	Sold 4,400 units of inventory on account for $0.90 per unit. (It sold 3,000 of the $0.60 units and 1,400 of the $0.72.)
	7	Granted the December 5 customer $180 credit for 200 units of inventory returned costing $120. These units were returned to inventory.
	17	Purchased 2,200 units of inventory for cash at $0.80 each.
	22	Sold 2,000 units of inventory on account for $0.95 per unit. (It sold 2,000 of the $0.72 units.)

Adjustment data:

1. Accrued salaries payable $400.
2. Depreciation $200 per month.

Instructions

(a) Journalize the December transactions and adjusting entries, assuming Matthias uses the perpetual inventory method.

(b) Enter the December 1 balances in the ledger T-accounts and post the December transactions. In addition to the accounts mentioned above, use the following additional accounts: Cost of Goods Sold, Depreciation Expense, Salaries and Wages Expense, Salaries and Wages Payable, Sales Revenue, and Sales Returns and Allowances.

(c) Prepare an adjusted trial balance as of December 31, 2015.

(d) Prepare an income statement for December 2015 and a classified balance sheet at December 31, 2015.

(e) Compute ending inventory and cost of goods sold under FIFO, assuming Matthias Company uses the periodic inventory system.

(f) Compute ending inventory and cost of goods sold under LIFO, assuming Matthias Company uses the periodic inventory system.

CONTINUING COOKIE CHRONICLE

(*Note:* This is a continuation of the Cookie Chronicle from Chapters 1 through 5.)

CCC6 Natalie is busy establishing both divisions of her business (cookie classes and mixer sales) and completing her business degree. Her goals for the next 11 months are to sell one mixer per month and to give two to three classes per week.

The cost of the fine European mixers is expected to increase. Natalie has just negotiated new terms with Kzinski that include shipping costs in the negotiated purchase price (mixers will be shipped FOB destination). Natalie must choose a cost flow assumption for her mixer inventory.

Go to the book's companion website, **www.wiley.com/college/weygandt**, *to see the completion of this problem.*

Broadening Your PERSPECTIVE

Financial Reporting and Analysis

Financial Reporting Problem: Apple Inc.

BYP6-1 The notes that accompany a company's financial statements provide informative details that would clutter the amounts and descriptions presented in the statements. Refer to the financial statements of Apple Inc. in Appendix A as well as its annual report. Instructions for accessing and using the company's complete annual report, including the notes to the financial statements, are also provided in Appendix A.

Instructions

Answer the following questions. Complete the requirements in millions of dollars, as shown in Apple's annual report.

(a) What did Apple report for the amount of inventories in its consolidated balance sheet at September 25, 2010? At September 24, 2011?

(b) Compute the dollar amount of change and the percentage change in inventories between 2010 and 2011. Compute inventory as a percentage of current assets at September 24, 2011.

(c) How does Apple value its inventories? Which inventory cost flow method does Apple use? (See Notes to the Financial Statements.)

(d) What is the cost of sales (cost of goods sold) reported by Apple for 2011, 2010, and 2009? Compute the percentage of cost of sales to net sales in 2011.

Comparative Analysis Problem:
PepsiCo, Inc. vs. The Coca-Cola Company

BYP6-2 PepsiCo's financial statements are presented in Appendix B. Financial statements of The Coca-Cola Company are presented in Appendix C. Instructions for accessing and using the complete annual reports of PepsiCo and Coca-Cola, including the notes to the financial statements, are also provided in Appendices B and C, respectively.

Instructions

(a) Based on the information contained in these financial statements, compute the following 2011 ratios for each company.

  (1) Inventory turnover.

  (2) Days in inventory.

(b) What conclusions concerning the management of the inventory can you draw from these data?

Comparative Analysis Problem:
Amazon.com, Inc. vs. Wal-Mart Stores, Inc.

BYP6-3 Amazon.com, Inc.'s financial statements are presented in Appendix D. Financial statements of Wal-Mart Stores, Inc. are presented in Appendix E. Instructions for accessing and using the complete annual reports of Amazon and Wal-Mart, including the notes to the financial statements, are also provided in Appendices D and E, respectively.

Instructions

(a) Based on the information contained in these financial statements, compute the following 2011 ratios for each company.

  (1) Inventory turnover.

  (2) Days in inventory.

(b) What conclusions concerning the management of the inventory can you draw from these data?

Real-World Focus

BYP6-4 A company's annual report usually will identify the inventory method used. Knowing that, you can analyze the effects of the inventory method on the income statement and balance sheet.

Address: **www.cisco.com**, or go to **www.wiley.com/college/weygandt**

Instructions

Answer the following questions based on the current year's annual report on Cisco's website.

(a) At Cisco's fiscal year-end, what was the inventory on the balance sheet?

(b) How has this changed from the previous fiscal year-end?

(c) How much of the inventory was finished goods?

(d) What inventory method does Cisco use?

Critical Thinking

Decision-Making Across the Organization

BYP6-5 On April 10, 2015, fire damaged the office and warehouse of Corvet Company. Most of the accounting records were destroyed, but the following account balances were determined as of March 31, 2015: Inventory (January 1, 2015), $80,000; Sales Revenue (January 1–March 31, 2015), $180,000; Purchases (January 1–March 31, 2015), $94,000.

   The company's fiscal year ends on December 31. It uses a periodic inventory system.

   From an analysis of the April bank statement, you discover cancelled checks of $4,200 for cash purchases during the period April 1–10. Deposits during the same period totaled $18,500. Of that amount, 60% were collections on accounts receivable, and the balance was cash sales.

Correspondence with the company's principal suppliers revealed $12,400 of purchases on account from April 1 to April 10. Of that amount, $1,600 was for merchandise in transit on April 10 that was shipped FOB destination.

Correspondence with the company's principal customers produced acknowledgments of credit sales totaling $37,000 from April 1 to April 10. It was estimated that $5,600 of credit sales will never be acknowledged or recovered from customers.

Corvet Company reached an agreement with the insurance company that its fire-loss claim should be based on the average of the gross profit rates for the preceding 2 years. The financial statements for 2013 and 2014 showed the following data.

	2014	2013
Net sales	$600,000	$480,000
Cost of goods purchased	404,000	356,000
Beginning inventory	60,000	40,000
Ending inventory	80,000	60,000

Inventory with a cost of $17,000 was salvaged from the fire.

Instructions

With the class divided into groups, answer the following.

(a) Determine the balances in (1) Sales Revenue and (2) Purchases at April 10.
*(b)** Determine the average gross profit rate for the years 2013 and 2014. (*Hint:* Find the gross profit rate for each year and divide the sum by 2.)
*(c)** Determine the inventory loss as a result of the fire, using the gross profit method.

Communication Activity

BYP6-6 You are the controller of Small Toys Inc. Marta Johns, the president, recently mentioned to you that she found an error in the 2014 financial statements which she believes has corrected itself. She determined, in discussions with the Purchasing Department, that 2014 ending inventory was overstated by $1 million. Marta says that the 2015 ending inventory is correct. Thus, she assumes that 2015 income is correct. Marta says to you, "What happened has happened—there's no point in worrying about it anymore."

Instructions

You conclude that Marta is incorrect. Write a brief, tactful memo to Marta, clarifying the situation.

Ethics Case

BYP6-7 R. J. Graziano Wholesale Corp. uses the LIFO method of inventory costing. In the current year, profit at R. J. Graziano is running unusually high. The corporate tax rate is also high this year, but it is scheduled to decline significantly next year. In an effort to lower the current year's net income and to take advantage of the changing income tax rate, the president of R. J. Graziano Wholesale instructs the plant accountant to recommend to the purchasing department a large purchase of inventory for delivery 3 days before the end of the year. The price of the inventory to be purchased has doubled during the year, and the purchase will represent a major portion of the ending inventory value.

Instructions

(a) What is the effect of this transaction on this year's and next year's income statement and income tax expense? Why?
(b) If R. J. Graziano Wholesale had been using the FIFO method of inventory costing, would the president give the same directive?
(c) Should the plant accountant order the inventory purchase to lower income? What are the ethical implications of this order?

All About You

BYP6-8 Some of the largest business frauds ever perpetrated have involved the misstatement of inventory. Two classics were at Leslie Fay and McKesson Corporation.

Instructions

There is considerable information regarding inventory frauds available on the Internet. Search for information about one of the two cases mentioned above, or inventory fraud at any other company, and prepare a short explanation of the nature of the inventory fraud.

FASB Codification Activity

BYP6-9 If your school has a subscription to the FASB Codification, go to **http://aaahq.org/ ascLogin.cfm** to log in and prepare responses to the following.

Instructions
(a) The primary basis for accounting for inventories is cost. How is cost defined in the Codification?
(b) What does the Codification state regarding the use of consistency in the selection or employment of a basis for inventory?
(c) What does the Codification indicate is a justification for the use of the lower-of-cost-or-market for inventory valuation?

Answers to Chapter Questions

Answers to Insight and Accounting Across the Organization Questions

p. 281 A Big Hiccup   Q: What steps might the companies take to avoid such a serious disruption in the future? **A:** The manufacturer of the piston rings should spread its manufacturing facilities across a few locations that are far enough apart that they would not all be at risk at once. In addition, the automakers might consider becoming less dependent on a single supplier as well as having weather contingency plans.

p. 282 Falsifying Inventory to Boost Income   Q: What effect does an overstatement of inventory have on a company's financial statements? **A:** The balance sheet looks stronger because inventory and retained earnings are overstated. The income statement looks better because cost of goods sold is understated and income is overstated.

p. 293 Is LIFO Fair?   Q: What are the arguments for and against the use of LIFO? **A:** Proponents of LIFO argue that it is conceptually superior because it matches the most recent cost with the most recent selling price. Critics contend that it artificially understates the company's net income and consequently reduces tax payments. Also, because most foreign companies are not allowed to use LIFO, its use by U.S. companies reduces the ability of investors to compare U.S. companies with foreign companies.

p. 297 Too Many TVs or Too Few?   Q: For Sony, what are the advantages and disadvantages of having a low days in inventory measure? **A:** If Sony has a low days in inventory, it reduces the amount of cash it has tied up in inventory. It also minimizes the risk it will be stuck with excess inventory that could force it to provide big discounts, resulting in punishing losses. Sony also faces the risk that the TVs will become obsolete before they are sold. However, Sony increases the risk that it will encounter "stock-outs," that is, it will not have adequate inventory to meet customer demand.

Answers to Self-Test Questions

1. a   **2.** b ($180,000 + $35,000)   **3.** b   **4.** c [(5,000 × $13) + (4,000 × $12)]   **5.** d [(8,000 × $11) + (1,000 × $12)]   **6.** d ((5,000 × $8) + (15,000 × $10) + (20,000 × $12)) ÷ 40,000 = $10.75; $10.75 × 7,000   **7.** c   **8.** d   **9.** d (200 × $80)   **10.** b   **11.** b   **12.** b $285,000 ÷ [($80,000 + $110,000) ÷ 2] = 3; 365 ÷ 3   **13.** d   ***14.** d   ***15.** b [$150,000 − (30% × $150,000)] = $105,000; $135,000 − $105,000

A Look at IFRS

The major IFRS requirements related to accounting and reporting for inventories are the same as GAAP. The major differences are that IFRS prohibits the use of the LIFO cost flow assumption and determines market in the lower-of-cost-or-market inventory valuation differently.

Key Points

- The requirements for accounting for and reporting inventories are more principles-based under IFRS. That is, GAAP provides more detailed guidelines in inventory accounting.

- The definitions for inventory are essentially similar under IFRS and GAAP. Both define inventory as assets held-for-sale in the ordinary course of business, in the process of production for sale (work in process), or to be consumed in the production of goods or services (e.g., raw materials).
- Who owns the goods—goods in transit or consigned goods—as well as the costs to include in inventory are accounted for the same under IFRS and GAAP.
- Both GAAP and IFRS permit specific identification where appropriate. IFRS actually requires that the specific identification method be used where the inventory items are not interchangeable (i.e., can be specifically identified). If the inventory items are not specifically identifiable, a cost flow assumption is used. GAAP does not specify situations in which specific identification must be used.
- A major difference between IFRS and GAAP relates to the LIFO cost flow assumption. GAAP permits the use of LIFO for inventory valuation. IFRS prohibits its use. FIFO and average-cost are the only two acceptable cost flow assumptions permitted under IFRS.
- IFRS requires companies to use the same cost flow assumption for all goods of a similar nature. GAAP has no specific requirement in this area.
- In the lower-of-cost-or-market test for inventory valuation, IFRS defines market as net realizable value. Net realizable value is the estimated selling price in the ordinary course of business, less the estimated costs of completion and estimated selling expenses. In other words, net realizable value is the best estimate of the net amounts that inventories are expected to realize. GAAP, on the other hand, defines market as essentially replacement cost.
- Under GAAP, if inventory is written down under the lower-of-cost-or-market valuation, the new basis is now considered its cost. As a result, the inventory may not be written back up to its original cost in a subsequent period. Under IFRS, the write-down may be reversed in a subsequent period up to the amount of the previous write-down. Both the write-down and any subsequent reversal should be reported on the income statement as an expense. An item-by-item approach is generally followed under IFRS.
- An example of the use of lower-of-cost-or-net realizable value (LCNRV) under IFRS follows.

Mendel Company has the following four items in its ending inventory as of December 31, 2015. The company uses the lower-of-cost-or-net realizable value approach for inventory valuation following IFRS.

Item No.	Cost	Net Realizable Value
1320	$3,600	$3,400
1333	4,000	4,100
1428	2,800	2,100
1510	5,000	4,700

The computation of the ending inventory value to be reported in the financial statements at December 31, 2015, is as follows.

Item No.	Cost	Net Realizable Value	LCNRV
1320	$ 3,600	$ 3,400	$ 3,400
1333	4,000	4,100	4,000
1428	2,800	2,100	2,100
1510	5,000	4,700	4,700
Total	$15,400	$14,300	$14,200

- Unlike property, plant, and equipment, IFRS does not permit the option of valuing inventories at fair value. As indicated above, IFRS requires inventory to be written down, but inventory cannot be written up above its original cost.
- Similar to GAAP, certain agricultural products and mineral products can be reported at net realizable value using IFRS.
- IFRS allows companies to report inventory at standard cost if it does not differ significantly from actual cost. Standard cost is addressed in managerial accounting courses.

Looking to the Future

One convergence issue that will be difficult to resolve relates to the use of the LIFO cost flow assumption. As indicated, IFRS specifically prohibits its use. Conversely, the LIFO cost flow assumption is widely used in the United States because of its favorable tax advantages. In addition, many argue that LIFO from a financial reporting point of view provides a better matching of current costs against revenue and, therefore, enables companies to compute a more realistic income.

IFRS Practice

IFRS Self-Test Questions

1. Which of the following should **not** be included in the inventory of a company using IFRS?
   (a) Goods held on consignment from another company.
   (b) Goods shipped on consignment to another company.
   (c) Goods in transit from another company shipped FOB shipping point.
   (d) None of the above.

2. Which method of inventory costing is prohibited under IFRS?
   (a) Specific identification.   (c) FIFO.
   (b) LIFO.   (d) Average-cost.

3. Yang Company purchased 2,000 widgets and has 400 widgets in its ending inventory at a cost of $90 each and a current replacement cost of $80 each. The net realizable value of each unit in the ending inventory is $70. The ending inventory under lower-of-cost-or-net realizable value is:
   (a) $36,000.   (c) $28,000.
   (b) $32,000.   (d) None of the above.

4. Specific identification:
   (a) must be used under IFRS if the inventory items are not interchangeable.
   (b) cannot be used under IFRS.
   (c) cannot be used under GAAP.
   (d) must be used under IFRS if it would result in the most conservative net income.

5. IFRS requires the following:
   (a) Ending inventory is written up and down to net realizable value each reporting period.
   (b) Ending inventory is written down to net realizable value but cannot be written up.
   (c) Ending inventory is written down to net realizable value and may be written up in future periods to its net realizable value but not above its original cost.
   (d) Ending inventory is written down to net realizable value and may be written up in future periods to its net realizable value.

IFRS Exercises

IFRS6-1 Briefly describe some of the similarities and differences between GAAP and IFRS with respect to the accounting for inventories.

IFRS6-2 LaTour Inc. is based in France and prepares its financial statements (in euros) in accordance with IFRS. In 2015, it reported cost of goods sold of €578 million and average inventory of €154 million. Briefly discuss how analysis of LaTour's inventory turnover (and comparisons to a company using GAAP) might be affected by differences in inventory accounting between IFRS and GAAP.

IFRS6-3 Franklin Company has the following four items in its ending inventory as of December 31, 2015. The company uses the lower-of-cost-or-net realizable value approach for inventory valuation following IFRS.

Item No.	Cost	Net Realizable Value
AB	$1,700	$1,400
TRX	2,200	2,300
NWA	7,800	7,100
SGH	3,000	3,700

Compute the lower-of-cost-or-net realizable value.

International Financial Reporting Problem: Zetar plc

IFRS6-4 The financial statements of Zetar plc are presented in Appendix F. Instructions for accessing and using the company's complete annual report, including the notes to its financial statements, are also provided in Appendix F.

Instructions

Using the notes to the company's financial statements, answer the following questions.

(a) What cost flow assumption does the company use to value inventory?
(b) What was the amount of expense that the company reported for inventory write-downs during 2011?
(c) What amount of raw materials, work in process, and finished goods inventory did the company report at April 30, 2011?

Answers to IFRS Self-Test Questions
1. a 2. b 3. c 4. a 5. c

✔ **The Navigator**

✔ Remember to go back to The Navigator box on the chapter opening page and check off your completed work.

7 | Fraud, Internal Control, and Cash

Feature Story

Minding the Money in Moose Jaw

If you're ever looking for a cappuccino in Moose Jaw, Saskatchewan, stop by Stephanie's Gourmet Coffee and More, located on Main Street. Staff there serve, on average, 650 cups of coffee a day, including both regular and specialty coffees, not to mention soups, Italian sandwiches, and a wide assortment of gourmet cheesecakes.

"We've got high school students who come here, and students from the community college," says owner/manager Stephanie Mintenko, who has run the place since opening it in 1995. "We have customers who are retired, and others who are working people and have only 30 minutes for lunch. We have to be pretty quick."

That means that the cashiers have to be efficient. Like most businesses where purchases are low-cost and high-volume, cash control has to be simple.

"We have an electronic cash register, but it's not the fancy new kind where you just punch in the item," explains Ms. Mintenko. "You have to punch in the prices." The machine does keep track of sales in several categories, however. Cashiers punch a button to indicate whether each item is a beverage, a meal, or other type of item. An internal tape in the machine keeps a record of all transactions. The customer receives a receipt only upon request.

There is only one cash register. "Up to three of us might operate it on any given shift, including myself," says Ms. Mintenko.

She and her staff do two "cashouts" each day—one with the shift change at 5:00 p.m. and one when the shop closes at 10:00 p.m. At each cashout, they count the cash in the register drawer. That amount, minus the cash change carried forward (the float), should match the shift total on the register tape. If there's a discrepancy, they do another count. Then, if necessary, "we go through the whole tape to find the mistake," she explains. "It usually turns out to be someone who punched in $18 instead of $1.80, or something like that."

Ms. Mintenko sends all the cash tapes and float totals to a bookkeeper, who double-checks everything and provides regular reports. "We try to keep the accounting simple, so we can concentrate on making great coffee and food."

✔ The Navigator

- Scan Learning Objectives
- Read Feature Story
- Read Preview
- Read text and answer **DO IT!** p. 343
  - p. 346 ■ p. 351 ■ p. 359
- Work Comprehensive **DO IT!** p. 361
- Review Summary of Learning Objectives
- Answer Self-Test Questions
- Complete Assignments
- Go to *WileyPLUS* for practice and tutorials
- Read **A Look at IFRS** p. 383

Learning Objectives ✔ The Navigator

After studying this chapter, you should be able to:

[1] Define fraud and internal control.
[2] Identify the principles of internal control activities.
[3] Explain the applications of internal control principles to cash receipts.
[4] Explain the applications of internal control principles to cash disbursements.
[5] Describe the operation of a petty cash fund.
[6] Indicate the control features of a bank account.
[7] Prepare a bank reconciliation.
[8] Explain the reporting of cash.

© James Pauls/iStockphoto

Preview of Chapter 7

✔ The Navigator

As the story about recording cash sales at Stephanie's Gourmet Coffee and More indicates, control of cash is important to ensure that fraud does not occur. Companies also need controls to safeguard other types of assets. For example, Stephanie's undoubtedly has controls to prevent the theft of food and supplies, and controls to prevent the theft of tableware and dishes from its kitchen.

In this chapter, we explain the essential features of an internal control system and how it prevents fraud. We also describe how those controls apply to a specific asset—cash. The applications include some controls with which you may be already familiar, such as the use of a bank.

The content and organization of Chapter 7 are as follows.

FRAUD, INTERNAL CONTROL, AND CASH

Fraud and Internal Control	Cash Controls	Control Features: Use of a Bank	Reporting Cash
• Fraud • The Sarbanes-Oxley Act • Internal control • Principles of internal control activities • Limitations	• Cash receipts controls • Cash disbursements controls • Petty cash fund	• Making bank deposits • Writing checks • Bank statements • Reconciling the bank account • Electronic funds transfer (EFT) system	• Cash equivalents • Restricted cash

Fraud and Internal Control

The Feature Story describes many of the internal control procedures used by Stephanie's Gourmet Coffee and More. These procedures are necessary to discourage employees from fraudulent activities.

Fraud

A **fraud** is a dishonest act by an employee that results in personal benefit to the employee at a cost to the employer. Examples of fraud reported in the financial press include:

- A bookkeeper in a small company diverted $750,000 of bill payments to a personal bank account over a three-year period.
- A shipping clerk with 28 years of service shipped $125,000 of merchandise to himself.
- A computer operator embezzled $21 million from Wells Fargo Bank over a two-year period.
- A church treasurer "borrowed" $150,000 of church funds to finance a friend's business dealings.

Why does fraud occur? The three main factors that contribute to fraudulent activity are depicted by the **fraud triangle** in Illustration 7-1 (in the margin).

Illustration 7-1
Fraud triangle

The most important element of the fraud triangle is **opportunity**. For an employee to commit fraud, the workplace environment must provide opportunities that an employee can take advantage of. Opportunities occur when the workplace lacks sufficient controls to deter and detect fraud. For example, inadequate monitoring of employee actions can create opportunities for theft and can embolden employees because they believe they will not be caught.

A second factor that contributes to fraud is **financial pressure**. Employees sometimes commit fraud because of personal financial problems caused by too much debt. Or, they might commit fraud because they want to lead a lifestyle that they cannot afford on their current salary.

The third factor that contributes to fraud is **rationalization**. In order to justify their fraud, employees rationalize their dishonest actions. For example, employees sometimes justify fraud because they believe they are underpaid while the employer is making lots of money. Employees feel justified in stealing because they believe they deserve to be paid more.

The Sarbanes-Oxley Act

What can be done to prevent or to detect fraud? After numerous corporate scandals came to light in the early 2000s, Congress addressed this issue by passing the **Sarbanes-Oxley Act (SOX)**. Under SOX, all publicly traded U.S. corporations are required to maintain an adequate system of internal control. Corporate executives and boards of directors must ensure that these controls are reliable and effective. In addition, independent outside auditors must attest to the adequacy of the internal control system. Companies that fail to comply are subject to fines, and company officers can be imprisoned. SOX also created the Public Company Accounting Oversight Board (PCAOB) to establish auditing standards and regulate auditor activity.

One poll found that 60% of investors believe that SOX helps safeguard their stock investments. Many say they would be unlikely to invest in a company that fails to follow SOX requirements. Although some corporate executives have criticized the time and expense involved in following the SOX requirements, SOX appears to be working well. For example, the chief accounting officer of Eli Lily noted that SOX triggered a comprehensive review of how the company documents its controls. This review uncovered redundancies and pointed out controls that needed to be added. In short, it added up to time and money well spent. And the finance chief at General Electric noted, "We have seen value in SOX. It helps build investors' trust and gives them more confidence."[1]

Internal Control

Internal control consists of all the related methods and measures adopted within an organization to safeguard assets, enhance the reliability of accounting records, increase efficiency of operations, and ensure compliance with laws and regulations. Internal control systems have five primary components as listed below.[2]

- **A control environment.** It is the responsibility of top management to make it clear that the organization values integrity and that unethical activity will not be tolerated. This component is often referred to as the "tone at the top."

- **Risk assessment.** Companies must identify and analyze the various factors that create risk for the business and must determine how to manage these risks.

- **Control activities.** To reduce the occurrence of fraud, management must design policies and procedures to address the specific risks faced by the company.

- **Information and communication.** The internal control system must capture and communicate all pertinent information both down and up the organization, as well as communicate information to appropriate external parties.

- **Monitoring.** Internal control systems must be monitored periodically for their adequacy. Significant deficiencies need to be reported to top management and/or the board of directors.

PEOPLE, PLANET, AND PROFIT INSIGHT

And the Controls Are . . .

Internal controls are important for an effective financial reporting system. The same is true for sustainability reporting. An effective system of internal controls for sustainability reporting will help in the following ways: (1) prevent the unauthorized use of data; (2) provide reasonable assurance that the information is accurate, valid, and complete; and (3) report information that is consistent with overall sustainability accounting policies. With these types of controls, users will have the confidence that they can use the sustainability information effectively.

Some regulators are calling for even more assurance through audits of this information. Companies that potentially can cause environmental damage through greenhouse gases are subject to reporting requirements as well as companies in the mining and extractive industries. And, as demand for more information in the sustainability area expands, the need for audits of this information will grow.

© Karl Dolenc/iStockphoto

 Why is sustainability information important to investors? (See page 382.)

---

[1]"Corporate Regulation Must Be Working—There's a Backlash," *Wall Street Journal* (June 16, 2004), p. C1; and Judith Burns, "Is Sarbanes-Oxley Working?" *Wall Street Journal* (June 21, 2004), pp. R8–R9.
[2]The Committee of Sponsoring Organizations of the Treadway Commission, "Internal Control—Integrated Framework," *www.coso.org/publications/executive_summary_integrated_framework.htm* (accessed March 2008).

Principles of Internal Control Activities

Each of the five components of an internal control system is important. Here, we will focus on one component, the control activities. The reason? These activities are the backbone of the company's efforts to address the risks it faces, such as fraud. The specific control activities used by a company will vary, depending on management's assessment of the risks faced. This assessment is heavily influenced by the size and nature of the company.

The six principles of control activities are as follows.

- Establishment of responsibility
- Segregation of duties
- Documentation procedures
- Physical controls
- Independent internal verification
- Human resource controls

We explain these principles in the following sections. You should recognize that they apply to most companies and are relevant to both manual and computerized accounting systems.

ESTABLISHMENT OF RESPONSIBILITY

An essential principle of internal control is to assign responsibility to specific employees. **Control is most effective when only one person is responsible for a given task.**

To illustrate, assume that the cash on hand at the end of the day in a Safeway supermarket is $10 short of the cash entered in the cash register. If only one person has operated the register, the shift manager can quickly determine responsibility for the shortage. If two or more individuals have worked the register, it may be impossible to determine who is responsible for the error. In the Feature Story, the principle of establishing responsibility does not appear to be strictly applied by Stephanie's Gourmet Coffee and More, since three people operate the cash register on any given shift.

Many retailers solve this problem by having registers with multiple drawers. This makes it possible for more than one person to operate a register but still allows identification of a particular employee with a specific drawer. Only the signed-in cashier has access to his or her drawer.

Establishing responsibility often requires limiting access only to authorized personnel, and then identifying those personnel. For example, the automated systems used by many companies have mechanisms such as identifying passcodes that keep track of who made a journal entry, who entered a sale, or who went into an inventory storeroom at a particular time. Use of identifying passcodes enables the company to establish responsibility by identifying the particular employee who carried out the activity.

It's your shift now. I'm turning in my cash drawer and heading home.

Transfer of cash drawers

ANATOMY OF A FRAUD

Maureen Frugali was a training supervisor for claims processing at Colossal Healthcare. As a standard part of the claims-processing training program, Maureen created fictitious claims for use by trainees. These fictitious claims were then sent to the accounts payable department. After the training claims had been processed, she was to notify Accounts Payable of all fictitious claims, so that they would not be paid. However, she did not inform Accounts Payable about every fictitious claim. She created some fictitious claims for entities that she controlled (that is, she would receive the payment), and she let Accounts Payable pay her.

Total take: $11 million

THE MISSING CONTROL
Establishment of responsibility. The health-care company did not adequately restrict the responsibility for authorizing and approving claims transactions. The training supervisor should not have been authorized to create claims in the company's "live" system.

Source: Adapted from Wells, *Fraud Casebook* (2007), pp. 61–70.

SEGREGATION OF DUTIES

Segregation of duties is indispensable in an internal control system. There are two common applications of this principle:

1. Different individuals should be responsible for related activities.
2. The responsibility for record-keeping for an asset should be separate from the physical custody of that asset.

The rationale for segregation of duties is this: **The work of one employee should, without a duplication of effort, provide a reliable basis for evaluating the work of another employee.** For example, the personnel that design and program computerized systems should not be assigned duties related to day-to-day use of the system. Otherwise, they could design the system to benefit them personally and conceal the fraud through day-to-day use.

SEGREGATION OF RELATED ACTIVITIES Making one individual responsible for related activities increases the potential for errors and irregularities. Instead, companies should, for example, assign related **purchasing activities** to different individuals. Related purchasing activities include ordering merchandise, order approval, receiving goods, authorizing payment, and paying for goods or services. Various frauds are possible when one person handles related purchasing activities:

- If a purchasing agent is allowed to order goods without obtaining supervisory approval, the likelihood of the purchasing agent receiving kickbacks from suppliers increases.
- If an employee who orders goods also handles receipt of the goods and invoice, as well as payment authorization, he or she might authorize payment for a fictitious invoice.

These abuses are less likely to occur when companies divide the purchasing tasks.

Similarly, companies should assign related **sales activities** to different individuals. Related selling activities include making a sale, shipping (or delivering) the goods to the customer, billing the customer, and receiving payment. Various frauds are possible when one person handles related sales activities:

- If a salesperson can make a sale without obtaining supervisory approval, he or she might make sales at unauthorized prices to increase sales commissions.
- A shipping clerk who also has access to accounting records could ship goods to himself.
- A billing clerk who handles billing and receipt could understate the amount billed for sales made to friends and relatives.

These abuses are less likely to occur when companies divide the sales tasks: The salespeople make the sale; the shipping department ships the goods on the basis of the sales order; and the billing department prepares the sales invoice after comparing the sales order with the report of goods shipped.

Lawrence Fairbanks, the assistant vice-chancellor of communications at Aesop University, was allowed to make purchases of under $2,500 for his department without external approval. Unfortunately, he also sometimes bought items for himself, such as expensive antiques and other collectibles. How did he do it? He replaced the vendor invoices he received with fake vendor invoices that he created. The fake invoices had descriptions that were more consistent with the communications department's purchases. He submitted these fake invoices to the accounting department as the basis for their journal entries and to the accounts payable department as the basis for payment.

Total take: $475,000

THE MISSING CONTROL

Segregation of duties. The university had not properly segregated related purchasing activities. Lawrence was ordering items, receiving the items, and receiving the invoice. By receiving the invoice, he had control over the documents that were used to account for the purchase and thus was able to substitute a fake invoice.

Source: Adapted from Wells, *Fraud Casebook* (2007), pp. 3–15.

Accounting Employee A
Maintains cash
balances per books

Segregation of Duties
(Accountability for Assets)

Assistant Cashier B
Maintains custody
of cash on hand

SEGREGATION OF RECORD-KEEPING FROM PHYSICAL CUSTODY The accountant should have neither physical custody of the asset nor access to it. Likewise, the custodian of the asset should not maintain or have access to the accounting records. **The custodian of the asset is not likely to convert the asset to personal use when one employee maintains the record of the asset, and a different employee has physical custody of the asset.** The separation of accounting responsibility from the custody of assets is especially important for cash and inventories because these assets are very vulnerable to fraud.

Angela Bauer was an accounts payable clerk for Aggasiz Construction Company. Angela prepared and issued checks to vendors and reconciled bank statements. She perpetrated a fraud in this way: She wrote checks for costs that the company had not actually incurred (e.g., fake taxes). A supervisor then approved and signed the checks. Before issuing the check, though, Angela would "white-out" the payee line on the check and change it to personal accounts that she controlled. She was able to conceal the theft because she also reconciled the bank account. That is, nobody else ever saw that the checks had been altered.

Total take: $570,000

THE MISSING CONTROL

Segregation of duties. Aggasiz Construction Company did not properly segregate record-keeping from physical custody. Angela had physical custody of the checks, which essentially was control of the cash. She also had record-keeping responsibility because she prepared the bank reconciliation.

Source: Adapted from Wells, *Fraud Casebook* (2007), pp. 100–107.

DOCUMENTATION PROCEDURES

Documents provide evidence that transactions and events have occurred. At Stephanie's Gourmet Coffee and More, the cash register tape is the restaurant's documentation for the sale and the amount of cash received. More sophisticated registers, called point-of-sale terminals, do not rely on tapes. Rather, they are networked with the company's computing and accounting records, which results in direct documentation.

Similarly, a shipping document indicates that the goods have been shipped, and a sales invoice indicates that the company has billed the customer for the goods. By requiring signatures (or initials) on the documents, the company can identify the individual(s) responsible for the transaction or event. Companies should document transactions when they occur.

Companies should establish procedures for documents. First, whenever possible, companies should use **prenumbered documents, and all documents should be accounted for**. Prenumbering helps to prevent a transaction from being recorded more than once, or conversely, from not being recorded at all. Second, the control system should require that employees **promptly forward source documents for accounting entries to the accounting department. This control measure helps to ensure timely recording of the transaction** and contributes directly to the accuracy and reliability of the accounting records.

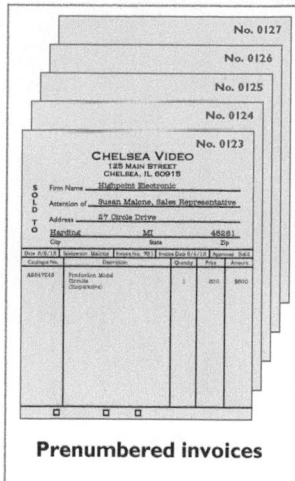

Prenumbered invoices

ANATOMY OF A FRAUD

To support their reimbursement requests for travel costs incurred, employees at Mod Fashions Corporation's design center were required to submit receipts. The receipts could include the detailed bill provided for a meal, the credit card receipt provided when the credit card payment is made, or a copy of the employee's monthly credit card bill that listed the item. A number of the designers who frequently traveled together came up with a fraud scheme: They submitted claims for the same expenses. For example, if they had a meal together that cost $200, one person submitted the detailed meal bill, another submitted the credit card receipt, and a third submitted a monthly credit card bill showing the meal as a line item. Thus, all three received a $200 reimbursement.

Total take: $75,000

THE MISSING CONTROL

Documentation procedures. Mod Fashions should require the original, detailed receipt. It should not accept photocopies, and it should not accept credit card statements. In addition, documentation procedures could be further improved by requiring the use of a corporate credit card (rather than a personal credit card) for all business expenses.

Source: Adapted from Wells, *Fraud Casebook* (2007), pp. 79–90.

PHYSICAL CONTROLS

Use of physical controls is essential. **Physical controls** relate to the safeguarding of assets and enhance the accuracy and reliability of the accounting records. Illustration 7-2 shows examples of these controls.

Illustration 7-2
Physical controls

Physical Controls

Safes, vaults, and safety deposit boxes for cash and business papers

Locked warehouses and storage cabinets for inventories and records

Computer facilities with pass-key access or fingerprint or eyeball scans

Alarms to prevent break-ins

Television monitors and garment sensors to deter theft

Time clocks for recording time worked

At Centerstone Health, a large insurance company, the mailroom each day received insurance applications from prospective customers. Mailroom employees scanned the applications into electronic documents before the applications were processed. Once the applications were scanned, they could be accessed online by authorized employees.

Insurance agents at Centerstone Health earn commissions based upon successful applications. The sales agent's name is listed on the application. However, roughly 15% of the applications are from customers who did not work with a sales agent. Two friends—Alex, an employee in record-keeping, and Parviz, a sales agent—thought up a way to perpetrate a fraud. Alex identified scanned applications that did not list a sales agent. After business hours, he entered the mailroom and found the hard-copy applications that did not show a sales agent. He wrote in Parviz's name as the sales agent and then rescanned the application for processing. Parviz received the commission, which the friends then split.

Total take: $240,000

THE MISSING CONTROL

Physical controls. Centerstone Health lacked two basic physical controls that could have prevented this fraud. First, the mailroom should have been locked during non-business hours, and access during business hours should have been tightly controlled. Second, the scanned applications supposedly could be accessed only by authorized employees using their passwords. However, the password for each employee was the same as the employee's user ID. Since employee user-ID numbers were available to all other employees, all employees knew all other employees' passwords. Unauthorized employees could access the scanned applications. Thus, Alex could enter the system using another employee's password and access the scanned applications.

Source: Adapted from Wells, *Fraud Casebook* (2007), pp. 316–326.

INDEPENDENT INTERNAL VERIFICATION

Most internal control systems provide for **independent internal verification**. This principle involves the review of data prepared by employees. To obtain maximum benefit from independent internal verification:

1. Companies should verify records periodically or on a surprise basis.
2. An employee who is independent of the personnel responsible for the information should make the verification.
3. Discrepancies and exceptions should be reported to a management level that can take appropriate corrective action.

Independent internal verification is especially useful in comparing recorded accountability with existing assets. The reconciliation of the cash register tape with the cash in the register at Stephanie's Gourmet Coffee and More is an example of this internal control principle. Other common examples are the reconciliation of a company's cash balance per books with the cash balance per bank, and the verification of the perpetual inventory records through a count of physical inventory. Illustration 7-3 shows the relationship between this principle and the segregation of duties principle.

Bobbi Jean Donnelly, the office manager for Mod Fashions Corporation's design center, was responsible for preparing the design center budget and reviewing expense reports submitted by design center employees. Her desire to upgrade her wardrobe got the better of her, and she enacted a fraud that involved filing expense-reimbursement requests for her own personal clothing purchases. Bobbi Jean was able to conceal the fraud because she was responsible for reviewing all expense reports, including her

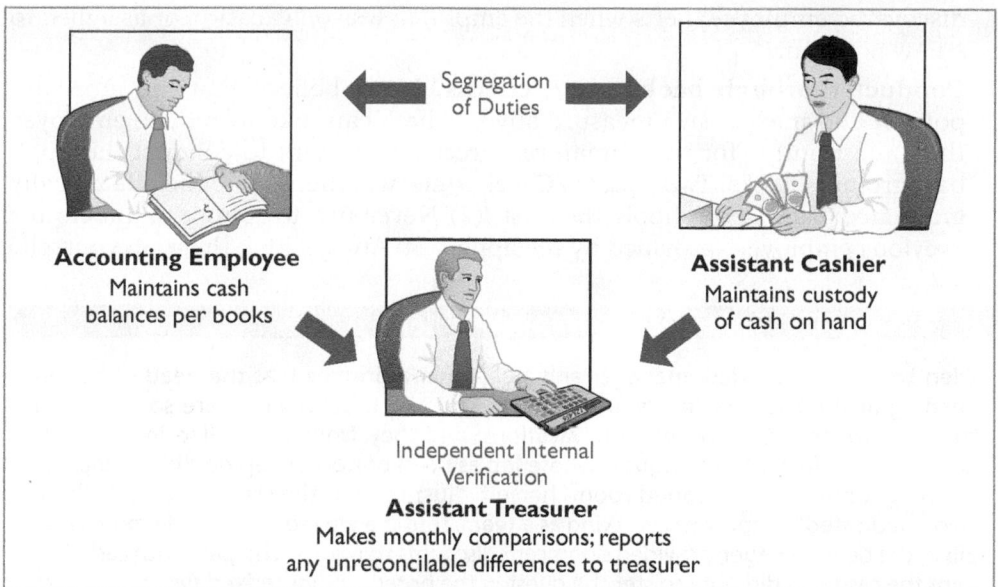

Illustration 7-3
Comparison of segregation of duties principle with independent internal verification principle

own. In addition, she sometimes was given ultimate responsibility for signing off on the expense reports when her boss was "too busy." Also, because she controlled the budget, when she submitted her expenses, she coded them to budget items that she knew were running under budget, so that they would not catch anyone's attention.

Total take: $275,000

THE MISSING CONTROL

Independent internal verification. Bobbi Jean's boss should have verified her expense reports. When asked what he thought her expenses for a year were, the boss said about $10,000. At $115,000 per year, her actual expenses were more than 10 times what would have been expected. However, because he was "too busy" to verify her expense reports or to review the budget, he never noticed.

Source: Adapted from Wells, *Fraud Casebook* (2007), pp. 79–90.

Large companies often assign independent internal verification to internal auditors. **Internal auditors** are company employees who continuously evaluate the effectiveness of the company's internal control systems. They review the activities of departments and individuals to determine whether prescribed internal controls are being followed. They also recommend improvements when needed. For example, WorldCom was at one time the second largest U.S. telecommunications company. The fraud that caused its bankruptcy (the largest ever when it occurred) involved billions of dollars. It was uncovered by an internal auditor.

HUMAN RESOURCE CONTROLS

Human resource control activities include the following.

1. **Bond employees who handle cash. Bonding** involves obtaining insurance protection against theft by employees. It contributes to the safeguarding of cash in two ways. First, the insurance company carefully screens all individuals before adding them to the policy and may reject risky applicants. Second, bonded employees know that the insurance company will vigorously prosecute all offenders.

2. **Rotate employees' duties and require employees to take vacations.** These measures deter employees from attempting thefts since they will not be able to permanently conceal their improper actions. Many banks, for example, have

discovered employee thefts when the employee was on vacation or assigned to a new position.

3. **Conduct thorough background checks.** Many believe that the most important and inexpensive measure any business can take to reduce employee theft and fraud is for the human resources department to conduct thorough background checks. Two tips: (1) Check to see whether job applicants actually graduated from the schools they list. (2) Never use telephone numbers for previous employers provided by the applicant. Always look them up yourself.

ANATOMY OF A FRAUD

Ellen Lowry was the desk manager and Josephine Rodriguez was the head of housekeeping at the Excelsior Inn, a luxury hotel. The two best friends were so dedicated to their jobs that they never took vacations, and they frequently filled in for other employees. In fact, Ms. Rodriguez, whose job as head of housekeeping did not include cleaning rooms, often cleaned rooms herself, "just to help the staff keep up." These two "dedicated" employees, working as a team, found a way to earn a little more cash. Ellen, the desk manager, provided significant discounts to guests who paid with cash. She kept the cash and did not register the guest in the hotel's computerized system. Instead, she took the room out of circulation "due to routine maintenance." Because the room did not show up as being used, it did not receive a normal housekeeping assignment. Instead, Josephine, the head of housekeeping, cleaned the rooms during the guests' stay.

Total take: $95,000

THE MISSING CONTROL

Human resource controls. Ellen, the desk manager, had been fired by a previous employer after being accused of fraud. If the Excelsior Inn had conducted a thorough background check, it would not have hired her. The hotel fraud was detected when Ellen missed work for a few days due to illness. A system of mandatory vacations and rotating days off would have increased the chances of detecting the fraud before it became so large.

Source: Adapted from Wells, *Fraud Casebook* (2007), pp. 145–155.

ACCOUNTING ACROSS THE ORGANIZATION

SOX Boosts the Role of Human Resources

Under SOX, a company needs to keep track of employees' degrees and certifications to ensure that employees continue to meet the specified requirements of a job. Also, to ensure proper employee supervision and proper separation of duties, companies must develop and monitor an organizational chart. When one corporation went through this exercise, it found that out of 17,000 employees, there were 400 people who did not report to anyone. The corporation also had 35 people who reported to each other. In addition, if an employee complains of an unfair firing and mentions financial issues at the company, HR should refer the case to the company audit committee and possibly to its legal counsel.

 Why would unsupervised employees or employees who report to each other represent potential internal control threats? (See page 382.)

Limitations of Internal Control

Companies generally design their systems of internal control to provide **reasonable assurance** of proper safeguarding of assets and reliability of the accounting records. The concept of reasonable assurance rests on the premise that the costs of establishing control procedures should not exceed their expected benefit.

To illustrate, consider shoplifting losses in retail stores. Stores could eliminate such losses by having a security guard stop and search customers as they leave the store. But store managers have concluded that the negative effects of such a procedure cannot be justified. Instead, they have attempted to control shoplifting losses by less costly procedures. They post signs saying, "We reserve the right to inspect all packages" and "All shoplifters will be prosecuted." They use hidden TV cameras and store detectives to monitor customer activity, and they install sensor equipment at exits.

The **human element** is an important factor in every system of internal control. A good system can become ineffective as a result of employee fatigue, carelessness, or indifference. For example, a receiving clerk may not bother to count goods received and may just "fudge" the counts. Occasionally, two or more individuals may work together to get around prescribed controls. Such **collusion** can significantly reduce the effectiveness of a system, eliminating the protection offered by segregation of duties. No system of internal control is perfect.

The **size of the business** also may impose limitations on internal control. Small companies often find it difficult to segregate duties or to provide for independent internal verification. A study by the Association of Certified Fraud Examiners (*2012 Report to the Nation on Occupational Fraud and Abuse*) indicates that businesses with fewer than 100 employees are most at risk for employee theft. In fact, 31% of frauds occurred at companies with fewer than 100 employees. The median loss at small companies was $147,000, which was higher than the median fraud at companies with more than 10,000 employees ($140,000). A $147,000 loss can threaten the very existence of a small company.

Helpful Hint
Controls may vary with the risk level of the activity. For example, management may consider cash to be high risk and maintaining inventories in the stockroom as low risk. Thus, management would have stricter controls for cash.

> DO IT!

Control Activities

Action Plan

✔ Familiarize yourself with each of the control activities summarized on page 336.

✔ Understand the nature of the frauds that each control activity is intended to address.

Identify which control activity is violated in each of the following situations, and explain how the situation creates an opportunity for a fraud.

1. The person with primary responsibility for reconciling the bank account and making all bank deposits is also the company's accountant.

2. Wellstone Company's treasurer received an award for distinguished service because he had not taken a vacation in 30 years.

3. In order to save money spent on order slips and to reduce time spent keeping track of order slips, a local bar/restaurant does not buy prenumbered order slips.

Solution

1. Violates the control activity of segregation of duties. Record-keeping should be separate from physical custody. As a consequence, the employee could embezzle cash and make journal entries to hide the theft.

2. Violates the control activity of human resource controls. Key employees must take vacations. Otherwise, the treasurer, who manages the company's cash, might embezzle cash and use his position to conceal the theft.

3. Violates the control activity of documentation procedures. If prenumbered documents are not used, then it is virtually impossible to account for the documents. As a consequence, an employee could write up a dinner sale, receive the cash from the customer, and then throw away the order slip and keep the cash.

Related exercise material: BE7-1, BE7-2, BE7-3, BE7-4, E7-1, **and** DO IT! 7-1.

 The Navigator

Cash Controls

LEARNING OBJECTIVE   **3**

Explain the applications
of internal control
principles to cash receipts.

Cash is the one asset that is readily convertible into any other type of asset. It also is easily concealed and transported, and is highly desired. Because of these characteristics, **cash is the asset most susceptible to fraudulent activities**. In addition, because of the large volume of cash transactions, numerous errors may occur in executing and recording them. To safeguard cash and to ensure the accuracy of the accounting records for cash, effective internal control over cash is critical.

Cash Receipts Controls

Illustration 7-4 shows how the internal control principles explained earlier apply to cash receipts transactions. As you might expect, companies vary considerably in how they apply these principles. To illustrate internal control over cash receipts, we will examine control activities for a retail store with both over-the-counter and mail receipts.

Illustration 7-4
Application of internal control
principles to cash receipts

Cash Receipts Controls

  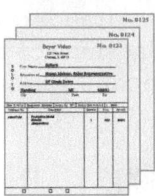

Establishment of Responsibility
Only designated personnel are authorized to handle cash receipts (cashiers)

Segregation of Duties
Different individuals receive cash, record cash receipts, and hold the cash

Documentation Procedures
Use remittance advice (mail receipts), cash register tapes or computer records, and deposit slips

Physical Controls
Store cash in safes and bank vaults; limit access to storage areas; use cash registers

Independent Internal Verification
Supervisors count cash receipts daily; assistant treasurer compares total receipts to bank deposits daily

Human Resource Controls
Bond personnel who handle cash; require employees to take vacations; conduct background checks

OVER-THE-COUNTER RECEIPTS

In retail businesses, control of over-the-counter receipts centers on cash registers that are visible to customers. A cash sale is entered in a cash register (or point-of-sale terminal), with the amount clearly visible to the customer. This activity prevents the sales clerk from entering a lower amount and pocketing the difference. The customer receives an itemized cash register receipt slip and is expected to count the change received. (One weakness at Stephanie's Gourmet Coffee and More in the Feature Story is that customers were only given a receipt if they requested it.) The cash register's tape is locked in the register until a supervisor removes it. This tape accumulates the daily transactions and totals.

At the end of the clerk's shift, the clerk counts the cash and sends the cash and the count to the cashier. The cashier counts the cash, prepares a deposit slip, and deposits the cash at the bank. The cashier also sends a duplicate of the deposit slip to the accounting department to indicate cash received. The supervisor removes the cash register tape and sends it to the accounting department as the basis for a journal entry to record the cash received. (For point-of-sale systems, the accounting department receives information on daily transactions and totals through the computer network.) Illustration 7-5 summarizes this process.

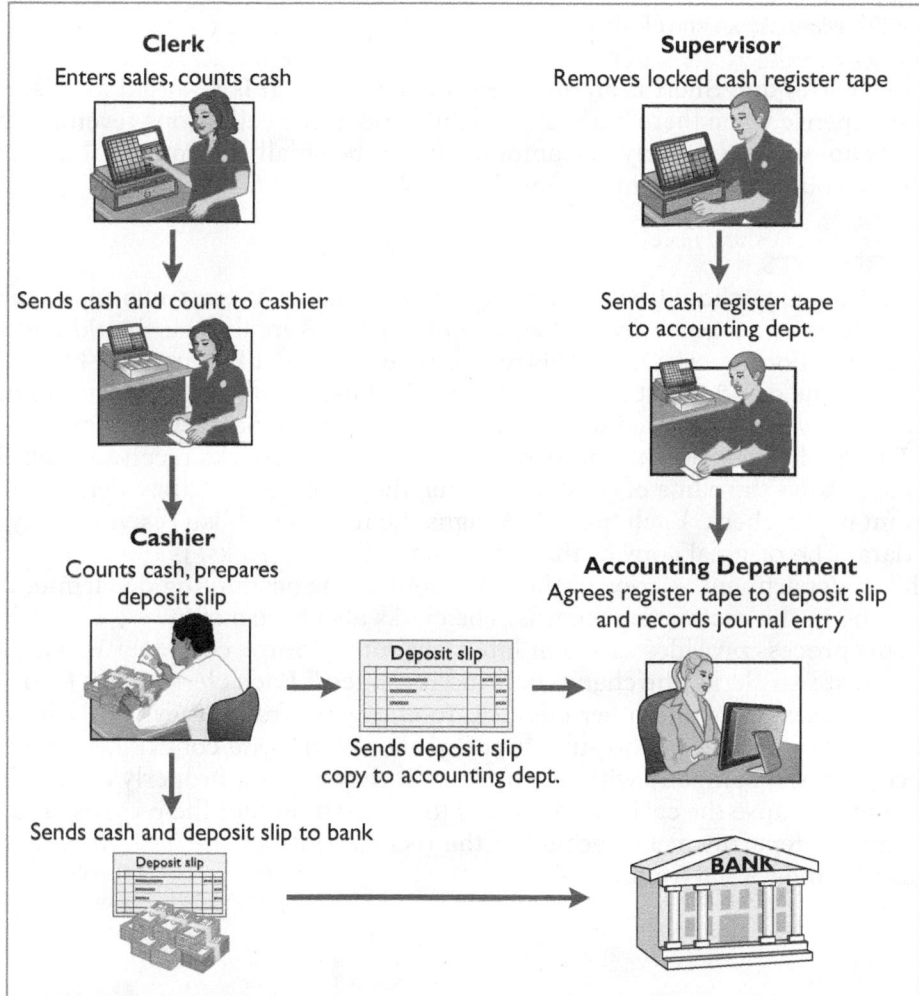

Illustration 7-5
Control of over-the-counter receipts

Helpful Hint
Flowcharts such as this one enhance the understanding of the flow of documents, the processing steps, and the internal control procedures.

This system for handling cash receipts uses an important internal control principle—segregation of record-keeping from physical custody. The supervisor has access to the cash register tape but **not** to the cash. The clerk and the cashier have access to the cash but **not** to the register tape. In addition, the cash register tape provides documentation and enables independent internal verification. Use of these three principles of internal control (segregation of record-keeping from physical custody, documentation, and independent internal verification) provides an effective system of internal control. Any attempt at fraudulent activity should be detected unless there is collusion among the employees.

In some instances, the amount deposited at the bank will not agree with the cash recorded in the accounting records based on the cash register tape. These differences often result because the clerk hands incorrect change back to the retail customer. In this case, the difference between the actual cash and the amount reported on the cash register tape is reported in a Cash Over and Short account. For example, suppose that the cash register tape indicated sales of $6,956.20 but the amount of cash was only $6,946.10. A cash shortfall of $10.10 exists. To account for this cash shortfall and related cash, the company makes the following entry.

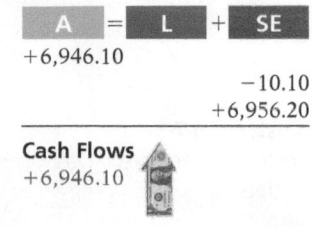

A = L + SE
+6,946.10
         −10.10
         +6,956.20

Cash Flows
+6,946.10

Cash	6,946.10	
Cash Over and Short	10.10	
Sales Revenue		6,956.20
(To record cash shortfall)		

Cash Over and Short is an income statement item. It is reported as miscellaneous expense when there is a cash shortfall, and as miscellaneous revenue when there is an overage. Clearly, the amount should be small. Any material amounts in this account should be investigated.

MAIL RECEIPTS

All mail receipts should be opened in the presence of at least two mail clerks. These receipts are generally in the form of checks. A mail clerk should endorse each check "For Deposit Only." This restrictive endorsement reduces the likelihood that someone could divert the check to personal use. Banks will not give an individual cash when presented with a check that has this type of endorsement.

The mail clerks prepare, in triplicate, a list of the checks received each day. This list shows the name of the check issuer, the purpose of the payment, and the amount of the check. Each mail clerk signs the list to establish responsibility for the data. The original copy of the list, along with the checks, is then sent to the cashier's department. A copy of the list is sent to the accounting department for recording in the accounting records. The clerks also keep a copy.

This process provides excellent internal control for the company. By employing at least two clerks, the chance of fraud is reduced. Each clerk knows he or she is being observed by the other clerk(s). To engage in fraud, they would have to collude. The customers who submit payments also provide control because they will contact the company with a complaint if they are not properly credited for payment. Because the cashier has access to the cash but not the records, and the accounting department has access to the records but not the cash, neither can engage in undetected fraud.

> **DO IT!**

Control over Cash Receipts

L. R. Cortez is concerned about the control over cash receipts in his fast-food restaurant, Big Cheese. The restaurant has two cash registers. At no time do more than two employees take customer orders and enter sales. Work shifts for employees range from 4 to 8 hours. Cortez asks your help in installing a good system of internal control over cash receipts.

Action Plan

✔ Differentiate among the internal control principles of (1) establishing responsibility, (2) using physical controls, and (3) independent internal verification.

✔ Design an effective system of internal control over cash receipts.

Solution

Cortez should assign a separate cash register drawer to each employee at the start of each work shift, with register totals set at zero. Each employee should have access to only the assigned register drawer to enter all sales. Each customer should be given a receipt. At the end of the shift, the employee should do a cash count. A separate employee should compare the cash count with the register tape to be sure they agree. In addition, Cortez should install an automated system that would enable the company to compare orders entered in the register to orders processed by the kitchen.

Related exercise material: BE7-5, BE7-6, BE7-7, E7-2, **and** DO IT! 7-2.

✔ **The Navigator**

Cash Disbursements Controls

Companies disburse cash for a variety of reasons, such as to pay expenses and liabilities or to purchase assets. **Generally, internal control over cash disbursements is more effective when companies pay by check or electronic funds transfer (EFT) rather than by cash.** One exception is **payments for incidental amounts that are paid out of petty cash.**[3]

Companies generally issue checks only after following specified control procedures. Illustration 7-6 (page 348) shows how principles of internal control apply to cash disbursements.

LEARNING OBJECTIVE 4

Explain the applications of internal control principles to cash disbursements.

VOUCHER SYSTEM CONTROLS

Most medium and large companies use vouchers as part of their internal control over cash disbursements. A **voucher system** is a network of approvals by authorized individuals, acting independently, to ensure that all disbursements by check are proper.

The system begins with the authorization to incur a cost or expense. It ends with the issuance of a check for the liability incurred. A **voucher** is an authorization form prepared for each expenditure. Companies require vouchers for all types of cash disbursements except those from petty cash.

The starting point in preparing a voucher is to fill in the appropriate information about the liability on the face of the voucher. The vendor's invoice provides most of the needed information. Then, an employee in the accounts payable department records the voucher (in a journal called a **voucher register**) and files it according to the date on which it is to be paid. The company issues and sends a check on that date, and stamps the voucher "paid." The paid voucher is sent to the accounting department for recording (in a journal called the **check register**). A voucher system involves two journal entries, one to record the liability when the voucher is issued and a second to pay the liability that relates to the voucher.

The use of a voucher system, whether done manually or electronically, improves internal control over cash disbursements. First, the authorization process inherent in a voucher system establishes responsibility. Each individual has responsibility to review the underlying documentation to ensure that it is correct. In addition, the voucher system keeps track of the documents that back up each transaction. By keeping these documents in one place, a supervisor can independently verify the authenticity of each transaction. Consider, for example, the case of Aesop University presented on page 338. Aesop did not use a voucher

---

[3]We explain the operation of a petty cash fund on pages 348–350.

Cash Disbursements Controls

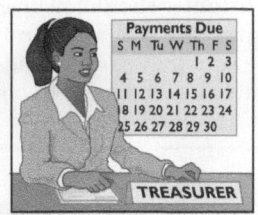

Establishment of Responsibility
Only designated personnel are
authorized to sign checks
(treasurer) and approve vendors

Segregation of Duties
Different individuals approve
and make payments; check-
signers do not record
disbursements

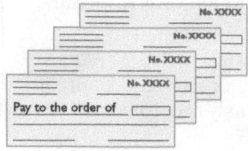

Documentation Procedures
Use prenumbered checks and
account for them in sequence;
each check must have an
approved invoice; require
employees to use corporate
credit cards for reimbursable
expenses; stamp invoices "paid"

Physical Controls
Store blank checks in safes,
with limited access; print
check amounts by machine
in indelible ink

Independent Internal Verification
Compare checks to invoices;
reconcile bank statement
monthly

Human Resource Controls
Bond personnel who handle
cash; require employees to
take vacations; conduct
background checks

Illustration 7-6
Application of internal
control principles to cash
disbursements

system for transactions under $2,500. As a consequence, there was no independent verification of the documents, which enabled the employee to submit fake invoices to hide his unauthorized purchases.

Petty Cash Fund

LEARNING OBJECTIVE   5

Describe the operation
of a petty cash fund.

As you just learned, better internal control over cash disbursements is possible when companies make payments by check. However, using checks to pay small amounts is both impractical and a nuisance. For instance, a company would not want to write checks to pay for postage due, working lunches, or taxi fares. A common way of handling such payments, while maintaining satisfactory control, is to use a **petty cash fund** to pay relatively small amounts. The operation of a petty cash fund, often called an **imprest system**, involves (1) establishing the fund, (2) making payments from the fund, and (3) replenishing the fund.[4]

---

[4]The term "imprest" means an advance of money for a designated purpose.

ESTABLISHING THE PETTY CASH FUND

Two essential steps in establishing a petty cash fund are (1) appointing a petty cash custodian who will be responsible for the fund, and (2) determining the size of the fund. Ordinarily, a company expects the amount in the fund to cover anticipated disbursements for a three- to four-week period.

To establish the fund, a company issues a check payable to the petty cash custodian for the stipulated amount. For example, if Laird Company decides to establish a $100 fund on March 1, the general journal entry is:

Mar. 1	Petty Cash	100	
	Cash		100
	(To establish a petty cash fund)		

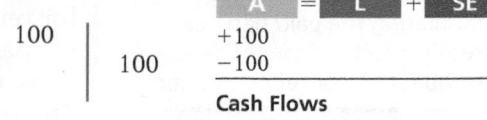

A	=	L	+	SE

+100
−100

Cash Flows
no effect

The fund custodian cashes the check and places the proceeds in a locked petty cash box or drawer. Most petty cash funds are established on a fixed-amount basis. The company will make no additional entries to the Petty Cash account unless management changes the stipulated amount of the fund. For example, if Laird Company decides on July 1 to increase the size of the fund to $250, it would debit Petty Cash $150 and credit Cash $150.

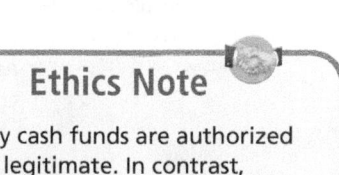

Ethics Note

Petty cash funds are authorized and legitimate. In contrast, "slush" funds are unauthorized and hidden (under the table).

MAKING PAYMENTS FROM THE PETTY CASH FUND

The petty cash custodian has the authority to make payments from the fund that conform to prescribed management policies. Usually, management limits the size of expenditures that come from petty cash. Likewise, it may not permit use of the fund for certain types of transactions (such as making short-term loans to employees).

Each payment from the fund must be documented on a prenumbered petty cash receipt (or petty cash voucher), as shown in Illustration 7-7. The signatures of both the fund custodian and the person receiving payment are required on the receipt. If other supporting documents such as a freight bill or invoice are available, they should be attached to the petty cash receipt.

Helpful Hint
The petty cash receipt satisfies two internal control procedures: (1) establishing responsibility (signature of custodian), and (2) documentation procedures.

Illustration 7-7
Petty cash receipt

No. 7   LAIRD COMPANY
                     Petty Cash Receipt

                                    Date___3/6/15___

Paid to___Acme Express Agency___   Amount___$18.00___

For___Collect Express Charges___

CHARGE TO___Freight-in___

Approved   Received Payment

L. A. Bird Custodian   _R. E. Meins_

The petty cash custodian keeps the receipts in the petty cash box until the fund is replenished. The sum of the petty cash receipts and the money in the fund should equal the established total at all times. Management can (and should) make surprise counts at any time to determine whether the fund is being maintained correctly.

Ethics Note

Internal control over a petty cash fund is strengthened by (1) having a supervisor make surprise counts of the fund to confirm whether the paid petty cash receipts and fund cash equal the imprest amount, and (2) canceling or mutilating the paid petty cash receipts so they cannot be resubmitted for reimbursement.

The company does not make an accounting entry to record a payment when it is made from petty cash. It is considered both inexpedient and unnecessary to do so. Instead, the company recognizes the accounting effects of each payment when it replenishes the fund.

REPLENISHING THE PETTY CASH FUND

When the money in the petty cash fund reaches a minimum level, the company replenishes the fund. The petty cash custodian initiates a request for reimbursement. The individual prepares a schedule (or summary) of the payments that have been made and sends the schedule, supported by petty cash receipts and other documentation, to the treasurer's office. The treasurer's office examines the receipts and supporting documents to verify that proper payments from the fund were made. The treasurer then approves the request and issues a check to restore the fund to its established amount. At the same time, all supporting documentation is stamped "paid" so that it cannot be submitted again for payment.

To illustrate, assume that on March 15 Laird's petty cash custodian requests a check for $87. The fund contains $13 cash and petty cash receipts for postage $44, freight-out $38, and miscellaneous expenses $5. The general journal entry to record the check is:

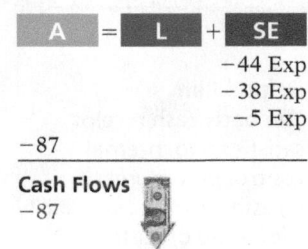

Mar. 15	Postage Expense	44	
	Freight-Out	38	
	Miscellaneous Expense	5	
	Cash		87
	(To replenish petty cash fund)		

Note that the reimbursement entry does not affect the Petty Cash account. Replenishment changes the composition of the fund by replacing the petty cash receipts with cash. It does not change the balance in the fund.

Occasionally, in replenishing a petty cash fund, the company may need to recognize a cash shortage or overage. This results when the total of the cash plus receipts in the petty cash box does not equal the established amount of the petty cash fund. To illustrate, assume that Laird's petty cash custodian has only $12 in cash in the fund plus the receipts as listed. The request for reimbursement would therefore be for $88, and Laird would make the following entry.

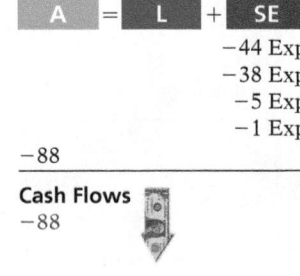

Mar. 15	Postage Expense	44	
	Freight-Out	38	
	Miscellaneous Expense	5	
	Cash Over and Short	1	
	Cash		88
	(To replenish petty cash fund)		

Conversely, if the custodian has $14 in cash, the reimbursement request would be for $86. The company would credit Cash Over and Short for $1 (overage). A company reports a debit balance in Cash Over and Short in the income statement as miscellaneous expense. It reports a credit balance in the account as miscellaneous revenue. The company closes Cash Over and Short to Income Summary at the end of the year.

Helpful Hint

Cash over and short situations result from mathematical errors or from failure to keep accurate records.

Companies should replenish a petty cash fund at the end of the accounting period, regardless of the cash in the fund. Replenishment at this time is necessary in order to recognize the effects of the petty cash payments on the financial statements.

ETHICS INSIGHT

How Employees Steal

A recent study by the Association of Certified Fraud Examiners found that two-thirds of all employee thefts involved a fraudulent disbursement by an employee. The most common form (24.9% of cases) was fraudulent billing schemes. In these, the employee causes the company to issue a payment to the employee by submitting a bill for nonexistent goods or services, purchases of personal goods by the employee, or inflated invoices. The graph below shows various types of fraudulent disbursements and the median loss from each.

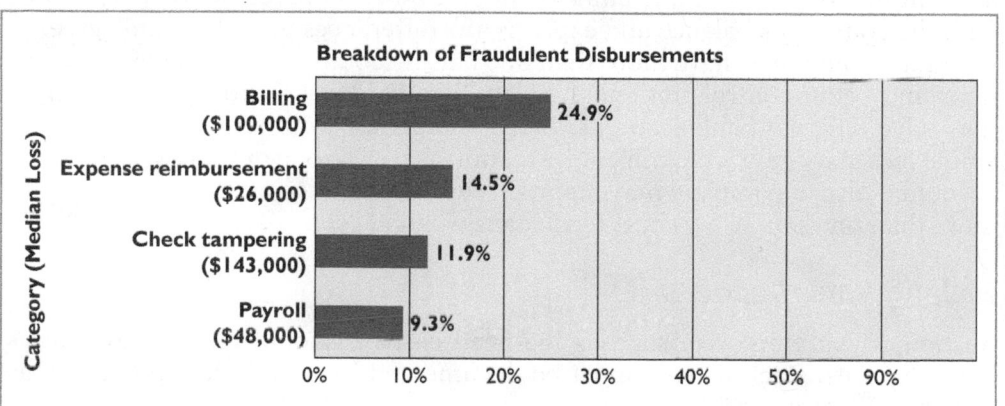

Source: *2012 Report to the Nation on Occupational Fraud and Abuse,* Association of Certified Fraud Examiners, *www.acfe.com/uploadedfiles/ACFE_website/content/rttn/2012-report-to-nations.pdf,* p. 12.

? How can companies reduce the likelihood of fraudulent disbursements? (See page 382.)

> DO IT!

Petty Cash Fund

Action Plan

✔ To establish the fund, set up a separate general ledger account.

✔ Determine how much cash is needed to replenish the fund: subtract the cash remaining from the petty cash fund balance.

✔ Total the petty cash receipts. Determine any cash over or short—the difference between the cash needed to replenish the fund and the total of the petty cash receipts.

✔ Record the expenses incurred according to the petty cash receipts when replenishing the fund.

Bateer Company established a $50 petty cash fund on July 1. On July 30, the fund had $12 cash remaining and petty cash receipts for postage $14, office supplies $10, and delivery expense $15. Prepare journal entries to establish the fund on July 1 and to replenish the fund on July 30.

Solution

July	1	Petty Cash	50	
		Cash		50
		(To establish petty cash fund)		
	30	Postage Expense	14	
		Supplies	10	
		Delivery Expense	15	
		Cash Over and Short		1
		Cash ($50 − $12)		38
		(To replenish petty cash)		

Related exercise material: **BE7-9, E7-7, E7-8, and DO IT! 7-3.**

✔ The Navigator

Control Features: Use of a Bank

The use of a bank contributes significantly to good internal control over cash. A company can safeguard its cash by using a bank as a depository and as a clearinghouse for checks received and written. Use of a bank minimizes the amount of currency that a company must keep on hand. Also, use of a bank facilitates the control of cash because it creates a double record of all bank transactions—one by the company and the other by the bank. The asset account Cash maintained by the company should have the same balance as the bank's liability account for that company. A **bank reconciliation** compares the bank's balance with the company's balance and explains any differences to make them agree.

Many companies have more than one bank account. For efficiency of operations and better control, national retailers like Wal-Mart Stores, Inc. and Target may have regional bank accounts. Large companies, with tens of thousands of employees, may have a payroll bank account, as well as one or more general bank accounts. Also, a company may maintain several bank accounts in order to have more than one source for short-term loans when needed.

Making Bank Deposits

An authorized employee, such as the head cashier, should make a company's bank deposits. Each deposit must be documented by a deposit slip (ticket), as shown in Illustration 7-8.

Illustration 7-8
Deposit slip

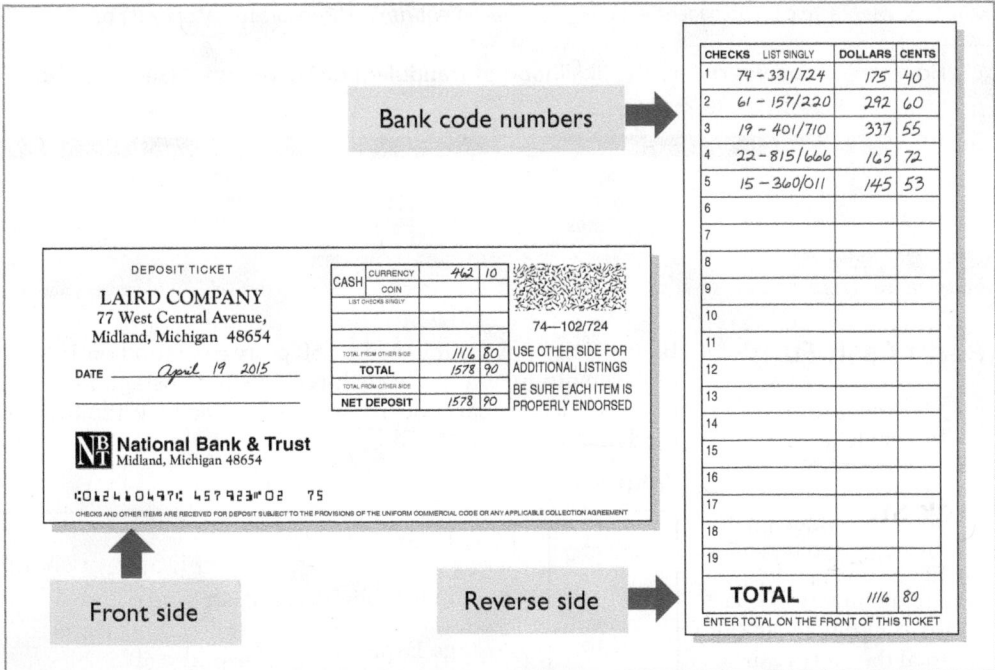

Deposit slips are prepared in duplicate. The bank retains the original; the depositor keeps the duplicate, machine-stamped by the bank to establish its authenticity.

Writing Checks

Most of us write checks without thinking very much about them. A **check** is a written order signed by the depositor directing the bank to pay a specified sum of money to a designated recipient. There are three parties to a check: (1) the **maker** (or drawer) who issues the check, (2) the **bank** (or payer) on which the check is drawn, and (3) the **payee** to whom the check is payable. A check is a **negotiable instrument** that one party can transfer to another party by endorsement. Each check should be accompanied by an explanation of its purpose. In many companies, a remittance advice attached to the check, as shown in Illustration 7-9, explains the check's purpose.

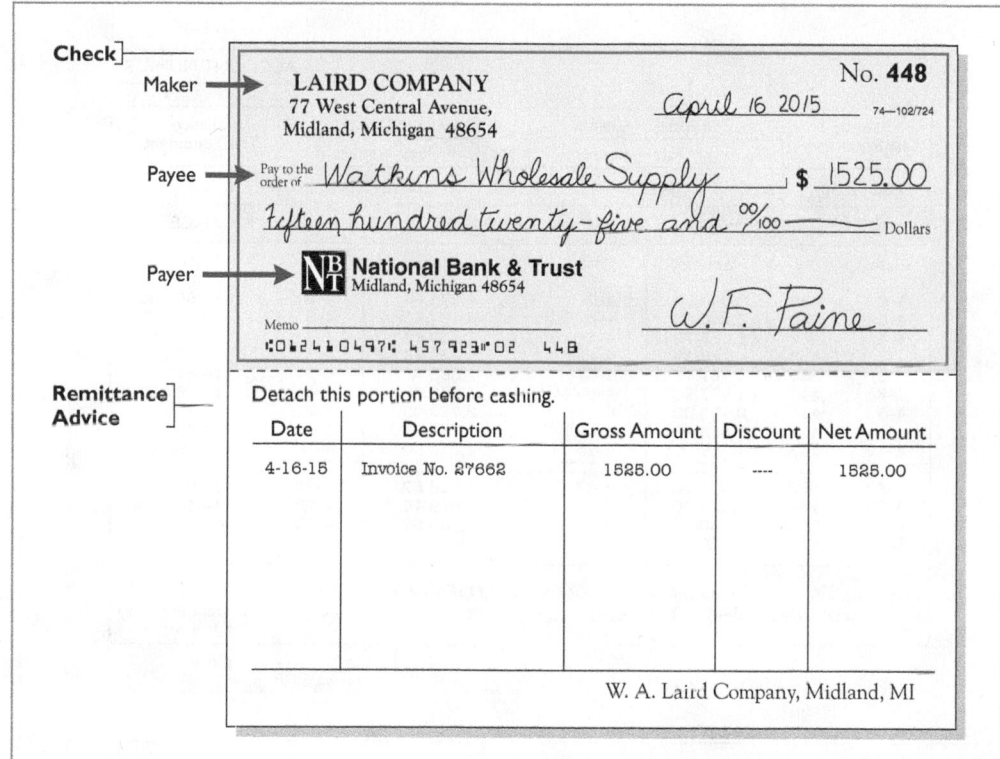

Illustration 7-9
Check with remittance advice

It is important to know the balance in the checking account at all times. To keep the balance current, the depositor should enter each deposit and check on running-balance memo forms (or online statements) provided by the bank or on the check stubs in the checkbook.

Bank Statements

If you have a personal checking account, you are probably familiar with bank statements. A **bank statement** shows the depositor's bank transactions and balances.[5] Each month, a depositor receives a statement from the bank. Illustration 7-10 (page 354) presents a typical bank statement for Laird Company. It shows (1) checks paid and other debits (such as debit card transactions or direct withdrawals for bill payments) that reduce the balance in the depositor's account, (2) deposits and other credits that increase the balance in the depositor's account, and (3) the account balance after each day's transactions.

Helpful Hint
Essentially, the bank statement is a copy of the bank's records sent to the customer (or available online) for review.

---

[5]Our presentation assumes that the depositor makes all adjustments at the end of the month. In practice, a company may also make journal entries during the month as it reviews information from the bank regarding its account.

Illustration 7-10
Bank statement

Helpful Hint
The bank *credits* to the customer's account every deposit it receives. The reverse occurs when the bank "pays" a check issued by a company on its checking account balance. Payment reduces the bank's liability. Thus, the bank *debits* check payments to the customer's account with the bank.

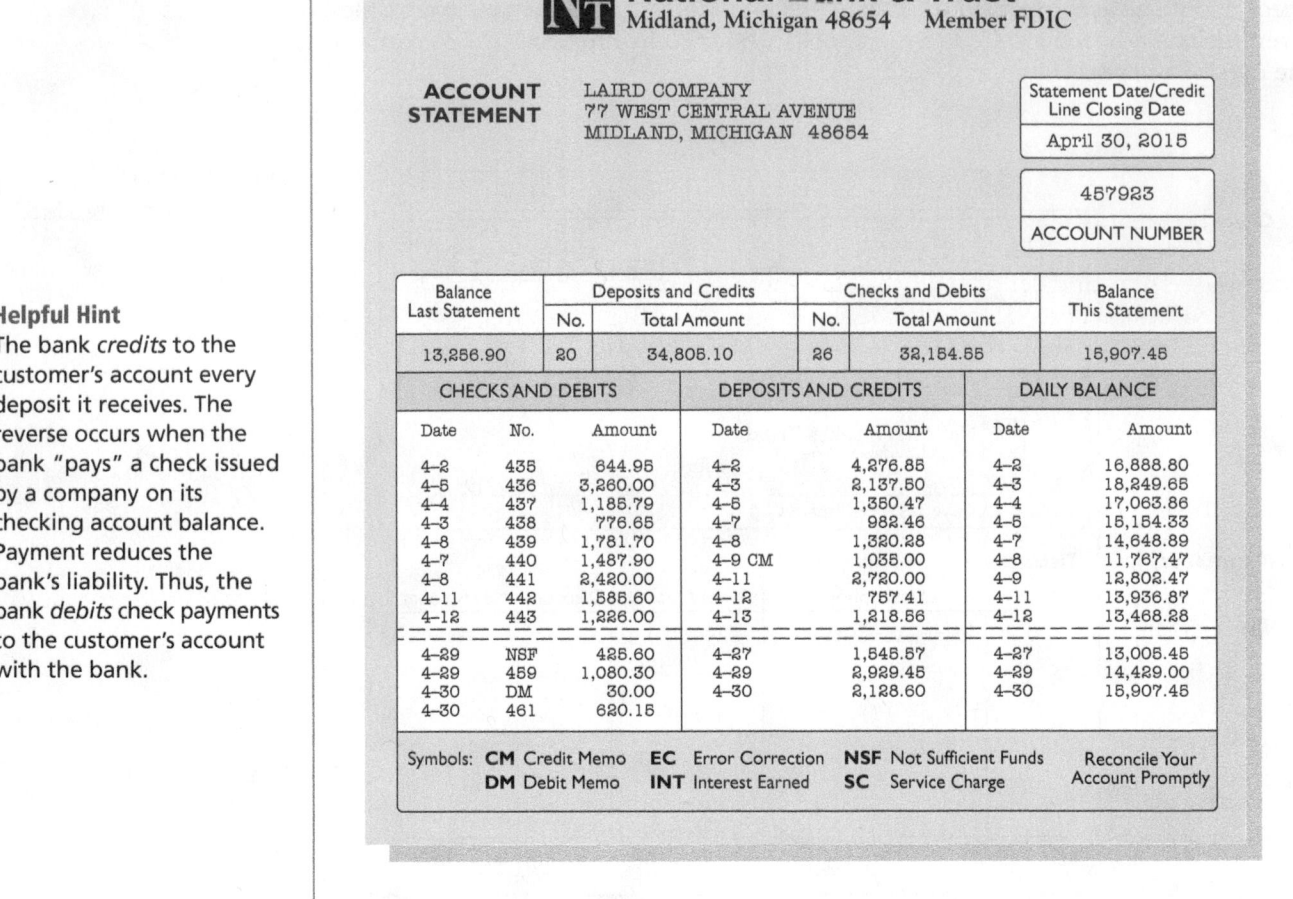

The bank statement lists in numerical sequence all "paid" checks, along with the date the check was paid and its amount. Upon paying a check, the bank stamps the check "paid"; a paid check is sometimes referred to as a **canceled** check. On the statement, the bank also includes memoranda explaining other debits and credits it made to the depositor's account.

DEBIT MEMORANDUM

Some banks charge a monthly fee for their services. Often, they charge this fee only when the average monthly balance in a checking account falls below a specified amount. They identify the fee, called a **bank service charge**, on the bank statement by a symbol such as **SC**. The bank also sends with the statement a debit memorandum explaining the charge noted on the statement. Other debit memoranda may also be issued for other bank services such as the cost of printing checks, issuing traveler's checks, and wiring funds to other locations. The symbol **DM** is often used for such charges.

Banks also use a debit memorandum when a deposited check from a customer "bounces" because of insufficient funds. For example, assume that J. R. Baron, a customer of Laird Company, sends a check for $425.60 to Laird Company for services performed. Unfortunately, Baron does not have sufficient funds at its bank to pay for these services. In such a case, Baron's bank marks the check

NSF (not sufficient funds) and returns it to Laird's (the depositor's) bank. Laird's bank then debits Laird's account, as shown by the symbol NSF on the bank statement in Illustration 7-10. The bank sends the NSF check and debit memorandum to Laird as notification of the charge. Laird then records an Account Receivable from J. R. Baron (the writer of the bad check) and reduces cash for the NSF check.

CREDIT MEMORANDUM

Sometimes a depositor asks the bank to collect its notes receivable. In such a case, the bank will credit the depositor's account for the cash proceeds of the note. This is illustrated by the symbol **CM** on the Laird Company bank statement. The bank issues and sends with the statement a credit memorandum to explain the entry. Many banks also offer interest on checking accounts. The interest earned may be indicated on the bank statement by the symbol **CM** or **INT**.

Reconciling the Bank Account

The bank and the depositor maintain independent records of the depositor's checking account. People tend to assume that the respective balances will always agree. In fact, the two balances are seldom the same at any given time, and both balances differ from the "correct" or "true" balance. Therefore, it is necessary to make the balance per books and the balance per bank agree with the correct or true amount—a process called **reconciling the bank account**. The need for agreement has two causes:

1. **Time lags** that prevent one of the parties from recording the transaction in the same period as the other party.
2. **Errors** by either party in recording transactions.

Time lags occur frequently. For example, several days may elapse between the time a company mails a check to a payee and the date the bank pays the check. Similarly, when the depositor uses the bank's night depository to make its deposits, there will be a difference of at least one day between the time the depositor records the deposit and the time the bank does so. A time lag also occurs whenever the bank mails a debit or credit memorandum to the depositor.

The incidence of errors depends on the effectiveness of the internal controls maintained by the company and the bank. Bank errors are infrequent. However, either party could accidentally record a $450 check as $45 or $540. In addition, the bank might mistakenly charge a check drawn by C. D. Berg to the account of C. D. Burg.

> **LEARNING OBJECTIVE   7**
>
> Prepare a bank reconciliation.

RECONCILIATION PROCEDURE

The bank reconciliation should be prepared by an employee who has no other responsibilities pertaining to cash. If a company fails to follow this internal control principle of independent internal verification, cash embezzlements may go unnoticed. For example, a cashier who prepares the reconciliation can embezzle cash and conceal the embezzlement by misstating the reconciliation. Thus, the bank accounts would reconcile, and the embezzlement would not be detected.

In reconciling the bank account, it is customary to reconcile the balance per books and balance per bank to their adjusted (correct or true) cash balances. The starting point in preparing the reconciliation is to enter the balance per bank statement and the balance per books on the reconciliation schedule. The company then makes various adjustments, as shown in Illustration 7-11 (page 356).

Illustration 7-11
Bank reconciliation
adjustments

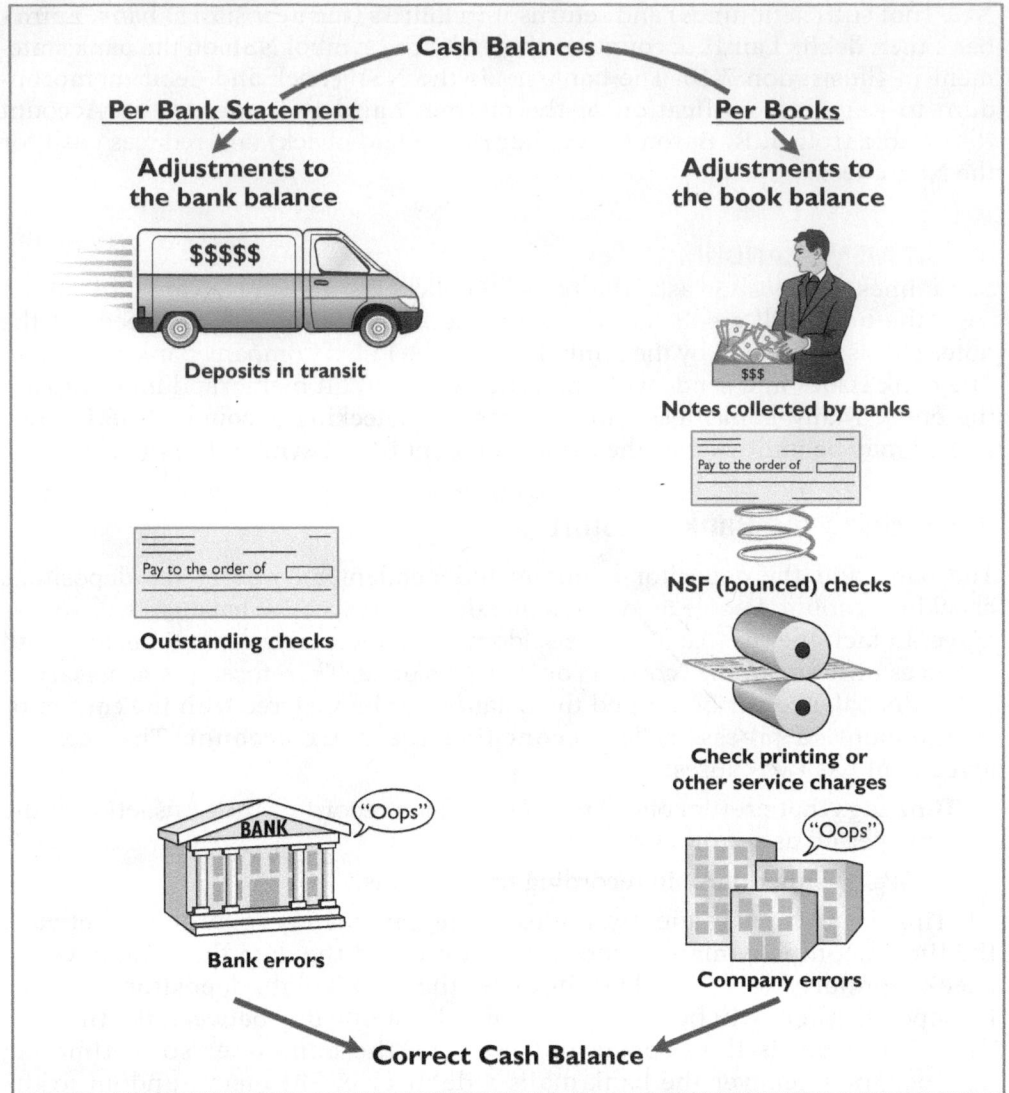

The following steps should reveal all the reconciling items that cause the difference between the two balances.

Step 1. **Deposits in transit.** Compare the individual deposits listed on the bank statement with deposits in transit from the preceding bank reconciliation and with the deposits per company records or duplicate deposit slips. Deposits recorded by the depositor that have not been recorded by the bank are the **deposits in transit**. Add these deposits to the balance per bank.

Step 2. **Outstanding checks.** Compare the paid checks shown on the bank statement with (a) checks outstanding from the previous bank reconciliation, and (b) checks issued by the company as recorded in the cash payments journal (or in the check register in your personal checkbook). Issued checks recorded by the company but that have not yet been paid by the bank are **outstanding checks**. Deduct outstanding checks from the balance per the bank.

Step 3. **Errors.** Note any errors discovered in the foregoing steps and list them in the appropriate section of the reconciliation schedule. For example, if the company mistakenly recorded as $169 a paid check correctly written for $196, it would deduct the error of $27 from the balance per books. All errors made by the depositor are reconciling items in determining the adjusted cash balance per books. In contrast, all errors made by the bank are reconciling items in determining the adjusted cash balance per bank.

Step 4. Bank memoranda. Trace bank memoranda to the depositor's records. List in the appropriate section of the reconciliation schedule any unrecorded memoranda. For example, the company would deduct from the balance per books a $5 debit memorandum for bank service charges. Similarly, it would add to the balance per books $32 of interest earned.

BANK RECONCILIATION ILLUSTRATED

The bank statement for Laird Company in Illustration 7-10 shows a balance per bank of $15,907.45 on April 30, 2015. On this date, the balance of cash per books is $11,589.45. Using the four reconciliation steps, Laird determines the following reconciling items.

Step 1. Deposits in transit: April 30 deposit (received by
bank on May 1). $2,201.40

Step 2. Outstanding checks: No. 453, $3,000.00; no. 457,
$1,401.30; no. 460, $1,502.70. 5,904.00

Step 3. Errors: Laird wrote check no. 443 for $1,226.00 and the bank correctly paid that amount. However, Laird recorded the check as $1,262.00. 36.00

Step 4. Bank memoranda:
  a. Debit—NSF check from J. R. Baron for $425.60. 425.60
  b. Debit—Charge for printing company checks $30.00. 30.00
  c. Credit—Collection of note receivable for $1,000
      plus interest earned $50, less bank collection fee $15.00. 1,035.00

Illustration 7-12 shows Laird's bank reconciliation.

Helpful Hint
Note in the bank statement in Illustration 7-10 that checks no. 459 and 461 have been paid but check no. 460 is not listed. Thus, this check is outstanding. If a complete bank statement were shown, checks no. 453 and 457 would also not be listed. The amounts for these three checks are obtained from the company's cash payments records.

Illustration 7-12
Bank reconciliation

LAIRD COMPANY Bank Reconciliation April 30, 2015		
Cash balance per bank statement		$ 15,907.45
Add: Deposits in transit		2,201.40
		18,108.85
Less: Outstanding checks		
No. 453	$3,000.00	
No. 457	1,401.30	
No. 460	1,502.70	5,904.00
Adjusted cash balance per bank		**$12,204.85**
Cash balance per books		$ 11,589.45
Add: Collection of note receivable $1,000, plus interest earned $50, less collection fee $15	$1,035.00	
Error in recording check no. 443	36.00	1,071.00
		12,660.45
Less: NSF check	425.60	
Bank service charge	30.00	455.60
Adjusted cash balance per books		**$12,204.85**

Alternative Terminology
The terms *adjusted cash balance*, *true cash balance*, and *correct cash balance* are used interchangeably.

Helpful Hint
The entries that follow are adjusting entries. In prior chapters, Cash was an account that did not require adjustment. That was a simplifying assumption for learning purposes because we had not yet explained a bank reconciliation.

ENTRIES FROM BANK RECONCILIATION

The company records each reconciling item used to determine the **adjusted cash balance per books. If the company does not journalize and post these items, the Cash account will not show the correct balance.** Laird Company would make the following entries on April 30.

COLLECTION OF NOTE RECEIVABLE This entry involves four accounts. Assuming that the interest of $50 has not been accrued and the collection fee is charged to Miscellaneous Expense, the entry is:

Apr. 30	Cash	1,035.00	
	Miscellaneous Expense	15.00	
	Notes Receivable		1,000.00
	Interest Revenue		50.00
	(To record collection of note		
	receivable by bank)		

BOOK ERROR The cash disbursements journal shows that check no. 443 was a payment on account to Andrea Company, a supplier. The correcting entry is:

Apr. 30	Cash	36.00	
	Accounts Payable—Andrea Company		36.00
	(To correct error in recording check		
	no. 443)		

NSF CHECK As indicated earlier, an NSF check becomes an account receivable to the depositor. The entry is:

Apr. 30	Accounts Receivable—J. R. Baron	425.60	
	Cash		425.60
	(To record NSF check)		

BANK SERVICE CHARGES Depositors debit check printing charges (DM) and other bank service charges (SC) to Miscellaneous Expense because they are usually nominal in amount. The entry is:

Apr. 30	Miscellaneous Expense	30.00	
	Cash		30.00
	(To record charge for printing company		
	checks)		

Instead of making four separate entries, Laird could combine them into one compound entry.

After Laird has posted the entries, the Cash account will show the following.

Illustration 7-13
Adjusted balance in Cash account

Cash					
Apr. 30 Bal.	11,589.45	Apr. 30			425.60
30	1,035.00	30			30.00
30	36.00				
Apr. 30 Bal.	**12,204.85**				

The adjusted cash balance in the ledger should agree with the adjusted cash balance per books in the bank reconciliation in Illustration 7-12 (page 357).

What entries does the bank make? If the company discovers any bank errors in preparing the reconciliation, it should notify the bank. The bank then can make the necessary corrections in its records. The bank does not make any entries for deposits in transit or outstanding checks. Only when these items reach the bank will the bank record these items.

Electronic Funds Transfer (EFT) System

It is not surprising that companies and banks have developed approaches to transfer funds among parties without the use of paper (deposit tickets, checks, etc.). Such procedures, called **electronic funds transfers (EFT)**, are disbursement systems that use wire, telephone, or computers to transfer cash balances from one location to another. Use of EFT is quite common. For example, many employees receive no formal payroll checks from their employers. Instead, employers send electronic payroll data to the appropriate banks. Also, individuals and companies now frequently make regular payments such as those for house, car, and utilities by EFT.

EFT transactions normally result in better internal control since no cash or checks are handled by company employees. This does not mean that opportunities for fraud are eliminated. In fact, the same basic principles related to internal control apply to EFT transactions. For example, without proper segregation of duties and authorizations, an employee might be able to redirect electronic payments into a personal bank account and conceal the theft with fraudulent accounting entries.

INVESTOR INSIGHT

Madoff's Ponzi Scheme

No recent fraud has generated more interest and rage than the one perpetrated by Bernard Madoff. Madoff was an elite New York investment fund manager who was highly regarded by securities regulators. Investors flocked to him because he delivered very steady returns of between 10% and 15%, no matter whether the market was going up or going down. However, for many years, Madoff did not actually invest the cash that people gave to him. Instead, he was running a Ponzi scheme: He paid returns to existing investors using cash received from new investors. As long as the size of his investment fund continued to grow from new investments at a rate that exceeded the amounts that he needed to pay out in returns, Madoff was able to operate his fraud smoothly. To conceal his misdeeds, he fabricated false investment statements that were provided to investors. In addition, Madoff hired an auditor that never verified the accuracy of the investment records but automatically issued unqualified opinions each year. Although a competing fund manager warned the SEC a number of times over a nearly 10-year period that he thought Madoff was engaged in fraud, the SEC never aggressively investigated the allegations. Investors, many of which were charitable organizations, lost more than $18 billion. Madoff was sentenced to a jail term of 150 years.

Mary Altaffer/©AP/Wide World Photos

 How was Madoff able to conceal such a giant fraud? (See page 382.)

> **DO IT!**

Bank Reconciliation

Sally Kist owns Linen Kist Fabrics. Sally asks you to explain how she should treat the following reconciling items when reconciling the company's bank account: (1) a debit memorandum for an NSF check, (2) a credit memorandum for a note collected by the bank, (3) outstanding checks, and (4) a deposit in transit.

Action Plan

✔ Understand the purpose of a bank reconciliation.

✔ Identify time lags and explain how they cause reconciling items.

Solution

Sally should treat the reconciling items as follows.

(1) NSF check: Deduct from balance per books.

(2) Collection of note: Add to balance per books.

(3) Outstanding checks: Deduct from balance per bank.

(4) Deposit in transit: Add to balance per bank.

Related exercise material: BE7-11, BE7-12, BE7-13, BE7-14, E7-9, E7-10, E7-11, E7-12, E7-13, **and** DO IT! 7-4.

✔ **The Navigator**

Reporting Cash

LEARNING OBJECTIVE 8

Explain the reporting of cash.

Cash consists of coins, currency (paper money), checks, money orders, and money on hand or on deposit in a bank or similar depository. Companies report cash in two different statements: the balance sheet and the statement of cash flows. The balance sheet reports the amount of cash available at a given point in time. The statement of cash flows shows the sources and uses of cash during a period of time. The statement of cash flows was introduced in Chapter 1 and will be discussed in much detail in Chapter 13. In this section, we discuss some important points regarding the presentation of cash in the balance sheet.

When presented in a balance sheet, cash on hand, cash in banks, and petty cash are often combined and reported simply as **Cash**. Because it is the most liquid asset owned by the company, cash is listed first in the current assets section of the balance sheet.

Cash Equivalents

Many companies use the designation "Cash and cash equivalents" in reporting cash. (See Illustration 7-14 for an example.) **Cash equivalents** are short-term, highly liquid investments that are both:

1. Readily convertible to known amounts of cash, and

2. So near their maturity that their market value is relatively insensitive to changes in interest rates.

Illustration 7-14
Balance sheet presentation of cash

DELTA AIR LINES, INC.
Balance Sheet (partial)
December 31, 2012 (in millions)

Assets	
Current assets	
Cash and cash equivalents	**$2,416**
Short-term investments	958
Restricted cash	375
Accounts receivable and other net	1,693
Parts inventories	404
Prepaid expenses and other	2,426
Total current assets	$ 8,272

Examples of cash equivalents are Treasury bills, commercial paper (short-term corporate notes), and money market funds. All typically are purchased with cash that is in excess of immediate needs.

Occasionally, a company will have a net negative balance in its bank account. In this case, the company should report the negative balance among current liabilities. For example, farm equipment manufacturer Ag-Chem recently reported "Checks outstanding in excess of cash balances" of $2,145,000 among its current liabilities.

Ethics Note

Recently, some companies were forced to restate their financial statements because they had too broadly interpreted which types of investments could be treated as cash equivalents. By reporting these items as cash equivalents, the companies made themselves look more liquid.

Restricted Cash

A company may have **restricted cash**, cash that is not available for general use but rather is restricted for a special purpose. For example, landfill companies are often required to maintain a fund of restricted cash to ensure they will have adequate resources to cover closing and clean-up costs at the end of a landfill site's useful life. McKesson Corp. recently reported restricted cash of $962 million to be paid out as the result of investor lawsuits.

Cash restricted in use should be reported separately on the balance sheet as restricted cash. If the company expects to use the restricted cash within the next year, it reports the amount as a current asset. When this is not the case, it reports the restricted funds as a noncurrent asset.

Illustration 7-14 shows restricted cash reported in the financial statements of Delta Air Lines. The company is required to maintain restricted cash as collateral to support insurance obligations related to workers' compensation claims. Delta does not have access to these funds for general use, and so it must report them separately, rather than as part of cash and cash equivalents.

> ## Comprehensive DO IT!

Poorten Company's bank statement for May 2015 shows the following data.

Balance 5/1	$12,650	Balance 5/31	$14,280
Debit memorandum:		Credit memorandum:	
NSF check	$175	Collection of note receivable	$505

The cash balance per books at May 31 is $13,319. Your review of the data reveals the following.

1. The NSF check was from Copple Co., a customer.
2. The note collected by the bank was a $500, 3-month, 12% note. The bank charged a $10 collection fee. No interest has been accrued.
3. Outstanding checks at May 31 total $2,410.
4. Deposits in transit at May 31 total $1,752.
5. A Poorten Company check for $352, dated May 10, cleared the bank on May 25. The company recorded this check, which was a payment on account, for $325.

Instructions
(a) Prepare a bank reconciliation at May 31.
(b) Journalize the entries required by the reconciliation.

Solution to Comprehensive DO IT!

Action Plan

✔ Follow the four steps in the reconciliation procedure (pp. 356–357).

✔ Work carefully to minimize mathematical errors in the reconciliation.

✔ Prepare entries from reconciling items per books.

✔ Make sure the cash ledger balance after posting the reconciling entries agrees with the adjusted cash balance per books.

(a)

POORTEN COMPANY
Bank Reconciliation
May 31, 2015

Cash balance per bank statement		$14,280
Add: Deposits in transit		1,752
		16,032
Less: Outstanding checks		2,410
Adjusted cash balance per bank		$13,622
Cash balance per books		$13,319
Add: Collection of note receivable $500, plus $15		
interest, less collection fee $10		505
		13,824
Less: NSF check	$175	
Error in recording check	27	202
Adjusted cash balance per books		$13,622

(b)

Date	Account	Debit	Credit
May 31	Cash	505	
	Miscellaneous Expense	10	
	Notes Receivable		500
	Interest Revenue		15
	(To record collection of note by bank)		
31	Accounts Receivable—Copple Co.	175	
	Cash		175
	(To record NSF check from Copple Co.)		
31	Accounts Payable	27	
	Cash		27
	(To correct error in recording check)		

✔ **The Navigator**

SUMMARY OF LEARNING OBJECTIVES   ✔ **The Navigator**

1 **Define fraud and internal control.** A fraud is a dishonest act by an employee that results in personal benefit to the employee at a cost to the employer. The fraud triangle refers to the three factors that contribute to fraudulent activity by employees: opportunity, financial pressure, and rationalization. Internal control consists of all the related methods and measures adopted within an organization to safeguard its assets, enhance the reliability of its accounting records, increase efficiency of operations, and ensure compliance with laws and regulations.

2 **Identify the principles of internal control activities.** The principles of internal control are establishment of responsibility; segregation of duties; documentation procedures; physical controls; independent internal verification; and human resource controls such as bonding and requiring employees to take vacations.

3 **Explain the applications of internal control principles to cash receipts.** Internal controls over cash receipts include (a) designating specific personnel to handle cash; (b) assigning different individuals to receive cash,

record cash, and maintain custody of cash; (c) using remittance advices for mail receipts, cash register tapes for over-the-counter receipts, and deposit slips for bank deposits; (d) using company safes and bank vaults to store cash with access limited to authorized personnel, and using cash registers in executing over-the-counter receipts; (e) making independent daily counts of register receipts and daily comparison of total receipts with total deposits; and (f) bonding personnel that handle cash and requiring them to take vacations.

4 **Explain the applications of internal control principles to cash disbursements.** Internal controls over cash disbursements include (a) having specific individuals such as the treasurer authorized to sign checks and approve invoices; (b) assigning different individuals to approve items for payment, make the payment, and record the payment; (c) using prenumbered checks and accounting for all checks, with each check supported by an approved invoice; (d) storing blank checks in a safe or vault with access restricted to authorized personnel,

and using a check-writing machine to imprint amounts on checks; (e) comparing each check with the approved invoice before issuing the check, and making monthly reconciliations of bank and book balances; and (f) bonding personnel who handle cash, requiring employees to take vacations, and conducting background checks.

5 **Describe the operation of a petty cash fund.** Companies operate a petty cash fund to pay relatively small amounts of cash. They must establish the fund, make payments from the fund, and replenish the fund when the cash in the fund reaches a minimum level.

6 **Indicate the control features of a bank account.** A bank account contributes to good internal control by providing physical controls for the storage of cash. It

minimizes the amount of currency that a company must keep on hand, and it creates a double record of a depositor's bank transactions.

7 **Prepare a bank reconciliation.** It is customary to reconcile the balance per books and balance per bank to their adjusted balances. The steps in the reconciling process are to determine deposits in transit, outstanding checks, errors by the depositor or the bank, and unrecorded bank memoranda.

8 **Explain the reporting of cash.** Companies list cash first in the current assets section of the balance sheet. In some cases, they report cash together with cash equivalents. Cash restricted for a special purpose is reported separately as a current asset or as a noncurrent asset, depending on when the cash is expected to be used.

GLOSSARY

Bank reconciliation The process of comparing the bank's balance of an account with the company's balance and explaining any differences to make them agree. (p. 352).

Bank service charge A fee charged by a bank for the use of its services. (p. 354).

Bank statement A monthly statement from the bank that shows the depositor's bank transactions and balances. (p. 353).

Bonding Obtaining insurance protection against misappropriation of assets by employees. (p. 341).

Cash Resources that consist of coins, currency, checks, money orders, and money on hand or on deposit in a bank or similar depository. (p. 360).

Cash equivalents Short-term, highly liquid investments that can be converted to a specific amount of cash. (p. 360).

Check A written order signed by a bank depositor, directing the bank to pay a specified sum of money to a designated recipient. (p. 352).

Deposits in transit Deposits recorded by the depositor but not yet recorded by the bank. (p. 356).

Electronic funds transfer (EFT) A disbursement system that uses wire, telephone, or computers to transfer funds from one location to another. (p. 359).

Fraud A dishonest act by an employee that results in personal benefit to the employee at a cost to the employer. (p. 334).

Fraud triangle The three factors that contribute to fraudulent activity by employees: opportunity, financial pressure, and rationalization. (p. 334).

Internal auditors Company employees who continuously evaluate the effectiveness of the company's internal control system. (p. 341).

Internal control All of the related methods and activities adopted within an organization to safeguard assets and enhance the accuracy and reliability of accounting records. (p. 335).

NSF check A check that is not paid by a bank because of insufficient funds in a customer's bank account. (p. 355).

Outstanding checks Checks issued and recorded by a company but not yet paid by the bank. (p. 356).

Petty cash fund A cash fund used to pay relatively small amounts. (p. 348).

Restricted cash Cash that must be used for a special purpose. (p. 361).

Sarbanes-Oxley Act (SOX) Regulations passed by Congress to try to reduce unethical corporate behavior. (p. 334).

Voucher An authorization form prepared for each payment in a voucher system. (p. 347).

Voucher system A network of approvals by authorized individuals acting independently to ensure that all disbursements by check are proper. (p. 347).

WileyPLUS Self-Test, Brief Exercises, Exercises, Problem Set A, and many more components are available for practice in *WileyPLUS*.

SELF-TEST QUESTIONS

Answers are on page 383.

(LO 1) **1.** Which of the following is **not** an element of the fraud triangle?

    (a) Rationalization.   (c) Segregation of duties.

    (b) Financial pressure.   (d) Opportunity.

2. An organization uses internal control to enhance (LO 1) the accuracy and reliability of accounting records and to:

    (a) safeguard assets.

    (b) eliminate fraud.

(c) produce correct financial statements.

(d) deter employee dishonesty.

(LO 1) **3.** Which of the following was **not** a result of the Sarbanes-Oxley Act?

(a) Companies must file financial statements with the Internal Revenue Service.

(b) All publicly traded companies must maintain adequate internal controls.

(c) The Public Company Accounting Oversight Board was created to establish auditing standards and regulate auditor activity.

(d) Corporate executives and board of directors must ensure that controls are reliable and effective, and they can be fined or imprisoned for failure to do so.

(LO 2) **4.** The principles of internal control do **not** include:

(a) establishment of responsibility.

(b) documentation procedures.

(c) management responsibility.

(d) independent internal verification.

(LO 2) **5.** Physical controls do **not** include:

(a) safes and vaults to store cash.

(b) independent bank reconciliations.

(c) locked warehouses for inventories.

(d) bank safety deposit boxes for important papers.

(LO 2) **6.** Which of the following control activities is **not** relevant when a company uses a computerized (rather than manual) accounting system?

(a) Establishment of responsibility.

(b) Segregation of duties.

(c) Independent internal verification.

(d) All of these control activities are relevant to a computerized system.

(LO 3) **7.** Permitting only designated personnel to handle cash receipts is an application of the principle of:

(a) segregation of duties.

(b) establishment of responsibility.

(c) independent internal verification.

(d) human resource controls.

(LO 4) **8.** The use of prenumbered checks in disbursing cash is an application of the principle of:

(a) establishment of responsibility.

(b) segregation of duties.

(c) physical controls.

(d) documentation procedures.

(LO 5) **9.** A company writes a check to replenish a $100 petty cash fund when the fund contains receipts of $94 and $4 in cash. In recording the check, the company should:

(a) debit Cash Over and Short for $2.

(b) debit Petty Cash for $94.

(c) credit Cash for $94.

(d) credit Petty Cash for $2.

(LO 6) **10.** The control features of a bank account do **not** include:

(a) having bank auditors verify the correctness of the bank balance per books.

(b) minimizing the amount of cash that must be kept on hand.

(c) providing a double record of all bank transactions.

(d) safeguarding cash by using a bank as a depository.

(LO 7) **11.** In a bank reconciliation, deposits in transit are:

(a) deducted from the book balance.

(b) added to the book balance.

(c) added to the bank balance.

(d) deducted from the bank balance.

(LO 7) **12.** The reconciling item in a bank reconciliation that will result in an adjusting entry by the depositor is:

(a) outstanding checks. **(c)** a bank error.

(b) deposit in transit. **(d)** bank service charges.

(LO 8) **13.** Which of the following items in a cash drawer at November 30 is **not** cash?

(a) Money orders.

(b) Coins and currency.

(c) An NSF check.

(d) A customer check dated November 28.

(LO 8) **14.** Which of the following statements correctly describes the reporting of cash?

(a) Cash cannot be combined with cash equivalents.

(b) Restricted cash funds may be combined with cash.

(c) Cash is listed first in the current assets section.

(d) Restricted cash funds cannot be reported as a current asset.

Go to the book's companion website, www.wiley.com/college/weygandt, for additional Self-Test Questions.

 ✔ **The Navigator**

QUESTIONS

1. A local bank reported that it lost $150,000 as the result of an employee fraud. Edward Jasso is not clear on what is meant by an "employee fraud." Explain the meaning of fraud to Edward and give an example of frauds that might occur at a bank.

2. Fraud experts often say that there are three primary factors that contribute to employee fraud. Identify the three factors and explain what is meant by each.

3. Identify and describe the five components of a good internal control system.

4. "Internal control is concerned only with enhancing the accuracy of the accounting records." Do you agree? Explain.

5. What principles of internal control apply to most organizations?

6. At the corner grocery store, all sales clerks make change out of one cash register drawer. Is this a violation of internal control? Why?

7. Liz Kelso is reviewing the principle of segregation of duties. What are the two common applications of this principle?

8. How do documentation procedures contribute to good internal control?

9. What internal control objectives are met by physical controls?

10. (a) Explain the control principle of independent internal verification. (b) What practices are important in applying this principle?

11. The management of Nickle Company asks you, as the company accountant, to explain (a) the concept of reasonable assurance in internal control and (b) the importance of the human factor in internal control.

12. Riverside Fertilizer Co. owns the following assets at the balance sheet date.

Cash in bank savings account	$ 8,000
Cash on hand	850
Cash refund due from the IRS	1,000
Checking account balance	14,000
Postdated checks	500

What amount should Riverside report as cash in the balance sheet?

13. What principle(s) of internal control is (are) involved in making daily cash counts of over-the-counter receipts?

14. Seaton Department Stores has just installed new electronic cash registers in its stores. How do cash registers improve internal control over cash receipts?

15. At Kellum Wholesale Company, two mail clerks open all mail receipts. How does this strengthen internal control?

16. "To have maximum effective internal control over cash disbursements, all payments should be made by check." Is this true? Explain.

17. Ken Deangelo Company's internal controls over cash disbursements provide for the treasurer to sign checks imprinted by a check-writing machine in indelible ink after comparing the check with the approved invoice. Identify the internal control principles that are present in these controls.

18. How do the principles of (a) physical controls and (b) documentation controls apply to cash disbursements?

19. (a) What is a voucher system? (b) What principles of internal control apply to a voucher system?

20. What is the essential feature of an electronic funds transfer (EFT) procedure?

21. (a) Identify the three activities that pertain to a petty cash fund, and indicate an internal control principle that is applicable to each activity. (b) When are journal entries required in the operation of a petty cash fund?

22. "The use of a bank contributes significantly to good internal control over cash." Is this true? Why or why not?

23. Anna Korte is confused about the lack of agreement between the cash balance per books and the balance per bank. Explain the causes for the lack of agreement to Anna, and give an example of each cause.

24. What are the four steps involved in finding differences between the balance per books and balance per bank?

25. Heather Kemp asks your help concerning an NSF check. Explain to Heather (a) what an NSF check is, (b) how it is treated in a bank reconciliation, and (c) whether it will require an adjusting entry.

26. (a) "Cash equivalents are the same as cash." Do you agree? Explain. (b) How should restricted cash funds be reported on the balance sheet?

27. At what amount does Apple report cash and cash equivalents in its 2011 consolidated balance sheet?

BRIEF EXERCISES

BE7-1 Match each situation with the fraud triangle factor—opportunity, financial pressure, or rationalization—that best describes it.

1. An employee's monthly credit card payments are nearly 75% of his or her monthly earnings.
2. An employee earns minimum wage at a firm that has reported record earnings for each of the last five years.
3. An employee has an expensive gambling habit.
4. An employee has check-writing and -signing responsibilities for a small company, as well as reconciling the bank account.

Identify fraud triangle concepts.
(LO 1)

BE7-2 Shelly Eckert has prepared the following list of statements about internal control.

1. One of the objectives of internal control is to safeguard assets from employee theft, robbery, and unauthorized use.
2. One of the objectives of internal control is to enhance the accuracy and reliability of the accounting records.
3. No laws require U.S. corporations to maintain an adequate system of internal control.

Identify each statement as true or false. If false, indicate how to correct the statement.

Indicate internal control concepts.
(LO 1)

Explain the importance of internal control.

(LO 1)

BE7-3 Jessica Mahan is the new owner of Penny Parking. She has heard about internal control but is not clear about its importance for her business. Explain to Jessica the four purposes of internal control and give her one application of each purpose for Penny Parking.

Identify internal control principles.

(LO 2)

BE7-4 The internal control procedures in Valentine Company provide that:

1. Employees who have physical custody of assets do not have access to the accounting records.
2. Each month, the assets on hand are compared to the accounting records by an internal auditor.
3. A prenumbered shipping document is prepared for each shipment of goods to customers.

Identify the principles of internal control that are being followed.

Identify the internal control principles applicable to cash receipts.

(LO 3)

BE7-5 Rosenquist Company has the following internal control procedures over cash receipts. Identify the internal control principle that is applicable to each procedure.

1. All over-the-counter receipts are entered in cash registers.
2. All cashiers are bonded.
3. Daily cash counts are made by cashier department supervisors.
4. The duties of receiving cash, recording cash, and custody of cash are assigned to different individuals.
5. Only cashiers may operate cash registers.

Make journal entries for cash overage and shortfall.

(LO 3)

BE7-6 The cash register tape for Bluestem Industries reported sales of $6,871.50. Record the journal entry that would be necessary for each of the following situations. (a) Cash to be accounted for exceeds cash on hand by $50.75. (b) Cash on hand exceeds cash to be accounted for by $28.32.

Make journal entry using cash count sheet.

(LO 3)

BE7-7 While examining cash receipts information, the accounting department determined the following information: opening cash balance $160, cash on hand $1,125.74, and cash sales per register tape $980.83. Prepare the required journal entry based upon the cash count sheet.

Identify the internal control principles applicable to cash disbursements.

(LO 4)

BE7-8 Pennington Company has the following internal control procedures over cash disbursements. Identify the internal control principle that is applicable to each procedure.

1. Company checks are prenumbered.
2. The bank statement is reconciled monthly by an internal auditor.
3. Blank checks are stored in a safe in the treasurer's office.
4. Only the treasurer or assistant treasurer may sign checks.
5. Check-signers are not allowed to record cash disbursement transactions.

Prepare entry to replenish a petty cash fund.

(LO 5)

BE7-9 On March 20, Dody's petty cash fund of $100 is replenished when the fund contains $9 in cash and receipts for postage $52, freight-out $26, and travel expense $10. Prepare the journal entry to record the replenishment of the petty cash fund.

Identify the control features of a bank account.

(LO 6)

BE7-10 Lance Bachman is uncertain about the control features of a bank account. Explain the control benefits of (a) a check and (b) a bank statement.

Indicate location of reconciling items in a bank reconciliation.

(LO 7)

BE7-11 The following reconciling items are applicable to the bank reconciliation for Ellington Company: (1) outstanding checks, (2) bank debit memorandum for service charge, (3) bank credit memorandum for collecting a note for the depositor, and (4) deposits in transit. Indicate how each item should be shown on a bank reconciliation.

Identify reconciling items that require adjusting entries.

(LO 7)

BE7-12 Using the data in BE7-11, indicate (a) the items that will result in an adjustment to the depositor's records and (b) why the other items do not require adjustment.

Prepare partial bank reconciliation.

(LO 7)

BE7-13 At July 31, Ramirez Company has the following bank information: cash balance per bank $7,420, outstanding checks $762, deposits in transit $1,620, and a bank service charge $20. Determine the adjusted cash balance per bank at July 31.

Prepare partial bank reconciliation.

(LO 7)

BE7-14 At August 31, Pratt Company has a cash balance per books of $9,500 and the following additional data from the bank statement: charge for printing Pratt Company checks $35, interest earned on checking account balance $40, and outstanding checks $800. Determine the adjusted cash balance per books at August 31.

Explain the statement presentation of cash balances.

(LO 8)

BE7-15 Zhang Company has the following cash balances: Cash in Bank $15,742, Payroll Bank Account $6,000, and Plant Expansion Fund Cash $25,000 to be used two years from now. Explain how each balance should be reported on the balance sheet.

> DO IT! Review

DO IT! 7-1 Identify which control activity is violated in each of the following situations, and explain how the situation creates an opportunity for fraud or inappropriate accounting practices.

1. Once a month, the sales department sends sales invoices to the accounting department to be recorded.
2. Leah Hutcherson orders merchandise for Rice Lake Company; she also receives merchandise and authorizes payment for merchandise.
3. Several clerks at Great Foods use the same cash register drawer.

Identify violations of control activities.
(LO 2)

DO IT! 7-2 Gary Stanten is concerned with control over mail receipts at Gary's Sporting Goods. All mail receipts are opened by Al Krane. Al sends the checks to the accounting department, where they are stamped "For Deposit Only." The accounting department records and deposits the mail receipts weekly. Gary asks for your help in installing a good system of internal control over mail receipts.

Design system of internal control over cash receipts.
(LO 3)

DO IT! 7-3 Wilkinson Company established a $100 petty cash fund on August 1. On August 31, the fund had $7 cash remaining and petty cash receipts for postage $31, office supplies $42, and miscellaneous expense $16. Prepare journal entries to establish the fund on August 1 and replenish the fund on August 31.

Make journal entries for petty cash fund.
(LO 5)

DO IT! 7-4 Roger Richman owns Richman Blankets. Richman asks you to explain how he should treat the following reconciling items when reconciling the company's bank account.

1. Outstanding checks.
2. A deposit in transit.
3. The bank charged to our account a check written by another company.
4. A debit memorandum for a bank service charge.

Explain treatment of items in bank reconciliation.
(LO 7)

EXERCISES

E7-1 Eve Herschel is the owner of Herschel's Pizza. Herschel's is operated strictly on a carryout basis. Customers pick up their orders at a counter where a clerk exchanges the pizza for cash. While at the counter, the customer can see other employees making the pizzas and the large ovens in which the pizzas are baked.

Identify the principles of internal control.
(LO 2)

Instructions
Identify the six principles of internal control and give an example of each principle that you might observe when picking up your pizza. (*Note:* It may not be possible to observe all the principles.)

E7-2 The following control procedures are used at Torres Company for over-the-counter cash receipts.

1. To minimize the risk of robbery, cash in excess of $100 is stored in an unlocked attaché case in the stockroom until it is deposited in the bank.
2. All over-the-counter receipts are registered by three clerks who use a cash register with a single cash drawer.
3. The company accountant makes the bank deposit and then records the day's receipts.
4. At the end of each day, the total receipts are counted by the cashier on duty and reconciled to the cash register total.
5. Cashiers are experienced; they are not bonded.

Identify internal control weaknesses over cash receipts and suggest improvements.
(LO 2, 3)

Instructions
(a) For each procedure, explain the weakness in internal control, and identify the control principle that is violated.
(b) For each weakness, suggest a change in procedure that will result in good internal control.

Identify internal control weaknesses over cash disbursements and suggest improvements.

(LO 2, 4)

E7-3 The following control procedures are used in Mendy Lang's Boutique Shoppe for cash disbursements.

1. The company accountant prepares the bank reconciliation and reports any discrepancies to the owner.
2. The store manager personally approves all payments before signing and issuing checks.
3. Each week, 100 company checks are left in an unmarked envelope on a shelf behind the cash register.
4. After payment, bills are filed in a paid invoice folder.
5. The company checks are unnumbered.

Instructions

(a) For each procedure, explain the weakness in internal control, and identify the internal control principle that is violated.
(b) For each weakness, suggest a change in the procedure that will result in good internal control.

Identify internal control weaknesses for cash disbursements and suggest improvements.

(LO 4)

E7-4 At Danner Company, checks are not prenumbered because both the purchasing agent and the treasurer are authorized to issue checks. Each signer has access to unissued checks kept in an unlocked file cabinet. The purchasing agent pays all bills pertaining to goods purchased for resale. Prior to payment, the purchasing agent determines that the goods have been received and verifies the mathematical accuracy of the vendor's invoice. After payment, the invoice is filed by the vendor name, and the purchasing agent records the payment in the cash disbursements journal. The treasurer pays all other bills following approval by authorized employees. After payment, the treasurer stamps all bills PAID, files them by payment date, and records the checks in the cash disbursements journal. Danner Company maintains one checking account that is reconciled by the treasurer.

Instructions

(a) List the weaknesses in internal control over cash disbursements.
(b) ⬤━━━ Write a memo to the company treasurer indicating your recommendations for improvement.

Indicate whether procedure is good or weak internal control.

(LO 2, 3, 4)

E7-5 Listed below are five procedures followed by Eikenberry Company.

1. Several individuals operate the cash register using the same register drawer.
2. A monthly bank reconciliation is prepared by someone who has no other cash responsibilities.
3. Joe Cockrell writes checks and also records cash payment journal entries.
4. One individual orders inventory, while a different individual authorizes payments.
5. Unnumbered sales invoices from credit sales are forwarded to the accounting department every four weeks for recording.

Instructions

Indicate whether each procedure is an example of good internal control or of weak internal control. If it is an example of good internal control, indicate which internal control principle is being followed. If it is an example of weak internal control, indicate which internal control principle is violated. Use the table below.

Procedure	IC Good or Weak?	Related Internal Control Principle
1.		
2.		
3.		
4.		
5.		

Indicate whether procedure is good or weak internal control.

(LO 2, 3, 4)

E7-6 Listed below are five procedures followed by Gilmore Company.

1. Employees are required to take vacations.
2. Any member of the sales department can approve credit sales.
3. Paul Jaggard ships goods to customers, bills customers, and receives payment from customers.
4. Total cash receipts are compared to bank deposits daily by someone who has no other cash responsibilities.
5. Time clocks are used for recording time worked by employees.

Instructions

Indicate whether each procedure is an example of good internal control or of weak internal control. If it is an example of good internal control, indicate which internal control principle is being followed. If it is an example of weak internal control, indicate which internal control principle is violated. Use the table below.

Procedure	IC Good or Weak?	Related Internal Control Principle
1.		
2.		
3.		
4.		
5.		

E7-7 Setterstrom Company established a petty cash fund on May 1, cashing a check for $100. The company reimbursed the fund on June 1 and July 1 with the following results.

> June 1: Cash in fund $1.75. Receipts: delivery expense $31.25; postage expense $39.00; and miscellaneous expense $25.00.
> July 1: Cash in fund $3.25. Receipts: delivery expense $21.00; entertainment expense $51.00; and miscellaneous expense $24.75.

On July 10, Setterstrom increased the fund from $100 to $130.

Prepare journal entries for a petty cash fund.
(LO 5)

Instructions

Prepare journal entries for Setterstrom Company for May 1, June 1, July 1, and July 10.

E7-8 Horvath Company uses an imprest petty cash system. The fund was established on March 1 with a balance of $100. During March, the following petty cash receipts were found in the petty cash box.

Prepare journal entries for a petty cash fund.
(LO 5)

Date	Receipt No.	For	Amount
3/5	1	Stamp Inventory	$39
7	2	Freight-Out	21
9	3	Miscellaneous Expense	6
11	4	Travel Expense	24
14	5	Miscellaneous Expense	5

The fund was replenished on March 15 when the fund contained $2 in cash. On March 20, the amount in the fund was increased to $175.

Instructions

Journalize the entries in March that pertain to the operation of the petty cash fund.

E7-9 Don Wyatt is unable to reconcile the bank balance at January 31. Don's reconciliation is as follows.

Prepare bank reconciliation and adjusting entries.
(LO 7)

Cash balance per bank	$3,560.20
Add: NSF check	490.00
Less: Bank service charge	25.00
Adjusted balance per bank	$4,025.20
Cash balance per books	$3,875.20
Less: Deposits in transit	530.00
Add: Outstanding checks	730.00
Adjusted balance per books	$4,075.20

Instructions

(a) Prepare a correct bank reconciliation.
(b) Journalize the entries required by the reconciliation.

E7-10 On April 30, the bank reconciliation of Westbrook Company shows three outstanding checks: no. 254, $650; no. 255, $620; and no. 257, $410. The May bank statement and the May cash payments journal are shown on page 370.

Determine outstanding checks.
(LO 7)

Bank Statement			Cash Payments Journal		
Checks Paid			Checks Issued		
Date	Check No.	Amount	Date	Check No.	Amount
5/4	254	$650	5/2	258	$159
5/2	257	410	5/5	259	275
5/17	258	159	5/10	260	890
5/12	259	275	5/15	261	500
5/20	261	500	5/22	262	750
5/29	263	480	5/24	263	480
5/30	262	750	5/29	264	560

Instructions

Using Step 2 in the reconciliation procedure, list the outstanding checks at May 31.

Prepare bank reconciliation and adjusting entries.

(LO 7)

E7-11 The following information pertains to Crane Video Company.

1. Cash balance per bank, July 31, $7,263.
2. July bank service charge not recorded by the depositor $28.
3. Cash balance per books, July 31, $7,284.
4. Deposits in transit, July 31, $1,300.
5. Bank collected $700 note for Crane in July, plus interest $36, less fee $20. The collection has not been recorded by Crane, and no interest has been accrued.
6. Outstanding checks, July 31, $591.

Instructions

(a) Prepare a bank reconciliation at July 31.
(b) Journalize the adjusting entries at July 31 on the books of Crane Video Company.

Prepare bank reconciliation and adjusting entries.

(LO 7)

E7-12 The information below relates to the Cash account in the ledger of Minton Company.

Balance September 1—$17,150; Cash deposited—$64,000.
Balance September 30—$17,404; Checks written—$63,746.

The September bank statement shows a balance of $16,422 on September 30 and the following memoranda.

Credits		Debits	
Collection of $2,500 note plus interest $30	$2,530	NSF check: Richard Nance	$425
Interest earned on checking account	$45	Safety deposit box rent	$65

At September 30, deposits in transit were $5,450, and outstanding checks totaled $2,383.

Instructions

(a) Prepare the bank reconciliation at September 30.
(b) Prepare the adjusting entries at September 30, assuming (1) the NSF check was from a customer on account, and (2) no interest had been accrued on the note.

Compute deposits in transit and outstanding checks for two bank reconciliations.

(LO 7)

E7-13 The cash records of Dawes Company show the following four situations.

1. The June 30 bank reconciliation indicated that deposits in transit total $920. During July, the general ledger account Cash shows deposits of $15,750, but the bank statement indicates that only $15,600 in deposits were received during the month.
2. The June 30 bank reconciliation also reported outstanding checks of $680. During the month of July, Dawes Company's books show that $17,200 of checks were issued. The bank statement showed that $16,400 of checks cleared the bank in July.
3. In September, deposits per the bank statement totaled $26,700, deposits per books were $26,400, and deposits in transit at September 30 were $2,100.
4. In September, cash disbursements per books were $23,700, checks clearing the bank were $25,000, and outstanding checks at September 30 were $2,100.

There were no bank debit or credit memoranda. No errors were made by either the bank or Dawes Company.

Instructions

Answer the following questions.

(a) In situation (1), what were the deposits in transit at July 31?
(b) In situation (2), what were the outstanding checks at July 31?

(c) In situation (3), what were the deposits in transit at August 31?

(d) In situation (4), what were the outstanding checks at August 31?

E7-14 Wynn Company has recorded the following items in its financial records.

Cash in bank	$ 42,000
Cash in plant expansion fund	100,000
Cash on hand	12,000
Highly liquid investments	34,000
Petty cash	500
Receivables from customers	89,000
Stock investments	61,000

Show presentation of cash in financial statements.

(LO 8)

The highly liquid investments had maturities of 3 months or less when they were purchased. The stock investments will be sold in the next 6 to 12 months. The plant expansion project will begin in 3 years.

Instructions

(a) What amount should Wynn report as "Cash and cash equivalents" on its balance sheet?

(b) Where should the items not included in part (a) be reported on the balance sheet?

(c) What disclosures should Wynn make in its financial statements concerning "cash and cash equivalents"?

EXERCISES: SET B AND CHALLENGE EXERCISES

Visit the book's companion website, at **www.wiley.com/college/weygandt**, and choose the Student Companion site to access Exercise Set B and Challenge Exercises.

PROBLEMS: SET A

P7-1A Bolz Office Supply Company recently changed its system of internal control over cash disbursements. The system includes the following features.

Instead of being unnumbered and manually prepared, all checks must now be pre-numbered and written by using the new check-writing machine purchased by the company. Before a check can be issued, each invoice must have the approval of Kathy Moon, the purchasing agent, and Robin Self, the receiving department supervisor. Checks must be signed by either Jennifer Edwards, the treasurer, or Rich Woodruff, the assistant treasurer. Before signing a check, the signer is expected to compare the amount of the check with the amount on the invoice.

After signing a check, the signer stamps the invoice PAID and inserts (within the stamp) the date, check number, and amount of the check. The "paid" invoice is then sent to the accounting department for recording.

Blank checks are stored in a safe in the treasurer's office. The combination to the safe is known only by the treasurer and assistant treasurer. Each month, the bank statement is reconciled with the bank balance per books by the assistant chief accountant. All employees who handle or account for cash are bonded.

Instructions

Identify the internal control principles and their application to cash disbursements of Bolz Office Supply Company.

Identify internal control principles over cash disbursements.

(LO 2, 4)

P7-2A Forney Company maintains a petty cash fund for small expenditures. The following transactions occurred over a 2-month period.

July 1   Established petty cash fund by writing a check on Scranton Bank for $200.

    15   Replenished the petty cash fund by writing a check for $196.00. On this date, the fund consisted of $4.00 in cash and the following petty cash receipts: freight-out $92.00, postage expense $42.40, entertainment expense $46.60, and miscellaneous expense $11.20.

Journalize and post petty cash fund transactions.

(LO 5)

31   Replenished the petty cash fund by writing a check for $192.00. At this date, the fund consisted of $8.00 in cash and the following petty cash receipts: freight-out $82.10, charitable contributions expense $45.00, postage expense $25.50, and miscellaneous expense $39.40.

Aug. 15   Replenished the petty cash fund by writing a check for $187.00. On this date, the fund consisted of $13.00 in cash and the following petty cash receipts: freight-out $77.60, entertainment expense $43.00, postage expense $33.00, and miscellaneous expense $37.00.

16   Increased the amount of the petty cash fund to $300 by writing a check for $100.

31   Replenished the petty cash fund by writing a check for $284.00. On this date, the fund consisted of $16 in cash and the following petty cash receipts: postage expense $140.00, travel expense $95.60, and freight-out $47.10.

Instructions

(a) July 15, Cash short $3.80

(b) Aug. 31 balance $300

(a) Journalize the petty cash transactions.

(b) Post to the Petty Cash account.

(c) What internal control features exist in a petty cash fund?

Prepare a bank reconciliation and adjusting entries.

(LO 7)

P7-3A On May 31, 2015, Reber Company had a cash balance per books of $6,781.50. The bank statement from New York State Bank on that date showed a balance of $6,404.60. A comparison of the statement with the Cash account revealed the following facts.

1. The statement included a debit memo of $40 for the printing of additional company checks.

2. Cash sales of $836.15 on May 12 were deposited in the bank. The cash receipts journal entry and the deposit slip were incorrectly made for $886.15. The bank credited Reber Company for the correct amount.

3. Outstanding checks at May 31 totaled $576.25. Deposits in transit were $2,416.15.

4. On May 18, the company issued check no. 1181 for $685 to Lynda Carsen on account. The check, which cleared the bank in May, was incorrectly journalized and posted by Reber Company for $658.

5. A $3,000 note receivable was collected by the bank for Reber Company on May 31 plus $80 interest. The bank charged a collection fee of $20. No interest has been accrued on the note.

6. Included with the canceled checks was a check issued by Stiner Company to Ted Cress for $800 that was incorrectly charged to Reber Company by the bank.

7. On May 31, the bank statement showed an NSF charge of $680 for a check issued by Sue Allison, a customer, to Reber Company on account.

Instructions

(a) Adjusted cash balance per bank $9,044.50

(a) Prepare the bank reconciliation at May 31, 2015.

(b) Prepare the necessary adjusting entries for Reber Company at May 31, 2015.

Prepare a bank reconciliation and adjusting entries from detailed data.

(LO 7)

P7-4A The bank portion of the bank reconciliation for Langer Company at November 30, 2015, was as follows.

LANGER COMPANY
Bank Reconciliation
November 30, 2015

Cash balance per bank		$14,367.90
Add: Deposits in transit		2,530.20
		16,898.10

Less: Outstanding checks		
Check Number	Check Amount	
3451	$2,260.40	
3470	720.10	
3471	844.50	
3472	1,426.80	
3474	1,050.00	6,301.80
Adjusted cash balance per bank		$10,596.30

The adjusted cash balance per bank agreed with the cash balance per books at November 30.

The December bank statement showed the following checks and deposits.

Bank Statement				
Checks			**Deposits**	
Date	**Number**	**Amount**	**Date**	**Amount**
12-1	3451	$ 2,260.40	12-1	$ 2,530.20
12-2	3471	844.50	12-4	1,211.60
12-7	3472	1,426.80	12-8	2,365.10
12-4	3475	1,640.70	12-16	2,672.70
12-8	3476	1,300.00	12-21	2,945.00
12-10	3477	2,130.00	12-26	2,567.30
12-15	3479	3,080.00	12-29	2,836.00
12-27	3480	600.00	12-30	1,025.00
12-30	3482	475.50	Total	$18,152.90
12-29	3483	1,140.00		
12-31	3485	540.80		
	Total	$15,438.70		

The cash records per books for December showed the following.

Cash Payments Journal						Cash Receipts Journal	
Date	**Number**	**Amount**	**Date**	**Number**	**Amount**	**Date**	**Amount**
12-1	3475	$1,640.70	12-20	3482	$ 475.50	12-3	$ 1,211.60
12-2	3476	1,300.00	12-22	3483	1,140.00	12-7	2,365.10
12-2	3477	2,130.00	12-23	3484	798.00	12-15	2,672.70
12-4	3478	621.30	12-24	3485	450.80	12-20	2,954.00
12-8	3479	3,080.00	12-30	3486	889.50	12-25	2,567.30
12-10	3480	600.00	Total		$13,933.20	12-28	2,836.00
12-17	3481	807.40				12-30	1,025.00
						12-31	1,690.40
						Total	$17,322.10

The bank statement contained two memoranda:

1. A credit of $5,145 for the collection of a $5,000 note for Langer Company plus interest of $160 and less a collection fee of $15. Langer Company has not accrued any interest on the note.

2. A debit of $572.80 for an NSF check written by L. Rees, a customer. At December 31, the check had not been redeposited in the bank.

At December 31, the cash balance per books was $12,485.20, and the cash balance per the bank statement was $20,154.30. The bank did not make any errors, but two errors were made by Langer Company.

Instructions

(a) Using the four steps in the reconciliation procedure, prepare a bank reconciliation at December 31.

(b) Prepare the adjusting entries based on the reconciliation. (*Hint:* The correction of any errors pertaining to recording checks should be made to Accounts Payable. The correction of any errors relating to recording cash receipts should be made to Accounts Receivable.)

(a) Adjusted balance per books $16,958.40

Prepare a bank reconciliation and adjusting entries.

(LO 7)

P7-5A Rodriguez Company maintains a checking account at the Imura Bank. At July 31, selected data from the ledger balance and the bank statement are shown below.

	Cash in Bank	
	Per Books	**Per Bank**
Balance, July 1	$17,600	$15,800
July receipts	81,400	
July credits		83,470
July disbursements	77,150	
July debits		74,756
Balance, July 31	$21,850	$24,514

Analysis of the bank data reveals that the credits consist of $79,000 of July deposits and a credit memorandum of $4,470 for the collection of a $4,400 note plus interest revenue of $70. The July debits per bank consist of checks cleared $74,700 and a debit memorandum of $56 for printing additional company checks.

You also discover the following errors involving July checks: (1) A check for $230 to a creditor on account that cleared the bank in July was journalized and posted as $320. (2) A salary check to an employee for $255 was recorded by the bank for $155.

The June 30 bank reconciliation contained only two reconciling items: deposits in transit $8,000 and outstanding checks of $6,200.

Instructions

(a) Adjusted balance per books $26,354

(a) Prepare a bank reconciliation at July 31, 2015.

(b) Journalize the adjusting entries to be made by Rodriguez Company. Assume that interest on the note has not been accrued.

Identify internal control weaknesses in cash receipts and cash disbursements.

(LO 2, 3, 4)

P7-6A Rondelli Middle School wants to raise money for a new sound system for its auditorium. The primary fund-raising event is a dance at which the famous disc jockey D.J. Sound will play classic and not-so-classic dance tunes. Matt Ballester, the music and theater instructor, has been given the responsibility for coordinating the fund-raising efforts. This is Matt's first experience with fund-raising. He decides to put the eighth-grade choir in charge of the event; he will be a relatively passive observer.

Matt had 500 unnumbered tickets printed for the dance. He left the tickets in a box on his desk and told the choir students to take as many tickets as they thought they could sell for $5 each. In order to ensure that no extra tickets would be floating around, he told them to dispose of any unsold tickets. When the students received payment for the tickets, they were to bring the cash back to Matt and he would put it in a locked box in his desk drawer.

Some of the students were responsible for decorating the gymnasium for the dance. Matt gave each of them a key to the money box and told them that if they took money out to purchase materials, they should put a note in the box saying how much they took and what it was used for. After 2 weeks, the money box appeared to be getting full, so Matt asked Jeff Kenney to count the money, prepare a deposit slip, and deposit the money in a bank account Matt had opened.

The day of the dance, Matt wrote a check from the account to pay the DJ. D.J. Sound, however, said that he accepted only cash and did not give receipts. So Matt took $200 out of the cash box and gave it to D.J. At the dance, Matt had Sam Cooper working at the entrance to the gymnasium, collecting tickets from students, and selling tickets to those who had not prepurchased them. Matt estimated that 400 students attended the dance.

The following day, Matt closed out the bank account, which had $250 in it, and gave that amount plus the $180 in the cash box to Principal Finke. Principal Finke seemed surprised that, after generating roughly $2,000 in sales, the dance netted only $430 in cash. Matt did not know how to respond.

Instructions

Identify as many internal control weaknesses as you can in this scenario, and suggest how each could be addressed.

PROBLEMS: SET B

P7-1B Granada Theater is located in the Brooklyn Mall. A cashier's booth is located near the entrance to the theater. Three cashiers are employed. One works from 1–5 p.m., another from 5–9 p.m. The shifts are rotated among the three cashiers. The cashiers receive cash from customers and operate a machine that ejects serially numbered tickets. The rolls of tickets are inserted and locked into the machine by the theater manager at the beginning of each cashier's shift.

Identify internal control weaknesses over cash receipts.

(LO 2, 3)

After purchasing a ticket, the customer takes the ticket to an usher stationed at the entrance of the theater lobby some 60 feet from the cashier's booth. The usher tears the ticket in half, admits the customer, and returns the ticket stub to the customer. The other half of the ticket is dropped into a locked box by the usher.

At the end of each cashier's shift, the theater manager removes the ticket rolls from the machine and makes a cash count. The cash count sheet is initialed by the cashier. At the end of the day, the manager deposits the receipts in total in a bank night deposit vault located in the mall. The manager also sends copies of the deposit slip and the initialed cash count sheets to the theater company treasurer for verification and to the company's accounting department. Receipts from the first shift are stored in a safe located in the manager's office.

Instructions

(a) Identify the internal control principles and their application to the cash receipts transactions of the Granada Theater.

(b) If the usher and cashier decide to collaborate to misappropriate cash, what actions might they take?

P7-2B Haig Company maintains a petty cash fund for small expenditures. The following transactions occurred over a 2-month period.

Journalize and post petty cash fund transactions.

(LO 5)

July 1   Established petty cash fund by writing a check on China Bank for $100.
    15   Replenished the petty cash fund by writing a check for $96.90. On this date, the fund consisted of $3.10 in cash and the following petty cash receipts: freight-out $51.00, postage expense $20.50, entertainment expense $23.10, and miscellaneous expense $6.10.
    31   Replenished the petty cash fund by writing a check for $95.90. At this date, the fund consisted of $4.10 in cash and the following petty cash receipts: freight-out $43.50, charitable contributions expense $20.00, postage expense $20.10, and miscellaneous expense $12.30.
Aug. 15   Replenished the petty cash fund by writing a check for $98.00. On this date, the fund consisted of $2.00 in cash and the following petty cash receipts: freight-out $40.20, entertainment expense $21.00, postage expense $16.00, and miscellaneous expense $19.80.
    16   Increased the amount of the petty cash fund to $150 by writing a check for $50.
    31   Replenished petty cash fund by writing a check for $137.00. On this date, the fund consisted of $13 in cash and the following petty cash receipts: freight-out $74.00, entertainment expense $43.20, and postage expense $17.70.

Instructions

(a) Journalize the petty cash transactions.

(b) Post to the Petty Cash account.

(c) What internal control features exist in a petty cash fund?

(a) July 15 Cash over $3.80

(b) Aug. 31 balance $150

P7-3B Davaney Genetics Company of Milwaukee, Wisconsin, spreads herbicides and applies liquid fertilizer for local farmers. On May 31, 2015, the company's Cash account per its general ledger showed the following balance.

Prepare a bank reconciliation and adjusting entries.

(LO 7)

	CASH				NO. 101
Date	Explanation	Ref.	Debit	Credit	Balance
May 31	Balance				13,287

The bank statement from Milwaukee State Bank on that date showed the following balance.

MILWAUKEE STATE BANK

Checks and Debits	Deposits and Credits	Daily Balance	
XXX	XXX	5/31	13,332

A comparison of the details on the bank statement with the details in the Cash account revealed the following facts.

1. The statement included a debit memo of $35 for the printing of additional company checks.
2. Cash sales of $1,720 on May 12 were deposited in the bank. The cash receipts journal entry and the deposit slip were incorrectly made for $1,820. The bank credited Davaney Genetics Company for the correct amount.
3. Outstanding checks at May 31 totaled $1,225, and deposits in transit were $2,600.
4. On May 18, the company issued check no. 1181 for $911 to J. Tallgrass on account. The check, which cleared the bank in May, was incorrectly journalized and posted by Davaney Genetics Company for $119.
5. A $4,500 note receivable was collected by the bank for Davaney Genetics Company on May 31 plus $80 interest. The bank charged a collection fee of $25. No interest has been accrued on the note.
6. Included with the canceled checks was a check issued by Morray Company to Terry Irvin for $900 that was incorrectly charged to Davaney Genetics Company by the bank.
7. On May 31, the bank statement showed an NSF charge of $1,308 for a check issued by Peter Reser, a customer, to Davaney Genetics Company on account.

Instructions
(a) Prepare the bank reconciliation at May 31, 2015.
(b) Prepare the necessary adjusting entries for Davaney Genetics Company at May 31, 2015.

(a) Adjusted cash balance per bank $15,607

Prepare a bank reconciliation and adjusting entries from detailed data.

(LO 7)

P7-4B The bank portion of the bank reconciliation for Phillips Company at October 31, 2015, was as follows.

PHILLIPS COMPANY
Bank Reconciliation
October 31, 2015

Cash balance per bank			$6,000
Add: Deposits in transit			842
			6,842
Less: Outstanding checks			
Check Number		Check Amount	
2451		$700	
2470		396	
2471		464	
2472		270	
2474		578	2,408
Adjusted cash balance per bank			$4,434

The adjusted cash balance per bank agreed with the cash balance per books at October 31. The November bank statement showed the following checks and deposits:

Bank Statement

Checks			Deposits	
Date	**Number**	**Amount**	**Date**	**Amount**
11-1	2470	$ 396	11-1	$ 842
11-2	2471	464	11-4	666
11-5	2474	578	11-8	545
11-4	2475	903	11-13	1,416
11-8	2476	1,556	11-18	810
11-10	2477	330	11-21	1,624
11-15	2479	980	11-25	1,412
11-18	2480	714	11-28	908
11-27	2481	382	11-30	652
11-30	2483	317	Total	$8,875
11-29	2486	495		
	Total	$7,115		

The cash records per books for November showed the following.

Cash Payments Journal

Date	Number	Amount	Date	Number	Amount
11-1	2475	$ 903	11-20	2483	$ 317
11-2	2476	1,556	11-22	2484	460
11-2	2477	330	11-23	2485	525
11-4	2478	300	11-24	2486	495
11-8	2479	890	11-29	2487	210
11-10	2480	714	11-30	2488	635
11-15	2481	382	Total		$8,067
11-18	2482	350			

Cash Receipts Journal

Date	Amount
11-3	$ 666
11-7	545
11-12	1,416
11-17	810
11-20	1,642
11-24	1,412
11-27	908
11-29	652
11-30	2,541
Total	$10,592

The bank statement contained two bank memoranda:

1. A credit of $2,375 for the collection of a $2,300 note for Phillips Company plus interest of $91 and less a collection fee of $16. Phillips Company has not accrued any interest on the note.
2. A debit for the printing of additional company checks $34.

At November 30, the cash balance per books was $5,958, and the cash balance per the bank statement was $9,100. The bank did not make any errors, but two errors were made by Phillips Company.

Instructions
(a) Using the four steps in the reconciliation procedure, prepare a bank reconciliation at November 30.
(b) Prepare the adjusting entries based on the reconciliation. (*Hint:* The correction of any errors pertaining to recording checks should be made to Accounts Payable. The correction of any errors relating to recording cash receipts should be made to Accounts Receivable.)

(a) Adjusted cash balance per bank $8,191

P7-5B Zhang Company's bank statement from Nguyen National Bank at August 31, 2015, shows the information below.

Prepare a bank reconciliation and adjusting entries.

(LO 7)

Balance, August 1	$11,284	Bank credit memoranda:	
August deposits	47,521	Collection of note	
Checks cleared in August	46,475	receivable plus $105	
Balance, August 31	16,856	interest	$5,105
		Interest earned	41
		Bank debit memorandum:	
		Safety deposit box rent	20

A summary of the Cash account in the ledger for August shows: balance, August 1, $10,959; receipts $50,050; disbursements $47,794; and balance, August 31, $13,215. Analysis reveals that the only reconciling items on the July 31 bank reconciliation were a deposit in transit for $3,200 and outstanding checks of $2,925. The deposit in transit was the first deposit recorded by the bank in August. In addition, you determine that there were two errors involving company checks drawn in August: (1) A check for $340 to a creditor on account that cleared the bank in August was journalized and posted for $430. (2) A salary check to an employee for $275 was recorded by the bank for $277.

Instructions

(a) Adjusted balance per books
$18,431

(a) Prepare a bank reconciliation at August 31.

(b) Journalize the adjusting entries to be made by Zhang Company at August 31. Assume that interest on the note has not been accrued by the company.

Prepare a comprehensive bank reconciliation with theft and internal control deficiencies.

(LO 2, 3, 4, 7)

P7-6B Gamel Company is a very profitable small business. It has not, however, given much consideration to internal control. For example, in an attempt to keep clerical and office expenses to a minimum, the company has combined the jobs of cashier and book-keeper. As a result, Jan Worthy handles all cash receipts, keeps the accounting records, and prepares the monthly bank reconciliations.

The balance per the bank statement on October 31, 2015, was $15,313. Outstanding checks were: no. 62 for $107.74, no. 183 for $127.50, no. 284 for $215.26, no. 862 for $132.10, no. 863 for $192.78, and no. 864 for $140.49. Included with the statement was a credit memorandum of $460 indicating the collection of a note receivable for Gamel Company by the bank on October 25. This memorandum has not been recorded by Gamel Company.

The company's ledger showed one cash account with a balance of $18,608.81. The balance included undeposited cash on hand. Because of the lack of internal controls, Jan took for personal use all of the undeposited receipts in excess of $3,226.18. She then prepared the following bank reconciliation in an effort to conceal her theft of cash.

BANK RECONCILIATION

Cash balance per books, October 31		$18,608.81
Add: Outstanding checks		
No. 862	$132.10	
No. 863	192.78	
No. 864	140.49	390.37
		18,999.18
Less: Undeposited receipts		3,226.18
Unadjusted balance per bank, October 31		15,773.00
Less: Bank credit memorandum		460.00
Cash balance per bank statement, October 31		$15,313.00

Instructions

(a) Adjusted balance per books
$17,623.31

(a) Prepare a correct bank reconciliation. (*Hint:* Deduct the amount of the theft from the adjusted balance per books.)

(b) Indicate the three ways that Jan attempted to conceal the theft and the dollar amount pertaining to each method.

(c) What principles of internal control were violated in this case?

PROBLEMS: SET C

Visit the book's companion website, at **www.wiley.com/college/weygandt**, and choose the Student Companion site to access Problem Set C.

COMPREHENSIVE PROBLEM

CP7 On December 1, 2015, Fullerton Company had the account balances shown on page 379.

	Debit		Credit
Cash	$18,200	Accumulated Depreciation—	
Notes Receivable	2,200	Equipment	$ 3,000
Accounts Receivable	7,500	Accounts Payable	6,100
Inventory	16,000	Common Stock	50,000
Prepaid Insurance	1,600	Retained Earnings	14,400
Equipment	28,000		$73,500
	$73,500		

During December, the company completed the following transactions.

Dec. 7   Received $3,600 cash from customers in payment of account (no discount allowed).
   12   Purchased merchandise on account from Vance Co. $12,000, terms 1/10, n/30.
   17   Sold merchandise on account $16,000, terms 2/10, n/30. The cost of the merchandise sold was $10,000.
   19   Paid salaries $2,200.
   22   Paid Vance Co. in full, less discount.
   26   Received collections in full, less discounts, from customers billed on December 17.
   31   Received $2,700 cash from customers in payment of account (no discount allowed).

Adjustment data:

1. Depreciation $200 per month.
2. Insurance expired $400.

Instructions
(a) Journalize the December transactions. (Assume a perpetual inventory system.)
(b) Enter the December 1 balances in the ledger T-accounts and post the December transactions. Use Cost of Goods Sold, Depreciation Expense, Insurance Expense, Salaries and Wages Expense, Sales Revenue, and Sales Discounts.
(c) The statement from Jackson County Bank on December 31 showed a balance of $26,130. A comparison of the bank statement with the Cash account revealed the following facts.
   1. The bank collected a note receivable of $2,200 for Fullerton Company on December 15.
   2. The December 31 receipts were deposited in a night deposit vault on December 31. These deposits were recorded by the bank in January.
   3. Checks outstanding on December 31 totaled $1,210.
   4. On December 31, the bank statement showed an NSF charge of $680 for a check received by the company from L. Bryan, a customer, on account.

   Prepare a bank reconciliation as of December 31 based on the available information. (*Hint:* The cash balance per books is $26,100. This can be proven by finding the balance in the Cash account from parts (a) and (b).)
(d) Journalize the adjusting entries resulting from the bank reconciliation and adjustment data.
(e) Post the adjusting entries to the ledger T-accounts.
(f) Prepare an adjusted trial balance.
(g) Prepare an income statement for December and a classified balance sheet at December 31.

CONTINUING COOKIE CHRONICLE

(*Note:* This is a continuation of the Cookie Chronicle from Chapters 1 through 6.)

CCC7   Part 1   Natalie is struggling to keep up with the recording of her accounting transactions. She is spending a lot of time marketing and selling mixers and giving her cookie classes. Her friend John is an accounting student who runs his own accounting service. He has asked Natalie if she would like to have him do her accounting. John and Natalie meet and discuss her business.

Part 2   Natalie decides that she cannot afford to hire John to do her accounting. One way that she can ensure that her cash account does not have any errors and is accurate and up-to-date is to prepare a bank reconciliation at the end of each month. Natalie would like you to help her.

Go to the book's companion website, **www.wiley.com/college/weygandt,** *to see the completion of this problem.*

Broadening Your **PERSPECTIVE**

Financial Reporting and Analysis

Financial Reporting Problem: Apple Inc.

BYP7-1 The financial statements of Apple Inc. are presented in Appendix A at the end of this textbook. Instructions for accessing and using the company's complete annual report, including the notes to the financial statements, are also provided in Appendix A.

Instructions
(a) What comments, if any, are made about cash in the report of the independent registered public accounting firm?
(b) What data about cash and cash equivalents are shown in the consolidated balance sheet?
(c) In its notes to Consolidated Financial Statements, how does Apple define cash equivalents?
(d) In management's Annual Report on Internal Control over Financial Reporting (Item 9), what does Apple's management say about internal control?

Comparative Analysis Problem:
PepsiCo, Inc. vs. The Coca-Cola Company

BYP7-2 PepsiCo's financial statements are presented in Appendix B. Financial statements of The Coca-Cola Company are presented in Appendix C. Instructions for accessing and using the complete annual reports of PepsiCo and Coca-Cola, including the notes to the financial statements, are also provided in Appendices B and C, respectively.

Instructions
(a) Based on the information contained in these financial statements, determine each of the following for each company:
  (1) Cash and cash equivalents balance at December 31, 2011, for PepsiCo and at December 31, 2011, for Coca-Cola.
  (2) Increase (decrease) in cash and cash equivalents from 2010 to 2011.
  (3) Cash provided by operating activities during the year ended December 2011 (from statement of cash flows).
(b) What conclusions concerning the management of cash can be drawn from these data?

Comparative Analysis Problem:
Amazon.com, Inc. vs. Wal-Mart Stores, Inc.

BYP7-3 Amazon.com, Inc.'s financial statements are presented in Appendix D. Financial statements of Wal-Mart Stores, Inc. are presented in Appendix E. Instructions for accessing and using the complete annual reports of Amazon and Wal-Mart, including the notes to the financial statements, are also provided in Appendices D and E, respectively.

Instructions
(a) Based on the information contained in these financial statements, determine each of the following for each company:
  (1) Cash and cash equivalents balance at December 31, 2011, for Amazon and at January 31, 2012, for Wal-Mart.
  (2) Increase (decrease) in cash and cash equivalents from 2011 to 2010.
  (3) Net cash provided by operating activities during the year ended December 31, 2011, for Amazon and January 31, 2012, for Wal-Mart from statement of cash flows.
(b) What conclusions concerning the management of cash can be drawn from these data?

Real-World Focus

BYP7-4 All organizations should have systems of internal control. Universities are no exception. This site discusses the basics of internal control in a university setting.

Address: **www.bc.edu/offices/audit/controls**, or go to **www.wiley.com/college/weygandt**

Steps: Go to the site shown above.

Instructions

The home page of this site provides links to pages that answer six critical questions. Use these links to answer the following questions.

(a) In a university setting, who has responsibility for evaluating the adequacy of the system of internal control?

(b) What are some red flags indicating white collar crime?

(c) What role does an internal audit play at Boston College?

(d) What are two IT controls over computer operations?

Critical Thinking

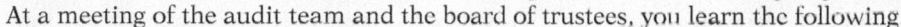

Decision-Making Across the Organization

BYP7-5 The board of trustees of a local church is concerned about the internal accounting controls for the offering collections made at weekly services. The trustees ask you to serve on a three-person audit team with the internal auditor of a local college and a CPA who has just joined the church.

At a meeting of the audit team and the board of trustees, you learn the following.

1. The church's board of trustees has delegated responsibility for the financial management and audit of the financial records to the finance committee. This group prepares the annual budget and approves major disbursements. It is not involved in collections or record-keeping. No audit has been made in recent years because the same trusted employee has kept church records and served as financial secretary for 15 years. The church does not carry any fidelity insurance.

2. The collection at the weekly service is taken by a team of ushers who volunteer to serve one month. The ushers take the collection plates to a basement office at the rear of the church. They hand their plates to the head usher and return to the church service. After all plates have been turned in, the head usher counts the cash received. The head usher then places the cash in the church safe along with a notation of the amount counted. The head usher volunteers to serve for 3 months.

3. The next morning, the financial secretary opens the safe and recounts the collection. The secretary withholds $150–$200 in cash, depending on the cash expenditures expected for the week, and deposits the remainder of the collections in the bank. To facilitate the deposit, church members who contribute by check are asked to make their checks payable to "Cash."

4. Each month, the financial secretary reconciles the bank statement and submits a copy of the reconciliation to the board of trustees. The reconciliations have rarely contained any bank errors and have never shown any errors per books.

Instructions

With the class divided into groups, answer the following.

(a) Indicate the weaknesses in internal accounting control over the handling of collections.

(b) List the improvements in internal control procedures that you plan to make at the next meeting of the audit team for (1) the ushers, (2) the head usher, (3) the financial secretary, and (4) the finance committee.

(c) What church policies should be changed to improve internal control?

Communication Activity

BYP7-6 As a new auditor for the CPA firm of Eaton, Quayle, and Hale, you have been assigned to review the internal controls over mail cash receipts of Pritchard Company. Your review reveals the following. Checks are promptly endorsed "For Deposit Only," but no list of the checks is prepared by the person opening the mail. The mail is opened either by the cashier or by the employee who maintains the accounts receivable records. Mail receipts are deposited in the bank weekly by the cashier.

Instructions

Write a letter to Danny Peak, owner of Pritchard Company, explaining the weaknesses in internal control and your recommendations for improving the system.

Ethics Case

BYP7-7 You are the assistant controller in charge of general ledger accounting at Linbarger Bottling Company. Your company has a large loan from an insurance company. The loan agreement requires that the company's cash account balance be maintained at $200,000 or more, as reported monthly.

At June 30, the cash balance is $80,000, which you report to Lisa Infante, the financial vice president. Lisa excitedly instructs you to keep the cash receipts book open for one additional day for purposes of the June 30 report to the insurance company. Lisa says, "If we don't get that cash balance over $200,000, we'll default on our loan agreement. They could close us down, put us all out of our jobs!" Lisa continues, "I talked to Oconto Distributors (one of Linbarger's largest customers) this morning. They said they sent us a check for $150,000 yesterday. We should receive it tomorrow. If we include just that one check in our cash balance, we'll be in the clear. It's in the mail!"

Instructions
(a) Who will suffer negative effects if you do not comply with Lisa Infante's instructions? Who will suffer if you do comply?
(b) What are the ethical considerations in this case?
(c) What alternatives do you have?

All About You

BYP7-8 The print and electronic media are full of stories about potential security risks that may arise from your personal computer. It is important to keep in mind, however, that there are also many other ways that your identity can be stolen other than from your computer. The federal government provides many resources to help protect you from identity thieves.

Instructions
Go to **http://onguardonline.gov/idtheft.html**, click **Video and Media**, and then click on **ID Theft Faceoff**. Complete the quiz provided there.

FASB Codification Activity

BYP7-9 If your school has a subscription to the FASB Codification, go to **http://aaahq.org/ascLogin.cfm** to log in and prepare responses to the following.

(a) How is cash defined in the Codification?
(b) How are cash equivalents defined in the Codification?
(c) What are the disclosure requirements related to cash and cash equivalents?

Answers to Chapter Questions

Answers to Insight and Accounting Across the Organization Questions

p. 335 And the Controls Are. . . Q: Why is sustainability information important to investors? **A:** Investors, customers, suppliers, and employees want more information about companies' long-term impact on society. There is a growing awareness that sustainability issues can affect a company's financial performance. Proper reporting on sustainability issues develops a solid reputation for transparency and provides confidence to shareholders.

p. 342 SOX Boosts the Role of Human Resources Q: Why would unsupervised employees or employees who report to each other represent potential internal control threats? **A:** An unsupervised employee may have a fraudulent job (or may even be a fictitious person), e.g., a person drawing a paycheck without working. Or, if two employees supervise each other, there is no real separation of duties, and they can conspire to defraud the company.

p. 351 How Employees Steal Q: How can companies reduce the likelihood of fraudulent disbursements? **A:** To reduce the occurrence of fraudulent disbursements, a company should follow the procedures discussed in this chapter. These include having only designated personnel sign checks; having different personnel approve payments and make payments; ensuring that check-signers do not record disbursements; using prenumbered checks and matching each check to an approved invoice; storing blank checks securely; reconciling the bank statement; and stamping invoices PAID.

p. 359 Madoff's Ponzi Scheme Q: How was Madoff able to conceal such a giant fraud? **A:** Madoff fabricated false investment statements that were provided to investors. In addition, his auditor never verified these investment statements even though the auditor issued an unqualified opinion each year.

A Look at IFRS

Fraud can occur anywhere. Because the three main factors that contribute to fraud are universal in nature, the principles of internal control activities are used globally by companies. While Sarbanes-Oxley (SOX) does not apply to non-U.S. companies, most large international companies have internal controls similar to those indicated in the chapter. IFRS and GAAP are also very similar in accounting for cash. *IAS No. 1 (revised)*, "Presentation of Financial Statements," is the only standard that discusses issues specifically related to cash.

> **LEARNING OBJECTIVE 9**
>
> **Compare the accounting procedures for fraud, internal control, and cash under GAAP and IFRS.**

Key Points

- The fraud triangle discussed in this chapter is applicable to all international companies. Some of the major frauds on an international basis are Parmalat (Italy), Royal Ahold (the Netherlands), and Satyam Computer Services (India).

- Rising economic crime poses a growing threat to companies, with 34% of all organizations worldwide being victims of fraud in a recent 12-month period. The survey data shows that the incidence of economic crime varies by industry sector, some (notably insurance, governmental, hospitality and leisure, and financial services) reporting higher levels of fraud than others, and by size and type of organization. However, no organization is immune (*PricewaterhouseCoopers' Global Economic Crime Survey*, 2011).

- Economic crime takes on many different forms, some more common than others. The chart below shows the types of economic crime reported by companies over a 12-month period.

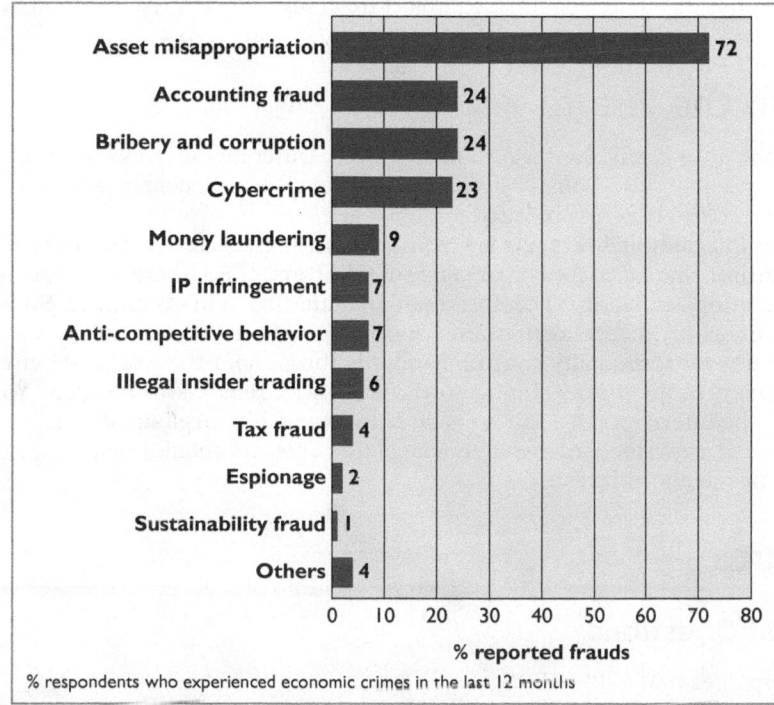

This chart shows that the four most common types of economic crimes experienced in the 12 months were asset misappropriation, accounting fraud, bribery and corruption, and cybercrime (*PricewaterhouseCoopers' Global Economic Crime Survey*, 2011).

- Accounting scandals both in the United States and internationally have re-ignited the debate over the relative merits of GAAP, which takes a "rules-based" approach to accounting, versus IFRS, which takes a "principles-based" approach. The FASB announced that it intends to introduce more principles-based standards.

- On a lighter note, at one time the Ig Nobel Prize in Economics went to the CEOs of those companies involved in the corporate accounting scandals of that year for "adapting the mathematical concept of imaginary numbers for use in the business world." A parody of the Nobel Prizes, the Ig Nobel Prizes (read Ignoble, as not noble) are given each year in early October for 10 achievements that "first make people laugh, and then make them think." Organized by the scientific humor magazine *Annals of Improbable Research* (*AIR*), they are presented by a group that includes genuine Nobel laureates at a ceremony at Harvard University's Sanders Theater (see **en.wikipedia.org/wiki/Ig_Nobel_Prize**).

- Internal controls are a system of checks and balances designed to prevent and detect fraud and errors. While most companies have these systems in place, many have never completely documented them, nor had an independent auditor attest to their effectiveness. Both of these actions are required under SOX.

- Companies find that internal control review is a costly process but badly needed. One study estimates the cost of SOX compliance for U.S. companies at over $35 billion, with audit fees doubling in the first year of compliance. At the same time, examination of internal controls indicates lingering problems in the way companies operate. One study of first compliance with the internal-control testing provisions documented material weaknesses for about 13% of companies reporting in a two-year period (*PricewaterhouseCoopers' Global Economic Crime Survey*, 2005).

- The SOX internal control standards apply only to companies listed on U.S. exchanges. There is continuing debate over whether foreign issuers should have to comply with this extra layer of regulation.

- The accounting and internal control procedures related to cash are essentially the same under both IFRS and this textbook. In addition, the definition used for cash equivalents is the same.

- Most companies report cash and cash equivalents together under IFRS, as shown in this textbook. In addition, IFRS follows the same accounting policies related to the reporting of restricted cash.

- IFRS defines cash and cash equivalents as follows.
  - ♦ **Cash** is comprised of cash on hand and demand deposits.
  - ♦ **Cash equivalents** are short-term, highly liquid investments that are readily convertible to known amounts of cash and which are subject to an insignificant risk of changes in value.

- Under IFRS, cash and cash equivalents are often shown in the statement of financial position.

Looking to the Future

Ethics has become a very important aspect of reporting. Different cultures have different perspectives on bribery and other questionable activities, and consequently penalties for engaging in such activities vary considerably across countries.

High-quality international accounting requires both high-quality accounting standards and high-quality auditing. Similar to the convergence of GAAP and IFRS, there is movement to improve international auditing standards. The International Auditing and Assurance Standards Board (IAASB) functions as an independent standard-setting body. It works to establish high-quality auditing and assurance and quality-control standards throughout the world. Whether the IAASB adopts internal control provisions similar to those in SOX remains to be seen. You can follow developments in the international audit arena at **http://www.ifac.org/iaasb/**.

Under proposed new standards for financial statements, companies would not be allowed to combine cash equivalents with cash.

IFRS Practice

IFRS Self-Test Questions

1. Non-U.S companies that follow IFRS:
   (a) do not normally use the principles of internal control activities described in this textbook.
   (b) often offset cash with accounts payable on the balance sheet.
   (c) are not required to follow SOX.
   (d) None of the above.

2. Which of the following is the correct accounting under IFRS for cash?
   (a) Cash cannot be combined with cash equivalents.
   (b) Restricted cash funds may be reported as a current or non-current asset depending on the circumstances.
   (c) Restricted cash funds cannot be reported as a current asset.
   (d) Cash on hand is not reported on the balance sheet as Cash.

3. The Sarbanes-Oxley Act applies to:
   (a) all U.S. companies listed on U.S. exchanges.
   (b) all companies that list stock on any stock exchange in any country.
   (c) all European companies listed on European exchanges.
   (d) Both (a) and (c).

4. High-quality international accounting requires both high-quality accounting standards and:
   (a) a reconsideration of SOX to make it less onerous.
   (b) high-quality auditing standards.
   (c) government intervention to ensure that the public interest is protected.
   (d) the development of new principles of internal control activities.

5. Cash equivalents under IFRS:
   (a) are significantly different than the cash equivalents discussed in the textbook.
   (b) are generally disclosed separately from cash.
   (c) may be required to be reported separately from cash in the future.
   (d) None of the above.

IFRS Exercises

IFRS7-1 Some people argue that the internal control requirements of the Sarbanes-Oxley Act (SOX) put U.S. companies at a competitive disadvantage to companies outside the United States. Discuss the competitive implications (both pros and cons) of SOX.

IFRS7-2 State whether each of the following is true or false. For those that are false, explain why.

(a) A proposed new financial accounting standard would not allow cash equivalents to be reported in combination with cash.
(b) Perspectives on bribery and penalties for engaging in bribery are the same across all countries.
(c) Cash equivalents are comprised of cash on hand and demand deposits.
(d) SOX was created by the International Accounting Standards Board.

International Financial Reporting Problem: Zetar plc

IFRS7–3 The financial statements of Zetar plc are presented in Appendix F. Instructions for accessing and using the company's complete annual report, including the notes to its financial statements, are also provided in Appendix F.

Instructions
Using the notes to the company's financial statements, answer the following questions.

(a) Which committee of the board of directors is responsible for considering management's reports on internal control?
(b) What are the company's key control procedures?
(c) Does the company have an internal audit department?
(d) In what section or sections does Zetar report its bank overdrafts?

Answers to IFRS Self-Test Questions
1. c 2. b 3. a 4. b 5. c

8 | Accounting for Receivables

Feature Story

A Dose of Careful Management Keeps Receivables Healthy

"Sometimes you have to know when to be very tough, and sometimes you can give them a bit of a break," says Vivi Su. She's not talking about her children but about the customers of a subsidiary of pharmaceutical company Whitehall-Robins, where she works as supervisor of credit and collections.

For example, while the company's regular terms are 1/15, n/30 (1% discount if paid within 15 days), a customer might ask for and receive a few days of grace and still get the discount. Or a customer might place orders above its credit limit, in which case, depending on its payment history and the circumstances, Ms. Su might authorize shipment of the goods anyway.

"It's not about drawing a line in the sand, and that's all," she explains. "You want a good relationship with your customers—but you also need to bring in the money."

"The money," in Whitehall-Robins' case, amounts to some $170 million in sales a year. Nearly all of it comes in through the credit accounts Ms. Su manages. The process starts with the decision to grant a customer an account in the first place, Ms. Su explains. The sales rep gives the customer a credit application. "My department reviews this application very carefully; a customer needs to supply three good references, and we also run a check with a credit firm like Equifax. If we accept them, then based on their size and history, we assign a credit limit."

Once accounts are established, "I get an aging report every single day," says Ms. Su. "The rule of thumb is that we should always have at least 85% of receivables current—meaning they were billed less than 30 days ago," she continues. "But we try to do even better than that—I like to see 90%."

At 15 days overdue, Whitehall-Robins phones the client. After 45 days, Ms. Su notes, "I send a letter. Then a second notice is sent in writing. After the third and final notice, the client has 10 days to pay, and then I hand it over to a collection agency, and it's out of my hands."

Ms. Su's boss, Terry Norton, records an estimate for bad debts every year, based on a percentage of receivables. The percentage depends on the current aging history. He also calculates and monitors the company's accounts receivable turnover, which the company reports in its financial statements.

✔ The Navigator

- Scan Learning Objectives
- Read Feature Story
- Read Preview
- Read text and answer **DO IT!** p. 396
  - p. 398   p. 404   p. 406
- Work Comprehensive **DO IT!** p. 406
- Review Summary of Learning Objectives
- Answer Self-Test Questions
- Complete Assignments
- Go to *WileyPLUS* for practice and tutorials
- Read **A Look at IFRS** p. 426

Learning Objectives   ✔ The Navigator

After studying this chapter, you should be able to:

[1] Identify the different types of receivables.

[2] Explain how companies recognize accounts receivable.

[3] Distinguish between the methods and bases companies use to value accounts receivable.

[4] Describe the entries to record the disposition of accounts receivable.

[5] Compute the maturity date of and interest on notes receivable.

[6] Explain how companies recognize notes receivable.

[7] Describe how companies value notes receivable.

[8] Describe the entries to record the disposition of notes receivable.

[9] Explain the statement presentation and analysis of receivables.

© Cogal/iStockphoto

Ms. Su knows that she and Mr. Norton are crucial to the profitability of Whitehall-Robins. "Receivables are generally the second-largest asset of any company (after its capital assets)," she points out. "So it's no wonder we keep a very close eye on them."

Preview of Chapter 8

✔ The Navigator

As indicated in the Feature Story, receivables are a significant asset for many pharmaceutical companies. Because a large portion of sales in the United States are done on credit, receivables are important to companies in other industries as well. As a consequence, companies must pay close attention to their receivables and manage them carefully. In this chapter, you will learn what journal entries companies make when they sell products, when they collect cash from those sales, and when they write off accounts they cannot collect.

The content and organization of the chapter are as follows.

ACCOUNTING FOR RECEIVABLES

Types of Receivables	Accounts Receivable	Notes Receivable	Statement Presentation and Analysis
• Accounts receivable • Notes receivable • Other receivables	• Recognizing accounts receivable • Valuing accounts receivable • Disposing of accounts receivable	• Determining maturity date • Computing interest • Recognizing notes receivable • Valuing notes receivable • Disposing of notes receivable	• Presentation • Analysis

Types of Receivables

The term **receivables** refers to amounts due from individuals and companies. Receivables are claims that are expected to be collected in cash. The management of receivables is a very important activity for any company that sells goods or services on credit.

Receivables are important because they represent one of a company's most liquid assets. For many companies, receivables are also one of the largest assets. For example, receivables represented 21.9% of the current assets of pharmaceutical giant Rite Aid in 2011. Illustration 8-1 lists receivables as a percentage of total assets for five other well-known companies in a recent year.

Illustration 8-1
Receivables as a percentage of assets

Company	Receivables as a Percentage of Total Assets
General Electric	52%
Ford Motor Company	42%
Minnesota Mining and Manufacturing Company (3M)	14%
DuPont Co.	17%
Intel Corporation	5%

The relative significance of a company's receivables as a percentage of its assets depends on various factors: its industry, the time of year, whether it extends long-term financing, and its credit policies. To reflect important differences among receivables, they are frequently classified as (1) accounts receivable, (2) notes receivable, and (3) other receivables.

Accounts receivable are amounts customers owe on account. They result from the sale of goods and services. Companies generally expect to collect accounts receivable within 30 to 60 days. They are usually the most significant type of claim held by a company.

Notes receivable are a written promise (as evidenced by a formal instrument) for amounts to be received. The note normally requires the collection of interest and extends for time periods of 60–90 days or longer. Notes and accounts receivable that result from sales transactions are often called **trade receivables**.

Other receivables include nontrade receivables such as interest receivable, loans to company officers, advances to employees, and income taxes refundable. These do not generally result from the operations of the business. Therefore, they are generally classified and reported as separate items in the balance sheet.

Ethics Note

Companies report receivables from employees separately in the financial statements. The reason: Sometimes those assets are not the result of an "arm's-length" transaction.

Accounts Receivable

Three accounting issues associated with accounts receivable are:

1. **Recognizing** accounts receivable.
2. **Valuing** accounts receivable.
3. **Disposing** of accounts receivable.

Recognizing Accounts Receivable

Recognizing accounts receivable is relatively straightforward. A service organization records a receivable when it performs a service on account. A merchandiser records accounts receivable at the point of sale of merchandise on account. When a merchandiser sells goods, it increases (debits) Accounts Receivable and increases (credits) Sales Revenue.

The seller may offer terms that encourage early payment by providing a discount. Sales returns also reduce receivables. The buyer might find some of the goods unacceptable and choose to return the unwanted goods.

To review, assume that Jordache Co. on July 1, 2015, sells merchandise on account to Polo Company for $1,000, terms 2/10, n/30. On July 5, Polo returns merchandise worth $100 to Jordache Co. On July 11, Jordache receives payment from Polo Company for the balance due. The journal entries to record these transactions on the books of Jordache Co. are as follows. **(Cost of goods sold entries are omitted.)**

Ethics Note

In exchange for lower interest rates, some companies have eliminated the 25-day grace period before finance charges kick in. Be sure you read the fine print in any credit agreement you sign.

July 1	Accounts Receivable—Polo Company	1,000	
	Sales Revenue		1,000
	(To record sales on account)		
July 5	Sales Returns and Allowances	100	
	Accounts Receivable—Polo Company		100
	(To record merchandise returned)		
July 11	Cash ($900 − $18)	882	
	Sales Discounts ($900 × .02)	18	
	Accounts Receivable—Polo Company		900
	(To record collection of accounts receivable)		

Helpful Hint
These entries are the same as those described in Chapter 5. For simplicity, we have omitted inventory and cost of goods sold from this set of journal entries and from end-of-chapter material.

Some retailers issue their own credit cards. When you use a retailer's credit card (JCPenney, for example), the retailer charges interest on the balance due if not paid within a specified period (usually 25–30 days).

To illustrate, assume that you use your JCPenney Company credit card to purchase clothing with a sales price of $300 on June 1, 2015. JCPenney will increase (debit) Accounts Receivable for $300 and increase (credit) Sales Revenue for $300 (cost of goods sold entry omitted) as follows.

June 1	Accounts Receivable	300	
	Sales Revenue		300
	(To record sale of merchandise)		

A = L + SE
+300
　　　　　+300 Rev

Cash Flows
no effect

Assuming that you owe $300 at the end of the month and JCPenney charges 1.5% per month on the balance due, the adjusting entry that JCPenney makes to record interest revenue of $4.50 ($300 × 1.5%) on June 30 is as follows.

June 30	Accounts Receivable	4.50	
	Interest Revenue		4.50
	(To record interest on amount due)		

A = L + SE
+4.50
　　　　　+4.50 Rev

Cash Flows
no effect

Interest revenue is often substantial for many retailers.

ANATOMY OF A FRAUD

Tasanee was the accounts receivable clerk for a large non-profit foundation that provided performance and exhibition space for the performing and visual arts. Her responsibilities included activities normally assigned to an accounts receivable clerk, such as recording revenues from various sources that included donations, facility rental fees, ticket revenue, and bar receipts. However, she was also responsible for handling all cash and checks from the time they were received until the time she deposited them, as well as preparing the bank reconciliation. Tasanee took advantage of her situation by falsifying bank deposits and bank reconciliations so that she could steal cash from the bar receipts. Since nobody else logged the donations or matched the donation receipts to pledges prior to Tasanee receiving them, she was able to offset the cash that was stolen against donations that she received but didn't record. Her crime was made easier by the fact that her boss, the company's controller, only did a very superficial review of the bank reconciliation and thus didn't notice that some numbers had been cut out from other documents and taped onto the bank reconciliation.

Total take: $1.5 million

THE MISSING CONTROLS
Segregation of duties. The foundation should not have allowed an accounts receivable clerk, whose job was to record receivables, to also handle cash, record cash, make deposits, and especially prepare the bank reconciliation.

Independent internal verification. The controller was supposed to perform a thorough review of the bank reconciliation. Because he did not, he was terminated from his position.

Source: Adapted from Wells, *Fraud Casebook* (2007), pp. 183–194.

Valuing Accounts Receivable

Once companies record receivables in the accounts, the next question is: How should they report receivables in the financial statements? Companies report accounts receivable on the balance sheet as an asset. But determining the **amount** to report is sometimes difficult because some receivables will become uncollectible.

Alternative Terminology
You will sometimes see *Bad Debt Expense* called *Uncollectible Accounts Expense.*

Each customer must satisfy the credit requirements of the seller before the credit sale is approved. Inevitably, though, some accounts receivable become uncollectible. For example, a customer may not be able to pay because of a decline in its sales revenue due to a downturn in the economy. Similarly, individuals may be laid off from their jobs or faced with unexpected hospital bills. Companies record credit losses as debits to **Bad Debt Expense** (or Uncollectible Accounts Expense). Such losses are a normal and necessary risk of doing business on a credit basis.

Recently, when U.S. home prices fell, home foreclosures rose and the economy in general slowed. As a result, lenders experienced huge increases in their bad debt expense. For example, during one quarter Wachovia (a large U.S. bank now owned by Wells Fargo) increased bad debt expense from $108 million to $408 million. Similarly, American Express increased its bad debt expense by 70%.

Two methods are used in accounting for uncollectible accounts: (1) the direct write-off method and (2) the allowance method. The following sections explain these methods.

DIRECT WRITE-OFF METHOD FOR UNCOLLECTIBLE ACCOUNTS
Under the **direct write-off method**, when a company determines a particular account to be uncollectible, it charges the loss to Bad Debt Expense. Assume, for example, that Warden Co. writes off as uncollectible M. E. Doran's $200 balance on December 12. Warden's entry is:

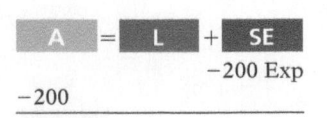

Dec. 12	Bad Debt Expense	200	
	Accounts Receivable—M. E. Doran		200
	(To record write-off of M. E. Doran account)		

Cash Flows
no effect

Under this method, Bad Debt Expense will show only **actual losses** from uncollectibles. The company will report accounts receivable at its gross amount.

Although this method is simple, its use can reduce the usefulness of both the income statement and balance sheet. Consider the following example. Assume that in 2015, Quick Buck Computer Company decided it could increase its revenues by offering computers to college students without requiring any money down and with no credit-approval process. On campuses across the country, it distributed one million computers with a selling price of $800 each. This increased Quick Buck's revenues and receivables by $800 million. The promotion was a huge success! The 2015 balance sheet and income statement looked great. Unfortunately, during 2016, nearly 40% of the customers defaulted on their loans. This made the 2016 income statement and balance sheet look terrible. Illustration 8-2 shows the effect of these events on the financial statements if the direct write-off method is used.

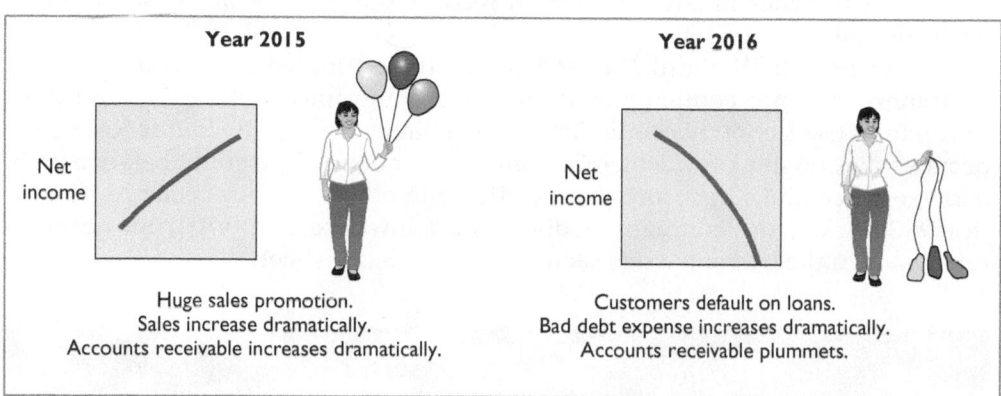

Illustration 8-2
Effects of direct write-off method

Under the direct write-off method, companies often record bad debt expense in a period different from the period in which they record the revenue. The method does not attempt to match bad debt expense to sales revenue in the income statement. Nor does the direct write-off method show accounts receivable in the balance sheet at the amount the company actually expects to receive. **Consequently, unless bad debt losses are insignificant, the direct write-off method is not acceptable for financial reporting purposes.**

ALLOWANCE METHOD FOR UNCOLLECTIBLE ACCOUNTS

The **allowance method** of accounting for bad debts involves estimating uncollectible accounts at the end of each period. This provides better matching on the income statement. It also ensures that companies state receivables on the balance sheet at their cash (net) realizable value. **Cash (net) realizable value** is the net amount the company expects to receive in cash. It excludes amounts that the company estimates it will not collect. Thus, this method reduces receivables in the balance sheet by the amount of estimated uncollectible receivables.

GAAP requires the allowance method for financial reporting purposes when bad debts are material in amount. This method has three essential features:

Helpful Hint
In this context, *material* means significant or important to financial statement users.

1. Companies **estimate** uncollectible accounts receivable. They match this estimated expense **against revenues** in the same accounting period in which they record the revenues.

2. Companies debit estimated uncollectibles to Bad Debt Expense and credit them to Allowance for Doubtful Accounts through an adjusting entry at the end of each period. Allowance for Doubtful Accounts is a contra account to Accounts Receivable.

3. When companies write off a specific account, they debit actual uncollectibles to Allowance for Doubtful Accounts and credit that amount to Accounts Receivable.

RECORDING ESTIMATED UNCOLLECTIBLES To illustrate the allowance method, assume that Hampson Furniture has credit sales of $1,200,000 in 2015. Of this amount, $200,000 remains uncollected at December 31. The credit manager estimates that $12,000 of these sales will be uncollectible. The adjusting entry to record the estimated uncollectibles increases (debits) Bad Debt Expense and increases (credits) Allowance for Doubtful Accounts, as follows.

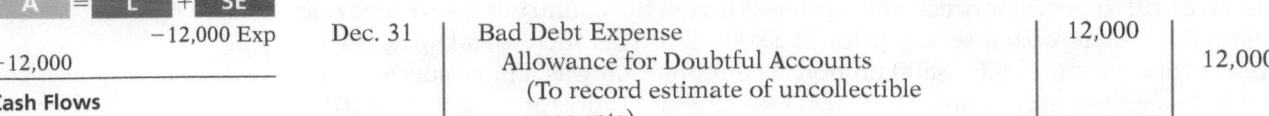

Dec. 31	Bad Debt Expense	12,000	
	Allowance for Doubtful Accounts		12,000
	(To record estimate of uncollectible accounts)		

A = L + SE
−12,000 Exp
−12,000

Cash Flows
no effect

Hampson reports Bad Debt Expense in the income statement as an operating expense (usually as a selling expense). Thus, the estimated uncollectibles are matched with sales in 2015. Hampson records the expense in the same year it made the sales.

Allowance for Doubtful Accounts shows the estimated amount of claims on customers that the company expects will become uncollectible in the future. Companies use a contra account instead of a direct credit to Accounts Receivable because they do not know which customers will not pay. The credit balance in the allowance account will absorb the specific write-offs when they occur. As Illustration 8-3 shows, the company deducts the allowance account from accounts receivable in the current assets section of the balance sheet.

Illustration 8-3
Presentation of allowance for doubtful accounts

HAMPSON FURNITURE		
Balance Sheet (partial)		
Current assets		
Cash		$ 14,800
Accounts receivable	$200,000	
Less: Allowance for doubtful accounts	12,000	188,000
Inventory		310,000
Supplies		25,000
Total current assets		$537,800

Helpful Hint
Cash realizable value is sometimes referred to as *accounts receivable (net)*.

The amount of $188,000 in Illustration 8-3 represents the expected **cash realizable value** of the accounts receivable at the statement date. **Companies do not close Allowance for Doubtful Accounts at the end of the fiscal year.**

RECORDING THE WRITE-OFF OF AN UNCOLLECTIBLE ACCOUNT As described in the Feature Story, companies use various methods of collecting past-due accounts, such as letters, calls, and legal action. When they have exhausted all means of collecting a past-due account and collection appears impossible, the company writes off the account. In the credit card industry, for example, it is standard practice to write off accounts that are 210 days past due. To prevent premature or unauthorized write-offs, authorized management personnel should formally approve each write-off. To maintain segregation of duties, the employee authorized to write off accounts should not have daily responsibilities related to cash or receivables.

To illustrate a receivables write-off, assume that the financial vice president of Hampson Furniture authorizes a write-off of the $500 balance owed by R. A. Ware on March 1, 2016. The entry to record the write-off is:

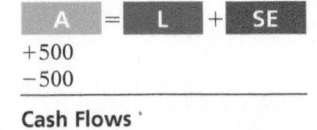

A = L + SE
+500
−500

Cash Flows
no effect

Mar. 1	Allowance for Doubtful Accounts	500	
	Accounts Receivable—R. A. Ware		500
	(Write-off of R. A. Ware account)		

Bad Debt Expense does not increase when the write-off occurs. **Under the allow-ance method, companies debit every bad debt write-off to the allowance account rather than to Bad Debt Expense.** A debit to Bad Debt Expense would be incorrect because the company has already recognized the expense when it made the adjusting entry for estimated bad debts. Instead, the entry to record the write-off of an uncollectible account reduces both Accounts Receivable and Allowance for Doubtful Accounts. After posting, the general ledger accounts appear as shown in Illustration 8-4.

Accounts Receivable				Allowance for Doubtful Accounts			
Jan. 1 Bal. 200,000	Mar. 1		500	Mar. 1	500	Jan. 1 Bal.	12,000
Mar. 1 Bal. 199,500						Mar. 1 Bal.	11,500

Illustration 8-4
General ledger balances after write-off

A write-off affects **only balance sheet accounts**—not income statement accounts. The write-off of the account reduces both Accounts Receivable and Allowance for Doubtful Accounts. Cash realizable value in the balance sheet, therefore, remains the same, as Illustration 8-5 shows.

	Before Write-Off	After Write-Off
Accounts receivable	$ 200,000	$ 199,500
Allowance for doubtful accounts	12,000	11,500
Cash realizable value	**$188,000**	**$188,000**

Illustration 8-5
Cash realizable value comparison

RECOVERY OF AN UNCOLLECTIBLE ACCOUNT Occasionally, a company col-lects from a customer after it has written off the account as uncollectible. The company makes two entries to record the recovery of a bad debt: (1) It reverses the entry made in writing off the account. This reinstates the customer's account. (2) It journalizes the collection in the usual manner.

To illustrate, assume that on July 1, R. A. Ware pays the $500 amount that Hampson had written off on March 1. Hampson makes these entries:

(1)

July 1	Accounts Receivable—R. A. Ware	500	
	Allowance for Doubtful Accounts		500
	(To reverse write-off of R. A. Ware account)		

A = L + SE
+500
−500

Cash Flows
no effect

(2)

July 1	Cash	500	
	Accounts Receivable—R. A. Ware		500
	(To record collection from R. A. Ware)		

A = L + SE
+500
−500

Cash Flows
+500

Note that the recovery of a bad debt, like the write-off of a bad debt, affects **only balance sheet accounts**. The net effect of the two entries above is a debit to Cash and a credit to Allowance for Doubtful Accounts for $500. Accounts Receivable and Allowance for Doubtful Accounts both increase in entry (1) for two reasons. First, the company made an error in judgment when it wrote off the account receivable. Second, after R. A. Ware did pay, Accounts Receivable in the general ledger and Ware's account in the subsidiary ledger should show the col-lection for possible future credit purposes.

ESTIMATING THE ALLOWANCE For Hampson Furniture in Illustration 8-3, the amount of the expected uncollectibles was given. However, in "real life," companies must estimate that amount when they use the allowance method. Two bases are used to determine this amount: **(1) percentage of sales** and **(2) percentage of receivables**. Both bases are generally accepted. The choice is a management decision. It depends on the relative emphasis that management wishes to give to expenses and revenues on the one hand or to cash realizable value of the accounts receivable on the other. The choice is whether to emphasize income statement or balance sheet relationships. Illustration 8-6 compares the two bases.

Illustration 8-6
Comparison of bases for estimating uncollectibles

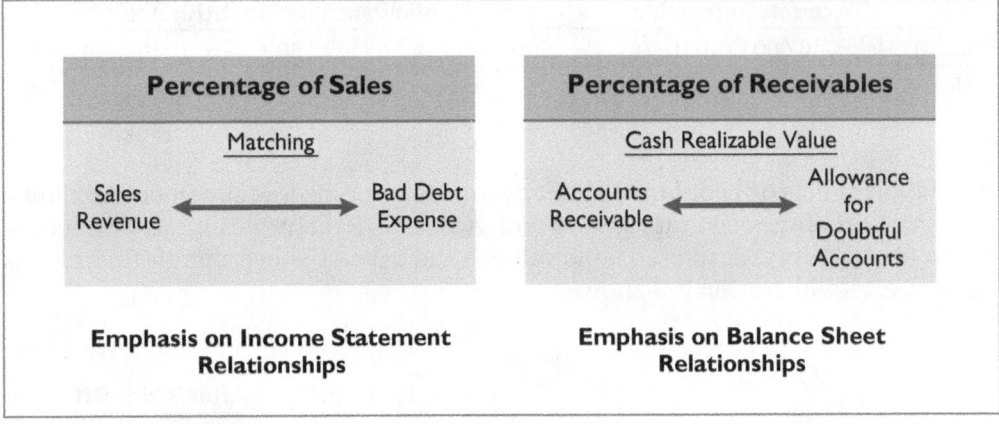

The percentage-of-sales basis results in a better matching of expenses with revenues—an income statement viewpoint. The percentage-of-receivables basis produces the better estimate of cash realizable value—a balance sheet viewpoint. Under both bases, the company must determine its past experience with bad debt losses.

Percentage-of-Sales. In the **percentage-of-sales basis**, management estimates what percentage of credit sales will be uncollectible. This percentage is based on past experience and anticipated credit policy.

The company applies this percentage to either total credit sales or net credit sales of the current year. To illustrate, assume that Gonzalez Company elects to use the percentage-of-sales basis. It concludes that 1% of net credit sales will become uncollectible. If net credit sales for 2015 are $800,000, the estimated bad debt expense is $8,000 (1% × $800,000). The adjusting entry is:

A = L + SE
−8,000 Exp
−8,000

Cash Flows
no effect

Dec. 31	Bad Debt Expense	8,000	
	Allowance for Doubtful Accounts		8,000
	(To record estimated bad debts for year)		

After the adjusting entry is posted, assuming the allowance account already has a credit balance of $1,723, the accounts of Gonzalez Company will show the following.

Illustration 8-7
Bad debt accounts after posting

Bad Debt Expense		Allowance for Doubtful Accounts	
Dec. 31 Adj. **8,000**			Jan. 1 Bal. 1,723
			Dec. 31 Adj. **8,000**
			Dec. 31 Bal. 9,723

This basis of estimating uncollectibles emphasizes the matching of expenses with revenues. As a result, Bad Debt Expense will show a direct percentage relationship to the sales base on which it is computed. **When the company**

makes the adjusting entry, it disregards the existing balance in Allowance for Doubtful Accounts. The adjusted balance in this account should be a reasonable approximation of the realizable value of the receivables. If actual write-offs differ significantly from the amount estimated, the company should modify the percentage for future years.

Percentage-of-Receivables. Under the **percentage-of-receivables basis**, management estimates what percentage of receivables will result in losses from uncollectible accounts. The company prepares an **aging schedule**, in which it classifies customer balances by the length of time they have been unpaid. Because of its emphasis on time, the analysis is often called **aging the accounts receivable**. In the Feature Story, Whitehall-Robins prepared an aging report daily.

After the company arranges the accounts by age, it determines the expected bad debt losses. It applies percentages based on past experience to the totals in each category. The longer a receivable is past due, the less likely it is to be collected. Thus, the estimated percentage of uncollectible debts increases as the number of days past due increases. Illustration 8-8 shows an aging schedule for Dart Company. Note that the estimated percentage uncollectible increases from 2% to 40% as the number of days past due increases.

Helpful Hint
Where appropriate, companies may use only a single percentage rate.

Illustration 8-8
Aging schedule

	Worksheet.xls					

Home | Insert | Page Layout | Formulas | Data | Review | View

P18   *fx*

	A	B	C	D	E	F	G
1				Number of Days Past Due			
2			Not				
3	Customer	Total	Yet Due	1–30	31–60	61–90	Over 90
4	T. E. Adert	$ 600		$ 300		$ 200	$ 100
5	R. C. Bortz	300	$ 300				
6	B. A. Carl	450		200	$ 250		
7	O. L. Diker	700	500			200	
8	T. O. Ebbet	600			300		300
9	Others	36,950	26,200	5,200	2,450	1,600	1,500
10		$39,600	$27,000	$5,700	$3,000	$2,000	$1,900
11	Estimated Percentage Uncollectible		2%	4%	10%	20%	40%
12	Total Estimated Bad Debts	$ 2,228	$ 540	$ 228	$ 300	$ 400	$ 760
13							

Helpful Hint
The older categories have higher percentages because the longer an account is past due, the less likely it is to be collected.

Total estimated bad debts for Dart Company ($2,228) represent the amount of existing customer claims the company expects will become uncollectible in the future. This amount represents the **required balance** in Allowance for Doubtful Accounts at the balance sheet date. **The amount of the bad debt adjusting entry is the difference between the required balance and the existing balance in the allowance account.** If the trial balance shows Allowance for Doubtful Accounts with a credit balance of $528, the company will make an adjusting entry for $1,700 ($2,228 − $528), as shown here.

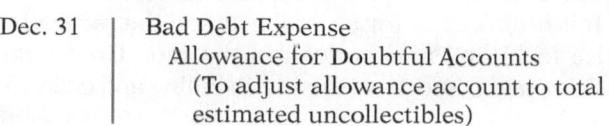

Dec. 31	Bad Debt Expense	1,700	
	Allowance for Doubtful Accounts		1,700
	(To adjust allowance account to total estimated uncollectibles)		

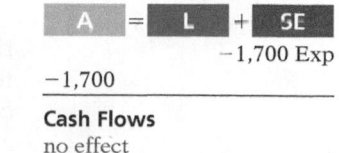

A = L + SE
             −1,700 Exp
−1,700

Cash Flows
no effect

After Dart posts its adjusting entry, its accounts will appear as follows.

Illustration 8-9
Bad debt accounts after posting

Bad Debt Expense		Allowance for Doubtful Accounts	
Dec. 31 Adj. **1,700**		Bal. 528	
		Dec. 31 Adj. **1,700**	
		Bal. 2,228	

Occasionally, the allowance account will have a **debit balance** prior to adjustment. This occurs when write-offs during the year have exceeded previous provisions for bad debts. In such a case, the company **adds the debit balance to the required balance** when it makes the adjusting entry. Thus, if there had been a $500 debit balance in the allowance account before adjustment, the adjusting entry would have been for $2,728 ($2,228 + $500) to arrive at a credit balance of $2,228 (see T-account in margin). The percentage-of-receivables basis will normally result in the better approximation of cash realizable value.

Allowance
for Doubtful Accounts

Dec. 31 Unadj. Bal. 500	Dec. 31 Adj. 2,728
	Dec. 31 Bal. 2,228

> **DO IT!**

Uncollectible Accounts Receivable

Brule Co. has been in business for five years. The unadjusted trial balance at the end of the current year shows:

Accounts Receivable	$30,000 Dr.
Sales Revenue	$180,000 Cr.
Allowance for Doubtful Accounts	$2,000 Dr.

Brule estimates bad debts to be 10% of receivables. Prepare the entry necessary to adjust Allowance for Doubtful Accounts.

Action Plan

✔ Report receivables at their cash (net) realizable value.

✔ Estimate the amount the company does not expect to collect.

✔ Consider the existing balance in the allowance account when using the percentage-of-receivables basis.

Solution

The following entry should be made to bring the balance in Allowance for Doubtful Accounts up to a normal credit balance of $3,000 (10% × $30,000):

Bad Debt Expense [(10% × $30,000) + $2,000]	5,000	
Allowance for Doubtful Accounts		5,000
(To record estimate of uncollectible accounts)		

Related exercise material: BE8-3, BE8-4, BE8-5, BE8-6, BE8-7, E8-3, E8-4, E8-5, E8-6, **and** DO IT! 8-1.

 The Navigator

Disposing of Accounts Receivable

LEARNING OBJECTIVE   4

Describe the entries to record the disposition of accounts receivable.

In the normal course of events, companies collect accounts receivable in cash and remove the receivables from the books. However, as credit sales and receivables have grown in significance, the "normal course of events" has changed. Companies now frequently sell their receivables to another company for cash, thereby shortening the cash-to-cash operating cycle.

Companies sell receivables for two major reasons. First, **they may be the only reasonable source of cash**. When money is tight, companies may not be able to borrow money in the usual credit markets. Or if money is available, the cost of borrowing may be prohibitive.

A second reason for selling receivables is that **billing and collection are often time-consuming and costly**. It is often easier for a retailer to sell the receivables to another party with expertise in billing and collection matters. Credit card companies such as MasterCard, Visa, and Discover specialize in billing and collecting accounts receivable.

SALE OF RECEIVABLES

A common sale of receivables is a sale to a factor. A **factor** is a finance company or bank that buys receivables from businesses and then collects the payments directly from the customers. Factoring is a multibillion dollar business.

Factoring arrangements vary widely. Typically, the factor charges a commission to the company that is selling the receivables. This fee ranges from 1–3% of the amount of receivables purchased. To illustrate, assume that Hendredon Furniture factors $600,000 of receivables to Federal Factors. Federal Factors assesses a service charge of 2% of the amount of receivables sold. The journal entry to record the sale by Hendredon Furniture on April 2, 2015, is as follows.

Apr. 2	Cash	588,000	
	Service Charge Expense (2% × $600,000)	12,000	
	Accounts Receivable		600,000
	(To record the sale of accounts receivable)		

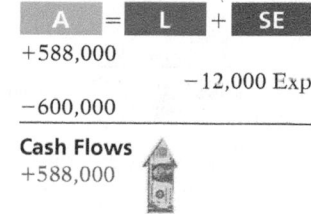

A = L + SE
+588,000
            −12,000 Exp
−600,000

Cash Flows
+588,000

If the company often sells its receivables, it records the service charge expense (such as that incurred by Hendredon) as a selling expense. If the company infrequently sells receivables, it may report this amount in the "Other expenses and losses" section of the income statement.

CREDIT CARD SALES

Over one billion credit cards are in use in the United States—more than three credit cards for every man, woman, and child in this country. Visa, MasterCard, and American Express are the national credit cards that most individuals use. Three parties are involved when national credit cards are used in retail sales: (1) the credit card issuer, who is independent of the retailer; (2) the retailer; and (3) the customer. A retailer's acceptance of a national credit card is another form of selling (factoring) the receivable.

Illustration 8-10 shows the major advantages of national credit cards to the retailer. In exchange for these advantages, the retailer pays the credit card issuer a fee of 2–6% of the invoice price for its services.

Illustration 8-10
Advantages of credit cards to the retailer

ACCOUNTING FOR CREDIT CARD SALES The retailer generally considers sales from the use of national credit card sales as **cash sales**. The retailer must pay to the bank that issues the card a fee for processing the transactions. The retailer records the credit card slips in a similar manner as checks deposited from a cash sale.

To illustrate, Anita Ferreri purchases $1,000 of compact discs for her restaurant from Karen Kerr Music Co., using her Visa First Bank Card. First Bank charges a service fee of 3%. The entry to record this transaction by Karen Kerr Music on March 22, 2015, is as follows.

A	=	L	+	SE
+970				
				−30 Exp
				+1,000 Rev

Cash Flows
+970

Mar. 22	Cash	970	
	Service Charge Expense	30	
	Sales Revenue		1,000
	(To record Visa credit card sales)		

ACCOUNTING ACROSS THE ORGANIZATION

How Does a Credit Card Work?

Most of you know how to use a credit card, but do you know what happens in the transaction and how the transaction is processed? Suppose that you use a Visa card to purchase some new ties at Nordstrom. The salesperson swipes your card, which allows the information on the magnetic strip on the back of the card to be read. The salesperson then enters in the amount of the purchase. The machine contacts the Visa computer, which routes the call back to the bank that issued your Visa card. The issuing bank verifies that the account exists, that the card is not stolen, and that you have not exceeded your credit limit. At this point, the slip is printed, which you sign.

Visa acts as the clearing agent for the transaction. It transfers funds from the issuing bank to Nordstrom's bank account. Generally this transfer of funds, from sale to the receipt of funds in the merchant's account, takes two to three days.

In the meantime, Visa puts a pending charge on your account for the amount of the tie purchase; that amount counts immediately against your available credit limit. At the end of the billing period, Visa sends you an invoice (your credit card bill) which shows the various charges you made, and the amounts that Visa expended on your behalf, for the month. You then must "pay the piper" for your stylish new ties.

© Zibedik/iStockphoto

 Assume that Nordstrom prepares a bank reconciliation at the end of each month. If some credit card sales have not been processed by the bank, how should Nordstrom treat these transactions on its bank reconciliation? (See page 425.)

> **DO IT!**

Disposition of Accounts Receivable

Mehl Wholesalers Co. has been expanding faster than it can raise capital. According to its local banker, the company has reached its debt ceiling. Mehl's suppliers (creditors) are demanding payment within 30 days of the invoice date for goods acquired, but Mehl's customers are slow in paying (60–90 days). As a result, Mehl has a cash flow problem.

Mehl needs $120,000 in cash to safely cover next Friday's payroll. Its balance of outstanding accounts receivable totals $750,000. To alleviate this cash crunch, Mehl sells $125,000 of its receivables on September 7, 2015. Record the entry that Mehl would make when it raises the needed cash. (Assume a 1% service charge.)

Action Plan

✔ To speed up the collection of cash, sell receivables to a factor.

✔ Calculate service charge expense as a percentage of the factored receivables.

Solution

If Mehl Wholesalers factors $125,000 of its accounts receivable at a 1% service charge, it would make the following entry.

Sept. 7	Cash	123,750	
	Service Charge Expense (1% × $125,000)	1,250	
	Accounts Receivable		125,000
	(To record sale of receivables to factor)		

Related exercise material: BE8-8, E8-7, E8-8, E8-9, **and** DO IT! 8-2.

✔ **The Navigator**

Notes Receivable

Companies may also grant credit in exchange for a formal credit instrument known as a promissory note. A **promissory note** is a written promise to pay a specified amount of money on demand or at a definite time. Promissory notes may be used (1) when individuals and companies lend or borrow money, (2) when the amount of the transaction and the credit period exceed normal limits, or (3) in settlement of accounts receivable.

In a promissory note, the party making the promise to pay is called the **maker**. The party to whom payment is to be made is called the **payee**. The note may specifically identify the payee by name or may designate the payee simply as the bearer of the note.

In the note shown in Illustration 8-11, Calhoun Company is the maker and Wilma Company is the payee. To Wilma Company, the promissory note is a note receivable. To Calhoun Company, it is a note payable.

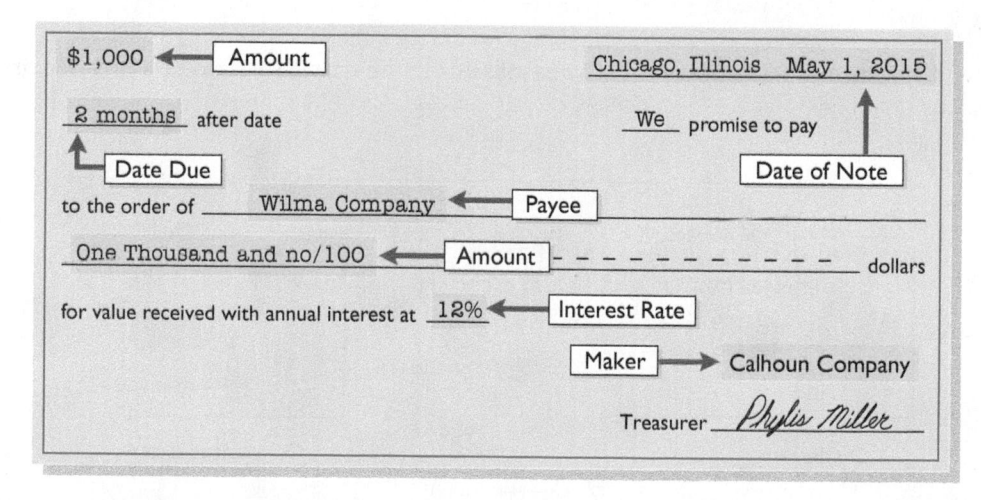

Illustration 8-11
Promissory note

Helpful Hint
Who are the two key parties to the note, and what entry does each party make when the note is issued?

Answer:
1. The maker, Calhoun Company, debits Cash and credits Notes Payable.
2. The payee, Wilma Company, debits Notes Receivable and credits Cash.

Notes receivable give the holder a stronger legal claim to assets than do accounts receivable. Like accounts receivable, notes receivable can be readily sold to another party. Promissory notes are negotiable instruments (as are checks), which means that they can be transferred to another party by endorsement.

Companies frequently accept notes receivable from customers who need to extend the payment of an outstanding account receivable. They often require such notes from high-risk customers. In some industries (such as the pleasure and sport boat industry), all credit sales are supported by notes. The majority of notes, however, originate from loans.

The basic issues in accounting for notes receivable are the same as those for accounts receivable:

1. **Recognizing** notes receivable.

2. **Valuing** notes receivable.

3. **Disposing** of notes receivable.

On the following pages, we will look at these issues. Before we do, we need to consider two issues that do not apply to accounts receivable: determining the maturity date and computing interest.

Determining the Maturity Date

When the life of a note is expressed in terms of months, you find the date when it matures by counting the months from the date of issue. For example, the maturity date of a three-month note dated May 1 is August 1. A note drawn on the last day of a month matures on the last day of a subsequent month. That is, a July 31 note due in two months matures on September 30.

When the due date is stated in terms of days, you need to count the exact number of days to determine the maturity date. In counting, **omit the date the note is issued but include the due date**. For example, the maturity date of a 60-day note dated July 17 is September 15, computed as follows.

Illustration 8-12
Computation of maturity date

Term of note		60 days
July (31 − 17)	14	
August	31	45
Maturity date: September		**15**

Illustration 8-13 shows three ways of stating the maturity date of a promissory note.

Illustration 8-13
Maturity date of different notes

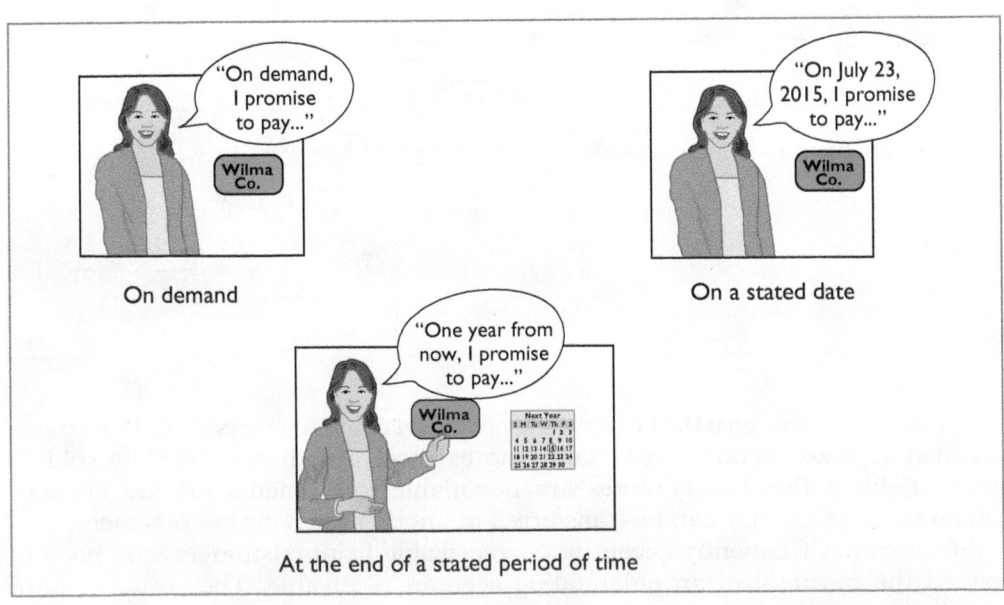

At the end of a stated period of time

Computing Interest

Illustration 8-14 gives the basic formula for computing interest on an interest-bearing note.

<table>
<tr><td>Face Value of Note</td><td>×</td><td>Annual Interest Rate</td><td>×</td><td>Time in Terms of One Year</td><td>=</td><td>Interest</td></tr>
</table>

Illustration 8-14
Formula for computing interest

The interest rate specified in a note is an **annual** rate of interest. The time factor in the formula in Illustration 8-14 expresses the fraction of a year that the note is outstanding. When the maturity date is stated in days, the time factor is often the number of days divided by 360. When counting days, omit the date that the note is issued but include the due date. When the due date is stated in months, the time factor is the number of months divided by 12. Illustration 8-15 shows computation of interest for various time periods.

Helpful Hint
The interest rate specified is the *annual* rate.

Terms of Note	Interest Computation
	Face × Rate × Time = Interest
$ 730, 12%, 120 days	$ 730 × 12% × 120/360 = $ 29.20
$1,000, 9%, 6 months	$1,000 × 9% × 6/12 = $ 45.00
$2,000, 6%, 1 year	$2,000 × 6% × 1/1 = $120.00

Illustration 8-15
Computation of interest

There are different ways to calculate interest. For example, the computation in Illustration 8-15 assumes 360 days for the length of the year. Most financial instruments use 365 days to compute interest. *For homework problems, assume 360 days to simplify computations.*

Recognizing Notes Receivable

LEARNING OBJECTIVE   6
Explain how companies recognize notes receivable.

To illustrate the basic entry for notes receivable, we will use Calhoun Company's $1,000, two-month, 12% promissory note dated May 1. Assuming that Calhoun Company wrote the note to settle an open account, Wilma Company makes the following entry for the receipt of the note.

May 1	Notes Receivable	1,000	
	Accounts Receivable—Calhoun Company		1,000
	(To record acceptance of Calhoun Company note)		

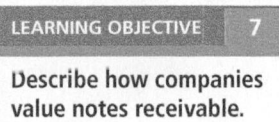

A = L + SE
+1,000
−1,000

Cash Flows
no effect

The company records the note receivable at its **face value**, the amount shown on the face of the note. No interest revenue is reported when the note is accepted because the revenue recognition principle does not recognize revenue until the performance obligation is satisfied. Interest is earned (accrued) as time passes.

If a company lends money using a note, the entry is a debit to Notes Receivable and a credit to Cash in the amount of the loan.

Valuing Notes Receivable

LEARNING OBJECTIVE   7
Describe how companies value notes receivable.

Valuing short-term notes receivable is the same as valuing accounts receivable. Like accounts receivable, companies report short-term notes receivable at their **cash (net) realizable value**. The notes receivable allowance account is Allowance for Doubtful Accounts. The estimations involved in determining cash realizable value and in recording bad debt expense and the related allowance are done similarly to accounts receivable.

INTERNATIONAL INSIGHT

Can Fair Value Be Unfair?

The FASB and the International Accounting Standards Board (IASB) are considering proposals for how to account for financial instruments. The FASB has proposed that loans and receivables be accounted for at their fair value (the amount they could currently be sold for), as are most investments. The FASB believes that this would provide a more accurate view of a company's financial position. It might be especially useful as an early warning when a bank is in trouble because of poor-quality loans. But, banks argue that fair values are difficult to estimate accurately. They are also concerned that volatile fair values could cause large swings in a bank's reported net income.

Source: David Reilly, "Banks Face a Mark-to-Market Challenge," *Wall Street Journal Online* (March 15, 2010).

 What are the arguments in favor of and against fair value accounting for loans and receivables? (See page 425.)

Disposing of Notes Receivable

Notes may be held to their maturity date, at which time the face value plus accrued interest is due. In some situations, the maker of the note defaults, and the payee must make an appropriate adjustment. In other situations, similar to accounts receivable, the holder of the note speeds up the conversion to cash by selling the receivables (as described later in this chapter).

HONOR OF NOTES RECEIVABLE

A note is **honored** when its maker pays in full at its maturity date. For each interest-bearing note, the **amount due at maturity** is the face value of the note plus interest for the length of time specified on the note.

To illustrate, assume that Wolder Co. lends Higley Co. $10,000 on June 1, accepting a five-month, 9% interest note. In this situation, interest is $375 ($10,000 × 9% × $\frac{5}{12}$). The amount due, **the maturity value**, is $10,375 ($10,000 + $375). To obtain payment, Wolder (the payee) must present the note either to Higley Co. (the maker) or to the maker's agent, such as a bank. If Wolder presents the note to Higley Co. on November 1, the maturity date, Wolder's entry to record the collection is:

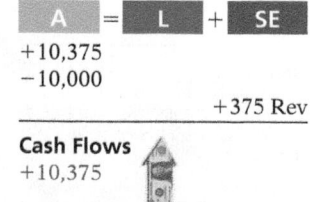

A = L + SE
+10,375
−10,000
+375 Rev

Cash Flows
+10,375

Nov. 1	Cash	10,375	
	Notes Receivable		10,000
	Interest Revenue ($10,000 × 9% × $\frac{5}{12}$)		375
	(To record collection of Higley note and interest)		

ACCRUAL OF INTEREST RECEIVABLE

Suppose instead that Wolder Co. prepares financial statements as of September 30. The timeline in Illustration 8-16 presents this situation.

Illustration 8-16
Timeline of interest earned

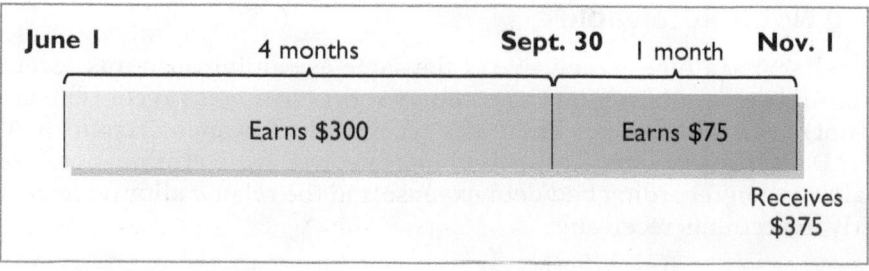

To reflect interest earned but not yet received, Wolder must accrue interest on September 30. In this case, the adjusting entry by Wolder is for four months of interest, or $300, as shown below.

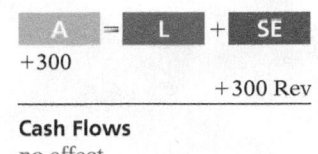

Sept. 30	Interest Receivable ($10,000 × 9% × $\frac{4}{12}$)	300	
	Interest Revenue		300
	(To accrue 4 months' interest on Higley note)		

Cash Flows
no effect

At the note's maturity on November 1, Wolder receives $10,375. This amount represents repayment of the $10,000 note as well as five months of interest, or $375, as shown below. The $375 is comprised of the $300 Interest Receivable accrued on September 30 plus $75 earned during October. Wolder's entry to record the honoring of the Higley note on November 1 is:

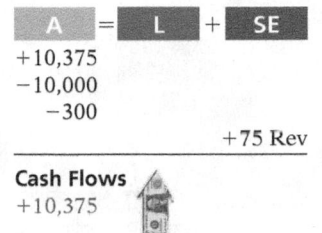

Nov. 1	Cash [$10,000 + ($10,000 × 9% × $\frac{5}{12}$)]	10,375	
	Notes Receivable		10,000
	Interest Receivable		300
	Interest Revenue ($10,000 × 9% × $\frac{1}{12}$)]		75
	(To record collection of Higley note and interest)		

Cash Flows
+10,375

In this case, Wolder credits Interest Receivable because the receivable was established in the adjusting entry on September 30.

DISHONOR OF NOTES RECEIVABLE

A **dishonored (defaulted) note** is a note that is not paid in full at maturity. A dishonored note receivable is no longer negotiable. However, the payee still has a claim against the maker of the note for both the note and the interest. Therefore, the note holder usually transfers the Notes Receivable account to an Accounts Receivable account.

To illustrate, assume that Higley Co. on November 1 indicates that it cannot pay at the present time. The entry to record the dishonor of the note depends on whether Wolder Co. expects eventual collection. If it does expect eventual collection, Wolder Co. debits the amount due (face value and interest) on the note to Accounts Receivable. It would make the following entry at the time the note is dishonored (assuming no previous accrual of interest).

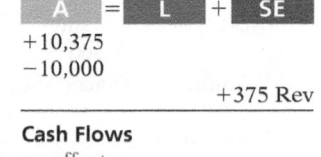

Nov. 1	Accounts Receivable—Higley	10,375	
	Notes Receivable		10,000
	Interest Revenue		375
	(To record the dishonor of Higley note)		

Cash Flows
no effect

If instead, on November 1, there is no hope of collection, the note holder would write off the face value of the note by debiting Allowance for Doubtful Accounts. No interest revenue would be recorded because collection will not occur.

SALE OF NOTES RECEIVABLE

The accounting for the sale of notes receivable is recorded similarly to the sale of accounts receivable. The accounting entries for the sale of notes receivable are left for a more advanced course.

ACCOUNTING ACROSS THE ORGANIZATION

Bad Information Can Lead to Bad Loans

Many factors have contributed to the recent credit crisis. One significant factor that resulted in many bad loans was a failure by lenders to investigate loan customers sufficiently. For example, Countrywide Financial Corporation wrote many loans under its "Fast and Easy" loan program. That program allowed borrowers to provide little or no documentation for their income or their assets. Other lenders had similar programs, which earned the nickname "liars' loans." One study found that in these situations, 60% of applicants overstated their incomes by more than 50% in order to qualify for a loan. Critics of the banking industry say that because loan officers were compensated for loan volume and because banks were selling the loans to investors rather than holding them, the lenders had little incentive to investigate the borrowers' creditworthiness.

Sources: Glenn R. Simpson and James R. Hagerty, "Countrywide Loss Focuses Attention on Underwriting," *Wall Street Journal* (April 30, 2008), p. B1; and Michael Corkery, "Fraud Seen as Driver in Wave of Foreclosures," *Wall Street Journal* (December 21, 2007), p. A1.

 What steps should the banks have taken to ensure the accuracy of financial information provided on loan applications? (See page 425.)

> DO IT!

Notes Receivable

Gambit Stores accepts from Leonard Co. a $3,400, 90-day, 6% note dated May 10 in settlement of Leonard's overdue account. (a) What is the maturity date of the note? (b) What entry does Gambit make at the maturity date, assuming Leonard pays the note and interest in full at that time?

Solution

(a) The maturity date is August 8, computed as follows.

Term of note:		90 days
May (31 − 10)	21	
June	30	
July	31	82
Maturity date: August		8

(b) The interest payable at the maturity date is $51, computed as follows.

Face	×	Rate	×	Time	=	Interest
$3,400	×	6%	×	90/360	=	$51

The entry recorded by Gambit Stores at the maturity date is:

Cash	3,451	
Notes Receivable		3,400
Interest Revenue		51
(To record collection of Leonard note)		

Action Plan

✔ Count the exact number of days to determine the maturity date. Omit the date the note is issued, but include the due date.

✔ Determine whether interest was accrued.

✔ Compute the accrued interest.

✔ Prepare the entry for payment of the note and interest.

✔ The entry to record interest at maturity in this solution assumes no interest has been previously accrued on this note.

Related exercise material: BE8-9, BE8-10, BE8-11, E8-10, E8-11, E8-12, E8-13, **and** DO IT! 8-3.

 The Navigator

Statement Presentation and Analysis

Presentation

Companies should identify in the balance sheet or in the notes to the financial statements each of the major types of receivables. Short-term receivables appear in the current assets section of the balance sheet. Short-term investments appear before short-term receivables because these investments are more liquid (nearer to cash). Companies report both the gross amount of receivables and the allowance for doubtful accounts.

In a multiple-step income statement, companies report bad debt expense and service charge expense as selling expenses in the operating expenses section. Interest revenue appears under "Other revenues and gains" in the nonoperating activities section of the income statement.

Analysis

Investors and corporate managers compute financial ratios to evaluate the liquidity of a company's accounts receivable. They use the **accounts receivable turnover** to assess the liquidity of the receivables. This ratio measures the number of times, on average, the company collects accounts receivable during the period. It is computed by dividing net credit sales (net sales less cash sales) by the average net accounts receivable during the year. Unless seasonal factors are significant, average net accounts receivable outstanding can be computed from the beginning and ending balances of net accounts receivable.

For example, in 2011 Cisco Systems had net sales of $34,526 million for the year. It had a beginning accounts receivable (net) balance of $4,929 million and an ending accounts receivable (net) balance of $4,698 million. Assuming that Cisco's sales were all on credit, its accounts receivable turnover is computed as follows.

Net Credit Sales	÷	Average Net Accounts Receivable	=	Accounts Receivable Turnover
$34,526	÷	$\dfrac{\$4{,}929 + \$4{,}698}{2}$	=	7.2 times

Illustration 8-17
Accounts receivable turnover and computation

The result indicates an accounts receivable turnover of 7.2 times per year. The higher the turnover, the more liquid the company's receivables.

A variant of the accounts receivable turnover that makes the liquidity even more evident is its conversion into an **average collection period** in terms of days. This is done by dividing the accounts receivable turnover into 365 days. For example, Cisco's turnover of 7.2 times is divided into 365 days, as shown in Illustration 8-18, to obtain approximately 51 days. This means that it takes Cisco 51 days to collect its accounts receivable.

Days in Year	÷	Accounts Receivable Turnover	=	Average Collection Period in Days
365 days	÷	7.2 times	=	51 days

Illustration 8-18
Average collection period for receivables formula and computation

Companies frequently use the average collection period to assess the effectiveness of a company's credit and collection policies. The general rule is that the collection period should not greatly exceed the credit term period (that is, the time allowed for payment).

> DO IT!

Analysis of Receivables

Action Plan

✔ Review the formula to compute the accounts receivable turnover.

✔ Make sure that both the beginning and ending accounts receivable balances are considered in the computation.

✔ Review the formula to compute the average collection period in days.

In 2015, Phil Mickelson Company has net credit sales of $923,795 for the year. It had a beginning accounts receivable (net) balance of $38,275 and an ending accounts receivable (net) balance of $35,988. Compute Phil Mickelson Company's (a) accounts receivable turnover and (b) average collection period in days.

Solution

(a)						
	Net credit sales	÷	Average net accounts receivable	=	Accounts receivable turnover	
	$923,795	÷	$\dfrac{\$38,275 + \$35,988}{2}$	=	24.9 times	
(b)	Days in year	÷	Accounts receivable turnover	=	Average collection period in days	
	365	÷	24.9 times	=	14.7 days	

Related exercise material: BE8-12, E8-14, **and** DO IT! 8-4.

✔ The Navigator

> Comprehensive DO IT!

The following selected transactions relate to Dylan Company.

Mar. 1 Sold $20,000 of merchandise to Potter Company, terms 2/10, n/30.
     11 Received payment in full from Potter Company for balance due on existing accounts receivable.
     12 Accepted Juno Company's $20,000, 6-month, 12% note for balance due.
     13 Made Dylan Company credit card sales for $13,200.
     15 Made Visa credit card sales totaling $6,700. A 3% service fee is charged by Visa.
Apr. 11 Sold accounts receivable of $8,000 to Harcot Factor. Harcot Factor assesses a service charge of 2% of the amount of receivables sold.
     13 Received collections of $8,200 on Dylan Company credit card sales and added finance charges of 1.5% to the remaining balances.
May 10   Wrote off as uncollectible $16,000 of accounts receivable. Dylan uses the percentage-of-sales basis to estimate bad debts.
June 30 Credit sales recorded during the first 6 months total $2,000,000. The bad debt percentage is 1% of credit sales. At June 30, the balance in the allowance account is $3,500 before adjustment.
July 16 One of the accounts receivable written off in May was from J. Simon, who pays the amount due, $4,000, in full.

Instructions
Prepare the journal entries for the transactions.

Solution to Comprehensive DO IT!

Action Plan

✔ Generally, record accounts receivable at invoice price.

✔ Recognize that sales returns and allowances and cash discounts reduce the amount received on accounts receivable.

Mar.	1	Accounts Receivable—Potter	20,000	
		Sales Revenue		20,000
		(To record sales on account)		
	11	Cash	19,600	
		Sales Discounts (2% × $20,000)	400	
		Accounts Receivable—Potter		20,000
		(To record collection of accounts receivable)		

Action Plan (cont'd.)	12	Notes Receivable	20,000	
✔ Record service charge expense on the seller's books when accounts receivable are sold.		Accounts Receivable—Juno		20,000
		(To record acceptance of Juno Company note)		
	13	Accounts Receivable	13,200	
✔ Prepare an adjusting entry for bad debt expense.		Sales Revenue		13,200
		(To record company credit card sales)		
✔ Ignore any balance in the allowance account under the percentage-of-sales basis. Recognize the balance in the allowance account under the percentage-of-receivables basis.	15	Cash	6,499	
		Service Charge Expense (3% × $6,700)	201	
		Sales Revenue		6,700
		(To record credit card sales)		
	Apr. 11	Cash	7,840	
		Service Charge Expense (2% × $8,000)	160	
		Accounts Receivable		8,000
		(To record sale of receivables to factor)		
✔ Record write-offs of accounts receivable only in balance sheet accounts.	13	Cash	8,200	
		Accounts Receivable		8,200
		(To record collection of accounts receivable)		
		Accounts Receivable [($13,200 − $8,200) × 1.5%]	75	
		Interest Revenue		75
		(To record interest on amount due)		
	May 10	Allowance for Doubtful Accounts	16,000	
		Accounts Receivable		16,000
		(To record write-off of accounts receivable)		
	June 30	Bad Debt Expense ($2,000,000 × 1%)	20,000	
		Allowance for Doubtful Accounts		20,000
		(To record estimate of uncollectible accounts)		
	July 16	Accounts Receivable—J. Simon	4,000	
		Allowance for Doubtful Accounts		4,000
		(To reverse write-off of accounts receivable)		
		Cash	4,000	
		Accounts Receivable—J. Simon		4,000
		(To record collection of accounts receivable)		

✔ **The Navigator**

SUMMARY OF LEARNING OBJECTIVES

 ✔ **The Navigator**

1 **Identify the different types of receivables.** Receivables are frequently classified as (1) accounts, (2) notes, and (3) other. Accounts receivable are amounts customers owe on account. Notes receivable are claims for which lenders issue formal instruments of credit as proof of the debt. Other receivables include nontrade receivables such as interest receivable, loans to company officers, advances to employees, and income taxes refundable.

2 **Explain how companies recognize accounts receivable.** Companies record accounts receivable when they perform a service on account or at the point of sale of merchandise on account. Accounts receivable are reduced by sales returns and allowances. Cash discounts reduce the amount received on accounts receivable.

When interest is charged on a past due receivable, the company adds this interest to the accounts receivable balance and recognizes it as interest revenue.

3 **Distinguish between the methods and bases companies use to value accounts receivable.** There are two methods of accounting for uncollectible accounts: the allowance method and the direct write-off method. Companies may use either the percentage-of-sales or the percentage-of-receivables basis to estimate uncollectible accounts using the allowance method. The percentage-of-sales basis emphasizes the expense recognition (matching) principle. The percentage-of-receivables basis emphasizes the cash realizable value of the accounts receivable. An aging schedule is often used with this basis.

4   **Describe the entries to record the disposition of accounts receivable.** When a company collects an account receivable, it credits Accounts Receivable. When a company sells (factors) an account receivable, a service charge expense reduces the amount received.

5   **Compute the maturity date of and interest on notes receivable.** For a note stated in months, the maturity date is found by counting the months from the date of issue. For a note stated in days, the number of days is counted, omitting the issue date and counting the due date. The formula for computing interest is Face value × Interest rate × Time.

6   **Explain how companies recognize notes receivable.** Companies record notes receivable at face value. In some cases, it is necessary to accrue interest prior to maturity. In this case, companies debit Interest Receivable and credit Interest Revenue.

7   **Describe how companies value notes receivable.** As with accounts receivable, companies report notes receivable at their cash (net) realizable value. The notes receivable allowance account is Allowance for Doubtful Accounts. The computation and estimations involved in valuing notes receivable at cash realizable value, and in recording the proper amount of bad debt expense and the related allowance, are similar to those for accounts receivable.

8   **Describe the entries to record the disposition of notes receivable.** Notes can be held to maturity. At that time the face value plus accrued interest is due, and the note is removed from the accounts. In many cases, the holder of the note speeds up the conversion by selling the receivable to another party (a factor). In some situations, the maker of the note dishonors the note (defaults), in which case the company transfers the note and accrued interest to an account receivable or writes off the note.

9   **Explain the statement presentation and analysis of receivables.** Companies should identify in the balance sheet or in the notes to the financial statements each major type of receivable. Short-term receivables are considered current assets. Companies report the gross amount of receivables and the allowance for doubtful accounts. They report bad debt and service charge expenses in the multiple-step income statement as operating (selling) expenses. Interest revenue appears under other revenues and gains in the nonoperating activities section of the statement. Managers and investors evaluate accounts receivable for liquidity by computing a turnover ratio and an average collection period.

GLOSSARY

Accounts receivable Amounts owed by customers on account. (p. 388).

Accounts receivable turnover A measure of the liquidity of accounts receivable; computed by dividing net credit sales by average net accounts receivable. (p. 405).

Aging the accounts receivable The analysis of customer balances by the length of time they have been unpaid. (p. 395).

Allowance method A method of accounting for bad debts that involves estimating uncollectible accounts at the end of each period. (p. 391).

Average collection period The average amount of time that a receivable is outstanding; calculated by dividing 365 days by the accounts receivable turnover. (p. 405).

Bad Debt Expense An expense account to record uncollectible receivables. (p. 390).

Cash (net) realizable value The net amount a company expects to receive in cash. (p. 391).

Direct write-off method A method of accounting for bad debts that involves expensing accounts at the time they are determined to be uncollectible. (p. 390).

Dishonored (defaulted) note A note that is not paid in full at maturity. (p. 403).

Factor A finance company or bank that buys receivables from businesses and then collects the payments directly from the customers. (p. 397).

Maker The party in a promissory note who is making the promise to pay. (p. 399).

Notes receivable Written promise (as evidenced by a formal instrument) for amounts to be received. (p. 388).

Other receivables Various forms of nontrade receivables, such as interest receivable and income taxes refundable. (p. 388).

Payee The party to whom payment of a promissory note is to be made. (p. 399).

Percentage-of-receivables basis Management estimates what percentage of receivables will result in losses from uncollectible accounts. (p. 395).

Percentage-of-sales basis Management estimates what percentage of credit sales will be uncollectible. (p. 394).

Promissory note A written promise to pay a specified amount of money on demand or at a definite time. (p. 399).

Receivables Amounts due from individuals and other companies. (p. 388).

Trade receivables Notes and accounts receivable that result from sales transactions. (p. 388).

SELF-TEST QUESTIONS

Answers are on page 425.

(LO 1) **1.** Receivables are frequently classified as:
  (a) accounts receivable, company receivables, and other receivables.
  (b) accounts receivable, notes receivable, and employee receivables.
  (c) accounts receivable and general receivables.
  (d) accounts receivable, notes receivable, and other receivables.

(LO 2) **2.** Buehler Company on June 15 sells merchandise on account to Chaz Co. for $1,000, terms 2/10, n/30. On June 20, Chaz Co. returns merchandise worth $300 to Buehler Company. On June 24, payment is received from Chaz Co. for the balance due. What is the amount of cash received?
  (a) $700.   **(c)** $686.
  (b) $680.   **(d)** None of the above.

(LO 3) **3.** Which of the following approaches for bad debts is best described as a balance sheet method?
  (a) Percentage-of-receivables basis.
  (b) Direct write-off method.
  (c) Percentage-of-sales basis.
  (d) Both percentage-of-receivables basis and direct write-off method.

(LO 3) **4.** Hughes Company has a credit balance of $5,000 in its Allowance for Doubtful Accounts before any adjustments are made at the end of the year. Based on review and aging of its accounts receivable at the end of the year, Hughes estimates that $60,000 of its receivables are uncollectible. The amount of bad debt expense which should be reported for the year is:
  (a) $5,000.   **(c)** $60,000.
  (b) $55,000.   **(d)** $65,000.

(LO 3) **5.** Use the same information as in Question 4, except that Hughes has a debit balance of $5,000 in its Allowance for Doubtful Accounts before any adjustments are made at the end of the year. In this situation, the amount of bad debt expense that should be reported for the year is:
  (a) $5,000.   **(c)** $60,000.
  (b) $55,000.   **(d)** $65,000.

(LO 3) **6.** Net sales for the month are $800,000, and bad debts are expected to be 1.5% of net sales. The company uses the percentage-of-sales basis. If Allowance for Doubtful Accounts has a credit balance of $15,000 before adjustment, what is the balance after adjustment?
  (a) $15,000.   **(c)** $23,000.
  (b) $27,000.   **(d)** $31,000.

(LO 3) **7.** In 2015, Roso Carlson Company had net credit sales of $750,000. On January 1, 2015, Allowance for Doubtful Accounts had a credit balance of $18,000. During 2015,

$30,000 of uncollectible accounts receivable were written off. Past experience indicates that 3% of net credit sales become uncollectible. What should be the adjusted balance of Allowance for Doubtful Accounts at December 31, 2015?
  (a) $10,050.   **(c)** $22,500.
  (b) $10,500.   **(d)** $40,500.

(LO 3) **8.** An analysis and aging of the accounts receivable of Prince Company at December 31 reveals the following data.

Accounts receivable	$800,000
Allowance for doubtful accounts per books before adjustment	50,000
Amounts expected to become uncollectible	65,000

The cash realizable value of the accounts receivable at December 31, after adjustment, is:
  (a) $685,000.   **(c)** $800,000.
  (b) $750,000.   **(d)** $735,000.

(LO 4) **9.** Which of the following statements about Visa credit card sales is **incorrect**?
  (a) The credit card issuer makes the credit investigation of the customer.
  (b) The retailer is not involved in the collection process.
  (c) Two parties are involved.
  (d) The retailer receives cash more quickly than it would from individual customers on account.

(LO 4) **10.** Blinka Retailers accepted $50,000 of Citibank Visa credit card charges for merchandise sold on July 1. Citibank charges 4% for its credit card use. The entry to record this transaction by Blinka Retailers will include a credit to Sales Revenue of $50,000 and a debit(s) to:

(a) Cash	$48,000
and Service Charge Expense	$2,000
(b) Accounts Receivable	$48,000
and Service Charge Expense	$2,000
(c) Cash	$50,000
(d) Accounts Receivable	$50,000

(LO 6) **11.** One of the following statements about promissory notes is incorrect. The **incorrect** statement is:
  (a) The party making the promise to pay is called the maker.
  (b) The party to whom payment is to be made is called the payee.
  (c) A promissory note is not a negotiable instrument.
  (d) A promissory note is often required from high-risk customers.

(LO 6) **12.** Foti Co. accepts a $1,000, 3-month, 6% promissory note in settlement of an account with Bartelt Co. The entry to record this transaction is as follows.

(a)	Notes Receivable	1,015	
	Accounts Receivable		1,015
(b)	Notes Receivable	1,000	
	Accounts Receivable		1,000
(c)	Notes Receivable	1,000	
	Sales Revenue		1,000
(d)	Notes Receivable	1,030	
	Accounts Receivable		1,030

(LO 8) **13.** Ginter Co. holds Kolar Inc.'s $10,000, 120-day, 9% note. The entry made by Ginter Co. when the note is collected, assuming no interest has been previously accrued, is:

(a)	Cash	10,300	
	Notes Receivable		10,300
(b)	Cash	10,000	
	Notes Receivable		10,000
(c)	Accounts Receivable	10,300	
	Notes Receivable		10,000
	Interest Revenue		300

(d)	Cash	10,300	
	Notes Receivable		10,000
	Interest Revenue		300

14. Accounts and notes receivable are reported in the cur- (LO 9) rent assets section of the balance sheet at:
(a) cash (net) realizable value.
(b) net book value.
(c) lower-of-cost-or-market value.
(d) invoice cost.

15. Oliveras Company had net credit sales during the year (LO 9) of $800,000 and cost of goods sold of $500,000. The balance in accounts receivable at the beginning of the year was $100,000, and the end of the year it was $150,000. What were the accounts receivable turnover and the average collection period in days?
(a) 4.0 and 91.3 days.
(b) 5.3 and 68.9 days.
(c) 6.4 and 57 days.
(d) 8.0 and 45.6 days.

Go to the book's companion website, www.wiley.com/college/weygandt, for additional Self-Test Questions.

 The Navigator

QUESTIONS

1. What is the difference between an account receivable and a note receivable?

2. What are some common types of receivables other than accounts receivable and notes receivable?

3. Texaco Oil Company issues its own credit cards. Assume that Texaco charges you $40 interest on an unpaid balance. Prepare the journal entry that Texaco makes to record this revenue.

4. What are the essential features of the allowance method of accounting for bad debts?

5. Roger Holloway cannot understand why cash realizable value does not decrease when an uncollectible account is written off under the allowance method. Clarify this point for Roger.

6. Distinguish between the two bases that may be used in estimating uncollectible accounts.

7. Borke Company has a credit balance of $3,000 in Allowance for Doubtful Accounts. The estimated bad debt expense under the percentage-of-sales basis is $4,100. The total estimated uncollectibles under the percentage-of-receivables basis is $5,800. Prepare the adjusting entry under each basis.

8. How are bad debts accounted for under the direct write-off method? What are the disadvantages of this method?

9. Freida Company accepts both its own credit cards and national credit cards. What are the advantages of accepting both types of cards?

10. An article recently appeared in the *Wall Street Journal* indicating that companies are selling their receivables at a record rate. Why are companies selling their receivables?

11. Westside Textiles decides to sell $800,000 of its accounts receivable to First Factors Inc. First Factors assesses a service charge of 3% of the amount of receivables sold. Prepare the journal entry that Westside Textiles makes to record this sale.

12. Your roommate is uncertain about the advantages of a promissory note. Compare the advantages of a note receivable with those of an account receivable.

13. How may the maturity date of a promissory note be stated?

14. Indicate the maturity date of each of the following promissory notes:

Date of Note	Terms
(a) March 13	one year after date of note
(b) May 4	3 months after date
(c) June 20	30 days after date
(d) July 1	60 days after date

15. Compute the missing amounts for each of the following notes.

	Principal	Annual Interest Rate	Time	Total Interest
(a)	?	9%	120 days	$ 450
(b)	$30,000	10%	3 years	?
(c)	$60,000	?	5 months	$1,500
(d)	$45,000	8%	?	$1,200

16. In determining interest revenue, some financial institutions use 365 days per year and others use 360 days. Why might a financial institution use 360 days?

17. Jana Company dishonors a note at maturity. What are the options available to the lender?

18. General Motors Corporation has accounts receivable and notes receivable. How should the receivables be reported on the balance sheet?

19. The accounts receivable turnover is 8.14, and average net accounts receivable during the period is $400,000. What is the amount of net credit sales for the period?

20. What percentage does Apple's 2011 allowance for doubtful accounts represent as a percentage of its gross receivables?

BRIEF EXERCISES

BE8-1 Presented below are three receivables transactions. Indicate whether these receivables are reported as accounts receivable, notes receivable, or other receivables on a balance sheet.

Identify different types of receivables.

(LO 1)

(a) Sold merchandise on account for $64,000 to a customer.
(b) Received a promissory note of $57,000 for services performed.
(c) Advanced $10,000 to an employee.

BE8-2 Record the following transactions on the books of RAS Co.

Record basic accounts receivable transactions.

(LO 2)

(a) On July 1, RAS Co. sold merchandise on account to Waegelein Inc. for $17,200, terms 2/10, n/30.
(b) On July 8, Waegelein Inc. returned merchandise worth $3,800 to RAS Co.
(c) On July 11, Waegelein Inc. paid for the merchandise.

BE8-3 During its first year of operations, Gavin Company had credit sales of $3,000,000; $600,000 remained uncollected at year-end. The credit manager estimates that $31,000 of these receivables will become uncollectible.

Prepare entry for allowance method and partial balance sheet.

(LO 3, 9)

(a) Prepare the journal entry to record the estimated uncollectibles.
(b) Prepare the current assets section of the balance sheet for Gavin Company. Assume that in addition to the receivables it has cash of $90,000, inventory of $130,000, and prepaid insurance of $7,500.

BE8-4 At the end of 2015, Carpenter Co. has accounts receivable of $700,000 and an allowance for doubtful accounts of $54,000. On January 24, 2016, the company learns that its receivable from Megan Gray is not collectible, and management authorizes a write-off of $6,200.

Prepare entry for write-off; determine cash realizable value.

(LO 3)

(a) Prepare the journal entry to record the write-off.
(b) What is the cash realizable value of the accounts receivable (1) before the write-off and (2) after the write-off?

BE8-5 Assume the same information as BE8-4. On March 4, 2016, Carpenter Co. receives payment of $6,200 in full from Megan Gray. Prepare the journal entries to record this transaction.

Prepare entries for collection of bad debt write-off.

(LO 3)

BE8-6 Farr Co. elects to use the percentage-of-sales basis in 2015 to record bad debt expense. It estimates that 2% of net credit sales will become uncollectible. Sales revenues are $800,000 for 2015, sales returns and allowances are $40,000, and the allowance for doubtful accounts has a credit balance of $9,000. Prepare the adjusting entry to record bad debt expense in 2015.

Prepare entry using percentage-of-sales method.

(LO 3)

BE8-7 Kingston Co. uses the percentage-of-receivables basis to record bad debt expense. It estimates that 1% of accounts receivable will become uncollectible. Accounts receivable are $420,000 at the end of the year, and the allowance for doubtful accounts has a credit balance of $1,500.

Prepare entry using percentage-of-receivables method.

(LO 3)

(a) Prepare the adjusting journal entry to record bad debt expense for the year.
(b) If the allowance for doubtful accounts had a debit balance of $800 instead of a credit balance of $1,500, determine the amount to be reported for bad debt expense.

BE8-8 Presented below and on page 412 are two independent transactions.

Prepare entries to dispose of accounts receivable.

(LO 4)

(a) Tony's Restaurant accepted a Visa card in payment of a $175 lunch bill. The bank charges a 4% fee. What entry should Tony's make?

(b) Larkin Company sold its accounts receivable of $60,000. What entry should Larkin make, given a service charge of 3% on the amount of receivables sold?

Compute interest and determine maturity dates on notes.

(LO 5)

BE8-9 Compute interest and find the maturity date for the following notes.

	Date of Note	Principal	Interest Rate (%)	Terms
(a)	June 10	$80,000	6%	60 days
(b)	July 14	$64,000	7%	90 days
(c)	April 27	$12,000	8%	75 days

Determine maturity dates and compute interest and rates on notes.

(LO 5)

BE8-10 Presented below are data on three promissory notes. Determine the missing amounts.

Date of Note	Terms	Maturity Date	Principal	Annual Interest Rate	Total Interest
(a) April 1	60 days	?	$600,000	6%	?
(b) July 2	30 days	?	90,000	?	$600
(c) March 7	6 months	?	120,000	10%	?

Prepare entry for note receivable exchanged for account receivable.

(LO 6)

BE8-11 On January 10, 2015, Perez Co. sold merchandise on account to Robertsen Co. for $15,600, n/30. On February 9, Robertsen Co. gave Perez Co. a 10% promissory note in settlement of this account. Prepare the journal entry to record the sale and the settlement of the account receivable.

Compute ratios to analyze receivables.

(LO 9)

BE8-12 The financial statements of Minnesota Mining and Manufacturing Company (3M) report net sales of $20.0 billion. Accounts receivable (net) are $2.7 billion at the beginning of the year and $2.8 billion at the end of the year. Compute 3M's accounts receivable turnover. Compute 3M's average collection period for accounts receivable in days.

> DO IT! Review

Prepare entry for uncollectible accounts.

(LO 3)

DO IT! 8-1 Gonzalez Company has been in business for several years. At the end of the current year, the ledger shows:

Accounts Receivable	$ 310,000 Dr.
Sales Revenue	2,200,000 Cr.
Allowance for Doubtful Accounts	6,100 Cr.

Bad debts are estimated to be 5% of receivables. Prepare the entry to adjust Allowance for Doubtful Accounts.

Prepare entry for factored accounts.

(LO 4)

DO IT! 8-2 Wynn Distributors is a growing company whose ability to raise capital has not been growing as quickly as its expanding assets and sales. Wynn's local banker has indicated that the company cannot increase its borrowing for the foreseeable future. Wynn's suppliers are demanding payment for goods acquired within 30 days of the invoice date, but Wynn's customers are slow in paying for their purchases (60–90 days). As a result, Wynn has a cash flow problem.

Wynn needs $160,000 to cover next Friday's payroll. Its balance of outstanding accounts receivable totals $1,000,000. To alleviate this cash crunch, Wynn sells $200,000 of its receivables. Record the entry that Wynn would make when it raises the needed cash. (Assume a 3% service charge.)

Prepare entries for notes receivable.

(LO 5, 8)

DO IT! 8-3 Gentry Wholesalers accepts from Benton Stores a $6,200, 4-month, 9% note dated May 31 in settlement of Benton's overdue account. (a) What is the maturity date of the note? (b) What is the entry made by Gentry at the maturity date, assuming Benton pays the note and interest in full at that time?

Compute ratios for receivables.

(LO 9)

DO IT! 8-4 In 2015, Wainwright Company has net credit sales of $1,300,000 for the year. It had a beginning accounts receivable (net) balance of $101,000 and an ending accounts receivable (net) balance of $107,000. Compute Wainwright Company's (a) accounts receivable turnover and (b) average collection period in days.

EXERCISES

E8-1 Presented below are selected transactions of Molina Company. Molina sells in large quantities to other companies and also sells its product in a small retail outlet.

Journalize entries related to accounts receivable.

(LO 2)

March 1 Sold merchandise on account to Dodson Company for $5,000, terms 2/10, n/30.

3 Dodson Company returned merchandise worth $500 to Molina.

9 Molina collected the amount due from Dodson Company from the March 1 sale.

15 Molina sold merchandise for $400 in its retail outlet. The customer used his Molina credit card.

31 Molina added 1.5% monthly interest to the customer's credit card balance.

Instructions

Prepare journal entries for the transactions above.

E8-2 Presented below are two independent situations.

Journalize entries for recognizing accounts receivable.

(LO 2)

(a) On January 6, Brumbaugh Co. sells merchandise on account to Pryor Inc. for $7,000, terms 2/10, n/30. On January 16, Pryor Inc. pays the amount due. Prepare the entries on Brumbaugh's books to record the sale and related collection.

(b) On January 10, Andrew Farley uses his Paltrow Co. credit card to purchase merchandise from Paltrow Co. for $9,000. On February 10, Farley is billed for the amount due of $9,000. On February 12, Farley pays $5,000 on the balance due. On March 10, Farley is billed for the amount due, including interest at 1% per month on the unpaid balance as of February 12. Prepare the entries on Paltrow Co.'s books related to the transactions that occurred on January 10, February 12, and March 10.

E8-3 The ledger of Costello Company at the end of the current year shows Accounts Receivable $110,000, Sales Revenue $840,000, and Sales Returns and Allowances $20,000.

Journalize entries to record allowance for doubtful accounts using two different bases.

(LO 3)

Instructions

(a) If Costello uses the direct write-off method to account for uncollectible accounts, journalize the adjusting entry at December 31, assuming Costello determines that L. Dole's $1,400 balance is uncollectible.

(b) If Allowance for Doubtful Accounts has a credit balance of $2,100 in the trial balance, journalize the adjusting entry at December 31, assuming bad debts are expected to be (1) 1% of net sales, and (2) 10% of accounts receivable.

(c) If Allowance for Doubtful Accounts has a debit balance of $200 in the trial balance, journalize the adjusting entry at December 31, assuming bad debts are expected to be (1) 0.75% of net sales and (2) 6% of accounts receivable.

E8-4 Menge Company has accounts receivable of $93,100 at March 31. An analysis of the accounts shows the following information.

Determine bad debt expense; prepare the adjusting entry for bad debt expense.

(LO 3)

Month of Sale	Balance, March 31
March	$60,000
February	17,600
January	8,500
Prior to January	7,000
	$93,100

Credit terms are 2/10, n/30. At March 31, Allowance for Doubtful Accounts has a credit balance of $1,200 prior to adjustment. The company uses the percentage-of-receivables basis for estimating uncollectible accounts. The company's estimate of bad debts is shown below.

Age of Accounts	Estimated Percentage Uncollectible
1–30 days	2.0%
31–60 days	5.0%
61–90 days	20.0%
Over 90 days	50.0%

Instructions

(a) Determine the total estimated uncollectibles.

(b) Prepare the adjusting entry at March 31 to record bad debt expense.

Journalize write-off and recovery.

(LO 3)

E8-5 At December 31, 2014, Finzelberg Company had a credit balance of $15,000 in Allowance for Doubtful Accounts. During 2015, Finzelberg wrote off accounts totaling $11,000. One of those accounts ($1,800) was later collected. At December 31, 2015, an aging schedule indicated that the balance in Allowance for Doubtful Accounts should be $19,000.

Instructions

Prepare journal entries to record the 2015 transactions of Finzelberg Company.

Journalize percentage-of-sales basis, write-off, recovery.

(LO 3)

E8-6 On December 31, 2015, Ling Co. estimated that 2% of its net sales of $450,000 will become uncollectible. The company recorded this amount as an addition to Allowance for Doubtful Accounts. On May 11, 2016, Ling Co. determined that the Jeff Shoemaker account was uncollectible and wrote off $1,100. On June 12, 2016, Shoemaker paid the amount previously written off.

Instructions

Prepare the journal entries on December 31, 2015, May 11, 2016, and June 12, 2016.

Journalize entries for the sale of accounts receivable.

(LO 4)

E8-7 Presented below are two independent situations.

(a) On March 3, Kitselman Appliances sells $650,000 of its receivables to Ervay Factors Inc. Ervay Factors assesses a finance charge of 3% of the amount of receivables sold. Prepare the entry on Kitselman Appliances' books to record the sale of the receivables.

(b) On May 10, Fillmore Company sold merchandise for $3,000 and accepted the customer's America Bank MasterCard. America Bank charges a 4% service charge for credit card sales. Prepare the entry on Fillmore Company's books to record the sale of merchandise.

Journalize entries for credit card sales.

(LO 4)

E8-8 Presented below are two independent situations.

(a) On April 2, Jennifer Elston uses her JCPenney Company credit card to purchase merchandise from a JCPenney store for $1,500. On May 1, Elston is billed for the $1,500 amount due. Elston pays $500 on the balance due on May 3. On June 1, Elston receives a bill for the amount due, including interest at 1.0% per month on the unpaid balance as of May 3. Prepare the entries on JCPenney Co.'s books related to the transactions that occurred on April 2, May 3, and June 1.

(b) On July 4, Spangler's Restaurant accepts a Visa card for a $200 dinner bill. Visa charges a 2% service fee. Prepare the entry on Spangler's books related to this transaction.

Journalize credit card sales, and indicate the statement presentation of financing charges and service charge expense.

(LO 4)

E8-9 Colaw Stores accepts both its own and national credit cards. During the year, the following selected summary transactions occurred.

Jan. 15 Made Colaw credit card sales totaling $18,000. (There were no balances prior to January 15.)

  20 Made Visa credit card sales (service charge fee 2%) totaling $4,500.

Feb. 10 Collected $10,000 on Colaw credit card sales.

  15 Added finance charges of 1.5% to Colaw credit card account balances.

Instructions

(a) Journalize the transactions for Colaw Stores.

(b) Indicate the statement presentation of the financing charges and the credit card service charge expense for Colaw Stores.

Journalize entries for notes receivable transactions.

(LO 5, 6)

E8-10 Elburn Supply Co. has the following transactions related to notes receivable during the last 2 months of 2015. The company does not make entries to accrue interest except at December 31.

Nov. 1 Loaned $30,000 cash to Manny Lopez on a 12 month, 10% note.

Dec. 11 Sold goods to Ralph Kremer, Inc., receiving a $6,750, 90-day, 8% note.

  16 Received a $4,000, 180 day, 9% note in exchange for Joe Fernetti's outstanding accounts receivable.

  31 Accrued interest revenue on all notes receivable.

Instructions

(a) Journalize the transactions for Elburn Supply Co.

(b) Record the collection of the Lopez note at its maturity in 2016.

E8-11 Record the following transactions for Redeker Co. in the general journal.

2015

May 1   Received a $9,000, 12-month, 10% note in exchange for Mark Chamber's outstanding accounts receivable.
Dec. 31   Accrued interest on the Chamber note.
Dec. 31   Closed the interest revenue account.

2016

May 1   Received principal plus interest on the Chamber note. (No interest has been accrued in 2016.)

Journalize entries for notes receivable.
(LO 5, 6, 8)

E8-12 Vandiver Company had the following select transactions.

Apr. 1, 2015   Accepted Goodwin Company's 12-month, 12% note in settlement of a $30,000 account receivable.
July 1, 2015   Loaned $25,000 cash to Thomas Slocombe on a 9-month, 10% note.
Dec. 31, 2015   Accrued interest on all notes receivable.
Apr. 1, 2016   Received principal plus interest on the Goodwin note.
Apr. 1, 2016   Thomas Slocombe dishonored its note; Vandiver expects it will eventually collect.

Prepare entries for notes receivable transactions.
(LO 5, 6, 8)

Instructions
Prepare journal entries to record the transactions. Vandiver prepares adjusting entries once a year on December 31.

E8-13 On May 2, McLain Company lends $9,000 to Chang, Inc., issuing a 6-month, 9% note. At the maturity date, November 2, Chang indicates that it cannot pay.

Journalize entries for dishonor of notes receivable.
(LO 5, 8)

Instructions
(a) Prepare the entry to record the issuance of the note.
(b) Prepare the entry to record the dishonor of the note, assuming that McLain Company expects collection will occur.
(c) Prepare the entry to record the dishonor of the note, assuming that McLain Company does not expect collection in the future.

E8-14 Kerwick Company had accounts receivable of $100,000 on January 1, 2015. The only transactions that affected accounts receivable during 2015 were net credit sales of $1,000,000, cash collections of $920,000, and accounts written off of $30,000.

Compute accounts receivable turnover and average collection period.
(LO 9)

Instructions
(a) Compute the ending balance of accounts receivable.
(b) Compute the accounts receivable turnover for 2015.
(c) Compute the average collection period in days.

EXERCISES: SET B AND CHALLENGE EXERCISES

Visit the book's companion website, at **www.wiley.com/college/weygandt**, and choose the Student Companion site to access Exercise Set B and Challenge Exercises.

PROBLEMS: SET A

P8-1A At December 31, 2014, House Co. reported the following information on its balance sheet.

Prepare journal entries related to bad debt expense.
(LO 2, 3, 9)

Accounts receivable	$960,000
Less: Allowance for doubtful accounts	80,000

During 2015, the company had the following transactions related to receivables.

1. Sales on account	$3,700,000
2. Sales returns and allowances	50,000
3. Collections of accounts receivable	2,810,000
4. Write-offs of accounts receivable deemed uncollectible	90,000
5. Recovery of bad debts previously written off as uncollectible	29,000

Instructions

(a) Prepare the journal entries to record each of these five transactions. Assume that no cash discounts were taken on the collections of accounts receivable.

(b) Accounts receivable
   $1,710,000
   ADA $19,000
(c) Bad debt expense $96,000

(b) Enter the January 1, 2015, balances in Accounts Receivable and Allowance for Doubtful Accounts, post the entries to the two accounts (use T-accounts), and determine the balances.

(c) Prepare the journal entry to record bad debt expense for 2015, assuming that an aging of accounts receivable indicates that expected bad debts are $115,000.

(d) Compute the accounts receivable turnover for 2015, assuming the expected bad debt information provided in (c).

Compute bad debt amounts.

(LO 3)

P8-2A Information related to Mingenback Company for 2015 is summarized below.

Total credit sales	$2,500,000
Accounts receivable at December 31	875,000
Bad debts written off	33,000

Instructions

(a) What amount of bad debt expense will Mingenback Company report if it uses the direct write-off method of accounting for bad debts?

(b) Assume that Mingenback Company estimates its bad debt expense to be 2% of credit sales. What amount of bad debt expense will Mingenback record if it has an Allowance for Doubtful Accounts credit balance of $4,000?

(c) Assume that Mingenback Company estimates its bad debt expense based on 6% of accounts receivable. What amount of bad debt expense will Mingenback record if it has an Allowance for Doubtful Accounts credit balance of $3,000?

(d) Assume the same facts as in (c), except that there is a $3,000 debit balance in Allowance for Doubtful Accounts. What amount of bad debt expense will Mingenback record?

(e) What is the weakness of the direct write-off method of reporting bad debt expense?

Journalize entries to record transactions related to bad debts.

(LO 3)

P8-3A Presented below is an aging schedule for Halleran Company.

	Worksheet.xls						
	Home Insert Page Layout Formulas Data Review View						
	P18	fx					
	A	B	C	D	E	F	G
1				Number of Days Past Due			
2			Not				
3	Customer	Total	Yet Due	1–30	31–60	61–90	Over 90
4	Anders	$ 22,000		$10,000	$12,000		
5	Blake	40,000	$ 40,000				
6	Coulson	57,000	16,000	6,000		$35,000	
7	Deleon	34,000					$34,000
8	Others	132,000	96,000	16,000	14,000		6,000
9		$285,000	$152,000	$32,000	$26,000	$35,000	$40,000
10	Estimated Percentage Uncollectible		3%	6%	13%	25%	50%
11	Total Estimated Bad Debts	$ 38,610	$ 4,560	$ 1,920	$ 3,380	$ 8,750	$20,000
12							

At December 31, 2015, the unadjusted balance in Allowance for Doubtful Accounts is a credit of $12,000.

Instructions

(a) Bad debt expense $26,610

(a) Journalize and post the adjusting entry for bad debts at December 31, 2015.

(b) Journalize and post to the allowance account the following events and transactions in the year 2016.

(1) On March 31, a $1,000 customer balance originating in 2015 is judged uncollectible.
(2) On May 31, a check for $1,000 is received from the customer whose account was written off as uncollectible on March 31.

(c) Journalize the adjusting entry for bad debts on December 31, 2016, assuming that the unadjusted balance in Allowance for Doubtful Accounts is a debit of $800 and the aging schedule indicates that total estimated bad debts will be $31,600.

(c) Bad debt expense $32,400

P8-4A Rigney Inc. uses the allowance method to estimate uncollectible accounts receivable. The company produced the following aging of the accounts receivable at year-end.

Journalize transactions related to bad debts.
(LO 3)

	Worksheet.xls					
Home Insert Page Layout Formulas Data Review View						
P18	fx					
	A	B	C	D	E	F	G

	A	B	C	D	E	F	G
1				Number of Days Outstanding			
2							
3		Total	0–30	31–60	61–90	91–120	Over 120
4	Accounts receivable	200,000	77,000	46,000	39,000	23,000	$15,000
5	% uncollectible		1%	4%	5%	8%	20%
6	Estimated bad debts						
7							

Instructions

(a) Calculate the total estimated bad debts based on the above information.

(a) Tot. est. bad debts $9,400

(b) Prepare the year-end adjusting journal entry to record the bad debts using the aged uncollectible accounts receivable determined in (a). Assume the current balance in Allowance for Doubtful Accounts is a $8,000 debit.

(c) Of the above accounts, $5,000 is determined to be specifically uncollectible. Prepare the journal entry to write off the uncollectible account.

(d) The company collects $5,000 subsequently on a specific account that had previously been determined to be uncollectible in (c). Prepare the journal entry(ies) necessary to restore the account and record the cash collection.

(e) Comment on how your answers to (a)–(d) would change if Rigney Inc. used 4% of **total** accounts receivable rather than aging the accounts receivable. What are the advantages to the company of aging the accounts receivable rather than applying a percentage to total accounts receivable?

P8-5A At December 31, 2015, the trial balance of Darby Company contained the following amounts before adjustment.

Journalize entries to record transactions related to bad debts.
(LO 3)

	Debit	Credit
Accounts Receivable	$385,000	
Allowance for Doubtful Accounts		$ 1,000
Sales Revenue		970,000

Instructions

(a) Based on the information given, which method of accounting for bad debts is Darby Company using—the direct write-off method or the allowance method? How can you tell?

(b) Prepare the adjusting entry at December 31, 2015, for bad debt expense under each of the following independent assumptions.
(1) An aging schedule indicates that $11,750 of accounts receivable will be uncollectible.
(2) The company estimates that 1% of sales will be uncollectible.

(b)(2) $9,700

(c) Repeat part (b) assuming that instead of a credit balance there is an $1,000 debit balance in Allowance for Doubtful Accounts.

(d) During the next month, January 2016, a $3,000 account receivable is written off as uncollectible. Prepare the journal entry to record the write-off.

(e) Repeat part (d) assuming that Darby uses the direct write-off method instead of the allowance method in accounting for uncollectible accounts receivable.

(f) ➤ What type of account is Allowance for Doubtful Accounts? How does it affect how accounts receivable is reported on the balance sheet at the end of the accounting period?

Prepare entries for various notes receivable transactions.

(LO 2, 4, 5, 8, 9)

P8-6A Farwell Company closes its books monthly. On September 30, selected ledger account balances are:

Notes Receivable	$37,000
Interest Receivable	183

Notes Receivable include the following.

Date	Maker	Face	Term	Interest
Aug. 16	K. Goza Inc.	$12,000	60 days	8%
Aug. 25	Holt Co.	9,000	60 days	7%
Sept. 30	Noblitt Corp.	16,000	6 months	9%

Interest is computed using a 360-day year. During October, the following transactions were completed.

Oct. 7   Made sales of $6,900 on Farwell credit cards.
     12   Made sales of $900 on MasterCard credit cards. The credit card service charge is 3%.
     15   Added $460 to Farwell customer balances for finance charges on unpaid balances.
     15   Received payment in full from K. Goza Inc. on the amount due.
     24   Received notice that the Holt note has been dishonored. (Assume that Holt is expected to pay in the future.)

Instructions
(a) Journalize the October transactions and the October 31 adjusting entry for accrued interest receivable.

(b) Accounts receivable $16,465

(c) Total receivables $32,585

(b) Enter the balances at October 1 in the receivable accounts. Post the entries to all of the receivable accounts.
(c) Show the balance sheet presentation of the receivable accounts at October 31.

Prepare entries for various receivable transactions.

(LO 2, 4, 5, 6, 8)

P8-7A On January 1, 2015, Harter Company had Accounts Receivable $139,000, Notes Receivable $25,000, and Allowance for Doubtful Accounts $13,200. The note receivable is from Willingham Company. It is a 4-month, 9% note dated December 31, 2014. Harter Company prepares financial statements annually at December 31. During the year, the following selected transactions occurred.

Jan. 5   Sold $20,000 of merchandise to Sheldon Company, terms n/15.
     20   Accepted Sheldon Company's $20,000, 3-month, 8% note for balance due.
Feb. 18   Sold $8,000 of merchandise to Patwary Company and accepted Patwary's $8,000, 6-month, 9% note for the amount due.
Apr. 20   Collected Sheldon Company note in full.
     30   Received payment in full from Willingham Company on the amount due.
May 25   Accepted Potter Inc.'s $6,000, 3-month, 7% note in settlement of a past-due balance on account.
Aug. 18   Received payment in full from Patwary Company on note due.
     25   The Potter Inc. note was dishonored. Potter Inc. is not bankrupt; future payment is anticipated.
Sept. 1   Sold $12,000 of merchandise to Stanbrough Company and accepted a $12,000, 6-month, 10% note for the amount due.

Instructions
Journalize the transactions.

PROBLEMS: SET B

Prepare journal entries related to bad debt expense.

(LO 2, 3, 9)

P8-1B At December 31, 2014, Obermeyer Imports reported the following information on its balance sheet.

Accounts receivable	$250,000
Less: Allowance for doubtful accounts	15,000

During 2015, the company had the following transactions related to receivables.

1. Sales on account	$2,600,000
2. Sales returns and allowances	45,000

3. Collections of accounts receivable   2,250,000
4. Write-offs of accounts receivable deemed uncollectible   10,000
5. Recovery of bad debts previously written off as uncollectible   3,000

Instructions

(a) Prepare the journal entries to record each of these five transactions. Assume that no cash discounts were taken on the collections of accounts receivable.

(b) Enter the January 1, 2015, balances in Accounts Receivable and Allowance for Doubtful Accounts. Post the entries to the two accounts (use T-accounts), and determine the balances.

(c) Prepare the journal entry to record bad debt expense for 2015, assuming that an aging of accounts receivable indicates that estimated bad debts are $22,000.

(d) Compute the accounts receivable turnover for the year 2015.

(b) Accounts receivable
$545,000
ADA $8,000
(c) Bad debt expense $14,000

P8-2B Information related to Miracle Company for 2015 is summarized below.

Total credit sales	$1,000,000
Accounts receivable at December 31	369,000
Bad debts written off	22,150

Compute bad debt amounts.
(LO 3)

Instructions

(a) What amount of bad debt expense will Miracle Company report if it uses the direct write-off method of accounting for bad debts?

(b) Assume that Miracle Company decides to estimate its bad debt expense to be 2% of credit sales. What amount of bad debt expense will Miracle record if Allowance for Doubtful Accounts has a credit balance of $3,000?

(c) Assume that Miracle Company decides to estimate its bad debt expense based on 5% of accounts receivable. What amount of bad debt expense will Miracle Company record if Allowance for Doubtful Accounts has a credit balance of $4,000?

(d) Assume the same facts as in (c), except that there is a $2,000 debit balance in Allowance for Doubtful Accounts. What amount of bad debt expense will Miracle record?

(e) ━━━━▶ What is the weakness of the direct write-off method of reporting bad debt expense?

P8-3B Presented below is an aging schedule for Loucks Company.

Journalize entries to record transactions related to bad debts.
(LO 3)

		Worksheet.xls				
Home Insert Page Layout Formulas Data Review View						
P18	*fx*					

	A	B	C	D	E	F	G
1					**Number of Days Past Due**		
2			**Not**				
3	**Customer**	**Total**	**Yet Due**	**1–30**	**31–60**	**61–90**	**Over 90**
4	Alma	$ 30,000		$ 13,500	$16,500		
5	Browne	45,000	$ 45,000				
6	Conlon	75,000	22,500	7,500		$45,000	
7	Dalton	57,000					$57,000
8	Others	189,000	138,000	22,500	19,500		9,000
9		$396,000	$205,500	$43,500	$36,000	$45,000	$66,000
10	Estimated Percentage Uncollectible		2%	6%	10%	25%	40%
11	Total Estimated Bad Debts	$ 47,970	$ 4,110	$ 2,610	$ 3,600	$ 11,250	$26,400
12							

At December 31, 2015, the unadjusted balance in Allowance for Doubtful Accounts is a credit of $16,000.

Instructions

(a) Journalize and post the adjusting entry for bad debts at December 31, 2015.

(a) Bad debt expense $31,970

(b) Journalize and post to the allowance account the following events and transactions in the year 2016.

  (1) March 1, a $1,900 customer balance originating in 2015 is judged uncollectible.

  (2) May 1, a check for $1,900 is received from the customer whose account was written off as uncollectible on March 1.

(c) Bad debt expense $40,300

(c) Journalize the adjusting entry for bad debts on December 31, 2016. Assume that the unadjusted balance in Allowance for Doubtful Accounts is a debit of $2,000, and the aging schedule indicates that total estimated bad debts will be $38,300.

Journalize transactions related to bad debts.

(LO 3)

P8-4B The following represents selected information taken from a company's aging schedule to estimate uncollectible accounts receivable at year-end.

		Worksheet.xls					
		Home Insert Page Layout Formulas Data Review View					
	P18		*fx*				
	A	B	C	D	E	F	G
1				**Number of Days Outstanding**			
2							
3		Total	0–30	31–60	61–90	91–120	Over 120
4	Accounts receivable	$375,000	$220,000	$90,000	$40,000	$10,000	$15,000
5	% uncollectible		1%	4%	5%	8%	20%
6	Estimated bad debts						
7							

Instructions

(a) Tot. est. bad debts $11,600

(a) Calculate the total estimated bad debts based on the above information.

(b) Prepare the year-end adjusting journal entry to record the bad debts using the allowance method and the aged uncollectible accounts receivable determined in (a). Assume the current balance in Allowance for Doubtful Accounts is a $3,000 credit.

(c) Of the above accounts, $1,600 is determined to be specifically uncollectible. Prepare the journal entry to write off the uncollectible accounts.

(d) The company subsequently collects $700 on a specific account that had previously been determined to be uncollectible in (c). Prepare the journal entry(ies) necessary to restore the account and record the cash collection.

(e) Explain how establishing an allowance account satisfies the expense recognition principle.

Journalize entries to record transactions related to bad debts.

(LO 3)

P8-5B At December 31, 2015, the trial balance of Markowitz Company contained the following amounts before adjustment.

	Debit	**Credit**
Accounts Receivable	$250,000	
Allowance for Doubtful Accounts		$ 1,100
Sales Revenue		650,000

Instructions

(a) Prepare the adjusting entry at December 31, 2015, to record bad debt expense under each of the following independent assumptions.

(1) An aging schedule indicates that $13,500 of accounts receivable will be uncollectible.

(a)(2) $13,000

(2) The company estimates that 2% of sales will be uncollectible.

(b) Repeat part (a) assuming that instead of a credit balance, there is a $1,100 debit balance in Allowance for Doubtful Accounts.

(c) During the next month, January 2016, a $3,200 account receivable is written off as uncollectible. Prepare the journal entry to record the write-off.

(d) Repeat part (c) assuming that Markowitz Company uses the direct write-off method instead of the allowance method in accounting for uncollectible accounts receivable.

(e) ──── What are the advantages of using the allowance method in accounting for uncollectible accounts as compared to the direct write-off method?

Prepare entries for various notes receivable transactions.

(LO 2, 4, 5, 8, 9)

P8-6B Sauer Co. closes its books monthly. On June 30, selected ledger account balances are:

Notes Receivable	$47,000
Interest Receivable	285

Notes Receivable include the following.

Date	Maker	Face	Term	Interest
May 16	Eddy Inc.	$12,000	60 days	7%
May 25	Masasi Co.	20,000	60 days	9%
June 30	Pelsma Corp.	15,000	6 months	8%

During July, the following transactions were completed.

July 5   Made sales of $7,200 on Sauer Co. credit cards.
     14   Made sales of $1,000 on Visa credit cards. The credit card service charge is 3%.
     14   Added $510 to Sauer Co. credit card customer balances for finance charges on unpaid balances.
     15   Received payment in full from Eddy Inc. on the amount due.
     24   Received notice that the Masasi Co. note has been dishonored. (Assume that Masasi Co. is expected to pay in the future.)

Instructions

(a) Journalize the July transactions and the July 31 adjusting entry for accrued interest receivable. (Interest is computed using 360 days.)

(b) Enter the balances at July 1 in the receivable accounts. Post the entries to all of the receivable accounts.

(c) Show the balance sheet presentation of the receivable accounts at July 31.

(b) Accounts receivable $28,010

(c) Total receivables $43,110

P8-7B On January 1, 2015, Morfitt Company had Accounts Receivable $98,000 and Allowance for Doubtful Accounts $8,100. Morfitt Company prepares financial statements annually. During the year, the following selected transactions occurred.

Prepare entries for various receivable transactions.

(LO 2, 4, 5, 6, 8)

Jan. 5   Sold $10,800 of merchandise to Motte Company, terms n/30.
Feb. 2   Accepted a $10,800, 4-month, 9% promissory note from Motte Company for the balance due.
     12   Sold $13,500 of merchandise to Gitchel Company and accepted Gitchel's $13,500, 2-month, 8% note for the balance due.
     26   Sold $9,000 of merchandise to Benedict Co., terms n/10.
Apr. 5   Accepted a $9,000, 3-month, 8% note from Benedict Co. for the balance due.
     12   Collected Gitchel Company note in full.
June 2   Collected Motte Company note in full.
July 5   Benedict Co. dishonors its note of April 5. It is expected that Benedict will eventually pay the amount owed.
     15   Sold $12,000 of merchandise to Kriley Co. and accepted Kriley's $12,000, 3-month, 12% note for the amount due.
Oct. 15   Kriley Co.'s note was dishonored. Kriley Co. is bankrupt, and there is no hope of future settlement.

Instructions

Journalize the transactions.

PROBLEMS: SET C

Visit the book's companion website, at **www.wiley.com/college/weygandt**, and choose the Student Companion site to access Problem Set C.

COMPREHENSIVE PROBLEM

CP8 Winter Company's balance sheet at December 31, 2014, is presented below.

WINTER COMPANY
Balance Sheet
December 31, 2014

Cash	$13,100	Accounts payable	$ 8,750
Accounts receivable	19,780	Common stock	20,000
Allowance for doubtful accounts	(800)	Retained earnings	12,730
Inventory	9,400		$41,480
	$41,480		

During January 2015, the following transactions occurred. Winter uses the perpetual inventory method.

Jan. 1 Winter accepted a 4-month, 8% note from Merando Company in payment of Merando's $1,200 account.

3 Winter wrote off as uncollectible the accounts of Inwood Corporation ($450) and Goza Company ($280).

8 Winter purchased $17,200 of inventory on account.

11 Winter sold for $28,000 on account inventory that cost $19,600.

15 Winter sold inventory that cost $700 to Mark Lauber for $1,000. Lauber charged this amount on his Visa First Bank card. The service fee charged Winter by First Bank is 3%.

17 Winter collected $22,900 from customers on account.

21 Winter paid $14,300 on accounts payable.

24 Winter received payment in full ($280) from Goza Company on the account written off on January 3.

27 Winter purchased supplies for $1,400 cash.

31 Winter paid other operating expenses, $3,718.

Adjustment data:

1. Interest is recorded for the month on the note from January 1.
2. Bad debts are expected to be 6% of the January 31, 2015, accounts receivable.
3. A count of supplies on January 31, 2015, reveals that $560 remains unused.

Instructions

(You may want to set up T-accounts to determine ending balances.)

(a) Prepare journal entries for the transactions listed above and adjusting entries. (Include entries for cost of goods sold using the perpetual system.)

(b) Prepare an adjusted trial balance at January 31, 2015.

(c) Prepare an income statement and a retained earnings statement for the month ending January 31, 2015, and a balance sheet as of January 31, 2015.

CONTINUING COOKIE CHRONICLE

(*Note:* This is a continuation of the Cookie Chronicle from Chapters 1 through 7.)

CCC8 One of Natalie's friends, Curtis Lesperance, runs a coffee shop where he sells specialty coffees and prepares and sells muffins and cookies. He is eager to buy one of Natalie's fine European mixers, which would enable him to make larger batches of muffins and cookies. However, Curtis cannot afford to pay for the mixer for at least 30 days. He asks Natalie if she would be willing to sell him the mixer on credit. Natalie comes to you for advice.

Go to the book's companion website, **www.wiley.com/college/weygandt**, *to see the completion of this problem.*

Broadening Your PERSPECTIVE

Financial Reporting and Analysis

Financial Reporting Problem: RLF Company

BYP8-1 RLF Company sells office equipment and supplies to many organizations in the city and surrounding area on contract terms of 2/10, n/30. In the past, over 75% of the credit customers have taken advantage of the discount by paying within 10 days of the invoice date.

The number of customers taking the full 30 days to pay has increased within the last year. Current indications are that less than 60% of the customers are now taking the discount. Bad debts as a percentage of gross credit sales have risen from the 2.5% provided in past years to about 4.5% in the current year.

The company's Finance Committee has requested more information on the collections of accounts receivable. The controller responded to this request with the report reproduced below.

RLF COMPANY
Accounts Receivable Collections
May 31, 2015

The fact that some credit accounts will prove uncollectible is normal. Annual bad debt write-offs have been 2.5% of gross credit sales over the past 5 years. During the last fiscal year, this percentage increased to slightly less than 4.5%. The current Accounts Receivable balance is $1,400,000. The condition of this balance in terms of age and probability of collection is as follows.

Proportion of Total	Age Categories	Probability of Collection
60%	not yet due	98%
22%	less than 30 days past due	96%
9%	30 to 60 days past due	94%
5%	61 to 120 days past due	91%
$2\frac{1}{2}$%	121 to 180 days past due	75%
$1\frac{1}{2}$%	over 180 days past due	30%

Allowance for Doubtful Accounts had a credit balance of $29,500 on June 1, 2014. RLF has provided for a monthly bad debt expense accrual during the current fiscal year based on the assumption that 4.5% of gross credit sales will be uncollectible. Total gross credit sales for the 2014–2015 fiscal year amounted to $2,900,000. Write-offs of bad accounts during the year totaled $102,000.

Instructions
(a) Prepare an accounts receivable aging schedule for RLF Company using the age categories identified in the controller's report to the Finance Committee showing the following.
  (1) The amount of accounts receivable outstanding for each age category and in total.
  (2) The estimated amount that is uncollectible for each category and in total.
(b) Compute the amount of the year-end adjustment necessary to bring Allowance for Doubtful Accounts to the balance indicated by the age analysis. Then prepare the necessary journal entry to adjust the accounting records.
(c) In a recessionary environment with tight credit and high interest rates:
  (1) Identify steps RLF Company might consider to improve the accounts receivable situation.
  (2) Then evaluate each step identified in terms of the risks and costs involved.

Comparative Analysis Problem:
PepsiCo, Inc. vs. The Coca-Cola Company

BYP8-2 PepsiCo, Inc.'s financial statements are presented in Appendix B. Financial statements of The Coca-Cola Company are presented in Appendix C. Instructions for accessing and using the complete annual reports of PepsiCo and Coca-Cola, including the notes to the financial statements, are also provided in Appendices B and C, respectively.

Instructions
(a) Based on the information in these financial statements, compute the following 2011 ratios for each company. (Assume all sales are credit sales and that PepsiCo's receivables on its balance sheet are all trade receivables.)
  (1) Accounts receivable turnover.
  (2) Average collection period for receivables.
(b) What conclusions about managing accounts receivable can you draw from these data?

Comparative Analysis Problem:
Amazon.com, Inc. vs. Wal-Mart Stores, Inc.

BYP8-3 Amazon.com, Inc.'s financial statements are presented in Appendix D. Financial statements of Wal-Mart Stores, Inc. are presented in Appendix E. Instructions for accessing and using the complete annual reports of Amazon and Wal-Mart, including the notes to the finanial statements, are also provided in Appendices D and E, respectively.

Instructions
(a) Based on the information in these financial statements, compute the following ratios for each company (for the most recent year shown). (Assume all sales are credit sales.)
  (1) Accounts receivable turnover.
  (2) Average collection period for receivables.

(b) What conclusions about managing accounts receivable can you draw from these data?

Real-World Focus

BYP8-4 Purpose: To learn more about factoring.

Address: **www.ccapital.net**, or go to **www.wiley.com/college/weygandt**

Steps: Go to the website, click on **Invoice Factoring**, and answer the following questions.
(a) What are some of the benefits of factoring?
(b) What is the range of the percentages of the typical discount rate?
(c) If a company factors its receivables, what percentage of the value of the receivables can it expect to receive from the factor in the form of cash, and how quickly will it receive the cash?

Critical Thinking

Decision-Making Across the Organization

BYP8-5 Carol and Sam Foyle own Campus Fashions. From its inception, Campus Fashions has sold merchandise on either a cash or credit basis, but no credit cards have been accepted. During the past several months, the Foyles have begun to question their sales policies. First, they have lost some sales because of refusing to accept credit cards. Second, representatives of two metropolitan banks have been persuasive in almost convincing them to accept their national credit cards. One bank, City National Bank, has stated that its credit card fee is 4%.

The Foyles decide that they should determine the cost of carrying their own credit sales. From the accounting records of the past 3 years, they accumulate the following data.

	2016	2015	2014
Net credit sales	$500,000	$550,000	$400,000
Collection agency fees for slow-paying customers	2,450	2,500	2,300
Salary of part-time accounts receivable clerk	4,100	4,100	4,100

Credit and collection expenses as a percentage of net credit sales are uncollectible accounts 1.6%, billing and mailing costs 0.5%, and credit investigation fee on new customers 0.15%.

Carol and Sam also determine that the average accounts receivable balance outstanding during the year is 5% of net credit sales. The Foyles estimate that they could earn an average of 8% annually on cash invested in other business opportunities.

Instructions
With the class divided into groups, answer the following.

(a) Prepare a table showing, for each year, total credit and collection expenses in dollars and as a percentage of net credit sales.
(b) Determine the net credit and collection expense in dollars and as a percentage of sales after considering the revenue not earned from other investment opportunities.
(c) Discuss both the financial and nonfinancial factors that are relevant to the decision.

Communication Activity

BYP8-6 Jill Epp, a friend of yours, overheard a discussion at work about changes her employer wants to make in accounting for uncollectible accounts. Jill knows little about accounting, and she asks you to help make sense of what she heard. Specifically, she asks you to explain the differences between the percentage-of-sales, percentage-of-receivables, and the direct write-off methods for uncollectible accounts.

Instructions
In a letter of one page (or less), explain to Jill the three methods of accounting for uncollectibles. Be sure to discuss differences among these methods.

Ethics Case

BYP8-7 The controller of Diaz Co. believes that the yearly allowance for doubtful accounts for Diaz Co. should be 2% of net credit sales. The president of Diaz Co., nervous that the stockholders might expect the company to sustain its 10% growth rate, suggests that the controller increase

the allowance for doubtful accounts to 4%. The president thinks that the lower net income, which reflects a 6% growth rate, will be a more sustainable rate for Diaz Co.

Instructions
(a) Who are the stakeholders in this case?
(b) Does the president's request pose an ethical dilemma for the controller?
(c) Should the controller be concerned with Diaz Co.'s growth rate? Explain your answer.

All About You

BYP8-8 Credit card usage in the United States is substantial. Many startup companies use credit cards as a way to help meet short-term financial needs. The most common forms of debt for startups are use of credit cards and loans from relatives.

Suppose that you start up Brothers Sandwich Shop. You invested your savings of $20,000 and borrowed $70,000 from your relatives. Although sales in the first few months are good, you see that you may not have sufficient cash to pay expenses and maintain your inventory at acceptable levels, at least in the short term. You decide you may need to use one or more credit cards to fund the possible cash shortfall.

Instructions
(a) Go to the Internet and find two sources that provide insight into how to compare credit card terms.
(b) Develop a list, in descending order of importance, as to what features are most important to you in selecting a credit card for your business.
(c) Examine the features of your present credit card. (If you do not have a credit card, select a likely one online for this exercise.) Given your analysis above, what are the three major disadvantages of your present credit card?

FASB Codification Activity

BYP8-9 If your school has a subscription to the FASB Codification, go to **http://aaahq.org/ascLogin.cfm** to log in and prepare responses to the following.

(a) How are receivables defined in the Codification?
(b) What are the conditions under which losses from uncollectible receivables (Bad Debt Expense) should be reported?

Answers to Chapter Questions

Answers to Insight and Accounting Across the Organization Questions

p. 398 How Does a Credit Card Work? Q: Assume that Nordstrom prepares a bank reconciliation at the end of each month. If some credit card sales have not been processed by the bank, how should Nordstrom treat these transactions on its bank reconciliation? **A:** Nordstrom would treat the credit card receipts as deposits in transit. It has already recorded the receipts as cash. Its bank will increase Nordstrom's cash account when it receives the receipts.

p. 402 Can Fair Value Be Unfair? Q: What are the arguments in favor of and against fair value accounting for loans and receivables? **A:** Arguments in favor of fair value accounting for loans and receivables are that fair value would provide a more accurate view of a company's financial position. This might provide a useful early warning of when a bank or other financial institution was in trouble because its loans were of poor quality. But, banks argue that estimating fair values is very difficult to do accurately. They are also concerned that volatile fair values could cause large swings in a bank's reported net income.

p. 404 Bad Information Can Lead to Bad Loans Q: What steps should the banks have taken to ensure the accuracy of financial information provided on loan applications? **A:** At a minimum, the bank should have requested copies of recent income tax forms and contacted the supposed employer to verify income. To verify ownership and value of assets, it should have examined bank statements, investment statements, and title documents, and should have employed appraisers.

Answers to Self-Test Questions

1. d **2.** c ($1,000 − $300) × (100% − 2%) **3.** a **4.** b ($60,000 − $5,000) **5.** d ($60,000 + $5,000) **6.** b ($800,000 × 1.5%) + $15,000 **7.** b ($750,000 × 3%) + ($18,000 − $30,000) **8.** d ($800,000 − $65,000) **9.** c **10.** a **11.** c **12.** b **13.** d $10,000 + ($10,000 × 120/360 × 9%) **14.** a **15.** c $800,000 ÷ [($100,000 + $150,000) ÷ 2] and 365 ÷ 6.4

A Look at IFRS

The basic accounting and reporting issues related to recognition and measurement of receivables, such as the use of allowance accounts, how to record discounts, use of the allowance method to account for bad debts, and factoring, are essentially the same between IFRS and GAAP.

Key Points

- IFRS requires that loans and receivables be accounted for at amortized cost, adjusted for allowances for doubtful accounts. IFRS sometimes refers to these allowances as **provisions**. The entry to record the allowance would be:

Bad Debt Expense	xxxxxx	
Allowance for Doubtful Accounts		xxxxxx

- Although IFRS implies that receivables with different characteristics should be reported separately, there is no standard that mandates this segregation.

- The FASB and IASB have worked to implement fair value measurement (the amount they currently could be sold for) for financial instruments. Both Boards have faced bitter opposition from various factions. As a consequence, the Boards have adopted a piecemeal approach. The first step is disclosure of fair value information in the notes. The second step is the fair value option, which permits but does not require companies to record some types of financial instruments at fair values in the financial statements.

- IFRS requires a two-tiered approach to test whether the value of loans and receivables are impaired (have a loss in value). First, a company should look at specific loans and receivables to determine whether they are impaired. Then, the loans and receivables as a group should be evaluated for impairment. GAAP does not prescribe a similar two-tiered approach.

- IFRS and GAAP differ in the criteria used to determine how to record a factoring transaction. IFRS uses a combination approach focused on risks and rewards and loss of control. GAAP uses loss of control as the primary criterion. In addition, IFRS permits partial derecognition of receivables; GAAP does not.

Looking to the Future

It appears likely that the question of recording fair values for financial instruments will continue to be an important issue to resolve as the Boards work toward convergence. Both the IASB and the FASB have indicated that they believe that financial statements would be more transparent and understandable if companies recorded and reported all financial instruments at fair value. That said, in *IFRS 9*, which was issued in 2009, the IASB created a split model, where some financial instruments are recorded at fair value, but other financial assets, such as loans and receivables, can be accounted for at amortized cost if certain criteria are met. Critics say that this can result in two companies with identical securities accounting for those securities in different ways. A proposal by the FASB would require that practically all equity instruments be reported at fair value, and that debt instruments may or may not be reported at fair value depending on whether certain criteria are met. It has been suggested that *IFRS 9* will likely be changed or replaced as the FASB and IASB continue to deliberate the best treatment for financial instruments. In fact, one past member of the IASB said that companies should ignore *IFRS 9* and continue to report under the old standard. In his opinion, it was extremely likely that it would be changed before 2015, the mandatory adoption date of the standard.

IFRS Practice

IFRS Self-Test Questions

1. Under IFRS, loans and receivables are to be reported on the balance sheet at:
   (a) amortized cost.
   (b) amortized cost adjusted for estimated loss provisions.

    (c) historical cost.
    (d) replacement cost.

2. Which of the following statements is **false**?
    (a) Loans and receivables include equity securities purchased by the company.
    (b) Loans and receivables include credit card receivables.
    (c) Loans and receivables include amounts owed by employees as a result of company loans to employees.
    (d) Loans and receivables include amounts resulting from transactions with customers.

3. In recording a factoring transaction:
    (a) IFRS focuses on loss of control.
    (b) GAAP focuses on loss of control and risks and rewards.
    (c) IFRS and GAAP allow partial derecognition.
    (d) IFRS allows partial derecognition

4. Under IFRS:
    (a) the entry to record estimated uncollected accounts is the same as GAAP.
    (b) loans and receivables should only be tested for impairment as a group.
    (c) it is always acceptable to use the direct write-off method.
    (d) all financial instruments are recorded at fair value.

5. Which of the following statements is **true**?
    (a) The fair value option requires that some types of financial instruments be recorded at fair value.
    (b) The fair value option allows, but does not require, that some types of financial instruments be recorded at amortized cost.
    (c) The fair value option allows, but does not require, that some types of financial instruments be recorded at fair value.
    (d) The FASB and IASB would like to reduce the reliance on fair value accounting for financial instruments in the future.

IFRS Exercise

IFRS8-1 What are some steps taken by both the FASB and IASB to move to fair value measurement for financial instruments? In what ways have some of the approaches differed?

International Financial Reporting Problem: Zetar plc

IFRS8-2 The financial statements of Zetar plc are presented in Appendix F. Instructions for accessing and using the company's complete annual report, including the notes to its financial statements, are also provided in Appendix F.

Instructions
Use the company's annual report to answer the following questions.

(a) According to Note 18, what was one reason why the balance in receivables increased relative to the previous year?
(b) According to the notes to the financial statements, how are loans and receivables defined?
(c) Using the notes to the financial statements, what amount of trade receivables were written off (utilised) during 2011?
(d) Using information in the notes to the financial statements, determine what percentage the provision for impairment of receivables was as a percentage of total trade receivables for 2011 and 2010. How did the ratio change from 2010 to 2011, and what does this suggest about the company's receivables?

Answers to IFRS Self-Test Questions
1. b   **2.** a   **3.** d   **4.** a   **5.** c

 The Navigator

 Remember to go back to The Navigator box on the chapter opening page and check off your completed work.

9 | Plant Assets, Natural Resources, and Intangible Assets

How Much for a Ride to the Beach?

It's spring break. Your plane has landed, you've finally found your bags, and you're dying to hit the beach—but first you need a "vehicular unit" to get you there. As you turn away from baggage claim, you see a long row of rental agency booths. Many are names you are familiar with—Hertz, Avis, and Budget. But a booth at the far end catches your eye—Rent-A-Wreck. Now there's a company making a clear statement!

Any company that relies on equipment to generate revenues must make decisions about what kind of equipment to buy, how long to keep it, and how vigorously to maintain it. Rent-A-Wreck has decided to rent used rather than new cars and trucks. It rents these vehicles across the United States, Europe, and Asia. While the big-name agencies push vehicles with that "new car smell," Rent-A-Wreck competes on price.

Rent-A-Wreck's message is simple: Rent a used car and save some cash. It's not a message that appeals to everyone. If you're a marketing executive wanting to impress a big client, you probably don't want to pull up in a Rent-A-Wreck car. But if you want to get from point A to point B for the minimum cash per mile, then Rent-A-Wreck is playing your tune. The company's message seems to be getting across to the right clientele. Revenues have increased significantly.

When you rent a car from Rent-A-Wreck, you are renting from an independent business person. This owner has paid a "franchise fee" for the right to use the Rent-A-Wreck name. In order to gain a franchise, he or she must meet financial and other criteria, and must agree to run the rental agency according to rules prescribed by Rent-A-Wreck. Some of these rules require that each franchise maintain its cars in a reasonable fashion. This ensures that, though you won't be cruising down Daytona Beach's Atlantic Avenue in a Mercedes convertible, you can be reasonably assured that you won't be calling a towtruck.

 The Navigator

- ■ Scan Learning Objectives
- ■ Read Feature Story
- ■ Read Preview
- ■ Read text and answer **DO IT!** p. 433
  - ■ p. 439 ■ p. 440 ■ p. 444 ■ p. 449
- ■ Work Comprehensive **DO IT!** 1 p. 452
  - ■ 2 p. 453
- ■ Review Summary of Learning Objectives
- ■ Answer Self-Test Questions
- ■ Complete Assignments
- ■ Go to *WileyPLUS* for practice and tutorials
- Read **A Look at IFRS** p. 475

Learning Objectives **The Navigator**

After studying this chapter, you should be able to:

[1] Describe how the historical cost principle applies to plant assets.

[2] Explain the concept of depreciation and how to compute it.

[3] Distinguish between revenue and capital expenditures, and explain the entries for each.

[4] Explain how to account for the disposal of a plant asset.

[5] Compute periodic depletion of natural resources.

[6] Explain the basic issues related to accounting for intangible assets.

[7] Indicate how plant assets, natural resources, and intangible assets are reported.

David Trood/Getty Images, Inc.

Preview of Chapter 9

✔ The Navigator

The accounting for long-term assets has important implications for a company's reported results. In this chapter, we explain the application of the historical cost principle of accounting to property, plant, and equipment, such as Rent-A-Wreck vehicles, as well as to natural resources and intangible assets such as the "Rent-A-Wreck" trademark. We also describe the methods that companies may use to allocate an asset's cost over its useful life. In addition, we discuss the accounting for expenditures incurred during the useful life of assets, such as the cost of replacing tires and brake pads on rental cars.

The content and organization of Chapter 9 are as follows.

PLANT ASSETS, NATURAL RESOURCES, AND INTANGIBLE ASSETS			
Plant Assets	**Natural Resources**	**Intangible Assets**	**Statement Presentation and Analysis**
• Determining the cost of plant assets • Depreciation • Expenditures during useful life • Plant asset disposals	• Depletion • Presentation	• Accounting for intangibles • Research and development costs	• Presentation • Analysis

Plant Assets

Plant assets are resources that have three characteristics. They have a physical substance (a definite size and shape), are used in the operations of a business, and are not intended for sale to customers. They are also called **property, plant, and equipment**; **plant and equipment**; and **fixed assets**. These assets are expected to be of use to the company for a number of years. Except for land, plant assets decline in service potential over their useful lives.

Because plant assets play a key role in ongoing operations, companies keep plant assets in good operating condition. They also replace worn-out or outdated plant assets, and expand productive resources as needed. Many companies have substantial investments in plant assets. Illustration 9-1 shows the percentages of plant assets in relation to total assets of companies in a number of industries.

Illustration 9-1
Percentages of plant assets
in relation to total assets

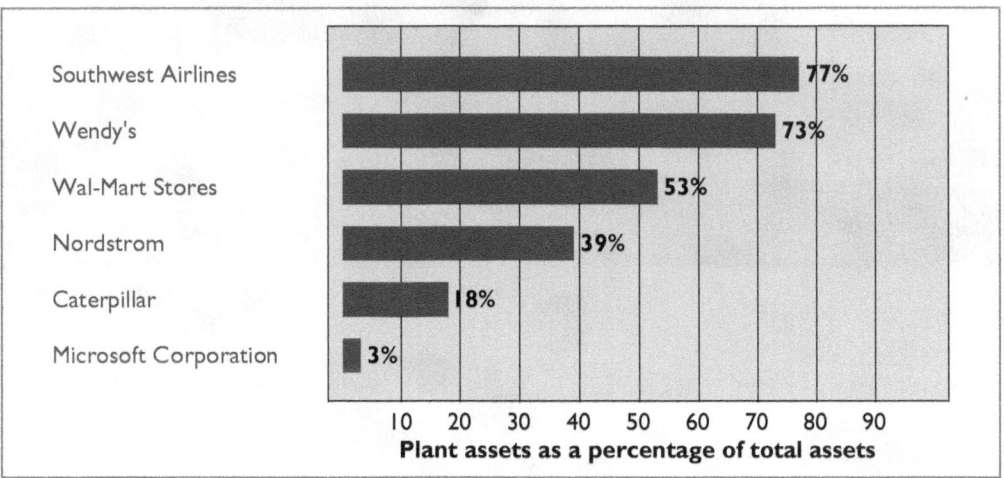

Plant assets as a percentage of total assets

Determining the Cost of Plant Assets

The historical cost principle requires that companies record plant assets at cost. Thus, Rent-A-Wreck records its vehicles at cost. **Cost consists of all expenditures necessary to acquire the asset and make it ready for its intended use.** For example, the cost of factory machinery includes the purchase price, freight costs paid by the purchaser, and installation costs. Once cost is established, the company uses that amount as the basis of accounting for the plant asset over its useful life.

In the following sections, we explain the application of the historical cost principle to each of the major classes of plant assets.

LAND

Companies often use **land** as a building site for a manufacturing plant or office building. The cost of land includes (1) the cash purchase price, (2) closing costs such as title and attorney's fees, (3) real estate brokers' commissions, and (4) accrued property taxes and other liens assumed by the purchaser. For example, if the cash price is $50,000 and the purchaser agrees to pay accrued taxes of $5,000, the cost of the land is $55,000.

Helpful Hint
Management's intended
use is important in applying
the historical cost principle.

Companies record as debits (increases) to the Land account all necessary costs incurred to make land **ready for its intended use**. When a company acquires vacant land, these costs include expenditures for clearing, draining, filling, and grading. Sometimes the land has a building on it that must be removed before construction of a new building. In this case, the company debits to the Land account all demolition and removal costs, less any proceeds from salvaged materials.

To illustrate, assume that Hayes Company acquires real estate at a cash cost of $100,000. The property contains an old warehouse that is razed at a net cost of $6,000 ($7,500 in costs less $1,500 proceeds from salvaged materials). Additional expenditures are the attorney's fee, $1,000, and the real estate broker's commission, $8,000. The cost of the land is $115,000, computed as shown in Illustration 9-2.

Illustration 9-2
Computation of cost of land

Land

Cash price of property	$ 100,000
Net removal cost of warehouse ($7,500 − $1,500)	6,000
Attorney's fee	1,000
Real estate broker's commission	8,000
Cost of land	**$115,000**

When Hayes records the acquisition, it debits Land for $115,000 and credits Cash for $115,000.

LAND IMPROVEMENTS

Land improvements are structural additions made to land. Examples are driveways, parking lots, fences, landscaping, and underground sprinklers. The cost of land improvements includes all expenditures necessary to make the improvements ready for their intended use. For example, the cost of a new parking lot for Home Depot includes the amount paid for paving, fencing, and lighting. Thus, Home Depot debits to Land Improvements the total of all of these costs.

Land improvements have limited useful lives. Even when well-maintained, they will eventually need to be replaced. As a result, companies expense (depreciate) the cost of land improvements over their useful lives.

BUILDINGS

Buildings are facilities used in operations, such as stores, offices, factories, warehouses, and airplane hangars. Companies debit to the Buildings account all necessary expenditures related to the purchase or construction of a building. When a building is **purchased**, such costs include the purchase price, closing costs (attorney's fee, title insurance, etc.), and the real estate broker's commission. Costs to make the building ready for its intended use include expenditures for remodeling and replacing or repairing the roof, floors, electrical wiring, and plumbing. When a new building is **constructed**, cost consists of the contract price plus payments for architects' fees, building permits, and excavation costs.

In addition, companies charge certain interest costs to the Buildings account. Interest costs incurred to finance the project are included in the cost of the building when a significant period of time is required to get the building ready for use. In these circumstances, interest costs are considered as necessary as materials and labor. However, the inclusion of interest costs in the cost of a constructed building is **limited to the construction period**. When construction has been completed, the company records subsequent interest payments on funds borrowed to finance the construction as debits (increases) to Interest Expense.

EQUIPMENT

Equipment includes assets used in operations, such as store check-out counters, office furniture, factory machinery, delivery trucks, and airplanes. The cost of equipment, such as Rent-A-Wreck vehicles, consists of the cash purchase price, sales taxes, freight charges, and insurance during transit paid by the purchaser. It also includes expenditures required in assembling, installing, and testing the unit. However, Rent-A-Wreck does not include motor vehicle licenses and accident insurance on company vehicles in the cost of equipment. These costs represent annual recurring expenditures and do not benefit future periods. Thus, they are treated as **expenses** as they are incurred.

To illustrate, assume Merten Company purchases factory machinery at a cash price of $50,000. Related expenditures are for sales taxes $3,000, insurance during shipping $500, and installation and testing $1,000. The cost of the factory machinery is $54,500, computed in Illustration 9-3.

Illustration 9-3
Computation of cost of factory machinery

Factory Machinery	
Cash price	$ 50,000
Sales taxes	3,000
Insurance during shipping	500
Installation and testing	1,000
Cost of factory machinery	**$54,500**

Merten makes the following summary entry to record the purchase and related expenditures.

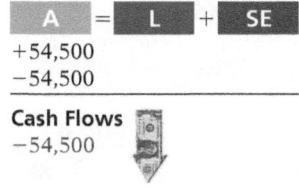

A	=	L	+	SE

+54,500
−54,500

Cash Flows
−54,500

Equipment	54,500	
Cash		54,500
(To record purchase of factory machine)		

For another example, assume that Lenard Company purchases a delivery truck at a cash price of $22,000. Related expenditures consist of sales taxes $1,320, painting and lettering $500, motor vehicle license $80, and a three-year accident insurance policy $1,600. The cost of the delivery truck is $23,820, computed as follows.

Illustration 9-4
Computation of cost of delivery truck

Delivery Truck	
Cash price	$ 22,000
Sales taxes	1,320
Painting and lettering	500
Cost of delivery truck	**$23,820**

Lenard treats the cost of the motor vehicle license as an expense, and the cost of the insurance policy as a prepaid asset. Thus, Lenard makes the following entry to record the purchase of the truck and related expenditures:

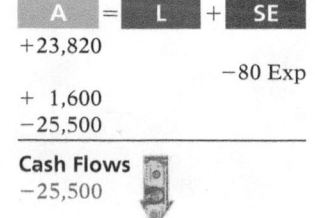

A	=	L	+	SE

+23,820
　　　　　−80 Exp
+ 1,600
−25,500

Cash Flows
−25,500

Equipment	23,820	
License Expense	80	
Prepaid Insurance	1,600	
Cash		25,500
(To record purchase of delivery truck and related expenditures)		

ACCOUNTING ACROSS THE ORGANIZATION

Many U.S. Firms Use Leases

Leasing is big business for U.S. companies. For example, business investment in equipment in a recent year totaled $709 billion. Leasing accounted for about 31% of all business investment ($218 billion).

Who does the most leasing? Interestingly, major banks such as Continental Bank, J.P. Morgan Leasing, and US Bancorp Equipment Finance are the major lessors. Also, many companies have established separate leasing companies, such as Boeing Capital Corporation, Dell Financial Services, and John Deere Capital Corporation. And, as an excellent example of the magnitude of leasing, leased planes account for nearly 40% of the U.S. fleet of commercial airlines. In addition, leasing is becoming increasingly common in the hotel industry. Marriott, Hilton, and InterContinental are increasingly choosing to lease hotels that are owned by someone else.

? Why might airline managers choose to lease rather than purchase their planes? (See page 475.)

> **DO IT!**

Cost of Plant Assets

Action Plan

✔ Identify expenditures made in order to get delivery equipment ready for its intended use.

✔ Treat operating costs as expenses.

Assume that Drummond Heating and Cooling Co. purchases a delivery truck for $15,000 cash, plus sales taxes of $900 and delivery costs of $500. The buyer also pays $200 for painting and lettering, $600 for an annual insurance policy, and $80 for a motor vehicle license. Explain how each of these costs would be accounted for.

Solution

The first four payments ($15,000, $900, $500, and $200) are expenditures necessary to make the truck ready for its intended use. Thus, the cost of the truck is $16,600. The payments for insurance and the license are operating costs and therefore are expensed.

Related exercise material: BE9-1, BE9-2, E9-1, E9-2, E9-3, **and** DO IT! 9-1.

✔ **The Navigator**

Depreciation

As explained in Chapter 3, **depreciation is the process of allocating to expense the cost of a plant asset over its useful (service) life in a rational and systematic manner**. Cost allocation enables companies to properly match expenses with revenues in accordance with the expense recognition principle, as shown in Illustration 9-5.

LEARNING OBJECTIVE 2

Explain the concept of depreciation and how to compute it.

Illustration 9-5
Depreciation as a cost allocation concept

Ethics Note

When a business is acquired, proper allocation of the purchase price to various asset classes is important since different depreciation treatments can materially affect income. For example, buildings are depreciated, but land is not.

It is important to understand that **depreciation is a process of cost allocation**. **It is not a process of asset valuation.** No attempt is made to measure the change in an asset's fair value during ownership. So, the **book value** (cost less accumulated depreciation) of a plant asset may be quite different from its fair value. In fact, if an asset is fully depreciated, it can have a zero book value but still have a significant fair value.

Depreciation applies to three classes of plant assets: land improvements, buildings, and equipment. Each asset in these classes is considered to be a **depreciable asset**. Why? Because the usefulness to the company and revenue-producing ability of each asset will decline over the asset's useful life. Depreciation **does not apply to land** because its usefulness and revenue-producing ability generally remain intact over time. In fact, in many cases, the usefulness of land is greater over time because of the scarcity of good land sites. Thus, **land is not a depreciable asset**.

During a depreciable asset's useful life, its revenue-producing ability declines because of **wear and tear**. A delivery truck that has been driven 100,000 miles will be less useful to a company than one driven only 800 miles.

Revenue-producing ability may also decline because of obsolescence. **Obsolescence** is the process of becoming out of date before the asset physically wears out. For example, major airlines moved from Chicago's Midway Airport to Chicago-O'Hare International Airport because Midway's runways were too short for jumbo jets. Similarly, many companies replace their computers long before they originally planned to do so because technological improvements make the old computers obsolete.

Recognizing depreciation on an asset does not result in an accumulation of cash for replacement of the asset. The balance in Accumulated Depreciation represents the total amount of the asset's cost that the company has charged to expense. It is not a cash fund.

Note that the concept of depreciation is consistent with the going concern assumption. The **going concern assumption** states that the company will continue in operation for the foreseeable future. If a company does not use a going concern assumption, then plant assets should be stated at their fair value. In that case, depreciation of these assets is not needed.

FACTORS IN COMPUTING DEPRECIATION

Three factors affect the computation of depreciation, as shown in Illustration 9-6.

Illustration 9-6
Three factors in computing depreciation

Helpful Hint
Depreciation expense is reported on the income statement. Accumulated depreciation is reported on the balance sheet as a deduction from plant assets.

Cost: all expenditures necessary to acquire the asset and make it ready for intended use

Useful life: estimate of the expected life based on need for repair, service life, and vulnerability to obsolescence

Salvage value: estimate of the asset's value at the end of its useful life

1. **Cost.** Earlier, we explained the issues affecting the cost of a depreciable asset. Recall that companies record plant assets at cost, in accordance with the historical cost principle.

2. **Useful life.** Useful life is an estimate of the expected productive life, also called service life, of the asset for its owner. Useful life may be expressed in terms of time, units of activity (such as machine hours), or units of output. Useful life is an estimate. In making the estimate, management considers such factors as the intended use of the asset, its expected repair and maintenance, and its vulnerability to obsolescence. Past experience with similar assets is often helpful in deciding on expected useful life. We might reasonably expect Rent-A-Wreck and Avis to use different estimated useful lives for their vehicles.

3. **Salvage value.** Salvage value is an estimate of the asset's value at the end of its useful life. This value may be based on the asset's worth as scrap or on its expected trade-in value. Like useful life, salvage value is an estimate. In making the estimate, management considers how it plans to dispose of the asset and its experience with similar assets.

Alternative Terminology
Another term sometimes used for salvage value is *residual value*.

DEPRECIATION METHODS
Depreciation is generally computed using one of the following methods:

1. Straight-line
2. Units-of-activity
3. Declining-balance

Each method is acceptable under generally accepted accounting principles. Management selects the method(s) it believes to be appropriate. The objective is to select the method that best measures an asset's contribution to revenue over its useful life. Once a company chooses a method, it should apply it consistently over the useful life of the asset. Consistency enhances the comparability of financial statements. Depreciation affects the balance sheet through accumulated depreciation and the income statement through depreciation expense.

We will compare the three depreciation methods using the following data for a small delivery truck purchased by Barb's Florists on January 1, 2015.

Cost	$13,000
Expected salvage value	$ 1,000
Estimated useful life in years	5
Estimated useful life in miles	100,000

Illustration 9-7
Delivery truck data

Illustration 9-8 (in the margin) shows the use of the primary depreciation methods in a sample of the largest companies in the United States. No matter what method is used, the total amount depreciated over the useful life of the asset is its depreciable cost. **Depreciable cost** is equal to the cost of the asset less its salvage value.

STRAIGHT-LINE Under the **straight-line method**, companies expense the same amount of depreciation for each year of the asset's useful life. It is measured solely by the passage of time.

To compute depreciation expense under the straight-line method, companies need to determine depreciable cost. As indicated above, depreciable cost is the cost of the asset less its salvage value. It represents the total amount subject to depreciation. Under the straight-line method, to determine annual depreciation expense, we divide depreciable cost by the asset's useful life. Illustration 9-9 (page 436) shows the computation of the first year's depreciation expense for Barb's Florists.

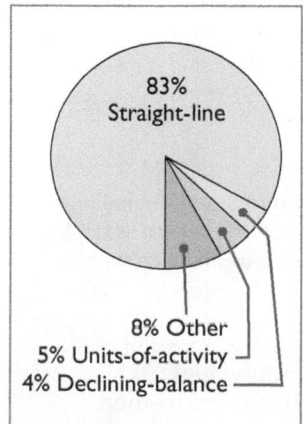

83% Straight-line

8% Other
5% Units-of-activity
4% Declining-balance

Illustration 9-8
Use of depreciation methods in large U.S. companies

Illustration 9-9
Formula for straight-line
method

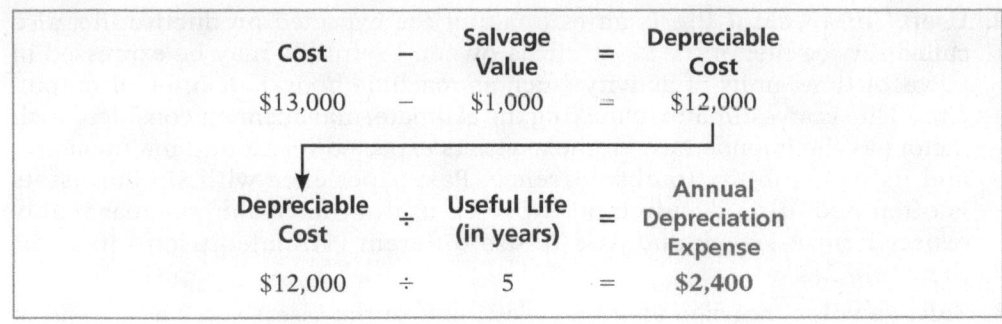

Alternatively, we also can compute an annual **rate** of depreciation. In this case, the rate is 20% (100% ÷ 5 years). When a company uses an annual straight-line rate, it applies the percentage rate to the depreciable cost of the asset. Illustration 9-10 shows a **depreciation schedule** using an annual rate.

Illustration 9-10
Straight-line depreciation
schedule

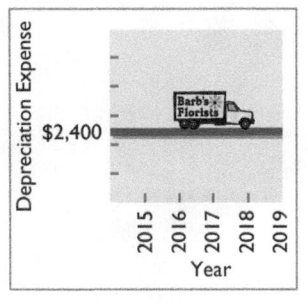

	Computation			Annual	End of Year	
Year	Depreciable Cost	×	Depreciation Rate	= Depreciation Expense	Accumulated Depreciation	Book Value
2015	$12,000		20%	$2,400	$ 2,400	$10,600*
2016	12,000		20	2,400	4,800	8,200
2017	12,000		20	2,400	7,200	5,800
2018	12,000		20	2,400	9,600	3,400
2019	12,000		20	2,400	12,000	1,000

BARB'S FLORISTS

*Book value = Cost − Accumulated depreciation = ($13,000 − $2,400).

Note that the depreciation expense of $2,400 is the same each year. The book value (computed as cost minus accumulated depreciation) at the end of the useful life is equal to the expected $1,000 salvage value.

What happens to these computations for an asset purchased **during** the year, rather than on January 1? In that case, it is necessary to **prorate the annual depreciation** on a time basis. If Barb's Florists had purchased the delivery truck on April 1, 2015, the company would own the truck for nine months of the first year (April–December). Thus, depreciation for 2015 would be $1,800 ($12,000 × 20% × 9/12 of a year).

The straight-line method predominates in practice. Such large companies as Campbell Soup, Marriott, and General Mills use the straight-line method. It is simple to apply, and it matches expenses with revenues when the use of the asset is reasonably uniform throughout the service life.

Alternative Terminology
Another term often used is the
units-of-production method.

UNITS-OF-ACTIVITY Under the **units-of-activity method**, useful life is expressed in terms of the total units of production or use expected from the asset, rather than as a time period. The units-of-activity method is ideally suited to factory machinery. Manufacturing companies can measure production in units of output or in machine hours. This method can also be used for such assets as delivery equipment (miles driven) and airplanes (hours in use). The units-of-activity method is generally not suitable for buildings or furniture because depreciation for these assets is more a function of time than of use.

Helpful Hint
Under any method,
depreciation stops when
the asset's book value
equals expected salvage
value.

To use this method, companies estimate the total units of activity for the entire useful life, and then divide these units into depreciable cost. The resulting number represents the depreciable cost per unit. The depreciable cost per unit is then applied to the units of activity during the year to determine the annual depreciation expense.

To illustrate, assume that Barb's Florists drives its delivery truck 15,000 miles in the first year. Illustration 9-11 shows the units-of-activity formula and the computation of the first year's depreciation expense.

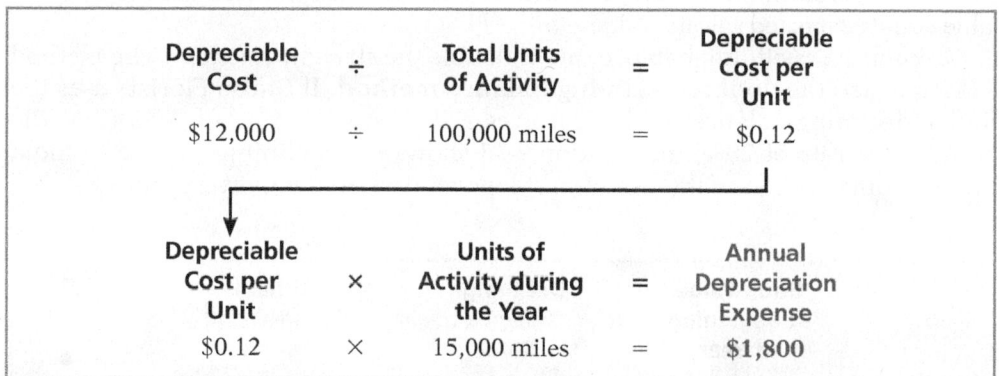

Depreciable Cost	÷	Total Units of Activity	=	Depreciable Cost per Unit
$12,000	÷	100,000 miles	=	$0.12

Depreciable Cost per Unit	×	Units of Activity during the Year	=	Annual Depreciation Expense
$0.12	×	15,000 miles	=	**$1,800**

Illustration 9-11
Formula for units-of-activity method

The units-of-activity depreciation schedule, using assumed mileage, is as follows.

Illustration 9-12
Units-of-activity depreciation schedule

BARB'S FLORISTS

| | Computation | | | Annual | End of Year | |
	Units of Activity	×	Depreciable Cost/Unit	=	Depreciation Expense	Accumulated Depreciation	Book Value
Year							
2015	15,000		$0.12		$1,800	$ 1,800	$11,200*
2016	30,000		0.12		3,600	5,400	7,600
2017	20,000		0.12		2,400	7,800	5,200
2018	25,000		0.12		3,000	10,800	2,200
2019	10,000		0.12		1,200	12,000	1,000

*($13,000 − $1,800).

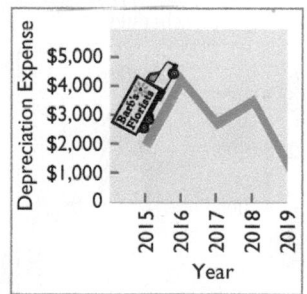

This method is easy to apply for assets purchased mid-year. In such a case, the company computes the depreciation using the productivity of the asset for the partial year.

The units-of-activity method is not nearly as popular as the straight-line method (see Illustration 9-8, page 435) primarily because it is often difficult for companies to reasonably estimate total activity. However, some very large companies, such as Chevron and Boise Cascade (a forestry company), do use this method. When the productivity of an asset varies significantly from one period to another, the units-of-activity method results in the best matching of expenses with revenues.

DECLINING-BALANCE The **declining-balance method** produces a decreasing annual depreciation expense over the asset's useful life. The method is so named because the periodic depreciation is based on a **declining book value** (cost less accumulated depreciation) of the asset. With this method, companies compute annual depreciation expense by multiplying the book value at the beginning of the year by the declining-balance depreciation rate. **The depreciation rate remains constant from year to year, but the book value to which the rate is applied declines each year.**

At the beginning of the first year, book value is the cost of the asset. This is because the balance in accumulated depreciation at the beginning of the asset's useful life is zero. In subsequent years, book value is the difference between cost and accumulated depreciation to date. Unlike the other depreciation methods, the declining-balance method **ignores salvage value in determining the amount to which the declining-balance rate is applied**. Salvage value, however, does limit the total depreciation that can be taken. Depreciation stops when the asset's book value equals expected salvage value.

A common declining-balance rate is double the straight-line rate. The method is often called the **double-declining-balance method**. If Barb's Florists uses the double-declining-balance method, it uses a depreciation rate of 40% (2 × the straight-line rate of 20%). Illustration 9-13 shows the declining-balance formula and the computation of the first year's depreciation on the delivery truck.

Illustration 9-13
Formula for declining-balance method

Book Value at Beginning of Year	×	Declining-Balance Rate	=	Annual Depreciation Expense
$13,000	×	40%	=	$5,200

The depreciation schedule under this method is as follows.

Illustration 9-14
Double-declining-balance depreciation schedule

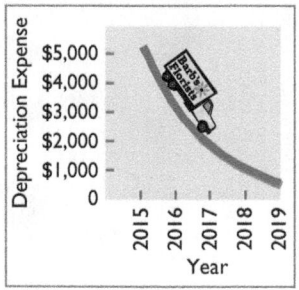

	BARB'S FLORISTS					
	Computation			**Annual**	**End of Year**	
Year	**Book Value Beginning of Year**	×	**Depreciation Rate**	= **Depreciation Expense**	**Accumulated Depreciation**	**Book Value**
2015	$13,000		40%	$5,200	$ 5,200	$7,800
2016	7,800		40	3,120	8,320	4,680
2017	4,680		40	1,872	10,192	2,808
2018	2,808		40	1,123	11,315	1,685
2019	1,685		40	685*	12,000	1,000

*Computation of $674 ($1,685 × 40%) is adjusted to $685 in order for book value to equal salvage value.

Helpful Hint
The method recommended for an asset that is expected to be significantly more productive in the first half of its useful life is the declining-balance method.

The delivery equipment is 69% depreciated ($8,320 ÷ $12,000) at the end of the second year. Under the straight-line method, the truck would be depreciated 40% ($4,800 ÷ $12,000) at that time. Because the declining-balance method produces higher depreciation expense in the early years than in the later years, it is considered an **accelerated-depreciation method**. The declining-balance method is compatible with the expense recognition principle. It matches the higher depreciation expense in early years with the higher benefits received in these years. It also recognizes lower depreciation expense in later years, when the asset's contribution to revenue is less. Some assets lose usefulness rapidly because of obsolescence. In these cases, the declining-balance method provides the most appropriate depreciation amount.

When a company purchases an asset during the year, it must prorate the first year's declining-balance depreciation on a time basis. For example, if Barb's Florists had purchased the truck on April 1, 2015, depreciation for 2015 would become $3,900 ($13,000 × 40% × 9/12). The book value at the beginning of 2016 is then $9,100 ($13,000 − $3,900), and the 2016 depreciation is $3,640 ($9,100 × 40%). Subsequent computations would follow from those amounts.

> DO IT!

Straight-Line Depreciation

On January 1, 2015, Iron Mountain Ski Corporation purchased a new snow-grooming machine for $50,000. The machine is estimated to have a 10-year life with a $2,000 salvage value. What journal entry would Iron Mountain Ski Corporation make at December 31, 2015, if it uses the straight-line method of depreciation?

Solution

Action Plan

✔ Calculate depreciable cost (Cost − Salvage value).

✔ Divide the depreciable cost by the asset's estimated useful life.

$$\text{Depreciation expense} = \frac{\text{Cost} - \text{Salvage value}}{\text{Useful life}} = \frac{\$50,000 - \$2,000}{10} = \$4,800$$

The entry to record the first year's depreciation would be:

Dec. 31	Depreciation Expense	4,800	
	Accumulated Depreciation—Equipment		4,800
	(To record annual depreciation on		
	snow-grooming machine)		

Related exercise material: BE9-3, BE9-4, E9-4, **and** DO IT! 9-2.

 The Navigator

COMPARISON OF METHODS Illustration 9-15 compares annual and total depreciation expense under each of the three methods for Barb's Florists.

Year	Straight-Line	Units-of-Activity	Declining-Balance
2015	$ 2,400	$ 1,800	$ 5,200
2016	2,400	3,600	3,120
2017	2,400	2,400	1,872
2018	2,400	3,000	1,123
2019	2,400	1,200	685
	$12,000	$12,000	$12,000

Illustration 9-15
Comparison of depreciation methods

Annual depreciation varies considerably among the methods, but **total depreciation expense is the same ($12,000) for the five-year period** under all three methods. Each method is acceptable in accounting because each recognizes in a rational and systematic manner the decline in service potential of the asset. Illustration 9-16 graphs the depreciation expense pattern under each method.

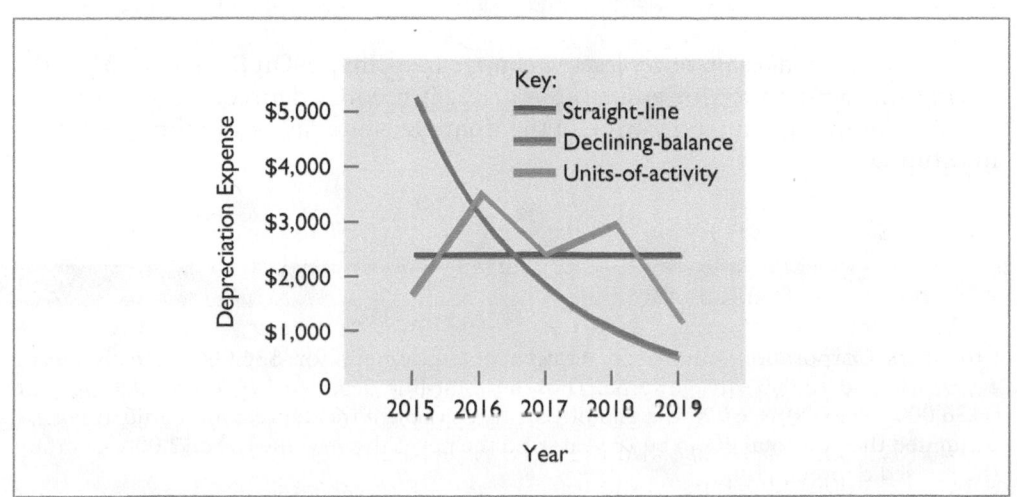

Illustration 9-16
Patterns of depreciation

DEPRECIATION AND INCOME TAXES

The Internal Revenue Service (IRS) allows taxpayers to deduct depreciation expense when they compute taxable income. However, the IRS does not require taxpayers to use the same depreciation method on the tax return that is used in preparing financial statements.

Many corporations use straight-line in their financial statements to maximize net income. At the same time, they use a special accelerated-depreciation method on their tax returns to minimize their income taxes. Taxpayers must use on their tax returns either the straight-line method or a special accelerated-depreciation method called the **Modified Accelerated Cost Recovery System** (MACRS).

REVISING PERIODIC DEPRECIATION

Depreciation is one example of the use of estimation in the accounting process. Management should periodically review annual depreciation expense. If wear and tear or obsolescence indicate that annual depreciation estimates are inadequate or excessive, the company should change the amount of depreciation expense.

When a change in an estimate is required, the company makes the change in **current and future years. It does not change depreciation in prior periods.** The rationale is that continual restatement of prior periods would adversely affect confidence in financial statements.

Helpful Hint
Use a step-by-step approach: (1) determine new depreciable cost; (2) divide by remaining useful life.

To determine the new annual depreciation expense, the company first computes the asset's depreciable cost at the time of the revision. It then allocates the revised depreciable cost to the remaining useful life.

To illustrate, assume that Barb's Florists decides on January 1, 2018, to extend the useful life of the truck by one year (a total life of six years) and increase its salvage value to $2,200. The company has used the straight-line method to depreciate the asset to date. Depreciation per year was $2,400 [($13,000 − $1,000) ÷ 5]. Accumulated depreciation after three years (2015–2017) is $7,200 ($2,400 × 3), and book value is $5,800 ($13,000 − $7,200). The new annual depreciation is $1,200, computed as shown in Illustration 9-17.

Illustration 9-17
Revised depreciation computation

Book value, 1/1/18	$ 5,800
Less: Salvage value	2,200
Remaining depreciable cost	$ 3,600
Remaining useful life	3 years (2018–2020)
Revised annual depreciation ($3,600 ÷ 3)	**$ 1,200**

Barb's Florists makes no entry for the change in estimate. On December 31, 2018, during the preparation of adjusting entries, it records depreciation expense of $1,200. Companies must describe in the financial statements significant changes in estimates.

> DO IT!

Revised Depreciation

Chambers Corporation purchased a piece of equipment for $36,000. It estimated a 6-year life and $6,000 salvage value. Thus, straight-line depreciation was $5,000 per year [($36,000 − $6,000) ÷ 6]. At the end of year three (before the depreciation adjustment), it estimated the new total life to be 10 years and the new salvage value to be $2,000. Compute the revised depreciation.

Action Plan

✔ Calculate remaining depreciable cost.

✔ Divide remaining depreciable cost by new remaining life.

Solution

Original depreciation expense = [($36,000 − $6,000) ÷ 6] = $5,000
Accumulated depreciation after 2 years = 2 × $5,000 = $10,000
Book value = $36,000 − $10,000 = $26,000

Book value after 2 years of depreciation	$26,000
Less: New salvage value	2,000
Remaining depreciable cost	$24,000
Remaining useful life	8 years
Revised annual depreciation ($24,000 ÷ 8)	$ 3,000

Related exercise material: BE9-7, E9-8, **and** DO IT! 9-3.

✔ **The Navigator**

Expenditures During Useful Life

During the useful life of a plant asset, a company may incur costs for ordinary repairs, additions, or improvements. **Ordinary repairs** are expenditures to **maintain** the operating efficiency and productive life of the unit. They usually are fairly small amounts that occur frequently. Examples are motor tune-ups and oil changes, the painting of buildings, and the replacing of worn-out gears on machinery. Companies record such repairs as debits to Maintenance and Repairs Expense as they are incurred. Because they are immediately charged as an expense against revenues, these costs are often referred to as **revenue expenditures**.

In contrast, **additions and improvements** are costs incurred to **increase** the operating efficiency, productive capacity, or useful life of a plant asset. They are usually material in amount and occur infrequently. Additions and improvements increase the company's investment in productive facilities. Companies generally debit these amounts to the plant asset affected. They are often referred to as **capital expenditures**.

Companies must use good judgment in deciding between a revenue expenditure and capital expenditure. For example, assume that Rodriguez Co. purchases a number of wastepaper baskets. Although the proper accounting would appear to be to capitalize and then depreciate these wastepaper baskets over their useful lives, it would be more usual for Rodriguez to expense them immediately. This practice is justified on the basis of **materiality**. Materiality refers to the impact of an item's size on a company's financial operations. The **materiality concept** states that if an item would not make a difference in decision-making, the company does not have to follow GAAP in reporting that item.

> **LEARNING OBJECTIVE 3**
>
> Distinguish between revenue and capital expenditures, and explain the entries for each.

ANATOMY OF A FRAUD

Bernie Ebbers was the founder and CEO of the phone company WorldCom. The company engaged in a series of increasingly large, debt-financed acquisitions of other companies. These acquisitions made the company grow quickly, which made the stock price increase dramatically. However, because the acquired companies all had different accounting systems, WorldCom's financial records were a mess. When WorldCom's performance started to flatten out, Bernie coerced WorldCom's accountants to engage in a number of fraudulent activities to make net income look better than it really was and thus prop up the stock price. One of these frauds involved treating $7 billion of line costs as capital expenditures. The line costs, which were rental fees paid to other phone companies to use their phone lines, had always been properly expensed in previous years. Capitalization delayed expense recognition to future periods and thus boosted current-period profits.

Total take: $7 billion

THE MISSING CONTROLS
Documentation procedures. The company's accounting system was a disorganized collection of non-integrated systems, which resulted from a series of corporate acquisitions. Top management took advantage of this disorganization to conceal its fraudulent activities.

Independent internal verification. A fraud of this size should have been detected by a routine comparison of the actual physical assets with the list of physical assets shown in the accounting records.

Plant Asset Disposals

Companies dispose of plant assets that are no longer useful to them. Illustration 9-18 shows the three ways in which companies make plant asset disposals.

Whatever the disposal method, the company must determine the book value of the plant asset at the disposal date to determine the gain or loss. Recall that the book value is the difference between the cost of the plant asset and the accumulated depreciation to date. If the disposal occurs at any time during the year, the company must record depreciation for the fraction of the year to the date of disposal. The company then eliminates the book value by reducing (debiting) Accumulated Depreciation for the total depreciation associated with that asset to the date of disposal and reducing (crediting) the asset account for the cost of the asset.

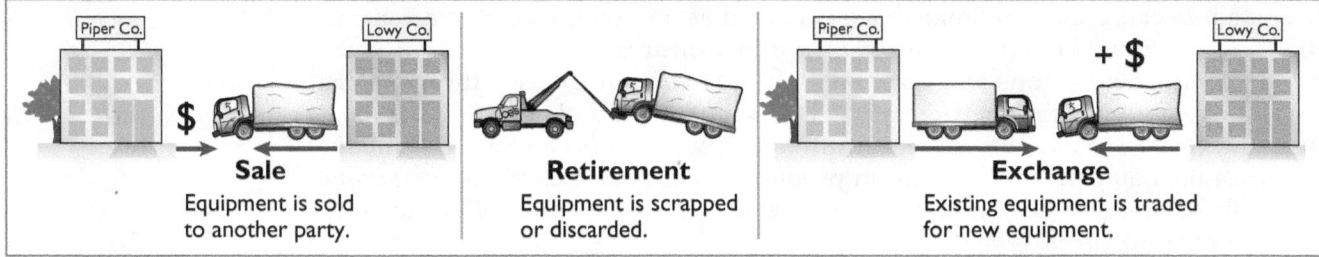

Sale	**Retirement**	**Exchange**
Equipment is sold to another party.	Equipment is scrapped or discarded.	Existing equipment is traded for new equipment.

Illustration 9-18
Methods of plant asset disposal

In this chapter, we examine the accounting for the retirement and sale of plant assets. In the appendix to the chapter, we discuss and illustrate the accounting for exchanges of plant assets.

RETIREMENT OF PLANT ASSETS

To illustrate the retirement of plant assets, assume that Hobart Company retires its computer printers, which cost $32,000. The accumulated depreciation on these printers is $32,000. The equipment, therefore, is fully depreciated (zero book value). The entry to record this retirement is as follows.

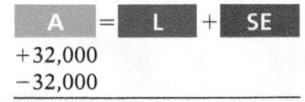

A	=	L	+	SE

+32,000
−32,000

Cash Flows
no effect

Helpful Hint
In disposing of a plant asset, the company removes all amounts related to the asset. This includes the original cost in the asset account and the total depreciation to date in the accumulated depreciation account.

Accumulated Depreciation—Equipment	32,000	
Equipment		32,000
(To record retirement of fully depreciated equipment)		

What happens if a fully depreciated plant asset is still useful to the company? In this case, the asset and its accumulated depreciation continue to be reported on the balance sheet, without further depreciation adjustment, until the company retires the asset. Reporting the asset and related accumulated depreciation on the balance sheet informs the financial statement reader that the asset is still in use. Once fully depreciated, no additional depreciation should be taken, even if an asset is still being used. In no situation can the accumulated depreciation on a plant asset exceed its cost.

If a company retires a plant asset before it is fully depreciated and no cash is received for scrap or salvage value, a loss on disposal occurs. For example, assume that Sunset Company discards delivery equipment that cost $18,000 and has accumulated depreciation of $14,000. The entry is as follows.

	Accumulated Depreciation—Equipment	14,000	
	Loss on Disposal of Plant Assets	4,000	
	Equipment		18,000
	(To record retirement of delivery equipment at a loss)		

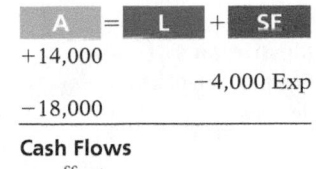

A = L + SE
+14,000
−4,000 Exp
−18,000

Cash Flows
no effect

Companies report a loss on disposal of plant assets in the "Other expenses and losses" section of the income statement.

SALE OF PLANT ASSETS

In a disposal by sale, the company compares the book value of the asset with the proceeds received from the sale. If the proceeds of the sale **exceed** the book value of the plant asset, **a gain on disposal occurs**. If the proceeds of the sale **are less than** the book value of the plant asset sold, **a loss on disposal occurs**.

Only by coincidence will the book value and the fair value of the asset be the same when the asset is sold. Gains and losses on sales of plant assets are therefore quite common. For example, Delta Airlines reported a $94,343,000 gain on the sale of five Boeing B727-200 aircraft and five Lockheed L-1011-1 aircraft.

GAIN ON SALE To illustrate a gain on sale of plant assets, assume that on July 1, 2015, Wright Company sells office furniture for $16,000 cash. The office furniture originally cost $60,000. As of January 1, 2015, it had accumulated depreciation of $41,000. Depreciation for the first six months of 2015 is $8,000. Wright records depreciation expense and updates accumulated depreciation to July 1 with the following entry.

July 1	Depreciation Expense	8,000	
	Accumulated Depreciation—Equipment		8,000
	(To record depreciation expense for the first 6 months of 2015)		

A = L + SE
−8,000 Exp
−8,000

Cash Flows
no effect

After the accumulated depreciation balance is updated, the company computes the gain or loss. The gain or loss is the difference between the proceeds from the sale and the book value at the date of disposal. Illustration 9-19 shows this computation for Wright Company, which has a gain on disposal of $5,000.

Cost of office furniture	$60,000
Less: Accumulated depreciation ($41,000 + $8,000)	49,000
Book value at date of disposal	11,000
Proceeds from sale	16,000
Gain on disposal of plant asset	**$ 5,000**

Illustration 9-19
Computation of gain on disposal

Wright records the sale and the gain on disposal of the plant asset as follows.

July 1	Cash	16,000	
	Accumulated Depreciation—Equipment	49,000	
	Equipment		60,000
	Gain on Disposal of Plant Assets		5,000
	(To record sale of office furniture at a gain)		

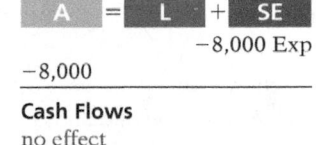

A = L + SE
+16,000
+49,000
−60,000
+5,000 Rev

Cash Flows
+16,000

Companies report a gain on disposal of plant assets in the "Other revenues and gains" section of the income statement.

LOSS ON SALE Assume that instead of selling the office furniture for $16,000, Wright sells it for $9,000. In this case, Wright computes a loss of $2,000 as follows.

Illustration 9-20
Computation of loss on disposal

Cost of office furniture	$60,000
Less: Accumulated depreciation	49,000
Book value at date of disposal	11,000
Proceeds from sale	9,000
Loss on disposal of plant asset	**$ 2,000**

Wright records the sale and the loss on disposal of the plant asset as follows.

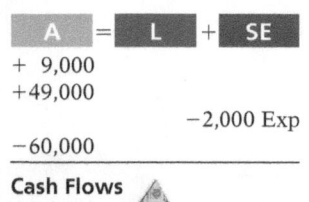

A	=	L	+	SE
+ 9,000				
+49,000				
				−2,000 Exp
−60,000				

Cash Flows
+9,000

July 1	Cash	9,000	
	Accumulated Depreciation—Equipment	49,000	
	Loss on Disposal of Plant Assets	2,000	
	Equipment		60,000
	(To record sale of office furniture at a loss)		

Companies report a loss on disposal of plant assets in the "Other expenses and losses" section of the income statement.

> DO IT!

Plant Asset Disposal

Overland Trucking has an old truck that cost $30,000, and it has accumulated depreciation of $16,000 on this truck. Overland has decided to sell the truck. (a) What entry would Overland Trucking make to record the sale of the truck for $17,000 cash? (b) What entry would Overland Trucking make to record the sale of the truck for $10,000 cash?

Solution

Action Plan

✔ At the time of disposal, determine the book value of the asset.

✔ Compare the asset's book value with the proceeds received to determine whether a gain or loss has occurred.

(a) Sale of truck for cash at a gain:

Cash	17,000	
Accumulated Depreciation—Equipment	16,000	
Equipment		30,000
Gain on Disposal of Plant Assets		
[$17,000 − ($30,000 − $16,000)]		3,000
(To record sale of truck at a gain)		

(b) Sale of truck for cash at a loss:

Cash	10,000	
Accumulated Depreciation—Equipment	16,000	
Loss on Disposal of Plant Assets		
[$10,000 − ($30,000 − $16,000)]	4,000	
Equipment		30,000
(To record sale of truck at a loss)		

Related exercise material: BE9-9, BE9-10, E9-9, E9-10, **and** DO IT! 9-4.

✔ **The Navigator**

Natural Resources

Natural resources consist of standing timber and underground deposits of oil, gas, and minerals. These long-lived productive assets have two distinguishing characteristics: (1) They are physically extracted in operations (such as mining, cutting, or pumping). (2) They are replaceable only by an act of nature.

The acquisition cost of a natural resource is the price needed to acquire the resource **and** prepare it for its intended use. For an already-discovered resource, such as an existing coal mine, cost is the price paid for the property.

Depletion

The allocation of the cost of natural resources to expense in a rational and systematic manner over the resource's useful life is called **depletion**. (That is, depletion is to natural resources as depreciation is to plant assets.) **Companies generally use the units-of-activity method** (learned earlier in the chapter) **to compute depletion**. The reason is that **depletion generally is a function of the units extracted during the year**.

Under the units-of-activity method, companies divide the total cost of the natural resource minus salvage value by the number of units estimated to be in the resource. The result is a **depletion cost per unit of product**. They then multiply the depletion cost per unit by the number of units extracted and sold. The result is the **annual depletion expense**. Illustration 9-21 shows the formula to compute depletion expense.

Helpful Hint
On a balance sheet, natural resources may be described more specifically as *timberlands, mineral deposits, oil reserves*, and so on.

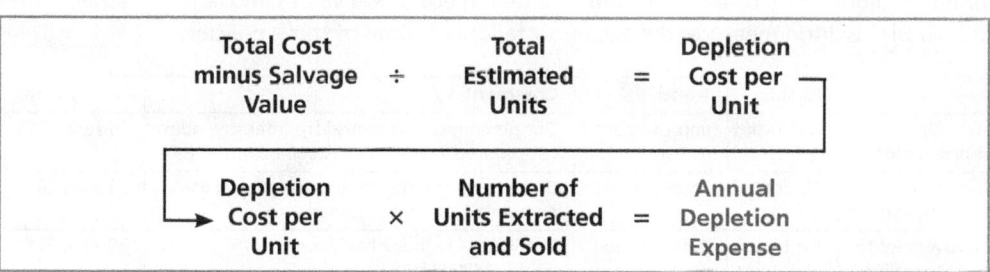

Illustration 9-21
Formula to compute depletion expense

To illustrate, assume that Lane Coal Company invests $5 million in a mine estimated to have 10 million tons of coal and no salvage value. In the first year, Lane extracts and sells 800,000 tons of coal. Using the formulas above, Lane computes the depletion expense as follows.

$$\$5,000,000 \div 10,000,000 = \$0.50 \text{ depletion cost per ton}$$

$$\$0.50 \times 800,000 = \$400,000 \text{ annual depletion expense}$$

Lane records depletion expense for the first year of operation as follows.

> **Ethics Note**
>
> Investors were stunned at news that Royal Dutch Shell had significantly overstated its reported oil reserves—and perhaps had done so intentionally.

Dec. 31	Depletion Expense	400,000	
	Accumulated Depletion		400,000
	(To record depletion expense on coal deposits)		

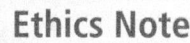

−400,000 Exp
−400,000

Cash Flows
no effect

Presentation

The company reports the account Depletion Expense as a part of the cost of producing the product. Accumulated Depletion is a contra asset account, similar to accumulated depreciation. It is deducted from the cost of the natural resource in the balance sheet, as Illustration 9-22 shows.

LANE COAL COMPANY		
Balance Sheet (partial)		
Coal mine	$5,000,000	
Less: Accumulated depletion	400,000	$4,600,000

Illustration 9-22
Statement presentation of accumulated depletion

Many companies do not use an accumulated depletion account. In such cases, the company credits the amount of depletion directly to the natural resources account.

Sometimes, a company will extract natural resources in one accounting period but not sell them until a later period. In this case, the company does not expense the depletion until it sells the resource. It reports the amount not sold as inventory in the current assets section.

© Christian Uhrig/iStockphoto

PEOPLE, PLANET, AND PROFIT INSIGHT

Sustainability Report Please

Sustainability reports identify how the company is meeting its corporate social responsibilities. Many companies, both large and small, are now issuing these reports. For example, companies such as Disney, Best Buy, Microsoft, Ford, and ConocoPhilips issue these reports. Presented below is an adapted section of BHP Billiton's (a global mining, oil, and gas company) sustainability report on its environmental policies. These policies are to (1) take action to address the challenges of climate change, (2) set and achieve targets that reduce pollution, and (3) enhance biodiversity by assessing and considering ecological values and land-use aspects. Here is how BHP Billiton measures the success or failure of some of these policies:

Environment	Result	Trend	Commentary	Target Date
Aggregate Group target of 6% reduction in greenhouse gas emissions per unit of production	On track	Improvement	Our greenhouse gas emissions intensity index has reduced 7% on our FY2006 baseline year	30 June 2012
Aggregate Group target of 13% reduction in carbon-based energy use per unit of production	On track	Improvement	Our energy intensity index has reduced 6% on our FY2006 baseline year	30 June 2012
Aggregate Group target of a 10% improvement in the ratio of water recycled/reused to high-quality water consumed	On track	Deterioration	Our water use index has improved 7% on our FY2007 baseline year	30 June 2012

In addition to the environment, BHP Billiton has sections in its sustainability report which discuss people, safety, health, and community.

Source: BHP Billiton, *2010 Sustainability Report.*

 Why do you believe companies issue sustainability reports? (See page 475.)

Intangible Assets

LEARNING OBJECTIVE   6

Explain the basic issues related to accounting for intangible assets.

Intangible assets are rights, privileges, and competitive advantages that result from the ownership of long-lived assets that do not possess physical substance. Evidence of intangibles may exist in the form of contracts or licenses. Intangibles may arise from the following sources:

1. Government grants, such as patents, copyrights, licenses, trademarks, and trade names.

2. Acquisition of another business, in which the purchase price includes a payment for **goodwill**.

3. Private monopolistic arrangements arising from contractual agreements, such as franchises and leases.

Some widely known intangibles are Microsoft's patents, McDonald's franchises, Apple's trade name iPod, J.K. Rowling's copyrights on the *Harry Potter* books, and the trademark Rent-A-Wreck in the Feature Story.

Accounting for Intangible Assets

Companies record intangible assets at cost. This cost consists of all expenditures necessary for the company to acquire the right, privilege, or competitive advantage. Intangibles are categorized as having either a limited life or an indefinite life. If an intangible has a **limited life**, the company allocates its cost over the asset's useful life using a process similar to depreciation. The process of allocating the cost of intangibles is referred to as **amortization**. The cost of intangible assets with **indefinite lives should not be amortized**.

To record amortization of an intangible asset, a company increases (debits) Amortization Expense and decreases (credits) the specific intangible asset. (Unlike depreciation, no contra account, such as Accumulated Amortization, is usually used.)

Intangible assets are typically amortized on a straight-line basis. For example, the legal life of a patent is 20 years. Companies **amortize the cost of a patent over its 20-year life or its useful life, whichever is shorter**. To illustrate the computation of patent amortization, assume that National Labs purchases a patent at a cost of $60,000. If National estimates the useful life of the patent to be eight years, the annual amortization expense is $7,500 ($60,000 ÷ 8). National records the annual amortization as follows.

Dec. 31	Amortization Expense	7,500	
	Patents		7,500
	(To record patent amortization)		

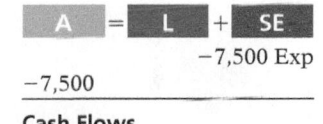

−7,500 Exp

−7,500

Cash Flows
no effect

Companies classify Amortization Expense as an operating expense in the income statement.

There is a difference between intangible assets and plant assets in determining cost. For plant assets, cost includes both the purchase price of the asset and the costs incurred in designing and constructing the asset. In contrast, the initial cost for an intangible asset includes **only the purchase price**. Companies expense any costs incurred in developing an intangible asset.

PATENTS

A **patent** is an exclusive right issued by the U.S. Patent Office that enables the recipient to manufacture, sell, or otherwise control an invention for a period of 20 years from the date of the grant. A patent is nonrenewable. But, companies can extend the legal life of a patent by obtaining new patents for improvements or other changes in the basic design. **The initial cost of a patent is the cash or cash equivalent price paid to acquire the patent.**

The saying, "A patent is only as good as the money you're prepared to spend defending it," is very true. Many patents are subject to litigation by competitors. Any legal costs an owner incurs in successfully defending a patent in an infringement suit are considered necessary to establish the patent's validity. **The owner adds those costs to the Patents account and amortizes them over the remaining life of the patent.**

The patent holder amortizes the cost of a patent over its 20-year legal life or its useful life, whichever is shorter. Companies consider obsolescence and inadequacy in determining useful life. These factors may cause a patent to become economically ineffective before the end of its legal life.

COPYRIGHTS

The federal government grants **copyrights**, which give the owner the exclusive right to reproduce and sell an artistic or published work. Copyrights extend for the life of the creator plus 70 years. The cost of a copyright is the **cost of acquiring and defending it**. The cost may be only the small fee paid to the U.S. Copyright Office. Or, it may amount to much more if an infringement suit is involved.

The useful life of a copyright generally is significantly shorter than its legal life. Therefore, copyrights usually are amortized over a relatively short period of time.

TRADEMARKS AND TRADE NAMES

A **trademark** or **trade name** is a word, phrase, jingle, or symbol that identifies a particular enterprise or product. Trade names like Wheaties, Monopoly, Big Mac, Kleenex, Coca-Cola, and Jeep create immediate product identification. They also generally enhance the sale of the product. The creator or original user may obtain exclusive legal right to the trademark or trade name by registering it with the U.S. Patent Office. Such registration provides 20 years of protection. The registration may be renewed indefinitely as long as the trademark or trade name is in use.

If a company purchases the trademark or trade name, its cost is the purchase price. If a company develops and maintains the trademark or trade name, any costs related to these activities are expensed as incurred. Because trademarks and trade names have indefinite lives, they are not amortized.

FRANCHISES

When you fill up your tank at the corner Shell station, eat lunch at Subway, or rent a car from Rent-A-Wreck, you are dealing with franchises. A **franchise** is a contractual arrangement between a franchisor and a franchisee. The franchisor grants the franchisee the right to sell certain products, perform specific services, or use certain trademarks or trade names, usually within a designated geographic area.

Another type of franchise is a **license**. A license granted by a governmental body permits a company to use public property in performing its services. Examples are the use of city streets for a bus line or taxi service, the use of public land for telephone and electric lines, and the use of airwaves for radio or TV broadcasting. In a recent license agreement, FOX, CBS, and NBC agreed to pay $27.9 billion for the right to broadcast NFL football games over an eight-year period. Franchises and licenses may by granted for a definite period of time, an indefinite period, or perpetually.

When a company incurs costs in connection with the purchase of a franchise or license, it should recognize an intangible asset. Companies should amortize the cost of a limited-life franchise (or license) over its useful life. If the life is indefinite, the cost is not amortized. Annual payments made under a franchise agreement are recorded as **operating expenses** in the period in which they are incurred.

GOODWILL

Usually, the largest intangible asset that appears on a company's balance sheet is goodwill. **Goodwill** represents the value of all favorable attributes that relate to a company that are not attributable to any other specific asset. These include exceptional management, desirable location, good customer relations, skilled employees, high-quality products, and harmonious relations with labor unions. Goodwill is unique. Unlike assets such as investments and plant assets, which can be sold **individually** in the marketplace, goodwill can be identified only with the business **as a whole**.

If goodwill can be identified only with the business as a whole, how can its amount be determined? One could try to put a dollar value on the factors listed above (exceptional management, desirable location, and so on). But, the results would be very subjective, and such subjective valuations would not contribute to the reliability of financial statements. **Therefore, companies record goodwill only when an entire business is purchased. In that case, goodwill is the excess of cost over the fair value of the net assets (assets less liabilities) acquired.**

In recording the purchase of a business, the company debits (increases) the identifiable acquired assets, credits liabilities at their fair values, credits cash for the purchase price, and records the difference as goodwill. **Goodwill is not amortized** because it is considered to have an indefinite life. Companies report goodwill in the balance sheet under intangible assets.

INTERNATIONAL INSIGHT

Should Companies Write Up Goodwill?

Softbank Corp. was Japan's biggest Internet company. At one time, it boosted the profit margin of its mobile-phone unit from 3.2% to 11.2% through what appeared to some as accounting tricks. What did it do? It wrote down the value of its mobile-phone-unit assets by half. This would normally result in a huge loss. But rather than take a loss, the company wrote up goodwill by the same amount. How did this move increase earnings? The assets were being depreciated over 10 years, but the company amortizes goodwill over 20 years. (Amortization of goodwill was allowed under the accounting standards it followed at that time.) While the new treatment did not break any rules, the company was criticized by investors for not providing sufficient justification or a detailed explanation for the sudden shift in policy.

Source: Andrew Morse and Yukari Iwatani Kane, "Softbank's Accounting Shift Raises Eyebrows," *Wall Street Journal* (August 28, 2007), p. C1.

 Do you think that this treatment would be allowed under U.S. GAAP? (See page 475.)

Research and Development Costs

Research and development costs are expenditures that may lead to patents, copyrights, new processes, and new products. Many companies spend considerable sums of money on research and development (R&D). For example, in a recent year, IBM spent over $5.1 billion on R&D.

Research and development costs present accounting problems. For one thing, it is sometimes difficult to assign the costs to specific projects. Also, there are uncertainties in identifying the extent and timing of future benefits. As a result, companies usually record R&D costs **as an expense when incurred**, whether the research and development is successful or not.

To illustrate, assume that Laser Scanner Company spent $3 million on R&D that resulted in two highly successful patents. It spent $20,000 on legal fees for the patents. The company would add the lawyers' fees to the Patents account. The R&D costs, however, cannot be included in the cost of the patents. Instead, the company would record the R&D costs as an expense when incurred.

Many disagree with this accounting approach. They argue that expensing R&D costs leads to understated assets and net income. Others, however, argue that capitalizing these costs will lead to highly speculative assets on the balance sheet. Who is right is difficult to determine.

Helpful Hint
Research and development (R&D) costs are not intangible assets. But because they may lead to patents and copyrights, we discuss them in this section.

> **DO IT!**

Classification Concepts

Match the statement with the term most directly associated with it.

Copyrights
Intangible assets
Research and development costs

Depletion
Franchises

1. _____ The allocation of the cost of a natural resource to expense in a rational and systematic manner.

2. _____ Rights, privileges, and competitive advantages that result from the ownership of long-lived assets that do not possess physical substance.

3. _____ An exclusive right granted by the federal government to reproduce and sell an artistic or published work.

4. _____ A right to sell certain products or services or to use certain trademarks or trade names within a designated geographic area.

5. _____ Costs incurred by a company that often lead to patents or new products. These costs must be expensed as incurred.

Action Plan

✔ Know that the accounting for intangibles often depends on whether the item has a finite or indefinite life.

✔ Recognize the many similarities and differences between the accounting for natural resources, plant assets, and intangible assets.

Solution

1. Depletion	4. Franchises
2. Intangible assets	5. Research and development costs
3. Copyrights	

Related exercise material: BE9-11, BE9-12, E9-11, E9-12, E9-13, **and** DO IT! 9-5.

✔ **The Navigator**

Statement Presentation and Analysis

Presentation

Usually, companies combine plant assets and natural resources under "Property, plant, and equipment" in the balance sheet. They show intangibles separately. Companies disclose either in the balance sheet or the notes the balances of the major classes of assets, such as land, buildings, and equipment, and accumulated depreciation by major classes or in total. In addition, they should describe the depreciation and amortization methods that were used, as well as disclose the amount of depreciation and amortization expense for the period.

Illustration 9-23 shows a typical financial statement presentation of property, plant, and equipment and intangibles for The Procter & Gamble Company

Illustration 9-23
P&G's presentation of property, plant, and equipment, and intangible assets

Real World

THE PROCTER & GAMBLE COMPANY
Balance Sheet (partial)
(in millions)

	June 30	
	2012	**2011**
Property, plant, and equipment		
Buildings	$ 7,324	$ 7,753
Machinery and equipment	32,029	32,820
Land	880	934
	40,233	41,507
Accumulated depreciation	(19,856)	(20,214)
Net property, plant, and equipment	20,377	21,293
Goodwill and other intangible assets		
Goodwill	53,773	57,562
Trademarks and other intangible assets, net	30,988	32,620
Net goodwill and other intangible assets	$84,761	$90,182

(P&G) in its 2012 balance sheet. The notes to P&G's financial statements present greater details about the accounting for its long-term tangible and intangible assets.

Illustration 9-24 shows another comprehensive presentation of property, plant, and equipment from the balance sheet of Owens-Illinois. The notes to the financial statements of Owens-Illinois identify the major classes of property, plant, and equipment. They also indicate that depreciation and amortization are by the straight-line method, and depletion is by the units-of-activity method.

Illustration 9-24
Owens-Illinois' presentation of property, plant, and equipment, and intangible assets

OWENS-ILLINOIS, INC. Balance Sheet (partial) (in millions)		
Property, plant, and equipment		
Timberlands, at cost, less accumulated depletion		$ 95.4
Buildings and equipment, at cost	$2,207.1	
Less: Accumulated depreciation	1,229.0	978.1
Total property, plant, and equipment		$1,073.5
Intangibles		
Patents		410.0
Total		$1,483.5

Analysis

Using ratios, we can analyze how efficiently a company uses its assets to generate sales. The **asset turnover** analyzes the productivity of a company's assets. It tells us how many dollars of sales a company generates for each dollar invested in assets. This ratio is computed by dividing net sales by average total assets for the period. Illustration 9-25 shows the computation of the asset turnover for The Procter & Gamble Company. P&G's net sales for 2012 were $83,680 million. Its total ending assets were $132,244 million, and beginning assets were $138,354 million.

Illustration 9-25
Asset turnover formula and computation

$$\text{Net Sales} \div \text{Average Total Assets} = \text{Asset Turnover}$$

$$\$83,680 \div \frac{\$138,354 + \$132,244}{2} = .62 \text{ times}$$

Thus, each dollar invested in assets produced $0.62 in sales for P&G. If a company is using its assets efficiently, each dollar of assets will create a high amount of sales. This ratio varies greatly among different industries—from those that are asset-intensive (utilities) to those that are not (services).

DuPage Company purchases a factory machine at a cost of $18,000 on January 1, 2015. DuPage expects the machine to have a salvage value of $2,000 at the end of its 4-year useful life.

During its useful life, the machine is expected to be used 160,000 hours. Actual annual hourly use was 2015, 40,000; 2016, 60,000; 2017, 35,000; and 2018, 25,000.

Instructions

Prepare depreciation schedules for the following methods: (a) straight-line, (b) units-of-activity, and (c) declining-balance using double the straight-line rate.

Solution to Comprehensive DO IT! 1

Action Plan

✔ Under the straight-line method, apply the depreciation rate to depreciable cost.

✔ Under the units-of-activity method, compute the depreciable cost per unit by dividing depreciable cost by total units of activity.

✔ Under the declining-balance method, apply the depreciation rate to **book value** at the beginning of the year.

(a)

Straight-Line Method

	Computation			Annual	End of Year	
Year	Depreciable Cost*	×	Depreciation Rate	=	Depreciation Expense	Accumulated Depreciation	Book Value
2015	$16,000		25%		$4,000	$ 4,000	$14,000**
2016	16,000		25%		4,000	8,000	10,000
2017	16,000		25%		4,000	12,000	6,000
2018	16,000		25%		4,000	16,000	2,000

*$18,000 − $2,000.
**$18,000 − $4,000.

(b)

Units-of-Activity Method

	Computation			Annual	End of Year	
Year	Units of Activity	×	Depreciable Cost/Unit	=	Depreciation Expense	Accumulated Depreciation	Book Value
2015	40,000		$0.10*		$4,000	$ 4,000	$14,000
2016	60,000		0.10		6,000	10,000	8,000
2017	35,000		0.10		3,500	13,500	4,500
2018	25,000		0.10		2,500	16,000	2,000

*($18,000 − $2,000) ÷ 160,000.

(c)

Declining-Balance Method

	Computation			Annual	End of Year	
Year	Book Value Beginning of Year	×	Depreciation Rate*	=	Depreciation Expense	Accumulated Depreciation	Book Value
2015	$18,000		50%		$9,000	$ 9,000	$9,000
2016	9,000		50%		4,500	13,500	4,500
2017	4,500		50%		2,250	15,750	2,250
2018	2,250		50%		250**	16,000	2,000

*¼ × 2.
**Adjusted to $250 because ending book value should not be less than expected salvage value.

✔ The Navigator

> Comprehensive DO IT! 2

On January 1, 2015, Skyline Limousine Co. purchased a limo at an acquisition cost of $28,000. The vehicle has been depreciated by the straight-line method using a 4-year service life and a $4,000 salvage value. The company's fiscal year ends on December 31.

Instructions

Prepare the journal entry or entries to record the disposal of the limousine assuming that it was:

(a) Retired and scrapped with no salvage value on January 1, 2019.
(b) Sold for $5,000 on July 1, 2018.

Solution to Comprehensive DO IT! 2

Action Plan

✔ At the time of disposal, determine the book value of the asset.

✔ Recognize any gain or loss from disposal of the asset.

✔ Remove the book value of the asset from the records by debiting Accumulated Depreciation for the total depreciation to date of disposal and crediting the asset account for the cost of the asset.

(a) 1/1/19	Accumulated Depreciation—Equipment		24,000	
	Loss on Disposal of Plant Assets		4,000	
	Equipment			28,000
	(To record retirement of limousine)			
(b) 7/1/18	Depreciation Expense		3,000	
	Accumulated Depreciation—Equipment			3,000
	(To record depreciation to date of disposal)			
	Cash		5,000	
	Accumulated Depreciation—Equipment		21,000	
	Loss on Disposal of Plant Assets		2,000	
	Equipment			28,000
	(To record sale of limousine)			

 The Navigator

SUMMARY OF LEARNING OBJECTIVES

 The Navigator

1 Describe how the historical cost principle applies to plant assets. The cost of plant assets includes all expenditures necessary to acquire the asset and make it ready for its intended use. Once cost is established, the company uses that amount as the basis of accounting for the plant assets over its useful life.

2 Explain the concept of depreciation and how to compute it. Depreciation is the allocation of the cost of a plant asset to expense over its useful (service) life in a rational and systematic manner. Depreciation is not a process of valuation, nor is it a process that results in an accumulation of cash.

Three depreciation methods are:

Method	Effect on Annual Depreciation	Formula
Straight-line	Constant amount	Depreciable cost ÷ Useful life (in years)
Units-of-activity	Varying amount	Depreciable cost per unit × Units of activity during the year
Declining-balance	Decreasing amount	Book value at beginning of year × Declining-balance rate

Companies make revisions of periodic depreciation in present and future periods, not retroactively. They determine the new annual depreciation by dividing the depreciable cost at the time of the revision by the remaining useful life.

3 Distinguish between revenue and capital expenditures, and explain the entries for each. Companies incur revenue expenditures to maintain the operating efficiency and productive life of an asset. They debit these expenditures to Maintenance and Repairs Expense as incurred. Capital expenditures increase the operating efficiency, productive capacity, or expected useful life of the asset. Companies generally debit these expenditures to the plant asset affected.

4 Explain how to account for the disposal of a plant asset. The accounting for disposal of a plant asset through retirement or sale is as follows. (a) Eliminate the book value of the plant asset at the date of disposal. (b) Record cash proceeds, if any. (c) Account for the difference between the book value and the cash proceeds as a gain or loss on disposal.

5 Compute periodic depletion of natural resources. Companies compute depletion cost per unit by dividing the total cost of the natural resource minus salvage value by the number of units estimated to be in the resource. They then multiply the depletion cost per unit by the number of units extracted and sold.

6 **Explain the basic issues related to accounting for intangible assets.** The process of allocating the cost of an intangible asset is referred to as amortization. The cost of intangible assets with indefinite lives is not amortized. Companies normally use the straight-line method for amortizing intangible assets.

7 **Indicate how plant assets, natural resources, and intangible assets are reported.** Companies usually combine plant assets and natural resources under property,

plant, and equipment. They show intangibles separately under intangible assets. Either within the balance sheet or in the notes, companies should disclose the balances of the major classes of assets, such as land, buildings, and equipment, and accumulated depreciation by major classes or in total. They also should describe the depreciation and amortization methods used, and should disclose the amount of depreciation and amortization expense for the period. The asset turnover measures the productivity of a company's assets in generating sales.

GLOSSARY

Accelerated-depreciation method Depreciation method that produces higher depreciation expense in the early years than in the later years. (p. 438).

Additions and improvements Costs incurred to increase the operating efficiency, productive capacity, or useful life of a plant asset. (p. 441).

Amortization The allocation of the cost of an intangible asset to expense over its useful life in a systematic and rational manner. (p. 447).

Asset turnover A measure of how efficiently a company uses its assets to generate sales; calculated as net sales divided by average total assets. (p. 451).

Capital expenditures Expenditures that increase the company's investment in productive facilities. (p. 441).

Copyrights Exclusive grant from the federal government that allows the owner to reproduce and sell an artistic or published work. (p. 447).

Declining-balance method Depreciation method that applies a constant rate to the declining book value of the asset and produces a decreasing annual depreciation expense over the useful life of the asset. (p. 437).

Depletion The allocation of the cost of a natural resource to expense in a rational and systematic manner over the resource's useful life. (p. 445).

Depreciable cost The cost of a plant asset less its salvage value. (p. 435).

Depreciation The process of allocating to expense the cost of a plant asset over its useful (service) life in a rational and systematic manner. (p. 433).

Franchise (license) A contractual arrangement under which the franchisor grants the franchisee the right to sell certain products, perform specific services, or use certain trademarks or trade names, usually within a designated geographic area. (p. 448).

Going concern assumption States that the company will continue in operation for the foreseeable future. (p. 434).

Goodwill The value of all favorable attributes that relate to a company that is not attributable to any other specific asset. (p. 448).

Intangible assets Rights, privileges, and competitive advantages that result from the ownership of long-lived assets that do not possess physical substance. (p. 446).

Materiality concept If an item would not make a difference in decision-making, a company does not have to follow GAAP in reporting it. (p. 441).

Natural resources Assets that consist of standing timber and underground deposits of oil, gas, and minerals. (p. 444).

Ordinary repairs Expenditures to maintain the operating efficiency and productive life of the unit. (p. 441).

Patent An exclusive right issued by the U.S. Patent Office that enables the recipient to manufacture, sell, or otherwise control an invention for a period of 20 years from the date of the grant. (p. 447).

Plant assets Tangible resources that are used in the operations of the business and are not intended for sale to customers. (p. 430).

Research and development (R&D) costs Expenditures that may lead to patents, copyrights, new processes, or new products. (p. 449).

Revenue expenditures Expenditures that are immediately charged against revenues as an expense. (p. 441).

Salvage value An estimate of an asset's value at the end of its useful life. (p. 435).

Straight-line method Depreciation method in which periodic depreciation is the same for each year of the asset's useful life. (p. 435).

Trademark (trade name) A word, phrase, jingle, or symbol that identifies a particular enterprise or product. (p. 448).

Units-of-activity method Depreciation method in which useful life is expressed in terms of the total units of production or use expected from an asset. (p. 436).

Useful life An estimate of the expected productive life, also called service life, of an asset. (p. 435).

APPENDIX 9A   Exchange of Plant Assets

Ordinarily, companies record a gain or loss on the exchange of plant assets. The rationale for recognizing a gain or loss is that most exchanges have **commercial substance**. An exchange has commercial substance if the future cash flows change as a result of the exchange.

LEARNING OBJECTIVE   8

Explain how to account for the exchange of plant assets.

To illustrate, Ramos Co. exchanges some of its equipment for land held by Brodhead Inc. It is likely that the timing and amount of the cash flows arising from the land will differ significantly from the cash flows arising from the equipment. As a result, both Ramos and Brodhead are in different economic positions. Therefore, **the exchange has commercial substance**, and the companies recognize a gain or loss in the exchange. Because most exchanges have commercial substance (even when similar assets are exchanged), we illustrate only this type of situation for both a loss and a gain.

Loss Treatment

To illustrate an exchange that results in a loss, assume that Roland Company exchanged a set of used trucks plus cash for a new semi-truck. The used trucks have a combined book value of $42,000 (cost $64,000 less $22,000 accumulated depreciation). Roland's purchasing agent, experienced in the secondhand market, indicates that the used trucks have a fair value of $26,000. In addition to the trucks, Roland must pay $17,000 for the semi-truck. Roland computes the cost of the semi-truck as follows.

Fair value of used trucks	$26,000
Cash paid	17,000
Cost of semi-truck	$43,000

Illustration 9A-1
Cost of semi-truck

Roland incurs a loss on disposal of plant assets of $16,000 on this exchange. The reason is that the book value of the used trucks is greater than the fair value of these trucks. The computation is as follows.

Book value of used trucks ($64,000 − $22,000)	$ 42,000
Fair value of used trucks	26,000
Loss on disposal of plant assets	$16,000

Illustration 9A-2
Computation of loss on disposal

In recording an exchange at a loss, three steps are required: (1) eliminate the book value of the asset given up, (2) record the cost of the asset acquired, and (3) recognize the loss on disposal of plant assets. Roland Company thus records the exchange on the loss as follows.

Equipment (new)	43,000		
Accumulated Depreciation—Equipment	22,000		
Loss on Disposal of Plant Assets	16,000		
Equipment (old)		64,000	
Cash		17,000	
(To record exchange of used trucks for semi-truck)			

A	=	L	+	SE
+43,000				
+22,000				
				−16,000 Exp
−64,000				
−17,000				

Cash Flows
−17,000

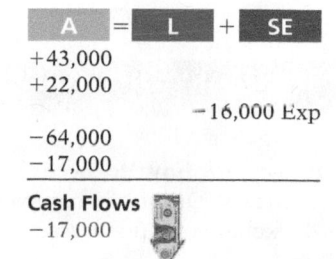

Gain Treatment

To illustrate a gain situation, assume that Mark Express Delivery decides to exchange its old delivery equipment plus cash of $3,000 for new delivery equipment. The book value of the old delivery equipment is $12,000 (cost $40,000 less accumulated depreciation $28,000). The fair value of the old delivery equipment is $19,000.

The cost of the new asset is the fair value of the old asset exchanged plus any cash paid (or other consideration given up). The cost of the new delivery equipment is $22,000, computed as follows.

Illustration 9A-3
Cost of new delivery equipment

Fair value of old delivery equipment	$ 19,000
Cash paid	3,000
Cost of new delivery equipment	**$22,000**

A gain results when the fair value of the old delivery equipment is greater than its book value. For Mark Express, there is a gain of $7,000 on disposal of plant assets, computed as follows.

Illustration 9A-4
Computation of gain on disposal

Fair value of old delivery equipment	$19,000
Book value of old delivery equipment ($40,000 − $28,000)	12,000
Gain on disposal of plant assets	**$ 7,000**

Mark Express Delivery records the exchange as follows.

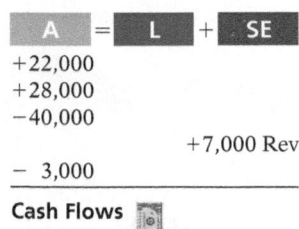

A = L + SE
+22,000
+28,000
−40,000
        +7,000 Rev
− 3,000

Cash Flows
− 3,000

Equipment (new)	22,000	
Accumulated Depreciation—Equipment (old)	28,000	
Equipment (old)		40,000
Gain on Disposal of Plant Assets		7,000
Cash		3,000
(To record exchange of old delivery equipment for new delivery equipment)		

In recording an exchange at a gain, the following three steps are involved: (1) eliminate the book value of the asset given up, (2) record the cost of the asset acquired, and (3) recognize the gain on disposal of plant assets. Accounting for exchanges of plant assets becomes more complex if the transaction does not have commercial substance. This issue is discussed in more advanced accounting classes.

8 Explain how to account for the exchange of plant assets. Ordinarily, companies record a gain or loss on the exchange of plant assets. The rationale for recognizing a gain or loss is that most exchanges have commercial substance. An exchange has commercial substance if the future cash flows change as a result of the exchange.

WileyPLUS   Self-Test, Brief Exercises, Exercises, Problem Set A, and many more components are available for practice in *WileyPLUS*.

Note: All asterisked Questions, Exercises, and Problems relate to material in the appendix to the chapter.

SELF-TEST QUESTIONS

Answers are on page 475.

(LO 1) **1.** Erin Danielle Company purchased equipment and incurred the following costs.

Cash price	$24,000
Sales taxes	1,200
Insurance during transit	200
Installation and testing	400
Total costs	$25,800

What amount should be recorded as the cost of the equipment?

(a) $24,000.
(b) $25,200.
(c) $25,400.
(d) $25,800.

(LO 2) **2.** Depreciation is a process of:

(a) valuation.
(b) cost allocation.
(c) cash accumulation.
(d) appraisal.

(LO 2) **3.** Micah Bartlett Company purchased equipment on January 1, 2014, at a total invoice cost of $400,000. The equipment has an estimated salvage value of $10,000 and an estimated useful life of 5 years. The amount of accumulated depreciation at December 31, 2015, if the straight-line method of depreciation is used, is:

(a) $80,000.
(b) $160,000.
(c) $78,000.
(d) $156,000.

(LO 2) **4.** Ann Torbert purchased a truck for $11,000 on January 1, 2014. The truck will have an estimated salvage value of $1,000 at the end of 5 years. Using the units-of-activity method, the balance in accumulated depreciation at December 31, 2015, can be computed by the following formula:

(a) ($11,000 ÷ Total estimated activity) × Units of activity for 2015.
(b) ($10,000 ÷ Total estimated activity) × Units of activity for 2015.
(c) ($11,000 ÷ Total estimated activity) × Units of activity for 2014 and 2015.
(d) ($10,000 ÷ Total estimated activity) × Units of activity for 2014 and 2015.

(LO 2) **5.** Jefferson Company purchased a piece of equipment on January 1, 2015. The equipment cost $60,000 and has an estimated life of 8 years and a salvage value of $8,000. What was the depreciation expense for the asset for 2016 under the double-declining-balance method?

(a) $6,500.
(b) $11,250.
(c) $15,000.
(d) $6,562.

(LO 2) **6.** When there is a change in estimated depreciation:

(a) previous depreciation should be corrected.
(b) current and future years' depreciation should be revised.

(c) only future years' depreciation should be revised.
(d) None of the above.

(LO 2) **7.** Able Towing Company purchased a tow truck for $60,000 on January 1, 2013. It was originally depreciated on a straight-line basis over 10 years with an assumed salvage value of $12,000. On December 31, 2015, before adjusting entries had been made, the company decided to change the remaining estimated life to 4 years (including 2015) and the salvage value to $2,000. What was the depreciation expense for 2015?

(a) $6,000.
(b) $4,800.
(c) $15,000.
(d) $12,100.

(LO 3) **8.** Additions to plant assets are:

(a) revenue expenditures.
(b) debited to the Maintenance and Repairs Expense account.
(c) debited to the Purchases account.
(d) capital expenditures.

(LO 4) **9.** Bennie Razor Company has decided to sell one of its old manufacturing machines on June 30, 2015. The machine was purchased for $80,000 on January 1, 2011, and was depreciated on a straight-line basis for 10 years assuming no salvage value. If the machine was sold for $26,000, what was the amount of the gain or loss recorded at the time of the sale?

(a) $18,000.
(b) $54,000.
(c) $22,000.
(d) $46,000.

(LO 5) **10.** Maggie Sharrer Company expects to extract 20 million tons of coal from a mine that cost $12 million. If no salvage value is expected and 2 million tons are mined and sold in the first year, the entry to record depletion will include a:

(a) debit to Accumulated Depletion of $2,000,000.
(b) credit to Depletion Expense of $1,200,000.
(c) debit to Depletion Expense of $1,200,000.
(d) credit to Accumulated Depletion of $2,000,000.

(LO 6) **11.** Which of the following statements is **false**?

(a) If an intangible asset has a finite life, it should be amortized.
(b) The amortization period of an intangible asset can exceed 20 years.
(c) Goodwill is recorded only when a business is purchased.
(d) Research and development costs are expensed when incurred, except when the research and development expenditures result in a successful patent.

(LO 6) **12.** Martha Beyerlein Company incurred $150,000 of research and development costs in its laboratory to develop a patent granted on January 2, 2015. On July 31, 2015, Beyerlein paid $35,000 for legal fees in a successful defense of the patent. The total amount debited to Patents through July 31, 2015, should be:
  (a) $150,000.   (c) $185,000.
  (b) $35,000.   (d) $170,000.

(LO 7) **13.** Indicate which of the following statements is **true**.
  (a) Since intangible assets lack physical substance, they need be disclosed only in the notes to the financial statements.
  (b) Goodwill should be reported as a contra account in the stockholders' equity section.
  (c) Totals of major classes of assets can be shown in the balance sheet, with asset details disclosed in the notes to the financial statements.
  (d) Intangible assets are typically combined with plant assets and natural resources, and shown in the property, plant, and equipment section.

(LO 7) **14.** Lake Coffee Company reported net sales of $180,000, net income of $54,000, beginning total assets of $200,000, and ending total assets of $300,000. What was the company's asset turnover?
  (a) 0.90.
  (b) 0.20.
  (c) 0.72.
  (d) 1.39.

*15. Schopenhauer Company exchanged an old machine, (LO 8) with a book value of $39,000 and a fair value of $35,000, and paid $10,000 cash for a similar new machine. The transaction has commercial substance. At what amount should the machine acquired in the exchange be recorded on Schopenhauer's books?
  (a) $45,000.
  (b) $46,000.
  (c) $49,000.
  (d) $50,000.

*16. In exchanges of assets in which the exchange has (LO 8) commercial substance:
  (a) neither gains nor losses are recognized immediately.
  (b) gains, but not losses, are recognized immediately.
  (c) losses, but not gains, are recognized immediately.
  (d) both gains and losses are recognized immediately.

Go to the book's companion website, www.wiley.com/college/weygandt, for additional Self-Test Questions.

 ✔ The Navigator

QUESTIONS

1. Sid Watney is uncertain about the applicability of the historical cost principle to plant assets. Explain the principle to Sid.
2. What are some examples of land improvements?
3. Lynn Company acquires the land and building owned by Noble Company. What types of costs may be incurred to make the asset ready for its intended use if Lynn Company wants to use (a) only the land, and (b) both the land and the building?
4. In a recent newspaper release, the president of Downs Company asserted that something has to be done about depreciation. The president said, "Depreciation does not come close to accumulating the cash needed to replace the asset at the end of its useful life." What is your response to the president?
5. Andrew is studying for the next accounting examination. He asks your help on two questions: (a) What is salvage value? (b) Is salvage value used in determining periodic depreciation under each depreciation method? Answer Andrew's questions.
6. Contrast the straight-line method and the units-of-activity method as to (a) useful life, and (b) the pattern of periodic depreciation over useful life.
7. Contrast the effects of the three depreciation methods on annual depreciation expense.
8. In the fourth year of an asset's 5-year useful life, the company decides that the asset will have a 6-year service life. How should the revision of depreciation be recorded? Why?
9. Distinguish between revenue expenditures and capital expenditures during useful life.

10. How is a gain or loss on the sale of a plant asset computed?
11. Romero Corporation owns a machine that is fully depreciated but is still being used. How should Romero account for this asset and report it in the financial statements?
12. What are natural resources, and what are their distinguishing characteristics?
13. Explain what depletion is and how it is computed.
14. What are the similarities and differences between the terms depreciation, depletion, and amortization?
15. Rowand Company hires an accounting intern who says that intangible assets should always be amortized over their legal lives. Is the intern correct? Explain.
16. Goodwill has been defined as the value of all favorable attributes that relate to a business. What types of attributes could result in goodwill?
17. Jimmy West, a business major, is working on a case problem for one of his classes. In the case problem, the company needs to raise cash to market a new product it developed. Ron Thayer, an engineering major, takes one look at the company's balance sheet and says, "This company has an awful lot of goodwill. Why don't you recommend that it sell some of it to raise cash?" How should Jimmy respond to Ron?
18. Under what conditions is goodwill recorded?
19. Often, research and development costs provide companies with benefits that last a number of years. (For example, these costs can lead to the development of a patent that will increase the company's income for many years.) However, generally accepted accounting principles require that such costs be recorded as an expense when incurred. Why?

20. McDonald's Corporation reports total average assets of $28.9 billion and net sales of $20.5 billion. What is the company's asset turnover?

21. Stark Corporation and Zuber Corporation operate in the same industry. Stark uses the straight-line method to account for depreciation; Zuber uses an accelerated method. Explain what complications might arise in trying to compare the results of these two companies.

22. Gomez Corporation uses straight-line depreciation for financial reporting purposes but an accelerated method for tax purposes. Is it acceptable to use different methods for the two purposes? What is Gomez's motivation for doing this?

23. You are comparing two companies in the same industry. You have determined that Ace Corp. depreciates its plant assets over a 40-year life, whereas Liu Corp. depreciates its plant assets over a 20-year life. Discuss the implications this has for comparing the results of the two companies.

24. Sosa Company is doing significant work to revitalize its warehouses. It is not sure whether it should capitalize these costs or expense them. What are the implications for current-year net income and future net income of expensing versus capitalizing these costs?

*25. When assets are exchanged in a transaction involving commercial substance, how is the gain or loss on disposal of plant assets computed?

*26. Unruh Refrigeration Company trades in an old machine on a new model when the fair value of the old machine is greater than its book value. The transaction has commercial substance. Should Unruh recognize a gain on disposal of plant assets? If the fair value of the old machine is less than its book value, should Unruh recognize a loss on disposal of plant assets?

BRIEF EXERCISES

BE9-1 The following expenditures were incurred by McCoy Company in purchasing land: cash price $50,000, accrued taxes $3,000, attorneys' fees $2,500, real estate broker's commission $2,000, and clearing and grading $3,500. What is the cost of the land?

Determine the cost of land. (LO 1)

BE9-2 Rich Castillo Company incurs the following expenditures in purchasing a truck: cash price $30,000, accident insurance $2,000, sales taxes $2,100, motor vehicle license $100, and painting and lettering $400. What is the cost of the truck?

Determine the cost of a truck. (LO 1)

BE9-3 Corales Company acquires a delivery truck at a cost of $38,000. The truck is expected to have a salvage value of $6,000 at the end of its 4-year useful life. Compute annual depreciation expense for the first and second years using the straight-line method.

Compute straight-line depreciation. (LO 2)

BE9-4 Chisenhall Company purchased land and a building on January 1, 2015. Management's best estimate of the value of the land was $100,000 and of the building $200,000. However, management told the accounting department to record the land at $220,000 and the building at $80,000. The building is being depreciated on a straight-line basis over 15 years with no salvage value. Why do you suppose management requested this accounting treatment? Is it ethical?

Compute depreciation and evaluate treatment. (LO 2)

BE9-5 Depreciation information for Corales Company is given in BE9-3. Assuming the declining-balance depreciation rate is double the straight-line rate, compute annual depreciation for the first and second years under the declining-balance method.

Compute declining-balance depreciation. (LO 2)

BE9-6 Rosco Taxi Service uses the units-of-activity method in computing depreciation on its taxicabs. Each cab is expected to be driven 150,000 miles. Taxi no. 10 cost $39,500 and is expected to have a salvage value of $500. Taxi no. 10 is driven 30,000 miles in year 1 and 20,000 miles in year 2. Compute the depreciation for each year.

Compute depreciation using the units-of-activity method. (LO 2)

BE9-7 On January 1, 2015, the Morgantown Company ledger shows Equipment $32,000 and Accumulated Depreciation—Equipment $9,000. The depreciation resulted from using the straight-line method with a useful life of 10 years and a salvage value of $2,000. On this date, the company concludes that the equipment has a remaining useful life of only 4 years with the same salvage value. Compute the revised annual depreciation.

Compute revised depreciation. (LO 2)

BE9-8 Flaherty Company had the following two transactions related to its delivery truck.
1. Paid $45 for an oil change.
2. Paid $400 to install a special gear unit, which increases the operating efficiency of the truck.
Prepare Flaherty's journal entries to record these two transactions.

Prepare entries for delivery truck costs. (LO 3)

BE9-9 Prepare journal entries to record the following.
(a) Sound Tracker Company retires its delivery equipment, which cost $41,000. Accumulated depreciation is also $41,000 on this delivery equipment. No salvage value is received.
(b) Assume the same information as (a), except that accumulated depreciation is $37,000, instead of $41,000, on the delivery equipment.

Prepare entries for disposal by retirement. (LO 4)

Prepare entries for disposal by sale.
(LO 4)

BE9-10 Gunkelson Company sells equipment on September 30, 2015, for $18,000 cash. The equipment originally cost $72,000 and as of January 1, 2015, had accumulated depreciation of $42,000. Depreciation for the first 9 months of 2015 is $5,250. Prepare the journal entries to (a) update depreciation to September 30, 2015, and (b) record the sale of the equipment.

Prepare depletion expense entry and balance sheet presentation for natural resources.
(LO 5)

BE9-11 Franceour Mining Co. purchased for $7 million a mine that is estimated to have 35 million tons of ore and no salvage value. In the first year, 5 million tons of ore are extracted and sold.

(a) Prepare the journal entry to record depletion expense for the first year.
(b) Show how this mine is reported on the balance sheet at the end of the first year.

Prepare amortization expense entry and balance sheet presentation for intangibles.
(LO 6)

BE9-12 Campanez Company purchases a patent for $140,000 on January 2, 2015. Its estimated useful life is 10 years.

(a) Prepare the journal entry to record amortization expense for the first year.
(b) Show how this patent is reported on the balance sheet at the end of the first year.

Classify long-lived assets on balance sheet.
(LO 7)

BE9-13 Information related to plant assets, natural resources, and intangibles at the end of 2015 for Dent Company is as follows: buildings $1,100,000; accumulated depreciation—buildings $600,000; goodwill $410,000; coal mine $500,000; accumulated depletion—coal mine $108,000. Prepare a partial balance sheet of Dent Company for these items.

Calculate asset turnover.
(LO 7)

BE9-14 In a recent annual report, Target reported beginning total assets of $44.1 billion; ending total assets of $44.5 billion; and net sales of $63.4 billion. Compute Target's asset turnover.

Prepare entry for disposal by exchange.
(LO 8)

*BE9-15 Olathe Company exchanges old delivery equipment for new delivery equipment. The book value of the old delivery equipment is $31,000 (cost $61,000 less accumulated depreciation $30,000). Its fair value is $24,000, and cash of $5,000 is paid. Prepare the entry to record the exchange, assuming the transaction has commercial substance.

Prepare entry for disposal by exchange.
(LO 8)

*BE9-16 Assume the same information as BE9-15, except that the fair value of the old delivery equipment is $33,000. Prepare the entry to record the exchange.

> DO IT! Review

Explain accounting for cost of plant assets.
(LO 1)

DO IT! 9-1 Lofton Company purchased a delivery truck. The total cash payment was $27,900, including the following items.

Negotiated purchase price	$24,000
Installation of special shelving	1,100
Painting and lettering	900
Motor vehicle license	100
Annual insurance policy	500
Sales tax	1,300
Total paid	$27,900

Explain how each of these costs would be accounted for.

Calculate depreciation expense and make journal entry.
(LO 2)

DO IT! 9-2 On January 1, 2015, Emporia Country Club purchased a new riding mower for $15,000. The mower is expected to have an 8-year life with a $3,000 salvage value. What journal entry would Emporia make at December 31, 2015, if it uses straight-line depreciation?

Calculate revised depreciation.
(LO 2)

DO IT! 9-3 Pinewood Corporation purchased a piece of equipment for $70,000. It estimated an 8-year life and a $2,000 salvage value. At the end of year four (before the depreciation adjustment), it estimated the new total life to be 10 years and the new salvage value to be $6,000. Compute the revised depreciation.

Make journal entries to record plant asset disposal.
(LO 4)

DO IT! 9-4 Napoli Manufacturing has old equipment that cost $52,000. The equipment has accumulated depreciation of $28,000. Napoli has decided to sell the equipment.

(a) What entry would Napoli make to record the sale of the equipment for $26,000 cash?
(b) What entry would Napoli make to record the sale of the equipment for $15,000 cash?

DO IT! 9-5 Match the statement with the term most directly associated with it.

Goodwill   Amortization
Intangible assets   Franchises
Research and development costs

1. _____ Rights, privileges, and competitive advantages that result from the ownership of long-lived assets that do not possess physical substance.

2. _____ The allocation of the cost of an intangible asset to expense in a rational and systematic manner.

3. _____ A right to sell certain products or services, or use certain trademarks or trade names, within a designated geographic area.

4. _____ Costs incurred by a company that often lead to patents or new products. These costs must be expensed as incurred.

5. _____ The excess of the cost of a company over the fair value of the net assets acquired.

EXERCISES

E9-1 The following expenditures relating to plant assets were made by Prather Company during the first 2 months of 2015.

1. Paid $5,000 of accrued taxes at time plant site was acquired.
2. Paid $200 insurance to cover possible accident loss on new factory machinery while the machinery was in transit.
3. Paid $850 sales taxes on new delivery truck.
4. Paid $17,500 for parking lots and driveways on new plant site.
5. Paid $250 to have company name and advertising slogan painted on new delivery truck.
6. Paid $8,000 for installation of new factory machinery.
7. Paid $900 for one-year accident insurance policy on new delivery truck.
8. Paid $75 motor vehicle license fee on the new truck.

Instructions
(a) ⬤➤ Explain the application of the historical cost principle in determining the acquisition cost of plant assets.
(b) List the numbers of the foregoing transactions, and opposite each indicate the account title to which each expenditure should be debited.

E9-2 Benedict Company incurred the following costs.

1. Sales tax on factory machinery purchased	$ 5,000
2. Painting of and lettering on truck immediately upon purchase	700
3. Installation and testing of factory machinery	2,000
4. Real estate broker's commission on land purchased	3,500
5. Insurance premium paid for first year's insurance on new truck	880
6. Cost of landscaping on property purchased	7,200
7. Cost of paving parking lot for new building constructed	17,900
8. Cost of clearing, draining, and filling land	13,300
9. Architect's fees on self-constructed building	10,000

Instructions
Indicate to which account Benedict would debit each of the costs.

E9-3 On March 1, 2015, Westmorlan Company acquired real estate on which it planned to construct a small office building. The company paid $75,000 in cash. An old warehouse on the property was razed at a cost of $8,600; the salvaged materials were sold for $1,700. Additional expenditures before construction began included $1,100 attorney's fee for work concerning the land purchase, $5,000 real estate broker's fee, $7,800 architect's fee, and $14,000 to put in driveways and a parking lot.

Instructions
(a) Determine the amount to be reported as the cost of the land.
(b) For each cost not used in part (a), indicate the account to be debited.

Understand depreciation concepts.

(LO 2)

E9-4 Tom Parkey has prepared the following list of statements about depreciation.

1. Depreciation is a process of asset valuation, not cost allocation.
2. Depreciation provides for the proper matching of expenses with revenues.
3. The book value of a plant asset should approximate its fair value.
4. Depreciation applies to three classes of plant assets: land, buildings, and equipment.
5. Depreciation does not apply to a building because its usefulness and revenue-producing ability generally remain intact over time.
6. The revenue-producing ability of a depreciable asset will decline due to wear and tear and to obsolescence.
7. Recognizing depreciation on an asset results in an accumulation of cash for replacement of the asset.
8. The balance in accumulated depreciation represents the total cost that has been charged to expense.
9. Depreciation expense and accumulated depreciation are reported on the income statement.
10. Four factors affect the computation of depreciation: cost, useful life, salvage value, and residual value.

Instructions

Identify each statement as true or false. If false, indicate how to correct the statement.

Compute depreciation under units-of-activity method.

(LO 2)

E9-5 Yello Bus Lines uses the units-of-activity method in depreciating its buses. One bus was purchased on January 1, 2015, at a cost of $148,000. Over its 4-year useful life, the bus is expected to be driven 100,000 miles. Salvage value is expected to be $8,000.

Instructions

(a) Compute the depreciable cost per unit.
(b) Prepare a depreciation schedule assuming actual mileage was: 2015, 26,000; 2016, 32,000; 2017, 25,000; and 2018, 17,000.

Determine depreciation for partial periods.

(LO 2)

E9-6 Rottino Company purchased a new machine on October 1, 2015, at a cost of $150,000. The company estimated that the machine will have a salvage value of $12,000. The machine is expected to be used for 10,000 working hours during its 5-year life.

Instructions

Compute the depreciation expense under the following methods for the year indicated.

(a) Straight-line for 2015.
(b) Units-of-activity for 2015, assuming machine usage was 1,700 hours.
(c) Declining-balance using double the straight-line rate for 2015 and 2016.

Compute depreciation using different methods.

(LO 2)

E9-7 Linton Company purchased a delivery truck for $34,000 on January 1, 2015. The truck has an expected salvage value of $2,000, and is expected to be driven 100,000 miles over its estimated useful life of 8 years. Actual miles driven were 15,000 in 2015 and 12,000 in 2016.

Instructions

(a) Compute depreciation expense for 2015 and 2016 using (1) the straight-line method, (2) the units-of-activity method, and (3) the double-declining-balance method.
(b) Assume that Linton uses the straight-line method.
  (1) Prepare the journal entry to record 2015 depreciation.
  (2) Show how the truck would be reported in the December 31, 2015, balance sheet.

Compute revised annual depreciation.

(LO 2)

E9-8 Terry Wade, the new controller of Hellickson Company, has reviewed the expected useful lives and salvage values of selected depreciable assets at the beginning of 2015. His findings are as follows.

Type of Asset	Date Acquired	Cost	Accumulated Depreciation 1/1/15	Useful Life in Years Old	Useful Life in Years Proposed	Salvage Value Old	Salvage Value Proposed
Building	1/1/09	$800,000	$114,000	40	50	$40,000	$26,000
Warehouse	1/1/10	100,000	19,000	25	20	5,000	6,000

All assets are depreciated by the straight-line method. Hellickson Company uses a calendar year in preparing annual financial statements. After discussion, management has agreed to accept Terry's proposed changes.

Instructions

(a) Compute the revised annual depreciation on each asset in 2015. (Show computations.)
(b) Prepare the entry (or entries) to record depreciation on the building in 2015.

E9-9 Presented below are selected transactions at Ridge Company for 2015.

Jan. 1   Retired a piece of machinery that was purchased on January 1, 2005. The machine cost $62,000 on that date. It had a useful life of 10 years with no salvage value.

June 30   Sold a computer that was purchased on January 1, 2012. The computer cost $45,000. It had a useful life of 5 years with no salvage value. The computer was sold for $14,000.

Dec. 31   Discarded a delivery truck that was purchased on January 1, 2011. The truck cost $33,000. It was depreciated based on a 6-year useful life with a $3,000 salvage value.

Journalize entries for disposal of plant assets.
(LO 4)

Instructions

Journalize all entries required on the above dates, including entries to update depreciation, where applicable, on assets disposed of. Ridge Company uses straight-line depreciation. (Assume depreciation is up to date as of December 31, 2014.)

E9-10 Pryce Company owns equipment that cost $65,000 when purchased on January 1, 2012. It has been depreciated using the straight-line method based on an estimated salvage value of $5,000 and an estimated useful life of 5 years.

Journalize entries for disposal of equipment.
(LO 4)

Instructions

Prepare Pryce Company's journal entries to record the sale of the equipment in these four independent situations.

(a) Sold for $31,000 on January 1, 2015.
(b) Sold for $31,000 on May 1, 2015.
(c) Sold for $11,000 on January 1, 2015.
(d) Sold for $11,000 on October 1, 2015.

E9-11 On July 1, 2015, Friedman Inc. invested $720,000 in a mine estimated to have 900,000 tons of ore of uniform grade. During the last 6 months of 2015, 100,000 tons of ore were mined and sold.

Journalize entries for natural resources depletion.
(LO 5)

Instructions

(a) Prepare the journal entry to record depletion expense.
(b) Assume that the 100,000 tons of ore were mined, but only 80,000 units were sold. How are the costs applicable to the 20,000 unsold units reported?

E9-12 The following are selected 2015 transactions of Pedigo Corporation.

Jan. 1   Purchased a small company and recorded goodwill of $150,000. Its useful life is indefinite.

May 1   Purchased for $75,000 a patent with an estimated useful life of 5 years and a legal life of 20 years.

Prepare adjusting entries for amortization.
(LO 6)

Instructions

Prepare necessary adjusting entries at December 31 to record amortization required by the events above.

E9-13 Gill Company, organized in 2015, has the following transactions related to intangible assets.

1/2/15	Purchased patent (7-year life)	$595,000
4/1/15	Goodwill purchased (indefinite life)	360,000
7/1/15	10-year franchise; expiration date 7/1/2025	480,000
9/1/15	Research and development costs	185,000

Prepare entries to set up appropriate accounts for different intangibles; amortize intangible assets.
(LO 6)

Instructions

Prepare the necessary entries to record these intangibles. All costs incurred were for cash. Make the adjusting entries as of December 31, 2015, recording any necessary amortization and reflecting all balances accurately as of that date.

E9-14 During 2015, Paola Corporation reported net sales of $3,500,000 and net income of $1,500,000. Its balance sheet reported average total assets of $1,400,000.

Calculate asset turnover.
(LO 7)

Instructions

Calculate the asset turnover.

Journalize entries for exchanges.

(LO 8)

*E9-15 Presented below are two independent transactions. Both transactions have commercial substance.

1. Mercy Co. exchanged old trucks (cost $64,000 less $22,000 accumulated depreciation) plus cash of $17,000 for new trucks. The old trucks had a fair value of $38,000.
2. Pence Inc. trades its used machine (cost $12,000 less $4,000 accumulated depreciation) for a new machine. In addition to exchanging the old machine (which had a fair value of $11,000), Pence also paid cash of $3,000.

Instructions

(a) Prepare the entry to record the exchange of assets by Mercy Co.
(b) Prepare the entry to record the exchange of assets by Pence Inc.

Journalize entries for the exchange of plant assets.

(LO 8)

*E9-16 Rizzo's Delivery Company and Overland's Express Delivery exchanged delivery trucks on January 1, 2015. Rizzo's truck cost $22,000. It has accumulated depreciation of $15,000 and a fair value of $3,000. Overland's truck cost $10,000. It has accumulated depreciation of $8,000 and a fair value of $3,000. The transaction has commercial substance.

Instructions

(a) Journalize the exchange for Rizzo's Delivery Company.
(b) Journalize the exchange for Overland's Express Delivery.

EXERCISES: SET B AND CHALLENGE EXERCISES

Visit the book's companion website, at **www.wiley.com/college/weygandt**, and choose the Student Companion site to access Exercise Set B and Challenge Exercises.

PROBLEMS: SET A

Determine acquisition costs of land and building.

(LO 1)

P9-1A Venable Company was organized on January 1. During the first year of operations, the following plant asset expenditures and receipts were recorded in random order.

Debit

1. Cost of filling and grading the land	$ 4,000
2. Full payment to building contractor	690,000
3. Real estate taxes on land paid for the current year	5,000
4. Cost of real estate purchased as a plant site (land $100,000 and building $45,000)	145,000
5. Excavation costs for new building	35,000
6. Architect's fees on building plans	10,000
7. Accrued real estate taxes paid at time of purchase of real estate	2,000
8. Cost of parking lots and driveways	14,000
9. Cost of demolishing building to make land suitable for construction of new building	25,000
	$930,000

Credit

10. Proceeds from salvage of demolished building	$ 3,500

Instructions

Analyze the foregoing transactions using the following column headings. Insert the number of each transaction in the Item column, and then insert the amounts in the other appropriate columns. For amounts entered in the Other Accounts column, also indicate the account titles.

Totals

Land $172,500
Buildings $735,000

Item	Land	Buildings	Other Accounts

Compute depreciation under different methods.

(LO 2)

P9-2A In recent years, Avery Transportation purchased three used buses. Because of frequent turnover in the accounting department, a different accountant selected the depreciation method for each bus, and various methods were selected. Information concerning the buses is shown on the next page.

Bus	Acquired	Cost	Salvage Value	Useful Life in Years	Depreciation Method
1	1/1/13	$ 96,000	$ 6,000	5	Straight-line
2	1/1/13	110,000	10,000	4	Declining-balance
3	1/1/14	92,000	8,000	5	Units-of-activity

For the declining-balance method, the company uses the double-declining rate. For the units-of-activity method, total miles are expected to be 120,000. Actual miles of use in the first 3 years were 2014, 24,000; 2015, 34,000; and 2016, 30,000.

Instructions

(a) Compute the amount of accumulated depreciation on each bus at December 31, 2015.

(b) If Bus 2 was purchased on April 1 instead of January 1, what is the depreciation expense for this bus in (1) 2013 and (2) 2014?

(a) Bus 2, 2014, $82,500

P9-3A On January 1, 2015, Evers Company purchased the following two machines for use in its production process.

Compute depreciation under different methods.

(LO 2)

Machine A: The cash price of this machine was $48,000. Related expenditures included: sales tax $1,700, shipping costs $150, insurance during shipping $80, installation and testing costs $70, and $100 of oil and lubricants to be used with the machinery during its first year of operations. Evers estimates that the useful life of the machine is 5 years with a $5,000 salvage value remaining at the end of that time period. Assume that the straight-line method of depreciation is used.

Machine B: The recorded cost of this machine was $180,000. Evers estimates that the useful life of the machine is 4 years with a $10,000 salvage value remaining at the end of that time period.

Instructions

(a) Prepare the following for Machine A.

(1) The journal entry to record its purchase on January 1, 2015.

(2) The journal entry to record annual depreciation at December 31, 2015.

(b) Calculate the amount of depreciation expense that Evers should record for Machine B each year of its useful life under the following assumptions.

(1) Evers uses the straight-line method of depreciation.

(2) Evers uses the declining-balance method. The rate used is twice the straight-line rate.

(3) Evers uses the units-of-activity method and estimates that the useful life of the machine is 125,000 units. Actual usage is as follows: 2015, 45,000 units; 2016, 35,000 units; 2017, 25,000 units; 2018, 20,000 units.

(b)(2) 2015 DDB depreciation $90,000

(c) Which method used to calculate depreciation on Machine B reports the highest amount of depreciation expense in year 1 (2015)? The highest amount in year 4 (2018)? The highest total amount over the 4-year period?

P9-4A At the beginning of 2013, Mazzaro Company acquired equipment costing $120,000. It was estimated that this equipment would have a useful life of 6 years and a salvage value of $12,000 at that time. The straight-line method of depreciation was considered the most appropriate to use with this type of equipment. Depreciation is to be recorded at the end of each year.

Calculate revisions to depreciation expense.

(LO 2)

During 2015 (the third year of the equipment's life), the company's engineers reconsidered their expectations and estimated that the equipment's useful life would probably be 7 years (in total) instead of 6 years. The estimated salvage value was not changed at that time. However, during 2018, the estimated salvage value was reduced to $5,000.

Instructions

Indicate how much depreciation expense should be recorded each year for this equipment, by completing the following table.

Year	Depreciation Expense	Accumulated Depreciation
2013		
2014		
2015		
2016		
2017		
2018		
2019		

2019 depreciation expense, $17,900

Journalize a series of equipment transactions related to purchase, sale, retirement, and depreciation.

(LO 2, 4, 7)

P9-5A At December 31, 2015, Grand Company reported the following as plant assets.

Land		$ 4,000,000
Buildings	$28,500,000	
Less: Accumulated depreciation—buildings	12,100,000	16,400,000
Equipment	48,000,000	
Less: Accumulated depreciation—equipment	5,000,000	43,000,000
Total plant assets		$63,400,000

During 2016, the following selected cash transactions occurred.

April 1   Purchased land for $2,130,000.
May   1   Sold equipment that cost $750,000 when purchased on January 1, 2012. The equipment was sold for $450,000.
June 1   Sold land purchased on June 1, 2006, for $1,500,000. The land cost $400,000.
July 1   Purchased equipment for $2,500,000.
Dec. 31   Retired equipment that cost $500,000 when purchased on December 31, 2006. No salvage value was received.

Instructions

(b) Depreciation Expense—Buildings $570,000; Equipment $4,800,000

(c) Total plant assets $61,760,000

(a) Journalize the above transactions. The company uses straight-line depreciation for buildings and equipment. The buildings are estimated to have a 50-year life and no salvage value. The equipment is estimated to have a 10-year useful life and no salvage value. Update depreciation on assets disposed of at the time of sale or retirement.
(b) Record adjusting entries for depreciation for 2016.
(c) Prepare the plant assets section of Grand's balance sheet at December 31, 2016.

Record disposals.

(LO 4)

(b) $9,000 loss

P9-6A Ceda Co. has equipment that cost $80,000 and that has been depreciated $50,000.

Instructions

Record the disposal under the following assumptions.

(a) It was scrapped as having no value.
(b) It was sold for $21,000.
(c) It was sold for $31,000.

Prepare entries to record transactions related to acquisition and amortization of intangibles; prepare the intangible assets section.

(LO 6, 7)

P9-7A The intangible assets section of Sappelt Company at December 31, 2015, is presented below.

Patents ($70,000 cost less $7,000 amortization)	$63,000
Franchises ($48,000 cost less $19,200 amortization)	28,800
Total	$91,800

The patent was acquired in January 2015 and has a useful life of 10 years. The franchise was acquired in January 2012 and also has a useful life of 10 years. The following cash transactions may have affected intangible assets during 2016.

Jan. 2   Paid $27,000 legal costs to successfully defend the patent against infringement by another company.
Jan.–June   Developed a new product, incurring $140,000 in research and development costs. A patent was granted for the product on July 1. Its useful life is equal to its legal life.
Sept. 1   Paid $50,000 to an extremely large defensive lineman to appear in commercials advertising the company's products. The commercials will air in September and October.

(b) Amortization Expense (patents) $10,000 Amortization Expense (franchises) $5,500

(c) Total intangible assets $243,300

Oct. 1   Acquired a franchise for $140,000. The franchise has a useful life of 50 years.

Instructions

(a) Prepare journal entries to record the transactions above.
(b) Prepare journal entries to record the 2016 amortization expense.
(c) Prepare the intangible assets section of the balance sheet at December 31, 2016.

Prepare entries to correct errors made in recording and amortizing intangible assets.

(LO 6)

P9-8A Due to rapid turnover in the accounting department, a number of transactions involving intangible assets were improperly recorded by Goins Company in 2015.

1. Goins developed a new manufacturing process, incurring research and development costs of $136,000. The company also purchased a patent for $60,000. In early January, Goins capitalized $196,000 as the cost of the patents. Patent amortization expense of $19,600 was recorded based on a 10-year useful life.

2. On July 1, 2015, Goins purchased a small company and as a result acquired goodwill of $92,000. Goins recorded a half-year's amortization in 2015, based on a 50-year life ($920 amortization). The goodwill has an indefinite life.

Instructions

Prepare all journal entries necessary to correct any errors made during 2015. Assume the books have not yet been closed for 2015.

1. R&D Exp. $136,000

P9-9A LaPorta Company and Lott Corporation, two corporations of roughly the same size, are both involved in the manufacture of in-line skates. Each company depreciates its plant assets using the straight-line approach. An investigation of their financial statements reveals the following information.

Calculate and comment on asset turnover.

(LO 7)

	LaPorta Co.	Lott Corp.
Net income	$ 800,000	$1,000,000
Sales revenue	1,300,000	1,180,000
Average total assets	2,500,000	2,000,000
Average plant assets	1,800,000	1,000,000

Instructions

(a) For each company, calculate the asset turnover.

(b) ▭▬► Based on your calculations in part (a), comment on the relative effectiveness of the two companies in using their assets to generate sales and produce net income.

PROBLEMS: SET B

P9-1B Russo Company was organized on January 1. During the first year of operations, the following plant asset expenditures and receipts were recorded in random order.

Determine acquisition costs of land and building.

(LO 1)

Debit

1. Accrued real estate taxes paid at time of purchase of real estate	$ 5,000
2. Real estate taxes on land paid for the current year	7,500
3. Full payment to building contractor	490,000
4. Excavation costs for new building	19,000
5. Cost of real estate purchased as a plant site (land $75,000 and building $25,000)	100,000
6. Cost of parking lots and driveways	18,000
7. Architect's fees on building plans	9,000
8. Installation cost of fences around property	6,000
9. Cost of demolishing building to make land suitable for construction of new building	27,000
	$681,500

Credit

10. Proceeds from salvage of demolished building	$ 3,500

Instructions

Analyze the foregoing transactions using the following column headings. Insert the number of each transaction in the Item column, and then insert the amounts in the other appropriate columns. For amounts entered in the Other Accounts column, also indicate the account title.

Item	Land	Buildings	Other Accounts

Totals

Land $128,500

Buildings $518,000

P9-2B In recent years, Darnell Company purchased three machines. Because of heavy turnover in the accounting department, a different accountant was in charge of selecting the depreciation method for each machine, and each selected a different method. Information concerning the machines is summarized below.

Compute depreciation under different methods.

(LO 2)

Machine	Acquired	Cost	Salvage Value	Useful Life in Years	Depreciation Method
1	1/1/12	$105,000	$ 5,000	10	Straight-line
2	1/1/13	180,000	10,000	8	Declining-balance
3	11/1/15	125,000	15,000	6	Units-of-activity

For the declining-balance method, the company uses the double-declining rate. For the units-of-activity method, total machine hours are expected to be 25,000. Actual hours of use in the first 3 years were 2015, 2,000; 2016, 4,500; and 2017, 5,500.

Instructions

(a) Machine 2, 2014, $78,750

(a) Compute the amount of accumulated depreciation on each machine at December 31, 2015.

(b) If Machine 2 had been purchased on May 1 instead of January 1, what would be the depreciation expense for this machine in (1) 2013 and (2) 2014?

Compute depreciation under different methods.

(LO 2)

P9-3B On January 1, 2015, Bourgeois Company purchased the following two machines for use in its production process.

Machine A: The cash price of this machine was $58,000. Related expenditures included: sales tax $2,750, shipping costs $100, insurance during shipping $75, installation and testing costs $75, and $90 of oil and lubricants to be used with the machinery during its first year of operation. Bourgeois estimates that the useful life of the machine is 4 years with a $5,000 salvage value remaining at the end of that time period.

Machine B: The recorded cost of this machine was $120,000. Bourgeois estimates that the useful life of the machine is 4 years with a $10,000 salvage value remaining at the end of that time period.

Instructions

(a) Prepare the following for Machine A.

(1) The journal entry to record its purchase on January 1, 2015.

(a) (2) $14,000

(2) The journal entry to record annual depreciation at December 31, 2015, assuming the straight-line method of depreciation is used.

(b) Calculate the amount of depreciation expense that Bourgeois should record for Machine B each year of its useful life under the following assumption.

(1) Bourgeois uses the straight-line method of depreciation.

(2) Bourgeois uses the declining-balance method. The rate used is twice the straight-line rate.

(3) Bourgeois uses the units-of-activity method and estimates the useful life of the machine is 25,000 units. Actual usage is as follows: 2015, 5,500 units; 2016, 7,000 units; 2017, 8,000 units; 2018, 4,500 units.

(c) Which method used to calculate depreciation on Machine B reports the lowest amount of depreciation expense in year 1 (2015)? The lowest amount in year 4 (2018)? The lowest total amount over the 4-year period?

Calculate revisions to depreciation expense.

(LO 2)

P9-4B At the beginning of 2013, Sullivan Company acquired equipment costing $300,000. It was estimated that this equipment would have a useful life of 6 years and a salvage value of $30,000 at that time. The straight-line method of depreciation was considered the most appropriate to use with this type of equipment. Depreciation is to be recorded at the end of each year.

During 2015 (the third year of the equipment's life), the company's engineers reconsidered their expectations and estimated that the equipment's useful life would probably be 7 years (in total) instead of 6 years. The estimated salvage value was not changed at that time. However, during 2018, the estimated salvage value was reduced to $5,000.

Instructions

Indicate how much depreciation expense should be recorded for this equipment each year by completing the following table.

Year	Depreciation Expense	Accumulated Depreciation
2013		
2014		
2015		
2016		
2017		
2018		
2019		

2019 depreciation expense, $48,500

P9-5B At December 31, 2015, Torrealba Company reported the following as plant assets.

Land		$ 2,000,000
Buildings	$20,000,000	
Less: Accumulated depreciation—buildings	8,000,000	12,000,000
Equipment	30,000,000	
Less: Accumulated depreciation—equipment	4,000,000	26,000,000
Total plant assets		$40,000,000

Journalize a series of equipment transactions related to purchase, sale, retirement, and depreciation.

(LO 2, 4, 7)

During 2016, the following selected cash transactions occurred.

April 1	Purchased land for $1,200,000.
May 1	Sold equipment that cost $450,000 when purchased on January 1, 2012. The equipment was sold for $260,000.
June 1	Sold land purchased on June 1, 2006, for $1,000,000. The land cost $340,000.
July 1	Purchased equipment for $1,500,000.
Dec. 31	Retired equipment that cost $300,000 when purchased on December 31, 2006. No salvage value was received.

Instructions
(a) Journalize the above transactions. Torrealba uses straight-line depreciation for buildings and equipment. The buildings are estimated to have a 50-year useful life and no salvage value. The equipment is estimated to have a 10-year useful life and no salvage value. Update depreciation on assets disposed of at the time of sale or retirement.
(b) Record adjusting entries for depreciation for 2016.
(c) Prepare the plant assets section of Torrealba's balance sheet at December 31, 2016.

(b) Depreciation Expense—Buildings $400,000; Equipment $3,000,000

(c) Total plant assets $38,660,000

P9-6B Dickey's has equipment that cost $45,000 and that has been depreciated $26,000.

Instructions
Record the disposal under the following assumptions.

(a) It was scrapped as having no value.
(b) It was sold for $29,000.
(c) It was sold for $10,000.

Record disposals.

(LO 4)

(b) $10,000 gain

P9-7B The intangible assets section of Willingham Company at December 31, 2015, is presented below.

Patents ($100,000 cost less $10,000 amortization)	$ 90,000
Copyrights ($60,000 cost less $24,000 amortization)	36,000
Total	$126,000

Prepare entries to record transactions related to acquisition and amortization of intangibles; prepare the intangible assets section.

(LO 6, 7)

The patent was acquired in January 2015 and has a useful life of 10 years. The copyright was acquired in January 2012 and also has a useful life of 10 years. The following cash transactions may have affected intangible assets during 2016.

Jan. 2	Paid $36,000 legal costs to successfully defend the patent against infringement by another company.
Jan.–June	Developed a new product, incurring $230,000 in research and development costs. A patent was granted for the product on July 1. Its useful life is equal to its legal life.
Sept. 1	Paid $125,000 to an X-Games star to appear in commercials advertising the company's products. The commercials will air in September and October.
Oct. 1	Acquired a copyright for $300,000. The copyright has a useful life of 50 years.

Instructions
(a) Prepare journal entries to record the transactions above.
(b) Prepare journal entries to record the 2016 amortization expense for intangible assets.
(c) Prepare the intangible assets section of the balance sheet at December 31, 2016.
(d) ———► Prepare the note to the financials on Willingham's intangibles as of December 31, 2016.

(b) Amortization Expense (patents) $14,000; Amortization Expense (copyrights) $7,500

(c) Total intangible assets, $440,500

P9-8B Due to rapid turnover in the accounting department, a number of transactions involving intangible assets were improperly recorded by Farnsworth Company in 2015.

1. Farnsworth developed a new manufacturing process, incurring research and development costs of $110,000. The company also purchased a patent for $50,000. In early January,

Prepare entries to correct errors made in recording and amortizing intangible assets.

(LO 6)

Farnsworth capitalized $160,000 as the cost of the patents. Patent amortization expense of $16,000 was recorded based on a 10-year useful life.

2. On July 1, 2015, Farnsworth purchased a small company and as a result acquired goodwill of $200,000. Farnsworth recorded a half-year's amortization in 2015, based on a 50-year life ($2,000 amortization). The goodwill has an indefinite life.

R&D Exp. $110,000

Instructions

Prepare all journal entries necessary to correct any errors made during 2015. Assume the books have not yet been closed for 2015.

Calculate and comment on asset turnover.

(LO 7)

P9-9B Auer Corporation and Marte Corporation, two corporations of roughly the same size, are both involved in the manufacture of canoes and sea kayaks. Each company depreciates its plant assets using the straight-line approach. An investigation of their financial statements reveals the following information.

	Auer Corp.	**Marte Corp.**
Net income	$ 300,000	$ 325,000
Sales revenue	1,050,000	945,000
Average total assets	1,000,000	1,050,000
Average plant assets	750,000	770,000

Instructions

(a) For each company, calculate the asset turnover.

(b) ━━━━━▶ Based on your calculations in part (a), comment on the relative effectiveness of the two companies in using their assets to generate sales and produce net income.

PROBLEMS: SET C

Visit the book's companion website, at **www.wiley.com/college/weygandt**, and choose the Student Companion site to access Problem Set C.

COMPREHENSIVE PROBLEM: CHAPTERS 3 TO 9

CP9 Hassellhouf Company's trial balance at December 31, 2015, is presented below and on page 471. All 2015 transactions have been recorded except for the items described on page 471.

	Debit	**Credit**
Cash	$ 28,000	
Accounts Receivable	36,800	
Notes Receivable	10,000	
Interest Receivable	–0–	
Inventory	36,200	
Prepaid Insurance	3,600	
Land	20,000	
Buildings	150,000	
Equipment	60,000	
Patents	9,000	
Allowance for Doubtful Accounts		$ 500
Accumulated Depreciation—Buildings		50,000
Accumulated Depreciation—Equipment		24,000
Accounts Payable		27,300
Salaries and Wages Payable		–0–
Unearned Rent Revenue		6,000
Notes Payable (due in 2016)		11,000
Interest Payable		–0–
Notes Payable (due after 2016)		30,000
Common Stock		50,000
Retained Earnings		63,600
Dividends	12,000	

	Debit	Credit
Sales Revenue		905,000
Interest Revenue		–0–
Rent Revenue		–0–
Gain on Disposal of Plant Assets		–0–
Bad Debt Expense	–0–	
Cost of Goods Sold	630,000	
Depreciation Expense	–0–	
Insurance Expense	–0–	
Interest Expense	–0–	
Other Operating Expenses	61,800	
Amortization Expense	–0–	
Salaries and Wages Expense	110,000	
Total	$1,167,400	$1,167,400

Unrecorded transactions:

1. On May 1, 2015, Hassellhouf purchased equipment for $21,200 plus sales taxes of $1,600 (all paid in cash).
2. On July 1, 2015, Hassellhouf sold for $3,500 equipment which originally cost $5,000. Accumulated depreciation on this equipment at January 1, 2015, was $1,800; 2015 depreciation prior to the sale of the equipment was $450.
3. On December 31, 2015, Hassellhouf sold for $9,000 on account inventory that cost $6,300.
4. Hassellhouf estimates that uncollectible accounts receivable at year-end is $4,000.
5. The note receivable is a one-year, 8% note dated April 1, 2015. No interest has been recorded.
6. The balance in prepaid insurance represents payment of a $3,600 6-month premium on September 1, 2015.
7. The building is being depreciated using the straight-line method over 30 years. The salvage value is $30,000.
8. The equipment owned prior to this year is being depreciated using the straight-line method over 5 years. The salvage value is 10% of cost.
9. The equipment purchased on May 1, 2015, is being depreciated using the straight-line method over 5 years, with a salvage value of $1,800.
10. The patent was acquired on January 1, 2015, and has a useful life of 10 years from that date.
11. Unpaid salaries and wages at December 31, 2015, total $5,200.
12. The unearned rent revenue of $6,000 was received on December 1, 2015, for 3 months' rent.
13. Both the short-term and long-term notes payable are dated January 1, 2015, and carry a 9% interest rate. All interest is payable in the next 12 months.

Instructions
(a) Prepare journal entries for the transactions listed above.
(b) Prepare an updated December 31, 2015, trial balance.   (b) Totals $1,205,040
(c) Prepare a 2015 income statement and a retained earnings statement.
(d) Prepare a December 31, 2015, classified balance sheet.   (d) Total assets $259,200

CONTINUING COOKIE CHRONICLE

(*Note:* This is a continuation of the Cookie Chronicle from Chapters 1 through 8.)

CCC9 Natalie is also thinking of buying a van that will be used only for business. Natalie is concerned about the impact of the van's cost on her income statement and balance sheet. She has come to you for advice on calculating the van's depreciation.

Go to the book's companion website, **www.wiley.com/college/weygandt**, *to see the completion of this problem.*

Financial Reporting and Analysis

Financial Reporting Problem: Apple Inc.

BYP9-1 The financial statements of Apple Inc. are presented in Appendix A. Instructions for accessing and using the company's complete annual report, including the notes to the financial statements, are also provided in Appendix A.

Instructions
Refer to Apple's financial statements and answer the following questions.

(a) What was the total cost and book value of property, plant, and equipment at September 24, 2011?
(b) What was the amount of depreciation and amortization expense for each of the three years 2009–2011?
(c) Using the statement of cash flows, what is the amount of capital spending in 2011 and 2010?
(d) Where does the company disclose its intangible assets, and what types of intangibles did it have at September 24, 2011?

Comparative Analysis Problem:
PepsiCo, Inc. vs. The Coca-Cola Company

BYP9-2 PepsiCo, Inc.'s financial statements are presented in Appendix B. Financial statements of The Coca-Cola Company are presented in Appendix C. Instructions for accessing and using the complete annual reports of PepsiCo and Coca-Cola, including the notes to the financial statements, are also provided in Appendices B and C, respectively.

Instructions
(a) Compute the asset turnover for each company for 2011.
(b) What conclusions concerning the efficiency of assets can be drawn from these data?

Comparative Analysis Problem:
Amazon.com, Inc. vs. Wal-Mart Stores, Inc.

BYP9-3 Amazon.com, Inc.'s financial statements are presented in Appendix D. Financial statements of Wal-Mart Stores, Inc. are presented in Appendix E. Instructions for accessing and using the complete annual reports of Amazon and Wal-Mart, including the notes to the financial statements, are also provided in Appendices D and E, respectively.

Instructions
(a) Compute the asset turnover for each company for 2011.
(b) What conclusions concerning the efficiency of assets can be drawn from these data?

Real-World Focus

BYP9-4 A company's annual report identifies the amount of its plant assets and the depreciation method used.

Address: **www.annualreports.com**, or go to **www.wiley.com/college/weygandt**

Steps
1. Select a particular company.
2. Search by company name.
3. Follow instructions below.

Instructions

Answer the following questions.

(a) What is the name of the company?
(b) What is the Internet address of the annual report?
(c) At fiscal year-end, what is the net amount of its plant assets?
(d) What is the accumulated depreciation?
(e) Which method of depreciation does the company use?

Critical Thinking

Decision-Making Across the Organization

BYP9-5 Pinson Company and Estes Company are two proprietorships that are similar in many respects. One difference is that Pinson Company uses the straight-line method and Estes Company uses the declining-balance method at double the straight-line rate. On January 2, 2013, both companies acquired the depreciable assets shown below.

Asset	Cost	Salvage Value	Useful Life
Buildings	$360,000	$20,000	40 years
Equipment	130,000	10,000	10 years

Including the appropriate depreciation charges, annual net income for the companies in the years 2013, 2014, and 2015 and total income for the 3 years were as follows.

	2013	2014	2015	Total
Pinson Company	$84,000	$88,400	$90,000	$262,400
Estes Company	68,000	76,000	85,000	229,000

At December 31, 2015, the balance sheets of the two companies are similar except that Estes Company has more cash than Pinson Company.

Lynda Peace is interested in buying one of the companies. She comes to you for advice.

Instructions

With the class divided into groups, answer the following.

(a) Determine the annual and total depreciation recorded by each company during the 3 years.
(b) Assuming that Estes Company also uses the straight-line method of depreciation instead of the declining-balance method as in (a), prepare comparative income data for the 3 years.
(c) Which company should Lynda Peace buy? Why?

Communication Activity

BYP9-6 The chapter presented some concerns regarding the current accounting standards for research and development expenditures.

Instructions

Assume that you are either (a) the president of a company that is very dependent on ongoing research and development, writing a memo to the FASB complaining about the current accounting standards regarding research and development, or (b) the FASB member defending the current standards regarding research and development. Your memo should address the following questions.

1. By requiring expensing of R&D, do you think companies will spend less on R&D? Why or why not? What are the possible implications for the competitiveness of U.S. companies?
2. If a company makes a commitment to spend money for R&D, it must believe it has future benefits. Shouldn't these costs therefore be capitalized just like the purchase of any long-lived asset that is believed to have future benefits?

Ethics Case

BYP9-7 Turner Container Company is suffering declining sales of its principal product, nonbio-degradeable plastic cartons. The president, Robert Griffin, instructs his controller, Alexis Landrum, to lengthen asset lives to reduce depreciation expense. A processing line of automated plastic extruding equipment, purchased for $3.5 million in January 2015, was originally estimated to have a useful life of 8 years and a salvage value of $300,000. Depreciation has been recorded for 2 years on that basis. Robert wants the estimated life changed to 12 years total, and the straight-line method continued. Alexis is hesitant to make the change, believing it is unethical to increase net income in this manner. Robert says, "Hey, the life is only an estimate, and I've heard that our competition uses a 12-year life on their production equipment."

Instructions
(a) Who are the stakeholders in this situation?
(b) Is the change in asset life unethical, or is it simply a good business practice by an astute president?
(c) What is the effect of Robert Griffin's proposed change on income before taxes in the year of change?

All About You

BYP9-8 The Feature Story at the beginning of the chapter discussed the company Rent-A-Wreck. Note that the trade name Rent-A-Wreck is a very important asset to the company, as it creates immediate product identification. As indicated in the chapter, companies invest substantial sums to ensure that their product is well-known to the consumer. Test your knowledge of who owns some famous brands and their impact on the financial statements.

Instructions
(a) Provide an answer to the five multiple-choice questions below.
    (1) Which company owns both Taco Bell and Pizza Hut?
        (a) McDonald's.   **(c)** Yum Brands.
        (b) CKE.   **(d)** Wendy's.
    (2) Dairy Queen belongs to:
        (a) Breyer.   **(c)** GE.
        (b) Berkshire Hathaway.   **(d)** The Coca-Cola Company.
    (3) Philip Morris, the cigarette maker, is owned by:
        (a) Altria.   **(c)** Boeing.
        (b) GE.   **(d)** ExxonMobil.
    (4) AOL, a major Internet provider, belongs to:
        (a) Microsoft.   **(c)** NBC.
        (b) Cisco.   **(d)** Time Warner.
    (5) ESPN, the sports broadcasting network, is owned by:
        (a) Procter & Gamble.   **(c)** Walt Disney.
        (b) Altria.   **(d)** The Coca-Cola Company.
(b) How do you think the value of these brands is reported on the appropriate company's balance sheet?

FASB Codification Activity

BYP9-9 If your school has a subscription to the FASB Codification, go to **http://aaahq.org/ascLogin.cfm** to log in and prepare responses to the following.

(a) What does it mean to capitalize an item?
(b) What is the definition provided for an intangible asset?
(c) Your great-uncle, who is a CPA, is impressed that you are taking an accounting class. Based on his experience, he believes that depreciation is something that companies do based on past practice, not on the basis of authoritative guidance. Provide the authoritative literature to support the practice of fixed-asset depreciation.

Answers to Chapter Questions

Answers to Insight and Accounting Across the Organization Questions

p. 433 Many U.S. Firms Use Leases **Q:** Why might airline managers choose to lease rather than purchase their planes? **A:** The reasons for leasing include favorable tax treatment, better financing options, increased flexibility, reduced risk of obsolescence, and often less debt shown on the balance sheet.

p. 446 Sustainability Report Please **Q:** Why do you believe companies issue sustainability reports? **A:** It is important that companies clearly describe the things they value in addition to overall profitability. Most companies recognize that the health, safety, and environmental protections of their workforce and community are important components in developing strategies for continued growth and longevity. Without a strong commitment to the principles of corporate social responsibility, it is unlikely that a company will be able to maintain long-term stability and profitability. The development of a sustainability report helps companies to consider these issues and develop measures to assess whether they are meeting their goals in this area.

p. 449 Should Companies Write Up Goodwill? **Q:** Do you think that this treatment would be allowed under U.S. GAAP? **A:** The write-down of assets would have been allowed if it could be shown that the assets had declined in value (an impairment). However, the creation of goodwill to offset the write-down would not have been allowed. Goodwill can be recorded only when it results from the acquisition of a business. It cannot be recorded as the result of being created internally.

Answers to Self-Test Questions

1. d ($24,000 + $1,200 + $200 + $400) **2.** b **3.** d [($400,000 − $10,000) ÷ 5] × 2 **4.** d **5.** b $60,000 × 25% = $15,000; ($60,000 − $15,000) × 25% = $11,250 **6.** b **7.** d [($60,000 − $12,000) ÷ 10] × 2 = $9,600; ($60,000 − $9,600 − $2,000) ÷ 4 **8.** d **9.** a [($80,000 ÷ 10) × 4.5] = $36,000; ($80,000 − $36,000) − $26,000 **10.** c ($12 million ÷ 20 million) × 2 million **11.** d **12.** b **13.** c **14.** c $180,000 ÷ [($200,000 + $300,000) ÷ 2] ***15.** a ($35,000 + $10,000) ***16.** d

A Look at IFRS

IFRS follows most of the same principles as GAAP in the accounting for property, plant, and equipment. There are, however, some significant differences in the implementation. IFRS allows the use of revaluation of property, plant, and equipment, and it also requires the use of component depreciation. In addition, there are some significant differences in the accounting for both intangible assets and impairments.

> **LEARNING OBJECTIVE 9**
>
> Compare the accounting procedure for long-lived assets under GAAP and IFRS.

Key Points

- The definition for plant assets for both IFRS and GAAP is essentially the same.

- Both IFRS and GAAP follow the historical cost principle when accounting for property, plant, and equipment at date of acquisition. Cost consists of all expenditures necessary to acquire the asset and make it ready for its intended use.

- Under both IFRS and GAAP, interest costs incurred during construction are capitalized. Recently, IFRS converged to GAAP requirements in this area.

- IFRS, like GAAP, capitalizes all direct costs in self-constructed assets such as raw materials and labor. IFRS does not address the capitalization of fixed overhead although in practice these costs are generally capitalized.

- IFRS also views depreciation as an allocation of cost over an asset's useful life. IFRS permits the same depreciation methods (e.g., straight-line, accelerated, and units-of-activity) as GAAP. However, a major difference is that IFRS requires component depreciation. **Component depreciation** specifies that any significant parts of a depreciable asset that have different estimated useful lives should be separately depreciated. Component depreciation is allowed under GAAP but is seldom used.

To illustrate, assume that Lexure Construction builds an office building for $4,000,000, not including the cost of the land. If the $4,000,000 is allocated over the 40-year useful life of the building, Lexure reports $100,000 of depreciation per year, assuming straight-line depreciation and no disposal value. However, assume that $320,000 of the cost of the building relates to personal property and $600,000 relates to land improvements. The personal property has a depreciable life of 5 years, and the land improvements have a depreciable life of 10 years. In accordance with IFRS, Lexure must use component depreciation. It must reclassify $320,000 of the cost of the building to personal property and $600,000 to the cost of land improvements. Assuming that Lexure uses straight-line depreciation, component depreciation for the first year of the office building is computed as follows.

Building cost adjusted ($4,000,000 − $320,000 − $600,000)	$3,080,000
Building cost depreciation per year ($3,080,000/40)	$ 77,000
Personal property depreciation ($320,000/5)	64,000
Land improvements depreciation ($600,000/10)	60,000
Total component depreciation in first year	$ 201,000

- IFRS uses the term **residual value** rather than salvage value to refer to an owner's estimate of an asset's value at the end of its useful life for that owner.

- IFRS allows companies to revalue plant assets to fair value at the reporting date. Companies that choose to use the revaluation framework must follow revaluation procedures. If revaluation is used, it must be applied to all assets in a class of assets. Assets that are experiencing rapid price changes must be revalued on an annual basis, otherwise less frequent revaluation is acceptable.

  To illustrate asset revaluation accounting, assume that Pernice Company applies revaluation to plant assets with a carrying value of $1,000,000, a useful life of 5 years, and no residual value. Pernice makes the following journal entries in year 1, assuming straight-line depreciation.

Depreciation Expense	200,000	
Accumulated Depreciation—Plant Assets		200,000
(To record depreciation expense in year 1)		

After this entry, Pernice's plant assets have a carrying amount of $800,000 ($1,000,000 − $200,000). At the end of year 1, independent appraisers determine that the asset has a fair value of $850,000. To report the plant assets at fair value, or $850,000, Pernice eliminates the Accumulated Depreciation—Plant Assets account, reduces Plant Assets to its fair value of $850,000, and records Revaluation Surplus of $50,000. The entry to record the revaluation is as follows.

Accumulated Depreciation—Plant Assets	200,000	
Plant Assets		150,000
Revaluation Surplus		50,000
(To record adjusting the plant assets to fair value)		

Thus, Pernice follows a two-step process. First, Pernice records depreciation based on the cost basis of $1,000,000. As a result, it reports depreciation expense of $200,000 on the income statement. Second, it records the revaluation. It does this by eliminating any accumulated depreciation, adjusting the recorded value of the plant assets to fair value, and debiting or crediting the Revaluation Surplus account. In this example, the revaluation surplus is $50,000, which is the difference between the fair value of $850,000 and the book value of $800,000. Revaluation surplus is an example of an item reported as other comprehensive income, as discussed in the *A Look at IFRS* section of Chapter 5. Pernice now reports the following information in its statement of financial position at the end of year 1.

Plant assets ($1,000,000 − $150,000)	$850,000
Accumulated depreciation—plant assets	0
	$850,000
Revaluation surplus (equity)	$ 50,000

As indicated, $850,000 is the new basis of the asset. Pernice reports depreciation expense of $200,000 in the income statement and $50,000 in other comprehensive income. Assuming no change in the total useful life, depreciation in year 2 will be $212,500 ($850,000 ÷ 4).

- Under both GAAP and IFRS, changes in the depreciation method used and changes in useful life are handled in current and future periods. Prior periods are not affected. GAAP recently conformed to international standards in the accounting for changes in depreciation methods.

- The accounting for subsequent expenditures, such as ordinary repairs and additions, are essentially the same under IFRS and GAAP.

- The accounting for plant asset disposals is essentially the same under IFRS and GAAP.

- Initial costs to acquire natural resources are essentially the same under IFRS and GAAP.

- The definition of intangible assets is essentially the same under IFRS and GAAP.

- As in GAAP, under IFRS the costs associated with research and development are segregated into the two components. Costs in the research phase are always expensed under both IFRS and GAAP. Under IFRS, however, costs in the development phase are capitalized as Development Costs once technological feasibility is achieved.

  To illustrate, assume that Laser Scanner Company spent $1 million on research and $2 million on development of new products. Of the $2 million in development costs, $500,000 was incurred prior to technological feasibility and $1,500,000 was incurred after technological feasibility had been demonstrated. The company would record these costs as follows.

Research Expense	1,000,000	
Development Expense	500,000	
Development Costs	1,500,000	
Cash		3,000,000
(To record research and development costs)		

- IFRS permits revaluation of intangible assets (except for goodwill). GAAP prohibits revaluation of intangible assets.

- IFRS requires an impairment test at each reporting date for plant assets and intangibles, and records an impairment if the asset's carrying amount exceeds its recoverable amount. The recoverable amount is the higher of the asset's fair value less costs to sell or its value-in-use. Value-in-use is the future cash flows to be derived from the particular asset, discounted to present value. Under GAAP, impairment loss is measured as the excess of the carrying amount over the asset's fair value.

- IFRS allows reversal of impairment losses when there has been a change in economic conditions or in the expected use of the asset. Under GAAP, impairment losses cannot be reversed for assets to be held and used; the impairment loss results in a new cost basis for the asset. IFRS and GAAP are similar in the accounting for impairments of assets held for disposal.

- The accounting for exchanges of nonmonetary assets has recently converged between IFRS and GAAP. GAAP now requires that gains on exchanges of nonmonetary assets be recognized if the exchange has commercial substance. This is the same framework used in IFRS.

Looking to the Future

With respect to revaluations, as part of the conceptual framework project, the Boards will examine the measurement bases used in accounting. It is too early to say whether a converged conceptual framework will recommend fair value measurement (and revaluation accounting) for plant assets and intangibles. However, this is likely to be one of the more contentious issues, given the long-standing use of historical cost as a measurement basis in GAAP.

The IASB and FASB have identified a project that would consider expanded recognition of internally generated intangible assets. IFRS permits more recognition of intangibles compared to GAAP. Thus, it will be challenging to develop converged standards for intangible assets, given the long-standing prohibition on capitalizing internally generated intangible assets and research and development costs in GAAP.

IFRS Practice

IFRS Self-Test Questions

1. Which of the following statements is **correct**?
   (a) Both IFRS and GAAP permit revaluation of property, plant, and equipment and intangible assets (except for goodwill).
   (b) IFRS permits revaluation of property, plant, and equipment and intangible assets (except for goodwill).
   (c) Both IFRS and GAAP permit revaluation of property, plant, and equipment but not intangible assets.
   (d) GAAP permits revaluation of property, plant, and equipment but not intangible assets.

2. International Company has land that cost $450,000 but now has a fair value of $600,000. International Company decides to use the revaluation method specified in IFRS to account for the land. Which of the following statements is **correct**?
   (a) International Company must continue to report the land at $450,000.
   (b) International Company would report a net income increase of $150,000 due to an increase in the value of the land.
   (c) International Company would debit Revaluation Surplus for $150,000.
   (d) International Company would credit Revaluation Surplus by $150,000.

3. Francisco Corporation is constructing a new building at a total initial cost of $10,000,000. The building is expected to have a useful life of 50 years with no residual value. The building's finished surfaces (e.g., roof cover and floor cover) are 5% of this cost and have a useful life of 20 years. Building services systems (e.g., electric, heating, and plumbing) are 20% of the cost and have a useful life of 25 years. The depreciation in the first year using component depreciation, assuming straight-line depreciation with no residual value, is:
   (a) $200,000.
   (b) $215,000.
   (c) $255,000.
   (d) None of the above.

4. Research and development costs are:
   (a) expensed under GAAP.
   (b) expensed under IFRS.
   (c) expensed under both GAAP and IFRS.
   (d) None of the above.

5. Under IFRS, value-in-use is defined as:
   (a) net realizable value.
   (b) fair value.
   (c) future cash flows discounted to present value.
   (d) total future undiscounted cash flows.

IFRS Exercises

IFRS9-1 What is component depreciation, and when must it be used?

IFRS9-2 What is revaluation of plant assets? When should revaluation be applied?

IFRS9-3 Some product development expenditures are recorded as development expenses and others as development costs. Explain the difference between these accounts and how a company decides which classification is appropriate.

IFRS9-4 Beckham Company constructed a warehouse for $280,000. Beckham estimates that the warehouse has a useful life of 20 years and no residual value. Construction records indicate that $50,000 of the cost of the warehouse relates to its heating, ventilation, and air conditioning (HVAC) system, which has an estimated useful life of only 10 years. Compute the first year of depreciation expense using straight-line component depreciation.

IFRS9-5 At the end of its first year of operations, Escobar Company chose to use the revaluation framework allowed under IFRS. Escobar's ledger shows Plant Assets $475,000 and Accumulated Depreciation—Plant Assets $60,000. Prepare journal entries to record the following.

(a) Independent appraisers determine that the plant assets have a fair value of $460,000.
(b) Independent appraisers determine that the plant assets have a fair value of $400,000.

IFRS9-6 Odessa Industries spent $350,000 on research and $600,000 on development of a new product. Of the $600,000 in development costs, $400,000 was incurred prior to technological feasibility and $200,000 after technological feasibility had been demonstrated. Prepare the journal entry to record research and development costs.

International Financial Statement Analysis: Zetar plc

IFRS9-7 The financial statements of Zetar plc are presented in Appendix F. Instructions for accessing and using the company's complete annual report, including the notes to its financial statements, are also provided in Appendix F.

Instructions
Use the company's annual report to answer the following questions.

(a) According to the notes to the financial statements, what method or methods does the company use to depreciate "plant and equipment?" What rate does it use to depreciate plant and equipment?

(b) According to the notes to the financial statements, how often is goodwill tested for impairment?

(c) Using the notes to the financial statements, as well as information from the statement of cash flows, prepare the journal entry to record the disposal of property, plant, and equipment during 2011. (Round your amounts to the nearest thousand.)

Answers to IFRS Self-Test Questions
1. b **2.** d **3.** c ($10,000,000 ×.05/20) + ($10,000,000 × .20/25) + ($10,000,000 × .75/50) **4.** a
5. c

 The Navigator

10 | Liabilities

Feature Story

Financing His Dreams

What would you do if you had a great idea for a new product but couldn't come up with the cash to get the business off the ground? Small businesses often cannot attract investors. Nor can they obtain traditional debt financing through bank loans or bond issuances. Instead, they often resort to unusual, and costly, forms of nontraditional financing.

Such was the case for Wilbert Murdock. Murdock grew up in a New York housing project and always had great ambitions. This ambitious spirit led him into some business ventures that failed: a medical diagnostic tool, a device to eliminate carpal tunnel syndrome, custom-designed sneakers, and a device to keep people from falling asleep while driving.

Another idea was computerized golf clubs that analyze a golfer's swing and provide immediate feedback. Murdock saw great potential in the idea. Many golfers are willing to shell out considerable sums of money for devices that might improve their game. But Murdock had no cash to develop his product, and banks and other lenders had shied away. Rather than give up,

Murdock resorted to credit cards—in a big way. He quickly owed $25,000 to credit card companies.

While funding a business with credit cards might sound unusual, it isn't. A recent study found that one-third of businesses with fewer than 20 employees financed at least part of their operations with credit cards. As Murdock explained, credit cards are an appealing way to finance a start-up because "credit-card companies don't care how the money is spent." However, they do care how they are paid. And so Murdock faced high interest charges and a barrage of credit card collection letters.

Murdock's debt forced him to sacrifice nearly everything in order to keep his business afloat. His car stopped running, he barely had enough money to buy food, and he lived and worked out of a dimly lit apartment in his mother's basement. Through it all he tried to maintain a positive spirit, joking that, if he becomes successful, he might some day get to appear in an American Express commercial.

Source: Rodney Ho, "Banking on Plastic: To Finance a Dream, Many Entrepreneurs Binge on Credit Cards," *Wall Street Journal* (March 9, 1998), p. A1.

✔ **The Navigator**

- Scan Learning Objectives
- Read Feature Story
- Read Preview
- Read text and answer **DO IT!** p. 486
  - p. 487 ■ p. 493 ■ p. 498 ■ p. 499
  - p. 502
- Work Comprehensive **DO IT!** p. 503
- Review Summary of Learning Objectives
- Answer Self-Test Questions
- Complete Assignments
- Go to *WileyPLUS* for practice and tutorials

 Read **A Look at IFRS** p. 539

Learning Objectives ✔ The Navigator

After studying this chapter, you should be able to:

[1] Explain a current liability, and identify the major types of current liabilities.

[2] Describe the accounting for notes payable.

[3] Explain the accounting for other current liabilities.

[4] Explain why bonds are issued, and identify the types of bonds.

[5] Prepare the entries for the issuance of bonds and interest expense.

[6] Describe the entries when bonds are redeemed or converted.

[7] Describe the accounting for long-term notes payable.

[8] Identify the methods for the presentation and analysis of long-term liabilities.

Cary Westfall/iStockphoto

Preview of Chapter 10

✔ **The Navigator**

Inventor-entrepreneur Wilbert Murdock, as you can tell from the Feature Story, had to use multiple credit cards to finance his business ventures. Murdock's credit card debts would be classified as **current liabilities** because they are due every month. Yet, by making minimal payments and paying high interest each month, Murdock used this credit source long-term. Some credit card balances remain outstanding for years as they accumulate interest.

Earlier, we defined liabilities as creditors' claims on total assets and as existing debts and obligations. These claims, debts, and obligations must be settled or paid at some time **in the future** by the transfer of assets or services. The future date on which they are due or payable (maturity date) is a significant feature of liabilities. This "future date" feature gives rise to two basic classifications of liabilities: (1) current liabilities and (2) long-term liabilities. Our discussion in this chapter is divided into these two classifications.

The content and organization of Chapter 10 are as follows.

LIABILITIES	
Current Liabilities	**Long-Term Liabilities**
• Notes payable	• Bond basics
• Sales taxes payable	• Accounting for bond issues
• Payroll and payroll taxes payable	• Accounting for bond redemptions
• Unearned revenues	• Accounting for long-term notes payable
• Current maturities of long-term debt	
• Statement presentation and analysis	• Statement presentation and analysis

Current Liabilities

LEARNING OBJECTIVE   1

Explain a current liability, and identify the major types of current liabilities.

As explained in Chapter 4, a **current liability** is a debt that a company expects to pay within one year or the operating cycle, whichever is longer. Debts that do not meet this criterion are classified as long-term liabilities.

Companies must carefully monitor the relationship of current liabilities to current assets. This relationship is critical in evaluating a company's short-term debt-paying ability. A company that has more current liabilities than current assets may not be able to meet its current obligations when they become due.

Current liabilities include notes payable, accounts payable, and unearned revenues. They also include accrued liabilities such as taxes, salaries and wages, and interest payable. In the sections that follow, we discuss a few of the common types of current liabilities.

Notes Payable

LEARNING OBJECTIVE   2

Describe the accounting for notes payable.

Companies record obligations in the form of written notes as **notes payable**. Notes payable are often used instead of accounts payable because they give the lender formal proof of the obligation in case legal remedies are needed to collect the debt. Companies frequently issue notes payable to meet short-term financing needs. Notes payable usually require the borrower to pay interest.

Notes are issued for varying periods of time. **Those due for payment within one year of the balance sheet date are usually classified as current liabilities.**

To illustrate the accounting for notes payable, assume that First National Bank agrees to lend $100,000 on September 1, 2015, if Cole Williams Co. signs a $100,000, 12%, four-month note maturing on January 1. When a company issues an interest-bearing note, the amount of assets it receives upon issuance of the note generally equals the note's face value. Cole Williams Co. therefore will receive $100,000 cash and will make the following journal entry.

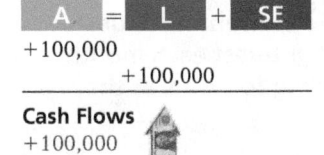

+100,000
    +100,000

Cash Flows
+100,000

Sept. 1	Cash	100,000	
	Notes Payable		100,000
	(To record issuance of 12%, 4-month note		
	to First National Bank)		

Interest accrues over the life of the note, and the company must periodically record that accrual. If Cole Williams Co. prepares financial statements annually, it makes an adjusting entry at December 31 to recognize interest expense and interest payable of $4,000 ($100,000 × 12% × 4/12). Illustration 10-1 shows the formula for computing interest and its application to Cole Williams Co.'s note.

Illustration 10-1
Formula for computing interest

Face Value of Note	×	Annual Interest Rate	×	Time in Terms of One Year	=	Interest
$100,000	×	12%	×	4/12	=	$4,000

Cole Williams makes an adjusting entry as follows.

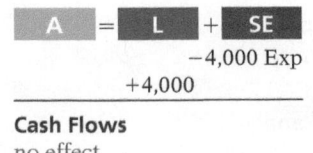

−4,000 Exp
    +4,000

Cash Flows
no effect

Dec. 31	Interest Expense	4,000	
	Interest Payable		4,000
	(To accrue interest for 4 months on		
	First National Bank note)		

In the December 31 financial statements, the current liabilities section of the balance sheet will show notes payable $100,000 and interest payable $4,000. In addition, the company will report interest expense of $4,000 under "Other expenses and losses" in the income statement. If Cole Williams Co. prepared financial statements monthly, the adjusting entry at the end of each month would be $1,000 ($100,000 × 12% × 1/12).

At maturity (January 1, 2016), Cole Williams Co. must pay the face value of the note ($100,000) plus $4,000 interest ($100,000 × 12% × 4/12). It records payment of the note and accrued interest as follows.

Jan. 1	Notes Payable	100,000	
	Interest Payable	4,000	
	Cash		104,000
	(To record payment of First National Bank interest-bearing note and accrued interest at maturity)		

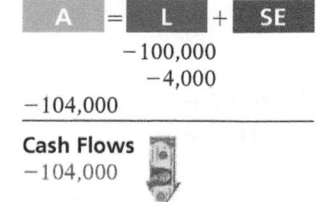

A = L + SE
−100,000
−4,000
−104,000

Cash Flows
−104,000

Sales Taxes Payable

As a consumer, you know that many of the products you purchase at retail stores are subject to sales taxes. Many states also are now collecting sales taxes on purchases made on the Internet as well. Sales taxes are expressed as a percentage of the sales price. The selling company collects the tax from the customer when the sale occurs. Periodically (usually monthly), the retailer remits the collections to the state's department of revenue. Collecting sales taxes is important. For example, the state of New York recently sued Sprint Corporation for $300 million for its alleged failure to collect sales taxes on phone calls.

Under most state sales tax laws, the selling company must enter separately in the cash register the amount of the sale and the amount of the sales tax collected. (Gasoline sales are a major exception.) The company then uses the cash register readings to credit Sales Revenue and Sales Taxes Payable. For example, if the March 25 cash register reading for Cooley Grocery shows sales of $10,000 and sales taxes of $600 (sales tax rate of 6%), the journal entry is:

Mar. 25	Cash	10,600	
	Sales Revenue		10,000
	Sales Taxes Payable		600
	(To record daily sales and sales taxes)		

> **LEARNING OBJECTIVE 3**
>
> **Explain the accounting for other current liabilities.**

> **Helpful Hint**
> For point-of-sale systems, the company receives sales information through the computer network.

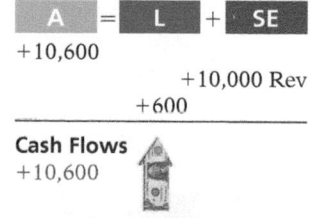

A = L + SE
+10,600
+10,000 Rev
+600

Cash Flows
+10,600

When the company remits the taxes to the taxing agency, it debits Sales Taxes Payable and credits Cash. The company does not report sales taxes as an expense. It simply forwards to the government the amount paid by the customers. Thus, Cooley Grocery serves only as a **collection agent** for the taxing authority.

Sometimes companies do not enter sales taxes separately in the cash register. To determine the amount of sales in such cases, divide total receipts by 100% plus the sales tax percentage. To illustrate, assume that in the above example Cooley Grocery enters total receipts of $10,600. The receipts from the sales are equal to the sales price (100%) plus the tax percentage (6% of sales), or 1.06 times the sales total. We can compute the sales amount as follows.

$$\$10,600 \div 1.06 = \$10,000$$

Thus, Cooley Grocery could find the sales tax amount it must remit to the state ($600) by subtracting sales from total receipts ($10,600 − $10,000).

> **Helpful Hint**
> Alternatively, Cooley could find the tax by multiplying sales by the sales tax rate ($10,000 × .06).

Payroll and Payroll Taxes Payable

Assume that Susan Alena works 40 hours this week for Pepitone Inc., earning a wage of $10 per hour. Will Susan receive a $400 check at the end of the week? Not likely. The reason: Pepitone is required to withhold amounts from her wages to pay various governmental authorities. For example, Pepitone will withhold amounts for Social Security taxes[1] and for federal and state income taxes. If these withholdings total $100, Susan will receive a check for only $300. Illustration 10-2 summarizes the types of payroll deductions that normally occur for most companies.

Illustration 10-2
Payroll deductions

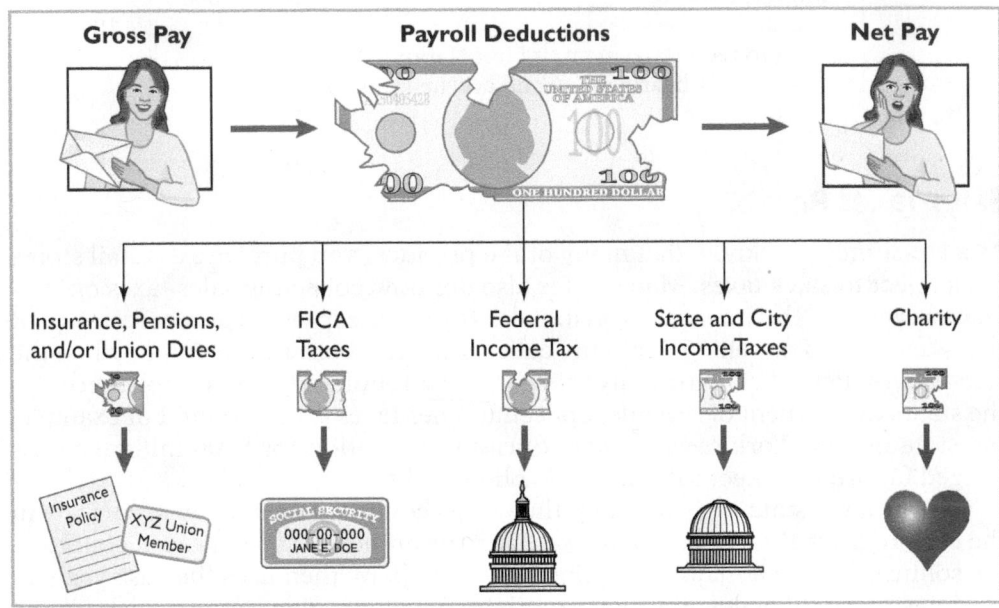

As a result of these deductions, companies withhold from employee pay-checks amounts that must be paid to other parties. Pepitone therefore has incurred a liability to pay these third parties and must report this liability in its balance sheet.

As a second illustration, assume that Cargo Corporation records its payroll for the week of March 7 with the journal entry shown below.

A	=	L	+	SE
				−100,000 Exp
		+7,650		
		+21,864		
		+2,922		
		+67,564		

Cash Flows
no effect

Mar. 7	Salaries and Wages Expense	100,000	
	FICA Taxes Payable		7,650
	Federal Income Taxes Payable		21,864
	State Income Taxes Payable		2,922
	Salaries and Wages Payable		67,564
	(To record payroll and withholding taxes for the week ending March 7)		

---

[1]Social Security taxes are commonly called FICA taxes. In 1937, Congress enacted the Federal Insurance Contribution Act (FICA). As can be seen in the journal entry and the payroll tax journal entry on the next page, the employee and employer must make equal contributions to Social Security. The Social Security rate in 2013 was 7.65%.

Cargo then records payment of this payroll on March 7 as follows.

Mar. 7	Salaries and Wages Payable	67,564	
	Cash		67,564
	(To record payment of the March 7 payroll)		

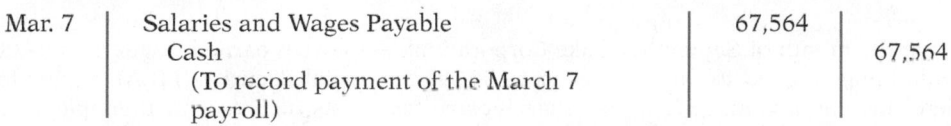

In this case, Cargo reports $100,000 in salaries and wages expense. In addition, it reports liabilities for the salaries and wages payable as well as liabilities to governmental agencies. Rather than pay the employees $100,000, Cargo instead must withhold the taxes and make the tax payments directly. In summary, Cargo is essentially serving as a tax collector.

In addition to the liabilities incurred as a result of withholdings, employers also incur a second type of payroll-related liability. With every payroll, the employer incurs liabilities to pay various **payroll taxes** levied upon the employer. These payroll taxes include the **employer's share** of Social Security (FICA) taxes and state and federal unemployment taxes. Based on Cargo Corp.'s $100,000 payroll, the company would record the employer's expense and liability for these payroll taxes as follows.

Mar. 7	Payroll Tax Expense	13,850	
	FICA Taxes Payable		7,650
	Federal Unemployment Taxes Payable		800
	State Unemployment Taxes Payable		5,400
	(To record employer's payroll taxes on March 7 payroll)		

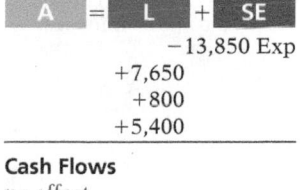

Companies classify the payroll and payroll tax liability accounts as current liabilities because they must be paid to employees or remitted to taxing authorities periodically and in the near term. Taxing authorities impose substantial fines and penalties on employers if the withholding and payroll taxes are not computed correctly and paid on time.

ANATOMY OF A FRAUD

Art was a custodial supervisor for a large school district. The district was supposed to employ between 35 and 40 regular custodians, as well as 3 or 4 substitute custodians to fill in when regular custodians were absent. Instead, in addition to the regular custodians, Art "hired" 77 substitutes. In fact, almost none of these people worked for the district. Instead, Art submitted time cards for these people, collected their checks at the district office, and personally distributed the checks to the "employees." If a substitute's check was for $1,200, that person would cash the check, keep $200, and pay Art $1,000.

Total take: $150,000

THE MISSING CONTROLS

Human resource controls. Thorough background checks should be performed. No employees should begin work until they have been approved by the Board of Education and entered into the payroll system. No employees should be entered into the payroll system until they have been approved by a supervisor. All paychecks should be distributed directly to employees at the official school locations by designated employees.

Independent internal verification. Budgets should be reviewed monthly to identify situations where actual costs significantly exceed budgeted amounts.

Source: Adapted from Wells, *Fraud Casebook* (2007), pp. 164–171.

Wages and Payroll Taxes

During the month of September, Lake Corporation's employees earned wages of $60,000. Withholdings related to these wages were $4,590 for Social Security (FICA), $6,500 for federal income tax, and $2,000 for state income tax. Costs incurred for unemployment taxes were $90 for federal and $150 for state.

Prepare the September 30 journal entries for (a) salaries and wages expense and salaries and wages payable, assuming that all September wages will be paid in October, and (b) the company's payroll tax expense.

Solution

Action Plan

✔ Remember that wages earned are an expense to the company, but withholdings reduce the amount due to be paid to the employee.

✔ Payroll taxes are taxes the company incurs related to its employees.

(a) To determine wages payable, reduce wages expense by the withholdings for FICA, federal income tax, and state income tax.

Sept. 30	Salaries and Wages Expense	60,000	
	FICA Taxes Payable		4,590
	Federal Income Taxes Payable		6,500
	State Income Taxes Payable		2,000
	Salaries and Wages Payable		46,910

(b) Payroll taxes would be for the company's share of FICA, as well as for federal and state unemployment tax.

Sept. 30	Payroll Tax Expense	4,830	
	FICA Taxes Payable		4,590
	Federal Unemployment Taxes Payable		90
	State Unemployment Taxes Payable		150

Related exercise material: BE10-6, E10-5, E10-6, **and** DO IT! 10-2.

 The Navigator

Unearned Revenues

A magazine publisher, such as Sports Illustrated, receives customers' checks when they order magazines. An airline company, such as Southwest Airlines, often receives cash when it sells tickets for future flights. Season tickets for concerts, sporting events, and theater programs are also paid for in advance. How do companies account for unearned revenues that are received before goods are delivered or services are performed?

1. When a company receives the advance payment, it debits Cash, and credits a current liability account identifying the source of the unearned revenue.

2. When the company recognizes revenue, it debits an unearned revenue account, and credits a revenue account.

To illustrate, assume that Superior University sells 10,000 season football tickets at $50 each for its five-game home schedule. The university makes the following entry for the sale of season tickets.

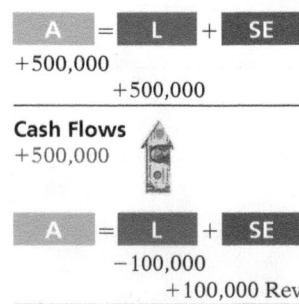

A = L + SE
+500,000
   +500,000

Cash Flows
+500,000

Aug. 6	Cash	500,000	
	Unearned Ticket Revenue		500,000
	(To record sale of 10,000 season tickets)		

As each game is completed, Superior records the recognition of revenue with the following entry.

A = L + SE
   −100,000
   +100,000 Rev

Cash Flows
no effect

Sept. 7	Unearned Ticket Revenue	100,000	
	Ticket Revenue		100,000
	(To record football ticket revenue)		

The account Unearned Ticket Revenue represents unearned revenue, and Superior reports it as a current liability. As the school recognizes revenue, it reclassifies the amount from unearned revenue to Ticket Revenue. Unearned revenue is substantial for some companies. In the airline industry, for example, tickets sold for future flights represent almost 50% of total current liabilities. At United Air Lines, unearned ticket revenue is its largest current liability, recently amounting to over $1 billion.

Illustration 10-3 shows specific unearned revenue and revenue accounts used in selected types of businesses.

Type of Business	Account Title	
	Unearned Revenue	Revenue
Airline	Unearned Ticket Revenue	Ticket Revenue
Magazine publisher	Unearned Subscription Revenue	Subscription Revenue
Hotel	Unearned Rent Revenue	Rent Revenue

Illustration 10-3
Unearned revenue and revenue accounts

Current Maturities of Long-Term Debt

Companies often have a portion of long-term debt that comes due in the current year. That amount is considered a current liability. As an example, assume that Wendy Construction issues a five-year, interest-bearing $25,000 note on January 1, 2014. This note specifies that each January 1, starting January 1, 2015, Wendy should pay $5,000 of the note. When the company prepares financial statements on December 31, 2014, it should report $5,000 as a current liability and $20,000 as a long-term liability. (The $5,000 amount is the portion of the note that is due to be paid within the next 12 months.) Companies often identify current maturities of long-term debt on the balance sheet as **long-term debt due within one year**.

It is not necessary to prepare an adjusting entry to recognize the current maturity of long-term debt. At the balance sheet date, all obligations due within one year are classified as current, and all other obligations as long-term.

> **DO IT!**

Current Liabilities

Action Plan

✔ Use the interest formula: Face value of note × Annual interest rate × Time in terms of one year.

✔ Divide total receipts by 100% plus the tax rate to determine sales revenue; then subtract sales revenue from the total receipts.

✔ Determine what fraction of the total unearned rent should be recognized this year.

You and several classmates are studying for the next accounting examination. They ask you to answer the following questions.

1. If cash is borrowed on a $50,000, 6-month, 12% note on September 1, how much interest expense would be incurred by December 31?

2. How is the sales tax amount determined when the cash register total includes sales taxes?

3. If $15,000 is collected in advance on November 1 for 3 months' rent, what amount of rent revenue should be recognized by December 31?

Solution

1. $50,000 × 12% × 4/12 = $2,000
2. First, divide the total cash register receipts by 100% plus the sales tax percentage to find the sales revenue amount. Second, subtract the sales revenue amount from the total cash register receipts to determine the sales taxes.
3. $15,000 × 2/3 = $10,000

Related exercise material: BE10-2, BE10-3, BE10-4, E10-1, E10-2, E10-3, E10-4, **and** DO IT! 10-1.

 The Navigator

Statement Presentation and Analysis

PRESENTATION

As indicated in Chapter 4, current liabilities are the first category under liabilities on the balance sheet. Each of the principal types of current liabilities is listed separately. In addition, companies disclose the terms of notes payable and other key information about the individual items in the notes to the financial statements.

Companies seldom list current liabilities in the order of liquidity. The reason is that varying maturity dates may exist for specific obligations such as notes payable. A more common method of presenting current liabilities is to list them by **order of magnitude**, with the largest ones first. Or, as a matter of custom, many companies show notes payable first and then accounts payable, regardless of amount. Then the remaining current liabilities are listed by magnitude. (*Use this approach in your homework*.) Illustration 10-4 provides an adapted excerpt from Caterpillar Inc.'s balance sheet, which illustrates its order of presentation.

Illustration 10-4
Balance sheet presentation of current liabilities

CATERPILLAR INC.
Balance Sheet
December 31, 2012
(in millions)

Real World

Assets

Current assets	$42,524
Property, plant and equipment (net)	16,461
Other long-term assets	30,371
Total assets	$89,356

Liabilities and Stockholders' Equity

Current liabilities	
Short-term borrowings (notes payable)	$ 5,287
Accounts payable	6,753
Accrued expenses	3,667
Accrued wages, salaries, and employee benefits	1,911
Customer advances	2,978
Other current liabilities	2,055
Long-term debt due within one year	7,104
Total current liabilities	29,755
Noncurrent liabilities	42,019
Total liabilities	71,774
Stockholders' equity	17,582
Total liabilities and stockholders' equity	$89,356

Helpful Hint
For other examples of current liabilities sections, refer to the PepsiCo and Coca-Cola balance sheets in Appendices B and C.

ANALYSIS

Use of current and noncurrent classifications makes it possible to analyze a company's liquidity. **Liquidity** refers to the ability to pay maturing obligations and meet unexpected needs for cash. The relationship of current assets to current liabilities is critical in analyzing liquidity. We can express this relationship as a dollar amount (working capital) and as a ratio (the current ratio).

The excess of current assets over current liabilities is **working capital**. Illustration 10-5 shows the formula for the computation of Caterpillar's working capital (dollar amounts in millions).

Illustration 10-5
Working capital formula and computation

Current Assets	−	Current Liabilities	=	Working Capital
$42,524	−	$29,755	=	$12,769

As an absolute dollar amount, working capital offers limited informational value. For example, $1 million of working capital may be more than needed for a small company but inadequate for a large corporation. Also, $1 million of working capital may be adequate for a company at one time but inadequate at another time.

The **current ratio** permits us to compare the liquidity of different-sized companies and of a single company at different times. The current ratio is calculated as current assets divided by current liabilities. Illustration 10-6 shows the formula for this ratio, along with its computation using Caterpillar's current asset and current liability data (dollar amounts in millions).

Current Assets	÷	Current Liabilities	=	Current Ratio
$42,524	÷	$29,755	=	1.43:1

Illustration 10-6
Current ratio formula and computation

Historically, companies and analysts considered a current ratio of 2:1 to be the standard for a good credit rating. In recent years, however, many healthy companies have maintained ratios well below 2:1 by improving management of their current assets and liabilities. Caterpillar's ratio of 1.43:1 is adequate but certainly below the standard of 2:1.

Long-Term Liabilities

Long-term liabilities are obligations that are expected to be paid after one year. In this section, we will explain the accounting for the principal types of obligations reported in the long-term liability section of the balance sheet. These obligations often are in the form of bonds or long-term notes.

LEARNING OBJECTIVE   4

Explain why bonds are issued, and identify the types of bonds.

Bond Basics

Bonds are a form of interest-bearing notes payable. To obtain **large amounts of long-term capital**, corporate management usually must decide whether to issue common stock (equity financing) or bonds (debt financing). Bonds offer three advantages over common stock, as shown in Illustration 10-7.

Bond Financing	Advantages
Ballot	1. **Stockholder control is not affected.** Bondholders do not have voting rights, so current owners (stockholders) retain full control of the company.
Tax Bill	2. **Tax savings result.** Bond interest is deductible for tax purposes; dividends on stock are not.
$ / STOCK	3. **Return on common stockholders' equity may be higher.** Although bond interest expense reduces net income, return on common stockholders' equity often is higher under bond financing because no additional shares of common stock are issued.

Illustration 10-7
Advantages of bond financing over common stock

As Illustration 10-7 shows, one reason to issue bonds is that they do not affect stockholder control. Because bondholders do not have voting rights, owners can raise capital with bonds and still maintain corporate control. In addition, bonds are attractive to corporations because the cost of bond interest is tax-deductible. As a result of this tax treatment, which stock dividends do not offer, bonds may result in a lower cost of financing than equity financing.

To illustrate another advantage of bond financing, assume that Microsystems, Inc. is considering two plans for financing the construction of a new $5 million plant. Plan A involves issuance of 200,000 shares of common stock at the current market price of $25 per share. Plan B involves issuance of $5 million, 8% bonds at face value. Income before interest and taxes on the new plant will be $1.5 million. Income taxes are expected to be 30%. Microsystems currently has 100,000 shares of common stock outstanding. Illustration 10-8 shows the alternative effects on earnings per share.

Illustration 10-8
Effects on earnings per share—stocks vs. bonds

	Plan A Issue Stock	Plan B Issue Bonds
Income before interest and taxes	$1,500,000	$1,500,000
Interest (8% × $5,000,000)	—	400,000
Income before income taxes	1,500,000	1,100,000
Income tax expense (30%)	450,000	330,000
Net income	$1,050,000	$ 770,000
Outstanding shares	300,000	100,000
Earnings per share	**$3.50**	**$7.70**

Note that net income is $280,000 less ($1,050,000 − $770,000) with long-term debt financing (bonds). However, earnings per share is higher because there are 200,000 fewer shares of common stock outstanding.

One disadvantage in using bonds is that the company must **pay interest** on a periodic basis. In addition, the company must also **repay the principal** at the due date. A company with fluctuating earnings and a relatively weak cash position may have great difficulty making interest payments when earnings are low.

Helpful Hint
Besides corporations, governmental agencies and universities also issue bonds to raise capital.

A corporation may also obtain long-term financing from notes payable and leasing. However, notes payable and leasing are seldom sufficient to furnish the amount of funds needed for plant expansion and major projects like new buildings.

Bonds are sold in relatively small denominations (usually $1,000 multiples). As a result of their size and the variety of their features, bonds attract many investors.

TYPES OF BONDS

Bonds may have many different features. In the following sections, we describe the types of bonds commonly issued.

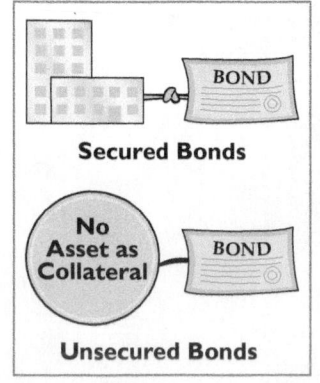

Secured Bonds

Unsecured Bonds

SECURED AND UNSECURED BONDS **Secured bonds** have specific assets of the issuer pledged as collateral for the bonds. A bond secured by real estate, for example, is called a **mortgage bond**. A bond secured by specific assets set aside to redeem (retire) the bonds is called a **sinking fund bond**.

Unsecured bonds, also called **debenture bonds**, are issued against the general credit of the borrower. Companies with good credit ratings use these bonds extensively. For example, at one time, DuPont reported over $2 billion of debenture bonds outstanding.

CONVERTIBLE AND CALLABLE BONDS Bonds that can be converted into common stock at the bondholder's option are **convertible bonds**. The conversion feature generally is attractive to bond buyers. Bonds that the issuing company can redeem (buy back) at a stated dollar amount prior to maturity are **callable bonds**. A call feature is included in nearly all corporate bond issues.

Convertible Bonds

Callable Bonds

ISSUING PROCEDURES

State laws grant corporations the power to issue bonds. Both the board of directors and stockholders usually must approve bond issues. **In authorizing the bond issue, the board of directors must stipulate the number of bonds to be authorized, total face value, and contractual interest rate.** The total bond authorization often exceeds the number of bonds the company originally issues. This gives the corporation the flexibility to issue more bonds, if needed, to meet future cash requirements.

The **face value** is the amount of principal due at the maturity date. The **maturity date** is the date that the final payment is due to the investor from the issuing company. The **contractual interest rate**, often referred to as the **stated rate**, is the rate used to determine the amount of cash interest the issuing company pays and the investor receives. Usually, the contractual rate is stated as an annual rate. Interest is generally paid semiannually.

The terms of the bond issue are set forth in a legal document called a **bond indenture**. The indenture shows the terms and summarizes the rights of the bondholders and their trustees, and the obligations of the issuing company. The **trustee** (usually a financial institution) keeps records of each bondholder, maintains custody of unissued bonds, and holds conditional title to pledged property.

In addition, the issuing company arranges for the printing of **bond certificates**. The indenture and the certificate are separate documents. As shown in Illustration 10-9, a bond certificate provides the following information: name of

Illustration 10-9
Bond certificate

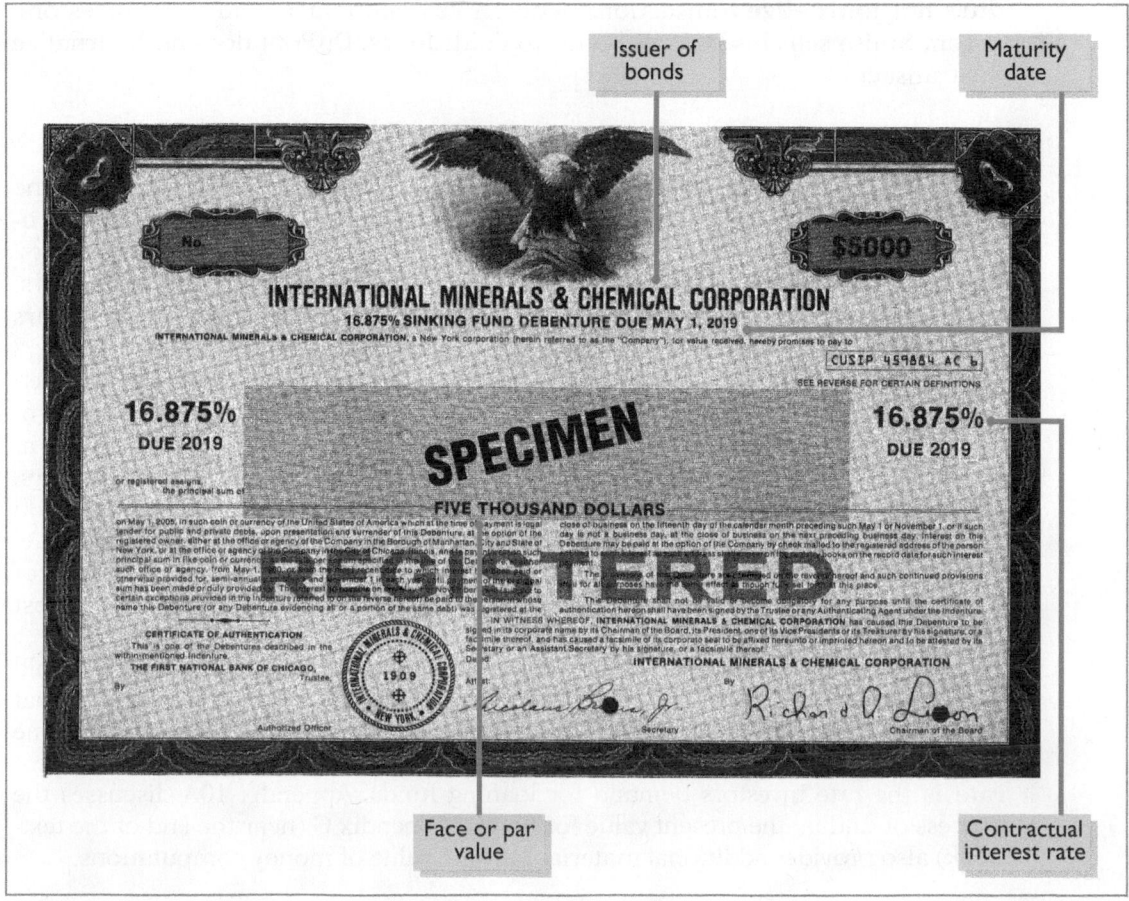

the issuer, face value, contractual interest rate, and maturity date. An investment company that specializes in selling securities generally sells the bonds for the issuing company.

BOND TRADING

Bondholders have the opportunity to convert their holdings into cash at any time by selling the bonds at the current market price on national securities exchanges. **Bond prices are quoted as a percentage of the face value of the bond, which is usually $1,000.** A $1,000 bond with a quoted price of 97 means that the selling price of the bond is 97% of face value, or $970. Newspapers and the financial press publish bond prices and trading activity daily, as shown in Illustration 10-10.

Illustration 10-10
Market information for bonds

Bonds	Maturity	Close	Yield	Est. Volume (000)
Boeing Co. 5.125	Feb. 15, 2014	96.595	5.747	33,965

Helpful Hint
(1) What is the price of a $1,000 bond trading at 95¼?
(2) What is the price of a $1,000 bond trading at 101⅞?
Answers: (1) $952.50.
(2) $1,018.75.

This bond listing indicates that Boeing Co. has outstanding 5.125%, $1,000 bonds that mature in 2014. They currently yield a 5.747% return. On this day, $33,965,000 of these bonds were traded. At the close of trading, the price was 96.595% of face value, or $965.95.

A corporation makes journal entries **only when it issues or buys back bonds**, or when bondholders convert bonds into common stock. For example, DuPont **does not journalize** transactions between its bondholders and other investors. If Tom Smith sells his DuPont bonds to Faith Jones, DuPont does not journalize the transaction.

DETERMINING THE MARKET PRICE OF A BOND

2015
$1 million
≠
2035
$1 million

Same dollars at different times are not equal.

If you were an investor wanting to purchase a bond, how would you determine how much to pay? To be more specific, assume that Coronet, Inc. issues a **zero-interest bond** (pays no interest) with a face value of $1,000,000 due in 20 years. For this bond, the only cash you receive is a million dollars at the end of 20 years. Would you pay a million dollars for this bond? We hope not! A million dollars received 20 years from now is not the same as a million dollars received today.

The term **time value of money** is used to indicate the relationship between time and money—that a dollar received today is worth more than a dollar promised at some time in the future. If you had $1 million today, you would invest it. From that investment, you would earn interest such that at the end of 20 years, you would have much more than $1 million. Thus, if someone is going to pay you $1 million 20 years from now, you would want to find its equivalent today, or its present value. In other words, you would want to determine the value today of the amount to be received in the future after taking into account current interest rates.

The current market price (present value) of a bond is the value at which it should sell in the marketplace. Market price therefore is a function of the three factors that determine present value: (1) the dollar amounts to be received, (2) the length of time until the amounts are received, and (3) the market rate of interest. The **market interest rate** is the rate investors demand for loaning funds. Appendix 10A discusses the process of finding the present value for bonds. Appendix G (near the end of the textbook) also provides additional material for time value of money computations.

ACCOUNTING ACROSS THE ORGANIZATION

How About Those 30-Year Bonds?

Companies like Philip Morris International, Medtronic Inc., Plains All American Pipeline LP, and Simon Properties Group all sold 30-year bonds in 2012. The chart below indicates that companies were on pace to issue a record number of investment-grade bonds of 30-year maturities in 2012.

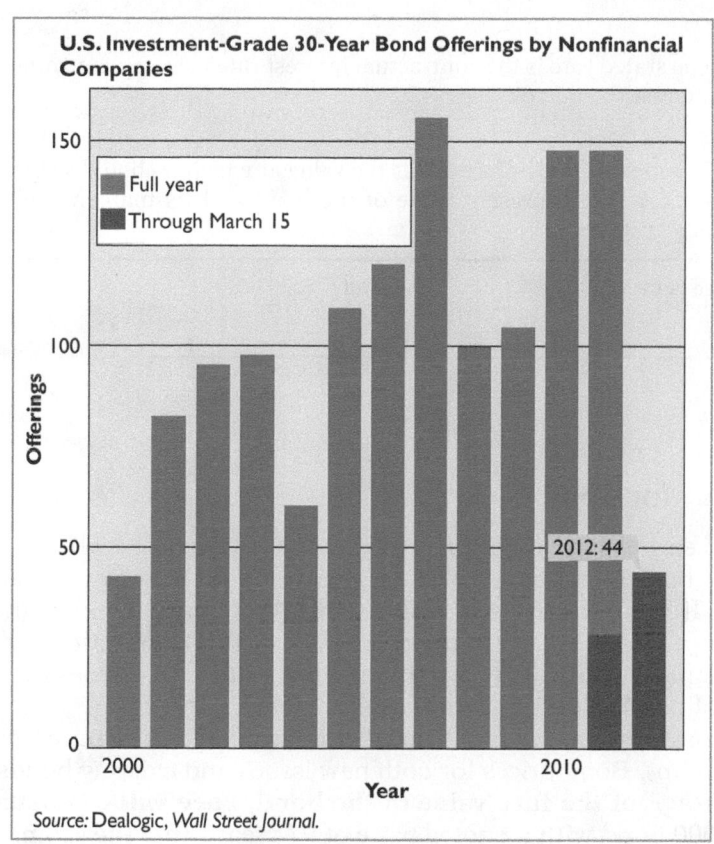

U.S. Investment-Grade 30-Year Bond Offerings by Nonfinancial Companies

Legend:
- Full year
- Through March 15

(y-axis: Offerings; x-axis: Year, 2000 to 2010; 2012: 44)

Source: Dealogic, *Wall Street Journal.*

© Eric Hood/iStockphoto

These companies are looking to extend their debt to lock in low interest rates and take advantage of investor demand.

The issuers of these bonds are benefitting from "a massive sentiment shift" says one bond expert. The belief that the economy will recover is making investors more comfortable holding longer-term bonds, as they search for investments that offer better returns than U.S. Treasury bonds.

Source: Vipal Monga, "The Big Number," *Wall Street Journal* (March 20, 2012), p. B5.

? What are the advantages for companies of issuing 30-year bonds instead of 5-year bonds? (See page 539.)

> **DO IT!**

Bond Terminology State whether each of the following statements is true or false. If false, indicate how to correct the statement.

_____ **1.** Mortgage bonds and sinking fund bonds are both examples of secured bonds.

_____ **2.** Unsecured bonds are also known as debenture bonds.

_____ **3.** The stated rate is the rate investors demand for loaning funds.

_____ **4.** The face value is the amount of principal the issuing company must pay at the maturity date.

_____ **5.** The market price of a bond is equal to its maturity value.

Solution

Action Plan

✔ Review the types of bonds and the basic terms associated with bonds.

1. True.

2. True.

3. False.   The stated rate is the contractual interest rate used to determine the amount of cash interest the borrower pays.

4. True.

5. False.   The market price of a bond is the value at which it should sell in the marketplace. As a result, the present value of the bond and its maturity value are often different.

Related exercise material: BE10-7, E10-8, E10-9, **and** DO IT! 10-3.

 The Navigator

Accounting for Bond Issues

LEARNING OBJECTIVE   5

Prepare the entries for the issuance of bonds and interest expense.

As indicated earlier, a corporation records bond transactions when it issues (sells) or redeems (buys back) bonds and when bondholders convert bonds into common stock. If bondholders sell their bond investments to other investors, the issuing company receives no further money on the transaction, **nor does the issuing company journalize the transaction** (although it does keep records of the names of bondholders in some cases).

Bonds may be issued at face value, below face value (discount), or above face value (premium). Bond prices for both new issues and existing bonds are quoted as **a percentage of the face value of the bond. Face value is usually $1,000.** Thus, a $1,000 bond with a quoted price of 97 means that the selling price of the bond is 97% of face value, or $970.

ISSUING BONDS AT FACE VALUE

To illustrate the accounting for bonds issued at face value, assume that on January 1, 2015, Candlestick, Inc. issues $100,000, five-year, 10% bonds at 100 (100% of face value). The entry to record the sale is:

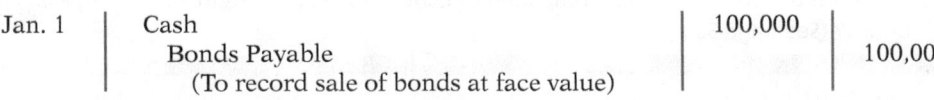

Jan. 1	Cash		100,000	
	Bonds Payable			100,000
	(To record sale of bonds at face value)			

Candlestick reports bonds payable in the long-term liabilities section of the balance sheet because the maturity date is January 1, 2020 (more than one year away).

Over the term (life) of the bonds, companies make entries to record bond interest. Interest on bonds payable is computed in the same manner as interest on notes payable, as explained on page 482. Assume that interest is payable semiannually on January 1 and July 1 on the Candlestick bonds. In that case, Candlestick must pay interest of $5,000 ($100,000 × 10% × 6/12) on July 1, 2015. The entry for the payment, assuming no previous accrual of interest, is:

July 1	Interest Expense	5,000	
	Cash		5,000
	(To record payment of bond interest)		

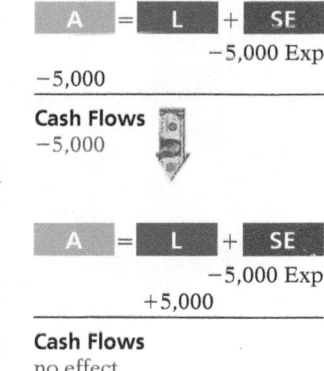

A = L + SE
−5,000 Exp
−5,000

Cash Flows
−5,000

At December 31, Candlestick recognizes the $5,000 of interest expense incurred since July 1 with the following adjusting entry:

Dec. 31	Interest Expense	5,000	
	Interest Payable		5,000
	(To accrue bond interest)		

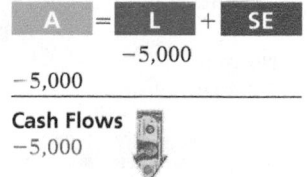

A = L + SE
−5,000 Exp
+5,000

Cash Flows
no effect

Companies classify interest payable as a current liability because it is scheduled for payment within the next year. When Candlestick pays the interest on January 1, 2016, it debits (decreases) Interest Payable and credits (decreases) Cash for $5,000.

Candlestick records the payment on January 1 as follows.

Jan. 1	Interest Payable	5,000	
	Cash		5,000
	(To record payment of bond interest)		

A = L + SE
−5,000
−5,000

Cash Flows
−5,000

DISCOUNT OR PREMIUM ON BONDS

The previous illustrations assumed that the contractual (stated) interest rate and the market (effective) interest rate paid on the bonds were the same. Recall that the **contractual interest rate** is the rate applied to the face (par) value to arrive at the interest paid in a year. The **market interest rate** is the rate investors demand for loaning funds to the corporation. When the contractual interest rate and the market interest rate are the same, bonds sell **at face value (par value)**.

However, market interest rates change daily. The type of bond issued, the state of the economy, current industry conditions, and the company's performance all affect market interest rates. As a result, contractual and market interest rates often differ. To make bonds salable when the two rates differ, bonds sell below or above face value.

To illustrate, suppose that a company issues 10% bonds at a time when other bonds of similar risk are paying 12%. Investors will not be interested in buying the 10% bonds, so their value will fall below their face value. When a bond is sold for less than its face value, the difference between the face value of a bond and its selling price is called a **discount**. As a result of the decline in the bonds' selling price, the actual interest rate incurred by the company increases to the level of the current market interest rate.

Conversely, if the market rate of interest is **lower than** the contractual interest rate, investors will have to pay more than face value for the bonds. That is, if the market rate of interest is 8% but the contractual interest rate on the bonds is 10%, the price of the bonds will be bid up. When a bond is sold for more than its face value, the difference between the face value and its selling price is called a **premium**. Illustration 10-11 (page 496) shows these relationships graphically.

Issuance of bonds at an amount different from face value is quite common. By the time a company prints the bond certificates and markets the bonds, it will be a coincidence if the market rate and the contractual rate are the same. Thus, the issuance of bonds at a discount does not mean that the issuer's financial

Illustration 10-11
Interest rates and bond prices

Helpful Hint

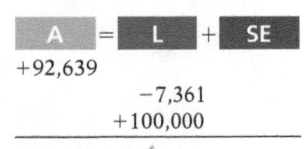

strength is suspect. Conversely, the sale of bonds at a premium does not indicate that the financial strength of the issuer is exceptional.

ISSUING BONDS AT A DISCOUNT

To illustrate issuance of bonds at a discount, assume that on January 1, 2015, Candlestick, Inc. sells $100,000, five-year, 10% bonds for $92,639 (92.639% of face value). Interest is payable on July 1 and January 1. The entry to record the issuance is:

Jan. 1	Cash	92,639	
	Discount on Bonds Payable	7,361	
	Bonds Payable		100,000
	(To record sale of bonds at a discount)		

Although Discount on Bonds Payable has a debit balance, **it is not an asset**. Rather, it is a **contra account**. This account is **deducted from bonds payable** on the balance sheet, as shown in Illustration 10-12.

Illustration 10-12
Statement presentation of discount on bonds payable

CANDLESTICK, INC.		
Balance Sheet (partial)		
Long-term liabilities		
Bonds payable	$100,000	
Less: Discount on bonds payable	**7,361**	$92,639

Helpful Hint
Carrying value (book value) of bonds issued at a discount is determined by subtracting the balance of the discount account from the balance of the Bonds Payable account.

The $92,639 represents the **carrying (or book) value** of the bonds. On the date of issue, this amount equals the market price of the bonds.

The issuance of bonds below face value—at a discount—causes the total cost of borrowing to differ from the bond interest paid. That is, the issuing corporation must pay not only the contractual interest rate over the term of the bonds but also the face value (rather than the issuance price) at maturity. Therefore, the difference between the issuance price and face value of the bonds—the discount—is an **additional cost of borrowing**. The company records this additional cost as **interest expense** over the life of the bonds. Appendices 10B and 10C show the procedures for recording this additional cost.

The total cost of borrowing $92,639 for Candlestick, Inc. is $57,361, computed as follows.

Bonds Issued at a Discount

Semiannual interest payments ($100,000 × 10% × ½ = $5,000; $5,000 × 10)	$ 50,000
Add: Bond discount ($100,000 − $92,639)	7,361
Total cost of borrowing	**$57,361**

Illustration 10-13
Total cost of borrowing—bonds issued at a discount

Alternatively, we can compute the total cost of borrowing as follows.

Bonds Issued at a Discount

Principal at maturity	$100,000
Semiannual interest payments ($5,000 × 10)	50,000
Cash to be paid to bondholders	150,000
Cash received from bondholders	92,639
Total cost of borrowing	**$ 57,361**

Illustration 10-14
Alternative computation of total cost of borrowing—bonds issued at a discount

ISSUING BONDS AT A PREMIUM

To illustrate the issuance of bonds at a premium, we now assume the Candlestick, Inc. bonds described above sell for $108,111 (108.111% of face value) rather than for $92,639. The entry to record the sale is:

Jan. 1	Cash	108,111	
	Bonds Payable		100,000
	Premium on Bonds Payable		8,111
	(To record sale of bonds at a premium)		

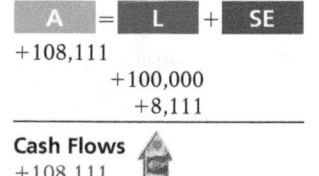

A = L + SE
+108,111
+100,000
+8,111

Cash Flows
+108,111

Candlestick adds the premium on bonds payable **to the bonds payable amount** on the balance sheet, as shown in Illustration 10-15.

CANDLESTICK, INC.
Balance Sheet (partial)

Long-term liabilities		
Bonds payable	$100,000	
Add: Premium on bonds payable	8,111	$108,111

Illustration 10-15
Statement presentation of bond premium

Helpful Hint
Premium on Bonds Payable

Decrease Debit	Increase Credit ↓ Normal Balance

The sale of bonds above face value causes the total cost of borrowing to be **less than the bond interest paid**. The reason: The borrower is not required to pay the bond premium at the maturity date of the bonds. Thus, the bond premium is considered to be **a reduction in the cost of borrowing**. The company credits the bond premium to Interest Expense over the life of the bonds. Appendices 10B and 10C show the procedures for recording this reduction in the cost of borrowing. The total cost of borrowing $108,111 for Candlestick, Inc. is shown in Illustrations 10-16 and 10-17 (page 498).

Illustration 10-16
Total cost of borrowing—
bonds issued at a premium

Bonds Issued at a Premium

Semiannual interest payments	
($100,000 × 10% × ½ = $5,000; $5,000 × 10)	$ 50,000
Less: Bond premium ($108,111 − $100,000)	8,111
Total cost of borrowing	**$41,889**

Alternatively, we can compute the cost of borrowing as follows.

Illustration 10-17
Alternative computation of
total cost of borrowing—bonds
issued at a premium

Bonds Issued at a Premium

Principal at maturity	$100,000
Semiannual interest payments ($5,000 × 10)	50,000
Cash to be paid to bondholders	150,000
Cash received from bondholders	108,111
Total cost of borrowing	**$ 41,889**

> DO IT!

Bond Issuance

Giant Corporation issues $200,000 of bonds for $189,000. (a) Prepare the journal entry to record the issuance of the bonds, and (b) show how the bonds would be reported on the balance sheet at the date of issuance.

Solution

Action Plan

✔ Record cash received, bonds payable at face value, and the difference as a discount or premium.

✔ Report discount as a deduction from bonds payable and premium as an addition to bonds payable.

(a)

Cash	189,000	
Discount on Bonds Payable	11,000	
Bonds Payable		200,000
(To record sale of bonds at a discount)		

(b)

Long-term liabilities		
Bonds payable	$200,000	
Less: Discount on bonds payable	11,000	$189,000

Related exercise material: BE10-8, BE10-9, BE10-10, E10-10, E10-11, E10-12, **and** DO IT 10-4.

 The Navigator

Accounting for Bond Redemptions

An issuing corporation retires bonds either when it buys back (redeems) the bonds or when bondholders convert them into common stock. We explain the entries for these transactions in the following sections.

REDEEMING BONDS AT MATURITY

Regardless of the issue price of bonds, the book value of the bonds at maturity will equal their face value. Assuming that the company pays and records separately the interest for the last interest period, Candlestick records the redemption of its bonds at maturity as follows.

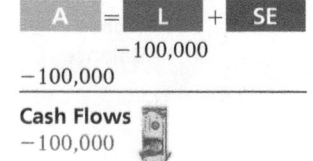

A = L + SE
−100,000
−100,000

Cash Flows
−100,000

Jan. 1	Bonds Payable	100,000	
	Cash		100,000
	(To record redemption of bonds at maturity)		

REDEEMING BONDS BEFORE MATURITY

Bonds also may be redeemed before maturity. A company may decide to redeem bonds before maturity to reduce interest cost and to remove debt from its balance sheet. A company should redeem debt early only if it has sufficient cash resources.

When a company redeems bonds before maturity, it is necessary to (1) eliminate the carrying value of the bonds at the redemption date, (2) record the cash paid, and (3) recognize the gain or loss on redemption. The **carrying value** of the bonds is the face value of the bonds less any remaining bond discount or plus any remaining bond premium at the redemption date.

To illustrate, assume that Candlestick, Inc. has sold its bonds at a premium. At the end of the eighth period, Candlestick redeems these bonds at 103 after paying the semiannual interest. Assume also that the carrying value of the bonds at the redemption date is $101,623. Candlestick makes the following entry to record the redemption at the end of the eighth interest period (January 1, 2019).

Helpful Hint

Question: A bond is redeemed prior to its maturity date. Its carrying value exceeds its redemption price. Will this result in a gain or a loss on redemption?

Answer: Gain.

Jan. 1	Bonds Payable	100,000	
	Premium on Bonds Payable	1,623	
	Loss on Bond Redemption	1,377	
	Cash		103,000
	(To record redemption of bonds at 103)		

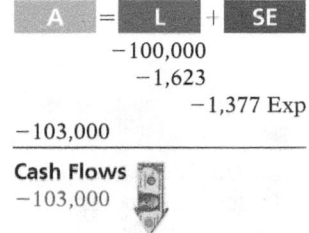

```
A  =  L  +  SE
      -100,000
      -1,623
                -1,377 Exp
-103,000
```

Cash Flows
-103,000

Note that the loss of $1,377 is the difference between the cash paid of $103,000 and the carrying value of the bonds of $101,623.

CONVERTING BONDS INTO COMMON STOCK

Convertible bonds have features that are attractive both to bondholders and to the issuer. The conversion often gives bondholders an opportunity to benefit if the market price of the common stock increases substantially. Until conversion, though, the bondholder receives interest on the bond. For the issuer of convertible bonds, the bonds sell at a higher price and pay a lower rate of interest than comparable debt securities without the conversion option. Many corporations, such as Intel, Ford, and Wells Fargo, have convertible bonds outstanding.

When the issuing company records a conversion, the company ignores the current market prices of the bonds and stock. Instead, the company transfers the **carrying value** of the bonds to paid-in capital accounts. **No gain or loss is recognized.**

To illustrate, assume that on July 1, Saunders Associates converts $100,000 bonds sold at face value into 2,000 shares of $10 par value common stock. Both the bonds and the common stock have a market value of $130,000. Saunders makes the following entry to record the conversion.

July 1	Bonds Payable	100,000	
	Common Stock		20,000
	Paid-in Capital in Excess of Par—		
	Common Stock		80,000
	(To record bond conversion)		

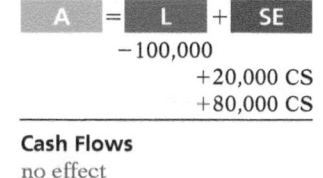

```
A  =  L  +  SE
      -100,000
                +20,000 CS
                +80,000 CS
```

Cash Flows
no effect

Note that the company does not consider the current market value of the bonds and stock ($130,000) in making the entry. This method of recording the bond conversion is often referred to as the **carrying (or book) value method**.

> **DO IT!**

Bond Redemption R & D Inc. Issued $500,000, 10-year bonds at a premium. Prior to maturity, when the carrying value of the bonds is $508,000, the company redeems the bonds at 102. Prepare the entry to record the redemption of the bonds.

Action Plan

✔ Determine and eliminate the carrying value of the bonds.

✔ Record the cash paid.

✔ Compute and record the gain or loss (the difference between the first two items).

Solution

There is a loss on redemption. The cash paid, $510,000 ($500,000 × 102%), is greater than the carrying value of $508,000. The entry is:

Bonds Payable	500,000	
Premium on Bonds Payable	8,000	
Loss on Bond Redemption	2,000	
Cash		510,000
(To record redemption of bonds at 102)		

Related exercise material: BE10-11, E10-13, E10-14, **and** DO IT 10-5.

 The Navigator

Accounting for Long-Term Notes Payable

LEARNING OBJECTIVE 7

Describe the accounting for long-term notes payable.

The use of notes payable in long-term debt financing is quite common. **Long-term notes payable** are similar to short-term interest-bearing notes payable except that the term of the notes exceeds one year. In periods of unstable interest rates, lenders may tie the interest rate on long-term notes to changes in the market rate for comparable loans. Examples are the 8.03% adjustable rate notes issued by General Motors and the floating-rate notes issued by American Express Company.

A long-term note may be secured by a **mortgage** that pledges title to specific assets as security for a loan. Individuals widely use **mortgage notes payable** to purchase homes, and many small and some large companies use them to acquire plant assets. At one time, approximately 18% of McDonald's long-term debt related to mortgage notes on land, buildings, and improvements.

Like other long-term notes payable, the mortgage loan terms may stipulate either a **fixed** or an **adjustable** interest rate. The interest rate on a fixed-rate mortgage remains the same over the life of the mortgage. The interest rate on an adjustable-rate mortgage is adjusted periodically to reflect changes in the market rate of interest. Typically, the terms require the borrower to make equal installment payments over the term of the loan. Each payment consists of (1) interest on the unpaid balance of the loan and (2) a reduction of loan principal. While the total amount of the payment remains constant, the interest decreases each period, and the portion applied to the loan principal increases.

Companies initially record mortgage notes payable at face value. They subsequently make entries for each installment payment. To illustrate, assume that Porter Technology Inc. issues a $500,000, 12%, 20-year mortgage note on December 31, 2015, to obtain needed financing for a new research laboratory. The terms provide for semiannual installment payments of $33,231 (not including real estate taxes and insurance). The installment payment schedule for the first two years is as follows.

Illustration 10-18
Mortgage installment payment schedule

Semiannual Interest Period	(A) Cash Payment	(B) Interest Expense (D) × 6%	(C) Reduction of Principal (A) − (B)	(D) Principal Balance (D) − (C)
12/31/15				$500,000
06/30/16	$33,231	$30,000	$3,231	496,769
12/31/16	33,231	29,806	3,425	493,344
06/30/17	33,231	29,601	3,630	489,714
12/31/17	33,231	29,383	3,848	485,866

Porter records the mortgage loan on December 31, 2015, as follows.

Dec. 31	Cash	500,000	
	Mortgage Payable		500,000
	(To record mortgage loan)		

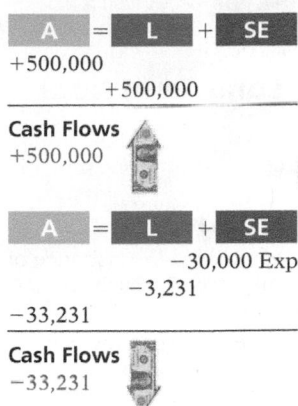

A = L + SE
+500,000
+500,000

Cash Flows
+500,000

On June 30, 2016, Porter records the first installment payment as follows.

June 30	Interest Expense	30,000	
	Mortgage Payable	3,231	
	Cash		33,231
	(To record semiannual payment on mortgage)		

A = L + SE
−30,000 Exp
−3,231
−33,231

Cash Flows
−33,231

In the balance sheet, the company reports the reduction in principal for the next year as a current liability, and it classifies the remaining unpaid principal balance as a long-term liability. At December 31, 2016, the total liability is $493,344. Of that amount, $7,478 ($3,630 + $3,848) is current, and $485,866 ($493,344 − $7,478) is long-term.

ACCOUNTING ACROSS THE ORGANIZATION

Bonds versus Notes?

Companies have a choice in the form of long-term borrowing they undertake—issue bonds or issue notes. Notes are generally issued to a single lender (usually through a loan from a bank). Bonds, on the other hand, allow the company to divide the borrowing into many small investing units, thereby enabling more than one investor to participate in the borrowing. As indicated in the graph below, companies are borrowing more from bond investors than from banks and other loan providers in a bid to lock in cheap, long-term funding.

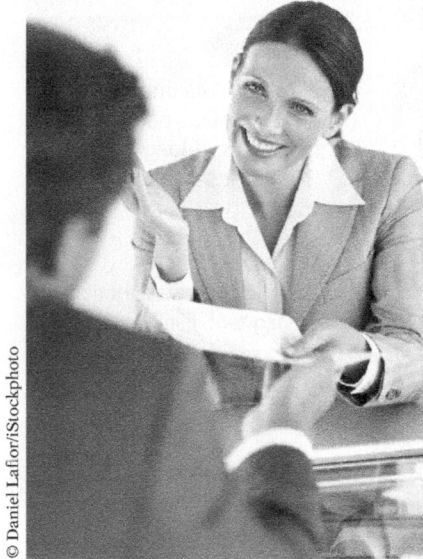

Why this trend? For one thing, low interest rates and rising inflows into fixed-income funds have triggered record bond issuances as banks cut back lending. In addition, for some high-rated companies, it can be riskier to borrow from a bank than the bond markets. The reason: High-rated companies tended to rely on short-term financing to fund working capital but were left stranded when these markets froze up. Some are now financing themselves with longer-term bonds instead.

Source: A. Sakoui and N. Bullock, "Companies Choose Bonds for Cheap Funds," *Financial Times* (October 12, 2009).

Why might companies prefer bond financing instead of short-term financing? (See page 539.)

> **DO IT!**

Long-Term Note

Cole Research issues a $250,000, 8%, 20-year mortgage note to obtain needed financing for a new lab. The terms call for semiannual payments of $12,631 each. Prepare the entries to record the mortgage loan and the first installment payment.

Solution

Action Plan

✔ Record the issuance of the note as a cash receipt and a liability.

✔ Each installment payment consists of interest and payment of principal.

Cash	250,000	
Mortgage Payable		250,000
(To record mortgage loan)		
Interest Expense	10,000*	
Mortgage Payable	2,361	
Cash		12,361
(To record semiannual payment on mortgage)		

*Interest expense = $250,000 × 8% × 6/12.

Related exercise material: BE10-12, E10-15, **and** DO IT! 10-6.

 The Navigator

Statement Presentation and Analysis

LEARNING OBJECTIVE 8

Identify the methods for the presentation and analysis of long-term liabilities.

PRESENTATION

Companies report long-term liabilities in a separate section of the balance sheet immediately following current liabilities, as shown in Illustration 10-19. Alternatively, companies may present summary data in the balance sheet, with detailed data (interest rates, maturity dates, conversion privileges, and assets pledged as collateral) shown in a supporting schedule.

Illustration 10-19
Balance sheet presentation of long-term liabilities

LAX CORPORATION		
Balance Sheet (partial)		
Long-term liabilities		
Bonds payable 10% due in 2020	$1,000,000	
Less: Discount on bonds payable	80,000	$ 920,000
Mortgage payable, 11%, due in 2026		
and secured by plant assets		500,000
Total long-term liabilities		$1,420,000

 Ethics Note

Some companies try to minimize the amount of debt reported on their balance sheet by not reporting certain types of commitments as liabilities. This subject is of intense interest in the financial community.

Companies report the current maturities of long-term debt under current liabilities if they are to be paid within one year or the operating cycle, whichever is longer.

ANALYSIS

Long-term creditors and stockholders are interested in a company's long-run solvency. Of particular interest is the company's ability to pay interest as it comes due and to repay the face value of the debt at maturity. Here we look at two ratios that provide information about debt-paying ability and long-run solvency.

The **debt to assets ratio** measures the percentage of the total assets provided by creditors. It is computed by dividing total liabilities (both current and long-term liabilities) by total assets. To illustrate, we use data from a recent Kellogg Company annual report. The company reported total liabilities of $8,925 million, total assets of $11,200 million, interest expense of $295 million, income taxes of $476 million, and net income of $1,208 million. As shown in Illustration 10-20, Kellogg's debt to assets ratio is 79.7%. The higher the percentage of debt to assets, the greater the risk that the company may be unable to meet its maturing obligation.

Total Liabilities	÷	Total Assets	=	Debt to Assets Ratio
$8,925	÷	$11,200	=	79.7%

Illustration 10-20
Debt to assets ratio

Times interest earned indicates the company's ability to meet interest payments as they come due. It is computed by dividing the sum of net income, interest expense, and income tax expense by interest expense. As shown in Illustration 10-21, Kellogg's times interest earned is 6.71 times. This interest coverage is considered safe.

Net Income + Interest Expense + Income Tax Expense	÷	Interest Expense	=	Times Interest Earned
$1,208 + $295 + $476	÷	$295	=	6.71 times

Illustration 10-21
Times interest earned

INVESTOR INSIGHT

"Covenant-Lite" Debt

In many corporate loans and bond issuances, the lending agreement specifies debt covenants. These covenants typically are specific financial measures, such as minimum levels of retained earnings, cash flows, times interest earned, or other measures that a company must maintain during the life of the loan. If the company violates a covenant, it is considered to have violated the loan agreement. The creditors can then demand immediate repayment, or they can renegotiate the loan's terms. Covenants protect lenders because they enable lenders to step in and try to get their money back before the borrower gets too deep into trouble.

During the 1990s, most traditional loans specified between three to six covenants or "triggers." In more recent years, when lots of cash was available, lenders began reducing or completely eliminating covenants from loan agreements in order to be more competitive with other lenders. When the economy declined, lenders lost big money when companies defaulted.

Source: Cynthia Koons, "Risky Business: Growth of 'Covenant-Lite' Debt," *Wall Street Journal* (June 18, 2007), p. C2.

? How can financial ratios such as those covered in this chapter provide protection for creditors? (See page 539.)

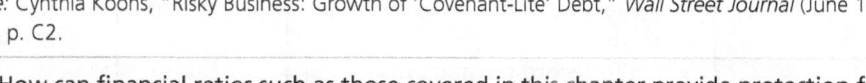

> Comprehensive DO IT!

Snyder Software Inc. has successfully developed a new spreadsheet program. To produce and market the program, the company needed $2 million of additional financing. On January 1, 2015, Snyder borrowed money as follows.

1. Snyder issued $500,000, 11%, 10-year convertible bonds. The bonds sold at face value and pay semiannual interest on January 1 and July 1. Each $1,000 bond is convertible into 30 shares of Snyder's $20 par value common stock.

2. Snyder issued $1 million, 10%, 10-year bonds at face value. Interest is payable semiannually on January 1 and July 1.

3. Snyder also issued a $500,000, 12%, 15-year mortgage payable. The terms provide for semiannual installment payments of $36,324 on June 30 and December 31.

Instructions

1. For the convertible bonds, prepare journal entries for:
   (a) The issuance of the bonds on January 1, 2015.
   (b) Interest expense on July 1 and December 31, 2015.
   (c) The payment of interest on January 1, 2016.
   (d) The conversion of all bonds into common stock on January 1, 2016, when the market price of the common stock was $67 per share.

2. For the 10-year, 10% bonds:
   (a) Journalize the issuance of the bonds on January 1, 2015.
   (b) Prepare the journal entries for interest expense in 2015. Assume no accrual of interest on June 30.
   (c) Prepare the entry for the redemption of the bonds at 101 on January 1, 2018, after paying the interest due on this date.

3. For the mortgage payable:
   (a) Prepare the entry for the issuance of the note on January 1, 2015.
   (b) Prepare a payment schedule for the first four installment payments.
   (c) Indicate the current and noncurrent amounts for the mortgage payable at December 31, 2015.

Solution to Comprehensive DO IT!

1. (a) 2015

Jan.	1	Cash		500,000	
		Bonds Payable			500,000
		(To record issue of 11%, 10-year convertible bonds at face value)			

(b) 2015

July	1	Interest Expense		27,500	
		Cash ($500,000 × 0.055)			27,500
		(To record payment of semiannual interest)			
Dec.	31	Interest Expense		27,500	
		Interest Payable			27,500
		(To record accrual of semiannual bond interest)			

(c) 2016

Jan.	1	Interest Payable		27,500	
		Cash			27,500
		(To record payment of accrued interest)			

(d)

Jan.	1	Bonds Payable		500,000	
		Common Stock			300,000*
		Paid-in Capital in Excess of Par—Common Stock			200,000
		(To record conversion of bonds into common stock)			

*($500,000 ÷ $1,000 = 500 bonds; 500 × 30 = 15,000 shares; 15,000 × $20 = $300,000)

2. (a) 2015

Jan.	1	Cash		1,000,000	
		Bonds Payable			1,000,000
		(To record issuance of bonds)			

(b) 2015

July 1	Interest Expense		50,000	
	Cash			50,000
	(To record payment of			
	semiannual interest)			
Dec. 31	Interest Expense		50,000	
	Interest Payable			50,000
	(To record accrual of			
	semiannual interest)			

(c) 2018

Jan. 1	Bonds Payable		1,000,000	
	Loss on Bond Redemption		10,000*	
	Cash			1,010,000
	(To record redemption			
	of bonds at 101)			

*($1,010,000 − $1,000,000)

3. (a) 2015

Jan. 1	Cash		500,000	
	Mortgage Payable			500,000
	(To record issuance of			
	mortgage payable)			

(b)

Semiannual Interest Period	Cash Payment	Interest Expense	Reduction of Principal	Principal Balance
Issue date				$500,000
1	$36,324	$30,000	$6,324	493,676
2	36,324	29,621	6,703	486,973
3	36,324	29,218	7,106	479,867
4	36,324	28,792	7,532	472,335

(c) Current liability: $14,638 ($7,106 + $7,532)
Long-term liability: $472,335

Action Plan

✔ Compute periodic interest expense on a mortgage payable, recognizing that as the principal amount decreases, so does the interest expense.

✔ Record mortgage payments, recognizing that each payment consists of (1) interest on the unpaid loan balance and (2) a reduction of the loan principal.

 The Navigator

SUMMARY OF LEARNING OBJECTIVES

✔ **The Navigator**

1 **Explain a current liability, and identify the major types of current liabilities.** A current liability is a debt that a company expects to pay within one year or the operating cycle, whichever is longer. The major types of current liabilities are notes payable, accounts payable, sales taxes payable, unearned revenues, and accrued liabilities such as taxes, salaries and wages, and interest payable.

2 **Describe the accounting for notes payable.** When a promissory note is interest-bearing, the amount of assets received upon the issuance of the note is generally equal to the face value of the note. Interest expense accrues over the life of the note. At maturity, the amount paid equals the face value of the note plus accrued interest.

3 **Explain the accounting for other current liabilities.** Companies record sales taxes payable at the time the related

sales occur. The company serves as a collection agent for the taxing authority. Sales taxes are not an expense to the company. Companies initially record unearned revenues in an unearned revenue account. As a company recognizes revenue, a transfer from unearned revenue to revenue occurs. Companies report the current maturities of long-term debt as a current liability in the balance sheet.

4 **Explain why bonds are issued, and identify the types of bonds.** Companies may sell bonds to investors to raise long-term capital. Bonds offer the following advantages over common stock: (a) stockholder control is not affected, (b) tax savings result, and (c) earnings per share of common stock may be higher. The following types of bonds may be issued: secured, unsecured (debenture), convertible, and callable bonds.

5 **Prepare the entries for the issuance of bonds and interest expense.** When companies issue bonds, they debit Cash for the cash proceeds and credit Bonds Payable for the face value of the bonds. The account Premium on Bonds Payable shows a bond premium. Discount on Bonds Payable shows a bond discount.

6 **Describe the entries when bonds are redeemed or converted.** When bondholders redeem bonds at maturity, the issuing company credits Cash and debits Bonds Payable for the face value of the bonds. When bonds are redeemed before maturity, the issuing company (a) eliminates the carrying value of the bonds at the redemption date, (b) records the cash paid, and (c) recognizes the gain or loss on redemption. When bonds are converted to common stock, the issuing company transfers the carrying (or book) value of the bonds to appropriate paid-in capital accounts. No gain or loss is recognized.

7 **Describe the accounting for long-term notes payable.** Each payment consists of (1) interest on the unpaid balance of the loan and (2) a reduction of loan principal. The interest decreases each period, while the portion applied to the loan principal increases.

8 **Identify the methods for the presentation and analysis of long-term liabilities.** Companies should report the nature and amount of each long-term debt in the balance sheet or in the notes accompanying the financial statements. Stockholders and long-term creditors are interested in a company's long-run solvency. Debt to assets and times interest earned are two ratios that provide information about debt-paying ability and long-run solvency.

GLOSSARY

Bond certificate A legal document that indicates the name of the issuer, the face value of the bonds, the contractual interest rate, and maturity date of the bonds. (p. 491).

Bond indenture A legal document that sets forth the terms of the bond issue. (p. 491).

Bonds A form of interest-bearing notes payable issued by corporations, universities, and governmental entities. (p. 489).

Callable bonds Bonds that are subject to redemption (buy back) at a stated dollar amount prior to maturity at the option of the issuer. (p. 490).

Contractual interest rate Rate used to determine the amount of cash interest the borrower pays and the investor receives. (p. 491).

Convertible bonds Bonds that permit bondholders to convert them into common stock at the bondholders' option. (p. 490).

Current ratio A measure of a company's liquidity; computed as current assets divided by current liabilities. (p. 489).

Debenture bonds Bonds issued against the general credit of the borrower. Also called unsecured bonds. (p. 490).

Debt to assets ratio A solvency measure that indicates the percentage of total assets provided by creditors; computed as total liabilities divided by total assets. (p. 502).

Discount (on a bond) The difference between the face value of a bond and its selling price, when the bond is sold for less than its face value. (p. 495).

Face value Amount of principal due at the maturity date of the bond. (p. 491).

Long-term liabilities Obligations expected to be paid more than one year in the future. (p. 489).

Market interest rate The rate investors demand for loaning funds to the corporation. (p. 492).

Maturity date The date on which the final payment on the bond is due from the bond issuer to the investor. (p. 491).

Mortgage bond A bond secured by real estate. (p. 490).

Mortgage notes payable A long-term note secured by a mortgage that pledges title to specific assets as security for a loan. (p. 500).

Notes payable Obligations in the form of written notes. (p. 482).

Premium (on a bond) The difference between the selling price and the face value of a bond, when the bond is sold for more than its face value. (p. 495).

Secured bonds Bonds that have specific assets of the issuer pledged as collateral. (p. 490).

Sinking fund bonds Bonds secured by specific assets set aside to redeem them. (p. 490).

Times interest earned A solvency measure that indicates a company's ability to meet interest payments; computed by dividing the sum of net income, interest expense, and income tax expense by interest expense. (p. 503).

Time value of money The relationship between time and money. A dollar received today is worth more than a dollar promised at some time in the future. (p. 492).

Unsecured bonds Bonds issued against the general credit of the borrower. Also called debenture bonds. (p. 490).

Working capital A measure of a company's liquidity; computed as current assets minus current liabilities. (p. 488).

APPENDIX 10A   Present Value Concepts Related to Bond Pricing

Congratulations! You have a winning lottery ticket and the state has provided you with three possible options for payment. They are:

1. Receive $10,000,000 in three years.
2. Receive $7,000,000 immediately.
3. Receive $3,500,000 at the end of each year for three years.

Which of these options would you select? The answer is not easy to determine at a glance. To make a dollar-maximizing choice, you must perform present value computations. A present value computation is based on the concept of time value of money. Time value of money concepts are useful for the lottery situation and for pricing other amounts to be received in the future. This appendix discusses how to use present value concepts to price bonds. It also will tell you how to determine what option you should take as a lottery winner.

Present Value of a Single Amount

To illustrate present value concepts, assume that you are willing to invest a sum of money that will yield $1,000 at the end of one year. In other words, what amount would you need to invest today to have $1,000 one year from now? If you want to earn 10%, the investment (or present value) is $909.09 ($1,000 ÷ 1.10). Illustration 10A-1 shows the computation.

Present Value	×	(1 + Interest Rate)	=	Future Amount
Present value	×	(1 + 10%)	=	$1,000
Present value			=	$1,000 ÷ 1.10
Present value			=	$909.09

Illustration 10A-1
Present value computation—$1,000 discounted at 10% for one year

The future amount ($1,000), the interest rate (10%), and the number of periods (1) are known. We can depict the variables in this situation as shown in the time diagram in Illustration 10A-2.

Illustration 10A-2
Finding present value if discounted for one period

If you are to receive the single future amount of $1,000 **in two years**, discounted at 10%, its present value is $826.45 [($1,000 ÷ 1.10) ÷ 1.10], depicted as follows.

Illustration 10A-3
Finding present value if discounted for two periods

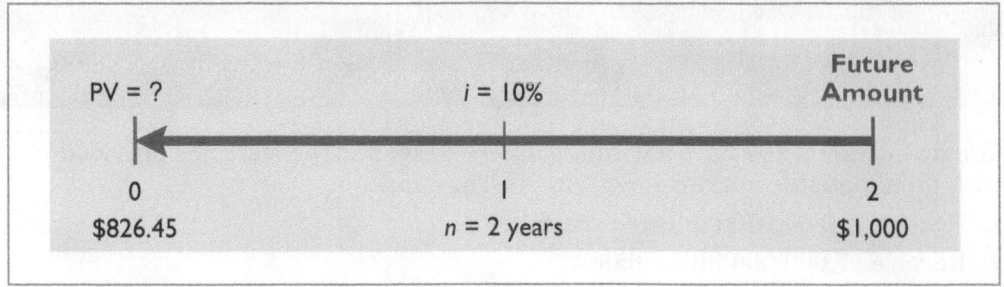

We also can determine the present value of 1 through tables that show the present value of 1 for *n* periods. In Table 10A-1, *n* is the number of discounting periods involved. The percentages are the periodic interest rates or discount rates, and the 5-digit decimal numbers in the respective columns are the present value of 1 factors.

When using Table 10A-1, we multiply the future amount by the present value factor specified at the intersection of the number of periods and the interest rate. For example, the present value factor for 1 period at an interest rate of 10% is .90909, which equals the $909.09 ($1,000 × .90909) computed in Illustration 10A-1.

TABLE 10A-1
Present Value of 1

(n) Periods	4%	5%	6%	7%	8%	9%	10%	11%	12%	15%
1	.96154	.95238	.94340	.93458	.92593	.91743	.90909	.90090	.89286	.86957
2	.92456	.90703	.89000	.87344	.85734	.84168	.82645	.81162	.79719	.75614
3	.88900	.86384	.83962	.81630	.79383	.77218	.75132	.73119	.71178	.65752
4	.85480	.82270	.79209	.76290	.73503	.70843	.68301	.65873	.63552	.57175
5	.82193	.78353	.74726	.71299	.68058	.64993	.62092	.59345	.56743	.49718
6	.79031	.74622	.70496	.66634	.63017	.59627	.56447	.53464	.50663	.43233
7	.75992	.71068	.66506	.62275	.58349	.54703	.51316	.48166	.45235	.37594
8	.73069	.67684	.62741	.58201	.54027	.50187	.46651	.43393	.40388	.32690
9	.70259	.64461	.59190	.54393	.50025	.46043	.42410	.39092	.36061	.28426
10	.67556	.61391	.55839	.50835	.46319	.42241	.38554	.35218	.32197	.24719

For two periods at an interest rate of 10%, the present value factor is .82645, which equals the $826.45 ($1,000 × .82645) computed previously.

Let's now go back to our lottery example. Given the present value concepts just learned, we can determine whether receiving $10,000,000 in three years is better than receiving $7,000,000 today, assuming the appropriate discount rate is 9%. The computation is as follows.

Illustration 10A-4
Present value of $10,000,000 to be received in three years

$10,000,000 × PV of 1 due in 3 years at 9% =	
$10,000,000 × .77218 (Table 10A-1)	$7,721,800
Amount to be received from state immediately	7,000,000
Difference	$ 721,800

What this computation shows you is that you would be $721,800 better off receiving the $10,000,000 at the end of three years rather than taking $7,000,000 immediately.

Present Value of Interest Payments (Annuities)

In addition to receiving the face value of a bond at maturity, an investor also receives periodic interest payments over the life of the bonds. These periodic payments are called **annuities**.

In order to compute the present value of an annuity, we need to know (1) the interest rate, (2) the number of interest periods, and (3) the amount of the periodic receipts or payments. To illustrate the computation of the present value of an annuity, assume that you will receive $1,000 cash annually for three years and the interest rate is 10%. The time diagram in Illustration 10A-5 depicts this situation.

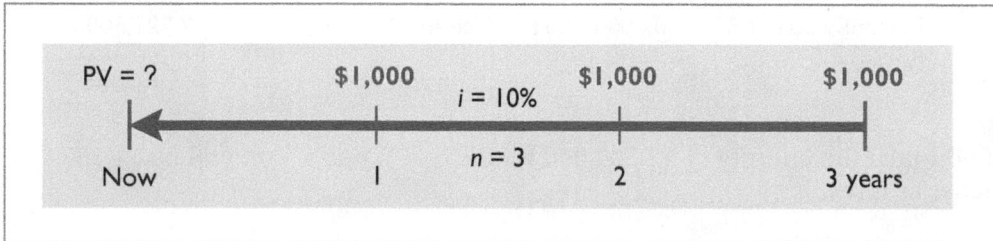

Illustration 10A-5
Time diagram for a three-year annuity

The present value in this situation may be computed as follows.

Future Amount	×	Present Value of 1 Factor at 10%	=	Present Value
$1,000 (1 year away)		.90909		$ 909.09
1,000 (2 years away)		.82645		826.45
1,000 (3 years away)		.75132		751.32
		2.48686		$2,486.86

Illustration 10A-6
Present value of a series of future amounts computation

We also can use annuity tables to value annuities. As illustrated in Table 10A-2 below, these tables show the present value of 1 to be received periodically for a given number of periods.

TABLE 10A-2										
Present Value of an Annuity of 1										

(n) Periods	4%	5%	6%	7%	8%	9%	10%	11%	12%	15%
1	.96154	.95238	.94340	.93458	.92593	.91743	.90909	.90090	.89286	.86957
2	1.88609	1.85941	1.83339	1.80802	1.78326	1.75911	1.73554	1.71252	1.69005	1.62571
3	2.77509	2.72325	2.67301	2.62432	2.57710	2.53130	2.48685	2.44371	2.40183	2.28323
4	3.62990	3.54595	3.46511	3.38721	3.31213	3.23972	3.16986	3.10245	3.03735	2.85498
5	4.45182	4.32948	4.21236	4.10020	3.99271	3.88965	3.79079	3.69590	3.60478	3.35216
6	5.24214	5.07569	4.91732	4.76654	4.62288	4.48592	4.35526	4.23054	4.11141	3.78448
7	6.00205	5.78637	5.58238	5.38929	5.20637	5.03295	4.86842	4.71220	4.56376	4.16042
8	6.73274	6.46321	6.20979	5.97130	5.74664	5.53482	5.33493	5.14612	4.96764	4.48732
9	7.43533	7.10782	6.80169	6.51523	6.24689	5.99525	5.75902	5.53705	5.32825	4.77158
10	8.11090	7.72173	7.36009	7.02358	6.71008	6.41766	6.14457	5.88923	5.65022	5.01877

From Table 10A-2 you can see that the present value factor of an annuity of 1 for three periods at 10% is 2.48685.[2] This present value factor is the total of the three individual present value factors as shown in Illustration 10A-6. Applying this amount to the annual cash flow of $1,000 produces a present value of $2,486.85.

Let's now go back to our lottery example. We determined that you would get more money if you wait and take the $10,000,000 in three years rather than take $7,000,000 immediately. But there is still another option—to receive $3,500,000 at the end of **each year** for three years (an annuity). The computation to evaluate this option (again assuming a 9% discount rate) is as follows.

Illustration 10A-7

Present value of lottery payments to be received over three years

$3,500,000 × PV of 1 due yearly for 3 years at 9% =	
$3,500,000 × 2.53130 (Table 10A-2)	$8,859,550
Present value of $10,000,000 to be received in 3 years	7,721,800
Difference	$1,137,750

If you take the annuity of $3,500,000 for each of 3 years, you will be $1,137,750 richer as a result.

Time Periods and Discounting

We have used an **annual** interest rate to determine present value. Present value computations may also be done over shorter periods of time, such as monthly, quarterly, or semiannually. When the time frame is less than one year, it is necessary to convert the annual interest rate to the shorter time frame.

Assume, for example, that the investor in Illustration 10A-6 received $500 **semiannually** for three years instead of $1,000 annually. In this case, the number of periods becomes 6 (3 × 2), the interest rate is 5% (10% ÷ 2), the present value factor from Table 10A-2 is 5.07569, and the present value of the future cash flows is $2,537.85 (5.07569 × $500). This amount is slightly higher than the $2,486.86 computed in Illustration 10A-6 because interest is computed twice during the same year. That is, interest is earned on the first half-year's interest.

Computing the Present Value of a Bond

The present value (or market price) of a bond is a function of three variables: (1) the payment amounts, (2) the length of time until the amounts are paid, and (3) the interest (discount) rate.

The first variable (dollars to be paid) is made up of two elements: (1) a series of interest payments (an annuity), and (2) the principal amount (a single sum). To compute the present value of the bond, we must discount both the interest payments and the principal amount.

When the investor's interest (discount) rate is equal to the bond's contractual interest rate, the present value of the bonds will equal the face value of the bonds. To illustrate, assume a bond issue of 10%, five-year bonds with a face value of $100,000 with interest payable **semiannually** on January 1 and July 1. If the discount rate is the same as the contractual rate, the bonds will sell **at face value**. In this case, the investor will receive (1) $100,000 at maturity and (2) a series of ten $5,000 interest payments [$100,000 × (10% ÷ 2)] over the term of the bonds. The length of time is expressed in terms of interest periods (in this case, 10) and the discount rate per interest period (5%). The time diagram in Illustration 10A-8 depicts the variables involved in this discounting situation.

---

[2]The difference of .00001 between 2.48686 and 2.48685 is due to rounding.

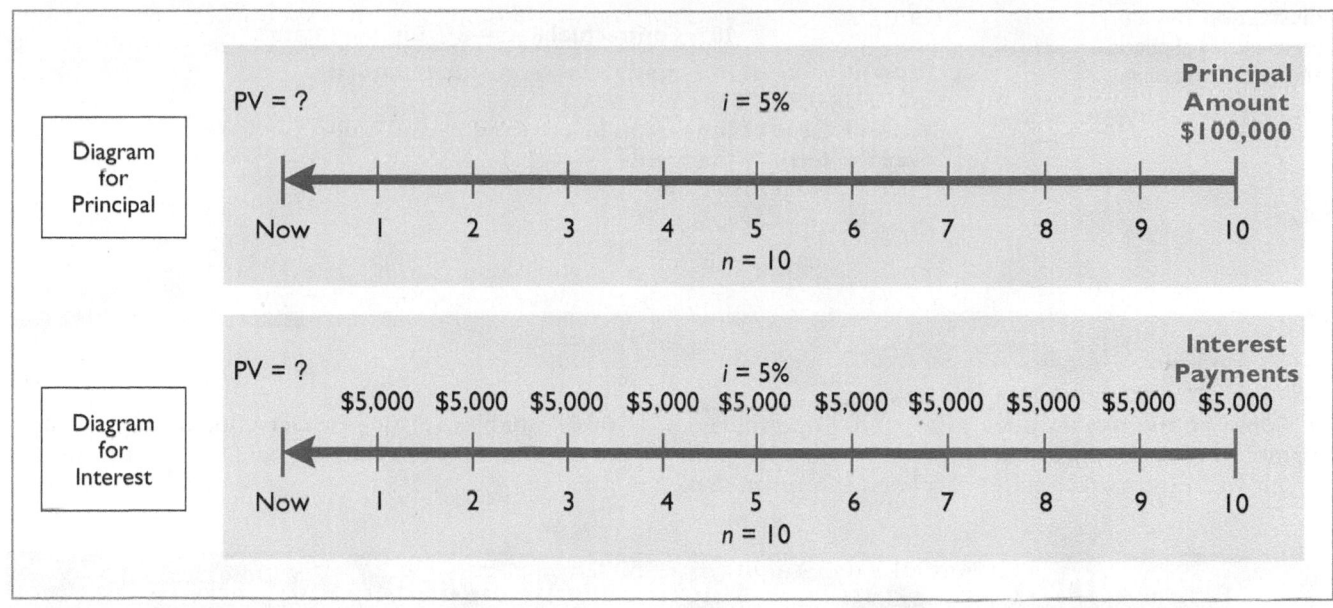

The computation of the present value of Candlestick's bonds, assuming they were issued at face value (page 494), is shown below.

Illustration 10A-9
Present value of principal and interest (face value)

10% Contractual Rate—10% Discount Rate

Present value of principal to be received at maturity
$100,000 × PV of 1 due in 10 periods at 5%
$100,000 × .61391 (Table 10A-1) $ 61,391
Present value of interest to be received periodically over the term of the bonds
$5,000 × PV of 1 due periodically for 10 periods at 5%
$5,000 × 7.72173 (Table 10A-2)   38,609*
Present value of bonds   **$100,000**

*Rounded.

Now assume that the investor's required rate of return is 12%, not 10%. The future amounts are again $100,000 and $5,000, respectively. But now we must use a discount rate of 6% (12% ÷ 2). The present value of Candlestick's bonds issued at a discount (page 496) is $92,639 as computed below.

Illustration 10A-10
Present value of principal and interest (discount)

10% Contractual Rate—12% Discount Rate

Present value of principal to be received at maturity
$100,000 × .55839 (Table 10A-1) $ 55,839
Present value of interest to be received periodically over the term of the bonds
$5,000 × 7.36009 (Table 10A-2)   36,800
Present value of bonds   **$92,639**

If the discount rate is 8% and the contractual rate is 10%, the present value of Candlestick's bonds issued at a premium (page 497) is $108,111, computed as shown in Illustration 10A-11 (page 512).

Illustration 10A-11
Present value of principal
and interest (premium)

<table>
<tr><td colspan="2" align="center">**10% Contractual Rate—8% Discount Rate**</td></tr>
<tr><td>Present value of principal to be received at maturity</td><td></td></tr>
<tr><td>$100,000 × .67556 (Table 10A-1)</td><td>$ 67,556</td></tr>
<tr><td>Present value of interest to be received periodically</td><td></td></tr>
<tr><td>over the term of the bonds</td><td></td></tr>
<tr><td>$5,000 × 8.11090 (Table 10A-2)</td><td>40,555</td></tr>
<tr><td>Present value of bonds</td><td>$108,111</td></tr>
</table>

SUMMARY OF LEARNING OBJECTIVE FOR APPENDIX 10A

9 Compute the market price of a bond. Time value of money concepts are useful for pricing bonds. The present value (or market price) of a bond is a function of three variables: (1) the payment amounts, (2) the length of time until the amounts are paid, and (3) the interest rate.

APPENDIX 10B   Effective-Interest Method of Bond Amortization

LEARNING OBJECTIVE   10

Apply the effective-interest method of amortizing bond discount and bond premium.

Under the **effective-interest method**, the amortization of bond discount or bond premium results in periodic interest expense equal to a **constant percentage** of the carrying value of the bonds. The effective-interest method results in varying amounts of amortization and interest expense per period but **a constant percentage rate**.

The following steps are required under the effective-interest method.

1. Compute the **bond interest expense**. To do so, multiply the carrying value of the bonds at the beginning of the interest period by the effective-interest rate.

2. Compute the **bond interest paid** (or accrued). To do so, multiply the face value of the bonds by the contractual interest rate.

3. Compute the **amortization amount**. To do so, determine the difference between the amounts computed in steps (1) and (2).

Illustration 10B-1 depicts these steps.

Illustration 10B-1
Computation of amortization—
effective-interest method

(1) Bond Interest Expense	(2) Bond Interest Paid	(3)
(Carrying Value of Bonds at Beginning of Period × Effective-Interest Rate)	− (Face Amount of Bonds × Contractual Interest Rate)	= Amortization Amount

When the difference between the straight-line method of amortization (Appendix 10C) and the effective-interest method is material, GAAP requires the use of the effective-interest method.

Amortizing Bond Discount

To illustrate the effective-interest method of bond discount amortization, assume that Candlestick, Inc. issues $100,000 of 10%, five-year bonds on January 1, 2015, with interest payable each July 1 and January 1 (pages 496–497). The bonds sell for $92,639 (92.639% of face value). This sales price results in a bond discount of $7,361 ($100,000 − $92,639) and an effective-interest rate of 12%. A bond discount amortization schedule, as shown in Illustration 10B-2, facilitates the recording of interest expense and the discount amortization. Note that interest expense as a percentage of carrying value remains constant at 6%.

		Candlestick Inc.xls			
Home Insert Page Layout Formulas Data Review View					
P18	*fx*				
	A	B	C	D	E	F

A	B	C	D	E	F
CANDLESTICK, INC.					
Bond Discount Amortization					
Effective-Interest Method—Semiannual Interest Payments					
10% Bonds Issued at 12%					
Semiannual Interest Periods	**(A) Interest to Be Paid (5% × $100,000)**	**(B) Interest Expense to Be Recorded (6% × Preceding Bond Carrying Value)**	**(C) Discount Amortization (B) – (A)**	**(D) Unamortized Discount (D) – (C)**	**(E) Bond Carrying Value ($100,000 – D)**
Issue date				$7,361	$ 92,639
1	$ 5,000	$ 5,558 (6% × $92,639)	$ 558	6,803	93,197
2	5,000	5,592 (6% × $93,197)	592	6,211	93,789
3	5,000	5,627 (6% × $93,789)	627	5,584	94,416
4	5,000	5,665 (6% × $94,416)	665	4,919	95,081
5	5,000	5,705 (6% × $95,081)	705	4,214	95,786
6	5,000	5,747 (6% × $95,786)	747	3,467	96,533
7	5,000	5,792 (6% × $96,533)	792	2,675	97,325
8	5,000	5,840 (6% × $97,325)	840	1,835	98,165
9	5,000	5,890 (6% × $98,165)	890	945	99,055
10	5,000	5,945* (6% × $99,055)	945	–0–	100,000
	$50,000	$57,361	$7,361		

Column **(A)** remains constant because the face value of the bonds ($100,000) is multiplied by the semiannual contractual interest rate (5%) each period.

Column **(B)** is computed as the preceding bond carrying value times the semiannual effective-interest rate (6%).

Column **(C)** indicates the discount amortization each period.

Column **(D)** decreases each period until it reaches zero at maturity.

Column **(E)** increases each period until it equals face value at maturity.

_____

*$2 difference due to rounding.

Illustration 10B-2
Bond discount amortization schedule

We have highlighted columns (A), (B), and (C) in the amortization schedule to emphasize their importance. These three columns provide the numbers for each period's journal entries. They are the primary reason for preparing the schedule.

For the first interest period, the computations of interest expense and the bond discount amortization are:

Illustration 10B-3
Computation of bond discount amortization

Interest expense ($92,639 × 6%)	$5,558
Contractual interest ($100,000 × 5%)	5,000
Bond discount amortization	**$ 558**

Candlestick records the payment of interest and amortization of bond discount on July 1, 2015, as follows.

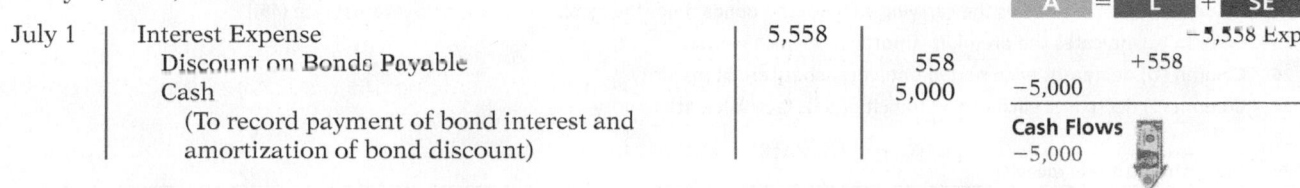

July 1	Interest Expense	5,558	
	Discount on Bonds Payable		558
	Cash		5,000
	(To record payment of bond interest and amortization of bond discount)		

A = L + SE
−5,558 Exp
+558
−5,000

Cash Flows
−5,000

For the second interest period, bond interest expense will be $5,592 ($93,197 × 6%), and the discount amortization will be $592. At December 31, Candlestick makes the following adjusting entry.

Cash Flows
no effect

Dec. 31	Interest Expense	5,592	
	Discount on Bonds Payable		592
	Interest Payable		5,000
	(To record accrued interest and		
	amortization of bond discount)		

A = L + SE
−5,592 Exp
+592
+5,000

Total interest expense for 2015 is $11,150 ($5,558 + $5,592). On January 1, Candlestick records payment of the interest by a debit to Interest Payable and a credit to Cash.

Amortizing Bond Premium

Helpful Hint
When a bond sells for $108,111, it is quoted as 108.111% of face value. Note that $108,111 can be proven as shown in Appendix 10A.

The amortization of bond premium by the effective-interest method is similar to the procedures described for bond discount. For example, assume that Candlestick, Inc. issues $100,000, 10%, five-year bonds on January 1, 2015, with interest payable on July 1 and January 1 (pages 497–498). In this case, the bonds sell for $108,111. This sales price results in bond premium of $8,111 and an effective-interest rate of 8%. Illustration 10B-4 shows the bond premium amortization schedule.

Illustration 10B-4
Bond premium amortization schedule

Candlestick Inc.xls

Home | Insert | Page Layout | Formulas | Data | Review | View

P18   fx

CANDLESTICK, INC.
Bond Premium Amortization
Effective-Interest Method—Semiannual Interest Payments
10% Bonds Issued at 8%

Semiannual Interest Periods	(A) Interest to Be Paid (5% × $100,000)	(B) Interest Expense to Be Recorded (4% × Preceding Bond Carrying Value)		(C) Premium Amortization (A) – (B)	(D) Unamortized Premium (D) – (C)	(E) Bond Carrying Value ($100,000 + D)
Issue date					$8,111	$108,111
1	$ 5,000	$ 4,324	(4% × $108,111)	$ 676	7,435	107,435
2	5,000	4,297	(4% × $107,435)	703	6,732	106,732
3	5,000	4,269	(4% × $106,732)	731	6,001	106,001
4	5,000	4,240	(4% × $106,001)	760	5,241	105,241
5	5,000	4,210	(4% × $105,241)	790	4,451	104,451
6	5,000	4,178	(4% × $104,451)	822	3,629	103,629
7	5,000	4,145	(4% × $103,629)	855	2,774	102,774
8	5,000	4,111	(4% × $102,774)	889	1,885	101,885
9	5,000	4,075	(4% × $101,885)	925	960	100,960
10	5,000	4,040*	(4% × $100,960)	960	–0–	100,000
	$50,000	$41,889		$8,111		

Column (A) remains constant because the face value of the bonds ($100,000) is multiplied by the semiannual contractual interest rate (5%) each period.

Column (B) is computed as the carrying value of the bonds times the semiannual effective-interest rate (4%).

Column (C) indicates the premium amortization each period.

Column (D) decreases each period until it reaches zero at maturity.

Column (E) decreases each period until it equals face value at maturity.

*$2 difference due to rounding.

For the first interest period, the computations of interest expense and the bond premium amortization are:

Interest expense ($108,111 × 4%)	$4,324	
Contractual interest ($100,000 × 5%)	5,000	
Bond premium amortization	**$ 676**	

Illustration 10B-5
Computation of bond premium amortization

Candlestick records payments on the first interest date as follows.

July 1	Interest Expense	4,324	
	Premium on Bonds Payable	676	
	Cash		5,000
	(To record payment of bond interest and amortization of bond premium)		

A	=	L	+	SE
				−4,324 Exp
				−676
−5,000				

Cash Flows
−5,000

For the second interest period, interest expense will be $4,297, and the premium amortization will be $703. Total bond interest expense for 2015 is $8,621 ($4,324 + $4,297).

> **DO IT!**

Gardner Corporation issues $1,750,000, 10-year, 12% bonds on January 1, 2015, at $1,968,090, to yield 10%. The bonds pay semiannual interest July 1 and January 1. Gardner uses the effective-interest method of amortization.

Instructions
(a) Prepare the journal entry to record the issuance of the bonds.
(b) Prepare the journal entry to record the payment of interest on July 1, 2015.

Solution

Action Plan

✔ Compute interest expense by multiplying bond carrying value at the beginning of the period by the effective-interest rate.

✔ Compute credit to cash (or interest payable) by multiplying the face value of the bonds by the contractual interest rate.

✔ Compute bond premium or discount amortization, which is the difference between interest expense and cash paid.

✔ Interest expense decreases when the effective-interest method is used for bonds issued at a premium. The reason is that a constant percentage is applied to a decreasing book value to compute interest expense.

(a) 2015			
Jan. 1	Cash	1,968,090	
	Bonds Payable		1,750,000
	Premium on Bonds Payable		218,090
	(To record issuance of bonds at a premium)		
(b) 2015			
July 1	Interest Expense	98,405*	
	Premium on Bonds Payable	6,595**	
	Cash		105,000
	(To record payment of semiannual interest and amortization of bond premium)		

*($1,968,090 × 5%)
**($105,000 − $98,405)

10 Apply the effective-interest method of amortizing bond discount and bond premium. The effective-interest method results in varying amounts of amortization and interest expense per period but a constant percentage rate of interest. When the difference between the straight-line and effective-interest method is material, GAAP requires the use of the effective-interest method.

Effective-interest method of amortization A method of amortizing bond discount or bond premium that results in periodic interest expense equal to a constant percentage of the carrying value of the bonds. (p. 512).

APPENDIX 10C Straight-Line Amortization

LEARNING OBJECTIVE 11

Apply the straight-line method of amortizing bond discount and bond premium.

Amortizing Bond Discount

Under the **straight-line method of amortization**, the amortization of bond discount or bond premium results in periodic interest expense of the same amount in each interest period. In other words, the straight-line method results in a constant amount of amortization and interest expense per period. The amount is determined using the formula in Illustration 10C-1.

Illustration 10C-1
Formula for straight-line method of bond discount amortization

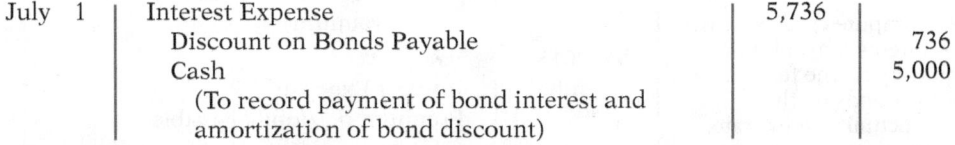

Bond Discount	÷	Number of Interest Periods	=	Bond Discount Amortization

In the Candlestick, Inc. example (pages 496–497), the company sold $100,000, five-year, 10% bonds on January 1, 2015, for $92,639. This price resulted in a $7,361 bond discount ($100,000 − $92,639). Interest is payable on July 1 and January 1. The bond discount amortization for each interest period is $736 ($7,361 ÷ 10). Candlestick records the payment of bond interest and the amortization of bond discount on the first interest date (July 1, 2015) as follows.

A = L + SE
                −5,736 Exp
        +736
−5,000
Cash Flows
−5,000

July 1	Interest Expense	5,736	
	Discount on Bonds Payable		736
	Cash		5,000
	(To record payment of bond interest and amortization of bond discount)		

At December 31, Candlestick makes the following adjusting entry.

A = L + SE
                −5,736 Exp
        +736
        +5,000
Cash Flows
no effect

Dec. 31	Interest Expense	5,736	
	Discount on Bonds Payable		736
	Interest Payable		5,000
	(To record accrued bond interest and amortization of bond discount)		

Over the term of the bonds, the balance in Discount on Bonds Payable will decrease annually by the **same amount** until it has a zero balance at the maturity date of the bonds. Thus, the carrying value of the bonds at maturity will be equal to the face value.

It is useful to prepare a bond discount amortization schedule as shown in Illustration 10C-2. The schedule shows interest expense, discount amortization, and the carrying value of the bond for each interest period. As indicated, the interest expense recorded **each period** for the Candlestick bond is $5,736. Also note that the carrying value of the bond increases $736 each period until it reaches its face value $100,000 at the end of period 10.

Illustration 10C-2
Bond discount amortization schedule

	Candlestick Inc.xls				
Home Insert Page Layout Formulas Data Review View					
P18 *fx*					
A	B	C	D	E	F

Semiannual Interest Periods	(A) Interest to Be Paid (5% × $100,000)	(B) Interest Expense to Be Recorded (A) + (C)	(C) Discount Amortization ($7,361 ÷ 10)	(D) Unamortized Discount (D) – (C)	(E) Bond Carrying Value ($100,000 – D)
CANDLESTICK, INC.					
Bond Discount Amortization					
Straight-Line Method—Semiannual Interest Payments					
Issue date				$7,361	$ 92,639
1	$ 5,000	$ 5,736	$ 736	6,625	93,375
2	5,000	5,736	736	5,889	94,111
3	5,000	5,736	736	5,153	94,847
4	5,000	5,736	736	4,417	95,583
5	5,000	5,736	736	3,681	96,319
6	5,000	5,736	736	2,945	97,055
7	5,000	5,736	736	2,209	97,791
8	5,000	5,736	736	1,473	98,527
9	5,000	5,736	736	737	99,263
10	5,000	5,737*	737*	–0–	100,000
	$50,000	$57,361	$7,361		

Column **(A)** remains constant because the face value of the bonds ($100,000) is multiplied by the semiannual contractual interest rate (5%) each period.

Column **(B)** is computed as the interest paid (Column A) plus the discount amortization (Column C).

Column **(C)** indicates the discount amortization each period.

Column **(D)** decreases each period by the same amount until it reaches zero at maturity.

Column **(E)** increases each period by the same amount of discount amortization until it equals the face value at maturity.

*$1 difference due to rounding.

We have highlighted columns (A), (B), and (C) in the amortization schedule to emphasize their importance. These three columns provide the numbers for each period's journal entries. They are the primary reason for preparing the schedule.

Amortizing Bond Premium

The amortization of bond premium parallels that of bond discount. Illustration 10C-3 presents the formula for determining bond premium amortization under the straight-line method.

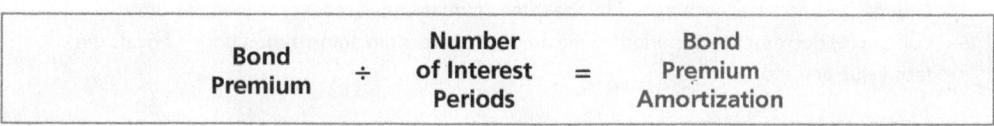

Illustration 10C-3
Formula for straight-line method of bond premium amortization

Continuing our example, assume that Candlestick sells the bonds for $108,111, rather than $92,639 (pages 497–498). This sale price results in a bond premium of $8,111 ($108,111 − $100,000). The bond premium amortization for each interest period is $811 ($8,111 ÷ 10). Candlestick records the first payment of interest on July 1 as follows.

A	=	L	+	SE

−4,189 Exp
−811
−5,000

Cash Flows
−5,000

July 1	Interest Expense	4,189	
	Premium on Bonds Payable	811	
	Cash		5,000
	(To record payment of bond interest and		
	amortization of bond premium)		

At December 31, the company makes the following adjusting entry.

A	=	L	+	SE

−4,189 Exp
−811
+5,000

Cash Flows
no effect

Dec. 31	Interest Expense	4,189	
	Premium on Bonds Payable	811	
	Interest Payable		5,000
	(To record accrued bond interest and		
	amortization of bond premium)		

Over the term of the bonds, the balance in Premium on Bonds Payable will decrease annually **by the same amount** until it has a zero balance at maturity.

It is useful to prepare a bond premium amortization schedule as shown in Illustration 10C-4. It shows interest expense, premium amortization, and the carrying

Illustration 10C-4
Bond premium amortization schedule

Candlestick Inc.xls

Home　Insert　Page Layout　Formulas　Data　Review　View

P18   fx

	A	B	C	D	E	F
1			**CANDLESTICK, INC.**			
2			**Bond Premium Amortization**			
3			**Straight-Line Method—Semiannual Interest Payments**			
4		**(A)**	**(B)**	**(C)**	**(D)**	**(E)**
5	**Semiannual**	**Interest to**	**Interest Expense**	**Premium**	**Unamortized**	**Bond**
6	**Interest**	**Be Paid**	**to Be Recorded**	**Amortization**	**Premium**	**Carrying Value**
7	**Periods**	**(5% × $100,000)**	**(A) – (C)**	**($8,111 ÷ 10)**	**(D) – (C)**	**($100,000 + D)**
8	Issue date				$8,111	$108,111
9	1	$ 5,000	$ 4,189	$ 811	7,300	107,300
10	2	5,000	4,189	811	6,489	106,489
11	3	5,000	4,189	811	5,678	105,678
12	4	5,000	4,189	811	4,867	104,867
13	5	5,000	4,189	811	4,056	104,056
14	6	5,000	4,189	811	3,245	103,245
15	7	5,000	4,189	811	2,434	102,434
16	8	5,000	4,189	811	1,623	101,623
17	9	5,000	4,189	811	812	100,812
18	10	5,000	4,188*	812*	–0–	100,000
19		$50,000	$41,889	$8,111		
20						
21	Column (A) remains constant because the face value of the bonds ($100,000) is multiplied by the semiannual contractual interest rate (5%) each period.					
22	Column (B) is computed as the interest paid (Column A) less the premium amortization (Column C).					
23	Column (C) indicates the premium amortization each period.					
24	Column (D) decreases each period by the same amount until it reaches zero at maturity.					
25	Column (E) decreases each period by the amount of premium amortization until it equals the face value at maturity.					
26						
27	*$1 difference due to rounding.					

value of the bond. The interest expense recorded each period for the Candlestick bond is $4,189. Also note that the carrying value of the bond decreases $811 each period until it reaches its face value ($100,000) at the end of period 10.

> DO IT!

Glenda Corporation issues $1,750,000, 10-year, 12% bonds on January 1, 2015, for $1,968,090 to yield 10%. The bonds pay semiannual interest July 1 and January 1. Glenda uses the straight-line method of amortization.

Action Plan

✔ Compute credit to cash (or interest payable) by multiplying the face value of the bonds by the contractual interest rate.

✔ Compute bond premium or discount amortization by dividing bond premium or discount by the total number of periods.

✔ Understand that interest expense decreases when bonds are issued at a premium. The reason is that the amortization of premium reduces the total cost of borrowing.

Instructions

(a) Prepare the journal entry to record the issuance of the bonds.

(b) Prepare the journal entry to record the payment of interest on July 1, 2015.

Solution

(a)	2015			
	Jan. 1	Cash	1,968,090	
		Bonds Payable		1,750,000
		Premium on Bonds Payable		218,090
(b)	2015			
	July 1	Interest Expense	94,095.50**	
		Premium on Bonds Payable	10,904.50*	
		Cash		105,000

*$218,090 ÷ 20
**$105,000 − $10,904.50

SUMMARY OF LEARNING OBJECTIVE FOR APPENDIX 10C

11 Apply the straight-line method of amortizing bond discount and bond premium. The straight-line method of amortization results in a constant amount of amortization and interest expense per period.

GLOSSARY FOR APPENDIX 10C

Straight-line method of amortization. A method of amortizing bond discount or bond premium that results in allocating the same amount to interest expense in each interest period. (p. 516).

WileyPLUS Self-Test, Brief Exercises, Exercises, Problem Set A, and many more components are available for practice in *WileyPLUS*.

*Note: All asterisked Questions, Exercises, and Problems relate to material in the appendices to the chapter.

SELF-TEST QUESTIONS

Answers are on page 539.

(LO 1) **1.** The time period for classifying a liability as current is one year or the operating cycle, whichever is:

(a) longer.

(b) shorter.

(c) probable.

(d) possible.

2. To be classified as a current liability, a debt must be (LO 1) expected to be paid within:

(a) one year.

(b) the operating cycle.

(c) 2 years.

(d) (a) or (b), whichever is longer.

(LO 2) **3.** Maggie Sharrer Company borrows $88,500 on September 1, 2015, from Sandwich State Bank by signing an $88,500, 12%, one-year note. What is the accrued interest at December 31, 2015?
(a) $2,655. (c) $4,425.
(b) $3,540. (d) $10,620.

(LO 3) **4.** Becky Sherrick Company has total proceeds from sales of $4,515. If the proceeds include sales taxes of 5%, the amount to be credited to Sales Revenue is:
(a) $4,000. (c) $4,289.25.
(b) $4,300. (d) No correct answer given.

(LO 3) **5.** Employer payroll taxes do **not** include:
(a) federal unemployment taxes.
(b) state unemployment taxes.
(c) federal income taxes.
(d) FICA taxes.

(LO 3) **6.** Sensible Insurance Company collected a premium of $18,000 for a 1-year insurance policy on April 1. What amount should Sensible report as a current liability for Unearned Service Revenue at December 31?
(a) $0. (c) $13,500.
(b) $4,500. (d) $18,000.

(LO 4) **7.** The term used for bonds that are unsecured is:
(a) callable bonds.
(b) indenture bonds.
(c) debenture bonds.
(d) bearer bonds.

(LO 5) **8.** Karson Inc. issues 10-year bonds with a maturity value of $200,000. If the bonds are issued at a premium, this indicates that:
(a) the contractual interest rate exceeds the market interest rate.
(b) the market interest rate exceeds the contractual interest rate.
(c) the contractual interest rate and the market interest rate are the same.
(d) no relationship exists between the two rates.

(LO 6) **9.** Gester Corporation redeems its $100,000 face value bonds at 105 on January 1, following the payment of semiannual interest. The carrying value of the bonds at the redemption date is $103,745. The entry to record the redemption will include a:
(a) credit of $3,745 to Loss on Bond Redemption.
(b) debit of $3,745 to Premium on Bonds Payable.
(c) credit of $1,255 to Gain on Bond Redemption.
(d) debit of $5,000 to Premium on Bonds Payable.

(LO 6) **10.** Colson Inc. converts $600,000 of bonds sold at face value into 10,000 shares of common stock, par value $1. Both the bonds and the stock have a market value of $760,000. What amount should be credited to Paid-in Capital in Excess of Par—Common Stock as a result of the conversion?
(a) $10,000. (c) $600,000.
(b) $160,000. (d) $590,000.

11. Andrews Inc. issues a $497,000, 10% 3-year mortgage (LO 7) note on January 1. The note will be paid in three annual installments of $200,000, each payable at the end of the year. What is the amount of interest expense that should be recognized by Andrews Inc. in the second year?
(a) $16,567. (c) $34,670.
(b) $49,700. (d) $346,700.

12. Howard Corporation issued a 20-year mortgage note (LO 7) payable on January 1, 2015. At December 31, 2015, the unpaid principal balance will be reported as:
(a) a current liability.
(b) a long-term liability.
(c) part current and part long-term liability.
(d) interest payable.

13. For 2015, Corn Flake Corporation reported net income (LO 8) of $300,000. Interest expense was $40,000 and income taxes were $100,000. The times interest earned was:
(a) 3 times. (c) 7.5 times.
(b) 4.4 times. (d) 11 times.

*14. The market price of a bond is dependent on: (LO 9)
(a) the payment amounts.
(b) the length of time until the amounts are paid.
(c) the interest rate.
(d) All of the above.

*15. On January 1, Besalius Inc. issued $1,000,000, 9% (LO 10) bonds for $938,554. The market rate of interest for these bonds is 10%. Interest is payable annually on December 31. Besalius uses the effective-interest method of amortizing bond discount. At the end of the first year, Besalius should report unamortized bond discount of:
(a) $54,900. (c) $51,610.
(b) $57,591. (d) $51,000.

*16. On January 1, Dias Corporation issued $1,000,000, (LO 10) 10%, 5-year bonds with interest payable on July 1 and January 1. The bonds sold for $1,081,105. The market rate of interest for these bonds was 8%. On the first interest date, using the effective-interest method, the debit entry to Interest Expense is for:
(a) $50,000. (c) $43,244.
(b) $54,055. (d) $100,811.

*17. On January 1, Hurley Corporation issues $500,000, (LO 11) 5-year, 12% bonds at 96 with interest payable on July 1 and January 1. The entry on July 1 to record payment of bond interest and the amortization of bond discount using the straight-line method will include a:
(a) debit to Interest Expense $30,000.
(b) debit to Interest Expense $60,000.
(c) credit to Discount on Bonds Payable $4,000.
(d) credit to Discount on Bonds Payable $2,000.

*18. For the bonds issued in Question 17 above, what is (LO 11) the carrying value of the bonds at the end of the third interest period?
(a) $486,000. (c) $472,000.
(b) $488,000. (d) $464,000.

Go to the book's companion website, www.wiley.com/college/weygandt, for additional Self-Test Questions.

✔ **The Navigator**

QUESTIONS

1. Lori Randle believes a current liability is a debt that can be expected to be paid in one year. Is Lori correct? Explain.

2. Petrocelli Company obtains $40,000 in cash by signing a 7%, 6-month, $40,000 note payable to First Bank on July 1. Petrocelli's fiscal year ends on September 30. What information should be reported for the note payable in the annual financial statements?

3. **(a)** Your roommate says, "Sales taxes are reported as an expense in the income statement." Do you agree? Explain.

   (b) Jensen Company has cash proceeds from sales of $8,400. This amount includes $400 of sales taxes. Give the entry to record the proceeds.

4. Ottawa University sold 15,000 season football tickets at $80 each for its six-game home schedule. What entries should be made (a) when the tickets were sold, and (b) after each game?

5. What is liquidity? What are two measures of liquidity?

6. Identify three taxes commonly withheld by the employer from an employee's gross pay.

7. (a) What are long-term liabilities? Give three examples. (b) What is a bond?

8. (a) As a source of long-term financing, what are the major advantages of bonds over common stock? (b) What are the major disadvantages in using bonds for long-term financing?

9. Contrast the following types of bonds: (a) secured and unsecured, and (b) convertible and callable.

10. The following terms are important in issuing bonds: (a) face value, (b) contractual interest rate, (c) bond indenture, and (d) bond certificate. Explain each of these terms.

11. Describe the two major obligations incurred by a company when bonds are issued.

12. Assume that Remington Inc. sold bonds with a face value of $100,000 for $104,000. Was the market interest rate equal to, less than, or greater than the bonds' contractual interest rate? Explain.

13. If a 7%, 10-year, $800,000 bond is issued at face value and interest is paid semiannually, what is the amount of the interest payment at the end of the first semiannual period?

14. If the Bonds Payable account has a balance of $900,000 and the Discount on Bonds Payable account has a balance of $120,000, what is the carrying value of the bonds?

15. Which accounts are debited and which are credited if a bond issue originally sold at a premium is redeemed before maturity at 97 immediately following the payment of interest?

16. Rattigan Corporation is considering issuing a convertible bond. What is a convertible bond? Discuss the advantages of a convertible bond from the standpoint of (a) the bondholders and (b) the issuing corporation.

17. Rob Grier, a friend of yours, has recently purchased a home for $125,000, paying $25,000 down and the remainder financed by a 10.5%, 20-year mortgage, payable at $998.38 per month. At the end of the first month, Rob receives a statement from the bank indicating that only $123.38 of principal was paid during the month. At this rate, he calculates that it will take over 67 years to pay off the mortgage. Is he right? Discuss.

18. In general, what are the requirements for the financial statement presentation of long-term liabilities?

*19. Kelli Deane is discussing the advantages of the effective-interest method of bond amortization with her accounting staff. What do you think Kelli is saying?

*20. Windsor Corporation issues $500,000 of 9%, 5-year bonds on January 1, 2015, at 104. If Windsor uses the effective-interest method in amortizing the premium, will the annual interest expense increase or decrease over the life of the bonds? Explain.

*21. Jill Grey and Mike Goreman are discussing how the market price of a bond is determined. Jill believes that the market price of a bond is solely a function of the amount of the principal payment at the end of the term of a bond. Is she right? Discuss.

*22. Explain the straight-line method of amortizing discount and premium on bonds payable.

*23. DeWeese Corporation issues $400,000 of 8%, 5-year bonds on January 1, 2015, at 105. Assuming that the straight-line method is used to amortize the premium, what is the total amount of interest expense for 2015?

BRIEF EXERCISES

BE10-1 Jamison Company has the following obligations at December 31: (a) a note payable for $100,000 due in 2 years, (b) a 10-year mortgage payable of $300,000 payable in ten $30,000 annual payments, (c) interest payable of $15,000 on the mortgage, and (d) accounts payable of $60,000. For each obligation, indicate whether it should be classified as a current liability. (Assume an operating cycle of less than one year.)

Identify whether obligations are current liabilities.

(LO 1)

BE10-2 Peralta Company borrows $60,000 on July 1 from the bank by signing a $60,000, 10%, one-year note payable.

Prepare entries for an interest-bearing note payable.

(LO 2)

(a) Prepare the journal entry to record the proceeds of the note.

(b) Prepare the journal entry to record accrued interest at December 31, assuming adjusting entries are made only at the end of the year.

Compute and record sales taxes payable.

(LO 3)

BE10-3 Coghlan Auto Supply does not segregate sales and sales taxes at the time of sale. The register total for March 16 is $16,380. All sales are subject to a 5% sales tax. Compute sales taxes payable, and make the entry to record sales taxes payable and sales revenue.

Prepare entries for unearned revenues.

(LO 3)

BE10-4 Derby University sells 4,000 season basketball tickets at $210 each for its 12-game home schedule. Give the entry to record (a) the sale of the season tickets and (b) the revenue recognized by playing the first home game.

Compute gross earnings and net pay.

(LO 3)

BE10-5 Beth Corbin's regular hourly wage rate is $16, and she receives an hourly rate of $24 for work in excess of 40 hours. During a January pay period, Beth works 45 hours. Beth's federal income tax withholding is $95, and she has no voluntary deductions. Compute Beth Corbin's gross earnings and net pay for the pay period.

Record a payroll and the payment of wages.

(LO 3)

BE10-6 Data for Beth Corbin are presented in BE10-5. Prepare the journal entries to record (a) Beth's pay for the period and (b) the payment of Beth's wages. Use January 15 for the end of the pay period and the payment date.

Compare bond versus stock financing.

(LO 4)

BE10-7 Moby Inc. is considering two alternatives to finance its construction of a new $2 million plant.

(a) Issuance of 200,000 shares of common stock at the market price of $10 per share.

(b) Issuance of $2 million, 8% bonds at face value.

Complete the following table, and indicate which alternative is preferable.

	Issue Stock	Issue Bond
Income before interest and taxes	$700,000	$700,000
Interest expense from bonds	_____	_____
Income before income taxes		
Income tax expense (30%)	_____	_____
Net income	$ _____	$ _____
Outstanding shares		500,000
Earnings per share	_____	_____

Prepare entries for bonds issued at face value.

(LO 5)

BE10-8 Meera Corporation issued 4,000, 8%, 5-year, $1,000 bonds dated January 1, 2015, at 100.

(a) Prepare the journal entry to record the sale of these bonds on January 1, 2015.

(b) Prepare the journal entry to record the first interest payment on July 1, 2015 (interest payable semiannually), assuming no previous accrual of interest.

(c) Prepare the adjusting journal entry on December 31, 2015, to record interest expense.

Prepare entries for bonds sold at a discount and a premium.

(LO 5)

BE10-9 Nasreen Company issues $2 million, 10-year, 8% bonds at 97, with interest payable on July 1 and January 1.

(a) Prepare the journal entry to record the sale of these bonds on January 1, 2015.

(b) Assuming instead that the above bonds sold for 104, prepare the journal entry to record the sale of these bonds on January 1, 2015.

Prepare entries for bonds issued.

(LO 5)

BE10-10 Frankum Company has issued three different bonds during 2015. Interest is payable semiannually on each of these bonds.

1. On January 1, 2015, 1,000, 8%, 5-year, $1,000 bonds dated January 1, 2015, were issued at face value.

2. On July 1, $900,000, 9%, 5-year bonds dated July 1, 2015, were issued at 102.

3. On September 1, $400,000, 7%, 5-year bonds dated September 1, 2015, were issued at 98.

Prepare the journal entry to record each bond transaction at the date of issuance.

Prepare entry for redemption of bonds.

(LO 6)

BE10-11 The balance sheet for Miley Consulting reports the following information on July 1, 2015.

Long-term liabilities		
Bonds payable	$1,000,000	
Less: Discount on bonds payable	60,000	$940,000

Miley decides to redeem these bonds at 101 after paying semiannual interest. Prepare the journal entry to record the redemption on July 1, 2015.

BE10-12 Hanschu Inc. issues an $800,000, 10%, 10-year mortgage note on December 31, 2015, to obtain financing for a new building. The terms provide for semiannual installment payments of $64,195. Prepare the entry to record the mortgage loan on December 31, 2015, and the first installment payment.

Prepare entries for long-term notes payable.
(LO 7)

BE10-13 Presented below are long-term liability items for Lind Company at December 31, 2015. Prepare the long-term liabilities section of the balance sheet for Lind Company.

Prepare statement presentation of long-term liabilities.
(LO 8)

Bonds payable, due 2017	$600,000
Notes payable, due 2020	80,000
Discount on bonds payable	45,000

*BE10-14 (a) What is the present value of $10,000 due 8 periods from now, discounted at 10%?

(b) What is the present value of $20,000 to be received at the end of each of 6 periods, discounted at 8%?

Determine present value.
(LO 9)

*BE10-15 Presented below is the partial bond discount amortization schedule for Ferree Corp. Ferree uses the effective-interest method of amortization.

Use effective-interest method of bond amortization.
(LO 10)

Semiannual Interest Periods	Interest to Be Paid	Interest Expense to Be Recorded	Discount Amortization	Unamortized Discount	Bond Carrying Value
Issue date				$62,311	$937,689
1	$45,000	$46,884	$1,884	60,427	939,573
2	45,000	46,979	1,979	58,448	941,552

(a) Prepare the journal entry to record the payment of interest and the discount amortization at the end of period 1.

(b) ⟶ Explain why interest expense is greater than interest paid.

(c) Explain why interest expense will increase each period.

*BE10-16 Sweetwood Company issues $5 million, 10-year, 9% bonds at 96, with interest payable on July 1 and January 1. The straight-line method is used to amortize bond discount.

Prepare entries for bonds issued at a discount.
(LO 11)

(a) Prepare the journal entry to record the sale of these bonds on January 1, 2015.

(b) Prepare the journal entry to record interest expense and bond discount amortization on July 1, 2015, assuming no previous accrual of interest.

*BE10-17 Golden Inc. issues $4 million, 5-year, 10% bonds at 102, with interest payable on July 1 and January 1. The straight-line method is used to amortize bond premium.

Prepare entries for bonds issued at a premium.
(LO 11)

(a) Prepare the journal entry to record the sale of these bonds on January 1, 2015.

(b) Prepare the journal entry to record interest expense and bond premium amortization on July 1, 2015, assuming no previous accrual of interest.

> DO IT! Review

DO IT! 10-1 You and several classmates are studying for the next accounting examination. They ask you to answer the following questions:

Answer questions about current liabilities.
(LO 2, 3)

1. If cash is borrowed on a $70,000, 9-month, 6% note on August 1, how much interest expense would be incurred by December 31?

2. The cash register total including sales taxes is $42,000, and the sales tax rate is 5%. What is the sales taxes payable?

3. If $45,000 is collected in advance on November 1 for 6-month magazine subscriptions, what amount of subscription revenue should be recognized by December 31?

DO IT! 10-2 During the month of February, Morrisey Corporation's employees earned wages of $74,000. Withholdings related to these wages were $5,661 for Social Security (FICA), $7,100 for federal income tax, and $1,900 for state income tax. Costs incurred for unemployment taxes were $110 for federal and $160 for state.

Prepare entries for payroll and payroll taxes.
(LO 3)

Prepare the February 28 journal entries for (a) salaries and wages expense and salaries and wages payable assuming that all February wages will be paid in March and (b) the company's payroll tax expense.

Evaluate statements about bonds.

(LO 4)

DO IT! 10-3 State whether each of the following statements is true or false. If false, indicate how to correct the statement.

_____ **1.** Mortgage bonds and sinking fund bonds are both examples of debenture bonds.

_____ **2.** Convertible bonds are also known as callable bonds.

_____ **3.** The market rate is the rate investors demand for loaning funds.

_____ **4.** Semiannual interest on bonds is equal to the face value times the stated rate times 6/12.

_____ **5.** The present value of a bond is the value at which it should sell in the market.

Prepare journal entry for bond issuance and show balance sheet presentation.

(LO 5)

DO IT! 10-4 Eubank Corporation issues $500,000 of bonds for $520,000. (a) Prepare the journal entry to record the issuance of the bonds, and (b) show how the bonds would be reported on the balance sheet at the date of issuance.

Prepare entry for bond redemption.

(LO 6)

DO IT! 10-5 Prater Corporation issued $400,000 of 10-year bonds at a discount. Prior to maturity, when the carrying value of the bonds was $390,000, the company redeemed the bonds at 99. Prepare the entry to record the redemption of the bonds.

Prepare entries for mortgage note and installment payment on note.

(LO 7)

DO IT! 10-6 Detwiler Orchard issues a $700,000, 6%, 15-year mortgage note to obtain needed financing for a new lab. The terms call for semiannual payments of $35,714 each. Prepare the entries to record the mortgage loan and the first installment payment.

EXERCISES

Prepare entries for interest-bearing notes.

(LO 2)

E10-1 C.S. Lewis Company had the following transactions involving notes payable.

July 1, 2015	Borrows $50,000 from First National Bank by signing a 9-month, 8% note.
Nov. 1, 2015	Borrows $60,000 from Lyon County State Bank by signing a 3-month, 6% note.
Dec. 31, 2015	Prepares adjusting entries.
Feb. 1, 2016	Pays principal and interest to Lyon County State Bank.
Apr. 1, 2016	Pays principal and interest to First National Bank.

Instructions

Prepare journal entries for each of the transactions.

Prepare entries for interest-bearing notes.

(LO 2)

E10-2 On June 1, Merando Company borrows $90,000 from First Bank on a 6-month, $90,000, 8% note.

Instructions

(a) Prepare the entry on June 1.

(b) Prepare the adjusting entry on June 30.

(c) Prepare the entry at maturity (December 1), assuming monthly adjusting entries have been made through November 30.

(d) What was the total financing cost (interest expense)?

Journalize sales and related taxes.

(LO 3)

E10-3 In performing accounting services for small businesses, you encounter the following situations pertaining to cash sales.

1. Poole Company enters sales and sales taxes separately in its cash register. On April 10, the register totals are sales $30,000 and sales taxes $1,500.

2. Waterman Company does not segregate sales and sales taxes. Its register total for April 15 is $25,680, which includes a 7% sales tax.

Instructions

Prepare the entry to record the sales transactions and related taxes for each client.

E10-4 Moreno Company publishes a monthly sports magazine, *Fishing Preview*. Subscriptions to the magazine cost $20 per year. During November 2015, Moreno sells 15,000 subscriptions beginning with the December issue. Moreno prepares financial statements quarterly and recognizes subscription revenue at the end of the quarter. The company uses the accounts Unearned Subscription Revenue and Subscription Revenue.

Instructions
(a) Prepare the entry in November for the receipt of the subscriptions.
(b) Prepare the adjusting entry at December 31, 2015, to record sales revenue recognized in December 2015.
(c) Prepare the adjusting entry at March 31, 2016, to record sales revenue recognized in the first quarter of 2016.

E10-5 Dan Noll's gross earnings for the week were $1,780, his federal income tax withholding was $303, and his FICA total was $136.

Instructions
(a) What was Noll's net pay for the week?
(b) Journalize the entry for the recording of his pay in the general journal. (*Note:* Use Salaries and Wages Payable: not Cash.)
(c) Record the issuing of the check for Noll's pay in the general journal.

E10-6 According to the accountant of Ulster Inc., its payroll taxes for the week were as follows: $137.68 for FICA taxes, $13.77 for federal unemployment taxes, and $92.93 for state unemployment taxes.

Instructions
Journalize the entry to record the accrual of the payroll taxes.

E10-7 Suppose the following financial data were reported by 3M Company for 2014 and 2015 (dollars in millions).

3M COMPANY
Balance Sheets (partial)

	2015	2014
Current assets		
Cash and cash equivalents	$ 3,040	$1,849
Accounts receivable, net	3,250	3,195
Inventories	2,639	3,013
Other current assets	1,866	1,541
Total current assets	$10,795	$9,598
Current liabilities	$ 4,897	$5,839

Instructions
(a) Calculate the current ratio and working capital for 3M for 2014 and 2015.
(b) Suppose that at the end of 2015, 3M management used $200 million cash to pay off $200 million of accounts payable. How would its current ratio and working capital have changed?

E10-8 Nick Bosch has prepared the following list of statements about bonds.

1. Bonds are a form of interest-bearing notes payable.
2. When seeking long-term financing, an advantage of issuing bonds over issuing common stock is that stockholder control is not affected.
3. When seeking long-term financing, an advantage of issuing common stock over issuing bonds is that tax savings result.
4. Secured bonds have specific assets of the issuer pledged as collateral for the bonds.
5. Secured bonds are also known as debenture bonds.
6. A conversion feature may be added to bonds to make them more attractive to bond buyers.
7. The rate used to determine the amount of cash interest the borrower pays is called the stated rate.
8. Bond prices are usually quoted as a percentage of the face value of the bond.
9. The present value of a bond is the value at which it should sell in the marketplace.

Instructions
Identify each statement as true or false. If false, indicate how to correct the statement.

Compare two alternatives of financing—issuance of common stock vs. issuance of bonds.

(LO 4)

E10-9 Gilliland Airlines is considering two alternatives for the financing of a purchase of a fleet of airplanes. These two alternatives are:

1. Issue 90,000 shares of common stock at $30 per share. (Cash dividends have not been paid nor is the payment of any contemplated.)
2. Issue 10%, 10-year bonds at face value for $2,700,000.

It is estimated that the company will earn $800,000 before interest and taxes as a result of this purchase. The company has an estimated tax rate of 30% and has 120,000 shares of common stock outstanding prior to the new financing.

Instructions

Determine the effect on net income and earnings per share for these two methods of financing.

Prepare entries for issuance of bonds, and payment and accrual of bond interest.

(LO 5)

E10-10 On January 1, Klosterman Company issued $500,000, 10%, 10-year bonds at face value. Interest is payable semiannually on July 1 and January 1.

Instructions

Prepare journal entries to record the following.

(a) The issuance of the bonds.
(b) The payment of interest on July 1, assuming that interest was not accrued on June 30.
(c) The accrual of interest on December 31.

Prepare entries for bonds issued at face value.

(LO 5)

E10-11 On January 1, Forrester Company issued $400,000, 8%, 5-year bonds at face value. Interest is payable semiannually on July 1 and January 1.

Instructions

Prepare journal entries to record the following events.

(a) The issuance of the bonds.
(b) The payment of interest on July 1, assuming no previous accrual of interest.
(c) The accrual of interest on December 31.

Prepare entries to record issuance of bonds at discount and premium.

(LO 5)

E10-12 Whitmore Company issued $500,000 of 5-year, 8% bonds at 97 on January 1, 2015. The bonds pay interest twice a year.

Instructions

(a) (1) Prepare the journal entry to record the issuance of the bonds.
    (2) Compute the total cost of borrowing for these bonds.
(b) Repeat the requirements from part (a), assuming the bonds were issued at 105.

Prepare entries for bond interest and redemption.

(LO 5, 6)

E10-13 The following section is taken from Ohlman Corp.'s balance sheet at December 31, 2014.

Current liabilities	
Interest payable	$ 56,000
Long-term liabilities	
Bonds payable, 7%, due January 1, 2019	1,600,000

Bond interest is payable semiannually on January 1 and July 1. The bonds are callable on any interest date.

Instructions

(a) Journalize the payment of the bond interest on January 1, 2015.
(b) Assume that on January 1, 2015, after paying interest, Ohlman calls bonds having a face value of $600,000. The call price is 103. Record the redemption of the bonds.
(c) Prepare the entry to record the payment of interest on July 1, 2015, assuming no previous accrual of interest on the remaining bonds.

Prepare entries for redemption of bonds and conversion of bonds into common stock.

(LO 6)

E10-14 Presented below and on page 527 are three independent situations.

1. Longbine Corporation redeemed $130,000 face value, 12% bonds on June 30, 2015, at 102. The carrying value of the bonds at the redemption date was $117,500. The bonds pay semiannual interest, and the interest payment due on June 30, 2015, has been made and recorded.
2. Tastove Inc. redeemed $150,000 face value, 12.5% bonds on June 30, 2015, at 98. The carrying value of the bonds at the redemption date was $151,000. The bonds pay semiannual interest, and the interest payment due on June 30, 2015, has been made and recorded.

3. Precision Company has $80,000, 8%, 12-year convertible bonds outstanding. These bonds were sold at face value and pay semiannual interest on June 30 and December 31 of each year. The bonds are convertible into 30 shares of Precision $5 par value common stock for each $1,000 worth of bonds. On December 31, 2015, after the bond interest has been paid, $20,000 face value bonds were converted. The market price of Precision common stock was $44 per share on December 31, 2015.

Instructions
For each independent situation above, prepare the appropriate journal entry for the redemption or conversion of the bonds.

E10-15 Jernigan Co. receives $300,000 when it issues a $300,000, 10%, mortgage note payable to finance the construction of a building at December 31, 2015. The terms provide for semiannual installment payments of $25,000 on June 30 and December 31.

Prepare entries to record mortgage note and installment payments.
(LO 7)

Instructions
Prepare the journal entries to record the mortgage loan and the first two installment payments.

E10-16 The adjusted trial balance for Karr Farm Corporation at the end of the current year contained the following accounts.

Prepare long-term liabilities section.
(LO 8)

Interest Payable	$ 9,000
Bonds Payable, due 2019	180,000
Premium on Bonds Payable	32,000

Instructions
Prepare the long-term liabilities section of the balance sheet.

*E10-17 England Corporation is issuing $200,000 of 8%, 5-year bonds when potential bond investors want a return of 10%. Interest is payable semiannually.

Compute market price of bonds.
(LO 9)

Instructions
Compute the market price (present value) of the bonds.

*E10-18 Lorance Corporation issued $800,000, 9%, 10-year bonds on January 1, 2015, for $750,150. This price resulted in an effective-interest rate of 10% on the bonds. Interest is payable semiannually on July 1 and January 1. Lorance uses the effective-interest method to amortize bond premium or discount.

Prepare entries for issuance of bonds, payment of interest, and amortization of discount using effective-interest method.
(LO 5, 10)

Instructions
Prepare the journal entries to record the following. (Round to the nearest dollar.)
(a) The issuance of the bonds.
(b) The payment of interest and the discount amortization on July 1, 2015, assuming that interest was not accrued on June 30.
(c) The accrual of interest and the discount amortization on December 31, 2015.

*E10-19 LRNA Company issued $300,000, 11%, 10-year bonds on January 1, 2015, for $318,694. This price resulted in an effective-interest rate of 10% on the bonds. Interest is payable semiannually on July 1 and January 1. LRNA uses the effective-interest method to amortize bond premium or discount.

Prepare entries for issuance of bonds, payment of interest, and amortization of discount using effective-interest method.
(LO 5, 10)

Instructions
Prepare the journal entries to record the following. (Round to the nearest dollar.)
(a) The issuance of the bonds.
(b) The payment of interest and the premium amortization on July 1, 2015, assuming that interest was not accrued on June 30.
(c) The accrual of interest and the premium amortization on December 31, 2015.

*E10-20 Adcock Company issued $600,000, 9%, 20-year bonds on January 1, 2015, at 103. Interest is payable semiannually on July 1 and January 1. Adcock uses straight-line amortization for bond premium or discount.

Prepare entries to record issuance of bonds, payment of interest, amortization of premium, and redemption at maturity.
(LO 5, 11)

Instructions
Prepare the journal entries to record the following.
(a) The issuance of the bonds.
(b) The payment of interest and the premium amortization on July 1, 2015, assuming that interest was not accrued on June 30.

(c) The accrual of interest and the premium amortization on December 31, 2015.

(d) The redemption of the bonds at maturity, assuming interest for the last interest period has been paid and recorded.

Prepare entries to record issuance of bonds, payment of interest, amortization of discount, and redemption at maturity.

(LO 5, 11)

*E10-21 Gridley Company issued $800,000, 11%, 10-year bonds on December 31, 2014, for $730,000. Interest is payable semiannually on June 30 and December 31. Gridley Company uses the straight-line method to amortize bond premium or discount.

Instructions

Prepare the journal entries to record the following.

(a) The issuance of the bonds.

(b) The payment of interest and the discount amortization on June 30, 2015.

(c) The payment of interest and the discount amortization on December 31, 2015.

(d) The redemption of the bonds at maturity, assuming interest for the last interest period has been paid and recorded.

EXERCISES: SET B AND CHALLENGE EXERCISES

Visit the book's companion website, at **www.wiley.com/college/weygandt**, and choose the Student Companion site to access Exercise Set B and Challenge Exercises.

PROBLEMS: SET A

Prepare current liability entries, adjusting entries, and current liabilities section.

(LO 1, 2, 3)

P10-1A On January 1, 2015, the ledger of Accardo Company contains the following liability accounts.

Accounts Payable	$52,000
Sales Taxes Payable	7,700
Unearned Service Revenue	16,000

During January, the following selected transactions occurred.

Jan. 5 Sold merchandise for cash totaling $20,520, which includes 8% sales taxes.

12 Performed services for customers who had made advance payments of $10,000. (Credit Service Revenue.)

14 Paid state revenue department for sales taxes collected in December 2014 ($7,700).

20 Sold 900 units of a new product on credit at $50 per unit, plus 8% sales tax.

21 Borrowed $27,000 from Girard Bank on a 3-month, 8%, $27,000 note.

25 Sold merchandise for cash totaling $12,420, which includes 8% sales taxes.

Instructions

(a) Journalize the January transactions.

(b) Journalize the adjusting entry at January 31 for the outstanding note payable. (*Hint:* Use one-third of a month for the Girard Bank note.)

(c) Current liability total $91,100

(c) Prepare the current liabilities section of the balance sheet at January 31, 2015. Assume no change in accounts payable.

Journalize and post note transactions; show balance sheet presentation.

(LO 2)

P10-2A The following are selected transactions of Blanco Company. Blanco prepares financial statements **quarterly**.

Jan. 2 Purchased merchandise on account from Nunez Company, $30,000, terms 2/10, n/30. (Blanco uses the perpetual inventory system.)

Feb. 1 Issued a 9%, 2-month, $30,000 note to Nunez in payment of account.

Mar. 31 Accrued interest for 2 months on Nunez note.

Apr. 1 Paid face value and interest on Nunez note.

July 1 Purchased equipment from Marson Equipment paying $11,000 in cash and signing a 10%, 3-month, $60,000 note.

Sept. 30 Accrued interest for 3 months on Marson note.

Oct. 1 Paid face value and interest on Marson note.

Dec. 1 Borrowed $24,000 from the Paola Bank by issuing a 3-month, 8% note with a face value of $24,000.

Dec. 31 Recognized interest expense for 1 month on Paola Bank note.

Instructions
(a) Prepare journal entries for the listed transactions and events.
(b) Post to the accounts Notes Payable, Interest Payable, and Interest Expense.
(c) Show the balance sheet presentation of notes and interest payable at December 31.
(d) What is total interest expense for the year?

(d) $2,110

P10-3A On May 1, 2015, Herron Corp. issued $600,000, 9%, 5-year bonds at face value. The bonds were dated May 1, 2015, and pay interest semiannually on May 1 and November 1. Financial statements are prepared annually on December 31.

Prepare entries to record issuance of bonds, interest accrual, and bond redemption.

(LO 5, 6, 8)

Instructions
(a) Prepare the journal entry to record the issuance of the bonds.
(b) Prepare the adjusting entry to record the accrual of interest on December 31, 2015.
(c) Show the balance sheet presentation on December 31, 2015.
(d) Prepare the journal entry to record payment of interest on May 1, 2016, assuming no accrual of interest from January 1, 2016, to May 1, 2016.

(d) Int. exp. $18,000

(e) Prepare the journal entry to record payment of interest on November 1, 2016.
(f) Assume that on November 1, 2016, Herron calls the bonds at 102. Record the redemption of the bonds.

(f) Loss $12,000

P10-4A Asquith Electric sold $750,000, 10%, 10-year bonds on January 1, 2015. The bonds were dated January 1 and paid interest on January 1 and July 1. The bonds were sold at 104.

Prepare entries to record issuance of bonds, interest accrual, and bond redemption.

(LO 5, 6, 8)

Instructions
(a) Prepare the journal entry to record the issuance of the bonds on January 1, 2015.
(b) At December 31, 2015, the balance in the Premium on Bonds Payable account is $27,000. Show the balance sheet presentation of accrued interest and the bond liability at December 31, 2015.
(c) On January 1, 2017, when the carrying value of the bonds was $774,000, the company redeemed the bonds at 105. Record the redemption of the bonds assuming that interest for the period has already been paid.

(c) Loss $13,500

P10-5A Talkington Electronics issues a $400,000, 8%, 10-year mortgage note on December 31, 2014. The proceeds from the note are to be used in financing a new research laboratory. The terms of the note provide for semiannual installment payments, exclusive of real estate taxes and insurance, of $29,433. Payments are due June 30 and December 31.

Prepare installment payments schedule and journal entries for a mortgage note payable.

(LO 7, 8)

Instructions
(a) Prepare an installment payments schedule for the first 2 years.
(b) Prepare the entries for (1) the loan and (2) the first two installment payments.
(c) Show how the total mortgage liability should be reported on the balance sheet at December 31, 2015.

(b) June 30 debit Mortgage Payable $13,433

(c) Current liability—2015 $29,639

***P10-6A** On July 1, 2015, Flanagin Corporation issued $2,000,000, 10%, 10-year bonds at $2,271,813. This price resulted in an effective-interest rate of 8% on the bonds. Flanagin uses the effective-interest method to amortize bond premium or discount. The bonds pay semiannual interest July 1 and January 1.

Prepare entries to record issuance of bonds, payment of interest, and amortization of bond premium using effective-interest method.

(LO 5, 10)

Instructions
(Round all computations to the nearest dollar.)
(a) Prepare the journal entry to record the issuance of the bonds on July 1, 2015.
(b) Prepare an amortization table through December 31, 2016 (3 interest periods), for this bond issue.
(c) Prepare the journal entry to record the accrual of interest and the amortization of the premium on December 31, 2015.

(c) Amortization $9,127

(d) Prepare the journal entry to record the payment of interest and the amortization of the premium on July 1, 2016, assuming no accrual of interest on June 30.

(d) Amortization $9,493

(e) Prepare the journal entry to record the accrual of interest and the amortization of the premium on December 31, 2016.

(e) Amortization $9,872

Prepare entries to record issuance of bonds, payment of interest, and amortization of discount using effective-interest method. In addition, answer questions.

(LO 5, 10)

***P10-7A** On July 1, 2015, Kellerman Company issued $5,000,000, 8%, 10-year bonds at $4,376,892. This price resulted in an effective-interest rate of 10% on the bonds. Kellerman uses the effective-interest method to amortize bond premium or discount. The bonds pay semiannual interest July 1 and January 1.

Instructions

(Round all computations to the nearest dollar.)

(a) Prepare the journal entries to record the following transactions.
   (1) The issuance of the bonds on July 1, 2015.
   (2) The accrual of interest and the amortization of the discount on December 31, 2015.
   (3) The payment of interest and the amortization of the discount on July 1, 2016, assuming no accrual of interest on June 30.
   (4) The accrual of interest and the amortization of the discount on December 31, 2016.

(b) Show the proper balance sheet presentation for the liability for bonds payable on the December 31, 2016, balance sheet.

(c) ━━━▶ Provide the answers to the following questions in letter form.
   (1) What amount of interest expense is reported for 2016?
   (2) Would the bond interest expense reported in 2016 be the same as, greater than, or less than the amount that would be reported if the straight-line method of amortization were used?
   (3) Determine the total cost of borrowing over the life of the bond.
   (4) Would the total bond interest expense be greater than, the same as, or less than the total interest expense that would be reported if the straight-line method of amortization were used?

(a)(3) Amortization $19,787

(a)(4) Amortization $20,776

(b) Bond carrying value $4,436,300

Prepare entries to record issuance of bonds, interest accrual, and straight-line amortization for 2 years.
(LO 5, 11)

(b) Amortization $6,000

(d) Premium on bonds payable $96,000

*P10-8A Wainwright Electric sold $3,000,000, 10%, 10-year bonds on January 1, 2015. The bonds were dated January 1 and pay interest July 1 and January 1. Wainwright Electric uses the straight-line method to amortize bond premium or discount. The bonds were sold at 104. Assume no interest is accrued on June 30.

Instructions

(a) Prepare the journal entry to record the issuance of the bonds on January 1, 2015.
(b) Prepare a bond premium amortization schedule for the first 4 interest periods.
(c) Prepare the journal entries for interest and the amortization of the premium in 2015 and 2016.
(d) Show the balance sheet presentation of the bond liability at December 31, 2016.

Prepare entries to record issuance of bonds, interest, and straight-line amortization of bond premium and discount.
(LO 5, 11)

(a) Amortization $7,000
(b) Amortization $3,500
(c) Premium on bonds payable $133,000
Discount on bonds payable $66,500

*P10-9A Saberhagen Company sold $3,500,000, 8%, 10-year bonds on July 1, 2015. The bonds were dated July 1, 2015, and pay interest July 1 and January 1. Saberhagen Company uses the straight-line method to amortize bond premium or discount. Assume no interest is accrued on June 30.

Instructions

(a) Prepare all the necessary journal entries to record the issuance of the bonds and bond interest expense for 2015, assuming that the bonds sold at 104.
(b) Prepare journal entries as in part (a) assuming that the bonds sold at 98.
(c) Show balance sheet presentation for the bonds at December 31, 2015.

Prepare entries to record interest payments, straight-line premium amortization, and redemption of bonds.
(LO 6, 11)

*P10-10A The following is taken from the Colaw Company balance sheet.

COLAW COMPANY
Balance Sheet (partial)
December 31, 2015

Current liabilities		
Interest payable (for 6 months from July 1 to December 31)		$ 105,000
Long-term liabilities		
Bonds payable, 7% due January 1, 2026	$3,000,000	
Add: Premium on bonds payable	200,000	3,200,000

Interest is payable semiannually on January 1 and July 1. The bonds are callable on any semiannual interest date. Colaw uses straight-line amortization for any bond premium or discount. From December 31, 2015, the bonds will be outstanding for an additional 10 years (120 months).

Instructions

(a) Journalize the payment of bond interest on January 1, 2016.

(b) Prepare the entry to amortize bond premium and to pay the interest due on July 1, 2016, assuming no accrual of interest on June 30.   (b) Amortization $10,000

(c) Assume that on July 1, 2016, after paying interest, Colaw Company calls bonds having a face value of $1,200,000. The call price is 101. Record the redemption of the bonds.   (c) Gain $64,000

(d) Prepare the adjusting entry at December 31, 2016, to amortize bond premium and to accrue interest on the remaining bonds.   (d) Amortization $6,000

PROBLEMS: SET B

P10-1B On January 1, 2015, the ledger of Werth Company contains the following liability accounts.

Prepare current liability entries, adjusting entries, and current liabilities section.

(LO 1, 2, 3)

Accounts Payable	$35,000
Sales Taxes Payable	5,000
Unearned Service Revenue	12,000

During January, the following selected transactions occurred.

Jan. 1 Borrowed $30,000 in cash from Platteville Bank on a 4-month, 6%, $30,000 note.

5 Sold merchandise for cash totaling $11,130, which includes 6% sales taxes.

12 Performed services for customers who had made advance payments of $8,000. (Credit Service Revenue.)

14 Paid state treasurer's department for sales taxes collected in December 2014, $5,000.

20 Sold 750 units of a new product on credit at $44 per unit, plus 6% sales tax.

25 Sold merchandise for cash totaling $16,536, which includes 6% sales taxes.

Instructions

(a) Journalize the January transactions.

(b) Journalize the adjusting entry at January 31 for the outstanding note payable.

(c) Prepare the current liabilities section of the balance sheet at January 31, 2015. Assume no change in accounts payable.   (c) Current liability total $72,696

P10-2B On June 1, 2015, Weller Corp. issued $2,000,000, 9%, 5-year bonds at face value. The bonds were dated June 1, 2015, and pay interest semiannually on June 1 and December 1. Financial statements are prepared annually on December 31.

Prepare entries to record issuance of bonds, interest accrual, and bond redemption.

(LO 5, 6, 8)

Instructions

(a) Prepare the journal entry to record the issuance of the bonds.

(b) Prepare the adjusting entry to record the accrual of interest on December 31, 2015.

(c) Show the balance sheet presentation on December 31, 2015.

(d) Prepare the journal entry to record payment of interest on June 1, 2016, assuming no accrual of interest from January 1, 2016, to June 1, 2016.   (d) Int. exp. $75,000

(e) Prepare the journal entry to record payment of interest on December 1, 2016.

(f) Assume that on December 1, 2016, Weller calls the bonds at 102. Record the redemption of the bonds.   (f) Loss $40,000

P10-3B Shonrock Co. sold $800,000, 9%, 10-year bonds on January 1, 2015. The bonds were dated January 1, and interest is paid on January 1 and July 1. The bonds were sold at 105.

Prepare entries to record issuance of bonds, interest accrual, and bond redemption.

(LO 5, 6, 8)

Instructions

(a) Prepare the journal entry to record the issuance of the bonds on January 1, 2015.

(b) At December 31, 2015, the balance in the Premium on Bonds Payable account is $36,000. Show the balance sheet presentation of accrued interest and the bond liability at December 31, 2015.

(c) On January 1, 2017, when the carrying value of the bonds was $832,000, the company redeemed the bonds at 105. Record the redemption of the bonds assuming that interest for the period has already been paid.   (c) Loss $8,000

Prepare installment payments schedule and journal entries for a mortgage note payable.
(LO 7, 8)

(b) June 30 debit Mortgage Payable $20,149
(c) Current liability—2016: $44,458

P10-4B Crosetti's Electronics issues a $600,000, 8%, 10-year mortgage note on December 31, 2015, to help finance a plant expansion program. The terms provide for semiannual installment payments, not including real estate taxes and insurance, of $44,149. Payments are due June 30 and December 31.

Instructions

(a) Prepare an installment payments schedule for the first 2 years.
(b) Prepare the entries for (1) the mortgage loan and (2) the first two installment payments.
(c) Show how the total mortgage liability should be reported on the balance sheet at December 31, 2016.

Prepare entries to record issuance of bonds, payment of interest, and amortization of bond discount using effective-interest method.
(LO 5, 10)

(c) Amortization $8,480

(d) Amortization $8,904

(e) Amortization $9,349

*P10-5B On July 1, 2015, Witherspoon Satellites issued $4,500,000, 9%, 10-year bonds at $4,219,600. This price resulted in an effective-interest rate of 10% on the bonds. Witherspoon uses the effective-interest method to amortize bond premium or discount. The bonds pay semiannual interest July 1 and January 1.

Instructions
(Round all computations to the nearest dollar.)

(a) Prepare the journal entry to record the issuance of the bonds on July 1, 2015.
(b) Prepare an amortization table through December 31, 2016 (3 interest periods), for this bond issue.
(c) Prepare the journal entry to record the accrual of interest and the amortization of the discount on December 31, 2015.
(d) Prepare the journal entry to record the payment of interest and the amortization of the discount on July 1, 2016, assuming that interest was not accrued on June 30.
(e) Prepare the journal entry to record the accrual of interest and the amortization of the discount on December 31, 2016.

Prepare entries to record issuance of bonds, payment of interest, and amortization of premium using effective-interest method. In addition, answer questions.
(LO 5, 10)

(a)(2) Amortization $18,255
(a)(3) Amortization $18,985

(a)(4) Amortization $19,745
(b) Bond carrying value $4,486,642

*P10-6B On July 1, 2015, Ashlock Chemical Company issued $4,000,000, 10%, 10 year bonds at $4,543,627. This price resulted in an 8% effective-interest rate on the bonds. Ashlock uses the effective-interest method to amortize bond premium or discount. The bonds pay semiannual interest on each July 1 and January 1.

Instructions
(Round all computations to the nearest dollar.)

(a) Prepare the journal entries to record the following transactions.
  (1) The issuance of the bonds on July 1, 2015.
  (2) The accrual of interest and the amortization of the premium on December 31, 2015.
  (3) The payment of interest and the amortization of the premium on July 1, 2016, assuming no accrual of interest on June 30.
  (4) The accrual of interest and the amortization of the premium on December 31, 2016.
(b) Show the proper balance sheet presentation for the liability for bonds payable on the December 31, 2016, balance sheet.
(c) ━━━━➤ Provide the answers to the following questions in letter form.
  (1) What amount of interest expense is reported for 2016?
  (2) Would the bond interest expense reported in 2016 be the same as, greater than, or less than the amount that would be reported if the straight-line method of amortization were used?
  (3) Determine the total cost of borrowing over the life of the bond.
  (4) Would the total bond interest expense be greater than, the same as, or less than the total interest expense if the straight-line method of amortization were used?

Prepare entries to record issuance of bonds, interest accrual, and straight-line amortization for 2 years.
(LO 5, 11)

(b) Amortization $6,000

(d) Discount on bonds payable $216,000

*P10-7B Fernetti Company sold $6,000,000, 9%, 20-year bonds on January 1, 2015. The bonds were dated January 1, 2015, and pay interest on January 1 and July 1. Fernetti Company uses the straight-line method to amortize bond premium or discount. The bonds were sold at 96. Assume no interest is accrued on June 30.

Instructions

(a) Prepare the journal entry to record the issuance of the bonds on January 1, 2015.
(b) Prepare a bond discount amortization schedule for the first 4 interest periods.
(c) Prepare the journal entries for interest and the amortization of the discount in 2015 and 2016.
(d) Show the balance sheet presentation of the bond liability at December 31, 2016.

*P10-8B Roswell Corporation sold $4,000,000, 8%, 10-year bonds on January 1, 2015. The bonds were dated January 1, 2015, and pay interest on July 1 and January 1. Roswell Corporation uses the straight-line method to amortize bond premium or discount. Assume no interest is accrued on June 30.

Prepare entries to record issuance of bonds, interest, and straight-line amortization of bond premium and discount.

(LO 5, 11)

Instructions

(a) Prepare all the necessary journal entries to record the issuance of the bonds and bond interest expense for 2015, assuming that the bonds sold at 103.

(b) Prepare journal entries as in part (a) assuming that the bonds sold at 96.

(c) Show balance sheet presentation for the bonds at December 31, 2015.

(a) Amortization $6,000
(b) Amortization $8,000
(c) Premium on bonds payable
    $108,000
    Discount on bonds payable
    $144,000

*P10-9B The following is taken from the Sinjh Corporation balance sheet.

Prepare entries to record interest payments, straight-line discount amortization, and redemption of bonds.

(LO 5, 6, 11)

SINJH CORPORATION
Balance Sheet (partial)
December 31, 2015

Current liabilities		
Interest payable (for 6 months		
from July 1 to December 31)		$ 108,000
Long-term liabilities		
Bonds payable, 9%, due		
January 1, 2026	$2,400,000	
Less: Discount on bonds payable	90,000	2,310,000

Interest is payable semiannually on January 1 and July 1. The bonds are callable on any semiannual interest date. Sinjh uses straight-line amortization for any bond premium or discount. From December 31, 2015, the bonds will be outstanding for an additional 10 years (120 months).

Instructions

(Round all computations to the nearest dollar).

(a) Journalize the payment of bond interest on January 1, 2016.

(b) Prepare the entry to amortize bond discount and to pay the interest due on July 1, 2016, assuming that interest was not accrued on June 30.

(b) Amortization $4,500

(c) Assume that on July 1, 2016, after paying interest, Sinjh Corp. calls bonds having a face value of $800,000. The call price is 102. Record the redemption of the bonds.

(c) Loss $44,500

(d) Prepare the adjusting entry at December 31, 2016, to amortize bond discount and to accrue interest on the remaining bonds.

(d) Amortization $3,000

PROBLEMS: SET C

Visit the book's companion website, at **www.wiley.com/college/weygandt**, and choose the Student Companion site to access Problem Set C.

COMPREHENSIVE PROBLEMS

CP10-1 James Corporation's balance sheet at December 31, 2014, is presented below.

JAMES CORPORATION
Balance Sheet
December 31, 2014

Cash	$ 30,500	Accounts payable	$ 13,750
Inventory	25,750	Interest payable	2,500
Prepaid insurance	5,600	Bonds payable	50,000
Equipment	43,000	Common stock	20,000
	$104,850	Retained earnings	18,600
			$104,850

During 2015, the following transactions occurred.

1. James paid $2,500 interest on the bonds on January 1, 2015.
2. James purchased $241,100 of inventory on account.
3. James sold for $450,000 cash inventory which cost $250,000. James also collected $31,500 sales taxes.
4. James paid $230,000 on accounts payable.
5. James paid $2,500 interest on the bonds on July 1, 2015.
6. The prepaid insurance ($5,600) expired on July 31.
7. On August 1, James paid $12,000 for insurance coverage from August 1, 2015, through July 31, 2016.
8. James paid $24,000 sales taxes to the state.
9. Paid other operating expenses, $91,000.
10. Retired the bonds on December 31, 2015, by paying $47,000 plus $2,500 interest.
11. Issued $90,000 of 8% bonds on December 31, 2015, at 104. The bonds pay interest every June 30 and December 31.

Adjustment data:

1. Recorded the insurance expired from item 7.
2. The equipment was acquired on December 31, 2014, and will be depreciated on a straight-line basis over 5 years with a $3,000 salvage value.
3. The income tax rate is 30%. (*Hint:* Prepare the income statement up to income before taxes and multiply by 30% to compute the amount.)

Instructions
(You may want to set up T-accounts to determine ending balances.)

(b) Totals $652,070
(c) N.I. $61,880

(a) Prepare journal entries for the transactions listed above and adjusting entries.
(b) Prepare an adjusted trial balance at December 31, 2015.
(c) Prepare an income statement and a retained earnings statement for the year ending December 31, 2015, and a classified balance sheet as of December 31, 2015.

CP10-2 Eastland Company and Westside Company are competing businesses. Both began operations 6 years ago and are quite similar in most respects. The current balance sheet data for the two companies are shown below.

	Eastland Company	Westside Company
Cash	$ 63,300	$ 48,400
Accounts receivable	304,700	302,500
Allowance for doubtful accounts	(13,600)	–0–
Inventory	463,900	515,200
Plant and equipment	255,300	257,300
Accumulated depreciation—plant and equipment	(112,650)	(189,850)
Total assets	$960,950	$933,550
Current liabilities	$440,200	$431,500
Long-term liabilities	78,000	82,000
Total liabilities	518,200	513,500
Stockholders' equity	442,750	420,050
Total liabilities and stockholders' equity	$960,950	$933,550

You have been engaged as a consultant to conduct a review of the two companies. Your goal is to determine which of them is in the stronger financial position.

Your review of their financial statements quickly reveals that the two companies have not followed the same accounting practices. The differences and your conclusions regarding them are summarized below.

1. Eastland Company has used the allowance method of accounting for bad debts. A review shows that the amount of its write-offs each year has been quite close to the allowances that have been provided. It therefore seems reasonable to have confidence in its current estimate of bad debts.

   Westside Company has used the direct write-off method for bad debts, and it has been somewhat slow to write off its uncollectible accounts. Based upon an aging analysis and review of its accounts receivable, it is estimated that $18,000 of its existing accounts will probably prove to be uncollectible.

2. Eastland Company has determined the cost of its merchandise inventory on a LIFO basis. The result is that its inventory appears on the balance sheet at an amount that is below its current replacement cost. Based upon a detailed physical examination of its merchandise on hand, the current replacement cost of its inventory is estimated at $513,000.

Westside Company has used the FIFO method of valuing its merchandise inventory. Its ending inventory appears on the balance sheet at an amount that quite closely approximates its current replacement cost.

3. Eastland Company estimated a useful life of 12 years and a salvage value of $30,000 for its plant and equipment. It has been depreciating them on a straight-line basis.

Westside Company has the same type of plant and equipment. However, it estimated a useful life of 10 years and a salvage value of $10,000. It has been depreciating its plant and equipment using the double-declining-balance method.

Based upon engineering studies of these types of plant and equipment, you conclude that Westside's estimates and method for calculating depreciation are the more appropriate.

4. Among its current liabilities, Eastland has included the portions of long-term liabilities that become due within the next year. Westside has not done so.

You find that $16,000 of Westside's $82,000 of long-term liabilities are due to be repaid in the current year.

Instructions

(a) Revise the balance sheets presented above so that the data are comparable and reflect the current financial position for each of the two companies.

(b) ━━━━▶ Prepare a brief report to your client stating your conclusions.

(a) Total assets:
   Eastland $934,325
   Westside $915,550

CONTINUING COOKIE CHRONICLE

(*Note:* This is a continuation of the Cookie Chronicle from Chapters 1 through 9.)

CCC10   Recall that Cookie Creations sells fine European mixers that it purchases from Kzinski Supply Co. Kzinski warrants the mixers to be free of defects in material and workmanship for a period of one year from the date of original purchase. If the mixer has such a defect, Kzinski will repair or replace the mixer free of charge for parts and labor.

Go to the book's companion website, **www.wiley.com/college/weygandt**, *to see the completion of this problem.*

Broadening Your **PERSPECTIVE**

Financial Reporting and Analysis

Financial Reporting Problem: Apple Inc.

BYP10-1   The financial statements of Apple Inc. and the notes to consolidated financial statements appear in Appendix A. Instructions for accessing and using the company's complete annual report, including the notes to the financial statements, are also provided in Appendix A.

Instructions

Refer to Apple's financial statements and answer the following questions about current and contingent liabilities and payroll costs.

(a) What were Apple's total current liabilities at September 24, 2011? What was the increase/ decrease in Apple's total current liabilities from the prior year?

(b) In Apple's Note 1 ("Summary of Significant Accounting Policies"), the company explains the nature of its contingencies. Under what conditions does Apple recognize (record and report) liabilities for contingencies?

(c) What were the components of total current liabilities on September 24, 2011?

(d) What were Apple's total long-term liabilities at September 24, 2011? What was the increase/decrease in total long-term liabilities from the prior year?

(e) Determine whether Apple redeemed (bought back) any long-term liabilities during the fiscal year ended September 24, 2011.

Comparative Analysis Problem:
PepsiCo, Inc. vs. The Coca-Cola Company

BYP10-2 PepsiCo, Inc.'s financial statements are presented in Appendix B. Financial statements of The Coca-Cola Company are presented in Appendix C. Instructions for accessing and using the complete annual reports of PepsiCo and Coca-Cola, including the notes to the financial statements, are also provided in Appendices B and C, respectively.

Instructions

(a) At December 31, 2011, what was PepsiCo's largest current liability account? What were its total current liabilities? At December 31, 2011, what was Coca-Cola's largest current liability account? What were its total current liabilities?

(b) Based on information contained in those financial statements, compute the following 2011 values for each company:

   (1) Working capital.

   (2) Current ratio.

(c) What conclusions concerning the relative liquidity of these companies can be drawn from these data?

(d) Based on the information contained in these financial statements, compute the following 2011 ratios for each company.

   (1) Debt to assets.

   (2) Times interest earned.

(e) What conclusions concerning the companies' long-run solvency can be drawn from these ratios?

Comparative Analysis Problem:
Amazon.com, Inc. vs. Wal-Mart Stores, Inc.

BYP10-3 Amazon.com, Inc.'s financial statements are presented in Appendix D. Financial statements for Wal-Mart Stores, Inc. are presented in Appendix E. Instructions for accessing and using the complete annual reports of Amazon and Wal-Mart, including the notes to the financial statements, are also provided in Appendices D and E, respectively.

Instructions

(a) At December 31, 2011, what was Amazon's largest current liability account? What were its total current liabilities? At January 31, 2012, what was Wal-Mart's largest current liability account? What were its total current liabilities?

(b) Based on information in these financial statements, compute the following 2011 values for Amazon and 2012 values for Wal-Mart:

   (1) Working capital.

   (2) Current ratio.

(c) What conclusions concerning the relative liquidity of these companies can be drawn from these data?

(d) Based on the information contained in these financial statements, compute the following 2011 ratios for Amazon and 2012 ratios for Wal-Mart.

   (1) Debt to assets.

   (2) Times interest earned.

(e) What conclusions concerning the companies' long-run solvency can be drawn from these ratios?

Real-World Focus

BYP10-4 Bond or debt securities pay a stated rate of interest. This rate of interest is dependent on the risk associated with the investment. Also, bond prices change when the risks associated with those bonds change. Standard & Poor's provides ratings for companies that issue debt securities.

Address: **www.img.en25.com/Web/StandardandPoors/GuidetoCreditRatingsCriteria.pdf**, or go to **www.wiley.com/college/weygandt**

Instructions
Go to the website shown and answer the following questions.

(a) Explain the meaning of an "A" rating. Explain the meaning of a "C" rating.
(b) What types of things can cause a change in a company's credit rating?
(c) Explain the relationship between a company's credit rating and the merit of an investment in that company's bonds.

Critical Thinking

Decision-Making Across the Organization

*BYP10-5 On January 1, 2013, Glover Corporation issued $2,400,000 of 5-year, 8% bonds at 95. The bonds pay interest semiannually on July 1 and January 1. By January 1, 2015, the market rate of interest for bonds of risk similar to those of Glover Corporation had risen. As a result, the market value of these bonds was $2,000,000 on January 1, 2015—below their carrying value. Joanna Glover, president of the company, suggests repurchasing all of these bonds in the open market at the $2,000,000 price. To do so, the company will have to issue $2,000,000 (face value) of new 10-year, 11% bonds at par. The president asks you, as controller, "What is the feasibility of my proposed repurchase plan?"

Instructions
With the class divided into groups, answer the following.

(a) What is the carrying value of the outstanding Glover Corporation 5-year bonds on January 1, 2015? (Assume straight-line amortization.)
(b) Prepare the journal entry to redeem the 5-year bonds on January 1, 2015. Prepare the journal entry to issue the new 10-year bonds.
(c) Prepare a short memo to the president in response to her request for advice. List the economic factors that you believe should be considered for her repurchase proposal.

Communication Activity

BYP10-6 Sam Masasi, president of Masasi Corporation, is considering the issuance of bonds to finance an expansion of his business. He has asked you to (1) discuss the advantages of bonds over common stock financing, (2) indicate the types of bonds he might issue, and (3) explain the issuing procedures used in bond transactions.

Instructions
Write a memo to the president, answering his request.

Ethics Case

BYP10-7 Ken Iwig is the president, founder, and majority owner of Olathe Medical Corporation, an emerging medical technology products company. Olathe is in dire need of additional capital to keep operating and to bring several promising products to final development, testing, and production. Ken, as owner of 51% of the outstanding stock, manages the company's operations. He places heavy emphasis on research and development and on long-term growth. The other principal stockholder is Barb Lowery who, as a nonemployee investor, owns 40% of the stock. Barb would like to deemphasize the R&D functions and emphasize the marketing function, to maximize short-run sales and profits from existing products. She believes this strategy would raise the market price of Olathe's stock.

All of Ken's personal capital and borrowing power is tied up in his 51% stock ownership. He knows that any offering of additional shares of stock will dilute his controlling interest because he won't be able to participate in such an issuance. But, Barb has money and would likely buy enough shares to gain control of Olathe. She then would dictate the company's future direction, even if it meant replacing Ken as president and CEO.

The company already has considerable debt. Raising additional debt will be costly, will adversely affect Olathe's credit rating, and will increase the company's reported losses due to the growth in interest expense. Barb and the other minority stockholders express opposition to the assumption of additional debt, fearing the company will be pushed to the brink of bankruptcy. Wanting to maintain his control and to preserve the direction of "his" company, Ken is doing everything to avoid a stock issuance. He is contemplating a large issuance of bonds, even if it means the bonds are issued with a high effective-interest rate.

Instructions
(a) Who are the stakeholders in this situation?
(b) What are the ethical issues in this case?
(c) What would you do if you were Ken?

All About You

BYP10-8 Medical costs are substantial and rising. But will they be the most substantial expense over your lifetime? Not likely. Will it be housing or food? Again, not likely. The answer is taxes. On average, Americans work 107 days per year to afford their taxes. Companies, too, have large tax burdens. They look very hard at tax issues in deciding where to build their plants and where to locate their administrative headquarters.

Instructions
(a) Determine what your state income taxes are if your taxable income is $60,000 and you file as a single taxpayer in the state in which you live.
(b) Assume that you own a home worth $200,000 in your community and the tax rate is 2.1%. Compute the property taxes you would pay.
(c) Assume that the total gasoline bill for your automobile is $1,200 a year (300 gallons at $4 per gallon). What are the amounts of state and federal taxes that you pay on the $1,200?
(d) Assume that your purchases for the year total $9,000. Of this amount, $5,000 was for food and prescription drugs. What is the amount of sales tax you would pay on these purchases? (Many states do not levy a sales tax on food or prescription drugs. Does yours?)
(e) Determine what your Social Security taxes are if your income is $60,000.
(f) Determine what your federal income taxes are if your taxable income is $60,000 and you file as a single taxpayer.
(g) Determine your total taxes paid based on the above calculations, and determine the percentage of income that you would pay in taxes based on the following formula: Total taxes paid ÷ Total income.

BYP10-9 Numerous articles have been written that identify early warning signs that you might be getting into trouble with your personal debt load. You can find many good articles on this topic on the Internet.

Instructions
Find an article that identifies early warning signs of personal debt trouble. Write a summary of the article and bring your summary and the article to class to share.

FASB Codification Activity

BYP10-10 If your school has a subscription to the FASB Codification, go to **http://aaahq.org/ascLogin.cfm** to log in and prepare responses to the following.
(a) What is the definition of current liabilities?
(b) What is the definition of long-term obligation?
(c) What guidance does the Codification provide for the disclosure of long-term liabilities?

Answers to Chapter Questions

Answers to Insight and Accounting Across the Organization Questions

p. 493 How About Those 30-Year Bonds? **Q:** What are the advantages for companies of issuing 30-year bonds instead of 5-year bonds? **A:** The major advantages for companies are to extend their debt and to pay low interest rates. This locks in these low rates for a considerable period of time.

p. 501 Bonds versus Notes? **Q:** Why might companies prefer bond financing instead of short-term financing? **A:** In some cases, it is difficult to get loans from banks. In addition, low interest rates have encouraged companies to go more long-term and fix their rate. Recently, short-term loans suddenly froze, leading to liquidity problems for certain companies.

p. 503 "Covenant-Lite" Debt **Q:** How can financial ratios such as those covered in this chapter provide protection for creditors? **A:** Financial ratios such as the current ratio, debt to assets ratio, and times interest earned provide indications of a company's liquidity and solvency. By specifying minimum levels of liquidity and solvency, as measured by these ratios, a creditor creates triggers that enable it to step in before a company's financial situation becomes too dire.

Answers to Self-Test Questions

1. a **2.** d **3.** b ($88,500 × 12% × 4/12) **4.** b ($4,515 ÷ 1.05) **5.** c **6.** b ($18,000 × 3/12) **7.** c **8.** a **9.** b **10.** d $600,000 − (10,000 × $1) **11.** c $200,000 − (10% × $497,000) = $150,300; ($497,000 − $150,300) × 10% **12.** c **13.** d ($300,000 + $40,000 + $100,000) ÷ $40,000 ***14.** d ***15.** b [($938,554 × 10%) − ($1,000,000 × 9%)] = $3,855; ($1,000,000 − $938,554) − $3,855 ***16.** c ($1,081,105 × 8%) ÷ 2 ***17.** d [$500,000 − (96% × $500,000)] = $20,000; ($20,000 ÷ 10) ***18.** a (500,000 × .96) = 480,000; ($480,000 + $2,000 + $2,000 + $2,000)

A Look at IFRS

IFRS and GAAP have similar definitions of liabilities. IFRS related to reporting and recognition of liabilities are found in *IAS 1 (revised)* ("Presentation of Financial Statements") and *IAS 37* ("Provisions, Contingent Liabilities, and Contingent Assets"). The general recording procedures for payroll are similar, although differences occur depending on the types of benefits that are provided in different countries. For example, companies in other countries often have different forms of pensions, unemployment benefits, welfare payments, and so on. The accounting for various forms of compensation plans under IFRS is found in *IAS 19* ("Employee Benefits") and *IFRS 2* ("Share-based Payments"). *IAS 19* addresses the accounting for a wide range of compensation elements, including wages, bonuses, post-employment benefits, and compensated absences. Both of these standards were recently amended, resulting in significant convergence between IFRS and GAAP.

LEARNING OBJECTIVE 12

Compare the accounting for liabilities under GAAP and IFRS.

Key Points

- The basic definition of a liability under GAAP and IFRS is very similar. In a more technical way, liabilities are defined by the IASB as a present obligation of the entity arising from past events, the settlement of which is expected to result in an outflow from the entity of resources embodying economic benefits. Liabilities may be legally enforceable via a contract or law but need not be; that is, they can arise due to normal business practice or customs.

- IFRS requires that companies classify liabilities as current or noncurrent on the face of the statement of financial position (balance sheet), except in industries where a **presentation** based on liquidity would be considered to provide more useful information (such as financial institutions). When current liabilities (also called short-term liabilities) are presented, they are generally presented in order of liquidity.

- Under IFRS, liabilities are classified as current if they are expected to be paid within 12 months.

- Similar to GAAP, items are normally reported in order of liquidity. Companies sometimes show liabilities before assets. Also, they will sometimes show long-term liabilities before current liabilities.

- Under IFRS, companies sometimes will net current liabilities against current assets to show working capital on the face of the statement of financial position. (This is evident in the Zetar financial statements in Appendix F.)
- The basic calculation for bond valuation is the same under GAAP and IFRS. In addition, the accounting for bond liability transactions is essentially the same between GAAP and IFRS.
- IFRS requires use of the effective-interest method for amortization of bond discounts and premiums. GAAP also requires the effective-interest method, except that it allows use of the straight-line method where the difference is not material. Under IFRS, companies do not use a premium or discount account but instead show the bond at its net amount. For example, if a $100,000 bond was issued at 97, under IFRS a company would record:

Cash	97,000	
Bonds Payable		97,000

- The accounting for convertible bonds differs between IFRS and GAAP. Unlike GAAP, IFRS splits the proceeds from the convertible bond between an equity component and a debt component. The equity conversion rights are reported in equity.

  To illustrate, assume that Harris Corp. issues convertible 7% bonds with a face value of $1,000,000 and receives $1,000,000. Comparable bonds without a conversion feature would have required a 9% rate of interest. To determine how much of the proceeds would be allocated to debt and how much to equity, the promised payments of the bond obligation would be discounted at the market rate of 9%. Suppose that this results in a present value of $850,000. The entry to record the issuance would be:

Cash	1,000,000	
Bonds Payable		850,000
Share Premium—Conversion Equity		150,000

Looking to the Future

The FASB and IASB are currently involved in two projects, each of which has implications for the accounting for liabilities. One project is investigating approaches to differentiate between debt and equity instruments. The other project, the elements phase of the conceptual framework project, will evaluate the definitions of the fundamental building blocks of accounting. The results of these projects could change the classification of many debt and equity securities.

IFRS Practice

IFRS Self-Test Questions

1. Which of the following is **false**?
   (a) Under IFRS, current liabilities must always be presented before noncurrent liabilities.
   (b) Under IFRS, an item is a current liability if it will be paid within the next 12 months.
   (c) Under IFRS, current liabilities are generally shown in order of liquidity.
   (d) Under IFRS, a liability is only recognized if it is a present obligation.

2. The accounting for bonds payable is:
   (a) essentially the same under IFRS and GAAP.
   (b) differs in that GAAP requires use of the straight-line method for amortization of bond premium and discount.
   (c) the same except that market prices may be different because the present value calculations are different between IFRS and GAAP.
   (d) not covered by IFRS.

3. Stevens Corporation issued 5% convertible bonds with a total face value of $3,000,000 for $3,000,000. If the bonds had not had a conversion feature, they would have sold for $2,600,000. Under IFRS, the entry to record the transaction would require a credit to:
   (a) Bonds Payable for $3,000,000.
   (b) Bonds Payable for $400,000.
   (c) Share Premium—Conversion Equity for $400,000.
   (d) Discount on Bonds Payable for $400,000.

4. Which of the following is **true** regarding accounting for amortization of bond discount and premium?
   (a) Both IFRS and GAAP must use the effective-interest method.
   (b) GAAP must use the effective interest method, but IFRS may use either the effective-interest method or the straight-line method.
   (c) IFRS is required to use the effective-interest method.
   (d) GAAP is required to use the straight-line method.

5. The joint projects of the FASB and IASB could potentially:
   (a) change the definition of liabilities.
   (b) change the definition of equity.
   (c) change the definition of assets.
   (d) All of the above.

IFRS Exercises

IFRS10-1 Briefly describe some of the similarities and differences between GAAP and IFRS with respect to the accounting for liabilities.

IFRS10-2 Ratzlaff Company issues (in euros) €2 million, 10-year, 8% bonds at 97, with interest payable on July 1 and January 1.

Instructions
(a) Prepare the journal entry to record the sale of these bonds on January 1, 2015.
(b) Assuming instead that the above bonds sold for 104, prepare the journal entry to record the sale of these bonds on January 1, 2015.

IFRS10-3 Archer Company issued (in pounds) £4,000,000 par value, 7% convertible bonds at 99 for cash. The net present value of the debt without the conversion feature is £3,800,000. Prepare the journal entry to record the issuance of the convertible bonds.

International Financial Statement Analysis: Zetar plc

IFRS10-4 The financial statements of Zetar plc are presented in Appendix F. Instructions for accessing and using the company's complete annual report, including the notes to its financial statements, are also provided in Appendix F.

Instructions
Use the company's annual report to answer the following questions.

(a) According to the notes to the financial statements, what types of transactions do trade payables relate to? What was the average amount of time it took the company to pay its payables?
(b) Note 4.2 discusses provisions that the company records for certain types of activities. What do the provisions relate to, what are the estimates based on, and what could cause those estimates to change in subsequent periods?
(c) What was the average interest rate paid on bank loans and overdrafts?

Answers to IFRS Self-Test Questions
1. a   2. a   3. c   4. c   5. d

 ✔ **The Navigator**

What's Cooking?

What major U.S. corporation got its start 41 years ago with a waffle iron? *Hint:* It doesn't sell food. *Another hint:* Swoosh. *Another hint:* "Just do it." That's right, Nike. In 1971, Nike co-founder Bill Bowerman put a piece of rubber into a kitchen waffle iron, and the trademark waffle sole was born. It seems fair to say that at Nike, "They don't make 'em like they used to."

Nike was co-founded by Bowerman and Phil Knight, a member of Bowerman's University of Oregon track team. Each began in the shoe business independently during the early 1960s. Bowerman got his start by making hand-crafted running shoes for his University of Oregon track team. Knight, after completing graduate school, started a small business importing low-cost, high-quality shoes from Japan. In 1964, the two joined forces, each contributing $500, and formed Blue Ribbon Sports, a partnership that marketed Japanese shoes.

It wasn't until 1971 that the company began manufacturing its own line of shoes. With the new shoes came a new corporate name–Nike–the Greek goddess of victory. It is hard to imagine that the company that now boasts a stable full of world-class athletes as promoters at one time had part-time employees selling shoes out of car trunks at track meets. Nike has achieved its success through relentless innovation combined with unbridled promotion.

By 1980, Nike was sufficiently established and issued its first stock to the public. That same year, it created a stock ownership program for its employees, allowing them to share in the company's success. Since then, Nike has enjoyed phenomenal growth, with 2012 sales reaching $24.1 billion and total dividends paid of $619 million.

Nike is not alone in its quest for the top of the sport shoe world. Reebok used to be Nike's arch rival (get it? "arch"), but then Reebok was acquired by the German company adidas. Now adidas pushes Nike every step of the way.

✔ **The Navigator**

- Scan Learning Objectives
- Read Feature Story
- Read Preview
- Read text and answer **DO IT!** p. 551
  - p. 553 ■ p. 556 ■ p. 560 ■ p. 565
  - p. 569 ■ p. 572 ■ p. 575
- Work Comprehensive **DO IT!** p. 575
- Review Summary of Learning Objectives
- Answer Self-Test Questions
- Complete Assignments
- Go to *WileyPLUS* for practice and tutorials
- Read **A Look at IFRS** p. 600

Learning Objectives ✔ The Navigator

After studying this chapter, you should be able to:

[1] Identify the major characteristics of a corporation.

[2] Record the issuance of common stock.

[3] Explain the accounting for treasury stock.

[4] Differentiate preferred stock from common stock.

[5] Prepare the entries for cash dividends and stock dividends.

[6] Identify the items reported in a retained earnings statement.

[7] Prepare and analyze a comprehensive stockholders' equity section.

Franck Fife/AFP/Getty Images, Inc.

The shoe market is fickle, with new styles becoming popular almost daily and vast international markets still lying untapped. Whether one of these two giants does eventually take control of the pedi-planet remains to be seen. Meanwhile, the shareholders sit anxiously in the stands as this Olympic-size drama unfolds.

Preview of Chapter 11

 The Navigator

Corporations like Nike and adidas have substantial resources at their disposal. In fact, the corporation is the dominant form of business organization in the United States in terms of sales, earnings, and number of employees. All of the 500 largest companies in the United States are corporations. In this chapter, we will explain the essential features of a corporation and the accounting for a corporation's capital stock transactions.

The content and organization of Chapter 11 are as follows.

CORPORATIONS: ORGANIZATION, STOCK TRANSACTIONS, DIVIDENDS, AND RETAINED EARNINGS

The Corporate Form of Organization	Accounting for Stock Transactions	Dividends	Retained Earnings	Statement Presentation and Analysis
• Characteristics • Formation • Stockholder rights • Stock issue considerations • Corporate capital	• Common stock • Treasury stock • Preferred stock	• Cash dividends • Stock dividends • Stock splits	• Retained earnings restrictions • Prior period adjustments • Retained earnings statement	• Presentation • Analysis

The Corporate Form of Organization

In 1819, Chief Justice John Marshall defined a corporation as "an artificial being, invisible, intangible, and existing only in contemplation of law." This definition is the foundation for the prevailing legal interpretation that a **corporation** is an **entity separate and distinct from its owners**.

A corporation is created by law, and its continued existence depends upon the statutes of the state in which it is incorporated. As a legal entity, a corporation has most of the rights and privileges of a person. The major exceptions relate to privileges that only a living person can exercise, such as the right to vote or to hold public office. A corporation is subject to the same duties and responsibilities as a person. For example, it must abide by the laws, and it must pay taxes.

Two common ways to classify corporations are by **purpose** and by **ownership**. A corporation may be organized for the purpose of making a profit, or it may be not-for-profit. For-profit corporations include such well-known companies as McDonald's, Nike, PepsiCo, and Google. Not-for-profit corporations are organized for charitable, medical, or educational purposes. Examples are the Salvation Army and the American Cancer Society.

Classification by ownership differentiates publicly held and privately held corporations. A **publicly held corporation** may have thousands of stockholders. Its stock is regularly traded on a national securities exchange such as the New York Stock Exchange. Examples are IBM, Caterpillar, and General Electric.

Alternative Terminology
Privately held corporations are also referred to as *closely held corporations*.

In contrast, a **privately held corporation** usually has only a few stockholders, and does not offer its stock for sale to the general public. Privately held companies are generally much smaller than publicly held companies, although some notable exceptions exist. Cargill Inc., a private corporation that trades in grain and other commodities, is one of the largest companies in the United States.

Characteristics of a Corporation

In 1964, when Nike's founders Phil Knight and Bill Bowerman were just getting started in the running shoe business, they formed their original organization as a partnership. In 1968, they reorganized the company as a corporation. A number of characteristics distinguish corporations from proprietorships and partnerships. We explain the most important of these characteristics below.

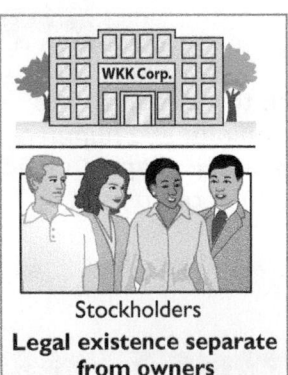

Stockholders
Legal existence separate from owners

SEPARATE LEGAL EXISTENCE

As an entity separate and distinct from its owners, the corporation acts under its own name rather than in the name of its stockholders. Nike may buy, own, and sell property. It may borrow money, and may enter into legally binding contracts in its own name. It may also sue or be sued, and it pays its own taxes.

In a partnership, the acts of the owners (partners) bind the partnership. In contrast, the acts of its owners (stockholders) do not bind the corporation unless such owners are **agents** of the corporation. For example, if you owned shares of Nike stock, you would not have the right to purchase inventory for the company unless you were designated as an agent of the corporation.

Stockholders
Limited liability of stockholders

LIMITED LIABILITY OF STOCKHOLDERS

Since a corporation is a separate legal entity, creditors have recourse only to corporate assets to satisfy their claims. The liability of stockholders is normally limited to their investment in the corporation. Creditors have no legal claim on the personal assets of the owners unless fraud has occurred. Even in the event of bankruptcy, stockholders' losses are generally limited to their capital investment in the corporation.

TRANSFERABLE OWNERSHIP RIGHTS

Shares of capital stock give ownership in a corporation. These shares are transferable units. Stockholders may dispose of part or all of their interest in a corporation simply by selling their stock. The transfer of an ownership interest in a partnership requires the consent of each owner. In contrast, the transfer of stock is entirely at the discretion of the stockholder. It does not require the approval of either the corporation or other stockholders.

Transferable ownership rights

The transfer of ownership rights between stockholders normally has no effect on the daily operating activities of the corporation. Nor does it affect the corporation's assets, liabilities, and total ownership equity. The transfer of these ownership rights is a transaction between individual owners. The company does not participate in the transfer of these ownership rights after the original sale of the capital stock.

ABILITY TO ACQUIRE CAPITAL

It is relatively easy for a corporation to obtain capital through the issuance of stock. Buying stock in a corporation is often attractive to an investor because a stockholder has limited liability and shares of stock are readily transferable. Also, numerous individuals can become stockholders by investing relatively small amounts of money.

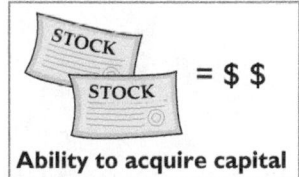

Ability to acquire capital

CONTINUOUS LIFE

The life of a corporation is stated in its charter. The life may be perpetual, or it may be limited to a specific number of years. If it is limited, the company can extend the life through renewal of the charter. Since a corporation is a separate legal entity, its continuance as a going concern is not affected by the withdrawal, death, or incapacity of a stockholder, employee, or officer. As a result, a successful company can have a continuous and perpetual life.

Continuous life

CORPORATION MANAGEMENT

Stockholders legally own the corporation. However, they manage the corporation indirectly through a board of directors they elect. Philip Knight is the chairman of the board for Nike. The board, in turn, formulates the operating policies for the company. The board also selects officers, such as a president and one or more vice presidents, to execute policy and to perform daily management functions. As a result of the Sarbanes-Oxley Act, the board is now required to monitor management's actions more closely. Many feel that the failures of Enron, WorldCom, and more recently MF Global could have been avoided by more diligent boards.

Illustration 11-1 (page 546) presents a typical organization chart showing the delegation of responsibility. The chief executive officer (CEO) has overall responsibility for managing the business. As the organization chart shows, the CEO delegates responsibility to other officers. The chief accounting officer is the **controller**. The controller's responsibilities include (1) maintaining the accounting records, (2) maintaining an adequate system of internal control, and (3) preparing financial statements, tax returns, and internal reports. The **treasurer** has custody of the corporation's funds and is responsible for maintaining the company's cash position.

Ethics Note

Managers who are not owners are often compensated based on the performance of the firm. They thus may be tempted to exaggerate firm performance by inflating income figures.

The organizational structure of a corporation enables a company to hire professional managers to run the business. On the other hand, the separation of ownership and management often reduces an owner's ability to actively manage the company.

Illustration 11-1
Corporation organization chart

GOVERNMENT REGULATIONS

A corporation is subject to numerous state and federal regulations. For example, state laws usually prescribe the requirements for issuing stock, the distributions of earnings permitted to stockholders, and the acceptable methods for buying back and retiring stock. Federal securities laws govern the sale of capital stock to the general public. Also, most publicly held corporations are required to make extensive disclosure of their financial affairs to the Securities and Exchange Commission (SEC) through quarterly and annual reports. In addition, when a corporation lists its stock on organized securities exchanges, it must comply with the reporting requirements of these exchanges. Government regulations are designed to protect the owners of the corporation.

ADDITIONAL TAXES

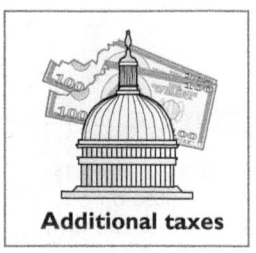

Owners of proprietorships and partnerships report their share of earnings on their personal income tax returns. The individual owner then pays taxes on this amount. Corporations, on the other hand, must pay federal and state income taxes **as a separate legal entity**. These taxes can be substantial. They can amount to as much as 40% of taxable income.

In addition, stockholders must pay taxes on cash dividends (pro rata distributions of net income). Thus, many argue that the government taxes corporate income **twice (double taxation)**—once at the corporate level and again at the individual level.

In summary, Illustration 11-2 shows the advantages and disadvantages of a corporation compared to a proprietorship and a partnership.

Forming a Corporation

A corporation is formed by grant of a state **charter**. The charter is a document that describes the name and purpose of the corporation, the types and number of shares of stock that are authorized to be issued, the names of the individuals that

Advantages	Disadvantages
Separate legal existence	Corporation management—separation of
Limited liability of stockholders	ownership and management
Transferable ownership rights	Government regulations
Ability to acquire capital	Additional taxes
Continuous life	
Corporation management—professional	
managers	

Illustration 11-2
Advantages and disadvantages of a corporation

formed the company, and the number of shares that these individuals agreed to purchase. Regardless of the number of states in which a corporation has operating divisions, it is incorporated in only one state.

It is to the company's advantage to incorporate in a state whose laws are favorable to the corporate form of business organization. For example, although General Motors has its headquarters in Michigan, it is incorporated in New Jersey. In fact, more and more corporations have been incorporating in states with rules that favor existing management. For example, Gulf Oil changed its state of incorporation to Delaware to thwart possible unfriendly takeovers. There, certain defensive tactics against takeovers can be approved by the board of directors alone, without a vote by shareholders.

Alternative Terminology
The charter is often referred to as the *articles of incorporation*.

Upon receipt of its charter from the state of incorporation, the corporation establishes **by-laws**. The by-laws establish the internal rules and procedures for conducting the affairs of the corporation. Corporations engaged in interstate commerce must also obtain a **license** from each state in which they do business. The license subjects the corporation's operating activities to the general corporation laws of the state.

Costs incurred in the formation of a corporation are called **organization costs**. These costs include legal and state fees, and promotional expenditures involved in the organization of the business. **Corporations expense organization costs as incurred.** Determining the amount and timing of future benefits is so difficult that it is standard procedure to take a conservative approach of expensing these costs immediately.

ACCOUNTING ACROSS THE ORGANIZATION

A Thousand Millionaires!

Traveling to space or embarking on an expedition to excavate lost Mayan ruins are normally the stuff of adventure novels. But for employees of Facebook, these and other lavish dreams moved closer to reality when the world's No. 1 online social network went public through an initial public offering (IPO) that may have created at least a thousand millionaires. The IPO was the largest in Internet history, valuing Facebook at over $104 billion.

With all these riches to be had, why did Mark Zuckerberg, the founder of Facebook, delay taking his company public? Consider that the main motivation for issuing shares to the public is to raise money so you can grow your business. However, unlike a manufacturer or even an online retailer, Facebook doesn't need major physical resources, it doesn't have inventory, and it doesn't really need much money for marketing. So in the past, the company hasn't had much need for additional cash beyond what it was already generating on its own. Finally, as head of a closely held, nonpublic company, Zuckerberg was subject to far fewer regulations than a public company.

Source: "Status Update: I'm Rich! Facebook Flotation to Create 1,000 Millionaires Among Company's Rank and File," *Daily Mail Reporter* (February 1, 2012)

 Why did Mark Zuckerberg, the CEO and founder of Facebook, delay taking his company's shares public through an initial public offering (IPO)? (See page 600.)

Stockholder Rights

When chartered, the corporation may begin selling shares of stock. When a corporation has only one class of stock, it is **common stock**. Each share of common stock gives the stockholder the ownership rights pictured in Illustration 11-3. The articles of incorporation or the by-laws state the ownership rights of a share of stock.

Illustration 11-3
Ownership rights of stockholders

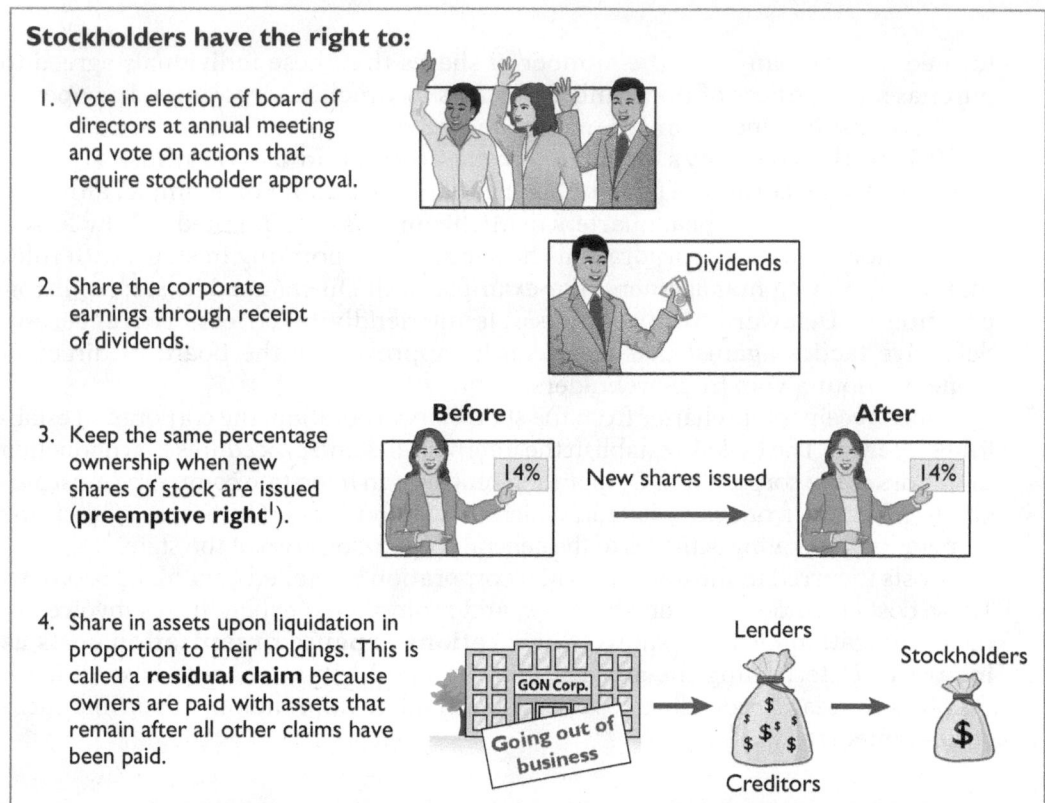

Stockholders have the right to:

1. Vote in election of board of directors at annual meeting and vote on actions that require stockholder approval.

2. Share the corporate earnings through receipt of dividends.

3. Keep the same percentage ownership when new shares of stock are issued (**preemptive right**[1]).

4. Share in assets upon liquidation in proportion to their holdings. This is called a **residual claim** because owners are paid with assets that remain after all other claims have been paid.

Proof of stock ownership is evidenced by a form known as a **stock certificate**. As Illustration 11-4 shows, the face of the certificate shows the name of the corporation, the stockholder's name, the class and special features of the stock, the number of shares owned, and the signatures of authorized corporate officials. Prenumbered certificates facilitate accountability. They may be issued for any quantity of shares.

Stock Issue Considerations

Although Nike incorporated in 1968, it did not sell stock to the public until 1980. At that time, Nike evidently decided it would benefit from the infusion of cash that a public sale would bring. When a corporation decides to issue stock, it must resolve a number of basic questions: How many shares should it authorize for sale? How should it issue the stock? What value should the corporation assign to the stock? We address these questions in the following sections.

---

[1]A number of companies have eliminated the preemptive right because they believe it makes an unnecessary and cumbersome demand on management. For example, by stockholder approval, IBM has dropped its preemptive right for stockholders.

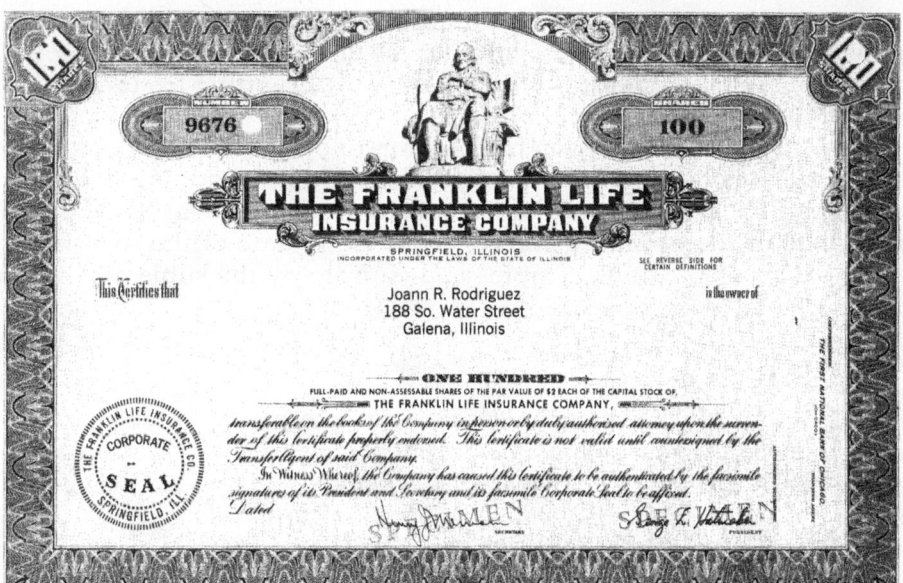

Illustration 11-4
A stock certificate

AUTHORIZED STOCK

The charter indicates the amount of stock that a corporation is **authorized** to sell. The total amount of **authorized stock** at the time of incorporation normally anticipates both initial and subsequent capital needs. As a result, the number of shares authorized generally exceeds the number initially sold. If it sells all authorized stock, a corporation must obtain consent of the state to amend its charter before it can issue additional shares.

The authorization of capital stock does not result in a formal accounting entry. The reason is that the event has no immediate effect on either corporate assets or stockholders' equity. However, the number of authorized shares is often reported in the stockholders' equity section. It is then simple to determine the number of unissued shares that the corporation can issue without amending the charter: subtract the total shares issued from the total authorized. For example, if Advanced Micro was authorized to sell 100,000 shares of common stock and issued 80,000 shares, 20,000 shares would remain unissued.

ISSUANCE OF STOCK

A corporation can issue common stock **directly** to investors. Alternatively, it can issue the stock **indirectly** through an investment banking firm that specializes in bringing securities to the attention of prospective investors. Direct issue is typical in closely held companies. Indirect issue is customary for a publicly held corporation.

In an indirect issue, the investment banking firm may agree to **underwrite** the entire stock issue. In this arrangement, the investment banker buys the stock from the corporation at a stipulated price and resells the shares to investors. The corporation thus avoids any risk of being unable to sell the shares. Also, it obtains immediate use of the cash received from the underwriter. The investment banking firm, in turn, assumes the risk of reselling the shares, in return for an underwriting fee.[2]

Indirect issuance

---

[2] Alternatively, the investment banking firm may agree only to enter into a **best-efforts contract** with the corporation. In such cases, the banker agrees to sell as many shares as possible at a specified price. The corporation bears the risk of unsold stock. Under a best-efforts arrangement, the banking firm is paid a fee or commission for its services.

For example, Google (the world's number-one Internet search engine) used underwriters when it issued a highly successful initial public offering, raising $1.67 billion. The underwriters charged a 3% underwriting fee (approximately $50 million) on Google's stock offering.

How does a corporation set the price for a new issue of stock? Among the factors to be considered are (1) the company's anticipated future earnings, (2) its expected dividend rate per share, (3) its current financial position, (4) the current state of the economy, and (5) the current state of the securities market. The calculation can be complex and is properly the subject of a finance course.

MARKET PRICE OF STOCK

The stock of publicly held companies is traded on organized exchanges. The interaction between buyers and sellers determines the prices per share. In general, the prices set by the marketplace tend to follow the trend of a company's earnings and dividends. But, factors beyond a company's control, such as an oil embargo, changes in interest rates, and the outcome of a presidential election, may cause day-to-day fluctuations in market prices.

The trading of capital stock on securities exchanges involves the transfer of **already issued shares** from an existing stockholder to another investor. These transactions have **no impact** on a corporation's stockholders' equity.

Joe Robbins/Getty Images, Inc.

INVESTOR INSIGHT

How to Read Stock Quotes

Organized exchanges trade the stock of publicly held companies at dollar prices per share established by the interaction between buyers and sellers. For each listed security, the financial press reports the high and low prices of the stock during the year, the total volume of stock traded on a given day, the high and low prices for the day, and the closing market price, with the net change for the day. Nike is listed on the New York Stock Exchange. Here is a listing for Nike:

	52 Weeks						
Stock	High	Low	Volume	High	Low	Close	Net Change
Nike	78.55	48.76	5,375,651	72.44	69.78	70.61	−1.69

These numbers indicate the following. The high and low market prices for the last 52 weeks have been $78.55 and $48.76. The trading volume for the day was 5,375,651 shares. The high, low, and closing prices for that date were $72.44, $69.78, and $70.61, respectively. The net change for the day was a decrease of $1.69 per share.

? For stocks traded on organized exchanges, how are the dollar prices per share established? What factors might influence the price of shares in the marketplace? (See page 600.)

PAR AND NO-PAR VALUE STOCKS

Par value stock is capital stock to which the charter has assigned a value per share. Years ago, par value determined the **legal capital** per share that a company must retain in the business for the protection of corporate creditors. That amount was not available for withdrawal by stockholders. Thus, in the past, most states required the corporation to sell its shares at par or above.

However, par value was often immaterial relative to the value of the company's stock—even at the time of issue. Thus, its usefulness as a protective device to creditors was questionable. For example, Loews Corporation's par value is $0.01 per share, yet a new issue in 2013 would have sold at a **market price** in the $46 per share range. Thus, par has no relationship with market price. In the vast majority of cases, it is an immaterial amount. As a consequence, today many states do not require a par value. Instead, they use other means to protect creditors.

No-par value stock is capital stock to which the charter has not assigned a value. No-par value stock is fairly common today. For example, Nike and Procter & Gamble both have no-par stock. In many states, the board of directors assigns a **stated value** to no-par shares.

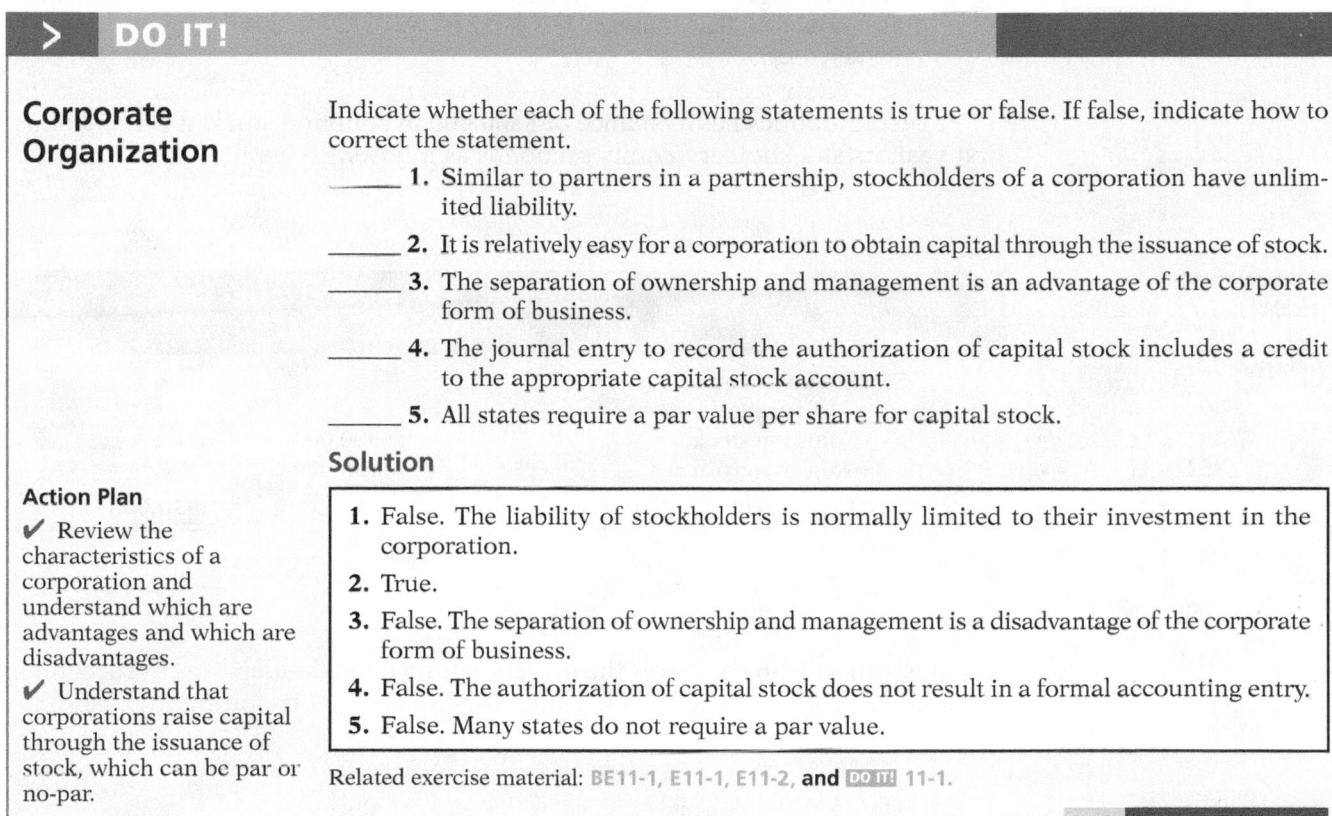

> DO IT!

Corporate Organization

Indicate whether each of the following statements is true or false. If false, indicate how to correct the statement.

_____ 1. Similar to partners in a partnership, stockholders of a corporation have unlimited liability.

_____ 2. It is relatively easy for a corporation to obtain capital through the issuance of stock.

_____ 3. The separation of ownership and management is an advantage of the corporate form of business.

_____ 4. The journal entry to record the authorization of capital stock includes a credit to the appropriate capital stock account.

_____ 5. All states require a par value per share for capital stock.

Solution

1. False. The liability of stockholders is normally limited to their investment in the corporation.
2. True.
3. False. The separation of ownership and management is a disadvantage of the corporate form of business.
4. False. The authorization of capital stock does not result in a formal accounting entry.
5. False. Many states do not require a par value.

Action Plan

✔ Review the characteristics of a corporation and understand which are advantages and which are disadvantages.

✔ Understand that corporations raise capital through the issuance of stock, which can be par or no-par.

Related exercise material: BE11-1, E11-1, E11-2, **and** DO IT! 11-1.

✔ The Navigator

Corporate Capital

Owners' equity is identified by various names: **stockholders' equity, shareholders' equity**, or **corporate capital**. The stockholders' equity section of a corporation's balance sheet consists of two parts: (1) paid-in (contributed) capital and (2) retained earnings (earned capital).

The distinction between **paid-in capital** and **retained earnings** is important from both a legal and a financial point of view. Legally, corporations can make distributions of earnings (declare dividends) out of retained earnings in all states. However, in many states they cannot declare dividends out of paid-in capital. Management, stockholders, and others often look to retained earnings for the continued existence and growth of the corporation.

PAID-IN CAPITAL

Paid-in capital is the total amount of cash and other assets paid in to the corporation by stockholders in exchange for capital stock. As noted earlier, when a corporation has only one class of stock, it is **common stock**.

RETAINED EARNINGS

Retained earnings is net income that a corporation retains for future use. Net income is recorded in Retained Earnings by a closing entry that debits Income Summary and credits Retained Earnings. For example, assuming that net income for Delta Robotics in its first year of operations is $130,000, the closing entry is:

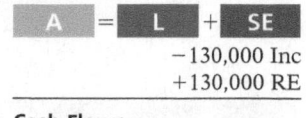

A	=	L	+	SE

−130,000 Inc
+130,000 RE

Cash Flows
no effect

Income Summary	130,000	
Retained Earnings		130,000
(To close Income Summary and transfer net income		
to Retained Earnings)		

If Delta Robotics has a balance of $800,000 in common stock at the end of its first year, its stockholders' equity section is as follows.

Illustration 11-5
Stockholders' equity section

DELTA ROBOTICS
Balance Sheet (partial)

Stockholders' equity
  Paid-in capital
    Common stock $800,000
  Retained earnings   130,000
    Total stockholders' equity   **$930,000**

Illustration 11-6 compares the owners' equity (stockholders' equity) accounts reported on a balance sheet for a proprietorship and a corporation.

Illustration 11-6
Comparison of owners' equity accounts

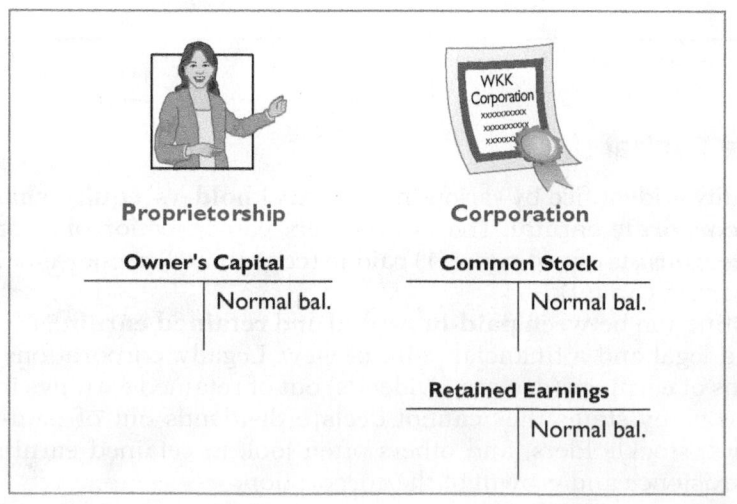

PEOPLE, PLANET, AND PROFIT INSIGHT

The Impact of Corporate Social Responsibility

A recent survey conducted by Institutional Shareholder Services, a proxy advisory firm, shows that 83% of investors now believe environmental and social factors can significantly impact shareholder value over the long term. This belief is clearly visible in the rising level of support for shareholder proposals requesting action related to social and environmental issues.

The following table shows that the number of corporate social responsibility (CSR)-related shareholder proposals rose from 150 in 2000 to 191 in 2010. Moreover, those proposals received average voting support of 18.4% of votes cast versus just 7.5% a decade earlier.

Trends in Shareholder Proposals on Corporate Responsibility

	2000	2005	2010
Number of proposals voted	150	155	191
Average voting support	7.5%	9.9%	18.4%
Percent proposals receiving >10% support	16.7%	31.2%	52.1%

Source: Investor Responsibility Research Center, Ernst & Young, *Seven Questions CEOs and Boards Should Ask About: "Triple Bottom Line" Reporting.*

©Robert Churchill/iStockphoto

? Why are CSR-related shareholder proposals increasing? (See page 600.)

> DO IT!

Corporate Capital

At the end of its first year of operation, Doral Corporation has $750,000 of common stock and net income of $122,000. Prepare (a) the closing entry for net income and (b) the stockholders' equity section at year-end.

Solution

Action Plan

✔ Record net income in Retained Earnings by a closing entry in which Income Summary is debited and Retained Earnings is credited.

✔ In the stockholders' equity section, show (1) paid-in capital and (2) retained earnings.

(a) Income Summary	122,000	
Retained Earnings		122,000
(To close Income Summary and transfer net income to Retained Earnings)		
(b) Stockholders' equity		
Paid-in capital		
Common stock	$750,000	
Retained earnings	122,000	
Total stockholders' equity		$872,000

Related exercise material: **DO IT!** 11-2.

 The Navigator

Accounting for Stock Transactions

Accounting for Common Stock

LEARNING OBJECTIVE 2

Let's now look at how to account for issues of common stock. The primary objectives in accounting for the issuance of common stock are (1) to identify the specific sources of paid-in capital, and (2) to maintain the distinction between paid-in

Record the issuance of common stock.

capital and retained earnings. **The issuance of common stock affects only paid-in capital accounts.**

ISSUING PAR VALUE COMMON STOCK FOR CASH

As discussed earlier, par value does not indicate a stock's market price. Therefore, the cash proceeds from issuing par value stock may be equal to, greater than, or less than par value. When the company records issuance of common stock for cash, it credits the par value of the shares to Common Stock. It also records in a separate paid-in capital account the portion of the proceeds that is above or below par value.

To illustrate, assume that Hydro-Slide, Inc. issues 1,000 shares of $1 par value common stock at par for cash. The entry to record this transaction is:

Cash	1,000	
Common Stock		1,000
(To record issuance of 1,000 shares of $1 par common stock at par)		

Now assume that Hydro-Slide issues an additional 1,000 shares of the $1 par value common stock for cash at $5 per share. The amount received above the par value, in this case $4 ($5 − $1), is credited to Paid-in Capital in Excess of Par—Common Stock. The entry is:

Cash	5,000	
Common Stock		1,000
Paid-in Capital in Excess of Par—Common Stock		4,000
(To record issuance of 1,000 shares of $1 par common stock)		

The total paid-in capital from these two transactions is $6,000, and the legal capital is $2,000. Assuming Hydro-Slide, Inc. has retained earnings of $27,000, Illustration 11-7 shows the company's stockholders' equity section.

Illustration 11-7
Stockholders' equity—paid-in capital in excess of par

HYDRO-SLIDE, INC.		
Balance Sheet (partial)		
Stockholders' equity		
Paid-in capital		
Common stock	$ 2,000	
Paid-in capital in excess of par— **common stock**	4,000	
Total paid-in capital	6,000	
Retained earnings	27,000	
Total stockholders' equity	$33,000	

Alternative Terminology
Paid-in Capital in Excess of Par is also called *Premium on Stock.*

When a corporation issues stock for less than par value, it debits the account Paid-in Capital in Excess of Par—Common Stock if a credit balance exists in this account. If a credit balance does not exist, then the corporation debits to Retained Earnings the amount less than par. This situation occurs only rarely. Most states do not permit the sale of common stock below par value because stockholders may be held personally liable for the difference between the price paid upon original sale and par value.

ISSUING NO-PAR COMMON STOCK FOR CASH

When no-par common stock has a stated value, the entries are similar to those illustrated for par value stock. The corporation credits the stated value to Common Stock. Also, when the selling price of no-par stock exceeds stated value, the corporation credits the excess to Paid-in Capital in Excess of Stated Value—Common Stock.

For example, assume that instead of $1 par value stock, Hydro-Slide, Inc. has $5 stated value no-par stock and the company issues 5,000 shares at $8 per share for cash. The entry is:

Cash	40,000	
Common Stock		25,000
Paid-in Capital in Excess of Stated Value—Common Stock		15,000
(To record issue of 5,000 shares of $5 stated		
value no-par stock)		

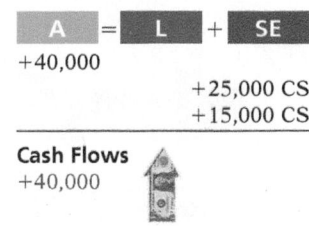

Hydro-Slide, Inc. reports Paid-in Capital in Excess of Stated Value—Common Stock as part of paid-in capital in the stockholders' equity section.

What happens when no-par stock does not have a stated value? In that case, the corporation credits the entire proceeds to Common Stock. Thus, if Hydro-Slide does not assign a stated value to its no-par stock, it records the issuance of the 5,000 shares at $8 per share for cash as follows.

Cash	40,000	
Common Stock		40,000
(To record issue of 5,000 shares of no-par stock)		

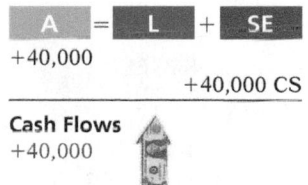

ISSUING COMMON STOCK FOR SERVICES OR NONCASH ASSETS

Corporations also may issue stock for services (compensation to attorneys or consultants) or for noncash assets (land, buildings, and equipment). In such cases, what cost should be recognized in the exchange transaction? To comply with the **historical cost principle**, in a noncash transaction **cost is the cash equivalent price**. Thus, **cost is either the fair value of the consideration given up or the fair value of the consideration received**, whichever is more clearly determinable.

To illustrate, assume that attorneys have helped Jordan Company incorporate. They have billed the company $5,000 for their services. They agree to accept 4,000 shares of $1 par value common stock in payment of their bill. At the time of the exchange, there is no established market price for the stock. In this case, the fair value of the consideration received, $5,000, is more clearly evident. Accordingly, Jordan Company makes the following entry.

Organization Expense	5,000	
Common Stock		4,000
Paid-in Capital in Excess of Par—Common Stock		1,000
(To record issuance of 4,000 shares of $1 par value		
stock to attorneys)		

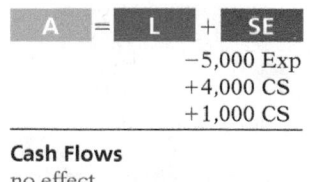

As explained on page 547, organization costs are expensed as incurred.

In contrast, assume that Athletic Research Inc. is an existing publicly held corporation. Its $5 par value stock is actively traded at $8 per share. The company issues 10,000 shares of stock to acquire land recently advertised for sale at $90,000. The most clearly evident value in this noncash transaction is the market price of the consideration given, $80,000. The company records the transaction as follows.

Land	80,000	
Common Stock		50,000
Paid-in Capital in Excess of Par—Common Stock		30,000
(To record issuance of 10,000 shares of $5 par value		
stock for land)		

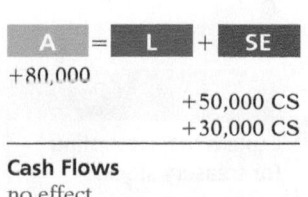

As illustrated in these examples, **the par value of the stock is never a factor in determining the cost of the assets received**. This is also true of the stated value of no-par stock.

ANATOMY OF A FRAUD

The president, chief operating officer, and chief financial officer of SafeNet, a software encryption company, were each awarded employee stock options by the company's board of directors as part of their compensation package. Stock options enable an employee to buy a company's stock sometime in the future at the price that existed when the stock option was awarded. For example, suppose that you received stock options today, when the stock price of your company was $30. Three years later, if the stock price rose to $100, you could "exercise" your options and buy the stock for $30 per share, thereby making $70 per share. After being awarded their stock options, the three employees changed the award dates in the company's records to dates in the past, when the company's stock was trading at historical lows. For instance, using the previous example, they would choose a past date when the stock was selling for $10 per share, rather than the $30 price on the actual award date. This would increase the profit from exercising the options to $90 per share.

Total take: $1.7 million

THE MISSING CONTROL

Independent internal verification. The company's board of directors should have ensured that the awards were properly administered. For example, the date on the minutes from the board meeting could be compared to the dates that were recorded for the awards. In addition, the dates should again be confirmed upon exercise.

> DO IT!

Issuance of Stock

Action Plan

✔ In issuing shares for cash, credit Common Stock for par value per share.

✔ Credit any additional proceeds in excess of par to a separate paid-in capital account.

✔ When stock is issued for services, use the cash equivalent price.

✔ For the cash equivalent price, use either the fair value of what is given up or the fair value of what is received, whichever is more clearly determinable.

Cayman Corporation begins operations on March 1 by issuing 100,000 shares of $10 par value common stock for cash at $12 per share. On March 15, it issues 5,000 shares of common stock to attorneys in settlement of their bill of $50,000 for organization costs. Journalize the issuance of the shares, assuming the stock is not publicly traded.

Solution

Mar. 1	Cash		1,200,000	
		Common Stock		1,000,000
		Paid-in Capital in Excess of Par—		
		Common Stock		200,000
		(To record issuance of 100,000 shares		
		at $12 per share)		
Mar. 15	Organization Expense		50,000	
		Common Stock		50,000
		(To record issuance of 5,000 shares		
		for attorneys' fees)		

Related exercise material: BE11-2, BE11-3, BE11-4, E11-3, E11-4, E11-8, **and** DO IT! 11-3.

✔ **The Navigator**

Accounting for Treasury Stock

LEARNING OBJECTIVE **3**

Explain the accounting for treasury stock.

Treasury stock is a corporation's own stock that it has issued and subsequently reacquired from shareholders but not retired. A corporation may acquire treasury stock for various reasons:

1. To reissue the shares to officers and employees under bonus and stock compensation plans.

2. To increase trading of the company's stock in the securities market. Companies expect that buying their own stock will signal that management believes the stock is underpriced, which they hope will enhance its market price.

3. To have additional shares available for use in the acquisition of other companies.

4. To reduce the number of shares outstanding and thereby increase earnings per share.

Helpful Hint
Treasury shares do not have dividend rights or voting rights.

Another infrequent reason for purchasing shares is that management may want to eliminate hostile shareholders by buying them out.

Many corporations have treasury stock. For example, approximately 68% of U.S. companies have treasury stock.[3] In a recent year, Nike purchased more than 6 million treasury shares.

PURCHASE OF TREASURY STOCK

Companies generally account for treasury stock by **the cost method**. This method uses the cost of the shares purchased to value the treasury stock. Under the cost method, the company debits **Treasury Stock** for the **price paid to reacquire the shares**. When the company disposes of the shares, it credits to Treasury Stock **the same amount** it paid to reacquire the shares.

To illustrate, assume that on January 1, 2015, the stockholders' equity section of Mead, Inc. has 400,000 shares authorized and 100,000 shares of $5 par value common stock outstanding (all issued at par value) and Retained Earnings of $200,000. The stockholders' equity section before purchase of treasury stock is as follows.

MEAD, INC.	
Balance Sheet (partial)	
Stockholders' equity	
Paid-in capital	
Common stock, $5 par value, 400,000 shares authorized, 100,000 shares issued and outstanding	$500,000
Retained earnings	200,000
Total stockholders' equity	$700,000

Illustration 11-8
Stockholders' equity with no treasury stock

On February 1, 2015, Mead acquires 4,000 shares of its stock at $8 per share. The entry is:

Feb. 1	Treasury Stock	32,000	
	Cash		32,000
	(To record purchase of 4,000 shares of treasury stock at $8 per share)		

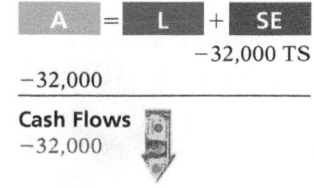

A = L + SE
−32,000 TS
−32,000

Cash Flows
−32,000

Mead debits Treasury Stock for the cost of the shares purchased ($32,000). Is the original paid-in capital account, Common Stock, affected? No, because the number of issued shares does not change.

In the stockholders' equity section of the balance sheet, Mead deducts treasury stock from total paid-in capital and retained earnings. Treasury Stock is a **contra stockholders' equity account**. Thus, the acquisition of treasury stock reduces

---

[3]*Accounting Trends and Techniques—2012* (New York: American Institute of Certified Public Accountants).

stockholders' equity. The stockholders' equity section of Mead, Inc. after purchase of treasury stock is as follows.

Illustration 11-9
Stockholders' equity with treasury stock

MEAD, INC.
Balance Sheet (partial)

Stockholders' equity	
Paid-in capital	
Common stock, $5 par value, 400,000 shares authorized,	
100,000 shares issued, and 96,000 shares outstanding	$500,000
Retained earnings	200,000
Total paid-in capital and retained earnings	700,000
Less: Treasury stock (4,000 shares)	**32,000**
Total stockholders' equity	$668,000

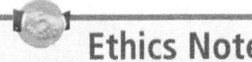

Ethics Note

The purchase of treasury stock reduces the cushion (cash available) for creditors and preferred stockholders. A restriction for the cost of treasury stock purchased is often required. The restriction is usually applied to retained earnings.

Mead discloses in the balance sheet both the number of shares issued (100,000) and the number in the treasury (4,000). The difference is the number of shares of stock outstanding (96,000). The term **outstanding stock** means the number of shares of issued stock that are being held by stockholders.

Some maintain that companies should report treasury stock as an asset because it can be sold for cash. But under this reasoning, companies would also show unissued stock as an asset, which is clearly incorrect. Rather than being an asset, treasury stock reduces stockholder claims on corporate assets. This effect is correctly shown by reporting treasury stock as a deduction from total paid-in capital and retained earnings.

ACCOUNTING ACROSS THE ORGANIZATION

Why Did Reebok Buy Its Own Stock?

In a bold (and some would say risky) move, Reebok at one time bought back nearly a third of its shares. This repurchase of shares dramatically reduced Reebok's available cash. In fact, the company borrowed significant funds to accomplish the repurchase. In a press release, management stated that it was repurchasing the shares because it believed its stock was severely underpriced. The repurchase of so many shares was meant to signal management's belief in good future earnings.

Skeptics, however, suggested that Reebok's management was repurchasing shares to make it less likely that another company would acquire Reebok (in which case Reebok's top managers would likely lose their jobs). By depleting its cash, Reebok became a less attractive acquisition target. Acquiring companies like to purchase companies with large cash balances so they can pay off debt used in the acquisition.

> What signal might a large stock repurchase send to investors regarding management's belief about the company's growth opportunities? (See page 600.)

Han Myung-Gu/WireImage/Getty Images, Inc.

DISPOSAL OF TREASURY STOCK

Treasury stock is usually sold or retired. The accounting for its sale differs when treasury stock is sold above cost than when it is sold below cost.

SALE OF TREASURY STOCK ABOVE COST If the selling price of the treasury shares is equal to their cost, the company records the sale of the shares by a debit to Cash and a credit to Treasury Stock. When the selling price of the shares is greater than their cost, the company credits the difference to Paid-in Capital from Treasury Stock.

To illustrate, assume that on July 1, Mead, Inc. sells for $10 per share the 1,000 shares of its treasury stock previously acquired at $8 per share. The entry is as follows.

July 1	Cash	10,000	
	Treasury Stock		8,000
	Paid-in Capital from Treasury Stock		2,000
	(To record sale of 1,000 shares of treasury stock above cost)		

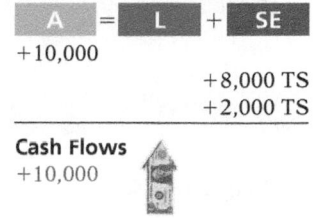

A = L + SE
+10,000
+8,000 TS
+2,000 TS

Cash Flows
+10,000

Mead does not record a $2,000 gain on sale of treasury stock because (1) gains on sales occur when **assets** are sold, and treasury stock is not an asset, and (2) a corporation does not realize a gain or suffer a loss from stock transactions with its own stockholders. Thus, companies should not include in net income any paid-in capital arising from the sale of treasury stock. Instead, they report Paid-in Capital from Treasury Stock separately on the balance sheet, as a part of paid-in capital.

SALE OF TREASURY STOCK BELOW COST When a company sells treasury stock below its cost, it usually debits to Paid-in Capital from Treasury Stock the excess of cost over selling price. Thus, if Mead, Inc. sells an additional 800 shares of treasury stock on October 1 at $7 per share, it makes the following entry.

Oct. 1	Cash	5,600	
	Paid-in Capital from Treasury Stock	800	
	Treasury Stock		6,400
	(To record sale of 800 shares of treasury stock below cost)		

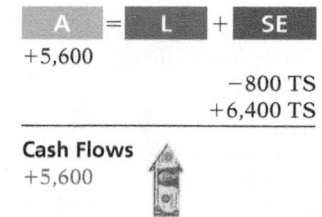

A = L + SE
+5,600
−800 TS
+6,400 TS

Cash Flows
+5,600

Observe the following from the two sales entries. (1) Mead credits Treasury Stock at cost in each entry. (2) Mead uses Paid-in Capital from Treasury Stock for the difference between cost and the resale price of the shares. (3) The original paid-in capital account, Common Stock, is not affected. **The sale of treasury stock increases both total assets and total stockholders' equity.**

After posting the foregoing entries, the treasury stock accounts will show the following balances on October 1.

Treasury Stock					Paid-in Capital from Treasury Stock				
Feb. 1	32,000	July 1	8,000		Oct. 1	800	July 1	2,000	
		Oct. 1	6,400						
							Oct. 1 Bal.	1,200	
Oct. 1 Bal.	17,600								

Illustration 11-10
Treasury stock accounts

When a company fully depletes the credit balance in Paid-in Capital from Treasury Stock, it debits to Retained Earnings any additional excess of cost over selling price. To illustrate, assume that Mead, Inc. sells its remaining 2,200 shares at $7 per share on December 1. The excess of cost over selling price is $2,200 [2,200 × ($8 − $7)]. In this case, Mead debits $1,200 of the excess to Paid-in

Capital from Treasury Stock. It debits the remainder to Retained Earnings. The entry is:

A = L + SE
+15,400

−1,200 TS
−1,000 RE
+17,600 TS

Cash Flows
+15,400

Dec. 1	Cash	15,400	
	Paid-in Capital from Treasury Stock	1,200	
	Retained Earnings	1,000	
	Treasury Stock		17,600
	(To record sale of 2,200 shares of treasury		
	stock at $7 per share)		

> DO IT!

Treasury Stock

Action Plan

✔ Record the purchase of treasury stock at cost.

✔ When treasury stock is sold above its cost, credit the excess of the selling price over cost to Paid-in Capital from Treasury Stock.

✔ When treasury stock is sold below its cost, debit the excess of cost over selling price to Paid-in Capital from Treasury Stock.

Santa Anita Inc. purchases 3,000 shares of its $50 par value common stock for $180,000 cash on July 1. It will hold the shares in the treasury until resold. On November 1, the corporation sells 1,000 shares of treasury stock for cash at $70 per share. Journalize the treasury stock transactions.

Solution

July 1	Treasury Stock	180,000	
	Cash		180,000
	(To record the purchase of 3,000 shares		
	at $60 per share)		
Nov. 1	Cash	70,000	
	Treasury Stock		60,000
	Paid-in Capital from Treasury Stock		10,000
	(To record the sale of 1,000 shares		
	at $70 per share)		

Related exercise material: BE11-5, E11-5, E11-7, E11-9, **and** DO IT! 11-4.

✔ **The Navigator**

Accounting for Preferred Stock

LEARNING OBJECTIVE 4

Differentiate preferred stock from common stock.

To appeal to a larger segment of potential investors, a corporation may issue an additional class of stock, called preferred stock. **Preferred stock** has contractual provisions that give it some preference or priority over common stock. Typically, preferred stockholders have a priority as to (1) distributions of earnings (dividends) and (2) assets in the event of liquidation. However, they generally do not have voting rights.

Like common stock, corporations may issue preferred stock for cash or for non-cash assets. The entries for these transactions are similar to the entries for common stock. When a corporation has more than one class of stock, each paid-in capital account title should identify the stock to which it relates. A company might have the following accounts: Preferred Stock, Common Stock, Paid-in Capital in Excess of Par—Preferred Stock, and Paid-in Capital in Excess of Par—Common Stock.

For example, if Stine Corporation issues 10,000 shares of $10 par value preferred stock for $12 cash per share, the entry to record the issuance is:

A = L + SE
+120,000

+100,000 PS
+20,000 PS

Cash Flows
+120,000

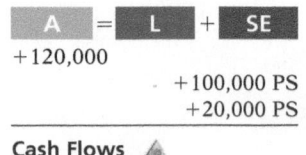

Cash	120,000	
Preferred Stock		100,000
Paid-in Capital in Excess of Par—Preferred Stock		20,000
(To record the issuance of 10,000 shares of $10 par		
value preferred stock)		

Preferred stock may have either a par value or no-par value. In the stockholders' equity section of the balance sheet, companies list preferred stock first because of its dividend and liquidation preferences over common stock.

DIVIDEND PREFERENCES

As indicated above, **preferred stockholders have the right to receive dividends before common stockholders**. For example, if the dividend rate on preferred stock is $5 per share, common shareholders will not receive any dividends in the current year until preferred stockholders have received $5 per share. The first claim to dividends does not, however, guarantee the payment of dividends. Dividends depend on many factors, such as adequate retained earnings and availability of cash. If a company does not pay dividends to preferred stockholders, it cannot of course pay dividends to common stockholders.

For preferred stock, companies state the per share dividend amount as a percentage of the par value or as a specified amount. For example, Earthlink specifies a 3% dividend on its $100 par value preferred. PepsiCo pays $4.56 per share on its no-par value stock.

Dividend preferences

CUMULATIVE DIVIDEND Preferred stock often contains a **cumulative dividend** feature. This right means that preferred stockholders must be paid both current-year dividends and any unpaid prior-year dividends before common stockholders receive dividends. When preferred stock is cumulative, preferred dividends not declared in a given period are called **dividends in arrears**.

To illustrate, assume that Scientific Leasing has 5,000 shares of 7%, $100 par value, cumulative preferred stock outstanding. Each $100 share pays a $7 dividend (.07 × $100). The annual dividend is $35,000 (5,000 × $7 per share). If dividends are two years in arrears, preferred stockholders are entitled to receive the following dividends in the current year.

Dividends in arrears ($35,000 × 2)	$ 70,000
Current-year dividends	35,000
Total preferred dividends	**$105,000**

Illustration 11-11
Computation of total dividends to preferred stock

The company cannot pay dividends to common stockholders until it pays the entire preferred dividend. In other words, companies cannot pay dividends to common stockholders while any preferred dividends are in arrears.

Are dividends in arrears considered a liability? **No—no payment obligation exists until the board of directors declares a dividend.** However, companies should disclose in the notes to the financial statements the amount of dividends in arrears. Doing so enables investors to assess the potential impact of this commitment on the corporation's financial position.

The investment community does not look favorably on companies that are unable to meet their dividend obligations. As a financial officer noted in discussing one company's failure to pay its cumulative preferred dividend for a period of time, "Not meeting your obligations on something like that is a major black mark on your record." The accounting entries for preferred stock dividends are explained later in this chapter.

LIQUIDATION PREFERENCE

Most preferred stocks also have a preference on corporate assets if the corporation fails. This feature provides security for the preferred stockholder. The preference to assets may be for the par value of the shares or for a specified liquidating value. For example, Commonwealth Edison's preferred stock entitles its holders to receive $31.80 per share, plus accrued and unpaid dividends, in the event of liquidation. The liquidation preference establishes the respective claims of creditors and preferred stockholders in litigation involving bankruptcy lawsuits.

Dividends

LEARNING OBJECTIVE   5

Prepare the entries for cash dividends and stock dividends.

A **dividend** is a corporation's distribution of cash or stock to its stockholders on a pro rata (proportional to ownership) basis. Pro rata means that if you own 10% of the common shares, you will receive 10% of the dividend. Dividends can take four forms: cash, property, scrip (a promissory note to pay cash), or stock. Cash dividends predominate in practice. Also, companies declare stock dividends with some frequency. These two forms of dividends are the focus of discussion in this chapter.

Investors are very interested in a company's dividend practices. In the financial press, **dividends are generally reported quarterly as a dollar amount per share**. (Sometimes they are reported on an annual basis.) For example, Nike's **quarterly** dividend rate in the fourth quarter of 2012 was 21 cents per share. The dividend rate for the fourth quarter of 2012 for GE was 19 cents, and for ConAgra Foods it was 25 cents.

Cash Dividends

A **cash dividend** is a pro rata distribution of cash to stockholders. Cash dividends are not paid on treasury shares. For a corporation to pay a cash dividend, it must have the following.

1. **Retained earnings.** The legality of a cash dividend depends on the laws of the state in which the company is incorporated. Payment of cash dividends from retained earnings is legal in all states. In general, cash dividend distributions from only the balance in common stock (legal capital) are illegal.

   A dividend declared out of paid-in capital is termed a **liquidating dividend**. Such a dividend reduces or "liquidates" the amount originally paid in by stockholders. Statutes vary considerably with respect to cash dividends based on paid-in capital in excess of par or stated value. Many states permit such dividends.

2. **Adequate cash.** The legality of a dividend and the ability to pay a dividend are two different things. For example, Nike, with retained earnings of over $5.8 billion, could legally declare a dividend of at least $5.8 billion. But Nike's cash balance is only $1.9 billion.

   Before declaring a cash dividend, a company's board of directors must carefully consider both current and future demands on the company's cash resources. In some cases, current liabilities may make a cash dividend inappropriate. In other cases, a major plant expansion program may warrant only a relatively small dividend.

3. **Declared dividends.** A company does not pay dividends unless its board of directors decides to do so, at which point the board "declares" the dividend. The board of directors has full authority to determine the amount of income to distribute in the form of a dividend and the amount to retain in the business. Dividends do not accrue like interest on a note payable, and they are not a liability until declared.

The amount and timing of a dividend are important issues for management to consider. The payment of a large cash dividend could lead to liquidity problems for the company. On the other hand, a small dividend or a missed dividend may cause unhappiness among stockholders. Many stockholders expect to receive a reasonable cash payment from the company on a periodic basis. Many companies declare and pay cash dividends quarterly. On the other hand, a number of high-growth companies pay no dividends, preferring to conserve cash to finance future capital expenditures.

ENTRIES FOR CASH DIVIDENDS

Three dates are important in connection with dividends: (1) the declaration date, (2) the record date, and (3) the payment date. Normally, there are two to four weeks between each date. Companies make accounting entries on the declaration date and the payment date.

On the **declaration date**, the board of directors formally declares (authorizes) the cash dividend and announces it to stockholders. The declaration of a cash dividend **commits the corporation to a legal obligation**. The company must make an entry to recognize the increase in Cash Dividends and the increase in the liability Dividends Payable.

To illustrate, assume that on December 1, 2015, the directors of Media General declare a 50 cents per share cash dividend on 100,000 shares of $10 par value common stock. The dividend is $50,000 (100,000 × $0.50). The entry to record the declaration is:

Declaration Date

Dec. 1	Cash Dividends	50,000	
	Dividends Payable		50,000
	(To record declaration of cash dividend)		

A	=	L	+	SE
				−50,000 Div
		+50,000		

Cash Flows
no effect

Media General debits the account Cash Dividends. Cash dividends decrease retained earnings. We use the specific title Cash Dividends to differentiate it from other types of dividends, such as stock dividends. Dividends Payable is a current liability. It will normally be paid within the next several months. When using a Cash Dividends account, the company transfers the balance of that account to Retained Earnings at the end of the year by a closing entry. *For homework problems, you should use the Cash Dividends account for recording dividend declarations.*

At the **record date**, the company determines ownership of the outstanding shares for dividend purposes. The stockholders' records maintained by the corporation supply this information. In the interval between the declaration date and the record date, the corporation updates its stock ownership records. For Media General, the record date is December 22. No entry is required on this date because the corporation's liability recognized on the declaration date is unchanged.

Helpful Hint
The purpose of the record date is to identify the persons or entities that will receive the dividend, not to determine the amount of the dividend liability.

Record Date

Dec. 22		No entry		

On the **payment date**, the company makes cash dividend payments to the stockholders of record (as of December 22) and records the payment of the dividend. If January 20 is the payment date for Media General, the entry on that date is:

Payment Date

Jan. 20	Dividends Payable	50,000	
	Cash		50,000
	(To record payment of cash dividend)		

A	=	L	+	SE
		−50,000		
−50,000				

Cash Flows
−50,000

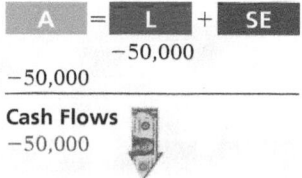

Note that payment of the dividend reduces both current assets and current liabilities. It has no effect on stockholders' equity. The cumulative effect of the declaration and payment of a cash dividend is to **decrease both stockholders' equity and total assets**. Illustration 11-12 (page 564) summarizes the three important dates associated with dividends for Media General.

Illustration 11-12
Key dividend dates

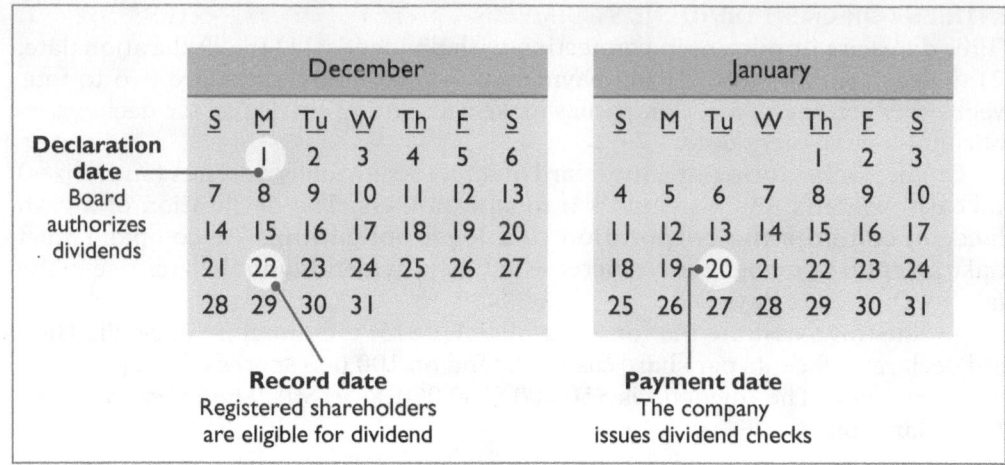

ALLOCATING CASH DIVIDENDS BETWEEN PREFERRED AND COMMON STOCK

As explained earlier in the chapter, preferred stock has priority over common stock in regard to dividends. Holders of cumulative preferred stock must be paid any unpaid prior-year dividends and their current year's dividend before common stockholders receive dividends.

To illustrate, assume that at December 31, 2015, IBR Inc. has 1,000 shares of 8%, $100 par value cumulative preferred stock. It also has 50,000 shares of $10 par value common stock outstanding. The dividend per share for preferred stock is $8 ($100 par value × 8%). The required annual dividend for preferred stock is therefore $8,000 (1,000 shares × $8). At December 31, 2015, the directors declare a $6,000 cash dividend. In this case, the entire dividend amount goes to preferred stockholders because of their dividend preference. The entry to record the declaration of the dividend is:

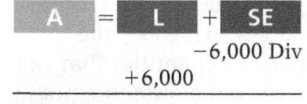

−6,000 Div
+6,000

Cash Flows
no effect

Dec. 31	Cash Dividends	6,000	
	Dividends Payable		6,000
	(To record $6 per share cash dividend		
	to preferred stockholders)		

Because of the cumulative feature, dividends of $2 ($8 − $6) per share are in arrears on preferred stock for 2015. IBR must pay these dividends to preferred stockholders before it can pay any future dividends to common stockholders. IBR should disclose dividends in arrears in the financial statements.

At December 31, 2016, IBR declares a $50,000 cash dividend. The allocation of the dividend to the two classes of stock is as follows.

Illustration 11-13
Allocating dividends to preferred and common stock

Total dividend		$50,000
Allocated to preferred stock		
Dividends in arrears, 2015 (1,000 × $2)	**$2,000**	
2016 dividend (1,000 × $8)	**8,000**	**10,000**
Remainder allocated to common stock		$40,000

The entry to record the declaration of the dividend is:

A	=	L	+	SE

−50,000 Div
+50,000

Cash Flows
no effect

Dec. 31	Cash Dividends	50,000	
	Dividends Payable		50,000
	(To record declaration of cash dividends of		
	$10,000 to preferred stock and $40,000		
	to common stock)		

If IBR's preferred stock is not cumulative, preferred stockholders receive only $8,000 in dividends in 2016. Common stockholders receive $42,000.

> **DO IT!**

Dividends on Preferred and Common Stock

MasterMind Corporation has 2,000 shares of 6%, $100 par value preferred stock outstanding at December 31, 2015. At December 31, 2015, the company declared a $60,000 cash dividend. Determine the dividend paid to preferred stockholders and common stockholders under each of the following scenarios.

1. The preferred stock is noncumulative, and the company has not missed any dividends in previous years.

2. The preferred stock is noncumulative, and the company did not pay a dividend in each of the two previous years.

3. The preferred stock is cumulative, and the company did not pay a dividend in each of the two previous years.

Action Plan

✔ Determine dividends on preferred shares by multiplying the dividend rate times the par value of the stock times the number of preferred shares.

✔ Understand the cumulative feature. If preferred stock is cumulative, then any missed dividends (dividends in arrears) and the current year's dividend must be paid to preferred stockholders before dividends are paid to common stockholders.

Solution

1. The company has not missed past dividends and the preferred stock is noncumulative. Thus, the preferred stockholders are paid only this year's dividend. The dividend paid to preferred stockholders would be $12,000 (2,000 × .06 × $100). The dividend paid to common stockholders would be $48,000 ($60,000 − $12,000).

2. The preferred stock is noncumulative. Thus, past unpaid dividends do not have to be paid. The dividend paid to preferred stockholders would be $12,000 (2,000 × .06 × $100). The dividend paid to common stockholders would be $48,000 ($60,000 − $12,000).

3. The preferred stock is cumulative. Thus, dividends that have been missed (dividends in arrears) must be paid. The dividend paid to preferred stockholders would be $36,000 (3 × 2,000 × .06 × $100). The dividend paid to common stockholders would be $24,000 ($60,000 − $36,000).

Related exercise material: BE11-7, E11-6, E11-13, **and** DO IT! 11-5.

 The Navigator

Stock Dividends

A **stock dividend** is a pro rata (proportional to ownership) distribution of the corporation's own stock to stockholders. Whereas a company pays cash in a cash dividend, a company issues shares of stock in a stock dividend. **A stock dividend results in a decrease in retained earnings and an increase in paid-in capital.** Unlike a cash dividend, a stock dividend does not decrease total stockholders' equity or total assets.

To illustrate, assume that you have a 2% ownership interest in Cetus Inc. That is, you own 20 of its 1,000 shares of common stock. If Cetus declares a 10% stock dividend, it would issue 100 shares (1,000 × 10%) of stock. You would receive two shares (2% × 100). Would your ownership interest change? No, it would remain at 2% (22 ÷ 1,100). **You now own more shares of stock, but your ownership interest has not changed.**

Cetus has disbursed no cash and has assumed no liabilities. What, then, are the purposes and benefits of a stock dividend? Corporations issue stock dividends generally for one or more of the following reasons.

1. To satisfy stockholders' dividend expectations without spending cash.

2. To increase the marketability of the corporation's stock. When the number of shares outstanding increases, the market price per share decreases. Decreasing

the market price of the stock makes it easier for smaller investors to purchase the shares.

3. To emphasize that a company has permanently reinvested in the business a portion of stockholders' equity, which therefore is unavailable for cash dividends.

When the dividend is declared, the board of directors determines the size of the stock dividend and the value assigned to each dividend.

Generally, if the company issues a **small stock dividend** (less than 20–25% of the corporation's issued stock), the value assigned to the dividend is the fair value per share. This treatment is based on the assumption that a small stock dividend will have little effect on the market price of the shares previously outstanding. Thus, many stockholders consider small stock dividends to be distributions of earnings equal to the market price of the shares distributed. If a company issues a **large stock dividend** (greater than 20–25%), the price assigned to the dividend is the par or stated value. Small stock dividends predominate in practice. Thus, we will illustrate only entries for small stock dividends.

ENTRIES FOR STOCK DIVIDENDS

To illustrate the accounting for small stock dividends, assume that Medland Corporation has a balance of $300,000 in retained earnings. It declares a 10% stock dividend on its 50,000 shares of $10 par value common stock. The current market price of its stock is $15 per share. The number of shares to be issued is 5,000 (10% × 50,000). Therefore, the total amount to be debited to Stock Dividends is $75,000 (5,000 × $15). The entry to record the declaration of the stock dividend is as follows.

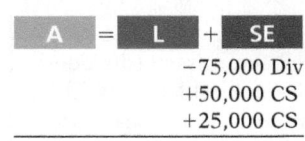

A = L + SE
−75,000 Div
+50,000 CS
+25,000 CS

Cash Flows
no effect

Stock Dividends	75,000	
Common Stock Dividends Distributable		50,000
Paid-in Capital in Excess of Par—Common Stock		25,000
(To record declaration of 10% stock dividend)		

Medland debits Stock Dividends for the market price of the stock issued ($15 × 5,000). (Similar to Cash Dividends, Stock Dividends decrease retained earnings.) Medland also credits Common Stock Dividends Distributable for the par value of the dividend shares ($10 × 5,000) and credits Paid-in Capital in Excess of Par—Common Stock for the excess of the market price over par ($5 × 5,000).

Common Stock Dividends Distributable is a **stockholders' equity account**. It is not a liability because assets will not be used to pay the dividend. If the company prepares a balance sheet before it issues the dividend shares, it reports the distributable account under paid-in capital as shown in Illustration 11-14.

Illustration 11-14
Statement presentation of common stock dividends distributable

Paid-in capital	
Common stock	$500,000
Common stock dividends distributable	50,000
Paid-in capital in excess of par—common stock	25,000
Total paid-in capital	$575,000

When Medland issues the dividend shares, it debits Common Stock Dividends Distributable and credits Common Stock, as follows.

A = L + SE
−50,000 CS
+50,000 CS

Cash Flows
no effect

Common Stock Dividends Distributable	50,000	
Common Stock		50,000
(To record issuance of 5,000 shares in a stock dividend)		

EFFECTS OF STOCK DIVIDENDS

How do stock dividends affect stockholders' equity? They **change the composition of stockholders' equity** because they transfer to paid-in capital a portion of retained earnings. However, **total stockholders' equity remains the same**. Stock dividends also have no effect on the par or stated value per share. But, the number of shares outstanding increases. Illustration 11-15 shows these effects for Medland Corporation.

	Before Dividend	After Dividend
Stockholders' equity		
Paid-in capital		
Common stock, $10 par	$ 500,000	$ 550,000
Paid-in capital in excess of par—common stock	—	25,000
Total paid-in capital	500,000	575,000
Retained earnings	300,000	225,000
Total stockholders' equity	$800,000	$800,000
Outstanding shares	50,000	55,000
Par value per share	$10.00	$10.00

Illustration 11-15
Stock dividend effects

In this example, total paid-in capital increases by $75,000 (50,000 shares × 10% × $15) and retained earnings decreases by the same amount. Note also that total stockholders' equity remains unchanged at $800,000. The number of shares increases by 5,000 (50,000 × 10%).

Stock Splits

A **stock split**, like a stock dividend, involves issuance of additional shares to stockholders according to their percentage ownership. **However, a stock split results in a reduction in the par or stated value per share.** The purpose of a stock split is to increase the marketability of the stock by lowering its market price per share. This, in turn, makes it easier for the corporation to issue additional stock.

The effect of a split on market price is generally **inversely proportional** to the size of the split. For example, after a 2-for-1 stock split, the market price of Nike's stock fell from $111 to approximately $55. The lower market price stimulated market activity. Within one year, the stock was trading above $100 again. Illustration 11-16 shows the effect of a 4-for-1 stock split for stockholders.

Helpful Hint
A stock split changes the par value per share but does not affect any balances in stockholders' equity.

Illustration 11-16
Effect of stock split for stockholders

In a stock split, the number of shares increases in the same proportion that par or stated value per share decreases. For example, in a 2-for-1 split, one share of $10 par value stock is exchanged for two shares of $5 par value stock. **A stock split does not have any effect on total paid-in capital, retained earnings, or total stockholders' equity.** But, the number of shares outstanding increases, and par value per share decreases. Illustration 11-17 shows these effects for Medland Corporation, assuming that it splits its 50,000 shares of common stock on a 2-for-1 basis.

Illustration 11-17
Stock split effects

	Before Stock Split	After Stock Split
Stockholders' equity		
Paid-in capital		
Common stock,	$ 500,000	$ 500,000
Paid-in capital in excess of par—common stock	–0–	–0–
Total paid-in capital	500,000	500,000
Retained earnings	300,000	300,000
Total stockholders' equity	$800,000	$800,000
Outstanding shares	50,000	100,000
Par value per share	$10.00	$5.00

A stock split does not affect the balances in any stockholders' equity accounts. Therefore, **it is not necessary to journalize a stock split.**

Illustration 11-18 summarizes the differences between stock splits and stock dividends.

Illustration 11-18
Differences between the effects of stock splits and stock dividends

Item	Stock Split	Stock Dividend
Total paid-in capital	No change	Increase
Total retained earnings	No change	Decrease
Total par value (common stock)	No change	Increase
Par value per share	Decrease	No change
Total stockholders' equity	No change	No change

Dietmar Klement/iStockphoto

INVESTOR INSIGHT

A No-Split Philosophy

Warren Buffett's company, Berkshire Hathaway, has two classes of shares. Until recently, the company had never split either class of stock. As a result, the class A stock had a market price of $97,000 and the class B sold for about $3,200 per share. Because the price per share is so high, the stock does not trade as frequently as the stock of other companies. Buffett has always opposed stock splits because he feels that a lower stock price attracts short-term investors. He appears to be correct. For example, while more than 6 million shares of IBM are exchanged on the average day, only about 1,000 class A shares of Berkshire are traded. Despite Buffett's aversion to splits, in order to accomplish a recent acquisition, Berkshire decided to split its class B shares 50 to 1.

Source: Scott Patterson, "Berkshire Nears Smaller Baby B's," *Wall Street Journal Online* (January 19, 2010).

? Why does Warren Buffett usually oppose stock splits? (See page 600.)

> DO IT!

Stock Dividends and Stock Splits

Sing CD Company has had five years of record earnings. Due to this success, the market price of its 500,000 shares of $2 par value common stock has tripled from $15 per share to $45. During this period, paid-in capital remained the same at $2,000,000. Retained earnings increased from $1,500,000 to $10,000,000. President Joan Elbert is considering either a 10% stock dividend or a 2-for-1 stock split. She asks you to show the before-and-after effects of each option on retained earnings and total stockholders' equity.

Action Plan

✔ Calculate the stock dividend's effect on retained earnings by multiplying the number of new shares times the market price of the stock (or par value for a large stock dividend).

✔ Recall that a stock dividend increases the number of shares without affecting total stockholders' equity.

✔ Recall that a stock split only increases the number of shares outstanding and decreases the par value per share.

Solution

The stock dividend amount is $2,250,000 [(500,000 × 10%) × $45]. The new balance in retained earnings is $7,750,000 ($10,000,000 − $2,250,000). The retained earnings balance after the stock split is the same as it was before the split: $10,000,000. Total stockholders' equity does not change. The effects on the stockholders' equity accounts are as follows.

	Original Balances	After Dividend	After Split
Paid-in capital	$ 2,000,000	$ 4,250,000	$ 2,000,000
Retained earnings	10,000,000	7,750,000	10,000,000
Total stockholders' equity	$12,000,000	$12,000,000	$12,000,000
Shares outstanding	500,000	550,000	1,000,000

Related exercise material: BE11-8, BE11-9, E11-14, E11-15, and DO IT! 11-6.

✔ The Navigator

Retained Earnings

Recall that **retained earnings** is net income that a company retains in the business. The balance in retained earnings is part of the stockholders' claim on the total assets of the corporation. It does not, though, represent a claim on any specific asset. Nor can the amount of retained earnings be associated with the balance of any asset account. For example, a $100,000 balance in retained earnings does not mean that there should be $100,000 in cash. The reason is that the company may have used the cash resulting from the excess of revenues over expenses to purchase buildings, equipment, and other assets.

To demonstrate that retained earnings and cash may be quite different, Illustration 11-19 shows recent amounts of retained earnings and cash in selected companies.

LEARNING OBJECTIVE **6**

Identify the items reported in a retained earnings statement.

Company	(in millions) Retained Earnings	Cash
Facebook	$ 1,606	$ 1,512
Google	20,082	10,198
Nike, Inc.	4,885	1,855
Starbucks Coffee Company	2,189	281
Amazon.com	(1,375)	2,539

Illustration 11-19
Retained earnings and cash balances

Remember that when a company has net income, it closes net income to retained earnings. The closing entry is a debit to Income Summary and a credit to Retained Earnings.

When a company has a **net loss** (expenses exceed revenues), it also closes this amount to retained earnings. The closing entry in this case is a debit to Retained

Helpful Hint
Remember that Retained Earnings is a stockholders' equity account, whose normal balance is a credit.

Earnings and a credit to Income Summary. This is done even if it results in a debit balance in Retained Earnings. **Companies do not debit net losses to paid-in capital accounts.** To do so would destroy the distinction between paid-in and earned capital. If cumulative losses exceed cumulative income over a company's life, a debit balance in Retained Earnings results. A debit balance in Retained Earnings is identified as a **deficit**. A company reports a deficit as a deduction in the stockholders' equity section, as shown below.

Illustration 11-20
Stockholders' equity with deficit

Balance Sheet (partial)

Stockholders' equity	
Paid-in capital	
Common stock	$800,000
Retained earnings (deficit)	(50,000)
Total stockholders' equity	$750,000

Retained Earnings Restrictions

The balance in retained earnings is generally available for dividend declarations. Some companies state this fact. For example, Lockheed Martin Corporation states the following in the notes to its financial statements.

Illustration 11-21
Disclosure of unrestricted retained earnings

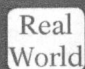 **Real World**   **LOCKHEED MARTIN CORPORATION**
Notes to the Financial Statements

At December 31, retained earnings were unrestricted and available for dividend payments.

In some cases, there may be **retained earnings restrictions**. These make a portion of the retained earnings balance currently unavailable for dividends. Restrictions result from one or more of the following causes.

1. **Legal restrictions.** Many states require a corporation to restrict retained earnings for the cost of treasury stock purchased. The restriction keeps intact the corporation's legal capital that is being temporarily held as treasury stock. When the company sells the treasury stock, the restriction is lifted.

2. **Contractual restrictions.** Long-term debt contracts may restrict retained earnings as a condition for the loan. The restriction limits the use of corporate assets for payment of dividends. Thus, it increases the likelihood that the corporation will be able to meet required loan payments.

3. **Voluntary restrictions.** The board of directors may voluntarily create retained earnings restrictions for specific purposes. For example, the board may authorize a restriction for future plant expansion. By reducing the amount of retained earnings available for dividends, the company makes more cash available for the planned expansion.

Companies generally disclose **retained earnings restrictions** in the notes to the financial statements. For example, as shown in Illustration 11-22, Tektronix Inc., a manufacturer of electronic measurement devices, had total retained earnings of $774 million, but the unrestricted portion was only $223.8 million.

Illustration 11-22
Disclosure of restriction

 Real World   **TEKTRONIX INC.**
Notes to the Financial Statements

Certain of the Company's debt agreements require compliance with debt covenants. Management believes that the Company is in compliance with such requirements. The Company had unrestricted retained earnings of $223.8 million after meeting those requirements.

Prior Period Adjustments

Suppose that a corporation has closed its books and issued financial statements. The corporation then discovers that it made a material error in reporting net income of a prior year. How should the company record this situation in the accounts and report it in the financial statements?

The correction of an error in previously issued financial statements is known as a **prior period adjustment**. The company makes the correction directly to Retained Earnings because the effect of the error is now in this account. The net income for the prior period has been recorded in retained earnings through the journalizing and posting of closing entries.

To illustrate, assume that General Microwave discovers in 2015 that it understated depreciation expense on equipment in 2014 by $300,000 due to computational errors. These errors overstated both net income for 2014 and the current balance in retained earnings. The entry for the prior period adjustment, ignoring all tax effects, is as follows.

Retained Earnings	300,000	
Accumulated Depreciation—Equipment		300,000
(To adjust for understatement of depreciation in a		
prior period)		

A	=	L	+	SE
				−300,000 RE
−300,000				

Cash Flows
no effect

A debit to an income statement account in 2015 is incorrect because the error pertains to a prior year.

Companies report prior period adjustments in the retained earnings statement.[4] They add (or deduct, as the case may be) these adjustments from the beginning retained earnings balance. This results in an adjusted beginning balance. For example, assuming a beginning balance of $800,000 in retained earnings, General Microwave reports the prior period adjustment as follows.

GENERAL MICROWAVE	
Retained Earnings Statement (partial)	
Balance, January 1, as reported	$ 800,000
Correction for overstatement of net income	
in prior period (depreciation error)	(300,000)
Balance, January 1, as adjusted	$ 500,000

Illustration 11-23
Statement presentation of prior period adjustments

Again, reporting the correction in the current year's income statement would be incorrect because it applies to a prior year's income statement.

Retained Earnings Statement

The **retained earnings statement** shows the changes in retained earnings during the year. The company prepares the statement from the Retained Earnings account. Illustration 11-24 shows (in T-account form) transactions that affect retained earnings.

Retained Earnings	
1. Net loss	1. Net income
2. Prior period adjustments for overstatement of net income	2. Prior period adjustments for understatement of net income
3. Cash dividends and stock dividends	
4. Some disposals of treasury stock	

Illustration 11-24
Debits and credits to retained earnings

---

[4]A complete retained earnings statement is shown in Illustration 11-25 on the next page.

As indicated, net income increases retained earnings, and a net loss decreases retained earnings. Prior period adjustments may either increase or decrease retained earnings. Both cash dividends and stock dividends decrease retained earnings. The circumstances under which treasury stock transactions decrease retained earnings are explained on page 559.

A complete retained earnings statement for Graber Inc., based on assumed data, is as follows.

Illustration 11-25
Retained earnings statement

GRABER INC.		
Retained Earnings Statement		
For the Year Ended December 31, 2015		
Balance, January 1, as reported		$1,050,000
Correction for understatement of net income in prior period (inventory error)		50,000
Balance, January 1, as adjusted		1,100,000
Add: Net income		360,000
		1,460,000
Less: Cash dividends	$100,000	
Stock dividends	200,000	300,000
Balance, December 31		$1,160,000

> **DO IT!**

Retained Earnings Statement

Vega Corporation has retained earnings of $5,130,000 on January 1, 2015. During the year, Vega earned $2,000,000 of net income. It declared and paid a $250,000 cash dividend. In 2015, Vega recorded an adjustment of $180,000 due to the understatement (from a mathematical error) of 2014 depreciation expense. Prepare a retained earnings statement for 2015.

Solution

Action Plan

✔ Recall that a retained earnings statement begins with retained earnings, as reported at the end of the previous year.

✔ Add or subtract any prior period adjustments to arrive at the adjusted beginning figure.

✔ Add net income and subtract dividends declared to arrive at the ending balance in retained earnings.

VEGA CORPORATION	
Retained Earnings Statement	
For the Year Ended December 31, 2015	
Balance, January 1, as reported	$5,130,000
Correction for overstatement of net income in prior period (depreciation error)	(180,000)
Balance, January 1, as adjusted	4,950,000
Add: Net income	2,000,000
	6,950,000
Less: Cash dividends	250,000
Balance, December 31	$6,700,000

Related exercise material: BE11-10, BE11-11, BE11-12, E11-17, E11-18, **and** DO IT! 11-7.

 The Navigator

Statement Presentation and Analysis

In the stockholders' equity section of the balance sheet, paid-in capital and retained earnings are reported. The specific sources of paid-in capital are identified. Within paid-in capital, two classifications are recognized:

1. **Capital stock.** This category consists of preferred and common stock. Preferred stock is shown before common stock because of its preferential rights. Par value, shares authorized, shares issued, and shares outstanding are reported for each class of stock.
2. **Additional paid-in capital.** This includes the excess of amounts paid over par or stated value and paid-in capital from treasury stock.

LEARNING OBJECTIVE 7

Prepare and analyze a comprehensive stockholders' equity section.

Presentation

Illustration 11-26 presents the stockholders' equity section of Graber Inc.'s balance sheet. Note the following: (1) "Common stock dividends distributable" is shown under "Capital stock," in "Paid-in capital." (2) A note (Note R) discloses a retained earnings restriction.

GRABER INC.
Balance Sheet (partial)

Illustration 11-26
Comprehensive stockholders' equity section

Stockholders' equity		
Paid-in capital		
Capital stock		
9% Preferred stock, $100 par value, cumulative, callable at $120, 10,000 shares authorized, 6,000 shares issued and outstanding		$ 600,000
Common stock, no par, $5 stated value, 500,000 shares authorized, 400,000 shares issued and 390,000 shares outstanding	$2,000,000	
Common stock dividends distributable	50,000	2,050,000
Total capital stock		2,650,000
Additional paid-in capital		
In excess of par—preferred stock	30,000	
In excess of stated value—common stock	1,050,000	
Total additional paid-in capital		1,080,000
Total paid-in capital		3,730,000
Retained earnings (see Note R)		1,160,000
Total paid-in capital and retained earnings		4,890,000
Less: Treasury stock (10,000 common shares)		80,000
Total stockholders' equity		$4,810,000

Note R: Retained earnings is restricted for the cost of treasury stock, $80,000.

The stockholders' equity section of Graber Inc. in Illustration 11-26 includes most of the accounts discussed in this chapter. The disclosures pertaining to Graber's common stock indicate that the company issued 400,000 shares; 100,000 shares are unissued (500,000 authorized less 400,000 issued); and 390,000 shares are outstanding (400,000 issued less 10,000 shares in treasury).

Published annual reports often combine and report as a single amount the individual sources of additional paid-in capital, as shown in Illustration 11-27 (page 574). In addition, authorized shares are sometimes not reported.

Illustration 11-27
Published stockholders' equity
section

Real World	KELLOGG COMPANY Balance Sheet (partial) ($ in millions)	
Stockholders' equity		
Common stock, $0.25 par value, 1,000,000,000 shares authorized		
Issued: 418,669,193 shares		$ 105
Capital in excess of par value		388
Retained earnings		4,217
Treasury stock, at cost 28,618,052 shares		(1,357)
Accumulated other comprehensive income (loss)		(827)
Total stockholders' equity		$ 2,526

In practice, companies sometimes use the term "Capital surplus" in place of "Additional paid-in capital," and "Earned surplus" in place of "Retained earnings." The use of the term "surplus" suggests that the company has available an excess amount of funds. Such is not necessarily the case. Therefore, **the term "surplus" should not be employed in accounting**. Unfortunately, a number of companies still do use it.

Instead of presenting a detailed stockholders' equity section in the balance sheet and a retained earnings statement, many companies prepare a **stockholders' equity statement**. This statement shows the changes (1) in each stockholders' equity account and (2) in total that occurred during the year. Examples of stockholders' equity statements appear for Apple in Appendix A and for Hampton Corporation in an appendix to this chapter (Illustration 11A-1).

Analysis

Investors and analysts can measure profitability from the viewpoint of the common stockholder by the **return on common stockholders' equity**. This ratio, as shown in Illustration 11-28, indicates how many dollars of net income the company earned for each dollar invested by the common stockholders. It is computed by dividing **net income available to common stockholders** (which is net income minus preferred dividends) by average common stockholders' equity.

To illustrate, Walt Disney Company's beginning-of-the-year and end-of-the-year common stockholders' equity were $31,820 and $30,753 million, respectively. Its net income was $4,687 million, and no preferred stock was outstanding. The return on common stockholders' equity is computed as follows.

Illustration 11-28
Return on common
stockholders' equity
and computation

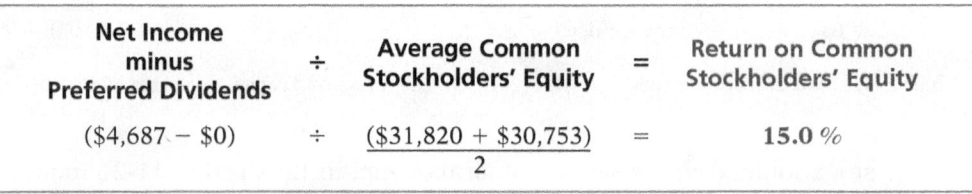

Net Income minus Preferred Dividends	÷	Average Common Stockholders' Equity	=	Return on Common Stockholders' Equity
($4,687 − $0)	÷	$\dfrac{(\$31{,}820 + \$30{,}753)}{2}$	=	15.0 %

As shown above, if a company has preferred stock, we would deduct the amount of **preferred dividends** from the company's net income to compute income available to common stockholders. Also, the par value of preferred stock is deducted from total stockholders' equity when computing the average common stockholders' equity.

Stockholders' Equity and EPS

On January 1, 2015, Siena Corporation purchased 2,000 shares of treasury stock. Other information regarding Siena Corporation is provided below.

	2014	2015
Net income	$110,000	$110,000
Dividends on preferred stock	$10,000	$10,000
Dividends on common stock	$2,000	$1,600
Common stockholders' equity, beginning of year	$500,000	$400,000*
Common stockholders' equity, end of year	$500,000	$400,000

*Adjusted for purchase of treasury stock.

Compute (a) return on common stockholders' equity for each year, and (b) discuss its change from 2014 to 2015.

Solution

Action Plan

✔ Determine return on common stockholders' equity by dividing net income available to common stockholders by average common stockholders' equity.

(a)

	2014		**2015**	
Return on common stockholders' equity	$\dfrac{(\$110{,}000 - \$10{,}000)}{(\$500{,}000 + \$500{,}000)/2}$	$= 20\%$	$\dfrac{(\$110{,}000 - \$10{,}000)}{(\$400{,}000 + \$400{,}000)/2}$	$= 25\%$

(b) Between 2014 and 2015, return on common stockholders' equity improved from 20% to 25%. While this would appear to be good news for the company's common stockholders, this increase should be carefully evaluated. It is important to note that net income did not change during this period. The increase in the ratio was due to the purchase of treasury shares, which reduced the denominator of the ratio. As the company repurchases its own shares, it becomes more reliant on debt and thus increases its risk.

Related exercise material: E11-22 **and** DO IT! 11-8.

 The Navigator

Rolman Corporation is authorized to issue 1,000,000 shares of $5 par value common stock. In its first year, the company has the following stock transactions.

Jan. 10	Issued 400,000 shares of stock at $8 per share.
July 1	Issued 100,000 shares of stock for land. The land had an asking price of $900,000. The stock is currently selling on a national exchange at $8.25 per share.
Sept. 1	Purchased 10,000 shares of common stock for the treasury at $9 per share.
Dec. 1	Sold 4,000 shares of the treasury stock at $10 per share.

Instructions

(a) Journalize the transactions.
(b) Prepare the stockholders' equity section assuming the company had retained earnings of $200,000 at December 31.

Solution to Comprehensive DO IT!

Action Plan

✔ When common stock has a par value, credit Common Stock for par value.

(a) Jan. 10	Cash	3,200,000	
	Common Stock		2,000,000
	Paid-in Capital in Excess of Par—Common Stock		1,200,000
	(To record issuance of 400,000 shares of $5 par value stock)		

Action Plan (cont'd.)

✔ Use fair value in a noncash transaction.

✔ Debit and credit the Treasury Stock account at cost.

✔ Record differences between the cost and selling price of treasury stock in stockholders' equity accounts, not as gains or losses.

July 1	Land	825,000	
	Common Stock		500,000
	Paid-in Capital in Excess		
	of Par—Common Stock		325,000
	(To record issuance of		
	100,000 shares of $5 par		
	value stock for land)		
Sept. 1	Treasury Stock	90,000	
	Cash		90,000
	(To record purchase of		
	10,000 shares of treasury		
	stock at cost)		
Dec. 1	Cash	40,000	
	Treasury Stock		36,000
	Paid-in Capital from Treasury		
	Stock		4,000
	(To record sale of 4,000 shares		
	of treasury stock above cost)		

(b)

ROLMAN CORPORATION
Balance Sheet (partial)

Stockholders' equity		
Paid-in capital		
Capital stock		
Common stock, $5 par value, 1,000,000 shares		
authorized, 500,000 shares issued, 494,000		
shares outstanding		$2,500,000
Additional paid-in capital		
In excess of par—common stock	$1,525,000	
From treasury stock	4,000	
Total additional paid-in capital		1,529,000
Total paid-in capital		4,029,000
Retained earnings		200,000
Total paid-in capital and retained earnings		4,229,000
Less: Treasury stock (6,000 shares)		54,000
Total stockholders' equity		$4,175,000

 The Navigator

SUMMARY OF LEARNING OBJECTIVES
 The Navigator

1 Identify the major characteristics of a corporation. The major characteristics of a corporation are separate legal existence, limited liability of stockholders, transferable ownership rights, ability to acquire capital, continuous life, corporation management, government regulations, and additional taxes.

2 Record the issuance of common stock. When companies record the issuance of common stock for cash, they credit the par value of the shares to Common Stock.

They record in a separate paid-in capital account the portion of the proceeds that is above or below par value. When no-par common stock has a stated value, the entries are similar to those for par value stock. When no-par stock does not have a stated value, companies credit the entire proceeds to Common Stock.

3 Explain the accounting for treasury stock. The cost method is generally used in accounting for treasury stock. Under this approach, companies debit Treasury

Stock at the price paid to reacquire the shares. They credit the same amount to Treasury Stock when they sell the shares. The difference between the sales price and cost is recorded in stockholders' equity accounts, not in income statement accounts.

4 **Differentiate preferred stock from common stock.** Preferred stock has contractual provisions that give it priority over common stock in certain areas. Typically, preferred stockholders have preferences (1) to dividends and (2) to assets in liquidation. They usually do not have voting rights.

5 **Prepare the entries for cash dividends and stock dividends.** Companies make entries for both cash and stock dividends at the declaration date and at the payment date. At the **declaration date**, the entries are: cash dividend—debit Cash Dividends and credit Dividends Payable; small stock dividend—debit Stock Dividends, credit Paid-in Capital in Excess of Par (or Stated Value)—Common Stock, and credit Common Stock Dividends Distributable. At the **payment date**, the entries for cash and stock dividends are: cash dividend—debit Dividends Payable and credit Cash; small stock dividend—debit Common Stock Dividends Distributable and credit Common Stock.

6 **Identify the items reported in a retained earnings statement.** Companies report each of the individual debits and credits to retained earnings in the retained earnings statement. Additions consist of net income and prior period adjustments to correct understatements of prior years' net income. Deductions consist of net loss, adjustments to correct overstatements of prior years' net income, cash and stock dividends, and some disposals of treasury stock.

7 **Prepare and analyze a comprehensive stockholders' equity section.** In the stockholders' equity section, paid-in capital and retained earnings are reported and specific sources of paid-in capital are identified. Within paid-in capital, two classifications are shown: capital stock and additional paid-in capital. If a corporation has treasury stock, the cost of treasury stock is deducted from total paid-in capital and retained earnings to obtain total stockholders' equity. One measure of profitability is the return on common stockholders' equity. It is calculated by dividing net income minus preferred dividends by average common stockholders' equity.

GLOSSARY

Authorized stock The amount of stock that a corporation is authorized to sell as indicated in its charter. (p. 549).

Cash dividend A pro rata distribution of cash to stockholders. (p. 562).

Charter A document that is issued by the state to set forth important terms and features regarding the creation of a corporation. (p. 546).

Corporation A business organized as a legal entity separate and distinct from its owners under state corporation law. (p. 544).

Cumulative dividend A feature of preferred stock entitling the stockholder to receive current and unpaid prior-year dividends before common stockholders receive dividends. (p. 561).

Declaration date The date the board of directors formally declares (authorizes) a dividend and announces it to stockholders. (p. 563).

Deficit A debit balance in Retained Earnings. (p. 570).

Dividend A corporation's distribution of cash or stock to its stockholders on a pro rata (proportional) basis. (p. 562).

Liquidating dividend A dividend declared out of paid-in capital. (p. 562).

No-par value stock Capital stock that has not been assigned a value in the corporate charter. (p. 551).

Organization costs Costs incurred in the formation of a corporation. (p. 547).

Outstanding stock Capital stock that has been issued and is being held by stockholders. (p. 558).

Paid-in capital Total amount of cash and other assets paid in to the corporation by stockholders in exchange for capital stock. (p. 552).

Par value stock Capital stock that has been assigned a value per share in the corporate charter. (p. 550).

Payment date The date dividends are transferred to stockholders. (p. 563).

Preferred stock Capital stock that has some preferences over common stock. (p. 560).

Prior period adjustment The correction of an error in previously issued financial statements. (p. 571).

Privately held corporation A corporation that has only a few stockholders and whose stock is not available for sale to the general public. (p. 544).

Publicly held corporation A corporation that may have thousands of stockholders and whose stock is regularly traded on a national securities exchange. (p. 544).

Record date The date when ownership of outstanding shares is determined for dividend purposes. (p. 563).

Retained earnings Net income that the corporation retains for future use. (p. 552).

Retained earnings restrictions Circumstances that make a portion of retained earnings currently unavailable for dividends. (p. 570).

Retained earnings statement A financial statement that shows the changes in retained earnings during the year. (p. 571).

Return on common stockholders' equity A measure of profitability that shows how many dollars of net income were earned for each dollar invested by the owners; computed as net income minus preferred dividends divided by average common stockholders' equity. (p. 574).

Stated value The amount per share assigned by the board of directors to no-par value stock. (p. 551).

Stock dividend A pro rata distribution to stockholders of the corporation's own stock. (p. 565).

Stockholders' equity statement A statement that shows the changes in each stockholders' equity account and in total stockholders' equity during the year. (p. 574).

Stock split The issuance of additional shares of stock to stockholders according to their percentage ownership. It is accompanied by a reduction in the par or stated value per share. (p. 567).

Treasury stock A corporation's own stock that has been issued and subsequently reacquired from shareholders by the corporation but not retired. (p. 556).

APPENDIX 11A   Stockholders' Equity Statement

LEARNING OBJECTIVE   8

Describe the use and content of the stockholders' equity statement.

When balance sheets and income statements are presented by a corporation, changes in the separate accounts comprising stockholders' equity should also be disclosed. Disclosure of such changes is necessary to make the financial statements sufficiently informative for users. The disclosures may be made in an additional statement or in the notes to the financial statements.

Many corporations make the disclosures in a **stockholders' equity statement**. The statement shows the changes in **each** stockholders' equity account and in **total** stockholders' equity during the year. As shown in Illustration 11A-1, the stockholders' equity statement is prepared in columnar form. It contains columns for each account and for total stockholders' equity. The transactions are then identified and their effects are shown in the appropriate columns.

Illustration 11A-1
Stockholders' equity statement

HAMPTON CORPORATION
Stockholders' Equity Statement
For the Year Ended December 31, 2015

	Common Stock ($5 Par)	Paid-in Capital in Excess of Par—Common Stock	Retained Earnings	Treasury Stock	Total
Balance January 1	$300,000	$200,000	$650,000	$(34,000)	$1,116,000
Issued 5,000 shares of common stock at $15	25,000	50,000			75,000
Declared a $40,000 cash dividend			(40,000)		(40,000)
Purchased 2,000 shares for treasury at $16				(32,000)	(32,000)
Net income for year			240,000		240,000
Balance December 31	$325,000	$250,000	$850,000	$(66,000)	$1,359,000

In practice, additional columns are usually provided to show the number of shares of issued stock and treasury stock. The stockholders' equity statement for PepsiCo, for a three-year period, is shown in Appendix B. **When a stockholders' equity statement is presented, a retained earnings statement is not necessary** because the retained earnings column explains the changes in this account.

SUMMARY OF LEARNING OBJECTIVE FOR APPENDIX 11A

 The Navigator

8   Describe the use and content of the stockholders' equity statement. Corporations must disclose changes in stockholders' equity accounts and may choose to do so by issuing a separate stockholders' equity statement. This statement, prepared in columnar form, shows changes in each stockholders' equity account and in total stockholders' equity during the accounting period. When this statement is presented, a retained earnings statement is not necessary.

APPENDIX 11B   Book Value—Another per Share Amount

Book Value per Share

LEARNING OBJECTIVE   9

Compute book value per share.

You have learned about a number of per share amounts in this chapter. Another per share amount of some importance is **book value per share**. It represents **the equity a common stockholder has in the net assets of the corporation** from owning one share of stock. Remember that the net assets (total assets minus total liabilities) of a corporation must be equal to total stockholders' equity. Therefore, the formula for computing book value per share when a company has only one class of stock outstanding is:

Total Stockholders' Equity	÷	Number of Common Shares Outstanding	=	Book Value per Share

Illustration 11B-1
Book value per share formula

Thus, if Marlo Corporation has total stockholders' equity of $1,500,000 (common stock $1,000,000 and retained earnings $500,000) and 50,000 shares of common stock outstanding, book value per share is $30 ($1,500,000 ÷ 50,000).

When a company has both preferred and common stock, the computation of book value is more complex. Since preferred stockholders have a prior claim on net assets over common stockholders, their equity must be deducted from total stockholders' equity. Then, we can determine the stockholders' equity that applies to the common stock. The computation of book value per share involves the following steps.

1. **Compute the preferred stock equity.** This equity is equal to the sum of the call price of preferred stock plus any cumulative dividends in arrears. If the preferred stock does not have a call price, the par value of the stock is used.

2. **Determine the common stock equity.** Subtract the preferred stock equity from total stockholders' equity.

3. **Determine book value per share.** Divide common stock equity by shares of common stock outstanding.

EXAMPLE

We will use the stockholders' equity section of Graber Inc. shown in Illustration 11-26. Graber's preferred stock is callable at $120 per share and is cumulative. Assume that dividends on Graber's preferred stock were in arrears for one year, $54,000 (6,000 × $9). The computation of preferred stock equity (Step 1 in the preceding list) is:

Call price (6,000 shares × $120)	$ 720,000
Dividends in arrears (6,000 shares × $9)	54,000
Preferred stock equity	**$774,000**

Illustration 11B-2
Computation of preferred stock equity—Step 1

The computation of book value (Steps 2 and 3) is as follows.

Total stockholders' equity	$4,810,000
Less: **Preferred stock equity**	774,000
Common stock equity	**$4,036,000**
Shares of common stock outstanding	390,000
Book value per share ($4,036,000 ÷ 390,000)	**$10.35**

Illustration 11B-3
Computation of book value per share with preferred stock—Steps 2 and 3

Note that we used the call price of $120 instead of the par value of $100. Note also that the paid-in capital in excess of par value of preferred stock, $30,000, **is**

not assigned to the preferred stock equity. Preferred stockholders ordinarily do not have a right to amounts paid-in in excess of par value. Therefore, such amounts are assigned to the common stock equity in computing book value.

Book Value versus Market Price

Be sure you understand that **book value per share may not equal market price per share**. Book value generally is based on recorded costs. Market price reflects the subjective judgments of thousands of stockholders and prospective investors about a company's potential for future earnings and dividends. Market price per share may exceed book value per share, but that fact does not necessarily mean that the stock is overpriced. The correlation between book value and the annual range of a company's market price per share is often remote, as indicated by the following recent data.

Illustration 11B-4
Book value and market prices compared

Company	Book Value (year-end)	Market Range (for the year)
The Limited, Inc.	$13.38	$31.03–$22.89
H. J. Heinz Company	$ 7.48	$40.61–$34.53
Cisco Systems	$ 3.66	$21.24–$17.01
Wal-Mart Stores, Inc.	$12.79	$50.87–$42.31

Book value per share **is useful** in determining the trend of a stockholder's per share equity in a corporation. It is also significant in many contracts and in court cases where the rights of individual parties are based on cost information.

SUMMARY OF LEARNING OBJECTIVE FOR APPENDIX 11B

 ✔ **The Navigator**

9 Compute book value per share. Book value per share represents the equity a common stockholder has in the net assets of a corporation from owning one share of stock. When there is only common stock outstanding, the formula for computing book value is: Total stockholders' equity ÷ Number of common shares outstanding = Book value per share.

GLOSSARY FOR APPENDIX 11B

Book value per share The equity a common stockholder has in the net assets of the corporation from owning one share of stock. (p. 579).

WileyPLUS   **Self-Test, Brief Exercises, Exercises, Problem Set A, and many more components are available for practice in *WileyPLUS*.**

*****Note:** All asterisked Questions, Exercises, and Problems relate to material in the appendices to the chapter.

SELF-TEST QUESTIONS

Answers are on page 600.

(LO 1) **1.** Which of the following is **not** a major advantage of a corporate form of organization?
   (a) Separate legal existence.
   (b) Continuous life.

   (c) Government regulations.
   (d) Transferable ownership rights.

2. A major disadvantage of a corporation is: (LO 1)
   (a) limited liability of stockholders.
   (b) additional taxes.

(c) transferable ownership rights.

(d) separate legal existence.

(LO 1) **3.** Which of the following statements is **false**?

(a) Ownership of common stock gives the owner a voting right.

(b) The stockholders' equity section begins with a paid-in capital section.

(c) The authorization of capital stock does not result in a formal accounting entry.

(d) Par value and market price of a company's stock are always the same.

(LO 2) **4.** ABC Corporation issues 1,000 shares of $10 par value common stock at $12 per share. In recording the transaction, credits are made to:

(a) Common Stock $10,000 and Paid-in Capital in Excess of Stated Value $2,000.

(b) Common Stock $12,000.

(c) Common Stock $10,000 and Paid-in Capital in Excess of Par $2,000.

(d) Common Stock $10,000 and Retained Earnings $2,000.

(LO 3) **5.** XYZ, Inc. sells 100 shares of $5 par value treasury stock at $13 per share. If the cost of acquiring the shares was $10 per share, the entry for the sale should include credits to:

(a) Treasury Stock $1,000 and Paid-in Capital from Treasury Stock $300.

(b) Treasury Stock $500 and Paid-in Capital from Treasury Stock $800.

(c) Treasury Stock $1,000 and Retained Earnings $300.

(d) Treasury Stock $500 and Paid-in Capital in Excess of Par $800.

(LO 3) **6.** In the stockholders' equity section, the cost of treasury stock is deducted from:

(a) total paid-in capital and retained earnings.

(b) retained earnings.

(c) total stockholders' equity.

(d) common stock in paid-in capital.

(LO 4) **7.** Preferred stock may have priority over common stock **except** in:

(a) dividends.

(b) assets in the event of liquidation.

(c) cumulative dividend features.

(d) voting.

(LO 4, 5) **8.** M-Bot Corporation has 10,000 shares of 8%, $100 par value, cumulative preferred stock outstanding at December 31, 2015. No dividends were declared in 2013 or 2014. If M-Bot wants to pay $375,000 of dividends in 2015, common stockholders will receive:

(a) $0.   (c) $215,000.

(b) $295,000.   (d) $135,000.

(LO 5) **9.** Entries for cash dividends are required on the:

(a) declaration date and the payment date.

(b) record date and the payment date.

(c) declaration date, record date, and payment date.

(d) declaration date and the record date.

(LO 5) **10.** Which of the following statements about small stock dividends is **true**?

(a) A debit to Retained Earnings for the par value of the shares issued should be made.

(b) A small stock dividend decreases total stockholders' equity.

(c) Market price per share should be assigned to the dividend shares.

(d) A small stock dividend ordinarily will have an effect on par value per share of stock.

(LO 6) **11.** All **but one** of the following is reported in a retained earnings statement. The exception is:

(a) cash and stock dividends.

(b) net income and net loss.

(c) sales revenue.

(d) prior period adjustments.

(LO 6) **12.** A prior period adjustment is:

(a) reported in the income statement as a nontypical item.

(b) a correction of an error that is recorded directly to retained earnings.

(c) reported directly in the stockholders' equity section.

(d) reported in the retained earnings statement as an adjustment of the ending balance of retained earnings.

(LO 7) **13.** In the stockholders' equity section of the balance sheet, common stock:

(a) is listed before preferred stock.

(b) is added to total capital stock.

(c) is part of paid-in capital.

(d) is part of additional paid-in capital.

(LO 7) **14.** Which of the following is **not** reported under additional paid-in capital?

(a) Paid-in capital in excess of par.

(b) Common stock.

(c) Paid-in capital in excess of stated value.

(d) Paid-in capital from treasury stock.

(LO 7) **15.** Katie Inc. reported net income of $186,000 during 2015 and paid dividends of $26,000 on common stock. It also has 10,000 shares of 6%, $100 par value, noncumulative preferred stock outstanding and paid dividends of $60,000 on preferred stock. Common stockholders' equity was $1,200,000 on January 1, 2015, and $1,600,000 on December 31, 2015. The company's return on common stockholders' equity for 2015 is:

(a) 10.0%.   (c) 7.1%.

(b) 9.0%.   (d) 13.3%.

(LO 8) *16. When a stockholders' equity statement is presented, it is not necessary to prepare a (an):

(a) retained earnings statement.

(b) balance sheet.

(c) income statement.

(d) None of the above.

(LO 9) *17. The ledger of JFK, Inc. shows common stock, common treasury stock, and no preferred stock. For this company, the formula for computing book value per share is:

(a) total paid-in capital and retained earnings divided by the number of shares of common stock issued.

(b) common stock divided by the number of shares of common stock issued.

(c) total stockholders' equity divided by the number of shares of common stock outstanding.

(d) total stockholders' equity divided by the number of shares of common stock issued.

Go to the book's companion website, www.wiley.com/college/weygandt, for additional Self-Test Questions.

✔ The Navigator

QUESTIONS

1. Mark Kemp, a student, asks your help in understanding the following characteristics of a corporation: (a) separate legal existence, (b) limited liability of stockholders, and (c) transferable ownership rights. Explain these characteristics to Mark.

2. (a) Your friend Katie Fehr cannot understand how the characteristic of corporation management is both an advantage and a disadvantage. Clarify this problem for Katie.
   (b) Identify and explain two other disadvantages of a corporation.

3. (a) The following terms pertain to the forming of a corporation: (1) charter, (2) by-laws, and (3) organization costs. Explain the terms.
   (b) Donna Fleming believes a corporation must be incorporated in the state in which its headquarters' office is located. Is Donna correct? Explain.

4. What are the basic ownership rights of common stockholders in the absence of restrictive provisions?

5. (a) What are the two principal components of stockholders' equity?
   (b) What is paid-in capital? Give three examples.

6. How do the financial statements for a corporation differ from the statements for a proprietorship?

7. The corporate charter of Luney Corporation allows the issuance of a maximum of 100,000 shares of common stock. During its first two years of operations, Luney sold 70,000 shares to shareholders and reacquired 7,000 of these shares. After these transactions, how many shares are authorized, issued, and outstanding?

8. Which is the better investment—common stock with a par value of $5 per share, or common stock with a par value of $20 per share? Why?

9. What factors help determine the market price of stock?

10. Why is common stock usually not issued at a price that is less than par value?

11. Land appraised at $80,000 is purchased by issuing 1,000 shares of $20 par value common stock. The market price of the shares at the time of the exchange, based on active trading in the securities market, is $95 per share. Should the land be recorded at $20,000, $80,000, or $95,000? Explain.

12. For what reasons might a company like IBM repurchase some of its stock (treasury stock)?

13. Meng, Inc. purchases 1,000 shares of its own previously issued $5 par common stock for $12,000. Assuming the shares are held in the treasury, what effect does this transaction have on (a) net income, (b) total assets, (c) total paid-in capital, and (d) total stockholders' equity?

14. The treasury stock purchased in Question 13 is resold by Meng, Inc. for $16,000. What effect does this transaction have on (a) net income, (b) total assets, (c) total paid-in capital, and (d) total stockholders' equity?

15. (a) What are the principal differences between common stock and preferred stock?
   (b) Preferred stock may be cumulative. Discuss this feature.
   (c) How are dividends in arrears presented in the financial statements?

16. Identify the events that result in credits and debits to retained earnings.

17. Indicate how each of the following accounts should be classified in the stockholders' equity section.
   (a) Common stock.
   (b) Paid-in capital in excess of par—common stock.
   (c) Retained earnings.
   (d) Treasury stock.
   (e) Paid-in capital from treasury stock.
   (f) Paid-in capital in excess of stated value—common stock.
   (g) Preferred stock.

18. Jan Kimler maintains that adequate cash is the only requirement for the declaration of a cash dividend. Is Jan correct? Explain.

19. (a) Three dates are important in connection with cash dividends. Identify these dates, and explain their significance to the corporation and its stockholders.
   (b) Identify the accounting entries that are made for a cash dividend and the date of each entry.

20. Contrast the effects of a cash dividend and a stock dividend on a corporation's balance sheet.

21. Rich Mordica asks, "Since stock dividends don't change anything, why declare them?" What is your answer to Rich?

22. Gorton Corporation has 30,000 shares of $10 par value common stock outstanding when it announces a 2-for-1 stock split. Before the split, the stock had a market price of $120 per share. After the split, how many shares of stock will be outstanding? What will be the approximate market price per share?

23. The board of directors is considering either a stock split or a stock dividend. They understand that total stockholders' equity will remain the same under either action. However, they are not sure of the different effects of the two types of actions on other aspects of stockholders' equity. Explain the differences to the directors.

24. What is a prior period adjustment, and how is it reported in the financial statements?

25. What is the purpose of a retained earnings restriction? Identify the possible causes of retained earnings restrictions.

*26. What is the formula for computing book value per share when a corporation has only common stock?

*27. Emko Inc.'s common stock has a par value of $1, a book value of $24, and a current market price of $18. Explain why these amounts are all different.

BRIEF EXERCISES

BE11-1 Angic Baden is studying for her accounting midterm examination. Identify for Angie the advantages and disadvantages of the corporate form of business organization.

List the advantages and disadvantages of a corporation.
(LO 1)

BE11-2 On May 10, Jack Corporation issues 2,000 shares of $10 par value common stock for cash at $18 per share. Journalize the issuance of the stock.

Prepare entries for issuance of par value common stock.
(LO 2)

BE11-3 On June 1, Noonan Inc. issues 4,000 shares of no-par common stock at a cash price of $6 per share. Journalize the issuance of the shares assuming the stock has a stated value of $1 per share.

Prepare entries for issuance of no-par value common stock.
(LO 2)

BE11-4 Lei Inc.'s $10 par value common stock is actively traded at a market price of $15 per share. Lei issues 5,000 shares to purchase land advertised for sale at $85,000. Journalize the issuance of the stock in acquiring the land.

Prepare entries for issuance of stock in a noncash transaction.
(LO 2)

BE11-5 On July 1, Raney Corporation purchases 500 shares of its $5 par value common stock for the treasury at a cash price of $9 per share. On September 1, it sells 300 shares of the treasury stock for cash at $11 per share. Journalize the two treasury stock transactions.

Prepare entries for treasury stock transactions.
(LO 3)

BE11-6 Garb Inc. issues 5,000 shares of $100 par value preferred stock for cash at $130 per share. Journalize the issuance of the preferred stock.

Prepare entries for issuance of preferred stock.
(LO 4)

BE11-7 Greenwood Corporation has 80,000 shares of common stock outstanding. It declares a $1 per share cash dividend on November 1 to stockholders of record on December 1. The dividend is paid on December 31. Prepare the entries on the appropriate dates to record the declaration and payment of the cash dividend.

Prepare entries for a cash dividend.
(LO 5)

BE11-8 Langley Corporation has 50,000 shares of $10 par value common stock outstanding. It declares a 15% stock dividend on December 1 when the market price per share is $16. The dividend shares are issued on December 31. Prepare the entries for the declaration and payment of the stock dividend.

Prepare entries for a stock dividend.
(LO 5)

BE11-9 The stockholders' equity section of Pretzer Corporation consists of common stock ($10 par) $2,000,000 and retained earnings $500,000. A 10% stock dividend (20,000 shares) is declared when the market price per share is $14. Show the before-and-after effects of the dividend on the following.

(a) The components of stockholders' equity.
(b) Shares outstanding.
(c) Par value per share.

Show before-and-after effects of a stock dividend.
(LO 5)

BE11-10 For the year ending December 31, 2015, Soto Inc. reports net income $170,000 and dividends $85,000. Prepare the retained earnings statement for the year assuming the balance in retained earnings on January 1, 2015, was $220,000.

Prepare a retained earnings statement.
(LO 6)

BE11-11 The balance in retained earnings on January 1, 2015, for Palmer Inc. was $800,000. During the year, the corporation paid cash dividends of $90,000 and distributed a stock dividend of $8,000. In addition, the company determined that it had understated its depreciation expense in prior years by $50,000. Net income for 2015 was $120,000. Prepare the retained earnings statement for 2015.

Prepare a retained earnings statement.
(LO 6)

BE11-12 Pine Corporation has the following accounts at December 31: Common Stock, $10 par, 5,000 shares issued, $50,000; Paid-in Capital in Excess of Par—Common Stock $30,000; Retained Earnings $45,000; and Treasury Stock, 500 shares, $11,000. Prepare the stockholders' equity section of the balance sheet.

Prepare stockholders' equity section.
(LO 7)

*BE11-13 The balance sheet for Lauren Inc. shows the following: total paid-in capital and retained earnings $877,000, total stockholders' equity $817,000, common stock issued 44,000 shares, and common stock outstanding 38,000 shares. Compute the book value per share. (No preferred stock is outstanding.)

Compute book value per share.
(LO 9)

> ## DO IT! Review

Analyze statements about corporate organization.

(LO 1)

DO IT! 11-1 Indicate whether each of the following statements is true or false. If false, indicate how to correct the statement.

_____ **1.** The corporation is an entity separate and distinct from its owners.

_____ **2.** The liability of stockholders is normally limited to their investment in the corporation.

_____ **3.** The relative lack of government regulation is an advantage of the corporate form of business.

_____ **4.** There is no journal entry to record the authorization of capital stock.

_____ **5.** No-par value stock is quite rare today.

Close net income and prepare stockholders' equity section.

(LO 1)

DO IT! 11-2 At the end of its first year of operation, Goss Corporation has $1,000,000 of common stock and net income of $236,000. Prepare (a) the closing entry for net income and (b) the stockholders' equity section at year-end.

Journalize issuance of stock.

(LO 2)

DO IT! 11-3 Beauty Island Corporation began operations on April 1 by issuing 60,000 shares of $5 par value common stock for cash at $13 per share. On April 19, it issued 2,000 shares of common stock to attorneys in settlement of their bill of $27,500 for organization costs. Journalize both issuances, assuming the stock is not publicly traded.

Journalize treasury stock transactions.

(LO 3)

DO IT! 11-4 Fouts Corporation purchased 2,000 shares of its $10 par value common stock for $130,000 on August 1. It will hold these shares in the treasury until resold. On December 1, the corporation sold 1,200 shares of treasury stock for cash at $72 per share. Journalize the treasury stock transactions.

Determine dividends paid to preferred and common stockholders.

(LO 5)

DO IT! 11-5 Herr Corporation has 3,000 shares of 7%, $100 par value preferred stock outstanding at December 31, 2015. At December 31, 2015, the company declared a $105,000 cash dividend. Determine the dividend paid to preferred stockholders and common stockholders under each of the following scenarios.

1. The preferred stock is noncumulative, and the company has not missed any dividends in previous years.

2. The preferred stock is noncumulative, and the company did not pay a dividend in each of the two previous years.

3. The preferred stock is cumulative, and the company did not pay a dividend in each of the two previous years.

Determine effects of stock dividend and stock split.

(LO 5)

DO IT! 11-6 Jurgens Company has had 4 years of net income. Due to this success, the market price of its 400,000 shares of $3 par value common stock has increased from $12 per share to $46. During this period, paid-in capital remained the same at $4,800,000. Retained earnings increased from $1,800,000 to $12,000,000. President E. Rife is considering either a 15% stock dividend or a 2-for-1 stock split. He asks you to show the before-and-after effects of each option on (a) retained earnings and (b) total stockholders' equity.

Prepare a retained earnings statement.

(LO 6)

DO IT! 11-7 Foley Corporation has retained earnings of $3,100,000 on January 1, 2015. During the year, Foley earned $1,200,000 of net income. It declared and paid a $150,000 cash dividend. In 2015, Foley recorded an adjustment of $110,000 due to the overstatement (from mathematical error) of 2014 depreciation expense. Prepare a retained earnings statement for 2015.

Compute return on stockholders' equity and discuss changes.

(LO 7)

DO IT! 11-8 On January 1, 2015, Vahsholtz Corporation purchased 5,000 shares of treasury stock. Other information regarding Vahsholtz Corporation is provided as follows.

	2014	2015
Net income	$100,000	$110,000
Dividends on preferred stock	$30,000	$30,000
Dividends on common stock	$20,000	$25,000
Weighted-average number of common shares outstanding	50,000	45,000
Common stockholders' equity beginning of year	$600,000	$750,000
Common stockholders' equity end of year	$750,000	$830,000

Compute (a) return on common stockholders' equity for each year, and (b) discuss the changes in each.

EXERCISES

E11-1 Andrea has prepared the following list of statements about corporations.

1. A corporation is an entity separate and distinct from its owners.
2. As a legal entity, a corporation has most of the rights and privileges of a person.
3. Most of the largest U.S. corporations are privately held corporations.
4. Corporations may buy, own, and sell property; borrow money; enter into legally binding contracts; and sue and be sued.
5. The net income of a corporation is not taxed as a separate entity.
6. Creditors have a legal claim on the personal assets of the owners of a corporation if the corporation does not pay its debts.
7. The transfer of stock from one owner to another requires the approval of either the corporation or other stockholders.
8. The board of directors of a corporation legally owns the corporation.
9. The chief accounting officer of a corporation is the controller.
10. Corporations are subject to fewer state and federal regulations than partnerships or proprietorships.

Identify characteristics of a corporation.

(LO 1)

Instructions
Identify each statement as true or false. If false, indicate how to correct the statement.

E11-2 Andrea (see E11-1) has studied the information you gave her in that exercise and has come to you with more statements about corporations.

1. Corporation management is both an advantage and a disadvantage of a corporation compared to a proprietorship or a partnership.
2. Limited liability of stockholders, government regulations, and additional taxes are the major disadvantages of a corporation.
3. When a corporation is formed, organization costs are recorded as an asset.
4. Each share of common stock gives the stockholder the ownership rights to vote at stockholder meetings, share in corporate earnings, keep the same percentage ownership when new shares of stock are issued, and share in assets upon liquidation.
5. The number of issued shares is always greater than or equal to the number of authorized shares.
6. A journal entry is required for the authorization of capital stock.
7. Publicly held corporations usually issue stock directly to investors.
8. The trading of capital stock on a securities exchange involves the transfer of already issued shares from an existing stockholder to another investor.
9. The market price of common stock is usually the same as its par value.
10. Retained earnings is the total amount of cash and other assets paid in to the corporation by stockholders in exchange for capital stock.

Identify characteristics of a corporation.

(LO 1, 2)

Instructions
Identify each statement as true or false. If false, indicate how to correct the statement.

E11-3 During its first year of operations, Foyle Corporation had the following transactions pertaining to its common stock.

Jan. 10   Issued 70,000 shares for cash at $5 per share.
July   1   Issued 40,000 shares for cash at $7 per share.

Journalize issuance of common stock.

(LO 2)

Instructions
(a) Journalize the transactions, assuming that the common stock has a par value of $5 per share.
(b) Journalize the transactions, assuming that the common stock is no-par with a stated value of $1 per share.

E11-4 Osage Corporation issued 2,000 shares of stock.

Instructions
Prepare the entry for the issuance under the following assumptions.

(a) The stock had a par value of $5 per share and was issued for a total of $52,000.
(b) The stock had a stated value of $5 per share and was issued for a total of $52,000.

Journalize issuance of common stock.

(LO 2)

(c) The stock had no par or stated value and was issued for a total of $52,000.
(d) The stock had a par value of $5 per share and was issued to attorneys for services dur-. ing incorporation valued at $52,000.
(e) The stock had a par value of $5 per share and was issued for land worth $52,000.

Journalize treasury stock transactions.

(LO 3)

E11-5 Rinehart Corporation purchased from its stockholders 5,000 shares of its own previously issued stock for $255,000. It later resold 2,000 shares for $54 per share, then 2,000 more shares for $49 per share, and finally 1,000 shares for $43 per share.

Instructions
Prepare journal entries for the purchase of the treasury stock and the three sales of treasury stock.

Differentiate between preferred and common stock.

(LO 4)

E11-6 Hodge Corporation issued 100,000 shares of $20 par value, cumulative, 6% preferred stock on January 1, 2014, for $2,300,000. In December 2016, Hodge declared its first dividend of $500,000.

Instructions
(a) Prepare Hodge's journal entry to record the issuance of the preferred stock.
(b) If the preferred stock is **not** cumulative, how much of the $500,000 would be paid to **common** stockholders?
(c) If the preferred stock is cumulative, how much of the $500,000 would be paid to **common** stockholders?

Journalize issuance of common and preferred stock and purchase of treasury stock.

(LO 2, 3, 4)

E11-7 Quay Co. had the following transactions during the current period.

Mar.	2	Issued 5,000 shares of $5 par value common stock to attorneys in payment of a bill for $30,000 for services performed in helping the company to incorporate.
June	12	Issued 60,000 shares of $5 par value common stock for cash of $375,000.
July	11	Issued 1,000 shares of $100 par value preferred stock for cash at $110 per share.
Nov.	28	Purchased 2,000 shares of treasury stock for $80,000.

Instructions
Journalize the transactions.

Journalize noncash common stock transactions.

(LO 2)

E11-8 As an auditor for the CPA firm of Hinkson and Calvert, you encounter the following situations in auditing different clients.

1. LR Corporation is a closely held corporation whose stock is not publicly traded. On December 5, the corporation acquired land by issuing 5,000 shares of its $20 par value common stock. The owners' asking price for the land was $120,000, and the fair value of the land was $110,000.
2. Vera Corporation is a publicly held corporation whose common stock is traded on the securities markets. On June 1, it acquired land by issuing 20,000 shares of its $10 par value stock. At the time of the exchange, the land was advertised for sale at $250,000. The stock was selling at $11 per share.

Instructions
Prepare the journal entries for each of the situations above.

Journalize treasury stock transactions.

(LO 3)

E11-9 On January 1, 2015, the stockholders' equity section of Newlin Corporation shows common stock ($5 par value) $1,500,000; paid-in capital in excess of par $1,000,000; and retained earnings $1,200,000. During the year, the following treasury stock transactions occurred.

Mar.	1	Purchased 50,000 shares for cash at $15 per share.
July	1	Sold 10,000 treasury shares for cash at $17 per share.
Sept.	1	Sold 8,000 treasury shares for cash at $14 per share.

Instructions
(a) Journalize the treasury stock transactions.
(b) Restate the entry for September 1, assuming the treasury shares were sold at $12 per share.

Journalize preferred stock transactions and indicate statement presentation.

(LO 4, 7)

E11-10 Tran Corporation is authorized to issue both preferred and common stock. The par value of the preferred is $50. During the first year of operations, the company had the following events and transactions pertaining to its preferred stock.

Feb. 1 Issued 20,000 shares for cash at $53 per share.
July 1 Issued 12,000 shares for cash at $57 per share.

Instructions
(a) Journalize the transactions.
(b) Post to the stockholders' equity accounts.
(c) Indicate the financial statement presentation of the related accounts.

E11-11 The stockholders' equity section of Haley Corporation at December 31 is as follows. *Answer questions about stockholders' equity section.*

(LO 2, 3, 4, 7)

HALEY CORPORATION
Balance Sheet (partial)

Paid-in capital	
Preferred stock, cumulative, 10,000 shares authorized, 6,000 shares issued and outstanding	$ 300,000
Common stock, no par, 750,000 shares authorized, 600,000 shares issued	1,200,000
Total paid-in capital	1,500,000
Retained earnings	1,858,000
Total paid-in capital and retained earnings	3,358,000
Less: Treasury stock (10,000 common shares)	64,000
Total stockholders' equity	$3,294,000

Instructions
From a review of the stockholders' equity section, as chief accountant, write a memo to the president of the company answering the following questions.

(a) How many shares of common stock are outstanding?
(b) Assuming there is a stated value, what is the stated value of the common stock?
(c) What is the par value of the preferred stock?
(d) If the annual dividend on preferred stock is $30,000, what is the dividend rate on preferred stock?
(e) If dividends of $60,000 were in arrears on preferred stock, what would be the balance in Retained Earnings?

E11-12 Gilliam Corporation recently hired a new accountant with extensive experience in accounting for partnerships. Because of the pressure of the new job, the accountant was unable to review his textbooks on the topic of corporation accounting. During the first month, the accountant made the following entries for the corporation's capital stock.

Prepare correct entries for capital stock transactions.

(LO 2, 3, 4)

May 2	Cash		130,000	
	Capital Stock			130,000
	(Issued 10,000 shares of $10 par value common stock at $13 per share)			
10	Cash		600,000	
	Capital Stock			600,000
	(Issued 10,000 shares of $50 par value preferred stock at $60 per share)			
15	Capital Stock		15,000	
	Cash			15,000
	(Purchased 1,000 shares of common stock for the treasury at $15 per share)			
31	Cash		8,000	
	Capital Stock			5,000
	Gain on Sale of Stock			3,000
	(Sold 500 shares of treasury stock at $16 per share)			

Instructions
On the basis of the explanation for each entry, prepare the entry that should have been made for the capital stock transactions.

Journalize cash dividends; indicate statement presentation.

(LO 5)

E11-13 On January 1, Guillen Corporation had 95,000 shares of no-par common stock issued and outstanding. The stock has a stated value of $5 per share. During the year, the following occurred.

Apr.	1	Issued 25,000 additional shares of common stock for $17 per share.
June	15	Declared a cash dividend of $1 per share to stockholders of record on June 30.
July	10	Paid the $1 cash dividend.
Dec.	1	Issued 2,000 additional shares of common stock for $19 per share.
	15	Declared a cash dividend on outstanding shares of $1.20 per share to stockholders of record on December 31.

Instructions

(a) Prepare the entries, if any, on each of the three dividend dates.

(b) How are dividends and dividends payable reported in the financial statements prepared at December 31?

Journalize stock dividends.

(LO 5)

E11-14 On January 1, 2015, Frontier Corporation had $1,000,000 of common stock outstanding that was issued at par. It also had retained earnings of $750,000. The company issued 40,000 shares of common stock at par on July 1 and earned net income of $400,000 for the year.

Instructions

Journalize the declaration of a 15% stock dividend on December 10, 2015, for the following independent assumptions.

(a) Par value is $10, and market price is $18.

(b) Par value is $5, and market price is $20.

Compare effects of a stock dividend and a stock split.

(LO 5)

E11-15 On October 31, the stockholders' equity section of Heins Company consists of common stock $500,000 and retained earnings $900,000. Heins is considering the following two courses of action: (1) declaring a 5% stock dividend on the 50,000, $10 par value shares outstanding, or (2) effecting a 2-for-1 stock split that will reduce par value to $5 per share. The current market price is $14 per share.

Instructions

Prepare a tabular summary of the effects of the alternative actions on the components of stockholders' equity, outstanding shares, and par value per share. Use the following column headings: Before Action, After Stock Dividend, and After Stock Split.

Prepare correcting entries for dividends and a stock split.

(LO 5)

E11-16 Before preparing financial statements for the current year, the chief accountant for Toso Company discovered the following errors in the accounts.

1. The declaration and payment of $50,000 cash dividend was recorded as a debit to Interest Expense $50,000 and a credit to Cash $50,000.

2. A 10% stock dividend (1,000 shares) was declared on the $10 par value stock when the market price per share was $18. The only entry made was Stock Dividends (Dr.) $10,000 and Dividend Payable (Cr.) $10,000. The shares have not been issued.

3. A 4-for-1 stock split involving the issue of 400,000 shares of $5 par value common stock for 100,000 shares of $20 par value common stock was recorded as a debit to Retained Earnings $2,000,000 and a credit to Common Stock $2,000,000.

Instructions

Prepare the correcting entries at December 31.

Prepare a retained earnings statement.

(LO 6)

E11-17 On January 1, 2015, Eddy Corporation had retained earnings of $650,000. During the year, Eddy had the following selected transactions.

1. Declared cash dividends $120,000.
2. Corrected overstatement of 2014 net income because of depreciation error $40,000.
3. Earned net income $350,000.
4. Declared stock dividends $90,000.

Instructions

Prepare a retained earnings statement for the year.

Prepare a retained earnings statement.

(LO 6)

E11-18 Newland Company reported retained earnings at December 31, 2014, of $310,000. Newland had 200,000 shares of common stock outstanding at the beginning of 2015.

The following transactions occurred during 2015.

1. An error was discovered. In 2013, depreciation expense was recorded at $70,000, but the correct amount was $50,000.
2. A cash dividend of $0.50 per share was declared and paid.
3. A 5% stock dividend was declared and distributed when the market price per share was $15 per share.
4. Net income was $285,000.

Instructions
Prepare a retained earnings statement for 2015.

E11-19 The ledger of Rolling Hills Corporation contains the following accounts: Common Stock, Preferred Stock, Treasury Stock, Paid-in Capital in Excess of Par—Preferred Stock, Paid-in Capital in Excess of Stated Value—Common Stock, Paid-in Capital from Treasury Stock, and Retained Earnings.

Classify stockholders' equity accounts.

(LO 7)

Instructions
Classify each account using the following table headings.

	Paid-in Capital			
	Capital		**Retained**	
Account	**Stock**	**Additional**	**Earnings**	**Other**

E11-20 The following accounts appear in the ledger of Horner Inc. after the books are closed at December 31.

Prepare a stockholders' equity section.

(LO 7)

Common Stock, no par, $1 stated value, 400,000 shares authorized;	
300,000 shares issued	$ 300,000
Common Stock Dividends Distributable	30,000
Paid-in Capital in Excess of Stated Value—Common Stock	1,200,000
Preferred Stock, $5 par value, 8%, 40,000 shares authorized;	
30,000 shares issued	150,000
Retained Earnings	800,000
Treasury Stock (10,000 common shares)	74,000
Paid-in Capital in Excess of Par—Preferred Stock	344,000

Instructions
Prepare the stockholders' equity section at December 31, assuming retained earnings is restricted for plant expansion in the amount of $100,000.

E11-21 Dirk Company reported the following balances at December 31, 2014: common stock $500,000, paid-in capital in excess of par value—common stock $100,000, and retained earnings $250,000. During 2015, the following transactions affected stockholders' equity.

Prepare a stockholders' equity section.

(LO 7)

1. Issued preferred stock with a par value of $125,000 for $200,000.
2. Purchased treasury stock (common) for $40,000.
3. Earned net income of $180,000.
4. Declared and paid cash dividends of $56,000.

Instructions
Prepare the stockholders' equity section of Dirk Company's December 31, 2015, balance sheet.

E11-22 In 2015, Pennington Corporation had net sales of $600,000 and cost of goods sold of $360,000. Operating expenses were $153,000, and interest expense was $7,500. The corporation's tax rate is 30%. The corporation declared preferred dividends of $15,000 in 2015, and its average common stockholders' equity during the year was $200,000.

Prepare an income statement and compute return on equity.

(LO 7)

Instructions
(a) Prepare an income statement for Pennington Corporation.
(b) Compute Pennington Corporation's return on common stockholders' equity for 2015.

***E11-23** The stockholders' equity section of Aluminum Company of America (Alcoa) showed the following (in alphabetical order): additional paid-in capital $6,101, common

Prepare a stockholders' equity section.

(LO 7, 9)

stock $925, preferred stock $56, retained earnings $7,428, and treasury stock $2,828. (All dollar data are in millions.)

The preferred stock has 557,740 shares authorized, with a par value of $100 and an annual $3.75 per share cumulative dividend preference. At December 31 of the current year, 557,649 shares of preferred are issued and 546,024 shares are outstanding. There are 1.8 billion shares of $1 par value common stock authorized, of which 924.6 million are issued and 844.8 million are outstanding at December 31.

Instructions
(a) Prepare the stockholders' equity section of the current year, including disclosure of all relevant data.
(b) Compute the book value per share of common stock, assuming there are no preferred dividends in arrears. (Round to two decimals.)

Compute book value per share with preferred stock.
(LO 4, 9)

*E11-24 At December 31, Gorden Corporation has total stockholders' equity of $3,200,000. Included in this total are preferred stock $500,000 and paid-in capital in excess of par— preferred stock $50,000. There are 10,000 shares of $50 par value, 8% cumulative preferred stock outstanding. At year-end, 200,000 shares of common stock are outstanding.

Instructions
Compute the book value per share of common stock under each of the following assumptions.
(a) There are no preferred dividends in arrears, and the preferred stock does not have a call price.
(b) Preferred dividends are one year in arrears, and the preferred stock has a call price of $60 per share.

EXERCISES: SET B AND CHALLENGE EXERCISES

Visit the book's companion website, at **www.wiley.com/college/weygandt**, and choose the Student Companion site to access Exercise Set B and Challenge Exercises.

PROBLEMS: SET A

Journalize stock transactions, post, and prepare paid-in capital section.
(LO 2, 4, 7)

P11-1A DeLong Corporation was organized on January 1, 2015. It is authorized to issue 10,000 shares of 8%, $100 par value preferred stock, and 500,000 shares of no-par common stock with a stated value of $2 per share. The following stock transactions were completed during the first year.

Jan. 10	Issued 80,000 shares of common stock for cash at $4 per share.
Mar. 1	Issued 5,000 shares of preferred stock for cash at $105 per share.
Apr. 1	Issued 24,000 shares of common stock for land. The asking price of the land was $90,000. The fair value of the land was $85,000.
May 1	Issued 80,000 shares of common stock for cash at $4.50 per share.
Aug. 1	Issued 10,000 shares of common stock to attorneys in payment of their bill of $30,000 for services performed in helping the company organize.
Sept. 1	Issued 10,000 shares of common stock for cash at $5 per share.
Nov. 1	Issued 1,000 shares of preferred stock for cash at $109 per share.

Instructions
(a) Journalize the transactions.
(b) Post to the stockholders' equity accounts. (Use J5 as the posting reference.)
(c) Prepare the paid-in capital section of stockholders' equity at December 31, 2015.

(c) Total paid-in capital
$1,479,000

Journalize and post treasury stock transactions, and prepare stockholders' equity section.
(LO 3, 7)

P11-2A Fechter Corporation had the following stockholders' equity accounts on January 1, 2015: Common Stock ($5 par) $500,000, Paid-in Capital in Excess of Par—Common Stock $200,000, and Retained Earnings $100,000. In 2015, the company had the following treasury stock transactions.

Mar. 1	Purchased 5,000 shares at $8 per share.
June 1	Sold 1,000 shares at $12 per share.

Sept. 1   Sold 2,000 shares at $10 per share.
Dec. 1   Sold 1,000 shares at $7 per share.

Fechter Corporation uses the cost method of accounting for treasury stock. In 2015, the company reported net income of $30,000.

Instructions

(a) Journalize the treasury stock transactions, and prepare the closing entry at December 31, 2015, for net income.
(b) Open accounts for (1) Paid-in Capital from Treasury Stock, (2) Treasury Stock, and (3) Retained Earnings. Post to these accounts using J10 as the posting reference.
(c) Prepare the stockholders' equity section for Fechter Corporation at December 31, 2015.

(b) Treasury Stock $8,000
(c) Total stockholders' equity
    $829,000

P11-3A The stockholders' equity accounts of Castle Corporation on January 1, 2015, were as follows.

Journalize and post transactions, and prepare stockholders' equity section.
(LO 2, 3, 4, 7)

Preferred Stock (8%, $50 par, cumulative, 10,000 shares authorized)	$ 400,000
Common Stock ($1 stated value, 2,000,000 shares authorized)	1,000,000
Paid-in Capital in Excess of Par—Preferred Stock	100,000
Paid-in Capital in Excess of Stated Value—Common Stock	1,450,000
Retained Earnings	1,816,000
Treasury Stock (10,000 common shares)	50,000

During 2015, the corporation had the following transactions and events pertaining to its stockholders' equity.

Feb. 1   Issued 25,000 shares of common stock for $120,000.
Apr. 14   Sold 6,000 shares of treasury stock—common for $33,000.
Sept. 3   Issued 5,000 shares of common stock for a patent valued at $35,000.
Nov. 10   Purchased 1,000 shares of common stock for the treasury at a cost of $6,000.
Dec. 31   Determined that net income for the year was $452,000.

No dividends were declared during the year.

Instructions

(a) Journalize the transactions and the closing entry for net income.
(b) Enter the beginning balances in the accounts, and post the journal entries to the stockholders' equity accounts. (Use J5 for the posting reference.)
(c) Prepare a stockholders' equity section at December 31, 2015, including the disclosure of the preferred dividends in arrears.

(c) Total stockholders' equity
    $5,350,000

P11-4A On January 1, 2015, Geffrey Corporation had the following stockholders' equity accounts.

Prepare dividend entries and stockholders' equity section.
(LO 5, 7)

Common Stock ($20 par value, 60,000 shares issued and outstanding)	$1,200,000
Paid-in Capital in Excess of Par—Common Stock	200,000
Retained Earnings	600,000

During the year, the following transactions occurred.

Feb. 1   Declared a $1 cash dividend per share to stockholders of record on February 15, payable March 1.
Mar. 1   Paid the dividend declared in February.
Apr. 1   Announced a 2-for-1 stock split. Prior to the split, the market price per share was $36.
July 1   Declared a 10% stock dividend to stockholders of record on July 15, distributable July 31. On July 1, the market price of the stock was $13 per share.
    31   Issued the shares for the stock dividend.
Dec. 1   Declared a $0.50 per share dividend to stockholders of record on December 15, payable January 5, 2016.
    31   Determined that net income for the year was $350,000.

Instructions

(a) Journalize the transactions and the closing entries for net income and dividends.
(b) Enter the beginning balances, and post the entries to the stockholders' equity accounts. (*Note:* Open additional stockholders' equity accounts as needed.)
(c) Prepare a stockholders' equity section at December 31.

(c) Total stockholders' equity
    $2,224,000

Prepare retained earnings statement and stockholders' equity section, and compute allocation of dividends.

(LO 5, 6, 7)

P11-5A The post-closing trial balance of Storey Corporation at December 31, 2015, contains the following stockholders' equity accounts.

Preferred Stock (15,000 shares issued)	$ 750,000
Common Stock (250,000 shares issued)	2,500,000
Paid-in Capital in Excess of Par—Preferred Stock	250,000
Paid-in Capital in Excess of Par—Common Stock	400,000
Common Stock Dividends Distributable	250,000
Retained Earnings	1,042,000

A review of the accounting records reveals the following.

1. No errors have been made in recording 2015 transactions or in preparing the closing entry for net income.
2. Preferred stock is $50 par, 6%, and cumulative; 15,000 shares have been outstanding since January 1, 2014.
3. Authorized stock is 20,000 shares of preferred, 500,000 shares of common with a $10 par value.
4. The January 1 balance in Retained Earnings was $1,170,000.
5. On July 1, 20,000 shares of common stock were issued for cash at $16 per share.
6. On September 1, the company discovered an understatement error of $90,000 in computing depreciation in 2014, which overstated net income. The net of tax effect of $63,000 was properly debited directly to Retained Earnings.
7. A cash dividend of $250,000 was declared and properly allocated to preferred and common stock on October 1. No dividends were paid to preferred stockholders in 2014.
8. On December 31, a 10% common stock dividend was declared out of retained earnings on common stock when the market price per share was $16.
9. Net income for the year was $585,000.
10. On December 31, 2015, the directors authorized disclosure of a $200,000 restriction of retained earnings for plant expansion. (Use Note X.)

Instructions
(a) Reproduce the Retained Earnings account (T-account) for 2015.
(b) Prepare a retained earnings statement for 2015.

(c) Total stockholders' equity
$5,192,000

(c) Prepare a stockholders' equity section at December 31, 2015.
(d) Compute the allocation of the cash dividend to preferred and common stock.

Prepare entries for stock transactions and prepare stockholders' equity section.

(LO 2, 3, 4, 7)

P11-6A Irwin Corporation has been authorized to issue 20,000 shares of $100 par value, 10%, noncumulative preferred stock and 1,000,000 shares of no-par common stock. The corporation assigned a $2.50 stated value to the common stock. At December 31, 2015, the ledger contained the following balances pertaining to stockholders' equity.

Preferred Stock	$ 120,000
Paid-in Capital in Excess of Par—Preferred Stock	20,000
Common Stock	1,000,000
Paid-in Capital in Excess of Stated Value—Common Stock	1,800,000
Treasury Stock (1,000 common shares)	11,000
Paid-in Capital from Treasury Stock	1,500
Retained Earnings	82,000

The preferred stock was issued for land having a fair value of $140,000. All common stock issued was for cash. In November, 1,500 shares of common stock were purchased for the treasury at a per share cost of $11. In December, 500 shares of treasury stock were sold for $14 per share. No dividends were declared in 2015.

Instructions
(a) Prepare the journal entries for the:
   (1) Issuance of preferred stock for land.
   (2) Issuance of common stock for cash.
   (3) Purchase of common treasury stock for cash.
   (4) Sale of treasury stock for cash.

(b) Total stockholders' equity
$3,012,500

(b) Prepare the stockholders' equity section at December 31, 2015.

P11-7A On January 1, 2015, Primo Corporation had the following stockholders' equity accounts.

Prepare dividend entries and stockholders' equity section.

(LO 5, 7)

Common Stock ($10 par value, 75,000 shares issued and outstanding)	$750,000
Paid-in Capital in Excess of Par—Common Stock	200,000
Retained Earnings	540,000

During the year, the following transactions occurred.

Jan. 15   Declared a $1 cash dividend per share to stockholders of record on January 31, payable February 15.

Feb. 15   Paid the dividend declared in January.

Apr. 15   Declared a 10% stock dividend to stockholders of record on April 30, distributable May 15. On April 15, the market price of the stock was $14 per share.

May 15   Issued the shares for the stock dividend.

July 1   Announced a 2-for-1 stock split. The market price per share prior to the announcement was $15. (The new par value is $5.)

Dec. 1   Declared a $0.60 per share cash dividend to stockholders of record on December 15, payable January 10, 2016.

31   Determined that net income for the year was $250,000.

Instructions

(a) Journalize the transactions and the closing entries for net income and dividends.

(b) Enter the beginning balances, and post the entries to the stockholders' equity accounts. (*Note:* Open additional stockholders' equity accounts as needed.)

(c) Prepare a stockholders' equity section at December 31.

(c) Total stockholders' equity $1,566,000

*P11-8A The following stockholders' equity accounts arranged alphabetically are in the ledger of Westin Corporation at December 31, 2015.

Prepare stockholders' equity section; compute book value per share.

(LO 7, 9)

Common Stock ($10 stated value)	$1,500,000
Paid-in Capital from Treasury Stock	6,000
Paid-in Capital in Excess of Par—Preferred Stock	42,400
Paid-in Capital in Excess of Stated Value—Common Stock	690,000
Preferred Stock (8%, $100 par, noncumulative)	360,000
Retained Earnings	776,000
Treasury Stock—Common (7,000 shares)	92,000

Instructions

(a) Prepare a stockholders' equity section at December 31, 2015.

(b) Compute the book value per share of the common stock, assuming the preferred stock has a call price of $110 per share.

(a) Total stockholders' equity $3,282,400

*P11-9A On January 1, 2015, Goodhue Inc. had the following stockholders' equity balances.

Prepare stockholders' equity statement.

(LO 7, 8)

Common Stock (400,000 shares issued)	$800,000
Paid-in Capital in Excess of Par—Common Stock	500,000
Common Stock Dividends Distributable	120,000
Retained Earnings	600,000

During 2015, the following transactions and events occurred.

1. Issued 60,000 shares of $2 par value common stock as a result of 15% stock dividend declared on December 15, 2014.
2. Issued 30,000 shares of common stock for cash at $4 per share.
3. Purchased 25,000 shares of common stock for the treasury at $5 per share.
4. Declared and paid a cash dividend of $111,000.
5. Sold 8,000 shares of treasury stock for cash at $5 per share.
6. Earned net income of $360,000.

Instructions

Prepare a stockholders' equity statement for the year.

Total stockholders' equity $2,304,000

PROBLEMS: SET B

Journalize stock transactions, post, and prepare paid-in capital section.

(LO 2, 4, 7)

P11-1B Mendoza Corporation was organized on January 1, 2015. It is authorized to issue 20,000 shares of 6%, $40 par value preferred stock, and 500,000 shares of no-par common stock with a stated value of $2 per share. The following stock transactions were completed during the first year.

Jan. 10 Issued 100,000 shares of common stock for cash at $3 per share.
Mar. 1 Issued 10,000 shares of preferred stock for cash at $55 per share.
Apr. 1 Issued 25,000 shares of common stock for land. The asking price of the land was $90,000. The company's estimate of fair value of the land was $75,000.
May 1 Issued 75,000 shares of common stock for cash at $4 per share.
Aug. 1 Issued 10,000 shares of common stock to attorneys in payment of their bill for $50,000 for services performed in helping the company organize.
Sept. 1 Issued 5,000 shares of common stock for cash at $6 per share.
Nov. 1 Issued 2,000 shares of preferred stock for cash at $60 per share.

Instructions

(c) Total paid-in capital $1,425,000

(a) Journalize the transactions.
(b) Post to the stockholders' equity accounts. (Use J1 as the posting reference.)
(c) Prepare the paid-in capital section of stockholders' equity at December 31, 2015.

Journalize and post treasury stock transactions, and prepare stockholders' equity section.

(LO 3, 7)

P11-2B Hawthorne Corporation had the following stockholders' equity accounts on January 1, 2015: Common Stock ($1 par) $400,000, Paid-in Capital in Excess of Par—Common Stock $500,000, and Retained Earnings $100,000. In 2015, the company had the following treasury stock transactions.

Mar. 1 Purchased 5,000 shares at $7 per share.
June 1 Sold 1,000 shares at $10 per share.
Sept. 1 Sold 2,000 shares at $9 per share.
Dec. 1 Sold 1,000 shares at $5 per share.

Hawthorne Corporation uses the cost method of accounting for treasury stock. In 2015, the company reported net income of $80,000.

Instructions

(a) Journalize the treasury stock transactions, and prepare the closing entry at December 31, 2015, for net income.

(b) Treasury Stock $7,000

(b) Open accounts for (1) Paid-in Capital from Treasury Stock, (2) Treasury Stock, and (3) Retained Earnings. Post to these accounts using J12 as the posting reference.

(c) Total stockholders' equity $1,078,000

(c) Prepare the stockholders' equity section for Hawthorne Corporation at December 31, 2015.

Journalize and post transactions, and prepare stockholders' equity section.

(LO 2, 3, 4, 7)

P11-3B The stockholders' equity accounts of Lore Corporation on January 1, 2015, were as follows.

Preferred Stock (10%, $100 par, noncumulative, 5,000 shares authorized)	$ 300,000
Common Stock ($5 stated value, 300,000 shares authorized)	1,000,000
Paid-in Capital in Excess of Par—Preferred Stock	20,000
Paid-in Capital in Excess of Stated Value—Common Stock	425,000
Retained Earnings	488,000
Treasury Stock (5,000 common shares)	40,000

During 2015, the corporation had the following transactions and events pertaining to its stockholders' equity.

Feb. 1 Issued 3,000 shares of common stock for $25,500.
Mar. 20 Purchased 1,500 additional shares of common treasury stock at $8 per share.
June 14 Sold 4,000 shares of treasury stock—common for $36,000.
Sept. 3 Issued 2,000 shares of common stock for a patent valued at $19,000.
Dec. 31 Determined that net income for the year was $350,000.

Instructions

(a) Journalize the transactions and the closing entry for net income.
(b) Enter the beginning balances in the accounts and post the journal entries to the stockholders' equity accounts. (Use J1 as the posting reference.)

(c) Total stockholders' equity $2,611,500

(c) Prepare a stockholders' equity section at December 31, 2015.

P11-4B On January 1, 2015, Chen Corporation had the following stockholders' equity accounts.

Common Stock ($5 par value, 200,000 shares issued and outstanding)	$1,000,000
Paid-In Capital in Excess of Par—Common Stock	200,000
Retained Earnings	840,000

Prepare dividend entries and stockholders' equity section.

(LO 5, 7)

During the year, the following transactions occurred.

Jan. 15	Declared a $1 cash dividend per share to stockholders of record on January 31, payable February 15.
Feb. 15	Paid the dividend declared in January.
Apr. 15	Declared a 10% stock dividend to stockholders of record on April 30, distributable May 15. On April 15, the market price of the stock was $15 per share.
May 15	Issued the shares for the stock dividend.
July 1	Announced a 2-for-1 stock split. The market price per share prior to the announcement was $17. (The new par value is $2.50.)
Dec. 1	Declared a $0.50 per share cash dividend to stockholders of record on December 15, payable January 10, 2016.
31	Determined that net income for the year was $250,000.

Instructions
(a) Journalize the transactions and the closing entries for net income and dividends.
(b) Enter the beginning balances, and post the entries to the stockholders' equity accounts. (*Note:* Open additional stockholders' equity accounts as needed.)
(c) Prepare a stockholders' equity section at December 31.

(c) Total stockholders' equity
$1,870,000

P11-5B On December 31, 2014, Andes Company had 1,500,000 shares of $10 par common stock issued and outstanding. The stockholders' equity accounts at December 31, 2014, had the following balances.

Prepare retained earnings statement and stockholders' equity section.

(LO 6, 7)

Common Stock	$15,000,000
Additional Paid-in Capital	1,500,000
Retained Earnings	900,000

Transactions during 2015 and other information related to stockholders' equity accounts were as follows.

1. On January 10, 2015, Andes issued at $105 per share 100,000 shares of $100 par value, 8% cumulative preferred stock.
2. On February 8, 2015, Andes reacquired 20,000 shares of its common stock for $14 per share.
3. On May 15, 2015, Andes declared the yearly cash dividend on preferred stock, payable June 10, 2015, to stockholders of record on May 15, 2015.
4. On June 8, 2015, Andes declared a cash dividend of $1 per share on the common stock outstanding, payable on July 10, 2015, to stockholders of record on July 1, 2015.
5. Net income for the year is $3,600,000.
6. It was discovered that depreciation expense had been understated in 2014 by $65,000.

Instructions
(a) Prepare a retained earnings statement for the year ended December 31, 2015.
(b) Prepare the stockholders' equity section of Andes' balance sheet at December 31, 2015.

(b) Total stockholders' equity
$28,875,000

P11-6B The ledger of Giffin Corporation at December 31, 2015, after the books have been closed, contains the following stockholders' equity accounts.

Prepare retained earnings statement and stockholders' equity section, and compute allocation of dividends.

(LO 5, 6, 7)

Preferred Stock (10,000 shares issued)	$1,000,000
Common Stock (400,000 shares issued)	2,000,000
Paid-in Capital in Excess of Par—Preferred Stock	200,000
Paid-in Capital in Excess of Stated Value—Common Stock	1,180,000
Common Stock Dividends Distributable	200,000
Retained Earnings	2,560,000

A review of the accounting records reveals the following.

1. No errors have been made in recording 2015 transactions or in preparing the closing entry for net income.
2. Preferred stock is 6%, $100 par value, noncumulative, and callable at $125. Since January 1, 2014, 10,000 shares have been outstanding; 20,000 shares are authorized.
3. Common stock is no-par with a stated value of $5 per share; 600,000 shares are authorized.
4. The January 1 balance in Retained Earnings was $2,450,000.
5. On October 1, 100,000 shares of common stock were sold for cash at $8 per share.
6. A cash dividend of $500,000 was declared and properly allocated to preferred and common stock on November 1. No dividends were paid to preferred stockholders in 2014.
7. On December 31, a 10% common stock dividend was declared out of retained earnings on common stock when the market price per share was $9.
8. Net income for the year was $970,000.
9. On December 31, 2015, the directors authorized disclosure of a $100,000 restriction of retained earnings for plant expansion. (Use Note A.)

Instructions

(c) Total stockholders' equity
$7,140,000

(a) Reproduce the Retained Earnings account (T-account) for 2015.
(b) Prepare a retained earnings statement for 2015.
(c) Prepare a stockholders' equity section at December 31, 2015.
(d) Compute the allocation of the cash dividend to preferred and common stock.

Prepare stockholders' equity section; compute book value per share.

(LO 7, 9)

*P11-7B The following stockholders' equity accounts arranged alphabetically are in the ledger of Crivello Corporation at December 31, 2015.

Common Stock ($3 stated value)	$2,400,000
Paid-in Capital from Treasury Stock	10,000
Paid-in Capital in Excess of Par—Preferred Stock	220,000
Paid-in Capital in Excess of Stated Value—Common Stock	1,600,000
Preferred Stock (8%, $50 par, noncumulative)	800,000
Retained Earnings	1,448,000
Treasury Stock—Common (10,000 shares)	75,000

Instructions

(a) Total stockholders' equity
$6,403,000

(a) Prepare a stockholders' equity section at December 31, 2015.
(b) Compute the book value per share of the common stock, assuming the preferred stock has a call price of $60 per share.

PROBLEMS: SET C

Visit the book's companion website, at **www.wiley.com/college/weygandt**, and choose the Student Companion site to access Problem Set C.

CONTINUING COOKIE CHRONICLE

(*Note:* This is a continuation of the Cookie Chronicle from Chapters 1 through 10.)

CCC11 After establishing their company's fiscal year-end to be October 31, Natalie and Curtis began operating Cookie & Coffee Creations Inc. on November 1, 2015. On that date, they issued both preferred and common stock. After the first year of operations, Natalie and Curtis want to prepare financial information for the year.

Go to the book's companion website, **www.wiley.com/college/weygandt**, *to see the completion of this problem.*

Broadening Your **PERSPECTIVE**

Financial Reporting and Analysis

Financial Reporting Problem: Apple Inc.

BYP11-1 The stockholders' equity section for Apple Inc. is shown in Appendix A. Instructions for accessing and using the company's complete annual report, including the notes to the financial statements, are also provided in Appendix A.

Instructions
(a) What is the par or stated value per share of Apple's common stock?
(b) What percentage of Apple's authorized common stock was issued at September 24, 2011?
(c) What amount, if any, did Apple declare in dividends on common stock in the year ended September 24, 2011?

Comparative Analysis Problem:
PepsiCo, Inc. vs. The Coca-Cola Company

BYP11-2 PepsiCo, Inc.'s financial statements are presented in Appendix B. Financial statements of The Coca-Cola Company are presented in Appendix C. Instructions for accessing and using the complete annual reports of PepsiCo and Coca-Cola, including the notes to the financial statements, are also provided in Appendices B and C, respectively.

Instructions
(a) What percentage of authorized shares was issued by Coca-Cola at December 31, 2011, and by PepsiCo at December 31, 2011?
(b) How many shares are held as treasury stock by Coca-Cola at December 31, 2011, and by PepsiCo at December 31, 2011?
(c) How many Coca-Cola common shares are outstanding at December 31, 2011? How many PepsiCo shares of common stock are outstanding at December 31, 2011?
(d) Compute earnings per share and return on common stockholders' equity for both companies for 2011. Assume PepsiCo's weighted-average shares were 1,580 million and Coca-Cola's weighted-average shares were 2,284 million. Can these measures be used to compare the profitability of the two companies? Why or why not?
(e) What was the total amount of dividends paid by each company in 2011?

Comparative Analysis Problem:
Amazon.com, Inc. vs. Wal-Mart Stores, Inc.

BYP11-3 Amazon.com, Inc.'s financial statements are presented in Appendix D. Financial statements of Wal-Mart Stores, Inc. are presented in Appendix E. Instructions for accessing and using the complete annual reports of Amazon and Wal-Mart, including the notes to the financial statements, are also provided in Appendices D and E, respectively.

Instructions
(a) What percentage of authorized shares was issued by Amazon at December 31, 2011, and by Wal-Mart at January 31, 2012?
(b) How many shares are held as treasury stock by Amazon at December 31, 2011, and by Wal-Mart at January 31, 2012?
(c) How many Amazon common shares are outstanding at December 31, 2011? How many Wal-Mart shares of common stock are outstanding at January 31, 2012?
(d) What are the basic earnings per share for both Amazon and Wal-Mart as of December 31, 2011, and January 31, 2012, respectively?
(e) What was the total amount of dividends, if any, paid by Amazon for the year ending December 31, 2011? What was the total dividends paid by Wal-Mart for the year ending January 31, 2012?

Real-World Focus

BYP11-4 Use the stockholders' equity section of an annual report and identify the major components.

Address: **www.annualreports.com**, or go to **www.wiley.com/college/weygandt**

Steps
1. From the Annual Reports Homepage, choose **Search by Alphabet**, and choose a letter.
2. Select a particular company.
3. Choose Annual Report.
4. Follow instructions below.

Instructions
Answer the following questions.

(a) What is the company's name?
(b) What classes of capital stock has the company issued?
(c) For each class of stock:
    (1) How many shares are authorized, issued, and/or outstanding?
    (2) What is the par value?
(d) What are the company's retained earnings?
(e) Has the company acquired treasury stock? How many shares?

Critical Thinking

Decision-Making Across the Organization

BYP11-5 The stockholders' meeting for Percival Corporation has been in progress for some time. The chief financial officer for Percival is presently reviewing the company's financial statements and is explaining the items that comprise the stockholders' equity section of the balance sheet for the current year. The stockholders' equity section of Percival Corporation at December 31, 2015, is as follows.

PERCIVAL CORPORATION
Balance Sheet (partial)
December 31, 2015

Paid-in capital		
Capital stock		
Preferred stock, authorized 1,000,000 shares		
cumulative, $100 par value, $8 per share, 6,000		
shares issued and outstanding		$ 600,000
Common stock, authorized 5,000,000 shares, $1 par		
value, 3,000,000 shares issued, and 2,700,000		
outstanding		3,000,000
Total capital stock		3,600,000
Additional paid-in capital		
In excess of par—preferred stock	$ 50,000	
In excess of par—common stock	25,000,000	
Total additional paid-in capital		25,050,000
Total paid-in capital		28,650,000
Retained earnings		900,000
Total paid-in capital and retained earnings		29,550,000
Less: Treasury stock (300,000 common shares)		9,300,000
Total stockholders' equity		$20,250,000

At the meeting, stockholders have raised a number of questions regarding the stockholders' equity section.

Instructions

With the class divided into groups, answer the following questions as if you were the chief financial officer for Percival Corporation.

(a) "What does the cumulative provision related to the preferred stock mean?"

(b) "I thought the common stock was presently selling at $29.75, but the company has the stock stated at $1 per share. How can that be?"

(c) "Why is the company buying back its common stock? Furthermore, the treasury stock has a debit balance because it is subtracted from stockholders' equity. Why is treasury stock not reported as an asset if it has a debit balance?"

Communication Activity

BYP11-6 Joe Moyer, your uncle, is an inventor who has decided to incorporate. Uncle Joe knows that you are an accounting major at U.N.O. In a recent letter to you, he ends with the question, "I'm filling out a state incorporation application. Can you tell me the difference in the following terms: (1) authorized stock, (2) issued stock, (3) outstanding stock, and (4) preferred stock?"

Instructions

In a brief note, differentiate for Uncle Joe among the four different stock terms. Write the letter to be friendly, yet professional.

Ethics Case

BYP11-7 The R&D division of Piqua Chemical Corp. has just developed a chemical for sterilizing the vicious Brazilian "killer bees" which are invading Mexico and the southern United States. The president of the company is anxious to get the chemical on the market to boost the company's profits. He believes his job is in jeopardy because of decreasing sales and profits. The company has an opportunity to sell this chemical in Central American countries, where the laws are much more relaxed than in the United States.

The director of Piqua's R&D division strongly recommends further testing in the laboratory for side-effects of this chemical on other insects, birds, animals, plants, and even humans. He cautions the president, "We could be sued from all sides if the chemical has tragic side-effects that we didn't even test for in the labs." The president answers, "We can't wait an additional year for your lab tests. We can avoid losses from such lawsuits by establishing a separate wholly owned corporation to shield Piqua Corp. from such lawsuits. We can't lose any more than our investment in the new corporation, and we'll invest in just the patent covering this chemical. We'll reap the benefits if the chemical works and is safe, and avoid the losses from lawsuits if it's a disaster." The following week, Piqua creates a new wholly owned corporation called Finlay Inc., sells the chemical patent to it for $10, and watches the spraying begin.

Instructions

(a) Who are the stakeholders in this situation?

(b) Are the president's motives and actions ethical?

(c) Can Piqua shield itself against losses of Finlay Inc.?

All About You

BYP11-8 A high percentage of Americans own stock in corporations. As a shareholder in a corporation, you will receive an annual report. One of the goals of this course is for you to learn how to navigate your way around an annual report.

Instructions

Use Apple's 2011 annual report (see Appendix A) to answer the following questions.

(a) What CPA firm performed the audit of Apple's financial statements?

(b) What was the amount of Apple's earnings per share in 2011?

(c) What were net sales in 2011?

(d) How much cash did Apple spend on capital expenditures in 2011?

(e) Over what life does the company depreciate its buildings?

(f) What were the proceeds from issuance of common stock in 2011?

FASB Codification Activity

BYP11-9 If your school has a subscription to the FASB Codification, go to **http://aaahq.org/ ascLogin.cfm** to log in and prepare responses to the following.

(a) What is the stock dividend?

(b) What is a stock split?

(c) At what percentage point does the issuance of additional shares qualify as a stock dividend, as opposed to a stock split?

Answers to Chapter Questions

Answers to Insight and Accounting Across the Organization Questions

p. 547 A Thousand Millionaires! Q: Why did Mark Zuckerberg, the CEO and founder of Facebook, delay taking his company's shares public through an initial public offering (IPO)? **A:** Facebook did not need to invest in factories, distribution systems, or even marketing, so it did not need to raise a lot of cash. Also, by delaying the decision to go public, Zuckerberg had more control over the direction of the company. In addition, publicly traded companies face many more financial reporting disclosure requirements.

p. 550 How to Read Stock Quotes Q: For stocks traded on organized exchanges, how are the dollar prices per share established? **A:** The dollar prices per share are established by the interaction between buyers and sellers of the shares.   **Q:** What factors might influence the price of shares in the marketplace? **A:** The price of shares is influenced by a company's earnings and dividends as well as by factors beyond a company's control, such as changes in interest rates, labor strikes, scarcity of supplies or resources, and politics. The number of willing buyers and sellers (demand and supply) also plays a part in the price of shares.

p. 553 The Impact of Corporate Social Responsibility Q: Why are CSR-related shareholder proposals increasing? **A:** The increase in shareholder proposals reflects a growing belief that a company's social and environmental policies correlate strongly with its risk-management strategy and ultimately its financial performance.

p. 558 Why Did Reebok Buy Its Own Stock? Q: What signal might a large stock repurchase send to investors regarding management's belief about the company's growth opportunities? **A:** When a company has many growth opportunities, it will normally conserve its cash in order to be better able to fund expansion. A large use of cash to buy back stock (and essentially shrink the company) would suggest that management was not optimistic about its growth opportunities.

p. 568 A No-Split Philosophy Q: Why does Warren Buffett usually oppose stock splits? **A:** Buffett prefers to attract shareholders who will make a long-term commitment to his company, as opposed to traders who will only hold their investment for a short period of time. He believes that a high stock price discourages short-term investment.

Answers to Self-Test Questions

1. c **2.** b **3.** d **4.** c **5.** a **6.** a **7.** d **8.** d **9.** a **10.** c **11.** c **12.** b **13.** c **14.** b **15.** b $186,000 − (6% × $100 × 10,000) = $126,000 ***16** a ***17** c

A Look at IFRS

LEARNING OBJECTIVE 10
Compare the accounting procedures for stockholders' equity under GAAP and IFRS.

The accounting for transactions related to stockholders' equity, such as issuance of shares and purchase of treasury stock, are similar under both IFRS and GAAP. Major differences relate to terminology used, introduction of items such as revaluation surplus, and presentation of stockholders' equity information.

Key Points

- Under IFRS, the term **reserves** is used to describe all equity accounts other than those arising from contributed (paid-in) capital. This would include, for example, reserves related to retained earnings, asset revaluations, and fair value differences.

- Many countries have a different mix of investor groups than in the United States. For example, in Germany, financial institutions like banks are not only major creditors of corporations but often are the largest corporate stockholders as well. In the United States, Asia, and the United Kingdom, many companies rely on substantial investment from private investors.
- There are often terminology differences for equity accounts. The following summarizes some of the common differences in terminology.

GAAP	IFRS
Common stock	Share capital—ordinary
Stockholders	Shareholders
Par value	Nominal or face value
Authorized stock	Authorized share capital
Preferred stock	Share capital—preference
Paid-in capital	Issued/allocated share capital
Paid-in capital in excess of par—common stock	Share premium—ordinary
Paid-in capital in excess of par—preferred stock	Share premium—preference
Retained earnings	Retained earnings or Retained profits
Retained earnings deficit	Accumulated losses
Accumulated other comprehensive income	General reserve and other reserve accounts

As an example of how similar transactions use different terminology under IFRS, consider the accounting for the issuance of 1,000 shares of $1 par value common stock for $5 per share. Under IFRS, the entry is as follows.

Cash	5,000	
Share Capital—Ordinary		1,000
Share Premium—Ordinary		4,000

- The accounting for treasury stock differs somewhat between IFRS and GAAP. (However, many of the differences are beyond the scope of this course.) Like GAAP, IFRS does not allow a company to record gains or losses on purchases of its own shares. One difference worth noting is that, when a company purchases its own shares, IFRS treats it as a reduction of stockholders' equity, but it does not specify which particular stockholders' equity accounts are to be affected. Therefore, it could be shown as an increase to a contra equity account (Treasury Stock) or a decrease to retained earnings or share capital.
- A major difference between IFRS and GAAP relates to the account Revaluation Surplus. Revaluation surplus arises under IFRS because companies are permitted to revalue their property, plant, and equipment to fair value under certain circumstances. This account is part of general reserves under IFRS and is not considered contributed capital.
- IFRS often uses terms such as **retained profits** or **accumulated profit or loss** to describe retained earnings. The term **retained earnings** is also often used.
- The accounting related to prior period adjustment is essentially the same under IFRS and GAAP. IFRS addresses the accounting for errors in *IAS 8* ("Accounting Policies, Changes in Accounting Estimates, and Errors"). One area where IFRS and GAAP differ in reporting relates to error corrections in previously issued financial statements. While IFRS requires restatement with some exceptions, GAAP does not permit any exceptions.
- Equity is given various descriptions under IFRS, such as shareholders' equity, owners' equity, capital and reserves, and shareholders' funds.
- The income statement using IFRS is called the **statement of comprehensive income**. A statement of comprehensive income is presented in a one- or two-statement format. The single-statement approach includes all items of income and expense, as well as each component of other comprehensive income or loss by its individual characteristic. In the two-statement approach, a traditional income statement is prepared. It is then followed by a statement of comprehensive income, which starts with net income or loss and then adds other comprehensive income or loss items. Regardless of which approach is reported, income tax expense is required to be reported.
- The computations related to earnings per share are essentially the same under IFRS and GAAP.

Looking to the Future

The IASB and the FASB are currently working on a project related to financial statement presentation. An important part of this study is to determine whether certain line items, subtotals, and totals should be clearly defined and required to be displayed in the financial statements. For example, it is likely that the statement of stockholders' equity and its presentation will be examined closely.

Both the IASB and FASB are working toward convergence of any remaining differences related to earnings per share computations. This convergence will deal with highly technical changes beyond the scope of this textbook.

IFRS Practice

IFRS Self-Test Questions

1. Under IFRS, a purchase by a company of its own shares is recorded by:
   (a) an increase in Treasury Stock.
   (b) a decrease in contributed capital.
   (c) a decrease in share capital.
   (d) All of these are acceptable treatments.

2. Which of the following is **true**?
   (a) In the United States, the primary corporate stockholders are financial institutions.
   (b) Share capital means total assets under IFRS.
   (c) The IASB and FASB are presently studying how financial statement information should be presented.
   (d) The accounting for treasury stock differs extensively between GAAP and IFRS.

3. Under IFRS, the amount of capital received in excess of par value would be credited to:
   (a) Retained Earnings.
   (b) Contributed Capital.
   (c) Share Premium.
   (d) Par value is not used under IFRS.

4. Which of the following is **false**?
   (a) Under GAAP, companies cannot record gains on transactions involving their own shares.
   (b) Under IFRS, companies cannot record gains on transactions involving their own shares.
   (c) Under IFRS, the statement of stockholders' equity is a required statement.
   (d) Under IFRS, a company records a revaluation surplus when it experiences an increase in the price of its common stock.

5. Which of the following does **not** represent a pair of GAAP/IFRS-comparable terms?
   (a) Additional paid-in capital/Share premium.
   (b) Treasury stock/Repurchase reserve.
   (c) Common stock/Share capital.
   (d) Preferred stock/Preference shares.

6. The basic accounting for cash dividends and stock dividends:
   (a) is different under IFRS versus GAAP.
   (b) is the same under IFRS and GAAP.
   (c) differs only for the accounting for cash dividends between GAAP and IFRS.
   (d) differs only for the accounting for stock dividends between GAAP and IFRS.

7. Which item in **not** considered part of reserves?
   (a) Unrealized loss on available-for-sale investments.
   (b) Revaluation surplus.
   (c) Retained earnings.
   (d) Issued shares.

8. Under IFRS, a statement of comprehensive income must include:
   (a) accounts payable.
   (b) retained earnings.
   (c) income tax expense.
   (d) preference stock.

9. Which set of terms can be used to describe total stockholders' equity under IFRS?
   (a) Shareholders' equity, capital and reserves, other comprehensive income.
   (b) Capital and reserves, shareholders' equity, shareholders' funds.
   (c) Capital and reserves, retained earnings, shareholders' equity.
   (d) All of the above.

10. Earnings per share computations related to IFRS and GAAP:
   (a) are essentially similar.
   (b) result in an amount referred to as earnings per share.
   (c) must deduct preferred (preference) dividends when computing earnings per share.
   (d) All of the above.

IFRS Exercises

IFRS11-1 On May 10, Jaurez Corporation issues 1,000 shares of $10 par value ordinary shares for cash at $18 per share. Journalize the issuance of the shares.

IFRS11-2 Meenen Corporation has the following accounts at December 31 (in euros): Share Capital—Ordinary, €10 par, 5,000 shares issued, €50,000; Share Premium—Ordinary €10,000; Retained Earnings €45,000; and Treasury Shares—Ordinary, 500 shares, €11,000. Prepare the equity section of the statement of financial position (balance sheet).

IFRS11-3 Overton Co. had the following transactions during the current period.

Mar. 2   Issued 5,000 shares of $1 par value ordinary shares to attorneys in payment of a bill for $30,000 for services provided in helping the company to incorporate.
June 12 Issued 60,000 shares of $1 par value ordinary shares for cash of $375,000.
July 11 Issued 1,000 shares of $100 par value preference shares for cash at $110 per share.
Nov. 28 Purchased 2,000 treasury shares for $80,000.

Instructions
Journalize the above transactions.

International Financial Reporting Problem: Zetar plc

IFRS11-4 The financial statements of Zetar plc are presented in Appendix F. Instructions for accessing and using the company's complete annual report, including the notes to its financial statements, are also provided in Appendix F.

Instructions
Use the company's annual report to answer the following questions.
(a) Using the information in the statement of changes in equity, prepare the journal entry to record the issuance of ordinary shares during the year ended April 30, 2010.
(b) Examine the equity section of the company's balance sheet. For each item in the equity section, provide the comparable label that would be used under GAAP.
(c) Did the company declare and pay any dividends for the year ended April 30, 2011?
(d) Compute the company's return on ordinary shareholders' equity for the year ended April 30, 2011.
(e) What was Zetar's earnings per share for the year ended April 30, 2011?

Answers to IFRS Self-Test Questions
1. d   2. c   3. c   4. d   5. b   6. b   7. d   8. c   9. b   10. d

 The Navigator

12 | Investments

Feature Story

"Is There Anything Else We Can Buy?"

In a rapidly changing world, you must keep up or suffer the consequences. In business, change requires investment.

A case in point is found in the entertainment industry. Technology is bringing about innovations so quickly that it is nearly impossible to guess which will last and which will soon fade away. For example, will both satellite TV and cable TV survive? Or, will both be replaced by something else?

Consider the publishing industry as well. Will paper newspapers and magazines be replaced completely by online news? If you are a publisher, you have to make your best guess about what the future holds and invest accordingly.

Time Warner Inc. lives at the center of this arena. It is not an environment for the timid, and Time Warner's philosophy is anything but that. Instead, it might be characterized as, "If we can't beat you, we will buy

you." Its mantra is "invest, invest, invest." A partial list of Time Warner's holdings gives an idea of its reach:

> ***Magazines:*** *People, Time, Life, Sports Illustrated,* and *Fortune.*
>
> ***Book publishers:*** Time-Life Books; Book-of-the-Month Club; Little, Brown & Co; and Sunset Books.
>
> ***Television and movies:*** Warner Bros. ("The Big Bang Theory" and "The Mentalist"), HBO, and movies like *Harry Potter and the Deathly Hollows: Part 2* and *The Dark Knight Rises.*
>
> ***Broadcasting:*** TNT, CNN news, and Turner's library of thousands of classic movies.
>
> ***Internet:*** America Online and AOL Anywhere.

Time Warner owns more information and entertainment copyrights and brands than any other company in the world.

The merger of America Online (AOL) with Time Warner, one of the biggest mergers ever, was originally perceived by many as the gateway to the future. In actuality, it was a financial disaster. It is largely responsible for much of the decline in Time Warner's stock price,

- ■ Scan Learning Objectives
- ■ Read Feature Story
- ■ Read Preview
- ■ Read text and answer **DO IT!** p. 608
  - ■ p. 613　■ p. 617　■ p. 620
- ■ Work Comprehensive **DO IT!** p. 622
- ■ Review Summary of Learning Objectives
- ■ Answer Self-Test Questions
- ■ Complete Assignments
- ■ Go to *WileyPLUS* for practice and tutorials
- 🌐 Read **A Look at IFRS** p. 645

Learning Objectives ✔ The Navigator

After studying this chapter, you should be able to:

[1] Discuss why corporations invest in debt and stock securities.

[2] Explain the accounting for debt investments.

[3] Explain the accounting for stock investments.

[4] Describe the use of consolidated financial statements.

[5] Indicate how debt and stock investments are reported in financial statements.

[6] Distinguish between short-term and long-term investments.

Warner Bros/Photofest

from a high of $95.80 to a level of $32. Ted Turner, who was at one time Time Warner's largest shareholder, lost billions of dollars on the deal and eventually sold most of his shares. In 2009, Time Warner completed a spin-off of AOL after years of trying to integrate the two companies. One analyst called the failed deal "a nine-year adventure akin to a marathon through mud."

Preview of Chapter 12

 ✔ **The Navigator**

Time Warner's management believes in aggressive growth through investing in the stock of existing companies. Besides purchasing stock, companies also purchase other securities such as bonds issued by corporations or by governments. Companies can make investments for a short or long period of time, as a passive investment, or with the intent to control another company. As you will see in this chapter, the way in which a company accounts for its investments is determined by a number of factors.

The content and organization of Chapter 12 are as follows.

INVESTMENTS			
Why Corporations Invest	**Accounting for Debt Investments**	**Accounting for Stock Investments**	**Valuing and Reporting Investments**
• Cash management • Investment income • Strategic reasons	• Recording acquisition of bonds • Recording bond interest • Recording sale of bonds	• Holdings of less than 20% • Holdings between 20% and 50% • Holdings of more than 50%	• Categories of securities • Balance sheet presentation • Realized and unrealized gain or loss • Classified balance sheet

Why Corporations Invest

LEARNING OBJECTIVE   **1**

Discuss why corporations invest in debt and stock securities.

Corporations purchase investments in debt or stock securities generally for one of three reasons. First, a corporation may **have excess cash** that it does not need for the immediate purchase of operating assets. For example, many companies experience seasonal fluctuations in sales. A Cape Cod marina has more sales in the spring and summer than in the fall and winter. The reverse is true for an Aspen ski shop. Thus, at the end of an operating cycle, many companies may have cash on hand that is temporarily idle until the start of another operating cycle. These companies may invest the excess funds to earn—through interest and dividends—a greater return than they would get by just holding the funds in the bank. The role that such temporary investments play in the operating cycle is shown in Illustration 12-1.

Illustration 12-1
Temporary investments and the operating cycle

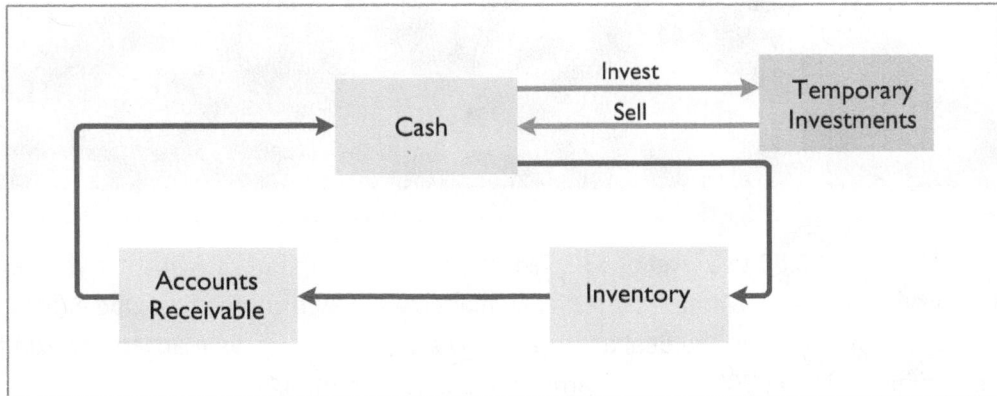

Excess cash may also result from economic cycles. For example, when the economy is booming, General Electric generates considerable excess cash. It uses some of this cash to purchase new plant and equipment, and pays out some of the cash in dividends. But, it may also invest excess cash in liquid assets in anticipation of a future downturn in the economy. It can then liquidate these investments during a recession, when sales slow and cash is scarce.

When investing excess cash for short periods of time, corporations invest in low-risk, highly liquid securities—most often short-term government securities. It is generally not wise to invest short-term excess cash in shares of common stock because stock investments can experience rapid price changes. If you did invest your short-term excess cash in stock and the price of the stock declined significantly just before you needed cash again, you would be forced to sell your stock investment at a loss.

A second reason some companies purchase investments is to generate **earnings from investment income**. For example, banks make most of their earnings by lending money, but they also generate earnings by investing in debt. Conversely, mutual stock funds invest primarily in equity securities in order to benefit from stock-price appreciation and dividend revenue.

Third, companies also invest for **strategic reasons**. A company can exercise some influence over a customer or supplier by purchasing a significant, but not controlling, interest in that company. Or, a company may purchase a noncontrolling interest in another company in a related industry in which it wishes to establish a presence. For example, Time Warner initially purchased an interest of less than 20% in Turner Broadcasting to have a stake in Turner's expanding business opportunities. At a later date, Time Warner acquired the remaining 80%. Subsequently, Time Warner merged with AOL and became AOL Time Warner, Inc. Now, it is again just Time Warner Inc., as indicated in the Feature Story.

A corporation may also choose to purchase a controlling interest in another company. For example, as the *Accounting Across the Organization* box on page 612 shows, Procter & Gamble purchased Gillette. Such purchases might be done to enter a new industry without incurring the tremendous costs and risks associated with starting from scratch. Or, a company might purchase another company in its same industry.

In summary, businesses invest in other companies for the reasons shown in Illustration 12-2.

Reason	Typical Investment
To house excess cash until needed	Low-risk, highly liquid, short-term securities such as government-issued securities
To generate earnings	Debt securities (banks and other financial institutions) and stock securities (mutual funds and pension funds)
To meet strategic goals	Stocks of companies in a related industry or in an unrelated industry that the company wishes to enter

Illustration 12-2
Why corporations invest

Accounting for Debt Investments

Debt investments are investments in government and corporation bonds. In accounting for debt investments, companies make entries to record (1) the acquisition, (2) the interest revenue, and (3) the sale.

LEARNING OBJECTIVE 2

Explain the accounting for debt investments.

Recording Acquisition of Bonds

At acquisition, debt investments are recorded at cost. Cost includes all expenditures necessary to acquire these investments, such as the price paid plus brokerage fees (commissions), if any.

For example, assume that Kuhl Corporation acquires 50 Doan Inc. 8%, 10-year, $1,000 bonds on January 1, 2015, for $50,000. Kuhl records the investment as:

Jan. 1	Debt Investments	50,000	
	Cash		50,000
	(To record purchase of 50 Doan Inc. bonds)		

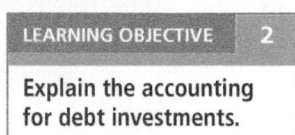

A = L + SE
+50,000
−50,000

Cash Flows
−50,000

Recording Bond Interest

The Doan Inc. bonds pay interest of $2,000 semiannually on July 1 and January 1 ($50,000 × 8% × ½). The entry for the receipt of interest on July 1 is:

July 1	Cash	2,000	
	Interest Revenue		2,000
	(To record receipt of interest on Doan Inc. bonds)		

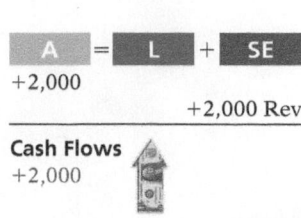

A = L + SE
+2,000
+2,000 Rev

Cash Flows
+2,000

If Kuhl Corporation's fiscal year ends on December 31, it accrues the interest of $2,000 earned since July 1. The adjusting entry is:

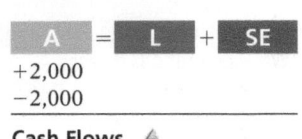

Cash Flows
no effect

Dec. 31	Interest Receivable	2,000	
	Interest Revenue		2,000
	(To accrue interest on Doan Inc. bonds)		

Kuhl reports Interest Receivable as a current asset in the balance sheet. It reports Interest Revenue under "Other revenues and gains" in the income statement.

Kuhl reports receipt of the interest on January 1 as follows.

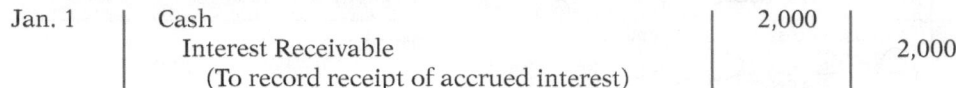

Cash Flows
+2,000

Jan. 1	Cash	2,000	
	Interest Receivable		2,000
	(To record receipt of accrued interest)		

A credit to Interest Revenue at this time is incorrect because the company earned and accrued interest revenue in the **preceding** accounting period.

Recording Sale of Bonds

When Kuhl sells the bonds, it credits the investment account for the cost of the bonds. Kuhl records as a gain or loss any difference between the net proceeds from the sale (sales price less brokerage fees) and the cost of the bonds.

Assume, for example, that Kuhl Corporation receives net proceeds of $54,000 on the sale of the Doan Inc. bonds on January 1, 2016, after receiving the interest due. Since the securities cost $50,000, the company realizes a gain of $4,000. It records the sale as:

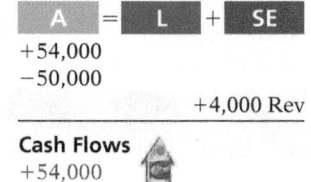

Cash Flows
+54,000

Jan. 1	Cash	54,000	
	Debt Investments		50,000
	Gain on Sale of Debt Investments		4,000
	(To record sale of Doan Inc. bonds)		

Kuhl reports the gain on sale of debt investments under "Other revenues and gains" in the income statement and reports losses under "Other expenses and losses."

> DO IT!

Debt Investments

Waldo Corporation had the following transactions pertaining to debt investments.

Jan. 1   Purchased 30, $1,000 Hillary Co. 10% bonds for $30,000. Interest is payable semiannually on July 1 and January 1.
July 1   Received semiannual interest on Hillary Co. bonds.
July 1   Sold 15 Hillary Co. bonds for $14,600.

(a) Journalize the transactions, and (b) prepare the adjusting entry for the accrual of interest on December 31.

Solution

(a) Jan. 1	Debt Investments	30,000	
	Cash		30,000
	(To record purchase of 30 Hillary Co. bonds)		

Action Plan

✔ Record bond investments at cost.

✔ Record interest when received and/or accrued.

✔ When bonds are sold, credit the investment account for the cost of the bonds.

✔ Record any difference between the cost and the net proceeds as a gain or loss.

July 1	Cash		1,500	
	Interest Revenue ($30,000 × 10% × 6/12)			1,500
	(To record receipt of interest on Hillary Co. bonds)			
July 1	Cash		14,600	
	Loss on Sale of Debt Investments		400	
	Debt Investments ($30,000 × 15/30)			15,000
	(To record sale of 15 Hillary Co. bonds)			
(b) Dec. 31	Interest Receivable		750	
	Interest Revenue ($15,000 × 10% × 6/12)			750
	(To accrue interest on Hillary Co. bonds)			

Related exercise material: BE12-1, E12-2, E12-3, **and** DO IT! 12-1.

✔ **The Navigator**

Accounting for Stock Investments

Stock investments are investments in the capital stock of other corporations. When a company holds stock (and/or debt) of several different corporations, the group of securities is identified as an **investment portfolio**.

The accounting for investments in common stock depends on the extent of the investor's influence over the operating and financial affairs of the issuing corporation (the **investee**). Illustration 12-3 shows the general guidelines.

LEARNING OBJECTIVE   3

Explain the accounting for stock investments.

Investor's Ownership Interest in Investee's Common Stock	Presumed Influence on Investee	Accounting Guidelines
Less than 20%	Insignificant	Cost method
Between 20% and 50%	Significant	Equity method
More than 50%	Controlling	Consolidated financial statements

Illustration 12-3
Accounting guidelines for stock investments

Companies are required to use judgment instead of blindly following the guidelines.[1] We explain the application of each guideline next.

Holdings of Less than 20%

In accounting for stock investments of less than 20%, companies use the cost method. Under the **cost method**, companies record the investment at cost and recognize revenue only when cash dividends are received.

Helpful Hint
The entries for investments in common stock also apply to investments in preferred stock.

---

[1] Among the questions that are considered in determining an investor's influence are these: (1) Does the investor have representation on the investee's board? (2) Does the investor participate in the investee's policy-making process? (3) Are there material transactions between the investor and investee? (4) Is the common stock held by other stockholders concentrated or dispersed?

RECORDING ACQUISITION OF STOCK INVESTMENTS

At acquisition, stock investments are recorded at cost. Cost includes all expenditures necessary to acquire these investments, such as the price paid plus any brokerage fees (commissions), if any.

For example, assume that on July 1, 2015, Sanchez Corporation acquires 1,000 shares (10% ownership) of Beal Corporation common stock. Sanchez pays $40 per share. The entry for the purchase is:

+40,000
−40,000
_____
Cash Flows
−40,000

July 1	Stock Investments	40,000	
	Cash		40,000
	(To record purchase of 1,000 shares of		
	Beal Corporation common stock)		

RECORDING DIVIDENDS

During the time Sanchez owns the stock, it makes entries for any cash dividends received. If Sanchez receives a $2 per share dividend on December 31, the entry is:

+2,000
_____
+2,000 Rev
_____
Cash Flows
+2,000

Dec. 31	Cash (1,000 × $2)	2,000	
	Dividend Revenue		2,000
	(To record receipt of a cash dividend)		

Sanchez reports Dividend Revenue under "Other revenues and gains" in the income statement. Unlike interest on notes and bonds, dividends do not accrue. Therefore, companies do not make adjusting entries to accrue dividends.

RECORDING SALE OF STOCK

When a company sells a stock investment, it recognizes as a gain or a loss the difference between the net proceeds from the sale (sales price less brokerage fees) and the cost of the stock.

Assume that Sanchez Corporation receives net proceeds of $39,000 on the sale of its Beal stock on February 10, 2016. Because the stock cost $40,000, Sanchez incurred a loss of $1,000. The entry to record the sale is:

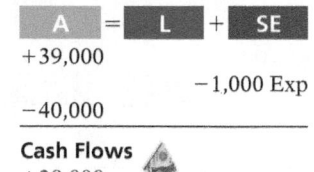

+39,000
_____
−1,000 Exp
_____
−40,000
_____
Cash Flows
+39,000

Feb. 10	Cash	39,000	
	Loss on Sale of Stock Investments	1,000	
	Stock Investments		40,000
	(To record sale of Beal common stock)		

Sanchez reports the loss under "Other expenses and losses" in the income statement. It would show a gain on sale under "Other revenues and gains."

Holdings Between 20% and 50%

When an investor company owns only a small portion of the shares of stock of another company, the investor cannot exercise control over the investee. But, when an investor owns between 20% and 50% of the common stock of a corporation, it is presumed that the investor has significant influence over the financial and operating activities of the investee. The investor probably has a representative on the investee's board of directors. Through that representative, the investor may exercise some control over the investee. The investee company in some sense becomes part of the investor company.

For example, even prior to purchasing all of Turner Broadcasting, Time Warner owned 20% of Turner. Because it exercised significant control over major decisions made by Turner, Time Warner used an approach called the equity method.

Under the equity method, **the investor records its share of the net income of the investee in the year when it is earned**. An alternative might be to delay recognizing the investor's share of net income until the investee declares a cash dividend. But, that approach would ignore the fact that the investor and investee are, in some sense, one company, making the investor better off by the investee's earned income.

Under the equity method, the investor company initially records the investment in common stock at cost. After that, it **adjusts** the investment account annually to show the investor's equity in the investee. Each year, the investor does the following. (1) It increases (debits) the investment account and increases (credits) revenue for its share of the investee's net income.[2] (2) The investor also decreases (credits) the investment account for the amount of dividends received. The investment account is reduced for dividends received because payment of a dividend decreases the net assets of the investee.

Helpful Hint
Under the equity method, the investor recognizes revenue on the accrual basis—i.e., when it is earned by the investee.

RECORDING ACQUISITION OF STOCK INVESTMENTS

Assume that Milar Corporation acquires 30% of the common stock of Beck Company for $120,000 on January 1, 2015. The entry to record this transaction is:

Jan. 1	Stock Investments	120,000	
	Cash		120,000
	(To record purchase of Beck common stock)		

A = L + SE
+120,000
−120,000

Cash Flows
−120,000

RECORDING REVENUE AND DIVIDENDS

For 2015, Beck reports net income of $100,000. It declares and pays a $40,000 cash dividend. Milar records (1) its share of Beck's income, $30,000 (30% × $100,000), and (2) the reduction in the investment account for the dividends received, $12,000 ($40,000 × 30%). The entries are:

(1)

Dec. 31	Stock Investments	30,000	
	Revenue from Stock Investments		30,000
	(To record 30% equity in Beck's 2015 net income)		

A = L + SE
+30,000
       +30,000 Rev

Cash Flows
no effect

(2)

Dec. 31	Cash	12,000	
	Stock Investments		12,000
	(To record dividends received)		

A = L + SE
+12,000
−12,000

Cash Flows
+12,000

After Milar posts the transactions for the year, its investment and revenue accounts will show the following.

Stock Investments				Revenue from Stock Investments		
Jan. 1	120,000	Dec. 31	12,000		Dec. 31	30,000
Dec. 31	30,000					
Dec. 31 Bal.	138,000					

Illustration 12-4
Investment and revenue accounts after posting

During the year, the net increase in the investment account was $18,000. As indicated above, the investment account increased by $30,000 due to Milar's share of Beck's income, and it decreased by $12,000 due to dividends received from Beck.

---

[2]Or, the investor increases (debits) a loss account and decreases (credits) the investment account for its share of the investee's net loss.

In addition, Milar reports $30,000 of revenue from its investment, which is 30% of Beck's net income of $100,000.

Note that the difference between reported revenue under the cost method and reported revenue under the equity method can be significant. For example, Milar would report only $12,000 of dividend revenue (30% × $40,000) if it used the cost method.

Holdings of More than 50%

LEARNING OBJECTIVE 4

Describe the use of consolidated financial statements.

A company that owns more than 50% of the common stock of another entity is known as the **parent company**. The entity whose stock the parent company owns is called the **subsidiary (affiliated) company**. Because of its stock ownership, the parent company has a **controlling interest** in the subsidiary.

When a company owns more than 50% of the common stock of another company, it usually prepares **consolidated financial statements**. These statements present the total assets and liabilities controlled by the parent company. They also present the total revenues and expenses of the subsidiary companies. Companies prepare consolidated statements **in addition to** the financial statements for the parent and individual subsidiary companies.

Helpful Hint
If parent (A) has three wholly owned subsidiaries (B, C, & D), there are four separate legal entities. From the viewpoint of the shareholders of the parent company, there is only one economic entity.

As noted earlier, when Time Warner had a 20% investment in Turner, it reported this investment in a single line item—Other Investments. After the merger, Time Warner instead consolidated Turner's results with its own. Under this approach, Time Warner included Turner's individual assets and liabilities with its own. Its plant and equipment were added to Time Warner's plant and equipment, its receivables were added to Time Warner's receivables, and so on.

ACCOUNTING ACROSS THE ORGANIZATION

How Procter & Gamble Accounts for Gillette

Several years ago, Procter & Gamble Company acquired Gillette Company for $53.4 billion. The common stockholders of Procter & Gamble elect the board of directors of the company, who, in turn, select the officers and managers of the company. Procter & Gamble's board of directors controls the property owned by the corporation, which includes the common stock of Gillette. Thus, they are in a position to elect the board of directors of Gillette and, in effect, control its operations. These relationships are graphically illustrated here.

© Stígur Karlsson/iStockphoto

 Where on Procter & Gamble's balance sheet will you find its investment in Gillette Company? (See page 645.)

Consolidated statements are useful to the stockholders, board of directors, and management of the parent company. These statements indicate the magnitude and scope of operations of the companies under common control. For example, regulators and the courts undoubtedly used the consolidated statements of AT&T to determine whether a breakup of the company was in the public interest. Illustration 12-5 lists three companies that prepare consolidated statements and some of the companies they have owned.

PepsiCo	Cendant	The Disney Company
Frito-Lay	Howard Johnson	Capital Cities/ABC, Inc.
Tropicana	Ramada Inn	Disneyland, Disney World
Quaker Oats	Century 21	Mighty Ducks
Pepsi-Cola	Coldwell Banker	Anaheim Angels
Gatorade	Avis	ESPN

Illustration 12-5
Examples of consolidated companies and their subsidiaries

> **DO IT!**

Stock Investments

Presented below are two independent situations.

1. Rho Jean Inc. acquired 5% of the 400,000 shares of common stock of Stillwater Corp. at a total cost of $6 per share on May 18, 2015. On August 30, Stillwater declared and paid a $75,000 dividend. On December 31, Stillwater reported net income of $244,000 for the year.

2. Debbie, Inc. obtained significant influence over North Sails by buying 40% of North Sails' 60,000 outstanding shares of common stock at a cost of $12 per share on January 1, 2015. On April 15, North Sails declared and paid a cash dividend of $45,000. On December 31, North Sails reported net income of $120,000 for the year.

Prepare all necessary journal entries for 2015 for (1) Rho Jean Inc. and (2) Debbie, Inc.

Solution

Action Plan

✔ Presume that the investor has relatively little influence over the investee when an investor owns less than 20% of the common stock of another corporation. In this case, net income earned by the investee is not considered a proper basis for recognizing income from the investment by the investor.

✔ Presume significant influence for investments of 20%–50%. Therefore, record the investor's share of the net income of the investee.

(1) May 18	Stock Investments (400,000 × 5% × $6)	120,000	
	Cash		120,000
	(To record purchase of 20,000 shares of Stillwater Co. stock)		
Aug. 30	Cash	3,750	
	Dividend Revenue ($75,000 × 5%)		3,750
	(To record receipt of cash dividend)		
(2) Jan. 1	Stock Investments (60,000 × 40% × $12)	288,000	
	Cash		288,000
	(To record purchase of 24,000 shares of North Sails' stock)		
Apr. 15	Cash	18,000	
	Stock Investments ($45,000 × 40%)		18,000
	(To record receipt of cash dividend)		
Dec. 31	Stock Investments ($120,000 × 40%)	48,000	
	Revenue from Stock Investments		48,000
	(To record 40% equity in North Sails' net income)		

Related exercise material: BE12-2, BE12-3, E12-4, E12-5, E12-6, E12-7, E12-8, **and** DO IT! 12-2.

 The Navigator

Valuing and Reporting Investments

LEARNING OBJECTIVE   5

Indicate how debt and stock investments are reported in financial statements.

The value of debt and stock investments may fluctuate greatly during the time they are held. For example, in one 12-month period, the stock price of Time Warner hit a high of $58.50 and a low of $9. In light of such price fluctuations, how should companies value investments at the balance sheet date? Valuation could be at cost, at fair value, or at the lower-of-cost-or-market value.

Many people argue that fair value offers the best approach because it represents the expected cash realizable value of securities. **Fair value** is the amount for which a security could be sold in a normal market. Others counter that unless a security is going to be sold soon, the fair value is not relevant because the price of the security will likely change again.

Categories of Securities

For purposes of valuation and reporting at a financial statement date, companies classify debt investments into three categories:

1. **Trading securities** are bought and held primarily for sale in the near term to generate income on short-term price differences.
2. **Available-for-sale securities** are held with the intent of selling them sometime in the future.
3. **Held-to-maturity securities** are debt securities that the investor has the intent and ability to hold to maturity.[3]

Stock investments are classified into two categories:

1. **Trading securities** (as defined above).
2. **Available-for-sale securities** (as defined above).

Stock investments have no maturity date. Therefore, they are never classified as held-to-maturity securities.

Illustration 12-6 shows the valuation guidelines for these securities. **These guidelines apply to all debt securities and all stock investments in which the holdings are less than 20%.**

Illustration 12-6
Valuation guidelines

---

[3]This category is provided for completeness. The accounting and valuation issues related to held-to-maturity securities are discussed in more advanced accounting courses.

TRADING SECURITIES

Companies hold trading securities with the intention of selling them in a short period (generally less than a month). **Trading** means frequent buying and selling. As indicated in Illustration 12-7, companies adjust trading securities to fair value at the end of each period. They report changes from cost as part of net income. The changes are reported as **unrealized gains or losses** because the securities have not been sold. The unrealized gain or loss is the difference between the **total cost** of trading securities and their **total fair value**. Companies classify trading securities as current assets.

Illustration 12-7 shows the cost and fair values for investments Pace Corporation classified as trading securities on December 31, 2015. Pace has an unrealized gain of $7,000 because total fair value of $147,000 is $7,000 greater than total cost of $140,000.

Trading Securities, December 31, 2015			
Investments	Cost	Fair Value	Unrealized Gain (Loss)
Yorkville Company bonds	$ 50,000	$ 48,000	$(2,000)
Kodak Company stock	90,000	99,000	9,000
Total	$140,000	$147,000	$ 7,000

Illustration 12-7
Valuation of trading securities

Pace records fair value and unrealized gain or loss through an adjusting entry at the time it prepares financial statements. In this entry, the company uses a valuation allowance account, Fair Value Adjustment—Trading, to record the difference between the total cost and the total fair value of the securities. The adjusting entry for Pace Corporation is:

Dec. 31	Fair Value Adjustment—Trading	7,000	
	Unrealized Gain—Income		7,000
	(To record unrealized gain on trading securities)		

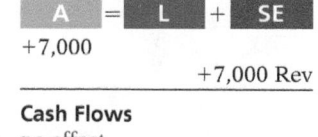

A	=	L	+	SE
+7,000				
				+7,000 Rev

Cash Flows
no effect

The use of a Fair Value Adjustment—Trading account enables Pace to maintain a record of the investment cost. It needs actual cost to determine the gain or loss realized when it sells the securities. Pace adds the debit balance (or subtracts a credit balance) of the Fair Value Adjustment—Trading account to the cost of the investments to arrive at a fair value for the trading securities.

The fair value of the securities is the amount Pace reports on its balance sheet. It reports the unrealized gain in the income statement in the "Other revenues and gains" section. The term "Income" in the account title indicates that the gain affects net income.

If the total cost of the trading securities is greater than total fair value, an unrealized loss has occurred. In such a case, the adjusting entry is a debit to Unrealized Loss—Income and a credit to Fair Value Adjustment—Trading. Companies report the unrealized loss under "Other expenses and losses" in the income statement.

The Fair Value Adjustment—Trading account is carried forward into future accounting periods. The company does not make any entry to the account until the end of each reporting period. At that time, the company adjusts the balance in the account to the difference between cost and fair value. For trading securities, it closes the Unrealized Gain (Loss)—Income account at the end of the reporting period.

ACCOUNTING ACROSS THE ORGANIZATION

And the Correct Way to Report Investments Is...?

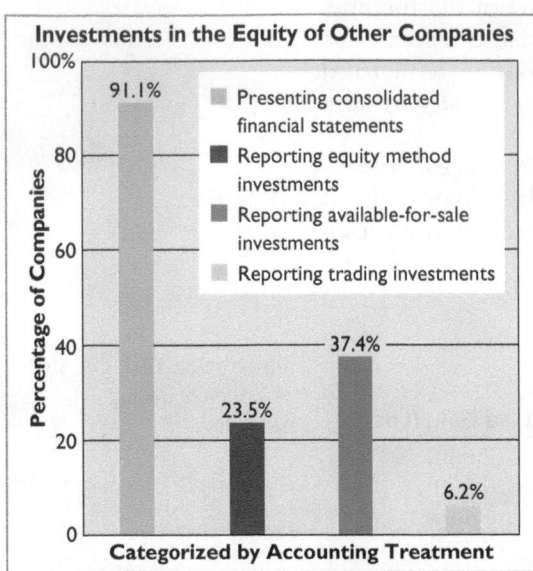

Investments in the Equity of Other Companies

- Presenting consolidated financial statements
- Reporting equity method investments
- Reporting available-for-sale investments
- Reporting trading investments

91.1%
23.5%
37.4%
6.2%

Percentage of Companies

Categorized by Accounting Treatment

The accompanying graph presents an estimate of the percentage of companies on the major exchanges that have investments in the equity of other entities.

As the graph indicates, many companies have equity investments of some type. These investments can be substantial. For example, the total amount of equity-method investments appearing on company balance sheets is approximately $403 billion, and the amount shown in the income statements in any one year for all companies is approximately $38 billion.

Source: "Report and Recommendations Pursuant to Section 401(c) of the Sarbanes-Oxley Act of 2002 on Arrangements with Off-Balance Sheet Implications, Special Purpose Entities, and Transparency of Filings by Issuers," United States Securities and Exchange Commission—Office of Chief Accountant, Office of Economic Analyses, Division of Corporation Finance (June 2005), pp. 36–39.

 Why might the use of the equity method not lead to full disclosure in the financial statements? (See page 645.)

AVAILABLE-FOR-SALE SECURITIES

As indicated earlier, companies hold available-for-sale securities with the intent of selling these investments sometime in the future. If the intent is to sell the securities within the next year or operating cycle, the investor classifies the securities as current assets in the balance sheet. Otherwise, it classifies them as long-term assets in the investments section of the balance sheet.

Ethics Note

Some managers seem to hold their available-for-sale securities that have experienced losses, while selling those that have gains, thus increasing income. Do you think this is ethical?

Companies report available-for-sale securities at fair value. The procedure for determining fair value and the unrealized gain or loss for these securities is the same as for trading securities. To illustrate, assume that Ingrao Corporation has two securities that it classifies as available-for-sale. Illustration 12-8 provides information on the cost, fair value, and amount of the unrealized gain or loss on December 31, 2015. There is an unrealized loss of $9,537 because total cost of $293,537 is $9,537 more than total fair value of $284,000.

Illustration 12-8
Valuation of available-for-sale securities

Available-for-Sale Securities, December 31, 2015

Investments	Cost	Fair Value	Unrealized Gain (Loss)
Campbell Soup Corporation 8% bonds	$ 93,537	$103,600	$10,063
Hershey Company stock	200,000	180,400	(19,600)
Total	$293,537	$284,000	$(9,537)

Both the adjusting entry and the reporting of the unrealized gain or loss for Ingrao's available-for-sale securities differ from those illustrated for trading securities. The differences result because Ingrao does not expect to sell these securities in the near term. Thus, prior to actual sale it is more likely that changes in fair value may change either unrealized gains or losses. Therefore, Ingrao does not report an unrealized gain or loss in the income statement. Instead, it reports it as a **separate component of stockholders' equity**.

In the adjusting entry, Ingrao identifies the fair value adjustment account with available-for-sale securities, and it identifies the unrealized gain or loss account with stockholders' equity. Ingrao records the unrealized loss of $9,537 as follows.

Dec. 31	Unrealized Gain or Loss—Equity	9,537	
	Fair Value Adjustment—Available-for-Sale		9,537
	(To record unrealized loss on available-for-sale securities)		

A	=	L	+	SE
				−9,537 Exp
−9,537				

Cash Flows
no effect

If total fair value exceeds total cost, Ingrao debits Fair Value Adjustment—Available-for-Sale and credits Unrealized Gain or Loss—Equity.

For available-for-sale securities, the company carries forward the Unrealized Gain or Loss—Equity account to future periods. At each future balance sheet date, Ingrao adjusts the Fair Value Adjustment—Available-for-Sale account and the Unrealized Gain or Loss—Equity account to show the difference between cost and fair value at that time.

> ### Ethics Note
>
> At one time, the SEC accused investment bank Morgan Stanley of overstating the value of certain bond investments by $75 million. The SEC stated that, in applying market value accounting, Morgan Stanley used its own more-optimistic assumptions rather than relying on external pricing sources.

> DO IT!

Trading and Available-for-Sale Securities

Some of Powderhorn Corporation's investment securities are classified as trading securities and some are classified as available-for-sale. The cost and fair value of each category at December 31, 2015, are shown below.

	Cost	Fair Value	Unrealized Gain (Loss)
Trading securities	$93,600	$94,900	$1,300
Available-for-sale securities	$48,800	$51,400	$2,600

At December 31, 2014, the Fair Value Adjustment—Trading account had a debit balance of $9,200, and the Fair Value Adjustment—Available-for-Sale account had a credit balance of $5,750. Prepare the required journal entries for each group of securities for December 31, 2015.

Solution

Action Plan

✔ Mark trading securities to fair value and report the adjustment in current-period income.

✔ Mark available-for-sale securities to fair value and report the adjustment as a separate component of stockholders' equity.

Trading securities:

Unrealized Loss—Income	7,900*	
Fair Value Adjustment—Trading		7,900
(To record unrealized loss on trading securities)		

    *$9,200 − $1,300

Available-for-sale securities:

Fair Value Adjustment—Available-for-Sale	8,350**	
Unrealized Gain or Loss—Equity		8,350
(To record unrealized gain on available-for-sale securities)		

    **$5,750 + $2,600

Related exercise material: BE12-4, BE12-5, BE12-6, BE12-7, E12-8, E12-10, E12-11, E12-12, **and** DO IT! 12-3.

 The Navigator

Balance Sheet Presentation

In the balance sheet, companies classify investments as either short-term or long-term.

SHORT-TERM INVESTMENTS

Short-term investments (also called **marketable securities**) are securities held by a company that are (1) **readily marketable** and (2) **intended to be converted into cash** within the next year or operating cycle, whichever is longer. Investments that do not meet **both criteria** are classified as **long-term investments**.

READILY MARKETABLE **An investment is readily marketable when it can be sold easily whenever the need for cash arises.** Short-term paper[4] meets this criterion. It can be readily sold to other investors. Stocks and bonds traded on organized securities exchanges, such as the New York Stock Exchange, are readily marketable. They can be bought and sold daily. In contrast, there may be only a limited market for the securities issued by small corporations, and no market for the securities of a privately held company.

INTENT TO CONVERT **Intent to convert means that management intends to sell the investment within the next year or operating cycle, whichever is longer.** Generally, this criterion is satisfied when the investment is considered a resource that the investor will use whenever the need for cash arises. For example, a ski resort may invest idle cash during the summer months with the intent to sell the securities to buy supplies and equipment shortly before the winter season. This investment is considered short-term even if lack of snow cancels the next ski season and eliminates the need to convert the securities into cash as intended.

Because of their high liquidity, short-term investments appear immediately below Cash in the "Current assets" section of the balance sheet. They are reported at fair value. For example, Pace Corporation would report its trading securities as shown in Illustration 12-9.

Illustration 12-9
Presentation of short-term
investments

PACE CORPORATION Balance Sheet (partial)	
Current assets	
Cash	$ 21,000
Short-term investments, at fair value	147,000

LONG-TERM INVESTMENTS

Companies generally report long-term investments in a separate section of the balance sheet immediately below "Current assets," as shown later in Illustration 12-12 (page 621). Long-term investments in available-for-sale securities are reported at

---

[4]**Short-term paper** includes (1) certificates of deposit (CDs) issued by banks, (2) money market certificates issued by banks and savings and loan associations, (3) Treasury bills issued by the U.S. government, and (4) commercial paper (notes) issued by corporations with good credit ratings.

fair value. Investments in common stock accounted for under the equity method are reported at equity.

Presentation of Realized and Unrealized Gain or Loss

Companies must present in the financial statements gains and losses on investments, whether realized or unrealized. In the income statement, companies report gains and losses in the nonoperating activities section under the categories listed in Illustration 12-10. Interest and dividend revenue are also reported in that section.

Other Revenues and Gains	Other Expenses and Losses
Interest Revenue	Loss on Sale of Investments
Dividend Revenue	Unrealized Loss—Income
Gain on Sale of Investments	
Unrealized Gain—Income	

Illustration 12-10
Nonoperating items related to investments

As indicated earlier, companies report an unrealized gain or loss on available-for-sale securities as a separate component of stockholders' equity. To illustrate, assume that Dawson Inc. has common stock of $3,000,000, retained earnings of $1,500,000, and an unrealized loss on available-for-sale securities of $100,000. Illustration 12-11 shows the balance sheet presentation of the unrealized loss.

Illustration 12-11
Unrealized loss in stockholders' equity section

DAWSON INC. Balance Sheet (partial)	
Stockholders' equity	
Common stock	$3,000,000
Retained earnings	1,500,000
Total paid-in capital and retained earnings	4,500,000
Less: Unrealized loss on available-for-sale securities	100,000
Total stockholders' equity	$4,400,000

Note that the loss decreases stockholders' equity. An unrealized gain is added to stockholders' equity. Reporting the unrealized gain or loss in the stockholders' equity section serves two purposes. (1) It reduces the volatility of net income due to fluctuations in fair value. (2) It informs the financial statement user of the gain or loss that would occur if the securities were sold at fair value.

Companies must report items such as this, which affect stockholders' equity but are not included in the calculation of net income, as part of a more inclusive measure called **comprehensive income**. We discuss comprehensive income more fully in Chapter 14.

Classified Balance Sheet

We have presented many sections of classified balance sheets in this and preceding chapters. The classified balance sheet in Illustration 12-12 includes, in one place, key topics from previous chapters: the issuance of par value common stock, restrictions of retained earnings, and issuance of long-term bonds. From this chapter, the statement includes (highlighted in red) short-term and long-term investments. The investments in short-term securities are considered trading securities. The long-term investments in stock of less than 20%-owned companies are considered available-for-sale securities. Illustration 12-12 also includes a long-term investment reported at equity and descriptive notations within the statement, such as the basis for valuing inventory and one note to the statement.

> **DO IT!**

Financial Statement Presentation of Investments

Identify where each of the following items would be reported in the financial statements.

1. Interest earned on investments in bonds.
2. Fair value adjustment—available-for-sale.
3. Unrealized loss on available-for-sale securities.
4. Gain on sale of investments in stock.
5. Unrealized gain on trading securities.

Use the following possible categories:

Balance sheet:

Current assets	Current liabilities
Investments	Long-term liabilities
Property, plant, and equipment	Stockholders' equity
Intangible assets	

Income statement:

Other revenues and gains	Other expenses and losses

Action Plan

✔ Classify investments as current assets if they will be held for less than one year.

✔ Report unrealized gains or losses on trading securities in income.

✔ Report unrealized gains or losses on available-for-sale securities in equity.

✔ Report realized earnings on investments in the income statement as "Other revenues and gains" or as "Other expenses and losses."

Solution

Item	Financial Statement	Category
1. Interest earned on investments in bonds	Income statement	Other revenues and gains
2. Fair value adjustment—available-for-sale	Balance sheet	Investments
3. Unrealized loss on available-for-sale securities	Balance sheet	Stockholders' equity
4. Gain on sale of investments in stock	Income statement	Other revenues and gains
5. Unrealized gain on trading securities	Income statement	Other revenues and gains

Related exercise material: BE12-5, BE12-7, BE12-8, E12-10, E12-11, E12-12, **and** DO IT! 12-4.

 The Navigator

Illustration 12-12
Classified balance sheet

PACE CORPORATION
Balance Sheet
December 31, 2015

Assets

Current assets			
Cash			$ 21,000
Short-term investments, at fair value			147,000
Accounts receivable		$ 84,000	
Less: Allowance for doubtful accounts		4,000	80,000
Inventory, at FIFO cost			43,000
Prepaid insurance			23,000
Total current assets			314,000
Investments			
Investment in stock of less than 20%			
owned companies, at fair value		50,000	
Investment in stock of 20–50% owned			
company, at equity		150,000	
Total investments			200,000
Property, plant, and equipment			
Land		200,000	
Buildings	$800,000		
Less: Accumulated depreciation—buildings	200,000	600,000	
Equipment	180,000		
Less: Accumulated depreciation—equipment	54,000	126,000	
Total property, plant, and equipment			926,000
Intangible assets			
Goodwill			270,000
Total assets			$1,710,000

Liabilities and Stockholders' Equity

Current liabilities			
Accounts payable			$ 185,000
Federal income taxes payable			60,000
Interest payable			10,000
Total current liabilities			255,000
Long-term liabilities			
Bonds payable, 10%, due 2021		$ 300,000	
Less: Discount on bonds		10,000	
Total long-term liabilities			290,000
Total liabilities			545,000
Stockholders' equity			
Paid-in capital			
Common stock, $10 par value,			
200,000 shares authorized, 80,000 shares			
issued and outstanding		800,000	
Paid-in capital in excess of par—			
common stock		100,000	
Total paid-in capital		900,000	
Retained earnings (Note 1)		255,000	
Total paid-in capital and retained earnings		1,155,000	
Add: Unrealized gain on available-for-sale			
securities		10,000	
Total stockholders' equity			1,165,000
Total liabilities and stockholders' equity			$1,710,000

Note 1. Retained earnings of $100,000 is restricted for plant expansion.

> **Comprehensive DO IT!**

In its first year of operations, DeMarco Company had the following selected transactions in stock investments that are considered trading securities.

June 1 Purchased for cash 600 shares of Sanburg common stock at $24 per share.
July 1 Purchased for cash 800 shares of Cey Corporation common stock at $33 per share.
Sept. 1 Received a $1 per share cash dividend from Cey Corporation.
Nov. 1 Sold 200 shares of Sanburg common stock for cash at $27 per share.
Dec. 15 Received a $0.50 per share cash dividend on Sanburg common stock.

At December 31, the fair values per share were Sanburg $25 and Cey $30.

Instructions
(a) Journalize the transactions.
(b) Prepare the adjusting entry at December 31 to report the securities at fair value.

Solution to Comprehensive DO IT!

Action Plan

✔ Record the price paid as the cost of the investment.

✔ Compute the gain or loss on sales as the difference between selling price and the cost of the securities.

✔ Base the adjustment to fair value on the total difference between the cost and the fair value of the securities.

(a)	June 1	Stock Investments	14,400	
		Cash (600 × $24)		14,400
		(To record purchase of 600 shares of Sanburg common stock)		
	July 1	Stock Investments	26,400	
		Cash (800 × $33)		26,400
		(To record purchase of 800 shares of Cey common stock)		
	Sept. 1	Cash (800 × $1.00)	800	
		Dividend Revenue		800
		(To record receipt of $1 per share cash dividend from Cey Corporation)		
	Nov. 1	Cash (200 × $27)	5,400	
		Stock Investments ($14,400 × 200/600)		4,800
		Gain on Sale of Stock Investments		600
		(To record sale of 200 shares of Sanburg common stock)		
	Dec. 15	Cash [(600 − 200) × $0.50]	200	
		Dividend Revenue		200
		(To record receipt of $0.50 per share dividend from Sanburg)		
(b)	Dec. 31	Unrealized Loss—Income	2,000	
		Fair Value Adjustment—Trading		2,000
		(To record unrealized loss on trading securities)		

Investment	Cost	Fair Value	Unrealized Gain (Loss)
Sanburg common stock	$ 9,600	$10,000	$ 400
Cey common stock	26,400	24,000	(2,400)
Total	$36,000	$34,000	$(2,000)

✔ **The Navigator**

✔ **The Navigator**

1 Discuss why corporations invest in debt and stock securities. Corporations invest for three primary reasons. (a) They have excess cash. (b) They view investments as a significant revenue source. (c) They have strategic goals such as gaining control of a competitor or moving into a new line of business.

2 Explain the accounting for debt investments. Companies record investments in debt securities when they purchase bonds, receive or accrue interest, and sell the bonds. They report gains or losses on the sale of bonds in the "Other revenues and gains" or "Other expenses and losses" sections of the income statement.

3 Explain the accounting for stock investments. Companies record investments in common stock when they purchase the stock, receive dividends, and sell the stock. When ownership is less than 20%, the cost method is used. When ownership is between 20% and 50%, the equity method should be used. When ownership is more than 50%, companies prepare consolidated financial statements.

4 Describe the use of consolidated financial statements. When a company owns more than 50% of the common stock of another company, it usually prepares consolidated financial statements. These statements indicate the magnitude and scope of operations of the companies under common control.

5 Indicate how debt and stock investments are reported in financial statements. Investments in debt securities are classified as trading, available-for-sale, or held-to-maturity securities for valuation and reporting purposes. Stock investments are classified either as trading or available-for-sale securities. Stock investments have no maturity date and therefore are never classified as held-to-maturity securities. Trading securities are reported as current assets at fair value, with changes from cost reported in net income. Available-for-sale securities are also reported at fair value, with the changes from cost reported in stockholders' equity. Available-for-sale securities are classified as short-term or long-term, depending on their expected future sale date.

6 Distinguish between short-term and long-term investments. Short-term investments are securities that are (a) readily marketable and (b) intended to be converted to cash within the next year or operating cycle, whichever is longer. Investments that do not meet both criteria are classified as long-term investments.

Available-for-sale securities Securities that are held with the intent of selling them sometime in the future. (p. 614).

Consolidated financial statements Financial statements that present the assets and liabilities controlled by the parent company and the total revenues and expenses of the subsidiary companies. (p. 612).

Controlling interest Ownership of more than 50% of the common stock of another entity. (p. 612).

Cost method An accounting method in which the investment in common stock is recorded at cost, and revenue is recognized only when cash dividends are received. (p. 609).

Debt investments Investments in government and corporation bonds. (p. 607).

Equity method An accounting method in which the investment in common stock is initially recorded at cost, and the investment account is then adjusted annually to show the investor's equity in the investee. (p. 611).

Fair value Amount for which a security could be sold in a normal market. (p. 614).

Held-to-maturity securities Debt securities that the investor has the intent and ability to hold to their maturity date. (p. 614).

Investment portfolio A group of stocks and/or debt securities in different corporations held for investment purposes. (p. 609).

Long-term investments Investments that are not readily marketable or that management does not intend to convert into cash within the next year or operating cycle, whichever is longer. (p. 618).

Parent company A company that owns more than 50% of the common stock of another entity. (p. 612).

Short-term investments Investments that are readily marketable and intended to be converted into cash within the next year or operating cycle, whichever is longer. (p. 618).

Stock investments Investments in the capital stock of other corporations. (p. 609).

Subsidiary (affiliated) company A company in which more than 50% of its stock is owned by another company. (p. 612).

Trading securities Securities bought and held primarily for sale in the near term to generate income on short-term price differences. (p. 614).

APPENDIX 12A   Preparing Consolidated Financial Statements

Most of the large U.S. corporations are holding companies that own other corporations. They therefore prepare **consolidated** financial statements that combine the separate companies.

Consolidated Balance Sheet

Companies prepare consolidated balance sheets from the individual balance sheets of their affiliated companies. They do not prepare consolidated statements from ledger accounts kept by the consolidated entity because only the separate legal entities maintain accounting records.

All items in the individual balance sheets are included in the consolidated balance sheet except amounts that pertain to transactions between the affiliated companies. Transactions between the affiliated companies are identified as **intercompany transactions**. The process of excluding these transactions in preparing consolidated statements is referred to as **intercompany eliminations**. These eliminations are necessary to avoid overstating assets, liabilities, and stockholders' equity in the consolidated balance sheet. For example, amounts owed by a subsidiary to a parent company and the related receivable reported by the parent company would be eliminated. The objective in a consolidated balance sheet is to show only obligations to and receivables from parties who are not part of the affiliated group of companies.

Helpful Hint
Eliminations are aptly named because they eliminate duplicate data. They are not adjustments.

To illustrate, assume that on January 1, 2015, Powers Construction Company pays $150,000 in cash for 100% of Serto Brick Company's common stock. Powers Company records the investment at cost, as required by the cost principle. Illustration 12A-1 presents the separate balance sheets of the two companies immediately after the purchase, together with combined and consolidated data.[5] Powers obtains the balances in the "combined" column by adding the items in the separate balance sheets of the affiliated companies. The combined totals do not represent a consolidated balance sheet because there has been a double-counting of assets and stockholders' equity in the amount of $150,000.

Illustration 12A-1
Combined and consolidated data

POWERS COMPANY AND SERTO COMPANY Balance Sheet January 1, 2015				
Assets	**Powers Company**	**Serto Company**	**Combined Data**	**Consolidated Data**
Current assets	$ 50,000	$ 80,000	$130,000	**$130,000**
Investment in Serto Company common stock	150,000		150,000	**–0–**
Plant and equipment (net)	325,000	145,000	470,000	**470,000**
Total assets	$525,000	$225,000	$750,000	**$600,000**
Liabilities and Stockholders' Equity				
Current liabilities	$ 50,000	$ 75,000	$125,000	**$125,000**
Common stock	300,000	100,000	400,000	**300,000**
Retained earnings	175,000	50,000	225,000	**175,000**
Total liabilities and stockholders' equity	$525,000	$225,000	$750,000	**$600,000**

---

[5]We use condensed data throughout this material to keep details at a minimum.

The Investment in Serto Company common stock that appears on the balance sheet of Powers Company represents an interest in the net assets of Serto. As a result, there has been a double-counting of assets. Similarly, there has been a double-counting in stockholders' equity because the common stock of Serto Company is completely owned by the stockholders of Powers Company.

The balances in the consolidated data column are the amounts that should appear in the consolidated balance sheet. The double-counting has been eliminated by showing Investment in Serto Company at zero and by reporting only the common stock and retained earnings of Powers Company as stockholders' equity.

USE OF A WORKSHEET—COST EQUAL TO BOOK VALUE

The preparation of consolidated balance sheets is usually facilitated by the use of a worksheet. As shown in Illustration 12A-2, the worksheet for a consolidated balance sheet contains columns for (1) the balance sheet data for the separate legal entities, (2) intercompany eliminations, and (3) consolidated data. All data in the worksheet relate to the preceding example in which Powers Company acquires 100% ownership of Serto Company for $150,000. In this case, the cost of the investment, $150,000, is equal to the book value [$150,000 ($225,000 − $75,000)] of the subsidiary's net assets. The intercompany elimination results in a credit to the investment account maintained by Powers Company for its balance, $150,000, and debits to the Common Stock and Retained Earnings accounts of Serto Company for their respective balances, $100,000 and $50,000.

POWERS COMPANY AND SUBSIDIARY
Worksheet—Consolidated Balance Sheet
January 1, 2015 (Acquisition Date)

Assets	Powers Company	Serto Company	Eliminations Dr.	Eliminations Cr.	Consolidated Data
Current assets	50,000	80,000			130,000
Investment in Serto Company common stock	150,000			150,000	–0–
Plant and equipment (net)	325,000	145,000			470,000
Totals	525,000	225,000			600,000
Liabilities and Stockholders' Equity					
Current liabilities	50,000	75,000			125,000
Common stock—Powers Company	300,000				300,000
Common stock—Serto Company		100,000	100,000		–0–
Retained earnings—Powers Company	175,000				175,000
Retained earnings—Serto Company		50,000	50,000		–0–
Totals	525,000	225,000	150,000	150,000	600,000

Illustration 12A-2
Worksheet—Cost equal to book value

It is important to recognize that companies make intercompany eliminations solely on the worksheet to present correct consolidated data. Neither of the affiliated companies journalizes or posts the eliminations. Therefore, eliminations do not affect the ledger accounts. Powers Company's investment account and Serto Company's common stock and retained earnings accounts are reported by the separate entities in preparing their own financial statements.

Helpful Hint
As in the case of the worksheets explained earlier in this textbook, consolidated worksheets are also optional.

Helpful Hint
The consolidated
worksheet is another
useful spreadsheet
application. This is an
easier worksheet to
attempt since the required
instructions are very
straightforward.

USE OF A WORKSHEET—COST ABOVE BOOK VALUE

The cost of acquiring the common stock of another company may be above or below its book value. The management of the parent company may pay more than book value for the stock. Why? Because it believes the fair values of identifiable assets such as land, buildings, and equipment are higher than their recorded book values. Or, it may believe the subsidiary's future earnings prospects warrant a payment for goodwill.

To illustrate, assume the same data used above, except that Powers Company pays $165,000 in cash for 100% of Serto's common stock. The excess of cost over book value is $15,000 ($165,000 − $150,000). Powers recognizes this amount separately in eliminating the parent company's investment account, as shown in Illustration 12A-3. Total assets and total liabilities and stockholders' equity are the same as in the preceding example ($600,000). However, in this case, total assets include $15,000 of Excess of Cost Over Book Value of Subsidiary. The disposition of the excess is explained in the next section.

Illustration 12A-3
Worksheet—Cost above
book value

	Powers Company	Serto Company	Eliminations Dr.	Eliminations Cr.	Consolidated Data
POWERS COMPANY AND SUBSIDIARY					
Worksheet—Consolidated Balance Sheet					
January 1, 2015 (Acquisition Date)					
Assets					
Current assets	35,000	80,000			115,000
Investment in Serto Company common stock	165,000			165,000	–0–
Plant and equipment (net)	325,000	145,000			470,000
Excess of cost over book value of subsidiary			15,000		15,000
Totals	525,000	225,000			600,000
Liabilities and Stockholders' Equity					
Current liabilities	50,000	75,000			125,000
Common stock—Powers Company	300,000				300,000
Common stock—Serto Company		100,000	100,000		–0–
Retained earnings—Powers Company	175,000				175,000
Retained earnings—Serto Company		50,000	50,000		–0–
Totals	525,000	225,000	165,000	165,000	600,000
Note that a separate line is added to the worksheet for the excess of cost over book value of subsidiary.					

CONTENT OF A CONSOLIDATED BALANCE SHEET

To illustrate a consolidated balance sheet, we will use the worksheet shown in Illustration 12A-3. This worksheet shows an excess of cost over book value of $15,000. In the consolidated balance sheet, Powers first allocates this amount to specific assets, such as plant and equipment and inventory, if their fair values on the acquisition date exceed their book values. Any remainder is considered to be goodwill. For Serto Company, assume that the fair value of the plant and equipment is $155,000. Thus, Powers allocates $10,000 of the excess of cost over book value to plant and equipment, and the remainder, $5,000, to goodwill. Illustration 12A-4 shows the condensed consolidated balance sheet of Powers Company.

Through innovative financial restructuring, The Coca-Cola Company at one time eliminated a substantial amount of non-intercompany debt. It sold to the public 51% of two bottling companies. The "49% solution," as insiders call the strategy, enabled Coca-Cola to keep effective control over the businesses, and it swept $3 billion of debt from its consolidated balance sheet. (It no longer consolidated the two bottling companies.) At the same time the new companies obtained independent access to equity markets to satisfy their own large appetites for capital.

Illustration 12A-4
Consolidated balance sheet

POWERS COMPANY		
Consolidated Balance Sheet		
January 1, 2015		
Assets		
Current assets		$115,000
Plant and equipment (net)		480,000
Goodwill		5,000
Total assets		$600,000
Liabilities and Stockholders' Equity		
Current liabilities		$125,000
Stockholders' equity		
Common stock	$300,000	
Retained earnings	175,000	475,000
Total liabilities and stockholders' equity		$600,000

Consolidated Income Statement

Affiliated companies also prepare a consolidated income statement. This statement shows the results of operations of affiliated companies as though they are one economic unit. This means that the statement shows only revenue and expense transactions between the consolidated entity and companies and individuals who are outside the affiliated group.

Consequently, all intercompany revenue and expense transactions must be eliminated. Intercompany transactions such as sales between affiliates and interest on loans charged by one affiliate to another must be eliminated. A worksheet facilitates the preparation of consolidated income statements in the same manner as it does for the balance sheet.

SUMMARY OF LEARNING OBJECTIVE FOR APPENDIX 12A

 The Navigator

7 Describe the form and content of consolidated financial statements as well as how to prepare them. Consolidated financial statements are similar in form and content to the financial statements of an individual corporation. A consolidated balance sheet shows the assets and liabilities controlled by the parent company.

A consolidated income statement shows the results of operations of affiliated companies as though they are one economic unit. The worksheet for a consolidated balance sheet contains columns for (a) the balance sheet data for the separate entities, (b) intercompany eliminations, and (c) consolidated data.

Intercompany eliminations Eliminations made to exclude the effects of intercompany transactions in preparing consolidated statements. (p. 624).

Intercompany transactions Transactions between affiliated companies. (p. 624).

WileyPLUS Self-Test, Brief Exercises, Exercises, Problem Set A, and many more components are available for practice in *WileyPLUS*.

*****Note:** All asterisked Questions, Exercises, and Problems relate to material in the appendix to the chapter.

SELF-TEST QUESTIONS

Answers are on page 645.

(LO 1) **1.** Which of the following is **not** a primary reason why corporations invest in debt and equity securities?
  (a) They wish to gain control of a competitor.
  (b) They have excess cash.
  (c) They wish to move into a new line of business.
  (d) They are required to by law.

(LO 2) **2.** Debt investments are initially recorded at:
  (a) cost.
  (b) cost plus accrued interest.
  (c) fair value.
  (d) face value.

(LO 2) **3.** Hanes Company sells debt investments costing $26,000 for $28,000. In journalizing the sale, credits are to:
  (a) Debt Investments and Loss on Sale of Debt Investments.
  (b) Debt Investments and Gain on Sale of Debt Investments.
  (c) Stock Investments and Gain on Sale of Stock Investments.
  (d) No correct answer is given.

(LO 3) **4.** Pryor Company receives net proceeds of $42,000 on the sale of stock investments that cost $39,500. This transaction will result in reporting in the income statement a:
  (a) loss of $2,500 under "Other expenses and losses."
  (b) loss of $2,500 under "Operating expenses."
  (c) gain of $2,500 under "Other revenues and gains."
  (d) gain of $2,500 under "Operating revenues."

(LO 3) **5.** The equity method of accounting for long-term investments in stock should be used when the investor has significant influence over an investee and owns:
  (a) between 20% and 50% of the investee's common stock.
  (b) 20% or more of the investee's common stock.
  (c) more than 50% of the investee's common stock.
  (d) less than 20% of the investee's common stock.

(LO 3) **6.** Assume that Horicon Corp acquired 25% of the common stock of Sheboygan Corp. on January 1, 2015, for $300,000. During 2015, Sheboygan Corp. reported net income of $160,000 and paid total dividends of $60,000. If Horicon uses the equity method to account for its investment, the balance in the investment account on December 31, 2015, will be:
  (a) $300,000.   **(c)** $400,000.
  (b) $325,000.   **(d)** $340,000.

7. Using the information in Self-Test Question 6, what (LO 3) entry would Horicon make to record the receipt of the dividend from Sheboygan?
  (a) Debit Cash and credit Revenue from Stock Investments.
  (b) Debit Cash Dividends and credit Revenue from Stock Investments.
  (c) Debit Cash and credit Stock Investments.
  (d) Debit Cash and credit Dividend Revenue.

8. You have a controlling interest if: (LO 3)
  (a) you own more than 20% of a company's stock.
  (b) you are the president of the company.
  (c) you use the equity method.
  (d) you own more than 50% of a company's stock.

9. Which of the following statements is **false**? Consoli- (LO 4) dated financial statements are useful to:
  (a) determine the profitability of specific subsidiaries.
  (b) determine the total profitability of companies under common control.
  (c) determine the breadth of a parent company's operations.
  (d) determine the full extent of total obligations of companies under common control.

10. At the end of the first year of operations, the total cost (LO 5) of the trading securities portfolio is $120,000. Total fair value is $115,000. The financial statements should show:
  (a) a reduction of an asset of $5,000 and a realized loss of $5,000.
  (b) a reduction of an asset of $5,000 and an unrealized loss of $5,000 in the stockholders' equity section.
  (c) a reduction of an asset of $5,000 in the current assets section and an unrealized loss of $5,000 in "Other expenses and losses."

(d) a reduction of an asset of $5,000 in the current assets section and a realized loss of $5,000 in "Other expenses and losses."

(LO 5) **11.** At December 31, 2015, the fair value of available-for-sale securities is $41,300 and the cost is $39,800. At January 1, 2015, there was a credit balance of $900 in the Fair Value Adjustment—Available-for-Sale account. The required adjusting entry would be:

(a) Debit Fair Value Adjustment—Available-for-Sale for $1,500 and credit Unrealized Gain or Loss—Equity for $1,500.

(b) Debit Fair Value Adjustment—Available-for-Sale for $600 and credit Unrealized Gain or Loss—Equity for $600.

(c) Debit Fair Value Adjustment—Available-for-Sale for $2,400 and credit Unrealized Gain or Loss—Equity for $2,400.

(d) Debit Unrealized Gain or Loss—Equity for $2,400 and credit Fair Value Adjustment—Available-for-Sale for $2,400.

(LO 5) **12.** In the balance sheet, a debit balance in Unrealized Gain or Loss—Equity is reported as a(n):

(a) increase to stockholders' equity.

(b) decrease to stockholders' equity.

(c) loss in the income statement.

(d) loss in the retained earnings statement.

(LO 6) **13.** Short-term debt investments must be readily marketable and expected to be sold within:

(a) 3 months from the date of purchase.

(b) the next year or operating cycle, whichever is shorter.

(c) the next year or operating cycle, whichever is longer.

(d) the operating cycle.

***14.** Pate Company pays $175,000 for 100% of Sinko's (LO 7) common stock when Sinko's stockholders' equity consists of Common Stock $100,000 and Retained Earnings $60,000. In the worksheet for the consolidated balance sheet, the eliminations will include a:

(a) credit to Investment in Sinko Common Stock $160,000.

(b) credit to Excess of Book Value over Cost of Subsidiary $15,000.

(c) debit to Retained Earnings $75,000.

(d) debit to Excess of Cost over Book Value of Subsidiary $15,000.

***15.** Which of the following statements about intercompany eliminations is **true**? (LO 7)

(a) They are not journalized or posted by any of the subsidiaries.

(b) They do not affect the ledger accounts of any of the subsidiaries.

(c) They are made solely on the worksheet to arrive at correct consolidated data.

(d) All of these statements are true.

***16.** Which one of the following statements about consolidated income statements is **false**? (LO 7)

(a) A worksheet facilitates the preparation of the statement.

(b) The consolidated income statement shows the results of operations of affiliated companies as a single economic unit.

(c) All revenue and expense transactions between parent and subsidiary companies are eliminated.

(d) When a subsidiary is wholly owned, the form and content of the statement will differ from the income statement of an individual corporation.

Go to the book's companion website, www.wiley.com/college/weygandt, for additional Self-Test Questions.

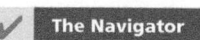 The Navigator

QUESTIONS

1. What are the reasons that corporations invest in securities?

2. (a) What is the cost of an investment in bonds?
(b) When is interest on bonds recorded?

3. Alex Ramirez is confused about losses and gains on the sale of debt investments. Explain to Alex (a) how the gain or loss is computed, and (b) the statement presentation of the gains and losses.

4. Seibel Company sells Mayo's bonds costing $40,000 for $45,000. Seibel records a $5,000 gain on this sale. Is this correct? Explain.

5. What is the cost of an investment in stock?

6. To acquire Peoples Corporation stock, J. Rich pays $62,000 in cash. What entry should be made for this investment?

7. (a) When should a long-term investment in common stock be accounted for by the equity method?
(b) When is revenue recognized under this method?

8. Ling Corporation uses the equity method to account for its ownership of 35% of the common stock of Gorman Packing. During 2015, Gorman reported a net income of $80,000 and declares and pays cash dividends of $10,000. What recognition should Ling Corporation give to these events?

9. What constitutes "significant influence" when an investor's financial interest is below the 50% level?

10. Distinguish between the cost and equity methods of accounting for investments in stocks.

11. What are consolidated financial statements?

12. What are the classification guidelines for investments at a balance sheet date?

13. Jill Hollern is the controller of Chavez Inc. At December 31, the company's investments in trading securities cost $74,000. They have a fair value of $72,000. Indicate how Jill would report these data in the financial statements prepared on December 31.

14. Using the data in Question 13, how would Jill report the data if the investments were long-term and the securities were classified as available-for-sale?

15. Culver Company's investments in available-for-sale securities at December 31 show total cost of $195,000 and total fair value of $205,000. Prepare the adjusting entry.

16. Using the data in Question 15, prepare the adjusting entry assuming the securities are classified as trading securities.

17. What is the proper statement presentation of the account Unrealized Loss—Equity?

18. What purposes are served by reporting Unrealized Gain or Loss—Equity in the stockholders' equity section?

19. Deering Wholesale Supply owns stock in Orr Corporation. Deering intends to hold the stock indefinitely because of some negative tax consequences if sold. Should the investment in Orr be classified as a short-term investment? Why or why not?

20. What does Apple state regarding its accounting policy involving consolidated financial statements?

*21. (a) What asset and stockholders' equity balances are eliminated in preparing a consolidated balance sheet for a parent and a wholly owned subsidiary? (b) Why are they eliminated?

*22. Roscoe Company pays $318,000 to purchase all the outstanding common stock of Lia Corporation. At the date of purchase, the net assets of Lia have a book value of $290,000. Roscoe's management allocates $20,000 of the excess cost to undervalued land on the books of Lia. What should be done with the rest of the excess?

BRIEF EXERCISES

Journalize entries for debt investments.
(LO 2)

BE12-1 Ownbey Corporation purchased debt investments for $52,000 on January 1, 2015. On July 1, 2015, Ownbey received cash interest of $2,340. Journalize the purchase and the receipt of interest. Assume that no interest has been accrued.

Journalize entries for stock investments.
(LO 3)

BE12-2 On August 1, Shaw Company buys 1,000 shares of Estrada common stock for $37,000 cash. On December 1, Shaw sells the stock investments for $40,000 in cash. Journalize the purchase and sale of the common stock.

Record transactions under the equity method of accounting.
(LO 3)

BE12-3 Noler Company owns 25% of Lauer Company. For the current year, Lauer reports net income of $180,000 and declares and pays a $50,000 cash dividend. Record Noler's equity in Lauer's net income and the receipt of dividends from Lauer.

Prepare adjusting entry using fair value.
(LO 5)

BE12-4 The cost of the trading securities of Munoz Company at December 31, 2015, is $64,000. At December 31, 2015, the fair value of the securities is $59,000. Prepare the adjusting entry to record the securities at fair value.

Indicate statement presentation using fair value.
(LO 5, 6)

BE12-5 For the data presented in BE12-4, show the financial statement presentation of the trading securities and related accounts.

Prepare adjusting entry using fair value.
(LO 5)

BE12-6 Godfrey Corporation holds, as a long-term investment, available-for-sale securities costing $72,000. At December 31, 2015, the fair value of the securities is $68,000. Prepare the adjusting entry to record the securities at fair value.

Indicate statements presentation using fair value.
(LO 5, 6)

BE12-7 For the data presented in BE12-6, show the financial statement presentation of the available-for-sale securities and related accounts. Assume the available-for-sale securities are noncurrent.

Prepare investments section of balance sheet.
(LO 5, 6)

BE12-8 Kruger Corporation has the following long-term investments. (1) Common stock of Eidman Co. (10% ownership) held as available-for-sale securities, cost $108,000, fair value $115,000. (2) Common stock of Pickerill Inc. (30% ownership), cost $210,000, equity $260,000. Prepare the investments section of the balance sheet.

Prepare partial consolidated worksheet when cost equals book value.
(LO 7)

*****BE12-9** Paula Company acquires 100% of the common stock of Shannon Company for $190,000 cash. On the acquisition date, Shannon's ledger shows Common Stock $120,000 and Retained Earnings $70,000. Complete the worksheet for the following accounts: Paula—Investment in Shannon Common Stock, Shannon—Common Stock, and Shannon—Retained Earnings.

Prepare partial consolidated worksheet when cost exceeds book value.
(LO 7)

*****BE12-10** Data for the Paula and Shannon companies are given in BE12-9. Instead of paying $190,000, assume that Paula pays $200,000 to acquire the 100% interest in Shannon Company. Complete the worksheet for the accounts identified in BE12-9 and for the excess of cost over book value.

> **DO IT! Review**

DO IT! 12-1 Kurtyka Corporation had the following transactions relating to debt investments:

Jan.   1   Purchased 50 $1,000, 10% Spiller Company bonds for $50,000. Interest is payable semiannually on January 1 and July 1.
July   1   Received semiannual interest from Spiller Company bonds.
July   1   Sold 30 Spiller Company bonds for $29,000.

(a) Journalize the transactions, and (b) prepare the adjusting entry for the accrual of interest on December 31.

Make journal entry for bond purchase and adjusting entry for interest accrual.
(LO 2)

DO IT! 12-2 Presented below are two independent situations:

1. Edelman Inc. acquired 10% of the 500,000 shares of common stock of Schuberger Corporation at a total cost of $11 per share on June 17, 2015. On September 3, Schuberger declared and paid a $160,000 dividend. On December 31, Schuberger reported net income of $550,000 for the year.
2. Wen Corporation obtained significant influence over Hunsaker Company by buying 30% of Hunsaker's 100,000 outstanding shares of common stock at a cost of $18 per share on January 1, 2015. On May 15, Hunsaker declared and paid a cash dividend of $150,000. On December 31, Hunsaker reported net income of $270,000 for the year.

Prepare all necessary journal entries for 2015 for (a) Edelman and (b) Wen.

Make journal entries for stock investments.
(LO 3)

DO IT! 12-3 Some of Tollakson Corporation's investment securities are classified as trading securities and some are classified as available-for-sale. The cost and fair value of each category at December 31, 2015, were as follows.

	Cost	Fair Value	Unrealized Gain (Loss)
Trading securities	$96,300	$84,900	$(11,400)
Available-for-sale securities	$59,000	$63,200	$ 4,200

At December 31, 2014, the Fair Value Adjustment—Trading account had a debit balance of $3,200, and the Fair Value Adjustment—Available-for-Sale account had a credit balance of $5,750. Prepare the required journal entries for each group of securities for December 31, 2015.

Make journal entries for trading and available-for-sale securities.
(LO 5)

DO IT! 12-4 Identify where each of the following items would be reported in the financial statements.

1. Loss on sale of investments in stock.
2. Unrealized gain on available-for-sale securities.
3. Fair value adjustment—trading.
4. Interest earned on investments in bonds.
5. Unrealized loss on trading securities.

Use the following possible categories:

Balance sheet:

Current assets   Current liabilities
Investments   Long-term liabilities
Property, plant, and equipment   Stockholders' equity
Intangible assets

Income statement:

Other revenues and gains   Other expenses and losses

Indicate financial statement presentation of investments.
(LO 6)

EXERCISES

E12-1 Mr. Taliaferro is studying for an accounting test and has developed the questions below and on page 632 about investments.

1. What are three reasons why companies purchase investments in debt or stock securities?
2. Why would a corporation have excess cash that it does not need for operations?
3. What is the typical investment when investing cash for short periods of time?

Understand debt and stock investments.
(LO 1)

4. What are the typical investments when investing cash to generate earnings?
5. Why would a company invest in securities that provide no current cash flows?
6. What is the typical stock investment when investing cash for strategic reasons?

Instructions
Provide answers for Mr. Taliaferro.

Journalize debt investment transactions and accrue interest.
(LO 2)

E12-2 Jenek Corporation had the following transactions pertaining to debt investments.

Jan. 1   Purchased 50 9%, $1,000 Leeds Co. bonds for $50,000 cash. Interest is payable semiannually on July 1 and January 1.
July 1   Received semiannual interest on Leeds Co. bonds.
July 1   Sold 30 Leeds Co. bonds for $33,000.

Instructions
(a) Journalize the transactions.
(b) Prepare the adjusting entry for the accrual of interest at December 31.

Journalize debt investment transactions, accrue interest, and record sale.
(LO 2)

E12-3 Flynn Company purchased 70 Rinehart Company 12%, 10-year, $1,000 bonds on January 1, 2015, for $70,000. The bonds pay interest semiannually on July 1 and January 1. On January 1, 2016, after receipt of interest, Flynn Company sold 40 of the bonds for $38,500.

Instructions
Prepare the journal entries to record the transactions described above.

Journalize stock investment transactions.
(LO 3)

E12-4 Hulse Company had the following transactions pertaining to stock investments.

Feb. 1   Purchased 600 shares of Wade common stock (2%) for $7,200 cash.
July 1   Received cash dividends of $1 per share on Wade common stock.
Sept. 1   Sold 300 shares of Wade common stock for $4,300.
Dec. 1   Received cash dividends of $1 per share on Wade common stock.

Instructions
(a) Journalize the transactions.
(b) Explain how dividend revenue and the gain (loss) on sale should be reported in the income statement.

Journalize transactions for investments in stocks.
(LO 3)

E12-5 Nosker Inc. had the following transactions pertaining to investments in common stock.

Jan. 1   Purchased 2,500 shares of Escalante Corporation common stock (5%) for $152,000 cash.
July 1   Received a cash dividend of $3 per share.
Dec. 1   Sold 500 shares of Escalante Corporation common stock for $32,000 cash.
Dec. 31   Received a cash dividend of $3 per share.

Instructions
Journalize the transactions.

Journalize transactions for investments in stocks.
(LO 3)

E12-6 On February 1, Rinehart Company purchased 500 shares (2% ownership) of Givens Company common stock for $32 per share. On March 20, Rinehart Company sold 100 shares of Givens stock for $2,900. Rinehart received a dividend of $1.00 per share on April 25. On June 15, Rinehart sold 200 shares of Givens stock for $7,600. On July 28, Rinehart received a dividend of $1.25 per share.

Instructions
Prepare the journal entries to record the transactions described above.

Journalize and post transactions, under the equity method.
(LO 3)

E12-7 On January 1, Zabel Corporation purchased a 25% equity in Helbert Corporation for $180,000. At December 31, Helbert declared and paid a $60,000 cash dividend and reported net income of $200,000.

Instructions
(a) Journalize the transactions.
(b) Determine the amount to be reported as an investment in Helbert stock at December 31.

E12-8 Presented below are two independent situations.

1. Gambino Cosmetics acquired 10% of the 200,000 shares of common stock of Nevins Fashion at a total cost of $13 per share on March 18, 2015. On June 30, Nevins declared and paid a $60,000 dividend. On December 31, Nevins reported net income of $122,000 for the year. At December 31, the market price of Nevins Fashion was $15 per share. The stock is classified as available-for-sale.

2. Kanza, Inc., obtained significant influence over Rogan Corporation by buying 40% of Rogan's 30,000 outstanding shares of common stock at a total cost of $9 per share on January 1, 2015. On June 15, Rogan declared and paid a cash dividend of $30,000. On December 31, Rogan reported a net income of $80,000 for the year.

Journalize entries under cost and equity methods.

(LO 3, 5)

Instructions
Prepare all the necessary journal entries for 2015 for (a) Gambino Cosmetics and (b) Kanza, Inc.

E12-9 Agee Company purchased 70% of the outstanding common stock of Himes Corporation.

Understand the usefulness of consolidated statements.

(LO 4)

Instructions
(a) Explain the relationship between Agee Company and Himes Corporation.
(b) How should Agee account for its investment in Himes?
(c) Why is the accounting treatment described in (b) useful?

E12-10 At December 31, 2015, the trading securities for Storrer, Inc. are as follows.

Prepare adjusting entry to record fair value, and indicate statement presentation.

(LO 5, 6)

Security	Cost	Fair Value
A	$17,500	$16,000
B	12,500	14,000
C	23,000	21,000
	$53,000	$51,000

Instructions
(a) Prepare the adjusting entry at December 31, 2015, to report the securities at fair value.
(b) Show the balance sheet and income statement presentation at December 31, 2015, after adjustment to fair value.

E12-11 Data for investments in stock classified as trading securities are presented in E12-10. Assume instead that the investments are classified as available-for-sale securities. They have the same cost and fair value. The securities are considered to be a long-term investment.

Prepare adjusting entry to record fair value, and indicate statement presentation.

(LO 5, 6)

Instructions
(a) Prepare the adjusting entry at December 31, 2015, to report the securities at fair value.
(b) Show the statement presentation at December 31, 2015, after adjustment to fair value.
(c) ▬▬▶ E. Kretsinger, a member of the board of directors, does not understand the reporting of the unrealized gains or losses. Write a letter to Ms. Kretsinger explaining the reporting and the purposes that it serves.

E12-12 Uttinger Company has the following data at December 31, 2015.

Prepare adjusting entries for fair value, and indicate statement presentation for two classes of securities.

(LO 5, 6)

Securities	Cost	Fair Value
Trading	$120,000	$126,000
Available-for-sale	100,000	96,000

The available-for-sale securities are held as a long-term investment.

Instructions
(a) Prepare the adjusting entries to report each class of securities at fair value.
(b) Indicate the statement presentation of each class of securities and the related unrealized gain (loss) accounts.

***E12-13** On January 1, 2015, Lennon Corporation acquires 100% of Ono Inc. for $220,000 in cash. The condensed balance sheets of the two corporations immediately following the acquisition are shown on page 634.

Prepare consolidated worksheet when cost equals book value.

(LO 7)

	Lennon Corporation	Ono Inc.
Current assets	$ 60,000	$ 50,000
Investment in Ono Inc. common stock	220,000	
Plant and equipment (net)	300,000	220,000
	$580,000	$270,000
Current liabilities	$180,000	$ 50,000
Common stock	230,000	80,000
Retained earnings	170,000	140,000
	$580,000	$270,000

Instructions
Prepare a worksheet for a consolidated balance sheet.

Prepare consolidated worksheet when cost exceeds book value.
(LO 7)

*E12-14 Data for the Lennon and Ono corporations are presented in E12-13. Assume that instead of paying $220,000 in cash for Ono Inc., Lennon Corporation pays $225,000 in cash. Thus, at the acquisition date, the assets of Lennon Corporation are current assets $55,000, investment in Ono Inc. common stock $225,000, and plant and equipment (net) $300,000.

Instructions
Prepare a worksheet for a consolidated balance sheet.

EXERCISES: SET B AND CHALLENGE EXERCISES

Visit the book's companion website, at **www.wiley.com/college/weygandt**, and choose the Student Companion site to access Exercise Set B and Challenge Exercises.

PROBLEMS: SET A

Journalize debt investment transactions and show financial statement presentation.
(LO 2, 5, 6)

P12-1A Vilander Carecenters Inc. provides financing and capital to the health-care industry, with a particular focus on nursing homes for the elderly. The following selected transactions relate to bonds acquired as an investment by Vilander, whose fiscal year ends on December 31.

2015

Jan. 1   Purchased at face value $2,000,000 of Javier Nursing Centers, Inc., 10-year, 8% bonds dated January 1, 2015, directly from Javier.
July 1   Received the semiannual interest on the Javier bonds.
Dec. 31   Accrual of interest at year-end on the Javier bonds.

(Assume that all intervening transactions and adjustments have been properly recorded and that the number of bonds owned has not changed from December 31, 2015, to December 31, 2017.)

2018

Jan. 1   Received the semiannual interest on the Javier bonds.
Jan. 1   Sold $1,000,000 Javier bonds at 106.
July 1   Received the semiannual interest on the Javier bonds.
Dec. 31   Accrual of interest at year-end on the Javier bonds.

Instructions

(a) Gain on sale of debt investment $60,000

(a) Journalize the listed transactions for the years 2015 and 2018.
(b) Assume that the fair value of the bonds at December 31, 2015, was $2,200,000. These bonds are classified as available-for-sale securities. Prepare the adjusting entry to record these bonds at fair value.
(c) Based on your analysis in part (b), show the balance sheet presentation of the bonds and interest receivable at December 31, 2015. Assume the investments are considered long-term. Indicate where any unrealized gain or loss is reported in the financial statements.

P12-2A In January 2015, the management of Kinzie Company concludes that it has sufficient cash to permit some short-term investments in debt and stock securities. During the year, the following transactions occurred.

Journalize investment transactions, prepare adjusting entry, and show statement presentation.

(LO 2, 3, 5, 6)

Feb. 1   Purchased 600 shares of Muninger common stock for $32,400.
Mar. 1   Purchased 800 shares of Tatman common stock for $20,000.
Apr. 1   Purchased 50 $1,000, 7% Yoakem bonds for $50,000. Interest is payable semiannually on April 1 and October 1.
July 1   Received a cash dividend of $0.60 per share on the Muninger common stock.
Aug. 1   Sold 200 shares of Muninger common stock at $58 per share.
Sept. 1   Received a $1 per share cash dividend on the Tatman common stock.
Oct. 1   Received the semiannual interest on the Yoakem bonds.
Oct. 1   Sold the Yoakem bonds for $49,000.

At December 31, the fair value of the Muninger common stock was $55 per share. The fair value of the Tatman common stock was $24 per share.

Instructions
(a) Journalize the transactions and post to the accounts Debt Investments and Stock Investments. (Post in T-account form.)
(b) Prepare the adjusting entry at December 31, 2015, to report the investments at fair value. All securities are considered to be trading securities.
(c) Show the balance sheet presentation of investments at December 31, 2015.
(d) Identify the income statement accounts and give the statement classification of each account.

(a) Gain on sale of stock investment $800

P12-3A On December 31, 2015, Turnball Associates owned the following securities, held as a long-term investment. The securities are not held for influence or control of the investee.

Journalize transactions and adjusting entry for stock investments.

(LO 3, 5, 6)

Common Stock	Shares	Cost
Gehring Co.	2,000	$60,000
Wooderson Co.	5,000	45,000
Kitselton Co.	1,500	30,000

On December 31, 2015, the total fair value of the securities was equal to its cost. In 2016, the following transactions occurred.

July 1   Received $1 per share semiannual cash dividend on Wooderson Co. common stock.
Aug. 1   Received $0.50 per share cash dividend on Gehring Co. common stock.
Sept. 1   Sold 1,500 shares of Wooderson Co. common stock for cash at $8 per share.
Oct. 1   Sold 800 shares of Gehring Co. common stock for cash at $33 per share.
Nov. 1   Received $1 per share cash dividend on Kitselton Co. common stock.
Dec. 15   Received $0.50 per share cash dividend on Gehring Co. common stock.
     31   Received $1 per share semiannual cash dividend on Wooderson Co. common stock.

At December 31, the fair values per share of the common stocks were Gehring Co. $32, Wooderson Co. $8, and Kitselton Co. $18.

Instructions
(a) Journalize the 2016 transactions and post to the account Stock Investments. (Post in T-account form.)
(b) Prepare the adjusting entry at December 31, 2016, to show the securities at fair value. The stock should be classified as available-for-sale securities.
(c) Show the balance sheet presentation of the investment-related accounts at December 31, 2016. At this date, Turnball Associates has common stock $1,500,000 and retained earnings $1,000,000.

(b) Unrealized loss $4,100

P12-4A Heidebrecht Design acquired 20% of the outstanding common stock of Quayle Company on January 1, 2015, by paying $800,000 for the 30,000 shares. Quayle declared and paid $0.30 per share cash dividends on March 15, June 15, September 15, and December 15, 2015. Quayle reported net income of $320,000 for the year. At December 31, 2015, the market price of Quayle common stock was $34 per share.

Prepare entries under the cost and equity methods, and tabulate differences.

(LO 3)

Instructions
(a) Prepare the journal entries for Heidebrecht Design for 2015 assuming Heidebrecht Design cannot exercise significant influence over Quayle. Use the cost method and assume that Quayle common stock should be classified as a trading security.
(b) Prepare the journal entries for Heidebrecht Design for 2015 assuming Heidebrecht Design can exercise significant influence over Quayle. Use the equity method.

(a) Total dividend revenue $36,000

(b) Revenue from stock investments $64,000

(c) Indicate the balance sheet and income statement account balances at December 31, 2015, under each method of accounting.

Journalize stock investment transactions and show statement presentation.

(LO 3, 5, 6)

P12-5A The following securities are in Frederick Company's portfolio of long-term available-for-sale securities at December 31, 2015.

	Cost
1,000 shares of Willhite Corporation common stock	$52,000
1,400 shares of Hutcherson Corporation common stock	84,000
1,200 shares of Downing Corporation preferred stock	33,600

On December 31, 2015, the total cost of the portfolio equaled total fair value. Frederick had the following transactions related to the securities during 2016.

Jan. 20	Sold all 1,000 shares of Willhite Corporation common stock at $55 per share.
28	Purchased 400 shares of $70 par value common stock of Liggett Corporation at $78 per share.
30	Received a cash dividend of $1.15 per share on Hutcherson Corporation common stock.
Feb. 8	Received cash dividends of $0.40 per share on Downing Corporation preferred stock.
18	Sold all 1,200 shares of Downing Corp. preferred stock at $27 per share.
July 30	Received a cash dividend of $1.00 per share on Hutcherson Corporation common stock.
Sept. 6	Purchased an additional 900 shares of $10 par value common stock of Liggett Corporation at $82 per share.
Dec. 1	Received a cash dividend of $1.50 per share on Liggett Corporation common stock.

At December 31, 2016, the fair values of the securities were:

Hutcherson Corporation common stock	$64 per share
Liggett Corporation common stock	$72 per share

Instructions

(a) Loss on sale of stock investment $1,200

(c) Unrealized loss $5,800

(a) Prepare journal entries to record the transactions.
(b) Post to the investment accounts. (Use T-accounts.)
(c) Prepare the adjusting entry at December 31, 2016 to report the portfolio at fair value.
(d) Show the balance sheet presentation at December 31, 2016, for the investment-related accounts.

Prepare a balance sheet.

(LO 5, 6)

P12-6A The following data, presented in alphabetical order, are taken from the records of Nieto Corporation.

Accounts payable	$ 260,000
Accounts receivable	140,000
Accumulated depreciation—buildings	180,000
Accumulated depreciation—equipment	52,000
Allowance for doubtful accounts	6,000
Bonds payable (10%, due 2023)	500,000
Buildings	950,000
Cash	62,000
Common stock ($10 par value; 500,000 shares authorized, 150,000 shares issued)	1,500,000
Dividends payable	80,000
Equipment	275,000
Fair value adjustment—available-for-sale securities (Dr)	8,000
Goodwill	200,000
Income taxes payable	120,000
Inventory	170,000
Investment in Mara common stock (30% ownership), at equity	380,000
Investment in Sasse common stock (10% ownership), at cost	278,000
Land	390,000
Notes payable (due 2016)	70,000
Paid-in capital in excess of par—common stock	130,000
Premium on bonds payable	40,000
Prepaid insurance	16,000
Retained earnings	103,000
Short-term investments, at fair value (and cost)	180,000
Unrealized gain—available-for-sale securities	8,000

The investment in Sasse common stock is considered to be a long-term available-for-sale security.

Instructions
Prepare a classified balance sheet at December 31, 2015.

Total assets $2,811,000

*P12-7A Robinson Corporation purchased all the outstanding common stock of Hoffman Plastics, Inc. on December 31, 2015. Just before the purchase, the condensed balance sheets of the two companies appeared as follows.

Prepare consolidated worksheet and balance sheet when cost exceeds book value.
(LO 7)

	Robinson Corporation	Hoffman Plastics, Inc.
Current assets	$1,480,000	$ 435,500
Plant and equipment (net)	2,100,000	676,000
	$3,580,000	$1,111,500
Current liabilities	$ 578,000	$ 92,500
Common stock	1,950,000	525,000
Retained earnings	1,052,000	494,000
	$3,580,000	$1,111,500

Robinson used current assets of $1,225,000 to acquire the stock of Hoffman Plastics. The excess of this purchase price over the book value of Hoffman Plastics' net assets is determined to be attributable $86,000 to Hoffman Plastics' plant and equipment and the remainder to goodwill.

Instructions
(a) Prepare the entry for Robinson's acquisition of Hoffman Plastics, Inc. stock.
(b) Prepare a consolidated worksheet at December 31, 2015.
(c) Prepare a consolidated balance sheet at December 31, 2015.

(b) Excess of cost over book value $120,000

PROBLEMS: SET B

P12-1B Cheese Farms is a grower of hybrid seed corn for Mukenthaler Genetics Corporation. It has had two exceptionally good years and has elected to invest its excess funds in bonds. The selected transactions, shown below, relate to bonds acquired as an investment by Cheese Farms, whose fiscal year ends on December 31.

Journalize debt investment transactions and show financial statement presentation.
(LO 2, 5, 6)

2015

Jan. 1 — Purchased at face value $400,000 of Wilkerson Corporation 10-year, 9% bonds dated January 1, 2015, directly from the issuing corporation.
July 1 — Received the semiannual interest on the Wilkerson bonds.
Dec. 31 — Accrual of interest at year-end on the Wilkerson bonds.

(Assume that all intervening transactions and adjustments have been properly recorded and the number of bonds owned has not changed from December 31, 2015, to December 31, 2017.)

2018

Jan. 1 — Received the semiannual interest on the Wilkerson bonds.
Jan. 1 — Sold $200,000 of Wilkerson bonds at 114.
July 1 — Received the semiannual interest on the Wilkerson bonds.
Dec. 31 — Accrual of interest at year-end on the Wilkerson bonds.

Instructions
(a) Journalize the listed transactions for the years 2015 and 2018.
(b) Assume that the fair value of the bonds at December 31, 2015, was $385,000. These bonds are classified as available-for-sale securities. Prepare the adjusting entry to record these bonds at fair value.
(c) Based on your analysis in part (b), show the balance sheet presentation of the bonds and interest receivable at December 31, 2015. Assume the investments are considered long-term. Indicate where any unrealized gain or loss is reported in the financial statements.

(a) Gain on sale of debt investments $28,000

P12-2B In January 2015, the management of Kord Company concludes that it has sufficient cash to purchase some short-term investments in debt and stock securities. During the year, the following transactions occurred.

Feb. 1   Purchased 500 shares of Day common stock for $30,800.
Mar. 1   Purchased 600 shares of Eldridge common stock for $20,300.
Apr. 1   Purchased 40 $1,000, 9% Lorenz bonds for $40,000. Interest is payable semiannually on April 1 and October 1.
July 1   Received a cash dividend of $0.60 per share on the Day common stock.
Aug. 1   Sold 300 shares of Day common stock at $69 per share.
Sept. 1 Received a $1 per share cash dividend on the Eldridge common stock.
Oct. 1   Received the semiannual interest on the Lorenz bonds.
Oct. 1   Sold the Lorenz bonds for $44,000.

At December 31, the fair value of the Day common stock was $66 per share. The fair value of the Eldridge common stock was $29 per share.

Instructions

(a) Journalize the transactions and post to the accounts Debt Investments and Stock Investments. (Post in T-account form.)

(b) Prepare the adjusting entry at December 31, 2015, to report the investments at fair value. All securities are considered to be trading securities.

(c) Show the balance sheet presentation of investments at December 31, 2015.

(d) Identify the income statement accounts and give the statement classification of each account.

P12-3B On December 31, 2015, Bly Associates owned the following securities, held as long-term investments.

Common Stock	Shares	Cost
Woolridge Co.	4,000	$100,000
Coria Co.	5,000	30,000
Sterling Motors Co.	3,000	60,000

On this date, the total fair value of the securities was equal to its cost. The securities are not held for influence or control over the investees. In 2016, the following transactions occurred.

July 1   Received $1 per share semiannual cash dividend on Coria Co. common stock.
Aug. 1   Received $0.50 per share cash dividend on Woolridge Co. common stock.
Sept. 1 Sold 1,500 shares of Coria Co. common stock for cash at $7 per share.
Oct. 1   Sold 600 shares of Woolridge Co. common stock for cash at $30 per share.
Nov. 1   Received $1 per share cash dividend on Sterling Motor Co. common stock.
Dec. 15 Received $0.50 per share cash dividend on Woolridge Co. common stock.
31   Received $1 per share semiannual cash dividend on Coria Co. common stock.

At December 31, the fair values per share of the common stocks were Woolridge Co. $23, Coria Co. $7, and Sterling Motors Co. $19.

Instructions

(a) Journalize the 2016 transactions and post to the account Stock Investments. (Post in T-account form.)

(b) Prepare the adjusting entry at December 31, 2016, to show the securities at fair value. The stock should be classified as available-for-sale securities.

(c) Show the balance sheet presentation of the investment-related accounts at December 31, 2016. At this date, Bly Associates has common stock $2,000,000 and retained earnings $1,200,000.

P12-4B Wooden's Concrete acquired 20% of the outstanding common stock of Hoag, Inc. on January 1, 2015, by paying $1,100,000 for 40,000 shares. Hoag declared and paid a $0.50 per share cash dividend on June 30 and again on December 31, 2015. Hoag reported net income of $600,000 for the year. At December 31, 2015, the market price of Hoag's common stock was $30 per share.

Instructions

(a) Prepare the journal entries for Wooden's Concrete for 2015 assuming Wooden's cannot exercise significant influence over Hoag. Use the cost method and assume Hoag common stock should be classified as available-for-sale.

(b) Prepare the journal entries for Wooden's Concrete for 2015 assuming Wooden's can exercise significant influence over Hoag. Use the equity method.

(c) Indicate the balance sheet and income statement account balances at December 31, 2015, under each method of accounting.

P12-5B The following are in Rodriguez Company's portfolio of long-term available-for-sale securities at December 31, 2015.

	Cost
700 shares of Parra Corporation common stock	$35,000
900 shares of Robison Corporation common stock	42,000
800 shares of Vega Corporation preferred stock	22,400

On December 31, the total cost of the portfolio equaled total fair value. Rodriguez Company had the following transactions related to the securities during 2016.

Jan. 7 Sold 700 shares of Parra Corporation common stock at $55 per share.

10 Purchased 300 shares, $70 par value common stock of Younker Corporation at $78 per share.

26 Received a cash dividend of $1.15 per share on Robison Corporation common stock.

Feb. 2 Received cash dividends of $0.40 per share on Vega Corporation preferred stock.

10 Sold all 800 shares of Vega Corporation preferred stock at $26 per share.

July 1 Received a cash dividend of $1.00 per share on Robison Corporation common stock.

Sept. 1 Purchased an additional 800 shares of the $70 par value common stock of Younker Corporation at $75 per share.

Dec. 15 Received a cash dividend of $1.50 per share on Younker Corporation common stock.

At December 31, 2016, the fair values of the securities were:

Robison Corporation common stock	$48 per share
Younker Corporation common stock	$72 per share

Instructions

(a) Prepare journal entries to record the transactions.

(b) Post to the investment accounts. (Use T-accounts.)

(c) Prepare the adjusting entry at December 31, 2016, to report the portfolio at fair value.

(d) Show the balance sheet presentation at December 31, 2016, for the investment-related accounts.

P12-6B The following data, presented in alphabetical order, are taken from the records of Mussatto Corporation.

Accounts payable	$ 375,000
Accounts receivable	135,000
Accumulated depreciation—buildings	270,000
Accumulated depreciation—equipment	80,000
Allowance for doubtful accounts	10,000
Bonds payable (10%, due 2025)	600,000
Buildings	1,350,000
Cash	210,000
Common stock ($5 par value; 500,000 shares authorized, 440,000 shares issued)	2,200,000
Discount on bonds payable	30,000
Dividends payable	75,000
Equipment	415,000
Goodwill	300,000
Income taxes payable	180,000
Inventory	255,000
Investment in Sanchez Inc. stock (30% ownership), at equity	900,000
Land	780,000
Notes payable (due 2016)	110,000

Paid-in capital in excess of par—common stock	$ 300,000
Prepaid insurance	25,000
Retained earnings	480,000
Short-term investments, at fair value (and cost)	280,000

Total assets $4,290,000

Instructions
Prepare a classified balance sheet at December 31, 2015.

Prepare consolidated worksheet and balance sheet when cost exceeds book value.

(LO 7)

*P12-7B Patel Company purchased all the outstanding common stock of Singh Company on December 31, 2015. Just before the purchase, the condensed balance sheets of the two companies were as follows.

	Patel Company	Singh Company
Current assets	$1,478,000	$379,000
Plant and equipment (net)	1,882,000	351,000
	$3,360,000	$730,000
Current liabilities	$ 870,000	$ 90,000
Common stock	1,947,000	360,000
Retained earnings	543,000	280,000
	$3,360,000	$730,000

Patel used current assets of $710,000 to acquire the stock of Singh. The excess of this purchase price over the book value of Patel's net assets is determined to be attributable $20,000 to Singh's plant and equipment and the remainder to goodwill.

Instructions
(a) Prepare the entry for Patel Company's acquisition of Singh Company stock.
(b) Prepare a consolidated worksheet at December 31, 2015.
(c) Prepare a consolidated balance sheet at December 31, 2015.

(b) Excess of cost over book value $50,000

PROBLEMS: SET C

Visit the book's companion website, at **www.wiley.com/college/weygandt**, and choose the Student Companion site to access Problem Set C.

COMPREHENSIVE PROBLEM: CHAPTERS 11 TO 12

CP12 Part I Debby Kauffman and her two colleagues, Jamie Hiatt and Ella Rincon, are personal trainers at an upscale health spa/resort in Tampa, Florida. They want to start a health club that specializes in health plans for people in the 50+ age range. The growing population in this age range and strong consumer interest in the health benefits of physical activity have convinced them they can profitably operate their own club. In addition to many other decisions, they need to determine what type of business organization they want. Jamie believes there are more advantages to the corporate form than a partnership, but he hasn't yet convinced Debby and Ella. They have come to you, a small-business consulting specialist, seeking information and advice regarding the choice of starting a partnership versus a corporation.

Instructions
(a) ━━━━▶ Prepare a memo (dated May 26, 2014) that describes the advantages and disadvantages of both partnerships and corporations. Advise Debby, Jamie, and Ella regarding which organizational form you believe would better serve their purposes. Make sure to include reasons supporting your advice.

Part II   After deciding to incorporate, each of the three investors receives 20,000 shares of $2 par common stock on June 12, 2014, in exchange for their co-owned building ($200,000 fair value) and $100,000 total cash they contributed to the business. The next decision that Debby, Jamie, and Ella need to make is how to obtain financing for renovation and equipment. They understand the difference between equity securities and debt securities, but do not understand the tax, net income, and earnings per share consequences of equity versus debt financing on the future of their business.

Instructions

(b) Prepare notes for a discussion with the three entrepreneurs in which you will compare the consequences of using equity versus debt financing. As part of your notes, show the differences in interest and tax expense assuming $1,400,000 is financed with common stock, and then alternatively with debt. Assume that when common stock is used, 140,000 shares will be issued. When debt is used, assume the interest rate on debt is 9%, the tax rate is 32%, and income before interest and taxes is $300,000. (You may want to use a computer spreadsheet.)

Part III   During the discussion about financing, Ella mentions that one of her clients, Timothy Hansen, has approached her about buying a significant interest in the new club. Having an interested investor sways the three to issue equity securities to provide the financing they need. On July 21, 2014, Mr. Hansen buys 90,000 shares at a price of $10 per share.

The club, LifePath Fitness, opens on January 12, 2015, and after a slow start begins to produce the revenue desired by the owners. The owners decide to pay themselves a stock dividend since cash has been less than abundant since they opened their doors. The 10% stock dividend is declared by the owners on July 27, 2015. The market price of the stock is $3 on the declaration date. The date of record is July 31, 2015 (there have been no changes in stock ownership since the initial issuance), and the issue date is August 15, 2015. By the middle of the fourth quarter of 2015, the cash flow of LifePath Fitness has improved to the point that the owners feel ready to pay themselves a cash dividend. They declare a $0.05 cash dividend on December 4, 2015. The record date is December 14, 2015, and the payment date is December 24, 2015.

Instructions

(c) (1) Record all of the transactions related to the common stock of LifePath Fitness during the years 2014 and 2015. (2) Indicate how many shares are issued and outstanding after the stock dividend is issued.

Part IV   Since the club opened, a major concern has been the pool facilities. Although the existing pool is adequate, Debby, Jamie, and Ella all desire to make LifePath a cutting-edge facility. Until the end of 2015, financing concerns prevented this improvement. However, because there has been steady growth in clientele, revenue, and income since the fourth quarter of 2015, the owners have explored possible financing options. They are hesitant to issue stock and change the ownership mix because they have been able to work together as a team with great effectiveness. They have formulated a plan to issue secured term bonds to raise the needed $600,000 for the pool facilities. By the end of April 2016, everything was in place for the bond issue to go ahead. On June 1, 2016, the bonds were issued for $548,000. The bonds pay semiannual interest of 3% (6% annual) on December 1 and June 1 of each year. The bonds mature in 10 years, and amortization is computed using the straight-line method.

Instructions

(d) Record (1) the issuance of the secured bonds, (2) the interest payment made on December 1, 2016, (3) the adjusting entry required at December 31, 2016, and (4) the interest payment made on June 1, 2017.

Part V   Mr. Hansen's purchase of the stock of LifePath Fitness was done through his business. The stock investment has always been accounted for using the cost method on his firm's books. However, early in 2017 he decided to take his company public. He is preparing an IPO (initial public offering), and he needs to have the firm's financial statements audited. One of the issues to be resolved is to restate the stock investment in LifePath Fitness using the equity method since Mr. Hansen's ownership percentage is greater than 20%.

Instructions

(e) (1) Give the entries that would have been made on Hansen's books if the equity method of accounting for investments had been used from the initial investment through 2016. Assume the following data for LifePath.

	2014	2015	2016
Net income	$30,000	$70,000	$105,000
Total cash dividends	$ 2,100	$20,000	$ 50,000

(2) Compute the balance in the Stock Investments account (as it relates to LifePath Fitness) at the end of 2016.

CONTINUING COOKIE CHRONICLE

(*Note:* This is a continuation of the Cookie Chronicle from Chapters 1 through 11.)

CCC12 Natalie has been approached by Ken Thornton, a shareholder of The Beanery Coffee Inc. Ken wants to retire and would like to sell his 1,000 shares in The Beanery, which represent 30% of all shares issued. The Beanery is currently operated by Ken's twin daughters, who each own 35% of the common shares. The Beanery not only operates a coffee shop but also roasts and sells beans to retailers under the name "Rocky Mountain Beanery."

Ken has met with Curtis and Natalie to discuss the business operation. All have concluded that there would be many advantages for Cookie & Coffee Creations Inc. to acquire an interest in The Beanery Coffee. Despite the apparent advantages, however, Natalie and Curtis are still not convinced that they should participate in this business venture.

Go to the book's companion website, **www.wiley.com/college/weygandt**, *to see the completion of this problem.*

Broadening Your PERSPECTIVE

Financial Reporting and Analysis

Financial Reporting Problem: Apple Inc.

BYP12-1 The annual report of Apple Inc. is presented in Appendix A. Instructions for accessing and using the company's complete annual report, including the notes to the financial statements, are also provided in Appendix A.

Instructions
(a) Determine the percentage increase for (1) short-term marketable securities from 2010 to 2011, and (2) long-term marketable securities from 2010 to 2011.
(b) Using Apple's consolidated statement of cash flows, determine:
  (1) Purchases of marketable securities during the current year.
  (2) How much was spent for business acquisitions, net of cash acquired during the current year.

Comparative Analysis Problem:
PepsiCo, Inc. vs. The Coca-Cola Company

BYP12-2 PepsiCo's financial statements are presented in Appendix B. Financial statements of The Coca-Cola Company are presented in Appendix C. Instructions for accessing and using the complete annual reports of PepsiCo and Coca-Cola, including the notes to the financial statements, are also provided in Appendices B and C, respectively.

Instructions

(a) Based on the information contained in these financial statements, determine the following for each company.

    (1) Net cash used in investing (investment) activities for the current year (from the statement of cash flows).

    (2) Cash used for capital expenditures during the current year.

(b) Each of PepsiCo's financial statements is labeled "consolidated." What has been consolidated? That is, from the contents of PepsiCo's annual report, identify by name the corporations that have been consolidated (parent and subsidiaries).

Comparative Analysis Problem: Amazon.com, Inc. vs. Wal-Mart Stores, Inc.

BYP12-3 Amazon.com, Inc.'s financial statements are presented in Appendix D. Financial statements of Wal-Mart Stores, Inc. are presented in Appendix E. Instructions for accessing and using the complete annual reports of Amazon and Wal-Mart, including the notes to the financial statements, are also provided in Appendices D and E, respectively.

Instructions

(a) Based on the information contained in these financial statements, determine the following for each company.

    (1) Net cash used for investing (investment) activities for the current year (from the statement of cash flows).

    (2) Cash used for business acquisitions, net of cash acquired during the current year.

(b) Each of Amazon's financial statements is labeled "consolidated." What has been consolidated? That is, from the contents of Amazon's annual report, identify by name the corporations that have been consolidated (parent and subsidiaries).

Real-World Focus

BYP12-4 Most publicly traded companies are examined by numerous analysts. These analysts often don't agree about a company's future prospects. In this exercise, you will find analysts' ratings about companies and make comparisons over time and across companies in the same industry. You will also see to what extent the analysts experienced "earnings surprises." Earnings surprises can cause changes in stock prices.

Address: **biz.yahoo.com/i**, or go to **www.wiley.com/college/weygandt**

Steps

1. Choose a company.
2. Use the index to find the company's name.
3. Choose **Research**.

Instructions

(a) How many analysts rated the company?

(b) What percentage rated it a strong buy?

(c) What was the average rating for the week?

(d) Did the average rating improve or decline relative to the previous week?

Critical Thinking

Decision-Making Across the Organization

BYP12-5 At the beginning of the question-and-answer portion of the annual stockholders' meeting of Neosho Corporation, stockholder John Linton asks, "Why did management sell the holdings in JMB Company at a loss when this company has been very profitable during the period Neosho held its stock?"

Since president Tony Cedeno has just concluded his speech on the recent success and bright future of Neosho, he is taken aback by this question and responds, "I remember we paid $1,300,000 for that stock some years ago. I am sure we sold that stock at a much higher price. You must be mistaken."

Linton retorts, "Well, right here in footnote number 7 to the annual report it shows that 240,000 shares, a 30% interest in JMB, were sold on the last day of the year. Also, it states that JMB earned $520,000 this year and paid out $160,000 in cash dividends. Further, a summary statement indicates that in past years, while Neosho held JMB stock, JMB earned $1,240,000 and paid out $440,000 in dividends. Finally, the income statement for this year shows a loss on the sale of JMB stock of $180,000. So, I doubt that I am mistaken."

Red-faced, president Cedeno turns to you.

Instructions

With the class divided into groups, answer the following.

(a) What dollar amount did Neosho receive upon the sale of the JMB stock?

(b) Explain why both stockholder Linton and president Cedeno are correct.

Communication Activity

BYP12-6 Fegan Corporation has purchased two securities for its portfolio. The first is a stock investment in Plummer Corporation, one of its suppliers. Fegan purchased 10% of Plummer with the intention of holding it for a number of years, but has no intention of purchasing more shares. The second investment was a purchase of debt securities. Fegan purchased the debt securities because its analysts believe that changes in market interest rates will cause these securities to increase in value in a short period of time. Fegan intends to sell the securities as soon as they have increased in value.

Instructions

Write a memo to Sam Nichols, the chief financial officer, explaining how to account for each of these investments. Explain what the implications for reported income are from this accounting treatment.

Ethics Case

BYP12-7 Harding Financial Services Company holds a large portfolio of debt and stock securities as an investment. The total fair value of the portfolio at December 31, 2015, is greater than total cost. Some securities have increased in value and others have decreased. Ann Bales, the financial vice president, and Kim Reeble, the controller, are in the process of classifying for the first time the securities in the portfolio.

Bales suggests classifying the securities that have increased in value as trading securities in order to increase net income for the year. She wants to classify the securities that have decreased in value as long-term available-for-sale securities, so that the decreases in value will not affect 2015 net income.

Reeble disagrees. She recommends classifying the securities that have decreased in value as trading securities and those that have increased in value as long-term available-for-sale securities. Reeble argues that the company is having a good earnings year and that recognizing the losses now will help to smooth income for this year. Moreover, for future years, when the company may not be as profitable, the company will have built-in gains.

Instructions

(a) Will classifying the securities as Bales and Reeble suggest actually affect earnings as each says it will?

(b) Is there anything unethical in what Bales and Reeble propose? Who are the stakeholders affected by their proposals?

(c) Assume that Bales and Reeble properly classify the portfolio. At year-end, Bales proposes to sell the securities that will increase 2015 net income, and Reeble proposes to sell the securities that will decrease 2015 net income. Is this unethical?

All About You

BYP12-8 The Securities and Exchange Commission (SEC) is the primary regulatory agency of U.S. financial markets. Its job is to ensure that the markets remain fair for all investors. The following SEC sites provide useful information for investors.

Address: **www.sec.gov/answers.shtml** and **http://www.sec.gov/investor/tools/quiz.htm**, or go to **www.wiley.com/college/weygandt.**

Instructions

(a) Go to the first SEC site and find the definition of the following terms.
   (i) Ask price.
   (ii) Margin.
   (iii) Prospectus.
   (iv) Index fund.

(b) Go to the second SEC site and take the short quiz.

FASB Codification Activity

BYP12-9 If your school has a subscription to the FASB Codification, go to **http://aaahq.org/ascLogin.cfm** to log in and prepare responses to the following.

(a) What is the definition of a trading security?
(b) What is the definition of an available-for-sale security?
(c) What is the definition of a held-to-maturity security?

Answers to Chapter Questions

Answers to Insight and Accounting Across the Organization Questions

p. 612 How Procter & Gamble Accounts for Gillette   Q: Where on Procter & Gamble's balance sheet will you find its investment in Gillette Company? **A:** Because Procter & Gamble owns 100% of Gillette, Procter & Gamble does not report Gillette in the investment section of its balance sheet. Instead, Gillette's assets and liabilities are included and commingled with the assets and liabilities of Procter & Gamble.

p. 616 And the Correct Way to Report Investments Is... ?   Q: Why might the use of the equity method not lead to full disclosure in the financial statements? **A:** Under the equity method, the investment in common stock of another company is initially recorded at cost. After that, the investment account is adjusted at each reporting date to show the investor's equity in the investee. However, on the investor's balance sheet, only the investment account is shown. The pro rata share of the investee's assets and liabilities are not reported. Because the pro rata share of the investee's assets and liabilities are not shown, some argue that the full disclosure principle is violated.

Answers to Self-Test Questions

1. d **2.** a **3.** b **4.** c **5.** a **6.** b $300,000 + [25\% \times (\$160,000 - \$60,000)]$ **7.** c **8.** d **9.** a **10.** c
11. c ($41,300 - \$39,800$) + $900 **12.** b **13.** c ***14.** d $175,000 - \$160,000$ ***15.** d ***16.** d

A Look at IFRS

Until recently, when the IASB issued *IFRS 9,* the accounting and reporting for investments under IFRS and GAAP were for the most part very similar. However, *IFRS 9* introduces new investment classifications and increases the situations when investments are accounted for at fair value, with gains and losses recorded in income.

LEARNING OBJECTIVE   8

Compare the accounting for investments under GAAP and IFRS.

Key Points

• The basic accounting entries to record the acquisition of debt securities, the receipt of interest, and the sale of debt securities are the same under IFRS and GAAP.

• The basic accounting entries to record the acquisition of stock investments, the receipt of dividends, and the sale of stock securities are the same under IFRS and GAAP.

- Both IFRS and GAAP use the same criteria to determine whether the equity method of accounting should be used—that is, significant influence with a general guide of over 20% ownership, IFRS uses the term **associate investment** rather than equity investment to describe its investment under the equity method.

- Under IFRS, both the investor and an associate company should follow the same accounting policies. As a result, in order to prepare financial information, adjustments are made to the associate's policies to conform to the investor's books. GAAP does not have that requirement.

- The basis for consolidation under IFRS is control. Under GAAP, a bipolar approach is used, which is a risk-and-reward model (often referred to as a variable-entity approach) and a voting-interest approach. However, under both systems, for consolidation to occur, the investor company must generally own 50% of another company.

- In general, IFRS requires that companies determine how to measure their financial assets based on two criteria:

   ♦ The company's business model for managing their financial assets; and

   ♦ The contractual cash flow characteristics of the financial asset.

   If a company has (1) a business model whose objective is to hold assets in order to collect contractual cash flows and (2) the contractual terms of the financial asset gives specified dates to cash flows that are solely payments of principal and interest on the principal amount outstanding, then the company should use cost (often referred to as amortized cost).

   For example, assume that Mitsubishi purchases a bond investment that it intends to hold to maturity (held-for-collection). Its business model for this type of investment is to collect interest and then principal at maturity. The payment dates for the interest rate and principal are stated on the bond. In this case, Mitsubishi accounts for the investment at cost. If, on the other hand, Mitsubishi purchased the bonds as part of a trading strategy to speculate on interest rate changes (a trading investment), then the debt investment is reported at fair value. As a result, only debt investments such as receivables, loans, and bond investments that meet the two criteria above are recorded at amortized cost. All other debt investments are recorded and reported at fair value.

- Equity investments are generally recorded and reported at fair value under IFRS. Equity investments do not have a fixed interest or principal payment schedule and therefore cannot be accounted for at amortized cost. In general, equity investments are valued at fair value, with all gains and losses reported in income.

- GAAP classifies investments as trading, available-for-sale (both debt and equity investments), and held-to-maturity (only for debt investments). IFRS uses held-for-collection (debt investments), trading (both debt and equity investments), and non-trading equity investment classifications. GAAP classifications are based on management's intent with respect to the investment. IFRS classifications are based on the business model used to manage the investments and the type of security.

- The accounting for trading investments is the same between GAAP and IFRS. Held-to-maturity (GAAP) and held-for-collection (IFRS) investments are accounted for at amortized cost. Gains and losses related to available-for-sale securities (GAAP) and non-trading equity investments (IFRS) are reported in other comprehensive income.

- Unrealized gains and losses related to available-for-sale securities are reported in other comprehensive income under GAAP and IFRS. These gains and losses that accumulate are then reported in the balance sheet.

- IFRS does not use "Other revenues and gains" or "Other expenses and losses" in its income statement presentation. It will generally classify these items as unusual items or financial items.

Looking to the Future

The FASB and IASB are close to developing a converged standard on the classification and measurement of financial instruments. It appears that companies will continue to classify financial instruments into three categories: trading, available-for-sale, and held-to-maturity (held-for-collection). In general, all equity investments will be reported at fair value and changes reported in net income. Debt investments will be reported at fair value unless held for collection. In that case, any gains or losses are reported in other comprehensive income.

IFRS Practice

IFRS Self-Test Questions

1. The following asset is **not** considered a financial asset under IFRS:
   (a) trading securities.
   (b) equity securities.
   (c) held-for-collection securities.
   (d) inventories.

2. Under IFRS, the equity method of accounting for long-term investments in common stock should be used when the investor has significant influence over an investee and owns:
   (a) between 20% and 50% of the investee's common stock.
   (b) 30% or more of the investee's common stock.
   (c) more than 50% of the investee's common stock.
   (d) less than 20% of the investee's common stock.

3. Under IFRS, at the end of the first year of operations, the total cost of the trading investments portfolio is $120,000. Total fair value is $115,000. The financial statement should show:
   (a) a reduction in the carrying value of the asset of $5,000 and an unrealized loss of $5,000 in unusual items or financial items.
   (b) a reduction in the carrying value of the asset of $5,000 and an unrealized loss of $5,000 in the stockholders' equity section.
   (c) a reduction in the carrying value of the asset of $5,000 in current assets and an unrealized loss of $5,000 in other comprehensive income.
   (d) a reduction in the carrying value of the asset of $5,000 in current assets and a realized loss of $5,000 in unusual items or financial items.

4. Under IFRS, unrealized gains on non-trading stock investments should:
   (a) be reported in the income statement as part of net income.
   (b) be reported as other gains on the income statement as part of net income.
   (c) not be reported on the income statement or balance sheet.
   (d) be reported as other comprehensive income.

5. Under IFRS, the unrealized loss on trading investments should be reported:
   (a) as part of other comprehensive loss reducing net income.
   (b) on the income statement reducing net income.
   (c) as part of other comprehensive loss not affecting net income.
   (d) directly to stockholders' equity bypassing the income statement.

✔ **The Navigator**

Answers to IFRS Self-Test Questions
1. d   **2.** a   **3.** a   **4.** d   **5.** b

13 | Statement of Cash Flows

Feature Story

Got Cash?

Companies must be ready to respond to changes quickly in order to survive and thrive. This requires careful management of cash. One company that managed cash successfully in its early years was Microsoft. During those years, the company paid much of its payroll with stock options (rights to purchase company stock in the future at a given price) instead of cash. This conserved cash and turned more than a thousand of its employees into millionaires.

In recent years, Microsoft has had a different kind of cash problem. Now that it has reached a more "mature" stage in life, it generates so much cash—roughly $1 billion per month—that it cannot always figure out what to do with it. At one time, Microsoft had accumulated $60 billion.

The company said it was accumulating cash to invest in new opportunities, buy other companies, and pay off pending lawsuits. Microsoft's stockholders complained that holding all this cash was putting a drag on the company's profitability. Why? Because Microsoft had the cash invested in very low-yielding government securities. Stockholders felt that the company either

should find new investment projects that would bring higher returns, or return some of the cash to stockholders.

Finally, Microsoft announced a plan to return cash to stockholders by paying a special one-time $32 billion dividend. This special dividend was so large that, according to the U.S. Commerce Department, it caused total personal income in the United States to rise by 3.7% in one month—the largest increase ever recorded by the agency. (It also made the holiday season brighter, especially for retailers in the Seattle area.) Microsoft also doubled its regular annual dividend to $3.50 per share. Further, it announced that it would spend another 30 billion buying treasury stock.

In recent years, Apple also encountered this cash "problem." At the end of 2011, Apple had nearly $100 billion in liquid assets (cash, cash equivalents, and investment securities). At that time, it was generating $37 billion of cash per year from its operating activities but spending only about $7 billion on plant assets and purchases of patents. Shareholders pressured Apple to unload some of this cash. In response, Apple announced that it would begin to pay a quarterly dividend of $2.65 per share and it would buy back up to $10 billion of its

✔ **The Navigator**

- ■ Scan Learning Objectives
- ■ Read Feature Story
- ■ Read Preview
- ■ Read text and answer **DO IT!** p. 653
  - ■ p. 660 ■ p. 663 ■ p. 667
- ■ Work Comprehensive **DO IT!** 1 p. 668
- ■ Review Summary of Learning Objectives
- ■ Work Comprehensive **DO IT!** 2 p. 677
- ■ Answer Self-Test Questions
- ■ Complete Assignments
- Go to *WileyPLUS* for practice and tutorials
- Read **A Look at IFRS** p. 709

Learning Objectives ✔ The Navigator

After studying this chapter, you should be able to:

[1] Indicate the usefulness of the statement of cash flows.

[2] Distinguish among operating, investing, and financing activities.

[3] Prepare a statement of cash flows using the indirect method.

[4] Analyze the statement of cash flows.

stock. Analysts noted that the dividend consumes only $10 billion of cash per year. This leaves Apple wallowing in cash. The rest of us should have such problems.

Source: "Business: An End to Growth? Microsoft's Cash Bonanza," *The Economist* (July 23, 2005), p. 61.

Preview of Chapter 13

✔ **The Navigator**

The balance sheet, income statement, and retained earnings statement do not always show the whole picture of the financial condition of a company or institution. In fact, looking at the financial statements of some well-known companies, a thoughtful investor might ask questions like these: How did Eastman Kodak finance cash dividends of $649 million in a year in which it earned only $17 million? How could United Air Lines purchase new planes that cost $1.9 billion in a year in which it reported a net loss of over $2 billion? How did the companies that spent a combined fantastic $3.4 trillion on mergers and acquisitions in a recent year finance those deals? Answers to these and similar questions can be found in this chapter, which presents the statement of cash flows.

The content and organization of this chapter are as follows.

STATEMENT OF CASH FLOWS		
The Statement of Cash Flows: Usefulness and Format	**Preparing the Statement of Cash Flows—Indirect Method**	**Using Cash Flows to Evaluate a Company**
• Usefulness • Classification • Significant noncash activities • Format • Preparation • Indirect and direct methods	• Step 1: Operating activities • Step 2: Investing and financing activities • Step 3: Net change in cash	• Free cash flow

The Statement of Cash Flows: Usefulness and Format

The balance sheet, income statement, and retained earnings statement provide only limited information about a company's cash flows (cash receipts and cash payments). For example, comparative balance sheets show the increase in property, plant, and equipment during the year. But, they do not show how the additions were financed or paid for. The income statement shows net income. But, it does not indicate the amount of cash generated by operating activities. The retained earnings statement shows cash dividends declared but not the cash dividends paid during the year. None of these statements presents a detailed summary of where cash came from and how it was used.

Usefulness of the Statement of Cash Flows

The **statement of cash flows** reports the cash receipts, cash payments, and net change in cash resulting from operating, investing, and financing activities during a period. The information in a statement of cash flows should help investors, creditors, and others assess:

1. **The entity's ability to generate future cash flows.** By examining relationships between items in the statement of cash flows, investors can make predictions of the amounts, timing, and uncertainty of future cash flows better than they can from accrual-basis data.

2. **The entity's ability to pay dividends and meet obligations.** If a company does not have adequate cash, it cannot pay employees, settle debts, or pay dividends. Employees, creditors, and stockholders should be particularly interested in this statement, because it alone shows the flows of cash in a business.

3. **The reasons for the difference between net income and net cash provided (used) by operating activities.** Net income provides information on the success or failure of a business. However, some financial statement users are critical of accrual-basis net income because it requires many estimates. As a result, users often challenge the reliability of the number. Such is not the case with cash. Many readers of the statement of cash flows want to know the reasons for the difference between net income and net cash provided by operating activities. Then they can assess for themselves the reliability of the income number.

4. **The cash investing and financing transactions during the period.** By examining a company's investing and financing transactions, a financial statement reader can better understand why assets and liabilities changed during the period.

Ethics Note

Though we would discourage reliance on cash flows to the exclusion of accrual accounting, comparing net cash provided by operating activities to net income can reveal important information about the "quality" of reported net income. Such a comparison can reveal the extent to which net income provides a good measure of actual performance.

Classification of Cash Flows

The statement of cash flows classifies cash receipts and cash payments as operating, investing, and financing activities. Transactions and other events characteristic of each kind of activity are as follows.

1. **Operating activities** include the cash effects of transactions that create revenues and expenses. They thus enter into the determination of net income.

2. **Investing activities** include (a) acquiring and disposing of investments and property, plant, and equipment, and (b) lending money and collecting the loans.

3. **Financing activities** include (a) obtaining cash from issuing debt and repaying the amounts borrowed, and (b) obtaining cash from stockholders, repurchasing shares, and paying dividends.

The operating activities category is the most important. It shows the cash provided by company operations. This source of cash is generally considered to be the best measure of a company's ability to generate sufficient cash to continue as a going concern.

Illustration 13-1 lists typical cash receipts and cash payments within each of the three classifications. **Study the list carefully.** It will prove very useful in solving homework exercises and problems.

Illustration 13-1
Typical receipt and payment classifications

TYPES OF CASH INFLOWS AND OUTFLOWS

Operating activities—Income statement items
Cash inflows:
  From sale of goods or services.
  From interest received and dividends received.
Cash outflows:
  To suppliers for inventory.
  To employees for wages.
  To government for taxes.
  To lenders for interest.
  To others for expenses.

Operating activities

Investing activities—Changes in investments and long-term assets
Cash inflows:
  From sale of property, plant, and equipment.
  From sale of investments in debt or equity securities of other entities.
  From collection of principal on loans to other entities.
Cash outflows:
  To purchase property, plant, and equipment.
  To purchase investments in debt or equity securities of other entities.
  To make loans to other entities.

Investing activities

Financing activities—Changes in long-term liabilities and stockholders' equity
Cash inflows:
  From sale of common stock.
  From issuance of debt (bonds and notes).
Cash outflows:
  To stockholders as dividends.
  To redeem long-term debt or reacquire capital stock (treasury stock).

Financing activities

Note the following general guidelines:

1. Operating activities involve income statement items.

2. Investing activities involve cash flows resulting from changes in investments and long-term asset items.

3. Financing activities involve cash flows resulting from changes in long-term liability and stockholders' equity items.

Companies classify as operating activities some cash flows related to investing or financing activities. For example, receipts of investment revenue (interest and dividends) are classified as operating activities. So are payments of interest to lenders. Why are these considered operating activities? **Because companies report these items in the income statement, where results of operations are shown.**

Significant Noncash Activities

Not all of a company's significant activities involve cash. Examples of significant noncash activities are:

1. Direct issuance of common stock to purchase assets.
2. Conversion of bonds into common stock.
3. Direct issuance of debt to purchase assets.
4. Exchanges of plant assets.

Companies do not report in the body of the statement of cash flows significant financing and investing activities that do not affect cash. Instead, they report these activities in either a **separate schedule** at the bottom of the statement of cash flows or in a **separate note or supplementary schedule** to the financial statements. The reporting of these noncash activities in a separate schedule satisfies the **full disclosure principle**.

In solving homework assignments, you should present significant noncash investing and financing activities in a separate schedule at the bottom of the statement of cash flows. (See the last entry in Illustration 13-2 on the next page for an example.)

ACCOUNTING ACROSS THE ORGANIZATION

Net *What?*

Net income is not the same as net cash provided by operating activities. Below are some results from recent annual reports (dollars in millions). Note the wide disparity among these companies, all of which engaged in retail merchandising.

Company	Net Income	Net Cash Provided by Operating Activities
Kohl's Corporation	$ 1,083	$ 1,234
Wal-Mart Stores, Inc.	11,284	20,169
J. C. Penney Company, Inc.	1,153	1,255
Costco Wholesale Corp.	1,082	2,076
Target Corporation	2,849	4,125

Darren McCollester/Getty Images, Inc.

In general, why do differences exist between net income and net cash provided by operating activities? (See page 709.)

Format of the Statement of Cash Flows

The general format of the statement of cash flows presents the results of the three activities discussed previously—operating, investing, and financing—plus the significant noncash investing and financing activities. Illustration 13-2 shows a widely used form of the statement of cash flows.

COMPANY NAME Statement of Cash Flows For the Period Covered		
Cash flows from operating activities		
(List of individual items)	XX	
Net cash provided (used) by operating activities		XXX
Cash flows from investing activities		
(List of individual inflows and outflows)	XX	
Net cash provided (used) by investing activities		XXX
Cash flows from financing activities		
(List of individual inflows and outflows)	XX	
Net cash provided (used) by financing activities		XXX
Net increase (decrease) in cash		XXX
Cash at beginning of period		XXX
Cash at end of period		XXX
Noncash investing and financing activities		
(List of individual noncash transactions)		XXX

Illustration 13-2
Format of statement of cash flows

The cash flows from operating activities section always appears first, followed by the investing activities section and then the financing activities section. The sum of the operating, investing, and financing sections equals the net increase or decrease in cash for the period. This amount is added to the beginning cash balance to arrive at the ending cash balance—the same amount reported on the balance sheet.

> **DO IT!**

Classification of Cash Flows

Action Plan

✔ Identify the three types of activities used to report all cash inflows and outflows.

✔ Report as operating activities the cash effects of transactions that create revenues and expenses and enter into the determination of net income.

✔ Report as investing activities transactions that (a) acquire and dispose of investments and long-term assets and (b) lend money and collect loans.

✔ Report as financing activities transactions that (a) obtain cash from issuing debt and repay the amounts borrowed and (b) obtain cash from stockholders and pay them dividends.

During its first week, Duffy & Stevenson Company had these transactions.

1. Issued 100,000 shares of $5 par value common stock for $800,000 cash.
2. Borrowed $200,000 from Castle Bank, signing a 5-year note bearing 8% interest.
3. Purchased two semi-trailer trucks for $170,000 cash.
4. Paid employees $12,000 for salaries and wages.
5. Collected $20,000 cash for services performed.

Classify each of these transactions by type of cash flow activity.

Solution

1. Financing activity	**4.** Operating activity
2. Financing activity	**5.** Operating activity
3. Investing activity	

Related exercise material: BE13-1, BE13-2, BE13-3, E13-1, E13-2, E13-3, **and** DO IT! 13-1.

 The Navigator

Preparing the Statement of Cash Flows

Companies prepare the statement of cash flows differently from the three other basic financial statements. First, it is not prepared from an adjusted trial balance. It requires detailed information concerning the changes in account balances that occurred between two points in time. An adjusted trial balance will not provide the necessary data. Second, the statement of cash flows deals with cash receipts and payments. As a result, the company **adjusts** the effects of the use of accrual accounting **to determine cash flows**.

The information to prepare this statement usually comes from three sources:

- **Comparative balance sheets.** Information in the comparative balance sheets indicates the amount of the changes in assets, liabilities, and stockholders' equities from the beginning to the end of the period.
- **Current income statement.** Information in this statement helps determine the amount of net cash provided or used by operating activities during the period.
- **Additional information.** Such information includes transaction data that are needed to determine how cash was provided or used during the period.

Preparing the statement of cash flows from these data sources involves three major steps, explained in Illustration 13-3.

Illustration 13-3
Three major steps in preparing the statement of cash flows

STEP 1: Determine net cash provided/used by operating activities by converting net income from an accrual basis to a cash basis.

Buying & selling goods

This step involves analyzing not only the current year's income statement but also comparative balance sheets and selected additional data.

STEP 2: Analyze changes in noncurrent asset and liability accounts and record as investing and financing activities, or disclose as noncash transactions.

Investing   Financing

This step involves analyzing comparative balance sheet data and selected additional information for their effects on cash.

STEP 3: Compare the net change in cash on the statement of cash flows with the change in the Cash account reported on the balance sheet to make sure the amounts agree.

Year 1   Year 2   Difference

The difference between the beginning and ending cash balances can be easily computed from comparative balance sheets.

Indirect and Direct Methods

In order to perform Step 1, a company **must convert net income from an accrual basis to a cash basis**. This conversion may be done by either of two methods: (1) the indirect method or (2) the direct method. **Both methods arrive at the same total amount** for "Net cash provided by operating activities." They differ in **how** they arrive at the amount.

The **indirect method** adjusts net income for items that do not affect cash. A great majority of companies (98%) use this method, as shown in the nearby chart.[1] Companies favor the indirect method for two reasons. (1) It is easier and less costly to prepare, and (2) it focuses on the differences between net income and net cash flow from operating activities.

The **direct method** shows operating cash receipts and payments. It is prepared by adjusting each item in the income statement from the accrual basis to the cash basis. The FASB has expressed a preference for the direct method, but allows the use of either method.

The next section illustrates the more popular indirect method. Appendix 13A illustrates the direct method.

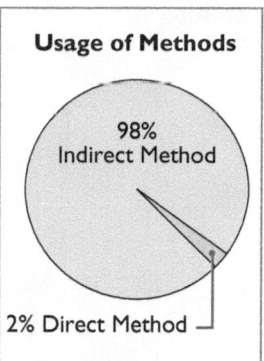

Usage of Methods

98% Indirect Method

2% Direct Method

Preparing the Statement of Cash Flows—Indirect Method

To explain how to prepare a statement of cash flows using the indirect method, we use financial information from Computer Services Company. Illustration 13-4 presents Computer Services' current and previous-year balance sheets, its current-year income statement, and related financial information for the current year.

LEARNING OBJECTIVE 3

Prepare a statement of cash flows using the indirect method.

Illustration 13-4
Comparative balance sheets, income statement, and additional information for Computer Services Company

COMPUTER SERVICES COMPANY
Comparative Balance Sheets
December 31

Assets	2015	2014	Change in Account Balance Increase/Decrease
Current assets			
Cash	$ 55,000	$ 33,000	$ 22,000 Increase
Accounts receivable	20,000	30,000	10,000 Decrease
Inventory	15,000	10,000	5,000 Increase
Prepaid expenses	5,000	1,000	4,000 Increase
Property, plant, and equipment			
Land	130,000	20,000	110,000 Increase
Buildings	160,000	40,000	120,000 Increase
Accumulated depreciation—buildings	(11,000)	(5,000)	6,000 Increase
Equipment	27,000	10,000	17,000 Increase
Accumulated depreciation—equipment	(3,000)	(1,000)	2,000 Increase
Total assets	$398,000	$138,000	
Liabilities and Stockholders' Equity			
Current liabilities			
Accounts payable	$ 28,000	$ 12,000	$ 16,000 Increase
Income taxes payable	6,000	8,000	2,000 Decrease
Long-term liabilities			
Bonds payable	130,000	20,000	110,000 Increase
Stockholders' equity			
Common stock	70,000	50,000	20,000 Increase
Retained earnings	164,000	48,000	116,000 Increase
Total liabilities and stockholders' equity	$398,000	$138,000	

(continued)

[1] *Accounting Trends and Techniques—2012* (New York: American Institute of Certified Public Accountants).

Illustration 13-4
(*continued*)

COMPUTER SERVICES COMPANY			
Income Statement			
For the Year Ended December 31, 2015			

Sales revenue		$507,000
Cost of goods sold	$150,000	
Operating expenses (excluding depreciation)	111,000	
Depreciation expense	9,000	
Loss on disposal of equipment	3,000	
Interest expense	42,000	315,000
Income before income tax		192,000
Income tax expense		47,000
Net income		$145,000

Additional information for 2015:
1. Depreciation expense was comprised of $6,000 for building and $3,000 for equipment.
2. The company sold equipment with a book value of $7,000 (cost $8,000, less accumulated depreciation $1,000) for $4,000 cash.
3. Issued $110,000 of long-term bonds in direct exchange for land.
4. A building costing $120,000 was purchased for cash. Equipment costing $25,000 was also purchased for cash.
5. Issued common stock for $20,000 cash.
6. The company declared and paid a $29,000 cash dividend.

We will now apply the three steps to the information provided for Computer Services Company.

Step 1: Operating Activities

DETERMINE NET CASH PROVIDED/USED BY OPERATING ACTIVITIES BY CONVERTING NET INCOME FROM AN ACCRUAL BASIS TO A CASH BASIS

To determine net cash provided by operating activities under the indirect method, companies **adjust net income in numerous ways**. A useful starting point is to understand **why** net income must be converted to net cash provided by operating activities.

Under generally accepted accounting principles, most companies use the accrual basis of accounting. This basis requires that companies record revenue when their performance obligation is satisfied and record expenses when incurred. Revenues include credit sales for which the company has not yet collected cash. Expenses incurred include some items that it has not yet paid in cash. Thus, under the accrual basis, net income is not the same as net cash provided by operating activities.

Therefore, under the **indirect method**, companies must adjust net income to convert certain items to the cash basis. The indirect method (or reconciliation method) starts with net income and converts it to net cash provided by operating activities. Illustration 13-5 lists the three types of adjustments.

Illustration 13-5
Three types of adjustments to convert net income to net cash provided by operating activities

Net Income	+/−	Adjustments	=	Net Cash Provided/ Used by Operating Activities
		• **Add back noncash expenses,** such as depreciation expense, amortization, or depletion.		
		• **Deduct gains and add losses** that resulted from investing and financing activities.		
		• **Analyze changes** to noncash current asset and current liability accounts.		

We explain the three types of adjustments in the next three sections.

DEPRECIATION EXPENSE

Computer Services' income statement reports depreciation expense of $9,000. Although depreciation expense reduces net income, it does not reduce cash. In other words, depreciation expense is a noncash charge. The company must add it back to net income to arrive at net cash provided by operating activities. Computer Services reports depreciation expense in the statement of cash flows as shown below.

Helpful Hint
Depreciation is similar to any other expense in that it reduces net income. It differs in that it does not involve a current cash outflow. That is why it must be *added back* to net income to arrive at net cash provided by operating activities.

Illustration 13-6
Adjustment for depreciation

Cash flows from operating activities	
Net income	$145,000
Adjustments to reconcile net income to net cash provided by operating activities:	
Depreciation expense	9,000
Net cash provided by operating activities	$154,000

As the first adjustment to net income in the statement of cash flows, companies frequently list depreciation and similar noncash charges such as amortization of intangible assets, depletion expense, and bad debt expense.

LOSS ON DISPOSAL OF EQUIPMENT

Illustration 13-1 states that cash received from the sale (disposal) of plant assets is reported in the investing activities section. Because of this, **companies eliminate from net income all gains and losses related to the disposal of plant assets, to arrive at net cash provided by operating activities**.

In our example, Computer Services' income statement reports a $3,000 loss on the disposal of equipment (book value $7,000, less $4,000 cash received from disposal of equipment). The company's loss of $3,000 should not be included in the operating activities section of the statement of cash flows. Illustration 13-7 shows that the $3,000 loss is eliminated by adding $3,000 back to net income to arrive at net cash provided by operating activities.

Illustration 13-7
Adjustment for loss on disposal of equipment

Cash flows from operating activities		
Net income		$145,000
Adjustments to reconcile net income to net cash provided by operating activities:		
Depreciation expense	$9,000	
Loss on disposal of equipment	3,000	12,000
Net cash provided by operating activities		$157,000

If a gain on disposal occurs, the company deducts the gain from net income in order to determine net cash provided by operating activities. **In the case of either a gain or a loss, companies report as a source of cash in the investing activities section of the statement of cash flows the actual amount of cash received from the sale.**

CHANGES TO NONCASH CURRENT ASSET AND CURRENT LIABILITY ACCOUNTS

A final adjustment in reconciling net income to net cash provided by operating activities involves examining all changes in current asset and current liability accounts. The accrual-accounting process records revenues in the period in which

658 Statement of Cash Flows

the performance obligation is satisfied and expenses in the period incurred. For example, Accounts Receivable reflects amounts owed to the company for sales that have been made but for which cash collections have not yet been received. Prepaid Insurance reflects insurance that has been paid for but which has not yet expired (therefore has not been expensed). Similarly, Salaries and Wages Payable reflects salaries and wages expense that has been incurred but has not been paid.

As a result, we need to adjust net income for these accruals and prepayments to determine net cash provided by operating activities. Thus, we must analyze the change in each current asset and current liability account to determine its impact on net income and cash.

CHANGES IN NONCASH CURRENT ASSETS. The adjustments required for changes in noncash current asset accounts are as follows. **Deduct from net income increases in current asset accounts, and add to net income decreases in current asset accounts, to arrive at net cash provided by operating activities.** We observe these relationships by analyzing the accounts of Computer Services Company.

DECREASE IN ACCOUNTS RECEIVABLE Computer Services Company's accounts receivable decreased by $10,000 (from $30,000 to $20,000) during the period. For Computer Services, this means that cash receipts were $10,000 higher than sales revenue. The Accounts Receivable account in Illustration 13-8 shows that Computer Services Company had $507,000 in sales revenue (as reported on the income statement), but it collected $517,000 in cash.

Illustration 13-8
Analysis of accounts receivable

Accounts Receivable				
1/1/15	Balance	30,000	**Receipts from customers**	**517,000**
	Sales revenue	**507,000**		
12/31/15	Balance	20,000		

As shown in Illustration 13-9 (page 659), to adjust net income to net cash provided by operating activities, the company adds to net income the decrease of $10,000 in accounts receivable. When the Accounts Receivable balance increases, cash receipts are lower than sales revenue earned under the accrual basis. Therefore, the company deducts from net income the amount of the increase in accounts receivable, to arrive at net cash provided by operating activities.

INCREASE IN INVENTORY Computer Services Company's inventory increased $5,000 (from $10,000 to $15,000) during the period. The change in the Inventory account reflects the difference between the amount of inventory purchased and the amount sold. For Computer Services, this means that the cost of merchandise purchased exceeded the cost of goods sold by $5,000. As a result, cost of goods sold does not reflect $5,000 of cash payments made for merchandise. The company deducts from net income this inventory increase of $5,000 during the period, to arrive at net cash provided by operating activities (see Illustration 13-9). If inventory decreases, the company adds to net income the amount of the change, to arrive at net cash provided by operating activities.

INCREASE IN PREPAID EXPENSES Computer Services' prepaid expenses increased during the period by $4,000. This means that cash paid for expenses is higher than expenses reported on an accrual basis. In other words, the company has made cash payments in the current period but will not charge expenses to income until future periods (as charges to the income statement). To adjust net income to net cash provided by operating activities, the company deducts from net income the $4,000 increase in prepaid expenses (see Illustration 13-9).

Cash flows from operating activities		
Net income		$145,000
Adjustments to reconcile net income to net cash provided by operating activities:		
Depreciation expense	$ 9,000	
Loss on disposal of equipment	3,000	
Decrease in accounts receivable	**10,000**	
Increase in inventory	**(5,000)**	
Increase in prepaid expenses	**(4,000)**	13,000
Net cash provided by operating activities		$158,000

Illustration 13-9
Adjustments for changes in current asset accounts

If prepaid expenses decrease, reported expenses are higher than the expenses paid. Therefore, the company adds to net income the decrease in prepaid expenses, to arrive at net cash provided by operating activities.

CHANGES IN CURRENT LIABILITIES. The adjustments required for changes in current liability accounts are as follows. **Add to net income increases in current liability accounts and deduct from net income decreases in current liability accounts, to arrive at net cash provided by operating activities.**

INCREASE IN ACCOUNTS PAYABLE For Computer Services Company, Accounts Payable increased by $16,000 (from $12,000 to $28,000) during the period. That means the company received $16,000 more in goods than it actually paid for. As shown in Illustration 13-10 (below), to adjust net income to determine net cash provided by operating activities, the company adds to net income the $16,000 increase in Accounts Payable.

DECREASE IN INCOME TAXES PAYABLE When a company incurs income tax expense but has not yet paid its taxes, it records income tax payable. A change in the Income Taxes Payable account reflects the difference between income tax expense incurred and income tax actually paid. Computer Services' Income Taxes Payable account decreased by $2,000. That means the $47,000 of income tax expense reported on the income statement was $2,000 less than the amount of taxes paid during the period of $49,000. As shown in Illustration 13-10, to adjust net income to a cash basis, the company must reduce net income by $2,000.

Cash flows from operating activities		
Net income		$145,000
Adjustments to reconcile net income to net cash provided by operating activities:		
Depreciation expense	$ 9,000	
Loss on disposal of equipment	3,000	
Decrease in accounts receivable	10,000	
Increase in inventory	(5,000)	
Increase in prepaid expenses	(4,000)	
Increase in accounts payable	**16,000**	
Decrease in income taxes payable	**(2,000)**	27,000
Net cash provided by operating activities		$172,000

Illustration 13-10
Adjustments for changes in current liability accounts

Illustration 13-10 shows that after starting with net income of $145,000 the sum of all of the adjustments to net income was $27,000. This resulted in net cash provided by operating activities of $172,000.

Summary of Conversion to Net Cash Provided by Operating Activities—Indirect Method

As shown in the previous illustrations, the statement of cash flows prepared by the indirect method starts with net income. It then adds or deducts items to arrive at net cash provided by operating activities. The required adjustments are of three types:

1. Noncash charges such as depreciation, amortization, and depletion.
2. Gains and losses on the disposal of plant assets.
3. Changes in noncash current asset and current liability accounts.

Illustration 13-11 provides a summary of these changes.

Illustration 13-11
Adjustments required to convert net income to net cash provided by operating activities

		Adjustments Required to Convert Net Income to Net Cash Provided by Operating Activities
Noncash Charges	Depreciation expense	Add
	Amortization expense	Add
	Depletion expense	Add
Gains and Losses	Loss on disposal of plant assets	Add
	Gain on disposal of plant assets	Deduct
Changes in Current Assets and Current Liabilities	Increase in current asset account	Deduct
	Decrease in current asset account	Add
	Increase in current liability account	Add
	Decrease in current liability account	Deduct

ANATOMY OF A FRAUD

For more than a decade, the top executives at the Italian dairy products company Parmalat engaged in multiple frauds that overstated cash and other assets by more than $1 billion while understating liabilities by between $8 and $12 billion. Much of the fraud involved creating fictitious sources and uses of cash. Some of these activities incorporated sophisticated financial transactions with subsidiaries created with the help of large international financial institutions. However, much of the fraud employed very basic, even sloppy, forgery of documents. For example, when outside auditors requested confirmation of bank accounts (such as a fake $4.8 billion account in the Cayman Islands), documents were created on scanners, with signatures that were cut and pasted from other documents. These were then passed through a fax machine numerous times to make them look real (if difficult to read). Similarly, fictitious bills were created in order to divert funds to other businesses owned by the Tanzi family (who controlled Parmalat).

Total take: Billions of dollars

THE MISSING CONTROL
Independent internal verification. Internal auditors at the company should have independently verified bank accounts and major transfers of cash to outside companies that were controlled by the Tanzi family.

> **DO IT!**

Cash from Operating Activities

Josh's PhotoPlus reported net income of $73,000 for 2015. Included in the income statement were depreciation expense of $7,000 and a gain on disposal of equipment of $2,500. Josh's comparative balance sheets show the following balances.

	12/31/14	12/31/15
Accounts receivable	$17,000	$21,000
Accounts payable	6,000	2,200

Action Plan

✔ Add noncash charges such as depreciation back to net income to compute net cash provided by operating activities.

✔ Deduct from net income gains on the disposal of plant assets, or add losses back to net income, to compute net cash provided by operating activities.

✔ Use changes in noncash current asset and current liability accounts to compute net cash provided by operating activities.

Calculate net cash provided by operating activities for Josh's PhotoPlus.

Solution

Cash flows from operating activities		
Net income		$73,000
Adjustments to reconcile net income to net cash provided by operating activities:		
Depreciation expense	$ 7,000	
Gain on disposal of equipment	(2,500)	
Increase in accounts receivable	(4,000)	
Decrease in accounts payable	(3,800)	(3,300)
Net cash provided by operating activities		$69,700

Related exercise material: BE13-4, BE13-5, BE13-6, E13-4, E13-5, E13-6, and DO IT! 13-2.

✔ **The Navigator**

Step 2: Investing and Financing Activities

ANALYZE CHANGES IN NONCURRENT ASSET AND LIABILITY ACCOUNTS AND RECORD AS INVESTING AND FINANCING ACTIVITIES, OR AS NONCASH INVESTING AND FINANCING ACTIVITIES

INCREASE IN LAND As indicated from the change in the Land account and the additional information, Computer Services Company purchased land of $110,000 by directly exchanging bonds for land. The issuance of bonds payable for land has no effect on cash. But, it is a significant noncash investing and financing activity that merits disclosure in a separate schedule. (See Illustration 13-13 on page 662.)

INCREASE IN BUILDINGS As the additional data indicate, Computer Services Company acquired a building for $120,000 cash. This is a cash outflow reported in the investing activities section. (See Illustration 13-13 on page 662.)

INCREASE IN EQUIPMENT The Equipment account increased $17,000. The additional information explains that this net increase resulted from two transactions: (1) a purchase of equipment of $25,000, and (2) the sale for $4,000 of equipment costing $8,000. These transactions are investing activities. The company should report each transaction separately. Thus, it reports the purchase of equipment as an outflow of cash for $25,000. It reports the sale as an inflow of cash for $4,000. The T-account below shows the reasons for the change in this account during the year.

Illustration 13-12
Analysis of equipment

Equipment			
1/1/15 Balance	10,000	Cost of equipment sold	8,000
Purchase of equipment	25,000		
12/31/15 Balance	27,000		

The following entry shows the details of the equipment sale transaction.

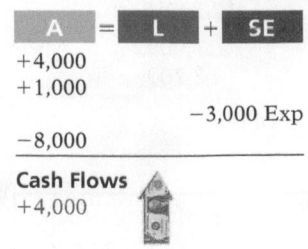

Cash	4,000	
Accumulated Depreciation—Equipment	1,000	
Loss on Disposal of Equipment	3,000	
Equipment		8,000

INCREASE IN BONDS PAYABLE The Bonds Payable account increased $110,000. As indicated in the additional information, the company acquired land from the issuance of these bonds. It reports this noncash transaction in a separate schedule at the bottom of the statement.

Helpful Hint
When companies issue stocks or bonds for cash, the actual proceeds will appear in the statement of cash flows as a financing inflow (rather than the par value of the stocks or face value of bonds).

INCREASE IN COMMON STOCK The balance sheet reports an increase in Common Stock of $20,000. The additional information section notes that this increase resulted from the issuance of new shares of stock. This is a cash inflow reported in the financing activities section.

INCREASE IN RETAINED EARNINGS Retained earnings increased $116,000 during the year. This increase can be explained by two factors. (1) Net income of $145,000 increased retained earnings. (2) Dividends of $29,000 decreased retained earnings. The company adjusts net income to net cash provided by operating activities in the operating activities section. Payment of the dividends (not the declaration) is a **cash outflow that the company reports as a financing activity**.

STATEMENT OF CASH FLOWS—2015

Using the previous information, we can now prepare a statement of cash flows for 2015 for Computer Services Company, as shown in Illustration 13-13.

Step 3: Net Change in Cash

COMPARE THE NET CHANGE IN CASH ON THE STATEMENT OF CASH FLOWS WITH THE CHANGE IN THE CASH ACCOUNT REPORTED ON THE BALANCE SHEET TO MAKE SURE THE AMOUNTS AGREE

Illustration 13-13 indicates that the net change in cash during the period was an increase of $22,000. This agrees with the change in Cash account reported on the balance sheet in Illustration 13-4 (page 655).

Illustration 13-13
Statement of cash flows, 2015—indirect method

Helpful Hint
Note that in the investing and financing activities sections, positive numbers indicate cash inflows (receipts), and negative numbers indicate cash outflows (payments).

COMPUTER SERVICES COMPANY		
Statement of Cash Flows—Indirect Method		
For the Year Ended December 31, 2015		
Cash flows from operating activities		
Net income		$145,000
Adjustments to reconcile net income to net cash		
provided by operating activities:		
Depreciation expense	$ 9,000	
Loss on disposal of equipment	3,000	
Decrease in accounts receivable	10,000	
Increase in inventory	(5,000)	
Increase in prepaid expenses	(4,000)	
Increase in accounts payable	16,000	
Decrease in income taxes payable	(2,000)	27,000
Net cash provided by operating activities		172,000

Cash flows from investing activities
  Purchase of building   (120,000)
  Purchase of equipment   (25,000)
  Sale of equipment   4,000
    Net cash used by investing activities   (141,000)
Cash flows from financing activities
  Issuance of common stock   20,000
  Payment of cash dividends   (29,000)
    Net cash used by financing activities   (9,000)
Net increase in cash   22,000
Cash at beginning of period   33,000
Cash at end of period $ 55,000

Noncash investing and financing activities
  Issuance of bonds payable to purchase land $110,000

Illustration 13-13
(*continued*)

> **DO IT!**

Indirect Method

Use the information below and on page 664 to prepare a statement of cash flows using the indirect method.

REYNOLDS COMPANY			
Comparative Balance Sheets			
December 31			
Assets	**2015**	**2014**	**Change Increase/Decrease**
Cash	$ 54,000	$ 37,000	$ 17,000 Increase
Accounts receivable	68,000	26,000	42,000 Increase
Inventory	54,000	–0–	54,000 Increase
Prepaid expenses	4,000	6,000	2,000 Decrease
Land	45,000	70,000	25,000 Decrease
Buildings	200,000	200,000	–0–
Accumulated depreciation—buildings	(21,000)	(11,000)	10,000 Increase
Equipment	193,000	68,000	125,000 Increase
Accumulated depreciation—equipment	(28,000)	(10,000)	18,000 Increase
Totals	$569,000	$386,000	
Liabilities and Stockholders' Equity			
Accounts payable	$ 23,000	$ 40,000	$ 17,000 Decrease
Accrued expenses payable	10,000	–0–	10,000 Increase
Bonds payable	110,000	150,000	40,000 Decrease
Common stock ($1 par)	220,000	60,000	160,000 Increase
Retained earnings	206,000	136,000	70,000 Increase
Totals	$569,000	$386,000	

REYNOLDS COMPANY		
Income Statement		
For the Year Ended December 31, 2015		
Sales revenue		$890,000
Cost of goods sold	$465,000	
Operating expenses	221,000	
Interest expense	12,000	
Loss on disposal of equipment	2,000	700,000
Income before income taxes		190,000
Income tax expense		65,000
Net income		$125,000

Additional information:

1. Operating expenses include depreciation expense of $33,000 and charges from prepaid expenses of $2,000.
2. Land was sold at its book value for cash.
3. Cash dividends of $55,000 were declared and paid in 2015.
4. Interest expense of $12,000 was paid in cash.
5. Equipment with a cost of $166,000 was purchased for cash. Equipment with a cost of $41,000 and a book value of $36,000 was sold for $34,000 cash.
6. Bonds of $10,000 were redeemed at their face value for cash. Bonds of $30,000 were converted into common stock.
7. Common stock ($1 par) of $130,000 was issued for cash.
8. Accounts payable pertain to merchandise suppliers.

Solution

Action Plan

✔ Determine net cash provided/used by operating activities by adjusting net income for items that did not affect cash.

✔ Determine net cash provided/used by investing activities and financing activities.

✔ Determine the net increase/decrease in cash.

Helpful Hint

1. Determine net cash provided/used by operating activities, recognizing that operating activities generally relate to changes in current assets and current liabilities.
2. Determine net cash provided/used by investing activities, recognizing that investing activities generally relate to changes in noncurrent assets.
3. Determine net cash provided/used by financing

REYNOLDS COMPANY		
Statement of Cash Flows—Indirect Method		
For the Year Ended December 31, 2015		
Cash flows from operating activities		
Net income		$ 125,000
Adjustments to reconcile net income to net cash provided by operating activities:		
Depreciation expense	$ 33,000	
Loss on disposal of equipment	2,000	
Increase in accounts receivable	(42,000)	
Increase in inventory	(54,000)	
Decrease in prepaid expenses	2,000	
Decrease in accounts payable	(17,000)	
Increase in accrued expenses payable	10,000	(66,000)
Net cash provided by operating activities		59,000
Cash flows from investing activities		
Sale of land	25,000	
Sale of equipment	34,000	
Purchase of equipment	(166,000)	
Net cash used by investing activities		(107,000)
Cash flows from financing activities		
Redemption of bonds	(10,000)	
Sale of common stock	130,000	
Payment of dividends	(55,000)	
Net cash provided by financing activities		65,000

activities, recognizing that financing activities generally relate to changes in long-term liabilities and stockholders' equity accounts.

Net increase in cash	17,000
Cash at beginning of period	37,000
Cash at end of period	$54,000
Noncash investing and financing activities	
Conversion of bonds into common stock	$30,000

Related exercise material: BE13-4, BE13-5, BE13-6, BE13-7, E13-4, E13-5, **and** E13-6.

✓ **The Navigator**

ACCOUNTING ACROSS THE ORGANIZATION

Burning Through Our Cash

Kodak used to dominate the market for photographic film—back when most cameras used film. But when digital cameras arrived, the company's cash flows steadily declined. Investors began to wonder whether Kodak's cash would run out before the company came up with an alternative source of income. Eventually, the company was forced to sell plant assets and intangibles such as patents in order to supplement its cash from operating activities. Finally, Kodak decided to borrow money against its line of credit. Investors in Kodak's stocks and bonds interpreted this as a desperate move (because it further increased the company's debt). The price of its stock and its bonds plummeted. Within months, Kodak had filed for bankruptcy.

Source: Dana Mattioli and Matt Marzemsky, "Clock Ticks as Kodak Burns Cash," *Wall Street Journal* (September 27, 2011).

© Soubrette/iStockphoto

? What impact did Kodak's sale of plant assets have on its net cash provided by investing activities? (See page 709.)

Using Cash Flows to Evaluate a Company

Traditionally, investors and creditors used ratios based on accrual accounting. These days, cash-based ratios are gaining increased acceptance among analysts.

LEARNING OBJECTIVE   4

Analyze the statement of cash flows.

Free Cash Flow

In the statement of cash flows, net cash provided by operating activities is intended to indicate the cash-generating capability of the company. Analysts have noted, however, that **net cash provided by operating activities fails to take into account that a company must invest in new fixed assets** just to maintain its current level of operations. Companies also must at least **maintain dividends at current levels** to satisfy investors. The measurement of free cash flow provides additional insight regarding a company's cash-generating ability. **Free cash flow** describes the net cash provided by operating activities after adjustment for capital expenditures and dividends.

Consider the following example. Suppose that MPC produced and sold 10,000 personal computers this year. It reported $100,000 net cash provided by operating activities. In order to maintain production at 10,000 computers, MPC invested $15,000 in equipment. It chose to pay $5,000 in dividends. Its free cash flow was $80,000 ($100,000 − $15,000 − $5,000). The company could use this $80,000 either to purchase new assets to expand the business or to pay an $80,000 dividend and continue to produce 10,000 computers. In practice, free cash flow is often calculated with the formula in Illustration 13-14. (Alternative definitions also exist.)

Illustration 13-14
Free cash flow

Free Cash Flow	=	Net Cash Provided by Operating Activities	−	Capital Expenditures	−	Cash Dividends

Illustration 13-15 provides basic information (in billions) excerpted from the 2012 statement of cash flows of Microsoft Corporation.

Illustration 13-15
Microsoft's cash flow information's ($ in millions)

Real World	MICROSOFT CORPORATION Statement of Cash Flows (partial) 2012		
Cash provided by operating activities			$31,626
Cash flows from investing activities			
Additions to property and equipment		$ (2,305)	
Purchases of investments		(57,250)	
Sales of investments		29,700	
Acquisitions of companies		(10,112)	
Maturities of investments		15,575	
Other		(394)	
Cash used by investing activities			(24,786)
Cash paid for dividends			(6,385)

Microsoft's free cash flow is calculated as shown in Illustration 13-16.

Illustration 13-16
Calculation of Microsoft's free cash flow ($ in millions)

Cash provided by operating activities	$31,626
Less: Expenditures on property, plant, and equipment	2,305
Dividends paid	6,385
Free cash flow	**$22,936**

Microsoft generated approximately $23 billion of free cash flow. This is a tremendous amount of cash generated in a single year. It is available for the acquisition of new assets, the retirement of stock or debt, or the payment of dividends.

Also note that Microsoft's cash from operations of $31.6 billion exceeds its 2012 net income of $17 billion. This lends additional credibility to Microsoft's income number as an indicator of potential future performance. If anything, Microsoft's net income might understate its actual performance.

Oracle Corporation is one of the world's largest sellers of database software and information management services. Like Microsoft, its success depends on continuing to improve its existing products while developing new products to keep pace with rapid changes in technology. Oracle's free cash flow for 2012 was $13.7 billion. This is also impressive but significantly less than Microsoft's amazing ability to generate cash.

> DO IT!

Free Cash Flow

Chicago Corporation issued the following statement of cash flows for 2015.

CHICAGO CORPORATION		
Statement of Cash Flows—Indirect Method		
For the Year Ended December 31, 2015		
Cash flows from operating activities		
Net income		$ 19,000
Adjustments to reconcile net income to net cash		
provided by operating activities:		
Depreciation expense	$ 8,100	
Loss on disposal of plant assets	1,300	
Decrease in accounts receivable	6,900	
Increase in inventory	(4,000)	
Decrease in accounts payable	(2,000)	10,300
Net cash provided by operating activities		29,300
Cash flows from investing activities		
Sale of investments	1,100	
Purchase of equipment	(19,000)	
Net cash used by investing activities		(17,900)
Cash flows from financing activities		
Issuance of stock	10,000	
Payment on long-term note payable	(5,000)	
Payment for dividends	(9,000)	
Net cash used by financing activities		(4,000)
Net increase in cash		7,400
Cash at beginning of year		10,000
Cash at end of year		$ 17,400

(a) Compute free cash flow for Chicago Corporation. (b) Explain why free cash flow often provides better information than "Net cash provided by operating activities."

Action Plan

✔ Compute free cash flow as: Net cash provided by operating activities – Capital expenditures – Cash dividends.

Solution

(a) Free cash flow = $29,300 – $19,000 – $9,000 = $1,300

(b) Net cash provided by operating activities fails to take into account that a company must invest in new plant assets just to maintain the current level of operations. Companies must also maintain dividends at current levels to satisfy investors. The measurement of free cash flow provides additional insight regarding a company's cash-generating ability.

Related exercise material: BE13-8, BE13-9, BE13-10, BE13-11, E13-7, E13-9, **and** DO IT 13-3.

 The Navigator

The income statement for the year ended December 31, 2015, for Kosinski Manufacturing Company contains the following condensed information.

KOSINSKI MANUFACTURING COMPANY		
Income Statement		
For the Year Ended December 31, 2015		
Sales revenue		$6,583,000
Operating expenses (excluding depreciation)	$4,920,000	
Depreciation expense	880,000	5,800,000
Income before income taxes		783,000
Income tax expense		353,000
Net income		$ 430,000

Included in operating expenses is a $24,000 loss resulting from the sale of equipment for $270,000 cash. Equipment was purchased at a cost of $750,000.

The following balances are reported on Kosinski's comparative balance sheets at December 31.

KOSINSKI MANUFACTURING COMPANY		
Comparative Balance Sheets (partial)		
	2015	**2014**
Cash	$672,000	$130,000
Accounts receivable	775,000	610,000
Inventory	834,000	867,000
Accounts payable	521,000	501,000

Income tax expense of $353,000 represents the amount paid in 2015. Dividends declared and paid in 2015 totaled $200,000.

Instructions

Prepare the statement of cash flows using the indirect method.

Action Plan

✔ Determine net cash from operating activities. Operating activities generally relate to changes in current assets and current liabilities.

✔ Determine net cash from investing activities. Investing activities generally relate to changes in noncurrent assets.

✔ Determine net cash from financing activities. Financing activities generally relate to changes in long-term liabilities and stockholders' equity accounts.

Solution to Comprehensive DO IT! 1

KOSINSKI MANUFACTURING COMPANY		
Statement of Cash Flows—Indirect Method		
For the Year Ended December 31, 2015		
Cash flows from operating activities		
Net income		$ 430,000
Adjustments to reconcile net income to net cash provided by operating activities:		
Depreciation expense	$ 880,000	
Loss on disposal of equipment	24,000	
Increase in accounts receivable	(165,000)	
Decrease in inventory	33,000	
Increase in accounts payable	20,000	792,000
Net cash provided by operating activities		1,222,000

Cash flows from investing activities		
Sale of equipment	270,000	
Purchase of equipment	(750,000)	
Net cash used by investing activities		(480,000)
Cash flows from financing activities		
Payment of cash dividends		(200,000)
Net increase in cash		542,000
Cash at beginning of period		130,000
Cash at end of period		$ 672,000

✔ **The Navigator**

SUMMARY OF LEARNING OBJECTIVES

 ✔ **The Navigator**

1 **Indicate the usefulness of the statement of cash flows.** The statement of cash flows provides information about the cash receipts, cash payments, and net change in cash resulting from the operating, investing, and financing activities of a company during the period.

2 **Distinguish among operating, investing, and financing activities.** Operating activities include the cash effects of transactions that enter into the determination of net income. Investing activities involve cash flows resulting from changes in investments and long-term asset items. Financing activities involve cash flows resulting from changes in long-term liability and stockholders' equity items.

3 **Prepare a statement of cash flows using the indirect method.** The preparation of a statement of cash flows

involves three major steps: (1) Determine net cash provided/used by operating activities by converting net income from an accrual basis to a cash basis. (2) Analyze changes in noncurrent asset and liability accounts and record as investing and financing activities, or disclose as noncash transactions. (3) Compare the net change in cash on the statement of cash flows with the change in the Cash account reported on the balance sheet to make sure the amounts agree.

4 **Analyze the statement of cash flows.** Free cash flow indicates the amount of cash a company generated during the current year that is available for the payment of additional dividends or for expansion.

GLOSSARY

Direct method A method that shows operating cash receipts and payments, making it more consistent with the objective of the statement of cash flows. (p. 655).

Financing activities Cash flow activities that include (a) obtaining cash from issuing debt and repaying the amounts borrowed and (b) obtaining cash from stockholders, repurchasing shares, and paying dividends. (p. 651).

Free cash flow Net cash provided by operating activities adjusted for capital expenditures and cash dividends paid. (p. 665).

Indirect method A method of preparing a statement of cash flows in which net income is adjusted for items that do not affect cash, to determine net cash provided by operating activities. (pp. 655, 656).

Investing activities Cash flow activities that include (a) purchasing and disposing of investments and property, plant, and equipment using cash and (b) lending money and collecting the loans. (p. 650).

Operating activities Cash flow activities that include the cash effects of transactions that create revenues and expenses and thus enter into the determination of net income. (p. 650).

Statement of cash flows A basic financial statement that provides information about the cash receipts, cash payments, and net change in cash during a period, resulting from operating, investing, and financing activities. (p. 650).

APPENDIX 13A   Statement of Cash Flows—Direct Method

LEARNING OBJECTIVE   5

Prepare a statement of cash flows using the direct method.

To explain and illustrate the direct method, we will use the transactions of Computer Services Company for 2015, to prepare a statement of cash flows. Illustration 13A-1 presents information related to 2015 for Computer Services Company.

Illustration 13A-1
Comparative balance sheets, income statement, and additional information for Computer Services Company

COMPUTER SERVICES COMPANY
Comparative Balance Sheets
December 31

Assets	2015	2014	Change in Account Balance Increase/Decrease
Current assets			
Cash	$ 55,000	$ 33,000	$ 22,000 Increase
Accounts receivable	20,000	30,000	10,000 Decrease
Inventory	15,000	10,000	5,000 Increase
Prepaid expenses	5,000	1,000	4,000 Increase
Property, plant, and equipment			
Land	130,000	20,000	110,000 Increase
Buildings	160,000	40,000	120,000 Increase
Accumulated depreciation—buildings	(11,000)	(5,000)	6,000 Increase
Equipment	27,000	10,000	17,000 Increase
Accumulated depreciation—equipment	(3,000)	(1,000)	2,000 Increase
Total assets	$398,000	$138,000	

Liabilities and Stockholders' Equity			
Current liabilities			
Accounts payable	$ 28,000	$ 12,000	$ 16,000 Increase
Income taxes payable	6,000	8,000	2,000 Decrease
Long-term liabilities			
Bonds payable	130,000	20,000	110,000 Increase
Stockholders' equity			
Common stock	70,000	50,000	20,000 Increase
Retained earnings	164,000	48,000	116,000 Increase
Total liabilities and stockholders' equity	$398,000	$138,000	

COMPUTER SERVICES COMPANY
Income Statement
For the Year Ended December 31, 2015

Sales revenue		$507,000
Cost of goods sold	$150,000	
Operating expenses (excluding depreciation)	111,000	
Depreciation expense	9,000	
Loss on disposal of equipment	3,000	
Interest expense	42,000	315,000
Income before income tax		192,000
Income tax expense		47,000
Net income		$145,000

Additional information for 2015:

1. Depreciation expense was comprised of $6,000 for building and $3,000 for equipment.
2. The company sold equipment with a book value of $7,000 (cost $8,000, less accumulated depreciation $1,000) for $4,000 cash.
3. Issued $110,000 of long-term bonds in direct exchange for land.
4. A building costing $120,000 was purchased for cash. Equipment costing $25,000 was also purchased for cash.
5. Issued common stock for $20,000 cash.
6. The company declared and paid a $29,000 cash dividend.

To prepare a statement of cash flows under the direct approach, we will apply the three steps outlined in Illustration 13-3 (page 654).

Step 1: Operating Activities

DETERMINE NET CASH PROVIDED/USED BY OPERATING ACTIVITIES BY CONVERTING NET INCOME FROM AN ACCRUAL BASIS TO A CASH BASIS

Under the **direct method**, companies compute net cash provided by operating activities by **adjusting each item in the income statement** from the accrual basis to the cash basis. To simplify and condense the operating activities section, companies **report only major classes of operating cash receipts and cash payments**. For these major classes, the difference between cash receipts and cash payments is the net cash provided by operating activities. These relationships are as shown in Illustration 13A-2.

Illustration 13A-2
Major classes of cash receipts and payments

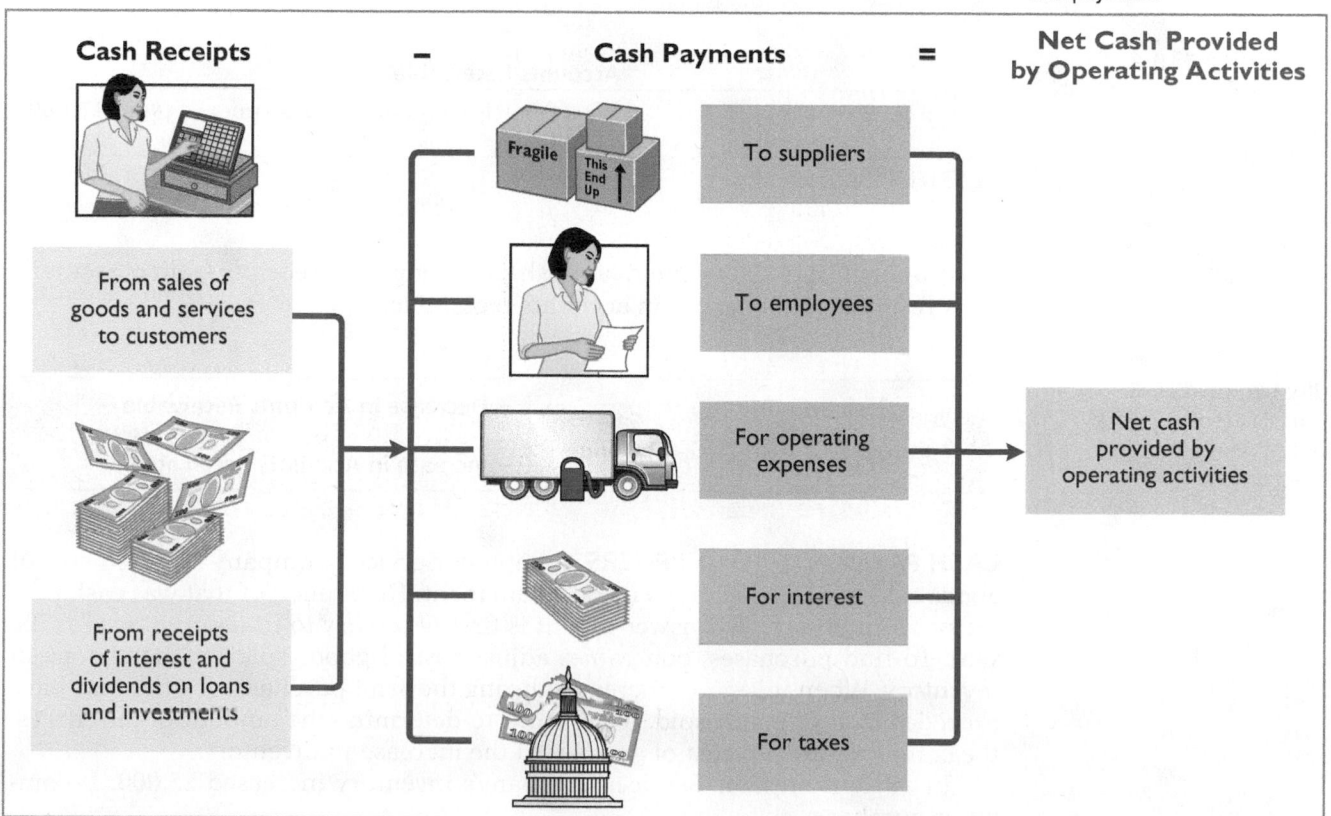

An efficient way to apply the direct method is to analyze the items reported in the income statement in the order in which they are listed. We then determine cash receipts and cash payments related to these revenues and expenses. The following pages present the adjustments required to prepare a statement of cash flows for Computer Services Company using the direct approach.

CASH RECEIPTS FROM CUSTOMERS The income statement for Computer Services Company reported sales revenue from customers of $507,000. How much of that was cash receipts? To answer that, companies need to consider the change in accounts receivable during the year. When accounts receivable increase during the year, revenues on an accrual basis are higher than cash receipts from customers. Operations led to revenues, but not all of those revenues resulted in cash receipts.

To determine the amount of cash receipts, the company deducts from sales revenue the increase in accounts receivable. On the other hand, there may be a decrease in accounts receivable. That would occur if cash receipts from customers exceeded sales revenue. In that case, the company adds to sales revenue the decrease in accounts receivable. For Computer Services Company, accounts receivable decreased $10,000. Thus, cash receipts from customers were $517,000, computed as shown in Illustration 13A-3.

Illustration 13A-3
Computation of cash receipts from customers

Sales revenue	$ 507,000
Add: Decrease in accounts receivable	10,000
Cash receipts from customers	**$517,000**

Computer Services can also determine cash receipts from customers from an analysis of the Accounts Receivable account, as shown in Illustration 13A-4.

Illustration 13A-4
Analysis of accounts receivable

Helpful Hint
The T-account shows that sales revenue plus decrease in accounts receivable equals cash receipts.

Accounts Receivable				
1/1/15	Balance	30,000	Receipts from customers	517,000
	Sales revenue	507,000		
12/31/15	Balance	20,000		

Illustration 13A-5 shows the relationships among cash receipts from customers, sales revenue, and changes in accounts receivable.

Illustration 13A-5
Formula to compute cash receipts from customers—direct method

Cash Receipts from Customers	=	Sales Revenue	+ Decrease in Accounts Receivable or − Increase in Accounts Receivable

CASH PAYMENTS TO SUPPLIERS Computer Services Company reported cost of goods sold of $150,000 on its income statement. How much of that was cash payments to suppliers? To answer that, it is first necessary to find purchases for the year. To find purchases, companies adjust cost of goods sold for the change in inventory. When inventory increases during the year, purchases for the year have exceeded cost of goods sold. As a result, to determine the amount of purchases, the company adds to cost of goods sold the increase in inventory.

In 2015, Computer Services Company's inventory increased $5,000. It computes purchases as follows.

Cost of goods sold	$ 150,000
Add: Increase in inventory	5,000
Purchases	**$155,000**

After computing purchases, a company can determine cash payments to suppliers. This is done by adjusting purchases for the change in accounts payable. When accounts payable increase during the year, purchases on an accrual basis are higher than they are on a cash basis. As a result, to determine cash payments to suppliers, a company deducts from purchases the increase in accounts payable. On the other hand, if cash payments to suppliers exceed purchases, there may be a decrease in accounts payable. In that case, a company adds to purchases the decrease in accounts payable. For Computer Services Company, cash payments to suppliers were $139,000, computed as follows.

Purchases	$ 155,000
Deduct: Increase in accounts payable	16,000
Cash payments to suppliers	**$139,000**

Computer Services also can determine cash payments to suppliers from an analysis of the Accounts Payable account, as shown in Illustration 13A-8

Accounts Payable

Payments to suppliers	139,000	1/1/15	Balance	12,000
			Purchases	155,000
		12/31/15	Balance	28,000

Illustration 13A-9 shows the relationships among cash payments to suppliers, cost of goods sold, changes in inventory, and changes in accounts payable.

Cash Payments to Suppliers	=	Cost of Goods Sold	+ Increase in Inventory or − Decrease in Inventory	+ Decrease in Accounts Payable or − Increase in Accounts Payable

CASH PAYMENTS FOR OPERATING EXPENSES Computer Services reported on its income statement operating expenses of $111,000. How much of that amount was cash paid for operating expenses? To answer that, we need to adjust this amount for any changes in prepaid expenses and accrued expenses payable. For example, if prepaid expenses increased during the year, cash paid for operating expenses is higher than operating expenses reported on the income statement. To convert operating expenses to cash payments for operating expenses, a company adds the increase in prepaid expenses to operating expenses. On the other hand, if prepaid expenses decrease during the year, it deducts the decrease from operating expenses.

Companies must also adjust operating expenses for changes in accrued expenses payable. When accrued expenses payable increase during the year, operating expenses on an accrual basis are higher than they are in a cash basis. As a result, to determine cash payments for operating expenses, a company deducts from operating expenses an increase in accrued expenses payable. On the other hand, a company adds to operating expenses a decrease in accrued expenses payable because cash payments exceed operating expenses.

Computer Services Company's cash payments for operating expenses were $115,000, computed as follows.

Illustration 13A-10
Computation of cash payments for operating expenses

Operating expenses	$ 111,000
Add: Increase in prepaid expenses	4,000
Cash payments for operating expenses	**$115,000**

Illustration 13A-11 shows the relationships among cash payments for operating expenses, changes in prepaid expenses, and changes in accrued expenses payable.

Illustration 13A-11
Formula to compute cash payments for operating expenses—direct method

Cash Payments for Operating Expenses	=	Operating Expenses	+ Increase in Prepaid Expenses or − Decrease in Prepaid Expenses	+ Decrease in Accrued Expenses Payable or − Increase in Accrued Expenses Payable

DEPRECIATION EXPENSE AND LOSS ON DISPOSAL OF EQUIPMENT Computer Services' depreciation expense in 2015 was $9,000. Depreciation expense is not shown on a statement of cash flows under the direct method because it is a noncash charge. If the amount for operating expenses includes depreciation expense, operating expenses must be reduced by the amount of depreciation to determine cash payments for operating expenses.

The loss on disposal of equipment of $3,000 is also a noncash charge. The loss on disposal of equipment reduces net income, but it does not reduce cash. Thus, the loss on disposal of equipment is not shown on the statement of cash flows under the direct method.

Other charges to expense that do not require the use of cash, such as the amortization of intangible assets, depletion expense, and bad debt expense, are treated in the same manner as depreciation.

CASH PAYMENTS FOR INTEREST Computer Services reported on the income statement interest expense of $42,000. Since the balance sheet did not include an accrual for interest payable for 2014 or 2015, the amount reported as expense is the same as the amount of interest paid.

CASH PAYMENTS FOR INCOME TAXES Computer Services reported income tax expense of $47,000 on the income statement. Income taxes payable, however, decreased $2,000. This decrease means that income taxes paid were more than income taxes reported in the income statement. Cash payments for income taxes were, therefore, $49,000 as shown below.

Illustration 13A-12
Computation of cash payments for income taxes

Income tax expense	$ 47,000
Add: Decrease in income taxes payable	2,000
Cash payments for income taxes	**$49,000**

Illustration 13A-13 shows the relationships among cash payments for income taxes, income tax expense, and changes in income taxes payable.

Cash Payments for Income Taxes	=	Income Tax Expense	$\Big\{$	+ Decrease in Income Taxes Payable or − Increase in Income Taxes Payable

Illustration 13A-13
Formula to compute cash payments for income taxes—direct method

The operating activities section of the statement of cash flows of Computer Services Company is shown in Illustration 13A-14.

Illustration 13A-14
Operating activities section of the statement of cash flows

Cash flows from operating activities		
Cash receipts from customers		$517,000
Less: Cash payments:		
To suppliers	$139,000	
For operating expenses	115,000	
For interest expense	42,000	
For income taxes	49,000	345,000
Net cash provided by operating activities		$172,000

When a company uses the direct method, it must also provide in a **separate schedule** (not shown here) the net cash flows from operating activities as computed under the indirect method.

Step 2: Investing and Financing Activities

ANALYZE CHANGES IN NONCURRENT ASSET AND LIABILITY ACCOUNTS AND RECORD AS INVESTING AND FINANCING ACTIVITIES, OR DISCLOSE AS NONCASH TRANSACTIONS

INCREASE IN LAND As indicated from the change in the Land account and the additional information, Computer Services Company purchased land of $110,000 by directly exchanging bonds for land. The exchange of bonds payable for land has no effect on cash. But, it is a significant noncash investing and financing activity that merits disclosure in a separate schedule. (See Illustration 13A-16.)

Helpful Hint
The investing and financing activities are measured and reported the same under both the direct and indirect methods.

INCREASE IN BUILDINGS As the additional data indicate, Computer Services Company acquired a building for $120,000 cash. This is a cash outflow reported in the investing activities section. (See Illustration 13A-16.)

INCREASE IN EQUIPMENT The Equipment account increased $17,000. The additional information explains that this was a net increase that resulted from two transactions: (1) a purchase of equipment of $25,000, and (2) the sale for $4,000 of equipment costing $8,000. These transactions are investing activities. The company should report each transaction separately. The statement in Illustration 13A-16 reports the purchase of equipment as an outflow of cash for $25,000. It reports the sale as an inflow of cash for $4,000. The T-account below shows the reasons for the change in this account during the year.

Illustration 13A-15
Analysis of equipment

Equipment			
1/1/15 Balance	10,000	Cost of equipment sold	8,000
Purchase of equipment	25,000		
12/31/15 Balance	27,000		

The following entry shows the details of the equipment sale transaction.

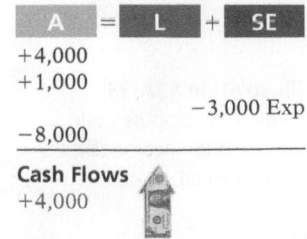

A = L + SE		
+4,000		
+1,000		
	−3,000 Exp	
−8,000		
Cash Flows		
+4,000		

Cash	4,000	
Accumulated Depreciation	1,000	
Loss on Disposal of Equipment	3,000	
Equipment		8,000

INCREASE IN BONDS PAYABLE The Bonds Payable account increased $110,000. As indicated in the additional information, the company acquired land by directly exchanging bonds for land. Illustration 13A-16 reports this noncash transaction in a separate schedule at the bottom of the statement.

INCREASE IN COMMON STOCK The balance sheet reports an increase in Common Stock of $20,000. The additional information section notes that this increase resulted from the issuance of new shares of stock. This is a cash inflow reported in the financing activities section in Illustration 13A-16.

Helpful Hint
When companies issue stocks or bonds for cash, the actual proceeds will appear in the statement of cash flows as a financing inflow (rather than the par value of the stocks or face value of bonds).

INCREASE IN RETAINED EARNINGS Retained earnings increased $116,000 during the year. This increase can be explained by two factors. (1) Net income of $145,000 increased retained earnings and (2) dividends of $29,000 decreased retained earnings. The company adjusts net income to net cash provided by operating activities in the operating activities section. **Payment** of the dividends (not the declaration) is a **cash outflow that the company reports as a financing activity in Illustration 13A-16**.

STATEMENT OF CASH FLOWS—2015
Illustration 13A-16 shows the statement of cash flows for Computer Services Company.

Illustration 13A-16
Statement of cash flows, 2015—direct method

COMPUTER SERVICES COMPANY
Statement of Cash Flows—Direct Method
For the Year Ended December 31, 2015

Cash flows from operating activities		
Cash receipts from customers		$ 517,000
Less: Cash payments:		
To suppliers	$ 139,000	
For operating expenses	115,000	
For income taxes	49,000	
For interest expense	42,000	345,000
Net cash provided by operating activities		172,000
Cash flows from investing activities		
Sale of equipment	4,000	
Purchase of building	(120,000)	
Purchase of equipment	(25,000)	
Net cash used by investing activities		(141,000)
Cash flows from financing activities		
Issuance of common stock	20,000	
Payment of cash dividends	(29,000)	
Net cash used by financing activities		(9,000)
Net increase in cash		22,000
Cash at beginning of period		33,000
Cash at end of period		$ 55,000
Noncash investing and financing activities		
Issuance of bonds payable to purchase land		$ 110,000

Step 3: Net Change in Cash

COMPARE THE NET CHANGE IN CASH ON THE STATEMENT OF CASH FLOWS WITH THE CHANGE IN THE CASH ACCOUNT REPORTED ON THE BALANCE SHEET TO MAKE SURE THE AMOUNTS AGREE

Illustration 13A-16 indicates that the net change in cash during the period was an increase of $22,000. This agrees with the change in balances in the Cash account reported on the balance sheets in Illustration 13A-1 (page 670).

SUMMARY OF LEARNING OBJECTIVE FOR APPENDIX 13A

5 **Prepare a statement of cash flows using the direct method.** The preparation of the statement of cash flows involves three major steps. (1) Determine net cash provided/used by operating activities by converting net income from an accrual basis to a cash basis. (2) Analyze changes in noncurrent asset and liability accounts and record as investing and financing activities, or disclose as noncash transactions. (3) Compare the net change in cash on the statement of cash flows with the change in the Cash account reported on the balance sheet to make sure the amounts agree. The direct method reports cash receipts less cash payments to arrive at net cash provided by operating activities.

> Comprehensive DO IT! 2

The income statement for Kosinski Manufacturing Company contains the following condensed information.

KOSINSKI MANUFACTURING COMPANY
Income Statement
For the Year Ended December 31, 2015

Sales revenue		$6,583,000
Operating expenses, excluding depreciation	$4,920,000	
Depreciation expense	880,000	5,800,000
Income before income taxes		783,000
Income tax expense		353,000
Net income		$ 430,000

Included in operating expenses is a $24,000 loss resulting from the sale of equipment for $270,000 cash. Equipment was purchased at a cost of $750,000. The following balances are reported on Kosinski's comparative balance sheet at December 31.

KOSINSKI MANUFACTURING COMPANY
Comparative Balance Sheets (partial)

	2015	2014
Cash	$672,000	$130,000
Accounts receivable	775,000	610,000
Inventory	834,000	867,000
Accounts payable	521,000	501,000

Income tax expense of $353,000 represents the amount paid in 2015. Dividends declared and paid in 2015 totaled $200,000.

Instructions
Prepare the statement of cash flows using the direct method.

Solution to Comprehensive DO IT! 2

KOSINSKI MANUFACTURING COMPANY
Statement of Cash Flows—Direct Method
For the Year Ended December 31, 2015

Cash flows from operating activities		
Cash collections from customers		$6,418,000*
Cash payments:		
For operating expenses	$4,843,000**	
For income taxes	353,000	5,196,000
Net cash provided by operating activities		1,222,000
Cash flows from investing activities		
Sale of equipment	270,000	
Purchase of equipment	(750,000)	
Net cash used by investing activities		(480,000)
Cash flows from financing activities		
Payment of cash dividends	(200,000)	
Net cash used by financing activities		(200,000)
Net increase in cash		542,000
Cash at beginning of period		130,000
Cash at end of period		$ 672,000

Direct-Method Computations:

*Computation of cash collections from customers:

Sales revenue	$6,583,000
Deduct: Increase in accounts receivable	(165,000)
Cash collections from customers	$6,418,000

**Computation of cash payments for operating expenses:

Operating expenses	$4,920,000
Deduct: Loss on disposal of equipment	(24,000)
Deduct: Decrease in inventories	(33,000)
Deduct: Increase in accounts payable	(20,000)
Cash payments for operating expenses	$4,843,000

✔ **The Navigator**

APPENDIX 13B   Using a Worksheet to Prepare the Statement of Cash Flows—Indirect Method

When preparing a statement of cash flows, companies may need to make numerous adjustments of net income. In such cases, they often use **a worksheet to assemble and classify the data that will appear on the statement**. The worksheet is merely an aid in preparing the statement. Its use is optional. Illustration 13B-1 shows the skeleton format of the worksheet for preparation of the statement of cash flows.

The following guidelines are important in preparing a worksheet.

1. In the balance sheet accounts section, **list accounts with debit balances separately from those with credit balances**. This means, for example, that Accumulated Depreciation appears under credit balances and not as a contra account under debit balances. Enter the beginning and ending balances of each account in the appropriate columns. Enter as reconciling items in the two middle columns the transactions that caused the change in the account balance during the year.

Illustration 13B-1
Format of worksheet

	XYZ Company.xls			
Home Insert Page Layout Formulas Data Review View				
P18	fx			

	A	B	C	D	E
1					
2		**XYZ COMPANY**			
3		**Worksheet**			
4		**Statement of Cash Flows For the Year Ended . . .**			
5					
6		**End of**			**End of**
7		**Last Year**	**Reconciling Items**		**Current Year**
8	**Balance Sheet Accounts**	**Balances**	**Debit**	**Credit**	**Balances**
9	Debit balance accounts	XX	XX	XX	XX
10		XX	XX	XX	XX
11	Totals	XXX			XXX
12	Credit balance accounts	XX	XX	XX	XX
13		XX	XX	XX	XX
14	Totals	XXX			XXX
15					
16	**Statement of Cash**				
17	**Flows Effects**				
18	Operating activities				
19	Net income		XX		
20	Adjustments to net income		XX	XX	
21	Investing activities				
22	Receipts and payments		XX	XX	
23	Financing activities				
24	Receipts and payments		XX	XX	
25	Totals		XXX	XXX	
26	Increase (decrease) in cash		(XX)	XX	
27	Totals		XXX	XXX	
28					

After all reconciling items have been entered, each line pertaining to a balance sheet account should "foot across." That is, the beginning balance plus or minus the reconciling item(s) must equal the ending balance. When this agreement exists for all balance sheet accounts, all changes in account balances have been reconciled.

2. The bottom portion of the worksheet consists of the operating, investing, and financing activities sections. It provides the information necessary to prepare the formal statement of cash flows. **Enter inflows of cash as debits in the reconciling columns. Enter outflows of cash as credits in the reconciling columns.** Thus, in this section, the sale of equipment for cash at book value appears as a debit under investing activities. Similarly, the purchase of land for cash appears as a credit under investing activities.

3. **The reconciling items shown in the worksheet are not entered in any journal or posted to any account.** They do not represent either adjustments or corrections of the balance sheet accounts. They are used only to facilitate the preparation of the statement of cash flows.

Preparing the Worksheet

As in the case of worksheets illustrated in earlier chapters, preparing a worksheet involves a series of prescribed steps. The steps in this case are:

1. Enter in the balance sheet accounts section the balance sheet accounts and their beginning and ending balances.

2. Enter in the reconciling columns of the worksheet the data that explain the changes in the balance sheet accounts other than cash and their effects on the statement of cash flows.

3. Enter on the cash line and at the bottom of the worksheet the increase or decrease in cash. This entry should enable the totals of the reconciling columns to be in agreement.

To illustrate the preparation of a worksheet, we will use the 2015 data for Computer Services Company. Your familiarity with these data (from the chapter) should help you understand the use of a worksheet. For ease of reference, the comparative balance sheets, income statement, and selected data for 2015 are presented in Illustration 13B-2.

Illustration 13B-2
Comparative balance sheets, income statement, and additional information for Computer Services Company

Computer Services Company.xls

Home   Insert   Page Layout   Formulas   Data   Review   View

P18   fx

	A	B	C	D
1	**COMPUTER SERVICES COMPANY**			
2	**Comparative Balance Sheets**			
3	**December 31**			
4				Change in
5				Account Balance
6	**Assets**	**2015**	**2014**	**Increase/Decrease**
7	Current assets			
8	Cash	$ 55,000	$ 33,000	$ 22,000 Increase
9	Accounts receivable	20,000	30,000	10,000 Decrease
10	Inventory	15,000	10,000	5,000 Increase
11	Prepaid expenses	5,000	1,000	4,000 Increase
12	Property, plant, and equipment			
13	Land	130,000	20,000	110,000 Increase
14	Buildings	160,000	40,000	120,000 Increase
15	Accumulated depreciation—buildings	(11,000)	(5,000)	6,000 Increase
16	Equipment	27,000	10,000	17,000 Increase
17	Accumulated depreciation—equipment	(3,000)	(1,000)	2,000 Increase
18	Total assets	$398,000	$138,000	
19				
20	**Liabilities and Stockholders' Equity**			
21	Current liabilities			
22	Accounts payable	$ 28,000	$ 12,000	$ 16,000 Increase
23	Income taxes payable	6,000	8,000	2,000 Decrease
24	Long-term liabilities			
25	Bonds payable	130,000	20,000	110,000 Increase
26	Stockholders' equity			
27	Common stock	70,000	50,000	20,000 Increase
28	Retained earnings	164,000	48,000	116,000 Increase
29	Total liabilities and stockholders' equity	$398,000	$138,000	

Computer Services Company.xls

Home   Insert   Page Layout   Formulas   Data   Review   View

P18   fx

	A	B	C	D
1	**COMPUTER SERVICES COMPANY**			
2	**Income Statement**			
3	**For the Year Ended December 31, 2015**			
4				
5	Sales revenue			$507,000
6	Cost of goods sold		$150,000	
7	Operating expenses (excluding depreciation)		111,000	
8	Depreciation expense		9,000	
9	Loss on disposal of equipment		3,000	
10	Interest expense		42,000	315,000
11	Income before income tax			192,000
12	Income tax expense			47,000
13	Net income			$145,000
14				

Additional information for 2015:

1. Depreciation expense was comprised of $6,000 for building and $3,000 for equipment.
2. The company sold equipment with a book value of $7,000 (cost $8,000, less accumulated depreciation $1,000) for $4,000 cash.
3. Issued $110,000 of long-term bonds in direct exchange for land.
4. A building costing $120,000 was purchased for cash. Equipment costing $25,000 was also purchased for cash.
5. Issued common stock for $20,000 cash.
6. The company declared and paid a $29,000 cash dividend.

DETERMINING THE RECONCILING ITEMS

Companies can use one of several approaches to determine the reconciling items. For example, they can first complete the changes affecting net cash provided by operating activities, and then can determine the effects of financing and investing transactions. Or, they can analyze the balance sheet accounts in the order in which they are listed on the worksheet. We will follow this latter approach for Computer Services, except for cash. As indicated in Step 3, **cash is handled last**.

ACCOUNTS RECEIVABLE The decrease of $10,000 in accounts receivable means that cash collections from sales revenue are higher than the sales revenue reported in the income statement. To convert net income to net cash provided by operating activities, we add the decrease of $10,000 to net income. The entry in the reconciling columns of the worksheet is:

| (a) | Operating—Decrease in Accounts Receivable | 10,000 | |
| | Accounts Receivable | | 10,000 |

INVENTORY Computer Services Company's inventory balance increases $5,000 during the period. The Inventory account reflects the difference between the amount of inventory that the company purchased and the amount that it sold. For Computer Services, this means that the cost of merchandise purchased exceeds the cost of goods sold by $5,000. As a result, cost of goods sold does not reflect $5,000 of cash payments made for merchandise. We deduct this inventory increase of $5,000 during the period from net income to arrive at net cash provided by operating activities. The worksheet entry is:

| (b) | Inventory | 5,000 | |
| | Operating—Increase in Inventory | | 5,000 |

PREPAID EXPENSES An increase of $4,000 in prepaid expenses means that expenses deducted in determining net income are less than expenses that were paid in cash. We deduct the increase of $4,000 from net income in determining net cash provided by operating activities. The worksheet entry is:

| (c) | Prepaid Expenses | 4,000 | |
| | Operating—Increase in Prepaid Expenses | | 4,000 |

LAND The increase in land of $110,000 resulted from a purchase through the issuance of long-term bonds. The company should report this transaction as a significant noncash investing and financing activity. The worksheet entry is:

| (d) | Land | 110,000 | |
| | Bonds Payable | | 110,000 |

Helpful Hint
These amounts are asterisked in the worksheet to indicate that they result from a significant noncash transaction.

BUILDINGS The cash purchase of a building for $120,000 is an investing activity cash outflow. The entry in the reconciling columns of the worksheet is:

| (e) | Buildings | 120,000 | |
| | Investing—Purchase of Building | | 120,000 |

EQUIPMENT The increase in equipment of $17,000 resulted from a cash purchase of $25,000 and the disposal of equipment costing $8,000. The book value of the equipment was $7,000, the cash proceeds were $4,000, and a loss of $3,000 was recorded. The worksheet entries are:

| (f) | Equipment | 25,000 | |
| | Investing—Purchase of Equipment | | 25,000 |

(g)	Investing—Sale of Equipment	4,000	
	Operating—Loss on Disposal of Equipment	3,000	
	Accumulated Depreciation—Equipment	1,000	
	Equipment		8,000

ACCOUNTS PAYABLE We must add the increase of $16,000 in accounts payable to net income to determine net cash provided by operating activities. The worksheet entry is:

| (h) | Operating—Increase in Accounts Payable | 16,000 | |
| | Accounts Payable | | 16,000 |

INCOME TAXES PAYABLE When a company incurs income tax expense but has not yet paid its taxes, it records income taxes payable. A change in the Income Taxes Payable account reflects the difference between income tax expense incurred and income tax actually paid. Computer Services' Income Taxes Payable account decreases by $2,000. That means the $47,000 of income tax expense reported on the income statement was $2,000 less than the amount of taxes paid during the period of $49,000. To adjust net income to a cash basis, we must reduce net income by $2,000. The worksheet entry is:

(i)	Income Taxes Payable	2,000	
	Operating—Decrease in Income Taxes		
	Payable		2,000

BONDS PAYABLE The increase of $110,000 in this account resulted from the issuance of bonds for land. This is a significant noncash investing and financing activity. Worksheet entry (d) above is the only entry necessary.

COMMON STOCK The balance sheet reports an increase in Common Stock of $20,000. The additional information section notes that this increase resulted from the issuance of new shares of stock. This is a cash inflow reported in the financing section. The worksheet entry is:

| (j) | Financing—Issuance of Common Stock | 20,000 | |
| | Common Stock | | 20,000 |

ACCUMULATED DEPRECIATION—BUILDINGS, AND ACCUMULATED DEPRECIATION—EQUIPMENT Increases in these accounts of $6,000 and $3,000, respectively, resulted from depreciation expense. Depreciation expense is a **noncash charge that we must add to net income** to determine net cash provided by operating activities. The worksheet entries are:

| (k) | Operating—Depreciation Expense | 6,000 | |
| | Accumulated Depreciation—Buildings | | 6,000 |

| (l) | Operating—Depreciation Expense | 3,000 | |
| | Accumulated Depreciation—Equipment | | 3,000 |

RETAINED EARNINGS The $116,000 increase in retained earnings resulted from net income of $145,000 and the declaration and payment of a $29,000 cash dividend. Net income is included in net cash provided by operating activities, and the dividends are a financing activity cash outflow. The entries in the reconciling columns of the worksheet are:

| (m) | Operating—Net Income | 145,000 | |
| | Retained Earnings | | 145,000 |

| (n) | Retained Earnings | 29,000 | |
| | Financing—Payment of Dividends | | 29,000 |

DISPOSITION OF CHANGE IN CASH The firm's cash increased $22,000 in 2015. The final entry on the worksheet, therefore, is:

| (o) | Cash | 22,000 | |
| | Increase in Cash | | 22,000 |

As shown in the worksheet, we enter the increase in cash in the reconciling credit column as a **balancing** amount. This entry should complete the reconciliation of the changes in the balance sheet accounts. Also, it should permit the totals of the reconciling columns to be in agreement. When all changes have been explained and the reconciling columns are in agreement, the reconciling columns are ruled to complete the worksheet. The completed worksheet for Computer Services Company is shown in Illustration 13B-3.

Illustration 13B-3
Completed worksheet—indirect method

	Computer Services Company.xls				
Home Insert Page Layout Formulas Data Review View					
P18	fx				
	A	B	C	D	E
1	COMPUTER SERVICES COMPANY				
2	Worksheet				
3	Statement of Cash Flows For the Year Ended December 31, 2015				
4					
5		Balance	Reconciling Items		Balance
6	**Balance Sheet Accounts**	12/31/14	Debit	Credit	12/31/15
7	Debits				
8	Cash	33,000	(o) 22,000		55,000
9	Accounts Receivable	30,000		(a) 10,000	20,000
10	Inventory	10,000	(b) 5,000		15,000
11	Prepaid Expenses	1,000	(c) 4,000		5,000
12	Land	20,000	(d) 110,000*		130,000
13	Buildings	40,000	(e) 120,000		160,000
14	Equipment	10,000	(f) 25,000	(g) 8,000	27,000
15	Total	144,000			412,000
16	Credits				
17	Accounts Payable	12,000		(h) 16,000	28,000
18	Income Taxes Payable	8,000	(i) 2,000		6,000
19	Bonds Payable	20,000		(d) 110,000*	130,000
20	Accumulated Depreciation—Buildings	5,000		(k) 6,000	11,000
21	Accumulated Depreciation—Equipment	1,000	(g) 1,000	(l) 3,000	3,000
22	Common Stock	50,000		(j) 20,000	70,000
23	Retained Earnings	48,000	(n) 29,000	(m) 145,000	164,000
24	Total	144,000			412,000
25					
26	**Statement of Cash Flows Effects**				
27	Operating activities				
28	Net income		(m) 145,000		
29	Decrease in accounts receivable		(a) 10,000		
30	Increase in inventory			(b) 5,000	
31	Increase in prepaid expenses			(c) 4,000	
32	Increase in accounts payable		(h) 16,000		
33	Decrease in income taxes payable			(i) 2,000	
34	Depreciation expense		(k) 6,000		
35			(l) 3,000		
36	Loss on disposal of equipment		(g) 3,000		
37	Investing activities				
38	Purchase of building			(e) 120,000	
39	Purchase of equipment			(f) 25,000	
40	Sale of equipment		(g) 4,000		
41	Financing activities				
42	Issuance of common stock		(j) 20,000		
43	Payment of dividends			(n) 29,000	
44	Totals		525,000	503,000	
45	Increase in cash			(o) 22,000	
46	Totals		525,000	525,000	
47					
	* Significant noncash investing and financing activity.				

6 **Explain how to use a worksheet to prepare the statement of cash flows using the indirect method.** When there are numerous adjustments, a worksheet can be a helpful tool in preparing the statement of cash flows. Key guidelines for using a worksheet are as follows. (1) List accounts with debit balances separately from those with credit balances. (2) In the reconciling columns in the bottom portion of the worksheet, show cash inflows as debits and cash outflows as credits. (3) Do not enter reconciling items in any journal or account, but use them only to help prepare the statement of cash flows.

The steps in preparing the worksheet are as follows. (1) Enter beginning and ending balances of balance sheet accounts. (2) Enter debits and credits in reconciling columns. (3) Enter the increase or decrease in cash in two places as a balancing amount.

APPENDIX 13C   Statement of Cash Flows—T-Account Approach

LEARNING OBJECTIVE   7

Use the T-account approach to prepare a statement of cash flows.

Many people like to use T-accounts to provide structure to the preparation of a statement of cash flows. The use of T-accounts is based on the accounting equation that you learned in Chapter 1. The basic equation is:

$$\text{Assets} = \text{Liabilities} + \text{Equity}$$

Now, let's rewrite the left-hand side as:

$$\text{Cash} + \text{Noncash Assets} = \text{Liabilities} + \text{Equity}$$

Next, rewrite the equation by subtracting Noncash Assets from each side to isolate Cash on the left-hand side:

$$\text{Cash} = \text{Liabilities} + \text{Equity} - \text{Noncash Assets}$$

Finally, if we insert the Δ symbol (which means "change in"), we have:

$$\Delta \text{ Cash} = \Delta \text{ Liabilities} + \Delta \text{ Equity} - \Delta \text{ Noncash Assets}$$

What this means is that the change in cash is equal to the change in all of the other balance sheet accounts. Another way to think about this is that if we analyze the changes in all of the noncash balance sheet accounts, we will explain the change in the Cash account. This, of course, is exactly what we are trying to do with the statement of cash flows.

To implement this approach, first prepare a large Cash T-account with sections for operating, investing, and financing activities. Then, prepare smaller T-accounts for all of the other noncash balance sheet accounts. Insert the beginning and ending balances for each of these accounts. Once you have done this, then walk through the steps outlined in Illustration 13-3 (page 654). As you walk through the steps, enter debit and credit amounts into the affected accounts. When all of the changes in the T-accounts have been explained, you are done. To demonstrate, we will apply this approach to the example of Computer Services Company that is presented in the chapter. Each of the adjustments in Illustration 13C-1 is numbered so you can follow them through the T-accounts.

1. Post net income as a debit to the operating section of the Cash T-account and a credit to Retained Earnings. Make sure to label all adjustments to the Cash T-account. It also helps to number each adjustment so you can trace all of them if you make an error.

2. Post depreciation expense as a debit to the operating section of Cash and a credit to each of the appropriate accumulated depreciation accounts.

3. Post any gains or losses on the sale of property, plant, and equipment. To do this, it is best to first prepare the journal entry that was recorded at the time

Cash

Operating			
(1) Net income	145,000	5,000	Inventory (5)
(2) Depreciation expense	9,000	4,000	Prepaid expenses (6)
(3) Loss on equipment	3,000	2,000	Income taxes payable (8)
(4) Accounts receivable	10,000		
(7) Accounts payable	16,000		
Net cash provided by operating activities	172,000		
Investing			
(3) Sold equipment	4,000	120,000	Purchased building (10)
		25,000	Purchased equipment (11)
		141,000	Net cash used by investing activities
Financing			
(12) Issued common stock	20,000	29,000	Dividend paid (13)
		9,000	Net cash used by financing activities
	22,000		

Accounts Receivable		Inventory		Prepaid Expenses		Land	
30,000		10,000		1,000		20,000	
	10,000 (4)	(5) 5,000		(6) 4,000		(9) 110,000	
20,000		15,000		5,000		130,000	

Buildings		Accumulated Depreciation—Buildings		Equipment		Accumulated Depreciation—Equipment	
40,000			5,000	10,000			1,000
(10) 120,000			6,000 (2)	(11) 25,000	8,000 (3)	(3) 1,000	3,000 (2)
160,000			11,000	27,000			3,000

Accounts Payable		Income Taxes Payable		Bonds Payable		Common Stock		Retained Earnings	
	12,000		8,000		20,000		50,000		48,000
	16,000 (7)	(8) 2,000			110,000 (9)		20,000 (12)		145,000 (1)
	28,000		6,000		130,000		70,000	(13) 29,000	
									164,000

Illustration 13C-1
T-account approach

of the sale and then post each element of the journal entry. For example, for Computer Services the entry was:

Cash	4,000	
Accumulated Depreciation—Equipment	1,000	
Loss on Disposal of Equipment	3,000	
Equipment		8,000

The $4,000 cash entry is a source of cash in the investing section of the Cash account. Accumulated Depreciation—Equipment is debited for $1,000. The Loss on Disposal of Equipment is a debit to the operating section of the Cash T-account. Finally, Equipment is credited for $8,000.

4–8. Next, post each of the changes to the noncash current asset and current liability accounts. For example, to explain the $10,000 decline in Computer Services' accounts receivable, credit Accounts Receivable for $10,000 and debit the operating section of the Cash T-account for $10,000.

9. Analyze the changes in the noncurrent accounts. Land was purchased by issuing bonds payable. This requires a debit to Land for $110,000 and a

credit to Bonds Payable for $110,000. Note that this is a significant noncash event that requires disclosure at the bottom of the statement of cash flows.

10. Buildings is debited for $120,000, and the investing section of the Cash T-account is credited for $120,000 as a use of cash from investing.

11. Equipment is debited for $25,000 and the investing section of the Cash T-account is credited for $25,000 as a use of cash from investing.

12. Common Stock is credited for $20,000 for the issuance of shares of stock, and the financing section of the Cash T-account is debited for $20,000.

13. Retained Earnings is debited to reflect the payment of the $29,000 dividend, and the financing section of the Cash T-account is credited to reflect the use of Cash.

At this point, all of the changes in the noncash accounts have been explained. All that remains is to subtotal each section of the Cash T-account and compare the total change in cash with the change shown on the balance sheet. Once this is done, the information in the Cash T-account can be used to prepare a statement of cash flows.

SUMMARY OF LEARNING OBJECTIVE FOR APPENDIX 13C

7 Use the T-account approach to prepare a statement of cash flows. To use T-accounts to prepare the statement of cash flows: (1) prepare a large Cash T-account with sections for operating, investing, and financing activities; (2) prepare smaller T-accounts for all other noncash accounts; (3) insert beginning and ending balances for all accounts; and (4) follows the steps in Illustration 13-3 (page 654), entering debit and credit amounts as needed.

WileyPLUS   **Self-Test, Brief Exercises, Exercises, Problem Set A, and many more components are available for practice in *WileyPLUS*.**

***Note:** All asterisked Questions, Exercises, and Problems relate to material in the appendices to the chapter.

SELF-TEST QUESTIONS

Answers are on page 709.

(LO 1) **1.** Which of the following is **incorrect** about the statement of cash flows?
  (a) It is a fourth basic financial statement.
  (b) It provides information about cash receipts and cash payments of an entity during a period.
  (c) It reconciles the ending cash account balance to the balance per the bank statement.
  (d) It provides information about the operating, investing, and financing activities of the business.

(LO 1) **2.** Which of the following will **not** be reported in the statement of cash flows?
  (a) The net change in stockholders' equity during the year.
  (b) Cash payments for plant assets during the year.
  (c) Cash receipts from sales of plant assets during the year.
  (d) How acquisitions of plant assets during the year were financed.

3. The statement of cash flows classifies cash receipts (LO 2) and cash payments by these activities:
  (a) operating and nonoperating.
  (b) investing, financing, and operating.
  (c) financing, operating, and nonoperating.
  (d) investing, financing, and nonoperating.

4. Which is an example of a cash flow from an operating (LO 2) activity?
  (a) Payment of cash to lenders for interest.
  (b) Receipt of cash from the sale of capital stock.
  (c) Payment of cash dividends to the company's stockholders.
  (d) None of the above.

5. Which is an example of a cash flow from an investing (LO 2) activity?
  (a) Receipt of cash from the issuance of bonds payable.
  (b) Payment of cash to repurchase outstanding capital stock.
  (c) Receipt of cash from the sale of equipment.
  (d) Payment of cash to suppliers for inventory.

(LO 2)   **6.** Cash dividends paid to stockholders are classified on the statement of cash flows as:
 (a) operating activities.
 (b) investing activities.
 (c) a combination of (a) and (b).
 (d) financing activities.

(LO 2)   **7.** Which is an example of a cash flow from a financing activity?
 (a) Receipt of cash from sale of land.
 (b) Issuance of debt for cash.
 (c) Purchase of equipment for cash.
 (d) None of the above

(LO 2)   **8.** Which of the following is **incorrect** about the statement of cash flows?
 (a) The direct method may be used to report cash provided by operations.
 (b) The statement shows the net cash provided (used) for three categories of activity.
 (c) The operating section is the last section of the statement.
 (d) The indirect method may be used to report net cash provided by operating activities.

Questions 9 through 11 apply only to the indirect method.

(LO 3)   **9.** Net income is $132,000, accounts payable increased $10,000 during the year, inventory decreased $6,000 during the year, and accounts receivable increased $12,000 during the year. Under the indirect method, what is net cash provided by operating activities?
 (a) $102,000.   **(c)** $124,000.
 (b) $112,000.   **(d)** $136,000.

(LO 3)   **10.** Items that are added back to net income in determining net cash provided by operating activities under the indirect method do **not** include:
 (a) depreciation expense.
 (b) an increase in inventory.
 (c) amortization expense.
 (d) loss on disposal of equipment.

(LO 3)   **11.** The following data are available for Allen Clapp Corporation.

Net income	$200,000
Depreciation expense	40,000
Dividends paid	60,000
Gain on disposal of land	10,000
Decrease in accounts receivable	20,000
Decrease in accounts payable	30,000

Net cash provided by operating activities is:
 (a) $160,000.   **(c)** $240,000.
 (b) $220,000.   **(d)** $280,000.

(LO 3)   **12.** The following data are available for Orange Peels Corporation.

Sale of land	$100,000
Sale of equipment	50,000
Issuance of common stock	70,000
Purchase of equipment	30,000
Payment of cash dividends	60,000

Net cash provided by investing activities is:
 (a) $120,000.   **(c)** $150,000.
 (b) $130,000.   **(d)** $190,000.

(LO 3)   **13.** The following data are available for Something Strange!

Increase in accounts payable	$ 40,000
Increase in bonds payable	100,000
Sale of investment	50,000
Issuance of common stock	60,000
Payment of cash dividends	30,000

Net cash provided by financing activities is:
 (a) $90,000.   **(c)** $160,000.
 (b) $130,000.   **(d)** $170,000.

(LO 4)   **14.** The statement of cash flows should **not** be used to evaluate an entity's ability to:
 (a) earn net income.
 (b) generate future cash flows.
 (c) pay dividends.
 (d) meet obligations.

(LO 4)   **15.** Free cash flow provides an indication of a company's ability to:
 (a) generate net income.
 (b) generate cash to pay dividends.
 (c) generate cash to invest in new capital expenditures.
 (d) Both (b) and (c).

Questions 16 and 17 apply only to the direct method.

(LO 5)   ***16.** The beginning balance in accounts receivable is $44,000, the ending balance is $42,000, and sales during the period are $129,000. What are cash receipts from customers?
 (a) $127,000.   **(c)** $131,000.
 (b) $129,000.   **(d)** $141,000.

(LO 5)   ***17.** Which of the following items is reported on a statement of cash flows prepared by the direct method?
 (a) Loss on disposal of building.
 (b) Increase in accounts receivable.
 (c) Depreciation expense.
 (d) Cash payments to suppliers.

(LO 6)   ***18.** In a worksheet for the statement of cash flows, a decrease in accounts receivable is entered in the reconciling columns as a credit to Accounts Receivable and a debit in the:
 (a) investing activities section.
 (b) operating activities section.
 (c) financing activities section.
 (d) None of the above.

(LO 6)   ***19.** In a worksheet for the statement of cash flows, a worksheet entry that includes a credit to accumulated depreciation will also include a:
 (a) credit in the operating activities section and a debit in another section.
 (b) debit in the operating activities section.
 (c) debit in the investing activities section.
 (d) debit in the financing activities section.

Go to the book's companion website, www.wiley.com/college/weygandt, for additional Self-Test Questions.

✔ **The Navigator**

QUESTIONS

1. **(a)** What is a statement of cash flows?
   (b) Mark Paxson maintains that the statement of cash flows is an optional financial statement. Do you agree? Explain.
2. What questions about cash are answered by the statement of cash flows?
3. Distinguish among the three types of activities reported in the statement of cash flows.
4. **(a)** What are the major sources (inflows) of cash in a statement of cash flows?
   (b) What are the major uses (outflows) of cash?
5. Why is it important to disclose certain noncash transactions? How should they be disclosed?
6. Diane Hollowell and Terry Parmenter were discussing the format of the statement of cash flows of Snow Candy Co. At the bottom of Snow Candy's statement of cash flows was a separate section entitled "Noncash investing and financing activities." Give three examples of significant noncash transactions that would be reported in this section.
7. Why is it necessary to use comparative balance sheets, a current income statement, and certain transaction data in preparing a statement of cash flows?
8. Contrast the advantages and disadvantages of the direct and indirect methods of preparing the statement of cash flows. Are both methods acceptable? Which method is preferred by the FASB? Which method is more popular?
9. When the total cash inflows exceed the total cash outflows in the statement of cash flows, how and where is this excess identified?
10. Describe the indirect method for determining net cash provided (used) by operating activities.
11. Why is it necessary to convert accrual-basis net income to cash-basis income when preparing a statement of cash flows?

12. The president of Merando Company is puzzled. During the last year, the company experienced a net loss of $800,000, yet its cash increased $300,000 during the same period of time. Explain to the president how this could occur.
13. Identify five items that are adjustments to convert net income to net cash provided by operating activities under the indirect method.
14. Why and how is depreciation expense reported in a statement prepared using the indirect method?
15. Why is the statement of cash flows useful?
16. During 2015, Doubleday Company converted $1,700,000 of its total $2,000,000 of bonds payable into common stock. Indicate how the transaction would be reported on a statement of cash flows, if at all.
17. In its 2011 statement of cash flows, what amount did Apple report for net cash (a) provided by operating activities, (b) used for investing activities, and (c) used for financing activities?
*18. Describe the direct method for determining net cash provided by operating activities.
*19. Give the formulas under the direct method for computing (a) cash receipts from customers and (b) cash payments to suppliers.
*20. Molino Inc. reported sales revenue of $2 million for 2015. Accounts receivable decreased $200,000 and accounts payable increased $300,000. Compute cash receipts from customers, assuming that the receivable and payable transactions related to operations.
*21. In the direct method, why is depreciation expense not reported in the cash flows from operating activities section?
*22. Why is it advantageous to use a worksheet when preparing a statement of cash flows? Is a worksheet required to prepare a statement of cash flows?

BRIEF EXERCISES

Indicate statement presentation of selected transactions.
(LO 2)

BE13-1 Each of the items below must be considered in preparing a statement of cash flows for Baskerville Co. for the year ended December 31, 2015. For each item, state how it should be shown in the statement of cash flows for 2015.

(a) Issued bonds for $200,000 cash.
(b) Purchased equipment for $150,000 cash.
(c) Sold land costing $20,000 for $20,000 cash.
(d) Declared and paid a $50,000 cash dividend.

Classify items by activities.
(LO 2)

BE13-2 Classify each item as an operating, investing, or financing activity. Assume all items involve cash unless there is information to the contrary.

(a) Purchase of equipment.
(b) Sale of building.
(c) Redemption of bonds.

(d) Depreciation.
(e) Payment of dividends.
(f) Issuance of capital stock.

BE13-3 The following T-account is a summary of the Cash account of Cuellar Company.

Identify financing activity transactions.

(LO 2)

Cash (Summary Form)

Balance, Jan. 1	8,000		
Receipts from customers	364,000	Payments for goods	200,000
Dividends on stock investments	6,000	Payments for operating expenses	140,000
Proceeds from sale of equipment	36,000	Interest paid	10,000
Proceeds from issuance of		Taxes paid	8,000
bonds payable	300,000	Dividends paid	50,000
Balance, Dec. 31	306,000		

What amount of net cash provided (used) by financing activities should be reported in the statement of cash flows?

BE13-4 Telfer, Inc. reported net income of $2.8 million in 2015. Depreciation for the year was $160,000, accounts receivable decreased $350,000, and accounts payable decreased $280,000. Compute net cash provided by operating activities using the indirect method.

Compute net cash provided by operating activities—indirect method.

(LO 3)

BE13-5 The net income for Metz Co. for 2015 was $280,000. For 2015, depreciation on plant assets was $70,000, and the company incurred a loss on disposal of plant assets of $12,000. Compute net cash provided by operating activities under the indirect method.

Compute net cash provided by operating activities—indirect method.

(LO 3)

BE13-6 The comparative balance sheets for Montalvo Company show these changes in noncash current asset accounts: accounts receivable decrease $80,000, prepaid expenses increase $28,000, and inventories increase $30,000. Compute net cash provided by operating activities using the indirect method assuming that net income is $300,000.

Compute net cash provided by operating activities—indirect method.

(LO 3)

BE13-7 The T-accounts for Equipment and the related Accumulated Depreciation—Equipment for Luo Company at the end of 2015 are shown here.

Determine cash received from sale of equipment.

(LO 3)

Equipment			
Beg. bal.	80,000	Disposals	22,000
Acquisitions	41,600		
End. bal.	99,600		

Accumulated Depreciation—Equipment			
Disposals	5,500	Beg. bal.	44,500
		Depr. exp.	12,000
		End. bal.	51,000

In addition, Luo Company's income statement reported a loss on the disposal of equipment of $6,500. What amount was reported on the statement of cash flows as "cash flow from sale of equipment"?

BE13-8 Assume that during 2015, Cypress Semiconductor Corporation reported net cash provided by operating activities of $155,793,000, net cash used in investing of $207,826,000, and net cash used in financing of $33,372,000. In addition, cash spent for fixed assets during the period was $132,280,000. No dividends were paid. Calculate free cash flow.

Calculate free cash flow.

(LO 4)

BE13-9 Hinck Corporation reported net cash provided by operating activities of $360,000, net cash used by investing activities of $250,000, and net cash provided by financing activities of $70,000. In addition, cash spent for capital assets during the period was $200,000. Dividends of $5,000 were paid. Calculate free cash flow.

Calculate free cash flow.

(LO 4)

BE13-10 Suppose in a recent quarter, Alliance Atlantis Communications Inc. reported net cash provided by operating activities of $45,600,000 and revenues of $264,800,000. Cash spent on plant asset additions during the quarter was $1,600,000. No dividends were paid. Calculate free cash flow.

Calculate free cash flow.

(LO 4)

BE13-11 The management of Morrow Inc. is trying to decide whether it can increase its dividend. During the current year, it reported net income of $875,000. It had net cash provided by operating activities of $734,000, paid cash dividends of $70,000, and had capital expenditures of $280,000. Compute the company's free cash flow, and discuss whether an increase in the dividend appears warranted. What other factors should be considered?

Calculate and analyze free cash flow.

(LO 4)

*BE13-12 Suppose Columbia Sportswear Company had accounts receivable of $206,024,000 at the beginning of a recent year, and $267,653,000 at year-end. Sales revenue was $1,095,307,000 for the year. What is the amount of cash receipts from customers?

Compute receipts from customers—direct method.

(LO 5)

Compute cash payments for income taxes—direct method.
(LO 5)

*BE13-13 Howell Corporation reported income taxes of $340,000,000 on its 2015 income statement and income taxes payable of $297,000,000 at December 31, 2014, and $522,000,000 at December 31, 2015. What amount of cash payments were made for income taxes during 2015?

Compute cash payments for operating expenses—direct method.
(LO 5)

*BE13-14 Sisson Corporation reports operating expenses of $80,000 excluding depreciation expense of $15,000 for 2015. During the year, prepaid expenses decreased $6,600 and accrued expenses payable increased $4,400. Compute the cash payments for operating expenses in 2015.

Indicate entries in worksheet.
(LO 6)

*BE13-15 During the year, prepaid expenses decreased $5,600, and accrued expenses increased $2,400. Indicate how the changes in prepaid expenses and accrued expenses payable should be entered in the reconciling columns of a worksheet. Assume that beginning balances were prepaid expenses $18,600 and accrued expenses payable $8,200.

> DO IT! Review

Classify transactions by type of cash flow activity.
(LO 2)

DO IT! 13-1 Ragsdell Corporation had the following transactions.

1. Issued $200,000 of bonds payable.
2. Paid utilities expense.
3. Issued 500 shares of preferred stock for $45,000.
4. Sold land and a building for $250,000.
5. Lent $30,000 to Tegtmeier Corporation, receiving Tegtmeier's 1-year, 12% note.

Classify each of these transactions by type of cash flow activity (operating, investing, or financing).

Calculate net cash from operating activities.
(LO 3)

DO IT! 13-2 Wise Photography reported net income of $130,000 for 2015. Included in the income statement were depreciation expense of $6,000, amortization expense of $2,000, and a gain on disposal of equipment of $3,600. Wise's comparative balance sheets show the following balances.

	12/31/14	12/31/15
Accounts receivable	$27,000	$21,000
Accounts payable	6,000	9,200

Calculate net cash provided by operating activities for Wise Photography.

Compute and discuss free cash flow.
(LO 4)

DO IT! 13-3 Obermeyer Corporation issued the following statement of cash flows for 2015.

OBERMEYER CORPORATION
Statement of Cash Flows—Indirect Method
For the Year Ended December 31, 2015

Cash flows from operating activities		
Net income		$59,000
Adjustments to reconcile net income to net cash provided by operating activities:		
Depreciation expense	$ 9,100	
Loss on disposal of equipment	9,500	
Increase in inventory	(5,000)	
Decrease in accounts receivable	3,300	
Decrease in accounts payable	(2,200)	14,700
Net cash provided by operating activities		73,700
Cash flows from investing activities		
Sale of investments	3,100	
Purchase of equipment	(27,000)	
Net cash used by investing activities		(23,900)

Cash flows from financing activities		
Issuance of stock	20,000	
Payment on long-term note payable	(10,000)	
Payment for dividends	(15,000)	
Net cash used by financing activities		(5,000)
Net increase in cash		44,800
Cash at beginning of year		13,000
Cash at end of year		$57,800

(a) Compute free cash flow for Obermeyer Corporation. (b) Explain why free cash flow often provides better information than "Net cash provided by operating activities."

EXERCISES

E13-1 Tabares Corporation had these transactions during 2015.

(a) Issued $50,000 par value common stock for cash.
(b) Purchased a machine for $30,000, giving a long-term note in exchange.
(c) Issued $200,000 par value common stock upon conversion of bonds having a face value of $200,000.
(d) Declared and paid a cash dividend of $18,000.
(e) Sold a long-term investment with a cost of $15,000 for $15,000 cash.
(f) Collected $16,000 of accounts receivable.
(g) Paid $18,000 on accounts payable.

Classify transactions by type of activity.

(LO 2)

Instructions

Analyze the transactions and indicate whether each transaction resulted in a cash flow from operating activities, investing activities, financing activities, or noncash investing and financing activities.

E13-2 An analysis of comparative balance sheets, the current year's income statement, and the general ledger accounts of Wellman Corp. uncovered the following items. Assume all items involve cash unless there is information to the contrary.

Classify transactions by type of activity.

(LO 2)

(a) Payment of interest on notes payable.
(b) Exchange of land for patent.
(c) Sale of building at book value.
(d) Payment of dividends.
(e) Depreciation.
(f) Receipt of dividends on investment in stock.
(g) Receipt of interest on notes receivable.
(h) Issuance of capital stock.
(i) Amortization of patent.
(j) Issuance of bonds for land.
(k) Purchase of land.
(l) Conversion of bonds into common stock.
(m) Loss on sale of land.
(n) Retirement of bonds.

Instructions

Indicate how each item should be classified in the statement of cash flows using these four major classifications: operating activity (indirect method), investing activity, financing activity, and significant noncash investing and financing activity.

E13-3 Cushenberry Corporation had the following transactions.

1. Sold land (cost $12,000) for $15,000.
2. Issued common stock at par for $20,000.
3. Recorded depreciation on buildings for $17,000.
4. Paid salaries of $9,000.
5. Issued 1,000 shares of $1 par value common stock for equipment worth $8,000.
6. Sold equipment (cost $10,000, accumulated depreciation $7,000) for $1,200.

Prepare journal entry and determine effect on cash flows.

(LO 2)

Instructions

For each transaction above, (a) prepare the journal entry, and (b) indicate how it would affect the statement of cash flows using the indirect method.

Prepare the operating activities section—indirect method.

(LO 3)

E13-4 Gutierrez Company reported net income of $225,000 for 2015. Gutierrez also reported depreciation expense of $45,000 and a loss of $5,000 on the disposal of equipment. The comparative balance sheet shows a decrease in accounts receivable of $15,000 for the year, a $17,000 increase in accounts payable, and a $4,000 decrease in prepaid expenses.

Instructions
Prepare the operating activities section of the statement of cash flows for 2015. Use the indirect method.

Prepare the operating activities section—indirect method.

(LO 3)

E13-5 The current sections of Scoggin Inc.'s balance sheets at December 31, 2014 and 2015, are presented here. Scoggin's net income for 2015 was $153,000. Depreciation expense was $24,000.

	2015	2014
Current assets		
Cash	$105,000	$ 99,000
Accounts receivable	110,000	89,000
Inventory	158,000	172,000
Prepaid expenses	27,000	22,000
Total current assets	$400,000	$382,000
Current liabilities		
Accrued expenses payable	$ 15,000	$ 5,000
Accounts payable	85,000	92,000
Total current liabilities	$100,000	$ 97,000

Instructions
Prepare the net cash provided by operating activities section of the company's statement of cash flows for the year ended December 31, 2015, using the indirect method.

Prepare partial statement of cash flows—indirect method.

(LO 3)

E13-6 The three accounts shown below appear in the general ledger of Herrick Corp. during 2015.

Equipment

Date		Debit	Credit	Balance
Jan. 1	Balance			160,000
July 31	Purchase of equipment	70,000		230,000
Sept. 2	Cost of equipment constructed	53,000		283,000
Nov. 10	Cost of equipment sold		49,000	234,000

Accumulated Depreciation—Equipment

Date		Debit	Credit	Balance
Jan. 1	Balance			71,000
Nov. 10	Accumulated depreciation on equipment sold	30,000		41,000
Dec. 31	Depreciation for year		28,000	69,000

Retained Earnings

Date		Debit	Credit	Balance
Jan. 1	Balance			105,000
Aug. 23	Dividends (cash)	14,000		91,000
Dec. 31	Net income		77,000	168,000

Instructions
From the postings in the accounts, indicate how the information is reported on a statement of cash flows using the indirect method. The loss on disposal of equipment was $7,000. (*Hint:* Cost of equipment constructed is reported in the investing activities section as a decrease in cash of $53,000.)

E13-7 Rojas Corporation's comparative balance sheets are presented below.

Prepare statement of cash flows and compute free cash flow.

(LO 3, 4)

ROJAS CORPORATION
Comparative Balance Sheets
December 31

	2015	2014
Cash	$ 14,300	$ 10,700
Accounts receivable	21,200	23,400
Land	20,000	26,000
Buildings	70,000	70,000
Accumulated depreciation—buildings	(15,000)	(10,000)
Total	$110,500	$120,100
Accounts payable	$ 12,370	$ 31,100
Common stock	75,000	69,000
Retained earnings	23,130	20,000
Total	$110,500	$120,100

Additional information:

1. Net income was $22,630. Dividends declared and paid were $19,500.
2. All other changes in noncurrent account balances had a direct effect on cash flows, except the change in accumulated depreciation. The land was sold for $4,900.

Instructions
(a) Prepare a statement of cash flows for 2015 using the indirect method.
(b) Compute free cash flow.

E13-8 Here are comparative balance sheets for Velo Company.

Prepare a statement of cash flows—indirect method.

(LO 3)

VELO COMPANY
Comparative Balance Sheets
December 31

Assets	2015	2014
Cash	$ 63,000	$ 22,000
Accounts receivable	85,000	76,000
Inventory	170,000	189,000
Land	75,000	100,000
Equipment	270,000	200,000
Accumulated depreciation—equipment	(66,000)	(32,000)
Total	$597,000	$555,000

Liabilities and Stockholders' Equity	2015	2014
Accounts payable	$ 39,000	$ 47,000
Bonds payable	150,000	200,000
Common stock ($1 par)	216,000	174,000
Retained earnings	192,000	134,000
Total	$597,000	$555,000

Additional information:

1. Net income for 2015 was $93,000.
2. Cash dividends of $35,000 were declared and paid.
3. Bonds payable amounting to $50,000 were redeemed for cash $50,000.
4. Common stock was issued for $42,000 cash.
5. No equipment was sold during 2015, but land was sold at cost.

Instructions
Prepare a statement of cash flows for 2015 using the indirect method.

694 13 Statement of Cash Flows

Prepare statement of cash flows and compute free cash flow.
(LO 3, 4)

E13-9 Rodriquez Corporation's comparative balance sheets are presented below.

RODRIQUEZ CORPORATION
Comparative Balance Sheets
December 31

	2015	2014
Cash	$ 15,200	$ 17,700
Accounts receivable	25,200	22,300
Investments	20,000	16,000
Equipment	60,000	70,000
Accumulated depreciation—equipment	(14,000)	(10,000)
Total	$106,400	$116,000
Accounts payable	$ 14,600	$ 11,100
Bonds payable	10,000	30,000
Common stock	50,000	45,000
Retained earnings	31,800	29,900
Total	$106,400	$116,000

Additional information:

1. Net income was $18,300. Dividends declared and paid were $16,400.
2. Equipment which cost $10,000 and had accumulated depreciation of $1,200 was sold for $3,300.
3. All other changes in noncurrent account balances had a direct effect on cash flows, except the change in accumulated depreciation.

Instructions
(a) Prepare a statement of cash flows for 2015 using the indirect method.
(b) Compute free cash flow.

Compute net cash provided by operating activities—direct method.
(LO 5)

*E13-10 Macgregor Company completed its first year of operations on December 31, 2015. Its initial income statement showed that Macgregor had revenues of $192,000 and operating expenses of $78,000. Accounts receivable and accounts payable at year-end were $60,000 and $23,000, respectively. Assume that accounts payable related to operating expenses. Ignore income taxes.

Instructions
Compute net cash provided by operating activities using the direct method.

Compute cash payments—direct method.
(LO 5)

*E13-11 Suppose a recent income statement for McDonald's Corporation shows cost of goods sold $4,852.7 million and operating expenses (including depreciation expense of $1,201 million) $10,671.5 million. The comparative balance sheet for the year shows that inventory increased $18.1 million, prepaid expenses increased $56.3 million, accounts payable (merchandise suppliers) increased $136.9 million, and accrued expenses payable increased $160.9 million.

Instructions
Using the direct method, compute (a) cash payments to suppliers and (b) cash payments for operating expenses.

Compute cash flow from operating activities—direct method.
(LO 5)

*E13-12 The 2015 accounting records of Blocker Transport reveal these transactions and events.

Payment of interest	$ 10,000	Collection of accounts receivable	$182,000
Cash sales	48,000	Payment of salaries and wages	53,000
Receipt of dividend revenue	18,000	Depreciation expense	16,000
Payment of income taxes	12,000	Proceeds from sale of vehicles	12,000
Net income	38,000	Purchase of equipment for cash	22,000
Payment of accounts payable		Loss on disposal of vehicles	3,000
for merchandise	115,000	Payment of dividends	14,000
Payment for land	74,000	Payment of operating expenses	28,000

Instructions
Prepare the cash flows from operating activities section using the direct method. (Not all of the items will be used.)

*E13-13 The following information is taken from the 2015 general ledger of Swisher Company.

Calculate cash flows—direct method.

(LO 5)

Rent	Rent expense	$ 48,000
	Prepaid rent, January 1	5,900
	Prepaid rent, December 31	9,000
Salaries	Salaries and wages expense	$ 54,000
	Salaries and wages payable, January 1	10,000
	Salaries and wages payable, December 31	8,000
Sales	Sales revenue	$175,000
	Accounts receivable, January 1	16,000
	Accounts receivable, December 31	7,000

Instructions

In each case, compute the amount that should be reported in the operating activities section of the statement of cash flows under the direct method.

*E13-14 Comparative balance sheets for International Company are presented below.

Prepare a worksheet.

(LO 6)

INTERNATIONAL COMPANY
Comparative Balance Sheets
December 31

Assets	2015	2014
Cash	$ 73,000	$ 22,000
Accounts receivable	85,000	76,000
Inventory	180,000	189,000
Land	75,000	100,000
Equipment	250,000	200,000
Accumulated depreciation—equipment	(66,000)	(42,000)
Total	$597,000	$545,000

Liabilities and Stockholders' Equity	2015	2014
Accounts payable	$ 34,000	$ 47,000
Bonds payable	150,000	200,000
Common stock ($1 par)	214,000	164,000
Retained earnings	199,000	134,000
Total	$597,000	$545,000

Additional information:

1. Net income for 2015 was $135,000.
2. Cash dividends of $70,000 were declared and paid.
3. Bonds payable amounting to $50,000 were redeemed for cash $50,000.
4. Common stock was issued for $50,000 cash.
5. Depreciation expense was $24,000.
6. Sales for the year were $978,000.

Instructions

Prepare a worksheet for a statement of cash flows for 2015 using the indirect method. Enter the reconciling items directly on the worksheet, using letters to cross-reference each entry.

EXERCISES: SET B AND CHALLENGE EXERCISES

Visit the book's companion website, at **www.wiley.com/college/weygandt**, and choose the Student Companion site to access Exercise Set B and Challenge Exercises.

PROBLEMS: SET A

P13-1A You are provided with the transactions shown on the next page that took place during a recent fiscal year.

Distinguish among operating, investing, and financing activities.

(LO 2)

Transaction	Statement of Cash Flow Activity Affected	Cash Inflow, Outflow, or No Effect?
(a) Recorded depreciation expense on the plant assets.		
(b) Recorded and paid interest expense.		
(c) Recorded cash proceeds from a disposal of plant assets.		
(d) Acquired land by issuing common stock.		
(e) Paid a cash dividend to preferred stockholders.		
(f) Paid a cash dividend to common stockholders.		
(g) Recorded cash sales.		
(h) Recorded sales on account.		
(i) Purchased inventory for cash.		
(j) Purchased inventory on account.		

Instructions

Complete the table indicating whether each item (1) affects operating (O) activities, investing (I) activities, financing (F) activities, or is a noncash (NC) transaction reported in a separate schedule, and (2) represents a cash inflow or cash outflow or has no cash flow effect. Assume use of the indirect approach.

Determine cash flow effects of changes in equity accounts.

(LO 3)

P13-2A The following account balances relate to the stockholders' equity accounts of Kerbs Corp. at year-end.

	2015	2014
Common stock, 10,500 and 10,000 shares, respectively, for 2015 and 2014	$170,000	$140,000
Preferred stock, 5,000 shares	125,000	125,000
Retained earnings	300,000	250,000

A small stock dividend was declared and issued in 2015. The market value of the shares was $10,500. Cash dividends were $15,000 in both 2015 and 2014. The common stock has no par or stated value.

(a) Net income $75,500

Instructions

(a) What was the amount of net income reported by Kerbs Corp. in 2015?

(b) Determine the amounts of any cash inflows or outflows related to the common stock and dividend accounts in 2015.

(c) Indicate where each of the cash inflows or outflows identified in (b) would be classified on the statement of cash flows.

Prepare the operating activities section—indirect method.

(LO 3)

P13-3A The income statement of Whitlock Company is presented here.

WHITLOCK COMPANY
Income Statement
For the Year Ended November 30, 2015

Sales revenue		$7,700,000
Cost of goods sold		
Beginning inventory	$1,900,000	
Purchases	4,400,000	
Goods available for sale	6,300,000	
Ending inventory	1,400,000	
Total cost of goods sold		4,900,000
Gross profit		2,800,000
Operating expenses		1,150,000
Net income		$1,650,000

Additional information:

1. Accounts receivable increased $200,000 during the year, and inventory decreased $500,000.
2. Prepaid expenses increased $150,000 during the year.

3. Accounts payable to suppliers of merchandise decreased $340,000 during the year.
4. Accrued expenses payable decreased $100,000 during the year.
5. Operating expenses include depreciation expense of $70,000.

Instructions

Prepare the operating activities section of the statement of cash flows for the year ended November 30, 2015, for Whitlock Company, using the indirect method.

*Cash from operations
$1,430,000*

*P13-4A Data for Whitlock Company are presented in P13-3A.

Instructions

Prepare the operating activities section of the statement of cash flows using the direct method.

Prepare the operating activities section—direct method.
(LO 5)

P13-5A Zumbrunn Company's income statement contained the condensed information below.

*Cash from operations
$1,430,000*

ZUMBRUNN COMPANY
Income Statement
For the Year Ended December 31, 2015

Service revenue		$970,000
Operating expenses, excluding depreciation	$624,000	
Depreciation expense	60,000	
Loss on disposal of equipment	16,000	700,000
Income before income taxes		270,000
Income tax expense		40,000
Net income		$230,000

Prepare the operating activities section—indirect method.
(LO 3)

Zumbrunn's balance sheet contained the comparative data at December 31, shown below.

	2015	2014
Accounts receivable	$75,000	$65,000
Accounts payable	46,000	28,000
Income taxes payable	11,000	7,000

Accounts payable pertain to operating expenses.

Instructions

Prepare the operating activities section of the statement of cash flows using the indirect method.

Cash from operations $318,000

*P13-6A Data for Zumbrunn Company are presented in P13-5A.

Instructions

Prepare the operating activities section of the statement of cash flows using the direct method.

Prepare the operating activities section—direct method.
(LO 5)

P13-7A Presented below are the financial statements of Nosker Company.

Cash from operations $318,000

NOSKER COMPANY
Comparative Balance Sheets
December 31

Prepare a statement of cash flows—indirect method, and compute free cash flow.
(LO 3, 4)

Assets	2015	2014
Cash	$ 38,000	$ 20,000
Accounts receivable	30,000	14,000
Inventory	27,000	20,000
Equipment	60,000	78,000
Accumulated depreciation—equipment	(29,000)	(24,000)
Total	$126,000	$108,000

Liabilities and Stockholders' Equity	2015	2014
Accounts payable	$ 24,000	$ 15,000
Income taxes payable	7,000	8,000
Bonds payable	27,000	33,000
Common stock	18,000	14,000
Retained earnings	50,000	38,000
Total	$126,000	$108,000

NOSKER COMPANY
Income Statement
For the Year Ended December 31, 2015

Sales revenue	$242,000
Cost of goods sold	175,000
Gross profit	67,000
Operating expenses	24,000
Income from operations	43,000
Interest expense	3,000
Income before income taxes	40,000
Income tax expense	8,000
Net income	$ 32,000

Additional data:

1. Dividends declared and paid were $20,000.
2. During the year equipment was sold for $8,500 cash. This equipment cost $18,000 originally and had a book value of $8,500 at the time of sale.
3. All depreciation expense, $14,500, is in the operating expenses.
4. All sales and purchases are on account.

Instructions

(a) Cash from operations $31,500

(a) Prepare a statement of cash flows using the indirect method.
(b) Compute free cash flow.

Prepare a statement of cash flows—direct method, and compute free cash flow.

(LO 4, 5)

XLS

(a) Cash from operations $31,500

*P13-8A Data for Nosker Company are presented in P13-7A. Further analysis reveals the following.

1. Accounts payable pertain to merchandise suppliers.
2. All operating expenses except for depreciation were paid in cash.

Instructions

(a) Prepare a statement of cash flows for Nosker Company using the direct method.
(b) Compute free cash flow.

Prepare a statement of cash flows—indirect method.

(LO 3)

P13-9A Condensed financial data of Cheng Inc. follow.

CHENG INC.
Comparative Balance Sheets
December 31

Assets	2015	2014
Cash	$ 80,800	$ 48,400
Accounts receivable	92,800	33,000
Inventory	117,500	102,850
Prepaid expenses	28,400	26,000
Investments	143,000	114,000
Equipment	270,000	242,500
Accumulated depreciation—equipment	(50,000)	(52,000)
Total	$682,500	$514,750

Liabilities and Stockholders' Equity		
Accounts payable	$112,000	$ 67,300
Accrued expenses payable	16,500	17,000
Bonds payable	110,000	150,000
Common stock	220,000	175,000
Retained earnings	224,000	105,450
Total	$682,500	$514,750

CHENG INC.
Income Statement
For the Year Ended December 31, 2015

Sales revenue		$392,780
Less:		
Cost of goods sold	$135,460	
Operating expenses, excluding depreciation	12,410	
Depreciation expense	46,500	
Income tax expense	27,280	
Interest expense	4,730	
˙Loss on disposal of plant assets	7,500	233,880
Net income		$158,900

Additional information:

1. New equipment costing $85,000 was purchased for cash during the year.
2. Old equipment having an original cost of $57,500 was sold for $1,500 cash.
3. Bonds matured and were paid off at face value for cash.
4. A cash dividend of $40,350 was declared and paid during the year.

Instructions

Prepare a statement of cash flows using the indirect method.

Cash from operations $180,250

*P13-10A Data for Cheng Inc. are presented in P13-9A. Further analysis reveals that accounts payable pertain to merchandise creditors.

Prepare a statement of cash flows—direct method.
(LO 5)

Instructions

Prepare a statement of cash flows for Cheng Inc. using the direct method.

Cash from operations $180,250

P13-11A The comparative balance sheets for Rothlisberger Company as of December 31 are presented below.

Prepare a statement of cash flows—indirect method.
(LO 3)

ROTHLISBERGER COMPANY
Comparative Balance Sheets
December 31

Assets	2015	2014
Cash	$ 81,000	$ 45,000
Accounts receivable	41,000	62,000
Inventory	151,450	142,000
Prepaid expenses	15,280	21,000
Land	105,000	130,000
Buildings	200,000	200,000
Accumulated depreciation—buildings	(60,000)	(40,000)
Equipment	221,000	155,000
Accumulated depreciation—equipment	(45,000)	(35,000)
Total	$709,730	$680,000

Liabilities and Stockholders' Equity		
Accounts payable	$ 47,730	$ 40,000
Bonds payable	260,000	300,000
Common stock, $1 par	200,000	160,000
Retained earnings	202,000	180,000
Total	$709,730	$680,000

Additional information:

1. Operating expenses include depreciation expense of $42,000 and charges from prepaid expenses of $5,720.
2. Land was sold for cash at book value.

3. Cash dividends of $20,000 were paid.

4. Net income for 2015 was $42,000.

5. Equipment was purchased for $88,000 cash. In addition, equipment costing $22,000 with a book value of $10,000 was sold for $6,000 cash.

6. Bonds were converted at face value by issuing 40,000 shares of $1 par value common stock.

Instructions

Cash from operations $113,000

Prepare a statement of cash flows for the year ended December 31, 2015, using the indirect method.

Prepare a worksheet—indirect method.

(LO 6)

*P13-12A Condensed financial data of Oakley Company appear below.

OAKLEY COMPANY
Comparative Balance Sheets
December 31

Assets	2015	2014
Cash	$ 82,700	$ 47,250
Accounts receivable	90,800	57,000
Inventory	126,900	102,650
Investments	84,500	87,000
Equipment	255,000	205,000
Accumulated depreciation—equipment	(49,500)	(40,000)
	$590,400	$458,900

Liabilities and Stockholders' Equity	2015	2014
Accounts payable	$ 57,700	$ 48,280
Accrued expenses payable	12,100	18,830
Bonds payable	100,000	70,000
Common stock	250,000	200,000
Retained earnings	170,600	121,790
	$590,400	$458,900

OAKLEY COMPANY
Income Statement
For the Year Ended December 31, 2015

Sales revenue		$297,500
Gain on disposal of equipment		8,750
		306,250
Less:		
Cost of goods sold	$99,460	
Operating expenses (excluding depreciation expense)	14,670	
Depreciation expense	49,700	
Income tax expense	7,270	
Interest expense	2,940	174,040
Net income		$132,210

Additional information:

1. Equipment costing $97,000 was purchased for cash during the year.

2. Investments were sold at cost.

3. Equipment costing $47,000 was sold for $15,550, resulting in gain of $8,750.

4. A cash dividend of $83,400 was declared and paid during the year.

Instructions

Reconciling items total

$610,210

Prepare a worksheet for the statement of cash flows using the indirect method. Enter the reconciling items directly in the worksheet columns, using letters to cross-reference each entry.

PROBLEMS: SET B

P13-1B You are provided with the following transactions that took place during a recent fiscal year.

Distinguish among operating, investing, and financing activities.

(LO 2)

Transaction	Statement of Cash Flow Activity Affected	Cash Inflow, Outflow, or No Effect?
(a) Recorded depreciation expense on the plant assets.		
(b) Incurred a loss on disposal of plant assets.		
(c) Acquired a building by paying cash.		
(d) Made principal repayments on a mortgage.		
(e) Issued common stock.		
(f) Purchased shares of another company to be held as a long-term equity investment.		
(g) Paid cash dividends to common stockholders.		
(h) Sold inventory on credit. The company uses a perpetual inventory system.		
(i) Purchased inventory on credit.		
(j) Paid wages to employees.		

Instructions
Complete the table indicating whether each item (1) affects operating (O) activities, investing (I) activities, financing (F) activities, or is a noncash (NC) transaction reported in a separate schedule, and (2) represents a cash inflow or cash outflow or has no cash flow effect. Assume use of the indirect approach.

P13-2B The following selected account balances relate to the plant asset accounts of Diaz Inc. at year-end.

Determine cash flow effects of changes in plant asset accounts.

(LO 3)

	2015	2014
Accumulated depreciation—buildings	$337,500	$300,000
Accumulated depreciation—equipment	144,000	96,000
Buildings	750,000	750,000
Depreciation expense	101,500	85,500
Equipment	300,000	240,000
Land	100,000	70,000
Loss on disposal of equipment	8,000	0

Additional information:

1. Diaz purchased $95,000 of equipment and $30,000 of land for cash in 2015.
2. Diaz also sold equipment in 2015.
3. Depreciation expense in 2015 was $37,500 on building and $64,000 on equipment.

Instructions
(a) Determine the amounts of any cash inflows or outflows related to the plant asset accounts in 2015.
(b) Indicate where each of the cash inflows or outflows identified in (a) would be classified on the statement of cash flows.

(a) Cash proceeds $11,000

P13-3B The income statement of Eichorn Company is presented on the next page.

Additional information:

1. Accounts receivable decreased $320,000 during the year, and inventory increased $120,000.
2. Prepaid expenses increased $175,000 during the year.

Prepare the operating activities section—indirect method.

(LO 3)

3. Accounts payable to merchandise suppliers increased $50,000 during the year.

4. Accrued expenses payable increased $155,000 during the year.

EICHORN COMPANY
Income Statement
For the Year Ended December 31, 2015

Sales revenue		$5,400,000
Cost of goods sold		
Beginning inventory	$1,780,000	
Purchases	3,430,000	
Goods available for sale	5,210,000	
Ending inventory	1,900,000	
Total cost of goods sold		3,310,000
Gross profit		2,090,000
Operating expenses		
Depreciation expense	105,000	
Amortization expense	20,000	
Other expenses	945,000	1,070,000
Net income		$1,020,000

Instructions

Cash from operations
$1,375,000

Prepare the operating activities section of the statement of cash flows for the year ended December 31, 2015, for Eichorn Company, using the indirect method.

Prepare the operating activities section—direct method.

(LO 5)

Cash from operations
$1,375,000

***P13-4B** Data for Eichorn Company are presented in P13-3B.

Instructions

Prepare the operating activities section of the statement of cash flows using the direct method.

Prepare the operating activities section—indirect method.

(LO 3)

P13-5B The income statement of Darbyshire Inc. reported the following condensed information.

DARBYSHIRE INC.
Income Statement
For the Year Ended December 31, 2015

Service revenue	$545,000
Operating expenses	400,000
Income from operations	145,000
Income tax expense	36,000
Net income	$109,000

Darbyshire's balance sheet contained these comparative data at December 31.

	2015	2014
Accounts receivable	$50,000	$70,000
Accounts payable	30,000	51,000
Income taxes payable	10,000	4,000

Darbyshire has no depreciable assets. Accounts payable pertain to operating expenses.

Cash from operations $114,000

Prepare the operating activities section—direct method.

(LO 5)

Cash from operations
$114,000

Instructions

Prepare the operating activities section of the statement of cash flows using the indirect method.

***P13-6B** Data for Darbyshire Inc. are presented in P13-5B.

Instructions

Prepare the operating activities section of the statement of cash flows using the direct method.

P13-7B Presented below are the financial statements of Johnston Company.

Prepare a statement of cash flows–indirect method, and compute free cash flow.

(LO 3, 4)

JOHNSTON COMPANY
Comparative Balance Sheets
December 31

Assets		2015		2014
Cash		$ 24,000		$ 33,000
Accounts receivable		25,000		14,000
Inventory		41,000		25,000
Equipment	$ 70,000		$ 78,000	
Less: Accumulated depreciation—				
equipment	(27,000)	43,000	(24,000)	54,000
Total		$133,000		$126,000

Liabilities and Stockholders' Equity	2015	2014
Accounts payable	$ 31,000	$ 43,000
Income taxes payable	24,000	20,000
Bonds payable	20,000	10,000
Common stock	25,000	25,000
Retained earnings	33,000	28,000
Total	$133,000	$126,000

JOHNSTON COMPANY
Income Statement
For the Year Ended December 31, 2015

Sales revenue	$286,000
Cost of goods sold	204,000
Gross profit	82,000
Operating expenses	37,000
Income from operations	45,000
Interest expense	7,000
Income before income taxes	38,000
Income tax expense	10,000
Net income	$ 28,000

Additional data:

1. Dividends of $23,000 were declared and paid.
2. During the year equipment was sold for $10,000 cash. This equipment cost $15,000 originally and had a book value of $10,000 at the time of sale.
3. All depreciation expense, $8,000, is in the operating expenses.
4. All sales and purchases are on account.
5. Additional equipment was purchased for $7,000 cash.

Instructions
(a) Prepare a statement of cash flows using the indirect method.
(b) Compute free cash flow.

(a) Cash from operations
$1,000

***P13-8B** Data for Johnston Company are presented in P13-7B. Further analysis reveals the following.

Prepare a statement of cash flows—direct method, and compute free cash flow.

(LO 4, 5)

1. Accounts payable pertains to merchandise creditors.
2. All operating expenses except for depreciation are paid in cash.

Instructions
(a) Prepare a statement of cash flows using the direct method.
(b) Compute free cash flow.

(a) Cash from operations
$1,000

Prepare a statement of cash flows—indirect method.
(LO 3)

P13-9B Condensed financial data of Saffordville Company are shown below.

SAFFORDVILLE COMPANY
Comparative Balance Sheets
December 31

Assets	2015	2014
Cash	$102,700	$ 33,400
Accounts receivable	60,800	37,000
Inventory	126,900	102,650
Investments	79,500	107,000
Equipment	315,000	205,000
Accumulated depreciation—equipment	(44,500)	(40,000)
Total	$640,400	$445,050

Liabilities and Stockholders' Equity	2015	2014
Accounts payable	$ 57,700	$ 48,280
Accrued expenses payable	15,100	18,830
Bonds payable	145,000	70,000
Common stock	250,000	200,000
Retained earnings	172,600	107,940
Total	$640,400	$445,050

SAFFORDVILLE COMPANY
Income Statement
For the Year Ended December 31, 2015

Sales revenue		$297,500
Gain on disposal of plant assets		5,000
		302,500
Less:		
Cost of goods sold	$99,460	
Operating expenses, excluding depreciation expense	19,670	
Depreciation expense	30,500	
Income tax expense	37,270	
Interest expense	2,940	189,840
Net income		$112,660

Additional information:

1. New equipment costing $146,000 was purchased for cash during the year.
2. Investments were sold at cost.
3. Equipment costing $36,000 was sold for $15,000, resulting in a gain of $5,000.
4. A cash dividend of $48,000 was declared and paid during the year.

Instructions

Cash from operations $95,800

Prepare a statement of cash flows using the indirect method.

Prepare a statement of cash flows—direct method.
(LO 5)
Cash from operations $95,800

*P13-10B Data for Saffordville Company are presented in P13-9B. Further analysis reveals that accounts payable pertain to merchandise creditors.

Instructions

Prepare a statement of cash flows for Saffordville Company using the direct method.

Prepare a statement of cash flows—indirect method.
(LO 3)

P13-11B Presented on the next page are the comparative balance sheets for Pester Company at December 31.

PESTER COMPANY
Comparative Balance Sheets
December 31

Assets	2015	2014
Cash	$ 41,000	$ 57,000
Accounts receivable	77,000	64,000
Inventory	172,000	140,000
Prepaid expenses	12,140	16,540
Land	110,000	150,000
Buildings	250,000	250,000
Accumulated depreciation—buildings	(70,000)	(50,000)
Equipment	215,000	175,000
Accumulated depreciation—equipment	(70,000)	(42,000)
Total	$737,140	$760,540
Liabilities and Stockholders' Equity		
Accounts payable	$ 58,000	$ 45,000
Bonds payable	235,000	265,000
Common stock, $1 par	280,000	250,000
Retained earnings	164,140	200,540
Total	$737,140	$760,540

Additional information:

1. Operating expenses include depreciation expense $55,000 and charges from prepaid expenses of $4,400.
2. Land was sold for cash at cost.
3. Cash dividends of $84,290 were paid.
4. Net income for 2015 was $47,890.
5. Equipment was purchased for $80,000 cash. In addition, equipment costing $40,000 with a book value of $33,000 was sold for $37,000 cash.
6. Bonds were converted at face value by issuing 30,000 shares of $1 par value common stock.

Instructions
Prepare a statement of cash flows for 2015 using the indirect method.

Cash from operations $71,290

PROBLEMS: SET C

Visit the book's companion website, at **www.wiley.com/college/weygandt**, and choose the Student Companion site to access Problem Set C.

CONTINUING COOKIE CHRONICLE

(*Note:* This is a continuation of the Cookie Chronicle from Chapters 1 through 12.)

CCC13 Natalie has prepared the balance sheet and income statement of Cookie & Coffee Creations Inc. and would like you to prepare the statement of cash flows.

Go to the book's companion website, **www.wiley.com/college/weygandt**, *to see the completion of this problem.*

Broadening Your **PERSPECTIVE**

Financial Reporting and Analysis

Financial Reporting Problem: Apple Inc.

BYP13-1 The financial statements of Apple Inc. are presented in Appendix A. Instructions for accessing and using the company's complete annual report, including the notes to the financial statements, are also provided in Appendix A.

Instructions
Answer the following questions.

(a) What was the amount of net cash provided by operating activities for the year ended September 24, 2011? For the year ended September 25, 2010?

(b) What was the amount of increase or decrease in cash and cash equivalents for the year ended September 24, 2011? For the year ended September 25, 2010?

(c) Which method of computing net cash provided by operating activities does Apple use?

(d) From your analysis of the 2011 statement of cash flows, did the change in accounts and notes receivable require or provide cash? Did the change in inventories require or provide cash? Did the change in accounts payable and other current liabilities require or provide cash?

(e) What was the net outflow or inflow of cash from investing activities for the year ended September 24, 2011?

(f) What was the amount of income taxes paid in the year ended September 24, 2011?

Comparative Analysis Problem:
PepsiCo, Inc. vs. The Coca-Cola Company

BYP13-2 PepsiCo's financial statements are presented in Appendix B. Financial statements of The Coca-Cola Company are presented in Appendix C. Instructions for accessing and using the complete annual reports of PepsiCo and Coca-Cola, including the notes to the financial statements, are also provided in Appendices B and C, respectively.

Instructions
(a) Based on the information contained in these financial statements, compute free cash flow for each company.

(b) What conclusions concerning the management of cash can be drawn from these data?

Comparative Analysis Problem:
Amazon.com, Inc. vs. Wal-Mart Stores, Inc.

BYP13-3 Amazon.com, Inc.'s financial statements are presented in Appendix D. Financial statements of Wal-Mart Stores, Inc. are presented in Appendix E. Instructions for accessing and using the complete annual reports of Amazon and Wal-Mart, including the notes to the financial statements, are also provided in Appendices D and E, respectively.

Instructions
(a) Based on the information contained in these financial statements, compute free cash flow for each company.

(b) What conclusions concerning the management of cash can be drawn from these data?

Real-World Focus

BYP13-4 Purpose: Learn about the SEC.

Address: **www.sec.gov/index.html**, or go to **www.wiley.com/college/weygandt**

From the SEC homepage, choose **About the SEC**.

Instructions

Answer the following questions.

(a) How many enforcement actions does the SEC take each year against securities law violators? What are typical infractions?

(b) After the Depression, Congress passed the Securities Acts of 1933 and 1934 to improve investor confidence in the markets. What two "common sense" notions are these laws based on?

(c) Who was the President of the United States at the time of the creation of the SEC? Who was the first SEC Chairperson?

BYP13-5 Purpose: Use the Internet to view SEC filings.

Address: **biz.yahoo.com/i**, or go to **www.wiley.com/college/weygandt**

Steps:
1. Type in a company name.
2. Choose **Profile**.
3. Choose **SEC Filings**. (This will take you to Yahoo-Edgar Online.)

Instructions

Answer the following questions.

(a) What company did you select?

(b) Which filing is the most recent? What is the date?

(c) What other recent SEC filings are available for your viewing?

Critical Thinking

Decision-Making Across the Organization

BYP13-6 Tom Epps and Mary Jones are examining the following statement of cash flows for Guthrie Company for the year ended January 31, 2015.

GUTHRIE COMPANY
Statement of Cash Flows
For the Year Ended January 31, 2015

Sources of cash	
From sales of merchandise	$380,000
From sale of capital stock	420,000
From sale of investment (purchased below)	80,000
From depreciation	55,000
From issuance of note for truck	20,000
From interest on investments	6,000
Total sources of cash	961,000
Uses of cash	
For purchase of fixtures and equipment	330,000
For merchandise purchased for resale	258,000
For operating expenses (including depreciation)	160,000
For purchase of investment	75,000
For purchase of truck by issuance of note	20,000
For purchase of treasury stock	10,000
For interest on note payable	3,000
Total uses of cash	856,000
Net increase in cash	$105,000

Tom claims that Guthrie's statement of cash flows is an excellent portrayal of a superb first year with cash increasing $105,000. Mary replies that it was not a superb first year. Rather, she says, the year was an operating failure, that the statement is presented incorrectly, and that $105,000 is not the actual increase in cash. The cash balance at the beginning of the year was $140,000.

Instructions

With the class divided into groups, answer the following.

(a) Using the data provided, prepare a statement of cash flows in proper form using the indirect method. The only noncash items in the income statement are depreciation and the gain from the sale of the investment.

(b) With whom do you agree, Tom or Mary? Explain your position.

Communication Activity

BYP13-7 Will Hardin, the owner-president of Computer Services Company, is unfamiliar with the statement of cash flows that you, as his accountant, prepared. He asks for further explanation.

Instructions

Write him a brief memo explaining the form and content of the statement of cash flows as shown in Illustration 13-13 (pages 662–663).

Ethics Case

BYP13-8 Wesley Corp. is a medium-sized wholesaler of automotive parts. It has 10 stockholders who have been paid a total of $1 million in cash dividends for 8 consecutive years. The board's policy requires that, for this dividend to be declared, net cash provided by operating activities as reported in Wesley's current year's statement of cash flows must exceed $1 million. President and CEO Samuel Gunkle's job is secure so long as he produces annual operating cash flows to support the usual dividend.

At the end of the current year, controller Gerald Rondelli presents president Samuel Gunkle with some disappointing news: The net cash provided by operating activities is calculated by the indirect method to be only $970,000. The president says to Gerald, "We must get that amount above $1 million. Isn't there some way to increase operating cash flow by another $30,000?" Gerald answers, "These figures were prepared by my assistant. I'll go back to my office and see what I can do." The president replies, "I know you won't let me down, Gerald."

Upon close scrutiny of the statement of cash flows, Gerald concludes that he can get the operating cash flows above $1 million by reclassifying a $60,000, 2-year note payable listed in the financing activities section as "Proceeds from bank loan—$60,000." He will report the note instead as "Increase in payables—$60,000" and treat it as an adjustment of net income in the operating activities section. He returns to the president, saying, "You can tell the board to declare their usual dividend. Our net cash provided by operating activities is $1,030,000." "Good man, Gerald! I knew I could count on you," exults the president.

Instructions

(a) Who are the stakeholders in this situation?

(b) Was there anything unethical about the president's actions? Was there anything unethical about the controller's actions?

(c) Are the board members or anyone else likely to discover the misclassification?

All About You

BYP13-9 In this chapter, you learned that companies prepare a statement of cash flows in order to keep track of their sources and uses of cash and to help them plan for their future cash needs. Planning for your own short- and long-term cash needs is every bit as important as it is for a company.

Instructions

Read the article ("Financial Uh-Oh? No Problem") provided at **www.fool.com/personal-finance/saving/index.aspx**, and answer the following questions.

(a) Describe the three factors that determine how much money you should set aside for short-term needs.

(b) How many months of living expenses does the article suggest to set aside?

(c) Estimate how much you should set aside based upon your current situation. Are you closer to Cliff's scenario or to Prudence's?

FASB Codification Activity

BYP13-10 If your school has a subscription to the FASB Codification, go to **http://aaahq.org/ascLogin.cfm** to log in and prepare responses to the following. Use the Master Glossary to determine the proper definitions.

(a) What are cash equivalents?
(b) What are financing activities?
(c) What are investing activities?
(d) What are operating activities?
(e) What is the primary objective for the statement of cash flow? Is working capital the basis for meeting this objective?
(f) Do companies need to disclose information about investing and financing activities that do not affect cash receipts or cash payments? If so, how should such information be disclosed?

Answers to Chapter Questions

Answers to Insight and Accounting Across the Organization Questions

p. 652 Net *What*? **Q:** In general, why do differences exist between net income and net cash provided by operating activities? **A:** The differences are explained by differences in the timing of the reporting of revenues and expenses under accrual accounting versus cash accounting. Under accrual accounting, companies report revenues when their performance obligation is satisfied, even if cash hasn't been received, and they report expenses when incurred, even if cash hasn't been paid.

p. 665 Burning Through Our Cash **Q:** What impact did Kodak's sale of plant assets have on its net cash provided by investing activities? **A:** Kodak sold its plant assets to increase its net cash provided by investing activities. This net cash increase allowed Kodak to then invest in new product ideas.

Answers to Self-Test Questions

1. c **2.** a **3.** b **4.** a **5.** c **6.** d **7.** b **8.** c **9.** d ($132,000 + $10,000 + $6,000 − $12,000) **10.** b **11.** b ($200,000 + $40,000 − $10,000 + $20,000 − $30,000) **12.** a ($100,000 + $50,000 − $30,000) **13.** b ($100,000 + $60,000 − $30,000) **14.** a **15.** d *16. c [$129,000 + ($44,000 − $42,000)] *17. d *18. b *19. b

A Look at IFRS

As in GAAP, the statement of cash flows is a required statement for IFRS. In addition, the content and presentation of an IFRS statement of cash flows is similar to the one used for GAAP. However, the disclosure requirements related to the statement of cash flows are more extensive under GAAP. *IAS 7* ("Cash Flow Statements") provides the overall IFRS requirements for cash flow information.

> **LEARNING OBJECTIVE 8**
>
> **Discuss the accounting procedures for the statement of cash flows under GAAP and IFRS.**

Key Points

- Companies preparing financial statements under IFRS must prepare a statement of cash flows as an integral part of the financial statements.

- Both IFRS and GAAP require that the statement of cash flows should have three major sections—operating, investing, and financing activities—along with changes in cash and cash equivalents.

- Similar to GAAP, the statement of cash flows can be prepared using either the indirect or direct method under IFRS. In both U.S. and international settings, companies choose for the most part to use the indirect method for reporting net cash flows from operating activities.

- The definition of cash equivalents used in IFRS is similar to that used in GAAP. A major difference is that in certain situations, bank overdrafts are considered part of cash and cash equivalents under IFRS (which is not the case in GAAP). Under GAAP, bank overdrafts are classified as financing activities in the statement of cash flows and are reported as liabilities on the balance sheet.

- IFRS requires that noncash investing and financing activities be excluded from the statement of cash flows. Instead, these noncash activities should be reported elsewhere. This requirement is interpreted to mean that noncash investing and financing activities should be disclosed in the notes to the financial statements instead of in the financial statements. Under GAAP, companies may present this information on the face of the statement of cash flows.

- One area where there can be substantial differences between IFRS and GAAP relates to the classification of interest, dividends, and taxes. The following table indicates the differences between the two approaches.

Item	IFRS	GAAP
Interest paid	Operating or financing	Operating
Interest received	Operating or investing	Operating
Dividends paid	Operating or financing	Financing
Dividends received	Operating or investing	Operating
Taxes paid	Operating—unless specific identification with financing or investing activity	Operating

- Under IFRS, some companies present the operating section in a single line item, with a full reconciliation provided in the notes to the financial statements. This presentation is not seen under GAAP.

- Similar to GAAP, under IFRS companies must disclose the amount of taxes and interest paid. Under GAAP, companies disclose this in the notes to the financial statements. Under IFRS, some companies disclose this information in the notes, but others provide individual line items on the face of the statement. In order to provide this information on the face of the statement, companies first add back the amount of interest expense and tax expense (similar to adding back depreciation expense) and then further down the statement they subtract the cash amount paid for interest and taxes. This treatment can be seen in the statement of cash flows provided for Zetar in Appendix F.

Looking to the Future

Presently, the FASB and the IASB are involved in a joint project on the presentation and organization of information in the financial statements. One interesting approach, revealed in a published proposal from that project, is that in the future the income statement and balance sheet would adopt headings similar to those of the statement of cash flows. That is, the income statement and balance sheet would be broken into operating, investing, and financing sections.

With respect to the statement of cash flows specifically, the notion of **cash equivalents** will probably not be retained. That is, cash equivalents will not be combined with cash but instead will be reported as a form of highly liquid, low-risk investment. The definition of cash in the existing literature would be retained, and the statement of cash flows would present information on changes in cash only. In addition, the FASB favors presentation of operating cash flows using the direct method only. However, the majority of IASB members express a preference for not requiring use of the direct method of reporting operating cash flows. The two Boards will have to resolve their differences in this area in order to issue a converged standard for the statement of cash flows.

IFRS Practice

IFRS Self-Test Questions

1. Under IFRS, interest paid can be reported as:
   (a) only a financing activity.
   (b) a financing activity or an investing activity.
   (c) a financing activity or an operating activity.
   (d) only an operating activity.

2. IFRS requires that noncash items:
   (a) be reported in the section to which they relate, that is, a noncash investing activity would be reported in the investing section.
   (b) be disclosed in the notes to the financial statements.

(c) do not need to be reported.

(d) be treated in a fashion similar to cash equivalents.

3. In the future, it appears likely that:

(a) the income statement and balance sheet will have headings of operating, investing, and financing, much like the statement of cash flows.

(b) cash and cash equivalents will be combined in a single line item.

(c) the IASB will not allow companies to use the direct approach to the statement of cash flows.

(d) None of the above.

4. Under IFRS:

(a) taxes are always treated as an operating activity.

(b) the income statement uses the headings operating, investing, and financing.

(c) dividends received can be either an operating or investing activity.

(d) dividends paid can be either an operating or investing activity.

5. Which of the following is **correct**?

(a) Under IFRS, the statement of cash flows is optional.

(b) IFRS requires use of the direct approach in preparing the statement of cash flows.

(c) The majority of companies following GAAP and the majority following IFRS employ the indirect approach to the statement of cash flows.

(d) Cash and cash equivalents are reported as separate line items under IFRS.

IFRS Exercises

IFRS13-1 Discuss the differences that exist in the treatment of bank overdrafts under GAAP and IFRS.

IFRS13-2 Describe the treatment of each of the following items under IFRS versus GAAP.

(a) Interest paid.

(b) Interest received.

(c) Dividends paid.

(d) Dividends received.

IFRS13-3 Explain how the treatment of cash equivalents will probably change in the future.

International Financial Reporting Problem: Zetar plc

IFRS13-4 The financial statements of Zetar plc are presented in Appendix F. Instructions for accessing and using the company's complete annual report, including the notes to its financial statements, are also provided in Appendix F.

Instructions

Use the company's annual report to answer the following questions.

(a) In which section (operating, investing, or financing) does Zetar report interest paid (finance costs)?

(b) Explain why the amount that Zetar reports for cash and cash equivalents in its statement of cash flows is negative.

(c) If Zetar reported under GAAP rather than IFRS, how would its treatment of bank overdrafts differ?

(d) Zetar's statement of cash flows reports negative "net movement in working capital" in 2011 of £(6,040) (in thousands). According to the statement of cash flows, what were the components of this "net movement"?

Answers to IFRS Self-Test Questions

1. c   2. b   3. a   4. c   5. c

 The Navigator

✔ Remember to go back to The Navigator box on the chapter opening page and check off your completed work.

14 | Financial Statement Analysis

It Pays to Be Patient

A recent issue of *Forbes* magazine listed Warren Buffett as the richest person in the world. His estimated wealth was $62 billion, give or take a few million. How much is $62 billion? If you invested $62 billion in an investment earning just 4%, you could spend $6.8 million per day—every day—forever.

So, how does Buffett spend his money? Basically, he doesn't! He still lives in the same house that he purchased in Omaha, Nebraska, in 1958 for $31,500. He still drives his own car (a Cadillac DTS). And, in case you were thinking that his kids are riding the road to Easy Street, think again. Buffett has committed to donate virtually all of his money to charity before he dies.

How did Buffett amass this wealth? Through careful investing. Buffett epitomizes a "value investor." He applies the basic techniques he learned in the 1950s from the great value investor Benjamin Graham. He looks for companies that have good long-term potential but are currently underpriced. He invests in companies that have low exposure to debt and that reinvest their earnings for future growth. He does not get caught up in fads or the latest trends.

For example, Buffett sat out on the dot-com mania in the 1990s. When other investors put lots of money into fledgling high-tech firms, Buffett didn't bite because he did not find dot-com companies that met his criteria. He didn't get to enjoy the stock price boom on the way up, but on the other hand, he didn't have to ride the price back down to Earth. When the dot-com bubble burst, everyone else was suffering from investment shock. Buffett swooped in and scooped up deals on companies that he had been following for years.

In 2012, the stock market had again reached near record highs. Buffett's returns had been significantly lagging the market. Only 26% of his investments at that time were in stock, and he was sitting on $38 billion in cash. One commentator noted that "if the past is any guide, just when Buffett seems to look most like a loser, the party is about to end."

If you think you want to follow Buffett's example and transform your humble nest egg into a mountain of cash, be warned. His techniques have been widely circulated and emulated, but never practiced with the same degree of success. You should probably start by honing your financial analysis skills. A good way for you to begin your

✔ The Navigator

- ■ Scan Learning Objectives
- ■ Read Feature Story
- ■ Read Preview
- ■ Read text and answer **DO IT!** p. 718
  - ■ p. 731   ■ p. 736   ■ p. 738
- ■ Work Comprehensive **DO IT!** p. 739
- ■ Review Summary of Learning Objectives
- ■ Answer Self-Test Questions
- ■ Complete Assignments
- ■ Go to *WileyPLUS* for practice and tutorials
- Read **A Look at IFRS** p. 761

Learning Objectives ✔ The Navigator

After studying this chapter, you should be able to:

[1] Discuss the need for comparative analysis.

[2] Identify the tools of financial statement analysis.

[3] Explain and apply horizontal analysis.

[4] Describe and apply vertical analysis.

[5] Identify and compute ratios used in analyzing a firm's liquidity, profitability, and solvency.

[6] Understand the concept of earning power, and how irregular items are presented.

[7] Understand the concept of quality of earnings.

career as a successful investor is to master the fundamentals of financial analysis discussed in this chapter.

Source: Jason Zweig, "Buffett Is Out of Step," *Wall Street Journal* (May 7, 2012).

Preview of Chapter 14

 ✔ The Navigator

We can all learn an important lesson from Warren Buffett. Study companies carefully if you wish to invest. Do not get caught up in fads but instead find companies that are financially healthy. Using some of the basic decision tools presented in this textbook, you can perform a rudimentary analysis on any U.S. company and draw basic conclusions about its financial health. Although it would not be wise for you to bet your life savings on a company's stock relying solely on your current level of knowledge, we strongly encourage you to practice your new skills wherever possible. Only with practice will you improve your ability to interpret financial numbers.

Before unleashing you on the world of high finance, we will present a few more important concepts and techniques, as well as provide you with one more comprehensive review of corporate financial statements. We use all of the decision tools presented in this text to analyze a single company—Macy's, Inc.—one of the country's oldest and largest retail store chains.

The content and organization of Chapter 14 are as follows.

FINANCIAL STATEMENT ANALYSIS

Basics of Financial Statement Analysis	Horizontal and Vertical Analysis	Ratio Analysis	Earning Power and Irregular Items	Quality of Earnings
• Need for comparative analysis • Tools of analysis	• Balance sheet • Income statement • Retained earnings statement	• Liquidity • Profitability • Solvency • Summary	• Discontinued operations • Extraordinary items • Changes in accounting principle • Comprehensive income	• Alternative accounting methods • Pro forma income • Improper recognition

Basics of Financial Statement Analysis

Analyzing financial statements involves evaluating three characteristics: a company's liquidity, profitability, and solvency. A **short-term creditor**, such as a bank, is primarily interested in liquidity—the ability of the borrower to pay obligations when they come due. The liquidity of the borrower is extremely important in evaluating the safety of a loan. A **long-term creditor**, such as a bondholder, looks to profitability and solvency measures that indicate the company's ability to survive over a long period of time. Long-term creditors consider such measures as the amount of debt in the company's capital structure and its ability to meet interest payments. Similarly, **stockholders** look at the profitability and solvency of the company. They want to assess the likelihood of dividends and the growth potential of the stock.

Need for Comparative Analysis

Every item reported in a financial statement has significance. When Macy's, Inc. reports cash and cash equivalents of $3 billion on its balance sheet, we know the company had that amount of cash on the balance sheet date. But, we do not know whether the amount represents an increase over prior years, or whether it is adequate in relation to the company's need for cash. To obtain such information, we need to compare the amount of cash with other financial statement data.

Comparisons can be made on a number of different bases. Three are illustrated in this chapter.

Intracompany

XYZ Co.

2014 ↔ 2015

1. **Intracompany basis.** Comparisons within a company are often useful to detect changes in financial relationships and significant trends. For example, a comparison of Macy's current year's cash amount with the prior year's cash amount shows either an increase or a decrease. Likewise, a comparison of Macy's year-end cash amount with the amount of its total assets at year-end shows the proportion of total assets in the form of cash.

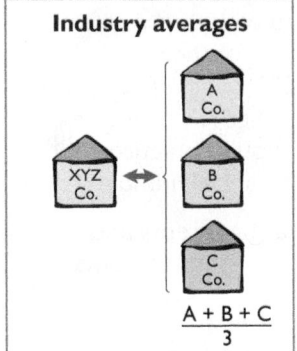

Industry averages

XYZ Co. ↔ A Co. / B Co. / C Co.

$\frac{A + B + C}{3}$

2. **Industry averages.** Comparisons with industry averages provide information about a company's relative position within the industry. For example, financial statement readers can compare Macy's financial data with the averages for its industry compiled by financial rating organizations such as Dun & Bradstreet, Moody's, and Standard & Poor's, or with information provided on the Internet by organizations such as Yahoo! on its financial site.

Intercompany

XYZ Co. ↔ A Co.

3. **Intercompany basis.** Comparisons with other companies provide insight into a company's competitive position. For example, investors can compare Macy's total sales for the year with the total sales of its competitors in retail, such as J.C. Penney.

Tools of Analysis

We use various tools to evaluate the significance of financial statement data. Three commonly used tools are as follows:

- **Horizontal analysis** evaluates a series of financial statement data over a period of time.
- **Vertical analysis** evaluates financial statement data by expressing each item in a financial statement as a percentage of a base amount.
- **Ratio analysis** expresses the relationship among selected items of financial statement data.

Horizontal analysis is used primarily in intracompany comparisons. Two features in published financial statements and annual report information facilitate this type of comparison. First, each of the basic financial statements presents comparative financial data for a minimum of two years. Second, a summary of selected financial data is presented for a series of five to 10 years or more. Vertical analysis is used in both intra- and intercompany comparisons. Ratio analysis is used in all three types of comparisons. In the following sections, we explain and illustrate each of the three types of analysis.

Horizontal Analysis

Horizontal analysis, also called **trend analysis**, is a technique for evaluating a series of financial statement data over a period of time. Its purpose is to determine the increase or decrease that has taken place. This change may be expressed as either an amount or a percentage. For example, Illustration 14-1 shows recent net sales figures of Macy's, Inc.

LEARNING OBJECTIVE 3

Explain and apply horizontal analysis.

Real World	MACY'S, INC. Net Sales (in millions)		
	2011	**2010**	**2009**
	$26,405	$25,003	$23,489

Illustration 14-1
Macy's, Inc.'s net sales

If we assume that 2009 is the base year, we can measure all percentage increases or decreases from this base period amount as follows.

$$\text{Change Since Base Period} = \frac{\text{Current Year Amount} - \text{Base Year Amount}}{\text{Base Year Amount}}$$

Illustration 14-2
Formula for horizontal analysis of changes since base period

For example, we can determine that net sales for Macy's increased from 2009 to 2010 approximately 6.4% [($25,003 − $23,489) ÷ $23,489]. Similarly, we can determine that net sales increased from 2009 to 2011 approximately 12.4% [($26,405 − $23,489) ÷ $23,489].

Alternatively, we can express current year sales as a percentage of the base period. We do this by dividing the current year amount by the base year amount, as shown below.

$$\text{Current Results in Relation to Base Period} = \frac{\text{Current Year Amount}}{\text{Base Year Amount}}$$

Illustration 14-3
Formula for horizontal analysis of current year in relation to base year

Illustration 14-4 presents this analysis for Macy's for a three-year period using 2009 as the base period.

Real World	MACY'S, INC. Net Sales (in millions) in relation to base period 2009		
	2011	**2010**	**2009**
	$26,405	$25,003	$23,489
	112.4%	106.4%	100%

Illustration 14-4
Horizontal analysis of Macy's, Inc.'s net sales in relation to base period

Balance Sheet

To further illustrate horizontal analysis, we will use the financial statements of Quality Department Store Inc., a fictional retailer. Illustration 14-5 presents a horizontal analysis of its two-year condensed balance sheets, showing dollar and percentage changes.

Illustration 14-5
Horizontal analysis of balance sheets

QUALITY DEPARTMENT STORE INC. Condensed Balance Sheets December 31				
			Increase or (Decrease) during 2011	
	2011	2010	Amount	Percent
Assets				
Current assets	$1,020,000	$ 945,000	$ 75,000	7.9%
Plant assets (net)	800,000	632,500	167,500	26.5%
Intangible assets	15,000	17,500	(2,500)	(14.3%)
Total assets	$1,835,000	$1,595,000	$240,000	15.0%
Liabilities				
Current liabilities	$ 344,500	$ 303,000	$ 41,500	13.7%
Long-term liabilities	487,500	497,000	(9,500)	(1.9%)
Total liabilities	832,000	800,000	32,000	4.0%
Stockholders' Equity				
Common stock, $1 par	275,400	270,000	5,400	2.0%
Retained earnings	727,600	525,000	202,600	38.6%
Total stockholders' equity	1,003,000	795,000	208,000	26.2%
Total liabilities and stockholders' equity	$1,835,000	$1,595,000	$240,000	15.0%

The comparative balance sheets in Illustration 14-5 show that a number of significant changes have occurred in Quality Department Store's financial structure from 2010 to 2011:

- In the assets section, plant assets (net) increased $167,500, or 26.5%.
- In the liabilities section, current liabilities increased $41,500, or 13.7%.
- In the stockholders' equity section, retained earnings increased $202,600, or 38.6%.

These changes suggest that the company expanded its asset base during 2011 and **financed this expansion primarily by retaining income** rather than assuming additional long-term debt.

Income Statement

Illustration 14-6 presents a horizontal analysis of the two-year condensed income statements of Quality Department Store Inc. for the years 2011 and 2010. Horizontal analysis of the income statements shows the following changes:

- Net sales increased $260,000, or 14.2% ($260,000 ÷ $1,837,000).
- Cost of goods sold increased $141,000, or 12.4% ($141,000 ÷ $1,140,000).
- Total operating expenses increased $37,000, or 11.6% ($37,000 ÷ $320,000).

Overall, gross profit and net income were up substantially. Gross profit increased 17.1%, and net income, 26.5%. Quality's profit trend appears favorable.

QUALITY DEPARTMENT STORE INC.
Condensed Income Statements
For the Years Ended December 31

	2011	2010	Increase or (Decrease) during 2011 Amount	Percent
Sales revenue	$2,195,000	$1,960,000	$235,000	12.0%
Sales returns and allowances	98,000	123,000	(25,000)	(20.3%)
Net sales	2,097,000	1,837,000	260,000	14.2%
Cost of goods sold	1,281,000	1,140,000	141,000	12.4%
Gross profit	816,000	697,000	119,000	17.1%
Selling expenses	253,000	211,500	41,500	19.6%
Administrative expenses	104,000	108,500	(4,500)	(4.1%)
Total operating expenses	357,000	320,000	37,000	11.6%
Income from operations	459,000	377,000	82,000	21.8%
Other revenues and gains Interest and dividends	9,000	11,000	(2,000)	(18.2%)
Other expenses and losses Interest expense	36,000	40,500	(4,500)	(11.1%)
Income before income taxes	432,000	347,500	84,500	24.3%
Income tax expense	168,200	139,000	29,200	21.0%
Net income	$ 263,800	$ 208,500	$ 55,300	26.5%

Illustration 14-6
Horizontal analysis of income statements

Helpful Hint
Note that though the amount column is additive (the total is $55,300), the percentage column is not additive (26.5% is not the column total). A separate percentage has been calculated for each item.

Retained Earnings Statement

Illustration 14-7 presents a horizontal analysis of Quality Department Store's comparative retained earnings statements. Analyzed horizontally, net income increased $55,300, or 26.5%, whereas dividends on the common stock increased only $1,200, or 2%. We saw in the horizontal analysis of the balance sheet that ending retained earnings increased 38.6%. As indicated earlier, the company retained a significant portion of net income to finance additional plant facilities.

QUALITY DEPARTMENT STORE INC.
Retained Earnings Statements
For the Years Ended December 31

	2011	2010	Increase or (Decrease) during 2011 Amount	Percent
Retained earnings, Jan. 1	$525,000	$376,500	$148,500	39.4%
Add: Net income	263,800	208,500	55,300	26.5%
	788,800	585,000	203,800	
Deduct: Dividends	61,200	60,000	1,200	2.0%
Retained earnings, Dec. 31	$727,600	$525,000	$202,600	38.6%

Illustration 14-7
Horizontal analysis of retained earnings statements

Horizontal analysis of changes from period to period is relatively straightforward and is quite useful. But, complications can occur in making the computations. If an item has no value in a base year or preceding year but does have a value in the next year, we cannot compute a percentage change. Similarly, if a negative amount appears in the base or preceding period and a positive amount exists the following year (or vice versa), no percentage change can be computed.

> **> DO IT!**

Horizontal Analysis

Action Plan

✔ Find the percentage change by dividing the amount of the increase by the 2014 amount (base year).

Summary financial information for Rosepatch Company is as follows.

	December 31, 2015	December 31, 2014
Current assets	$234,000	$180,000
Plant assets (net)	756,000	420,000
Total assets	$990,000	$600,000

Compute the amount and percentage changes in 2015 using horizontal analysis, assuming 2014 is the base year.

Solution

	Increase in 2015	
	Amount	**Percent**
Current assets	$ 54,000	30% [($234,000 − $180,000) ÷ $180,000]
Plant assets (net)	336,000	80% [($756,000 − $420,000) ÷ $420,000]
Total assets	$390,000	65% [($990,000 − $600,000) ÷ $600,000]

Related exercise material: BE14-2, BE14-3, BE14-5, BE14-6, BE14-7, E14-1, E14-3, E14-4, **and** DO IT! 14-1.

✔ **The Navigator**

Vertical Analysis

LEARNING OBJECTIVE   4

Describe and apply vertical analysis.

Vertical analysis, also called **common-size analysis**, is a technique that expresses each financial statement item as a percentage of a base amount. On a balance sheet, we might say that current assets are 22% of total assets—total assets being the base amount. Or on an income statement, we might say that selling expenses are 16% of net sales—net sales being the base amount.

Balance Sheet

Illustration 14-8 presents the vertical analysis of Quality Department Store Inc.'s comparative balance sheets. The base for the asset items is **total assets**. The base for the liability and stockholders' equity items is **total liabilities and stockholders' equity**.

Vertical analysis shows the relative size of each category in the balance sheet. It also can show the **percentage change** in the individual asset, liability, and stockholders' equity items. For example, we can see that current assets decreased from 59.2% of total assets in 2010 to 55.6% in 2011 (even though the absolute dollar amount increased $75,000 in that time). Plant assets (net) have increased from 39.7% to 43.6% of total assets. Retained earnings have increased from 32.9% to 39.7% of total liabilities and stockholders' equity. These results reinforce the earlier observations that **Quality Department Store is choosing to finance its growth through retention of earnings rather than through issuing additional debt.**

Illustration 14-8
Vertical analysis of balance sheets

QUALITY DEPARTMENT STORE INC.
Condensed Balance Sheets
December 31

	2011 Amount	2011 Percent	2010 Amount	2010 Percent
Assets				
Current assets	$1,020,000	55.6%	$ 945,000	59.2%
Plant assets (net)	800,000	43.6%	632,500	39.7%
Intangible assets	15,000	0.8%	17,500	1.1%
Total assets	$1,835,000	100.0%	$1,595,000	100.0%
Liabilities				
Current liabilities	$ 344,500	18.8%	$ 303,000	19.0%
Long-term liabilities	487,500	26.5%	497,000	31.2%
Total liabilities	832,000	45.3%	800,000	50.2%
Stockholders' Equity				
Common stock, $1 par	275,400	15.0%	270,000	16.9%
Retained earnings	727,600	39.7%	525,000	32.9%
Total stockholders' equity	1,003,000	54.7%	795,000	49.8%
Total liabilities and stockholders' equity	$1,835,000	100.0%	$1,595,000	100.0%

Helpful Hint
The formula for calculating these balance sheet percentages is:
$$\frac{\text{Each item on B/S}}{\text{Total assets}} = \%$$

Income Statement

Illustration 14-9 shows vertical analysis of Quality Department Store's income statements. Cost of goods sold as a percentage of net sales declined 1% (62.1% vs. 61.1%), and total operating expenses declined 0.4% (17.4% vs. 17.0%). As a result,

Illustration 14-9
Vertical analysis of income statements

QUALITY DEPARTMENT STORE INC.
Condensed Income Statements
For the Years Ended December 31

	2011 Amount	2011 Percent	2010 Amount	2010 Percent
Sales revenue	$2,195,000	104.7%	$1,960,000	106.7%
Sales returns and allowances	98,000	4.7%	123,000	6.7%
Net sales	2,097,000	100.0%	1,837,000	100.0%
Cost of goods sold	1,281,000	61.1%	1,140,000	62.1%
Gross profit	816,000	38.9%	697,000	37.9%
Selling expenses	253,000	12.0%	211,500	11.5%
Administrative expenses	104,000	5.0%	108,500	5.9%
Total operating expenses	357,000	17.0%	320,000	17.4%
Income from operations	459,000	21.9%	377,000	20.5%
Other revenues and gains				
Interest and dividends	9,000	0.4%	11,000	0.6%
Other expenses and losses				
Interest expense	36,000	1.7%	40,500	2.2%
Income before income taxes	432,000	20.6%	347,500	18.9%
Income tax expense	168,200	8.0%	139,000	7.5%
Net income	$ 263,800	12.6%	$ 208,500	11.4%

Helpful Hint
The formula for calculating these income statement percentages is:
$$\frac{\text{Each item on I/S}}{\text{Net sales}} = \%$$

it is not surprising to see net income as a percentage of net sales increase from 11.4% to 12.6%. Quality Department Store appears to be a profitable business that is becoming even more successful.

An associated benefit of vertical analysis is that it enables you to compare companies of different sizes. For example, Quality Department Store's main competitor is a Macy's store in a nearby town. Using vertical analysis, we can compare the condensed income statements of Quality Department Store Inc. (a small retail company) with Macy's, Inc.[1] (a giant international retailer), as shown in Illustration 14-10.

Illustration 14-10
Intercompany income statement comparison

Condensed Income Statements (in thousands)				
	Quality Department Store Inc.		**Macy's, Inc.**	
	Dollars	**Percent**	**Dollars**	**Percent**
Net sales	$2,097	100.0%	$26,405,000	100.0%
Cost of goods sold	1,281	61.1%	15,738,000	59.6%
Gross profit	816	38.9%	10,667,000	40.4%
Selling and administrative expenses	357	17.0%	8,256,000	31.3%
Income from operations	459	21.9%	2,411,000	9.1%
Other expenses and revenues (including income taxes)	195	9.3%	1,155,000	4.4%
Net income	$ 264	12.6%	$ 1,256,000	4.7%

Macy's net sales are 12,592 times greater than the net sales of relatively tiny Quality Department Store. But vertical analysis eliminates this difference in size. The percentages show that Quality's and Macy's gross profit rates were comparable at 38.9% and 40.4%, respectively. However, the percentages related to income from operations were significantly different at 21.9% and 9.1%, respectively. This disparity can be attributed to Quality's selling and administrative expense percentage (17%) which is much lower than Macy's (31.3%). Although Macy's earned net income more than 4,757 times larger than Quality's, Macy's net income as a **percentage of each sales dollar** (4.7%) is only 37% of Quality's (12.6%).

Ratio Analysis

LEARNING OBJECTIVE   5

Identify and compute ratios used in analyzing a firm's liquidity, profitability, and solvency.

Ratio analysis expresses the relationship among selected items of financial statement data. A **ratio** expresses the mathematical relationship between one quantity and another. The relationship is expressed in terms of either a percentage, a rate, or a simple proportion. To illustrate, in 2011 Nike, Inc. had current assets of $11,297 million and current liabilities of $3,958 million. We can find the relationship between these two measures by dividing current assets by current liabilities. The alternative means of expression are:

Percentage: Current assets are 285% of current liabilities.
Rate: Current assets are 2.85 times current liabilities.
Proportion: The relationship of current assets to liabilities is 2.85:1.

To analyze the primary financial statements, we can use ratios to evaluate liquidity, profitability, and solvency. Illustration 14-11 describes these classifications.

---

[1]*2011 Annual Report,* Macy's, Inc. (Cincinnati, Ohio).

Illustration 14-11
Financial ratio classifications

Liquidity Ratios

Measure short-term ability of the company to pay its maturing obligations and to meet unexpected needs for cash

Profitability Ratios

Measure the income or operating success of a company for a given period of time

Solvency Ratios

Measure the ability of the company to survive over a long period of time

Ratios can provide clues to underlying conditions that may not be apparent from individual financial statement components. However, a single ratio by itself is not very meaningful. Thus, in the discussion of ratios we will use the following types of comparisons.

1. **Intracompany comparisons** for two years for Quality Department Store.
2. **Industry average comparisons** based on median ratios for department stores.
3. **Intercompany comparisons** based on Macy's, Inc. as Quality Department Store's principal competitor.

ANATOMY OF A FRAUD

This final *Anatomy of a Fraud* box demonstrates that sometimes relationships between numbers can be used by companies to detect fraud. The numeric relationships that can reveal fraud can be such things as financial ratios that appear abnormal, or statistical abnormalities in the numbers themselves. For example, the fact that WorldCom's line costs, as a percentage of either total expenses or revenues, differed very significantly from its competitors should have alerted people to the possibility of fraud. Or, consider the case of a bank manager, who cooperated with a group of his friends to defraud the bank's credit card department. The manager's friends would apply for credit cards and then run up balances of slightly less than $5,000. The bank had a policy of allowing bank personnel to write-off balances of less than $5,000 without seeking supervisor approval. The fraud was detected by applying statistical analysis based on Benford's Law. Benford's Law states that in a random collection of numbers, the frequency of lower digits (e.g., 1, 2, or 3) should be much higher than higher digits (e.g., 7, 8, or 9). In this case, bank auditors analyzed the first two digits of amounts written off. There was a spike at 48 and 49, which was not consistent with what would be expected if the numbers were random.

Total take: Thousands of dollars

THE MISSING CONTROL
Independent internal verification. While it might be efficient to allow employees to write off accounts below a certain level, it is important that these write-offs be reviewed and verified periodically. Such a review would likely call attention to an employee with large amounts of write-offs, or in this case, write-offs that were frequently very close to the approval threshold.

Source: Mark J. Nigrini, "I've Got Your Number," *Journal of Accountancy Online* (May 1999).

Liquidity Ratios

Liquidity ratios measure the short-term ability of the company to pay its maturing obligations and to meet unexpected needs for cash. Short-term creditors such as bankers and suppliers are particularly interested in assessing liquidity. The ratios we can use to determine the company's short-term debt-paying ability are the current ratio, the acid-test ratio, accounts receivable turnover, and inventory turnover.

1. CURRENT RATIO

The **current ratio** is a widely used measure for evaluating a company's liquidity and short-term debt-paying ability. The ratio is computed by dividing current assets by current liabilities. Illustration 14-12 shows the 2011 and 2010 current ratios for Quality Department Store and comparative data.

Illustration 14-12
Current ratio

$$\text{Current Ratio} = \frac{\text{Current Assets}}{\text{Current Liabilities}}$$

Quality Department Store

2011	**2010**
$\dfrac{\$1,020,000}{\$344,500} = 2.96:1$	$\dfrac{\$945,000}{\$303,000} = 3.12:1$
Industry average	Macy's, Inc.
1.70:1	**1.40:1**

Helpful Hint
Can any company operate successfully without working capital? Yes, if it has very predictable cash flows and solid earnings. A number of companies (e.g., Whirlpool, American Standard, and Campbell's Soup) are pursuing this goal. The rationale: Less money tied up in working capital means more money to invest in the business.

What does the ratio actually mean? The 2011 ratio of 2.96:1 means that for every dollar of current liabilities, Quality has $2.96 of current assets. Quality's current ratio has decreased in the current year. But, compared to the industry average of 1.70:1, Quality appears to be reasonably liquid. Macy's has a current ratio of 1.40:1, which indicates it has adequate current assets relative to its current liabilities.

The current ratio is sometimes referred to as the **working capital ratio**. **Working capital** is current assets minus current liabilities. The current ratio is a more dependable indicator of liquidity than working capital. Two companies with the same amount of working capital may have significantly different current ratios.

The current ratio is only one measure of liquidity. It does not take into account the **composition** of the current assets. For example, a satisfactory current ratio does not disclose the fact that a portion of the current assets may be tied up in slow-moving inventory. A dollar of cash would be more readily available to pay the bills than a dollar of slow-moving inventory.

2. ACID-TEST RATIO

The **acid-test (quick) ratio** is a measure of a company's immediate short-term liquidity. We compute this ratio by dividing the sum of cash, short-term investments, and net accounts receivable by current liabilities. Thus, it is an important complement to the current ratio. For example, assume that the current assets of Quality Department Store for 2011 and 2010 consist of the items shown in Illustration 14-13.

QUALITY DEPARTMENT STORE INC. Balance Sheet (partial)		
	2011	**2010**
Current assets		
Cash	$ 100,000	$155,000
Short-term investments	20,000	70,000
Accounts receivable (net*)	230,000	180,000
Inventory	620,000	500,000
Prepaid expenses	50,000	40,000
Total current assets	$1,020,000	$ 945,000

*Allowance for doubtful accounts is $10,000 at the end of each year.

Illustration 14-13
Current assets of Quality Department Store

Cash, short-term investments, and accounts receivable (net) are highly liquid compared to inventory and prepaid expenses. The inventory may not be readily saleable, and the prepaid expenses may not be transferable to others. Thus, the acid-test ratio measures **immediate** liquidity. The 2011 and 2010 acid-test ratios for Quality Department Store and comparative data are as follows.

Illustration 14-14
Acid-test ratio

$$\text{Acid-Test Ratio} = \frac{\text{Cash + Short-Term Investments + Accounts Receivable (Net)}}{\text{Current Liabilities}}$$

Quality Department Store

2011

$$\frac{\$100,000 + \$20,000 + \$230,000}{\$344,500} = 1.02{:}1$$

Industry average
0.70:1

2010

$$\frac{\$155,000 + \$70,000 + \$180,000}{\$303,000} = 1.34{:}1$$

Macy's, Inc.
0.51:1

The ratio has declined in 2011. Is an acid-test ratio of 1.02:1 adequate? This depends on the industry and the economy. When compared with the industry average of 0.70:1 and Macy's of 0.51:1, Quality's acid-test ratio seems adequate.

INVESTOR INSIGHT %

How to Manage the Current Ratio

The apparent simplicity of the current ratio can have real-world limitations because adding equal amounts to both the numerator and the denominator causes the ratio to decrease.

Assume, for example, that a company has $2,000,000 of current assets and $1,000,000 of current liabilities. Thus, its current ratio is 2:1. If the company purchases $1,000,000 of inventory on account, it will have $3,000,000 of current assets and $2,000,000 of current liabilities. Its current ratio therefore decreases to 1.5:1. If, instead, the company pays off $500,000 of its current liabilities, it will have $1,500,000 of current assets and $500,000 of current liabilities. Its current ratio then increases to 3:1. Thus, any trend analysis should be done with care because the ratio is susceptible to quick changes and is easily influenced by management.

? How might management influence a company's current ratio? (See page 761.)

3. ACCOUNTS RECEIVABLE TURNOVER

We can measure liquidity by how quickly a company can convert certain assets to cash. How liquid, for example, are the accounts receivable? The ratio used to assess the liquidity of the receivables is **accounts receivable turnover**. It measures the number of times, on average, the company collects receivables during the period. We compute accounts receivable turnover by dividing net credit sales (net sales less cash sales) by the average net accounts receivable. Unless seasonal factors are significant, average net accounts receivable can be computed from the beginning and ending balances of the net accounts receivable.[2]

Assume that all sales are credit sales. The balance of net accounts receivable at the beginning of 2010 is $200,000. Illustration 14-15 shows the accounts receivable turnover for Quality Department Store and comparative data. Quality's accounts receivable turnover improved in 2011. The turnover of 10.2 times is substantially lower than Macy's 74.8 times, and is also lower than the department store industry's average of 46.4 times.

Illustration 14-15
Accounts receivable turnover

$$\text{Accounts Receivable Turnover} = \frac{\text{Net Credit Sales}}{\text{Average Net Accounts Receivable}}$$

Quality Department Store

2011	2010
$\dfrac{\$2,097,000}{\left[\dfrac{\$180,000 + \$230,000}{2}\right]} = 10.2 \text{ times}$	$\dfrac{\$1,837,000}{\left[\dfrac{\$200,000 + \$180,000}{2}\right]} = 9.7 \text{ times}$
Industry average	Macy's, Inc.
46.4 times	**74.8 times**

AVERAGE COLLECTION PERIOD A popular variant of the accounts receivable turnover is to convert it to an **average collection period** in terms of days. To do so, we divide the accounts receivable turnover into 365 days. For example, the accounts receivable turnover of 10.2 times divided into 365 days gives an average collection period of approximately 36 days. This means that accounts receivable are collected on average every 36 days, or about every 5 weeks. Analysts frequently use the average collection period to assess the effectiveness of a company's credit and collection policies. The general rule is that the collection period should not greatly exceed the credit term period (the time allowed for payment).

4. INVENTORY TURNOVER

Inventory turnover measures the number of times, on average, the inventory is sold during the period. Its purpose is to measure the liquidity of the inventory. We compute the inventory turnover by dividing cost of goods sold by the average inventory. Unless seasonal factors are significant, we can use the beginning and ending inventory balances to compute average inventory.

Assuming that the inventory balance for Quality Department Store at the beginning of 2010 was $450,000, its inventory turnover and comparative data are as shown in Illustration 14-16. Quality's inventory turnover declined slightly in 2011. The turnover of 2.3 times is low compared with the industry average of 4.3

---

[2]If seasonal factors are significant, the average accounts receivable balance might be determined by using monthly amounts.

and Macy's 3.2. Generally, the faster the inventory turnover, the less cash a company has tied up in inventory and the less the chance of inventory obsolescence.

Illustration 14-16
Inventory turnover

DAYS IN INVENTORY A variant of inventory turnover is the **days in inventory**. We calculate it by dividing the inventory turnover into 365. For example, Quality's 2011 inventory turnover of 2.3 times divided into 365 is approximately 159 days. An average selling time of 159 days is also high compared with the industry average of 84.9 days (365 ÷ 4.3) and Macy's 114.1 days (365 ÷ 3.2).

Inventory turnovers vary considerably among industries. For example, grocery store chains have a turnover of 17.1 times and an average selling period of 21 days. In contrast, jewelry stores have an average turnover of 0.80 times and an average selling period of 456 days.

Profitability Ratios

Profitability ratios measure the income or operating success of a company for a given period of time. Income, or the lack of it, affects the company's ability to obtain debt and equity financing. It also affects the company's liquidity position and the company's ability to grow. As a consequence, both creditors and investors are interested in evaluating earning power—profitability. Analysts frequently use profitability as the ultimate test of management's operating effectiveness.

5. PROFIT MARGIN

Profit margin is a measure of the percentage of each dollar of sales that results in net income. We can compute it by dividing net income by net sales. Illustration 14-17 shows Quality Department Store's profit margin and comparative data.

Alternative Terminology
Profit margin is also called the *rate of return on sales.*

Illustration 14-17
Profit margin

Quality experienced an increase in its profit margin from 2010 to 2011. Its profit margin is unusually high in comparison with the industry average of 8% and Macy's 4.8%.

High-volume (high inventory turnover) businesses, such as grocery stores (Safeway or Kroger) and discount stores (Kmart or Wal-Mart), generally experience low profit margins. In contrast, low-volume businesses, such as jewelry stores (Tiffany & Co.) or airplane manufacturers (Boeing Co.), have high profit margins.

6. ASSET TURNOVER

Asset turnover measures how efficiently a company uses its assets to generate sales. It is determined by dividing net sales by average total assets. The resulting number shows the dollars of sales produced by each dollar invested in assets. Unless seasonal factors are significant, we can use the beginning and ending balance of total assets to determine average total assets. Assuming that total assets at the beginning of 2010 were $1,446,000, the 2011 and 2010 asset turnover for Quality Department Store and comparative data are shown in Illustration 14-18.

Illustration 14-18
Asset turnover

Asset turnover shows that in 2011 Quality generated sales of $1.20 for each dollar it had invested in assets. The ratio changed very little from 2010 to 2011. Quality's asset turnover is below the industry average of 1.4 times and equal to Macy's ratio of 1.2 times.

Asset turnovers vary considerably among industries. For example, a large utility company like Consolidated Edison (New York) has a ratio of 0.4 times, and the large grocery chain Kroger Stores has a ratio of 3.4 times.

7. RETURN ON ASSETS

An overall measure of profitability is **return on assets**. We compute this ratio by dividing net income by average total assets. The 2011 and 2010 return on assets for Quality Department Store and comparative data are shown below.

Illustration 14-19
Return on assets

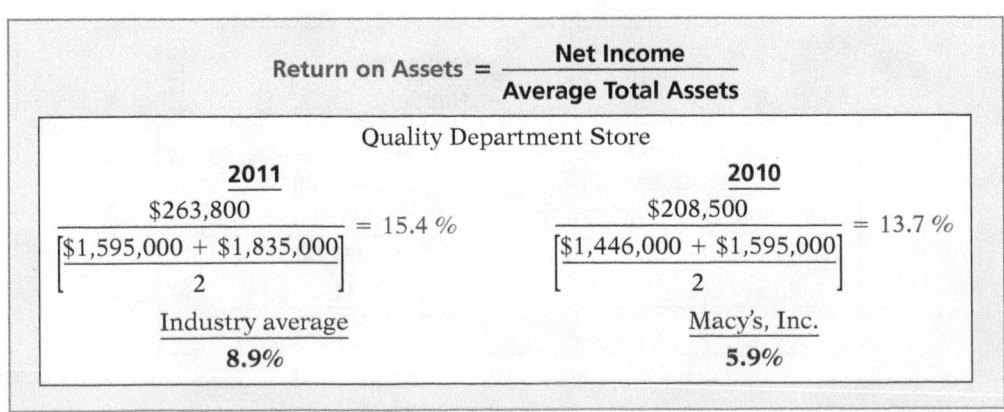

Quality's return on assets improved from 2010 to 2011. Its return of 15.4% is very high compared with the department store industry average of 8.9% and Macy's 5.9%.

8. RETURN ON COMMON STOCKHOLDERS' EQUITY

Another widely used profitability ratio is **return on common stockholders' equity**. It measures profitability from the common stockholders' viewpoint. This ratio shows how many dollars of net income the company earned for each dollar invested by the owners. We compute it by dividing net income by average common stockholders' equity. Assuming that common stockholders' equity at the beginning of 2010 was $667,000, Illustration 14-20 shows the 2011 and 2010 ratios for Quality Department Store and comparative data.

Illustration 14-20
Return on common stockholders' equity

Quality's rate of return on common stockholders' equity is high at 29.3%, considering an industry average of 18.3% and a rate of 21.9% for Macy's.

WITH PREFERRED STOCK When a company has preferred stock, we must deduct **preferred dividend** requirements from net income to compute income available to common stockholders. Similarly, we deduct the par value of preferred stock (or call price, if applicable) from total stockholders' equity to determine the amount of common stockholders' equity used in this ratio. The ratio then appears as follows.

$$\text{Return on Common Stockholders' Equity} = \frac{\text{Net Income} - \text{Preferred Dividends}}{\text{Average Common Stockholders' Equity}}$$

Illustration 14-21
Return on common stockholders' equity with preferred stock

Note that Quality's rate of return on stockholders' equity (29.3%) is substantially higher than its rate of return on assets (15.4%). The reason is that Quality has made effective use of **leverage**. **Leveraging** or **trading on the equity** at a gain means that the company has borrowed money at a lower rate of interest than it is able to earn by using the borrowed money. Leverage enables Quality Department Store to use money supplied by nonowners to increase the return to the owners. A comparison of the rate of return on total assets with the rate of interest paid for borrowed money indicates the profitability of trading on the equity. Quality Department Store earns more on its borrowed funds than it has to pay in the form of interest. Thus, the return to stockholders exceeds the return on the assets, due to benefits from the positive leveraging.

9. EARNINGS PER SHARE (EPS)

Earnings per share (EPS) is a measure of the net income earned on each share of common stock. It is computed by dividing net income less preferred dividends by the number of weighted-average common shares outstanding during the year. A measure of net income earned on a per share basis provides a useful perspective for determining profitability. Assuming that there is no change in the number of outstanding shares during 2010 and that the 2011 increase occurred midyear, Illustration 14-22 shows the net income per share for Quality Department Store for 2011 and 2010, assuming no preferred dividends.

Illustration 14-22
Earnings per share

$$\text{Earnings per Share} = \frac{\text{Net Income} - \text{Preferred Dividends}}{\text{Weighted-Average Common Shares Outstanding}}$$

Quality Department Store

2011	2010
$\dfrac{\$263,800}{\left[\dfrac{270,000 + 275,400}{2}\right]} = \$0.97$	$\dfrac{\$208,500}{270,000} = \$0.77$

Note that no industry or Macy's data are presented. Such comparisons are not meaningful because of the wide variations in the number of shares of outstanding stock among companies. The only meaningful EPS comparison is an intracompany trend comparison: Quality's earnings per share increased 20 cents per share in 2011. This represents a 26% increase over the 2010 earnings per share of 77 cents.

The terms "earnings per share" and "net income per share" refer to the amount of net income applicable to each share of **common stock**. Therefore, in computing EPS, if there are preferred dividends declared for the period, we must deduct them from net income to determine income available to the common stockholders.

10. PRICE-EARNINGS RATIO

The **price-earnings (P-E) ratio** is an oft-quoted measure of the ratio of the market price of each share of common stock to the earnings per share. The price-earnings (P-E) ratio reflects investors' assessments of a company's future earnings. We compute it by dividing the market price per share of the stock by earnings per share. Assuming that the market price of Quality Department Store Inc. stock is $8 in 2010 and $12 in 2011, the price-earnings ratio computation is as follows.

Illustration 14-23
Price-earnings ratio

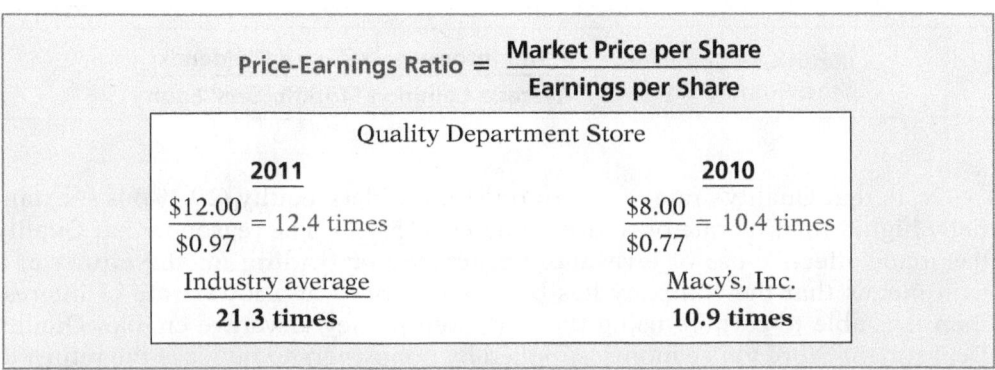

$$\text{Price-Earnings Ratio} = \frac{\text{Market Price per Share}}{\text{Earnings per Share}}$$

Quality Department Store

2011	2010
$\dfrac{\$12.00}{\$0.97} = 12.4$ times	$\dfrac{\$8.00}{\$0.77} = 10.4$ times
Industry average	Macy's, Inc.
21.3 times	**10.9 times**

In 2011, each share of Quality's stock sold for 12.4 times the amount that the company earned on each share. Quality's price-earnings ratio is lower than the industry average of 21.3 times but higher than the ratio of 10.9 times for Macy's.

For overall comparison to the market, the average price-earnings ratio for the stocks that constitute the Standard and Poor's 500 Index (500 largest U.S. firms) in late 2012 was approximately 15.9 times.

11. PAYOUT RATIO

The **payout ratio** measures the percentage of earnings distributed in the form of cash dividends. We compute it by dividing cash dividends declared on common stock by net income. Companies that have high growth rates generally have low payout ratios because they reinvest most of their net income into the business. The 2011 and 2010 payout ratios for Quality Department Store are computed as shown in Illustration 14-24.

Illustration 14-24
Payout ratio

$$\text{Payout Ratio} = \frac{\text{Cash Dividends Declared on Common Stock}}{\text{Net Income}}$$

Quality Department Store

2011	2010
$\dfrac{\$61,200}{\$263,800} = 23.2\%$	$\dfrac{\$60,000}{\$208,500} = 28.8\%$
Industry average	Macy's, Inc.
16.1%	**11.8%**

Quality's payout ratio is higher than the industry average payout ratio of 16.1%.

Solvency Ratios

Solvency ratios measure the ability of a company to survive over a long period of time. Long-term creditors and stockholders are particularly interested in a company's ability to pay interest as it comes due and to repay the face value of debt at maturity. Debt to assets and times interest earned are two ratios that provide information about debt-paying ability.

12. DEBT TO ASSETS RATIO

The **debt to assets ratio** measures the percentage of the total assets that creditors provide. We compute it by dividing total liabilities (both current and long-term liabilities) by total assets. This ratio indicates the company's degree of leverage. It also provides some indication of the company's ability to withstand losses without impairing the interests of creditors. The higher the percentage of total liabilities to total assets, the greater the risk that the company may be unable to meet its maturing obligations. The 2011 and 2010 ratios for Quality Department Store and comparative data are as follows.

Illustration 14-25
Debt to assets ratio

$$\text{Debt to Assets Ratio} = \frac{\text{Total Liabilities}}{\text{Total Assets}}$$

Quality Department Store

2011	2010
$\dfrac{\$832,000}{\$1,835,000} = 45.3\%$	$\dfrac{\$800,000}{\$1,595,000} = 50.2\%$
Industry average	Macy's, Inc.
34.2%	**73.1%**

A ratio of 45.3% means that creditors have provided 45.3% of Quality Department Store's total assets. Quality's 45.3% is above the industry average of 34.2%.

It is considerably below the high 73.1% ratio of Macy's. The lower the ratio, the more equity "buffer" there is available to the creditors. Thus, from the creditors' point of view, a low ratio of debt to assets is usually desirable.

The adequacy of this ratio is often judged in the light of the company's earnings. Generally, companies with relatively stable earnings (such as public utilities) have higher debt to assets ratios than cyclical companies with widely fluctuating earnings (such as many high-tech companies).

13. TIMES INTEREST EARNED

Times interest earned provides an indication of the company's ability to meet interest payments as they come due. We compute it by dividing the sum of net income, interest expense, and income tax expense by interest expense. Illustration 14-26 shows the 2011 and 2010 ratios for Quality Department Store and comparative data. Note that times interest earned uses net income before income tax expense and interest expense. This represents the amount available to cover interest. For Quality Department Store, the 2011 amount of $468,000 is computed by taking the income before income taxes of $432,000 and adding back the $36,000 of interest expense.

Illustration 14-26
Times interest earned

$$\text{Times Interest Earned} = \frac{\text{Net Income} + \text{Interest Expense} + \text{Income Tax Expense}}{\text{Interest Expense}}$$

Quality Department Store

2011	2010
$\dfrac{\$263,800 + \$36,000 + \$168,200}{\$36,000} = 13 \text{ times}$	$\dfrac{\$208,500 + \$40,500 + \$139,000}{\$40,500} = 9.6 \text{ times}$
Industry average	Macy's, Inc.
16.1 times	**5.4 times**

Quality's interest expense is well covered at 13 times, compared with the industry average of 16.1 times and Macy's 5.4 times.

Summary of Ratios

Illustration 14-27
Summary of liquidity, profitability, and solvency ratios

Illustration 14-27 summarizes the ratios discussed in this chapter. The summary includes the formula and purpose or use of each ratio.

Ratio	Formula	Purpose or Use
Liquidity Ratios		
1. Current ratio	$\dfrac{\text{Current assets}}{\text{Current liabilities}}$	Measures short-term debt-paying ability.
2. Acid-test (quick) ratio	$\dfrac{\text{Cash} + \text{Short-term investments} + \text{Accounts receivable (net)}}{\text{Current liabilities}}$	Measures immediate short-term liquidity.
3. Accounts receivable turnover	$\dfrac{\text{Net credit sales}}{\text{Average net accounts receivable}}$	Measures liquidity of accounts receivable.
4. Inventory turnover	$\dfrac{\text{Cost of goods sold}}{\text{Average inventory}}$	Measures liquidity of inventory.
Profitability Ratios		
5. Profit margin	$\dfrac{\text{Net income}}{\text{Net sales}}$	Measures net income generated by each dollar of sales.
6. Asset turnover	$\dfrac{\text{Net sales}}{\text{Average total assets}}$	Measures how efficiently assets are used to generate sales.

Ratio	Formula	Purpose or Use
7. Return on assets	$\dfrac{\text{Net income}}{\text{Average total assets}}$	Measures overall profitability of assets.
8. Return on common stockholders' equity	$\dfrac{\text{Net income} - \text{Preferred dividends}}{\text{Average common stockholders' equity}}$	Measures profitability of owners' investment.
9. Earnings per share (EPS)	$\dfrac{\text{Net income} - \text{Preferred dividends}}{\text{Weighted-average common shares outstanding}}$	Measures net income earned on each share of common stock.
10. Price-earnings (P-E) ratio	$\dfrac{\text{Market price per share}}{\text{Earnings per share}}$	Measures the ratio of the market price per share to earnings per share.
11. Payout ratio	$\dfrac{\text{Cash dividends declared on common stock}}{\text{Net income}}$	Measures percentage of earnings distributed in the form of cash dividends.
Solvency Ratios		
12. Debt to assets ratio	$\dfrac{\text{Total liabilities}}{\text{Total assets}}$	Measures the percentage of total assets provided by creditors.
13. Times interest earned	$\dfrac{\text{Net income} + \text{Interest expense} + \text{Income tax expense}}{\text{Interest expense}}$	Measures ability to meet interest payments as they come due.

> DO IT!

Ratio Analysis

The condensed financial statements of John Cully Company, for the years ended June 30, 2015 and 2014, are presented below.

JOHN CULLY COMPANY
Balance Sheets
June 30

	(in thousands)	
Assets	**2015**	**2014**
Current assets		
Cash and cash equivalents	$ 553.3	$ 611.6
Accounts receivable (net)	776.6	664.9
Inventory	768.3	653.5
Prepaid expenses and other current assets	204.4	269.2
Total current assets	2,302.6	2,199.2
Investments	12.3	12.6
Property, plant, and equipment (net)	694.2	647.0
Intangibles and other assets	876.7	849.3
Total assets	$3,885.8	$3,708.1
Liabilities and Stockholders' Equity		
Current liabilities	$1,497.7	$1,322.0
Long-term liabilities	679.5	637.1
Stockholders' equity—common	1,708.6	1,749.0
Total liabilities and stockholders' equity	$3,885.8	$3,708.1

JOHN CULLY COMPANY
Income Statements
For the Year Ended June 30

	(in thousands)	
	2015	**2014**
Sales revenue	$6,336.3	$5,790.4
Costs and expenses		
Cost of goods sold	1,617.4	1,476.3
Selling and administrative expenses	4,007.6	3,679.0
Interest expense	13.9	27.1
Total costs and expenses	5,638.9	5,182.4
Income before income taxes	697.4	608.0
Income tax expense	291.3	232.6
Net income	$ 406.1	$ 375.4

Compute the following ratios for 2015 and 2014.

(a) Current ratio.
(b) Inventory turnover. (Inventory on 6/30/13 was $599.0.)
(c) Profit margin.
(d) Return on assets. (Assets on 6/30/13 were $3,349.9.)
(e) Return on common stockholders' equity. (Stockholders' equity on 6/30/13 was $1,795.9.)
(f) Debt to assets ratio.
(g) Times interest earned.

Solution

Action Plan

✔ Remember that the current ratio includes all current assets. The acid-test ratio uses only cash, short-term investments, and net accounts receivable.

✔ Use average balances for turnover ratios like inventory, accounts receivable, and asset.

	2015	**2014**
(a) Current ratio:		
$2,302.6 ÷ $1,497.7 =	1.5:1	
$2,199.2 ÷ $1,322.0 =		1.7:1
(b) Inventory turnover:		
$1,617.4 ÷ [($768.3 + $653.5) ÷ 2] =	2.3 times	
$1,476.3 ÷ [($653.5 + $599.0) ÷ 2] =		2.4 times
(c) Profit margin:		
$406.1 ÷ $6,336.3 =	6.4%	
$375.4 ÷ $5,790.4 =		6.5%
(d) Return on assets:		
$406.1 ÷ [($3,885.8 + $3,708.1) ÷ 2] =	10.7%	
$375.4 ÷ [($3,708.1 + $3,349.9) ÷ 2] =		10.6%
(e) Return on common stockholders' equity:		
($406.1 − $0) ÷ [($1,708.6 + $1,749.0) ÷ 2] =	23.5%	
($375.4 − $0) ÷ [($1,749.0 + $1,795.9) ÷ 2] =		21.2%
(f) Debt to assets ratio:		
($1,497.7 + $679.5) ÷ $3,885.8 =	56.0%	
($1,322.0 + $637.1) ÷ $3,708.1 =		52.8%
(g) Times interest earned:		
($406.1 + $13.9 + $291.3) ÷ $13.9 =	51.2 times	
($375.4 + $27.1 + $232.6) ÷ $27.1 =		23.4 times

Related exercise material: BE14-9, BE14-10, BE14-12, BE14-13, E14-5, E14-6, E14-7, E14-8, E14-9, E14-10, E14-11, **and** DO IT! 14-2.

✔ **The Navigator**

Earning Power and Irregular Items

Users of financial statements are interested in the concept of earning power. **Earning power** means the normal level of income to be obtained in the future. Earning power differs from actual net income by the amount of irregular revenues, expenses, gains, and losses. Users are interested in earning power because it helps them derive an estimate of future earnings without the "noise" of irregular items.

For users of financial statements to determine earning power or regular income, the "irregular" items are separately identified on the income statement. Companies report two types of "irregular" items.

1. Discontinued operations.
2. Extraordinary items.

These "irregular" items are reported net of income taxes. That is, the income statement first reports income tax on the income before "irregular" items. Then the amount of tax for each of the listed "irregular" items is computed. The general concept is "let the tax follow income or loss."

LEARNING OBJECTIVE   6

Understand the concept of earning power, and how irregular items are presented.

Discontinued Operations

Discontinued operations refers to the disposal of a **significant component** of a business, such as the elimination of a major class of customers, or an entire activity. For example, to downsize its operations, General Dynamics Corp. sold its missile business to Hughes Aircraft Co. for $450 million. In its income statement, General Dynamics reported the sale in a separate section entitled "Discontinued operations."

Following the disposal of a significant component, the company should report on its income statement both income from continuing operations and income (or loss) from discontinued operations. **The income (loss) from discontinued operations consists of two parts: the income (loss) from operations** and **the gain (loss) on disposal of the component**.

To illustrate, assume that during 2015 Acro Energy Inc. has income before income taxes of $800,000. During 2015, Acro discontinued and sold its unprofitable chemical division. The loss in 2015 from chemical operations (net of $60,000 taxes) was $140,000. The loss on disposal of the chemical division (net of $30,000 taxes) was $70,000. Assuming a 30% tax rate on income, Illustration 14-28 shows Acro's income statement presentation.

ACRO ENERGY INC. Income Statement (partial) For the Year Ended December 31, 2015		
Income before income taxes		$ 800,000
Income tax expense		240,000
Income from continuing operations		560,000
Discontinued operations		
Loss from operations of chemical division, net of $60,000 income tax saving	$140,000	
Loss from disposal of chemical division, net of $30,000 income tax saving	70,000	210,000
Net income		$ 350,000

Illustration 14-28
Statement presentation of discontinued operations

Helpful Hint
Observe the dual disclosures. (1) The results of operations of the discontinued division must be eliminated from the results of continuing operations. (2) The company must also report the disposal of the operation.

Note that the statement uses the caption "Income from continuing operations" and adds a new section "Discontinued operations." **The new section reports both the operating loss and the loss on disposal net of applicable income taxes.** This presentation clearly indicates the separate effects of continuing operations and discontinued operations on net income.

Extraordinary Items

Extraordinary items are events and transactions that meet two conditions. They are (1) **unusual in nature,** and (2) **infrequent in occurrence**. To be unusual, the item should be abnormal and only incidentally related to the company's customary activities. To be infrequent, the item should not be reasonably expected to recur in the foreseeable future.

A company must evaluate both criteria in terms of its operating environment. Thus, Weyerhaeuser Co. reported the $36 million in damages to its timberland caused by the volcanic eruption of Mount St. Helens as an extraordinary item. The eruption was both unusual and infrequent. In contrast, Florida Citrus Company does not report frost damage to its citrus crop as an extraordinary item, because frost damage is not infrequent. Illustration 14-29 shows the classification of extraordinary and ordinary items.

Extraordinary items

1. Effects of major natural casualties, if rare in the area.

2. Expropriation (takeover) of property by a foreign government.

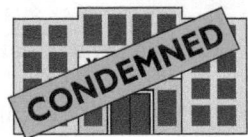

3. Effects of a newly enacted law or regulation, such as a condemnation action.

Ordinary items

1. Effects of major natural casualties, not uncommon in the area.

2. Write-down of inventories or write-off of receivables.

3. Losses attributable to labor strikes.

4. Gains or losses from sales of property, plant, or equipment.

Illustration 14-29
Examples of extraordinary and ordinary items

Companies report extraordinary items net of taxes in a separate section of the income statement, immediately below discontinued operations. To illustrate, assume that in 2015 a foreign government expropriated property held as an investment by Acro Energy Inc. If the loss is $70,000 before applicable income taxes of $21,000, the income statement will report a deduction of $49,000, as shown in Illustration 14-30. When there is an extraordinary item to report, the company adds the caption "Income before extraordinary item" immediately before the section for the extraordinary item. This presentation clearly indicates the effect of the extraordinary item on net income.

ACRO ENERGY INC. Income Statement (partial) For the Year Ended December 31, 2015		
Income before income taxes		$800,000
Income tax expense		240,000
Income from continuing operations		560,000
Discontinued operations		
Loss from operations of chemical division, net of $60,000 income tax saving	$140,000	
Loss from disposal of chemical division, net of $30,000 income tax saving	70,000	210,000
Income before extraordinary item		350,000
Extraordinary item		
Expropriation of investment, net of $21,000 income tax saving		49,000
Net income		$301,000

Illustration 14-30
Statement presentation of extraordinary items

Helpful Hint
If there are no discontinued operations, the third line of the income statement would be labeled "Income before extraordinary item."

What if a transaction or event meets one (but not both) of the criteria for an extraordinary item? In that case, the company reports it under either "Other revenues and gains" or "Other expenses and losses" at its gross amount (not net of tax). This is true, for example, of gains (losses) resulting from the sale of property, plant, and equipment, as explained in Chapter 9. It is quite common for companies to use the label "Non-recurring charges" for losses that do not meet the extraordinary item criteria.

INVESTOR INSIGHT %

© Andrey Armyagov/iStockphoto

What Does "Non-Recurring" Really Mean?

Many companies incur restructuring charges as they attempt to reduce costs. They often label these items in the income statement as "non-recurring" charges to suggest that they are isolated events which are unlikely to occur in future periods. The question for analysts is, are these costs really one-time, "non-recurring" events, or do they reflect problems that the company will be facing for many periods in the future? If they are one-time events, they can be largely ignored when trying to predict future earnings.

But some companies report "one-time" restructuring charges over and over again. For example, toothpaste and other consumer-goods giant Procter & Gamble Co. reported a restructuring charge in 12 consecutive quarters. Motorola had "special" charges in 14 consecutive quarters. On the other hand, other companies have a restructuring charge only once in a 5- or 10-year period. There appears to be no substitute for careful analysis of the numbers that comprise net income.

 If a company takes a large restructuring charge, what is the effect on the company's current income statement versus future ones? (See page 761.)

Changes in Accounting Principle

For ease of comparison, users of financial statements expect companies to prepare such statements on a basis **consistent** with the preceding period. A **change in accounting principle** occurs when the principle used in the current year is different from the one used in the preceding year. Accounting rules permit a change when management can show that the new principle is preferable to the old principle. An example is a change in inventory costing methods (such as FIFO to average-cost).

Ethics Note

Changes in accounting principle should result in financial statements that are more informative for statement users. They should *not* be used to artificially improve the reported performance or financial position of the corporation.

Companies report most changes in accounting principle retroactively. That is, they report both the current period and previous periods using the new principle. As a result, the same principle applies in all periods. This treatment improves the ability to compare results across years.

Comprehensive Income

The income statement reports most revenues, expenses, gains, and losses recognized during the period. However, over time, specific exceptions to this general practice have developed. Certain items now bypass income and are reported directly in stockholders' equity.

For example, in Chapter 12 you learned that companies do not include in income any unrealized gains and losses on available-for-sale securities. Instead, they report such gains and losses in the balance sheet as adjustments to stockholders' equity. Why are these gains and losses on available-for-sale securities excluded from net income? Because disclosing them separately (1) reduces the volatility of net income due to fluctuations in fair value, yet (2) informs the financial statement user of the gain or loss that would be incurred if the securities were sold at fair value.

Many analysts have expressed concern over the significant increase in the number of items that bypass the income statement. They feel that such reporting has reduced the usefulness of the income statement. To address this concern, in addition to reporting net income, a company must also report comprehensive income. **Comprehensive income** includes all changes in stockholders' equity during a period except those resulting from investments by stockholders and distributions to stockholders. A number of alternative formats for reporting comprehensive income are allowed. These formats are discussed in advanced accounting courses.

> DO IT!

Irregular Items

In its proposed 2015 income statement, AIR Corporation reports income before income taxes $400,000, extraordinary loss due to earthquake $100,000, income taxes $120,000 (not including irregular items), loss on operation of discontinued flower division $50,000, and loss on disposal of discontinued flower division $90,000. The income tax rate is 30%. Prepare a correct income statement, beginning with "Income before income taxes."

Solution

Action Plan

✔ Recall that a loss is extraordinary if it is both unusual and infrequent.

✔ Disclose the income tax effect of each component of income, beginning with income before any irregular items.

✔ Show discontinued operations before extraordinary items.

AIR CORPORATION		
Income Statement (partial)		
For the Year Ended December 31, 2015		
Income before income taxes		$400,000
Income tax expense		120,000
Income from continuing operations		280,000
Discontinued operations		
Loss from operation of flower division, net of $15,000 tax saving	$35,000	
Loss on disposal of flower division, net of $27,000 tax saving	63,000	98,000
Income before extraordinary item		182,000
Extraordinary earthquake loss, net of $30,000 tax saving		70,000
Net income		$112,000

Related exercise material: BE14-14, BE14-15, E14-12, E14-13, **and** DO IT! 14-3.

 The Navigator

Quality of Earnings

In evaluating the financial performance of a company, the quality of a company's earnings is of extreme importance to analysts. A company that has a high **quality of earnings** provides full and transparent information that will not confuse or mislead users of the financial statements.

The issue of quality of earnings has taken on increasing importance because recent accounting scandals suggest that some companies are spending too much time managing their income and not enough time managing their business. Here are some of the factors affecting quality of earnings.

Alternative Accounting Methods

Variations among companies in the application of generally accepted accounting principles may hamper comparability and reduce quality of earnings. For example, one company may use the FIFO method of inventory costing, while another company in the same industry may use LIFO. If inventory is a significant asset to both companies, it is unlikely that their current ratios are comparable. For example, if General Motors Corporation had used FIFO instead of LIFO for inventory valuation, its inventories in a recent year would have been 26% higher, which significantly affects the current ratio (and other ratios as well).

In addition to differences in inventory costing methods, differences also exist in reporting such items as depreciation, depletion, and amortization. Although these differences in accounting methods might be detectable from reading the notes to the financial statements, adjusting the financial data to compensate for the different methods is often difficult, if not impossible.

Pro Forma Income

Companies whose stock is publicly traded are required to present their income statement following generally accepted accounting principles (GAAP). In recent years, many companies have also reported a second measure of income, called pro forma income. **Pro forma income** usually excludes items that the company thinks are unusual or non-recurring. For example, at one time, Cisco Systems (a high-tech company) reported a quarterly net loss under GAAP of $2.7 billion. Cisco reported pro forma income for the same quarter as a profit of $230 million. This large difference in profits between GAAP income numbers and pro forma income is not unusual these days. For example, during one 9-month period the 100 largest firms on the Nasdaq stock exchange reported a total pro forma income of $19.1 billion but a total loss as measured by GAAP of $82.3 billion—a difference of about $100 billion!

To compute pro forma income, companies generally can exclude any items they deem inappropriate for measuring their performance. Many analysts and investors are critical of the practice of using pro forma income because these numbers often make companies look better than they really are. As the financial press noted, pro forma numbers might be called EBS, which stands for "earnings before bad stuff." Companies, on the other hand, argue that pro forma numbers more clearly indicate sustainable income because they exclude unusual and non-recurring expenses. "Cisco's technique gives readers of financial statements a clear picture of Cisco's normal business activities," the company said in a statement issued in response to questions about its pro forma income accounting.

The SEC has provided guidance on how companies should present pro forma information. Stay tuned: Everyone seems to agree that pro forma numbers can be useful if they provide insights into determining a company's sustainable income. However, many companies have abused the flexibility that pro forma numbers allow and have used the measure as a way to put their companies in a good light.

Improper Recognition

Due to pressure from Wall Street to continually increase earnings, some managers have manipulated the earnings numbers to meet these expectations. The most common abuse is the improper recognition of revenue. One practice that companies are using is **channel stuffing**. Offering deep discounts on their products to customers, companies encourage their customers to buy early (stuff the channel) rather than later. This lets the company report good earnings in the current period, but it often leads to a disaster in subsequent periods because customers have no need for additional goods. To illustrate, Bristol-Myers Squibb at one time indicated that it used sales incentives to encourage wholesalers to buy more drugs than needed to meet patients' demands. As a result, the company had to issue revised financial statements showing corrected revenues and income.

Another practice is the improper capitalization of operating expenses. The classic case is WorldCom. It capitalized over $7 billion of operating expenses so that it would report positive net income. In other situations, companies fail to report all their liabilities. Enron had promised to make payments on certain contracts if financial difficulty developed, but these guarantees were not reported as liabilities. In addition, disclosure was so lacking in transparency that it was impossible to understand what was happening at the company.

> **DO IT!**

Quality of Earnings, Financial Statement Analysis

Match each of the following terms with the phrase that best describes it.

Comprehensive income	Vertical analysis
Quality of earnings	Pro forma income
Solvency ratio	Extraordinary item

1. _____ Measures the ability of the company to survive over a long period of time.

2. _____ Usually excludes items that a company thinks are unusual or non-recurring.

3. _____ Includes all changes in stockholders' equity during a period except those resulting from investments by stockholders and distributions to stockholders.

4. _____ Indicates the level of full and transparent information provided to users of the financial statements.

5. _____ Describes events and transactions that are unusual in nature and infrequent in occurrence.

6. _____ Expresses each item within a financial statement as a percentage of a base amount.

Solution

1. Solvency ratio: Measures the ability of the company to survive over a long period of time.

2. Pro forma income: Usually excludes items that a company thinks are unusual or non-recurring.

3. Comprehensive income: Includes all changes in stockholders' equity during a period except those resulting from investments by stockholders and distributions to stockholders.

4. Quality of earnings: Indicates the level of full and transparent information provided to users of the financial statements.

5. Extraordinary item: Describes events and transactions that are unusual in nature and infrequent in occurrence.

6. Vertical analysis: Expresses each item within a financial statement as a percentage of a base amount.

Action Plan

✔ Develop a sound understanding of basic methods used for financial reporting.

✔ Understand the use of fundamental analysis techniques.

Related exercise material: **DO IT!** 14-4.

✔ **The Navigator**

The events and transactions of Dever Corporation for the year ending December 31, 2015, resulted in the following data.

Cost of goods sold	$2,600,000
Net sales	4,400,000
Other expenses and losses	9,600
Other revenues and gains	5,600
Selling and administrative expenses	1,100,000
Income from operations of plastics division	70,000
Gain from disposal of plastics division	500,000
Loss from tornado disaster (extraordinary loss)	600,000

Analysis reveals that:

1. All items are before the applicable income tax rate of 30%.

2. The plastics division was sold on July 1.

3. All operating data for the plastics division have been segregated.

Instructions
Prepare an income statement for the year.

Solution to Comprehensive DO IT!

Action Plan

✔ Report material items not typical of continuing operations in separate sections, net of taxes.

✔ Associate income taxes with the item that affects the taxes.

✔ Apply the corporate tax rate to income before income taxes to determine income tax expense.

DEVER CORPORATION
Income Statement
For the Year Ended December 31, 2015

Net sales		$4,400,000
Cost of goods sold		2,600,000
Gross profit		1,800,000
Selling and administrative expenses		1,100,000
Income from operations		700,000
Other revenues and gains	$ 5,600	
Other expenses and losses	9,600	4,000
Income before income taxes		696,000
Income tax expense ($696,000 × 30%)		208,800
Income from continuing operations		487,200
Discontinued operations		
Income from operations of plastics division, net of		
$21,000 income taxes ($70,000 × 30%)	49,000	
Gain from disposal of plastics division, net of $150,000		
income taxes ($500,000 × 30%)	350,000	399,000
Income before extraordinary item		886,200
Extraordinary item		
Tornado loss, net of $180,000 income tax saving		
($600,000 × 30%)		420,000
Net income		$ 466,200

 The Navigator

SUMMARY OF LEARNING OBJECTIVES

✔ The Navigator

1 Discuss the need for comparative analysis. There are three bases of comparison: (1) intracompany, which compares an item or financial relationship with other data within a company; (2) industry, which compares company data with industry averages; and (3) intercompany, which compares an item or financial relationship of a company with data of one or more competing companies.

2 Identify the tools of financial statement analysis. Financial statements can be analyzed horizontally, vertically, and with ratios.

3 Explain and apply horizontal analysis. Horizontal analysis is a technique for evaluating a series of data over a period of time to determine the increase or decrease that has taken place, expressed as either an amount or a percentage.

4 Describe and apply vertical analysis. Vertical analysis is a technique that expresses each item within a financial statement in terms of a percentage of a relevant total or a base amount.

5 Identify and compute ratios used in analyzing a firm's liquidity, profitability, and solvency. The formula and purpose of each ratio is presented in Illustration 14-27 (pages 730–731).

6 Understand the concept of earning power, and how irregular items are presented. Earning power refers to a company's ability to sustain its profits from operations. "Irregular items"—discontinued operations and extraordinary items—are presented net of tax below income from continuing operations to highlight their unusual nature.

7 Understand the concept of quality of earnings. A high quality of earnings provides full and transparent information that will not confuse or mislead users of the financial statements. Issues related to quality of earnings are (1) alternative accounting methods, (2) pro forma income, and (3) improper recognition.

GLOSSARY

Accounts receivable turnover A measure of the liquidity of accounts receivable; computed by dividing net credit sales by average net accounts receivable. (p. 724).

Acid-test (quick) ratio A measure of a company's immediate short-term liquidity; computed by dividing the sum of cash, short-term investments, and net accounts receivable by current liabilities. (p. 722).

Asset turnover A measure of how efficiently a company uses its assets to generate sales; computed by dividing net sales by average total assets. (p. 726).

Change in accounting principle The use of a principle in the current year that is different from the one used in the preceding year. (p. 735).

Comprehensive income Includes all changes in stockholders' equity during a period except those resulting from investments by stockholders and distributions to stockholders. (p. 736).

Current ratio A measure used to evaluate a company's liquidity and short-term debt-paying ability; computed by dividing current assets by current liabilities. (p. 722).

Debt to assets ratio Measures the percentage of assets provided by creditors; computed by dividing total liabilities by total assets. (p. 729).

Discontinued operations The disposal of a significant component of a business. (p. 733).

Earnings per share (EPS) The net income earned on each share of common stock; computed by dividing net income minus preferred dividends (if any) by the number of weighted-average common shares outstanding. (p. 728).

Extraordinary items Events and transactions that are unusual in nature and infrequent in occurrence. (p. 734).

Horizontal analysis A technique for evaluating a series of financial statement data over a period of time, to determine the increase (decrease) that has taken place, expressed as either an amount or a percentage. (p. 715).

Inventory turnover A measure of the liquidity of inventory; computed by dividing cost of goods sold by average inventory. (p. 724).

Leveraging See *Trading on the equity*. (p. 727).

Liquidity ratios Measures of the short-term ability of the company to pay its maturing obligations and to meet unexpected needs for cash. (p. 722).

Payout ratio Measures the percentage of earnings distributed in the form of cash dividends; computed by dividing cash dividends declared on common stock by net income. (p. 729).

Price-earnings (P-E) ratio Measures the ratio of the market price of each share of common stock to the earnings per share; computed by dividing the market price per share by earnings per share. (p. 728).

Profit margin Measures the percentage of each dollar of sales that results in net income; computed by dividing net income by net sales. (p. 725).

Profitability ratios Measures of the income or operating success of a company for a given period of time. (p. 725).

Pro forma income A measure of income that usually excludes items that a company thinks are unusual or non-recurring. (p. 737).

Quality of earnings Indicates the level of full and transparent information provided to users of the financial statements. (p. 737).

Ratio An expression of the mathematical relationship between one quantity and another. The relationship may be expressed either as a percentage, a rate, or a simple proportion. (p. 720).

Ratio analysis A technique for evaluating financial statements that expresses the relationship between selected financial statement data. (p. 720).

Return on assets An overall measure of profitability; computed by dividing net income by average total assets. (p. 726).

Return on common stockholders' equity Measures the dollars of net income earned for each dollar invested by the owners; computed by dividing net income minus preferred dividends (if any) by average common stockholders' equity. (p. 727).

Solvency ratios Measures of the ability of the company to survive over a long period of time. (p. 729).

Times interest earned Measures a company's ability to meet interest payments as they come due; computed by dividing the sum of net income, interest expense, and income tax expense by interest expense. (p. 730).

Trading on the equity Borrowing money at a lower rate of interest than can be earned by using the borrowed money. (p. 727).

Vertical analysis A technique for evaluating financial statement data that expresses each item within a financial statement as a percentage of a base amount. (p. 718).

WileyPLUS Self-Test, Brief Exercises, Exercises, Problem Set A, and many more components are available for practice in *WileyPLUS*.

SELF-TEST QUESTIONS

Answers are on page 761.

(LO 1) **1.** Comparisons of data within a company are an example of the following comparative basis:
 (a) Industry averages.
 (b) Intracompany.
 (c) Intercompany.
 (d) Both (b) and (c).

(LO 3) **2.** In horizontal analysis, each item is expressed as a percentage of the:
 (a) net income amount.
 (b) stockholders' equity amount.
 (c) total assets amount.
 (d) base year amount.

(LO 3) **3.** Sammy Corporation reported net sales of $300,000, $330,000, and $360,000 in the years, 2013, 2014, and 2015, respectively. If 2013 is the base year, what is the trend percentage for 2015?
 (a) 77%.
 (b) 108%.
 (c) 120%.
 (d) 130%.

(LO 4) **4.** The following schedule is a display of what type of analysis?

	Amount	Percent
Current assets	$200,000	25%
Property, plant, and equipment	600,000	75%
Total assets	$800,000	

 (a) Horizontal analysis.
 (b) Differential analysis.
 (c) Vertical analysis.
 (d) Ratio analysis.

(LO 4) **5.** In vertical analysis, the base amount for depreciation expense is generally:
 (a) net sales.
 (b) depreciation expense in a previous year.
 (c) gross profit.
 (d) fixed assets.

(LO 5) **6.** Which of the following measures is an evaluation of a firm's ability to pay current liabilities?
 (a) Acid-test ratio.
 (b) Current ratio.
 (c) Both (a) and (b).
 (d) None of the above.

(LO 5) **7.** A measure useful in evaluating the efficiency in managing inventories is:
 (a) inventory turnover.
 (b) days in inventory.
 (c) Both (a) and (b).
 (d) None of the above.

Use the following financial statement information as of the end of each year to answer Self-Test Questions 8-12.

	2015	2014
Inventory	$ 54,000	$ 48,000
Current assets	81,000	106,000
Total assets	382,000	326,000
Current liabilities	27,000	36,000
Total liabilities	102,000	88,000
Preferred stock	40,000	40,000
Common stockholders' equity	240,000	198,000
Net sales	784,000	697,000
Cost of goods sold	306,000	277,000
Net income	134,000	90,000
Income tax expense	22,000	18,000
Interest expense	12,000	12,000
Dividends paid to preferred stockholders	4,000	4,000
Dividends paid to common stockholders	15,000	10,000

(LO 5)　**8.** Compute the days in inventory for 2015.
　　(a) 64.4 days.　　　　　**(c)** 6 days.
　　(b) 60.8 days.　　　　　**(d)** 24 days.

(LO 5)　**9.** Compute the current ratio for 2015.
　　(a) 1.26:1.　　　　　　**(c)** .80:1.
　　(b) 3.0:1.　　　　　　**(d)** 3.75:1.

(LO 5)　**10.** Compute the profit margin for 2015.
　　(a) 17.1%.　　　　　　**(c)** 37.9%.
　　(b) 18.1%.　　　　　　**(d)** 5.9%.

(LO 5)　**11.** Compute the return on common stockholders' equity for 2015.
　　(a) 47.9%.　　　　　　**(c)** 61.2%.
　　(b) 51.7%.　　　　　　**(d)** 59.4%.

(LO 5)　**12.** Compute the times interest earned for 2015.
　　(a) 11.2 times.　　　　**(c)** 14.0 times.
　　(b) 65.3 times.　　　　**(d)** 13.0 times.

(LO 6)　**13.** In reporting discontinued operations, the income statement should show in a special section:
　　(a) gains and losses on the disposal of the discontinued component.

(b) gains and losses from operations of the discontinued component.
(c) Both (a) and (b).
(d) None of these answer choices are correct.

14. Scout Corporation has income before taxes of (LO 6) $400,000 and an extraordinary loss of $100,000. If the income tax rate is 25% on all items, the income statement should show income before extraordinary items and extraordinary items, respectively, of:
　　(a) $325,000 and $100,000.
　　(b) $325,000 and $75,000.
　　(c) $300,000 and $100,000.
　　(d) $300,000 and $75,000.

15. Which situation below might indicate a company has (LO 7) a low quality of earnings?
　　(a) The same accounting principles are used each year.
　　(b) Revenue is recognized when earned.
　　(c) Maintenance costs are expensed as incurred.
　　(d) The company is continually reporting pro forma income numbers.

Go to the book's companion website, www.wiley.com/college/weygandt, for additional Self-Test Questions.

 ✔ **The Navigator**

QUESTIONS

1. (a) Jose Ramirez believes that the analysis of financial statements is directed at two characteristics of a company: liquidity and profitability. Is Jose correct? Explain.
(b) Are short-term creditors, long-term creditors, and stockholders interested primarily in the same characteristics of a company? Explain.

2. (a) Distinguish among the following bases of comparison: (1) intracompany, (2) industry averages, and (3) intercompany.
(b) Give the principal value of using each of the three bases of comparison.

3. Two popular methods of financial statement analysis are horizontal analysis and vertical analysis. Explain the difference between these two methods.

4. (a) If Peoples Company had net income of $390,000 in 2015 and it experienced a 24.5% increase in net income for 2016, what is its net income for 2016?
(b) If six cents of every dollar of Peoples' revenue is net income in 2015, what is the dollar amount of 2015 revenue?

5. What is a ratio? What are the different ways of expressing the relationship of two amounts? What information does a ratio provide?

6. Name the major ratios useful in assessing (a) liquidity and (b) solvency.

7. Roberto Perez is puzzled. His company had a profit margin of 10% in 2015. He feels that this is an indication that the company is doing well. Julie Beck, his accountant, says that more information is needed to determine the firm's financial well-being. Who is correct? Why?

8. What do the following classes of ratios measure? (a) Liquidity ratios. (b) Profitability ratios. (c) Solvency ratios.

9. What is the difference between the current ratio and the acid-test ratio?

10. Hizar Company, a retail store, has an accounts receivable turnover of 4.5 times. The industry average is 12.5 times. Does Hizar have a collection problem with its accounts receivable?

11. Which ratios should be used to help answer the following questions?
(a) How efficient is a company in using its assets to produce sales?
(b) How near to sale is the inventory on hand?
(c) How many dollars of net income were earned for each dollar invested by the owners?
(d) How able is a company to meet interest charges as they fall due?

12. The price-earnings ratio of General Motors (automobile builder) was 8, and the price-earnings ratio of Microsoft (computer software) was 38. Which company did the stock market favor? Explain.

13. What is the formula for computing the payout ratio? Would you expect this ratio to be high or low for a growth company?

14. Holding all other factors constant, indicate whether each of the following changes generally signals good or bad news about a company.
(a) Increase in profit margin.
(b) Decrease in inventory turnover.
(c) Increase in the current ratio.

(d) Decrease in earnings per share.

(e) Increase in price-earnings ratio.

(f) Increase in debt to assets ratio.

(g) Decrease in times interest earned.

15. The return on assets for Zhang Corporation is 7.6%. During the same year, Zhang's return on common stockholders' equity is 12.8%. What is the explanation for the difference in the two rates?

16. Which two ratios do you think should be of greatest interest to:

(a) A pension fund considering the purchase of 20-year bonds?

(b) A bank contemplating a short-term loan?

(c) A common stockholder?

17. Why must preferred dividends be subtracted from net income in computing earnings per share?

18. (a) What is meant by trading on the equity?

(b) How would you determine the profitability of trading on the equity?

19. Lippert Inc. has net income of $160,000, weighted-average shares of common stock outstanding of 50,000, and preferred dividends for the period of $40,000. What is Lippert's earnings per share of common stock? Kate Lippert, the president of Lippert Inc., believes the computed EPS of the company is high. Comment.

20. Why is it important to report discontinued operations separately from income from continuing operations?

21. You are considering investing in Wingert Transportation. The company reports 2015 earnings per share of $6.50 on income before extraordinary items and $4.75 on net income. Which EPS figure would you consider more relevant to your investment decision? Why?

22. RAF Inc. reported 2014 earnings per share of $3.20 and had no extraordinary items. In 2015, EPS on income before extraordinary items was $2.99, and EPS on net income was $3.49. Is this a favorable trend?

23. Indicate which of the following items would be reported as an extraordinary item in Stumfol Corporation's income statement.

(a) Loss from damages caused by volcano eruption.

(b) Loss from sale of temporary investments.

(c) Loss attributable to a labor strike.

(d) Loss caused when manufacture of a product was prohibited by the Food and Drug Administration.

(e) Loss from flood damage. (The nearby Black River floods every 2 to 3 years.)

(f) Write-down of obsolete inventory.

(g) Expropriation of a factory by a foreign government.

24. Identify and explain factors that affect quality of earnings.

25. Identify the specific sections in Apple's 2011 annual report where horizontal and vertical analyses of financial data are presented.

BRIEF EXERCISES

Follow the rounding procedures used in the chapter.

BE14-1 You recently received a letter from your Uncle Sammy. A portion of the letter is presented below.

Discuss need for comparative analysis.

(LO 1)

You know that I have a significant amount of money I saved over the years. I am thinking about starting an investment program. I want to do the investing myself, based on my own research and analysis of financial statements. I know that you are studying accounting, so I have a couple of questions for you. I have heard that different users of financial statements are interested in different characteristics of companies. Is this true and, if so, why? Also, some of my friends who are already investing have told me that comparisons involving a company's financial data can be made on a number of different bases. Can you explain these bases to me?

Instructions

→ Write a letter to your Uncle Sammy which answers his questions.

BE14-2 Schellhammer Corporation reported the following amounts in 2014, 2015, and 2016.

Identify and use tools of financial statement analysis.

(LO 2, 3, 4, 5)

	2014	2015	2016
Current assets	$200,000	$210,000	$240,000
Current liabilities	150,000	168,000	184,000
Total assets	500,000	600,000	620,000

Instructions

(a) Identify and describe the three tools of financial statement analysis. (b) Perform each of the three types of analysis on Schellhammer's current assets.

Prepare horizontal analysis.
(LO 3)

BE14-3 Using the following data from the comparative balance sheet of Goody Company, illustrate horizontal analysis.

	December 31, 2015	December 31, 2014
Accounts receivable	$ 520,000	$ 400,000
Inventory	840,000	600,000
Total assets	3,000,000	2,500,000

Prepare vertical analysis.
(LO 4)

BE14-4 Using the same data presented above in BE14-3 for Goody Company, illustrate vertical analysis.

Calculate percentage of change.
(LO 3)

BE14-5 Net income was $500,000 in 2014, $450,000 in 2015, and $522,000 in 2016. What is the percentage of change from (a) 2014 to 2015 and (b) 2015 to 2016? Is the change an increase or a decrease?

Calculate net income.
(LO 3)

BE14-6 If Sappington Company had net income of $585,000 in 2015 and it experienced a 20% increase in net income over 2014, what was its 2014 net income?

Calculate change in net income.
(LO 3)

BE14-7 Horizontal analysis (trend analysis) percentages for Dody Company's sales revenue, cost of goods sold, and expenses are shown below.

Horizontal Analysis	2016	2015	2014
Sales revenue	96.2%	106.8%	100.0%
Cost of goods sold	102.0	97.0	100.0
Expenses	109.6	98.4	100.0

Did Dody's net income increase, decrease, or remain unchanged over the 3-year period?

Calculate change in net income.
(LO 4)

BE14-8 Vertical analysis (common size) percentages for Kochheim Company's sales revenue, cost of goods sold, and expenses are shown below.

Vertical Analysis	2016	2015	2014
Sales revenue	100.0%	100.0%	100.0%
Cost of goods sold	60.2	62.4	63.5
Expenses	25.0	25.6	27.5

Did Kochheim's net income as a percentage of sales increase, decrease, or remain unchanged over the 3-year period? Provide numerical support for your answer.

Calculate liquidity ratios.
(LO 5)

BE14-9 Selected condensed data taken from a recent balance sheet of Heidebrecht Inc. are as follows.

HEIDEBRECHT INC.
Balance Sheet (partial)

Cash	$ 8,041,000
Short-term investments	4,947,000
Accounts receivable	12,545,000
Inventory	14,814,000
Other current assets	5,571,000
Total current assets	$45,918,000
Total current liabilities	$40,644,000

What are the (a) working capital, (b) current ratio, and (c) acid-test ratio?

Calculate profitability ratios.
(LO 5)

BE14-10 Linebarger Corporation has net income of $11.44 million and net revenue of $95 million in 2015. Its assets are $14 million at the beginning of the year and $18 million at the end of the year. What are Linebarger's (a) asset turnover and (b) profit margin?

Evaluate collection of accounts receivable.
(LO 5)

BE14-11 The following data are taken from the financial statements of Rainsberger Company.

	2016	2015
Accounts receivable (net), end of year	$ 550,000	$ 520,000
Net sales on account	3,960,000	3,100,000
Terms for all sales are 1/10, n/60.		

(a) Compute for each year (1) the accounts receivable turnover and (2) the average collection period. At the end of 2014, accounts receivable (net) was $480,000.

(b) ——— What conclusions about the management of accounts receivable can be drawn from these data?

BE14-12 The following data are from the income statements of Haskin Company.

	2015	2014
Sales revenue	$6,420,000	$6,240,000
Beginning inventory	940,000	860,000
Purchases	4,340,000	4,661,000
Ending inventory	1,020,000	940,000

(a) Compute for each year (1) the inventory turnover and (2) the days in inventory.
(b) ━━━━ What conclusions concerning the management of the inventory can be drawn from these data?

BE14-13 Guo Company has stockholders' equity of $400,000 and net income of $66,000. It has a payout ratio of 20% and a return on assets of 15%. How much did Guo pay in cash dividends, and what were its average assets?

BE14-14 An inexperienced accountant for Silva Corporation showed the following in the income statement: income before income taxes and extraordinary item $450,000, and extraordinary loss from flood (before taxes) $70,000. The extraordinary loss and taxable income are both subject to a 30% tax rate. Prepare a correct income statement.

BE14-15 On June 30, Holloway Corporation discontinued its operations in Europe. During the year, the operating loss was $300,000 before taxes. On September 1, Holloway disposed of its European facilities at a pretax loss of $120,000. The applicable tax rate is 30%. Show the discontinued operations section of the income statement.

Evaluate management of inventory.
(LO 5)

Calculate amounts from profitability ratios.
(LO 5)

Prepare income statement including extraordinary items.
(LO 6)

Prepare discontinued operations section of income statement.
(LO 6)

> ## DO IT! Review

DO IT! 14-1 Summary financial information for Wolford Company is as follows.

	December 31, 2015	December 31, 2014
Current assets	$ 199,000	$ 220,000
Plant assets	821,000	780,000
Total assets	$1,020,000	$1,000,000

Compute the amount and percentage changes in 2015 using horizontal analysis, assuming 2014 is the base year.

DO IT! 14-2 The condensed financial statements of Murawski Company for the years 2014 and 2015 are presented below and on page 746. (Amounts in thousands.)

Prepare horizontal analysis.
(LO 3)

Compute ratios.
(LO 5)

MURAWSKI COMPANY
Balance Sheets
December 31

	2015	2014
Current assets		
Cash and cash equivalents	$ 330	$ 360
Accounts receivable (net)	470	400
Inventory	460	390
Prepaid expenses	120	160
Total current assets	1,380	1,310
Investments	10	10
Property, plant, and equipment	420	380
Intangibles and other assets	530	510
Total assets	$2,340	$2,210
Current liabilities	$ 900	$ 790
Long-term liabilities	410	380
Stockholders' equity—common	1,030	1,040
Total liabilities and stockholders' equity	$2,340	$2,210

MURAWSKI COMPANY
Income Statements
For the Years Ended December 31

	2015	2014
Sales revenue	$3,800	$3,460
Costs and expenses		
Cost of goods sold	955	890
Selling & administrative expenses	2,400	2,330
Interest expense	25	20
Total costs and expenses	3,380	3,240
Income before income taxes	420	220
Income tax expense	126	66
Net income	$ 294	$ 154

Compute the following ratios for 2015 and 2014.

(a) Current ratio.
(b) Inventory turnover. (Inventory on 12/31/13 was $340.)
(c) Profit margin.
(d) Return on assets. (Assets on 12/31/13 were $1,900.)
(e) Return on common stockholders' equity. (Stockholders' equity on 12/31/13 was $900.)
(f) Debt to assets ratio.
(g) Times interest earned.

Prepare income statement, including irregular items.
(LO 6)

DO IT! 14-3 In its proposed 2015 income statement, Hrabik Corporation reports income before income taxes $500,000, extraordinary loss due to earthquake $150,000, income taxes $200,000 (not including irregular items), loss on operation of discontinued music division $60,000, and gain on disposal of discontinued music division $40,000. The income tax rate is 30%. Prepare a correct income statement, beginning with income before income taxes.

Match terms relating to quality of earnings and financial statement analysis.
(LO 3, 4, 5, 6, 7)

DO IT! 14-4 Match each of the following terms with the phrase that best describes it.

Quality of earnings   Pro forma income
Current ratio   Discontinued operations
Horizontal analysis   Comprehensive income

1. _____ A measure used to evaluate a company's liquidity.
2. _____ Usually excludes items that a company thinks are unusual or non-recurring.
3. _____ Indicates the level of full and transparent information provided to users of the financial statements.
4. _____ The disposal of a significant component of a business.
5. _____ Determines increases or decreases in a series of financial statement data.
6. _____ Includes all changes in stockholders' equity during a period except those resulting from investments by stockholders and distributions to stockholders.

EXERCISES

Follow the rounding procedures used in the chapter.

Prepare horizontal analysis.
(LO 3)

E14-1 Financial information for Kurzen Inc. is presented below.

	December 31, 2015	December 31, 2014
Current assets	$125,000	$100,000
Plant assets (net)	396,000	330,000
Current liabilities	91,000	70,000
Long-term liabilities	133,000	95,000
Common stock, $1 par	161,000	115,000
Retained earnings	136,000	150,000

Instructions
Prepare a schedule showing a horizontal analysis for 2015 using 2014 as the base year.

E14-2 Operating data for Navarro Corporation are presented below.

Prepare vertical analysis.
(LO 4)

	2015	2014
Net sales	$750,000	$600,000
Cost of goods sold	465,000	390,000
Selling expenses	105,000	66,000
Administrative expenses	60,000	54,000
Income tax expense	36,000	27,000
Net income	84,000	63,000

Instructions
Prepare a schedule showing a vertical analysis for 2015 and 2014.

E14-3 The comparative condensed balance sheets of Gurley Corporation are presented below.

Prepare horizontal and vertical analyses.
(LO 3, 4)

GURLEY CORPORATION
Comparative Condensed Balance Sheets
December 31

	2015	2014
Assets		
Current assets	$ 74,000	$ 80,000
Property, plant, and equipment (net)	99,000	90,000
Intangibles	27,000	40,000
Total assets	$200,000	$210,000
Liabilities and stockholders' equity		
Current liabilities	$ 42,000	$ 48,000
Long-term liabilities	143,000	150,000
Stockholders' equity	15,000	12,000
Total liabilities and stockholders' equity	$200,000	$210,000

Instructions
(a) Prepare a horizontal analysis of the balance sheet data for Gurley Corporation using 2014 as a base.
(b) Prepare a vertical analysis of the balance sheet data for Gurley Corporation in columnar form for 2015.

E14-4 The comparative condensed income statements of Emley Corporation are shown below.

Prepare horizontal and vertical analyses.
(LO 3, 4)

EMLEY CORPORATION
Comparative Condensed Income Statements
For the Years Ended December 31

	2015	2014
Net sales	$660,000	$600,000
Cost of goods sold	483,000	420,000
Gross profit	177,000	180,000
Operating expenses	125,000	120,000
Net income	$ 52,000	$ 60,000

Instructions
(a) Prepare a horizontal analysis of the income statement data for Emley Corporation using 2014 as a base. (Show the amounts of increase or decrease.)
(b) Prepare a vertical analysis of the income statement data for Emley Corporation in columnar form for both years.

Compute liquidity ratios and compare results.

(LO 5)

E14-5 Suppose Nordstrom, Inc., which operates department stores in numerous states, has the following selected financial statement data for the year ending January 30, 2012.

NORDSTROM, INC.
Balance Sheet (partial)

(in millions)	End-of-Year	Beginning-of-Year
Cash and cash equivalents	$ 795	$ 72
Accounts receivable (net)	2,035	1,942
Inventory	898	900
Prepaid expenses	88	93
Other current assets	238	210
Total current assets	$4,054	$3,217
Total current liabilities	$2,014	$1,601

For the year, net sales were $8,258 and cost of goods sold was $5,328 (in millions).

Instructions

(a) Compute the four liquidity ratios at the end of the year.

(b) Using the data in the chapter, compare Nordstrom's liquidity with (1) that of Macy's, Inc., and (2) the industry averages for department stores.

Perform current and acid-test ratio analysis.

(LO 5)

E14-6 Keener Incorporated had the following transactions occur involving current assets and current liabilities during February 2015.

Feb. 3 Accounts receivable of $15,000 are collected.
     7 Equipment is purchased for $28,000 cash.
    11 Paid $3,000 for a 3-year insurance policy.
    14 Accounts payable of $12,000 are paid.
    18 Cash dividends of $5,000 are declared.

Additional information:

1. As of February 1, 2015, current assets were $110,000, and current liabilities were $50,000.

2. As of February 1, 2015, current assets included $15,000 of inventory and $2,000 of prepaid expenses.

Instructions

(a) Compute the current ratio as of the beginning of the month and after each transaction.

(b) Compute the acid-test ratio as of the beginning of the month and after each transaction.

Compute selected ratios.

(LO 5)

E14-7 Frizell Company has the following comparative balance sheet data.

FRIZELL COMPANY
Balance Sheets
December 31

	2015	2014
Cash	$ 15,000	$ 30,000
Accounts receivable (net)	70,000	60,000
Inventory	60,000	50,000
Plant assets (net)	200,000	180,000
	$345,000	$320,000
Accounts payable	$ 50,000	$ 60,000
Mortgage payable (6%)	100,000	100,000
Common stock, $10 par	140,000	120,000
Retained earnings	55,000	40,000
	$345,000	$320,000

Additional information for 2015:

1. Net income was $25,000.

2. Sales on account were $410,000. Sales returns and allowances were $20,000.

3. Cost of goods sold was $198,000.

Instructions

Compute the following ratios at December 31, 2015.

(a) Current ratio.
(b) Acid-test ratio.
(c) Accounts receivable turnover.
(d) Inventory turnover.

E14-8 Selected comparative statement data for Queen Products Company are presented below. All balance sheet data are as of December 31.

Compute selected ratios.
(LO 5)

	2015	2014
Net sales	$750,000	$720,000
Cost of goods sold	480,000	440,000
Interest expense	7,000	5,000
Net income	45,000	42,000
Accounts receivable	120,000	100,000
Inventory	85,000	75,000
Total assets	580,000	500,000
Total common stockholders' equity	430,000	325,000

Instructions

Compute the following ratios for 2015.

(a) Profit margin.
(b) Asset turnover.
(c) Return on assets.
(d) Return on common stockholders' equity.

E14-9 The income statement for Sutherland, Inc., appears below.

Compute selected ratios.
(LO 5)

SUTHERLAND, INC.
Income Statement
For the Year Ended December 31, 2015

Net sales	$400,000
Cost of goods sold	230,000
Gross profit	170,000
Expenses (including $16,000 interest and $24,000 income taxes)	105,000
Net income	$ 65,000

Additional information:

1. The weighted-average common shares outstanding in 2015 were 30,000 shares.
2. The market price of Sutherland, Inc. stock was $13 in 2015.
3. Cash dividends of $26,000 were paid, $5,000 of which were to preferred stockholders.

Instructions

Compute the following ratios for 2015.

(a) Earnings per share.
(b) Price-earnings ratio.
(c) Payout ratio.
(d) Times interest earned.

E14-10 Lingenfelter Corporation experienced a fire on December 31, 2015, in which its financial records were partially destroyed. It has been able to salvage some of the records and has ascertained the following balances.

Compute amounts from ratios.
(LO 5)

	December 31, 2015	December 31, 2014
Cash	$ 30,000	$ 10,000
Accounts receivable (net)	72,500	126,000
Inventory	200,000	180,000
Accounts payable	50,000	90,000
Notes payable	30,000	60,000
Common stock, $100 par	400,000	400,000
Retained earnings	113,500	101,000

Additional information:

1. The inventory turnover is 4.5 times.
2. The return on common stockholders' equity is 16%. The company had no additional paid-in capital.
3. The accounts receivable turnover is 8.8 times.
4. The return on assets is 12.5%.
5. Total assets at December 31, 2014, were $655,000.

Instructions
Compute the following for Lingenfelter Corporation.

(a) Cost of goods sold for 2015.
(b) Net sales (credit) for 2015.
(c) Net income for 2015.
(d) Total assets at December 31, 2015.

Compute ratios.
(LO 5)

E14-11 Wiemers Corporation's comparative balance sheets are presented below.

WIEMERS CORPORATION
Balance Sheets
December 31

	2015	2014
Cash	$ 4,300	$ 3,700
Accounts receivable (net)	21,200	23,400
Inventory	10,000	7,000
Land	20,000	26,000
Buildings	70,000	70,000
Accumulated depreciation—buildings	(15,000)	(10,000)
Total	$110,500	$120,100
Accounts payable	$ 12,370	$ 31,100
Common stock	75,000	69,000
Retained earnings	23,130	20,000
Total	$110,500	$120,100

Wiemers's 2015 income statement included net sales of $100,000, cost of goods sold of $60,000, and net income of $15,000.

Instructions
Compute the following ratios for 2015.

(a) Current ratio.
(b) Acid-test ratio.
(c) Accounts receivable turnover.
(d) Inventory turnover.
(e) Profit margin.
(f) Asset turnover.
(g) Return on assets.
(h) Return on common stockholders' equity.
(i) Debt to assets ratio.

Prepare a correct income statement.
(LO 6)

E14-12 For its fiscal year ending October 31, 2015, Haas Corporation reports the following partial data shown below.

Income before income taxes	$540,000
Income tax expense (30% × $420,000)	126,000
Income before extraordinary items	414,000
Extraordinary loss from flood	120,000
Net income	$294,000

The flood loss is considered an extraordinary item. The income tax rate is 30% on all items.

Instructions
(a) Prepare a correct income statement, beginning with income before income taxes.
(b) ⟶ Explain in memo form why the income statement data are misleading.

Prepare income statement.
(LO 6)

E14-13 Trayer Corporation has income from continuing operations of $290,000 for the year ended December 31, 2015. It also has the following items (before considering income taxes).

1. An extraordinary loss of $80,000.
2. A gain of $30,000 on the discontinuance of a division.
3. A correction of an error in last year's financial statements that resulted in a $20,000 understatement of 2014 net income.

Assume all items are subject to income taxes at a 30% tax rate.

Instructions
(a) Prepare an income statement, beginning with income from continuing operations.
(b) Indicate the statement presentation of any item not included in (a) above.

EXERCISES: SET B AND CHALLENGE EXERCISES

Visit the book's companion website, at **www.wiley.com/college/weygandt**, and choose the Student Companion site to access Exercise Set B and Challenge Exercises.

PROBLEMS

Follow the rounding procedures used in the chapter.

P14-1 Comparative statement data for Farris Company and Ratzlaff Company, two competitors, appear below. All balance sheet data are as of December 31, 2015, and December 31, 2014.

Prepare vertical analysis and comment on profitability.
(LO 4, 5)

	Farris Company		Ratzlaff Company	
	2015	**2014**	**2015**	**2014**
Net sales	$1,549,035		$339,038	
Cost of goods sold	1,080,490		241,000	
Operating expenses	302,275		79,000	
Interest expense	8,980		2,252	
Income tax expense	54,500		6,650	
Current assets	325,975	$312,410	83,336	$ 79,467
Plant assets (net)	521,310	500,000	139,728	125,812
Current liabilities	65,325	75,815	35,348	30,281
Long-term liabilities	108,500	90,000	29,620	25,000
Common stock, $10 par	500,000	500,000	120,000	120,000
Retained earnings	173,460	146,595	38,096	29,998

Instructions
(a) Prepare a vertical analysis of the 2015 income statement data for Farris Company and Ratzlaff Company in columnar form.
(b) ━━━► Comment on the relative profitability of the companies by computing the return on assets and the return on common stockholders' equity for both companies.

P14-2 The comparative statements of Painter Tool Company are presented below and on page 752.

Compute ratios from balance sheet and income statement.
(LO 5)

PAINTER TOOL COMPANY
Income Statement
For the Years Ended December 31

	2015	2014
Net sales	$1,818,500	$1,750,500
Cost of goods sold	1,011,500	996,000
Gross profit	807,000	754,500
Selling and administrative expenses	499,000	479,000
Income from operations	308,000	275,500
Other expenses and losses		
Interest expense	18,000	14,000
Income before income taxes	290,000	261,500
Income tax expense	87,000	77,000
Net income	$ 203,000	$ 184,500

PAINTER TOOL COMPANY
Balance Sheets
December 31

Assets	2015	2014
Current assets		
Cash	$ 60,100	$ 64,200
Short-term investments	69,000	50,000
Accounts receivable (net)	107,800	102,800
Inventory	133,000	115,500
Total current assets	369,900	332,500
Plant assets (net)	600,300	520,300
Total assets	$970,200	$852,800
Liabilities and Stockholders' Equity		
Current liabilities		
Accounts payable	$160,000	$145,400
Income taxes payable	43,500	42,000
Total current liabilities	203,500	187,400
Bonds payable	200,000	200,000
Total liabilities	403,500	387,400
Stockholders' equity		
Common stock ($5 par)	280,000	300,000
Retained earnings	286,700	165,400
Total stockholders' equity	566,700	465,400
Total liabilities and stockholders' equity	$970,200	$852,800

All sales were on account.

Instructions
Compute the following ratios for 2015. (Weighted-average common shares in 2015 were 57,000.)

(a) Earnings per share.
(b) Return on common stockholders' equity.
(c) Return on assets.
(d) Current ratio.
(e) Acid-test ratio.

(f) Accounts receivable turnover.
(g) Inventory turnover.
(h) Times interest earned.
(i) Asset turnover.
(j) Debt to assets ratio.

Perform ratio analysis, and evaluate financial position and operating results.

(LO 5)

P14-3 Condensed balance sheet and income statement data for Landwehr Corporation appear below and on page 753.

LANDWEHR CORPORATION
Balance Sheets
December 31

	2016	2015	2014
Cash	$ 25,000	$ 20,000	$ 18,000
Accounts receivable (net)	50,000	45,000	48,000
Other current assets	90,000	95,000	64,000
Investments	75,000	70,000	45,000
Plant and equipment (net)	400,000	370,000	358,000
	$640,000	$600,000	$533,000
Current liabilities	$ 75,000	$ 80,000	$ 70,000
Long-term debt	80,000	85,000	50,000
Common stock, $10 par	340,000	310,000	300,000
Retained earnings	145,000	125,000	113,000
	$640,000	$600,000	$533,000

LANDWEHR CORPORATION
Income Statement
For the Years Ended December 31

	2016	2015
Sales revenue	$740,000	$700,000
Less: Sales returns and allowances	40,000	50,000
Net sales	700,000	650,000
Cost of goods sold	420,000	400,000
Gross profit	280,000	250,000
Operating expenses (including income taxes)	235,000	220,000
Net income	$ 45,000	$ 30,000

Additional information:

1. The market price of Landwehr's common stock was $4.00, $5.00, and $8.00 for 2014, 2015, and 2016, respectively.
2. All dividends were paid in cash.

Instructions
(a) Compute the following ratios for 2015 and 2016.
   (1) Profit margin.
   (2) Asset turnover.
   (3) Earnings per share. (Weighted-average common shares in 2016 were 32,000 and in 2015 were 31,000.)
   (4) Price-earnings ratio.
   (5) Payout ratio.
   (6) Debt to assets ratio.
(b) ⟶ Based on the ratios calculated, discuss briefly the improvement or lack thereof in financial position and operating results from 2015 to 2016 of Landwehr Corporation.

P14-4 Financial information for Messersmith Company is presented below and on page 754.

Compute ratios, and comment on overall liquidity and profitability.

(LO 5)

MESSERSMITH COMPANY
Balance Sheets
December 31

Assets	2015	2014
Cash	$ 70,000	$ 65,000
Short-term investments	52,000	40,000
Accounts receivable (net)	98,000	80,000
Inventory	125,000	135,000
Prepaid expenses	29,000	23,000
Land	130,000	130,000
Building and equipment (net)	180,000	175,000
	$684,000	$648,000

Liabilities and Stockholders' Equity		
Notes payable	$100,000	$100,000
Accounts payable	48,000	42,000
Accrued liabilities	50,000	40,000
Bonds payable, due 2018	150,000	150,000
Common stock, $10 par	200,000	200,000
Retained earnings	136,000	116,000
	$684,000	$648,000

MESSERSMITH COMPANY
Income Statement
For the Years Ended December 31

	2015	2014
Net sales	$850,000	$790,000
Cost of goods sold	620,000	575,000
Gross profit	230,000	215,000
Operating expenses	187,000	173,000
Net income	$ 43,000	$ 42,000

Additional information:

1. Inventory at the beginning of 2014 was $118,000.
2. Total assets at the beginning of 2014 were $630,000.
3. No common stock transactions occurred during 2014 or 2015.
4. All sales were on account. Accounts receivable, net at the beginning of 2014, were $88,000.
5. Notes payable are classified as current liabilities.

Instructions
(a) Indicate, by using ratios, the change in liquidity and profitability of Messersmith Company from 2014 to 2015. (*Note:* Not all profitability ratios can be computed.)
(b) Given below are three independent situations and a ratio that may be affected. For each situation, compute the affected ratio (1) as of December 31, 2015, and (2) as of December 31, 2016, after giving effect to the situation. Net income for 2016 was $50,000. Total assets on December 31, 2016, were $700,000.

Situation	Ratio
(1) 18,000 shares of common stock were sold at par on July 1, 2016.	Return on common stockholders' equity
(2) All of the notes payable were paid in 2016. The only change in liabilities was that the notes payable were paid.	Debt to assets ratio
(3) Market price of common stock was $9 on December 31, 2015, and $12.80 on December 31, 2016.	Price-earnings ratio

Compute selected ratios, and compare liquidity, profitability, and solvency for two companies.

(LO 5)

P14-5 Selected financial data of Target and Wal-Mart for a recent year are presented here (in millions).

	Target Corporation	Wal-Mart Stores, Inc.
	Income Statement Data for Year	
Net sales	$61,471	$374,526
Cost of goods sold	41,895	286,515
Selling and administrative expenses	16,200	70,847
Interest expense	647	1,798
Other income (expense)	1,896	4,273
Income tax expense	1,776	6,908
Net income	$ 2,849	$ 12,731
	Balance Sheet Data (End of Year)	
Current assets	$18,906	$ 47,585
Noncurrent assets	25,654	115,929
Total assets	$44,560	$163,514
Current liabilities	$11,782	$ 58,454
Long-term debt	17,471	40,452
Total stockholders' equity	15,307	64,608
Total liabilities and stockholders' equity	$44,560	$163,514

	Target Corporation	Wal-Mart Stores, Inc.
	Beginning-of-Year Balances	
Total assets	$37,349	$151,587
Total stockholders' equity	15,633	61,573
Current liabilities	11,117	52,148
Total liabilities	21,716	90,014
	Other Data	
Average net accounts receivable	$ 7,124	$ 3,247
Average inventory	6,517	34,433
Net cash provided by operating activities	4,125	20,354

Instructions

(a) For each company, compute the following ratios.

(1) Current ratio.
(2) Accounts receivable turnover.
(3) Average collection period.
(4) Inventory turnover.
(5) Days in inventory.
(6) Profit margin.
(7) Asset turnover.
(8) Return on assets.
(9) Return on common stockholders' equity.
(10) Debt to assets ratio.
(11) Times interest earned.

(b) Compare the liquidity, profitability, and solvency of the two companies.

P14-6 The comparative statements of Corbin Company are presented below and on page 756. *Compute numerous ratios.* (LO 5)

CORBIN COMPANY
Income Statement
For the Years Ended December 31

	2015	2014
Net sales (all on account)	$595,000	$520,000
Expenses		
Cost of goods sold	415,000	354,000
Selling and administrative	120,800	114,800
Interest expense	7,800	6,000
Income tax expense	15,000	14,000
Total expenses	558,600	488,800
Net income	$ 36,400	$ 31,200

CORBIN COMPANY
Balance Sheets
December 31

Assets	2015	2014
Current assets		
Cash	$ 21,000	$ 18,000
Short-term investments	18,000	15,000
Accounts receivable (net)	91,000	74,000
Inventory	85,000	70,000
Total current assets	215,000	177,000
Plant assets (net)	423,000	383,000
Total assets	$638,000	$560,000

Liabilities and Stockholders' Equity	2015	2014
Current liabilities		
Accounts payable	$122,000	$110,000
Income taxes payable	23,000	20,000
Total current liabilities	145,000	130,000
Long-term liabilities		
Bonds payable	120,000	80,000
Total liabilities	265,000	210,000
Stockholders' equity		
Common stock ($5 par)	150,000	150,000
Retained earnings	223,000	200,000
Total stockholders' equity	373,000	350,000
Total liabilities and stockholders' equity	$638,000	$560,000

Additional data:

The common stock recently sold at $19.50 per share.

Instructions

Compute the following ratios for 2015.

(a) Current ratio.
(b) Acid-test ratio.
(c) Accounts receivable turnover.
(d) Inventory turnover.
(e) Profit margin.
(f) Asset turnover.
(g) Return on assets.

(h) Return on common stockholders' equity.
(i) Earnings per share.
(j) Price-earnings ratio.
(k) Payout ratio.
(l) Debt to assets ratio.
(m) Times interest earned.

Compute missing information given a set of ratios.

(LO 5)

P14-7 An incomplete income statement and an incomplete comparative balance sheet of Deines Corporation are presented below and on page 757.

DEINES CORPORATION
Income Statement
For the Year Ended December 31, 2015

Net sales	$11,000,000
Cost of goods sold	?
Gross profit	?
Operating expenses	1,665,000
Income from operations	?
Other expenses and losses	
Interest expense	?
Income before income taxes	?
Income tax expense	560,000
Net income	$?

DEINES CORPORATION
Balance Sheets
December 31

Assets	2015	2014
Current assets		
Cash	$ 450,000	$ 375,000
Accounts receivable (net)	?	950,000
Inventory	?	1,720,000
Total current assets	?	3,045,000
Plant assets (net)	4,620,000	3,955,000
Total assets	$?	$7,000,000

Liabilities and Stockholders' Equity	2015	2014
Current liabilities	$?	$ 825,000
Long-term notes payable	?	2,800,000
Total liabilities	?	3,625,000
Common stock, $1 par	3,000,000	3,000,000
Retained earnings	400,000	375,000
Total stockholders' equity	3,400,000	3,375,000
Total liabilities and stockholders' equity	$?	$7,000,000

Additional information:

1. The accounts receivable turnover for 2015 is 10 times.
2. All sales are on account.
3. The profit margin for 2015 is 14.5%.
4. Return on assets is 22% for 2015.
5. The current ratio on December 31, 2015, is 3.0.
6. The inventory turnover for 2015 is 4.8 times.

Instructions

Compute the missing information given the ratios above. Show computations. (*Note:* Start with one ratio and derive as much information as possible from it before trying another ratio. List all missing amounts under the ratio used to find the information.)

P14-8 Terwilliger Corporation owns a number of cruise ships and a chain of hotels. The hotels, which have not been profitable, were discontinued on September 1, 2015. The 2015 operating results for the company were as follows.

Prepare income statement with discontinued operations and extraordinary loss.

(LO 6)

Operating revenues	$12,850,000
Operating expenses	8,700,000
Operating income	$ 4,150,000

Analysis discloses that these data include the operating results of the hotel chain, which were operating revenues $1,500,000 and operating expenses $2,400,000. The hotels were sold at a gain of $200,000 before taxes. This gain is not included in the operating results. During the year, Terwilliger suffered an extraordinary loss of $600,000 before taxes, which is not included in the operating results. In 2015, the company had other revenues and gains of $100,000, which are not included in the operating results. The corporation is in the 30% income tax bracket.

Instructions

Prepare a condensed income statement.

P14-9 The ledger of Jaime Corporation at December 31, 2015, contains the following summary data.

Prepare income statement with nontypical items.

(LO 6)

Net sales	$1,700,000	Cost of goods sold	$1,100,000
Selling expenses	120,000	Administrative expenses	150,000
Other revenues and gains	20,000	Other expenses and losses	28,000

Your analysis reveals the following additional information that is not included in the above data.

1. The entire Puzzles Division was discontinued on August 31. The income from operations for this division before income taxes was $20,000. The Puzzles Division was sold at a loss of $90,000 before income taxes.
2. On May 15, company property was expropriated for an interstate highway. The settlement resulted in an extraordinary gain of $120,000 before income taxes.
3. The income tax rate on all items is 30%.

Instructions

Prepare an income statement for the year ended December 31, 2015. Use the format illustrated in the Comprehensive DO IT! (page 739).

PROBLEMS: SET B

Visit the book's companion website, at **www.wiley.com/college/weygandt**, and choose the Student Companion site to access Problem Set B.

CONTINUING COOKIE CHRONICLE

(*Note:* This is a continuation of the Cookie Chronicle from Chapters 1 through 13.)

CCC14 Natalie and Curtis have the balance sheet and income statement for the first year of operations for Cookie & Coffee Creations Inc. They have been told that they can use these financial statements to prepare horizontal and vertical analyses, and to calculate financial ratios, to determine how their business is doing and to make some decisions they have been considering.

Go to the book's companion website, **www.wiley.com/college/weygandt**, *to see the completion of this problem.*

Broadening Your **PERSPECTIVE**

Financial Reporting and Analysis

Financial Reporting Problem: Apple Inc.

BYP14-1 Your parents are considering investing in Apple Inc. common stock. They ask you, as an accounting expert, to make an analysis of the company for them. Apple's financial statements are presented in Appendix A. Instructions for accessing and using Apple's complete annual report, including the notes to the financial statements, are also provided in Appendix A.

Instructions
(Follow the approach in the chapter for rounding numbers.)

(a) Make a 3-year trend analysis, using 2009 as the base year, of (1) net sales and (2) net income. Comment on the significance of the trend results.

(b) Compute for 2011 and 2010 the (1) profit margin, (2) asset turnover, (3) return on assets, and (4) return on common stockholders' equity. How would you evaluate Apple's profitability? Total assets at September 26, 2009, were $47,501 and total stockholders' equity at September 26, 2009, was $31,640.

(c) Compute for 2011 and 2010 the (1) debt to assets ratio and (2) times interest earned. How would you evaluate Apple's long-term solvency?

(d) What information outside the annual report may also be useful to your parents in making a decision about Apple?

Comparative Analysis Problem:
PepsiCo, Inc. vs. The Coca-Cola Company

BYP14-2 PepsiCo's financial statements are presented in Appendix B. Financial statements of The Coca-Cola Company are presented in Appendix C. Instructions for accessing and using the complete annual reports of PepsiCo and Coca-Cola, including the notes to the financial statements, are also provided in Appendices B and C, respectively.

Instructions

(a) Based on the information contained in these financial statements, determine each of the following for each company.

    (1) The percentage increase (decrease) in (i) net sales and (ii) net income from 2010 to 2011.

    (2) The percentage increase in (i) total assets and (ii) total common stockholders' (shareholders') equity from 2010 to 2011.

    (3) The basic earnings per share and price-earnings ratio for 2011. (For both PepsiCo and Coca-Cola, use the basic earnings per share.) Coca-Cola's common stock had a market price of $75.05 at the end of fiscal-year 2011, and PepsiCo's common stock had a market price of $66.35.

(b) What conclusions concerning the two companies can be drawn from these data?

Comparative Analysis Problem:
Amazon.com, Inc. vs. Wal-Mart Stores, Inc.

BYP14-3 Amazon.com, Inc.'s financial statements are presented in Appendix D. Financial statements of Wal-Mart Stores, Inc. are presented in Appendix E. Instructions for accessing and using the complete annual reports of Amazon and Wal-Mart, including the notes to the financial statements, are also provided in Appendices D and E, respectively.

Instructions

(a) Based on the information contained in these financial statements, determine each of the following for each company.

    (1) The percentage increase (decrease) in (i) net sales and (ii) net income from 2010 to 2011.

    (2) The percentage increase in (i) total assets and (ii) total common stockholders' (shareholders') equity from 2010 to 2011.

    (3) The basic earnings per share and price-earnings ratio for 2011. (For both Amazon and Wal-Mart, use the basic earnings per share.) Amazon's common stock had a market price of $214.75 at the end of fiscal-year 2011, and Wal-Mart's common stock had a market price of $57.90.

(b) What conclusions concerning the two companies can be drawn from these data?

Real-World Focus

BYP14-4 The Management Discussion and Analysis section of an annual report addresses corporate performance for the year and sometimes uses financial ratios to support its claims.

Address: **www.ibm.com/investor/tools/index.phtml**, or go to **www.wiley.com/college/weygandt**

Steps

1. Choose **How to read annual reports** (in the Guides section).
2. Choose **Anatomy**.

Instructions

Using the information from the above site, answer the following questions.

(a) What are the optional elements that are often included in an annual report?

(b) What are the elements of an annual report that are required by the SEC?

(c) Describe the contents of the Management Discussion.

(d) Describe the contents of the Auditors' Report.

(e) Describe the contents of the Selected Financial Data.

Critical Thinking

Decision-Making Across the Organization

BYP14-5 As the CPA for Gandara Manufacturing Inc., you have been asked to develop some key ratios from the comparative financial statements. This information is to be used to convince creditors that the company is solvent and will continue as a going concern. The data requested and the computations developed from the financial statements follow.

	2015	2014
Current ratio	3.1 times	2.1 times
Acid-test ratio	.8 times	1.4 times
Asset turnover	2.8 times	2.2 times
Net income	Up 32%	Down 8%
Earnings per share	$3.30	$2.50

Instructions
With the class divided into groups, complete the following.

Gandara Manufacturing Inc. asks you to prepare a list of brief comments stating how each of these items supports the solvency and going-concern potential of the business. The company wishes to use these comments to support its presentation of data to its creditors. You are to prepare the comments as requested, giving the implications and the limitations of each item separately. Then prepare a collective inference that may be drawn from the individual items about Gandara's solvency and going-concern potential.

Communication Activity

BYP14-6 Abby Landis is the CEO of Pletcher's Electronics. Landis is an expert engineer but a novice in accounting. She asks you to explain (1) the bases for comparison in analyzing Pletcher's financial statements, and (2) the factors affecting quality of earnings.

Instructions
Write a letter to Abby Landis that explains the bases for comparison and factors affecting quality of earnings.

Ethics Case

BYP14-7 Dave Schonhardt, president of Schonhardt Industries, wishes to issue a press release to bolster his company's image and maybe even its stock price, which has been gradually falling. As controller, you have been asked to provide a list of 20 financial ratios along with some other operating statistics relative to Schonhardt Industries' first quarter financials and operations.

Two days after you provide the ratios and data requested, Steven Verlin, the public relations director of Schonhardt, asks you to prove the accuracy of the financial and operating data contained in the press release written by the president and edited by Steven. In the press release, the president highlights the sales increase of 25% over last year's first quarter and the positive change in the current ratio from 1.5:1 last year to 3:1 this year. He also emphasizes that production was up 50% over the prior year's first quarter.

You note that the press release contains only positive or improved ratios and none of the negative or deteriorated ratios. For instance, no mention is made that the debt to assets ratio has increased from 35% to 55%, that inventories are up 89%, and that while the current ratio improved, the acid-test ratio fell from 1:1 to 0.5:1. Nor is there any mention that the reported profit for the quarter would have been a loss had not the estimated lives of Schonhardt's plant and machinery been increased by 30%. Steven emphasizes, "The prez wants this release by early this afternoon."

Instructions
(a) Who are the stakeholders in this situation?
(b) Is there anything unethical in president Schonhardt's actions?
(c) Should you as controller remain silent? Does Steven have any responsibility?

All About You

BYP14-8 In this chapter, you learned how to use many tools for performing a financial analysis of a company. When making personal investments, however, it is most likely that you won't be buying stocks and bonds in individual companies. Instead, when most people want to invest in stock, they buy mutual funds. By investing in a mutual fund, you reduce your risk because the fund diversifies by buying the stock of a variety of different companies, bonds, and other investments, depending on the stated goals of the fund.

Before you invest in a fund, you will need to decide what type of fund you want. For example, do you want a fund that has the potential of high growth (but also high risk), or are you looking for lower risk and a steady stream of income? Do you want a fund that invests only in U.S. companies, or do you want one that invests globally? Many resources are available to help you with these types of decisions.

Instructions

Go to **http://web.archive.org/web/20050210200843/http://www.cnb1.com/invallocmdl.htm** and complete the investment allocation questionnaire. Add up your total points to determine the type of investment fund that would be appropriate for you.

FASB Codification Activity

BYP14-9 If your school has a subscription to the FASB Codification, go to **http://aaahq.org/ascLogin.cfm** to log in and prepare responses to the following. Use the Master Glossary for determining the proper definitions.

(a) Discontinued operations.
(b) Extraordinary items.
(c) Comprehensive income.

Answers to Chapter Questions

Answers to Insight and Accounting Across the Organization Questions

p. 723 How to Manage the Current Ratio   Q: How might management influence a company's current ratio? **A:** Management can affect the current ratio by speeding up or withholding payments on accounts payable just before the balance sheet date. Management can alter the cash balance by increasing or decreasing long-term assets or long-term debt, or by issuing or purchasing common stock.

p. 735 What Does "Non-Recurring" Really Mean?   Q: If a company takes a large restructuring charge, what is the effect on the company's current income statement versus future ones? **A:** The current period's net income can be greatly diminished by a large restructuring charge. The net incomes in future periods can be enhanced because they are relieved of costs (i.e., depreciation and labor expenses) that would have been charged to them.

Answers to Self-Test Questions

1. b **2.** d **3.** c ($360,000 ÷ 300,000) **4.** c **5.** a **6.** c **7.** c **8.** b $306,000 ÷ [($54,000 + $48,000) ÷ 2] = 6; 365 ÷ 6 **9.** b ($81,000 ÷ $27,000) **10.** a $134,000 ÷ $784,000 **11.** d ($134,000 − $4,000) ÷ [($240,000 + $198,000) ÷ 2] **12.** c ($134,000 + $22,000 + $12,000) ÷ $12,000 **13.** c **14.** d ($400,000 − (25% × $400,000); $300,000 − [$100,000 − (25% × $100,000)] **15.** d

A Look at IFRS

The tools of financial statement analysis, covered in the first section of this chapter, are the same throughout the world. Techniques such as vertical and horizontal analysis, for example, are tools used by analysts regardless of whether GAAP- or IFRS-related financial statements are being evaluated. In addition, the ratios provided in the textbook are the same ones that are used internationally.

The latter part of this chapter relates to the income statement and irregular items. As in GAAP, the income statement is a required statement under IFRS. In addition, the content and presentation of an IFRS income statement is similar to the one used for GAAP. *IAS 1* (revised), "Presentation of Financial Statements," provides general guidelines for the reporting of income statement information. In general, the differences in the presentation of financial statement information are relatively minor.

> **LEARNING OBJECTIVE   8**
>
> Compare financial statement analysis and income statement presentation under GAAP and IFRS.

Key Points

- The tools of financial statement analysis covered in this chapter are universal and therefore no significant differences exist in the analysis methods used.
- The basic objectives of the income statement are the same under both GAAP and IFRS. As indicated in the textbook, a very important objective is to ensure that users of the income statement can evaluate the earning power of the company. Earning power is the normal level of income to be obtained in the future. Thus, both the IASB and the FASB are interested in distinguishing normal levels of income from irregular items in order to better predict a company's future profitability.
- The basic accounting for discontinued operations is the same under IFRS and GAAP.
- Under IFRS, there is no classification for extraordinary items. In other words, extraordinary item treatment is prohibited under IFRS. All revenue and expense items are considered ordinary in nature. Disclosure, however, is extensive for items that are considered material to the financial results. Examples are write-downs of inventory or plant assets, or gains and losses on the sale of plant assets.
- The accounting for changes in accounting principles and changes in accounting estimates are the same for both GAAP and IFRS.
- Both GAAP and IFRS follow the same approach in reporting comprehensive income. The statement of comprehensive income can be prepared under the one-statement approach or the two-statement approach.
- The issues related to quality of earnings are the same under both GAAP and IFRS. It is hoped that by adopting a more principles-based approach, as found in IFRS, that many of the earning quality issues will disappear.

Looking to the Future

The FASB and the IASB are working on a project that would rework the structure of financial statements. Recently, the IASB decided to require a statement of comprehensive income, similar to what was required under GAAP. In addition, another part of this project addresses the issue of how to classify various items in the income statement. A main goal of this new approach is to provide information that better represents how businesses are run. In addition, the approach draws attention away from one number—net income.

IFRS Practice

IFRS Self-Test Questions

1. The basic tools of financial analysis are the same under both GAAP and IFRS **except** that:
   (a) horizontal analysis cannot be done because the format of the statements is sometimes different.
   (b) analysis is different because vertical analysis cannot be done under IFRS.
   (c) the current ratio cannot be computed because current liabilities are often reported before current assets in IFRS statements of position.
   (d) None of the above.

2. Under IFRS:
   (a) the reporting of discontinued items is different than under GAAP.
   (b) the reporting of extraordinary items is prohibited.
   (c) the reporting of changes in accounting principles is different than under GAAP.
   (d) None of the above.

3. Presentation of comprehensive income must be reported under IFRS in:
   (a) the statement of stockholders' equity.
   (b) the income statement ending with net income.
   (c) the notes to the financial statements.
   (d) a statement of comprehensive income.

4. In preparing its income statement for 2015, Parmalane assembles the following information.

Sales revenue	$500,000
Cost of goods sold	300,000
Operating expenses	40,000
Loss on discontinued operations	20,000
Loss from flood disaster (an extraordinary item under GAAP)	10,000

Ignoring income taxes, what is Parmalane's income from continuing operations for 2015 under IFRS?

(a) $260,000.　　　　　　**(c)** $240,000.

(b) $250,000　　　　　　**(d)** $150,000.

5. Using the same information as Question 4, which statement is **incorrect**?

(a) Net income under GAAP and IFRS are the same.

(b) Under GAAP, special reporting is provided for extraordinary items.

(c) Both GAAP and IFRS report the same amount for income from continuing operations.

(d) IFRS would not provide separate disclosure for discontinued operations.

International Financial Reporting Problem: Zetar plc

IFRS14-1 The financial statements of Zetar plc are presented in Appendix F. Instructions for accessing and using the company's complete annual report, including the notes to its financial statements, are also provided in Appendix F.

Instructions

Use the company's **2009 annual report** to answer the following questions.

(a) The company's income statement reports a loss on discontinued operations. What business did the company discontinue, and why did it choose to discontinue the business?

(b) For the year ended April 30, 2009, what amount did the company lose on the operation of the discontinued business, and what amount did it lose on disposal?

(c) What was the total recorded value of the net assets at the date of disposal, and what was the amount of costs incurred to dispose of the business?

Answers to IFRS Self-Test Questions
1. d   2. b   3. d   4. d   5. d

 The Navigator

Appendix A | Specimen Financial Statements: Apple Inc.

Once each year, a corporation communicates to its stockholders and other interested parties by issuing a complete set of audited financial statements. The **annual report**, as this communication is called, summarizes the financial results of the company's operations for the year and its plans for the future. Many annual reports are attractive, multicolored, glossy public relations pieces, containing pictures of corporate officers and directors as well as photos and descriptions of new products and new buildings. Yet the basic function of every annual report is to report financial information, almost all of which is a product of the corporation's accounting system.

The content and organization of corporate annual reports have become fairly standardized. Excluding the public relations part of the report (pictures, products, etc.), the following are the traditional financial portions of the annual report:

- Financial Highlights
- Letter to the Stockholders
- Management's Discussion and Analysis
- Financial Statements
- Notes to the Financial Statements

- Management's Responsibility for Financial Reporting
- Management's Report on Internal Control over Financial Reporting
- Report of Independent Registered Public Accounting Firm
- Selected Financial Data

The official SEC filing of the annual report is called a **Form 10-K**, which often omits the public relations pieces found in most standard annual reports. On the following pages, we present Apple Inc.'s financial statements taken from the company's 2011 Form 10-K. To access Apple's Form 10-K, including notes to the financial statements, follow these steps:

1. Go to **http://investor.apple.com**.
2. Select the SEC Filings tab.
3. Enter "10-K" in the SEC Filing Keyword Search box, select Annual in the Groupings Filter drop-down list, and then press Search.
4. Select the 10-K Annual Report filed Oct 26, 2011.
5. Item 8, on page 42, provides an index to the consolidated financial statements and notes. The Notes to Consolidated Financial Statements, for example, begin on page 47.

CONSOLIDATED STATEMENTS OF OPERATIONS
(In millions, except number of shares which are reflected in thousands and per share amounts)

Three years ended September 24, 2011	2011	2010	2009
Net sales	$108,249	$ 65,225	$ 42,905
Cost of sales	64,431	39,541	25,683
Gross margin	43,818	25,684	17,222
Operating expenses:			
Research and development	2,429	1,782	1,333
Selling, general and administrative	7,599	5,517	4,149
Total operating expenses	10,028	7,299	5,482
Operating income	33,790	18,385	11,740
Other income and expense	415	155	326
Income before provision for income taxes	34,205	18,540	12,066
Provision for income taxes	8,283	4,527	3,831
Net income	$ 25,922	$ 14,013	$ 8,235
Earnings per common share:			
Basic	$ 28.05	$ 15.41	$ 9.22
Diluted	$ 27.68	$ 15.15	$ 9.08
Shares used in computing earnings per share:			
Basic	924,258	909,461	893,016
Diluted	936,645	924,712	907,005

See accompanying Notes to Consolidated Financial Statements.

CONSOLIDATED BALANCE SHEETS
(In millions, except number of shares which are reflected in thousands)

	September 24, 2011	September 25, 2010
ASSETS:		
Current assets:		
Cash and cash equivalents	$ 9,815	$ 11,261
Short-term marketable securities	16,137	14,359
Accounts receivable, less allowances of $53 and $55, respectively	5,369	5,510
Inventories	776	1,051
Deferred tax assets	2,014	1,636
Vendor non-trade receivables	6,348	4,414
Other current assets	4,529	3,447
Total current assets	44,988	41,678
Long-term marketable securities	55,618	25,391
Property, plant and equipment, net	7,777	4,768
Goodwill	896	741
Acquired intangible assets, net	3,536	342
Other assets	3,556	2,263
Total assets	$ 116,371	$ 75,183
LIABILITIES AND SHAREHOLDERS' EQUITY:		
Current liabilities:		
Accounts payable	$ 14,632	$ 12,015
Accrued expenses	9,247	5,723
Deferred revenue	4,091	2,984
Total current liabilities	27,970	20,722
Deferred revenue – non-current	1,686	1,139
Other non-current liabilities	10,100	5,531
Total liabilities	39,756	27,392
Commitments and contingencies		
Shareholders' equity:		
Common stock, no par value; 1,800,000 shares authorized; 929,277 and 915,970 shares issued and outstanding, respectively	13,331	10,668
Retained earnings	62,841	37,169
Accumulated other comprehensive income/(loss)	443	(46)
Total shareholders' equity	76,615	47,791
Total liabilities and shareholders' equity	$ 116,371	$ 75,183

See accompanying Notes to Consolidated Financial Statements.

CONSOLIDATED STATEMENTS OF SHAREHOLDERS' EQUITY
(In millions, except number of shares which are reflected in thousands)

	Common Stock		Retained Earnings	Accumulated Other Comprehensive Income/ (Loss)	Total Shareholders' Equity
	Shares	Amount			
Balances as of September 27, 2008	888,326	$ 7,177	$ 15,129	$ (9)	$22,297
Components of comprehensive income:					
Net income	0	0	8,235	0	8,235
Change in foreign currency translation	0	0	0	(14)	(14)
Change in unrealized gains/losses on marketable securities, net of tax	0	0	0	118	118
Change in unrecognized gains/losses on derivative instruments, net of tax	0	0	0	(18)	(18)
Total comprehensive income					8,321
Share-based compensation	0	707	0	0	707
Common stock issued under stock plans, net of shares withheld for employee taxes	11,480	404	(11)	0	393
Tax benefit from equity awards, including transfer pricing adjustments	0	(78)	0	0	(78)
Balances as of September 26, 2009	899,806	8,210	23,353	77	31,640
Components of comprehensive income:					
Net income	0	0	14,013	0	14,013
Change in foreign currency translation	0	0	0	7	7
Change in unrealized gains/losses on marketable securities, net of tax	0	0	0	123	123
Change in unrecognized gains/losses on derivative instruments, net of tax	0	0	0	(253)	(253)
Total comprehensive income					13,890
Share-based compensation	0	876	0	0	876
Common stock issued under stock plans, net of shares withheld for employee taxes	16,164	703	(197)	0	506
Tax benefit from equity awards, including transfer pricing adjustments	0	879	0	0	879
Balances as of September 25, 2010	915,970	10,668	37,169	(46)	47,791
Components of comprehensive income:					
Net income	0	0	25,922	0	25,922
Change in foreign currency translation	0	0	0	(12)	(12)
Change in unrealized gains/losses on marketable securities, net of tax	0	0	0	(41)	(41)
Change in unrecognized gains/losses on derivative instruments, net of tax	0	0	0	542	542
Total comprehensive income					26,411
Share-based compensation	0	1,168	0	0	1,168
Common stock issued under stock plans, net of shares withheld for employee taxes	13,307	561	(250)	0	311
Tax benefit from equity awards, including transfer pricing adjustments	0	934	0	0	934
Balances as of September 24, 2011	929,277	$13,331	$ 62,841	$ 443	$76,615

See accompanying Notes to Consolidated Financial Statements.

CONSOLIDATED STATEMENTS OF CASH FLOWS
(In millions)

Three years ended September 24, 2011	2011	2010	2009
Cash and cash equivalents, beginning of the year	$ 11,261	$ 5,263	$ 11,875
Operating activities:			
Net income	25,922	14,013	8,235
Adjustments to reconcile net income to cash generated by operating activities:			
Depreciation, amortization and accretion	1,814	1,027	734
Share-based compensation expense	1,168	879	710
Deferred income tax expense	2,868	1,440	1,040
Changes in operating assets and liabilities:			
Accounts receivable, net	143	(2,142)	(939)
Inventories	275	(596)	54
Vendor non-trade receivables	(1,934)	(2,718)	586
Other current and non-current assets	(1,391)	(1,610)	(713)
Accounts payable	2,515	6,307	92
Deferred revenue	1,654	1,217	521
Other current and non-current liabilities	4,495	778	(161)
Cash generated by operating activities	37,529	18,595	10,159
Investing activities:			
Purchases of marketable securities	(102,317)	(57,793)	(46,724)
Proceeds from maturities of marketable securities	20,437	24,930	19,790
Proceeds from sales of marketable securities	49,416	21,788	10,888
Payments made in connection with business acquisitions, net of cash acquired	(244)	(638)	0
Payments for acquisition of property, plant and equipment	(4,260)	(2,005)	(1,144)
Payments for acquisition of intangible assets	(3,192)	(116)	(69)
Other	(259)	(20)	(175)
Cash used in investing activities	(40,419)	(13,854)	(17,434)
Financing activities:			
Proceeds from issuance of common stock	831	912	475
Excess tax benefits from equity awards	1,133	751	270
Taxes paid related to net share settlement of equity awards	(520)	(406)	(82)
Cash generated by financing activities	1,444	1,257	663
(Decrease)/increase in cash and cash equivalents	(1,446)	5,998	(6,612)
Cash and cash equivalents, end of the year	$ 9,815	$ 11,261	$ 5,263
Supplemental cash flow disclosure:			
Cash paid for income taxes, net	$ 3,338	$ 2,697	$ 2,997

See accompanying Notes to Consolidated Financial Statements.

Appendix B | Specimen Financial Statements: PepsiCo, Inc.

PepsiCo, Inc. is a world leader in convenient snacks, foods, and beverages. The following are PepsiCo's financial statements as presented in its 2011 annual report. To access PepsiCo's complete annual report, including notes to the financial statements, follow these steps:

1. Go to **www.pepsico.com**.
2. Select Annual Reports & Proxy Information under the Investors tab.
3. Select the 2011 Annual Report.
4. An index to the company's financials is provided on page 23. The Notes to Consolidated Financial Statements, for example, begin on page 56.

Consolidated Statement of Income

Fiscal years ended December 31, 2011, December 25, 2010 and December 26, 2009
(in millions except per share amounts)

	2011	2010	2009
Net Revenue	$66,504	$57,838	$43,232
Cost of sales	31,593	26,575	20,099
Selling, general and administrative expenses	25,145	22,814	15,026
Amortization of intangible assets	133	117	63
Operating Profit	9,633	8,332	8,044
Bottling equity income	–	735	365
Interest expense	(856)	(903)	(397)
Interest income and other	57	68	67
Income before income taxes	8,834	8,232	8,079
Provision for income taxes	2,372	1,894	2,100
Net income	6,462	6,338	5,979
Less: Net income attributable to noncontrolling interests	19	18	33
Net Income Attributable to PepsiCo	$ 6,443	$ 6,320	$ 5,946
Net Income Attributable to PepsiCo per Common Share			
Basic	$ 4.08	$ 3.97	$ 3.81
Diluted	$ 4.03	$ 3.91	$ 3.77
Weighted-average common shares outstanding			
Basic	1,576	1,590	1,558
Diluted	1,597	1,614	1,577
Cash dividends declared per common share	$ 2.025	$ 1.89	$ 1.775

See accompanying notes to consolidated financial statements

Consolidated Statement of Cash Flows

Fiscal years ended December 31, 2011, December 25, 2010 and December 26, 2009
(in millions)

	2011	2010	2009
Operating Activities			
Net income	$ 6,462	$ 6,338	$ 5,979
Depreciation and amortization	2,737	2,327	1,635
Stock-based compensation expense	326	299	227
Restructuring and impairment charges	383	–	36
Cash payments for restructuring charges	(31)	(31)	(196)
Merger and integration costs	329	808	50
Cash payments for merger and integration costs	(377)	(385)	(49)
Gain on previously held equity interests in PBG and PAS	–	(958)	–
Asset write-off	–	145	–
Non-cash foreign exchange loss related to Venezuela devaluation	–	120	–
Excess tax benefits from share-based payment arrangements	(70)	(107)	(42)
Pension and retiree medical plan contributions	(349)	(1,734)	(1,299)
Pension and retiree medical plan expenses	571	453	423
Bottling equity income, net of dividends	–	42	(235)
Deferred income taxes and other tax charges and credits	495	500	284
Change in accounts and notes receivable	(666)	(268)	188
Change in inventories	(331)	276	17
Change in prepaid expenses and other current assets	(27)	144	(127)
Change in accounts payable and other current liabilities	520	488	(133)
Change in income taxes payable	(340)	123	319
Other, net	(688)	(132)	(281)
Net Cash Provided by Operating Activities	8,944	8,448	6,796
Investing Activities			
Capital spending	(3,339)	(3,253)	(2,128)
Sales of property, plant and equipment	84	81	58
Acquisitions of PBG and PAS, net of cash and cash equivalents acquired	–	(2,833)	–
Acquisition of manufacturing and distribution rights from DPSG	–	(900)	–
Acquisition of WBD, net of cash and cash equivalents acquired	(2,428)	–	–
Investment in WBD	(164)	(463)	–
Other acquisitions and investments in noncontrolled affiliates	(601)	(83)	(500)
Divestitures	780	12	99
Cash restricted for pending acquisitions	–	–	15
Short-term investments, by original maturity			
More than three months—purchases	–	(12)	(29)
More than three months—maturities	21	29	71
Three months or less, net	45	(229)	13
Other investing, net	(16)	(17)	–
Net Cash Used for Investing Activities	(5,618)	(7,668)	(2,401)
Financing Activities			
Proceeds from issuances of long-term debt	$ 3,000	$ 6,451	$ 1,057
Payments of long-term debt	(1,596)	(59)	(226)
Debt repurchase	(771)	(500)	–
Short-term borrowings, by original maturity			
More than three months—proceeds	523	227	26
More than three months—payments	(559)	(96)	(81)
Three months or less, net	339	2,351	(963)
Cash dividends paid	(3,157)	(2,978)	(2,732)
Share repurchases—common	(2,489)	(4,978)	–
Share repurchases—preferred	(7)	(5)	(7)
Proceeds from exercises of stock options	945	1,038	413
Excess tax benefits from share-based payment arrangements	70	107	42
Acquisition of noncontrolling interests	(1,406)	(159)	–
Other financing	(27)	(13)	(26)
Net Cash (Used for)/Provided by Financing Activities	(5,135)	1,386	(2,497)
Effect of exchange rate changes on cash and cash equivalents	(67)	(166)	(19)
Net (Decrease)/Increase in Cash and Cash Equivalents	(1,876)	2,000	1,879
Cash and Cash Equivalents, Beginning of Year	5,943	3,943	2,064
Cash and Cash Equivalents, End of Year	$ 4,067	$ 5,943	$ 3,943
Non-cash activity:			
Issuance of common stock and equity awards in connection with our acquisitions of PBG and PAS, as reflected in investing and financing activities	–	$ 4,451	–

See accompanying notes to consolidated financial statements.

Consolidated Balance Sheet

December 31, 2011 and December 25, 2010 (in millions except per share amounts)	2011	2010
ASSETS		
Current Assets		
Cash and cash equivalents	$ 4,067	$ 5,943
Short-term investments	358	426
Accounts and notes receivable, net	6,912	6,323
Inventories	3,827	3,372
Prepaid expenses and other current assets	2,277	1,505
Total Current Assets	17,441	17,569
Property, Plant and Equipment, net	19,698	19,058
Amortizable Intangible Assets, net	1,888	2,025
Goodwill	16,800	14,661
Other nonamortizable intangible assets	14,557	11,783
Nonamortizable Intangible Assets	31,357	26,444
Investments in Noncontrolled Affiliates	1,477	1,368
Other Assets	1,021	1,689
Total Assets	$ 72,882	$ 68,153
LIABILITIES AND EQUITY		
Current Liabilities		
Short-term obligations	$ 6,205	$ 4,898
Accounts payable and other current liabilities	11,757	10,923
Income taxes payable	192	71
Total Current Liabilities	18,154	15,892
Long-Term Debt Obligations	20,568	19,999
Other Liabilities	8,266	6,729
Deferred Income Taxes	4,995	4,057
Total Liabilities	51,983	46,677
Commitments and Contingencies		
Preferred Stock, no par value	41	41
Repurchased Preferred Stock	(157)	(150)
PepsiCo Common Shareholders' Equity		
Common stock, par value 1²/₃¢ per share (authorized 3,600 shares, issued 1,865 shares)	31	31
Capital in excess of par value	4,461	4,527
Retained earnings	40,316	37,090
Accumulated other comprehensive loss	(6,229)	(3,630)
Repurchased common stock, at cost (301 and 284 shares, respectively)	(17,875)	(16,745)
Total PepsiCo Common Shareholders' Equity	20,704	21,273
Noncontrolling interests	311	312
Total Equity	20,899	21,476
Total Liabilities and Equity	$ 72,882	$ 68,153

See accompanying notes to consolidated financial statements

Consolidated Statement of Equity

Fiscal years ended December 31, 2011, December 25, 2010 and December 26, 2009
(in millions)

	2011		2010		2009	
	Shares	Amount	Shares	Amount	Shares	Amount
Preferred Stock	0.8	$ 41	0.8	$ 41	0.8	$ 41
Repurchased Preferred Stock						
Balance, beginning of year	(0.6)	(150)	(0.6)	(145)	(0.5)	(138)
Redemptions	(–)	(7)	(–)	(5)	(0.1)	(7)
Balance, end of year	(0.6)	(157)	(0.6)	(150)	(0.6)	(145)
Common Stock						
Balance, beginning of year	1,865	31	1,782	30	1,782	30
Shares issued in connection with our acquisitions of PBG and PAS	–	–	83	1	–	–
Balance, end of year	1,865	31	1,865	31	1,782	30
Capital in Excess of Par Value						
Balance, beginning of year		4,527		250		351
Stock-based compensation expense		326		299		227
Stock option exercises/RSUs converted(a)		(361)		(500)		(292)
Withholding tax on RSUs converted		(56)		(68)		(36)
Equity issued in connection with our acquisitions of PBG and PAS		–		4,451		–
Other		25		95		–
Balance, end of year		4,461		4,527		250
Retained Earnings						
Balance, beginning of year		37,090		33,805		30,638
Net income attributable to PepsiCo		6,443		6,320		5,946
Cash dividends declared — common		(3,192)		(3,028)		(2,768)
Cash dividends declared — preferred		(1)		(1)		(2)
Cash dividends declared — RSUs		(24)		(12)		(9)
Other		–		6		–
Balance, end of year		40,316		37,090		33,805
Accumulated Other Comprehensive Loss						
Balance, beginning of year		(3,630)		(3,794)		(4,694)
Currency translation adjustment		(1,529)		312		800
Cash flow hedges, net of tax:						
Net derivative losses		(83)		(111)		(55)
Reclassification of net losses to net income		14		53		28
Pension and retiree medical, net of tax:						
Net pension and retiree medical (losses)/gains		(1,110)		(280)		21
Reclassification of net losses to net income		133		166		86
Unrealized (losses)/gains on securities, net of tax		(8)		23		20
Other		(16)		1		–
Balance, end of year		(6,229)		(3,630)		(3,794)
Repurchased Common Stock						
Balance, beginning of year	(284)	(16,745)	(217)	(13,383)	(229)	(14,122)
Share repurchases	(39)	(2,489)	(76)	(4,978)	–	–
Stock option exercises	20	1,251	24	1,487	11	649
Other	2	108	(15)	129	1	90
Balance, end of year	(301)	(17,875)	(284)	(16,745)	(217)	(13,383)
Total Common Shareholders' Equity		20,704		21,273		16,908
Noncontrolling Interests						
Balance, beginning of year		312		638		476
Net income attributable to noncontrolling interests		19		18		33
Distributions to noncontrolling interests, net		(24)		(6)		–
Currency translation adjustment		65		(13)		(12)
Acquisitions and divestitures		(57)		(326)		150
Other, net		(4)		1		(9)
Balance, end of year		311		312		638
Total Equity		$ 20,899		$ 21,476		$ 17,442

(a) Includes total tax benefits of $43 million in 2011, $75 million in 2010 and $31 million in 2009.

(Continued on following page)

Consolidated Statement of Equity
(continued)

Fiscal years ended December 31, 2011, December 25, 2010 and December 26, 2009
(in millions)

	2011	2010	2009
Comprehensive Income			
Net income	$ 6,462	$6,338	$5,979
Other comprehensive (loss)/income			
Currency translation adjustment	(1,464)	299	788
Cash flow hedges, net of tax	(69)	(58)	(27)
Pension and retiree medical, net of tax:			
Net prior service (cost)/credit	(10)	22	(3)
Net (losses)/gains	(967)	(136)	110
Unrealized (losses)/gains on securities, net of tax	(8)	23	20
Other	(16)	1	–
	(2,534)	151	888
Comprehensive income	3,928	6,489	6,867
Comprehensive income attributable to noncontrolling interests	(84)	(5)	(21)
Comprehensive Income Attributable to PepsiCo	$ 3,844	$6,484	$6,846

See accompanying notes to consolidated financial statements

Appendix C | Specimen Financial Statements: The Coca-Cola Company

The Coca-Cola Company is a global leader in the beverage industry. It offers hundreds of brands, including soft drinks, fruit juices, sports drinks and other beverages in more than 200 countries. The following are Coca-Cola's financial statements as presented in its 2011 annual report. To access Coca-Cola's complete annual report, including notes to the financial statements, follow these steps:

1. Go to **www.coca-colacompany.com**.
2. Select the Investors link, and then select Annual & Other Reports under Financial Reports & Information.
3. Select the 2011 Annual Report on Form 10-K.
4. Use the Bookmarks section on the left to find specific information. The Notes to Consolidated Financial Statements, for example, begin on page 82.

THE COCA-COLA COMPANY AND SUBSIDIARIES
CONSOLIDATED STATEMENTS OF INCOME

Year Ended December 31,	2011	2010	2009
(In millions except per share data)			
NET OPERATING REVENUES	**$ 46,542**	$ 35,119	$ 30,990
Cost of goods sold	**18,216**	12,693	11,088
GROSS PROFIT	**28,326**	22,426	19,902
Selling, general and administrative expenses	**17,440**	13,158	11,358
Other operating charges	**732**	819	313
OPERATING INCOME	**10,154**	8,449	8,231
Interest income	**483**	317	249
Interest expense	**417**	733	355
Equity income (loss) — net	**690**	1,025	781
Other income (loss) — net	**529**	5,185	40
INCOME BEFORE INCOME TAXES	**11,439**	14,243	8,946
Income taxes	**2,805**	2,384	2,040
CONSOLIDATED NET INCOME	**8,634**	11,859	6,906
Less: Net income attributable to noncontrolling interests	**62**	50	82
NET INCOME ATTRIBUTABLE TO SHAREOWNERS OF THE COCA-COLA COMPANY	**$ 8,572**	$ 11,809	$ 6,824
BASIC NET INCOME PER SHARE[1]	**$ 3.75**	$ 5.12	$ 2.95
DILUTED NET INCOME PER SHARE[1]	**$ 3.69**	$ 5.06	$ 2.93
AVERAGE SHARES OUTSTANDING	**2,284**	2,308	2,314
Effect of dilutive securities	**39**	25	15
AVERAGE SHARES OUTSTANDING ASSUMING DILUTION	**2,323**	2,333	2,329

[1] Basic net income per share and diluted net income per share are calculated based on net income attributable to shareowners of The Coca-Cola Company.

Refer to Notes to Consolidated Financial Statements.

THE COCA-COLA COMPANY AND SUBSIDIARIES

CONSOLIDATED BALANCE SHEETS

December 31,	2011	2010
(In millions except par value)		
ASSETS		
CURRENT ASSETS		
Cash and cash equivalents	$ 12,803	$ 8,517
Short-term investments	1,088	2,682
TOTAL CASH, CASH EQUIVALENTS AND SHORT-TERM INVESTMENTS	13,891	11,199
Marketable securities	144	138
Trade accounts receivable, less allowances of $83 and $48, respectively	4,920	4,430
Inventories	3,092	2,650
Prepaid expenses and other assets	3,450	3,162
TOTAL CURRENT ASSETS	25,497	21,579
EQUITY METHOD INVESTMENTS	7,233	6,954
OTHER INVESTMENTS, PRINCIPALLY BOTTLING COMPANIES	1,141	631
OTHER ASSETS	3,495	2,121
PROPERTY, PLANT AND EQUIPMENT — net	14,939	14,727
TRADEMARKS WITH INDEFINITE LIVES	6,430	6,356
BOTTLERS' FRANCHISE RIGHTS WITH INDEFINITE LIVES	7,770	7,511
GOODWILL	12,219	11,665
OTHER INTANGIBLE ASSETS	1,250	1,377
TOTAL ASSETS	$ 79,974	$ 72,921
LIABILITIES AND EQUITY		
CURRENT LIABILITIES		
Accounts payable and accrued expenses	$ 9,009	$ 8,859
Loans and notes payable	12,871	8,100
Current maturities of long-term debt	2,041	1,276
Accrued income taxes	362	273
TOTAL CURRENT LIABILITIES	24,283	18,508
LONG-TERM DEBT	13,656	14,041
OTHER LIABILITIES	5,420	4,794
DEFERRED INCOME TAXES	4,694	4,261
THE COCA-COLA COMPANY SHAREOWNERS' EQUITY		
Common stock, $0.25 par value; Authorized — 5,600 shares;		
Issued — 3,520 and 3,520 shares, respectively	880	880
Capital surplus	11,212	10,057
Reinvested earnings	53,550	49,278
Accumulated other comprehensive income (loss)	(2,703)	(1,450)
Treasury stock, at cost — 1,257 and 1,228 shares, respectively	(31,304)	(27,762)
EQUITY ATTRIBUTABLE TO SHAREOWNERS OF THE COCA-COLA COMPANY	31,635	31,003
EQUITY ATTRIBUTABLE TO NONCONTROLLING INTERESTS	286	314
TOTAL EQUITY	31,921	31,317
TOTAL LIABILITIES AND EQUITY	$ 79,974	$ 72,921

Refer to Notes to Consolidated Financial Statements.

THE COCA-COLA COMPANY AND SUBSIDIARIES
CONSOLIDATED STATEMENTS OF CASH FLOWS

Year Ended December 31,	2011	2010	2009
(In millions)			
OPERATING ACTIVITIES			
Consolidated net income	$ 8,634	$ 11,859	$ 6,906
Depreciation and amortization	1,954	1,443	1,236
Stock-based compensation expense	354	380	241
Deferred income taxes	1,028	617	353
Equity (income) loss — net of dividends	(269)	(671)	(359)
Foreign currency adjustments	7	151	61
Significant (gains) losses on sales of assets — net	(220)	(645)	(43)
Other significant (gains) losses — net	—	(4,713)	—
Other operating charges	214	264	134
Other items	(335)	477	221
Net change in operating assets and liabilities	(1,893)	370	(564)
Net cash provided by operating activities	9,474	9,532	8,186
INVESTING ACTIVITIES			
Purchases of short-term investments	(4,057)	(4,579)	(2,130)
Proceeds from disposals of short-term investments	5,647	4,032	—
Acquisitions and investments	(977)	(2,511)	(300)
Purchases of other investments	(787)	(132)	(22)
Proceeds from disposals of bottling companies and other investments	562	972	240
Purchases of property, plant and equipment	(2,920)	(2,215)	(1,993)
Proceeds from disposals of property, plant and equipment	101	134	104
Other investing activities	(93)	(106)	(48)
Net cash provided by (used in) investing activities	(2,524)	(4,405)	(4,149)
FINANCING ACTIVITIES			
Issuances of debt	27,495	15,251	14,689
Payments of debt	(22,530)	(13,403)	(12,326)
Issuances of stock	1,569	1,666	664
Purchases of stock for treasury	(4,513)	(2,961)	(1,518)
Dividends	(4,300)	(4,068)	(3,800)
Other financing activities	45	50	(2)
Net cash provided by (used in) financing activities	(2,234)	(3,465)	(2,293)
EFFECT OF EXCHANGE RATE CHANGES ON CASH AND CASH EQUIVALENTS	(430)	(166)	576
CASH AND CASH EQUIVALENTS			
Net increase (decrease) during the year	4,286	1,496	2,320
Balance at beginning of year	8,517	7,021	4,701
Balance at end of year	$ 12,803	$ 8,517	$ 7,021

Refer to Notes to Consolidated Financial Statements.

THE COCA-COLA COMPANY AND SUBSIDIARIES
CONSOLIDATED STATEMENTS OF SHAREOWNERS' EQUITY

Year Ended December 31,	2011	2010	2009
(In millions except per share data)			
EQUITY ATTRIBUTABLE TO SHAREOWNERS OF THE COCA-COLA COMPANY			
NUMBER OF COMMON SHARES OUTSTANDING			
Balance at beginning of year	2,292	2,303	2,312
Purchases of treasury stock	(63)	(49)	(26)
Treasury stock issued to employees related to stock compensation plans	34	38	17
Balance at end of year	2,263	2,292	2,303
COMMON STOCK	$ 880	$ 880	$ 880
CAPITAL SURPLUS			
Balance at beginning of year	10,057	8,537	7,966
Stock issued to employees related to stock compensation plans	724	855	339
Replacement share-based awards issued in connection with an acquisition	—	237	—
Tax benefit (charge) from employees' stock option and restricted stock plans	79	48	(6)
Stock-based compensation	354	380	238
Other activities	(2)	—	—
Balance at end of year	11,212	10,057	8,537
REINVESTED EARNINGS			
Balance at beginning of year	49,278	41,537	38,513
Net income attributable to shareowners of The Coca-Cola Company	8,572	11,809	6,824
Dividends (per share — $1.88, $1.76 and $1.64 in 2011, 2010 and 2009, respectively)	(4,300)	(4,068)	(3,800)
Balance at end of year	53,550	49,278	41,537
ACCUMULATED OTHER COMPREHENSIVE INCOME (LOSS)			
Balance at beginning of year	(1,450)	(757)	(2,674)
Net foreign currency translation adjustment	(640)	(935)	1,824
Net gain (loss) on derivatives	145	(120)	34
Net change in unrealized gain on available-for-sale securities	(7)	102	(52)
Net change in pension and other benefit liabilities	(751)	260	111
Net other comprehensive income (loss)	(1,253)	(693)	1,917
Balance at end of year	(2,703)	(1,450)	(757)
TREASURY STOCK			
Balance at beginning of year	(27,762)	(25,398)	(24,213)
Stock issued to employees related to stock compensation plans	830	824	333
Purchases of treasury stock	(4,372)	(3,188)	(1,518)
Balance at end of year	(31,304)	(27,762)	(25,398)
TOTAL EQUITY ATTRIBUTABLE TO SHAREOWNERS OF THE COCA-COLA COMPANY	$ 31,635	$ 31,003	$ 24,799
EQUITY ATTRIBUTABLE TO NONCONTROLLING INTERESTS			
Balance at beginning of year	$ 314	$ 547	$ 390
Net income attributable to noncontrolling interests	62	50	82
Net foreign currency translation adjustment	(52)	(12)	49
Dividends paid to noncontrolling interests	(38)	(32)	(14)
Contributions by noncontrolling interests	—	1	40
Increase due to business combinations	—	13	—
Deconsolidation of certain variable interest entities	—	(253)	—
TOTAL EQUITY ATTRIBUTABLE TO NONCONTROLLING INTERESTS	$ 286	$ 314	$ 547
COMPREHENSIVE INCOME			
Consolidated net income	$ 8,634	$ 11,859	$ 6,906
Consolidated net other comprehensive income (loss)	(1,305)	(705)	1,966
CONSOLIDATED COMPREHENSIVE INCOME	$ 7,329	$ 11,154	$ 8,872

Refer to Notes to Consolidated Financial Statements.

Amazon.com, Inc. is the world's largest online retailer. It also produces consumer electronics—notably the Kindle e-book reader and the Kindle Fire Tablet computer—and is a major provider of cloud computing services. The following are Amazon's financial statements as presented in the company's 2011 annual report. To access Amazon's complete annual report, including notes to the financial statements, follow these steps:

1. Go to **www.amazon.com**.

2. Select the Investor Relations link at the bottom of the page and then select the 2011 Annual Report under Annual Reports and Proxies.

3. Use the Bookmarks section on the left to find specific information. The Notes to Consolidated Financial Statements, for example, begin on page 40.

AMAZON.COM, INC.

CONSOLIDATED STATEMENTS OF CASH FLOWS

(in millions)

	Year Ended December 31,		
	2011	2010	2009
CASH AND CASH EQUIVALENTS, BEGINNING OF PERIOD	$ 3,777	$ 3,444	$ 2,769
OPERATING ACTIVITIES:			
Net income	631	1,152	902
Adjustments to reconcile net income to net cash from operating activities:			
Depreciation of fixed assets, including internal-use software and website development, and other amortization	1,083	568	378
Stock-based compensation	557	424	341
Other operating expense (income), net	154	106	103
Losses (gains) on sales of marketable securities, net	(4)	(2)	(4)
Other expense (income), net	(56)	(79)	(15)
Deferred income taxes	136	4	81
Excess tax benefits from stock-based compensation	(62)	(259)	(105)
Changes in operating assets and liabilities:			
Inventories	(1,777)	(1,019)	(531)
Accounts receivable, net and other	(866)	(295)	(481)
Accounts payable	2,997	2,373	1,859
Accrued expenses and other	1,067	740	300
Additions to unearned revenue	1,064	687	1,054
Amortization of previously unearned revenue	(1,021)	(905)	(589)
Net cash provided by operating activities	3,903	3,495	3,293
INVESTING ACTIVITIES:			
Purchases of fixed assets, including internal-use software and website development	(1,811)	(979)	(373)
Acquisitions, net of cash acquired, and other	(705)	(352)	(40)
Sales and maturities of marketable securities and other investments	6,843	4,250	1,966
Purchases of marketable securities and other investments	(6,257)	(6,279)	(3,890)
Net cash used in investing activities	(1,930)	(3,360)	(2,337)
FINANCING ACTIVITIES:			
Excess tax benefits from stock-based compensation	62	259	105
Common stock repurchased	(277)	—	—
Proceeds from long-term debt and other	177	143	87
Repayments of long-term debt, capital lease, and finance lease obligations	(444)	(221)	(472)
Net cash provided by (used in) financing activities	(482)	181	(280)
Foreign-currency effect on cash and cash equivalents	1	17	(1)
Net increase in cash and cash equivalents	1,492	333	675
CASH AND CASH EQUIVALENTS, END OF PERIOD	$ 5,269	$ 3,777	$ 3,444
SUPPLEMENTAL CASH FLOW INFORMATION:			
Cash paid for interest on long term debt	$ 14	$ 11	$ 32
Cash paid for income taxes (net of refunds)	33	75	48
Fixed assets acquired under capital leases	753	405	147
Fixed assets acquired under build-to-suit leases	259	172	188

See accompanying notes to consolidated financial statements.

AMAZON.COM, INC.

CONSOLIDATED STATEMENTS OF OPERATIONS
(in millions, except per share data)

	Year Ended December 31,		
	2011	2010	2009
Net product sales	$42,000	$30,792	$22,273
Net services sales	6,077	3,412	2,236
Total net sales	48,077	34,204	24,509
Operating expenses (1):			
Cost of sales	37,288	26,561	18,978
Fulfillment	4,576	2,898	2,052
Marketing	1,630	1,029	680
Technology and content	2,909	1,734	1,240
General and administrative	658	470	328
Other operating expense (income), net	154	106	102
Total operating expenses	47,215	32,798	23,380
Income from operations	862	1,406	1,129
Interest income	61	51	37
Interest expense	(65)	(39)	(34)
Other income (expense), net	76	79	29
Total non-operating income (expense)	72	91	32
Income before income taxes	934	1,497	1,161
Provision for income taxes	(291)	(352)	(253)
Equity-method investment activity, net of tax	(12)	7	(6)
Net income	$ 631	$ 1,152	$ 902
Basic earnings per share	$ 1.39	$ 2.58	$ 2.08
Diluted earnings per share	$ 1.37	$ 2.53	$ 2.04
Weighted average shares used in computation of earnings per share:			
Basic	453	447	433
Diluted	461	456	442

---

(1) Includes stock-based compensation as follows:

Fulfillment	$ 133	$ 90	$ 79
Marketing	39	27	20
Technology and content	292	223	182
General and administrative	93	84	60

See accompanying notes to consolidated financial statements.

AMAZON.COM, INC.

CONSOLIDATED BALANCE SHEETS
(in millions, except per share data)

	December 31,	
	2011	**2010**
ASSETS		
Current assets:		
Cash and cash equivalents	$ 5,269	$ 3,777
Marketable securities	4,307	4,985
Inventories	4,992	3,202
Accounts receivable, net and other	2,571	1,587
Deferred tax assets	351	196
Total current assets	17,490	13,747
Fixed assets, net	4,417	2,414
Deferred tax assets	28	22
Goodwill	1,955	1,349
Other assets	1,388	1,265
Total assets	$25,278	$18,797
LIABILITIES AND STOCKHOLDERS' EQUITY		
Current liabilities:		
Accounts payable	$11,145	$ 8,051
Accrued expenses and other	3,751	2,321
Total current liabilities	14,896	10,372
Long-term liabilities	2,625	1,561
Commitments and contingencies		
Stockholders' equity:		
Preferred stock, $0.01 par value:		
Authorized shares — 500		
Issued and outstanding shares — none	0	0
Common stock, $0.01 par value:		
Authorized shares — 5,000		
Issued shares — 473 and 468		
Outstanding shares — 455 and 451	5	5
Treasury stock, at cost	(877)	(600)
Additional paid-in capital	6,990	6,325
Accumulated other comprehensive loss	(316)	(190)
Retained earnings	1,955	1,324
Total stockholders' equity	7,757	6,864
Total liabilities and stockholders' equity	$25,278	$18,797

See accompanying notes to consolidated financial statements.

AMAZON.COM, INC.

CONSOLIDATED STATEMENTS OF STOCKHOLDERS' EQUITY

(in millions)

	Common Stock Shares	Common Stock Amount	Treasury Stock	Additional Paid-In Capital	Accumulated Other Comprehensive Income (Loss)	Retained Earnings (Accumulated Deficit)	Total Stockholders' Equity
Balance at December 31, 2008	428	$ 4	$(600)	$4,121	$(123)	$ (730)	$2,672
Net income	—	—	—	—	—	902	902
Foreign currency translation gains, net of tax	—	—	—	—	62	—	62
Change in unrealized gains on available-for-sale securities, net of tax	—	—	—	—	4	—	4
Amortization of unrealized loss on terminated Euro Currency Swap, net of tax	—	—	—	—	1	—	1
Comprehensive income							969
Exercise of common stock options	7	—	—	19	—	—	19
Issuance of common stock for acquisition activity	9	1	—	1,144	—	—	1,145
Excess tax benefits from stock-based compensation	—	—	—	103	—	—	103
Stock-based compensation and issuance of employee benefit plan stock	—	—	—	349	—	—	349
Balance at December 31, 2009	444	5	(600)	5,736	(56)	172	5,257
Net income	—	—	—	—	—	1,152	1,152
Foreign currency translation gains, net of tax	—	—	—	—	(137)	—	(137)
Change in unrealized gains on available-for-sale securities, net of tax	—	—	—	—	3	—	3
Comprehensive income							1,018
Exercise of common stock options	7	—	—	16	—	—	16
Excess tax benefits from stock-based compensation	—	—	—	145	—	—	145
Stock-based compensation and issuance of employee benefit plan stock	—	—	—	428	—	—	428
Balance at December 31, 2010	451	5	(600)	6,325	(190)	1,324	6,864
Net income	—	—	—	—	—	631	631
Foreign currency translation gains, net of tax	—	—	—	—	(123)	—	(123)
Change in unrealized gains on available-for-sale securities, net of tax	—	—	—	—	(3)	—	(3)
Comprehensive income							505
Exercise of common stock options	5	—	—	7	—	—	7
Repurchase of common stock	(1)	—	(277)	—	—	—	(277)
Excess tax benefits from stock-based compensation	—	—	—	62	—	—	62
Stock-based compensation and issuance of employee benefit plan stock	—	—	—	569	—	—	569
Issuance of common stock for acquisition activity	—	—	—	27	—	—	27
Balance at December 31, 2011	455	$ 5	$(877)	$6,990	$(316)	$1,955	$7,757

See accompanying notes to consolidated financial statements.

Specimen Financial Statements: Wal-Mart Stores, Inc.

In 2012, Wal-Mart Stores, Inc. celebrated "50 years of helping customers save money and live better." The following are Wal-Mart's financial statements as presented in the company's 2012 annual report. To access Wal-Mart's complete annual report, including notes to the financial statements, follow these steps:

1. Go to **http://corporate.walmart.com**.
2. Select Annual Reports under the Investors tab.
3. Select 2010–2012 under Annual Report Archives, and then select the 2012 Annual Report (Wal-Mart's fiscal year ends January 31).
4. The Notes to Consolidated Financial Statements begin on page 38.

Consolidated Statements of Income

	Fiscal Years Ended January 31,		
(Amounts in millions except per share data)	2012	2011	2010
Revenues:			
Net sales	$443,854	$418,952	$405,132
Membership and other income	3,096	2,897	2,953
	446,950	421,849	408,085
Costs and expenses:			
Cost of sales	335,127	314,946	304,106
Operating, selling, general and administrative expenses	85,265	81,361	79,977
Operating income	26,558	25,542	24,002
Interest:			
Debt	2,034	1,928	1,787
Capital leases	288	277	278
Interest income	(162)	(201)	(181)
Interest, net	2,160	2,004	1,884
Income from continuing operations before income taxes	24,398	23,538	22,118
Provision for income taxes:			
Current	6,742	6,703	7,643
Deferred	1,202	876	(487)
	7,944	7,579	7,156
Income from continuing operations	16,454	15,959	14,962
Income (loss) from discontinued operations, net of tax	(67)	1,034	(79)
Consolidated net income	16,387	16,993	14,883
Less consolidated net income attributable to noncontrolling interest	(688)	(604)	(513)
Consolidated net income attributable to Walmart	$ 15,699	$ 16,389	$ 14,370
Basic net income per common share:			
Basic income per common share from continuing operations attributable to Walmart	$ 4.56	$ 4.20	$ 3.74
Basic income (loss) per common share from discontinued operations attributable to Walmart	(0.02)	0.28	(0.02)
Basic net income per common share attributable to Walmart	$ 4.54	$ 4.48	$ 3.72
Diluted net income per common share:			
Diluted income per common share from continuing operations attributable to Walmart	$ 4.54	$ 4.18	$ 3.73
Diluted income (loss) per common share from discontinued operations attributable to Walmart	(0.02)	0.29	(0.02)
Diluted net income per common share attributable to Walmart	$ 4.52	$ 4.47	$ 3.71
Weighted-average common shares outstanding:			
Basic	3,460	3,656	3,866
Diluted	3,474	3,670	3,877
Dividends declared per common share	$ 1.46	$ 1.21	$ 1.09

See accompanying notes.

Consolidated Balance Sheets

	As of January 31,	
(Amounts in millions except per share data)	2012	2011
ASSETS		
Current assets:		
Cash and cash equivalents	$ 6,550	$ 7,395
Receivables, net	5,937	5,089
Inventories	40,714	36,437
Prepaid expenses and other	1,685	2,960
Current assets of discontinued operations	89	131
Total current assets	54,975	52,012
Property and equipment:		
Property and equipment	155,002	148,584
Less accumulated depreciation	(45,399)	(43,486)
Property and equipment, net	109,603	105,098
Property under capital lease:		
Property under capital lease	5,936	5,905
Less accumulated amortization	(3,215)	(3,125)
Property under capital lease, net	2,721	2,780
Goodwill	20,651	16,763
Other assets and deferred charges	5,456	4,129
Total assets	$193,406	$180,782
LIABILITIES AND EQUITY		
Current liabilities:		
Short-term borrowings	$ 4,047	$ 1,031
Accounts payable	36,608	33,676
Accrued liabilities	18,154	18,701
Accrued income taxes	1,164	157
Long-term debt due within one year	1,975	4,655
Obligations under capital leases due within one year	326	336
Current liabilities of discontinued operations	26	47
Total current liabilities	62,300	58,603
Long-term debt	44,070	40,692
Long-term obligations under capital leases	3,009	3,150
Deferred income taxes and other	7,862	6,682
Redeemable noncontrolling interest	404	408
Commitments and contingencies		
Equity:		
Preferred stock ($0.10 par value; 100 shares authorized, none issued)	—	—
Common stock ($0.10 par value; 11,000 shares authorized, 3,418 and 3,516 issued and outstanding at January 31, 2012 and 2011, respectively)	342	352
Capital in excess of par value	3,692	3,577
Retained earnings	68,691	63,967
Accumulated other comprehensive income (loss)	(1,410)	646
Total Walmart shareholders' equity	71,315	68,542
Noncontrolling interest	4,446	2,705
Total equity	75,761	71,247
Total liabilities and equity	$193,406	$180,782

See accompanying notes.

Consolidated Statements of Shareholders' Equity

(Amounts in millions, except per share data)	Common Stock Shares	Common Stock Amount	Capital in Excess of Par Value	Retained Earnings	Accumulated Other Comprehensive Income (Loss)	Total Walmart Shareholders' Equity	Noncontrolling Interest	Total Equity
Balances — February 1, 2009	3,925	$ 393	$3,920	$ 63,344	$(2,688)	$ 64,969	$1,794	$ 66,763
Consolidated net income (excludes redeemable noncontrolling interest)	—	—	—	14,370	—	14,370	499	14,869
Other comprehensive income	—	—	—	—	2,618	2,618	64	2,682
Cash dividends ($1.09 per share)	—	—	—	(4,217)	—	(4,217)	—	(4,217)
Purchase of Company stock	(145)	(15)	(246)	(7,136)	—	(7,397)	—	(7,397)
Purchase of redeemable noncontrolling interest	—	—	(288)	—	—	(288)	—	(288)
Other	6	—	417	(4)	—	413	(177)	236
Balances — January 31, 2010	3,786	378	3,803	66,357	(70)	70,468	2,180	72,648
Consolidated net income (excludes redeemable noncontrolling interest)	—	—	—	16,389	—	16,389	584	16,973
Other comprehensive income	—	—	—	—	716	716	162	878
Cash dividends ($1.21 per share)	—	—	—	(4,437)	—	(4,437)	—	(4,437)
Purchase of Company stock	(280)	(28)	(487)	(14,319)	—	(14,834)	—	(14,834)
Other	10	2	261	(23)	—	240	(221)	19
Balances — January 31, 2011	3,516	352	3,577	63,967	646	68,542	2,705	71,247
Consolidated net income (excludes redeemable noncontrolling interest)	—	—	—	15,699	—	15,699	627	16,326
Other comprehensive loss	—	—	—	—	(2,056)	(2,056)	(660)	(2,716)
Cash dividends ($1.46 per share)	—	—	—	(5,048)	—	(5,048)	—	(5,048)
Purchase of Company stock	(113)	(11)	(229)	(5,930)	—	(6,170)	—	(6,170)
Noncontrolling interest of acquired entity	—	—	—	—	—	—	1,988	1,988
Other	15	1	344	3	—	348	(214)	134
Balances — January 31, 2012	3,418	$ 342	$3,692	$ 68,691	$(1,410)	$ 71,315	$4,446	$ 75,761

See accompanying notes.

Consolidated Statements of Comprehensive Income

(Amounts in millions)	Fiscal Years Ended January 31, 2012	2011	2010
Consolidated net income:			
Consolidated net income [1]	$16,387	$16,993	$14,883
Other comprehensive income:			
Currency translation [2]	(2,758)	1,137	2,854
Net change in fair values of derivatives	(67)	(17)	94
Change in minimum pension liability	43	(145)	(220)
Total comprehensive income	13,605	17,968	17,611
Less amounts attributable to the noncontrolling interest:			
Consolidated net income [1]	(688)	(604)	(513)
Currency translation [2]	726	(259)	(110)
Amounts attributable to the noncontrolling interest	38	(863)	(623)
Comprehensive income attributable to Walmart	$13,643	$17,105	$16,988

(1) Includes $61 million, $20 million and $14 million in fiscal 2012, 2011 and 2010, respectively, related to the redeemable noncontrolling interest.

(2) Includes $(66) million, $97 million and $46 million in fiscal 2012, 2011 and 2010, respectively, related to the redeemable noncontrolling interest.

See accompanying notes.

Consolidated Statements of Cash Flows

	Fiscal Years Ended January 31,		
(Amounts in millions)	2012	2011	2010
Cash flows from operating activities:			
Consolidated net income	$ 16,387	$ 16,993	$ 14,883
Loss (income) from discontinued operations, net of tax	67	(1,034)	79
Income from continuing operations	16,454	15,959	14,962
Adjustments to reconcile income from continuing operations to net cash provided by operating activities:			
Depreciation and amortization	8,130	7,641	7,157
Deferred income taxes	1,050	651	(504)
Other operating activities	398	1,087	318
Changes in certain assets and liabilities, net of effects of acquisitions:			
Accounts receivable	(796)	(733)	(297)
Inventories	(3,727)	(3,205)	2,213
Accounts payable	2,687	2,676	1,052
Accrued liabilities	59	(433)	1,348
Net cash provided by operating activities	24,255	23,643	26,249
Cash flows from investing activities:			
Payments for property and equipment	(13,510)	(12,699)	(12,184)
Proceeds from disposal of property and equipment	580	489	1,002
Investments and business acquisitions, net of cash acquired	(3,548)	(202)	—
Other investing activities	(131)	219	(438)
Net cash used in investing activities	(16,609)	(12,193)	(11,620)
Cash flows from financing activities:			
Net change in short-term borrowings	3,019	503	(1,033)
Proceeds from issuance of long-term debt	5,050	11,396	5,546
Payments of long-term debt	(4,584)	(4,080)	(6,033)
Dividends paid	(5,048)	(4,437)	(4,217)
Purchase of Company stock	(6,298)	(14,776)	(7,276)
Purchase of redeemable noncontrolling interest	—	—	(436)
Payment of capital lease obligations	(355)	(363)	(346)
Other financing activities	(242)	(271)	(396)
Net cash used in financing activities	(8,458)	(12,028)	(14,191)
Effect of exchange rates on cash and cash equivalents	(33)	66	194
Net increase (decrease) in cash and cash equivalents	(845)	(512)	632
Cash and cash equivalents at beginning of year	7,395	7,907	7,275
Cash and cash equivalents at end of year	$ 6,550	$ 7,395	$ 7,907
Supplemental disclosure of cash flow information:			
Income tax paid	$ 5,899	$ 6,984	$ 7,389
Interest paid	2,346	2,163	2,141

See accompanying notes.

Specimen Financial Statements: Zetar plc

Zetar plc is a leading U.K. manufacturer of confectionery and natural snacks with a reputation for quality and product innovation. Note that its financial statements are IFRS-based and are presented in British pounds (£). To access the company's complete 2011 annual report, including notes to the financial statements, follow these steps:

1. Go to **www.zetarplc.com**.
2. Select Download Library under the Archive tab.
3. Select Report & Accounts for the year ended 30th April 2011.
4. Use the Bookmarks sections on the left to navigate through the annual report. The Notes to the consolidated financial statements, for example, begin on page 28.

Consolidated income statement

FOR THE YEAR ENDED 30 APRIL 2011

	Note	2011 Adjusted¹ results £'000	2011 Adjusting items £'000	2011 Total £'000	2010 Adjusted¹ results £'000	2010 Adjusting items £'000	2010 Total £'000
Revenue	5	134,998	–	134,998	131,922	–	131,922
Cost of sales		(107,677)	–	(107,677)	(105,112)	–	(105,112)
Gross profit		27,321	–	27,321	26,810	–	26,810
Distribution costs		(5,550)	–	(5,550)	(5,495)	–	(5,495)
Administrative expenses:							
– other administrative expenses		(14,271)	(267)	(14,538)	(14,003)	–	(14,003)
– amortisation of intangible assets	15	–	(170)	(170)	–	(299)	(299)
– share-based payments	10	–	(330)	(330)	–	(287)	(287)
Operating profit		7,500	(767)	6,733	7,312	(586)	6,726
Finance income	9	3	–	3	11	–	11
Finance costs	9	(793)	(308)	(1,101)	(968)	201	(767)
Profit from continuing operations before taxation		6,710	(1,075)	5,635	6,355	(385)	5,970
Tax on profit from continuing activities	11	(1,764)	108	(1,656)	(1,722)	20	(1,702)
Net result from continuing operations		4,946	(967)	3,979	4,633	(365)	4,268
Net result from discontinued operations	34	–	503	503	–	–	–
Profit for the year		4,946	(464)	4,482	4,633	(365)	4,268
Basic earnings per share (p)	13			35.1			32.6
Diluted earnings/per share (p)	13			34.9			32.6
Adjusted basic earnings per share (p)¹	13	38.7			35.4		
Adjusted diluted earnings per share (p)¹	13	38.5			35.4		

¹ Adjusted operating profit and adjusted earnings per share are stated before one-off items, amortisation of intangible assets, share-based payments and the fair value movement on financial instruments.

Consolidated statement of comprehensive income

FOR THE YEAR ENDED 30 APRIL 2011

	2011 Total £'000	2010 Total £'000
Profit for the year	4,482	4,268
Other comprehensive income:		
– currency translation differences	245	(917)
Other comprehensive income	245	(917)
Total comprehensive income for the year	4,727	3,351
Attributable to:		
– owners of the parent	4,727	3,351

Consolidated balance sheet
AT 30 APRIL 2011

	Note	2011 £'000	2010 £'000
Non-current assets			
Goodwill	14	30,520	30,342
Other intangible assets	15	140	309
Property, plant and equipment	16	16,583	14,886
Deferred tax asset	22	149	213
		47,392	45,750
Current assets			
Inventories	17	16,453	16,039
Trade and other receivables	18	24,935	19,062
Cash at bank	27	4,282	4,257
		45,670	39,358
Total assets		93,062	85,108
Current liabilities			
Trade and other payables	19	(25,075)	(25,176)
Deferred consideration	12	(38)	–
Current tax liabilities		(620)	(524)
Obligations under finance leases	20	(75)	(90)
Derivative financial instruments	30	(157)	(406)
Borrowings and overdrafts	21	(14,509)	(12,885)
		(40,474)	(39,081)
Net current assets		5,196	277
Non-current liabilities			
Deferred consideration		–	(300)
Deferred tax liabilities	22	(1,750)	(1,605)
Obligations under finance leases	20	(15)	(77)
Borrowings and overdrafts	21	(4,536)	(2,290)
		(6,301)	(4,272)
Total liabilities		(46,775)	(43,353)
Net assets		46,287	41,755
Equity			
Share capital	23	1,324	1,324
Share premium account	24	28,266	28,266
Merger reserve		3,411	3,411
Equity reserve	25	2,664	2,089
Retained earnings	25	10,622	6,665
Total equity attributable to equity holders of the parent		46,287	41,755

The financial statements were approved by the Board for issue on 20 July 2011.

Consolidated cash flow statement

FOR THE YEAR ENDED 30 APRIL 2011

	Note	2011 £'000	2010 £'000
Cash flow from operating activities			
Profit from continuing operations before taxation		5,635	5,970
Finance costs		1,101	767
Interest income		(3)	(11)
Share-based payments		330	287
Depreciation	6	2,267	2,337
Loss/(profit) on sale of plant and equipment	6	9	(113)
Amortisation of intangible assets	6	170	299
Net movement in working capital		(6,040)	(179)
Decrease/(increase) in inventories		72	(1,720)
(Increase)/decrease in receivables		(5,295)	128
(Decrease)/increase in payables		(817)	1,413
Total cash flow from operations		3,469	9,357
Net interest paid	9	(1,347)	(957)
Tax paid		(1,369)	(1,415)
Total cash flow from operating activities		753	6,985
Cash flow from investing activities			
Purchase of property, plant and equipment		(3,789)	(2,098)
Proceeds from sale of plant and equipment		45	259
Disposal of subsidiary		500	–
Total cash impact of acquisitions		(848)	(220)
Acquisition of business		(483)	(220)
Net borrowings assumed on acquisition		(365)	–
Net cash flow from investing activities		(4,092)	(2,059)
Cash flow from financing activities			
Net proceeds from issue of ordinary share capital		–	14
Purchase of own shares		(525)	(250)
Proceeds from new borrowings		7,000	–
Repayment of borrowings		(5,174)	(2,545)
Finance lease repayments		(91)	(214)
Net cash flow from financing activities		1,210	(2,995)
Net (decrease)/increase in cash and cash equivalents		(2,129)	1,931
Cash and cash equivalents at beginning of the year		(6,608)	(8,127)
Effect of foreign exchange rate movements		96	(412)
Cash and cash equivalents at the end of the year		(8,641)	(6,608)
Cash and cash equivalents comprise:			
– cash at bank	27	4,282	4,257
– bank overdraft	27	(12,923)	(10,865)
		(8,641)	(6,608)

Consolidated statement of changes in equity

FOR THE YEAR ENDED 30 APRIL 2011

			Attributable to equity holders of the parent			
	Share capital £'000	Share premium account £'000	Merger reserve £'000	Equity reserve £'000	Retained earnings £'000	Total £'000
Balance at 1 May 2009	1,324	28,252	3,411	2,719	2,647	38,353
Comprehensive income						
Profit for the year	–	–	–	–	4,268	4,268
Other comprehensive income						
Exchange (loss) on translation of foreign operations	–	–	–	(917)	–	(917)
Total other comprehensive income	–	–	–	(917)	–	(917)
Total comprehensive income	–	–	–	(917)	4,268	3,351
Transactions with owners:						
– issue of new ordinary shares	–	14	–	–	–	14
– purchase of own shares	–	–	–	–	(250)	(250)
– share-based payment charge	–	–	–	287	–	287
Total transactions with owners	–	14	–	287	(250)	51
Balance at 30 April 2010	1,324	28,266	3,411	2,089	6,665	41,755
Comprehensive income						
Profit for the year	–	–	–	–	4,482	4,482
Other comprehensive income						
Exchange gain on translation of foreign operations	–	–	–	245	–	245
Total other comprehensive income	–	–	–	245	–	245
Total comprehensive income	–	–	–	245	4,482	4,727
Transactions with owners:						
– purchase of own shares	–	–	–	–	(525)	(525)
– share-based payment charge	–	–	–	330	–	330
Total transactions with owners	–	–	–	330	(525)	(195)
Balance at 30 April 2011	1,324	28,266	3,411	2,664	10,622	46,287

Appendix G | Time Value of Money

Learning Objectives

After studying this appendix, you should be able to:

[1] Distinguish between simple and compound interest.

[2] Solve for future value of a single amount.

[3] Solve for future value of an annuity.

[4] Identify the variables fundamental to solving present value problems.

[5] Solve for present value of a single amount.

[6] Solve for present value of an annuity.

[7] Compute the present value of notes and bonds.

[8] Compute the present values in capital budgeting situations.

[9] Use a financial calculator to solve time value of money problems.

Would you rather receive $1,000 today or a year from now? You should prefer to receive the $1,000 today because you can invest the $1,000 and earn interest on it. As a result, you will have more than $1,000 a year from now. What this example illustrates is the concept of the **time value of money**. Everyone prefers to receive money today rather than in the future because of the interest factor.

Nature of Interest

Interest is payment for the use of another person's money. It is the difference between the amount borrowed or invested (called the **principal**) and the amount repaid or collected. The amount of interest to be paid or collected is usually stated as a rate over a specific period of time. The rate of interest is generally stated as an annual rate.

> **LEARNING OBJECTIVE 1**
>
> Distinguish between simple and compound interest.

The amount of interest involved in any financing transaction is based on three elements:

1. **Principal (p):** The original amount borrowed or invested.
2. **Interest Rate (i):** An annual percentage of the principal.
3. **Time (n):** The number of years that the principal is borrowed or invested.

Simple Interest

Simple interest is computed on the principal amount only. It is the return on the principal for one period. Simple interest is usually expressed as shown in Illustration G-1.

$$\text{Interest} = \underset{p}{\text{Principal}} \times \underset{i}{\text{Rate}} \times \underset{n}{\text{Time}}$$

Illustration G-1
Interest computation

For example, if you borrowed $5,000 for 2 years at a simple interest rate of 12% annually, you would pay $1,200 in total interest, computed as follows.

$$
\begin{aligned}
\text{Interest} &= p \times i \times n \\
&= \$5{,}000 \times .12 \times 2 \\
&= \$1{,}200
\end{aligned}
$$

Compound Interest

Compound interest is computed on principal **and** on any interest earned that has not been paid or withdrawn. It is the return on (or growth of) the principal for two or more time periods. Compounding computes interest not only on the principal but also on the interest earned to date on that principal, assuming the interest is left on deposit.

To illustrate the difference between simple and compound interest, assume that you deposit $1,000 in Bank Two, where it will earn simple interest of 9% per year, and you deposit another $1,000 in Citizens Bank, where it will earn compound interest of 9% per year compounded annually. Also assume that in both cases you will not withdraw any cash until three years from the date of deposit. Illustration G-2 shows the computation of interest to be received and the accumulated year-end balances.

Illustration G-2
Simple versus compound interest

Bank Two				Citizens Bank		
Simple Interest Calculation	Simple Interest	Accumulated Year-End Balance		Compound Interest Calculation	Compound Interest	Accumulated Year-End Balance
Year 1 $1,000.00 × 9%	$ 90.00	$1,090.00		Year 1 $1,000.00 × 9%	$ 90.00	$1,090.00
Year 2 $1,000.00 × 9%	90.00	$1,180.00		Year 2 $1,090.00 × 9%	98.10	$1,188.10
Year 3 $1,000.00 × 9%	90.00	$1,270.00		Year 3 $1,188.10 × 9%	106.93	$1,295.03
	$ 270.00				$ 295.03	

$25.03 Difference

Note in Illustration G-2 that simple interest uses the initial principal of $1,000 to compute the interest in all three years. Compound interest uses the accumulated balance (principal plus interest to date) at each year-end to compute interest in the succeeding year—which explains why your compound interest account is larger.

Obviously, if you had a choice between investing your money at simple interest or at compound interest, you would choose compound interest, all other things—especially risk—being equal. In the example, compounding provides $25.03 of additional interest income. For practical purposes, compounding assumes that unpaid interest earned becomes a part of the principal, and the accumulated balance at the end of each year becomes the new principal on which interest is earned during the next year.

Illustration G-2 indicates that you should invest your money at the bank that compounds interest. Most business situations use compound interest. Simple interest is generally applicable only to short-term situations of one year or less.

Future Value Concepts

Future Value of a Single Amount

The **future value of a single amount** is the value at a future date of a given amount invested, assuming compound interest. For example, in Illustration G-2, $1,295.03 is the future value of the $1,000 investment earning 9% for three years. The $1,295.03 could be determined more easily by using the following formula.

$FV = p \times (1 + i)^n$	**Illustration G-3** Formula for future value

where:

FV = future value of a single amount
p = principal (or present value; the value today)
i = interest rate for one period
n = number of periods

The $1,295.03 is computed as follows.

$$
\begin{aligned}
FV &= p \times (1 + i)^n \\
&= \$1{,}000 \times (1 + .09)^3 \\
&= \$1{,}000 \times 1.29503 \\
&= \$1{,}295.03
\end{aligned}
$$

The 1.29503 is computed by multiplying ($1.09 \times 1.09 \times 1.09$). The amounts in this example can be depicted in the time diagram shown in Illustration G-4.

Illustration G-4
Time diagram

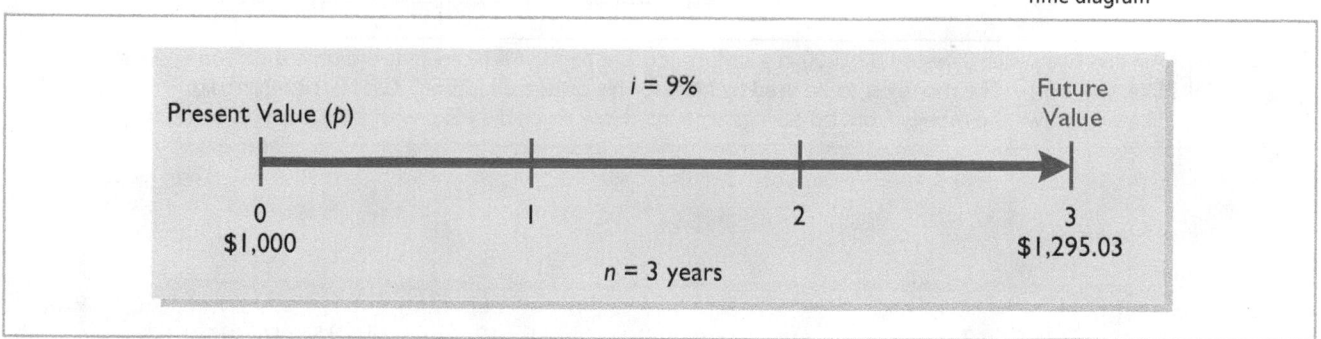

Another method used to compute the future value of a single amount involves a compound interest table. This table shows the future value of 1 for n periods. Table 1 on the next page is such a table.

In Table 1, n is the number of compounding periods, the percentages are the periodic interest rates, and the 5-digit decimal numbers in the respective columns are the future value of 1 factors. In using Table 1, you would multiply the principal amount by the future value factor for the specified number of periods and interest rate. For example, the future value factor for two periods at 9% is 1.18810. Multiplying this factor by $1,000 equals $1,188.10—which is the accumulated balance at the end of year 2 in the Citizens Bank example in Illustration G-2. The $1,295.03 accumulated balance at the end of the third year can be calculated from Table 1 by multiplying the future value factor for three periods (1.29503) by the $1,000.

The demonstration problem in Illustration G-5 (page G4) shows how to use Table 1.

TABLE 1   Future Value of 1

(n) Periods	4%	5%	6%	7%	8%	9%	10%	11%	12%	15%
0	1.00000	1.00000	1.00000	1.00000	1.00000	1.00000	1.00000	1.00000	1.00000	1.00000
1	1.04000	1.05000	1.06000	1.07000	1.08000	1.09000	1.10000	1.11000	1.12000	1.15000
2	1.08160	1.10250	1.12360	1.14490	1.16640	1.18810	1.21000	1.23210	1.25440	1.32250
3	1.12486	1.15763	1.19102	1.22504	1.25971	1.29503	1.33100	1.36763	1.40493	1.52088
4	1.16986	1.21551	1.26248	1.31080	1.36049	1.41158	1.46410	1.51807	1.57352	1.74901
5	1.21665	1.27628	1.33823	1.40255	1.46933	1.53862	1.61051	1.68506	1.76234	2.01136
6	1.26532	1.34010	1.41852	1.50073	1.58687	1.67710	1.77156	1.87041	1.97382	2.31306
7	1.31593	1.40710	1.50363	1.60578	1.71382	1.82804	1.94872	2.07616	2.21068	2.66002
8	1.36857	1.47746	1.59385	1.71819	1.85093	1.99256	2.14359	2.30454	2.47596	3.05902
9	1.42331	1.55133	1.68948	1.83846	1.99900	2.17189	2.35795	2.55803	2.77308	3.51788
10	1.48024	1.62889	1.79085	1.96715	2.15892	2.36736	2.59374	2.83942	3.10585	4.04556
11	1.53945	1.71034	1.89830	2.10485	2.33164	2.58043	2.85312	3.15176	3.47855	4.65239
12	1.60103	1.79586	2.01220	2.25219	2.51817	2.81267	3.13843	3.49845	3.89598	5.35025
13	1.66507	1.88565	2.13293	2.40985	2.71962	3.06581	3.45227	3.88328	4.36349	6.15279
14	1.73168	1.97993	2.26090	2.57853	2.93719	3.34173	3.79750	4.31044	4.88711	7.07571
15	1.80094	2.07893	2.39656	2.75903	3.17217	3.64248	4.17725	4.78459	5.47357	8.13706
16	1.87298	2.18287	2.54035	2.95216	3.42594	3.97031	4.59497	5.31089	6.13039	9.35762
17	1.94790	2.29202	2.69277	3.15882	3.70002	4.32763	5.05447	5.89509	6.86604	10.76126
18	2.02582	2.40662	2.85434	3.37993	3.99602	4.71712	5.55992	6.54355	7.68997	12.37545
19	2.10685	2.52695	3.02560	3.61653	4.31570	5.14166	6.11591	7.26334	8.61276	14.23177
20	2.19112	2.65330	3.20714	3.86968	4.66096	5.60441	6.72750	8.06231	9.64629	16.36654

John and Mary Rich invested $20,000 in a savings account paying 6% interest at the time their son, Mike, was born. The money is to be used by Mike for his college education. On his 18th birthday, Mike withdraws the money from his savings account. How much did Mike withdraw from his account?

Present Value (p)   i = 6%   Future Value = ?

0 1 2 3 4 5 6 7 8 9 10 11 12 13 14 15 16 17 18
$20,000

n = 18 years

Answer: The future value factor from Table 1 is 2.85434 (18 periods at 6%). The future value of $20,000 earning 6% per year for 18 years is **$57,086.80** ($20,000 × 2.85434).

Illustration G-5
Demonstration problem—
Using Table 1 for *FV* of 1

Future Value of an Annuity

The preceding discussion involved the accumulation of only a single principal sum. Individuals and businesses frequently encounter situations in which a **series** of equal dollar amounts are to be paid or received at evenly spaced time intervals (periodically), such as loans or lease (rental) contracts. A series of payments or receipts of equal dollar amounts is referred to as an **annuity**.

The **future value of an annuity** is the sum of all the payments (receipts) plus the accumulated compound interest on them. In computing the future value of an annuity, it is necessary to know (1) the interest rate, (2) the number of payments (receipts), and (3) the amount of the periodic payments (receipts).

To illustrate the computation of the future value of an annuity, assume that you invest $2,000 at the end of each year for three years at 5% interest compounded annually. This situation is depicted in the time diagram in Illustration G-6.

Illustration G-6
Time diagram for a three-year annuity

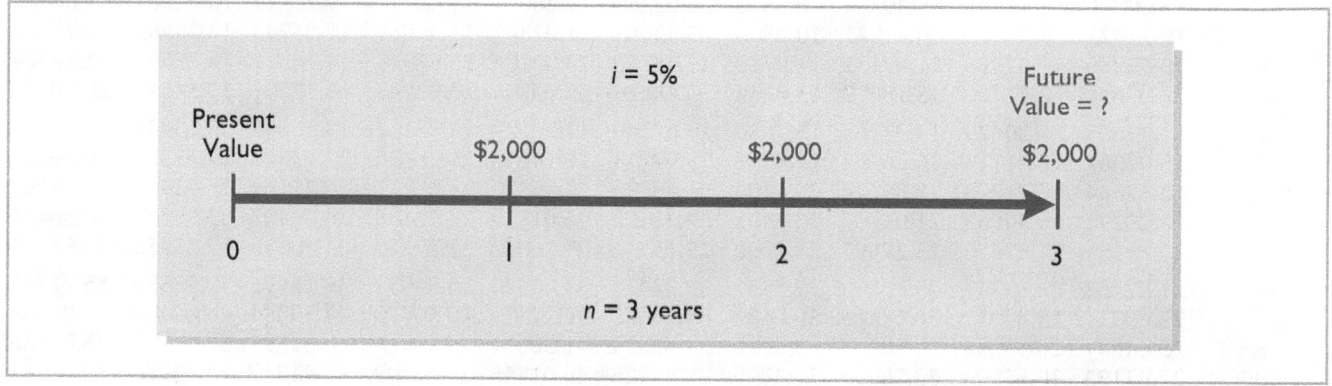

The $2,000 invested at the end of year 1 will earn interest for two years (years 2 and 3), and the $2,000 invested at the end of year 2 will earn interest for one year (year 3). However, the last $2,000 investment (made at the end of year 3) will not earn any interest. The future value of these periodic payments could be computed using the future value factors from Table 1, as shown in Illustration G-7.

Illustration G-7
Future value of periodic payment computation

Invested at End of Year	Number of Compounding Periods	Amount Invested	×	Future Value of 1 Factor at 5%	=	Future Value
1	2	$2,000	×	1.10250		$ 2,205
2	1	$2,000	×	1.05000		2,100
3	0	$2,000	×	1.00000		2,000
				3.15250		**$6,305**

The first $2,000 investment is multiplied by the future value factor for two periods (1.1025) because two years' interest will accumulate on it (in years 2 and 3). The second $2,000 investment will earn only one year's interest (in year 3) and therefore is multiplied by the future value factor for one year (1.0500). The final $2,000 investment is made at the end of the third year and will not earn any interest. Thus $n = 0$ and the future value factor is 1.00000. Consequently, the future value of the last $2,000 invested is only $2,000 since it does not accumulate any interest.

Calculating the future value of each individual cash flow is required when the periodic payments or receipts are not equal in each period. However, when the periodic payments (receipts) are **the same in each period**, the future value can be computed by using a future value of an annuity of 1 table. Table 2 (page G6) is such a table.

TABLE 2   Future Value of an Annuity of 1

(n) Payments	4%	5%	6%	7%	8%	9%	10%	11%	12%	15%
1	1.00000	1.00000	1.00000	1.0000	1.00000	1.00000	1.00000	1.00000	1.00000	1.00000
2	2.04000	2.05000	2.06000	2.0700	2.08000	2.09000	2.10000	2.11000	2.12000	2.15000
3	3.12160	3.15250	3.18360	3.2149	3.24640	3.27810	3.31000	3.34210	3.37440	3.47250
4	4.24646	4.31013	4.37462	4.4399	4.50611	4.57313	4.64100	4.70973	4.77933	4.99338
5	5.41632	5.52563	5.63709	5.7507	5.86660	5.98471	6.10510	6.22780	6.35285	6.74238
6	6.63298	6.80191	6.97532	7.1533	7.33592	7.52334	7.71561	7.91286	8.11519	8.75374
7	7.89829	8.14201	8.39384	8.6540	8.92280	9.20044	9.48717	9.78327	10.08901	11.06680
8	9.21423	9.54911	9.89747	10.2598	10.63663	11.02847	11.43589	11.85943	12.29969	13.72682
9	10.58280	11.02656	11.49132	11.9780	12.48756	13.02104	13.57948	14.16397	14.77566	16.78584
10	12.00611	12.57789	13.18079	13.8164	14.48656	15.19293	15.93743	16.72201	17.54874	20.30372
11	13.48635	14.20679	14.97164	15.7836	16.64549	17.56029	18.53117	19.56143	20.65458	24.34928
12	15.02581	15.91713	16.86994	17.8885	18.97713	20.14072	21.38428	22.71319	24.13313	29.00167
13	16.62684	17.71298	18.88214	20.1406	21.49530	22.95339	24.52271	26.21164	28.02911	34.35192
14	18.29191	19.59863	21.01507	22.5505	24.21492	26.01919	27.97498	30.09492	32.39260	40.50471
15	20.02359	21.57856	23.27597	25.1290	27.15211	29.36092	31.77248	34.40536	37.27972	47.58041
16	21.82453	23.65749	25.67253	27.8881	30.32428	33.00340	35.94973	39.18995	42.75328	55.71747
17	23.69751	25.84037	28.21288	30.8402	33.75023	36.97351	40.54470	44.50084	48.88367	65.07509
18	25.64541	28.13238	30.90565	33.9990	37.45024	41.30134	45.59917	50.39593	55.74972	75.83636
19	27.67123	30.53900	33.75999	37.3790	41.44626	46.01846	51.15909	56.93949	63.43968	88.21181
20	29.77808	33.06595	36.78559	40.9955	45.76196	51.16012	57.27500	64.20283	72.05244	102.44358

Illustration G-8

Demonstration problem— Using Table 2 for *FV* of an annuity of 1

Table 2 shows the future value of 1 to be received periodically for a given number of payments. It assumes that each payment is made at the **end** of each period. We can see from Table 2 that the future value of an annuity of 1 factor for three payments at 5% is 3.15250. The future value factor is the total of the three individual future value factors was shown in Illustration G-7. Multiplying this amount by the annual investment of $2,000 produces a future value of $6,305.

The demonstration problem in Illustration G-8 shows how to use Table 2.

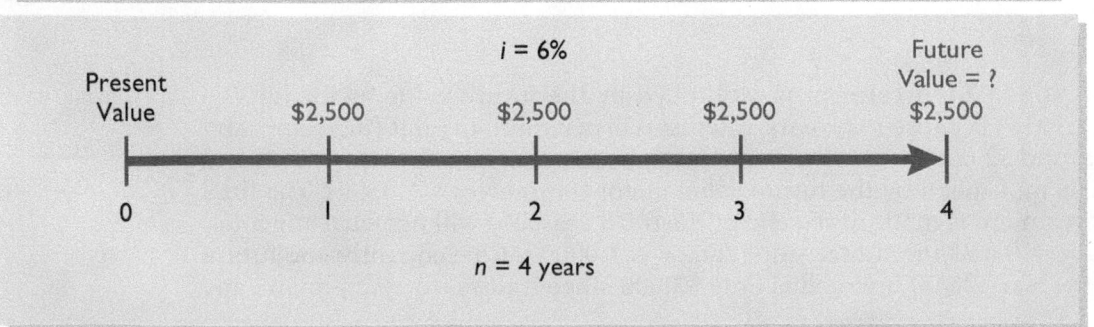

John and Char Lewis' daughter, Debra, has just started high school. They decide to start a college fund for her and will invest $2,500 in a savings account at the end of each year she is in high school (4 payments total). The account will earn 6% interest compounded annually. How much will be in the college fund at the time Debra graduates from high school?

Answer: The future value factor from Table 2 is 4.37462 (4 payments at 6%). The future value of $2,500 invested each year for 4 years at 6% interest is **$10,936.55** ($2,500 × 4.37462).

Present Value Concepts

Present Value Variables

The **present value** is the value now of a given amount to be paid or received in the future, assuming compound interest. The present value, like the future value, is based on three variables: (1) the dollar amount to be received (future amount), (2) the length of time until the amount is received (number of periods), and (3) the interest rate (the discount rate). The process of determining the present value is referred to as **discounting the future amount**.

Present value computations are used in measuring many items. For example, the present value of principal and interest payments is used to determine the market price of a bond. Determining the amount to be reported for notes payable and lease liabilities also involves present value computations. In addition, capital budgeting and other investment proposals are evaluated using present value computations. Finally, all rate of return and internal rate of return computations involve present value techniques.

LEARNING OBJECTIVE   4

Identify the variables fundamental to solving present value problems.

Present Value of a Single Amount

To illustrate present value, assume that you want to invest a sum of money today that will provide $1,000 at the end of one year. What amount would you need to invest today to have $1,000 one year from now? If you want a 10% rate of return, the investment or present value is $909.09 ($1,000 ÷ 1.10). The formula for calculating present value is shown in Illustration G-9.

LEARNING OBJECTIVE   5

Solve for present value of a single amount.

$$\text{Present Value} = \text{Future Value} \div (1 + i)^n$$

Illustration G-9
Formula for present value

The computation of $1,000 discounted at 10% for one year is as follows.

$$
\begin{aligned}
PV &= FV \div (1 + i)^n \\
&= \$1,000 \div (1 + .10)^1 \\
&= \$1,000 \div 1.10 \\
&= \$909.09
\end{aligned}
$$

The future amount ($1,000), the discount rate (10%), and the number of periods (1) are known. The variables in this situation can be depicted in the time diagram in Illustration G-10.

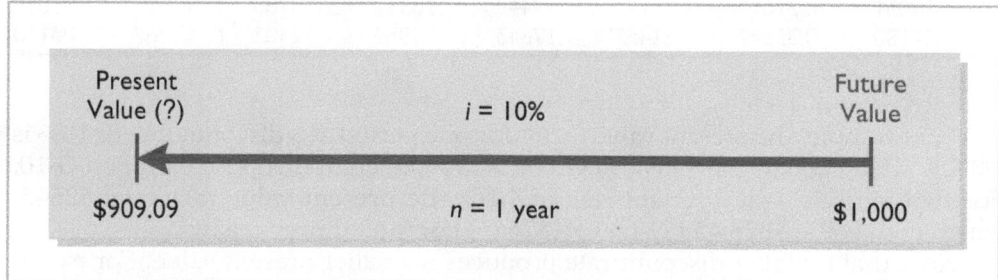

Illustration G-10
Finding present value if discounted for one period

If the single amount of $1,000 is to be received **in two years** and discounted at 10% [$PV = \$1,000 \div (1 + .10)^2$], its present value is $826.45 [($1,000 ÷ 1.21), depicted as shown in Illustration G-11 on the next page.

Illustration G-11
Finding present value if
discounted for two periods

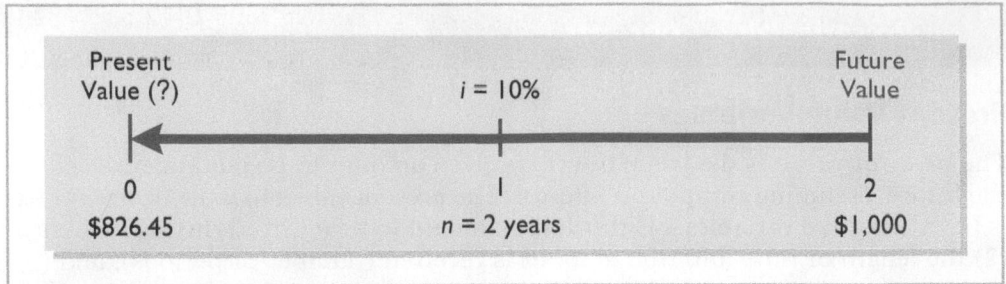

The present value of 1 may also be determined through tables that show the present value of 1 for n periods. In Table 3, below, n is the number of discounting periods involved. The percentages are the periodic interest rates or discount rates, and the 5-digit decimal numbers in the respective columns are the present value of 1 factors.

When using Table 3, the future value is multiplied by the present value factor specified at the intersection of the number of periods and the discount rate.

TABLE 3   Present Value of 1

(n) Periods	4%	5%	6%	7%	8%	9%	10%	11%	12%	15%
1	.96154	.95238	.94340	0.93458	.92593	.91743	.90909	.90090	.89286	.86957
2	.92456	.90703	.89000	0.87344	.85734	.84168	.82645	.81162	.79719	.75614
3	.88900	.86384	.83962	0.81630	.79383	.77218	.75132	.73119	.71178	.65752
4	.85480	.82270	.79209	0.76290	.73503	.70843	.68301	.65873	.63552	.57175
5	.82193	.78353	.74726	0.71299	.68058	.64993	.62092	.59345	.56743	.49718
6	.79031	.74622	.70496	0.66634	.63017	.59627	.56447	.53464	.50663	.43233
7	.75992	.71068	.66506	0.62275	.58349	.54703	.51316	.48166	.45235	.37594
8	.73069	.67684	.62741	0.58201	.54027	.50187	.46651	.43393	.40388	.32690
9	.70259	.64461	.59190	0.54393	.50025	.46043	.42410	.39092	.36061	.28426
10	.67556	.61391	.55839	0.50835	.46319	.42241	.38554	.35218	.32197	.24719
11	.64958	.58468	.52679	0.47509	.42888	.38753	.35049	.31728	.28748	.21494
12	.62460	.55684	.49697	0.44401	.39711	.35554	.31863	.28584	.25668	.18691
13	.60057	.53032	.46884	0.41496	.36770	.32618	.28966	.25751	.22917	.16253
14	.57748	.50507	.44230	0.38782	.34046	.29925	.26333	.23199	.20462	.14133
15	.55526	.48102	.41727	0.36245	.31524	.27454	.23939	.20900	.18270	.12289
16	.53391	.45811	.39365	0.33873	.29189	.25187	.21763	.18829	.16312	.10687
17	.51337	.43630	.37136	0.31657	.27027	.23107	.19785	.16963	.14564	.09293
18	.49363	.41552	.35034	0.29586	.25025	.21199	.17986	.15282	.13004	.08081
19	.47464	.39573	.33051	0.27615	.23171	.19449	.16351	.13768	.11611	.07027
20	.45639	.37689	.31180	0.25842	.21455	.17843	.14864	.12403	.10367	.06110

For example, the present value factor for one period at a discount rate of 10% is .90909, which equals the $909.09 ($1,000 × .90909) computed in Illustration G-10. For two periods at a discount rate of 10%, the present value factor is .82645, which equals the $826.45 ($1,000 × .82645) computed previously.

Note that a higher discount rate produces a smaller present value. For example, using a 15% discount rate, the present value of $1,000 due one year from now is $869.57, versus $909.09 at 10%. Also note that the further removed from the present the future value is, the smaller the present value. For example, using the same discount rate of 10%, the present value of $1,000 due in **five years** is $620.92. The present value of $1,000 due in **one year** is $909.09, a difference of $288.17.

The following two demonstration problems (Illustrations G-12 and G-13) illustrate how to use Table 3.

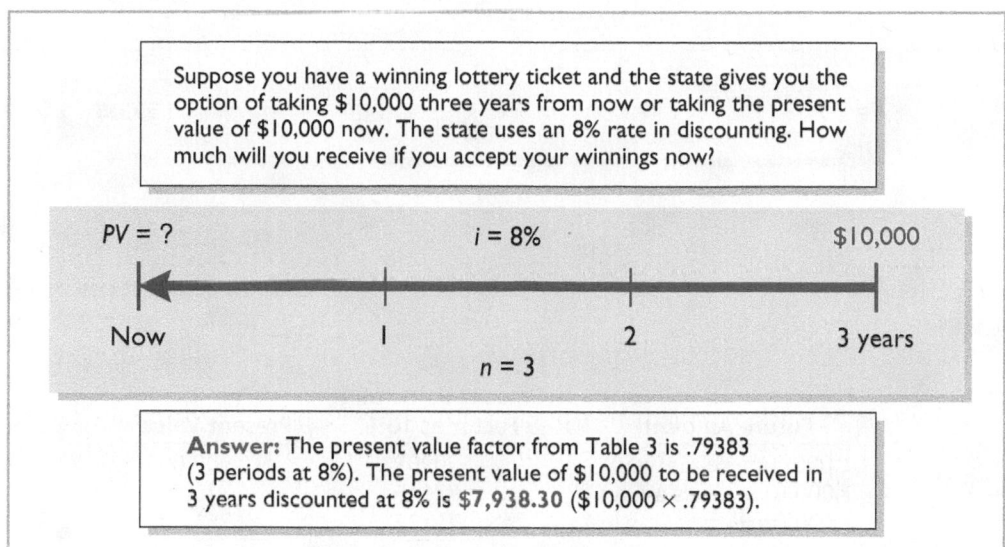

Illustration G-12
Demonstration problem—
Using Table 3 for *PV* of 1

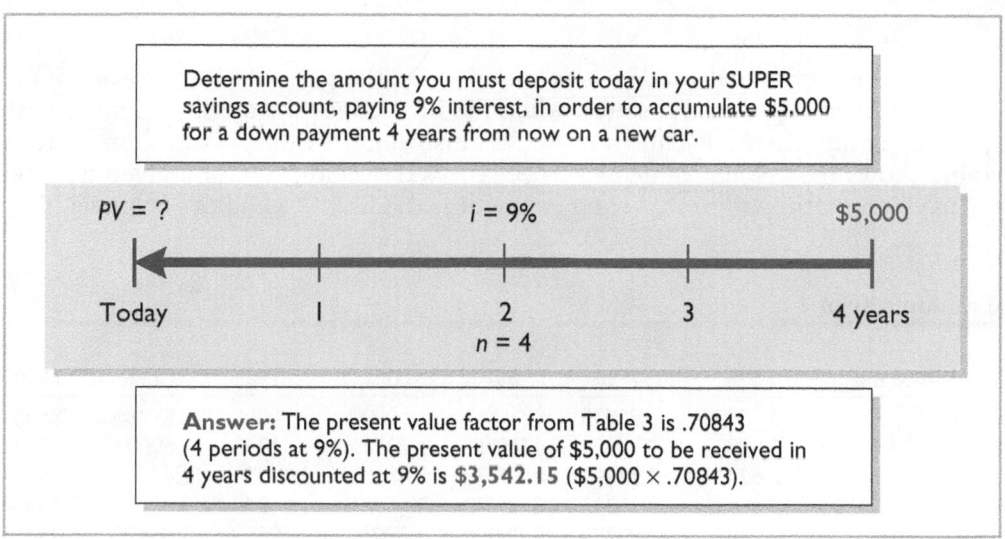

Illustration G-13
Demonstration problem—
Using Table 3 for *PV* of 1

Present Value of an Annuity

The preceding discussion involved the discounting of only a single future amount. Businesses and individuals frequently engage in transactions in which a series of equal dollar amounts are to be received or paid at evenly spaced time intervals (periodically). Examples of a series of periodic receipts or payments are loan agreements, installment sales, mortgage notes, lease (rental) contracts, and pension obligations. As discussed earlier, these periodic receipts or payments are **annuities**.

The **present value of an annuity** is the value now of a series of future receipts or payments, discounted assuming compound interest. In computing the present value of an annuity, it is necessary to know (1) the discount rate, (2) the number of payments (receipts), and (3) the amount of the periodic payments or receipts. To illustrate the computation of the present value of an annuity, assume that you

LEARNING OBJECTIVE 6

Solve for present value of an annuity.

will receive $1,000 cash annually for three years at a time when the discount rate is 10%. This situation is depicted in the time diagram in Illustration G-14. Illustration G-15 shows the computation of its present value in this situation.

Illustration G-14
Time diagram for a three-year annuity

Illustration G-15
Present value of a series of future amounts computation

Future Amount	×	Present Value of 1 Factor at 10%	=	Present Value
$1,000 (one year away)		.90909		$ 909.09
1,000 (two years away)		.82645		826.45
1,000 (three years away)		.75132		751.32
		2.48686		$2,486.86

This method of calculation is required when the periodic cash flows are not uniform in each period. However, when the future receipts are the same in each period, an annuity table can be used. As illustrated in Table 4 below, an annuity table shows the present value of 1 to be received periodically for a given number of payments. It assumes that each payment is made at the end of each period.

TABLE 4   Present Value of an Annuity of 1

(n) Payments	4%	5%	6%	7%	8%	9%	10%	11%	12%	15%
1	.96154	.95238	.94340	0.93458	.92593	.91743	.90909	.90090	.89286	.86957
2	1.88609	1.85941	1.83339	1.80802	1.78326	1.75911	1.73554	1.71252	1.69005	1.62571
3	2.77509	2.72325	2.67301	2.62432	2.57710	2.53130	2.48685	2.44371	2.40183	2.28323
4	3.62990	3.54595	3.46511	3.38721	3.31213	3.23972	3.16986	3.10245	3.03735	2.85498
5	4.45182	4.32948	4.21236	4.10020	3.99271	3.88965	3.79079	3.69590	3.60478	3.35216
6	5.24214	5.07569	4.91732	4.76654	4.62288	4.48592	4.35526	4.23054	4.11141	3.78448
7	6.00205	5.78637	5.58238	5.38929	5.20637	5.03295	4.86842	4.71220	4.56376	4.16042
8	6.73274	6.46321	6.20979	5.97130	5.74664	5.53482	5.33493	5.14612	4.96764	4.48732
9	7.43533	7.10782	6.80169	6.51523	6.24689	5.99525	5.75902	5.53705	5.32825	4.77158
10	8.11090	7.72173	7.36009	7.02358	6.71008	6.41766	6.14457	5.88923	5.65022	5.01877
11	8.76048	8.30641	7.88687	7.49867	7.13896	6.80519	6.49506	6.20652	5.93770	5.23371
12	9.38507	8.86325	8.38384	7.94269	7.53608	7.16073	6.81369	6.49236	6.19437	5.42062
13	9.98565	9.39357	8.85268	8.35765	7.90378	7.48690	7.10336	6.74987	6.42355	5.58315
14	10.56312	9.89864	9.29498	8.74547	8.24424	7.78615	7.36669	6.98187	6.62817	5.72448
15	11.11839	10.37966	9.71225	9.10791	8.55948	8.06069	7.60608	7.19087	6.81086	5.84737
16	11.65230	10.83777	10.10590	9.44665	8.85137	8.31256	7.82371	7.37916	6.97399	5.95424
17	12.16567	11.27407	10.47726	9.76322	9.12164	8.54363	8.02155	7.54879	7.11963	6.04716
18	12.65930	11.68959	10.82760	10.05909	9.37189	8.75563	8.2 0141	7.70162	7.24967	6.12797
19	13.13394	12.08532	11.15812	10.33560	9.60360	8.95012	8.36492	7.83929	7.36578	6.19823
20	13.59033	12.46221	11.46992	10.59401	9.81815	9.12855	8.51356	7.96333	7.46944	6.25933

Table 4 shows that the present value of an annuity of 1 factor for three payments at 10% is 2.48685.[1] This present value factor is the total of the three individual present value factors, as shown in Illustration G-15. Applying this amount to the annual cash flow of $1,000 produces a present value of $2,486.85.

The following demonstration problem (Illustration G-16) illustrates how to use Table 4.

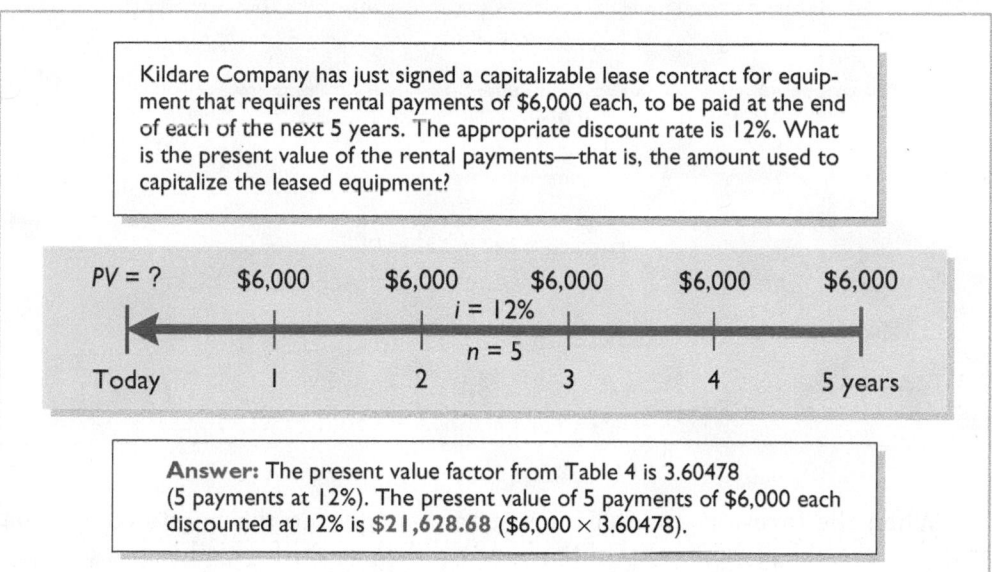

Illustration G-16
Demonstration problem—
Using Table 4 for *PV* of an annuity of 1

Kildare Company has just signed a capitalizable lease contract for equipment that requires rental payments of $6,000 each, to be paid at the end of each of the next 5 years. The appropriate discount rate is 12%. What is the present value of the rental payments—that is, the amount used to capitalize the leased equipment?

Answer: The present value factor from Table 4 is 3.60478 (5 payments at 12%). The present value of 5 payments of $6,000 each discounted at 12% is **$21,628.68** ($6,000 × 3.60478).

Time Periods and Discounting

In the preceding calculations, the discounting was done on an annual basis using an annual interest rate. Discounting may also be done over shorter periods of time such as monthly, quarterly, or semiannually.

When the time frame is less than one year, it is necessary to convert the annual interest rate to the applicable time frame. Assume, for example, that the investor in Illustration G-14 received $500 **semiannually** for three years instead of $1,000 annually. In this case, the number of periods becomes six (3 × 2), the discount rate is 5% (10% ÷ 2), the present value factor from Table 4 is 5.07569 (6 periods at 5%), and the present value of the future cash flows is $2,537.85 (5.07569 × $500). This amount is slightly higher than the $2,486.86 computed in Illustration G-15 because interest is computed twice during the same year. That is, during the second half of the year, interest is earned on the first half-year's interest.

Computing the Present Value of a Long-Term Note or Bond

The present value (or market price) of a long-term note or bond is a function of three variables: (1) the payment amounts, (2) the length of time until the amounts are paid, and (3) the discount rate. Our illustration (on the next page) uses a five-year bond issue.

LEARNING OBJECTIVE 7

Compute the present value of notes and bonds.

---

[1]The difference of .00001 between 2.48686 and 2.48685 is due to rounding.

G12 **Appendix G** Time Value of Money

The first variable (dollars to be paid) is made up of two elements: (1) a series of interest payments (an annuity) and (2) the principal amount (a single sum). To compute the present value of the bond, both the interest payments and the principal amount must be discounted—two different computations. The time diagrams for a bond due in five years are shown in Illustration G-17.

Illustration G-17
Present value of a bond time diagram

When the investor's market interest rate is equal to the bond's contractual interest rate, the present value of the bonds will equal the face value of the bonds. To illustrate, assume a bond issue of 10%, five-year bonds with a face value of $100,000 with interest payable **semiannually** on January 1 and July 1. If the discount rate is the same as the contractual rate, the bonds will sell at face value. In this case, the investor will receive (1) $100,000 at maturity and (2) a series of ten $5,000 interest payments [($100,000 × 10%) ÷ 2] over the term of the bonds. The length of time is expressed in terms of interest periods—in this case—10, and the discount rate per interest period, 5%. The following time diagram (Illustration G-18) depicts the variables involved in this discounting situation.

Illustration G-18
Time diagram for present value of a 10%, five-year bond paying interest semiannually

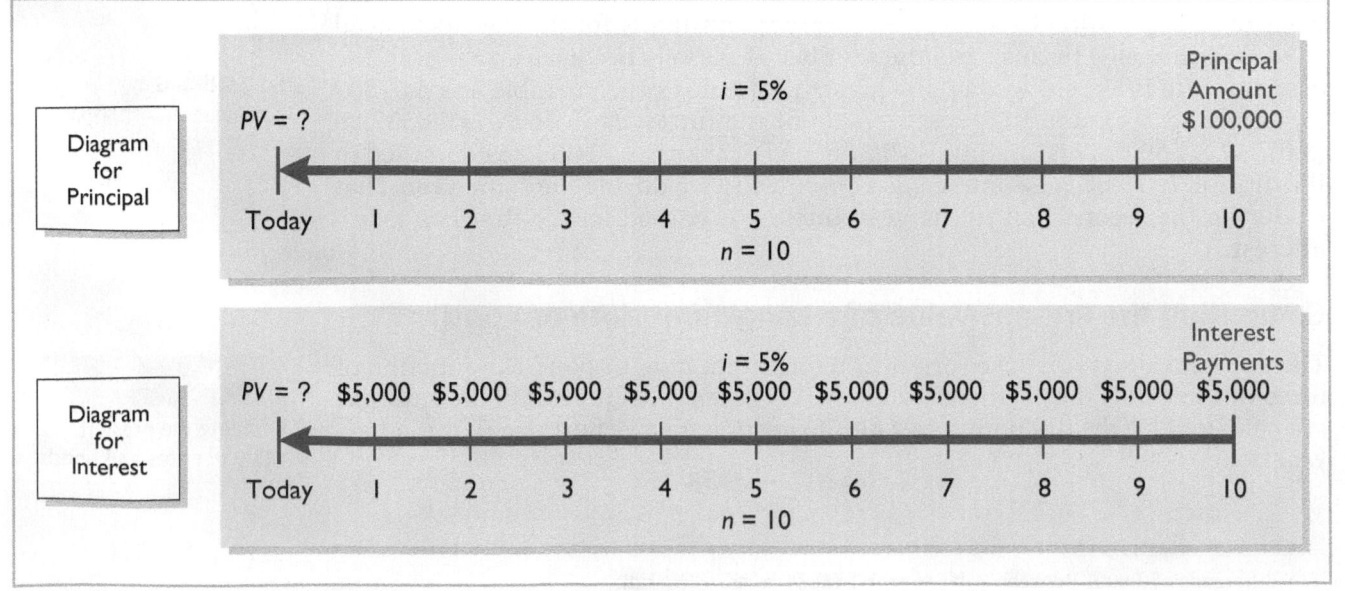

Illustration G-19 shows the computation of the present value of these bonds.

Illustration G-19
Present value of principal and interest—face value

10% Contractual Rate—10% Discount Rate

Present value of principal to be received at maturity	
$100,000 × PV of 1 due in 10 periods at 5%	
$100,000 × .61391 (Table 3)	$ 61,391
Present value of interest to be received periodically	
over the term of the bonds	
$5,000 × PV of 1 due periodically for 10 periods at 5%	
$5,000 × 7.72173 (Table 4)	38,609*
Present value of bonds	**$100,000**

*Rounded

Now assume that the investor's required rate of return is 12%, not 10%. The future amounts are again $100,000 and $5,000, respectively, but now a discount rate of 6% (12% ÷ 2) must be used. The present value of the bonds is $92,639, as computed in Illustration G-20.

Illustration G-20
Present value of principal and interest—discount

10% Contractual Rate—12% Discount Rate

Present value of principal to be received at maturity	
$100,000 × .55839 (Table 3)	$ 55,839
Present value of interest to be received periodically	
over the term of the bonds	
$5,000 × 7.36009 (Table 4)	36,800
Present value of bonds	**$92,639**

Conversely, if the discount rate is 8% and the contractual rate is 10%, the present value of the bonds is $108,111, computed as shown in Illustration G-21.

Illustration G-21
Present value of principal and interest—premium

10% Contractual Rate—8% Discount Rate

Present value of principal to be received at maturity	
$100,000 × .67556 (Table 3)	$ 67,556
Present value of interest to be received periodically	
over the term of the bonds	
$5,000 × 8.11090 (Table 4)	40,555
Present value of bonds	**$108,111**

The above discussion relied on present value tables in solving present value problems. Calculators may also be used to compute present values without the use of these tables. Many calculators, especially financial calculators, have present value (PV) functions that allow you to calculate present values by merely inputting the proper amount, discount rate, periods, and pressing the PV key. We discuss the use of financial calculators in a later section.

G14   **Appendix G** Time Value of Money

Computing the Present Values in a Capital Budgeting Decision

LEARNING OBJECTIVE   8

Compute the present values in capital budgeting situations.

The decision to make long-term capital investments is best evaluated using discounting techniques that recognize the time value of money. To do this, many companies calculate the present value of the cash flows involved in a capital investment.

To illustrate, Nagel-Siebert Trucking Company, a cross-country freight carrier in Montgomery, Illinois, is considering adding another truck to its fleet because of a purchasing opportunity. Navistar Inc., Nagel-Siebert's primary supplier of overland rigs, is overstocked and offers to sell its biggest rig for $154,000 cash payable upon delivery. Nagel-Siebert knows that the rig will produce a net cash flow per year of $40,000 for five years (received at the end of each year), at which time it will be sold for an estimated salvage value of $35,000. Nagel-Siebert's discount rate in evaluating capital expenditures is 10%. Should Nagel-Siebert commit to the purchase of this rig?

The cash flows that must be discounted to present value by Nagel-Siebert are as follows.

Cash payable on delivery (today): $154,000.
Net cash flow from operating the rig: $40,000 for 5 years (at the end of each year).
Cash received from sale of rig at the end of 5 years: $35,000.

The time diagrams for the latter two cash flows are shown in Illustration G-22.

Illustration G-22
Time diagrams for Nagel-Siebert Trucking Company

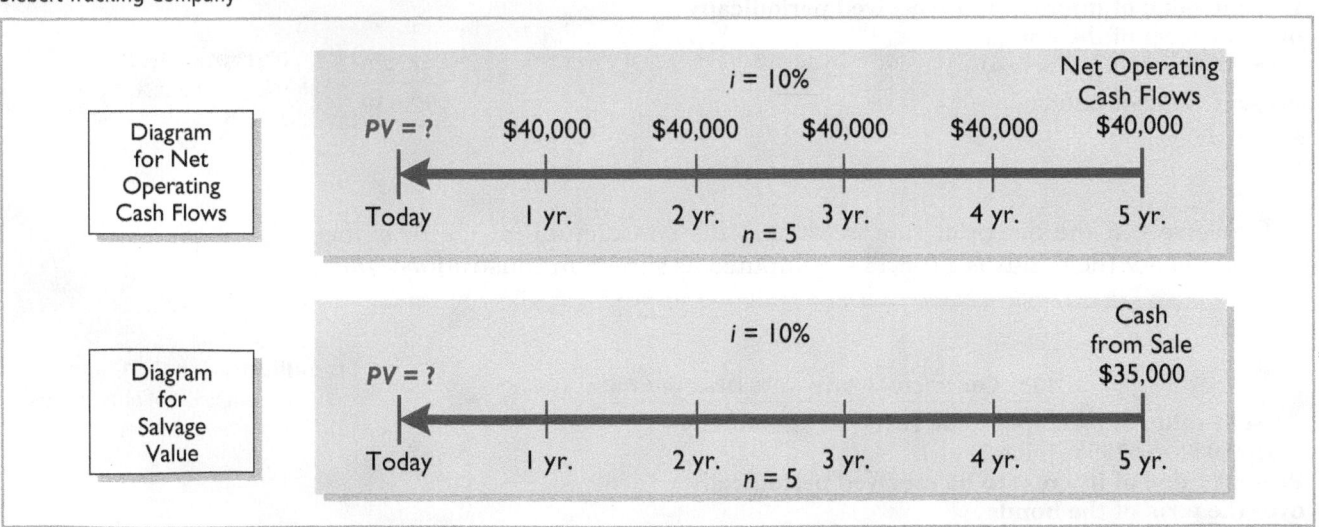

Notice from the diagrams that computing the present value of the net operating cash flows ($40,000 at the end of each year) is **discounting an annuity** (Table 4), while computing the present value of the $35,000 salvage value is **discounting a single sum** (Table 3). The computation of these present values is shown in Illustration G-23.

Present Values—10% Discount Rate

Present value of net operating cash flows received annually over 5 years:
 $40,000 × PV of 1 received annually for 5 years at 10%
 $40,000 × 3.79079 $ 151,631.60
Present value of salvage value (cash) to be received in 5 years:
 $35,000 × PV of 1 received in 5 years at 10%
 $35,000 × .62092   21,732.20

Present value of cash **inflows**   173,363.80
Present value cash **outflows** (purchase price due today at 10%):
 $154,000 × PV of 1 due today
 $154,000 × 1.00000   (154,000.00)

Net present value $ 19,363.80

Because the present value of the cash receipts (inflows) of $173,363.80 ($151,631.60 + $21,732.20) exceeds the present value of the cash payments (outflows) of $154,000.00, the net present value of $19,363.80 is positive, and **the decision to invest should be accepted**.

Now assume that Nagle-Siebert uses a discount rate of 15%, not 10%, because it wants a greater return on it investments in capital assets. The cash receipts and cash payments by Nagel-Siebert are the same. The present values of these receipts and cash payments discounted at 15% are shown in Illustration G-24.

Present Values—15% Discount Rate

Present value of net operating cash flows received annually
over 5 years at 15%:
 $40,000 × 3.35216 $ 134,086.40
Present value of salvage value (cash) to be received in 5 years at 15%:
 $35,000 × .49718   17,401.30

Present value of cash **inflows**   151,487.70
Present value of cash **outflows** (purchase price due today at 15%):
 $154,000 × 1.00000   (154,000.00)

Net present value $ (2,512.30)

Because the present value of the cash payments (outflows) of $154,000 exceeds the present value of the cash receipts (inflows) of $151,487.70 ($134,086.40 + $17,401.30), the net present value of $2,512.30 is negative, and **the investment should be rejected**.

The above discussion relied on present value tables in solving present value problems. As we show in the next section, calculators may also be used to compute present values without the use of these tables. Some calculators, especially the "business" or financial calculators, have present value (PV) functions that allow you to calculate present values by merely identifying the proper amount, discount rate, periods, and pressing the PV key.

Using Financial Calculators

Business professionals, once they have mastered the underlying future and present value concepts, often use a financial calculator to solve time value of money problems. In many cases, they must use calculators if interest rates or time periods do not correspond with the information provided in the compound interest tables.

To use financial calculators, you enter the time value of money variables into the calculator. Illustration G-25 shows the five most common keys used to solve time value of money problems.[2]

Illustration G-25
Financial calculator keys

where:

N = number of periods
I = interest rate per period (some calculators use I/YR or i)
PV = present value (occurs at the beginning of the first period)
PMT = payment (all payments are equal, and none are skipped)
FV = future value (occurs at the end of the last period)

In solving time value of money problems in this appendix, you will generally be given three of four variables and will have to solve for the remaining variable. The fifth key (the key not used) is given a value of zero to ensure that this variable is not used in the computation.

Present Value of a Single Sum

To illustrate how to solve a present value problem using a financial calculator, assume that you want to know the present value of $84,253 to be received in five years, discounted at 11% compounded annually. Illustration G-26 depicts this problem.

Illustration G-26
Calculator solution for present value of a single sum

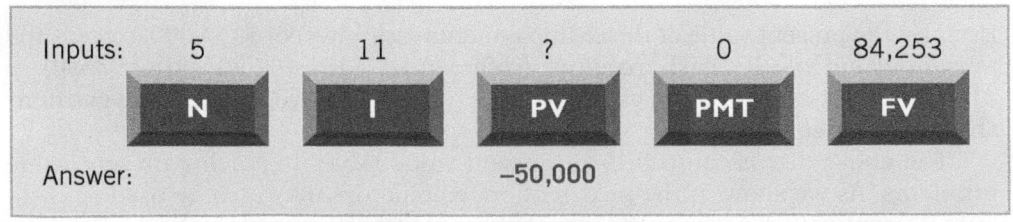

Inputs: 5   11   ?   0   84,253
             N   I   PV   PMT   FV

Answer: −50,000

---

[2]On many calculators, these keys are actual buttons on the face of the calculator; on others, they appear on the display after the user accesses a present value menu.

Illustration G-26 shows you the information (inputs) to enter into the calculator: N = 5, I = 11, PMT = 0, and FV = 84,253. You then press PV for the answer: −$50,000. As indicated, the PMT key was given a value of zero because a series of payments did not occur in this problem.

PLUS AND MINUS

The use of plus and minus signs in time value of money problems with a financial calculator can be confusing. Most financial calculators are programmed so that the positive and negative cash flows in any problem offset each other. In the present value problem above, we identified the $84,253 initial investment as a positive (inflow); the answer −$50,000 was shown as a negative amount, reflecting a cash outflow. If the 84,253 were entered as a negative, then the final answer would have been reported as a positive 50,000.

Hopefully, the sign convention will not cause confusion. If you understand what is required in a problem, you should be able to interpret a positive or negative amount in determining the solution to a problem.

COMPOUNDING PERIODS

In the problem above, we assumed that compounding occurs once a year. Some financial calculators have a default setting, which assumes that compounding occurs 12 times a year. You must determine what default period has been programmed into your calculator and change it as necessary to arrive at the proper compounding period.

ROUNDING

Most financial calculators store and calculate using 12 decimal places. As a result, because compound interest tables generally have factors only up to five decimal places, a slight difference in the final answer can result. In most time value of money problems, the final answer will not include more than two decimal places.

Present Value of an Annuity

To illustrate how to solve a present value of an annuity problem using a financial calculator, assume that you are asked to determine the present value of rental receipts of $6,000 each to be received at the end of each of the next five years, when discounted at 12%, as pictured in Illustration G-27.

Illustration G-27
Calculator solution for present value of an annuity

In this case, you enter N = 5, I = 12, PMT = 6,000, FV = 0, and then press PV to arrive at the answer of −$21,628.66.

Useful Applications of the Financial Calculator

With a financial calculator, you can solve for any interest rate or for any number of periods in a time value of money problem. Here are some examples of these applications.

AUTO LOAN

Assume you are financing the purchase of a used car with a three-year loan. The loan has a 9.5% stated annual interest rate, compounded monthly. The price of the car is $6,000, and you want to determine the monthly payments, assuming that the payments start one month after the purchase. This problem is pictured in Illustration G-28.

Illustration G-28

Calculator solution for auto loan payments

To solve this problem, you enter N = 36 (12 × 3), I = 9.5, PV = 6,000, FV = 0, and than press PMT. You will find that the monthly payments will be $192.20. Note that the payment key is usually programmed for 12 payments per year. Thus, you must change the default (compounding period) if the payments are other than monthly.

MORTGAGE LOAN AMOUNT

Let's say you evaluating financing options for a loan on a house. You decide that the maximum mortgage payment you can afford is $700 per month. The annual interest rate is 8.4%. If you get a mortgage that requires you to make monthly payments over a 15-year period, what is the maximum home loan you can afford? Illustration G-29 depicts this problem.

Illustration G-29

Calculator solution for mortgage amount

You enter N = 180 (12 × 15 years), I = 8.4, PMT = −700, FV = 0, and press PV. With the payments-per-year key set at 12, you find a present value of $71,509.81— the maximum home loan you can afford, given that you want to keep your mortgage payments at $700. Note that by changing any of the variables, you can quickly conduct "what-if" analyses for different situations.

SUMMARY OF LEARNING OBJECTIVES

1 Distinguish between simple and compound interest. Simple interest is computed on the principal only, while compound interest is computed on the principal and any interest earned that has not been withdrawn.

2 Solve for future value of a single amount. Prepare a time diagram of the problem. Identify the principal amount, the number of compounding periods, and the interest rate. Using the future value of 1 table, multiply the principal amount by the future value factor specified at the intersection of the number of periods and the interest rate.

3 Solve for future value of an annuity. Prepare a time diagram of the problem. Identify the amount of the periodic payments (receipts), the number of payments (receipts), and the interest rate. Using the future value of an annuity of 1 table, multiply the amount of the payments by the future value factor specified at the intersection of the number of payments and the interest rate.

4 Identify the variables fundamental to solving present value problems. The following three variables are fundamental to solving present value problems: (1) the future amount, (2) the number of periods, and (3) the interest rate (the discount rate).

5 Solve for present value of a single amount. Prepare a time diagram of the problem. Identify the future amount, the number of discounting periods, and the discount (interest) rate. Using the present value of a single amount table, multiply the future amount by the present value factor specified at the intersection of the number of periods and the discount rate.

6 Solve for present value of an annuity. Prepare a time diagram of the problem. Identify the amount of future periodic receipts or payment (annuities), the number of payments (receipts), and the discount (interest) rate.

Using the present value of an annuity of 1 table, multiply the amount of the annuity by the present value factor specified at the intersection of the number of payments and the interest rate.

7 Compute the present value of notes and bonds. Determine the present value of the principal amount: Multiply the principal amount (a single future amount) by the present value factor (from the present value of 1 table) intersecting at the number of periods (number of interest payments) and the discount rate. Determine the present value of the series of interest payments: Multiply the amount of the interest payment by the present value factor (from the present value of an annuity of 1 table) intersecting at the number of periods (number of interest payments) and the discount rate. Add the present value of the principal amount to the present value of the interest payments to arrive at the present value of the note or bond.

8 Compute the present values in capital budgeting situations. Compute the present values of all cash inflows and all cash outflows related to the capital budgeting proposal (an investment-type decision). If the **net** present value is positive, accept the proposal (make the investment). If the **net** present value is negative, reject the proposal (do not make the investment).

9 Use a financial calculator to solve time value of money problems. Financial calculators can be used to solve the same and additional problems as those solved with time value of money tables. Enter into the financial calculator the amounts for all of the known elements of a time value of money problem (periods, interest rate, payments, future or present value), and it solves for the unknown element. Particularly useful situations involve interest rates and compounding periods not presented in the tables.

GLOSSARY

Annuity A series of equal dollar amounts to be paid or received at evenly spaced time intervals (periodically). (p. G4).

Compound interest The interest computed on the principal and any interest earned that has not been paid or withdrawn. (p. G2).

Discounting the future amount(s) The process of determining present value. (p. G7).

Future value of a single amount The value at a future date of a given amount invested, assuming compound interest. (p. G2).

Future value of an annuity The sum of all the payments (receipts) plus the accumulated compound interest on them. (p. G5).

Interest Payment for the use of another person's money. (p. G1).

Present value The value now of a given amount to be paid or received in the future assuming compound interest. (p. G7).

Present value of an annuity The value now of a series of future receipts or payments, discounted assuming compound interest. (p. G9).

Principal The amount borrowed or invested. (p. G1).

Simple interest The interest computed on the principal only. (p. G1).

BRIEF EXERCISES

(Use tables to solve exercises BEG-1 to BEG-25.)

Compute the future value of a single amount.

(LO 1, 2)

BEG-1 Terry Nele invested $9,000 at 5% annual interest, and left the money invested without withdrawing any of the interest for 12 years. At the end of the 12 years, Terry withdrew the accumulated amount of money. (a) What amount did Terry withdraw, assuming the investment earns simple interest? (b) What amount did Terry withdraw, assuming the investment earns interest compounded annually?

Use future value tables.

(LO 2, 3)

BEG-2 For each of the following cases, indicate (a) to what interest rate columns and (b) to what number of periods you would refer in looking up the future value factor.

(1) In Table 1 (future value of 1):

	Annual Rate	Number of Years Invested	Compounded
Case A	5%	3	Annually
Case B	12%	4	Semiannually

(2) In Table 2 (future value of an annuity of 1):

	Annual Rate	Number of Years Invested	Compounded
Case A	3%	8	Annually
Case B	8%	6	Semiannually

Compute the future value of a single amount.

(LO 2)

BEG-3 Kiner Company signed a lease for an office building for a period of 12 years. Under the lease agreement, a security deposit of $8,400 is made. The deposit will be returned at the expiration of the lease with interest compounded at 4% per year. What amount will Kiner receive at the time the lease expires?

Compute the future value of an annuity.

(LO 3)

BEG-4 Dugan Company issued $1,000,000, 12-year bonds and agreed to make annual sinking fund deposits of $78,000. The deposits are made at the end of each year into an account paying 6% annual interest. What amount will be in the sinking fund at the end of 12 years?

Compute the future value of a single amount and of an annuity.

(LO 2, 3)

BEG-5 Steve and Martha Fernetti invested $5,000 in a savings account paying 5% annual interest when their daughter, Kristy, was born. They also deposited $1,000 on each of her birthdays until she was 18 (including her 18th birthday). How much was in the savings account on her 18th birthday (after the last deposit)?

Compute the future value of a single amount.

(LO 2)

BEG-6 Andy Finley borrowed $35,000 on July 1, 2015. This amount plus accrued interest at 8% compounded annually is to be repaid on July 1, 2020. How much will Andy have to repay on July 1, 2020?

Use present value tables.

(LO 5, 6)

BEG-7 For each of the following cases, indicate (a) to what interest rate columns and (b) to what number of periods you would refer in looking up the discount rate.

(1) In Table 3 (present value of 1):

	Annual Rate	Number of Years Involved	Discounts per Year
Case A	12%	7	Annually
Case B	8%	11	Annually
Case C	6%	8	Semiannually

(2) In Table 4 (present value of an annuity of 1):

	Annual Rate	Number of Years Involved	Number of Payments Involved	Frequency of Payments
Case A	10%	20	20	Annually
Case B	10%	7	7	Annually
Case C	8%	5	10	Semiannually

BEG-8 (a) What is the present value of $25,000 due 9 periods from now, discounted at 10%?
Determine present values.
(LO 5, 6)

(b) What is the present value of $25,000 to be received at the end of each of 6 periods, discounted at 9%?

BEG-9 Lincoln Company is considering an investment that will return a lump sum of $750,000 six years from now. What amount should Lincoln Company pay for this investment to earn an 8% return?
Compute the present value of a single amount investment.
(LO 5)

BEG-10 Foley Company earns 6% on an investment that will return $450,000 eight years from now. What is the amount Foley should invest now to earn this rate of return?
Compute the present value of a single amount investment.
(LO 5)

BEG-11 Slaton Company is considering investing in an annuity contract that will return $46,000 annually at the end of each year for 15 years. What amount should Slaton Company pay for this investment if it earns an 8% return?
Compute the present value of an annuity investment.
(LO 6)

BEG-12 Trenton Enterprises earns 5% on an investment that pays back $80,000 at the end of each of the next 6 years. What is the amount Trenton Enterprises invested to earn the 5% rate of return?
Compute the present value of an annual investment.
(LO 6)

BEG-13 Miley Railroad Co. is about to issue $300,000 of 10-year bonds paying an 11% interest rate, with interest payable semiannually. The discount rate for such securities is 10%. How much can Miley expect to receive for the sale of these bonds?
Compute the present value of bonds.
(LO 5, 6, 7)

BEG-14 Assume the same information as BEG-13 except that the discount rate is 12% instead of 10%. In this case, how much can Miley expect to receive from the sale of these bonds?
Compute the present value of bonds.
(LO 5, 6, 7)

BEG-15 Ramos Taco Company receives a $65,000, 6-year note bearing interest of 4% (paid annually) from a customer at a time when the discount rate is 6%. What is the present value of the note received by Ramos?
Compute the present value of a note.
(LO 5, 6, 7)

BEG-16 Beltran Enterprises issued 6%, 8-year, $2,500,000 par value bonds that pay interest semiannually on October 1 and April 1. The bonds are dated April 1, 2015, and are issued on that date. The discount rate of interest for such bonds on April 1, 2015, is 8%. What cash proceeds did Beltran receive from issuance of the bonds?
Compute the present value of bonds.
(LO 5, 6, 7)

BEG-17 Nick Heller owns a garage and is contemplating purchasing a tire retreading machine for $18,000. After estimating costs and revenues, Nick projects a net cash flow from the retreading machine of $3,200 annually for 8 years. Nick hopes to earn a return of 9% on such investments. What is the present value of the retreading operation? Should Nick purchase the retreading machine?
Compute the present value of a machine for purposes of making a purchase decision.
(LO 6, 8)

BEG-18 Bentley Company issues a 10%, 5-year mortgage note on January 1, 2015, to obtain financing for new equipment. Land is used as collateral for the note. The terms provide for semiannual installment payments of $48,850. What were the cash proceeds received from the issuance of the note?
Compute the present value of a note.
(LO 7)

BEG-19 Coleman Company is considering purchasing equipment. The equipment will produce the following cash flows: Year 1, $40,000; Year 2, $45,000; and Year 3, $50,000. Coleman requires a minimum rate of return of 8%. What is the maximum price Coleman should pay for this equipment?
Compute the maximum price to pay for a machine.
(LO 6, 8)

BEG-20 If Britney Cozart invests $4,765.50 now and she will receive $12,000 at the end of 12 years, what annual rate of interest will Britney earn on her investment? (*Hint:* Use Table 3.)
Compute the interest rate on a single amount.
(LO 5)

BEG-21 Romeo Cruz has been offered the opportunity of investing $29,319 now. The investment will earn 11% per year and at the end of that time will return Romeo $75,000. How many years must Romeo wait to receive $75,000? (*Hint:* Use Table 3.)
Compute the number of periods of a single amount.
(LO 5)

BEG-22 Andrea Stone made an investment of $10,271.38. From this investment, she will receive $1,200 annually for the next 15 years starting one year from now. What rate of interest will Andrea's investment be earning for her? (*Hint:* Use Table 4.)

BEG-23 Karen Hartman invests $6,542.83 now for a series of $1,300 annual returns beginning one year from now. Karen will earn a return of 9% on the initial investment. How many annual payments of $1,300 will Karen receive? (*Hint:* Use Table 4.)

BEG-24 George Dinkel owns a garage and is contemplating purchasing a tire retreading machine for $12,820. After estimating costs and revenues, George projects a net cash inflow from the retreading machine of $2,700 annually for 7 years. George hopes to earn a return of 9% on such investments. What is the present value of the retreading operation? Should George Dinkel purchase the retreading machine?

BEG-25 Gomez Company is considering purchasing equipment. The equipment will produce the following cash flows: Year 1, $20,000; Year 2, $30,000; Year 3, $40,000. Gomez requires a minimum rate of return of 11%. What is the maximum price Gomez should pay for this equipment?

BEG-26 Cindy Stein wishes to invest $18,000 on July 1, 2015, and have it accumulate to $50,000 by July 1, 2025. Use a financial calculator to determine at what exact annual rate of interest Cindy must invest the $18,000.

BEG-27 On July 17, 2015, Craig Horton borrowed $60,000 from his grandfather to open a clothing store. Starting July 17, 2016, Craig has to make 10 equal annual payments of $8,860 each to repay the loan. Use a financial calculator to determine what interest rate Craig is paying.

BEG-28 As the purchaser of a new house, Leslie Carpenter has signed a mortgage note to pay the Nashville National Bank and Trust Co. $8,400 every 6 months for 20 years, at the end of which time she will own the house. At the date the mortgage is signed, the purchase price was $198,000 and Carpenter made a down payment of $20,000. The first payment will be made 6 months after the date the mortgage is signed. Using a financial calculator, compute the exact rate of interest earned on the mortgage by the bank.

BEG-29 Using a financial calculator, solve for the unknowns in each of the following situations.

(a) On June 1, 2015, Holly Brennaman purchases lakefront property from her neighbor, George Coulter, and agrees to pay the purchase price in seven payments of $16,000 each, the first payment to be payable June 1, 2016. (Assume that interest compounded at an annual rate of 6.9% is implicit in the payments.) What is the purchase price of the property?

(b) On January 1, 2015, Renfro Corporation purchased 200 of the $1,000 face value, 7% coupon, 10-year bonds of Malone Inc. The bonds mature on January 1, 2025, and pay interest annually beginning January 1, 2016. Renfro purchased the bonds to yield 8.65%. How much did Renfro pay for the bonds?

BEG-30 Using a financial calculator, provide a solution to each of the following situations.

(a) Kate Morley owes a debt of $42,000 from the purchase of her new sport utility vehicle. The debt bears annual interest of 7.8% compounded monthly. Kate wishes to pay the debt and interest in equal monthly payments over 8 years, beginning one month hence. What equal monthly payments will pay off the debt and interest?

(b) On January 1, 2015, Roger Kimler offers to buy Dave Garner's used snowmobile for $8,000, payable in five equal annual installments, which are to include 7.25% interest on the unpaid balance and a portion of the principal. If the first payment is to be made on December 31, 2015, how much will each payment be?

Company Index

Subject Index

BASIC ACCOUNTING EQUATION (Chapter 2)

Basic Equation	Assets = Liabilities +			Stockholders' Equity			
Expanded Equation	Assets = Liabilities +	Common Stock +	Retained Earnings +	Revenues −	Expenses −	Dividends
Debit/Credit Effects	Dr. + Cr. −	Dr. − Cr. +	Dr. − Cr. +	Dr. − Cr. +	Dr. − Cr. +	Dr. + Cr. −	Dr. + Cr. −

ADJUSTING ENTRIES (Chapter 3)

	Type	Adjusting Entry	
Deferrals	1. Prepaid expenses	Dr. Expenses	Cr. Assets
	2. Unearned revenues	Dr. Liabilities	Cr. Revenues
Accruals	1. Accrued revenues	Dr. Assets	Cr. Revenues
	2. Accrued expenses	Dr. Expenses	Cr. Liabilities

Note: Each adjusting entry will affect one or more income statement accounts and one or more balance sheet accounts.

Interest Computation

Interest = Face value of note × Annual interest rate × Time in terms of one year

CLOSING ENTRIES (Chapter 4)

Purpose: (1) Update the Retained Earnings account in the ledger by transferring net income (loss) and dividends to retained earnings. (2) Prepare the temporary accounts (revenue, expense, dividends) for the next period's postings by reducing their balances to zero.

Process

1. Debit each revenue account for its balance (assuming normal balances) and credit Income Summary for total revenues.
2. Debit Income Summary for total expenses and credit each expense account for its balance (assuming normal balances).

    STOP AND CHECK: Does the balance in your Income Summary account equal the net income (loss) reported in the income statement?

3. Debit (credit) Income Summary and credit (debit) Retained Earnings for the amount of net income (loss).
4. Debit Retained Earnings for the balance in the Dividends account and credit Dividends for the same amount.

    STOP AND CHECK: Does the balance in your Retained Earnings account equal the ending balance reported in the balance sheet and the retained earnings statement? Are all of your temporary account balances zero?

ACCOUNTING CYCLE (Chapter 4)

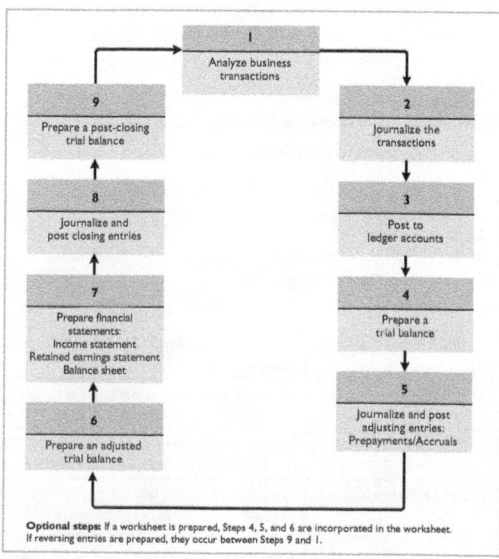

Optional steps: If a worksheet is prepared, Steps 4, 5, and 6 are incorporated in the worksheet. If reversing entries are prepared, they occur between Steps 9 and 1.

INVENTORY (Chapters 5 and 6)

Ownership

Freight Terms	Ownership of goods on public carrier resides with:	Who pays freight costs:
FOB shipping point	Buyer	Buyer
FOB destination	Seller	Seller

Perpetual vs. Periodic Journal Entries

Event	Perpetual	Periodic*

Purchase of goods	Inventory
	  Cash (A/P)
		Purchases
		  Cash (A/P)

Freight (shipping point)	Inventory
	  Cash
		Freight In
		  Cash

Return of goods	Cash (or A/P)
	  Inventory
		Cash (or A/P)
		  Purchase Returns and
		  Allowances

Sale of goods	Cash (or A/R)
	  Sales Revenue
	Cost of Goods Sold
	  Inventory
		Cash (or A/R)
		  Sales Revenue
		No entry

Sales returns and allowances	Sales Ret. and All.
	  Accounts Receivable
	Inventory
	  Cost of Goods Sold
		Sales Ret. and All.
		  Accounts Receivable
		No entry

Sales discounts	Cash
	Sales Discounts
	  Accounts Receivable
		Cash
		Sales Discounts
		  Accounts Receivable

End of period	No entry	Closing or adjusting entry required

*Covered in Appendix 5B.

Cost Flow Methods

- Specific identification
- First-in, first-out (FIFO)
- Weighted-average
- Last-in, first-out (LIFO)

FRAUD, INTERNAL CONTROL, AND CASH (Chapter 7)

The Fraud Triangle

Financial pressure △ Rationalization
Opportunity

Principles of Internal Control Activities

- Establishment of responsibility
- Segregation of duties
- Documentation procedures
- Physical controls
- Independent internal verification
- Human resource controls

Bank Reconciliation

Bank	Books
Balance per bank statement Add: Deposits in transit	Balance per books Add: Unrecorded credit memoranda from bank statement
Deduct: Outstanding checks	Deduct: Unrecorded debit memoranda from bank statement
Adjusted cash balance	Adjusted cash balance

Note: 1. Errors should be offset (added or deducted) on the side that made the error.
2. Adjusting journal entries should only be made on the books.

STOP AND CHECK: Does the adjusted cash balance in the Cash account equal the reconciled balance?

RAPID REVIEW
Chapter Content

RECEIVABLES (Chapter 8)

Methods to Account for Uncollectible Accounts

Direct write-off method	Record bad debt expense when the company determines a particular account to be uncollectible.
Allowance methods: Percentage-of-sales	At the end of each period, estimate the amount of credit sales uncollectible. Debit Bad Debt Expense and credit Allowance for Doubtful Accounts for this amount. As specific accounts become uncollectible, debit Allowance for Doubtful Accounts and credit Accounts Receivable.
Percentage-of-receivables	At the end of each period, estimate the amount of uncollectible receivables. Debit Bad Debt Expense and credit Allowance for Doubtful Accounts in an amount that results in a balance in the allowance account equal to the estimate of uncollectibles. As specific accounts become uncollectible, debit Allowance for Doubtful Accounts and credit Accounts Receivable.

PLANT ASSETS (Chapter 9)

Presentation

Tangible Assets	Intangible Assets
Property, plant, and equipment	Intangible assets (patents, copyrights, trademarks, franchises, goodwill)
Natural resources	

Computation of Annual Depreciation Expense

Straight-line	$\dfrac{\text{Cost} - \text{Salvage value}}{\text{Useful life (in years)}}$
Units-of-activity	$\dfrac{\text{Depreciable cost}}{\text{Useful life (in units)}} \times$ Units of activity during year
Declining-balance	Book value at beginning of year × Declining-balance rate* *Declining-balance rate = 1 ÷ Useful life (in years)

Note: If depreciation is calculated for partial periods, the straight-line and declining-balance methods must be adjusted for the relevant proportion of the year. Multiply the annual depreciation expense by the number of months expired in the year divided by 12 months.

BONDS (Chapter 10)

Premium	Market interest rate < Contractual interest rate
Face value	Market interest rate = Contractual interest rate
Discount	Market interest rate > Contractual interest rate

Computation of Annual Bond Interest Expense

Interest expense = Interest paid (payable) + Amortization of discount
(OR − Amortization of premium)

Straight-line amortization	$\dfrac{\text{Bond discount (premium)}}{\text{Number of interest periods}}$	
Effective-interest amortization (preferred method)	Bond interest expense	Bond interest paid
	Carrying value of bonds at beginning of period × Effective-interest rate	Face amount of bonds × Contractual interest rate

STOCKHOLDERS' EQUITY (Chapter 11)

No-Par Value vs. Par Value Stock Journal Entries

No-Par Value	Par Value
Cash Common Stock	Cash Common Stock (par value) Paid-in Capital in Excess of Par

Comparison of Dividend Effects

	Cash	Common Stock	Retained Earnings
Cash dividend	↓	No effect	↓
Stock dividend	No effect	↑	↓
Stock split	No effect	No effect	No effect

Debits and Credits to Retained Earnings

Retained Earnings	
Debits (Decreases)	Credits (Increases)
1. Net loss 2. Prior period adjustments for overstatement of net income 3. Cash dividends and stock dividends 4. Some disposals of treasury stock	1. Net income 2. Prior period adjustments for understatement of net income

INVESTMENTS (Chapter 12)

Comparison of Long-Term Bond Investment and Liability Journal Entries

Event	Investor	Investee
Purchase / issue of bonds	Debt Investments Cash	Cash Bonds Payable
Interest receipt / payment	Cash Interest Revenue	Interest Expense Cash

Comparison of Cost and Equity Methods of Accounting for Long-Term Stock Investments

Event	Cost	Equity
Acquisition	Stock Investments Cash	Stock Investments Cash
Investee reports earnings	No entry	Stock Investments Revenue from Stock Investments
Investee pays dividends	Cash Dividend Revenue	Cash Stock Investments

Trading and Available-for-Sale Securities

Trading	Report at fair value with changes reported in net income.
Available-for-sale	Report at fair value with changes reported in the stockholders' equity section.

STATEMENT OF CASH FLOWS (Chapter 13)

Cash flows from operating activities (**indirect method**)
Net income

Add:	Losses on disposals of assets	$ X
	Amortization and depreciation	X
	Decreases in noncash current assets	X
	Increases in current liabilities	X
Deduct:	Gains on disposals of assets	(X)
	Increases in noncash current assets	(X)
	Decreases in current liabilities	(X)
Net cash provided (used) by operating activities		$ X

Cash flows from operating activities (**direct method**)
Cash receipts
(Examples: from sales of goods and services to customers, from receipts of interest and dividends on loans and investments) $ X
Cash payments
(Examples: to suppliers, for operating expenses, for interest, for taxes)   (X)
Net cash provided (used) by operating activities $ X

PRESENTATION OF NON-TYPICAL ITEMS (Chapter 14)

Prior period adjustments (Chapter 11)	Retained earnings statement (adjustment of beginning retained earnings)
Discontinued operations	Income statement (presented separately after "Income from continuing operations")
Extraordinary items	Income statement (presented separately after "Income before extraordinary items")
Changes in accounting principle	In most instances, use the new method in current period and restate previous years' results using new method. For changes in depreciation and amortization methods, use the new method in the current period but do not restate previous periods.

RAPID REVIEW
Financial Statements

Order of Preparation

Statement Type	Date
1. Income statement	For the period ended
2. Retained earnings statement	For the period ended
3. Balance sheet	As of the end of the period
4. Statement of cash flows	For the period ended

Income Statement (perpetual inventory system)

COMPANY NAME Income Statement For the Period Ended		
Sales		
Sales revenue	$ X	
Less: Sales returns and allowances	X	
Sales discounts	X	
Net sales		$ X
Cost of goods sold		X
Gross profit		X
Operating expenses		
(Examples: salaries and wages, advertising, rent, depreciation, utilities, insurance)		X
Income from operations		X
Other revenues and gains		
(Examples: interest, gains)	X	
Other expenses and losses		
(Examples: interest, losses)	X	X
Income before income taxes		X
Income tax expense		X
Net income		$ X

Income Statement (periodic inventory system)

COMPANY NAME Income Statement For the Period Ended		
Sales		
Sales revenue	$ X	
Less: Sales returns and allowances	X	
Sales discounts	X	
Net sales		$ X
Cost of goods sold		
Beginning inventory	X	
Purchases	$ X	
Less: Purchase returns and allowances	X	
Net purchases	X	
Add: Freight-in	X	
Cost of goods purchased	X	
Cost of goods available for sale	X	
Less: Ending inventory	X	
Cost of goods sold		X
Gross profit		X
Operating expenses		
(Examples: salaries and wages, advertising, rent, depreciation, utilities, insurance)		X
Income from operations		X
Other revenues and gains		
(Examples: interest, gains)	X	
Other expenses and losses		
(Examples: interest, losses)	X	X
Income before income taxes		X
Income tax expense		X
Net income		$ X

Retained Earnings Statement

COMPANY NAME Retained Earnings Statement For the Period Ended	
Retained earnings, beginning of period	$ X
Add: Net income (or deduct net loss)	X
	X
Deduct: Dividends	X
Retained earnings, end of period	$ X

STOP AND CHECK: Net income (loss) presented on the retained earnings statement must equal the net income (loss) presented on the income statement.

Balance Sheet

COMPANY NAME Balance Sheet As of the End of the Period			
Assets			
Current assets			
(Examples: cash, short-term investments, accounts receivable, inventory, prepaid expenses)			$ X
Long-term investments			
(Examples: investments in bonds, investments in stocks)			X
Property, plant, and equipment			
Land		$ X	
Buildings and equipment	$ X		
Less: Accumulated depreciation	X	X	X
Intangible assets			X
Total assets			$ X
Liabilities and Stockholders' Equity			
Liabilities			
Current liabilities			
(Examples: notes payable, accounts payable, accruals, unearned revenues, current portion of notes payable)			$ X
Long-term liabilities			
(Examples: notes payable, bonds payable)			X
Total liabilities			X
Stockholders' equity			
Common stock			X
Retained earnings			X
Total liabilities and stockholders' equity			$ X

STOP AND CHECK: Total assets on the balance sheet must equal total liabilities and stockholders' equity, and ending retained earnings on the balance sheet must equal ending retained earnings on the retained earnings statement.

Statement of Cash Flows

COMPANY NAME Statement of Cash Flows For the Period Ended	
Cash flows from operating activities	
(*Note:* May be prepared using the direct or indirect method)	
Net cash provided (used) by operating activities	$ X
Cash flows from investing activities	
(Examples: purchase/sale of long-term assets)	
Net cash provided (used) by investing activities	X
Cash flows from financing activities	
(Examples: issue/repayment of long-term liabilities, issue of stock, payment of dividends)	
Net cash provided (used) by financing activities	X
Net increase (decrease) in cash	X
Cash, beginning of the period	X
Cash, end of the period	$ X

STOP AND CHECK: Cash, end of the period, on the statement of cash flows must equal cash presented on the balance sheet.

RAPID REVIEW
Using the Information in the Financial Statements

Ratio	Formula	Purpose or Use
Liquidity Ratios		
1. Current ratio	$$\frac{\text{Current assets}}{\text{Current liabilities}}$$	Measures short-term debt-paying ability.
2. Acid-test (quick) ratio	$$\frac{\text{Cash + Short-term investments + Accounts receivable (net)}}{\text{Current liabilities}}$$	Measures immediate short-term liquidity.
3. Accounts receivable turnover	$$\frac{\text{Net credit sales}}{\text{Average net accounts receivable}}$$	Measures liquidity of accounts receivable.
4. Inventory turnover	$$\frac{\text{Cost of goods sold}}{\text{Average inventory}}$$	Measures liquidity of inventory.
Profitability Ratios		
5. Profit margin	$$\frac{\text{Net income}}{\text{Net sales}}$$	Measures net income generated by each dollar of sales.
6. Asset turnover	$$\frac{\text{Net sales}}{\text{Average total assets}}$$	Measures how efficiently assets are used to generate sales.
7. Return on assets	$$\frac{\text{Net income}}{\text{Average total assets}}$$	Measures overall profitability of assets.
8. Return on common stockholders' equity	$$\frac{\text{Net income} - \text{Preferred dividends}}{\text{Average common stockholders' equity}}$$	Measures profitability of stockholders' investment.
9. Earnings per share (EPS)	$$\frac{\text{Net income} - \text{Preferred dividends}}{\text{Weighted-average common shares outstanding}}$$	Measures net income earned on each share of common stock.
10. Price-earnings (P-E) ratio	$$\frac{\text{Market price per share}}{\text{Earnings per share}}$$	Measures ratio of the market price per share to earnings per share.
11. Payout ratio	$$\frac{\text{Cash dividends declared on common stock}}{\text{Net income}}$$	Measures percentage of earnings distributed in the form of cash dividends.
Solvency Ratios		
12. Debt to assets ratio	$$\frac{\text{Total liabilities}}{\text{Total assets}}$$	Measures percentage of total assets provided by creditors.
13. Times interest earned	$$\frac{\text{Net income + Interest expense + Income tax expense}}{\text{Interest expense}}$$	Measures ability to meet interest payments as they come due.
14. Free cash flow	Net cash provided by operating activities − Capital expenditures − Cash dividends	Measures the amount of cash generated during the current year that is available for the payment of additional dividends or for expansion.

NOTES

NOTES

NOTES

NOTES

NOTES

NOTES

NOTES

NOTES